THE AMERICAN PEOPLE: A HISTORY

THE AMERICAN PEOPLE: A HISTORY

ARTHUR S. LINK
Princeton University

STANLEY COBEN
University of California, Los Angeles

ROBERT V. REMINI
University of Illinois, Chicago Circle

DOUGLAS GREENBERG
Princeton University

ROBERT C. MCMATH, JR.
Georgia Institute of Technology

AHM Publishing Corporation
Arlington Heights, Illinois 60004

Copyright © 1981

AHM PUBLISHING CORPORATION

ISBN 0-88295-804-6

Library of Congress Card Number: 80-69272

PRINTED IN THE UNITED STATES OF AMERICA

8120

PREFACE

The shattering changes in our social, political, and cultural institutions of the past quarter of a century make the study of the history of the United States particularly imperative—and rewarding—for a generation of young people who face the problems of the 1980s. Americans are understandably concerned about the future of their country—its physical and spiritual resources, its ability to satisfy legitimate demands for racial, sexual, and civil justice and equality, and the role that the United States should play in helping to shape the destiny of all humankind. No people can meet the challenges of their own time successfully without a thorough knowledge of their past. It is impossible to know where we are going without knowing where we came from. We commend this simple homily to a generation who will soon be called upon to take command of the destiny of the United States. And we commend it in the deep conviction that history does teach lessons for the present and future if only we be wise enough to heed them.

We also deeply believe that history is a profoundly moral discipline and teaches moral lessons. We can be set free to deal with the problems of the present and future only if we confront the truth that our nation has been guilty of genocide, slavery, continuing racism and sexism, aggression, persecution, and other violations of our own best historic ideals. We have discussed these matters frankly and, we hope, without self-righteousness, because we believe that we cannot truly love our country unless we are willing to know the truth which alone can energize us to continue to strive for a government and society that our noblest women and men have sacrificed so much to achieve.

The history of the United States is also instructive for other reasons. The United States, in the Declaration of Independence, struck a blow for the liberty of all humankind. The American people did prove that people could govern themselves without kings and a hereditary aristocracy. The history of the United States (with the exception of the Civil War, which seems to have been necessary in order to create a united nation) has demonstrated that constructive change is possible without recourse to violence and totalitarian rule. Most remarkable of all, the history of the United States has proved that it *is* possible for divers races, religions, and cultures to live peacefully together; not only that, it has also shown that the strongest nation is the one that treasures diversity.

We hope that readers will agree with us that the title of this book is truly descriptive of its contents. We have of course given due attention to the development of American political institutions, political history, and foreign policy. But we have also written in the deep conviction that it is just as important to record the significant contributions of women and all ethnic groups to the weaving of the rich social and cultural history which we have tried to relate. We have dealt with these groups throughout this book, not as isolated entities, but as integral participants and prime movers.

The American People: A History is the product of many minds and hands. We owe our greatest debt to the thousands of historians, both our forerunners and our contemporaries, whose work has made this book possible. We are especially indebted to the present generation of scholars who have so greatly expanded the frontiers of knowledge in economic, women's, family, demographic, labor, and other fields of history. Harlan Davidson, president of AHM Publishing Corporation, has helped in more ways than we can mention. Margaret D. Link edited the manuscript and saved us from many dangling participles, unclear antecedents, and passive constructions. Maureen Trobec, executive editor of AHM Publishing Corporation, also edited the manuscript, prepared the pictorial section on the struggle for women's rights, and oversaw the production of the book. Phyllis Marchand prepared the comprehensive index. Professor Ricardo Romo, director of the Center for Mexican American Studies at the University of Texas at Austin, prepared the pictorial section on Mexican Americans.

Stephen Rapley designed the book and he and Peter Coveney managed many phases of production; Herb Gotsch drew the splendid maps. Alan Wendt laid out the pictorial sections. Timothy Taylor coordinated manufacture of the book, and Natalie Salat did much of the work involved with the acquisition of pictures. All these persons helped to make this a better book; we, alone, are responsible for whatever errors remain in it.

We know that errors remain, and we would be grateful if readers would be good enough to call our attention to them by writing to Arthur S. Link, Firestone Library, Princeton, N.J. 08544.

The Authors

Princeton, N.J.
July 22, 1980

CONTENTS

PICTORIAL SECTIONS

APPENDICES

INDEX

THE AMERICAN PEOPLE: A HISTORY

CHAPTER 1
THE OLD WORLD AND THE NEW: THE CONTEXT OF COLONIZATION

1. THE CONTACT OF CULTURES

Two Worlds, Both Old

One of the most momentous events in human history was the explosive expansion of the nations along the Atlantic rim of western Europe in the fifteenth and sixteenth centuries. The discovery, conquest, and settlement of what is now the United States constituted part of this singular extension of western influence and power. In the fifteenth century, the European powers took control of the world's oceans and, subsequently, of most lands that these oceans washed. Within four centuries, they had imposed European civilization in some measure upon nearly all the earth.

The voyages of Columbus were the first tentative steps toward the eventual conquest and colonization of the Americas by Europeans of many nationalities. In subsequent years, Americans of European ancestry came to think of this hemisphere as the "new" world and referred to the eastern hemisphere as the "old" world. People in Europe shared this usage, but such designations reflected a profoundly ethnocentric perspective, one that has continued to influence our understanding of the early years of colonization and, indeed, the rest of American history. Such a perspective pits "civilized" Europeans against "savage" natives, and it is very meretricious. The Americas were empty neither of people nor of civilization when the Europeans arrived; the two continents were not, in the classic phrase, "virgin lands." They were, instead, already populated by the descendants of Asians who had come to the Americas across Bering Strait around 30,000 B.C. — the peoples whom Columbus called Indians. Indian civilization, like that of Europe, was not only very old, but it was also very diverse. The differences among the various Indian societies were at least as great, and probably, at some periods, greater, than those among the nations of Europe. Thus, the discovery of America by Columbus was not the first step in linking the old world with the new. Instead, it represented the first contact between two worlds that were both old.

Ultimately, of course, a "new" world did evolve in the Americas, but it was not simply an offshoot of European civilization. Rather, it was composed of the many hybrid strains that grew from the cross-fertilization, not only of European and native American cultures, but also of African ones as well. The arrival of Columbus, therefore, did not merely mark the discovery of America by Europe; it also signified the discovery of Europe by America. This dramatic contact of cultures had far-reaching consequences for both groups; moreover, when the Europeans began to traffic in African slaves, the situation became even more complex.

The meeting of cultures in this hemisphere did not occur in a peaceful or harmonious fashion. Just as it is incorrect to think of the Americas as the "new" world in 1492, so, too, it is an error to describe European colonization as "settlement" without being conscious that other things were involved. It is true that Europeans of many nations did ultimately settle in America, but, before they could do so, they had to gain control of land on which other people already lived. Such control was rarely granted easily or automatically by the Indians, who often struggled against the encroachments of the invading Europeans. Before Spaniards, Frenchmen, Dutchmen, or Englishmen could settle an area of the Americas, therefore, they first had to invade it, conquer its inhabitants, and evict them from their land. Such a struggle for the control of land and resources was, by its very nature, a brutal one that cost many thousands of lives.

In the long run, the Europeans emerged victorious from this struggle, and this raises questions about who the real savages were. The result of the European triumph has been that the dominant cultures of both Americas appear to be more like those of Europe than those of the native Indians or the Africans. But the experience of invasion, conquest, and settlement altered the world view of the Europeans in at least two ways. First, it forced them to construct elaborate justifications for seizing Indian lands and enslaving Africans. Such rationales for European behavior provided the ideological foundations of racism. Second, despite their belief in the superiority of their way of life, the Europeans absorbed and assimilated a variety of elements from Indian and African cultures and thereby altered their own languages, agriculture, religion, and art — to name just four things. Indians and Africans also adapted and adopted a variety of European cultural characteristics in their contact with the invaders. The ultimate result was that the descendants of the first Europeans, Indians, and Africans to come into contact with each other in this hemisphere shared as much — and as little — with each other as with their ancestors. The world in which they lived truly was new in the most fundamental sense, for it was neither European, nor Indian, nor African. It was instead American — a peculiar and unique culture formed in the experience of conquest and out of the contact of many peoples in the aftermath of 1492.

2. THE EXPANSION OF EUROPE

The Impulse for Discovery

It is not easy to account for an impulse as powerful as the one which sent Europeans streaming across the Atlantic and, ultimately, over the entire globe. However, it is possible to identify certain essential attributes of European history and culture that impelled people to move beyond the Atlantic coasts of Portugal, Spain, France, the Netherlands, and England. Indeed, despite the differences among these nations, they shared a set of common experiences that powerfully disposed them toward overseas exploration and territorial expan-

Voyages of Discovery

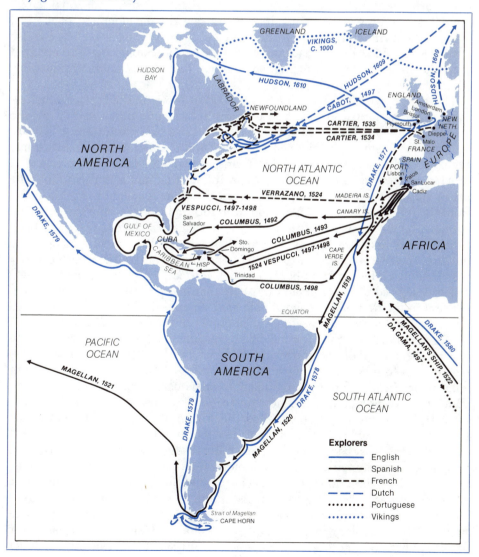

Explorers

———————	English
———————	Spanish
- - - - - - -	French
– – – – –	Dutch
• • • • • • •	Portuguese
• • • • • • •	Vikings

sion. Those experiences went far back into the European past and involved demographic as well as political and economic transformations.

The most fundamental characteristic of European society in the high Middle Ages was a sustained increase in population from which a variety of other changes flowed. Population pressures encouraged an unprecedented movement of people and goods over the whole of Europe and into Asia. The resultant exploitation of new sources of raw materials and new markets for finished products prompted alterations in economic organization. The growth of urban trading centers offered opportunities for a new class of men who derived their wealth, not from the ownership of land, but from the control of commerce. Thus a healthy biological environment, which permitted rapid population growth, also created a healthy economy.

The needs of this commercial economy were strikingly different from those of the land-based economy of an earlier era. It required new technologies to ease the passage of persons and materials from one place to another; it also demanded a more flexible form of social organization than traditional feudal arrangements allowed. As a result, this era saw the development of marked improvements in navigational techniques and shipbuilding, as well as the rise of new legal and political institutions that were more appropriate to changed conditions — for example, the English common law and economic innovations such as banking and insurance.

This period, which lasted from about 1000 to 1350, marked the commencement of a long-term revolution in western history, one that was to continue gradually for many hundreds of years. But it was no less revolutionary because its pace was leisurely. It involved a fundamental reorientation of institutions, behavior, and values that moved Europeans, their descendants, and, eventually, much of the rest of humanity along a continuum that ran from the rural to the urban, from the agrarian to the commercial, from the feudal to the capitalistic, from the religious to the secular, and from the traditional to the modern. The speed with which this revolution occurred varied from place to place and from time to time and was largely governed by demographic factors. In fact, the whole process slowed almost to a halt in the middle of the fourteenth century when the Black Death (or Bubonic Plague), carried by rats in the overcrowded cities, destroyed the very population base that had permitted commercial expansion in the first place. As available food supplies declined, warfare erupted all over Europe between peasants and landlords and among feuding dynasties.

The economic growth of Europe did not resume until the end of the fifteenth and the beginning of the sixteenth centuries, when population growth also regained its former vitality. By then, Europe was a very different place from what it had been before the demographic crisis began. Each of the European countries, except Holland, was now united under a powerful monarch. In Holland, the great merchants controlled the nation and made it a commercial force to be reckoned with throughout the continent. Equally important, while Europe's economy had stagnated, its cultural life had flourished, and the Renaissance continued even as the biological and economic health of Europe returned. The artistic and intellectual ferment of the Renaissance and dynamic economies provided the requisite tools for the maritime expansion of Europe. The scientific and cultural advances of the age provided the plotting instruments that made long ocean voyages possible and also an expansionistic ideology that counterposed European superiority to the "savagery" of other peoples. Similarly, burgeoning economic activity and population provided the material and human fuel for the enterprise.

The Portuguese undertook the first systematic voyages of exploration. The Portuguese, led by Prince Henry the Navigator, from the maritime province of the Algarve, sought gold, trade, and converts to Christianity in a series of unique overseas voyages. Portuguese sailors explored not only the western coast of Africa, but also the Azores, the Canaries, and the Cape Verde Islands. They may even have reached Brazil. The most dramatic of the Portuguese voyages was that of Vasco da Gama, who sailed for over three months in 1497 without seeing land and then steered around the Cape of Good Hope and on to India. The contributions of the Portuguese were, therefore, vital. They improved construction of ships by increasing the number of masts and sails and by enlarging and strengthening hulls. They also helped to insure success by outfitting their vessels with more destructive weapons. In addition, they began a commerce in human flesh—the African slave trade—that would continue until the middle of the nineteenth century. Ultimately, imperial preeminence would elude them, but, under Henry and his successors, the Portuguese—a nation of only 1,250,000 people—discovered half the world in less than a century.

The Voyages of Columbus

Before they sailed westward, European explorers had to conquer the terror aroused in sailors by the unknown North Atlantic. Although Viking ships had reached the coast of North America as early as 986 A.D., these voyages had been ignored outside of Scandinavia, where they continued to be the subject of a vivid folklore. Improvements in shipbuilding and navigation, and a reasonably accurate knowledge of Atlantic trade winds and currents, contributed to the courage of fifteenth-century ship captains—a courage that their sailors did

". . . in 33 days I passed over to the Indies . . . where I found very many islands peopled with inhabitants without number. . . . To the first which I found I gave the name Sant Salvadore." Christopher Columbus' first report of his discovery of America written to Luis de Santangel, the royal treasurer of Spain. (The Bettmann Archive)

not always share. However, it was the conviction that the shortest route to the Orient lay to the west that caused Christopher Columbus to plan, and Ferdinand and Isabella of Spain to finance, the great expedition of 1492. Ferdinand and Isabella had united Spain under their joint control and had succeeded in expelling the last Moslems from Europe. Having done so, they sought new commerce and new wealth for their nation. Isabella, in particular, was fascinated by Columbus and his enterprise.

The Orient was so important in Columbus' thinking that he carried with him a marked volume (which described Marco Polo's travels) to guide him to his expected destination of China. Geographers had warned, accurately, that China was much further away than three or four thousand miles; but both the explorer and his sponsors were too fascinated by the lure of eastern treasure to heed these warnings.

With three ships and a crew of eighty-eight, Columbus left Palos, Spain, on August 3, 1492, and expected to land first in Japan. With the aid of trade winds, the voyage was accomplished before the increasingly frightened sailors could mutiny. On October 12, the man whom Isabella had dubbed "Admiral of the Ocean Sea" stepped ashore on Watling Island in the Bahamas. He named it San Salvador and took possession of the land in the name of *"los reyes catolicos,"* the Spanish King and Queen. Columbus, thinking that he had arrived on an island off the Asian coast, sailed on to Cuba, which he believed was the storied land of Cathay.

In three subsequent voyages, Columbus explored the area more thoroughly. He left a small colony on the island of Hispaniola, where his men had discovered traces of gold. Although he explored the coasts of both Central and South America, he maintained until his death that he had reached the outposts of China and Japan. His widely publicized descriptions of imaginary golden cities, combined with reports of the real gold that his sailors found, led directly to the conquest and exploitation of lands that provided riches far greater than those of Cathay.

3. THE AMERICAS WHEN COLUMBUS ARRIVED

Indian Society and Civilization

It is difficult to generalize about the many peoples and civilizations that the early explorers found. The exact size of the native population of the Americas when Columbus landed is impossible to gauge. However, the best estimates suggest that as many as 110,000,000 people lived in the Americas in 1492. Of these, approximately 10,000,000 to 12,000,000 lived north of the Rio Grande River, 30,000,000 to 35,000,000 lived between the Rio Grande River and the Isthmus of Panama, and the rest lived in South America and on the Caribbean Islands.

The differences among the many native societies were considerable. Indian cultures were spread over an enormous expanse of land; many of them had developed in relative isolation. The linguistic diversity was striking. There were twelve basic stem languages—as different from one another as they were from the Romance languages of western Europe. Each of these twelve stem languages was itself subject to wide variations, and scholars now estimate that

Indian Tribes of North America in the 17th Century

there were as many as 2,000 distinct languages spoken by native Americans when the first Europeans arrived. In the area north of Mexico alone, there were 300 different languages—to say nothing of countless local dialects. Moreover, this linguistic variety was also symbolic of equally heterogeneous cultures.

The differences among Indian societies and civilizations were as wide as the range of geographical and climatological situations in which they lived. Everywhere, however, they engaged in agriculture of one form or another. Some, like the Hopis and Zuñis of the Southwest, used irrigation and terracing to transform the desert into productive farmland. Others, like the Cayugas and Senecas of the Iroquois Confederacy, tended vast orchards. Along the northeastern coast, Algonquin tribes, such as the Pequots and Wampanoags, developed great skills as fishermen and used the heads and bones of fish to fertilize their corn fields. To the south, such tribes as the Susquehannocks and Tuscaroras had a mixed economy of hunting, gathering, and agriculture. Although tended crops provided about 75 per cent of the pre-Columbian food supply, aboriginal peoples also spent a substantial proportion of their time in hunting game. Only among the Aztecs and Incas of Central and South America did agriculture satisfy virtually all basic dietary needs and permit the growth of a very large and densely settled population. There, and in other areas with intensive agriculture, trade also flourished.

The range of political and social organization among Indian societies was also remarkably broad. For example, the society of the Iroquois tribes — the Mohawks, Senecas, Cayugas, Onondagas, and Oneidas — was organized through family ties and was unusually egalitarian. Communal cooperation, diffusely exercised authority, and a lack of social hierarchy constituted the hallmarks of Iroquois life. One of the most distinctive traits of the Iroquois was their matrilineal family structure, which located individuals in families on the basis of their female ancestry. Moreover, women were accorded real social, economic, and political power: for example, they chose the representatives to tribal councils. Other eastern tribes like the Cherokees had confederacies similar to that of the Iroquois. Cherokee family organization was also matrilineal, and members of the tribe were gathered into a loose alliance.

Other Indian societies had other sorts of institutions and living arrangements. The ancestors of the Creeks and Choctaws — whom anthropologists call the Moundbuilders — lived in urban trading centers in the Ohio River Valley. Such cities had populations as large as 30,000. The Aztecs of the central Valley of Mexico were united under a single autocratic Emperor and lived in great ceremonial cities like Tenochtitlan (present-day Mexico City), which had a population of some 60,000. These cities, dominating the surrounding countryside, thrived on trade and warfare to enrich the Emperor. The great nobles of Aztec society — the *pipiltin* — advised the Emperor and exercised absolute control over those beneath them in the social order — the *macehuatlin*. Such urban civilizations invariably had advanced technologies and elaborate architectural styles.

The religious life of the Indians often reflected other aspects of their culture and society. The Iroquois evolved an elaborate code of behavior which centered around the revivalistic figure of Hiawatha who — according to legend — had unified the Iroquois tribes under the symbol of "the white roots of the tree of peace." Hiawatha had a vision in which a powerful spirit, Deganiwidah, had described and mandated the communitarian ideals that were the distinguishing traits of the Iroquois system of values. Hiawatha had also prophesied the conversion of the rest of humanity to these ideals, and the Iroquois did not hesitate to proselytize among surrounding peoples, just as missionaries would later attempt to convert the Iroquois, themselves, to Christianity. The Aztecs also practiced an extremely complex religion. In general, the complexity of ritual and spiritual life among the Indians paralleled the complexity of their political and social arrangements. Religious ceremonies were characteristically elaborate and numerous and provided symbolic reinforcement of social hierarchy among urban groups who were technologically oriented. In groups whose social organization was less complex, religion involved a more direct connection with the daily experience of the people; and the pantheon of gods and spirits was invariably smaller.

The Europeans who first encountered the natives of the Americas tended either to romanticize them or to portray them as brutish savages. Later historians have been inclined to do the same thing. But Indian societies were no more utopian and no more barbaric than those of Europe. It is true that Iroquois social values were less competitive, and Iroquois child rearing more indulgent, than comparable values and practices in Europe. But it is also true that the Iroquois were among the most feared warriors in the eastern woodlands. The Aztecs achieved advances in astronomy, engineering, and manual arts that were awesome, but they were also among the most militaristic peoples in the entire world. Or, to take another example, the Indians of the Great Plains lived in close-knit and harmonious villages, but the rites through which they initiated young men into manhood involved painful mutilation.

It is not useful, therefore, either to attempt to assess the relative superiority and inferiority of Indians and Europeans or to try to categorize some Indian civilizations as "advanced" and others as "primitive." Were the Hopis and Zuñis, who lived in pueblos, more "advanced" than the Sioux or Cheyenne, who lived in tepees? Were the Aztecs, with a religion that emphasized human sacrifice, more "primitive" than the Iroquois? Such questions are unanswerable precisely because they involve judgments about past societies that reflect our own cultural biases and values. The pre-Columbian world, which the Europeans altered forever in 1492, was a world of infinite variety and texture, one inhabited by many different peoples sometimes in conflict with each other and sometimes living together in peace. It was a world with many histories and many cultures all its own. The nature of those histories and the qualities of those cultures very much influenced the character of the new societies that the Europeans attempted to create and the speed with which they were established. In sum, the "new" world was a world neither more nor less civilized than Europe. It was only different.

4. SPAIN IN AMERICA

Montezuma and Cortés: The Conquest of Mexico

Nowhere were the differences between Europeans and native Americans more dramatically highlighted than in the Valley of Mexico, where the Aztec Emperor, Montezuma, faced an invading band of *conquistadores* under Hernan Cortés in the second decade of the sixteenth century. In order to understand the results of this clash of personality and culture, it is first necessary to understand the two men and the societies that had produced them.

The Spain from which Hernan Cortés came was a country whose entire history had been influenced by the experience of intercultural contact and conquest. For most of the Middle Ages, the southern half of Spain had been under the control of Muslims from North Africa, whom the Spanish called Moors. Arabs, Christians, and Jews lived in an uneasy peace in those areas of Spain dominated by the Moors. As these groups intermarried, a diverse and cosmopolitan society emerged, one that utilized the most dynamic elements of the three cultures which it comprised. Gradually, but inexorably, the Catholic kingdoms of the North were able to "reconquer" much of the southern half of the Iberian Peninsula. When Ferdinand of Aragon and Isabella of Castile married in 1469, they united the two most powerful Catholic states and forged an alliance that ultimately pushed the Moors out of Europe entirely. In 1492, the last Arab outpost, Granada, fell to Spanish troops. Of course, the Spanish culture was not transformed just because of a change in the political situation, but Isabella was determined to make the conquest of the non-Spaniards total. With the aid of her advisers, particularly the Dominican priest, Tomás de Torquemada, she devised a policy in 1492 designed to expunge all non-Catholic elements—whether Arab or Jewish—from Spanish culture. That policy was the Inquisition. Antonio de Nebrija also wrote the first grammar of the Spanish language in 1492. When Isabella asked him what its purpose was, he replied that it was "the perfect instrument of empire."

Thus, the culture into which Cortés was born in 1484 was one profoundly shaped by recent experience with conquest and its aftermath. When Spaniards like Cortés arrived in the new world, they came from a nation that had just completed a successful conquest in Europe; and they had very explicit notions about how a conquest should proceed and how conquered peoples should be treated. The discovery of America provided an outlet for the enormous military energy which the "reconquest" of Spain had released. New fields opened for the cultural nationalism and imperialism that were embodied in the Inquisition and summarized in Nebrija's reply to Isabella. Thus, the men who conquered America had an intense religious zeal and were eager to spread Spanish influence and dominion. Whatever else may be said of the *conquistadores*, they came to America convinced that they were doing God's work by bringing the Gospel to heathens. Not incidentally, they also came to seek wealth and the honors that they knew military success would bring. No Spaniard more clearly epitomized this triad of gold, glory, and the Gospel than the conqueror of Mexico, Hernan Cortés.

Almost as much has been written about Cortés as about the conquest itself. He was, in many ways, the typical *conquistador*. Nothing in his background suggested that he was destined for greatness. The son of a poor man of genteel birth, Cortés began, but did not complete, his studies at the University of Salamanca. As a result, he was a literate but not an especially learned man. Indeed, he was suspicious of men with university training and was much enamored of the life of a soldier. Cortés arrived in Hispaniola in 1504 and participated in the conquest of Cuba. Although he achieved some small wealth in Cuba, that did not satisfy him. He left Cuba late in 1518 with about 600 men in search of further conquest. He had heard rumors of a fabulous empire on the mainland, but he had no clear idea of where he was going.

On the other hand, the man who was to be Cortés' major adversary, Montezuma, was a very special man, indeed. He was the absolute ruler of the most powerful empire in Central America, had been reared for greatness, and believed himself to be a god. The role that he played in the fall of the Aztec empire derived directly from his historical traditions and culture.

The Aztecs, or *Mexica*, controlled the last in a series of successor states that had dominated central Mexico for centuries. The Aztecs had arrived in the Valley of Mexico from the mountains to the north some time during the thirteenth or fourteenth centuries. Ultimately, they dominated the other city-states of the valley, and established their own capital city in the middle of a lake at Tenochtitlan. Each of the emperors who engineered Aztec hegemony in the sixteenth century was blessed with an extraordinarily forceful personality and great military and political skills. When Montezuma came to the throne in 1502, he was the heir of a great dynasty that had survived through terror, cunning, and ruthless military might. Montezuma doubted that he possessed these traits.

The center of Montezuma's world view—and that of other Aztecs—was an apocalyptic religion with many gods. Among these, the two most important were Quetzalcoatl (the Feathered Serpent) and Huitzilopochtli (the Hummingbird). Quetzalcoatl was an ancient king who had been driven from his kingdom in the valley to the coast, where he had sailed off to the east, promising some day to return. The Hummingbird was the dominant Aztec god, however. He was bloodthirsty and violent; he mandated frequent wars and required great human sacrifice. In one four-day period alone, the Aztecs sacrificed 80,000 people at his altar in Tenochtitlan.

The combination of Montezuma's personal insecurities and a religion that forecast a cosmic struggle between the Feathered Serpent and the Hummingbird predisposed Montezuma to react in a disastrously indecisive way when he heard the news that strange creatures with white skins and beards, who rode on deerlike animals and held tubes that spat thunder and lightning, had arrived on the coast. These creatures came from precisely the direction that, according to predictions, Quetzalcoatl would come. For several years, rumors of their presence in the Caribbean had been filtering back to Montezuma's court. A series of famines and unsuccessful wars had seemed to foretell a crisis, and, in recent months, Montezuma's astrologers and priests had perceived omens of disaster. The orgy of human sacrifice and hunger had begun to take its toll in the disaffection of many of Montezuma's subjects, and he felt his empire slipping from his grasp. To Montezuma, therefore, the arrival of the Spaniards portended the commencement of the final battle between the Hummingbird and the Serpent. To forestall it, Montezuma increased the pace of ritual murder.

The Spaniards had the good fortune to land in Central America when the Aztec empire was approaching a decisive moment in its history. Cortés soon discovered this and exploited his knowledge in his dealings with Montezuma and with other Indian leaders, who attached themselves to the Spanish cause. Eventually, the Emperor overcame his initial hesitation and resisted the Spanish invasion forcefully when he realized that Cortés and his men were not gods. By this time, however, it was too late; Tenochtitlan fell to a combined Spanish and Indian army. However, the Spanish victory was not quickly and easily accomplished. It took the Spaniards a very long time to subdue Aztec resistance. In fact, there is some question as to whether Cortés could have succeeded at all or preserved his victory had he not possessed an ally infinitely more powerful than any army and one virtually invulnerable to counterattack. That ally was one which all the European invaders in the Americas possessed, and it accelerated their victories immeasurably. Its name was smallpox.

Spanish Disease, Indian Death

The most important characteristic of native Americans in 1492 was their isolation from the rest of the world over a period of many thousands of years. Not only had Indians had no contact with Europe, they had also been quarantined by geography from Asia and Africa. As a result, none of the epidemic diseases that had been perennial killers in other parts of the world had been encountered in the Americas. Indian peoples had virtually no immunities to protect them from sicknesses that were devastating, even sicknesses that had existed for centuries in other regions. In Europe, smallpox annually killed between 3 and 10 per cent of the population; after the initial contact between Europeans and American natives, that same disease killed between 30 and 40 per cent of the Indians.

Some examples may provide at least a glimpse of the demographic catastrophe which European disease set off in the Americas. The population of Santo Domingo was approximately 1,000,000 when the Spaniards arrived; some forty years later, one two-thousandth of the population—only 500 people—remained. In the area that is now Panama, 2,000,000 people died of disease in the sixteen years between 1514 and 1530. The best current estimate is that, at the very outset of conquest, between one third and one half of the native population died of smallpox, typhus, influenza, or some other epidemic disease unknown in America until the Europeans arrived. The preconquest population of New Spain was approximately 25,000,000. In 1532 it was 8,000,000; by 1548 it had declined to 6,000,000; twenty years later, in 1568, it was 3,000,000; by the end of the sixteenth century the Indian population was only 1,000,000. In other words, for every twenty-five Indians alive in 1500, there was only one alive in 1600. The population had suffered a decrease of 96 per cent.

It is impossible to grasp the meaning of figures like these in terms of human suffering and anguish. As one man put it in 1699, "The Indians die so easily that the bare look and smell of a Spaniard causes them to give up the ghost." Wherever the Spaniards and, later, the French, Dutch, and English went in the new world, they were horrified by the rapidity with which the Indians were decimated by disease. They had come for empire, after all, not for genocide. There were fourteen major epidemics in Mexico between the conquest and 1600, and seventeen such outbreaks in Peru during the same period. Not only whole families, but entire societies, were wiped out within the space of a few weeks. In fact, it is virtually certain that Cortés would never have been able to conquer Tenochtitlan if an epidemic had not swept the city before and during the seventy-five days that he held it under siege. When Cortés finally entered the capital, one chronicler wrote, "The streets, squares, houses, and courts were filled with bodies, so that it was almost impossible to pass. Even Cortés was sick from the stench in his nostrils." Cortés' experience was duplicated by Francisco Pizarro in Peru and by other Europeans in following centuries.

In the years after the conquest, English and other Protestant critics blamed the depopulation of Spanish America on the cruelty and cold-bloodedness of the Spanish, and some later historians adopted similar views. *La Leyenda Negra*—the Black Legend—thus surrounds the history of the conquest with an aura of Indian innocence and Spanish barbarity. Barbarity there was, but, however cruel the Spaniards were, they could never have achieved the ascendancy that they did without the aid of the microbes which spread disease and destroyed human lives in such terrifying numbers. Rather than say that the Spaniards conquered the Aztecs and other Indian civilizations, perhaps it would be more accurate to say that the native Americans were conquered *for* the Spaniards by a plague of sickness of almost incomprehensible proportions.

The Organization of Spanish America

The Spaniards still had to face the problem of organizing and governing the natives who survived. The political and cultural conquests of the diverse native American societies were more difficult than the military conquest. Because of their experience in the reconquest of their own country, the Spaniards possessed a number of tools that proved useful in securing their dominion in the new world.

Spanish law, for example, contained a substantial body of juridical theory that concerned itself with the legitimacy of conquest. Spanish law required that certain conditions be met before a conquest could be justified. The Catholic Spaniards never doubted their right—indeed, their obligation—to convert native peoples to Christianity, but they did worry about whether their duty of conversion carried with it a right to take possession of Indian land. No other colonizing power devoted as much intellectual or administrative energy to protecting the rights of aboriginal peoples. A great debate about the "nature" of the Indians and the Spanish right to conquer them raged in Spain throughout the sixteenth century. Many of the more rapacious *conquistadores* faced powerful opposition from members of the religious orders and imperial bureaucrats who sought to protect the Indians. Foremost among these Spanish advocates of Indian rights was Bartolomé de Las Casas, a friar who mounted a sustained attack on Spanish behavior and policy toward the Indians.

In the end, reformers like Las Casas did not succeed in overturning prevailing policy, although they did temper it with their calls for justice. Essentially, Spanish policymakers were torn between the limitations imposed upon them by Spanish law and the imperatives of the conquest experience itself. Two examples may indicate how the Spaniards bent their legal rules to accommodate their desire to seize Indian land and exploit Indian labor. The first example is that the Requirement, a solemn legal document written in 1510, had to be read to Indians before any military action could be undertaken against them. It asked the Indians to lay down their arms, convert to Catholicism, and accept Spanish dominion. Needless to say, this was not the most effective means to guarantee Indian rights. The document was read in Spanish on the field of battle; the Indians could not hear a document that they would not have been able to understand in any case. Moreover, even if they had been able to hear and understand the Requirement, what reason would they have had to obey it? For the Spaniards, however, these were not the crucial issues. It was most important that the Indians be offered—and reject—an opportunity to convert to Christianity. If they did reject the opportunity, the theory went, the Spaniards would be entirely justified in conquering them in a "just" war. Thus, the Requirement permitted the Spaniards to conquer the Indians even while it satisfied the demands of a humanitarianism that was more legalistic than real.

Another example of the relationship between the predispositions of Spanish law and the imperatives of conquest was the most crucial institution of government and labor in Spanish America: the *encomienda*. Because Spanish law seemed explicitly to forbid the outright enslavement of the Indians and the seizure of their lands, the Spaniards created a mechanism that ultimately provided all the benefits of slavery and seizure but avoided their formal institutionalization. The *encomienda* was an Indian village, or group of villages, granted under specific terms to a Spaniard called the *encomendero*. He was responsible for protecting the Indians from attack, for providing for their religious instruction, and for the maintenance of the church and clergy. In return, the *encomendero* received tribute in the form of labor and crops. The idea was to protect the Indians from exploitation through a contractual relationship defined by the *encomendero's* grant from the crown. In practice, however, the *encomendero* was subject to very little regulation, and he was able to enjoy many of the benefits of seizing the land and enslaving the people without actually having done so in law. In short, the Spanish legal system, although humane in theory, failed to protect the Indians with any consistency. In some places and at some times, to be sure, specific Indian groups managed to avoid the most brutal excesses of the system. But the over-all record was one of harsh exploitation.

The men who conquered the Americas and their superiors still faced the problem of organizing and administering a vast empire that continued to grow throughout the sixteenth century. Such organization and administration occurred in two separate spheres. One was local, the other, imperial. In other words, Spaniards *in America* faced one sort of task, while officials *in Spain* faced another. The former sought institutional arrangements that would enrich themselves and secure social control over a restive native population and an increasing number of enslaved Africans. Authorities in Spain, driven by different priorities, sought to regularize the imperial hierarchy and to transfer royal authority from Europe to America without any loss of control. Neither task was easily or quickly accomplished.

One of the most successful attempts to reconstruct society on a new foundation occurred in Mexico, where Cortés exercised the same cunning that had served him so well in his dealings with Montezuma. Cortés, first of all, seized control of Tenochtitlan in 1521, executed Montezuma, and gathered together the surviving Indian nobles—the *pipiltin*. He told them that they would be required to become Catholics and that they would have to pay the same tribute to the King that they had formerly paid to Montezuma. He assured them, however, that their rights and privileges as aristocrats of Mexico would be respected. When the *pipiltin* refused to cooperate, Cortés simply ignored them and put new men, formerly their social inferiors, in their places. He offered Indian collaborators special legal privileges and powerful offices in the reorganized structure of the city. He also provided exemptions from tribute for those who cooperated. The result was that the city was rebuilt very rapidly; some 100,000 new houses were constructed in about two months. The long-range effect of Cortés' maneuvers was to give many Indians who survived the conquest a stake in the maintenance of a new social order which had raised them from social obscurity to positions of influence and power.

This social and political hierarchy, with Cortés at its head, provided the foundation for social stability in colonial Mexico. As time went on, moreover, other such local centers of power developed throughout Spanish America. Simultaneously, imperial officials created an elaborate system for the administration of all of Spain's American possessions. In conception, the Spanish Empire was ruled by a highly centralized bureaucratic system designed to do the bidding of the King. At the top of the institutional pyramid was the Council of the Indies, which oversaw virtually every aspect of life in America. The two major arms of the Council in the new world were the Viceroys of New Spain and Peru. Beneath the Viceroys were nine *audiencias,* who governed particular parts of each vice-royalty. Inferior officials governed even the smallest Indian villages. In addition, the numerous ecclesiastical officers of the Catholic Church exercised substantial influence and power.

All of the many men who served in the various sectors of the bureaucracy were charged with enforcing a comprehensive series of regulations designed to see that virtually every aspect of life was carefully supervised. However, the system was too elaborate for its own good. It created a situation in which political authority was diffuse and overlapping rather than centralized and rationally delimited. Royal officials frequently competed with one another or with local *encomenderos.* As a result, the empire tended either to set different groups of imperial or ecclesiastical bureaucrats against each other or, with equal frequency, to counterpose men whose authority derived from local sources against those who had the approbation of the imperial bureaucracy.

In the long term, this system created powerful imperatives for instability and conflict in the empire, but the fact remains that the Spaniards succeeded in creating the largest empire in European history long before Englishmen even attempted to conquer and settle the new world. The Spaniards explored lands as far to the north as Oregon and as far to the south as Tierra del Fuego at the tip of South America. They established great cities in Mexico and at Lima, Peru, where they built a great university almost a hundred years before the founding of Harvard College in 1636. The Spanish domain contained the entire Caribbean basin (including Florida) and extended westward to California. In fact, the Spaniards at one time possessed more than half the territory of what is today the continental United States. Further, the mark of Spanish civilization has not disappeared. It is still apparent throughout the American West, where place names like California and Colorado, as well as styles of dress and architecture, reflect the enduring influence of Spain—even in lands that have been under the political control of English-speaking people for more than a century.

Culture and Religion in Spanish America

Given the veritable army of Spanish officials—religious and secular alike—who flocked to the Americas in the colonial period, one might well expect that the society and culture of the empire would have come close to duplicating those of Spain. In a variety of ways and for a variety of reasons, however, this did not happen. Moreover, it is as impossible to generalize about postconquest society as to identify a uniform preconquest culture. And the cultures of postconquest America did not duplicate those of the Indians any more than those of the Spaniards. Instead, they were neither Spanish nor Indian; they were each quite unique—more than the sum of their parts.

The factors that influenced social and cultural development were varied, but among the most important were age and sex. Almost everywhere that the Spaniards went, young men between the ages of eighteen and forty made up the most numerous group. Spanish women almost never accompanied these men in their initial contacts with the Indians. Like all conquerors, the Spaniards treated native women with great brutality. The rape of Indian women was so common that some historians suggest that the Spaniards left more pregnancies in the Indian villages than they did casualties on the battlefields. Moreover, such institutions as the *encomienda* created an environment in which such behavior could continue with impunity. Because the *conquistadores* and *encomenderos* very rarely provided for their children by Indian women, an entirely new cultural type of mixed Spanish and Indian parentage emerged: the *mestizo.*

The *mestizo* became the biological symbol for cultural Spanish America—a mixture of the Spanish and the Indian, but not precisely identified with either. Ultimately, "pure" Spaniards and "pure" Indians would be outnumbered by *mestizos* and mulattoes, and all the other permutations of "mixed blood" that issued from the sexual exploitation of Indian and African women by European men.

In addition, intentional attempts by the Spaniards to graft their own way of life on to that of the Indians often had unanticipated consequences for Hispanic cultural and social development. For example, the Spaniards were very energetic in their attempts to convert the Indians to Catholicism. However, the Spaniards often failed to understand the extent to which native peoples simply assimilated Catholic and Indian religious practices into a larger system of belief. In Mexico, where the bloodthirsty cult of the Hummingbird had ruled religious life under the Aztecs, the benevolent figure of the Virgin Mary attracted huge numbers of voluntary converts. Indeed, it was because the Virgin served as a kind of protective mother goddess that the Spaniards had relatively little difficulty in proselytizing the Mexican Indians. The Indians flocked to the Virgin in such numbers that the priests and friars could hardly keep up with the demand. Finally, they gave up trying to instruct the Indians in the complexities of the faith and simply engaged in wholesale conversions and sometimes baptized as many as 15,000 persons in a single day. The Indians were, of course, very susceptible to a religion that promised salvation without human sacrifice. They were refugees from the Hummingbird more than genuine converts to Christianity. As a result, Mexican Catholicism, both in the colonial period and since then, has borne only a superficial similarity to the "official" Catholicism of the Roman Church. Mexican Catholicism centers on the cult of the Virgin, but it also contains much of the traditional Indian emphasis on mysticism and the occult.

The results of the conquest were, therefore, ambiguous. The society, culture, politics, and religion that developed did not represent the complete conquest of one people by another so much as they represented the submersion of two peoples—the Indians and the Spaniards—among a third people who were neither Indian nor Spanish. Of course, this process did not have precisely the same results throughout all of Spanish America. In some areas, Spanish elements never had much impact on the cultural life of the natives; in others, Indian influences disappeared almost entirely.

The determining factors derived from the ways in which the Indians and the Spaniards related to one another. The Spaniards held the upper hand in the military sense, but governmental options were defined by the Indians themselves. Wherever the Spaniards found urban and densely populated Indian societies—like that of the Aztecs—they were more successful in gaining political, although not always cultural, control than in areas where they found hunting and gathering tribal societies.

Thus, the differences among the Indians were crucial in shaping the differences among the "new" societies that emerged in the aftermath of conquest. The direct cultural contributions of the Indians were, for reasons which we shall examine, less important in English than in Spanish America, where even

THE FIRST AMERICANS

Portrait of Red Cloud (c. 1822–1909), chief of the Oglala Sioux. A celebrated warrior who took eighty coups, Red Cloud was one of the few Indian leaders to score military victories against the U.S. Army. Asked to sign a treaty in 1865 to allow passage through Indian lands, Red Cloud refused. When forts were built along the trail, the Sioux and Cheyenne allies cut off supplies and forced the army to abandon all of the posts in the Powder River country by 1868. Red Cloud became an eminent and forceful statesman from the time of his first visit to Washington in 1870. Thereafter his life was spent in pursuit of peace and preservation of Indian values. If you wish to possess the white man's things, he cautioned his people, "you must begin anew and put away the wisdom of your fathers. You must lay up food and forget the hungry. When your house is built, your storeroom filled, then look around for a neighbor whom you can take advantage of and seize all he has." (Smithsonian Institution, National Anthropological Archives, Bureau of American Ethnology Collection)

Top: They take much pleasure in hunting of deer, whereof there is great store in the country, for it is fruitful, pleasant, and full of goodly woods.

Middle: The manner of making their boats in Virginia is very wonderful. . . . They make a fire according to the length of the body of the tree, saving at both the ends. That which they think is sufficiently burned they quench and scrape-away with shells, and making a new fire they burn it again, and so they continue, sometimes burning and sometimes scraping, until the boat have sufficient bottom. Thus god induceth these savage people with sufficient reason to make things necessary to serve their turns.

Bottom: A Florida cacique or chief and his queen, c 1565. Sometimes, in the evening the king goes for a walk in the neighbouring forest with his first wife. He wears a stag skin, most elegantly prepared and painted in incomparable colours. . . . The queen and her handmaidens wear a kind of moss that grows on trees.

Engravings by Theodore de Bry whose Historia Americae *was one of the first sophisticated attempts to illustrate travels in America. (Illustrations from the library of William H. Scheide, Princeton, N.J.: quotations from* Discovering the New World, *based on the works of Theodore de Bry, edited by Michael Alexander, Harper & Row, 1976, pages 56, 66, 75.)*

Ætatis suæ 21. Aᵒ. 1616.

Above: Powhatan, chief of a confederacy of Algonquian tribes in Virginia (1550?–1618). (The New York Public Library)

Right: Pocahontas. The daughter of Powhatan, credited by John Smith with saving his life in 1608, was later captured by the English and baptized Rebecca. She died in England at the age of 21 but was a frequent subject of idealized literature and paintings in the nineteenth century. (The National Portrait Gallery, Smithsonian Institution)

I have seen two generations of my people die. Not a man of the two generations is alive now but myself. I know the difference between peace and war better than any man in my country. I am now grown old, and must die soon; my authority must descend to my brothers, Opitchapan, Opechancanough and Catatough;—then to my two sisters, and then to my two daughters. I wish them to know as much as I do, and that your love to them may be like mine to you. Why will you take by force what you may have quietly by love? Why will you destroy us who supply you with food? What can you get by war? We can hide our provisions and run into the woods; then you will starve for wronging your friends. Why are you jealous of us? We are unarmed, and willing to give you what you ask, if you come in a friendly manner, and not with swords and guns, as if to make war upon an enemy. I am not so simple as not to know that it is much better to eat good meat, sleep comfortably, live quietly with my wives and children, laugh and be merry with the English, and trade for their copper and hatchets, than to run away from them, and to lie cold in the woods, feed on acorns, roots and such trash, and be so hunted that I can neither eat nor sleep. In these wars, my men must sit up watching, and, if a twig break, they all cry out, "Here comes Captain Smith!" So I must end my miserable life. Take away your guns and swords, the cause of all our jealousy, or you may all die in the same manner. Powhatan's speech to Captain John Smith, Virginia, 1609.
From Lives of Celebrated American Indians, *Geo. C. Rand, Cornhill, Wm. J. Reynolds, and Co., Boston, 1852, pp. 179–80.*

Assiniboin Indians at Fort Union,
painted by Charles Bodmer, 1833.
(Rare Book Division, The New
York Public Library; Astor, Lenox
and Tilden Foundations)

Fort Mackenzie, August 28, 1833.
(Smithsonian Institution, National
Anthropological Archives, Bureau of
American Ethnology Collection)

To kill an enemy from a
distance bespeaks no courage,
is not regarded as the deed
of a hero, is not accredited as
a "coup"; on the other hand,
to strike down your foe in
hand-to-hand combat requires
force, skill, bravery, and
cunning.

Inasmuch as some proof is
demanded of the victor's
having touched his van-
quished enemy, if no one is
present to bear witness to the
fact, he takes off the scalp
of the one slain. . . . To do
that requires time, and to
expose himself so long to the
rage or vengeance of enemies
demands courage.
*A note on the motives of
Plains Indian warfare from
the journal of the explorer
Rudolph Kurz, 1851.* From
Journal of Rudolph Friederich
Kurz, *trans. by Myrtis Jarrell, ed.
by J. N. B. Hewitt, Bureau of
American Ethnology Bulletin 115,
Smithsonian Inst., 1937, p. 142.*

*I appeal to any white man to
say, if ever he entered Logan's
camp hungry, and he gave
him not meat; if ever he
came cold and naked, and he
clothed him not. During the
course of the last long and
bloody war, Logan remained
idle in his cabin, an advocate
for peace. Such was my love
for the whites, that my
countrymen pointed as they
passed, and said, "Logan is
the friend of white man." I
had even thought to have
lived with you but for the
injuries of one man. Colonel
Cresap, the last spring, in
cold blood and unprovoked,
murdered all the relations*
*of Logan, not even sparing
my women and children.
There runs not a drop of my
blood in the veins of any
living creature. This called
on me for revenge. I have
sought it; I have killed many;
I have fully glutted my
vengeance. For my country, I
rejoice at the beams of peace.
But do not harbor a thought
that this is the joy of fear.
Logan never felt fear. He will
not turn on his heel to save
his life. Who is there to
mourn for Logan?—Not one!*
Chief Logan at the end of Dunmore's War, 1774. From Lives of
Celebrated American Indians, *pp.
230–31.*

Tecumseh (1768? – 1813), Shawnee (Ohio Valley) Indian chief. His plan to unite the Indian tribes of the Old Northwest, the South, and the eastern Mississippi collapsed after the Battle of Tippecanoe (1811). The British made him a brigadier general in the War of 1812, but he was killed in action in the Battle of the Thames. After a pencil sketch by Pierre Le Dru, a French trader at Vincennes, ca. 1808. (Smithsonian Institution National Anthropological Archives, Bureau of American Ethnology Collection)

Left: Three Cherokee (Southeast) chiefs in London, 1762. (Trustees of the British Museum)

Before the revolution, the Indians were in the habit of coming often and in great numbers of the seat of government [in Virginia] where I was very much with them. I knew much the great Outacite, the warrior and orator of the Cherokees; he was always the guest of my father, on his journeys to and from Williamsburg. I was in his camp when he made his great farewell oration to his people the evening before his departure for England. . . .his sounding voice, distinct articulation, animated action, and the solemn silence of his people at their several fires, filled me with awe and veneration, although I did not understand a word he uttered.

A letter of Thomas Jefferson to John Adams, March 1812. From The Indian in America's Past, *ed. by Jack D. Forbes, Prentice-Hall, Inc., Englewood Cliffs, N.J., 1964, p. 54.*

. . . once, nor until lately, there was no Whiteman on this continent, that it then all belonged to the Redman, children of the same parents, placed on it by the Great Spirit that made them to keep it, to traverse it, to enjoy its productions, and to fill it with the same race, once a happy race; since made miserable by the White people, who are never contented but always encroaching

The way, and the only way, to check and to stop this evil, is for all the Redmen to unite in claiming a common and equal right in the land, as it was at first and should be yet; for it was never divided, but belongs to all for the use of each. That no part has a right to sell, even to each other, much less to strangers – those who want all and will not do with less. The White people have no right to take the land from the Indians, because they had it first, it is theirs.

Tecumseh's speech to Governor W. H. Harrison, August 12, 1810. From The Indian in America's Past, *ed. by J. D. Forbes, pp. 59 – 60.*

One of the principal denunciations against the custom of taking the scalp, is on account of its alleged *cruelty*, which it certainly has not; as the cruelty would be in the *killing*, and not in the cutting the skin from a man's head after he is dead.

If the reader thinks that I am taking too much pains to defend the Indians for this, and others of their seemingly abominable customs, he will bear it in mind, that I have lived with these people, until I have learned the necessities of Indian life in which these customs are founded; and also, that I have met with so many acts of kindness and hospitality at the hands of the poor Indian, that I feel bound, when I can do it, to render what excuse I can for a people, who are dying with broken hearts, and never can speak in the civilized world in their own defence.

And even yet, reader, if your education, and your reading of Indian cruelties and Indian barbarities—of scalps and scalping-knives, and scalping, should have ossified a corner of your heart against these unfortunate people, and would shut out their advocate, I will annoy you no longer on this subject, but with-draw, and leave you to cherish the very beautiful, humane, and parental moral that was carried out by the United States and British Governments during the last, and the revolutionary wars, when they mutually employed thousands of their *"Red children,"* to aid and to bleed, in fighting their battles, and paid them, according to contract, so many pounds, shillings, and pence or so many dollars and cents for every *"scalp"* of a "red" or a "blue coat" they could bring in!

Letters (concerning Plains Indians) of George Catlin, artist and explorer, 1796–1872. From George Catlin, North American Indians, being letters & notes on their manners, customs, conditions, written during eight year's travel among the wildest tribes of Indians in North America, 1832–1839, John Grant, Edinburgh, 1926, pp. 269–70.

It may well have been a gang of Yavapai [Southwest] hoodlums who in 1851 commited a famous massacre usually credited to the Tonto Apaches: the killing of the Oatman family of emigrants along the Gila, at what has been known since as Oatman Flat. Olive Oatman, 12-year-old daughter of the family, was sold into slavery to the Mohaves. She was rescued by a Yuma five years later and returned to civilization, which made a sensation of her story and her Mohave tattooing.
From The American Heritage Book of Indians, *ed. by Alvin M. Josephy, Jr., American Heritage Publishing Co., Inc., New York, 1961, p. 384.*

Left: Catlin's drawing of a scalping. (George Catlin, Letters and Notes on the Manners, Customs and Condition of the North American Indians, London, 1841)

Above: Olive Oatman. (Yale University Library)

I am the Sun's son.
I sat on the turquoise horse.
He went to the opening in the sky.
He went with me to the opening.
The turquoise horse prances with me.
From where we start the turquoise horse is seen.
The lightning flashes from the turquoise horse.
The turquoise horse is terrifying.
He stands on the upper circle of the rainbow.
The sunbeam is in his mouth for his bridle.
He circles around all the peoples on the earth
With their goods.
Today he is on my side
And I shall win with him.

Navaho (Southwest) Song of the Horse. From Aileen O'Bryan, The Dine:
Origin Myths of the Navaho Indians, *Bureau of American Ethnology
Bulletin 163, Smithsonian Inst., 1956, pp. 179–80.*

*Above: Four Bears (Ma-to-toh-pe),
a great Mandan chief (Plains Indians),
painted by George Catlin, 1832. Four
Bears, who was said to have made
the greatest Okeepas (endurance of
ritual torture) in Mandan history,
suffered even more intensely when
he died with most of his tribe during
a devastating smallpox epidemic.
(National Collection of Fine Arts,
Smithsonian Institution; gift of Mrs.
Sarah Harrison)*

*Above left: Buffalo Dance, Mandan
rite. Painted by George Catlin.
(National Collection of Fine Arts,
Smithsonian Institution; gift of Mrs.
Sarah Harrison)*

*Left: Sioux horserace, by Charles
Bodmer, 1833–1834. (Rare Book
Division, The New York Public
Library; Astor, Lenox and Tilden
Foundations)*

Buffaloes . . . are a sort of
roaming creatures . . .
strolling away about the
country . . . just where their
whims or strange fancies may
lead them; and the Mandans
are sometimes . . . most
unceremoniously left without
anything to eat. . . . In an
emergency of this kind, every
man musters and brings out
of his lodge his mask (the
skin of a buffalo's head with
the horns on) . . . and then
commences the buffalo dance
. . . which is held for the
purpose of making the
"buffalo come" . . . this
dance . . . cannot be stopped
(but is going incessantly day
and night) until "buffalo
come."
From George Catlin, Letters and
Notes on the Manners, Customs
and Condition of the North
American Indians, *London, 1841.*

Helpless orphans pite ous cries
Scalding tears from widows eyes
Cool'd with tyrants daintiest food
Murder'd soldiers clotted blood

Tseg'sgin' Sells His Deer

I'll also tell you another one of the things I heard. I'll tell about Tseg'sgin' and what he did. He was evil and irresponsible—or maybe he was clever. We just don't know.

Tseg'sgin' owned a deer. Someone from afar came to Tseg'sgin''s house and wanted the deer. So he [Tseg'sgin'] sold it to him, and he was well paid for it.

The next morning the man left Tseg'sgin''s house and led the deer away. Tseg'sgin' ran ahead of the man, and, as soon as he had passed the man, took off one of his shoes, and put it down in the road.

When the man with the deer came to the shoe, he looked at it awhile, and then he went on. Then after a while he found another shoe where Tseg'sgin' had laid it. The man with the deer arrived there, looked at the shoe, and thought to himself, "This is the same kind of shoe as the other one. This would make a pair. If I had gotten the other one, now I would have had a pair." So he tied his deer by the road and went back for the other shoe.

When he arrived where the first shoe had been, it had disappeared. Tseg'sgin' had already gotten it. So he went back to where he had tied the deer. The shoe that had been there had disappeared, and his deer had disappeared Tseg'sgin' had gotten the shoe and the deer.

He [the man] ran about hunting his deer. After a while he thought to himself, "Maybe it ran back home." He returned toward Tseg'sgin''s house, but Tseg'sgin' had the deer tied in another place. Every time the man walked toward where the deer was tied, Tseg'sgin' would walk in the opposite direction and make a sound like a deer. Each time he [the man] heard this noise, he would go in that direction. Finally the man had hunted so long that he gave up and went to Tseg'sgin''s house.

Tseg'sgin' said, "I have another deer. You can have it if you'll pay for it." (But it was the deer that he had previously sold but had recovered and tied up.)

So Tseg'sgin' brought it to him [the man], and the man bought it again. He [Tseg'sgin'] had sold it twice by the time the man took the deer away.

Yan'sa

From Kilpatrick, Friends of Thunder, pp. 107–8.

There is a similarity too obvious to disregard between the two words Tseg'sin', Jackson, and Tseg'sgin', "Jack the Devil." To this day among the conservatives where one finds Tseg'sgin' stories being exchanged, the name of Andrew Jackson, the man who repaid Cherokee friendship and valor at Horseshoe Bend with the horrors of the Trail of Tears, is the symbol of trickery and deceit and of opportunism at the expense of others.

Opposite: Caricature of Andrew Jackson entitled "Richard III," 1836. (Courtesy of the New-York Historical Society, New York City)

Sequoya (1770?–1843), inventor of the Cherokee alphabet. Sequoya's alphabet was approved by the Cherokee council in 1821 and was effective in teaching thousands of Cherokee people to read and write. (Library of Congress)

SE-QUO-YAH

"The Things They Told Long Ago"

The things they told long ago are very interesting to hear. It is almost impossible to remember it [what was told] all. It seems that one can remember only a small amount of it. When people can remember all of it, they can tell very interesting things.

Many people do not tell the stories right: they get them all mixed up. That is the reason why these stories sometimes vary. Some people know more of the stories, some less.

Siquanid'

"When I Am Sitting Here Alone"

When I am sitting here alone, I can remember most of it [what I once knew], but when I have to do it [tell stories] very quickly [on short notice], I can't remember. It is only when I can sit down and think a long time that I can do it. That's the way it is.

Asudi

Cherokee (Southeast) storytellers on their art. From Jack F. and Anna G. Kilpatrick, Friends of Thunder: Folktales of the Oklahoma Cherokee, *Southern Methodist University Press, Dallas, 1964, pp. 4–5.*

*Stand Watie, Cherokee, 19th century.
Prominent in the Cherokee Nation
as an educated man and a lawyer,
he organized a regiment of Cherokees
for the Confederacy in 1861 and
became an officer in the Confederate
Army. (Library of Congress)*

Fayetteville, Ark.
May 18th, 1861

Capt. Stand Watie,
DR. SIR:

Several of our citizens addressed lately a letter to you on behalf
of a meeting of the County held in this place, on the 6th of
May last, and on behalf of the County and State, urging you,
as a private and public citizen of the Cherokee Nation, to join
us in our efforts for mutual defence.

Every day strengthens the probability that the soil of the
Cherokee People will be wrested from them unless they bow
down to Abolitionism and every day convinces us that it is
very important that the Cherokee be up and doing to defend
their soil, their homes, their firesides, aye their very existence.
To this end the State of Arkansas and the Confederate
Government will also strive, and bloodless will not be any
victory over us. The integrity of the soil of the Southern
Indians must and shall be maintained. We shall do all that
men can do to so maintain them.

It is reported that Jim Lane, the notorious Abolitionist, robber,
murderer and rascal now disgracing a seat in the old U.S.
Senate from Kansas has been recently appointed Cherokee
Agent. If this be true, you will know what it portends[:] The
subjugation of the Cherokee to the rule of Abolition. . . . The
interest[s] of the Cherokees are identical with ours, we feel
them to be so and we will do all in our power to aid and
protect them.

Respectfully,
Your Obt. Servt.
J. W. WASHBOURNE
A. M. WILSON

From Edward Everett Dale and Gaston Litton, Cherokee Cavaliers,
University of Oklahoma Press, Norman, 1939, pp. 106–7.

ARTICLE I.

DECLARATION OF RIGHTS.—
That general, great and
essential principles of liberty
and free government may be
recognized and established,
we declare:

SEC. 1.—That all free men,
when the general, great and
essential they form a social
compact, are equal in rights,
and that no man or set of
men are entitled to exclusive,
separate public emolument or
privileges from the com-
munity, but in consideration
of public services.

SEC. 2.—That all political
power is inherent in the
people, and all free government[s] are founded on their
authority and established for
their benefit, and therefore
they have at all times an
inalienable and indefeasible
right to alter, reform, or
abolish their form of
government in such manner
as they may think proper
or expedient.

SEC. 3.—There shall be no
establishment of religion by
law. No preference shall ever
be given by law to any
religious sects, society,
denomination or mode of
worship. And no religious test
shall ever be allowed as a
qualification to any public
trust under this government.

*A meeting of the Grand Council at
the Creek Indian Capitol, Okmulgee,
Oklahoma, 1920. (By permission of
The Huntington Library, San Marino
Calif.)*

*Oglala Sioux Indian Chiefs: From
left, Little Wound, Red Cloud, and
American Horse pose for a studio
portrait in Washington, D.C., with
their interpreter, John Bridgeman.*

SEC. 6.—No person shall ever
be appointed or elected to any
office in this nation for life
or during good behaviour, but
the tenure of all offices shall
be for some limited period
of time, if the person
appointed or elected thereto
so long behave well.

SEC. 9.—That the printing-
press shall be free to every
person, and no law shall ever
be made to restrain the rights
thereof. The free communication of opinion is one of the
inviolable rights of man, and
every citizen may freely
speak, write, and print on any
subject, being responsible for
abuse of that liberty.

SEC. 10.—That the people
shall be secure in their
persons, houses, papers and
possessions from unreasonable
seizures and searches, and
that no warrant to search any
place or to seize any person
or thing shall issue, without
describing the place to be
searched and the person or
thing to be seized as nearly
as may be, nor without
probable cause supported by
oath or affirmation. But in
all cases where suspicion rests
on any person or persons of
conveying or secreting whisky
or other intoxicating liquors,
the same shall be liable to
search or seizure as may be
hereafter provided by law.
**Sections of Article I of the
Constitution of the Choctaw
Nation, 1859.**
From Constitution and Laws of
the Choctaw Nation; together
with the Treaties of 1855, 1865 &
1866, *Wm. P. Lyon and Son,
New York, 1869, pp. 7–8.*

After having removed the *sanctum sanctorum*, or little scaffold, . . . and having removed also the buffalo and human skulls from the floor, and attached them to the posts of the lodge; and two men having taken their positions near the middle of the lodge, for the purpose of inflicting the tortures — the one with the scalping-knife, and the other with [a] bunch of splints . . . in his hand; one at a time of the young fellows, already emaciated with fasting, and thirsting, and waking, for nearly four days and nights, advanced from the side of the lodge, and placed himself on his hands and feet, or otherwise, as best suited for the performance of the operation, where he submitted to the cruelties in the following manner: — An inch or more of the flesh on each shoulder, or each breast was taken up between the thumb and finger by the man who held the knife in his right hand; and the knife, which had been ground sharp on both edges, and then hacked and notched with the blade of another, to make it produce as much pain as possible, was forced through the flesh below the fingers, and being withdrawn, was followed with a splint or skewer from the other, who held a bunch of such in his left hand, and was ready to force them through the wound. There were then two cords lowered down from the top of the lodge (by men who were placed on the lodge outside for the purpose), which were fastened to these splints or skewers, and they instantly began to haul him up; he was thus raised until his body was just suspended from the ground where he rested, until the knife and a splint were passed through the flesh or integuments in a similar manner on each arm below the shoulder (over the *brachialis externus*), below the elbow (over the *extensor carpi radialis*), on the thighs (over the *vastus externus*), and below the knees (over the *peroneus*).

George Catlin's account of a Mandan sun dance. The sun dance was one of the most important religious ceremonies among Plains Indians. From Catlin, North American Indians, *p. 192.*

A Sioux sun dance held on the Pine Ridge Reservation, July 29, 1883. (S. D. Butcher Collection, Nebraska State Historical Society)

"When the earth had been made, Killer of Enemies put us down right here in the vicinity of White Mountain," say the modern Mescaleros. *" 'That which lies on this mountain will be the land of the Mescalero,' he said. Killer of Enemies put us down right here. We are still here. Still poverty-stricken, we live just so. But then God created us that way. He created us without anything. We still go on in that way."* Mescalero Apache in the 20th century. From C. L. Sonnichsen, The Mescalero Apaches, University of Oklahoma Press, Norman, 1958, p. 16.

Seneca man and wife from the Tonawanda Reservation, New York, 1900. (Photograph courtesy of Museum of the American Indian, Heye Foundation)

Seneca man from the Allegheny Reservation, New York, 1908. (Photograph courtesy of Museum of the American Indian, Heye Foundation)

Indian log cabin in "Lame Deer" camp, Montana. (Gabriel D. Hackett)

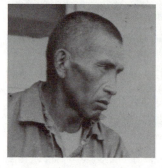 

George D. Heron, Seneca president, before the House Subcommittee on Indian Affairs, 1960. From The Kinzua Dam Controversy, Philadelphia Yearly Meeting of Friends, Philadelphia, as quoted in The Indian in America's Past, ed. by J. D. Forbes, p. 70.

My name is George D. Heron. I live on the Allegheny Reservation in New York, and I am president of the Seneca Nation of Indians. . . . my friends from Pennsylvania have said that the Treaty of November 11, 1794, was abrogated when all Indians became citizens in 1924. I would like to point out that the 1794 Treaty was signed by the *Seneca Nation*, not by individual Seneca Indians, and the Nation has not yet become a citizen. It remains today exactly what it was 165 years ago— in the words of the courts as reported to us by our attorney, Mr. [Arthur] Lazarus, a "quasi-sovereign dependent nation." More important, our tribal lawyer tells me that the Supreme Court of the United States has held not once, but at least a dozen times, that the grant of citizenship does not affect any Indian treaty rights or in any other way change the special relationship of Indians and their property to the Federal government. I am not an educated man, but it seems very strange to me that these lawyers from Pennsylvania are willing to say that the Supreme Court ruled against the Senecas, when it did not even hear the case, while at the same time they are ignoring a whole series of actual Supreme Court decisions which go against their arguments.

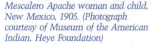

Mescalero Apache woman and child,
New Mexico, 1905. (Photograph
courtesy of Museum of the American
Indian, Heye Foundation)

Grey Mountain, age 91, telling his
grandchildren of early Navajo
legends, central Arizona, 1948.
(Leonard McCombe, Life Magazine
© 1948, Time Inc.)

NAHUATL: *To an Aztec daughter*

Hear well O my daughter O my child
the earth is not a good place

It is not a place of joy it is not a place of contentment

It is merely said it is a place of joy
      a place of joy with fatigue
      a place of joy with pain
      so the old men went saying

In order that we may not go forever weeping
      in order that we may not die of sorrow
      our creator gave us laughter

sleep

sustenance

strength

force

and carnal knowledge

*From Sahugan, Book VI, Rhetoric and Philosophy, adapted by William
Brandon and Betty Lou Frost in* The Last Americans: The Indian in
American Culture, *by William Brandon, McGraw Hill Publishing Co.,
1973, p. 451.*

American Indian Movement leader
Russell Means (left) shakes hands
with U.S. Assistant Attorney General
Kent Frizzell on April 5, 1973, as
AIM agreed to end their sixty-seven
day occupation of Wounded Knee,
South Dakota. The pact was signed
outside a ceremonial tepee on the
site of the 1890 massacre where U.S.
Cavalry killed 200 Sioux. The dispute
with federal officers over U.S.-Indian
treaty obligations won no significant
victory but dramatized the Indians'
continuing anger and frustration over
broken promises. More and more,
Indians looked to the courts.
Litigation is still in progress for the
return of or compensation for lost
tribal lands around the country, with
one of the most recent favorable
decisions rendered in June of 1980
(U.S. vs Sioux Nations). (United
Press International Photos)

Indians dancing during "Liberation
Day" ceremonies on Alcatraz Island,
April 31, 1970. Indians occupied the
former prison island in November
1969 and claimed that as abandoned
Federal property the island by treaty
should revert to the Indian. The
Interior Department later announced
plans to turn the island into a
national park. (United Press
International Photos)

For over a century now the
Sioux Nation has claimed that
the United States unlawfully
abrogated the Fort Laramie
Treaty of April 29, 1868 . . . in
Art. II of which the United
States pledged that the Great
Sioux Reservation, including
the Black Hills, would be ' "set
apart for the absolute and
undisturbed use and occupation
of the Indians herein
named. . . . The Fort Laramie
Treaty was concluded at the
culmination of the Powder River

War of 1866–1867, a series of
military engagements in which
the Sioux tribes, led by their
great chief, Red Cloud, fought to
protect the integrity of earlier-
recognized treaty lands from the
incursion of white settlers. . . .
    The years following the treaty
brought relative peace to the
Dakotas, an era of tranquility
that was disturbed, however, by
renewed speculation that the
Black Hills, which were included
in the Great Sioux Reservation,
contained vast quantities of gold
and silver. . . .

    In sum, we conclude that the
legal analysis and factual
findings of the Court of Claims
fully support its conclusion that

the terms of the 1877 Act did
not effect 'a mere change in the
form of investment of Indian
tribal property. . . .' Rather,
the 1877 Act effected a taking of
tribal property, property which
had been set aside for the
exclusive occupation of the
Sioux by the Fort Laramie Treaty
of 1868. That taking implied an
obligation on the part of the
Government to make just
compensation to the Sioux
Nation, and that obligation,
including an award of interest,
must now, at last, be paid.
From the majority opinion of
the Supreme Court, delivered by
Mr. Justice Blackmun in United
States v. Sioux Nation of
Indians, June 30, 1980.

today the heritage of Indian habits of thought and behavior lives on with remarkable vitality.

In Mexico, it is said that the Hummingbird still lives in a cave in the mountains and awaits an opportunity to revenge himself and reclaim his people. But his people and their culture are long since dead, vanquished by gods more powerful than the soldiers of Cortés or the warriors of Montezuma. In their stead, the Hummingbird would find a culture of rich diversity for which the conquest remains the formative historical experience.

5. OTHER DISCOVERIES, OTHER EMPIRES

Europe Takes to the Sea

The great European empire of the sixteenth century was Spanish. The treasures of Indian civilizations enriched the Spanish monarchy and permanently altered the economy of the West. For most of the century, the Spaniards achieved a naval preeminence that no other European country could approximate. Yet the social, economic, and demographic changes of the period affected the other nations of Europe, too. They also experienced increases in population; they, too, were improving their shipbuilding techniques and navigational skills; they, too, wished to reap the commercial benefits of an empire. The Spaniards, much as they might have desired it, could not keep other western nations out of the Americas indefinitely. All the major powers sent explorers to America and laid claims to land. Although they argued among themselves about the validity of these claims, they only rarely noticed that the land was already occupied by the Indians who, of course, had the best claims of all.

When English, French, and Dutch sailors arrived in America, they did not find the lavish and technologically sophisticated civilizations that the Spaniards had found among the Aztecs and the Incas. The new conquerors, who landed in the northern reaches of the hemisphere, more frequently met members of Algonquin or Iroquois tribes, whose economies either did not value or did not possess the precious metals that were so dear to the Europeans and the Indians further south. As a result, the northern nations of Europe were slower to establish empires in North America. This was true mainly because the other European monarchs were less inclined to finance voyages of exploration and conquest once it became apparent that great wealth would not be easily obtained in North America. Thus, although John Cabot undertook a voyage in the service of Henry VII of England in 1497, and Giovanni Verrazanno and Jacques Cartier sailed for America at the behest of Francis I of France in the 1520s and 1530s, little in the way of permanent conquests or settlements resulted from their exploits. In addition, domestic troubles in both France and England during the sixteenth century absorbed interest and energy that otherwise might have been expended in the establishment of American colonies.

For all these reasons, then, Spain reigned supreme — and alone — among European nations seeking empire in America. Along the Grand Bank off the coast of North America, European fishermen of many nations spent their springs and summers fishing for cod. In the autumn, they returned to sell the fish. They had some occasional contact with the Indians — enough to spread European diseases in North America as they had been spread in Central and South America. As a result, when the other nations of Europe finally did undertake conquest and settlement in the seventeenth century, they faced Indian societies already decimated and weakened by smallpox and influenza. In any case, these fishermen paid little attention to the claims of their respective nations. Their numbers were small enough, and the cod plentiful enough, that such competition was of no consequence to them. In their occasional exchanges with the Indians, these independent seamen purchased or, more accurately, bartered for the pelts of beavers, deer, and other forest animals. They offered European cloth or metal tools in exchange for the furs, and merchants at home soon saw possibilities for new wealth in the Indian fur trade. As turmoil calmed in England and France at the end of the century, the French, Dutch, and English increasingly began to appreciate the commercial potential that North America offered, even if it did not hold out the promise of the gold and silver of Mexico and Peru.

The French and the Dutch in North America

Although the other nations of Europe did eventually establish colonies in the new world, they did so in a way quite unlike the Spaniards. From the beginning, the Spanish Empire was a public and national enterprise financed and controlled by the King. In contrast, the French, Dutch, and English ventures in America were, at least at first, undertaken by private trading companies created by groups of investors whose interest was not in empire or national glory, but in personal profit. For example, when Henry IV of France secured his power in 1590, he did not himself outfit an expedition to conquer and settle America and further French claims there. Instead, he granted trading monopolies to companies which, at their own expense, attempted to establish fur-trading posts in the new world. These companies met with only indifferent success until Samuel de Champlain explored the St. Lawrence River Valley and founded the villages that are today the cities of Quebec and Montreal. By the time of his death in 1635, Champlain had succeeded in forging an alliance with the Hurons, the traditional enemies of the Iroquois, and had also firmly situated the French as the middlemen in the fur trade of the Great Lakes region.

Along with efforts to convert the Indians, the fur trade remained the central activity of French settlers in the new world for the next century and a half. The French crown, which took over New France in 1663, never succeeded in attracting many settlers to America as permanent farmers and residents. Thus, although France was more populous and wealthier than England in the seventeenth century, yet the vast French Empire in the new world remained underpopulated (by whites) and militarily vulnerable throughout its existence.

The Dutch also evinced an early interest in exploiting the fur trade. Just as French settlement had followed upon Champlain's exploration of the St. Lawrence, so Dutch trading posts were established in the wake of Henry Hudson's voyage in 1609 up the river which now bears his name. By the 1630s, the Dutch West India Company had several trading posts: most important were Fort Orange (Albany) and New Amsterdam (New York). The Dutch maintained a flourishing trade with the Iroquois and reaped huge profits from it, but they treated the Algonquin tribes of the lower Hudson Valley and Long Island with a viciousness that is difficult to comprehend. The result was intermittent warfare for most of the period of Dutch tenure and several massacres of peaceful Indian tribes. William Kieft and Peter Stuyvesant, both governors appointed by the Dutch West India Company, bore primary responsibility for this policy, as well as for the shape of life in New Netherland. Like the French, the Dutch were almost entirely dependent upon the fur trade and had trouble attracting permanent settlers. Also like the French, the Dutch created quasi-feudal arrangements for the distribution of land—called *seigneuries* in New France and patroonships in New Netherland. But such anachronistic institutions did little to encourage settlers. The Dutch even annexed the tiny colony of New Sweden, founded in 1638 on the Delaware River, and they tried to lure settlers to Long Island from the English colony of Connecticut. In the long run, however, the Dutch and their French neighbors were no match—either as conquerors or as settlers—for the men and women from England who would ultimately subdue the Indians, conquer their imperial rivals, and gain control of the whole of North America.

6. THE SOURCES OF ENGLISH CONQUEST AND COLONIZATION

Sixteenth-Century England

How and why did the English manage to dominate the eastern shore of North America? How did they manage to attract so many settlers when the French and Dutch could not? What was the nature of the societies which the English settlers established? In order to answer questions like these, it is first necessary to know something of the society from which the English colonists came and the social, political, and economic forces that shaped their views of the world. Indeed, Englishmen established their first permanent colonies in America at the end of one of the most tumultuous centuries in their history, one during which virtually every facet of English life—from religion and politics to population and economy—underwent fundamental transformation.

In 1500, England was a Catholic nation united under the rule of the first Tudor king, Henry VII. His son, Henry VIII, firmly resisted the Reformation, at least at first. While Luther and his followers began to change European Christianity forever, Henry remained staunchly loyal to Rome. Then, in 1534, Henry decided to dissolve his marriage to Catherine of Aragon, his Spanish Queen, who had not borne him the male heir he so desperately wanted. When the Pope refused his request, Henry broke with Rome, created the Church of England, and made himself not only the head of English government, but also the head of the English church as well. In 1539, his break with Rome complete, Henry seized the vast acreage and property of the religious orders in England. Thus, the separation of English Catholics from the rest of the Roman Church provided an opportunity for Protestantism to gain a foothold in England, one that became increasingly firm during the reign of Henry's daughter, Elizabeth I. Certain English Protestants, strongly influenced by the Protestant reformer, John Calvin, would eventually settle in America armed with an ideology that emphasized the special role and mission of the English nation to save the world from the Antichrist. Henry's divorce of Catherine also engendered a deep antagonism between Spain and England that continued under Elizabeth and culminated in the defeat of the Spanish Armada in 1588, an event which opened the way for English colonization because it destroyed Spanish naval dominance in the Atlantic.

Henry's break with Rome thus altered England's position in international relations as well as her internal religious life. But other changes were also occurring in England which would have a profound effect upon the nation's efforts at colonization. First, the population of England almost doubled in the sixteenth century. Simultaneously, prices rose dramatically. The combination of these two developments prompted an enormous social upheaval in English rural life. The price rise and the population boom, along with the sale of monastic lands, disrupted the entire English agrarian society. Some men managed to gain huge fortunes; others found themselves unable to survive economically in villages where their families had lived for generations. As a result, both social and geographic mobility increased sharply. People rose and fell very rapidly in the social order and also moved from place to place in greater numbers and with greater frequency than ever before. In this way, socioeconomic change provided both the people and the private capital that fueled the enterprise of colonization.

English merchants, many of whom benefited substantially from the price rise, began in this period to seek an outlet for their accumulated wealth. They frequently joined together in economic undertakings that they could not afford individually. The joint-stock trading companies that they formed for such purposes proliferated to such an extent that, by 1600, there were more than 200 of them—there had not been any at all in 1500—doing business all over Europe and Asia as well. The primary commodity that they sold was English cloth. As the profits of this expanded commerce increased, these merchants became more willing to take risks with their capital, and the wealth that might be generated by American colonies became more and more attractive to them.

In the end, therefore, a variety of factors combined to encourage and support the creation of a vast overseas English empire. Religious changes intensified England's rivalry with Spain and also created a group of religious dissenters who ultimately came to the new world. Economic and demographic changes produced substantial capital resources and opened opportunities for new profits, even while they sent poor people off their family land to seek their fortunes elsewhere. Finally, Elizabeth, who ruled from 1558 to 1603, managed to calm a turbulent political situation and looked favorably, as her father had not, upon efforts to explore and exploit the bounty of North America. However, despite this extraordinary blend of forces, which all impelled England in the same direction, the first steps toward creating an English empire in the Americas were cautious and tentative, and the success of that empire was by no means assured for many years.

The Impulse for Colonization and Early Failures

The ascension of Elizabeth to the throne marked the beginning of one of the most dynamic periods in English history. It was an era during which England's economy grew and modernized and her culture flourished. It was also the age when Englishmen began to consider seriously the possibility of explorations and settlement overseas for the first time since Cabot's voyages late in the sixteenth century. English privateers had been conducting raids on the Spanish colonies since the 1540s, and they continued to do so throughout Elizabeth's reign. Simultaneously, however, Englishmen began to contemplate the utility of permanent settlements in America. Some of these men had connections with the privateers and envisaged the new colonies as potential supply bases for pirating expeditions. Many men involved in these early ventures were also related to each other. They tended to be the younger sons of gentry families who found access to great wealth difficult to achieve in more traditional careers. Elizabeth favored such ventures, and, in 1578, she granted a charter to Sir Humphrey Gilbert which authorized him to "inhabit and possess all remote and heathen lands not in the actual possession of any Christian prince." As was customary among the Europeans, Elizabeth was not concerned about Indian claims. Gilbert sailed from Plymouth in 1583 armed with his charter, a copy of Thomas More's *Utopia*, and little else. He hoped to establish a colony in America and discover a passage through the continent to the Orient. Both attempts were unsuccessful — the latter because it was impossible, the former because Gilbert himself disappeared at sea soon after he had claimed Newfoundland for the English crown.

Sir Walter Raleigh, Gilbert's half-brother and one of Elizabeth's favorite courtiers, inherited the charter. Raleigh's friend, Richard Hakluyt, already the foremost publicist of the new world, was persuaded to write additional propaganda which encouraged emigration. In his *Discourse Concerning Western Planting* and other writings, Hakluyt extolled the value of America to England's future. He was genuinely enraptured by the idea of English colonization and kept the subject before the eyes of the public for the next thirty years.

In 1585, Raleigh sent more than 100 men to Roanoke Island off the coast of North Carolina. The settlement lasted only a year. Raleigh's adventurers, instead of settling down to work, started hunting for gold and a passage to the Indies. They quarreled among themselves and made war on the Indians. Finally, they deserted the settlement and sailed home on one of Sir Francis Drake's ships, which had returned from a successful raid on Spanish galleons.

Raleigh sent a second expedition of men, women, and children to Roanoke in 1587. With a little luck, this colony might have survived, but support from England was not forthcoming. When supplies finally did arrive in 1590, the settlers had disappeared. To this day no one knows what happened to the lost colony at Roanoke. Perhaps the colonists starved, perhaps they were killed by the Indians, who had been antagonized by the earlier settlers. Whatever happened, the experience did not bode well for English colonization efforts. Nor, it seems, did the English learn anything from it. Their next major attempt at colonization, although ultimately successful, suffered many of the same difficulties.

Another Attempt

The first permanent English colony at Jamestown was hardly an immediate success. The first steps toward creating the Virginia settlement were taken in 1606, with the formation of two new joint-stock companies — one in London and one in the western port of Plymouth — for the purpose of planting settlements in North America. James I, Elizabeth's successor, granted charters permitting the Virginia Company (the name "Virginia" honored Elizabeth who had never married and was known as the Virgin Queen) of Plymouth to settle the northern section of the continent, and the Virginia Company of London, the southern part. A council in England, appointed by the King, would manage the companies, although local councils in America were empowered to preserve order. Significantly, the charters promised the colonists "the same liberties, franchises, and immunities as if they had been abiding and born within our realm of England."

In the summer of 1607, the Plymouth Company sent out 120 colonists under George Popham, who started a settlement on the Sagadahoc (Kennebec) River in Maine. A single winter of disease and starvation reduced the colony by half and sent the survivors back to England with "their former hopes frozen to death." The Plymouth Company made no further attempts at colonization.

The London Company was only slightly more successful. Three small ships packed with 104 colonists, mostly former soldiers and fortune hunters, proceeded up the river which they named the James after their King. About thirty miles from the mouth of the river, they erected crude dwellings and a fort at a place they called Jamestown. During their five-month voyage, they had nearly exhausted their provisions; apparently they had thought that there would be plenty of food for the taking in Virginia. Moreover, they did no honor to James in their choice of a location. They settled on low-lying land ideal for malaria-carrying mosquitos rather than on high ground, as they had been instructed to do.

Like their predecessors at Roanoke, the Jamestown settlers searched for gold and dreamed of a water route to China. They quarreled among themselves and antagonized the Powhatan Indians upon whom they became dependent for food. They were fortunate to have in John Smith a leader of energy, ingenuity, and stern discipline. He reduced their squabbling, secured supplies of corn from the natives, and kept the settlement alive. Even then, more than half the colonists died before the first winter mercifully ended.

New recruits and supplies arrived from England in 1608 and 1609, but still the colonists failed to provide themselves with adequate food and shelter. Of the 900 immigrants who had come to Virginia since the granting of the charter, only 150 remained alive at the end of 1609. During the awful "starving time" of the third winter, ninety more of them died, and conditions were so bad that there was some cannibalism among the settlers. The remaining sixty people were on their way back to England in June 1610 when they met their new governor, Lord De La Warr, coming up the river with 300 new colonists and fresh supplies. Under De La Warr's orders, they returned to Jamestown.

Meanwhile the London Company in England realized that the colony would expire without better support. In 1609, as a result of new inducements and glowing advertisements that described the wealth and promise of Virginia, the number of stockholders increased to over 650 and included noblemen, gentry, tradesmen, and a number of the London industrial guilds. Soon another 600 settlers had arrived and, for the first time, it seemed that the colony might actually survive.

A Permanent Colony

The King surrendered his right to participate directly in the government of the company and the colony. An appointed governor now replaced the quarrelsome council in Virginia, and a "general court" in London, representing the stockholders, managed the colony's affairs. Under the severe rule of the *Lawes*,

Divine, Morall, and Martiall, imposed by De La Warr's deputy, Sir Thomas Dale, the colony achieved some prosperity. Even so, the company's finances remained weak, and the colony's agriculture was not productive enough even to feed all the settlers. By 1616, the population of the colony was only 350. Finally, in 1618 a new group, led by Sir Edwin Sandys, took control of the company. The new management devised a clever scheme to attract colonists to Virginia. Any person who transported himself or others to the colony would receive a grant of fifty acres — a "headright" — for each person so transported.

There were other important developments in this period as well. In 1619, the company ordered the governor to summon two representatives from each of the tiny Virginia settlements to Jamestown. This little assembly of twenty-two (called the House of Burgesses) met first in the crude church at Jamestown, ignored the company's instructions to give advice only, and devoted a few days to the passage of laws against idleness, gambling, drunkenness, Sabbath breaking, and excess in apparel. Then it adjourned "by reason of extreme heat both past and likely to ensue."

Also in 1619, a Dutch vessel arrived from the West Indies with "twenty Negars," or Africans. At first, such captives seem to have worked as indentured servants. In the long run, however, they would lose their freedom, work as slaves, and provide the labor upon which southern agriculture would come to depend. Substantial numbers of women had also arrived in Virginia by this time (see pp. 44–45), and their presence contributed to the organization of the colony along familial rather than military lines.

All these developments, combined with the importation of tobacco plants from the West Indies, provided new stability for the colony. Tobacco provided the colony with a profitable commodity for export and became the basis of Virginia's prosperity throughout the colonial period. In 1620, however, these seeds of stability had yet to bear fruit. Virginia and the English company that oversaw it were very fragile, so much so that King James withdrew the charter and took over the colony in 1624 — a development about which we will say more in the next chapter.

England in America

By the second decade of the seventeenth century, therefore, the English had established themselves in America. Their numbers were still small, and it had been forty years since Gilbert had received his charter from Elizabeth. However, the English were now in America to stay. There were several reasons for the slow pace of successful English colonization. One reason involved the internal difficulties that England suffered during the sixteenth century. Another was the use of English resources in warfare with the Spaniards and trade with the rest of Europe, rather than in American settlements. Most fundamentally, though, the English simply were not very interested in America. They were unwilling to devote money and energy to an empire in the new world because they could foresee only marginal economic benefits. The nature of Indian civilizations in North America was basic to such a judgment, as were the climate and the terrain. Moreover, the model for the earliest colonists was a military one. They likened their efforts to those of the Spaniards in Latin America and their own English brethren in Ireland. They came as an army of conquerors, not as a community of farmers. Without the staple crop of tobacco, which brought some wealth to the colony, it is doubtful that Jamestown would have survived at all.

The sixteenth century had been the golden age of Spanish imperialism, but the English, with their tiny settlement along the James River, began to recover lost time. Before the seventeenth century had come to an end, the Spaniards had been eclipsed by the English in the Atlantic world. Ironically, although the short-term returns of Indian wealth brought immediate treasure to the Spaniards, it was the commerce of Jamestown and its successors that eventually provided the English with the most powerful of all the Atlantic empires. What the English lacked in speed during the sixteenth century, they made up for in manpower, ingenuity, and military might during the seventeenth century.

SUGGESTED READINGS

The expansion of Europe has been vividly described by J. H. Parry in *The Establishment of European Hegemony* (1949) and *The Age of Reconnaissance* (1963). The master historian of the voyages of exploration is Samuel Eliot Morison. His biography of *Columbus, Admiral of the Ocean Sea* (1942), and his two-volume study of *The European Discovery of America* (*The Northern Voyages* [1971] and *The Southern Voyages* [1975]) set standards of scholarship and prose style that few other historians can equal. Also of interest are J. R. Hale, *Renaissance Exploration* (1968); J. B. Brebner, *The Explorers of North America, 1492–1806* (1933); and the early chapters of Ralph Davis, *The Rise of the Atlantic Economies* (1973).

The societies and cultures of American Indians were so diverse that they defy easy categorization. On the Aztecs, the two best studies are R. C. Padden, *The Hummingbird and the Hawk* (1967), and Eric Wolf, *Sons of the Shaking Earth* (1962). The more general work of A. L. Kroeber, *Cultural and Natural Areas of Native North America* (1939), is encyclopedic and an indispensable source of information. James Mooney, *The Aboriginal Population of America North of Mexico* (1928), is a vital contribution to demographic history, but Henry F. Dobyns, *Native American Historical Demography: A Critical Bibliography* (1976), should also be consulted. Among other treatments of Indian life are Robert Spencer and Jesse Jennings, *The Native Americans: Prehistory and Ethnology of the North American Indians* (1965); Alvin M. Josephy, *The Indian Heritage of America* (1968); Harold E. Driver, *The Indians of North America* (1961); William T. Hagan, *American Indians* (1961); and Wilcomb Washburn, *The Indian in America* (1975). The best recent summary of the results of the contact of European and Amerindian peoples and societies is Alfred W. Crosby, *The Columbian Exchange: Biological and Cultural Consequences of 1492* (1972).

The Spanish conquests of the Aztecs and the Incas have been a subject of intense interest among historians since the sixteenth century. The Padden and Wolf volumes cited above both treat the conquest of the Aztecs, but they should be supplemented by two extraordinary contemporary accounts from the Spanish and Aztec perspectives respectively: Hernan Cortés, *Letters from Mexico*, A. R. Padgen, trans. and ed. (1971), and Miguel Leon-Portilla, ed., *The Broken Spears* (1962). The definitive narrative of Spanish conquest in Peru is John Hemming, *The Conquest of the Incas* (1970). Charles Gibson, *The Inca Concept of Sovereignty and the Spanish Administration in Peru* (1948), is more limited in scope, but is an excellent discussion of the results of the contact of cultures. Louis B. Wright has discussed the *conquistadores* in more general terms in *Gold, Glory, and the Gospel* (1970).

In *The Spanish Seaborne Empire* (1966), J. H. Parry provides a masterful account of the Spanish experience in the Americas, while C. R. Boxer has performed the same service for the Portuguese in *The Portuguese Seaborne Empire* (1969). Charles Gibson, *Spain in America* (1966), is the best brief treatment of colonial Spanish America, although Clarence H. Haring, *The Spanish Empire in America* (1947), unravels the complexities of imperial administration with unusual effectiveness. Lewis Hanke offers a powerful examination of the moral dilemmas posed by Spanish conquest in *The Spanish Struggle for Justice in the Conquest of the Americas* (1949) and *Aristotle and the American Indians* (1959), while the actual operation of Spanish hegemony is explained in Charles Gibson, *The Aztecs Under Spanish Rule* (1964). The finest study of social institutions and class structure in the Spanish colonies is James Lockhart, *Spanish Peru, 1532–1560: A Colonial Society* (1968). On Mexico, see François Chevalier, *Land and Society in Colonial Mexico: The Great Hacienda*, Alvin Eustis, trans. (1963), and John Chance, *Race and Class in Colonial Oaxaca* (1978). Caio Prado, *The Colonial Background of Modern Brazil* (1967), discusses early Brazilian history with intelligence and authority. Anyone interested in colonial Latin America can benefit from the fresh interpretive focus of Stanley and Barbara Stein, *The Colonial Heritage of Latin America* (1970).

The French colonies have attracted far less interest among historians. W. J. Eccles, *France in America* (1972), is the best brief treatment, but George M. Wrong, *The Rise and Fall of New France* (1928), offers insights and information that can be found nowhere else.

The literature on the socioeconomic changes in sixteenth- and seventeenth-century England and the religious and political transformations which accompanied them is vast. For the sixteenth century, G. R. Elton, *England Under the Tudors* (1955), is the standard work. The best introductions to the human background of colonization are Wallace Notestein, *The English People on the Eve of Colonization, 1603–1630* (1951), and Carl Bridenbaugh, *Vexed and Troubled Englishmen, 1590–1642* (1968). Peter Laslett's *The World We Have Lost* (1965) is also vital reading for anyone interested in the social and economic instability of the period, while Lawrence Stone's magisterial *The Crisis of the Aristocracy* (1965) is also essential. Theodore K. Rabb analyzes the economic basis of commercial investment in *Enterprise and Empire* (1967), while David B. Quinn's collection of essays, *England and the Discovery of America, 1481–1620* (1974), demonstrates why he is the leading historian of early English settlement and discovery.

The most authoritative single volume treatment of the early years of the English colonies is John E. Pomfret and Floyd M. Shumway, *Founding the American Colonies, 1583–1660* (1970). On Virginia, Wesley Frank Craven, *The Southern Colonies in the Seventeenth Century, 1607–1689* (1949), is testimony to its author's unrivaled learning and control of his subject. Alden Vaughan's briefer and more narrowly gauged volume *American Genesis: Captain John Smith and the Founding of Virginia* (1975), is also worthy of close examination, as are the early chapters of Edmund S. Morgan's *American Slavery, American Freedom: The Ordeal of Colonial Virginia* (1975). The most complete account of the entire history of English colonization is Charles M. Andrews, *The Colonial Period of American History*, Vols. I–III (1934–1937).

Finally, students interested in the general issues of colonization, conquest, and cultural contact discussed in this chapter should consult the following representative works: Howard Mumford Jones, *O Strange New World* (1964); J. H. Elliott, *The Old World and the New, 1492–1650* (1970); Louis B. Hartz, ed., *The Founding of New Societies* (1969); and Gary B. Nash, *Red, White, and Black: The Peoples of Early America* (1974).

CHAPTER 2
THE ENGLISH COLONIES IN THE SEVENTEENTH CENTURY

1. LIFE IN SEVENTEENTH-CENTURY VIRGINIA

Conquering the Powhatan Confederacy

Apart from their other problems, the Virginia colonists faced the difficulty of establishing amicable relations with the Indians. Although the native Americans in the vicinity of Jamestown were not as numerous as those whom Cortés had confronted in Mexico a century before, they were nonetheless a formidable force. The most important Indian leader in Virginia was Powhatan, usually remembered as the father of Pocahontas. It is less well known, although far more significant, that Powhatan was in the process of building his own empire when the first English colonists sailed up the James River in 1607. Powhatan dominated virtually all the Indian tribes along the Virginia coast, and his influence extended from Maryland to the Carolinas. The population of Powhatan's domain was perhaps 10,000. The Powhatan Confederacy, as Thomas Jefferson later called it, boasted very productive agriculture, sophisticated and complex political arrangements, and substantial military capabilities.

Powhatan knew something about the Europeans when they appeared, exhausted and starving, on the banks of the James River. He was probably aware that the Jamestown settlement was but another outpost of a civilization which, from the Indian point of view, seemed to have considerable difficulty in surviving on land that supported the Indians quite well. Moreover, Powhatan certainly realized that he enjoyed an overwhelming numerical superiority over the first English settlers. He had no reason to regard them as a serious threat to his primacy, and he seems to have viewed them as potential allies in his attempts to subdue other Indian tribes. Despite his power, Powhatan's control over his subjects was not entirely secure, and, although he was cautious in his dealings with the invaders from across the sea, he was generally tolerant of these rather inept men with white skins, who seemed to know nothing of even the most rudimentary agriculture. Of course, there were occasional outbreaks of violence, but Powhatan hardly saw these Englishmen as ominous forerunners of conquest. He established a peaceful relationship with the English in 1614; he helped them when it suited his purposes and ignored them when it did not.

For their part, the colonists expected a hostile reaction from the Indians and came prepared for warfare, which they hoped would end in the subjugation of the Indians and their use as laborers to grow food for the settlers. When the Indians turned out to be relatively pacific, the settlers were mystified and attributed Indian generosity to the protection of God. However, a suspicion remained that the Indians, heathens that they were, could only be engaged in some diabolical treachery. Equally important, the English could not fail to know that their increasing encroachments on Indian land for tobacco cultivation would ultimately antagonize the natives.

So long as the English colony appeared to be floundering, Powhatan was content to use its presence to secure political goals of his own. However, when the colony began to achieve some stability and to expand, Powhatan and his brother and successor, Opechancanough, voiced their discontent to the English authorities in Jamestown. When the chiefs received no satisfaction, the Indians decided that the time had come to let the English know that they did not intend to yield their land without a fight.

In 1622, therefore, Opechancanough (Powhatan died in 1618) launched a surprise attack which took the lives of nearly 350 white settlers. The English, responding with unexpected fury, adopted a policy of "perpetual enmity" toward the Indians. Heretofore, the Virginia Company had tried to restrain the settlers. Now, however, all the forces of greed and conquest were unleashed. As one Englishman put it, "Our hands, which before were tied with gentlenesse and fair usage, are now set at liberty by [the Indians'] treacherous violence." A war ensued, and extermination and enslavement became the colony's main policies toward the Indians.

Treaties were negotiated and then broken just before harvest time; entire Indian villages were wiped out and the residents of others were scattered. On one occasion, the English poisoned the wine of Indian emissaries while they were negotiating a peace treaty. Whatever Opechancanough had hoped to accomplish in 1622, the long-term result was the decimation of the Powhatan Confederacy. Opechancanough attempted another uprising in 1644 and did impressive damage to the English settlements with a relatively small force. But by this time Virginia was firmly in English hands, and a new treaty in 1646 only confirmed what both Englishmen and Indians already knew: although sporadic warfare might continue for many years, the era of Indian dominance was at an end.

Virginia as a Royal Province

The violence between whites and Indians cost many lives in the early 1620s, but the attack of 1622 was not nearly so devastating as a continuation of the high death rate among whites from starvation and disease. Between 1619 and 1622, more than 3,000 English colonists, out of a total of a little more than 4,000, died in Virginia from causes other than Indian attacks. Moreover, in their desire for revenge, the colonists neglected their crops, and the harvests of 1622 and 1623 were disastrous failures. By 1624, despite all the efforts that had been made to secure the colony's stability, only a little more than 1,000 of the more than 8,000 people who had come to Virginia since 1607 remained alive. Disgruntled stockholders in London demanded an investigation by a royal commission. It discovered what all too many people knew firsthand: the colony had been badly mismanaged from the beginning and had failed even to provide adequate food supplies for itself, much less make a profit. As a result, James decided to put an end to the company. His judges annulled the charter, and the King again took the government into his own hands.

The status of the House of Burgesses that had met under the company's auspices was for a time not very clear under the King's rule. Occasional conventions of settlers did assemble to advise royal governors in the late 1620s. Although they had no formal authority to do so, similar conventions began to legislate on a regular basis in the 1630s. When the King instructed the governor in 1639 to call an assembly every year, he was merely validating in law a situation that had existed in fact for nearly a decade. However, the real power in Virginia in these early years rested in the council appointed by the King and composed of the leading planters of the colony. The council was so influential, in fact, that it succeeded in "thrusting out" Governor John Harvey in 1635 because he had tried to retard settlement in order to prevent clashes with the Indians.

The leading men of Virginia were a willful lot. They had survived significant hardship and were bent upon the economic success that tobacco cultivation was bringing to the still struggling colony. They were hardly aristocrats in the English sense; rather, they were an intensively competitive and, by English standards, ill-mannered group. Above all, they sought to expand their own holdings and to drive the Indians off the land. Their continued prosperity depended on tobacco, and tobacco exhausted the soil very rapidly. Without new land, tobacco production would decline and, with it, the incomes which supported an extravagant life-style characterized by drinking, horse-racing, and gambling.

Women in Early Virginia

The ambitious men of seventeenth-century Virginia had to compete for more than land; they also had to compete for wives. In 1625, the ratio of men to women was four to one. The proportion of women increased gradually thereafter, but even in 1700 only about 40 per cent of Virginia's population was female. This unequal sex ratio had dramatic effects upon Virginia society and, later, upon that of Maryland, where similar conditions existed. For one thing, it meant that a very large percentage of the men in the colony would be bachelors. As one historian has observed, "Bachelors are notoriously more reckless and rebellious than men surrounded by women and children, and these bachelors were a particularly wild lot." Thus, the numerical imbalance between the sexes imparted a continuing instability to Virginia society that distinguished it from other colonies where the sex ratio was more equal.

Another result of the scarcity of women in Virginia was that those women who did hazard the terrors of a transatlantic crossing and the rigors of life in the colony possessed considerable economic advantage. Although most women originally came to Virginia as indentured servants, their small numbers meant that they could quickly marry and escape their bonded status. In addition, a woman who outlived her husband automatically inherited one third of her husband's estate, and many men willed their wives more than that share of their holdings. Further, upon her husband's death (and women frequently outlived their menfolk in Virginia), a woman would be immediately courted by the numerous local bachelors attracted not only by her beauty but also by her estate. In her new marriage, a woman might be able to obtain guarantees of a larger inheritance from her new husband than he might otherwise have been willing to grant and, when he died, the process would repeat itself. The result was a society in which wealth became concentrated in the hands of women. In the apt description of a leading scholar, early Virginia was not so much a patriarchy or a matriarchy as it was a "widowarchy," in which women enjoyed higher status and greater economic power than they would have had in England during the same period.

Tobacco, Servitude, and Slavery

The first great fortunes and estates in colonial Virginia were acquired in the 1620s. Despite the colony's other troubles, tobacco prices reached high levels in that decade and provided the economic foundation for future growth and expansion. Population also finally began to grow in the latter half of the decade; it perhaps doubled by 1630 and reached approximately 8,000 in 1640. The relatively small number of women in the population meant that only a small percentage of this demographic growth came from natural increase. The majority was accounted for by immigrants from England, more than half of whom came as servants. Some were simply poor people, who sold their services in return for passage across the Atlantic; others were vagrants picked up by agents of the "poor laws," or offenders against the harsh criminal laws of England. The latter were often sentenced to be transported to the colonies rather than to be delivered over to the executioner for committing petty crimes. All of them, however, were treated quite harshly by their masters. Moreover, their indentures—the contracts that bound servants to masters—were bought and sold on a regular basis. Servants were thus powerless to control their own labor. In fact, masters were even known to use their servants as stakes in card games!

The brutal treatment of servants in seventeenth-century Virginia continued in spite of the colony's most salient difference from England, an economic condition experienced by all the English colonies well into the eighteenth century. In England, labor was plentiful and land was scarce. In Virginia, land was plentiful and labor was scarce. Ordinarily, workers in such a situation would receive high wages and privileged treatment because their labor is at a premium, but the indenture system served to undermine the market forces that would have improved conditions for Virginia servants.

This labor shortage played a vital role in the development of chattel slavery. In the short term, Africans were a much more expensive source of labor than white indentured servants. But indentures eventually expired, and white servants became free men and women, able to obtain their own property in land-rich Virginia as well as servants of their own. At first, black servants seem to have enjoyed the same legal status that white indentured servants enjoyed. By the middle of the seventeenth century, this relatively equal racial situation had changed. White servants continued to serve out their indentures, but a new and unique legal status had developed for blacks, one which held them in permanent servitude and saw to it that they were treated differently from whites when they appeared before the courts of the colony. Furthermore, their legal position was passed on to their children and their children's children. This meant that they, and all their descendants, would be treated, not as people, but as property. This "unthinking decision" was unprecedented in English law, and it proceeded directly from the profits that planters made by holding blacks in permanent rather than in temporary servitude.

The institution of slavery developed gradually, and it is difficult to ascribe an exact date to its definitive emergence. As the number of blacks in Virginia increased, so too did the legal differences between them and their white counterparts. A legal system to establish slavery was not fully developed until late in the century, although some blacks were held in permanent servitude as early as the 1650s. Simultaneously, an ideology also developed to justify the harsh requirements of the law. That ideology is now called racism, and the specific lines of its development are very difficult to identify. To some extent, it grew from preexisting English attitudes toward Africa, but it also partook of traditional European responses to all persons whose cultures seemed to be in some way alien or strange. Most essentially, though, racism grew from a psychological need to justify an activity that fundamentally contradicted basic human feelings of justice and compassion and the most sacred ethical tenets of Christianity.

By 1700, then, slavery had begun to provide a solution to Virginia's labor shortage. By adopting slavery as completely as they did and by making it the foundation of their social and economic system, the planters of Virginia also made themselves utterly dependent upon the labor of captured and enslaved Africans. In so doing, they created a dilemma more critical, morally and economically, then the labor shortage that they had originally sought to overcome.

2. PILGRIMS AND PURITANS

Religious Dissent in Old England

Few groups in American history have been so frequently written about and so widely misunderstood as the religious dissenters who established the first colonies in New England. Because the impulse that sent the Pilgrims and Puritans to the new world was so different from that which motivated the Virginia colonists, it is important to know something of the religious background against which the drama of their venture in North America was played out.

Henry VIII's break with the Roman Catholic Church set in motion a chain of events that had far-reaching consequences for English religion. By the end of Elizabeth's reign in 1603, many of the most radical religious ideas of continental Protestantism had deeply influenced significant numbers of people in an England already in social and economic turmoil caused by the price rise and population increase of the sixteenth century. In particular, the ideas of John Calvin, who had established a model religious community in Geneva, Switzerland, had been adopted by a group of English divines and intellectuals. These dissenters shared an intense dissatisfaction with the organization and ritual of the Church of England as it had emerged under Elizabeth's usually benign rule. Moreover, this dissatisfaction turned to outright enmity under James I, who was unwilling to let the people of England have their own way in matters of religion. Persuaded of his own divine right to govern, James was determined to insure conformity to his wishes in matters of religion. Insofar as the dissenters were concerned, James promised to "harry them out of the land" if they would not bend to his will.

Although they disagreed among themselves on a number of issues, theological and otherwise, all dissenters despised James and the church that he headed. The most radical among them — the Separatists — withdrew entirely from the Church of England. They did so, not only because they regarded it as hopelessly corrupt and "popish," but also because they denied the validity of the very concept of a "national" church. Rather, they believed that each congregation ought to be totally autonomous and free to govern itself without interference from any superior body or individual. In the Church of England, which had an elaborate hierarchy of bishops, with the King at its head, such an attitude constituted blasphemy of the worst sort, especially to the imperious James, who would brook no questioning of his authority in any matter whatsoever. It was among the Separatists that the second English colony in North America had its origins. A group of Separatists — the so-called Pilgrims — fled to Holland in 1608 and ultimately founded the colony of Plymouth in 1620.

The Puritans were more moderate in their views and more numerous. Like the Separatists, they heartily disapproved of the rituals of the Church of England. They regarded such things as organ music and the wearing of priestly vestments as the corrupt remnants of Roman Catholicism. They were called Puritans because they sought to "purify" the church of these sinful practices. Unlike the Separatists, they did not deny the legitimacy of a national church or want to leave it. They continued to acknowledge the Church of England and even thought that it, and the English people, had a special role to play in defeating the Antichrist and securing the salvation of all mankind. They tried to dissociate themselves from the church's current policies by governing their churches at the level of the individual congregation. Therefore, they said that they were nonseparating Congregationalists — a description which James regarded as a contradiction in terms. Indeed, the difficulty of walking the line between Separatism and loyalty to the Anglican establishment was partly responsible for sending a large number of Puritans to America.

For all their dissent, both the Pilgrims and the Puritans were still men and women of their age. Like most other Europeans in the early seventeenth century, they did not believe either in democracy or equality, as we understand those terms. They fully accepted the contemporary conception of society as a carefully ordered and hierarchically arranged network of relationships that depended upon consistently exercised and absolutely unquestioned authority by superiors over inferiors. When they used the term "body politic," they did so quite literally; they believed that the social body, like the physical body, had a head to coordinate and direct the use of every part. They differed with other Englishmen about what the precise nature of the social hierarchy ought to be, but they did not disagree about the need to have a hierarchy of some sort. They came to America not so much in search of liberty, as in hope of escaping the disorder that they saw all around them in England, and this motive was reflected in the new societies that they established.

The Pilgrims

By the end of their first decade in Holland, the Separatists, who had gone there in 1608, began to feel uneasy in their new home. The exiles were mostly farmers from the village of Scrooby, and they found it difficult to adapt themselves to the urban life-style of the city of Leyden where they had settled. In addition, they were Englishmen and did not want their children raised in a foreign land, where they might forget their native tongue and be tempted to neglect strict observance of the Sabbath by the multiplicity of religious groups in the tolerant Netherlands. They longed for a home, under the English flag, which would still permit them to practice their religion according to their own lights. America beckoned, but the Pilgrims had neither money, supplies, nor friends at the English court.

At length, the Pilgrims obtained permission from the Virginia Company of London to settle within its territory and found London investors who were willing to finance a voyage. They purchased *Mayflower*, a leaky vessel of 180 tons, and sailed from Plymouth on September 16, 1620. In addition to the crew, thirty-five of the Leyden congregation were on board and nearly twice that number of Londoners who were not Separatists. After a terrible voyage of sixty-five days, the dangerously overcrowded *Mayflower* reached the shores of Cape Cod.

The Pilgrims first stepped ashore on November 21, 1620, at what is now Provincetown, far north of the limits of the Virginia Company's land. Instead of proceeding southward, however, they spent a month exploring Cape Cod for a suitable place to settle. They took on fresh water, fish, and Indian corn. On December 21, the Pilgrims moved off the Cape to the low, sandy shore of Plymouth harbor and began to build their first permanent settlement. They had by now received permission to remain from the new Council for New England (successor to the Plymouth Company).

While *Mayflower* lay in Provincetown harbor, a group of forty-one men had gathered in the cabin of the ship and signed the so-called Mayflower Compact. In this document, they pledged allegiance to their "dread sovereign, the King," and bound themselves to obey "whatever laws . . . should be thought most meet and convenient for the general good of the Colony." This agreement was designed primarily to keep the non-Pilgrims, or Strangers, from disrupting the community.

The Mayflower Compact did not answer a fundamental difficulty that the colonists faced: gaining secure title to the land. The settlement had no charter from the King and, therefore, could not rely on his authority to dispossess the Wampanoag Indians who lived in the area. To solve the problem, the Pilgrims signed a treaty with the Wampanoags that the Pilgrims came to regard as the legal ground for the seizure of Indian land. The Wampanoags had already been weakened by an epidemic and were not inclined to attempt to repel the English invaders. In addition, the English proved useful allies to the Wampanoags against their traditional enemies, the Narragansetts. The result was that the settlers were able to establish themselves without having to fight the Wampa-noags, while the Indians were able to maintain a modicum of territorial inde-pendence until the 1670s. The process of cultural adjustment was thus quite different from what had occurred in Virginia because the Wampanoags, unlike the Powhatans, simply did not have sufficient manpower resources to defend their land.

Plymouth Colony

Just as their lack of a charter from the King helped to dictate the manner in which the Pilgrims would deal with the Indians, so, too, did it affect the nature of their early government. The Mayflower Compact became their authority to make their own laws and choose their own officials. Initially, every member of the colony had the right to vote, and, while the settlement remained small, most colonists took part in deciding important policies. The first elected gov-ernor of the colony, John Carver, died during the first year. He was succeeded in 1621 by William Bradford, who served as governor, with only occasional lapses, until his death in 1657. William Brewster, a magistrate, also exercised important leadership in the little colony until his death in 1644.

The Pilgrims had other pressing and more immediate concerns. In the first winter of settlement, more than half of the colonists died, and disease and star-vation remained a problem for several more years. Animated by their intense religious convictions, however, the Plymouth colonists were determined to make a life for themselves in America. Their profits from fish and furs enabled them to pay off their debt to the London merchants by 1627. This freed them from interference by a group that had little sympathy with their desire to found a religious community.

The Plymouth Colony consisted of only a few thousand people scattered in ten small towns. The settlement was never very prosperous and played only a minor part in the subsequent history of New England. It was overshadowed by its more populous and powerful neighbor of Massachusetts Bay and was ab-sorbed by that colony in 1691. A distinctive trait of the Plymouth settlers was their utopian attempt to establish a commonwealth in which the Bible would provide the foundation of all human relationships. They did not desire worldly success, for they were not worldly people. They had been simple farmers in England and remained so in America.

Massachusetts Bay Colony

The establishment of the Plymouth Colony did not herald an immediate exo-dus of dissenters from England to America. John Winthrop, later Governor of Massachusetts, was furious when he heard that Bradford and the Pilgrims had gone to America. In his eyes, the purpose of dissent was to change the Church of England. To go to America was to abandon the church in her hour of need. After all, how could the church be purified if the purifiers were across the sea?

In addition, the Puritans possessed considerable strength in Parliament and had been able to hold their own against James and his erratic policies. But when James died in 1625 and was succeeded by his son, Charles I, conditions began to change. In matters of politics and religion alike, Charles and his Bishop of London (and, later, Archbishop of Canterbury), William Laud, adopted policies that were simply intolerable from the Puritan point of view. Charles fought with Parliament constantly and then tried to rule without it. Worse still, his wife was a Roman Catholic, and Laud seemed determined to silence Puritan ministers altogether. As things went from bad to worse, even so staunch a Puritan as John Winthrop had to reconsider his views about settling in America.

Unlike the Pilgrims, the Puritans were well educated and possessed substantial political and financial resources. In part because they recognized the economic opportunities that America might offer, and in part because they feared the outcome of Charles' policies, a group of merchants, ministers, and country squires, most of them Puritans, formed the New England Company and obtained a grant of land from the Council for New England in 1628. The company immediately sent over about forty men, who settled at Salem. The next spring, the company reorganized itself as the Massachusetts Bay Company under a charter from the King which gave it powers of government like those of the old Virginia Company. Thus the Massachusetts Bay Company was freed from any political dependence upon the Council for New England.

By 1629, many Puritans, including John Winthrop, could see little hope for England so long as Charles remained on the throne. America was a logical refuge for them because they could continue to profess their loyalty to the King and Church of England (thereby remaining "nonseparating") without having to suffer the interference of Charles and Laud. The result would be a religious community of their own design and under their own control. Still, the decision to leave England was momentous, and men like Winthrop agonized about it. Once the decision was made, however, they pursued their goal to begin anew in America with remarkable persistence and energy. A dozen such men, all prominent members of the Massachusetts Bay Company, met at Cambridge, England, in the late summer of 1629. They covenanted, in the so-called Cambridge Agreement, to go to New England themselves, provided that they could take the charter and the company with them. The stockholders agreed and thus changed the charter of a trading company in England into the constitution of a virtually autonomous colony in America.

Winthrop was elected first governor of the colony and led the first Great Migration of seventeen vessels and 1,000 persons who landed at Boston in 1630. From the beginning, the Puritans envisaged a society that would be composed, not of individuals, but of families. Therefore, women and children were present from the outset, as they had not been in Virginia. In Winthrop, the men and women who founded Massachusetts had a leader of extraordinary talent and intelligence, one who participated in every detail of social, political, and religious life. A man of deep and unwavering conviction, Winthrop laid out his conception of society even before the settlers had landed.

In his justly renowned lay sermon, *A Model of Christian Charity*, delivered aboard *Arbella* as the Puritans were about to disembark, Winthrop argued that the Puritans had come to America on a special mission and under a covenant with God. In order to satisfy the terms of the covenant, the settlers would have to "be knit together in this work as one man . . . always having before our eyes our commission and community in the work, our community as members of the same body." If the colonists kept their part of the bargain, Winthrop said, God would keep His and would protect them and insure their prosperity. He went on to warn his fellow settlers to "consider that we shall be as a city upon a hill, the eyes of all people are upon us."

The Puritans were thus deeply convinced of the unique role that they had been assigned to play in human history. They hoped to be an example to the rest of the world, particularly England. The new colony, with educated and relatively wealthy leaders, went through no starving times such as those that had decimated Jamestown and Plymouth. With astonishing speed, the Puritans founded towns and laid the basis for a successful economy. During the troubled 1630s, when Charles I and Laud ruled without Parliament and intensified the persecution of the Puritans, an additional fifteen to twenty thousand colonists came to the haven in Massachusetts Bay. By 1640, it was the largest and richest of all the English settlements in America.

A Covenanted Society

The Puritans had an opportunity literally to remake society. Unlike their Virginia neighbors, they came to the new world with goals more transcendent than financial rewards. The leaders of the colony believed that God had led them to New England to found a Zion where mankind might make a new beginning. They thought of themselves as a Chosen People—"God's New English Israel"—and they believed that, if they succeeded, all the world would imitate them. Convictions like these did not lead to the creation of a society where people could think, worship, and do as they pleased. As Winthrop put it, true liberty was "a liberty to do that which is good, just, and honest." He contended that the enjoyment of such liberty required a perfect subjection to authority; it did not include the right to violate the laws of God, as the ministers and magistrates of the colony understood them.

The Puritans took their cue in this thinking from John Calvin, who had taught that man existed to enjoy God and glorify Him forever. They also agreed with Calvin that state and church should cooperate to see that people did glorify God. Societies that failed to punish infractions of God's laws, they believed, violated their covenant with Him and would be subject to harsh retribution. In order to insure conformity with their collective covenant, the Puritans modeled their commonwealth as much as possible on ancient Israel under the judges. They even briefly attempted to live under a law code based entirely on Biblical precepts.

The covenant idea was more than the organizing principle of the society's collective relationship to God; it was also the central conception that the Puritans used to describe individual religious experience. Although all members of the society shared in the obligation to try to be obedient to God's laws, the Puritans knew that most people, because they were tainted by original sin, would continue to be less than perfect in their submission to God's will. Puritans believed that God had singled out some people for what they called the covenant of grace. A person who shared in this covenant underwent a profound conversion experience that guaranteed the perfect obedience of which most people were incapable. Although all Puritans were required to attend church services, only those persons who had been given the covenant of grace—called the Saints or the Elect—were full members of the congregation. Since many people did not share in the covenant of grace, the Puritan leaders took great care to avoid the corruption of their churches by the admission of members who were not truly among the Elect.

As disciples of Calvin, the Puritans believed that God had elected some persons for the covenant of grace and consigned others to damnation. But Puritan theology, unlike that of the more rigid Calvinists, made a genuine effort to reduce the actions of God to logic and order. They accomplished this by emphasizing God's willingness to follow certain rules in bestowing grace on His children. The very idea of a covenant between the Saints and God made His actions in this world seem less arbitrary and more predictable. When Massachusetts experienced social or political problems, they were explained as manifestations of God's wrath against violations of the social covenant; similarly, prosperity reflected God's approbation of His people.

The Puritans believed that their entire society was bound together by a series of covenants or contracts: one between the entire society and God, another among the members of society, yet another that held certain predestined individuals in a uniquely protected relationship both to other people and to the Lord. So pervasive was this contractual way of thinking that, when new towns were founded in Massachusetts, the document of incorporation was called a covenant. At least in theory, these overlapping covenants provided the cement that held society together. There could be no place among the Puritans for those who would not adhere to the convenanted relationships that their theology required. Among men and women who saw themselves as the vanguard of history, how could there be a place for those who, by definition, were doing the work of Satan?

The Covenanted Family

The most important Puritan covenants were those which governed institutions, and one of the most important institutions was the family. The family, as the Puritans understood it, was a miniature of the entire society. Just as all members of the society were bound in a contractual relation, so, too, were the members of the family. A society composed of what the Puritans called "well-ordered" families would also be well ordered and, therefore, in better conformity to God's will. In addition, because Puritan ministers believed that families were the essential foundation stones of the entire social order, they also believed that it was dangerous for people to live outside what they called family government. They urged widows and widowers to remarry soon after a spouse's death and also encouraged parents to keep their children under their control until they began families of their own.

The ministers described the ideal family in very exacting terms. At the center was their view of the proper relationship between husband and wife. Just as individuals had to acknowledge the authority of the civil and religious leaders, so Puritan women were enjoined to acknowledge the authority of their husbands. A woman's choice to marry, the Puritans said, was a decision to subject herself to her husband. As Winthrop put it, "He is her lord." Yet this relationship was contractual; wives owed husbands absolute obedience, but husbands owed their wives support, protection, and love. The husband was the absolute master of the household, but he was expected to act responsibly. If he failed to do so, Puritan courts did not hesitate to step in to protect a woman who was being abused.

Moreover, the Puritans presumed that members of both sexes would love each other above all others (except God, of course) and that they would take pleasure from their sexual relations. The Puritans were not, as is often supposed, excessively prudish about sex. Quite the contrary, they regarded sexual intercourse—like all physical pleasure—as a gift from God, which was meant to be enjoyed, not only because it brought new life into the world, but also for its own sake. The only qualification of this view was the conviction that nothing should ever become more important than obedience and devotion to God. If the Puritans were sometimes harsh with persons who committed acts of adultery or fornication, it was only because such individuals had placed their own pleasure above the sanctity of the covenant, not because men like Winthrop disapproved of a healthy sexuality. In any case, sexual pleasure by both partners was an important condition of the marriage covenant, and either party might be punished for abstaining.

Children were bound by law to obey their parents in accordance with the Fifth Commandment: "Honor thy Father and thy Mother." Children could even be legally executed for showing disrespect to their elders. Only one person—a man forty-one years old, who had struck his father—was ever executed under this law. Parents, on the other hand, were required to love and protect their children and, particularly, to provide for their religious instruction. Failure to do so was a serious breach of the law. Provisions similar to those regulating relationships between parents and children governed masters and servants. The male head of a household thus carried a vitally important social responsibility: he was not only the civil and religious authority in the home; he was also empowered to enforce the laws of God. Just as magistrates and ministers drew their authority from the Almighty in government and the church, so men derived legitimacy from God in household affairs. In this way, the social covenant of Puritan society extended even to the most intimate of human relationships and obliged all parties to behave in accordance with the prevailing order.

Puritanism and Politics

Political relationships among the Puritans, like those within the family, were covenanted; but as in the family, contractual obligations did not imply equality between the parties. In the minds of the Puritan leaders, equality contradicted and defied God's natural order for the world. In Winthrop's words, "In all times some must be rich, some poor; some high and eminent in power and dignity; others mean and in subjection." It naturally followed that democracies were inherently weak and corrupt, and that the best form of government was an oligarchy of talent and character. After all, if some men were naturally superior to others, it would be the height of folly to give political power to persons unfit to exercise it.

Under its charter, the Massachusetts Bay Colony was to be ruled by a governor and eighteen assistants elected by the freemen, or company stockholders, who were to meet in a "general court" four times a year to enact legislation. Winthrop and nine assistants constituted the entire body of freemen, or General Court, in 1630. They would have preferred to govern the colony without having to consult its inhabitants. However, when the General Court met in October 1630, 100 persons presented a petition asking to be admitted as freemen. Winthrop and the assistants yielded in 1631, mainly to prevent the petitioners from leaving the colony. They admitted 118 new freemen, but they also decreed that, hereafter, only church members should be freemen and thus have the right to vote for assistants, and that the assistants alone should enact laws. In 1634, however, dissatisfaction with rule by the few was so great that the General Court made further concessions. It agreed that the towns should elect deputies to sit with the assistants in the General Court in making laws. Ten years later, the General Court divided into two houses. In this fashion, the people of Massachusetts transformed a trading company into a commonwealth with a representative government.

To allow greater flexibility and to avoid publicizing their deviations from English law (which might have led the King to nullify the charter), the leaders of the colony delayed the adoption of a formal code of laws. However, in 1641, the more important laws already enacted by the General Court were published as the "Body of Liberties," which became the basic law of the commonwealth. They were based both on the Mosaic code and the English common law and were the first published laws of any English colony in North America. This code remained a cornerstone of Massachusetts law for much of the rest of the colonial period.

Life in seventeenth-century Massachusetts centered in the town, and it was there that the most important political activity took place. The town residents had almost complete control over their local affairs. They, or their representatives, made land allotments, maintained order, executed justice, and exercised a close watch over the behavior of the inhabitants. The towns reinforced the collective ideals of the social covenant. No one was permitted to dwell alone; all unmarried people were required to live with some family. There was little overt conflict in the towns; the same men tended to be elected to office repeatedly, without much opposition, and the ideal of a community governed by consensus remained very strong for a good portion of the century.

The town also became the primary instrument of frontier expansion. In the seventeenth century, New Englanders migrated in groups and usually chose a minister to accompany them before leaving the older towns. The image of the solitary pioneer, alone in the wilderness, reflected the values of a later period in American history. In the seventeenth century, when New Englanders moved, they moved as groups of families who hoped to duplicate the life that they had known in their old communities.

Church and state in the Massachusetts Bay Colony were separate and yet closely intertwined. Only church members could vote in colony-wide elections; and it was the congregation, led by its ministers and elders, which determined whether an applicant had shown sufficient evidences of grace to be admitted to full membership in the local church. The Puritans who settled New England were Congregationalists, and they fervently believed that the church should exclude the unworthy from membership. Ministers did not hold political office themselves; indeed, they were prohibited from doing so. However, they were always among the most influential people in the colony and often served as informal advisers to the civil leaders.

The Conquest of the Pequots

Despite their number and elaborate design, the institutions of Massachusetts Bay were as subject to challenge as those of Virginia. In the first decade of its existence, Massachusetts Bay had to deal with several such challenges; one was the attempt of the Indians to defend their lands; others came from citizens of the colony itself.

Like other European invaders, the Puritans had no choice but to deal with the presence of other people on the land that they wished to settle. In contrast to their neighbors in Plymouth, the people of Massachusetts possessed a royal charter that granted them title to a specified area. As in Plymouth, epidemics had weakened the local Indians and, despite an occasional skirmish, the natives did not at first attempt to expel the Europeans because they did not have the military strength to do so. The white population of the colony grew very rapidly in the 1630s, however, and settlers were soon moving beyond the geographical limits set by the charter and into lands that the Indians had been assured would be theirs in perpetuity.

The Puritans were nothing if not legalists, and they required some legal principle to legitimize their encroachment on Indian lands. As in other things, John Winthrop was the principal theoretician of Puritan conquest. He argued that legal possession of land required that the inhabitants "subdue it" by using it for agricultural purposes. By this reasoning, lands that the Indians had used for hunting were "the Lord's waste" and might be seized for tillage by white settlers. Such an argument protected Indian farmland from confiscation, unless the English could persuade the Indians to cede it through what one historian has called the "deed game." On the other hand, Winthrop's argument opened vast tracts of Indian hunting grounds (particularly in the Connecticut Valley) to confiscation by whites.

The legal justification thus found, settlers began to stream into lands that the Indians had regarded as theirs and anything but waste. The Pequot Indians, until the mid-1630s a relatively peaceful tribe, struck back by murdering two disruptive English traders. To revenge these deaths, Massachusetts dispatched John Endecott in 1636 with a war party commissioned to "put to death the men of Block Island, but to spare the women and children." The raid succeeded only in arousing further Indian resistance; the Pequots made peace with their traditional enemies, the Narragansetts, and attacked Saybrook and Wethersfield. By 1637, the English had determined that the Pequots must be taught a lesson. A party of ninety men surprised the Indians and set fire to their main town. This time, women and children were not spared. As they ran to escape the flames, the Englishmen shot them or cut them down with swords. When it was over, between 300 and 700 Pequots were dead or wounded. There were fewer than twenty-five English casualties.

The conquest of the Pequots began a truce between Indians and whites in New England that lasted for almost forty years. In the aftermath of the war against the Pequots, the English concentrated on converting the Indians and isolating their towns. For their part, the Indians had learned that the English meant to expand, and that they would resort to violence if necessary. More than that, the Indians of the region realized that their relatively small populations and — by European standards — their unsophisticated weaponry were no match for a burgeoning white population armed with muskets. The Pequots were virtually exterminated by the English; other New England tribes tried to avoid a similar fate by suing for peace.

Challenges from Within

Winthrop's argument regarding English rights to Indian land was opposed by Roger Williams, a man who deviated from the prevailing order in a variety of other ways. Williams arrived in Massachusetts in 1631 and served as assistant pastor, and then pastor, of the church at Salem. Not only did he reject Winthrop's rationale for the expropriation of Indian hunting grounds; he also contended that the land grants in the charter itself were invalid because the King had no legal title to any land in America that had not been purchased directly from the Indians. Without such purchases, he said, no European had any right to American land. Needless to say, men like Winthrop were not inclined to take such views lightly, since news of their free expression might lead the King to revoke the charter altogether.

Williams was also a Separatist who contended that, by refusing to break entirely with the Church of England, the Puritans had defiled and corrupted their own congregations. He also taught that church and state should be entirely separate, because concern with political offices would inevitably taint the church with the sins of the secular world. Williams saw no reason to bar non-church members from voting. He thought that the leaders of Massachusetts had things backwards: they made everyone attend church and allowed only the Saints to vote; he would permit only the Saints to go to church and allow everyone to vote!

In short, Roger Williams saw no reason why the church should meddle in the affairs of the state, or why the state should interfere with the individual

A thorn in the flesh of the Puritans for his liberal views, Roger Williams, a Separatist, was banished from Massachusetts and founded Providence in 1636. (The Bettmann Archive)

churches, regardless of their religious viewpoint. For Williams, religion was a matter of private conscience, not to be mediated by any human agency. God knew who the truly regenerate were, and that was enough. The men who ran Massachusetts, although they were much taken with Williams' personal charm, deemed all these opinions to be heretical and subversive of the order that they had labored so carefully to build. Williams was simply carrying the essential principles of Puritanism to their logical conclusions, but the colony banished him for his dissent in the bitter winter of 1635.

Williams made his way southward from one Indian tribe to another and arrived at the head of Narragansett Bay. There he purchased a tract of land from the Indians and began a settlement which he called Providence, in recognition of God's guidance through the wilderness. Other dissenters from Massachusetts followed, and soon four small towns were established. Williams' mark on the colony was decisive, and it remained a haven for dissenters of all kinds throughout the colonial period.

One of those who followed Williams to Rhode Island was Anne Hutchinson, whom Winthrop described as a woman of "nimble wit and active spirit and very voluble tongue more bold than a man." Like Williams, Hutchinson was especially dangerous in Massachusetts Bay because she, too, carried certain aspects of Puritan theology to their logical conclusions. She denied that Christian conduct was a sign of salvation and asserted that believers in whom the Holy Spirit dwelt were above both the law and the control of the church (antinomianism). Moreover, she accused all the ministers of the colony, except John Cotton (whom she had followed to the new world) and John Wheelwright (who was her brother-in-law), of preaching the heresy that good works were by themselves sufficient for salvation.

Hutchinson attracted so much support among men and women alike that the authorities felt constrained to silence her and brought her to trial. In the dramatic trial, she confronted Winthrop and virtually every leading minister and magistrate in Massachusetts. She defended herself with extraordinary intelligence and showed herself to be the theological match of all her accusers. However, Anne Hutchinson's fate was sealed before her trial began. Her preaching violated every Puritan standard for proper female behavior and upset, not only the established structures of authority in the church and the state, but also those within the family. In other words, she threatened to overturn all the cherished covenanted relationships upon which the edifice of Puritan society rested. Such a threat could not be tolerated in the Bay Colony, and Hutchinson and many of her supporters were banished in 1638. She fled to Rhode Island, where she knew that she could express her views openly and without fear of persecution.

The scornful orthodox Puritans in Massachusetts called the Rhode Island population "the Lord's debris." They sneered that if any man lost his religion he would certainly find it in some Rhode Island village. They refused to admit the little colony into the New England Confederation of Massachusetts, Connecticut, Plymouth, and New Haven, which was formed in 1643 for defense against the Indians and the Dutch. Nevertheless, Rhode Island grew and prospered. The land that Williams settled included one of the finest natural harbors in New England. Williams obtained a charter from Parliament in 1644. By then, Puritans who had remained in England controlled Parliament and were embroiled in a civil war that would ultimately lead to the beheading of Charles I in 1649. When Charles II was restored to the throne in 1660, he granted Rhode Island a royal charter that guaranteed its continued existence. Rhode Island's government under these charters closely resembled that of Massachusetts Bay, except that suffrage was not confined to church members.

3. NEW COLONIES, NEW SOCIETIES

The Expansion of New England

Rhode Island was not the only new settlement established by former residents of Massachusetts during the 1630s. In 1636, people from several Massachusetts towns received permission to "transport themselves and their estates unto the River of Connecticut there to reside and inhabit." This exodus from Massachusetts Bay was caused by overcrowding in the towns around the bay (most of the choice land had been taken up by the middle of the 1630s), the attraction of fertile land in the Connecticut River Valley, and personality clashes among the colony's ministers. John Cotton had established himself as the leading minister in the colony, and his major rival, Thomas Hooker of Cambridge, led the immigrants across the wooded wilderness from the Charles River to the Connecticut River. They drove their cattle before them, carried their household goods on wagons, and founded the towns of Hartford, Windsor, and Wethersfield.

The settlers adopted a set of bylaws for their government called "The Fundamental Orders of Connecticut." As in Rhode Island, church membership was not a condition for voting; nor were ministers allowed to take part in politics. For the most part, however, Connecticut modeled itself on Massachusetts. A royal charter confirmed this political arrangement in 1662 and joined to Connecticut the colony of New Haven, founded in 1638 by English Puritans who had stopped briefly in Boston before they established their colony on Long Island Sound. Some of the New Haven people, resentful of the incorporation of their colony by Connecticut, soon pulled up stakes and settled the town of Newark in the colony of New Jersey.

The process through which new Puritan settlements were established foreshadowed a pattern of migration that was repeated over and over again and reached enormous proportions in the nineteenth century: a small group of people, either dissatisfied with conditions where they lived or eager to try their luck in a new place, would pick up all that they owned and start again elsewhere. New dissatisfactions might then arise, and the new settlement would generate yet another. In time, much of North America was settled by whites in an infinite repetition of this pattern. And, at each point along the way, the whites paused to subdue and conquer the Indians whose own towns stood in their paths.

The Puritans were not alone in bringing English dominance to the rocky soil of New England. Non-Puritans also took part. Sir Ferdinando Gorges, a courtier active earlier in the Council for New England, obtained a royal charter in 1639 to settle the area which now is Maine. Gorges wanted a settlement, faithful to the King and the Anglican Church, to act as a rival to Massachusetts. He died before he could stock his colony with loyal settlers, and his heirs complet-

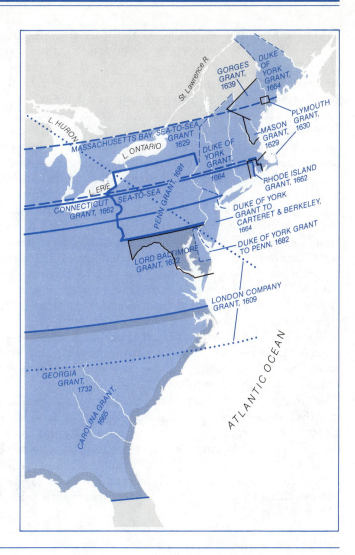

**Colonial Land
Grants, 1609-1732**

ed the demolition of Gorges' dream by selling their rights to the Bay Company. Another area north of Massachusetts was granted to Captain John Mason in 1629; but Mason and his heirs enjoyed no more success than Gorges in attracting Anglican settlers. Indeed, the first group to occupy the area was led by Anne Hutchinson's brother-in-law, John Wheelwright, who departed from Massachusetts with a party of fellow heretics in 1638. Charles II gathered the settlements within Mason's grant into the royal province of New Hampshire in 1679.

A Catholic Haven in a Protestant World

Another settlement, different from the Puritan venture, emerged along the Chesapeake Bay in what is now Maryland. There George Calvert, Lord Baltimore, obtained for his family a charter to 10,000,000 acres on which he hoped to establish a refuge for English Catholics. Calvert had served as a close adviser to James I until 1625, when he converted to Catholicism and resigned his offices. Nevertheless, his objectives in Maryland were not altogether religious; he also expected to increase his family's fortune. Under the charter, Calvert was to make a token payment of two Indian arrows at Easter for the land, and no taxes were to be levied by the King thereafter. Settlers, however, were to pay a land tax, called a quit-rent, to the proprietor. In general, Calvert had the right to treat the colony like a private feudal estate: he appointed the governor, judges, and councillors, organized the courts, and authorized lawmaking assemblies. Thus, if the Puritan vision was somewhat nostalgic in its desire to create a society based on consensual harmony, Calvert's was no less backward looking in its hopes to establish a feudal society and a Catholic refuge.

Calvert died before Maryland's charter received the King's seal, and it was finally issued to his son Cecilius, the second Lord Baltimore, in 1632. A year later, Cecilius organized an expedition of about 300 colonists, including twenty gentlemen, mostly Catholics, who expected to become manorial lords under Calvert. They founded a settlement at St. Mary's, near the mouth of the Potomac River, on land which proved as suitable as that of Virginia for the cultivation of tobacco.

The Maryland colonists had relatively little conflict with the already weakened Indians of the area, and, at least at the beginning, the settlement seemed a model of careful planning and stability. But the Marylanders did face new difficulties unlike those that had plagued their neighbors to the north and south. The Stuart monarchs had a careless habit of granting land to courtiers which they had already granted to someone else. Maryland lay wholly within the territory of the Virginia Company as defined by the Charter of 1609, and Lord Baltimore had to resort to armed force to drive Virginia fur traders from Kent Island in Chesapeake Bay. He had trouble with his own settlers, too. He interpreted the charter to mean that the proprietor was to propose laws and the freemen were to accept them; this, indeed, was exactly what the charter did mean. However, the very first assembly in Maryland, which met in 1635, insisted on the right to pass its own laws and to organize itself along lines similar to those of the House of Commons in England. Baltimore tactfully yielded to these demands, and the Maryland assembly became a real legislature.

Despite the Calvert family's high hopes for Maryland as a religious refuge, Catholics numbered less than one fourth the population before the colony was ten years old. Moreover, when Calvert, in 1640, instituted a headright system similar to Virginia's in an effort to attract new settlers, he succeeded only too well. Most persons who came were Protestant, and they resented the political power wielded by Baltimore's appointees, almost all of whom were Catholic. By the end of the century, Protestants outnumbered Catholics ten to one. To protect the Roman Catholic minority from the very sort of persecution that they had come to Maryland to escape, Baltimore persuaded the assembly to pass a Toleration Act in 1649. It read: "No person in this province professing the belief in Jesus Christ shall be in any ways troubled . . . for his or her religion." However, by excluding non-Christians, and by providing the death penalty for persons guilty of blasphemy against any part of the Trinity, Maryland somewhat diminished its claim to a special spirit of tolerance.

The Toleration Act failed, in any event, to appease the large numbers of Protestants and Puritans in Maryland. Baltimore feared the loss of his colony after the Puritan triumph in England and appointed a Protestant governor in 1652. But strife between Baltimore and his Protestant colonists continued for much of the century. The Protestant assembly was continually at odds with proprietary officials, and violence between Catholic and Protestant settlers was common. In sum, although tobacco made Maryland an economic success, the colony did not develop as George Calvert had intended it to. It was difficult to maintain feudal privileges in an environment where land was so much more plentiful than labor, and it was equally difficult to afford special protections to Catholics when they were so vastly outnumbered. As a result, both tenantry on proprietary lands and religion remained volatile issues in Maryland for the rest of the colonial period.

Another Kind of South

Between 1641 and 1660, there was a hiatus in the English colonization of America, while the people of England attempted to sort out the political and religious consequences of socioeconomic change. When the dust had settled and Charles II was restored to the throne in 1660, English interest in America renewed in dramatic fashion. Charles owed debts of gratitude and money to the men who had helped him regain his kingdom. To repay these debts, he began to distribute American land to his creditors. As a result, the pattern of colonization that emerged in the aftermath of the Restoration was like that in Maryland, rather than in Virginia and Massachusetts. Settlement and conquest were undertaken, not by joint-stock companies or by the crown, but by individuals or groups of individuals, called proprietors. The King granted huge tracts of American land to these men, and they possessed distinct feudal privileges.

The first of these new proprietary colonies was located in a vast stretch of land between Virginia and Spanish Florida. The group of royalist leaders to whom Charles granted the land in 1663 intended to foster a prosperous trade in silk, wine, ginger, rice, and indigo. The leader of the group who founded the colony (named Carolina after Charles' wife, Queen Caroline) was Sir John Colleton. A royalist, Colleton had fled from England when Charles I was beheaded in 1649. Colleton had gone to the West Indian island of Barbados, where he found a large group of English planters who had become increasingly reliant upon slave labor to grow and market sugar. Since Barbados was already overcrowded, Colleton hoped to attract enterprising Barbadians to the abundant Carolina land.

Colleton and the other proprietors immediately set out to populate their colony. Like other promoters of American colonies, they advertised. They published *A Brief Description* of the province with a map setting forth "the Healthfulness of the Air, the Fertility of the Earth and Waters, and the great Pleasure and Profit that will accrue to those that shall go thither to enjoy the same." Slowly at first, and then in increasing numbers, settlers from Barbados, as well as from Virginia, New England, England, Scotland, Ireland, France, and Germany were attracted to the colony. By 1700, it had an extremely diverse population of more than 50,000.

One of the distinctive features of the Carolina venture was an extraordinary plan of government and settlement called the "Fundamental Constitutions of Carolina," which was drafted by one of the proprietors, Anthony Ashley Cooper (Earl of Shaftesbury), and his secretary, John Locke. The Constitutions sought to create a feudal order with an elaborately defined social structure and a parallel system of manorial courts. For the first time in the history of English colonization, the Fundamental Constitutions also explicitly recognized and legitimized black slavery. However, except for slavery (to which few white colonists would object), this archaic and inflexible system of government and society could never be enforced. Yet the Fundamental Constitutions also permitted religious freedom and established a representative assembly. Settlers who came to the colony simply ignored the archaic provisions of the Fundamental Constitutions and took advantage of its more liberal provisions. Like Calvert in Maryland, the Carolina proprietors had a very specific notion of the sort of society that they wished to create. The outcome was quite different from what they had expected, because they faced a heterogeneous and land-hungry population represented by an aggressive assembly. This assembly would tolerate no limitations on its privileges and even succeeded in expanding its powers.

The Carolina grant was huge; naturally, the settlers were widely dispersed. There were two major clusters of population. One was located on Albemarle Sound, in what is now North Carolina, while the other centered around what is today Charleston, South Carolina. The two enclaves were 300 miles apart, and they went their own ways. The settlers in the North grew tobacco, traded with the Indians, and supplied naval stores to the shipbuilders of old and New England. The Southerners discovered (with the help of the Africans whom they held as slaves) that rice grew well in the rich and moist soil. In time, the wealth generated by the trade in rice, indigo, and slaves enabled Charleston to become the only important city in the colonial South and one of the most cosmopolitan cities in the entire hemisphere.

Relations between the Carolinians and the Indian tribes of the region were extraordinarily complex. The proprietors forbade the colonists to trade with the Indians. (The proprietors hoped to avoid unnecessary warfare and, not incidentally, to secure the most lucrative segment of the trade for themselves.) Like their other plans, this one ran afoul of settlers who wanted a piece of the trading pie or who wanted to establish plantations on Indian lands. The settlers managed to turn one local group of Savannah Indians against the Westos, who were allied with the proprietors. By 1683, with the Savannahs acting as surrogates for the whites, the Westos had been all but wiped out. Later, the colonists would turn the Catawbas against the Savannahs in a similar strategy. In addition, the whites used their Indian allies to conquer still other groups of Indians, whom they frequently sold into slavery. It was a cruel policy that depended upon treachery of many kinds, and it left the Indians of the Carolinas exterminated, enslaved, or utterly dependent upon the invading whites. In this, as in other things, the plans of the proprietors had results that these would-be feudal lords did not desire and could not anticipate.

The Conquest of New York

While the Carolina proprietors were making plans for a feudal regime in the South, Charles II and his brother, James, Duke of York, cast their eyes northward to the still struggling Dutch colony of New Netherland. With a splendid harbor at New Amsterdam and a great river flowing from the heart of the fur country, the Dutch province enjoyed perhaps the best location on the entire Atlantic coast. Agriculture and overseas commerce should both have thrived there, but the Dutch had done very little to attract settlers from their own nation. Unlike the English, with their intricate plans for new societies, the Dutch cared only for the profits of the fur trade; settlement did not interest them much.

By the middle of the century, the colony was populated by a strange mixture of people: Dutch fur traders in Albany and among the Iroquois, merchants of several nations in New Amsterdam, some Spanish and Portuguese Jews, Puritan farmers who had moved westward and southward from Connecticut into the Hudson River Valley and on to Long Island, and a variety of other groups, including some African slaves. Most of these people cared little for the rule of the Dutch West India Company and its autocratic governors. On Long Island, towns settled by Puritans from Connecticut enjoyed virtual independence from the company, and lines of authority were everywhere as vague as they were weak. In addition, with the exception of the Iroquois, relations with the Indians were not good. In the Hudson River Valley, things were so bad that the settlers had to flee to New Amsterdam in the mid-1650s when the Indians sought retribution for three decades of Dutch brutality. New Amsterdam itself was almost overrun. In short, the Dutch had not exploited the advantages that location offered. The English hoped to do better.

The Dutch and English nations were intense commercial rivals, and the English were only too aware of the weakness of New Netherland. In 1664, England was on the brink of one of its periodic commercial wars with Holland, and Charles quietly granted to James all the land between the Connecticut and Delaware rivers. No one informed the Dutch of this transfer until a British fleet appeared in the harbor and issued a curt summons for the surrender of the fort at the foot of Manhattan Island. Governor Peter Stuyvesant, surprised by this demand, stormed, fumed, and declared that he would never surrender, but he had no choice. The leading citizens, knowing that resistance was hopeless, finally persuaded him to yield, and New Netherland fell without a shot. The Duke of York, now the proprietor, renamed the colony New York.

For a very long time, the English did not do much better than the Dutch on the banks of the Hudson. The surrender changed very little. The Dutch settlers were permitted to keep their property, and, because James was hardly an admirer of representative assemblies, he attempted to govern the province directly through a governor without seeking the advice of the inhabitants. English colonists already in New York protested against this arrangement, and potential immigrants saw no reason to go to a colony where they would have no say in the government and where the feudal privileges of the patroonship system would be maintained on a series of manors in the Hudson Valley. In 1683, James finally yielded to pressure from the residents and permitted an assembly to meet; however, when he became King James II, two years later, he revoked the concession. If the Carolinas ultimately prospered because the proprietors were too weak to impose the restrictions embodied in the Fundamental Constitutions, New York failed to do so because James succeeded too well in ignoring the needs and desires of the colonists.

There were other problems in New York. As a conquered people, the Dutch were antipathetic to English rule and resentful because they had been displaced from positions of social and economic prestige. As a result, ethnic antagonism was a significant factor in the social life of New York from the beginning. Dutch merchants in New York and Dutch fur traders in Albany continued to regard the English with a suspicion bordering on contempt, and the feeling was reciprocated. In addition, New York's semifeudal land arrangements not only drove new settlers away; they also antagonized the people already there. New York also had a growing population of black slaves, and Indian relations remained very sensitive and volatile. In general, the colony was characterized by a disruptive and bewildering pluralism of religious, racial, and ethnic groups. New York's most serious problem was, in the words of one Englishman, "too great a mixture of nations."

Proprietary New Jersey

The Duke of York gave the lower part of his province between the Delaware River and the Atlantic Ocean to two friends, Lord John Berkeley and Sir George Carteret. Since the latter had served as governor of the island of Jersey in the English Channel, the province was named New Jersey in his honor. Both men were part of the proprietary group then attempting to establish Carolina, and they had similar hopes for New Jersey. What they did not know, however, was that James' first governor of New York, Richard Nicolls, had already given part of their northern colony to a group of Puritan settlers from New York. Berkeley and Carteret proceeded to dole out some of the same lands to other people. The result was a confusion about land titles that was a persistent problem for New Jersey.

The new proprietors immediately published a liberal constitution which granted religious liberty and created a popular assembly with control of taxation. Both measures were designed to bring settlers into the colony. The proprietors divided their province into East Jersey (Carteret's) and West Jersey (Berkeley's). The governors of New York constantly disputed their right to establish a government, and the settlers (many of them Puritans accustomed to owning their own land) resisted their attempts to collect rents. Both proprietors grew tired of the strife and finally sold their claims in 1674 and 1682. West Jersey went to members of the Society of Friends, or Quakers. Among them was William Penn, who would soon have a colony of his own. The West Jersey group established a tolerant constitution called the "West Jersey Concessions and Agreements." Meanwhile, East Jersey passed into the hands of a group of Anglican land speculators. In both areas, Puritans were numerous, and Puritans loved neither Quakers nor Anglicans. In addition, the population of New Jersey was almost as diverse as that of New York. This heterogeneity, along with the chaotic state of land titles, made New Jersey one of the most unstable of all the colonies.

East and West Jersey were united into a single royal colony in 1702. For the next thirty-six years, it had the same governor as New York but elected its own legislature and courts. Apart from its tumultuous political life, New Jersey never acquired a distinct character of its own. East Jersey lived within the orbit, and often under the influence, of New York. West Jersey found itself similarly affected by events and personalities in the last of the proprietary colonies to be founded in the seventeenth century—Pennsylvania.

William Penn's Holy Experiment

Many English colonies were founded in a spirit of renewal and idealism, but in none were these traits more apparent than in Pennsylvania. In virtually every

Scene in a Quaker meeting house. Allowed to shape their own laws, Quakers were determined that no one "be compelled to frequent or maintain any religious worship, place, or ministry contrary to his or their mind, or to do or suffer any other act or things contrary to their religious persuasion." (Courtesy, Museum of Fine Arts, Boston, M. & M. Karolik Collection)

aspect — from government to religion to Indian affairs — the colony exemplified some of the highest aspirations of the age. The founder of the settlement was, of course, William Penn, a young friend of Charles II, and the story of the colony's early years is also his personal story.

While a student at Oxford, Penn was converted to the beliefs of the Society of Friends, one of the most radical offshoots of the religious ferment that had been sweeping England since the late sixteenth century. The Quakers rejected all ceremonies of religious worship and all authority of priests, bishops, or ministers. They obeyed only the "inner light" of conscience. They believed in complete equality and would not bow or kneel or remove their hats, even in the presence of the King's officials. Not only did they profess brotherly love, as did all Christians; they also attempted to practice it by refusing to take part in wars.

Penn adopted all these beliefs with great fervor. Neither the anger of his father, Admiral William Penn, nor imprisonment by the state could make him abandon them. William Penn, Jr.'s, famous paper, "The Great Case of Liberty of Conscience," was written in jail. On his release, Penn traveled as a missionary in Holland and Germany, where he organized Quaker societies.

Through it all, Penn maintained his friendship with Charles II, and it was probably this personal tie that led the King to discharge his debt of £16,000 to the elder Penn by granting the son a huge tract of land in America. There Penn planned to establish a shelter for the persecuted Quakers. In 1681, he received a royal charter that made him the proprietor of a territory roughly corresponding to the present state of Pennsylvania. Penn called the area "Sylvania" (Woodland), but the King insisted on adding "Penn" as a prefix in honor of the old Admiral. From the outset, Penn was embroiled in border controversies with the Calvert family over the boundary between Pennsylvania and Maryland. The dispute was not settled until 1764–1767, when two English surveyors, Charles Mason and Jeremiah Dixon, ran the present line at 39° 43′ 26″ northern latitude.

In 1682, Penn persuaded the Duke of York to cede him the land on the Delaware that the Dutch had seized from the Swedes many years before. He governed the territory as the "Three Lower Counties" through a deputy until 1702. It remained part of the proprietary domain of the Penn family, under the authority of Pennsylvania's governor, until the American Revolution, when it became the state of Delaware.

Like the Puritans, Penn proposed to conduct a "holy experiment" which would provide a model of amity and harmony for all humankind. Unlike Massachusetts, Pennsylvania was to be an experiment in religious liberty as well as in Christian living. Penn welcomed people of all nationalities and tolerated all creeds. In addition, at a time when scores of offenses were punished by death in England, Penn's "Great Law" made murder and treason the only capital crimes in the colony. The criminal law of Pennsylvania was, as a consequence, probably the most liberal in the western world. Later, after Penn's death in 1718, this policy would change, since it had the unfortunate effect of attracting lawbreakers to the colony; however, it was nonetheless a tribute to Penn's humanitarianism.

Penn's idealism extended to other areas as well. Only Roger Williams was Penn's equal in his careful relations with the Indians. Penn learned the language of the Delawares, the most important tribe in the area; he granted no land to whites that had not first been purchased from the natives; and he treated them with a respect that was unheard of among other Europeans. The Delawares, like all the coastal tribes, had already suffered serious depopulation as a result of smallpox and other European diseases, but Penn made every effort to treat them with scrupulous justice and did his best to protect them from the rapacious land hunger of white settlers. In the end, Pennsylvania would have its Indian troubles because its white population could be neither contained nor controlled in the rush for good farmland. Penn's idealism simply postponed the conquest of the Delawares and the other local tribes.

Penn was an aristocrat and made no effort to prohibit slavery. For many years it flourished in Pennsylvania, where there was a substantial black population, as in neighboring New Jersey and New York. But Quaker humanitarianism could not long tolerate so oppressive an institution. In the eighteenth century, Quakers led the early attempts to abolish slavery, and Quaker meetings expelled members who continued to hold other human beings in permanent bondage.

Quaker idealism also showed itself in Penn's political plans. He was no democrat in political matters, and he never doubted that some men were fit to rule while others were not. His first Frame of Government (1682) established a

COLONIAL SOCIETY

*. . . the eies of all people are
uppon us; soe that if wee
shall deal falsely with our
god in this worke wee have
undertaken and soe cause
him to withdrawe his present
help from us, wee shall be
made a story and a by-word
through the world, wee shall
open the mouthes of enemies
to speake evill of the wayes
of god and all professours for
Gods sake; wee shall shame
the faces of many of gods
worthy servants, and cause
theire prayers to be turned
into Cursses upon us till wee
be consumed out of the
good land whither wee are
goeing.*
John Winthrop, 1630. From
Edmund S. Morgan, The Puritan
Dilemma, *Little, Brown and Co.,
1958.*

John Winthrop, first governor of
Massachusetts Bay colony. (Courtesy
of the American Antiquarian
Society)

Frontispiece for Part Two of Saducismus Triumphatus, or a Full and Plain Evidence concerning Witches and Apparitions, by Joseph Glanvill, London, 1726. (Rare Book Division, The New York Public Library, Astor, Lenox and Tilden Foundations)

If any Man or Woman after legal conviction shall Have or Worship any other God but the Lord God, he shal be put to death. *Deu.* **13-6.17, 21.** *Ex.* **22.2.**
2. If any person within this Colony shall Blaspheme the Name of God the Father, Son or Holy Ghost, with dirct, express, presumptuous or high-handed Blasphemy, or shall Curse in the like manner, he shall be put to death, *Levit.* **24. 15, 16.**
3. If any Man or Woman be a Witch, that is, hath or consulteth with a Familiar Spirit, they shall be put to death, *Exo.* **22. 18.** *Lev.* **20. 27.** *Deu.* **18. 10. 11.**
From The Laws of Connecti *1673.*

O the horrid Suggestions that Satan has, Day after Day, follow'ed me with! He has endeavoured to cast a Cloud over all the Manifestations I have had of the Divine Favour . . . Satan had the Impudence, in the midst of my Prayers this Day, to suggest to me, that I was not one of God's Elect and therefore my Prayers were an Abomination. He is generally so busy with me in Prayer, that my Time is chiefly spent in keeping him off; so that I am often Three Hours about those Intercessions, which might otherwise be offered in one Sixth Part of that Space.
From William Seward, Journal of a Voyage from Savannah to Philadelphia and from Philadelphia to England, J. Oswald, London, 1740.

Religious zeal too, like smothered fire, is secretly burning in the hearts of the different sectaries that inhabit them [the colonies], and were it not restrained by laws and superior authority, would soon burst out into a flame of universal persecution. Even the peaceable Quakers struggle hard for pre-eminence, and evince in a very striking manner, that passions of mankind are much stronger than any principles of religion.
From Travels Through the Middle Settlements in North America in the Years 1759 and 1760 with Observations upon the State of the Colonies, *by the Reverend Andrew Burnaby, Vicar of Greenwich, England.*

Our conversation run chiefly upon religion. He gave me a short account of the spirit of enthusiasim that had lately poss[ess]ed the inhabitants of the forrests there [Maryland] and informed me that it had been a common practise for companys of 20 or 30 hair brained fanaticks to ride thro' the woods singing of psalms.

Dr. Alexander Hamilton, colonial physician. From his work Hamilton's Itinerarium, being a Narritive of a Journey . . . from May to September, 1744, ed. by Albert Bushnell Hart, 1907.

George Whitefield preaching, 1742, by John Wollaston. (National Portrait Gallery, London)

He [George Whitefield] had a loud and clear voice, and articulated his words and sentences so perfectly, that he might be heard and understood at a great distance, especially as his auditories, however numerous, observ'd the most exact silence. He preach'd one evening from the top of the Court-house steps, which are in the middle of Market-street, and on the west side of Second-street, which crosses it at right angles. Both streets were fill'd with his hearers to a considerable distance. Being among the hindmost in Market-street, I had the curiosity to learn how far he could be heard, by retiring backwards down the street towards the river; and I found his voice distinct till I came near Front-street, when some noise in that street obscur'd it. Imagining then a semicircle, of which my distance should be the radius, and that it were fill'd with auditors, to each of whom I allow'd two square feet, I computed that he might well be heard by more than thirty thousand. This reconcil'd me to the newspaper accounts of his having preach'd to twenty-five thousand people in the fields, and to the antient histories of generals haranguing whole armies, of which I had sometimes doubted. . . .

I happened soon after to attend one of his sermons, in the course of which I perceived he intended to finish with a collection, and I silently resolved he should get nothing from me. I had in my pocket a handful of copper money, three or four silver dollars, and five pistoles in gold. As he proceeded I began to soften, and concluded to give the coppers. Another stroke of his oratory made me ashamed of that, and determined me to give the silver. And he finished so admirably that I emptied my pocket wholly into the collector's dish, gold and all.

From The Life of Benjamin Franklin, Written by Himself, *1739.*

The Great God commands thee to love her, How vile then are those who don't love their Wives. . . . This duty of love is mutual, it should be performed by each, to each of them. They should endeavour to have their affections really, cordially and closely knit, to each other. If therefore the *Husband* is bitter against his wife, beating or striking of her (as some vile wretches do) or in any unkind carriage, ill language, hard words, morose, peevish, surly behaviour; nay if he is not kind, loving, tender in his words and carriage to her; he then shames his profession of Christianity, he breaks the Divine Law, he dishonours God.

From The Well-Ordered Family, *by Benjamin Wadsworth, 1712.*

Mrs. Elizabeth Clarke Freake and baby Mary, 1674. (Worcester Art Museum)

Oct. 30, [1713] Sam. and his Wife dine here, go home together in the Calash. William Ilsly rode and pass'd by them. My son warn'd him not to lodge at his house; Daughter said she had as much to doe with the house as he. Ilsly lodged there.

From Samuel Sewall, "Diary," as quoted in Edmund S. Morgan, The Puritan Family, Harper, 1944.

MY DEARE WIFE, — *Thy sweet Lettres . . . how welcome they were to me I canot expresse: both in regard of the continuance of thy health & thy little ones, my mother & o^r whole familye, for wch I humbly blesse & prayse o^r good God & Heavenly father, & doe heartyly begge of him & trust in him for the continuance of the same mercie to thyselfe & all the rest: as also in respect of the manifestation of the constancie & increase of thy true love wherein (I seariously professe) I doe more reioyce then in any earthly blessinge: O how I prize the sweet societye of so modest & faithfull a spouse! O that I could be wise to be thankfull & improve it, according to that esteeme wch I have of it when I want it! I am heere where I have all outward content, most kinde entertainment, good companye & good fare, &c: onely the want of thy presence & amiable society makes me weary of all other accomplem^{ts}, so deare is thy love to me, & so confident am I of the like entertainem^t my true affection findes wth thee: O that the consideration of these things could make us raise up o^r spirits to a like conformitye of sinceritye & fervencie in the Love of Christ o^r Lord & heavenly husband; that we could delight in him as we doe in each other, & that his absence were like greivous to us. . . . Thus embracinge thee in the true affection of a faithful husband, I will so remain Thine*

JOHN WINTHROP.

I have nothinge to send thee but my love, neither shall I bringe thee anythinge but my selfe, wch I knowe wilbe best welcome.

From Some Old Puritan Love Letters: John and Margaret Winthrop, *1618–1638, ed. by John Hopkins Twichell, New York, 1894.*

Simon Bradstreet (husband of Anne Bradstreet), Governor of Massachusetts, 1679–86, 1689–92. Engraving by H. W. Smith from a painting in the Senate chamber of the State House, Massachusetts. (Historical Pictures Service, Inc., Chicago)

MOST DEARE AND LOVEINGE HUSBAND, —I can not expres my love to you as I desire. in these poore livelesse lines, but I doe hartily wish you did see my harte how true and faythfull it is to you, and how much I doe desire to be allwayes with you. to injoy the sweet comfort of your presence. and those helps from you in sperituall and temperall dutyes wch I am so unfite to performe without you. It makes me to see the want of you and wish my selfe with you, but I desire wee may be gided by God in all our wayes who is able to derect us for the best and so I will wayt upon him with pacience who is all sufficient for me. I shall not need to right much to you at this time. My brother Goslinge can tel you any thinge by word of mouth, I prayse God we are all heare in health as you left us, and are glad to heare the same of you and all the rest of our frends at London. My mother and my selfe remember our best love to you and all the rest. our children remember theare duty to you. and thus desirnge to be remembred in your prayers I bid my good Husband god-night, littell Samerwell [Samuel] thinkes it is time for me to goe to bed, and so I beseech the Lord to keepe you in safety and us all heare. Farwell, my sweete husband.

Your obediente wife

Margaret Winthrope.

From Some Old Puritan Love Letters: John and Margaret Winthrop, *1618–1638, ed. by John Hopkins Twichell, New York, 1894.*

To My Dear Loving Husband

If ever two were one, then surely we.
If ever man were lov'd by wife, then thee;
If ever wife was happy in a man,
Compare with me ye women if you can.
I prize thy love more than whole mines of gold.
Or all the riches that the East doth hold.
My love is such that rivers cannot quench,
Nor aught but love from thee, give recompence.
Thy love is such I can no way repay,
The heavens reward thee manifold, I pray!
Then while we live, in love lets go persever,
That when we live no longer, we may live ever.

Anne Bradstreet, 1650. From Works of Anne Bradstreet, *ed. by John H. Ellis, Massachusetts, 1867.*

Undutiful Children soon become horrible Creatures, for Unchastity, for Dishonesty, for Lying, and all manner of Abominations ... Mind the most Scandalous Instances of Wickedness and Villainy; You'll ordinarily find, they were first Undutiful Children, before they fell into the rest of their atrocious Wickedness ... Yea, an Early Death, and a Woeful Death, is not seldom the Curse of God upon Undutiful Children.
From A Family Well Ordered, *by Cotton Mather, 1699.*

Their Hearts naturally, are a meer nest, root, fountain of Sin, and wickedness; and *evil Treasure* from whence proceed *evil things,* viz. *Evil Thoughts, Murders, Adulteries &c.* In deed, as sharers in the guilt of *Adam's* first Sin, they're *Children of Wrath by Nature,* liable to Eternal Vengeance, the Unquencheable Flames of Hell. But besides this, their Hearts (as hath been said) are unspeakably wicked, estrang'd from God, enmity against Him, eagerly set in pursuing Vanities, on provoking God by actual Personal transgressions, whereby they merit and deserve *greater measures* of Wrath.
From A Course of Sermons on Early Piety, *by Benjamin Wadsworth, 1702.*

Forgive me dearest Lord for Thy dear Son
The many ills that I this day have done,
Teach me to live that I may ever dread
The Grave, as little as I do my Bed.
Keep me this night, O keep me King of Kings
Secure under thy own Almighty Wings.
Evening prayer for children, *c.* **1755.**

From John Taylor, Verbum Sempiternum, The Third Edition with Amendments, *as quoted in Monica Kiefer,* American Children Through Their Books, *University of Pennsylvania Press, 1948.*

The Word Written and Preacht is the ordinary Medium of Conversion and Sanctification. Now in order to obtaining these Benefits by the Word, it is requisite, that Persons be diligent in *Reading and Hearing* of it; And in order to these, how expedient and necessary is it, that there be Schools of Learning; those of a Lower Character, for the instructing of Youth in Reading, and those of an Higher, for the more Liberal Education of such, as may be devoted to the Work of the Ministry?
From Cleansing Our Way in Youth, *by Thomas Foxcraft, 1719.*

She is a godly young woman of special parts who was fallen into a sad infirmity the loss of her understanding and reason, ... by occasion of her giving herself wholly to reading and writing and had written many books ... if she had attended her household affairs, and such things as belong to women, and not gone out of her way to meddle with such things as are proper for men, whose minds are stonger, etc., she had kept her wits, and might have improved them usefully and honorably in the place God had set her.

John Winthrop about Governor Edward Hopkins' wife, 1645. From John Winthrop, The History of New England, *ed. by James Savage, Boston, 1853.*

... a serious, *virtuous*, and *industrious* Course of Life, being first provided for, it is further the Design of this College, to instruct and perfect the Youth in the learned Languages, and in the Arts of *reasoning* exactly, of *writing* correctly, and *speaking* eloquently; and in the Arts of *numbering* and *measuring*; of *Surveying* and *Navigation*, of *Geography* and *History*, of *Husbandry*, *Commerce* and *Government*, and in the Knowledge of *all Nature* in the *Heavens* above us, and in the *Air*, *Water* and *Earth* around us, and the various kinds of *Meteors*, *Stones*, *Mines* and *Minerals*, *Plants* and *Animals*, and of every Thing *useful* for the Comfort, the Convenience and Elegance of Life, in the chief *Manufactures* relating to any of these Things: And, finally, to lead them from the Study of Nature to the Knowledge of themselves, and of the God of Nature, and their Duty to him, themselves, and one another, and every Thing that can contribute to their true Happiness, both here and hereafter.
From an early advertisement for King's College, June 1754.

After God had carried us safe to *New-England*, and wee had builded our houses, provided necessaries for our liveli-hood, rear'd convenient places for Gods worship, and setled the Civill Government: One of the next things we longed for, and looked after was to advance *Learning* and perpetuate it to Posterity; dreading to leave an illiterate Ministery to the Churches, when our present Ministers shall lie in the Dust. And as wee were thinking and consulting how to effect this great Work; it pleased God to stir up the heart of one Mr. *Harvard* (a godly Gentleman and a lover of Learning, there living amongst us) to give the one halfe of his Estate (it being in all about 1700. 1.[£]) towards the erecting of a Colledge, and all his Library.
Anonymous. From New England's First Fruits, *1643.*

Top: Southeast view of New York City, showing King's (Columbia) College, c. 1763. (I. N. Phelps Stokes Collection, The New York Public Library)

Above: Old College, Harvard, built 1638–42. (Massachusetts Historical Society)

Douglass, the physician here [in Boston], is a man of good learning, but mischievously given to criticism, and the most compleat snarler I ever knew. He is loath to allow learning, merit, or a character to anybody. He is of the clinical class of physicians, and laughs at all theory and practise founded upon it, looking upon empiricism or bare experience as the only firm basis upon which practise ought to be founded. ... This man I esteem a notorious physical heretic, capable to corrupt and vitiate the practise of the place by spreading his erroneous doctrines among his shallow brethren.

From Hamilton, Hamilton's Itinerarium . . . 1744, *1907.*

Capon Ale ... [is] good for any who are in consumption, & it is restorative for any other weakness. ... Take an old Capon with yellow Leggs pull him and crush ye bones, but keep ye scin whole and then take an ounce of carraway seeds, and an ounce of anny seeds and two ounces of harts horne and one handful of rosemary tops, a piece or 2 of mace and a Leamon pill, Sow all these into ye bellie of your Capon & Chop him into hot mash or hot water and put him into two gallons of strong ale when it is working, after let it stand for two or three dayes & put a lump of sugar into every bottle wh will make it drink brisker.

From Martha Washington's Cookbook.

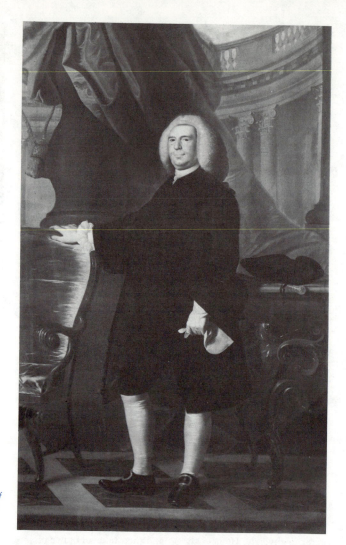

Portrait of Thomas Hancock, uncle of the patriot, by John Singleton Copley, painted 1764–66. (Courtesy of Harvard University)

Some gentlemen of Boston who have long served the government, because they have not the supplying of everything, have done all the mischief they could. Their substance ... enables them to distress and domineer. Without them, they say, we can't do and so must comply with what terms they think proper to impose. These are Messrs. Apthorp and Hancock, the two richest merchants in Boston—made so by the public money and now wanton in their insolent demands.

From a letter of Governor Cornwallis to the English Lords of Trade, November 1750.

The antediluvians were all very sober,
For they had no wine and they brewed no October;
All wicked, bad livers, on mischief still thinking,
For there can't be good living where there is not good drinking.
                                             Derry-down.

'Twas honest old Noah first planted the vine,
And mended his morals by drinking its wine;
And thenceforth justly the drinking of water decried;
For he knew that all mankind by drinking it died.
                                             Derry-down.

Benjamin Franklin, c. 1745. From Carl Van Doren, Benjamin Franklin, *Viking Press, New York, 1938.*

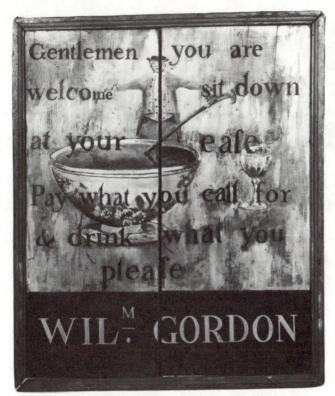

The people of New York at the first appearance of a stranger, are seemingly civil and courteous, but this civility and complaisance soon relaxes if he be not either highly recommended or a good toaper. To drink stoutly with the Hungarian Club, who are all bumper men, is the readiest way for a stranger to recommend himself, and a set among them are very fond of making a stranger drunk. To talk bawdy and to have a knack at punning passes among some there for good sterling wit. Governour Clinton himself is a jolly toaper and gives good example, and for that one quality is esteemed among these Dons.

From Hamilton, Hamilton's Itinerarium . . . 1744, *1907.*

"A Prospective View of Part of the (Boston) Commons," 1768, engraved after a watercolor by Christian Remick. (Concord Antiquarian Museum, Concord, Mass.)

What they call the Mall is a walk on a fine green Common adjoining to the south-west side of the town. It is near half a mile over, with two rows of young trees planted opposite to each other, with a fine footway between, in imitation of St. James's Park; and part of the bay of the sea which encircles the town, taking its course along the north-west side of the Common,—by which it is bounded on the one side, and by the country on the other, — forms a beautiful canal, in view of the walk.... Both the ladies and gentlemen dress and appear as gay, in common, as courtiers in England on a coronation or birthday. And the ladies here visit, drink tea, and indulge every little piece of gentility, to the height of the mode; and neglect the affairs of their families with as good a grace as the finest ladies in London.

From an account by Joseph Bennett of his travels in New England, 1740.

March 6. This day was to have been spent with Thomas Loughton Smith Esqr. at his country seat. Bad weather prevents, and I take what is called a family dinner with him. A prodigious fine pudding made of what they call rice flour. Nicknacks brought on table after removal of meats. Ladies ask the gentlemen to drink a glass of wine with them: Upon a gentleman's asking a lady to do the like, she replies "G — bless you, I thought you never would ask. I have been waiting for you this half hour."

First toast, Our Boston friend and your good health. Sir: the unmarried lady (of nineteen) at my right, "your good health and best affections Sir!" Miss —— your toast, madam. "Love and friendship and they who feel them!" Toasts called for from the guests, etc., till coffee, etc. Mr. Smith's house furniture, pictures, plate etc. very elegant—wines very fine.

An account of his visit to Charleston, South Carolina, by Josiah Quincy, Jr., 1773. From Josiah Quincy, Memoirs of the life of Josiah Quincy, jun., of Mass.; by his son, Josiah Quincy, Boston, 1825.

The lower ferry of the Susquehanna, which I crossed is above a mile broad. It is kept by a little old man whom I found att vittles with his wife and family upon a homely dish of fish without any kind of sauce. They desired me to eat, but I told them I had no stomach. They had no cloth upon the table, and their mess was in a dirty, deep wooden dish which they evacuated with their hands, cramming down skins, scales, and all. They used neither knife, fork, spoon, plate, or napkin because, I suppose, they had none to use. I looked upon this as a picture of that primitive simplicity practiced by our forefathers long before the mechanic arts had supplied them with instruments for the luxury and elegance of life.

From Hamilton, Hamilton's Itinerarium . . . 1744, *1907.*

On special occasions a dinner or supper was given, and of one of these feasts the story has been handed down. The occasion was the surrender of Cornwallis; the giver was a stanch patriot and captain in the New York line, Cornelius Dubois; the place was his stone cottage on the right bank of the Catskill, near its mouth; the time was a Sunday afternoon, late in the autumn of 1781, after the chickens and the turkeys had been fattened, the hams cured, and the cider ripened. The house was filled: the sitting-room above with the Whigs of the neighborhood the kitchen beneath with the uninvited but not unwelcome slaves of the yeomen. There was loud and hearty talking; there was fiddling by the negroes; there was a long table covered with savory food; there was an abundance of flip and toddy in *bockjes,* or wooden bowls. A prominent figure in the assembled company was the figure of a repentant Tory, who went about with a large pitcher of milk punch, asking each guest to drink with him to the final success of the American arms. The party broke up late; and it is said that a venerable elder of the united churches of Catskill and Coxsackie went home, for the first time in his life, in a state of unnatural exhilaration.

From "Old Catskill," Harper's New Monthly Magazine, *No. CCCLX, Vol. LX, (May, 1880), pp. 818–826.*

Dinner at Cornelius Dubois'.
Engraving by Howard Pyle, 1879, for
Harper's New Monthly Magazine.
(Historical Pictures Service, Inc.,
Chicago)

Half after eight we were rung in to Supper. The room looked luminous and splendid; four very large candles burning on the table where we supped; three others in different parts of the Room; a gay, sociable Assembly, & four well instructed waiters! —— So soon as we rose from supper, the Company formed into a semicircle round the fire.... Description in a journal kept by Philip Fithian, tutor to the children of Robert Carter, 1767–74. From Journal and letters of Philip Vickers Fithian, 1773–1774, a plantation tutor of the Old Dominion, ed. by Hunter Dickinson Farish, Williamsburg, 1943.

They [the Virginians] are immoderately fond of dancing, and indeed it is almost the only amusement they partake of: but even in this they discover great want to taste and elegance, and seldom appear with that gracefullness and ease, which these movements are so calculated to display. Towards the close of an evening, when the company are pretty well tired with country dances, it is usual to dance jiggs; a practice originally borrowed [,] I am informed, from the Negroes.... The ladies, excepting these amusements, and now and then a party of pleasure into the woods to partake of a barbacue, chiefly spend their time in sewing and taking care of their families: they seldom read, or endeavour to improve their minds.... *From Burnaby,* Travels Through the Middle Settlements. . ., in 1759.

Above: Detail from "An Old-Time Sewing-Room." From a color drawing by Anna Whelan Betts. (Historical Pictures Service, Inc., Chicago)

Top: Title page from Thompson's Compleat Collection of 200 Favourite Country Dances, *an 18th-century English dance manual. (John Carter Brown Library, Brown University)*

"The Bostonians Paying the Excise-Man, or Tarring and Feathering," 1774. (Courtesy of The New-York Historical Society, New York City)

Left: Page from the New England Primer showing George III, 1727 (Rare Book Division, The New York Public Library, Astor, Lenox and Tilden Foundations)

Unhappy Boston! see thy Sons deplore,
Thy hallow'd Walks besmear'd with guiltless Gore:
While faithless P—n and his savage Bands,
With murd'rous Rancour stretch their bloody Hands;
Like fierce Barbarians grinning o'er their Prey,
Approve the Carnage, and enjoy the Day.

If scalding drops from Rage from Anguish Wrung
If speechless Sorrows lab'ring for a Tongue,
Or if a weeping World can ought appease
The plaintive Ghosts of Victims such as these;
The Patriot's copious Tears for each are shed,
A glorious Tribute which embalms the Dead.

But know, Fate summons to that awful Goal,
Where Justice strips the Murd'rer of his Soul:
Should venal C—ts the scandal of the Land,
Snatch the relentless Villain from her Hand.
Keen Execrations on this Plate inscrib'd,
Shall reach a Judge who never can be brib'd.

From a broadside about the Boston Massacre by Paul Revere, 1770.

**This bumper I crown for
our sovereign's health
And this for Britania's glory
and wealth;
That wealth and that glory
immortal may be,
If she is but just—and we
are but free.**

**In Freedom we're born, and
in freedom we'll live,
Our purses are ready,
Steady, friends, steady,
Not as slaves, but as freemen
our money we'll give.**

Anonymous, 1768.

Rouse, America! your danger is great,—great from a quarter where you least expect it. The Tories, the Tories will yet be the ruin of you! 'Tis high time they were separated from among you. They are now busy engaged in undermining your liberties. They have a thousand ways of doing it, and they make use of them all. Who were the occasion of this war? The Tories! Who persuaded the tyrant of Britain to prosecute it in a manner before unknown to civilized nations, and shocking even to barbarians? The Tories! Who prevailed on the savages of the wilderness to join the standard of the enemy? The Tories! Who have assisted the Indians in taking the scalp from the aged matron, the blooming fair one, the helpless infant and the dying hero? The Tories! Who advised and who assisted in burning your towns, ravaging your country and violating the chastity of your women? The Tories!... Who prevent your battalions from being filled? The Tories! Who dissade men from entering the army? The Tories! Who persuade those who have enlisted to desert? The Tories! Who harbor those who do desert? The Tories! In short, who wish to see us conquered, to see us slaves, to see us hewers of wood and drawers of water? The Tories!

From a Philadelphia newspaper, 1779.

"The Procession" and "The Tory's Day of Judgment," engravings by E. Tisdale from the first illustrated edition of John Trumbull's M'Fingal, *a burlesque on the Loyalists, 1795. (Rare Book Division, The New York Public Library, Astor, Lenox and Tilden Foundations)*

government composed of an appointed governor and council, who originated all laws. There was also an assembly, chosen only by those who owned property, but it was relatively powerless. Penn apparently believed that this sort of enlightened government would attract relatively little opposition. He was wrong in that judgment, for, over the years, the Pennsylvania assembly proved to be one of the most assertive of all the colonial legislatures. It slowly eroded the power of the proprietor and his governors and correspondingly increased its own.

However, Pennsylvania's early history was not characterized by disappointed ideals. Penn showed considerable skill at the business of attracting settlers. He advertised his province in attractive pamphlets, distributed both in England and on the Continent, in which he offered land for sale on easy terms and for rent as low as a penny an acre. Although sincere in his convictions, Penn exploited the obvious attraction of the colony's liberal constitution to potential settlers. He came to America himself in 1682 and laid out the town of Philadelphia. By the end of the seventeenth century, Pennsylvania was the largest and most prosperous colony in America, and it continued to attract more immigrants than any other colony because of its reputation as the "Best Poor Man's Country." Equally important—although the politics of the colony were often acrimonious—the ethnic tensions that were so divisive in the other Middle Colonies (New York and New Jersey) seem only rarely to have been present in Pennsylvania. Yet it had a polyglot population of French, German, Swedish, Dutch, Welsh, and English settlers, all of whom made their homes there in relative peace and harmony.

The English Colonies Established

The establishment of Pennsylvania marked the culmination of the first phase of the conquest and colonization of English North America. As we have seen, there were many differences among the various colonies. Some, like those in New England and Pennsylvania, had been founded to achieve religious and idealistic purposes. Others, like Virginia, New Jersey, and New York, resulted from a desire to exploit the potential wealth of America; and still others, like Maryland and the Carolinas, were founded to fulfill a vision of social perfection and also for material gain. Nor were these the only disparities among the early settlements. Virginia and the New England colonies (except Rhode Island) were ethnically and religiously homogeneous, while the populations of the Carolinas, New York, New Jersey, and Pennsylvania were quite diverse, and settlers in Maryland were sharply divided along religious lines. Moreover, even in these early years, differences between the North and the South had already begun to emerge. Provinces in the South tended to rely upon a single staple crop—usually tobacco or rice—while those in the North were oriented toward more diversified agriculture and commerce.

The governments of the colonies varied as well. Virginia and Massachusetts had begun as the enterprises of trading companies; one had become a royal colony, while the other had been able to chart a relatively independent course. Maryland, the Carolinas, New Jersey, and Pennsylvania were proprietary colonies, theoretically controlled neither by the colonists nor by the King, but rather by private individuals. Yet the manner and extent of proprietary influence was quite unique in each of them. New York had the most peculiar history of all. It was begun by a Dutch trading company. It then became an English proprietary colony, and, then, when the proprietor became the King, was transformed into a royal colony.

These many differences among the colonies gave each one a peculiar character of its own. Yet all of the English colonists shared significant common experiences. All of them, for example, had to deal with the difficult problem of Indian relations. Although some colonizers, like Roger Williams and William Penn, hoped to treat the Indians justly, the presence of Englishmen in North America drastically altered and frequently destroyed the cultures of the coastal Indians. However, native Americans remained a vital factor in the development of all the colonies well into the eighteenth century. Similarly, all the colonists enslaved Africans, although such slavery was more important in some colonies than in others. From the very beginning of American history, therefore, race was a factor of considerable significance. In this, as in other respects, English colonists shared more in common among themselves than with their countrymen in England.

One general common characteristic of the colonies was that representative political institutions of some sort had not only emerged in all of them, but also exercised an important influence on the direction of provincial life. In some colonies, such institutions had been conceded to quiet the complaints of disgruntled inhabitants. In others, they had been created in an effort to attract new immigrants. Some of the assemblies were quite powerful; others were less so. Even so, they were everywhere regarded as a check upon arbitrary power and as instrumentalities through which colonists could achieve a measure of self-government.

Moreover, the major institutions of the English government—Parliament and the King—took little direct part in the founding of the colonies and made little effort to oversee their growth and development. This lack of centralized control and regulation partially accounted for the differences among the settlements, since no one in England was charged with insuring their uniformity. By the 1660s, leaders in the English government began to see the disadvantages of such a policy, and important changes (which we will discuss in the next chapter) were instituted. For much of the century, however, English colonization was haphazard and free from the imperial institutions and bureaucratic organization that were characteristic of New Spain. Over the long term, this early autonomy would have critical ramifications for the history of the American colonies.

The colonies were all alike in that they turned out differently from what their founders had expected them to be. Everyone responsible for these first settlements had seen in America an opportunity to create a world that would be quite literally "new,"—a world that would somehow be free of the constraining forces of history. To be sure, the sort of new world that the various colonizers hoped to create varied enormously from one group to another. However, all of them believed that, in America, they might exert some control over the social changes that were continuing to transform England even as colonization got under way. Whether the impulse to go to America came from the Virginia Company or from the Puritans, from William Penn or from the Carolina proprietors, America seemed to offer the chance to establish societies in which social change might, at the very least, be controlled and directed. And some of the most ambitious colonizers hoped to halt social change altogether by creating static and utopian worlds.

Everywhere, though, such hopes were frustrated by developments that the founders did not anticipate. The new American societies were, in some ways, even more unstable and fluid than the English one that had spawned them. The first colonists were correct in believing that they would create unique so· cieties in America, but they were wrong in predicting what the nature of those societies would be. In the last quarter of the seventeenth century, as Englishmen on both sides of the Atlantic came to appreciate and understand the effects of colonization, American society would undergo a crisis which simultaneously embodied the changes of the seventeenth century and pointed the way toward the equally dramatic transformations of the eighteenth.

SUGGESTED READINGS

As the first of the English colonies in North America, Virginia has properly occupied a central place in studies of early American history. The best general discussion of the colony is Wesley Frank Craven, *The Southern Colonies in the Seventeenth Century* (1949). Craven's slender, but critically important, volume, *White, Red, and Black: The Seventeenth Century Virginian* (1975), should be read in conjunction with Alden Vaughan, *American Genesis* (1975), and Edmund S. Morgan, *American Slavery, American Freedom* (1975). Philip Barbour's biographies, *The Three Worlds of Captain John Smith* (1964), and *Pocahontas and Her World* (1969), make pleasant reading. Frank G. Speck, *Chapters on the Ethnology of the Powhatan Tribes of Virginia* (1928), provides good background for the confrontation of white man and Indian in the Chesapeake area, while Ben C. McCrary, *Indians in Seventeenth-Century Virginia* (1957), describes that conflict. Morgan's volume on slavery and Abbot E. Smith, *Colonists in Bondage* (1947), provide the best introductions to black slavery and white servitude. However, the ideology of racism cannot be understood without reference to Winthrop Jordan's magnificent *White Over Black* (1968). Thomas J. Wertenbaker, *Virginia Under the Stuarts, 1607–1688* (1914), and Richard L. Morton, *Colonial Virginia: The Tidewater Period, 1607–1710* (1960), are both useful one-volume histories. A variety of specific topics in Virginia's early history receive careful discussion in Darrett B. Rutman, ed., *The Old Dominion: Essays for Thomas Perkins Abernethy* (1964).

The English background of Puritanism is a complex subject, but the essential lines of development may be gleaned from Patrick Collinson, *The Elizabethan Puritan Movement* (1967); William Haller, *The Rise of Puritanism* (1957); and Christopher Hill, *Society and Puritanism in Pre-Revolutionary England* (1969). Alan Simpson, *Puritanism in Old and New England* (1955), is an interesting attempt to deal with the comparative dimensions of Puritan thought.

John Demos, *A Little Commonwealth* (1970); George Langdon, *Pilgrim Colony* (1966); and Darrett B. Rutman, *Husbandmen of Plymouth* (1967), examine life in Plymouth, but they do not supersede William Bradford's own moving narrative, which is still the best history of the colony: *Of Plymouth Plantation*, Samuel Eliot Morison, ed. (1952). Edmund S. Morgan, *The Puritan Dilemma: The Story of John Winthrop* (1958), is the most informative and lively book on the Bay Colony's early years and the life of its most prominent citizen. Older interpretations like those of Brooks Adams, *The Emancipation of Massachusetts* (1886); James T. Adams, *The Founding of New England* (1921); Thomas J. Wertenbaker, *The Puritan Oligarchy* (1947); and Samuel Eliot Morison, *Builders of the Bay Colony* (1930), differ substantially in perspective, but can still be read with profit.

The study of New England Puritanism has been the single most active field in early American colonial studies. This is due almost entirely to the influence of Perry Miller, whose extraordinary distillations of New England life and thought remain the most brilliant corpus of work yet produced by an American historian. In particular, his *The New England Mind: From Colony to Province* (1953) reveals all the fascinating complexity of Puritan thought. However, Miller's superb collection of essays, *Errand Into the Wilderness* (1956), is also illuminating, as are his many other books and articles. Edmund S. Morgan, Miller's outstanding student, is responsible for a series of carefully conceived studies that no one interested in the Puritans should overlook. In addition to *The Puritan Dilemma*, his *Roger Williams* (1967), *Visible Saints* (1963), and *The Puritan Family* (1944) are all wonderfully written and succinct books. The leading critic of the approach of Miller and Morgan is Darrett Rutman, whose two books, *American Puritanism* (1970), and *Winthrop's Boston* (1965), provide a different methodological perspective and interpretive emphasis. In addition, various aspects of Puritanism's variant in the new world receive intelligent coverage in David D. Hall, *The Faithful Shepherd* (1972); Timothy H. Breen, *The Character of the Good Ruler* (1970); Stephen Foster, *Their Solitary Way* (1971); Robert Pope, *The Half-Way Covenant* (1969); and Sacvan Bercovitch, *The Puritan Origins of the American Self* (1975).

There is no good modern biography of Anne Hutchinson, but Emery Battis, *Saints and Sectaries* (1962), offers an arresting and controversial account of the Antinomian Crisis that emphasizes Hutchinson's psychological motives and social divisions within the colony. The social history of New England towns, which was almost unknown a generation ago, now occupies a central place in the historical literature. Among the best of the local studies are Kenneth A. Lockridge, *A New England Town* [Dedham] (1970); Philip J. Greven, Jr., *Four Generations* [Andover] (1970); and Sumner Chilton Powell, *Puritan Village* [Sudbury] (1963). Paul Boyer and Stephen Nissenbaum, *Salem Possessed* (1974), is a penetrating attempt to explain the witchcraft trials within the context of the town's social history.

Those interested in the economic and commercial development of New England should turn to Bernard Bailyn's perceptive book, *The New England Merchants in the Seventeenth Century* (1955). Two elegantly conceived histories of leading New England families shed light on the entire history of the region: Richard S. Dunn, *Puritans and Yankees* [the Winthrops] (1962), and Robert Middlekauff, *The Mathers* (1971). The best single-volume synthesis of American Puritanism (and one which takes advantage of recent, as well as more traditional interpretations) is Francis J. Bremer, *The Puritan Experiment* (1976).

No other colony has received the sort of attention that Virginia and Massachusetts have. In general, see the relevant sections of Charles M. Andrews, *The Colonial Period in American History*, Vols. I–III (1934–1937). Among the best histories of Connecticut are Mary J. A. Jones, *Congregational Commonwealth* (1968), and Paul R. Lucas, *Valley of Discord* (1976). Maryland's early years still await a modern book-length treatment, but Matthew P. Andrews, *The Founding of Maryland* (1933), and Newton D. Mereness, *Maryland as a Proprietary Province* (1932), both provide detailed narratives. The most exciting recent work on Maryland has appeared in article form. Some outstanding examples may be found in Aubrey C. Land, ed., *Law, Society, and Politics in Early Maryland* (1977). M. Eugene Sirmans, *Colonial South Carolina* (1966), is the best history of that colony, while Peter Wood, *Black Majority* (1974) highlights the contributions of African slaves to South Carolina culture and society.

Sidney V. James, *Colonial Rhode Island* (1975); Hugh T. Lefler and William S. Powell, *Colonial North Carolina* (1973); John E. Pomfret, *Colonial New Jersey* (1973); and Joseph Illick, *Colonial Pennsylvania* (1976), are all volumes in a superb series on the colonies edited by Milton M. Klein and Jacob E. Cooke. Each provides basic information in clear prose, as well as bibliographies for the colonies with which they are concerned. Michael Kammen, *Colonial New York* (1975), is in the same series, and is also the best one-volume history of any colony available. Owing to their social and political peculiarities, New York and Pennsylvania have each spawned a rather considerable body of scholarly work. Among the most useful recent contributions to Pennsylvania's early history are Edwin B. Bronner, *William Penn's Holy Experiment* (1962), and Mary Maples Dunn, *William Penn: Politics and Conscience* (1967). For New York's earliest years, see Thomas J. Condon, *New York Beginnings* 1968); Van Cleaf Bachman, *Peltries or Plantations* (1969); and George L. Smith, *Religion and Trade in New Netherland* (1973).

CHAPTER 3
IMPERIAL REFORM, SOCIAL CHANGE, AND THE CRISIS OF SEVENTEENTH-CENTURY COLONIAL SOCIETY

1. THE SEVENTEENTH-CENTURY ECONOMY

An English Empire

When Charles II returned in triumph to London in 1660, he also regained England's American colonies. He quickly discovered that his throne was more securely under his control than his empire. Virginia was the only royal colony. New England was ruled by the very Puritans who had beheaded his father, and Maryland belonged to the Catholic Calvert family. If this disparate collection of settlements could be called an empire at all, it was hardly one over which Charles could exert a ready and direct influence. Moreover, he had to give up additional lands to proprietors in New York, New Jersey, the Carolinas, and Pennsylvania in order to pay his huge debts.

Diffuse and varied though they were, the colonies were not independent entities that could completely ignore the mother country. The colonists were still subjects of the King and under Parliament's jurisdiction. True, the charters of trading companies, proprietors, and the so-called charter colonies (like Rhode Island and Connecticut) authorized them to make laws for the conduct of their own affairs. However, they had not been given such authority with any idea of freeing them from royal or parliamentary control. Nor was the colonists' authority complete. Their charters had precisely the same legal standing as those of any other English corporation: they could be amended or taken away as, indeed, they sometimes were. To be sure, the charters guaranteed that the settlers should enjoy all the rights of Englishmen. No one ever doubted that these included such basic protections as due process and the free enjoyment of private property. But the charters did not grant to the colonists exclusive control over their internal affairs; all the charters included the proviso that any legislation contrary to the laws of England was strictly prohibited.

The question of colonial home rule was confused throughout the seventeenth century by the long and bitter struggle between the Stuart Kings and Parliament for supremacy within the British constitutional system. The early Stuarts, James I and Charles I, were eager to encourage, though not to finance, settlement in America. As a result, they granted liberal charters to persons willing to undertake the costs of colonization. Yet the annulment of the Virginia Company's charter and the transformation of Virginia into a royal colony in 1624 were early signs that James did not intend to yield his prerogative in the new world. Charles I had so much political and religious trouble at home that he had little time for colonial affairs. It was during his turbulent reign that the American provinces began to go their own way. Parliament and the King were so busy fighting each other that they had little reason to be concerned about the affairs of a few colonists 3,000 miles across the Atlantic. In any event, America was generating too little wealth to attract the attention of men fighting a civil war which involved issues of transcendent importance.

However, things had changed by the time of the Restoration. An uneasy peace between the King and Parliament had been attained, and the potential of American wealth was far more alluring than it had ever been before. Unfortunately for Charles II, it was now too late to impose the sort of rigid and hierarchical controls on his empire that had enriched the Spanish Kings in the previous century. But some changes were within reach, and Charles took administrative action to strengthen his control. For example, in the very first year of his reign, he created a Council of Trade and a Council of Foreign Plantations to keep himself informed about the conduct of his distant subjects. Among the members of these two committees, which were combined in 1672 as the Joint Council of Trade and Foreign Plantations, were a number of the Carolina proprietors, including Colleton, Shaftesbury, Berkeley, and Carteret. John Locke was the secretary of the council, which the King used as a source of advice as well as information. Charles was thus not unmindful of the value of his American colonies. For example, when he granted William Penn a charter in 1681, he was careful to include a provision that laws enacted by the provincial legislature had to be sent to England every five years for approval.

However, it was Charles II's brother and successor, James II, who carried royal rule in America to its most extreme limits. James annulled the charters of all the New England colonies in 1686 and combined them into one unit—the Dominion of New England—to which New York and New Jersey were soon added. More important, James eliminated all local and provincial self-government and attempted to impose his own rule through a governor who acted as his personal representative.

These new imperial policies were part of a larger move by James to extend his personal rule at home. Neither effort succeeded. In the bloodless Glorious Revolution of 1688, the King's opponents in Parliament forced him into exile and instituted constitutional changes that eventually assured the supremacy of Parliament over the King. But parliamentary supremacy did not mean that the colonists thereafter enjoyed sovereignty over their own affairs. On the contrary, Parliament was too sensitive to its own recently acquired importance to let the colonies go their own way. Although it was many years before Parliament would devote much concerted attention to America, sporadic legislation gave evidence, time and again, that Parliament believed that it had the right to control the empire, even if it did not always seek to exercise that control.

A Mercantilist World

Charles and James did not seek closer regulation of the colonies simply to satisfy prideful political ambitions. On the contrary, the economic importance of the colonies was central to their thinking and to the calculations of all English policymakers in the period. Better political control of the colonies would mean greater economic efficiency and an expanded overseas commerce. Colonies were essential links in a commercial chain that would enrich England and permit it to dominate the Atlantic world.

This drive to make better economic use of the colonies derived its ideological underpinnings from the prevailing economic "philosophy" of the day—mercantilism. Although it was never formally articulated, this concept was used to justify the many conflicting policies that English merchants, as well as English Kings, found expedient to further their own ends. It was based on the premise that a country's wealth was to be measured by the amount of gold and silver in its coffers. National policies were, therefore, supposed to aim at favorable balances of trade in order to increase the national stock of bullion. Colonies were desirable because they would furnish the raw materials and staples that the mother country would otherwise have to purchase from rival states. Tobacco, furs, naval stores, indigo, rice, and sugar were such products for seventeenth-century England. The growing population of the colonies would not only supply an increasing trade in these raw materials to English merchants; the colonies would also provide a growing market for the goods manufactured by the home country. Accordingly, England and every other imperial power did everything possible to monopolize the trade of their colonies and to exclude foreign ships from that trade.

Economic regulation was, of course, accepted practice in late medieval Europe. The English government had attempted to restrict certain types of trade for centuries. The interloping of Dutch merchants in the tobacco trade in the 1630s and 1640s led Parliament to enact a series of navigation laws designed to strengthen the English merchant marine. A comprehensive Act of Navigation, passed in 1651, required that all goods shipped from the colonies to England or from one colony to another be carried in English (including colonial) bottoms. Moreover, all goods brought into England or the colonies had to be transported either in English vessels or on ships from the countries that produced the goods being imported. This provision was designed to eliminate Dutch vessels from English imperial trade. Following the Restoration, Parliament reenacted this statute in 1660 and 1661 and added a provision which stipulated that certain "enumerated" articles could be exported from the colonies only to England. The original list named, among others, sugar and tobacco. Rice was added in 1704, naval stores in 1705, and furs in 1722. The Staple Act of 1663 required that European goods which were destined for the colonies should first be landed at an English port for payment of customs duties. A measure adopted in 1672 added new safeguards against the shipment of articles on the enumerated list directly from colonial ports to Europe.

Increasingly stringent legislation was accompanied by the development of administrative machinery. The Joint Council of Trade and Foreign Plantations never had much coercive power. The first administrative body that seriously attempted to administer colonial affairs and enforce the Navigation Acts was the Lords of Trade, a committee of the Privy Council created in 1675. Under the enthusiastic leadership of its first secretary, William Balthwayt, the Lords of Trade proved to be a body with energy and vision. In 1696, it was reorganized, strengthened, and renamed the Board of Trade and Plantations. A Navigation Act in 1696 also strengthened the customs service. It authorized the establishment of special admiralty courts for the trial, without jury, of merchants accused of smuggling and other violations of the Navigation Acts.

The Lords of Trade, and then the Board of Trade, became extremely active in colonial administration after 1675. As advisers to the King, the Lords of Trade favored the centralization of the empire, supported the revocation of the charter of Massachusetts Bay, and attempted to prevent the bestowal of private proprietary charters. They succeeded in making New Hampshire a royal colony in 1679, but were unable to keep Charles II from awarding Pennsylvania to William Penn. During this period, a rudimentary imperial bureaucracy began to evolve. Colonial administrators favored strict enforcement of the acts of trade and even proposed the revocation of all colonial charters. By the early eighteenth century, however, most English politicians were more interested in English affairs than imperial matters. Many questions remained unresolved until the middle of the eighteenth century, when the colonies once again occupied a position of central importance in imperial policymaking.

Patterns of Economic Growth

The interest of empire-minded men in England in developing and exploiting the possibilities of American wealth late in the 1600s was no mere coincidence. There was more involved than the disappearance of the distractions that convulsed England's volatile political life before 1660. Equally important was the realization in England that, although North America might not provide huge direct supplies of precious metals, the commercial potential of the continent was enormous. Moreover, as new colonies were founded and began to thrive, this realization grew in significance. To a considerable extent, events in America were responsible for the changed English perspective, since economic growth was one of the most salient characteristics of life in the seventeenth-century colonies.

Neither the nature nor the extent of economic change was uniform among all the colonies. Some regions and some sectors of the economy grew quite rapidly; the pace of development was slower in others. Everywhere, however, America offered opportunities for individual and collective prosperity that were quite unlike those available either in England or in the rest of Europe. The fundamental condition that made such opportunities available was, of course, a relative scarcity of labor in comparison to a relative abundance of unimproved land. Such a statement ignores the Indians, but so, too, did most of the white settlers ignore the Indians. Once they conquered, exterminated, or removed Indian tribes along the coast, whites found themselves in a situation that had no precedent in their experience: there was more land available than there were people to farm it.

The fertility of the land varied significantly from place to place and helped to govern the extent and nature of economic growth. In most of New England, the soil was rocky and not especially fertile. This did not particularly disturb the Puritans. They had come to America not so much for material profit as for spiritual gain. The soil of New England was certainly good enough to support them and their families, even if it did not offer the possibility of huge agricultural surpluses. Notwithstanding their hope to establish a perfect religious community, they still had to engage in economic activity of some sort. Their original goal was to achieve economic self-sufficiency by producing everything that they needed to survive on family farms in closely knit agricultural villages, and many New Englanders did exactly that. But there were some things that were not easily made in small farming towns—metal tools and household implements, for example. And there were also some services—like blacksmithing and carpentry—that farmers were not always able to perform themselves. To pay for such things, Puritan farms had to produce more food than they or their families could consume.

Very early in New England history, these agricultural products combined with furs, fish, and naval stores to produce the foundation of a thriving commerce. In Boston, a merchant community grew up which fostered and profited from this trade. Moreover, Boston's commerce soon became international. The merchants took advantage of the availability of naval stores and lumber, built their own ships, and traded furs, foodstuffs, and other products throughout the Atlantic world. The sugar islands of the West Indies were particularly important in this trade because they had to import much of what they needed to survive. The ships of the New England merchants carried food and other needed commodities to the islands in exchange for sugar and molasses. The latter, distilled into rum, might then be traded for Chesapeake tobacco or fish from Newfoundland. These, in turn, might be carried to England or the continent, where they would be exchanged for wine or manufactured items. This commerce was extremely complex. It brought New England merchants, sailors, and sea captains to Africa (where they became involved in the slave trade), Europe, the Caribbean, Spanish America, the Mediterranean, and, of course, all of England's American colonies. After the Restoration, much of this trade was carried on in violation of the Navigation Acts, but it enriched the New England merchants enormously and continued to do so for many years.

The economic strength of the New England merchants lay in their diversification and their refusal to rely on one commodity. Because they bought and sold so many different products in so many different locales, they were able to weather rapid changes in the market for any single item. By the last quarter of the seventeenth century, New England merchants, shipbuilders, and shipowners (and many men were all three) had achieved a preeminence both in their home colonies and in the Atlantic economy which John Winthrop could never have envisioned and probably would not have desired. The intercoastal and transatlantic voyages of the merchant ships not only brought new products to the New England marketplace; they also brought New Englanders into contact with the values, fashions, and ideas of a wider and more cosmopolitan world.

While the commercial economy of New England boomed, another pattern of

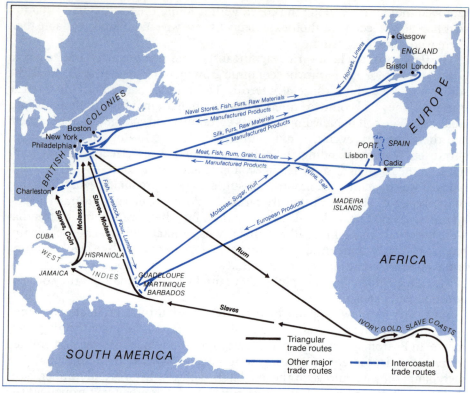

Colonial Overseas Trade

economic development was emerging in the Chesapeake region. There, tobacco became the foundation upon which the economic life of the society was built. Unlike the New Englanders, the Chesapeake colonists had not come to America to create a heaven on earth. They came instead for individual gain of the most basic sort, and they cared little for careful social organization or for lofty social ideals. The fertile land of Virginia and Maryland gave them access to the wealth that they sought. Although the soil of the region might have been used to produce any number of crops, the first settlers came to rely almost exclusively upon tobacco. The reasons for this reliance and the results of it played a critical role in the subsequent history of the area.

No one ever planned that tobacco should dominate the Chesapeake economy. Tobacco was only one of a number of crops that the early Virginians tried in their attempt to find a profitable staple. But the introduction of the weed coincided with a boom in tobacco prices during the 1620s, which was the result of the fad of tobacco smoking that was then sweeping England. Tobacco prices were so high that there was little incentive for planters to seek other sources of revenue; indeed, they would have lost money if they had turned to other crops. When the bottom dropped out of the market in the 1630s, as it occasionally did for the rest of the colonial period, the Virginians simply put more acres under cultivation. Although prices did rise again, Virginia (like neighboring Maryland and the Albemarle region of Carolina) was firmly locked into a cycle which virtually guaranteed both that tobacco cultivation would expand and that overproduction would be a chronic problem.

On account of the vagaries of the price of tobacco, competition for land and markets was fierce in the Chesapeake area. The best land was along the river banks, not only because the soil was rich, but also because river transportation permitted easy access to the sea. The boom and bust pattern in the economy, like competition for the best land, hardly encouraged social stability. Moreover, even the wealthiest planters often became indebted to merchants in Scotland and England who advanced them the capital necessary for planting against the potential profits that the crop would bring. However, if the crop failed, the planters, with no resources to pay off their creditors, fell heavily into dept. Consequently, the "plantations" of the tobacco men were hardly the elegant and lavish country homes that are usually associated with the colonial South. Such ostentatious wealth would not appear until a later period in southern history. In the seventeenth century, the planters were an aggressive and competitive lot who worked very hard to maintain their always fragile economic position.

Tobacco affected every aspect of Chesapeake life. Not only did it lend a precariousness to socioeconomic status; it also had long-term effects on the texture of the entire society. Unlike other staple crops — for example, wheat and, to some extent, rice and sugar — tobacco did not promote the development of subsidiary economic activities such as milling or light industry. The only work that it created for society was on the plantations themselves, which grew as much grain and livestock as possible in order to be self-sufficient, but which usually wound up importing some foodstuffs. The plantations rarely exported anything except tobacco. This lack of secondary economies not only inhibited the development of Chesapeake agriculture but also discouraged the development of urban centers. Each plantation had its own wharves and docks and had no need for the services of a port city. Not until late in the next century did major towns like Baltimore and Annapolis emerge in the Chesapeake region. Even then, their growth can be attributed more to the rise of wheat cultivation in the region than to any other cause.

In sum, the tobacco economy was, like the crop it produced, an addictive drug. It could provide an effusive feeling of well-being, but it created needs that became increasingly difficult to satisfy. Since it isolated the planters from one another, it undercut and eroded social stability. Although it did little to support the long-range economic health of the area, it created secondary addictions — first to white indentured labor, then to black slave labor. In addition, repeated tobacco planting soon exhausted the soil; hence more land had to be put under cultivation. This, in turn, encouraged further conflict between the Indians and the whites.

The other seventeenth-century southern colonies came into existence later than those in New England and the Chesapeake area, and their economies were comparably less developed. Still, some common traits of economic life were apparent everywhere by the 1680s and 1690s. In North Carolina, the tobacco farmers of the Albemarle eked out a living, but they had relatively little contact with the outside world and lived in a frontier environment in which the emphasis was on self-sufficiency rather than commerce. Their neighbors to the south fared much better. Charleston, situated at the confluence of the

Ashley and Cooper rivers, quickly became a major port with a diversified merchant class, many of whom also owned sizable rice plantations in the interior. The Charleston merchant-planters pursued a vigorous trade in local agricultural and forest products — rice, indigo, furs, and naval stores. They also captured Indians in the interior and sold them as slaves in the West Indies. The South Carolinians were, by all accounts, more aristocratic, cosmopolitan, and economically diversified than the Chesapeake settlers. In the long run, however, they proved equally land-hungry and even more dependent upon slavery for their prosperity.

The Middle Colonies exhibited still other patterns of economic development. In New York, the fur trade continued to be the mainstay of the economy under the English, just as it had been under the Dutch. There was relatively little commercial agriculture, and New York lagged behind Boston and Philadelphia in shipbuilding. However, the Iroquois remained a reliable source of the skins and pelts of forest animals that were so much in demand among upper-class Europeans. A new group of merchants, composed not only of Englishmen, but also of French Huguenots, slowly but surely supplanted the Dutch grandees who had held sway under the Dutch West India Company's ineffectual rule. The antagonisms between the two groups were strong, especially in New York City. The most prosperous and diversified economy in North America emerged in Pennsylvania, and the Quaker merchants of Philadelphia soon became the wealthiest and most secure economic group on the continent. The agricultural products of the Jerseys filtered through the ports of New York and Philadelphia, but in economic matters, as in other things, New Jersey was dominated by its larger neighbors.

2. SOCIAL CHANGE

The Structure of Society

Patterns of economic growth and development in the seventeenth-century colonies were accompanied by an equally striking configuration of social relationships and institutions. Of course, social change both influences and is influenced by economic change, and it is sometimes difficult to distinguish cause and effect. However, certain social changes occurred in the colonies which, when combined with the economic changes just discussed, created a volatile and potentially explosive mixture.

In the competitive world of seventeenth-century America, inevitably some people were more successful than others. Each colony — indeed, each town and county — had a group of men whose economic position exceeded that of the other members of society. Of course, success in the economic sphere bred other sorts of distinctions. Members of elite economic groups dominated religious and political institutions, set styles and fashions, exercised informal influence on the behavior of the rest of society, and, generally speaking, set the tone for relationships of all kinds.

The development of an economic upper class with special social and political prerogatives upset very few people in the seventeenth century and surprised no one. Everyone assumed that social relationships would be hierarchical, and most persons believed that society and government benefited from clearly demarcated lines of authority. Moreover, in an age in which God's influence was thought to be present, even in the most minute details of daily life, the preeminence of some men over others could not fail to seem to be an indication of God's approbation of the former. In this limited sense, therefore, class relationships paralleled those in England.

But America was not England, and social conditions were very different in the colonies. First, and most important, the English aristocracy was a legally defined group. It derived its status not simply from wealth, but also from social and political roles that stretched by hereditary right deep into the English past. Whatever the economic fortunes of his family, a member of the English aristocracy remained a nobleman and passed that status on to his eldest son. It is true that the English aristocracy underwent a crisis in the seventeenth century, partly due to competition from members of the gentry with less distinguished lineage. Even so, the peers of England still occupied a special and legally protected position of dignity and honor.

In contrast, there were no noblemen in America. There were only men of wealth. Their social status depended entirely upon their economic fortunes which, by English standards, were not very great. Equally important, members of the colonial elite did not enjoy the security of the English aristocrats. Members of the colonial elite could not be sure that their own preeminence would be passed down to their children and their children's children. In addition, they could not always expect automatic deference from their social inferiors, and they were far more dependent on the vagaries of the marketplace than members of the English aristocracy. Finally, they faced direct competition for their prerogatives from other ambitious men immediately below them in the social structure. Consequently, the American elite of the seventeenth century was hardly a leisure class. Its members were jealous of their privileges and careful to protect their position, because they knew that upward and downward mobility were complementary processes. That is to say, a man might fall from wealth and status as quickly as he had risen.

So general a portrait of the American upper classes inevitably obscures the complexity and variety that existed among them. Although competition and insecurity were present everywhere, the pattern differed from place to place. In New England, the merchants were gradually replacing the old Puritan elite of the founders' generation. In New York, English merchants were in the process of overturning the Dutch traders. In Pennsylvania, the Philadelphia merchants quickly came into conflict with William Penn and his family. In Maryland, Protestant settlers resented the Catholic proprietor and his local supporters. In Virginia, the men who had made their fortunes on the eastern rivers in the 1630s faced a challenge from new men who sought western expansion. The Carolina proprietors met similar difficulties in the Albemarle area. Only in South Carolina did the leading men achieve a measure of security, and problems remained even there.

The fluidity of class relationships in the colonies bred significant and diverse conflicts. For one thing, members of elite groups throughout America used political instrumentalities to exert power for their own purposes. The most important of these instrumentalities were the representative assemblies of the various colonies. As a result, social and economic competition invariably led to intense political wrangling within the elite that focused in the assemblies.

What of people on the lower rungs of the social ladder? Less can be said of them. Most were farmers; few had much contact with the world beyond their own communities. Once the various colonies had established themselves, relatively few people were in dire economic circumstances. Servants, to be sure, often suffered horribly at the hands of their masters (especially in the South), but eventually many of them could acquire their own land when their indentures expired. Slaves, of course, enjoyed no such luxury, but their numbers were relatively small in the seventeenth century. Skilled workers—wheelwrights, coopers, carpenters, shoemakers, and the like—were the most prosperous group outside the elite. Skilled workers could also command higher wages in America than in England. Generally speaking, the social, economic, and physical distance between those at the top of society and those at the bottom was relatively small in most places—especially in comparison with England. Political and social relationships, as a result, were usually characterized by the deferential pattern associated with face-to-face societies. Put another way, although class conflict existed in the colonies, it usually occurred within the upper ranks of society rather than between the rich and the poor.

Yet it is precisely because the range of socioeconomic statuses was much narrower in America, and because labor was at such a premium, that those in the upper strata sought to distinguish themselves in symbolic fashion from others. In New England, sumptuary laws prohibited persons who did not possess great wealth from dressing ostentatiously and expensively. Such laws were difficult to enforce, but their passage reflects a perception among the elite that their social prestige was undermined when those whom they called "the meaner sort" wore apparel that belied their status and thus blurred lines of social authority.

In the Chesapeake region, social position was defined by what we would today call "life-style." The truly eminent men owned and raced horses, had freewheeling sexual habits, drank to excess, and gambled for huge stakes. Such activities delineated them from their fellow colonists who could not afford such extravagance and hedonism. Symbolic reinforcements of the social hierarchy like these were quite common and reflected the precarious position of men whose prestige was neither guaranteed by law nor protected by economic sanction.

Religious Institutions and Social Development: Two Examples

Sumptuary laws and a life-style like that of the Virginia planters were improvised responses to an unanticipated vagueness in patterns of social organization. In other areas of life as well, expectations and reality did not always coincide. Religion was one such area, and two examples—developments in New England and Virginia—indicate in what a startling way institutional arrangements could diverge from the plans of the founders of the colonies. The hope for Virginia had been that it would be an Anglican colony where the ecclesiastical hierarchy of the Church of England would exercise firm control over religious life. In contrast, the founders of Massachusetts had regarded congregational government as one of the major tenets of their faith; they abhorred the idea of religious decrees by officials who had no knowledge of local needs and desires. Yet it was in Virginia that individual churches had the most independence and in Massachusetts that church policy was more frequently controlled from

above. Such an ironic reversal owed its occurrence to social differences between the two colonies.

Virginia was not settled by pious men — and, at the beginning, almost all the
colonists *were* men. Rather, it was established by ambitious individuals who
sought personal gain. Still, even men such as these lived in an age that took religion very seriously, and few of them were dissenters from the Church of England. Yet the elaborate institutions and bishops of the Anglican Church never
found a home in the colony; as late as the decade before the outbreak of the
American Revolution, Virginians were unsuccessful in their efforts to establish an American episcopate.

There were several reasons why the Anglican hierarchy was never able to
sink its roots into the soil of Virginia. The first was that it was difficult to attract ministers and church officials to a crude settlement which was first disease-ridden and later dominated by men of a distinctly impious cast of mind.
In 1650, there were only six ministers in the entire colony of Virginia. According to the calculations of one historian, this was a ratio of one minister to every 3,239 persons. A group so small could hardly expect to stand up to the planters of the colony and impose the rigid dogma and standards of behavior of the
Church of England. In addition, tobacco cultivation served to spread the population of the colony very widely over the landscape rather than to concentrate
it in communities where the church might have more easily exercised its authority. Finally, ministers in Virginia did not occupy a position of acknowledged leadership and dignity. They were, themselves, dependent on local
planters for financial support. These factors — all of them tied to the social circumstances of settlement — combined to weaken the authority of the church
generally, and to make religious life a matter of local, even individual, concern.

In New England, where the diffusion of religious authority was a goal to be
sought rather than a pitfall to be avoided, social developments also worked to
achieve an unforeseen result. Ministers were leaders in the colonization of
New England from the outset. They were not only numerous — the ratio of
people to ministers in Massachusetts in 1650 was 415 to one — but also influential, especially so in their individual towns and churches. Moreover, they
continued to articulate the predominant values of the communities of the area
for many years. Furthermore, the Puritans settled in family-centered villages
that supported their ministers and other leaders without much question for
much of the seventeenth century. As long as settlement centered in the core of
these agrarian communities, most of the colonists had frequent contact with
the minister and tended to grant him considerable social authority and a decent income.

On the face of things, such a situation should have permitted the Puritans to
govern their churches along congregational lines. In the end, however, hierarchical religious authority was more pervasive in New England than in Virginia. Almost from the beginning, Puritan ministers perceived a falling away
from the high ideals of the first settlers. Over the years, fewer and fewer New
Englanders underwent the conversion experience that was so central to Puritan theology. Moreover, the growing commerce of New England brought new
values, often antithetical to those of Puritanism, into the region and thus diluted the original zeal of the founders. Or at least so the ministers thought.
There is some question whether the ministers' perception was accurate. In all

likelihood, they were unduly sensitive to such developments. Perhaps they were simply defending themselves against what they perceived to be the ascendancy of commercial values emanating from the merchant community.

In any event, the ministers organized themselves against what they saw as a threat to orthodoxy by attempting to insure greater uniformity of doctrine and religious practice. Because the population was concentrated within relatively narrow boundaries, it was easy for the ministers of the various churches to meet to make decisions about church policy. As early as the 1630s, they gathered in such meetings—the most important of these were called synods—to identify the common problems of the churches, point out doctrinal errors, and insure conformity to their understanding of God's will. In the Boston area, there were more than 160 ministerial meetings between 1633 and 1672. One such meeting eased the requirements for church membership with the so-called Halfway Covenant of 1662. It admitted the grandchildren of Saints to "halfway" membership, even if their parents had failed to have a conversion experience. In 1679, the General Court of Massachusetts called the ministers together to deal with "the provoking evils of New England." This gathering—the Synod of 1679—drew up a long list of evils, and the ministers returned to their congregations with plenty of materials in hand for jeremiads—sermons that berated congregations for their sins and were designed to inspire them to emulate the holy ways of the early colonists.

In both Virginia and New England, therefore, local social situations significantly affected religious life. To be sure, the Church of England was never entirely powerless in Virginia; indeed, it gained influence as the colonial period progressed. Nor was the authority of the New England ministers always accepted; on the contrary, many church members, true to their belief in congregational government, resisted the encroachments of the ministerial organizations. Some of them, for example, refused to adopt the Halfway Covenant. Yet even when such deviations occurred, their causes were embedded in social and economic conditions; they did not flow directly from the articulated intentions of the colonists. In religion, as in other facets of provincial life, social change and social goals interacted to form a complex and frequently surprising reality.

Population and Family Structure

No aspects of early American society more sharply highlighted the differences between the colonists and Englishmen than the most basic physical realities of their existence. For example, most colonists lived longer and healthier lives than their cousins in England or other parts of Europe. The average life expectancy varied, but in New England towns such as Plymouth, Andover, and Salem, a man who reached the age of twenty could expect to live from his late fifties to his late sixties; a very large percentage lived much longer. Among the second generation of Andover settlers, more than half of the men lived past the age of seventy. Not only do such statistics compare favorably with our own day; they were startlingly better than comparable calculations for England in the same period. Data for other regions are less striking—especially in the disease-prone Chesapeake area. However, in one North Carolina county, a man who reached the age of twenty could expect to live into his fifties, and almost 40 per cent lived past the age of sixty. In addition, infant mortality was lower

MAINE
(Part of Mass.)

Ft. Western
(Augusta)

N.H.

Falmouth
(Portland)

Portsmouth

Boston

Ft. Oswego

L. ONTARIO

Albany
Ft.
Stanwix

MASS.

Providence

R.I.

CONN.

N.Y.

Hartford

L. ERIE

New York
Perth Amboy

PA.

Harris
Ferry
(Harrisburg)

Burlington

Philadelphia

New Castle

Ft.
Bedford

Ft. Cumberland

Baltimore

MD.

DEL.

Ohio R.

Charlottesville

Richmond

V A.

Williamsburg

PROCLAMATION LINE OF 1763

Hillsboro

Salem
(Winston-Salem)

New Bern

N.C.

Wilmington

Camden

S.C.

Ft. Augusta
(Augusta)

Charles Town

GA.

Savannah

St. Lawrence R.

	1760
	1700
	1660

**Colonial Settlement
and Population,
1660-1760**

in America than in England, so that more children survived to adulthood. Data for colonial women indicate that their lives were shorter than their male counterparts because childbirth was more dangerous than it is today. However, if a woman survived her childbearing years, she, too, could look forward to a long life. In any event, colonial women lived longer lives than did their contemporaries in England.

Several factors seem to have been responsible for the longevity of the American colonists. First, they lived in a favorable "disease environment." The colonies were relatively isolated from the rest of the world. As a result, they had fewer opportunities to come into contact with the epidemic diseases that continued to kill large numbers of Europeans every year. Not only that, but the colonists were isolated from each other. Thus when epidemics did occur, they tended to be localized and of brief duration. In addition, although there were cities of a sort in America, they were few, far apart, and hardly more than large towns by European standards. Consequently, the poor sanitation that characterized early modern urban life had no impact on the health of most seventeenth-century American colonists. Furthermore, although the Indians were disastrously susceptible to European diseases like smallpox and influenza, there were no comparable native infections to ravage the health of Europeans in America. In the eighteenth century, as the isolation of the colonists from each other and from the outside world declined, and as their cities grew, the death rate increased. The seventeenth century was, therefore, one of the healthiest periods in American history.

Comparatively long lives and low rates of infant mortality had important consequences for early American society. One was that colonial families were quite large—often twice as large as families in England. This was a natural concomitant of low infant mortality, of course, but it also resulted from the fact that colonial women married at an early age. Since eligible men outnumbered eligible women in the colonies, women became likely marriage partners at an average of between nineteen and twenty-two years of age (depending on the locality)—a younger age than in England at the same time. As the sex ratio equalized over time, this average rose accordingly, but this was a gradual development. In the meantime, younger marriages meant more pregnancies per marriage. Larger families with more children surviving to adulthood meant that colonial population grew quite rapidly. Annual rates of increase were approximately 5 per cent, and the population doubled about every thirty years. By 1700, there were 250,000 people living in English North America. In turn, rising population prompted greater agricultural productivity and more active commerce and investment. It also created significant pressures for more land, which inevitably brought the colonists into conflict with the Indians.

A Society in Flux

As the end of the seventeenth century approached, the English colonies in North America could take some satisfaction in having achieved high levels of population growth and substantial economic prosperity. Yet both growth and prosperity had occurred very rapidly, and the institutions of the colonies had not kept pace with the rate of social change. A transformation of profound importance was in progress, one that would ultimately propel the colonists into a world more modern and less traditional than the one that they had known. Imperial reorganization, competition among ambitious entrepreneurs and planters, weakened structures of authority, rising population, and conflict with the Indians and with each other were all part of the transformation of the world in which the settlers lived. But none of these experiences could be absorbed as quickly as they occurred. The anxieties and tensions bred by so radical a departure from expectations and so fundamental an alteration in daily life required a period of readjustment, and just such a readjustment occurred between about 1675 and 1700. The result was a crisis whose dimensions differed from one colony to another. But everywhere it highlighted the most conspicuous features of seventeenth-century social development.

3. THE CRISIS OF SEVENTEENTH-CENTURY SOCIETY

Bacon's Rebellion

Virginia, the first colony to be founded, was also the first colony where conflict caused by socioeconomic change erupted. After 1660, when the passage of the first Navigation Act restricted the market for American tobacco to England, prices fell precipitately. As in the past, Virginia's response was to grow more tobacco in order to make up for lower prices. Newly freed white servants and new immigrants to Virginia (whose population was about 25,000 in 1660) found that the best land was already in the hands of the great planters and that they enjoyed much less economic opportunity than before. The only way to increase such opportunity was to acquire fresh land, and the only way to acquire fresh land was to move deeper into the interior and closer to the areas inhabited by Indian tribes, such as the Susquehannocks. Such westward movement was bound to inflame the Indians and destroy the relatively peaceful relations between whites and Indians which had been maintained since the last great battle with Opechancanough in 1644. The wealthy planters in the coastal areas wanted to avoid conflict with the Indians. They controlled the House of Burgesses; Governor William Berkeley and his council agreed with them. Thus the government adopted a policy of limiting or prohibiting settlement beyond the existing frontier.

Several forces then came together to breed conflict among white Virginians. One group of men — with secure political, social, and economic power — had been able to thwart another group which wanted to emulate and share in their success. These frustrations exploded in 1676 in Bacon's Rebellion. The immediate cause of the crisis was symptomatic of its more long-range causes. Berkeley refused to initiate a war against the Susquehannocks in order to permit settlers on the upper James River to seize Indian land. The frontiersmen (many were young men recently freed from servitude) took matters into their own hands. They made war, not only on the Susquehannocks, but also on the Appomattoxes, the Pamunkeys, and the Occaneechees. Led by a newly arrived planter, Nathaniel Bacon, who had achieved some economic success, they not only conducted a bloody war against the Indians; they also drove Berkeley out of Jamestown, set the town on fire, and took the government into their own hands.

Bacon was symbolic of the movement that he led. He was not desperately poor, but he found his ambitions blocked on two fronts: first, by the Indians;

second, by Berkeley and the clique that surrounded him. Bacon sought to remove both obstacles with violence, but he died of fever (or poison) at the moment of his victory. His rebellion collapsed. Twenty-three of Bacon's supporters were hanged by the vengeful Berkeley before the Governor was removed from office by commissioners sent by Charles II to find out why his authority had been challenged in the first place.

For all its brevity and lack of specific political accomplishments, Bacon's Rebellion was a critically important event. The war against the Indians was brutal, and Indian casualties were high enough to open considerably more land for tobacco cultivation. When prices rose again in the 1680s, new settlers moved in, took advantage of Indian weakness, and made new fortunes that rivaled and sometimes exceeded those of the old elite. The central issue of the rebellion had been whether or not white settlers would permit the Indian presence to prevent the satisfaction of their hunger for land and the prosperity and power that such land would bring. Although Bacon himself did not live to see the results, the two conflicts that he initiated — the one among the whites and the other between whites and Indians — were both resolved in favor of the land-hungry men whom he represented. Thus Virginia society would continue on the social and economic course that had been set in the 1620s.

Empire, War, and Rebellion in Seventeenth-Century New England

The crisis of the late 1600s in New England was more intricate than that in Virginia, and it was longer in coming. But it was equally significant and similarly indicative of fundamental difficulties in New England society and the empire as a whole. New England's troubles began with the Restoration. Charles II wanted no repetition of the religious controversies that had cost his father his head. Charles sent word that the execution of Quakers in Massachusetts and the expulsion of Anglicans (practices that had become all too common in the 1650s) had to cease. He made it clear that he intended to keep a careful eye on the Puritans to see that they discontinued their practice of passing laws that flouted royal prerogatives.

Charles had reason to be suspicious. The Massachusetts leaders had always made it clear that they were determined to "obey God rather than man." They coined their own money and omitted the King's name from legal documents. They winked at violations of the Navigation Acts and seemed in general to pay little heed to the fact that they were the King's subjects. In addition, New England (and Massachusetts in particular) was the most populous and prosperous region in North America. The King saw no reason why he and the empire should not benefit from that prosperity. And so, in 1664, hard upon the heels of their participation in the conquest of New Netherland, four royal commissioners came to Boston to investigate. The populace insulted them, the government rebuffed them, and their chairman wrote home, "Our time is lost upon men puffed up with the spirit of independence." The commissioners advised the King to revoke the Massachusetts charter. Had the colony made token gestures of submission, as many moderates in New England suggested, a direct confrontation with the King might have been avoided. But more stubborn conservatives prevailed, and a collector of revenue reported from Boston a few years later: "The King's letters are of no more account in Massachusetts than an old number of the *London Gazette*."

While the New Englanders were thus resisting royal authority, their own imperious behavior prompted resistance from another source—the Indians. The Indians had not resisted the slow encroachment of white men on their lands. They had put up with white missionaries who sought to destroy sacred tribal traditions. They had tolerated the random violence of white settlers and had tried, without success, to live in peace with the men who had shown their savage capacity for conquest during the Pequot War. But there was a limit to Indian tolerance, and that limit was reached in the mid-1670s. The Indians of New England struck back with a vengeance that threw white settlers throughout the region into panic.

The leader of this bold attempt to expel the invaders was Metacom or, as the English dubbed him, King Philip. Metacom was a Wampanoag, a member of the very tribe that had greeted the Pilgrims at Plymouth and shared in the first Thanksgiving. He had seen the fortunes of his people decline over the years and concluded that something had to be done to restore their dignity, if not their land. When the English hanged three Wampanoags on a trumped-up murder charge in 1675, Metacom launched a war which centered in Plymouth, in the beginning. He met with immediate success, and, soon, most of the surviving tribes of New England had risen in rebellion. The line of English settlement, which had been moving steadily westward, was now pushed back toward the coast. Even in Boston, people had reason to fear for their lives. But the Indians simply could not sustain their victories. In the end, they were outnumbered and outsupplied by the English colonists who proved again that they were not to be denied what they still believed was a God-given right to Indian land.

Metacom died in the war; his severed head was displayed on a stake by the men who killed him as a warning to other Indians. But Metacom's struggle and that of the Wampanoags and other coastal Indians to maintain their independence had profound repercussions. First, the war retarded English settlement considerably. Second, Metacom's War marked the last time that the tribes of the eastern coast of New England would be able to attempt resistance, for it left them decimated. Finally, the war had vital consequences for white society that fed directly into the continuing friction between the King and the colonists. Perhaps one tenth of the adult white males in New England died in the conflict, and a large number of towns on the frontier were entirely wiped out. These casualties, and the fury of the Indian attack, provoked a deep crisis of confidence in the leadership of New England. Ministers railed against sin and warned that further disasters would surely come if the people continued their impious ways.

The preachers were better prophets than they realized, for, hard upon the end of Metacom's War, another series of actions by the King brought new tumult to a New England not fully recovered from its battle with the Indians. Charles II had suffered the insolent behavior of the Puritans for over twenty years, and his patience was exhausted. He had the Massachusetts charter nullified in court in 1684 because of persistent violations of the original contract, and the colony became, like Virginia, a royal province. But death in 1685 prevented Charles from imposing his will on the recalcitrant New Englanders.

James II succeeded his brother Charles. On the advice of the Lords of Trade, James united New York, New Jersey, and all of New England into one great province called the Dominion of New England. The alleged purpose of the move was to improve defense against French and Indian invasion. Such a union would also facilitate colonial administration and insure the enforcement of the Navigation Acts. James sent Sir Edmund Andros to establish royal authority as the first governor of the Dominion.

Andros, though an experienced administrator, unfortunately depended upon forcefulness rather than diplomacy in dealing with his wards. He followed the instructions of the Lords of Trade and tried to seize the charters of Connecticut and Rhode Island, but failed. He dismissed the representative assemblies, abolished the colonial courts, and introduced Anglican worship in Boston. These actions raised the specter of popery in the Puritan sanctuary. Landowners were compelled to pay fees for titles to land which had been allotted to them by the towns and which their families had inhabited for several generations. A tax was levied on land without the people's consent. Andros also questioned the deeds of some wealthy land speculators and forbade the holding of town meetings except to elect local officials. When the New Englanders protested and insisted upon their rights as Englishmen, Andros informed them that they had no such rights. He next proceeded to wage a wasteful and costly war against the Indians.

After almost sixty years of doing things their own way, the Puritans would have been less than human if they had not resented actions that struck at all their most cherished political rights and privileges. A small group of merchants, tired of the rule of the Saints, at first welcomed the new government. But the merchants soon discovered that Andros would not permit the smuggling that had helped to enrich them. And they resented the campaign that he began to suppress piracy, for the pirates had been big spenders, and Massachusetts suffered from a chronic shortage of hard currency. Moreover, Andros showed no sign of a willingness to share his power with any of the colonists, whether they supported his policies or not.

Anger against Andros was already running high when news arrived in Boston that William of Orange had landed in England in 1688. Even before the Puritans heard that William had succeeded in ousting James in the Glorious Revolution, they rose in rebellion in April 1689 and imprisoned Andros. The town meeting of Boston took over the government and then waited the approval of William and his wife, Mary, whom they now knew to be the new monarchs of England. William recalled Andros, permitted Connecticut and Rhode Island to resume self-government under their old charters, and allowed Massachusetts to return, temporarily, to Puritan rule. New York and New Jersey eventually received new royal governors.

The great Puritan divine, Increase Mather, sailed for England to negotiate for a new charter. He was forced to accept one from William in 1691 which altered the political structure of the colony in three important respects: the governor was to be appointed by the King instead of elected by the colony's freemen; freedom of worship was guaranteed to all Protestants; and ownership of property, rather than membership in a Puritan church, became the basis of political rights. The royal charter altered the nature of Massachusetts life in critical ways. It undercut the political influence of Puritanism and opened the way for the ascendance of the merchant elite into the highest echelons of political and social power. Thus, as had been the case in Virginia, New England's experience at the end of the century reflected internal and imperial changes and served to emphasize the impact of Indian affairs on provincial life. Also, as in Virginia, the final outcome of the crisis paved the way for a new configuration of socio-economic and institutional relationships which would guide the development of New England in the eighteenth century.

Leisler's Rebellion

In New York, tensions that had been accumulating since the English conquest of 1664 erupted into violence when news of the toppling of the Andros regime arrived in April 1689. New York was then governed by Andros' lieutenant, Francis Nicholson, who had no more endeared himself to the people than had his superior in New England. Andros' ouster left Nicholson without secure authority for his rule. The people of New York City, as well as in some of the outlying counties, discovered that Nicholson had suppressed the news of William's landing in England. Soon they let their feelings be known in a series of petitions and public meetings. Rumors of an impending Indian attack and a Catholic conspiracy to take over the province (James II was a Catholic and Andros was suspected of being one) combined to create extraordinary unrest. Nicholson's response was less than diplomatic; he threatened to burn the fort at the head of Manhattan Island, but the threat was to no avail. Under pressure, he abdicated, sailed for England, and left three members of his council in charge. However, the militia of the city would not accept the council's authority. Under the leadership of Captain Jacob Leisler, a dissatisfied merchant, the militia took control of the province, and Leisler declared himself to be the governor in the name of William and Mary. He held power for almost two years and finally surrendered to William's and Mary's own agent, Henry Sloughter, who had to put the city under naval siege before Leisler gave up. Leisler was tried and hanged for treason, but the Leislerian and anti-Leislerian parties remained the major divisions in New York's volatile political life for the next twenty-five years.

On the face of it, Leisler's Rebellion was a natural response to the unsettled situation in English and American politics that followed upon the Glorious Revolution, and Leisler himself was simply an ambitious man who took advantage of that situation. But the rebellion was more complex and so, too, was its leader. It will be remembered that the English and the Dutch in New York had never got along very well and that there were serious economic rivalries between the two groups. These antagonisms had been exacerbated by events in the years immediately preceding the rebellion. Andros had been James' governor of New York when James was still the Duke of York and the proprietor of the colony. Andros had made a vigorous effort to purge the province of Dutch influences by granting political offices and economic favors to leading Englishmen and by imposing a loyalty oath on all the Dutch residents. This attempt to anglicize the colony only heightened ethnic tensions. Andros was succeeded by a more liberal governor, Thomas Dongan. However, when Andros became Governor of the Dominion of New England, into which New York was incorporated, all the old fears revived. For the Dutch residents of New York, therefore, the rebellion against Andros provided an opportunity to restore the status and influence that had been lost in a quarter-century of English rule.

Jacob Leisler was an ideal choice to articulate the discontent of Dutch New

Yorkers. Although a German, he married into a prominent Dutch family and had mostly Dutch business connections. He was a devout, even slightly fanatical, Calvinist with an intense dislike for Catholics and Anglicans. Unlike Nathaniel Bacon, Leisler did not represent an ambitious group of men on their way up. Instead, he stood for an old elite that had been displaced by interloping Englishmen and was on its way down. When Leisler came to power, moreover, most of his immediate lieutenants were Dutch, and much of his appeal was directed toward Dutch residents. He assured them that William (a Dutchman who married into the English royal family) would restore them to their old positions of power. He renamed the fort in New York City Fort Amsterdam and did everything that he could to restore Dutch influence. In addition, although Leisler called a representative assembly, he disbanded it when it refused to cooperate with his every whim. All these measures aroused the ire of Englishmen, who were relieved when Colonel Henry Sloughter finally seized control in 1691 and transformed the colony into a royal province with a regular assembly.

New Yorkers did not divide over the Glorious Revolution, and most of them supported Leisler in his initial seizure of power. Ultimately, though, New Yorkers divided over whether Leisler was the legitimate representative of the principles that the Glorious Revolution had vindicated. The hangman's rope settled the immediate issue, but ethnic conflict, encouraged by economic change, remained characteristic of New York life throughout the colonial period. As late as 1765, one Englishman could write that the Dutch showed "an unwearied attention to their own and particular Interests and abhorrence of all superiour powers." In the end, however, Leisler's Rebellion established English rule once and for all and created real incentives for the Dutch to adopt English ways lest they be victimized as Leisler's generation had been. Leisler's Rebellion thus reflected the socioeconomic changes of the era that preceded it and also colored the subsequent social history of New York in the eighteenth century.

Coode's Rebellion

In Maryland, Protestant colonists had always resented the Catholic proprietor. As the percentage of Catholics in the population declined over the course of the seventeenth century, moreover, Protestants were increasingly embittered by a political system which failed to reflect their numbers. Violence had broken out several times, and life in the colony was further destabilized by its reliance on tobacco and by border disputes with William Penn. Despite these difficulties, the Calvert family had maintained control, and Protestant leaders had few avenues to political power beyond their own counties. But when news of the accession of the Protestants, William and Mary, arrived in Maryland, new hopes and possibilities suddenly appeared.

Lord Baltimore's governor, William Joseph, was slow to acknowledge the rule of the new King and Queen. He postponed a meeting of the assembly and relied instead on his Catholic-dominated council. As the summer of 1689 progressed and news of the rebellions in Massachusetts and New York reached Maryland, a group of disgruntled planters organized themselves into the Protestant Association. Led by John Coode, a veteran of another uprising in 1681, the rebels seized control of the province in a bloodless coup that finally opened the political doors that had been closed against them for so long. They called a representative assembly which promptly declared that William and Mary were King and Queen. In addition, they established a committee to investigate what they believed was yet another Catholic-Indian conspiracy to take over the colony.

The new Protestant rulers of Maryland were all too aware that the Calvert family still possessed a proprietary charter to the colony and that, in a technical sense, the rebellion had no foundation in law. They wrote to London and, after some wrangling, managed to have the proprietary charter revoked. Maryland, like Massachusetts and New York, became a royal colony with a governor appointed by the crown and a popularly elected assembly. The Calverts were permitted to retain their land in Maryland, but Catholics were disfranchised and Anglicanism became the established religion. Political feelings continued to run high, even under the more benign rule of Protestant officials, and Maryland was anything but stable in the next two decades. Finally, the fifth Lord Baltimore, Charles Calvert, regained political control of Maryland in 1715. However, he was a Protestant and so inspired less antagonism from the local elite than his Catholic ancestors had evoked. Thereafter, religious tensions subsided in the colony, although conflict between the proprietor and the people simmered for the rest of the colonial period. Even so, Coode's rebellion had accomplished its goal of opening opportunities to Protestant colonists who had been unable to translate their economic achievements into political power so long as the province was ruled by Catholics.

Chaos in the Carolinas

The situation in the Carolinas was the most complex of all. The crisis began in 1677 with a confused little rebellion in the Albemarle. It continued intermittently until 1729, when North Carolina was purchased from the proprietors and became a royal colony. The basic cause of the discontent was dissatisfaction with proprietary rule. However, the vagaries of the tobacco economy, ethnic and religious strife, and conflict with the Indians also played a rule in translating turbulent social and economic relations into political chaos.

The first sign of trouble in the Carolinas came with Culpeper's Rebellion in 1677. John Culpeper, who had been in Jamestown during Bacon's Rebellion, was one of a group of relatively recent arrivals. The newcomers attempted to displace the more established planters who had enjoyed the favor of the proprietors. As in Virginia, North Carolina's tobacco economy was very precarious, and there was considerable pressure among the newcomers to seize more Indian land. In any event, the rebels seized power with the help of a Boston ship captain who was smuggling North Carolina tobacco. They organized an elected government and managed to secure tacit approval from the proprietors for their actions. We know little of the anarchical period that followed, but in 1683 the proprietors sent a new governor, Seth Sothel, to the province. As news of rebellions in other colonies spread to the Carolinas in 1689, armed colonists expelled the arbitrary and imperious Sothel from North Carolina. He fled southward to Charleston, where he found himself in the midst of an ongoing conflict between religious dissenters attached to the proprietors and a group of Anglican settlers from Barbados. Sothel allied himself with the latter group, but the conflict was so confusing that not even the participants were sure who had won.

In other colonies the events surrounding the Glorious Revolution set the tone for eighteenth-century politics, which were carried on without much violence. But pandemonium in the Carolinas continued. There was another antiproprietary rebellion in North Carolina in 1711; then came a bloody war against the Tuscarora Indians, for which the North Carolinians required the aid of their southern neighbors. In turn, the South Carolina planters launched a vicious campaign against the Yamasee Indians without proprietary approval. Both wars were manifestations of a desire to put more land under cultivation for rice and tobacco, whatever the cost. Then, in 1719, the South Carolinians, impatient with the proprietors' refusal to finance their exploits of conquest, forced the governor from office and formally requested that their settlement be made a royal colony. The crown agreed, and a royal governor arrived in 1720. North Carolina, in the meantime, continued to squabble with the proprietors until it, too, became a crown province in 1729. In sum, the crisis lingered on longer in the Carolinas than in some colonies, but it flowed from many of the same sources of social, economic, and political discontent.

Unrest in New Jersey and Pennsylvania

In contrast, New Jersey and Pennsylvania suffered no outbreaks of violence or overt rebellion at the end of the century. Yet they came perilously close to doing so. Significant conflict appeared in the two colonies, and new institutional arrangements were devised in both to calm political strife. New Jersey's story is quickly told. In East Jersey and West Jersey, controversy over land titles combined with religious and ethnic antagonisms to create almost constant turmoil. Proprietary and antiproprietary groups struggled without success to achieve political dominance, and the two Jerseys had been reduced to near anarchy by the end of the century. The amalgamation of the two proprietaries into a single royal colony in 1702 settled basic constitutional questions by creating a representative assembly and a shared governorship with New York. However, social and economic competition continued to spill over into politics, even after New Jersey got its own governor in 1738.

In Pennsylvania, different circumstances yielded similar results. William Penn, who had returned to England after getting the colony started, was beset on several fronts by opponents who sought to deprive him of his power. Within the colony, he faced attacks throughout the 1680s and 1690s by several groups of insurgents, led by Quaker merchants and landowners, who sought to limit the proprietor's power and exalt that of the assembly. In England, Penn was also besieged since he had failed to support the Glorious Revolution and was commonly thought to be a secret agent of James II. He even lost control of the colony briefly in 1692.

In the last ten years of the seventeenth century, Penn struggled to hold on to his dream of a "holy experiment," even as that dream was slipping from his grasp. He returned to Pennsylvania in 1699 in an effort to establish the harmony that his appointees had failed to achieve. But his efforts only resulted in his being forced to give up more of his power. In 1701, the very colonists whom Penn's liberal policies had attracted pressed him to draft a new constitutional framework for Pennsylvania—the so-called Charter of Privileges. It granted greater legislative power to the assembly and limited the proprietor's control over the distribution of land. It did nothing, however, to lessen antiproprietary feeling, which continued to run high during Penn's lifetime and even increased under the less adroit administration of his heirs. Pennsylvania's politics, like those of the other Middle Colonies, reflected the frustrated ambitions of men who had benefited from the economic development of the late seventeenth century. New constitutional provisions did not eliminate that frustration; they only provided an institutional outlet for its expression.

The American Colonies at the Opening of the Eighteenth Century

The rebellions and constitutional crises of the late 1600s were as diverse as the colonies themselves. Each had its own peculiar characteristics, and each revealed particular traits of social and economic development in the colony where it occurred. But the similarities among the various outbreaks are even more striking than their differences. First, the outbreaks all involved competition among elite groups struggling either to maintain or to achieve political power. Second, the poorer members of society did little to initiate political action, although they frequently supported it. Third, all the outbreaks of unrest embodied antiauthoritarian attitudes that focused upon officials from England appointed either by the King or by the proprietors. (None of the rebellions challenged English rule *per se;* rather, they mirrored antagonisms to specific representatives of English power.) Fourth, the conflicting groups utilized the political instrumentality of a representative assembly in one way or another and thereby associated the assembly with the defense of political rights and liberties. Fifth, Indian affairs were critically important in shaping events in all the colonies. Moreover, despite the differing results of the conflict among white settlers, the coastal Indian tribes were all either wiped out or driven further to the West. Finally, there was a lingering fear of an alliance between the Catholics and Indians. As the latter were pushed further westward, they moved toward the French along the northern frontier and the Spaniards in the South.

The many disturbances also gave evidence of a process of change that was occurring everywhere in provincial America. The rapid growth of population and commerce after the Restoration caused far-reaching alterations in fundamental patterns of attitude and behavior and engendered conflicts for which there were few appropriate outlets. The central cause of these conflicts was the involvement of the colonists in a wider commercial world that had transformed the American settlements from isolated outposts of European civilization into integral parts of a larger network of economic and political relationships. Even in the tiny village of Salem, Massachusetts, where the witchcraft trials occurred, the town divided into two factions, one supporting the trials, the other opposing them. The first group represented a traditional and insular agrarian order; the second stood for the modern and commercial world that was emerging everywhere in the colonies. By 1700, therefore, there truly was a new world on the western rim of the Atlantic. The peoples and societies of English North America had undergone a transition of enduring significance. The eighteenth century would bring still other changes to American life, but they would be continuations of the process of socioeconomic and political transformation that had so unsettled colonial life at the end of the seventeenth century.

SUGGESTED READINGS

Charles M. Andrews, *The Colonial Period in American History*, Vol. IV (1938), provides a solid summary of the formulation, administration, and interpretation of the Navigation Acts. More recently, Stephen S. Webb has offered another view of the organizational and ideological foundations of the empire. His *The Governors-General* (1979) represents a striking revision of what has been the conventional wisdom: that the early empire was primarily mercantile rather than imperial in focus. The tangled threads of imperial politics are clearly and imaginatively unraveled in Michael Kammen, *Empire and Interest* (1970), while Michael G. Hall discusses the career of one prototypical imperial official in *Edward Randolph and the American Colonies* (1960). Alison G. Olson, *Anglo-American Politics, 1660–1775* (1973); I. K. Steele, *The Politics of Colonial Policy* (1968); and James A. Henretta, *Salutary Neglect* (1972), all treat various aspects of the mercantile world with care and intelligence. Customs administration is deftly handled by Thomas C. Barrow, *Trade and Empire* (1967). Two radically different views of the economic impact of the mercantile system are contained in Lawrence A. Harper, *The English Navigation Laws* (1939), and Oliver M. Dickerson, *The Navigation Acts and the American Revolution* (1951), but the most reliable data have been collected by James F. Shepherd and Gary M. Walton in *Shipping, Maritime Trade, and the Economic Development of Colonial North America* (1972). The most readable general treatment of the economic growth of the English Empire is Charles Wilson, *England's Apprenticeship* (1965).

Stuart Bruchey, *Roots of American Economic Growth, 1607–1861* (1965), contains a good account of early American economic history, and Curtis Nettels, *The Money Supply of the American Colonies Before 1720* (1934), is more wide-ranging than its title indicates. Carl Bridenbaugh, *Cities in the Wilderness* (1938), is the standard account of early American urban life, while Michael Kammen, *Deputyes and Libertyes* (1969), narrates and interprets the rise of representative political institutions in the colonies.

The dealings of the colonists with the Indians are among the most tragic episodes in our history, as Francis Jennings demonstrates in his searing indictment of the Puritans, *The Invasion of America* (1975). For other views, see Alden T. Vaughan, *The New England Frontier* (1965), and Douglas E. Leach, *Flintlock and Tomahawk* (1958). In *Indian Affairs in Colonial New York* (1960) and *Fraud, Politics, and the Dispossession of the American Indian* (1969), Allen Trelease and Georgiana C. Nammack, respectively, analyze the relationships between the European invaders

and the Iroquois tribes. In addition, the following studies each treat subjects of vital importance to any understanding of the dynamics of European conquest: David H. Corkran, *The Creek Frontier* (1967); Douglas Rights, *The American Indian in North Carolina* (1947); Paul Wallace, *Indians in Pennsylvania* (1961); Ted J. Brasser, *Riding on the Frontier's Crest* (1974); C. A. Weslager, *The Delaware Indians* (1972); Anthony F. C. Wallace, *King of the Delawares* (1949); and Verner W. Crane, *The Southern Frontier* (1929). Important as these studies are, they are limited in scope. A more capacious interpretive overview can be obtained by reading Wilcomb Washburn, *Red Man's Land—White Man's Law* (1971); Calvin Martin, *Keepers of the Game* (1978); and Anthony F. C. Wallace's masterpiece, *The Death and Rebirth of the Seneca* (1969).

The rebellions and other disturbances of the late seventeenth century reflected deep underlying tensions in colonial society. As a result, any understanding of them must be grounded in the preceding history of the individual colonies. Still, several more specific studies are available. On Bacon's Rebellion, the interpretations of Craven in *The Southern Colonies in the Seventeenth Century* and Wilcomb Washburn in *The Governor and the Rebel* (1957) should be compared with the perspective contained in the relevant chapters of Morgan's *American Slavery, American Freedom*. The best general account of the late seventeenth-century colonies is Wesley Frank Craven, *The Colonies in Transition* (1968). David S. Lovejoy, *The Glorious Revolution in America* (1972), is the definitive work on the American side of the transatlantic crisis. In addition, several colonies have received more extensive individual study. On New England, see Viola F. Barnes, *The Dominion of New England* (1923), and the appropriate chapters in Dunn, *Puritan and Yankee*, and Bailyn, *The New England Merchants in the Seventeenth Century*. The best recent discussions of Leisler's Rebellion are Robert C. Ritchie, *The Duke's Province* (1977), and Thomas J. Archdeacon, *New York City, 1664–1710* (1975). Lois G. Carr and David W. Jordan, *Maryland's Revolution of Government, 1689–1692* (1973), analyzes the conflicts in that colony in minute detail, but John Barth's bawdy and brilliant novel, *The Sot-Weed Factor* (1967), recreates the texture and tone of provincial life with unmatched fidelity and insight. Gary Nash, *Quakers and Politics* (1968), contains the best account of Pennsylvania's chaotic 1690s, while the results in England of the Glorious Revolution are thoughtfully outlined in J. H. Plumb, *The Growth of Political Stability in England* (1967).

Anyone interested in seventeenth-century America will benefit from reading the essays in two outstanding anthologies: Stanley N. Katz, ed., *Colonial America: Essays in Politics and Social Development* (2nd edition, 1976), and James M. Smith, ed., *Seventeenth-Century America* (1959). Indeed, these two books by themselves constitute an excellent point of departure for further study. Finally, all of the topics discussed in this chapter can be pursued in greater depth by reference to the best available bibliography, Alden T. Vaughan's *The American Colonies in the Seventeenth Century* (1971).

CHAPTER 4
AMERICAN SOCIETY IN THE EIGHTEENTH CENTURY

1. THE DIMENSIONS OF GROWTH

Population

The burgeoning of American population in the eighteenth century was both rapid and constant. Only 250,000 people lived in the mainland colonies in 1700. By 1720, that number had jumped to 466,000; in 1740 it was close to 1,000,000; in 1760 it had passed the million-and-a-half mark; and when the colonies declared their independence in 1776, their population probably exceeded 2,500,000 people. In other words, between 1700 and 1776 the population of British North America increased tenfold. The rate of increase was about 35 per cent every ten years, or between 3 and 4 per cent every year. Generally speaking, population growth was most rapid in the Lower South, where it reached an annual rate of 6.7 per cent in the fifteen years before the Revolution. In the Chesapeake region, the highest rate of growth was attained early in the century but declined later on. In the Middle Colonies and New England, growth continued at a relatively constant rate.

The vast majority of this increase came from natural growth. Many of the same factors that had permitted rapid population growth in the seventeenth century—a young age at first marriage for women, greater longevity, and lower death rates—continued to be significant in the eighteenth century. In the South, particularly, conditions seem to have improved markedly, as the ratio of men to women became more equal over time. In New England, however, eighteenth-century conditions were less, rather than more, conducive to population growth. Nonetheless, population was on the rise everywhere, and the rate of natural increase was probably the highest in American history. The population of England in this period was growing at a much slower rate—less than 1 per cent a year for the whole of the eighteenth century. As a result, while Englishmen outnumbered American colonists by a ratio of twenty to one in 1700, there were only three Englishmen for every colonist (including slaves) at the outbreak of the Revolution.

The second most important source of population growth was immigration. Because neither imperial nor local officials kept immigration statistics, it is difficult to know what proportion of the American population in the eighteenth century was composed of European immigrants. The best recent estimates suggest that between 450,000 and 500,000 new immigrants arrived in America between the turn of the century and 1776. About 20 per cent of the total population increase was thus caused by immigration. The largest number of immigrants went to the Middle Colonies and the Carolinas—one reason why their over-all rate of increase was higher than in New England or the Chesapeake region.

Of course, immigration was hardly a new or strange experience in eighteenth-century America. Except for the Indians (whose population continued to decline under the pressure of increasing numbers of whites), every man, woman, and child in the colonies was either an immigrant or the descendant of immigrants. Yet eighteenth-century immigration was fundamentally different from that of the earlier era. Before 1690, the newcomers had been mainly English; after that date they came largely from other countries. As happened with other immigrants later in American history, these people were both "pushed" and "pulled" to the new world. Poor economic conditions or political oppression in their countries of origin pushed them; the economic opportunity and political liberty that America seemed to offer pulled them.

European Immigrants

Probably the largest group of immigrants were the Scotch-Irish, descendants of English and Scottish Protestants who had colonized Ireland in the sixteenth and seventeenth centuries much as they colonized America in the eighteenth century. The Scotch-Irish came from northern Ireland, or Ulster, and the numbers of Scotch-Irish immigrants increased dramatically after about 1718. English laws which discriminated against Irish Presbyterians and Irish agricultural exports, as well as high rents, pushed them out of Ulster, while the attraction of being able to own their own land "pulled" them to America.

Some Scotch-Irish settled in New York and New Jersey, but most of them went to Pennsylvania. There they settled in the river valleys in the central part of that province. They also flooded down the valleys of Maryland and Virginia and spilled over on to the Piedmont plateau in Virginia and the Carolinas. In America, they made ideal frontiersmen. After they had fought the English and the Irish Catholics for a century and a half, they turned easily to the conquest of Indians and struggles against landlords and the agents of the proprietors in America. Perhaps as many as 300,000 Scotch-Irish came to America during the colonial period.

Germany was the second major source of new immigrants. German immigration began in 1683, when the Reverend Daniel Francis Pastorius led a group of German Mennonites, a pietistic sect, to Philadelphia. But the great German migration commenced only in about 1710, after the devastation of the Rhineland by French armies in the War of the Spanish Succession. Three thousand Germans came to New York in 1710. They were so badly treated by the provincial government that many left for Pennsylvania. That colony, because of its liberal policies and the vigorous publicity given it by William Penn, attracted the main stream of German immigrants. Their density in the eighteenth century led Benjamin Franklin to propose a program of education for the Germans to keep the colony from being "Germanized." They populated the eastern counties, where evidence of their culture and language still survives among the so-called Pennsylvania Dutch. When the best land in eastern Pennsylvania was taken, they moved, like the Scotch-Irish, down the valleys of the Appalachians into western Maryland, Virginia, and the Carolinas. The Germans were efficient farmers with a keen eye for good land, but many of them were also skilled artisans. Statistics for the colonial period are unreliable; however, some 270,000 Americans (about 9 per cent of the population) were listed as being of German extraction by the First Census of the United States in 1790.

The Scotch-Irish and the Germans were only the most numerous of the immigrant groups. About 1,000,000 Huguenots fled France following Louis XIV's revocation of the Edict of Nantes in 1685. Thousands of them came to New England, New York, and South Carolina, and an exceptional number of them rose in social and economic status because of their high level of education and industriousness. The defeat of the Scottish Highlanders in the Stuart Rebellion at the Battle of Culloden Moor in 1746, along with subsequent poverty and English oppression, drove several thousand Highlanders to America. They settled principally in eastern North Carolina, around Fayetteville, and developed a thriving commerce in naval stores. Thousands of southern Irish also came to America in the eighteenth century. They settled everywhere, quickly assimilated, and, for the most part, lost their Roman Catholic faith. Such choices were a matter of survival more than of conviction since the Irish, like all Catholics, were regarded with deep suspicion and antagonism by the English Protestants who dominated politics and society. Small groups of Jews from Spain, Portugal, and the West Indies settled in New York, Philadelphia, Newport, and Charleston. A sizable colony of Welsh settled in eastern Pennsylvania. Extreme poverty in Switzerland drove some 12,000 persons from the German cantons to America between 1734 and 1744. Most of them moved to the frontier of South Carolina.

All immigrants shared one experience—the terrors of crossing the North Atlantic in slow moving sailing ships. That crossing was hazardous under the best of conditions. The immigrants, plagued by fierce storms and insanitary conditions, suffered terribly on the voyage to America. Young children rarely survived on these disease-laden, rat-infested vessels. Mortality on immigrant ships probably averaged about 20 per cent. In addition, if they survived the trip to America, the immigrants faced yet another adjustment when they arrived in a new country whose language and customs were often very different from their own.

Assimilation, Americanization, and Anglicization

The non-English immigration of the pre-Revolutionary period had several major consequences. In addition to a substantial increase in population growth, it contributed to the cultural heterogeneity of American society and made the colonies even more different from England than they had been in the seventeenth century. American culture in the eighteenth century was perhaps the most varied in the western world. There was nothing in Europe, for example, to compare to the diversity of such pluralistic colonies as Pennsylvania and New York.

The process of cultural adaptation and assimilation among the various groups was quite complex. Some non-English colonists adjusted to their new environment by rapidly assimilating. They intermarried with the English, anglicized their names, and converted to English religious sects. Others maintained their ethnic identities and came into sharp conflict with each other and with the English authorities. This was especially true of groups living on the frontier, where they could be relatively free of the influence of English culture but had to cope with the political dominance of coastal inhabitants of English descent.

Thus, immigration simultaneously made Americans different both from Englishmen and from each other. On the one hand, the flood of European immigrants created a unique, polyglot American culture. On the other hand, the prevailing trait of that culture was that it lacked the underlying cohesion and unity characteristic of European societies and was, as a result, more prone to internal conflict. Indeed, English settlers worried in the eighteenth century about what they believed were the deleterious effects of extensive immigration from outside Great Britain (created in 1707 by the Act of Union, which united Scotland and England). The nativism and antiimmigrant feelings that appeared at several later points in American history existed well before the Revolution.

Whatever forces may have separated Americans of many different national backgrounds from each other, they frequently shared an antipathy to the British. By 1775, several hundred thousand people in the colonies either had no historical or cultural attachment to England, or hated the English government for one reason or another. It was no accident that Scotch-Irish people often led the resistance to English authority in areas where they were an important element of the population.

Even so, English institutions and values dominated the American landscape. Virtually no one in America foresaw the possibility of American independence until the very eve of the Revolution. In fact, many colonists regarded their connection with the British Empire and the powerful influence of English law and culture as their only protections against the disruption that cultural diversity promised to create. This side-by-side relationship among peoples of varied origins was unprecedented. Social and political theory continued to prescribe homogeneity as the essential basis of order. The heterogeneity of the American population was thus very threatening, and many Americans in the eighteenth century were *more*, not less, attached to English values than earlier colonists had been. Americanization—the unconscious social process through which a distinctive American culture was created—and anglicization ran in contradictory directions, and American society was frequently at odds with itself in the eighteenth century. Not until the Revolution would Americans come to terms with and, to some degree, resolve the contradiction.

African Immigrants

A final and critical component of American population growth was the rise of chattel slavery, which became the central institution of labor and production throughout the South in the eighteenth century and also achieved substantial importance in the North. The ascendance of slavery meant a phenomenal rise in black population everywhere. In 1680, there were no more than 7,000 slaves on the mainland of North America; as late as 1700, Africans numbered slightly over 25,000, or about 10 per cent of the total population of the colonies. In the 1700s, however, black population increased about twice as fast as the general population. By 1720, slaves accounted for 15 per cent of the people living in colonial America; by the time of the Revolution, their proportion had increased to more than 20 per cent. Most of this increase came from rising imports from Africa and the West Indies, which reached their height in the 1760s, but there was also substantial natural increase. Generally speaking, natural increase was more important in the Upper South and in the North than in the Carolinas, where mortality was much higher among blacks forced to tend rice fields often infested with malaria-carrying mosquitos.

General statistics on the growth of black population conceal significant regional differences. Slavery existed in all the colonies, but it was more important in some than in others. In New England, for example, the enslaved population was never more than 3 or 4 per cent of the total. In the Middle Colonies, on the other hand, black slaves rose from a little more than 8 per cent of the region's people to more than 16 per cent in 1770. In New York City, slavery was particularly important; blacks there constituted almost 20 per cent of the city's population at mid-century.

Not surprisingly, the most phenomenal growth took place in the South, where blacks were a little more than 20 per cent of the population in 1700 and almost 40 per cent in 1770. By 1770, almost 90 per cent of all the blacks in America lived in the southern colonies. This growth was especially striking in South Carolina. There were only 1,200 black slaves there in 1680, when they constituted about 17 per cent of the population. By 1720, that number had risen to 12,000 slaves, who comprised more than 70 per cent of the population.

It is easier to describe the growth of slavery than it is to explain it. However, several factors seem to have been involved. One was that white indentured servitude was economically inefficient when compared to black slavery. Southern planters who held whites under indentures had to replace them when the indentures expired, and such replacement required an additional outlay of money. Planters who owned slaves, in contrast, might have a higher initial cost, but a slave served for life once he or she had been purchased. More than that, the master owned or could sell to others all the slave's descendants. In addition, Englishmen already regarded Africans as inferior to whites, and this made it easier to justify holding black people as property. At the end of the seventeenth century, therefore, the economic attraction of slavery became too great to resist, and it replaced indentured servitude as the dominant labor system in the staple-producing southern colonies. Parliament opened the slave trade to all English subjects in 1697. Commerce in slaves grew rapidly from that point on and became the biggest business in the Atlantic world in the eighteenth century. Colonial merchants, especially in Boston, Newport, Salem, Providence, and New York, rushed to get their share of the profits and supplied slaves, not only to the southern colonies, but to the sugar islands of the West Indies as well. Slave traders were even less concerned about their passengers than other ship captains, and the death rate was appallingly high on the terrifying Middle Passage between Africa and the New World. Sometimes it reached 50 per cent. The captives were packed into unventilated and filthy holds, where they died of disease, starvation, and maltreatment. But the profits of the trade overwhelmed any concern for the human beings who were its most crucial commodity.

Economic Growth

Population increases in the eighteenth-century colonies were both a cause and an effect of economic development. On the one hand, burgeoning populations increased the output of American agriculture by making more labor available while, on the other hand, a thriving economy permitted people to have larger families and attracted greater numbers of immigrants. In any case, the extent of economic growth was very impressive. The agricultural output of the colonies grew by 600 per cent between 1700 and 1770. During the same period, imports rose by 800 per cent, and exports quadrupled. As a result, per capita income also increased at a rate of about a half a percentage point every year between 1720 and 1775.

There were several reasons for this sustained growth. First, certain innovations in the techniques of production improved agricultural yields. Second, the demand in England and in Europe for colonial products such as rice, indigo, naval stores, and wheat increased more rapidly than the colonial demand for English finished products. As a consequence, Americans trading overseas could expect to get good prices for what they produced for most of the eighteenth century. More important, those prices rose, and they rose faster than prices for English products. For example, 100 bushels of American wheat were equivalent in value to 150 yards of English cloth in the mid-1740s. By the early 1760s, the same 100 bushels of wheat would buy 250 yards of cloth. Third, European merchants, eager to garner a share of the fortune being made in the colonial trade, served as sources of capital and credit to the colonists (particularly those in the South) and thereby permitted them to expand their production more rapidly than they could have done otherwise.

American economic growth in the eighteenth century took many forms. Although the vast majority of America's production was agricultural, there was some industry as well. The easy availability of forest products had always provided the resources for a vigorous shipbuilding industry, and Americans not only exported naval stores to England but also produced ships of their own. By 1775 one third of the entire British merchant fleet had been constructed in America.

The colonial iron industry also thrived in the eighteenth century. Iron ore and wood for charcoal were abundant, and even the absence of sufficient capital or a large domestic market could not prevent the development of a sizable pig and bar iron industry. Despite British legislation in 1750, which prohibited the construction of factories to produce finished and semifinished iron products, the American iron industry was one of the largest in the world before the Revolution. Milling products and New England rum, which played a major role in the slave trade, were other important colonial industries, but American production of such items as shoes, clothing, and furniture began to rise markedly in the 1760s.

All of this growth took place within the context of the trading arrangements that had been established in the seventeenth century. What distinguished the eighteenth-century colonies from their predecessors was not so much the pattern of their commerce as the amount of commerce in which they engaged. New Englanders still caught fish and traded in furs. Virginians and Marylanders remained enmeshed in the risky but profitable tobacco economy. South Carolinians produced rice and indigo, while Pennsylvanians and New Yorkers marketed flour, wheat, and lumber. Few planters and fewer merchants paid much attention to the Navigation Acts, and things continued much as they always had, although on a larger scale. The difference was that patterns of trade hardened. Americans and Englishmen alike became more dependent than ever before on each other; by the early 1770s, American overseas trade constituted one third of the entire commerce of the British Empire. At the opening of the eighteenth century, the colonies made up only one of many links in the growing chain of the empire; by its seventh decade, they constituted the crucial link without which the chain would completely shatter.

2. PATTERNS OF COMMUNITY

The New England Town

To the colonists, growth did not occur in the abstract, but rather within the context of the individual communities in which they lived. These communities were of several types, each shaped by the intentions of the first settlers and the subsequent history of the community. Probably the best-known type of colonial community was the New England town—a peculiar form of social, economic, and political organization that Puritans took with them wherever they went. The New England town has often been regarded as the birthplace of American democracy. This is probably an exaggeration, but it is true that certain changes took place in the eighteenth century that provided opportunities for the expression of democratic values that would have been anathema to the people who had established the towns during the seventeenth century.

The first towns were founded by groups of settlers who received a grant of land from the General Court. They distributed the land among themselves, established house lots, built a church, or meetinghouse, to which they all belonged, and governed themselves through a town meeting. The original grants of land made to the town were typically quite large, and only a portion of the land was distributed among the original settlers. As new families arrived in the community, they might purchase land of their own. Long-time residents might also receive additional grants. At first, all the inhabitants lived close to the town center, where the meetinghouse was the focus of religious and secular life. These arrangements made for close-knit, consensually oriented communities in which there was little conflict and where most people knew each other and many were related by marriage. The leading men of the town possessed sufficient authority to shape the direction of town life without much dissent. Furthermore, they usually exercised that authority responsibly, and the life of the towns was orderly and harmonious, if somewhat isolated from the outside world.

Late in the seventeenth century, and increasingly in the eighteenth century, this pattern began to change. The old values of order and community were voiced as fervently as ever, but a variety of factors undercut the relatively stable relationships of the past. All of these factors were tied to the most essential phenomenon of the period—growth.

The key to understanding the consequences of growth in New England is an understanding of how land was transferred from one generation to the next. Ordinarily, a father did not leave all his land to his oldest son. Instead, he distributed his property among all his male heirs. Thus, if a man owned 100 acres of land and doled it out equally among five sons, each of them would receive twenty acres. If each of them had five sons and followed the same pattern, members of the next generation would have only four acres each. Members of the third generation had large families just as their grandparents had, but they possessed less land with which to support those families. The New England system of inheritance thus helped to keep children close to home in the early years, but, over the long term, it also made it more difficult for them to survive. Of course, things were rarely as simple as this example suggests. A father might give a portion of his land to his sons-in-law as a dowry, or one of his own sons might, in similar fashion, receive additional land for his children.

Generally speaking, however, successive generations of New Englanders found increasingly less land available to them than had been available to their fathers, and the land that was available was of lower quality. The original town grants were large, but they were not unlimited, and not all the land was equally fertile. A growing population meant that more and more land, some of it very poor, had to be used for agriculture. Eventually, all the land was in use, and no new land was available within the town boundaries. At that point, even if a man could afford to buy more land for his children's use, none remained. In the face of the declining availability of good land, the members of a young family starting out had several options. They might move away from their families to another town, where some land was still open; they might move westward across the Berkshires into New York; they might go to Boston or another port city in the hope of finding nonagricultural work; or, if their situation was truly desperate, they might be forced to accept poor relief from their neighbors. As a result, high levels of geographical mobility were characteristic of eighteenth-century New England. Equally important, such mobility eroded the cooperative patterns of behavior that had been the hallmark of town life, for it meant that people frequently found themselves among strangers rather than among the trusted family and friends whom they had known since childhood.

The filling up of the original town grants had other effects as well. It became very difficult for those living on the outskirts of the town to attend church and to market their produce. Such people came to resent being required to pay taxes to support a church that they could not attend. Peripheral centers soon developed with churches of their own, and residents clamored to separate themselves entirely from the original town. The town fathers frequently resisted such attempts to secede, and this resulted in protracted and bitter disputes in which the General Court served as arbiter. In the end, people living in the outlying parts of a town usually succeeded in breaking away, but they did so at the cost of serious conflict that hardly conformed to the old values of harmony and deference.

Other forces also changed the nature of town life. Better communication and transportation brought strangers into towns that had been islands unto themselves. Increased commerce encouraged economic competition among neighbors that led to disputes over land, which flooded the courts with lawsuits. Religious issues created deep rifts between antagonistic factions who struggled over the choice of a minister. In short, the concerns of the first settlers — survival in a threatening natural world and the creation of a perfect religious society — gave way to a new set of interests that turned people toward individualism and away from communalism. New Englanders bravely continued to vaunt consensus, conformity, and cooperation, but social and economic reality mocked their ideals. The stable, deferential, family-oriented world of the New England town had been transformed. In this transformation to a competitive structure of values and expectations, democratic political values were born.

The Plantation

The plantation was the dominant social organization in the South. While the stability of New England towns declined over time, the viciously competitive and almost anarchical society of the seventeenth-century South achieved a modicum of stability in the eighteenth century. In the coastal areas, which had been settled earliest, networks of interconnected families emerged to dominate every aspect of life. These families intermarried over several generations and managed to engross most of the best land. Their plantations were the centers of social, economic, and political life. Although most white Southerners neither lived on nor owned large plantations, they were nonetheless critically influenced by the great planters who, through their economic power, achieved a dominance that no other elite group in the colonies could match.

The extent of planter control in the colonial South resulted from the nature of the plantation itself. Because there were few towns, and plantations had the best access to river transportation, local farmers frequently used the planter as their middleman. In addition, the plantation was the only place where a small landholder could find skilled laborers such as wheelwrights, coopers, and blacksmiths who, as often as not, were also slaves. The plantation thus served the same function for Southerners that the town center served for New Englanders. The difference was that the plantation was owned by one man who controlled all the goods and services, while economic control was more diffuse in a New England town. As is usually the case with monopolies, the great planters possessed influence out of all proportion to their numbers. They were unchallenged in their leadership of society and were repeatedly reelected to local and provincial offices. They dispensed justice and ruled the plantations and the surrounding countryside absolutely.

This is not to imply that southern planters were harsh and cruel in their relations with their poorer white neighbors. On the contrary, they had no need to be. Moreover, planters were genuinely public-spirited men of a distinctly patriarchal cast of mind. They fancied themselves country squires on the English model, and they took their responsibilities quite seriously. Although they expected complete deference from those beneath them, they were frequently benevolent. They extended credit to local people who had fallen on hard times. They distributed large quantities of cider when election day rolled around and were rarely irresponsible in their use of power. In return, the people of the county acknowledged the planters' superior social position and accepted their rule without much question. It was a system based on mutual obligation and trust. Its successful operation imparted an extraordinary stability to all social relations among whites.

Much as the planters might have wished to emulate the English aristocracy, and as stable as their society seemed, there were two lingering problems with which they were never able to deal adequately. The first was their reliance upon staple crops, which made them extremely vulnerable to changes in market conditions. Especially in the Chesapeake area, where tobacco overproduction continued in the eighteenth century, planters were heavily dependent upon Scottish and English merchants or their American representatives. These merchants not only purchased and shipped tobacco; they also served as the planters' bankers and commission agents. Many planters, unable or unwilling to adjust the level of their purchases to the fluctuations in their incomes, fell deeply into debt. They became, as Thomas Jefferson later observed, a species of property owned by merchants in London and Edinburgh. The South Carolina planters fared somewhat better because they frequently owned their own ships and because the market for rice, which was removed from the enumerated list in 1731, was more constant and less subject to rapid fluctuation.

South Carolinians, however, were more dependent on the second flaw in the plantation system — its reliance on the labor of blacks who were permanent slaves. Of course, the southern colonists did not invent slavery. The ruling classes of most earlier civilizations had held slaves, and the Africans who came to America usually began their journey as the bondsmen of other Africans. In West Africa, the losers at war and perpetrators of certain crimes usually suffered enslavement. Although slavery in Africa placed captives in positions of low status within society and the family in which they resided, individuals could rise from that status and even marry into a higher social class. Equally important, slavery in Africa was not a permanent and unalterable condition, nor was it racially defined. The permanent legal bondage of one race by another, known as chattel slavery in America, was unknown in West Africa.

Once slaves had arrived in the colonies, they were systematically separated from others who spoke their language. The luckiest of them came to the continental settlements of Great Britain, where mortality was lowest and they had the best chance of survival. Only about 5 per cent of the total ended up on North American plantations; the rest went to South America and the West Indies, where conditions were unspeakably brutal and the death rate was appallingly high. Even when slaves did survive the ocean voyage, therefore, most of them could not anticipate living longer than ten years in the disease-ridden and harshly oppressive plantations of the English, French, and Spanish sugar colonies.

Even in North America, slaves faced a dismal prospect. They were sent off to work for white masters whose language and culture were completely foreign to them. Slaves were cast adrift in a society that regarded them as hopelessly inferior and barbaric. Blacks in the colonial South were accorded virtually no civil or political rights. Everywhere, slave codes controlled their behavior; the severity of such codes and white fears of slave rebellion increased in direct propor-

Colonists bargaining with a trader who has received new merchandise from an incoming ship. This engraving shows evidence of early black slaves who, by the middle of the eighteenth century, comprised close to half of the entire population of such southern colonies as Georgia, Maryland, South Carolina, and Virginia. (The Bettmann Archive)

tion to the number of slaves in the population. South Carolina thus had the harshest slave code, and the racism of South Carolinians was easily the most virulent in the colonies.

Masters, themselves, usually disciplined their slaves. Although such discipline was frequently violent, most masters could not afford to treat their slaves too harshly because, from the master's point of view, the slave represented an investment of substantial capital which would be lost if a slave was crippled or killed. Nonetheless, masters possessed the right to be as arbitrary and as cruel as they wished. Black women, particularly, suffered at the hands of masters who could rape them without any fear of legal consequences. However benign a master's treatment of his slaves might be, the entire system depended upon the implicit ability of the master to treat his slaves as property rather than as human beings. In that sense, violence was at the core of American race relations from the very beginning.

Little is known about how slaves reacted to the brutality of plantation labor. Some adapted quickly and learned the white man's language and skills. Others retained their African ways, despite the severities under which they were forced to live. There were probably as many reactions as there were slaves. However, a vital and creative culture emerged from the experience of enslavement, one that possessed its own music, art, social structure, and dialect. It has continued to shape and influence the culture of white as well as black Americans in many ways. It helped slaves to maintain their humanity and dignity in the face of a systematic attempt to deprive them of those qualities. It also gave them the courage to resist their master's authority where and when they could—by running away, disobedience, lying, stealing, malingering, destroying crops, breaking tools, or attacking masters and overseers. Occasionally, slaves also organized rebellions. One such rebellion occurred along the Stono River in South Carolina in 1739; it resulted in the death of twenty whites and sent the entire white population of the colony into a panic that led to even harsher restrictions on slave behavior. Try as they might, however, whites could neither persuade nor coerce slaves into accommodating themselves easily or quietly to the loss of their liberty.

Slaves also made positive contributions to white culture. In South Carolina, especially, whites depended on the superior knowledge and ability of their slaves in certain crucial areas. It was African slaves who taught Englishmen how to grow rice, for example. Slaves were also expert shepherds, fishermen, and fur traders. They were excellent sailors and valiant soldiers. South Carolina might well have lost its war of conquest against the Yamasee Indians in 1715 without the aid of black troops. Blacks were, in short, the people who made the settlement of South Carolina possible. As one white man put it in 1737, "Carolina looks more like a negro country than like a country settled by white people."

For all its outward signs of health and stability, therefore, the system of plantation agriculture had two crucial flaws. It would be many years before those flaws became fully apparent, however, and in the 1700s the planters reigned supreme in a world where they accounted for only a very small percentage of the population. In the years ahead, the internal contradictions of their way of life would plague them and cause serious upheavals, but in the Chesapeake area and the Carolinas of the eighteenth century, those contradictions had yet to make themselves felt.

The Cities

The growth of cities in the colonies was another consequence of economic prosperity and increases in population. There were five major colonial cities in the eighteenth century: Boston, Newport, New York, Philadelphia, and Charles Town (Charleston). At the opening of the century, none of them was more than a small trading outpost. Even in 1720, the largest of them, Boston, had a population of only 12,000. In 1770, when the population of London was 750,000, the largest city of America was Philadelphia, with some 35,000 inhabitants. By European standards, therefore, American cities were hardly more than small towns, and only a little less than 5 per cent of the colonists lived in cities in 1770. Yet these facts conceal a very important pattern of growth and expansion. Between 1700 and 1775, Philadelphia's population grew by at least 700 per cent. The populations of New York and Charleston grew at only slightly slower rates, while Newport quadrupled in size. Only Boston showed signs of stagnation. It more than doubled in population between 1700 and 1740, but after 1740 the number of Bostonians rose very little and may even have declined slightly.

The increase in urban population outside of Massachusetts and its slackening in Boston were caused by the changing trade patterns of the British Empire. When the century began, Boston merchants virtually monopolized the carry-

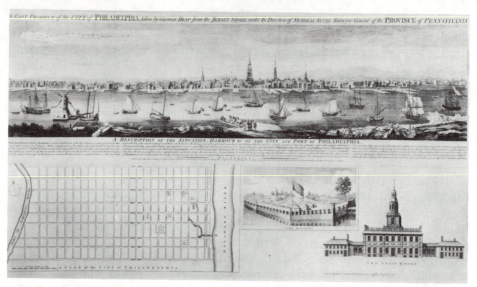

Its bustling harbor and rich trade enabled Philadelphia to experience rapid growth in size and wealth. This print, which appeared in London Magazine, *October 1761, served to lure settlers and capital to this major American city. (I. N. Phelps Stokes Collection, The New York Public Library)*

ing trade to the West Indies. As time progressed, however, ambitious men in the newer cities of New York and Philadelphia entered the trade and competed with the Bostonians. The merchants of the Middle Colonies overtook their New England neighbors for a variety of reasons. One of the most important reasons was that the Hudson and Delaware valleys were more productive than the rocky soil of New England, and farmers of the Middle Colonies produced larger surpluses of foodstuffs that could be exported to the Caribbean. In fact, food production in the Middle Colonies was so great that Boston itself began to import wheat and corn from New York and Philadelphia. The success of the New York and Philadelphia merchants brought new business and new people to their cities. In addition, Boston remained a Puritan town, while the cities of the Middle Colonies were more open and welcomed people of every nationality and religious persuasion. Boston as a result was not only less prosperous than New York and Philadelphia; it was also more homogeneous.

In any event, cities became increasingly important in American life in the eighteenth century, far more important than their percentage of the total colonial population would at first suggest. They served as centers of commerce and hubs of transportation and communication. They were the focus of provincial political activity. The colonial newspapers were published in the cities, and news from the rest of the empire and the world arrived first in urban areas. The leading men of the individual colonies lived in cities and used them as a base for wide-ranging economic and political activities. Such men also set standards of culture and fashion for the rest of the province and generally possessed a more cosmopolitan world view than persons in rural areas. Like the plantation owners of the South, such men sought to imitate the English upper classes.

They prided themselves on their sophistication and consciously adopted English fads and fashions. The wealthiest of them wore wigs and purchased their clothing from English tailors and their tableware from English silversmiths. They read English books, followed English politics, and aspired to enter the highest echelons of English society. When they traveled to Great Britain, however, they were disappointed to discover that the great men of the realm contemptuously regarded them as crude provincials hardly worthy of notice.

Whatever Englishmen thought, Americans were proud of their cities and saw their development as a manifestation of the growing maturity of their society. Yet growth also had its costs. Sanitation and epidemic disease became problems for the first time as the cities grew. Fire protection was inefficient and ineffective. Poverty, too, began to appear, and all the colonial cities had to make provisions to care for the poor. And, in times of economic distress, the cities became crowded with unemployed seamen and transients from the countryside who could not support themselves. Poverty bred crime, and theft was a continuing problem with which the colonists were unequipped to deal because they had only the most rudimentary police forces. Prostitution and other crimes also flourished in busy ports filled with sailors seeking alcohol and companionship after long and lonely weeks and months at sea.

Slavery in the cities also created new difficulties, since the urban environment offered bondsmen a freedom of movement that they could not enjoy on isolated farms and plantations. New York, with the largest slave population, lived in constant fear of rebellions and undertook prosecutions of major slave conspiracies in 1712 and 1741, only to find that slaves could engage in more subtle forms of resistance such as arson and theft. As was the case among southern planters, New York merchants found that it was easier to buy slaves than to control them.

Colonial cities thus lacked the coherent sense of organization and purpose that was apparent in the New England town and on the southern plantation. Colonial cities were bustling and frequently chaotic places undergoing unusually rapid growth and change for which they were not institutionally prepared. Their transformation from tiny trading villages to major ports was one of the most significant developments in early American history. Urbanization helped to move the cities and the colonies in the direction of capitalism and modernity. Although Englishmen might scoff at them, the cities of eighteenth-century America did succeed in making colonial society more English than it had ever been before. Both the achievements and the problems of American cities were characteristic of English urban life, too. This fact was not lost on Americans, who could see that the gap between them and the mother country was narrowing as the century wore on.

The Countryside

Of course many Americans lived neither in cities, nor on plantations, nor in New England towns. They were small farmers who produced enough to support their families and perhaps a surplus that could be sold. Such people lived a difficult and isolated existence in windowless log cabins and tilled fields that they had cleared themselves. They lacked easy access to churches, schools, government, and legal institutions, and they knew little about the sophisticated life of the cities and almost nothing of the larger world of the British Empire. Their lives revolved around the cycle of the seasons, which dictated when they would work and what work they would do, where they would travel and how long it would take to get there, what they would eat and how much, and when they were born and how long they would live. They were poor folk, suspicious of strangers and contemptuous of the cities.

Most of these backcountry farmers owned their own farms, but in some areas they rented their land from great landlords. Particularly in New York and New Jersey, but also in Maryland, Virginia, and Pennsylvania, many people lived in a semifeudal relationship to a man who owned the land that they farmed and probably the land of all their neighbors as well. Such a relationship was bound to breed resentment, and many tenants simply refused to pay their rents. When Massachusetts farmers, accustomed to owning their own land, moved into New York at mid-century, they sparked tenant rebellions of substantial proportions. Indeed, wherever men were bound by leasing arrangements, serious class antagonisms emerged. Such conflicts were often characterized by armed violence and made for considerable instability throughout the colonies.

Even in areas where small farmers owned their own land, they frequently clashed with the wealthier and more influential men who controlled the provincial government. Such conflict usually set poor farmers in the western and relatively unsettled portions of a colony against wealthy planters and merchants along the coast. In New York, New Jersey, Pennsylvania, and the Carolinas, sectional violence of this sort exploded at several points during the century. And even in areas where there was no violence, Easterners and Westerners were continually at odds with each other over such issues as representation in the assemblies, taxation, and relations with the Indians.

The Founding of Georgia

Even while the older colonies were undergoing considerable growth, a new colony came into existence in the Southeast. Georgia was the last colony settled of the thirteen that became the original states of the Union. In 1732, James Oglethorpe obtained a charter from George II which granted the southern, unsettled, part of the old Carolina territory lying between the Savannah and Altamaha rivers to a body of trustees. Oglethorpe was a philanthropist who wished to provide a home in the new world for the victims of harsh English laws that threw a man into prison for a small debt and held him there even though he could earn no money to pay his creditors. The Anglican Church, eager to convert the Creek and Cherokee Indians on the Carolina borders, cooperated. Capitalists hoped to make profits out of the silk and wine industries to be introduced into the province. And the British government, drifting into war with Spain, was glad to have the frontier extended southward to Spanish Florida. The charter was granted for the unusual term of twenty-one years, after which control of Georgia would pass to the King.

Parliament, along with the proselytizing arm of the Church of England (the Society for the Propagation of the Gospel), the Bank of England, and many private citizens contributed toward founding the new colony. The trustees collected enough money and debtors to give the colony a promising start, and other settlers, not debtors, responded to declarations that Georgia was at least the equal of the Garden of Eden. Oglethorpe and 120 colonists arrived in Amer-

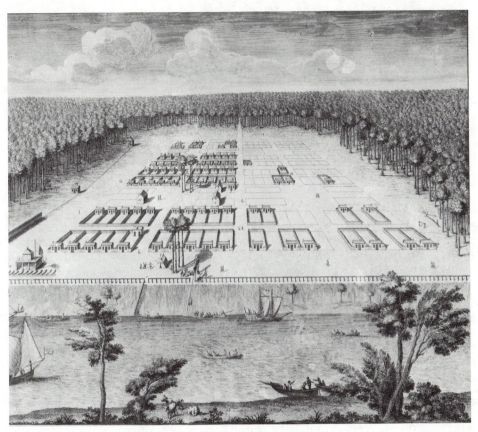

A view of Savannah, 1734. This idealized image reflects the utopian ideals of the founder of Georgia, James Oglethorpe. (I. N. Phelps Stokes Collection, The New York Public Library)

ica in January 1733 and established a settlement where the city of Savannah now stands.

The Georgia trustees forbade slavery and the traffic in rum, and they prohibited land sales without their permission. Settlers, therefore, had no choice but to work the soil. When silk and wine culture proved unsuited to the land, the colonists, faced with dwindling supplies and the prospect of difficult work, demanded their rights as English colonists to hold slaves. At the very least, they insisted on drinking rum to ease their living conditions. The trustees gave in, permitted slavery and rum, and gladly handed their unprosperous colony over to the King in 1752, a year before their charter expired.

The settlement of Georgia was really nothing more than the final footnote in the history of English colonization, but it was an instructive one. In the 1730s and 1740s, Georgia duplicated two crucial patterns of development that had first appeared in other colonies during the seventeenth century. First, the Georgia trustees began their colony with the specific utopian intention of creating a perfect society and an ideal community. They believed, as many earlier colonizers had, that America might provide an opportunity to discard the archaic institutions of Europe and start over again. But, as had been the case with the seventeenth-century colonies, conditions in the new world interfered with the plans of the founders, and Georgia turned out to be quite a different kind of place from what they had planned it to be. Second, the men who founded Georgia did not decide to establish slavery as the dominant system of labor in their colony; indeed, they hoped to prohibit it entirely. But slavery offered the same economic incentives to Georgians that it had to Marylanders, Virginians, and Carolinians; the Georgians were no more successful in resisting those inducements than other whites. Soon Georgia was bound to the institution of slavery and the ideology of racism, much as the Carolinas and the Chesapeake area had been in the previous century.

Social Structure

Despite the many different kinds of communities in which eighteenth-century Americans lived, economic expansion and demographic growth made it inevitable that they would all share certain common experiences. One of the most important of these was the development of a more stratified social structure. In the seventeenth century, the gap between the wealthiest and poorest members of society was relatively narrow, but the gap widened over the course of the eighteenth century. In Boston, for example, the richest 10 per cent controlled 46 per cent of the taxable property in 1687. In 1771, the upper tenth owned 63 per cent of the wealth. Concurrently, the poorest 10 per cent, which had owned only 2.6 per cent of the wealth in 1687, was virtually propertyless by 1771. Similar changes in the distribution of wealth occurred everywhere in the colonies. Although both the rate and the extent of change varied from one area to another, every colonial community that has been studied evidences the same pattern of the rich getting richer and the poor getting poorer. The heaviest concentrations of wealth occurred in the South, followed by the cities and commercial towns of New England and the Middle Colonies. Generally speaking, economic inequality declined as one traveled away from the older and more developed coastal regions.

The increasingly inequitable distribution of wealth had different effects upon relationships among social classes. The dominance of the southern plantation owners was such that they were able to tighten their control. The challenges that they faced came from their slaves and the poor farmers of the West; simple class conflict among white Southerners was the exception, not the rule. In the cities, on the other hand, there was considerable conflict that stemmed primarily from class antagonisms. Unemployed laborers and seamen resented the wealth and ostentatious life-style of the merchants, and they made their feelings known in the press and in occasional rioting as well. Thus, just as the maldistribution of wealth enhanced the stability of southern society, it undermined stability in the urban areas. Westerners, as we have seen, had no love for the Easterners who controlled the political and economic systems, and their antagonism derived from both class and sectional feelings.

The increasing stratification of early American society thus had ambiguous effects. The process through which wealth became more concentrated in the upper ranks of society may be viewed from several perspectives. As compared to the seventeenth century, there is no question but that the eighteenth century brought a lessening of economic opportunity and an increase in the political and social influence of the wealthy. There were also more poor people, proportionately, in the eighteenth century than in the seventeenth. Fathers frequently failed to guarantee their sons a decent income, and a growing percentage of the colonists were never able to purchase land of their own; between 40 and 50 per cent of the Maryland colonists, for example, were tenants.

However, this somewhat gloomy picture can be misleading. From another point of view, social stratification may be seen as the natural consequence of an economic boom from which most, though not all, Americans benefited. If conditions in eighteenth-century America are compared to those in eighteenth-century England, rather than to those in the America of an earlier generation, another sort of judgment emerges. Per capita income rose throughout the pre-Revolutionary era, and economic opportunity, although declining, remained more available in America than in England or the rest of Europe. The American standard of living was one of the highest in the world in the eighteenth century. Even among the poor, conditions were better in the colonies than in England. America *was* the "best poor man's country," even though the number of poor men was increasing. By almost any standard of comparison, except that of the seventeenth-century colonies, therefore, America still offered considerably more economic opportunity than Europe.

Finally, the stratification of American society in the eighteenth century and the rising number of poor people and tenants were the results of a larger process of development. The relatively egalitarian conditions of an earlier era could not survive an expanding capitalistic economy. The trend away from traditional social arrangements, which was so apparent in other sectors of colonial life, reflected the extent to which American society was becoming more similar to English society. So, too, with social stratification. Anglicization was more than the intentional imitation of English fashions by the American upper classes. It also involved less self-conscious sorts of social change. Social stratification gave the American colonies the "look" of the English society that had spawned them, as the upper classes came to enjoy both more luxury and more power than they had ever possessed before. Indeed, the most important general change that took place in British North America in the eighteenth century was the extent to which the many societies of America came more and more to resemble English society in every way. The rise of economic inequality was but one of many aspects of this larger process of change and modernization.

3. POLITICS IN PROVINCIAL AMERICA

The Structure of Colonial Government

Growth also wrought changes in and brought new complexity to political life in the colonies. The basic institutional system had been set by the end of the seventeenth century. At the apex of the political pyramid in all the colonies stood the governor. The King appointed him in the royal colonies; the proprietor chose him in the proprietary colonies; and the people elected him in the charter colonies of Connecticut and Rhode Island. Everywhere, the governor was the central figure of political life. In most colonies, the governor appointed his council, judges, sheriffs, and justices of the peace. He could veto legislation, control the distribution of land, and call and dismiss the assembly. Beneath him sat the council. For the most part, councillors were closely tied to the governor and were chosen from among the wealthiest men in the colony. In theory, the council was the upper house of the colonial legislature.

Next came the assembly. Although the formal powers of the assemblies varied considerably, all of them were true lawmaking bodies and genuine representative institutions. Moreover, a far higher proportion of the people participated in the governmental process in the colonies than in any European nation. By the late seventeenth century, almost all free, adult males who owned property could vote. This property qualification varied from colony to colony, but a common requirement was ownership of fifty acres of land or possession of personal property worth fifty pounds. Women and slaves were not allowed to vote, and indentured servants usually were excluded because they owned no property. Catholics and Jews were disfranchised in most colonies on religious grounds after 1688. Most historians believe that about 50 per cent of the adult white males in the southern colonies and about 75 per cent in the middle and northern colonies were qualified to vote. In the late colonial period, a large percentage of the eligible voters exercised that right. Members of the assembly, therefore, spoke for a relatively small proportion of the total population, but they represented a far larger percentage of white males than members of the House of Commons did.

Beneath the province-wide structures of governor, council, and assembly were the county and town governments, which regulated local affairs. In many ways, these were the most democratic of colonial political institutions. Persons who held office were immediately responsible to the people who elected them, and they could be carefully observed in the performance of their duties. At the other extreme, of course, there were the King and Parliament. Most Americans knew very little about them and had virtually no contact with them. Ultimately, the King could veto any colonial legislation, and parliamentary regulations could have a significant impact upon provincial life. However, both the monarch and his legislature were very distant from the colonies, both psychologically and geographically. The governmental structures that mattered most to Americans were those in their own individual communities and colonies.

The Reality of Colonial Politics

In theory, the institutional structure of politics in colonial America served as a guarantee of stability and harmony. Governors possessed substantial formal powers, and the tripartite division of governor, upper house, and lower house duplicated a similar division in England. The hallmark of English political life in the eighteenth century was its stability, and everyone in America and England expected that colonial politics would assume a similar character. But the structural parallels between England and America concealed underlying differences that made the politics of the colonies as unstable and cacophonous as those of England were stable and harmonious.

The primary reason for political strife in eighteenth-century America was an ongoing struggle for power between governors and assemblies that was not unlike that which had occurred between Parliament and the Stuart Kings in seventeenth-century England. Despite their rather considerable formal powers, the governors lacked access to the patronage which was the key to political stability in Great Britain. Without patronage to distribute, the governors were unable to disarm political opposition, and the lower houses acquired greater power as a result. The power of the lower houses derived from their control over taxation and the expenditure of tax monies. These legislatures, imitating the development of the power of Parliament, were usually able to bend governors to their wills by their control over the purse strings — a power that included the ability to refuse to pay the governor's salary. Through these means, the assemblies in all the colonies became more and more powerful in the eighteenth century and acquired control over matters that were theoretically beyond their jurisdiction.

Many of the governors were exceptionally maladroit. They resented limitations placed on powers that they thought were obviously their own, and they were, in any event, not the ablest men in the huge bureaucracy of the British Empire. For example, Edward Hyde, Lord Cornbury, served as Governor of New York early in the eighteenth century. Not only did he succeed in alienating virtually everyone in the colony through his imperious behavior; he was also a transvestite who walked the battlements of the fort dressed as a woman. He had his portrait painted in similar garb because he believed that his resemblance to his cousin, Queen Anne, would augment his power and dignity. Needless to say, such behavior did not endear him to the people of the colony.

Edward Hyde, Lord Cornbury, was governor of New York at the beginning of the eighteenth century. To increase his authority he dressed in the manner of his cousin, Queen Anne. (Courtesy of the New-York Historical Society, New York City)

Cornbury was an extreme case, but he was symbolic of the lack of skill and tact from which many a colonial governor suffered. Even the most skillful governors, however, faced almost constant opposition from the assemblies. The theoretical balance of colonial government simply did not operate as it was supposed to operate.

The issues that divided governors and assemblies were numerous, and they varied from one colony to another. They included the nature of representation and the distribution of seats among the various constituencies, the allotment of land, the issuance of paper money, and the granting of governmental contracts. The mutual suspicion of governors and legislatures appeared whenever there was power to be exercised or money to be made, which is to say that such strife was almost constant. It was through the assemblies that the elites of the colonies could translate their socioeconomic positions into political power that would further enhance their influence, status, and wealth. However, in many colonies the elites were divided among themselves and not at all unanimous in their views, or in their opposition to the governor. As a result, political conflict usually set the leaders of an opposition party in the assembly against the governor and his party of *local* supporters. The trial in New York of John Peter Zenger for seditious libel in 1735, usually remembered as a vindication of the freedom of the press, was actually part of a larger political confrontation. The governor, William Cosby, and his supporters opposed Lewis Morris (whom Cosby had removed from office as Chief Justice of the Supreme Court) and Morris' supporters. Zenger's newspaper, the spokesman of the Morris party, had published a vicious attack against Cosby. Zenger's acquittal was not justified by the legal definition of seditious libel. It represented a victory of Morris over Cosby, not a triumph of liberty. The Morris-Cosby dispute was typical of political confrontations in the colonies because it arrayed a "popular" party (the Morrisites) against another faction associated with the governor (the Cosbyites).

Still other factors exacerbated political instability in the colonies. Within the assemblies, there were also rival factions who sought policies that would benefit the interests that they represented. Ethnic heterogeneity, religious diversity, landlord-tenant antagonisms, debtor-creditor relations, and sectional differences all further splintered the already contentious assemblies. In addition, frequent elections—annual in New England, every two or three years elsewhere—kept political temperatures high, and the enlarged electorate participated actively and vociferously in the entire process. Colonial politics were, to use the eighteenth-century word, "factious." They drew their animated character from population growth—more people were taking part in politics—and from economic prosperity—there were more politics in which to take part. Access to office meant access to control over the fruits of economic growth. Moreover, the nature of eighteenth-century political life was additional evidence of anglicization, since the process of political change paralleled that through which Parliament had gained control over English political life in the previous century. The experiences of the elites in organizing for political purposes and of the populace in making political choices were vitally important, moreover, in providing colonists of every social strata with concrete training in the realities of modern interest-group politics, training that familiarized them with techniques of organization and action that would prove very useful in the 1760s and 1770s.

Political Ideology

The antiauthoritarian bent of colonial politicians was not at all new. However, they did adopt a new ideology to explain and justify their behavior. The major tenets of that ideology originated in England among a group of pamphleteers and politicians who were variously called Commonwealthmen, Country Whigs, Opposition Whigs, or Real Whigs. They attacked the administration of Robert Walpole, the great Prime Minister of the era, for its corruption and venality. They claimed to represent the true spirit of the Glorious Revolution, and they elaborated their ideas in books, newspapers, and pamphlets that Americans read avidly.

Two of the most important of the Real or Opposition Whig writers were John Trenchard and William Gordon. In a series of essays published in *The Independent Whig* and *Cato's Letters*, Trenchard and Gordon articulated a series of political maxims that the colonists would ultimately use to make intelligible their own tumultuous political world. The premise upon which all Real Whig, or "country" ideology was based was the principle that power and liberty were incompatible. Trenchard and Gordon argued that people who held power were naturally inclined to suppress liberty, and that conspiracies to destroy the rights of the people were everywhere rampant in government. To defend themselves, the people had to be ever wary and watchful of those who held power, lest they lose their liberty altogether. In addition, Trenchard and Gordon regarded corruption as power's greatest weapon and virtue as liberty's greatest defense. Such a view led them quite naturally to condemn Walpole's management of Parliament through bribery, corruption, and the appointment of incompetent "placemen." The Walpolean system, they argued, relied upon a corrupt conspiracy that had undermined the liberty of the people by destroying the virtue of the House of Commons—the only protection against despotism that the people of Great Britain possessed.

Trenchard's and Gordon's ideas about government and politics had a powerful appeal to Americans, who associated their own assemblies with the defense of liberty and their governors with the tyranny of power. *Cato's Letters* and *The Independent Whig* were reprinted repeatedly in the colonies, and they were frequently plagiarized as well. Whenever and wherever colonial assemblies and colonial governors became embroiled in controversy, assembly leaders cried out against corruption and vowed to check the spread of arbitrary power. It is difficult to exaggerate the attraction that Real or Opposition Whig ideas held for men whose political lives had been devoted to limiting the power of governors who frequently owed their positions to the corrupt system of officeholding in Walpolean England. The persistent application of these ideas over many years eventually led many Americans to associate their assemblies with liberty and all imperial officialdom with conspiratorial power. In such a context, control over the governor's salary became a crucial defense against tyranny, and the prerogatives of the assembly became the only barrier to the "enslavement" of the American people. The colonists also came to regard their assemblies as the American equivalent of Parliament. Saving those legislatures from corruption was as vital to American liberty as the protection of the House of Commons was to the rights of Englishmen.

The use of Real Whig ideas by colonial politicians was yet another example of the extent to which Americans were coming to see themselves as more similar to, than different from, their English cousins. American political ideology was in the process of anglicization, just as American political behavior was. Of course, only a relatively small group of Americans possessed the leisure to familiarize themselves fully with English writers, and an even smaller group associated their personal well-being with the assemblies. Urban workers, for example, were more concerned with finding work at decent wages than they were with the rights of assemblies that were controlled by wealthy merchants in any case. Similarly, seamen worried more about the immediate problem of being impressed into the Royal Navy than the abstract philosophical issue of liberty versus power. And western farmers who objected to heavy taxes or high rents saw the assembly as the enemy as frequently as they did the governor.

On the other hand, these "country" or Opposition Whig ideas might be adapted to the concerns of day laborers, seamen, or farmers, who had their own views about who represented the corruption of power and who represented the virtue of liberty. The ideas of the eighteenth-century Real or Opposition Whigs proved marvelously flexible and were thus very well suited to the disparate political interests of many Americans. In addition, literacy was very high in the colonies. Historians now estimate that 85 per cent of the people in New England could read and write by 1776. The proportion was lower in other colonies—between 60 and 70 per cent—but it was nonetheless quite high by European standards. Literacy rates like these accelerated the diffusion of Opposition Whig political ideology through the newspapers. As a result, even if a day laborer in the city had not read *Cato's Letters* and had never heard of John Trenchard and William Gordon, he might well have been exposed to some of their ideas. Literacy, therefore, not only encouraged wider political participation among people who were outside the elite; it also provided such people with ideological support for their political activity.

4. RELIGION AND CULTURE IN PROVINCIAL AMERICA

The Great Awakening

Nothing that happened in the pre-Revolutionary era so divided the colonists as the religious revival known as the Great Awakening. Rich and poor, planters and merchants, farmers and storekeepers, Easterners and Westerners, and Northerners and Southerners were all caught up in the intense emotionalism and bitter controversy that accompanied the Awakening. By the early eighteenth century, American religion had already splintered into many factions. But the Great Awakening fractured even the sectarian unity that had developed within the various religious groups.

The Great Awakening was actually a series of revivals rather than a single unified movement. It began in New Jersey and New England in the 1720s and spread throughout Anglo-America. Theodorus Jacobus Frelinghuysen, a Reformed Dutch clergyman, began the ferment in the Raritan Valley of New Jersey. Jonathan Edwards, the pastor of the church in Northampton, Massachusetts, and one of the most brilliant thinkers in American history, reaped another "harvest of souls" in 1734. He remained one of the Awakening's most ardent defenders for the rest of his life. Edwards and other revivalists, called New Lights in New England, believed that the religious life of their church members had become emotionally sterile. The conversion process that should have been a profoundly moving experience had, they believed, been replaced by an overintellectualized ritual with no genuine religious meaning. The revivalists called for a more feeling approach and warned their parishioners of the fiery torment that awaited them if they failed to enliven their souls with God's grace. They demanded that church members examine their faith and renew their commitment to achieve an understanding of God's power. To Edwards, New Englanders were "sinners in the hands of an angry God" who would destroy them utterly if they continued in their unholy ways.

The Awakening continued in fits and starts until the arrival of the English evangelist, George Whitefield, in 1739. Whitefield toured all the colonies from South Carolina to New England. By all accounts, he was a speaker of unusual magnetism, and, wherever he went, huge crowds turned out to hear him. Benjamin Franklin estimated that Whitefield preached to 10,000 people in Philadelphia alone. Franklin was a skeptic in religious matters, but even he was deeply affected by Whitefield and emptied his purse when the collection was taken. Whitefield's tour sparked renewed revivalistic fervor. In its aftermath, American religious life was animated as it had never been before.

Jonathan Edwards, one of the most profound theologians in American history and the leader of the Great Awakening in New England. Portrait by Joseph Badger. (Courtesy, Yale University Art Gallery. Bequest of Eugene Phelps Edwards, B. A. 1938)

The Awakening also aroused powerful opposition. Established ministers frequently condemned the emotionalism of the revival as "enthusiasm" and hysteria. Such men, much influenced by the rationalistic philosophy of the Enlightenment, viewed the Awakening as an embarrassing outburst of emotions that were better left alone. And it is true that the Awakening had its excesses. One minister, James Davenport, was so carried away that he stripped and threw his clothes into a bonfire because they were signs of the material cares of the secular world; he demanded that the listening crowd do the same, and many of them complied. But excesses like Davenport's were hardly typical of the Awakening, and he was roundly condemned by the more sober voices among the evangelical ministry.

The emotional fervor of the Awakening was certainly responsible for much of the fire that it drew from "Old Light" ministers, but more was involved than a disagreement over behavior in church or preaching methods. The Great Awakening threatened the Old Light clergy in several more specific ways. First, the revivalists were frequently itinerants who held meetings in the open air, supervised conversions, and castigated the local minister for his failure to shepherd his flock properly. Many congregations were shattered by the conflict between New Lights and Old Lights, with part of the church supporting the old minister and part opposing him for his failure to take part in the revival.

Evangelical theology emphasized a personal relationship between the individual and God. New Light preachers hammered away at this theme repeatedly and told their congregations that no man could intervene between God and a person in search of salvation. To Old Light clerics, such a doctrine had disastrous implications since it specifically demanded that individuals reject the minister's authority and substitute their own judgment in place of the minister's in religious affairs. In short, the Old Light ministers had good reason to perceive a threat to their power in the Great Awakening. Indeed, one of the revivals' most important effects was to alter permanently the status and power of ministers in American society.

Causes and Consequences of the Great Awakening

The Great Awakening was a phenomenal success. It is more difficult to account for this great movement than it is to describe it. To some extent, it drew its strength from those segments of the population to whom the established churches had paid little attention. Poor people, in city and countryside alike, flocked to hear men like Whitefield, but they were not alone, as many people of higher station also responded to his appeal. Immigrants (especially among the Germans and Scotch-Irish), Westerners, and other disaffected elements of the population also drew comfort from the New Light assertion of the promise of salvation, but so, also, did many merchants and planters. Economic difficulty, earthquakes in New England, slave conspiracies in South Carolina and New York, epidemics in the cities, warfare with the French, and other seeming omens of doom may also have created the kinds of anxieties that prompt people to seek solace in religion. All of these factors — and others — were somehow involved in causing the Great Awakening. But its appeal was finally as individualistic as its message, and a simple explanation for its pervasive influence is beyond the historian's grasp.

The consequences of the Awakening are more easily summarized. First, it permanently eroded the influence of the clergy in secular as well as religious affairs. Second, the theological controversies of the Awakening spilled over into politics and further inflamed an already heated political situation. Third, the Awakening prompted an extraordinary outburst of religious sectarianism and denominationalism. The antagonisms that it engendered divided and redivided churches like so many amoebae. Even the great Edwards was driven from his church by Old Light members who were furious at his attack upon their religious status. By 1750, the number of religious sects in America was bewildering, and the doctrines that they espoused varied enormously as well. Fourth, the Great Awakening prompted the founding of a group of new colleges. The establishment of Princeton, Brown, Dartmouth, Rutgers, and Columbia represented attempts by various sectarian groups to assure better and more "correct" education. Princeton, in particular, was established for the express purpose of training New Light ministers, and Jonathan Edwards was soon called to serve as its president.

A final consequence of the Great Awakening is more elusive, but nonetheless important. It was the first experience in their entire history that all the colonies shared, and, despite its similarities to other outbursts of evangelical activity in Europe, it had a peculiar significance in America. The message of the Awakening was, above all else, individualistic. It was also explicitly antiauthoritarian. To a people whose social circumstances had always inclined them to challenge established authority, such a message had profound effects that were not immediately apparent. The New Light preachers told their audiences to follow their consciences in seeking God's grace and to ignore the formulaic preaching of Old Light clergymen. Although such an approach had no explicit political or social purpose, it did have social and political implications. The Awakening told people that they could depend upon their own experiences, and that wealth and high position were of no value in God's eyes. If the authority of a minister in religious matters might be questioned, so might the authority of a magistrate in secular affairs. If independent religious judgment might be valid, why should independent political judgment be prohibited? In this sense, the Great Awakening undermined the deferential pattern of American social and political life and further contributed to the instability of American society and the insecurity of authority of all kinds.

Anglo-American Culture

The increasing anglicization of American society and politics had its parallel in American cultural life. In the eighteenth century, American culture came more and more to resemble that of England. The economic growth of the 1700s, combined with the stratification of the colonial social structure, created leisure time and excess income that could be devoted to cultural activities that had been only secondary concerns during the perilous early years of colonization. The upper and middle classes were the arbiters of a cultural explosion which manifested itself as an aggressive attempt to transport the artistic and intellectual forms of England to America without significant alteration. American authors imitated the styles and the ideas of English writers; American newspapers reprinted the latest pamphlets published in London; American scientists corresponded with the Royal Society, the English scientific guild; American readers read English books; American artists emulated English styles of portraiture; American merchants sat in English-style coffee houses and discussed English ideas; and Americans, generally, looked to London for models of every form of cultural expression.

The anglicization of eighteenth-century American culture was also notable in education. The modern system of tax-supported public education is not of colonial origin. Only Massachusetts and Connecticut required that every town with fifty inhabitants or more support a public school, and even these laws were ignored by most communities. Boston alone complied with the requirements for any length of time. As a result, most children in colonial America received their education at home. Few families could afford more formal education than some slight training in reading, writing, and arithmetic, and some religious instruction. Generally, a higher proportion of children attended school in the North than in the South, and a higher proportion in urban areas than rural. Children in well-to-do families were trained in private "dame" schools, academies, and by tutors. Young men learned a trade or profession as apprentices or clerks. Training for girls was limited to household skills under the direction of mothers and older sisters, although religious instruction enabled a high proportion of women to become literate.

Regardless of what sort of education a colonist received, its content was English. Even for people whose only education was to learn to read the Bible, the version that they read was the King James version. And the more advanced an education was, the more likely it was to include still other aspects of the English cultural tradition. A young man entering the law might well travel to England to hone his skills at the Inns of Court. Another might go off to study at Cambridge or Oxford, while still others stayed at home to be trained at the colonial colleges. Until the 1740s only three colleges offered a semblance of higher education: Harvard, founded in 1636, William and Mary, founded in 1693, and Yale, founded in 1701. The flurry of college founding that followed the Great Awakening increased the number of colonial colleges to nine. Although all the colleges, with the exception of the University of Pennsylvania, were founded as religious seminaries, by the 1760s the central concerns of English higher education—natural science and natural philosophy—had deeply influenced curricula. The modern secular learning of the Enlightenment was at least as important as the more traditional theological subjects in American higher education.

Even an American without much formal educational background would find signs of anglicization everywhere at mid-century. Colonial newspapers, which increased in number and circulation throughout the 1700s, were the major media of communication. They were published weekly and usually included more news of events in Europe and England than of happenings in North America. They frequently did little more than reprint dispatches from the London papers. Almanacs, although more mundane in their concerns than newspapers, were similarly derivative in form. As compendia of weather forecasts, calendars, and proverbs, the almanacs provided information as well as advice. To be sure, Benjamin Franklin's *Poor Richard's Almanack* bore the unique stamp of its author and editor, but the layout and form of the publication followed an English model.

The theater was another aspect of English culture that made its first appearance in America during the eighteenth century. In New England and Philadelphia, the religious scruples of Puritans and Quakers sometimes stood in the way of theatrical productions, but amusements of this sort flourished in the South. Williamsburg, Virginia, had its own theater as early as 1722. Charleston, South Carolina, the most anglicized city in the colonies, boasted of musical societies and regular concerts, opera, fairs, and race tracks—all of them specifically imitative of English models. In 1750, Lewis Hallam brought over an excellent dramatic company from London. For twenty years it entertained all the colonies except those in New England with the plays of Shakespeare, Addison, Steele, and other English playwrights. Significantly, though, indigenous American plays were rarely produced and were generally disdained as unsophisticated copies of English originals.

Other signs of cultural anglicization appeared in such areas as the law. Eighteenth-century American lawyers and judges, in an effort to augment their authority and dignity, began to wear robes and wigs in court, as their English counterparts did. American attorneys made a greater effort to familiarize themselves with the complex procedures of the common law, and they also attempted to duplicate the correct technical language of English legal documents in their own writs and warrants. Similar evidences of anglicization were apparent in every aspect of culture. If these signs are taken individually, they are curiosities, but together they reveal the insecurities that many Americans of the upper classes felt in the face of English contempt for the uncultivated character of colonial life. Americans took great pains to prove their "Englishness," because they were embarrassed and defensive about their provincialism. During the Revolutionary era they would ultimately come to regard their provincialism as a virtue rather than as a failing. However, in the earlier part of the century they sought anglicization as a way to demonstrate that they were a civilized people with mature institutions and a cosmopolitan world view.

Benjamin Franklin and the American Enlightenment

No aspect of English culture was more admired in America than the cross-cultural intellectual ferment known as the Enlightenment. Central to the Enlightenment was an empirical approach to the physical world and a rationalistic view of human society. The work of scientists such as Isaac Newton seemed to unlock the secrets of the universe, while the writings of philosophers such as John Locke helped to divorce society from the religious traditions by which it had been bound for centuries. The Enlightenment's confidence in human reason and its cautious optimism had a significant impact in America. Although many Americans were isolated from this great intellectual transformation, which marked the emergence of the modern world, many others were acutely aware of it. Literary and scientific clubs sprang up in every colonial city. Men met in them to debate political theories and discuss recent European scientific discoveries, as well as the astronomical, botanical, and geological observations of their own members. Benjamin Franklin, in 1743, founded the prototype and most important of these associations—the American Philosophical Society of Philadelphia.

In Franklin, Enlightenment ideals, American opportunity, and exceptional talents came together to form a unique character. Franklin, born in Boston into a large family of Puritan origins, had little schooling before he went to work, first in his father's tallow shop, then as an apprentice in his brother's printing business. At seventeen, he broke his apprenticeship and ran away to Philadelphia. Thereafter he enjoyed unparalleled success in everything that he undertook. He became America's most popular author. The newspapers that he founded prospered, and he was on the verge of establishing a chain of colonial newspapers when he decided to retire in order to devote himself to his various hobbies. He became one of the recognized political leaders of the American colonies, their foremost diplomatic representative and agent, a prolific inventor, and a world-famous scientist. His speculation about the nature of electricity and his experimental verification of his theories was by far the greatest scientific achievement of colonial America, and his *Autobiography* is one of the classics of American literature.

Franklin was the only American of pre-Revolutionary times who not only observed the Enlightenment, but was also one of its foremost participants. Other Americans might read Locke's *Essay on Human Understanding*, Newton's *Principia Mathematica,* or the tracts of other Enlightenment writers and scientists. Franklin not only read and understood the work of such people, but his own writings were of equal stature. His experiments in electricity, especially, earned him the respect of learned men in England and on the continent. No other American of his generation won the prominence or acceptance that

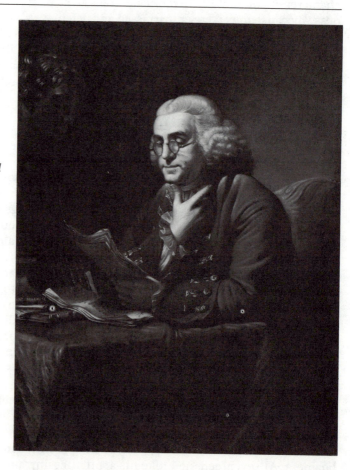

As a son of the Enlightenment, Benjamin Franklin—printer, scientist, and diplomat—desired to "read, study, (and) make Experiments . . . on such Points as may produce something for the common Benefit of Mankind. . . ." The most cosmopolitan American of his age was painted here by Charles Willson Peale. "He snatched the lightning from heaven and the scepter from tyrants." (American Philosophical Society Library)

Franklin did among Europeans of every station. Ironically, the greatest man that the anglicized culture of eighteenth-century America produced was himself no anglophile. Unlike many of his fellow colonists, Franklin made no attempt to ape English styles of dress and behavior. He walked around London in his American homespun clothing and fur hat and paraded his provincialism as a mark of distinction. In shaping his public image, Franklin thus exploited English prejudices about Americans and turned them to his own advantage. Self-consciously anglicized Americans appeared foolish to English eyes, but Franklin was hailed as a great genius and evidence of the "new-ness" of the new world.

Franklin's exceptionalism only highlights the derivative character of vast segments of American culture in the middle of the eighteenth century. The colonists drew considerable comfort from their ties to England and its powerful empire and cosmopolitan culture. In the next twenty-five years, moreover, the pace of anglicization of all sorts—social and political, as well as cultural—would accelerate. In 1750, Franklin and other Americans could look forward to the next fifty years of the eighteenth century with genuine optimism and confidence. They had every reason to expect that the phenomenal growth that their societies had experienced in the first half of the century would continue in the second half under the protection of the greatest empire in the world. They could not know that twenty-five years later they would be on the verge of declaring their independence from that empire. How they reached that point and moved successively from optimism to frustration to anger to revolution is the subject of the next chapter.

SUGGESTED READINGS

Population growth and change as the subjects of historical demography have only recently come to occupy a central place in the study of early American society. Such topics can be investigated both in individual localities and in larger aggregates, and a number of works of both types are available. Robert V. Wells, *The Population of the British Colonies in America before 1776* (1975), is now the standard reference, but useful information can still be found in Stella H. Sutherland, *Population Distribution in Colonial America* (1936), and Evarts B. Greene and Virginia D. Harrington, *American Population before the Federal Census of 1790* (1932). The two most careful local studies are Philip J. Greven, *Four Generations* [Andover, Mass.] (1970), and Stephanie G. Wolf, *Urban Village* [Germantown, Pa.] (1976). In addition, several older works contain important data and information: John Brush, *The Population of New Jersey* (1956); Albert L. Olson, *Agricultural Economy and the Population of Eighteenth-Century Connecticut* (1935); and Julian J. Petty, *The Growth and Distribution of Population in South Carolina* (1943). The work of historical geographers like James T. Lemon, *The Best*

Poor Man's Country (1972), and Harry R. Merrens, *Colonial North Carolina* (1964), is also extraordinarily valuable for the light that it sheds on population movements.

As this chapter indicates, immigrants to the colonies came not only from the British Isles, but from continental Europe and Africa as well. Although there is no general history of colonial immigration, there are several studies of particular groups. R. J. Dickson, *Ulster Emigration to Colonial America* (1968); Ian C. Graham, *Colonists from Scotland* (1956); James G. Leburn, *The Scotch-Irish* (1962); and Duane Meyer, *The Highland Scots of North Carolina* (1961), all treat British ethnic groups. George W. Baird, *History of the Huguenot Emigration to America*, 2 vols. (1885), discusses the effects on America of the revocation of the Edict of Nantes. Jacob R. Marcus, *Early American Jewry*, 2 vols. (1951–1953), is the standard history of colonial Jews, while the Germans have been chronicled in Dieter Cunz, *The Maryland Germans* (1948); Frederic Klees, *The Pennsylvania Dutch* (1950); and Gillian L. Gollin, *Moravians in Two Worlds* (1967). The very important problem of naturalization receives brilliant analysis in James H. Kettner, *The Development of American Citizenship* (1978). Philip D. Curtin, *The Atlantic Slave Trade* (1969), contains the most comprehensive data on the forced migration of Africans to the New World.

Americans who are attached to the mythic image of the independent yeoman farmer will find little comfort in two recent books on tenantry in the colonies: Gregory A. Stiverson, *Poverty in a Land of Plenty* [on Maryland] (1978), and Sung Bok Kim, *Landlord and Tenant in Colonial New York* (1978). Abbot E. Smith, *Colonists in Bondage* (1947), is the outstanding study of white servitude in the colonies, but the subject still demands further investigation. Slavery in early America has been surprisingly neglected in favor of the later decades of its history. However, Gerald Mullin, *Flight and Rebellion* (1972), and Peter Wood, *Black Majority* (1974), are striking attempts to interpret black experience in the provinces of Virginia and South Carolina. The relation of black Americans to the law in the colonial period is the subject of A. Leon Higginbotham's comprehensive volume, *In the Matter of Color* (1978), while Winthrop Jordan, *White Over Black* (1968), is an analysis of the ideology of racism that underlay the legal oppression of Africans in the new world.

Studies of slavery in the northern colonies include Lorenzo J. Greene, *The Negro in Colonial New England* (1942), and Edgar J. McManus' two books: *Negro Slavery in New York* (1966) and *Black Bondage in the North* (1973). The comparative study of slavery in Latin America and the English-speaking colonies has done much to expand our understanding of the many forms that the institution took in this hemisphere. Frank Tannenbaum, *Slave and Citizen* (1946), is the seminal work on the subject, although Stanley Elkins, *Slavery* (1959), has probably done more than any other book to inspire carefully conceived comparative research. Carl N. Degler, *Neither Black Nor White* (1971), which compares the United States with Brazil, and Herbert S. Klein, *Slavery in the Americas* (1967), which compares Virginia with Cuba, are both significant contributions to that body of scholarship. In addition, Eugene Genovese and Laura Foner have edited *Slavery in the New World* (1969), a fine collection of essays. Last, David Brion Davis, *The Problem of Slavery in Western Culture* (1966), will reward the reader with luminous prose and a searching examination of a dilemma of fundamental and enduring importance.

The social structure of early America was infinitely complex, emerging as it did in a congeries of societies with differing demographic, cultural, and economic foundations. The best synthesis of recent scholarship is James A. Henretta, *The Evolution of American Society* (1973). Jackson T. Main, *The So-cial Structure of Revolutionary America* (1965), is a pioneering work of immense value, and Carl Bridenbaugh, *Myths and Realities* (1963), is an impressionistic, but very useful discussion of social development in the colonial South. Richard Hofstadter, *America at 1750* (1971), is evidence of its author's customary thoughtful analysis and felicitous writing. It offers an excellent summary of eighteenth-century social change. The outstanding interpretive social history of colonial America is Gary B. Nash, *Red, White, and Black* (1974).

Carl Bridenbaugh, *Cities in the Wilderness* (1938) and *Cities in Revolt* (1956), are the standard volumes on colonial urbanization, but they have been recently superseded by Gary Nash's *The Urban Crucible* (1979). G. B. Warden, *Boston, 1687–1776* (1970), is the only recent history of an individual city. Developments in the backcountry of the various colonies have not received due attention from scholars. The Kim and Stiverson volumes noted above contain considerable useful information, but much more remains to be done.

The study of American legal history has undergone a renaissance in recent years, but the colonial period still awaits fuller examination. George A. Billias, ed., *Law and Authority in Colonial America* (1965); Richard B. Morris, *Studies in the History of American Law*; and David H. Flaherty, ed., *Essays in the History of Early American Law* (1969), are all good introductions. The only systematic study of the relationship between legal institutions and social control is Douglas Greenberg, *Crime and Law Enforcement in the Colony of New York* (1976).

There is no general discussion of the eighteenth-century merchant community, but there are a variety of more narrowly focused volumes that bear on the development of early American commerce. Frederick Tolles, *Meeting House and Counting House* (1948), is a readable and thoughtful book on the Quaker merchants that does much the same thing for the Quakers that Bernard Bailyn does for the Puritans in *The New England Merchants* (1955). The Tolles book should be supplemented by Arthur L. Jensen, *The Maritime Commerce of Colonial Philadelphia* (1963). The merchants of all the colonial cities receive attention in Bridenbaugh, *Cities in the Wilderness* and *Cities in Revolt*, but one of the most pleasant ways to achieve an understanding of early American commerce is to study the fortunes of the great merchant families. Among the best works in this category are Philip L. White, *The Beekmans of New York* (1956); William T. Baxter, *The House of Hancock* (1945); James B. Hedges, *The Browns of Providence Plantations* (1952); and Randolph S. Klein, *Portrait of an Early American Family* [on the Shippens of Pennsylvania] (1975). The work of Richard Pares also deserves careful reading since it has done so much to clarify patterns of trade and commerce among the colonies of the new world. See his *Yankees and Creoles* (1956) and *Merchants and Planters* (1960).

The master work on the tobacco trade is Jacob M. Price, *France and the Chesapeake*, 2 vols. (1973). Surprisingly, there is no single book on the outlook and behavior of the southern elite in the eighteenth century, although Robert E. and B. Katherine Brown, *Virginia, 1705–1786* (1964), and Aubrey C. Land, *The Dulanys of Maryland* (1955), are helpful. Harry R. Merrens, *Colonial North Carolina in the Eighteenth Century* (1964), offers the fresh perspective of a geographer. However, the definitive history of southern agriculture is still Lewis C. Gray, *History of Agriculture in the Southern United States to 1860*, 2 vols. (1933). For the North, see Percy W. Bidwell and John I. Falconer, *History of Agriculture in the Northern United States, 1620–1860* (1925). James T. Lemon, *The Best Poor Man's Country* (1972), is a study of the agricultural communities of southeastern Pennsylvania which brilliantly combines the methods of history and geography.

Very few topics in American history have been so minutely examined as eighteenth-century politics. Too often, however, historians of this subject look forward to the American Revolution and fail thereby to discuss colonial political life on its own terms. Still, the local studies that have appeared in the last decade or so have done much to illuminate the backdrop against which eighteenth-century contests for power were played. In addition to Kenneth Lockridge's study of Dedham, *A New England Town* (1970), Charles S. Grant, *Democracy in the Connecticut Frontier Town of Kent* (1961), is an outstanding example of carefully conceived and lucidly composed historical research and writing. Patterns of leadership in New England towns receive exhaustive treatment in Edward M. Cook, Jr., *The Fathers of the Towns* (1976), whose generalizations should be compared to those of Michael Zuckerman, *Peaceable Kingdoms* (1970).

Most of the book-length studies of local government outside New England are still unpublished, but there are a variety of excellent studies of politics at the provincial level. Patricia Bonomi, *A Factious People* (1971), is the best study of New York's unusually intricate political life, while specific problems in that colony's political history are gracefully analyzed in Milton M. Klein's book of essays, *The Politics of Diversity* (1974), and Stanley N. Katz, *Newcastle's New York* (1968). Taken together, Gary Nash, *Quakers and Politics* (1968), and Alan Tully, *William Penn's Legacy* (1977), tell the story of eighteenth-century Pennsylvania with great thoroughness. The standard discussion of politics in the colonial South is Jack P. Greene, *The Quest for Power* (1963), an encyclopedic discussion of the rise

of the assemblies and their relationships with the royal governors. Charles S. Sydnor, *Gentleman Freeholders* (1952), remains a wonderfully suggestive study of Virginia politics, while Jack P. Greene, *Landon Carter* (1965), is a probing analysis of the world view of a Virginia planter. M. Eugene Sirmans, *Colonial South Carolina* (1966), and the Bonomi volume cited above are the best studies of politics in individual colonies. Remarkably, we do not possess very many good one-volume narrative political histories of the New England colonies, although Robert Zemsky, *Merchants, Farmers, and River Gods* (1971), and Richard Bushman, *From Puritan to Yankee* (1967), offer original interpretations of Massachusetts and Connecticut, respectively.

Bernard Bailyn, *The Origins of American Politics* (1968) is a controversial, but essential, interpretive overview of the politics of all the colonies in the eighteenth century. The conclusions of this brief and extraordinarily influential book should be compared to those of Greene, *The Quest for Power*, as well as to those of the more specialized studies mentioned here. The ideological and intellectual context of political thought in eighteenth-century America is a topic that has generated intense debate among contemporary historians. Among the most important books touching on such questions are Caroline Robbins, *The Eighteenth-Century Commonwealthman* (1959), and J. G. A. Pocock, *The Machiavellian Moment* (1975).

The history of religion in the eighteenth-century colonies invariably involves a discussion of the Great Awakening. Yet there is no single book that provides a comprehensive history of the revival, nor is there general agreement among historians about the causes and consequences of this outburst of evangelical activity. Sydney E. Ahlstrom's *A Religious History of the American People* (1972), is a monumental work that displays remarkable erudition and contains some excellent chapters on colonial religion. Richard Bushman, *From Puritan to Yankee* (1967), is a brilliant history of the Awakening (among other things) in Connecticut. Edwin S. Gaustad, *The Great Awakening in New England* (1957); Charles H. Maxson, *The Great Awakening in the Middle Colonies* (1920); and Wesley M. Gewehr, *The Great Awakening in Virginia* (1930), are all complete in their coverage of the regional dimensions of revivalism. Alan Heimert, *Religion and the American Mind from the Great Awakening to the Revolution* (1966), has inspired a wealth of criticism. Perry Miller, *Jonathan Edwards* (1949), is the best intellectual biography of one of the most important thinkers in American history. But Ola E. Winslow, *Jonathan Edwards* (1940), and Conrad Cherry, *The Theology of Jonathan Edwards* (1966), also deserve careful scrutiny.

Education in the colonies was intimately

related to issues of religious import. Lawrence Cremin, *American Education: The Colonial Experience* (1970), reaches into many areas of culture and should be supplemented by Robert Middlekauff, *Ancients and Axioms* (1963), as well as by the numerous histories of the colonial colleges. Of these, the most thoughtful is Richard Warch, *School of the Prophets* (1973), a history of Yale. Philip J. Greven, *The Protestant Temperament* (1978), is an extraordinarily original interpretation of the relationship between religious conviction, child-rearing practices, and personality formation in the colonies. Each of these books owes something of its inspiration to Bernard Bailyn, *Education in the Forming of American Society* (1960), a book whose brevity belies its influence on the study of early American history.

Daniel Boorstin, *The Americans: The Colonial Experience* (1955), contains numerous insights on the nature of early American culture. Michael Kraus, *The Atlantic Civilization* (1949), is a sensitive portrait of the relationship between European and American culture in the eighteenth century. The most creative attempt to discover the colonial origins of an "American style" is Michael Kammen, *People of Paradox* (1972), a delightfully playful and imaginative book. Many of the topics discussed in this chapter can be pursued in greater depth by consulting two fine anthologies of recent essays: James K. Martin, ed., *Interpreting Colonial America* (2nd ed., 1978), and Stanley N. Katz, ed., *Colonial America* (2nd ed., 1976). The best bibliography of works on eighteenth-century American history is Jack P. Greene, *The American Colonies in the Eighteenth Century* (1969).

CHAPTER 5
THE IMPERIAL CRISIS AND AMERICAN RESISTANCE

1. THE BRITISH EMPIRE IN THE EIGHTEENTH CENTURY

Salutary Neglect

British mercantilism and the Navigation Acts, which supported it, had a single purpose—to protect the interests of the mother country. The system, if rigorously enforced, would have kept the colonies in a subservient and disadvantageous position; it would have given British merchants a monopoly on colonial staples. At the same time, it would have prohibited the colonists from selling directly to other nations of Europe, which might be willing to pay higher prices for American products. In addition, the system would have inhibited domestic industry by insuring that the colonists did not produce and export such finished goods as textiles and iron which might compete with more expensive English commodities. But British mercantilism rarely performed as intended. Partly by design and partly by accident, the administration of the eighteenth-century imperial system was indifferent, and enforcement was haphazard. Throughout the first half of the eighteenth century, Parliament added new laws and regulations in the hope of increasing the economic value of the colonies. However, the imperial bureaucracy possessed neither the will nor the manpower to enforce the new regulations. Colonial merchants thrived under this policy of "salutary neglect" and violated the Navigation Acts with impunity, while they engaged in a smuggling trade that would have been interrupted and halted if the law had been rigorously and consistently enforced.

Indigo processing on a South Carolina plantation during the 1740s. Indigo became second only to rice in its importance to the economy of this colony. The large-scale cultivation of indigo was made possible by the agricultural experiments of Eliza Lucas Pinckney, who began to run her father's three plantations at the age of seventeen. She raised seed and encouraged neighboring planters to adopt the new crop. The profitability of indigo ultimately encouraged development of the plantation system and slavery. (Courtesy of the Charleston Library Society)

Perhaps the best example of salutary neglect was the Molasses Act of 1733. British sugar planters in the West Indies, who had a powerful lobby in London, persuaded Parliament to adopt a law that put heavy duties on sugar and molasses imported from the French, Dutch, and Spanish islands of the West Indies into the ports of the American mainland. The obvious purpose of the Molasses Act was to protect the market for the higher priced British West Indian sugar. The effect of the new law in the North American colonies would have been to interdict a very profitable trade in the less expensive sugar and molasses of the non-English islands and to raise the costs of rum distillers and sugar refiners by prohibiting them from buying raw sugar at the lowest available prices. Like much imperial legislation, however, the Molasses Act was never enforced. London authorities knew that American prosperity largely depended upon the West Indian trade as a whole and that the Molasses Act would have seriously constricted that trade. In any case, even if they had wanted to enforce the Molasses Act, it would have been very difficult for the British to do so.

Salutary neglect thus provided the colonists with all the benefits of being a part of the British Empire at a cheap price. The Navigation Acts, which required all commerce with the colonies to be carried on by Englishmen in English ships, benefited colonial shipbuilders and merchants as much, if not more, than their English counterparts. The same acts of trade that required certain colonial products to be shipped only to England also gave colonial producers a monopoly on the large English market for these products. Finally, the English government offered generous bounties to encourage colonial production of naval stores, indigo, and other crucial commodities.

Imperial Warfare

One of the reasons why the British paid so little attention to implementing all the regulations of the mercantilist system was that they were preoccupied with the more serious problem of fighting a series of wars with other imperial powers—particularly France—for military dominance in Europe and North America and naval preeminence on the high seas. From the very beginning of European colonization in the sixteenth century, of course, the rivalry among the European nations had been very intense, but, at the end of the seventeenth century, rivals turned to warfare that continued intermittently until 1763.

France and England had now emerged as the premier contestants in the struggle to control North America. They might have gone to war earlier, but the last two Stuart Kings, Charles II and James II, were close friends of Louis XIV of France and at times were financially dependent on their French friend. As a result, they were naturally reluctant to go to war with him. But the policies of Louis and his leading adviser, Jean Baptiste Colbert, engendered conflict between English and French interests in the new world. Under Colbert's direction, the French government sought to extend its influence in America. The arrival of Count Louis de Buade Frontenac in New France in 1672 signaled France's intention to expand and reap a profit from its struggling colony. Frontenac commissioned an expedition to explore the Mississippi River Valley, which he claimed in Louis XIV's name. In the late 1670s, the French began to exploit this claim by building a series of forts and trading posts along the rivers of the West. By the beginning of the 1690s, French settlers—although still less numerous than the English—were firmly entrenched along the St. Lawrence River, the Great Lakes, and the Mississippi River and its tributaries. The result was that the English settlers, always sensitive to the Catholic "menace," were encircled by the French and their Indian allies along the northern and western borders of the British colonies.

While antagonism grew between the French and English colonists in the new world, their countrymen at home were also preparing for war. When James was chased from the English throne in the Glorious Revolution, he fled to France, and warfare erupted almost immediately between the Protestant, William, and the Catholic, Louis. In America, fighting had actually begun on an intermittent basis as early as 1680. However, William's arrival on the English throne gave the conflict a new legitimacy. Between 1689 and 1697, and, then, again, between 1702 and 1713, the American colonies joined the mother country in fighting King William's and Queen Anne's Wars. In the Peace of Utrecht, which ended the latter conflict, England seemed to make considerable headway in establishing its hegemony in North America. The French ceded territory in eastern Canada to the English; the French were also forced to permit more extensive trading between Englishmen and the interior Indian tribes with whom the French had heretofore enjoyed a virtual monopoly.

In America, the experience of more than twenty years of almost continuous war had a different meaning. For the colonists, these wars were formative experiences. The British had devoted most of their military might to the European front and had been unwilling to commit their army to an American campaign. As a result, the Americans had to fight the French on their own or through Indian surrogates. Especially for New Englanders, who attacked Quebec and several other French outposts, the warfare of the late seventeenth and early eighteenth centuries reinforced already powerful fears of the Catholic French and "heathen" Indians on their borders. Moreover, such fears, which had always been a part of New England life, gained new cogency with the realization that British troops might not be available to protect the colonists. Despite English victories, therefore, the Americans remained deeply fearful and suspicious of a combined French and Indian invasion which would destroy their dearly won religious and civil liberties.

The Anglo-French rivalry became increasingly serious toward the middle of the eighteenth century, when Great Britain and France began a worldwide struggle for military and naval supremacy. From 1740 to 1748 another war, King George's War, or the War of the Austrian Succession, raged between the English and the French. But now the stakes were higher. Great Britain's colonies and New France were both growing and seeking to expand. English settlers, land speculators, and fur traders were beginning to cross the Appalachians into the Mississippi River basin. The French were simultaneously seeking to restrict English settlement to the narrow coastal strip in which it had previously been confined. Although the English settlers vastly outnumbered the French, the Frenchmen were unwilling to surrender their claims without a fight. Both sides found again that fighting in America was more difficult than warfare in Europe. Lines of supply and communication were longer, the enemy was more difficult to locate, and the whole affair was enormously more expensive. The only major victory of King George's War was the capture by New Englanders of the French fortress at Louisbourg on Cape Breton Island in 1745. For New Englanders, this was a crowning triumph over the hated French, one that might at last protect them from a Catholic invasion. Much to their chagrin, Britain returned Louisbourg to France in the Treaty of Aix-la-Chapelle which ended the war in 1748.

Although the treaty returned matters to where they had stood in 1740 (the *status quo antebellum*), it did not end the competition between France and Britain in America and throughout the world. The rich lands between the Appalachian Mountains and the Mississippi River now became the prize in a worldwide struggle between England and France. The French sent an expedition down the Ohio River to claim the land around it for Louis XV in 1749. In that same year, the Ohio Company, formed by English capitalists and Virginia planters still hungry for land, sent an agent to find sites for new settlements on the "western waters." A final struggle for control of North America was beginning to take shape.

The French, the English, and the Indians

The Europeans were not battling for control of empty land, of course. The structure of all the imperial wars was triangular, and the various Indian tribes played a vitally important role in shaping the outcome of the European contest for American empire. In the North, the Iroquois quickly recognized that they occupied a crucial strategic position between the French and the English. They exploited this position to great advantage and often succeeded in playing the two groups of Europeans off against each other. They maintained their neutrality, which pleased the French, who could ill afford the enmity of the powerful Iroquois. However, they continued to serve as middlemen in the profitable English fur trade. The Iroquois shrewdly realized that neither the French nor the English could dare to alienate them. As a result, the Iroquois were able to maintain their political and territorial independence far longer than the coastal tribes who had possessed neither their strategic advantages nor their diplomatic and commercial skills.

The two major Indian confederacies of the South—the Creeks and the Cherokees—adopted similar tactics in dealing with the Europeans. The Creeks served as powerful allies of the English against the French and Spaniards in King William's and Queen Anne's Wars. On the other hand, they joined the Yamasees in their attack on the South Carolina settlers during the second decade of the eighteenth century. When the Yamasee War ended, the Creeks turned to the Spaniards whom they had earlier fought. Although the English and the Spaniards both attempted to secure the dependence of the Creeks for many years, they never succeeded. Like the Iroquois, the Creeks were able to prevent the conquest or seizure of their lands by either group. The Cherokees played a similar game with equal skill. The English depended upon the Cherokees for aid in defeating their Indian enemies (such as the Yamasees and the Creeks), and, as a result, they dared not alienate the Cherokees. Throughout the century, the Cherokees maintained a nominal allegiance to the English, but both parties realized that such allegiance was conditional. In exchange for English aid, the Cherokees required a measure of independence that the English would never otherwise have granted.

When the English gained complete hegemony along the eastern coast of North America in 1763, however, the Cherokees and Creeks, as well as the Iroquois, lost a crucial diplomatic advantage. Eventually, this loss would spell their doom.

The Albany Plan of Union

By the early 1750s, despite the Treaty of Aix-la-Chapelle in 1748, the Anglo-French rivalry was reaching a crucial turning point. English settlers were streaming across the Appalachians into land claimed by the French King. The French, who could not begin to match the size of the English colonial population, struck back by building a series of forts along the frontier and by encouraging their Indian allies to resist the encroaching Englishmen. To repel this threat to the expansion of their empire, officials in London tried to secure cooperation among the colonies and their major Indian supporters in the North—the Iroquois. On instructions from the English Privy Council, representatives from seven colonies met at Albany in June 1754 with 150 Iroquois chiefs. The Indians, experienced at operating a confederation of their own, insisted that the white men should observe the formalities to which they were accustomed, which included lengthy exchanges of compliments and gifts. Then they listened as the colonial delegates discussed a plan of union devised by Benjamin Franklin.

Franklin recommended the establishment of a colonial "general government," with representatives chosen by each of the legislatures. It would meet annually to regulate Indian affairs, maintain a colonial army, and control public lands. It might pass laws for the general welfare of the colonists and levy taxes for the common defense. A President-General, appointed by the King, would name high officials and military commanders. The President-General might also veto bills passed by the council. The Albany Congress agreed upon a plan based on Franklin's proposals. However, French military power impressed the Iroquois chiefs more than English plans. They were ever wary to protect their autonomy and left the meeting with no commitments.

Franklin was furious when both the colonial legislatures and the crown rejected his plan. "Everyone cries a union," he wrote, "but when they come to the manner and form of the union, their weak noodles are perfectly distracted." He also compared the English colonies rather uncharitably to the Iroquois and observed that the power of the natives grew from the strength and cohesion of their confederacy. Franklin noted sarcastically that the Iroquois were "ignorant Savages." If they could forge themselves into a union, why should it be so difficult for a group of presumably civilized English people to do the same? Franklin's frustration was indicative of the extent to which most Americans still thought of themselves in rather narrow and parochial terms. Franklin was a man of vision, but most of his contemporaries were unable to see the advantages of a new continental alliance because they still thought of themselves as Virginians, New Yorkers, or New Englanders and failed to attach much significance to their common bond as Americans.

The French and Indian War

While the delegates met at Albany, Virginia, which had ignored the call to the conference, sent a military force to establish a fort at the fork of the Ohio River. The Virginia militia, under the command of a twenty-two year old colonel, George Washington, arrived in the Ohio country, only to discover that the French had already constructed a major fortification—Fort Duquesne—at the river fork on the present site of Pittsburgh. The Virginians built a small stockade fifty miles away, which they called Fort Necessity; but the French quickly obliged them to surrender their position. The French then turned the prisoners loose to walk back over the mountains and report on the French strength.

Governor Robert Dinwiddie of Virginia now called for help from England. Despite the fact that they were officially still at peace with France, the British recognized that their enemies were preparing for a major military effort in America and sent General Edward Braddock and 1,500 soldiers to the colonies. In July 1755, Braddock, reinforced by about 1,200 colonial militiamen, set off to capture Fort Duquesne. The French and Indians ambushed them about eight miles from the fort; they destroyed the British force and killed Braddock.

For the next two years, the war went badly for the British and the Americans. London officials, preoccupied with European campaigns against the French, sent unskilled generals to America. Colonial assemblies refused to vote sufficient money or troops for successful defense against the French. The Scotch-Irish on the Pennsylvania frontier, seriously menaced by Indian warriors and French troops, forced the pacifist Quakers to withdraw from the colonial legislature so that the more bellicose representatives could vote for military appropriations. Nevertheless, the key forts fell to the French and the

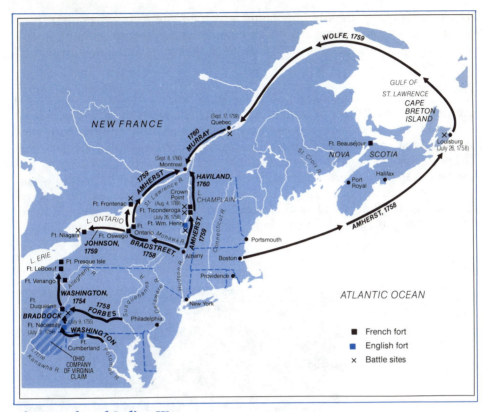

The French and Indian War

Indians, and the whole frontier was exposed to attack. Defeat seemed near for a while.

The tide turned in 1757, when the British finally found a statesman, William Pitt, who could implement the government's determination to wage all-out war against the French around the world. Pitt, who came to the cabinet convinced that British world mastery depended upon control of both India and America, completely shifted England's military policy. He left the war against France on the continent to his Prussian allies and sent England's finest soldiers and best young generals to America. Arguments with colonial legislatures ceased when Pitt promised that Britain would repay the cost of raising the troops.

British and American armies won victories almost everywhere. Under the leadership of Generals James Wolfe and Jeffrey Amherst (who was known for sending smallpox-infected blankets to the Indians), English forces recaptured Louisbourg. Another army took Fort Frontenac at the other end of the St. Lawrence River; this forced the French to abandon Fort Duquesne, which was renamed Fort Pitt. Only a temporary setback at Ticonderoga slowed the British and American advance. In the final battles between the British and the French in America, Ticonderoga was captured by an army under Amherst, and then the two major Canadian cities of Quebec and Montreal fell to the British in 1759 and 1760. In the dramatic siege of Quebec, both Wolfe and the valiant

French commander, the Marquis Louis Joseph de Montcalm, gave their lives. During the next three years, England completed the destruction of France's overseas empire by capturing the French territories in India and the Caribbean.

The Peace of Paris

Shortly after the British victories in Canada, George II died; his grandson, George III, succeeded him. Pitt soon resigned as a result of conflict both with the new King and with English politicians who were jealous of Pitt's power. The peace treaty, the Treaty of Paris, 1763, drawn up without Pitt's help and against his advice, permitted France to keep her West Indian possessions and to give Louisiana to her ally, Spain. England, however, retained Canada and most of India and acquired Florida from Spain. Influential British politicians wanted to keep the French sugar islands of Guadeloupe and Martinique and to

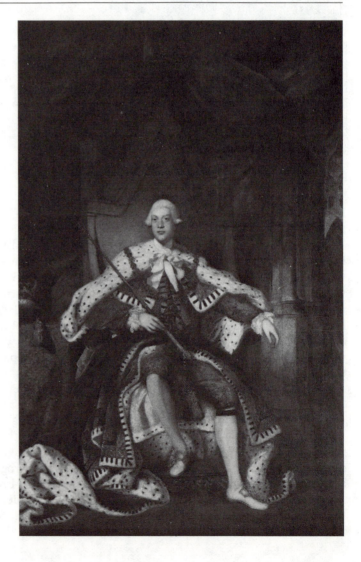

George III, who had the misfortune to oversee the loss of Britain's American colonies, came to the throne in 1760. He did not leave it until his death sixty years later in 1820. (Courtesy of the Royal Academy of Arts, London)

permit France to retain Canada instead. They argued that the trade of the two islands was much greater than that of Canada, and they pointed out that it would be harder to keep the American colonies in submission if the French threat disappeared altogether from colonial frontiers. The French minister, François Etienne de Choiseul, predicted that the colonies would "shake off their dependence" on Great Britain "as soon as Canada was ceded." But British West Indian sugar planters opposed the acquisition of colonies that produced sugar more cheaply than they could. British fur traders wanted Canada to replenish their diminishing sources of supply.

The acquisition of Canada would also fulfill one of the basic aims of the war: the assurance of military security along the colonial frontier. Benjamin Franklin reminded the British government that the colonists had put much blood and treasure into the war effort to eliminate the French menace. He declared that the colonists' pride in seeing the British flag float from the northern seas to the Gulf of Mexico would double their loyalty to the mother country. And, for a time, Franklin's prediction seemed correct. Great enthusiasm over both the victory and the British government's decision to hold Canada swept through the colonies. Congratulations poured into England from the colonial assemblies. Pulpits rang with sermons of joy, and statues were erected to William Pitt and George III. But the Duke de Choiseul turned out to be an excellent prophet after all. Two years after the Treaty of Paris had been signed, the colonists were quarreling with England over taxation. Ten years later they were firing on His Majesty's troops from Concord Bridge to Boston.

2. THE FIRST CRISIS OF EMPIRE

Britain and the American Colonies in 1763

It is difficult to exaggerate the importance that Englishmen on both sides of the Atlantic attached to the victory over France. For the colonists, it secured their borders against invasion for the first time in the eighteenth century. The Boston clergyman, Jonathan Mayhew, had written fearfully of the French in 1754: "The continent is not wide enough for both of us and they are resolved to have the whole. . . . Do I see Christianity banished for popery! . . . Do I see a Protestant there stealing a look at his Bible, and, being taken in the fact, punished like a felon!" With the signing of the Treaty of Paris, however, Mayhew could write more securely of a continent filled with Protestants, who would flourish without fear of threats by "savage nations" or Catholics. Equally important, Americans took pride in their participation in the war and their demonstrated military capacities. It was, after all, a victory which American troops had helped to win. Finally, the French defeat opened paths of settlement that had previously been blocked. A new empire of land was now available, and the impulse for westward expansion that had been present from the earliest days of colonial history could now be given free rein.

The English could also look upon the end of the war with deep satisfaction. The French and Indian War has rightly been called the Great War for Empire, since it settled the long contest for overseas empire that had begun when Columbus first arrived in the Americas in 1492. Great Britain's most threatening and powerful rival had been eliminated from the imperial contest; the British army and navy stood virtually unchallenged as the premier fighting forces in the world; and the newly secure colonies promised to produce ever more wealth to enrich the mother country. Americans and Britons alike now saw their historical sense of the superiority of England and English institutions vindicated. They knew that they were citizens of the greatest empire in the world and could see nothing in their future but continued prosperity and strength.

Yet, underlying the extraordinary arrogance of Anglo-American culture, there were unrecognized problems that would gain new significance in the ensuing years. One was that American and English perceptions of the place of the colonies in the empire were radically different. To English political leaders, the Americans were subordinate to Great Britain and subject to its authority. As individuals, the colonists possessed certain civil rights; however, their political institutions were inferior to Parliament, which could alter them to suit

The Colonies in 1763

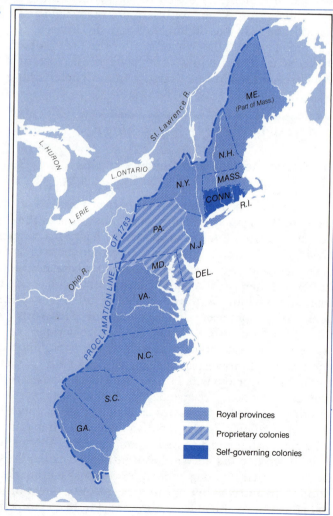

Royal provinces

Proprietary colonies

Self-governing colonies

imperial needs. The existence of representative assemblies in the colonies was a privilege, not a right. The colonists, in contrast, thought of themselves as citizens of Great Britain, with the same fundamental political rights as Englishmen in Liverpool or East Anglia, except that they enjoyed a greater degree of self-government because of their distance from the mother country. As the colonists saw it, their assemblies were not mere products of parliamentary generosity. Their rights and privileges were as inviolate as those of Parliament itself. Any interference with those prerogatives would be a violation of the British Constitution.

Two such divergent perspectives were by themselves dangerous to the stability of the empire, especially if Parliament should attempt to supersede the lower houses. However, the situation was further complicated by an analogy used by both Americans and Englishmen to explain the imperial relationship. People throughout the empire regarded the colonies as children and England as the parent. The phrase "mother country" was not an incidental usage; it bespoke a fundamental understanding of the relationship between Britain and the colonies. The colonies, all parties agreed, owed filial obedience and loyalty to the parent who had protected and nourished them from infancy. Similarly, the mother country had an obligation to continue its parental policies and to behave with the benevolence that was characteristic of all good parents. On this point, both parent and child could concur; they disagreed in their view of the ongoing nature of their relationship. For the British, the parent-child metaphor perfectly expressed the perpetual dependence of the colonies. In their thinking, the imperial relationship was a static one. Americans, on the other hand, were more likely to see the metaphor in more dynamic terms and to believe that the colonies, like all children, would some day reach maturity and strike out on their own.

On the other hand, very few Americans in 1763 could anticipate independence in the near future. The pervasive and differing use of the parent-child metaphor by both Englishmen and Americans did mean, however, that, given the proper circumstances, the colonists might come to regard Great Britain with the same rebellious attitude that characterizes other children on the verge of adulthood. And, indeed, the social changes and aggressive anglicization of the first half of the eighteenth century were signs of a growing sophistication and maturity in colonial society, just as American victories in wartime indicated that the colonies could take care of themselves in a military sense. Furthermore, if Great Britain had been a parent to the colonies, it had been a rather permissive one. After 1763 that permissiveness—the policy of salutary neglect—changed to a much stricter attitude. From the English point of view, such a change was well within the limits set both by the parent-child metaphor and the British Constitution. For many Americans, however, the same changes in policy seemed to violate a sacred familial trust and could not be tolerated.

The Imperatives of British Policy

Great Britain faced new and serious problems in the aftermath of the Great War for Empire. The French threat had been removed, but other difficulties took its place. Whatever errors they may have made subsequently, English officials in 1763 had to devise ways to administer and govern an empire that was

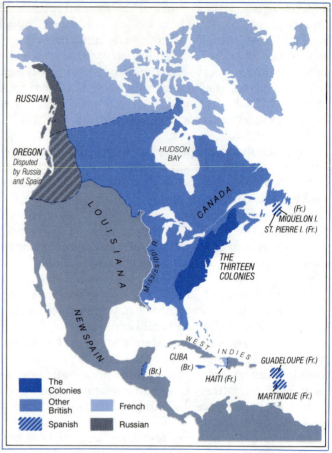

North America in 1763

vastly larger and more complex than the one they had occupied before they entered the war. Canada, the entire eastern basin of the Mississippi, and Florida were all now British possessions. They constituted a territory more than three times as large as the colonies along the Atlantic seaboard. How would these new lands be settled, and by whom? Who would control the expanded and more lucrative fur trade? How would the British deal with the Indians in the West? All these questions (and others) demanded quick answers.

The most immediate difficulty which faced imperial policymakers was the presence of more than 200,000 Indians who lived in the region west of the Appalachians. Many of them knew all too well what the English victory over the French augured for their own futures: English settlers would soon oust them from their own hunting grounds and farmlands unless they resisted. In the summer of 1763, the great Ottawa chieftain, Pontiac, roused the Indian tribes from Lake Superior to the Gulf of Mexico in an attempt to repel the European invaders and keep them contained along the coast. He captured ten of the fourteen English frontier posts. Although Pontiac's movement eventually collapsed, the interior tribes were able to maintain considerable independence for some time to come because England and, later, the United States, was not immediately prepared to devote the resources necessary to conquer the powerful tribes of the West.

In any case, the British government decided that it would be necessary to keep a standing army of 10,000 men in North America. The trans-Appalachian country, the newly organized provinces of Canada, and Florida needed protection. This task could not be entrusted to the individual colonies, since they had revealed a remarkable unwillingness to cooperate during the recent war. It was also essential to supervise the fur trade, regulate the purchase of land, and maintain law and order in the vast and unruly West, if costly Indian wars were to be avoided in the future. Indeed, during the French and Indian War, British officials had assured the natives that England would attempt to restrict frontier expansion, and their failure to keep that promise accounted in part for Pontiac's Rebellion. In the past, separate colonies had done an inadequate job of policing their own frontier areas. Consequently, serious security problems had emerged in wartime, and English officials resolved to avoid a repetition of this confusion by establishing a uniform policy for the western region.

The second major set of problems that the British faced was financial. The war had been extremely expensive. The national debt had doubled during the war; the interest on it alone amounted to £5 million a year. Domestic taxes had risen 20 per cent, and the people of Great Britain were probably the most heavily taxed people in the world. Why should the rapidly growing colonies not help to bear the burdens of a war which had relieved them of danger from the French and Indians? In turn, the colonists argued that England had fought the war for reasons of self-interest, not to benefit the people of America. Admittedly, some of the colonies had been generous in their supplies of men and money. Massachusetts, for example, had gone into debt £818,000 because of the war. Virginia had spent £385,000; Pennsylvania, £313,000; and so on. Still, these contributions had not been forthcoming until Pitt promised the colonial legislatures partial reimbursement. Even then, some had refused to give any aid at all. The matter, British leaders decided, could no longer be left to the individual colonies. There must be some uniform plan for raising revenue in America.

The two major difficulties created by the end of hostilities with the French—administration of the West and payment of the costs of the war—prompted English officials to devise a new and more coherent approach to colonial affairs. As early as the 1740s and 1750s, the Earl of Halifax, president of the Board of Trade, had pushed for more careful supervision of the colonies. What he had failed to realize, and what his successors in the 1760s and 1770s refused to learn, was that any movement of imperial reform would have to be very carefully proposed because it would upset the precarious balance between colonial autonomy and imperial oversight that had been established during the preceding 150 years. In addition, efforts to alter the structure of relations between the mother country and the colonies were usually more ambitious than they were practical. English power and enforcement abilities in America were too weak to do the job that the new policies required of them. Moreover, attempts to shore up British authority antagonized the colonists and created still other problems. Whenever and wherever British officials confronted Americans in the 1760s and 1770s, they lacked both the power and the legitimacy to perform their tasks successfully.

The Proclamation Line of 1763

The impotence of English authority in America was apparent in the American response to the first of the new measures promulgated at the end of the war. A royal proclamation, prepared by the Board of Trade and issued by George III in October 1763, forbade the colonists to move west of an imaginary line drawn along the crest of the Appalachians. The land west of the line was to be reserved for the Indians, and British agents were to have exclusive control over relations with them. Although there already were a considerable number of colonists in the prohibited territory, the proclamation was an attempt to pacify Indians who were justifiably concerned about the consequences of continued white settlement. The English did not intend to keep the Americans out of the interior permanently, but they thought it wise not to give the Indians further cause for immediate discontent. As it turned out, the announcement of the new policy came too late to prevent or even to dampen Pontiac's Rebellion.

The Proclamation of 1763 dashed the hopes of certain Americans who had already formed land companies to exploit the West. But the policy inaugurated by the Proclamation of 1763 was not itself a major cause of trouble between the colonies and the mother country because the colonists simply ignored it, and the British were powerless to stop them. The Americans knew that it would be impossible to patrol the line, and they knew, too, that, once they had settled in the trans-Appalachian West, it would be difficult to dislodge them. On its face, the Proclamation Line was a reasonable response to the problem of the West. However, it revealed a misperception in England about how easily the colonists might be controlled—a misperception that survived in one way or another until the colonies had become completely independent of England in 1783.

Ironically, as truly imaginary as the Proclamation Line turned out to be, the ineffective British attempt to enforce it prompted considerable disgruntlement among the colonists. British troops were to patrol the line, and the colonists objected to the presence of a standing army in their midst for the first time in their history. For members of the colonial elite, the presence of such an army had significant implications. The ideology of Whig oppositionism, which was fundamental to their political thought, warned them that standing armies in time of peace were the first weapons of power in a conspiracy to destroy liberty. In more concrete terms, the physical presence of British regulars on the frontier and in their cities and towns represented a threat to the capacity of colonial leaders to govern themselves without interference, as they had always done. For the working people of the cities, the army posed even more dangerous threats. First, the soldiers were notoriously violent and abusive in their dealings with civilians. Soldiers had also been used to impress American seamen into the British navy, a practice that prompted major riots in several colonial ports. Second, off-duty soldiers often competed with American workers in the labor market, and they were frequently willing to accept lower wages. Unemployment was already high in 1763; the competition of the soldiers for jobs did much to alienate colonial workers. Finally, all the colonists knew that it would be expensive to maintain the army in America—in fact, it cost more than £400,000 a year. For many Americans, therefore, the tax measures that soon followed the army across the Atlantic seemed designed to force them to pay for an army that would be an instrument of their own oppression. The

Proclamation of 1763 was thus a double failure. It did not accomplish its purpose — to contain colonial settlement — and the army charged with its enforcement succeeded only in arousing colonial suspicions about English intentions.

The Grenville Program

George Grenville became Prime Minister in 1763. He was a fiscal conservative, determined to pay off Britain's £147 million national debt, or at least to reduce it. He began by raising taxes in England and by trying to reduce governmental expenditures; but he was also determined that Americans should share the financial burdens of a war that had been fought, at least in part, to protect them. Grenville's plan had several components. The first was to bring salutary neglect to an end through enforcement of the existing acts of trade. Customs officials — many accustomed to drawing their salaries and enjoying their leisure in London — were ordered to report to their posts in America and to attend strictly to their duties. Judges who winked at the unlawful commerce that Americans carried on with Europe and the West Indies were eliminated. In general, Grenville sought to correct the faults that the Privy Council had noted in October 1763, when it complained that "through Neglect, Connivance and Fraud, not only the Revenue is impaired, but the Commerce of the Colonies is diverted from its natural Course and the salutary Provisions of many wise Laws to secure it to the Mother Country are in great Measure defeated."

Grenville knew that, even if the current laws were perfectly enforced, the revenues that they generated would be insufficient. It was clear to the Prime Minister that the colonies would have to be taxed. He considered a stamp tax on legal documents but temporarily rejected the idea because of the resistance that it might arouse in America. He settled instead on new customs duties and changes in the institutions and methods of enforcement. Parliament passed a measure called the Revenue Act of 1764 (dubbed the Sugar Act in the colonies). The new law had two crucial provisions. First, it reduced the duty on foreign molasses by half, from the six-pence-a-gallon levy of the still unenforced Molasses Act of 1733. But a clear intention to see that the new duty would be collected accompanied this reduction. In addition, there was a direct statement that the purpose of the duty was to raise revenue rather than to regulate trade. The bill also reorganized and strengthened the system for trying smugglers by creating new vice admiralty courts, where suspects could be tried without a jury. The vice admiralty courts, along with the presence of increased naval patrols along the coast, suggested an entirely new state of affairs for colonial merchants.

In these circumstances, the three-pence-per-gallon duty on foreign molasses was onerous, indeed. In order to avoid paying it, colonial importers would have to rely exclusively on British sugar growers. But the British West Indies could furnish less than two thirds of the molasses necessary for the thirty rum distilleries of Rhode Island alone, to say nothing of the sixty distilleries of Massachusetts. Without rum, the African slave trade would be disrupted, and without slaves, bills of credit would be more difficult to obtain in the West Indies. Furthermore, colonial merchants very much needed the money that they received from the French, Spanish, and Dutch islands. Otherwise, they could not settle the large debts that they owed to their British creditors for imported articles. Critics warned that the ministry was killing the goose that laid the golden egg by shutting off the colonial trade with the foreign West Indies. If they were deprived of their best market, well-to-do Americans would have to stop importing British goods.

In short, the Sugar Act was more than just another customs duty; it threatened to disrupt the entire trade upon which American prosperity had been based. But it was only part of Grenville's program. He also pushed another bill through Parliament: the Currency Act, whose provisions increased the economic hardships imposed by the Sugar Act. This second piece of legislation outlawed the issuance of paper money in the colonies. A similar measure, which applied only to New England, had been passed in 1751 as part of the Halifax reforms; it had been indifferently enforced during the war. Parliament now alerted the colonies to take the prohibition seriously. The Sugar Act most immediately affected the northern merchants, but the Currency Act hurt everyone.

The colonists were exporters of raw materials and importers of finished products and had always suffered from a shortage of gold and silver. Paper money had been their solution to their inadequate supply of hard money. Many groups of colonists had come to depend on paper currency, and the Currency Act was potentially disastrous for them — especially if they were in debt. For example, the indebtedness of southern planters to Scottish factors had been increasing for many years. Similarly, northern merchants had been facing a rising debt for English manufactured goods since the 1740s. Paper money was equally important to artisans and shopkeepers, who were frequently in debt to the merchants. The whole structure of commercial credit thus depended upon paper money. Moreover, the colonists pointed out that the measure would eventually hurt British merchants. How were the Americans to pay for imported items if they had no money for domestic commerce?

Neither the Sugar Act nor the Currency Act was well received in the colonies. Individually, and in tandem, they threatened the prosperity of significant sectors of colonial society. Few colonists tried to hide the fact that their grievances were economic. But there were constitutional issues involved as well. The Sugar Act, the colonists contended, was an attempt by the British to tax the colonies. They did not object to the regulation by Parliament of their trade, but the Sugar Act was explicitly a revenue measure, and, worse still, a tax levied without the consent of those who would pay it. Because the colonies were not represented in Parliament, and because no Englishman could be taxed without representation, the Sugar Act violated the British Constitution. The Americans acknowledged that Parliament could legislate for the better administration of the empire, but they denied that it had any right to raise revenue through taxes of *any* kind.

Beyond the economic and constitutional issues that the Grenville program raised, there were other, more symbolic questions that troubled the Americans. The Sugar and Currency Acts seemed only portents of things to come. The colonists knew that, even if it was enforced, the Sugar Act would not supply half the revenue that Grenville hoped to raise; and the Currency Act interfered with a legislative right that the colonial assemblies had always been able to exercise. In 1764, therefore, while Parliament considered still other measures, the Americans made it clear that they regarded their assemblies as virtually sovereign in internal affairs and their exemption from parliamentary taxation as a right "the Deprivation of which, will dispirit the People, abate their Industry, discourage Trade, introduce Discord, Poverty and Slavery . . . and shake the Power and Independency of the most opulent and flourishing Empire in the World."

The Stamp Act Crisis

Parliament eventually amended the Sugar Act in 1766 by substituting a very low duty on all molasses—British and foreign—imported into the colonies, in place of the original act's high duty on foreign molasses. By then, however, the situation was far more complicated. Grenville had never intended to stop with the Sugar Act. Even while news of it was being communicated to the colonies, the Prime Minister and his staff were preparing another measure that would raise more revenue. While these preparations continued, Grenville called in the colonial agents and asked for their suggestions. The agents all strongly opposed direct taxes and suggested a system of requisitions whereby imperial officials would request colonial legislatures to furnish money and supplies according to need. Grenville seemed amenable to such a plan, but he never pursued it thoroughly. When the time came, he ignored altogether the agents' warnings of vigorous American opposition to direct taxation.

In March 1765, Parliament passed a Stamp Act which would take effect on the first of November of that year. It required that tax stamps be affixed to all colonial deeds, leases, bills of sale, pamphlets, newspapers, advertisements, mortgages, wills, contracts, playing cards, dice, almanacs, liquor licenses, and academic diplomas. In other words, it forced colonists of all stations to pay a tax on virtually any public use of paper. Such taxes had long existed in England, but they were completely unprecedented in the colonies. Unlike the Sugar Act, the effect of the Stamp Act would be direct and immediate. One did not need a sophisticated understanding of the imperial economy or any extensive involvement in the world of commerce to understand the Stamp Act. This was not a case of merchants who grumbled about a high duty or overzealous measures of enforcement. Every lawyer who drew up a legal paper had to place a stamp on the document. Every publisher of a newspaper or pamphlet would have to attach a stamp which represented a tax of so many pence per page; every person who purchased such items would find the cost of the stamps added to the price. Ordinary people who bought almanacs, dice, or playing cards would be as directly affected by the tax as members of the elite, and everyone would find the price of liquor raised. Before the autumn frosts set in, agents would arrive from England with bundles of stamps and stamped paper to be distributed throughout the colonies. And if the Stamp Act was not enough, Parliament also passed the Quartering Act in May, which provided for the housing of British troops in the colonies at American expense.

The response of the colonists was immediate. Antagonistic Americans forced almost all the stamp distributors to resign before November. Only in Georgia were the stamps actually used. Americans resisted on several fronts. Members of the educated elite drafted pamphlets that once again argued that the colonies could not be taxed without representation. When English pamphleteers argued that the colonists were *virtually* represented in Parliament, as were the large majority of the people of Great Britain who could not vote, the colonists replied that only *actual* representation would do. For their entire history, Americans had been represented directly by their own chosen representatives in their own legislatures; they did not intend to surrender that prerogative simply because some citizens of Great Britain did not enjoy similar rights. As one writer put it, "The colonies have a complete and adequate legislative authority, and are not only represented in their assemblies, but in *no* other manner." In other words, the notion of virtual representation was anachronistic to Americans. The colonies must be represented actually, or they would not be represented at all.

The colonists repeated this argument in every available forum. Speaker after speaker in the assemblies denounced the tyranny of taxation without representation. Parliament's assumption of a taxing power over the colonies led American spokesmen, all schooled in the ideas of Opposition Whiggery, to declare that the new legislation was part of a larger conspiracy to crush American liberty. One such orator was an eloquent young lawyer, Patrick Henry, who had just been elected from a backcountry county to the Virginia House of Burgesses. He defended the rights of Americans to levy their own taxes in a speech so hostile to King George that someone in the chamber cried "Treason!" Henry also attempted to introduce a series of seven resolutions that denounced the authority of King and Parliament. But a majority of the representatives had already left the assembly, and the remaining delegates agreed to only four of Henry's resolutions. They rejected his more extreme demands, but newspapers published all seven resolutions and circulated them throughout the colonies.

The debate over taxation was crucial, but it was not subject to definitive resolution. Both sides agreed that taxation without representation was tyranny; they disagreed about precisely what representation meant. Moreover, both the Americans and their English opponents revered the British Constitution and claimed that it supported their argument. But the British Constitution was unwritten; as a result, there was no way for either side to validate its case by reference to a particular provision of a written document. Even more important, each party to the debate saw the other as involved in an attempt to destroy the Constitution completely. The controversy over the Stamp Act did not simply involve an issue of policy; it raised questions of the most fundamental kind. The importance that each side attached to the outcome was greater than it would otherwise have been because the Stamp Act itself was only the precipitating cause. At stake was the very nature of the British Empire.

Patterns of Resistance

Pamphlets and assembly resolutions constituted only one manifestation of colonial reactions to the Stamp Act. Crowds, rallying to the cry of "Liberty, Property, and No Stamps," took to the streets in many colonial communities. In doing so, they continued a tradition of rioting for political purposes that had long been an accepted feature of colonial life. Rather than a departure from normal politics, rioting was the political weapon of last resort. Even the archenemy of the Boston crowds, Thomas Hutchinson, wrote that "Mobs, a sort of them at least, are constitutional." When all other means of redress had failed, crowd action was a legitimate tactic so long as it was intended to seek redress for a specific grievance and did not threaten to overturn the entire social order. Members of the elite who opposed the Stamp Act did not hesitate, therefore, to approve violent attacks on stamp distributors and other imperial officials. However, they sought to control the crowds and to direct their actions in ways that did not challenge the existing social structure or threaten their own positions.

Members of the elite were not always as successful as they would have liked in their attempts to control the crowds that filled the streets after news of the Stamp Act arrived in America. Nowhere was this more apparent than in Boston, where there were several different riots, each with its own peculiar character. The first took place on August 14, 1765. It was a carefully organized affair that had the backing of the leaders of the assembly. Early in the morning of the fourteenth, the crowd hanged an effigy of Andrew Oliver, who had been appointed as the stamp distributor. Later in the day, a crowd of about 2,000 people marched to Oliver's house, where they beheaded the effigy and demanded Oliver's resignation. Oliver was not at home, and the leaders tried to disperse the crowd. But the crowd refused to leave and broke into Oliver's house. The lieutenant governor of the colony, Thomas Hutchinson, arrived with a sheriff, but the crowd drove them away in a hail of stones. Oliver, who apparently preferred to hang in effigy rather than in reality, resigned his position on the following day.

Oliver's resignation accomplished the major goal of the assembly leaders, but twelve days later—on August 26—another crowd paraded to Hutchinson's house and sacked it. Hutchinson had long been an object of considerable contempt among the citizens of Boston. He had been a proponent of the act of 1751 which prohibited paper currency in New England and, although he had opposed the Stamp Act as unwise, he categorically defended Britain's right to tax the colonies. He was also a supporter of writs of assistance. These writs were general search warrants and were frequently used to enforce the customs laws in Great Britain. They had been introduced in America in 1761 in an effort to curb wartime smuggling. With these writs in hand, royal customs officers could search any warehouse or private residence where they suspected the concealment of smuggled goods. James Otis of Boston had attacked these writs in a fiery speech, which John Adams later called the opening act of the Revolution.

The crowd's attack on Hutchinson's mansion on August 26, 1765, drew the uniform disapproval of the group (which included John Adams and James Otis) which had organized the demonstration at Oliver's home on August 14. John Adams' cousin, Samuel Adams, led the Boston town meeting in adopting a resolution which condemned the attack on Hutchinson's home. The leaders of Boston were, in other words, willing to support crowd action, but only if they could choose the time and place, and also target and steer the violence in the "proper" direction. In any case, it was clear by November 1 that the Stamp Act would never be enforced in Boston. On November 5, or Pope's Day—an annual celebration among the working people of Boston that was tinged with anti-catholicism, evangelical religion, and class antagonism—another crowd gathered. Still another congregated at Oliver's house on December 17 to force the stamp distributor to renounce his office a second time. Elite leaders were not always able to control crowd activity in other parts of America. One group marched on the home of Benjamin Franklin in Philadelphia; another gathered at the home of South Carolina's Henry Laurens, one of the wealthiest men in

America and, later, President of the Second Continental Congress. A crowd marched on the Rhode Island assembly itself and demanded more aggressive opposition to the Stamp Act. In New York, the stamp distributor was twice forced by crowds to resign when his first resignation was judged to be insincere. Resistance was complex all over the colonies, and the elite had to struggle everywhere, often unsuccessfully, to maintain control of crowds that usually had more radical ideas about resistance and its targets.

The colonists had other weapons in their arsenal. One was nonimportation—the refusal by colonial merchants to buy English manufactured goods in the hope that their boycott would prompt their English suppliers to press for the repeal of the Stamp Act. Another was to give the resistance an institutional arm in a new organization—the Sons of Liberty—which was begun in New York in the autumn of 1765. It was initially composed of the politically active members of the elite, but the Sons of Liberty sought to broaden the base of the resistance. They established a communications network among the leaders in the various colonies and attempted to draw a broad spectrum of the population into resistance activities. They operated in public because they wished to make the people aware of the conspiracy against American liberty which they believed was gaining ground in England. In addition, they hoped to control what they thought were the excesses of the crowds.

A final expression of colonial protest was the Stamp Act Congress, called by the Massachusetts legislature in June 1765. Delegates from nine colonies met in New York during the following October. They drew up a declaration that reasserted their loyalty to the King and Parliament but also claimed that they possessed "all the inherent rights and privileges of His natural born subjects in the kingdom of Great Britain." Therefore, they could not be denied their constitutional right to be taxed only by their own assemblies. Any attempt to do otherwise would be "unreasonable and inconsistent with the principles and spirit of the British constitution." The declaration also protested against the Sugar, Currency, and Quartering Acts and rejected as impractical any scheme to send American representatives to Parliament.

The widespread, violent, and unexpected resistance from the colonies and complaints from British merchants, whose business was being hurt by the colonial boycott, moved Parliament to repeal the Stamp Act in 1766. The colonies hailed the repeal with great rejoicing and professions of loyalty to King George. They had not, however, won the constitutional argument, for the repeal was accompanied by a Declaratory Act. This measure asserted that Parliament had "full power and authority . . . to bind the colonies and people of America, subjects of the crown of Great Britain, in all cases whatsoever." The members of Parliament, therefore, did not repeal the Stamp Act because they had been persuaded by the colonial argument. On the contrary, the Declaratory Act made it quite clear that they regarded the colonists' constitutional position as indefensible—as nothing more than propaganda and rhetoric. Rather, Parliament acted as it did because the colonists had given it no choice. The American resistance had made it impossible to enforce the Stamp Act, and Parliament was not yet ready to send soldiers to America for that purpose. Moreover, as Benjamin Franklin informed the House of Commons, although such an army would not find a rebellion in America, it might well make one.

3. THE SECOND CRISIS OF EMPIRE

The Townshend Duties

Parliament soon provided another opportunity for the colonists to hone their skills as rebels. The Grenville ministry fell from power in the summer of 1766 and was replaced by a new government headed by the American hero, William Pitt, now the Earl of Chatham. Unfortunately, Chatham suffered a physical and mental collapse soon after he took office. Charles Townshend, Chancellor of the Exchequer, took his place. Townshend had no love for Americans, whose objections to being taxed by Parliament he regarded as "so much nonsense." He believed that Americans opposed internal taxes only. Therefore, the King could raise revenue by taxing trade, and the Americans would be forced to accept the tax by the logic of their own arguments. Actually, Townshend had completely misread the colonial protests. Since the passage of the Sugar Act, Americans had objected to *all* parliamentary taxation, however disguised. The only distinction that they drew was between laws designed to regulate trade and duties which were levied simply to raise money. They denied that there was any distinction between internal and external taxes.

In January 1767, Townshend, operating from his erroneous assumption, proposed that Parliament begin a new system to raise revenue in America that would rely primarily upon high customs duties or "external" taxes. At first, even his own supporters were reluctant to stir up another hornet's nest in the colonies. However, late in the spring of 1767, Townshend persuaded Parliament to impose duties on glass, painters' colors, red and white lead, paper, and tea imported into America. This bill also reaffirmed the legality of writs of assistance. But the most menacing feature, in colonial eyes, was a provision which stated that part of the revenue raised might be used to pay the salaries of royal governors and judges so that they would not have to depend upon the assemblies. Another Townshend-sponsored measure established a board of customs commissioners in Boston to oversee the collection of duties in all American ports. At the same time, an act of Parliament suspended the New York assembly for refusing to furnish supplies to British troops quartered in the province. Finally, the Privy Council, in mid-1768, established three new vice admiralty courts at Boston, New York, and Philadelphia.

The reaction in the colonies to Townshend's program was as immediate as it was vitriolic. Not only were the Americans to be taxed without their consent, but also the taxes would be used to eliminate the most important lever of control that their assemblies possessed — the appropriation of the salaries of royal officials. In addition, the new laws violated other fundamental liberties to which the colonists attached great importance. Their rights against unwarranted search and to a jury trial were now in jeopardy. Worst of all, the suspension of the New York assembly was a frontal assault on the most cherished of all their political institutions. If Parliament could suspend the New York legislature, it could suspend or abolish all of them; and if this was true, then all colonial liberty was in danger. Many Americans now believed that power and corruption had so pervaded the ministry that the final conspiracy against liberty and virtue was about to accomplish its evil purposes.

The immediate reactions of Americans were similar to the reactions to the Stamp Act. When the new customs commissioners arrived in Boston on Pope's Day, November 5, 1767, a crowd greeted them crying "Liberty, Property, and No Commissioners!" The premier American pamphlet of the period, *Letters from an American Farmer*, by John Dickinson of Pennsylvania, spelled out the colonial position in terms that not even Charles Townshend could mistake. The suspension of the New York assembly, Dickinson wrote, was a "dreadful stroke aimed at the liberty of these colonies . . . for the cause of one is the cause of all." And why had the New York assembly been suspended? Because it had insisted upon the people's right to be taxed only by their own representatives! There could be no distinction between internal and external taxes, Dickinson said. Parliament had no right at all to tax the colonies without their consent, and the Townshend duties *were* taxes. "*Those* who are *taxed* without their own consent," Dickinson cried, "are *slaves.* We are taxed without our own consent. . . . We are therefore — SLAVES."

Dickinson's pamphlet brought many new adherents to the cause of resistance. However, actions as well as words were required if the protests were to succeed. Sam Adams was already convinced that the only remedy for the colonies was complete independence from Great Britain. Adams, a master politician and tireless organizer, persuaded the Massachusetts legislature to send a Circular Letter to all the towns in the province and to invite them to unite in protest. When the governor ordered the legislature to recall the letter and make apologies, it refused by a vote of ninety-two to seventeen.

Hard on the heels of the Massachusetts Circular Letter there came another incident that inflamed passions on both sides. In June 1768, the customs commissioners seized a sloop owned by John Hancock, one of the wealthiest of the Boston merchants and, in the words of one of the commissioners, "the Idol of the Mob." The sloop, all too appropriately named *Liberty*, was seized by a British warship, *Romney*, which had recently been involved in attempts to impress American sailors into the Royal Navy. Soon after the seizure of *Liberty*, a crowd went to the streets with the express intention of driving the commissioners out of the city. Three of the commissioners suffered severe beatings, much of their property was destroyed, and they barely escaped with their lives. The combination of the *Liberty* riot and the Massachusetts Circular Letter infuriated imperial officials. They now acceded to a request from the commissioners and ignored Franklin's warning during the Stamp Act crisis. They sent four regiments of Redcoats to enforce the law in Boston.

Nonimportation

Pamphlets, speeches, letters, petitions, and crowd violence all caused the crisis to deepen, but the colonists also exploited the method that had served them so well in 1765 — an economic boycott. By the spring of 1769, merchants in the colonial cities had agreed not to import British goods. George Washington presented the Virginia agreement to the royal governor, together with the statement that the right of taxation belonged to the House of Burgesses alone. The reply of the governor was to dissolve the House, but the members met at a private home and adopted the nonimportation agreement.

Nonimportation was an extremely effective tactic, but it could cause hardship for Americans as well as for English merchants. As a result, many importers of English goods hesitated to cooperate. In fact, the boycott might have begun sooner if the Philadelphia merchants had not initially refused to cooperate. Once the agreements were adopted, however, the Sons of Liberty reemerged to enforce them. They painted the windows of persons who did not cooperate, threatened them and their families, and generally made it clear that there would be unpleasant consequences for those who did not support the American cause. In addition, as quasi-judicial bodies, they meted out punishment to offenders.

But more was involved in the success of nonimportation than coercion. The colonists, like other people, had no wish to act in ways detrimental to their own economic interests. Merchants who specialized in imports, for example, might have been seriously hurt by nonimportation. As it happened, many of them had built large inventories in the period before the Townshend crisis and could thus afford to cease their importing activities temporarily. When their inventories were exhausted, they resumed their business with English merchants, and the boycott collapsed. Southern planters acted out of similar motives. Rice and tobacco prices were so low in the late 1760s that many planters could not afford the imported items on which they ordinarily depended. When prices rose again in the early 1770s, they used their new profits to resume buying British goods. Poor people in the cities were perhaps most consistent in their support for nonimportation because they had the least to lose from it. They had never been able to afford expensive imported commodities and therefore suffered no hardship by refusing to buy things which they could not purchase in any case.

In 1769, importers had high inventories, planters were suffering low prices for their staples, working people in the cities were angry over the presence of British troops, and the Sons of Liberty were enforcing the nonimportation agreements as though they had the force of law. The result was a remarkably effective boycott. British exports to the colonies fell in value from £2,157,218 in 1768 to £1,336,122 in 1769.

The Boston Massacre

As the boycott began to take effect and the British regiments settled down in Boston, tensions began to ease. By the summer of 1769, half the troops in Boston had been withdrawn to Halifax in Nova Scotia. But the calm was deceptive. The Massachusetts legislature continued to refuse to provide quarters for the troops or furnish supplies to them. The presence of the Redcoats was a constant irritation to the citizens — especially those who had to compete with idle soldiers for scarce jobs.

On March 5, 1770, the antagonism between the soldiers and citizens erupted into tragic violence. Some British soldiers, taunted and pelted by snowballs by a crowd of jeering men and boys, fired into the group and killed five men and wounded six more. The first to fall was a mulatto seaman, Crispus Attucks. This act of bloodshed roused the town and the surrounding country to fury. Samuel Adams hastened to Acting Governor Thomas Hutchinson's house and demanded the immediate removal of the soldiers from the town. Hutchinson yielded, and the troops were taken down the harbor to Castle William. The customs commissioners, who knew the Boston crowd all too well, wisely decided to accompany them. Two Bostonians, John Adams and Josiah Quincy,

"The Bloody Massacre perpetrated in King-Street Boston on March 5th 1770, by a party of the 29th Reg." Engraving by Paul Revere after Henry Pelham. (Courtesy of The Metropolitan Museum of Art. Gift of Mrs. Russell Sage, 1910.)

acted as lawyers for the British officer in command, Captain Preston, and his men when they were tried by a Boston jury. The jury acquitted Preston and convicted two of the soldiers of manslaughter, but they were let off with nominal punishment. Despite the outcome of the trial, the anniversary of the Boston Massacre became a solemn holiday in Massachusetts—a palpable reminder of the danger of standing armies to the liberties of a free people.

The British Back Down

Edmund Burke, one of the wisest political philosophers of the eighteenth century and one of the defenders of the American cause in the House of Commons in the 1770s, accused the British government of "blundering into a policy one day and backing out of it the next." That is what it had done during the Stamp Act crisis, and that is what it was about to do again. Lord North, who became Prime Minister in 1770, believed that the Townshend duties were not in line with sound colonial policy because they taxed articles of British manufacture. It was costing far more money to collect the taxes than they yielded in revenue. In addition, the American boycott was severely injuring British trade.

Lord North therefore secured the repeal of all the Townshend duties except a trifling tax of three pence a pound on tea. King George insisted that it should be kept in order to vindicate Parliament's right to tax the colonies. The tea tax actually counted for little because the colonists smuggled most of their tea from Holland. Friendly relations between the mother country and the colonies seemed to be restored at once. The nonimportation agreements collapsed, and colonial merchants sent large orders to British firms. Colonial imports from England rose from £1,336,122 in 1769 to £4,200,000 in 1771.

The years between 1770 and 1773 were generally peaceful. The only trouble originated with some Americans who attempted to exercise their traditional right to smuggle. In June 1772, a group of Rhode Islanders boarded and burned a revenue vessel, *Gaspee*, when it ran aground in Narragansett Bay. With this exception, Anglo-American relations were better than they had been since before the passage of the Sugar Act, and the colonial trade was booming. The merchants, who heretofore had been at the forefront of the resistance, were giving up protests and attending to profitmaking, although importers once again sought to build inventories in anticipation of more trouble. However, permanent damage had been done to American trust in the British Empire. After all, the repeal of the Stamp Act had not solved anything; why should the repeal of the Townshend duties? The colonists and the ministry in London were as far apart as they had ever been on the question of taxation. Furthermore, many Americans had come to believe that the problem did not involve specific acts of Parliament, but a coherent attempt to tax the colonies and suppress American liberty. The corrupt system of English government had encouraged the formation of a ministerial conspiracy, and the colonists knew that conspiracies could be devious in achieving their goals.

Although some people believed that hostilities were at an end, radical leaders like Sam Adams warned the colonists to be watchful and urged them not to be complacent. Adams sought to keep the people stirred up with letters and articles in newspapers. "It is high time," he wrote, "for the people of this country explicitly to declare whether they will be Freemen or Slaves. . . . Let it be the topic of conversation in every Social Club. Let every Town assemble. Let Associations & Combinations be everywhere set up to consult and recover our just rights." In 1772, Adams organized committees of correspondence in all the towns of Massachusetts. The next year, Thomas Jefferson of Virginia extended the committees of correspondence to all the colonies.

Furthermore, Adams, Jefferson, and other colonial leaders could point to additional evidence that the crisis had abated only temporarily. For some years, an English radical, John Wilkes, had led a popular movement to reform the English government. He was several times elected to Parliament and several times expelled by that body's conservative leadership. Wilkes was even jailed for attacking the government in a pamphlet, *The North Briton #45*. A friendly crowd gathered outside his cell. Troops, called to the scene to maintain order, fired into the crowd and killed several persons. To Americans, the persecution of Wilkes proved that a ministerial conspiracy did in fact exist to suppress liberty throughout the empire. The number *45* became a symbol in the colonies of resistance to the conspiracy. When a New York radical, Alexander McDougall, was jailed on charges similar to those that had led to Wilkes' imprisonment, forty-five men visited him on the forty-fifth day of his incarceration and dined with him on forty-five pounds of beef from a steer that was forty-five months old. When the South Carolina assembly appropriated money to help pay Wilkes' debts, such a controversy ensued that royal government in the colony broke down altogether. The colonists, in other words, adopted Wilkes' cause as their own. His difficulties proved to them that the plot against liberty was continuing even though the Townshend duties had been repealed. Even worse, the expulsion of Wilkes from the House of Commons seemed to demonstrate that even that bastion of the British Constitution was implicated in the plot.

A final blow to colonial trust during the deceptively quiet period after 1770 came from the King, whom Americans had long thought to be sympathetic to their cause but misled by the ministry. George made it clear that he regarded the rebellious behavior of his American subjects to be unacceptable. When presented with a colonial petition for relief, he said that, although he was always ready to listen to the complaints of his subjects, he looked upon the American "Address and Remonstrance" as "disrespectful to me, injurious to Parliament, and irreconcilable to the Principles of the Constitution." The King's statement was widely publicized in America. To many colonists, the loss of the King's protection was a disaster. It was proof that every sector of the British government was now infected by the contagion of corruption and conspiracy. Calm might prevail momentarily, but Americans knew that they could not survive the evil machinations of a scheme to reduce them to slavery. News from London soon seemed to confirm their worst suspicions.

4. TOWARD REVOLUTION

A Tempest Over Tea

By the spring of 1773, the colonists had had more than eight years of experience in resisting what they believed to be imperial encroachments upon their historic liberties. They possessed a substantial repertoire of constitutional arguments and an articulate group of spokesmen and pamphleteers to express them. They had an arsenal of tactical weapons, including intercolonial meetings, crowd actions, and economic boycotts. These weapons had all proved effective. The committees of correspondence and the Sons of Liberty were also two powerful and effective instruments able to communicate information rapidly and organize resistance with equal speed.

In May 1773, two months after Thomas Jefferson organized the intercolonial committees of correspondence, Lord North provided them with their first piece of news. At North's and the King's behest, Parliament had passed the Tea Act, a measure directed more toward salvaging the faltering East India Company than taxing the colonies. The East India Company had a monopoly on the importation of tea into England, for which it paid a duty of a shilling a pound.

The company was in financial distress in 1773—it had 17,000,000 pounds of tea stored in England on which it could not pay the duty, and it could not sell the tea until the duty had been paid. Lord North and the King settled on the clever scheme of permitting the company to ship its tea directly to America and to sell it there. Thus it would not have to pay the shilling duty. In this way, the government could accomplish three objectives: the company would have a large market in which to dispose of its tea; it could afford to sell the tea in America at a lower price than was paid for tea smuggled from Holland; and the duty of three pence a pound collected in America would bring a neat sum to the British Treasury. These provisions were embodied in the Tea Act, and several ships loaded with East India tea sailed for the colonies in the autumn of 1773.

Unfortunately, both Lord North and the King overlooked two very important questions in devising their plan: first, would the colonists be bribed to buy British tea at the cheaper price and be willing to pay the three-pence duty? This would imply acceptance of Parliament's right to tax them. Second, would the merchants, who profited by handling smuggled tea, be content to be replaced by agents of the East India Company? In effect, this would mean granting outsiders a monopoly on the sale of tea in the colonies. The answers to both these questions were negative. The colonists feared that if one monopoly was established, others would follow. Merchants who had dropped out of the resistance now returned to it in even larger numbers, and colonists everywhere found their local committees determined that not a drop of East India tea would be drunk in North America. When tea ships reached New York and Phil-

"The Able Doctor; Or, America Swallowing the Bitter Draught." This cartoon, typical of eighteenth-century Anglo-American satire, depicts Liberty being assaulted by the British Ministry and forced to drink tea. (Courtesy of the Trustees of the British Museum, London)

adelphia, radicals persuaded their captains to return to England without unloading their cargo. At Charleston the tea was landed, but it was stored in the
cellar of the exchange building (three years later it was sold at auction to support the Revolution). Colonists in Annapolis, Maryland, burned a tea ship and
its cargo, but it was in Boston that the Tea Act set off the most dramatic confrontation.

The Boston Tea Party

As they had been doing since the Stamp Act, the colonists simply made it
impossible for British officials to enforce the law. In Boston, Thomas Hutchinson, now Governor of Massachusetts, had run out of patience. He was determined that parliamentary and royal authority should be obeyed. The Boston
tea consignment had been entered at the customs, and Hutchinson, whose two
sons and nephew were among the agents assigned to sell the shipment, refused
to permit customs officers to release the ships. For their part, Bostonians regarded the Tea Act and Hutchinson's stubbornness as attempts to test their
devotion to liberty and virtue. In a mass meeting at Old South Church on November 29, 1773, they made it abundantly clear that they would not permit the
tea to be landed.

An impasse had been reached. Hutchinson intended to have a showdown. As
he had put it earlier in the year: "I know of no line that can be drawn between
the supreme authority of parliament and the total independence of the colonies." He paid no heed to the demand that the tea be returned to England. The
tea would rot before he would permit the ships to leave the harbor without
unloading their cargoes. Finally, on December 16, a band of Indians—who
looked remarkably like costumed Bostonians—obliged the governor. They
ripped open 342 chests of tea valued at £90,000 and dumped the contents into
the harbor.

The radical leaders in Boston had met the Tea Act with the same kind of
measured resistance that had characterized their behavior since 1765. The Boston Tea Party was the last resort—an attempt to secure objectives that could
be achieved in no other way. In fact, the tea resistance was, for the most part,
less violent than the Stamp Act resistance had been. But tempers were shorter
in 1773 than they had been eight years earlier. British officials now believed
that there was a conspiracy in America, which centered in Boston, and that the
conspiracy's purpose was to secure the independence of the colonies by resisting imperial authority at every turn and by inciting the people to violence.
Such officials regarded the Boston Tea Party as an act of mob violence that
simply could not be tolerated if the colonies were to remain in the empire. The
colonists would obey the law or pay the consequences.

The Intolerable Acts

Even so great a friend of America as William Pitt was shocked by the Boston
Tea Party. British power might soon be at an end throughout America if the
authors of the Tea Party went unpunished. Parliament now decided to bring all
resistance to a halt by making examples of Massachusetts and of Boston. In the
early months of 1774, Parliament replied with what were called in America
the "Intolerable Acts" or the "Coercive Acts." They closed the port of Boston

to all trade until the destroyed tea had been paid for. They forbade town meetings—except for the annual election of officers—without the governor's consent. The Massachusetts assembly lost its right to elect the upper house. British soldiers accused of committing capital crimes in the performance of their duties henceforth could be sent to another colony or to England for trial—beyond the reach of Boston juries. Finally, a new Quartering Act, which applied to all the colonies, empowered colonial governors to requisition vacant buildings for the quartering of British troops.

To Americans everywhere, the Intolerable Acts represented a dire threat to colonial liberty. Parliament, after all, had unilaterally changed the government of Massachusetts without the consent of its citizens. Moreover, the closing of the port of Boston punished all the inhabitants of the colony—the innocent along with the guilty. Memories of the Boston Massacre were very much alive, too. Bostonians could only interpret the provision for trying soldiers outside of Boston as preparation for a physical assault on their homes and their lives. The implications of these decisions were clear to all Americans. If Parliament could terminate the existing political system of one colony, it could do the same in others. For those writers who had warned of a secret plot against America, the Intolerable Acts offered unimpeachable evidence that the conspiracy had entered its climatic phase. It seemed that liberty was about to be destroyed, just as they had predicted.

The Quebec Act

Parliament soon adopted yet another measure that the colonists found obnoxious—the Quebec Act. Partly because of the suspicious timing, American radicals regarded this legislation as an outrageous violation of colonial rights. It extended the boundaries of the province of Quebec to include the territory between the Ohio and Mississippi rivers and south of the Great Lakes. Moreover, it established French civil law, which had no provision for jury trials, and authorized Catholic priests to collect tithes from their people. Actually, Parliament passed the Quebec Act with no other intention than to recognize the rights of the 80,000 French-speaking inhabitants of Canada. The seeming establishment of the Roman Catholic Church, however, frightened many Protestant colonists, who had long been suspicious of a "popish" plot. In addition, the new boundaries abrogated the claims of New York, Pennsylvania, and Virginia to western lands; they would now be reserved for Indians and Catholics. The Quebec Act, innocuous as it may have seemed to Parliament, was extraordinarily threatening to Americans. In New England, all these measures had the ring of the hated regime of Sir Edmund Andros in the previous century. Then, too, traditional political institutions and liberties had been abolished, and the threat of a Catholic tyranny had been only narrowly avoided. In city and countryside alike, the people of Massachusetts began to resist or ignore the Intolerable Acts. In the other colonies, the British strategy backfired completely. Instead of becoming an example, Massachusetts became a martyr to the cause of American liberty and proof positive that the English intended to enslave the people of America. Wagonloads of food and expressions of sympathy poured into Boston from every colony. The Virginia House of Burgesses met in defiance of Governor John Murray Dunmore's orders and appointed June 1, 1774— the day on which the port of Boston was to be closed—as a day of fasting, humiliation, and prayer. It also proposed that the colonies hold an annual congress to consider common interests. A few days later, the Massachusetts assembly invited all the colonies to send delegates to such a congress.

In August 1774, Thomas Jefferson published a pamphlet entitled *A Summary View of the Rights of British America.* Jefferson recounted the history of American resistance to British tyranny and defended the Boston Tea Party as the act of an "exasperated people." The pamphlet addressed the King and condemned his "wanton exercise of power." *A Summary View* was direct, learned, and powerful, and it firmly established Jefferson as the leading spokesman of colonial rights and interests. But it had little impact in England. While the colonists were preparing to resist, General Thomas Gage replaced Governor Hutchinson, who departed for England. Gage brought with him an army of about 4,000 men and intended to deal with the colonists as severely as necessary. Gage was a military man and fully expected to apply military solutions. King George agreed with him. "The die is cast," he told Lord North. "The colonies must either triumph or submit."

The First Continental Congress

Delegates from all colonies except Georgia met in the First Continental Congress in Carpenter's Hall in Philadelphia on September 5, 1774. They first adopted the Suffolk Resolves—so named because they were drafted in Suffolk County, Massachusetts. The Suffolk Resolves declared the Intolerable Acts null and void, but they stopped short of a complete denial of all parliamentary authority. The more radical members of Congress, including Sam and John Adams from Massachusetts and Patrick Henry and Richard Henry Lee of Virginia, wanted Congress to reject the authority of Parliament explicitly and absolutely and to adopt a more militant program of immediate nonintercourse with Great Britain. Not all the delegates, particularly those from the Middle Colonies, were willing to move that quickly. A group of moderates, led by Joseph Galloway, a conservative Pennsylvanian, sought a more conciliatory policy.

Galloway proposed a plan similar to the one that Franklin had offered to the Albany Congress twenty years before. Congress narrowly defeated it, and the radicals made sure that all mention of the scheme was deleted from the journals of Congress. The delegates finally adopted a compromise resolution written by John Adams—the Declaration and Resolves. It asserted the colonists' right to "life, liberty, & property" and vigorously condemned all the recent imperial legislation as "unconstitutional, dangerous, and destructive." It demanded the repeal of all tax measures and the Intolerable Acts and a return to the situation that had prevailed before 1763. In addition, Congress recommended that the individual colonies institute a system of military training to prepare for the common defense. The members of Congress also addressed messages to the King and the people of Great Britain. They said that the colonies were fundamentally loyal. But people on both sides of the Atlantic knew that the conflict had entered an entirely new phase.

The most important measure adopted by the Continental Congress was a timetable for economic action. It approved resolutions asking that nonimportation begin on December 1, 1774, nonconsumption on March 1, 1775, and nonexportation on September 1, 1775. This was a slower schedule than the more radical members had wanted, but Southerners wanted time to market their next crop. This agreement for economic action, called the Continental Association, was crucial. In every city, town, county, and village, local committees, chosen by those qualified to vote in assembly elections, were authorized to enforce the Association just as if it was law and they were courts. The committees adopted careful procedural rules which gave violators the same rights that they would have enjoyed in a court of law. The committees issued summonses, called witnesses, and adjudged innocence and guilt. Because they were popularly chosen, moreover, they helped to bring the entire electorate into the resistance movement and raised political consciousness to new heights. Together, the Continental Congress and the local committees constituted a sort of *de facto* government for the colonies. When the First Continental Congress adjourned with a call for another similar meeting to be held the following May, its members could take pride in the achievement of a unified course of action to vindicate American rights.

However, the illusion of colonial unity was quickly shattered. The conservative New York assembly, in January 1775, refused to endorse the proposals of Congress. In fact, nonimportation was less than a rousing success among merchants in New York and Philadelphia and among southern planters, who signed nonimportation agreements but frequently failed to live up to their promises. In the months before the Second Continental Congress was due to meet, the radical and conservative factions of the resistance began to prepare for the inevitable debate on independence. Meanwhile, British friends of the colonies, like William Pitt and Edmund Burke, tried to obtain a compromise and have the Intolerable Acts repealed, but Parliament was in no mood to yield. It rejected all attempts to soften colonial policy; indeed, on March 30, 1775, it forbade New Englanders to trade with any part of the world but Great Britain, or to fish off the Grand Bank. English policy was hardening just as the resistance was beginning to falter. A dramatic event would soon alter the situation once again.

Armed Resistance

While British and American leaders struggled to gain control of a situation which, in New England, bordered on civil war, colonial militiamen had been training for the possibility of open violence. Bands of "minutemen" had organized and were ready to march at a minute's notice to meet a British attack. Late in the night of April 18, 1775, General Gage sent a thousand men under Lieutenant Colonel Francis Smith and Major John Pitcairn to seize supplies of guns and powder at Concord, about twenty miles from Boston. But the patriots learned of the plan. Paul Revere and William Dawes rode by different routes and aroused the countryside. Church bells and signal shots warned everyone, including the British soldiers, that serious trouble lay ahead. Pitcairn reached Lexington at early dawn to find a company of about seventy minutemen drawn up on the common to dispute his passage. He ordered the rebels to disperse. A shot fired by an unknown person rang out, and the British fired a volley which killed eight minutemen.

Pitcairn's troops immediately marched on to Concord. After they burned the few guns that the colonists had neglected to remove from their arsenal, the British started back toward Boston. During the long, hot afternoon, three to

Engraving of the Battle of Bunker Hill by Phillibrown after the original painting by Chappel. The rebels used clubbed guns, nails, rocks, and musket balls to meet the advancing British army. (Library of Congress)

four thousand Americans harassed them by deadly fire from behind trees and stone walls. By the time that the last Redcoats had reached Charlestown, Pitcairn's force had lost nearly 300 men.

All New England now rallied to the cause of liberty. Farmers took down their old flintlocks and hastened to join the militiamen surrounding Boston. They came, not only from Massachusetts, but also from New Hampshire, Connecticut, and Rhode Island. Within a few days, a disorganized army of 16,000 besieged Gage in Boston. A few weeks later, on May 10, Ethan Allen and his Green Mountain Boys seized the British fort at Ticonderoga, on Lake Champlain. That events were now entirely out of control was demonstrated a month later, when British regulars and colonial militiamen met in the bloodiest conflict that had ever been fought on American soil. It was the Battle of Bunker Hill.

During the night of June 16, 1,600 colonials under Colonel William Prescott fortified Breed's Hill, about a mile across the water from Boston. For some reason, the ensuing battle was named for nearby Bunker Hill. In any case, Gage decided to begin to break the siege of Boston by driving the Americans from the strategic hill. A bombardment on June 17 from British warships in the harbor failed to dislodge the Americans. Then General William Howe who, with Generals Henry Clinton and John Burgoyne, had recently arrived in Boston with reinforcements for Gage, attempted to storm the American position. The Redcoats charged up the hill twice in the face of deadly fire. Each time, as they neared the trenches, the Americans drove them back with terrible losses. On the third attack, the colonials, their powder gone, were driven from the position with bayonets. But Howe had lost over 1,000 men, double the casualties that the Americans suffered. One eighth of all the British officers killed in the Revolutionary War fell at Bunker Hill. "Another such victory," wrote General Clinton, "would have ruined us."

The Second Continental Congress

When Congress reassembled on May 10, 1775, the situation was entirely different from what it had been during the previous autumn. The conflict between Britain and her colonies was now taking place, not only on paper, but also on the field of battle. It would be difficult for the conservative delegates to resist the momentum of the movement for independence. On May 15, Congress put all the colonies in a state of defense; a month later, it took over the troops around Boston and dubbed them the Continental Army. It also initiated an attempt to raise six additional companies and, on the suggestion of John Adams, appointed George Washington of Virginia as commander in chief.

Congress also issued two statements early in July—the Olive Branch Petition and the Declaration of the Causes of Taking Up Arms. The first, written by John Dickinson, was addressed to the King and sought his aid in reestablishing peaceful relations between the colonies and the empire. The second, drafted by Thomas Jefferson, summarized the injuries that the colonies had suffered and asserted that justice, not independence, was their goal. Nonetheless, the Declaration was a militant document. "Our cause is just," Jefferson wrote. "Our union is perfect. Our internal resources are great, and, if necessary, foreign assistance is undoubtedly obtainable. . . . We are resolved to die Freemen rather than live Slaves."

To the King, it was now obvious that the colonists would be satisfied only with independence, despite all their protestations to the contrary. The Declaration of the Causes of Taking Up Arms was a declaration of war and nothing less, and George responded with a bellicose document of his own. He proclaimed that the colonists had been "misled by dangerous and ill-designing Men" who had succeeded in bringing the colonies into "open and avowed Rebellion." Such men were traitors and would be punished with utmost severity. Parliament voted to send an additional 25,000 troops to America.

By the summer of 1775, therefore, events had conspired virtually to shatter the ties that bound the American colonies to Great Britain. People who had shared the glory of defeating the French in 1763 were now, only twelve years later, killing each other on the rocky soil of New England. Preparations for a larger war continued on both sides of the Atlantic, and the colonies would declare their independence within less than a year. How had thirteen disparate colonies, which were more closely united to the mother country than to each other in 1763, achieved sufficient unity and self-confidence to make war on the most powerful nation in the world? What had caused the deep affection of the colonists for their mother country to turn into bitter resentment and violent enmity?

In part, the outbreak of hostilities was the result of two self-fulfilling prophecies. The colonists believed that there was a conspiracy in Great Britain to destroy their liberties. By acting on their beliefs, they had encouraged the formation of such a conspiracy. The British, on the other hand, believed that there was a plot in America to obtain independence. That perception caused the British to adopt policies that further aroused colonial anger and prompted the Americans to consider leaving the empire.

The crucial issue throughout all the controversies was, of course, taxation. The colonists sincerely believed that Great Britain had no constitutional right to tax them, but the issue of taxation involved more than ideological principles. The material interests of the Americans would have been immediately and detrimentally affected by the implementation of the various measures which Grenville and his successors hoped to use to acquire money in North America. When Americans rose in defense of the principle of no taxation without representation, they sought to protect their incomes as well as their political beliefs.

Yet there were deeper causes of the Revolution. The isolated and unsophisticated world of the first settlers had gradually given way to a more modern, cosmopolitan, and anglicized society. The colonists believed that their impressive achievements were the direct result of their unique position in an empire that had benefited from their growth and had permitted them to prosper without much interference. When British imperial policy changed after 1763, many Americans regarded the new legislation as an unjust attempt to change the rules in the middle of the game. It seemed to colonial leaders that the ministry, Parliament, and, in the end, the King were engaged in an act of parental betrayal, whose first manifestation was an attack on the rights of the colonial assemblies. The analogy between their own legislatures and the experience of the House of Commons in the 1600s was only too clear. When Americans resisted British assaults against their assemblies, they believed that they were acting like good Englishmen.

And all the while, Americans had discovered resources and power that they had never realized they possessed. Their victories against the Stamp Act, the Townshend duties, the Tea Act, and the Intolerable Acts reinforced a conviction that they could resist the very empire they had so long emulated. By the summer of 1775, the success of their resistance during the previous decade persuaded them that they had to choose to leave the empire altogether if they could not remain in it on their own terms. Many Americans had learned from experience that they were no longer children, and they were determined that they should no longer be treated as such. They had survived a sometimes painful adolescence and were ready to assume the responsibilities of adulthood. But first they would have to defeat the most powerful army and navy in the world.

SUGGESTED READINGS

With the possible exception of the Civil War, the American Revolution has been the subject of more historical research and writing than any other event in our national past. This is as it should be, of course, since the Revolution's influence has been so pervasive. However, it also means that any suggestions for further reading must be very abbreviated and will necessarily pass over a number of significant books. In addition to the books described in succeeding paragraphs, the interested reader can obtain a deeper knowledge of the Revolution, its causes, and its consequences by consulting John Shy's outstanding bibliography, *The American Revolution* (1973). Four recent brief histories of the Revolution also deserve notice: Robert M. Calhoon, *Revolutionary America: An Interpretive Overview* (1976); E. James Ferguson, *The American Revolution: A General History* (2nd ed.,

1978); Esmond Wright, *Fabric of Freedom* (1961); and James Kirby Martin, *In the Course of Human Events: An Interpretive Exploration of the American Revolution* (1979). A longer general history by one of the acknowledged masters of this formative era is Merrill Jensen, *The Founding of a Nation* (1968). Ian R. Christie and Benjamin W. Labaree, *Empire or Independence* (1976), is an excellent collaborative effort by an English and an American historian. In addition, two fine anthologies of original essays are filled with judicious insights: Stephen G. Kurtz and James H. Hutson, eds., *Essays on the American Revolution* (1973), and Alfred F. Young, ed., *The American Revolution* (1976). The latter presents several superb contributions to the history of social and economic conflict in the Revolutionary period. Edmund S. Morgan, *The Challenge of the American Revolution* (1976), is eloquent evidence of the author's vital contributions to American historical writing, for the essays in this book point up the most difficult problems of interpretation in Revolutionary historiography.

The premier historian of the imperial context of the rebellion was Lawrence H. Gipson, whose fifteen-volume *The British Empire Before the American Revolution* (1936–1972), will be too difficult and intimidating for any but the most energetic reader. Fortunately, Gipson compressed his ideas in *The Coming of the Revolution* (1954). Charles M. Andrews, *The Colonial Background of the American Revolution* (rev. ed., 1931), is another brief book with a similar point of view. The decade or so preceding the passage of the Stamp Act was crucial in shaping both British policy and American responses to it in subsequent years. Robert C. Newbold, *The Albany Congress and Plan of Union of 1754* (1955); Alan Rogers, *Empire and Liberty* (1974); and Bernhard Knollenberg, *Origin of the American Revolution* (1960), are all useful in establishing the immediate background of colonial resistance to British authority.

The politics of England during the age of George III were among the most complicated in British history. From the perspective of the twentieth century, in fact, they can be quite bewildering. A good and mercifully succinct introduction is Richard Pares, *King George III and the Politicians* (1953), but Sir Lewis Namier's meticulous reconstructions of English political life in this period are deservedly regarded as the most important corpus of scholarship on the subject. In particular, his *England in the Age of the American Revolution* (2nd ed., 1962) and *The Structure of Politics at the Accession of George III* (2nd ed., 1957), are monuments of diligent research. The place of the colonial agents in British politics is the subject of Michael Kammen's important *A Rope of Sand* (1968). Kammen's *Empire and Interest* (1970) is an excellent guide to the nature of Anglo-American poli-

tics throughout the eighteenth century, while P. D. G. Thomas, *British Politics and the Stamp Act Crisis* (1975), is a cogent discussion of an important topic.

The history of the American resistance that culminated in the Declaration of Independence has been a source of enduring fascination to historians. Bernard Bailyn, *The Ideological Origins of the American Revolution* (1967), is a historiographical landmark. One of the most influential books ever written on the revolt, it delineates the ideological underpinnings of the American reaction with uncommon grace and originality. Edmund S. and Helen M. Morgan, *The Stamp Act Crisis* (1953), is an eminently readable and persuasive account of the first confrontation between American principles and British policy. Joseph Ernst, *Money and Politics in America, 1755–1775* (1973), eschews the "idealist" approach associated with Bailyn and concentrates instead on economic issues. Pauline Maier, *From Resistance to Revolution* (1972), examines the relationship between the Revolutionary leaders and Revolutionary crowds. For the relationship between religious and political ideas, see Nathan Hatch, *The Sacred Cause of Liberty* (1977). The career of John Wilkes can be followed in Ian R. Christie, *Wilkes, Wyvil, and Reform* (1962), and George Rude, *Wilkes and Liberty* (1962).

Hiller B. Zobel, *The Boston Massacre* (1970), should be read with a critical eye, but it does succeed in evoking the charged atmosphere in Boston during the period before and following the Massacre. The organizational and institutional side of the resistance in Massachusetts is faithfully rendered in Richard D. Brown, *Revolutionary Politics in Massachusetts* (1970), while Benjamin W. Labaree, *The Boston Tea Party* (1964), is a solid account of that crucial event. The definitive analysis of the American response to the Coercive Acts is David Ammerman, *In The Common Cause* (1974). Edmund C. Burnett's *The Continental Congress* (1941) is somewhat outdated in several points of interpretation, but it is written in a charming style and makes very entertaining reading. The interpretation of Arthur M. Schlesinger in *The Colonial Merchants and the American Revolution* (1918) is problematic, but the book remains an essential one. Robert A. Gross, *The Minutemen and Their World* (1976), is an elegant portrait of Concord, Massachusetts, that contains fine narrative of the battle that began the Revolution. John Shy, *Toward Lexington* (1965), is a book of the first importance on the role of the British army.

There are studies of the Revolution in all the states. Among the best of these are Larry R. Gerlach, *Prologue to Independence* [on New Jersey] (1976); Roger Champagne, *Alexander McDougall and the American Revolution in New York* (1975); Richard A. Ryerson, *The Revolution Is Now Begun* [on

Pennsylvania] (1978); Ronald Hoffman, *A Spirit of Dissension* [on Maryland] (1973); David S. Lovejoy, *Rhode Island Politics and the American Revolution* (1958); Jere R. Daniell, *Experiment in Republicanism* [on New Hampshire] (1970); Richard Walsh, *Charleston's Sons of Liberty* [on South Carolina] (1959); and the essays on New York, Massachusetts, and Virginia in Richard M. Jellison, ed., *Society, Freedom, and Conscience* (1976). In *Men in Rebellion* (1973), James Kirby Martin provides a careful quantitative analysis of the relationship between the political institutions of the colonies and patterns of leadership in the Revolution itself. J. R. Pole, *Political Representation in England and the Origins of the American Republic* (1966), also examines a very important problem. Finally, Gordon S. Wood, *The Creation of the American Republic* (1969), is a book that anyone interested in the origins of American political attitudes and institutions simply must read, while Michael Kammen, *A Season of Youth* (1978), is a perceptive interpretation of the larger significance of the Revolution in American cultural history.

CHAPTER 6
AN AMERICAN REVOLUTION

1. THE DECISION FOR INDEPENDENCE

The Breach Widens

By the early autumn of 1775, a good many members of the Second Continental Congress had become convinced that a declaration of independence would eventually be necessary. They well knew, however, that such a step could be taken only if the colonies were unified. The radicals in Congress moved slowly because they wanted to present a united front, not only to England, but also to France, whose aid they would almost certainly require. Conservative members from the Middle Colonies still resisted the idea of independence, and those who desired a break with England, although frustrated by the recalcitrance of their colleagues, had no wish to bring the division out into the open. Instead, they operated behind the scenes and attempted to persuade the more reluctant delegates. While this process of informal debate continued, the breach between the King and his American subjects widened.

George III hired 20,000 German mercenaries to help subdue the rebellion in America. Parliament shared the King's determination to bring the conflict to a rapid conclusion. It passed acts strengthening the King's forces in America and, on December 22, 1775, cut off all trade with the American colonies. Parliament further declared that all American ships should be seized and their crews impressed into the Royal Navy. Both these actions played into the hands of the radicals in Congress. Planters and merchants who had hesitated to cooperate with the Continental Association now had no choice but to go along, and the threat of impressment only exacerbated the antagonisms that American seamen had always felt toward the British navy. Moreover, these new policies were adopted by large majorities in Parliament, while a proposal for conciliation, sponsored by Edmund Burke, failed by a two-to-one margin. Few Americans could now see much hope that Britain might be turned from her course of tyranny.

On the American side of the water, too, the ties that bound the colonies to the mother country were snapping. Royal governors from New Hampshire to Georgia were taking refuge in warships off the coast. Their legislatures were refusing to obey them and were converting themselves into popular conventions controlled by radical leaders. The Continental Congress, after it adjourned briefly at the end of the summer, reconvened and labored to increase the army and provide it with food, clothing, and money.

Captains of American sloops and schooners began to attack British supply ships and to seize barrels of flour and gunpowder. The cannon captured at Fort Ticonderoga were dragged by eighty yoke of oxen over the December snow 300 miles to Cambridge, where Washington held Boston under seige. This artillery helped to keep Sir William Howe (who had succeeded Gage) shut up in the city. The American generals, Richard Montgomery and Benedict Arnold, invaded Canada at the same time — Montgomery by way of Lake Champlain and Arnold through the Maine wilderness. Their purpose was to win the French settlers to the American cause. On the last day of the year, in the midst of a blinding snowstorm, Montgomery was killed and Arnold severely wounded in a vain attempt to capture Quebec.

"Common Sense" and the Movement for Independence

All these events narrowed options considerably for leaders on both sides. In the first six months of 1776, there was really only one question before the Continental Congress: independence. Several factors impelled the delegates, inexorably, in that direction. The first was the publication in January of a pamphlet, *Common Sense*, written by Thomas Paine, a recent immigrant to Philadelphia. *Common Sense* was not an elegant or learned piece of political theorizing. It was, instead, an emotional essay written in a plain style that made the argument for independence in the most effective terms. Paine bypassed Parliament almost entirely and focused his attack on George III, whom he attacked as a "Royal Brute." Unlike so many previous American writers, Paine made no obligatory show of loyalty to Great Britain or to the British Constitution. Indeed, he said that the problem was the monarchy itself, and that the entire Constitution was "rotten." The only remedy for Americans, he said, was independence.

Paine seized upon the central metaphor of colonial history and turned it to his advantage. He acknowledged that many people believed Britain was the "parent country," but he argued that, if this was true, then her behavior was all the more shameful. "Even brutes do not devour their young, nor savages make war upon their families," Paine wrote, but the King of England, the father of his people, could "unflinchingly hear of their slaughter, and composedly sleep with their blood upon his soul." God had destined America for republican liberty, not for monarchical tyranny. In any case, Europe, not England, was the

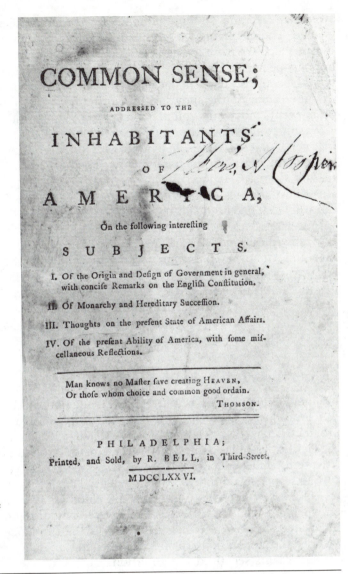

COMMON SENSE;

ADDRESSED TO THE

INHABITANTS

OF

AMERICA,

On the following interesting

SUBJECTS.

I. Of the Origin and Design of Government in general,
with concise Remarks on the English Constitution.

II. Of Monarchy and Hereditary Succession.

III. Thoughts on the present State of American Affairs.

IV. Of the present Ability of America, with some mis-
cellaneous Reflections.

Man knows no Master save creating HEAVEN,
Or those whom choice and common good ordain.

THOMSON.

PHILADELPHIA;
Printed, and Sold, by R. BELL, in Third-Street.

MDCCLXXVI.

Title page of Thomas Paine's famous pamphlet Common Sense, *published in 1776. In strong, moving language, he urged: "Everything that is right or reasonable pleads for separation. The blood of the slain, the weeping voice of nature cries 'TIS TIME TO PART." (Picture collection, The New York Public Library)*

parent country of America: "This new world hath been the asylum for the persecuted lovers of civil and religious liberty from *every part* of Europe." Paine described the unique qualities of American society, not as vices, but as virtues. He asserted that it was the destiny of Americans to break their connection with corrupt Great Britain and establish their own "continental" government on a republican model.

Common Sense had an immediate impact upon American public opinion. Although some leaders of Congress did not like Paine—John Adams said that he was a "mongrel between a pig and a puppy, begotten by a wild boar on a bitch wolf"—there was no denying the power of his argument. More than 100,000 copies of the pamphlet were sold, and it went through twenty-five printings in 1776 alone. Washington spoke of its "sound doctrine and unanswerable reasoning." Edmund Randolph of Virginia declared that, next to King George, Thomas Paine was the man most responsible for the Declaration of Independence. Within one month after the publication of *Common Sense,* the ordinary people of America, to whom Paine had appealed directly, began to rally to the cause of independence and to push even the most reluctant leaders in that direction. As the snows of the winter of 1775–1776 began to thaw, still other events moved the colonies ever closer to independence.

Washington brought the long seige of Boston to an end in March. During the nights of March 4 and 5, his troops seized Dorchester Heights, which commanded the town and the harbor. Howe had his back to the sea and was forced to sail away to Halifax. Eleven hundred Tory refugees from some of the wealthiest families in the colony accompanied Howe. Boston was now free of the army that had been stationed there for so long. For the rest of the war, Massachusetts and northern New England saw no more of the Redcoats.

Meanwhile, Congress was busy. It sent Silas Deane of Connecticut to seek men and money from Britain's foremost enemy, France. Benjamin Franklin and Arthur Lee joined Deane in Paris about six months later to assist in the negotiations. In April, Congress opened the ports of America to all the nations of the world and thereby abolished the Acts of Trade. A month later, Congress took a momentous step and advised all the colonies to adopt new governments to succeed the now defunct royal administrations.

Congress Debates Independence

In Philadelphia, as well as in the individual colonies, the pressures for a declaration of independence mounted in the spring of 1776. North Carolina held a provincial congress at Halifax in April. It adopted a series of resolutions, called the Halifax Resolves, which instructed North Carolina's delegates in Congress to vote for independence at the earliest opportunity. Virginia soon followed suit. In response, on June 7, Richard Henry Lee of Virginia offered a resolution to Congress which, first, absolved the colonists of allegiance to the British crown and declared that the colonies were "and of right ought to be, free and independent states"; second, called for foreign alliances; and, third, recommended the preparation of a plan of confederation.

John Adams seconded Lee's motion. Debate in the Congress was spirited. Some members, long tied to the mother country, were not ready to close the door finally to reconciliation. They argued that a declaration of independence would both divide the colonies and unite the British. These cautious members feared also that Englishmen like Pitt and Burke, who sympathized with Americans fighting for their liberties as British subjects, might cease to support Americans fighting to establish an independent nation.

The radicals replied that, so long as the colonies remained a part of Great Britain, they could not expect help from France. Furthermore, a bold declaration of their independence might be the best way to secure their firm union. If the members of Congress did not all "hang together," exclaimed Benjamin Franklin, they would "all hang separately." In the end, the supporters of independence prevailed because both the momentum of events and the pressure from the populace helped to guarantee their victory. As Thomas Jefferson put it, "The question was not whether, by a declaration or independence, we should make ourselves what we are not; but whether we should declare a fact which already exists."

Congress adopted Lee's resolutions on July 2, 1776, by a vote of twelve to nothing. The New York delegates did not vote because they had no instructions from home. Five days later, they received permission to join the other delegates and made the vote unanimous. Ironically, John Dickinson, the great pamphleteer, was the only delegate who refused to sign the Declaration of Independence. On July 3, John Adams wrote to his wife Abigail: "Yesterday the greatest question was decided, which ever was debated in America, and a greater perhaps, never was or will be decided among men." Adams knew that declaring independence and securing it were different matters, and he told his wife that he was "well aware of the Toil and Blood and Treasure, that will cost us to maintain this Declaration, and support and defend these States."

The Declaration of Independence

Before the adoption of Lee's resolutions, a committee composed of Jefferson, Franklin, Adams, Roger Sherman of Connecticut, and Robert R. Livingston of New York had been elected to prepare a public paper to justify the action of Congress in case it should vote for independence. Adams later remembered that, when he and Jefferson were chosen as a subcommittee actually to write the document, he had prevailed upon the Virginian to prepare the first draft by telling him that Jefferson's writing style was ten times better than his own. Indeed, Jefferson was a master of clear and forceful prose. At his desk in a Philadelphia lodging room, "without reference to book or pamphlet," he produced the document which, with some amendments by Franklin and Adams, was adopted by Congress on July 4, 1776.

The Declaration of Independence attempted to justify the Revolution—for that is what the war now was—as a legitimate and necessary rebellion against a despot who had violated his most sacred obligations. Jefferson drew upon the ideas of a variety of Enlightenment thinkers for his argument; they included Scottish Common Sense philosophers like Francis Hutcheson as well as the better known Englishman, John Locke. However, Jefferson applied these ideas in his own, and in a peculiarly American, way. The Declaration insisted that the basis of government was the consent of the governed. When a ruler broke his side of the civil compact, the people had the right to abolish the government and form a new one. In this case, the King was to blame and bore sole responsibility for the tyranny that Americans had been suffering since 1763. In fact, the Declaration made no mention at all of Parliament and adopted Tom Paine's tactic when it attacked the King and the monarchy exclusively.

One of the passages of Jefferson's draft that the members of Congress agreed to delete was what John Adams called "a vehement phillipic against negro slavery." Jefferson condemned George for waging "cruel war against human nature, violating its most sacred rights of life and liberty in the persons of a distant people who never offended him." Slavery, Jefferson said, was the result of "a piratical warfare." The institution was an "assemblage of horrors." The delegates from South Carolina and Georgia wanted no mention of slavery in the Declaration and demanded that the offending passage be eliminated from the final copy. The other delegates agreed, lest they quarrel and divide at just the moment when unity was crucial.

Notwithstanding the deletion of Jefferson's attack on slavery, there was something hypocritical about Americans who condemned George III for enslaving them when they owned slaves or profited from the slave trade. Jefferson himself, despite his revulsion at the institution, owned slaves and continued to do so long after George III had passed from the scene. Jefferson's pathetic attempt to maintain some consistency on the question of human rights only highlighted the most fundamental contradiction of the American Revolution. Indeed, it is a contradiction that has yet to be fully resolved. The British never ceased to delight in pointing out that American complaints about being enslaved were somewhat less persuasive when viewed in light of American support of chattel slavery.

Whatever the hypocrisy of Jefferson and his contemporaries on the subject of slavery, the Declaration of Independence remains a passionate statement of human liberty and equality. Its powerful prose gave white Americans a cause for which to fight in 1776, and it has provided a standard against which they have had to measure their performance ever since. The literary grace and philosophical depth of the Declaration were recognized in its own time, and the document had important political consequences, too. It offered France and Spain the opportunity to help shatter the proud empire that had humiliated them in recent wars, and it also helped to unify the American people and inspire the Continental Army. Washington had the Declaration read to his troops in New York on July 9. "The General hopes," stated the order of the day, "this important event will serve as a fresh incentive to every officer and soldier to act with fidelity and courage, as knowing that now the peace and safety of his country depends, under God, solely on the success of our arms."

Ideas and Interests in the Coming of the Revolution

As eloquent as *Common Sense* and the Declaration of Independence were, they did not by themselves carry all the people of America into the patriot ranks. Many remained deeply loyal to England and chose to continue that loyalty by supporting British arms during the war. Others adopted a wait-and-see attitude and tried to avoid commitment to either side. Still others had been active members of the resistance throughout the 1760s and 1770s but balked at joining the Revolution. Even among the patriots, there was considerable disagreement about the ultimate shape that the new confederation should take. Despite these qualifications, it is still true that a substantial number of Americans were willing to risk their lives, their fortunes, and their sacred honor in a war for independence which they might well have lost. Why?

Ideology was critical in shaping American political behavior in the decade or so before independence was declared. Colonists came to the crises of the 1760s and 1770s with a variety of ideas which aided them in interpreting British colonial policy and which ultimately impelled them to break with the mother country altogether. The most important of these ideas were those associated with Opposition or Real Whiggery and seventeenth-century English libertarianism. As has been said, this ideology emphasized the eternal struggle between power and liberty as it was reflected in a battle between executive and legislative institutions.

A second strain of ideology was related to, but distinct from, Opposition Whiggery. It emphasized antagonism to the British army, all ill-begotten wealth, excessive taxation, and hard money. Such ideas were most popular among the urban working classes and had no regular institutional vehicle for their expression. When crowds took to the streets, both before and during the

Revolutionary era, they were often motivated by views like these, which were as rooted in class antagonisms as in opposition to parliamentary taxation. A third component was religious in origin. These ideas were most powerful in New England, where the Puritan heritage remained significant, but they were present everywhere. Their central assumption was a virulent anti-Catholic prejudice. As we have seen, the Quebec Act intensified such sentiments.

A fourth ideological thread in the Revolution was also religious and grew out of the intense millenial fervor generated by the Great Awakening. It harked back to the profound religious struggles of seventeenth-century England. Moreover, it appeared in several different forms. In New England, it associated the coming of the millenium with the growth and prosperity of America and the unique religious liberty that it offered. In the South, it gave an emotional cast to quests for political liberty. Everywhere, it gave the Revolution the character of a religious revival.

A final ideological component of the Revolution was the Enlightenment. Educated Americans had read Enlightenment authors like John Locke and were deeply influenced by them. This was especially true of such men as John Adams and Thomas Jefferson. However, Enlightenment ideas became energizing only when the time came to justify a bid for independence. Enlightenment writings did not move people emotionally. Enlightenment ideas played their most important role in providing the theoretical basis for the creation of republican governments after independence had been declared.

In any event, these ideas constituted the frame of reference by which various Americans viewed the events of their times. In that sense, they were causes of the American Revolution because each, in its own way, helped to persuade people that British policy toward America was not simply mistaken or based on erroneous information. On the contrary, that policy was a concerted effort to suppress political and religious liberty in the colonies. These ideas were neither new nor mere rationalizations adopted to suit the propaganda needs of the leaders of the resistance. The ideas filtered reality so as to lead people to believe that their most essential freedoms were at stake in the controversy.

But ideas alone do not make a revolution. The 3,000,000 Americans were not paranoids. British policies toward the colonies after 1763 posed real threats to the interests of many Americans. For example, the great merchants and planters at the top of the class structure were generally conservative. They had no wish to arouse an internal struggle for power in the colonies from which they had a great deal to lose. Despite their ideas about power and liberty, they had reason to support cautiously a resistance movement whose consequences they could not foresee and whose direction they could not completely control. They tended to respond, therefore, in ways which simultaneously vindicated their political ideas and served their economic interests.

The southern planters depended upon the export of their staples at good prices if they were to continue to live in the lavish style to which they had become accustomed. Planters cooperated with nonimportation only when, as during the resistance to the Townshend duties, the price of staples was so low that they could not make a profit. When prices improved, as they did in the 1770s, many southern planters followed their ideals by signing nonimportation agreements, but they followed their interests by violating those agreements. When the time came to decide on the question of independence, planters tended to support independence because it would both vindicate their ideals and enhance their future well-being. A successful revolution would open the market for southern tobacco beyond the British Isles, where it had been confined by the Acts of Trade. It would also permit other European countries to engage in the competitive sale of goods that Southerners imported.

Many northern merchants similarly found the resistance congenial to their economic interests. Merchants who were primarily importers supported non-importation only when their inventories were so high that they would benefit from a temporary suspension of overseas commerce. They also tended to oppose a declaration of independence which would cut them off entirely from their English suppliers. Exporters, on the other hand, were more consistent in their support of resistance because they would lose nothing from nonimportation and, like Southerners, would gain from the expanded market opportunities that independence would bring.

What of those who were on the lower rungs of the socioeconomic ladder? In the South, the traditionally deferential pattern of political life frequently carried over into the Revolutionary period. One group of "respectable but uninformed" Virginians told their local delegate to the Continental Congress that they had complete trust in his leadership. "You assert that there is a fixed intention to invade our rights and privileges," they said. "We own that we do not see this clearly, but since you assure us that it is so, we believe it. We are about to take a dangerous step, but we have confidence in you and will do anything you think proper."Of course not all Southerners were so responsive to their leaders' call to revolution. Some settlers in the western sections of the southern colonies had strong reservations about independence, and there were pockets of loyalism among poor people throughout the South. On the whole, however, southern resistance was remarkable for its unity and for the shared assumptions of both leaders and followers.

In New England and the Middle Colonies, where social divisions were closer to the surface, the appeal of independence to farmers and urban workers was more diffuse. In the New England countryside, imperial reform in general, and the Intolerable Acts, in particular, raised the specter of insecure land titles, abrogated town charters, and the oppression of the Andros regime at the end of the seventeenth century. In Boston, New York, and Philadelphia, the resistance movement attracted considerable support from workers with real grievances against British troops. Furthermore, the various acts of Parliament in the ten years before Lexington and Concord all tended to drive prices up and hurt city residents. Nonimportation also raised the prices of imported goods, but most urban workers could not afford such luxuries in any case. More important was the fact that nonimportation generated employment for skilled workers and artisans in the cities and raised their wages by eliminating English competition. In all the cities, therefore, skilled laborers played a vital role in enforcing the nonimportation agreements. Moreover, the Revolution offered an opportunity for artisans and skilled workers to transfer the power that they exercised in local committees to the new political institutions created after the Declaration of Independence.

The relationship between ideas and interests in the coming of the American Revolution was a complex one. The real grievances that Americans suffered confirmed the lessons taught by their ideologies, while their ideologies helped to explain their grievances in comprehensible terms. In this way, ideas and interests were mutually supportive. An individual's support of the resistance, and then of the Revolution, derived from a combination of factors. Like other people, Americans acted both from high idealism and realistic self-interest. Although frequently divided among themselves, they were able to agree on independence because it expressed their varying needs in different ways, rather than because it appealed to all of them in the same way. Before those varying needs could be satisfied, however, Americans faced a military struggle unlike any that they or their British enemies had known before, one which would demand fervent and committed idealism, as well as enlightened and rational practicality.

2. THE REVOLUTIONARY WAR

The Opposing Forces

Superficially, the American decision to try to win independence by force seemed foolhardy. Great Britain was the world's richest nation, with a population three times that of the United States. Britain was also the world's greatest military power, with a disciplined regular army and a navy capable of dominating American waters while guarding the sea lanes to the homeland. In contrast, the young American republic had no central government able to marshal resources, maintain a sound currency, or adequately supply an army. Its army consisted only of raw, undisciplined troops, many of whom were "summer soldiers," who went home once the firing grew hot or the weather cold. The United States owned only the nucleus of a seagoing navy when the Declaration of Independence was adopted, and not much more than a nucleus when the war ended. Americans were not even united in their bid for independence. John Adams later estimated that one third of the population supported the American cause, one third opposed it, and one third did not care one way or the other.

But appearances were deceiving in 1776. The British suffered disadvantages as severe as those that plagued their foes. Their greatest handicap was the necessity to transport troops and military supplies over 3,000 miles of rough ocean by slow-moving vessels. Of forty transports dispatched from England to Boston in the winter of 1775–1776, only eight reached their destination. Most of the rest barely limped into the West Indies. A sizable proportion of officers sent to America were incompetent—and of those who were not, some secretly sympathized with the rebels. Most of the politicians who planned British strategy were inept and consistently underestimated American strength. Even Britain's military might worked against her. She had eliminated all the other ambitious western European nations; now they welcomed a chance for revenge. America found powerful allies in Europe; the British had none.

Even with a large margin of military and naval superiority, it still would have been difficult for the British to win the war in America by force of arms. They could easily have triumphed if their object had been a few great centers of American population and industry, but there were no such centers. In order to win, the British either had to destroy Washington's slippery army, or occupy most of America. Even more important, the British objective was not strictly military; it was also political. The opposing armies were not merely fighting for territory, but also for control of a civilian population that was instinctively more loyal to local leaders than to Redcoats and mercenaries sent by the King.

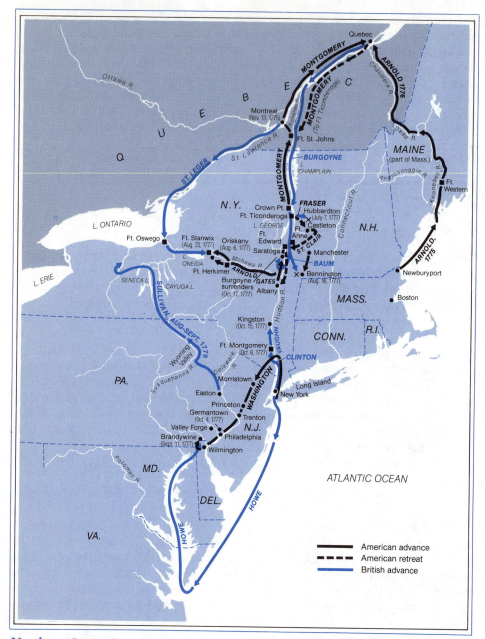

Northern Campaigns, 1775–1779

A massive application of armed force might win temporary military victories, but it could not alleviate the political resentments that had caused the war in the first place. Indeed, the British army did more to arouse the anger of otherwise indifferent Americans than to encourage them to remain loyal to English authority.

The occupation of a rebellious foreign nation is never an easy task, and the problems in America were especially formidable. The same absence of adequate roads that handicapped colonial commerce made America a nightmare for British soldiers. Woods and mountains in the North and creeks and swamps in the South enabled the Americans to set ambushes every half mile. Because of local hostility, the British had to carry supplies with them — in slow-moving wagons when they could get them — so that the Americans could almost always choose their own battlegrounds. Loyalists helped the royal armies at first, but commanders in America and politicians in England arrogantly ignored the advice of the Loyalists, whose knowledge of America was far superior to their own. In addition, when the British withdrew from occupied territory, as from Boston in 1776 and Philadelphia in 1778, the Loyalists were left to the tender mercies of local patriots — a plight that few people were willing to risk.

The Americans enjoyed other important advantages. When the war began, they owned a large and daring merchant marine. American merchantmen, turned into privateers, made life miserable for British shippers. The American vessels were always able to maintain a steady flow of vital military supplies from abroad because the British could not blockade the entire American coast. Many ship captains, of course, had carried on a bit of smuggling even before it became a patriotic duty.

A final American advantage was psychological. The patriots fought for a cause. Not only their leaders, but also ordinary members of the militia and the Continental Army knew that they were fighting for their own future and for that of their children. British soldiers and German mercenaries, on the other hand, had no such commitments. They were invaders with no personal stakes in the ultimate outcome of the war. In addition, the leaders of the American war effort, both military and civilian, were a remarkable group. Their chief, George Washington, was not a great military genius, but he was a daring tactician, and his devotion and courage sustained his followers through many discouraging days.

Washington At Bay

On July 12, 1776, Admiral Lord Richard Howe landed on Staten Island in New York harbor. Howe brought British reinforcements and Hessian mercenaries for his brother, Sir William, who had already brought his army down from Halifax. The troops of General Henry Clinton, just returned from an unsuccessful attempt to capture Fort Moultrie at Charleston, South Carolina, rendezvoused with the other British forces in New York. Opposed to this well-trained British army of 35,000 men was Washington's force of half that number, composed of inexperienced troops with short-term enlistments.

Washington knew that he could not hold New York, but he was determined to make the British fight for every inch of ground. He met them first on Long Island on August 27. After the inevitable defeat on the following day, Washington ferried his whole army, with its provisions and military equipment, across the East River to Manhattan Island under the cover of fog. Howe forced him out of the city and up the Hudson River Valley. New York remained in British hands until the end of the war.

Washington was unable to hold the forts along the Hudson River against

Howe's superior forces. He crossed to the New Jersey side and led his dwindling army southward across New Jersey with the armies of General Howe and General Lord Cornwallis at his heels. Washington had just got his last boat-loads of men over the Delaware River at Trenton when the Hessians entered the town. The American army by this time had been reduced to 3,000 effectives, who shivered on the banks of the Delaware in the December frosts. Their cause looked hopeless, and Washington begged the Continental Congress for aid. Thomas Paine sat down in the gloomy American camp to write, in the first number of *The Crisis:* "These are the times that try men's souls." Even the great commander himself nearly lost courage. "If every nerve is not strained to recruit a new army," he wrote, "I think the game is pretty well up."

The Tide Begins to Turn

Before the river could freeze, and the British could cross it to wipe out his little army, Washington embarked on a daring campaign. Late on Christmas night, in the midst of a driving sleet storm, he transported about 2,300 men across the ice-filled Delaware River some nine miles northwest of Trenton. At daybreak they fell upon the Hessians, who were sleeping after their Christmas celebration. Washington's men stormed the town, killed the Hessian commander, and took more than 900 prisoners. Washington had been in retreat since abandoning New York; now he was on the attack.

Lord Cornwallis hastened to repair the disaster, but Washington outwitted him. The Americans struck the British rear guard at Princeton, defeated three regiments, and forced Cornwallis to retreat in panic to protect his military stores. Washington then moved up to Morristown, about thirty miles from New York, to go into winter quarters. In a brilliant campaign of ten days he had recovered New Jersey and, more important, convinced his soldiers that they had a chance to win. Desertions from the American army decreased to a tolerable rate, and the local population was more generous in supplying the troops. The British had permitted Washington to slip through their fingers and, in the process, had lost an opportunity to bring the war to a swift end.

Lord George Germain, the new British Minister of War, sadly confessed that all his hopes "were blasted by the unhappy affair at Trenton." However, the British government now planned to conquer the State of New York and so cut off New England from the states to the south. The plan had three spearheads: General John Burgoyne, with an army of 8,000 British regulars, Hessians, Canadians, and Indians, was to march down to Albany from the St. Lawrence via Lake Champlain and the Hudson; Lieutenant Colonel Barry St. Leger was to bring his army eastward from Lake Ontario through the Mohawk Valley to join Burgoyne at Albany. General Howe, in New York, was to support Burgoyne and St. Leger.

The plan was a dismal failure in every respect. Howe hoped to end the war by capturing Philadelphia. He asked for and received permission from London to move against that city and to keep only part of his force at New York, ready to aid Burgoyne. So Howe set sail with the greater part of his army for Chesapeake Bay—just as Burgoyne was starting from Canada. St. Leger's force was turned back at the bloody battle of Oriskany before it got halfway to Albany. Burgoyne confidently marched southward with his great baggage trains and host of camp followers. But he soon found himself tangled in the forests be-

Washington at the Battle of Princeton. Charles Willson Peale, who painted this dramatic portrait, was a soldier in Washington's army. The painting portrays the death of General Hugh Mercer, who fell in the attack. (Courtesy of The Art Museum, Princeton University)

tween Lake Champlain and the Hudson River. American woodsmen had felled hundreds of trees across his line of march, and militiamen from New York and New England swarmed about him. Burgoyne was far from his base of supplies. Neither Howe nor St. Leger was near enough to help him, while the force left at New York was too weak to break through. Heavy forces sent to seize supplies at Bennington met with disaster. Burgoyne, brought to bay and decisively beaten, surrendered his entire army (reduced to 5,800 men by casualties and desertions) to General Horatio Gates on October 17, 1777.

Meanwhile, Washington hastened to meet Howe, who landed at the head of Chesapeake Bay and marched on Philadelphia. The Americans were defeated and driven off at the battles of Brandywine Creek and Germantown, and the British-occupied Philadelphia. Howe's victory, however, hardly compensated for the loss of Burgoyne's army. And Washington, although defeated, had not been destroyed. As 1777 came to an end, British policymakers and strategists had good reason for concern.

The French Alliance

The American victory at Saratoga made the greatest continental power in Europe an ally of America. The French had welcomed the Declaration of Independence. From an early stage in the war, they had secretly supplied the rebels with arms and provisions through an adventurous courtier and playwright, Pierre Augustin Caronde Beaumarchais. The wealthy young Marquis de Lafayette went so far as to fit out a ship at his own expense to aid the American cause. In April 1777, in spite of Louis XVI's disapproval, Lafayette sailed to America and carried a dozen French officers with him. Benjamin Franklin, who was to be as successful in Paris as he had been unsuccessful in London, daily reminded the French of the advantages that they would reap from American independence. He also did not harm the American cause by winning the hearts of a number of ladies of the French court.

But the Count de Vergennnes, the clever French Foreign Minister, was wary of bringing on a war with Great Britain until his Spanish allies were willing to help, and until the Americans had proved that they had a good chance to win. The news of Saratoga arrived in Paris in December and satisfied Vergennes on the second point. It also caused him to worry that the British might make proposals for peace and reconciliation which, if accepted by the Americans, would leave the French out in the cold. In addition, the American victory enabled Vergennes to persuade Spain secretly to furnish the Americans with money. Spain waited another year and then joined the war against Great Britain.

On February 6, 1778, France entered into treaties of alliance and commerce with the United States. The two nations agreed to open their ports to each other for prizes taken from the enemy. Each guaranteed forever the other's possessions in the new world. Neither was to lay down its arms until Great Britain acknowledged the independence of the United States. There was some irony in this alliance in view of the traditional American distrust of both the French and the Spaniards that went back to the very beginning of the English settlements in America. In 1778, however, both parties could see the advantages of a coordinated effort against the British.

The British Offer Concessions

News of Saratoga changed the attitudes of officials in London as well as in Paris. Even Lord North and the King were ready to make concessions to the Americans. The Prime Minister introduced a bill for reconciliation in November 1777. But Parliament dallied, and North's bill did not pass until February 17, 1778, eleven days after the American alliance with France had been signed. North's bill granted the Americans all that they had asked before their separation from the empire. Parliament would levy no taxes in America, and all objectionable laws since 1763 would be repealed. Those who had been branded as rebels would be pardoned. A commission would also be authorized to negotiate with Congress, the provincial assemblies, or with General Washington himself. The British rulers were ready to grant full dominion status to the

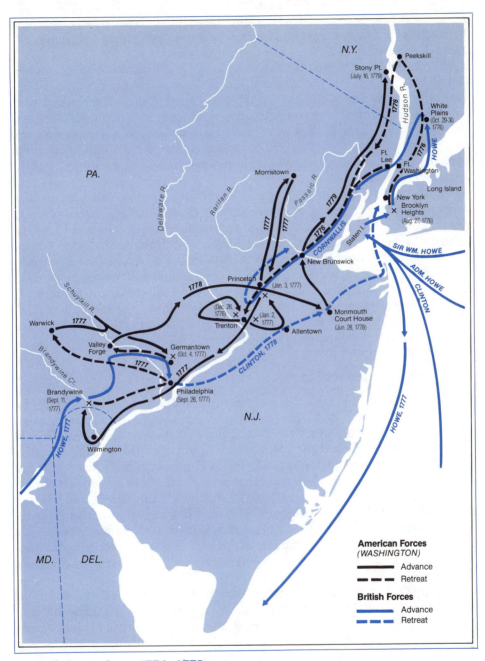

Central Campaigns, 1776–1779

former American colonies and would retain control only over foreign relations and defense.

But the Americans now had a powerful ally in the French and, even if the treaty had not been sealed, they probably would not have accepted North's offer. Before July 2, 1776, North's terms might well have been enough. But now the rebels would be content with nothing less than complete independence — and even their old friend, Pitt, was unwilling to grant that.

While Franklin negotiated in Paris and Lord North maneuvered in London, George Washington was encamped at Valley Forge, some twenty miles northwest of Philadelphia. While the British were making the winter merry with dances and pageants in the captured city, Washington's 8,000 men were in a dreadful state of distress. They were housed in rude huts built of trees from the surrounding forests. They shivered, sickened, and died from lack of clothing, blankets, food, and medicine. Washington beseeched Congress for aid, but little was forthcoming.

Still, there were encouraging signs to offset the gloom at Valley Forge. The sympathy of Europe for the American cause was growing stronger every month. Frederick the Great of Prussia forbade German troops hired by King George to march through his territory. Frederick declared that the chances were a hundred to one that the Americans would win their independence. Friedrich von Steuben, a veteran of the European part of the Seven Years' War, arrived at Valley Forge to drill the troops into an efficient army. Franklin, at Paris, won more support daily from Louis and Vergennes. In the spring of 1778, Count Charles Hector d'Estaing sailed for America with twelve French ships of the line and several regiments of French troops.

The Changed Character of the War

The first effect of the French alliance was the abandonment of Philadelphia by Howe's successor, General Clinton, because the forts on the Delaware were not strong enough to protect the city against d'Estaing's fleet. With 17,000 men and a baggage train eight miles long, Clinton marched through New Jersey to New York. Washington met Clinton at Monmouth, New Jersey, on June 28, 1778. There seemed to be a good chance to strike the extended British column on the flank, but General Charles Lee bungled the attack, and Clinton counterattacked sharply. Washington appeared just in time to organize a defense that repulsed the British. Monmouth was the last major battle of the war north of Virginia. It was also the last major battle in which Washington took part until he led the combined forces of America and France to the final victory at Yorktown in 1781.

D'Estaing's French fleet departed to defend the French West Indies late in 1778. This left the Americans with only small privateers and a few fighting ships, mostly overaged and undermanned, to combat the Royal Navy. However, one of the American vessels, commanded by John Paul Jones, captured more than 300 British vessels and raided English coastal towns. Although the contribution of such raids to the war effort was slight, even small victories like these boosted American morale tremendously.

The British government adopted a new military strategy in 1778. It decided to transfer the seat of war to the South in the belief that Loyalists and runaway slaves in large numbers were ready to join the British army there. Moreover, the government resolved to carry on the war without mercy to punish the Americans for allying themselves with the French. Americans henceforth would be treated, not as disobedient subjects, but as foreign foes to be utterly crushed.

GREAT ENCOURAGEMENT FOR SEAMEN.

ALL GENTLEMEN SEAMEN and able-bodied LANDSMEN who have a Mind to diſtinguiſh themſelves in the GLORIOUS CAUSE of their COUNTRY, and make their Fortunes, an Opportunity now offers on board the Ship RANGER, of Twenty Guns, (for FRANCE) now laying in PORTSMOUTH, in the State of NEW-HAMPSHIRE, commanded by JOHN PAUL JONES Eſq; let them repair to the Ship's Rendezvous in PORTSMOUTH, or at the Sign of Commodore MANLEY, in SALEM, where they will be kindly entertained, and receive the greateſt Encouragement.---The Ship RANGER, in the Opinion of every Perſon who has ſeen her is looked upon to be one of the beſt Cruizers in AMERICA.---She will be always able to Fight her Guns under a moſt excellent Cover ; and no Veſſel yet built was ever calculated for ſailing faſter, and making good Weather.

Any GENTLEMEN VOLUNTEERS who have a Mind to take an agreable Voyage in this pleaſant Seaſon of the Year, may, by entering on board the above Ship RANGER, meet with every Civility they can poſſibly expect, and for a further Encouragement depend on the firſt Opportunity being embraced to reward each one agreable to his Merit.

All reaſonable Travelling Expences will be allowed, and the Advance-Money be paid on their Appearance on Board.

IN CONGRESS, MARCH 29, 1777.

RESOLVED,

THAT the MARINE COMMITTEE be authoriſed to advance to every able Seaman, that enters into the CONTINENTAL SERVICE, any Sum not exceeding FORTY DOLLARS, and to every ordinary Seaman or Landſman, any Sum not exceeding TWENTY DOLLARS, to be deducted from their future Prize-Money.

By Order of CONGRESS,

JOHN-HANCOCK, PRESIDENT.

DANVERS: Printed by E. RUSSELL, at the Houſe late the Bell-Tavern.

Broadside seeking volunteers for the ship Ranger *under the command of John Paul Jones. (Courtesy of Essex Institute, Salem, Massachusetts)*

The British campaign began with the capture of Savannah in December 1778. The British went on easily to overrun the State of Georgia. They restored the old royal governor to office and declared the state to be reunited with the empire. Then, in December 1779, General Clinton sailed from New York with an army of some 8,500 men for the conquest of South Carolina. The following May, he took Charleston and compelled General Benjamin Lincoln to surrender his whole army of almost 5,500 men. This was practically the entire regular American army south of the Potomac, although irregular militia units continued to harass the British in both Georgia and South Carolina.

Both states felt the full fury of the British army and its Loyalist reinforcements. The troops burned houses and barns, killed livestock, destroyed crops, and drove rebel sympathizers into prison camps. Then Clinton returned to New York, and left Lord Cornwallis in command in the South. Clinton wrote smugly to Germain, "Few men are not either our prisoners or in arms with us." Clinton's confidence received another boost when Congress, in spite of

Washington's preference for General Nathanael Greene, sent Gates to supersede Lincoln. The hero of Saratoga suffered the worst defeat of the war at the hands of Cornwallis at Camden, South Carolina, on August 16, 1780. His militiamen "ran like a torrent" before the charges of the British regulars, and Gates ran with them. The Bavarian, Baron Johann de Kalb, who had come over with Lafayette in 1777, died in the attempt to save the day for the Americans.

No sooner did the news of the British victory at Camden arrive at Washington's headquarters than yet another disaster overtook the American cause. On September 25, Benedict Arnold, a brilliant young commander who had been instrumental in defeating the British at Saratoga, turned traitor and renounced his allegiance to the United States. It later turned out that he had been in the pay of Sir Henry Clinton for over a year and had been providing the British commander with military intelligence. With the capture of Major John André, who had carried messages between Arnold and Clinton, Arnold was forced to declare openly his allegiance to the King. He later became a British general and served under Cornwallis in the Virginia campaign.

The Collapse of the Southern Campaign

It looked as though the southern states were lost for good to the patriot cause. "Three or four hundred good soldiers would finish the business," wrote Colonel Patrick Ferguson to his chief, Cornwallis. Then, on October 7, 1780, several regiments of American backwoodsmen from both sides of the Appalachians gathered under John Sevier. They caught Ferguson's force of 1,200 Loyalists at King's Mountain near the border of South Carolina and annihilated it in the bloodiest battle of the war since Bunker Hill. King's Mountain, said Jefferson, was "the turn of the tide." It struck terror into Cornwallis' army and stirred up patriots throughout the Carolinas. Guerilla bands under General Thomas Sumter, Andrew Pickens, and Francis Marion, the "Swamp Fox," struck the British at every turn.

Nathanael Greene, who was, next to Washington, the ablest of the American generals, arrived to replace Gates. With him went the fiery Daniel Morgan, who had won fame at Saratoga. Morgan made up for the defeat at Camden with a brilliant victory at Cowpens, South Carolina, on January 17, 1781. Then he and Greene skillfully maneuvered Cornwallis northward until he was far removed from his base at Charleston. At Guilford Court House, North Carolina, a mixed force of American militiamen and regulars faced the British. The Americans inflicted heavy casualties and then retired.

American prospects were improving but the war was not yet over. Despite their successes in the South and the conquest of the Illinois territory by a small force under George Rogers Clark, the opening of the year 1781 found the American cause floundering. Continental money was worthless, and the soldiers were in rags. Washington wrote in his diary that he could hardly begin another campaign without help from France. A special envoy sailed for Paris, and Louis responded with two million francs in gold and 7,000 men led by Count Jean Baptiste de Rochambeau. They were carried across the Atlantic by a fleet of twenty warships commanded by Admiral François Joseph Paul de Grasse.

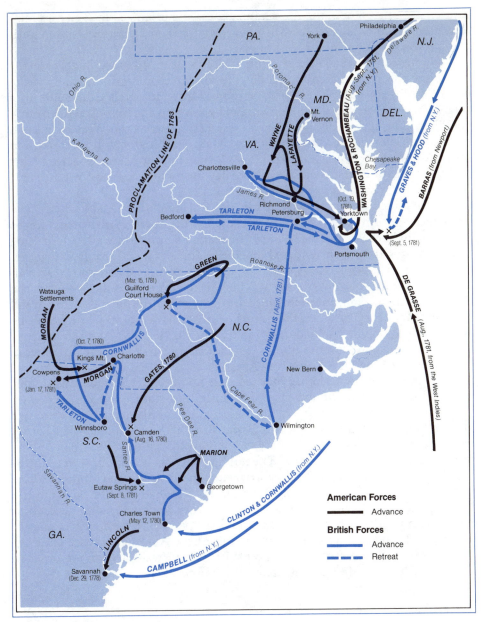

Southern Campaigns, 1778–1781

Cornwallis Surrenders at Yorktown

Cornwallis abandoned the Carolinas and now attempted to crush "that boy," Lafayette, who was defending Virginia with a small army of regulars aided by militiamen. Clinton meantime feared a combined attack on New York by Washington's army and De Grasse. He therefore ordered Cornwallis to fortify himself at some point along the Virginia coast and promised to send him reinforcements. Cornwallis reluctantly obeyed and gathered his army behind fortifications on the peninsula at Yorktown.

Word arrived in New York that De Grasse's fleet, intended largely for the defense of the West Indies, would be able to help temporarily in Chesapeake Bay. Washington quickly grasped the opportunity to catch Cornwallis in a trap. A French fleet could cut off his relief by sea, and a Franco-American army could close in on him by land. De Grasse arrived from the West Indies and blocked the entrance to Chesapeake Bay. Then Washington, who pretended to move toward New York, hurried his and Rochambeau's armies across New Jersey. He was at the head of Chesapeake Bay, ready to be ferried down to Yorktown, before Clinton was aware of the move.

The combined forces of Washington and Rochambeau, 16,000 strong, now drew the siege lines closer and closer about Yorktown. British naval forces tried to help but were turned back by the French ships. Cornwallis, despairing of help from Clinton, surrendered his entire army of 7,250 regulars, together with 850 sailors, 244 cannons, and a large supply of military stores on October 19, 1781. Scottish bagpipers played "The World Turned Upside Down" as the British regiments, some of them quite drunk, marched through the French and American ranks to lay down their arms. Cornwallis wrote to Clinton that he was mortified that he had had to surrender, but that he had had no alternative. The war dragged on for more than a year, but, after Yorktown, the British gave up any serious attempt to reconquer America.

King George still stubbornly insisted that no difficulties would make him consent to peace "at the expense of a separation from America." He even threatened to abdicate and retire to his Kingdom of Hanover if he were not supported in the continuation of the war. But the King's majority in Parliament rapidly melted away. The City of London pleaded with him to end "this unnatural and unfortunate war." The public debt was increasing at a frightful rate. French, Spanish, and Dutch ports were closed to British commerce. The headstrong King finally gave way. Lord North, who had tried to carry out the King's policies, resigned in March 1782, and Lord Rockingham came back to power with the condition that there should be "no veto to the independence of America." In his cabinet were many friends of the American cause. The next month, the new ministry sent its agent, Richard Oswald, to Paris in order to consult with Benjamin Franklin on terms of peace.

Independence Achieved

The American victory in the Revolutionary War was not so much a consequence of military miscalculation by the British as it was the result of their political misperception. The English lost the war because, at every stage, they failed to understand the political dimensions of the problems that they faced. Early in the war, when the fighting centered in New England, generals and bureaucrats alike believed that a massive show of force would bring the rebels to their knees. To their dismay, the English discovered that the presence of an army in Boston neither quelled the resistance there nor discouraged other colonies from joining it.

Then the British moved their base of operations to the more strategically located Middle Colonies, where they believed that the people were friendlier to England. They further assumed that victory in the region would split the Americans in two by isolating Virginia and Massachusetts from each other. But again they failed. They suffered unnecessary losses at Trenton and Princeton, but, equally important, the behavior of the British army in New Jersey was brutal and indiscriminate. Atrocities against civilians did not suppress resistance so much as encourage it. As in New England, England's military assessment was unaccompanied by any understanding of the political consequences of military strategy.

In 1778, after they had failed in New England and the Middle Colonies, British strategists turned toward the South, where they believed that they might yet crush the rebel forces. Although the southern campaign succeeded at first, it suffered from the same sort of misguided appraisal of political realities that had disabled the campaigns in the North. Wherever it went, the British army taught Americans a lesson that they could have learned in no other way. The behavior of British soldiers in the punitive southern campaign gave Americans day-to-day experience with British tyranny that went far beyond anything that they might have suffered from the legislation of the pre-Revolutionary decade.

In one sense, therefore, British military strategy between 1775 and 1783 was merely an extension of British political strategy between 1763 and 1775. In both cases, English politicians and generals found that their attempts at coercion backfired. They consistently underestimated American strength, but, even more significantly, they never learned that their efforts to impose their will upon the colonies only inspired further resistance. As Benjamin Franklin had predicted in 1765, the British army did more to bring support to the American cause than the efforts of the radical leaders ever did. Every American who suffered at the hands of British troops, no matter how politically uninformed or passive, had concrete reason to join the fight for independence. The British thereby did what no amount of American propaganda could have achieved: they persuaded the one third of the colonists, whom John Adams believed to be apathetic, that it had a vital stake in the success of the Revolution.

Moreover, the politicization of Americans that resulted from their experiences during the war had important consequences for American society once the fighting was over. Between 150,000 and 200,000 men served actively in either the local militias or in the Continental Army. Put another way, between one third and one half of all the eligible adult white males who were not Loyalists participated in the fighting at some time during the war. Of these, approximately 10 per cent died in battle, of disease, or as prisoners of war, while another 25,000 were wounded. A higher percentage of the American population was killed or injured in the American Revolution than in any other war in the nation's history except the Civil War. In 1973, Israel, with a population approximately equal to that of the United States in 1780, suffered only one tenth as many casualties in its war against Egypt and her allies. In other words, virtually every white family in America was touched directly by the Revolution. People who fought, died, and killed for the cause of independence or who had lost loved ones in the war had a real stake in the course that the new nation would take in the 1780s. Their voices would be heard in American politics as they had never been heard before.

The Treaty of Paris

Congress had appointed Franklin, John Adams, John Jay, Henry Laurens, and Thomas Jefferson as peace commissioners in June 1781 and instructed them to take no step "without the knowledge and agreement" of the French ministry. Jefferson declined the appointment, and Laurens was captured by the British on his way to Europe. Franklin, Adams, and Jay therefore conducted the negotiations. The commissioners violated their instructions and concluded a preliminary treaty with the British on November 30, 1782, without consulting Vergennes. It took all of Franklin's tact to smooth the ruffled feelings of the French Foreign Minister. Vergennes accused the American commissioners of bad faith, but he finally agreed to the peace treaty, which was signed at Paris on September 3, 1783.

The American commissioners obtained their most important objectives. England acknowledged the independence of the United States, with the Mississippi River as its western boundary. The great river was to be open to the shipping of both nations, and Americans were to share the Newfoundland fisheries. The British demanded that Congress restore the estates taken from Loyalists and guarantee the payment of debts owed by Americans to British merchants. All that the American commissioners would or, for that matter, could promise was that Congress would "earnestly recommend" to the states that they restore the property. Similarly, British creditors would not be hindered from the collection of their debts through the courts. In addition, the treaty returned Florida, which had been an English possession for twenty years, to Spain. Finally, islands in the West Indies captured by the British reverted to France and Spain.

3. THE REVOLUTION WITHIN

Indians and the Revolution

The Treaty of Paris settled the claims of England, France, and Spain in America and gave firm international recognition to the United States. The treaty thus closed a chapter in the history of European colonization and imperialism. However, it made no mention of the Indians, who had participated in the Revolution, just as they had taken part in all the struggles to control North America during the previous two hundred years. For them, the Revolution was a catastrophe—the culmination of an invasion that had slowly deprived them of their land and independence for generations. The American Revolution left the major eastern tribes divided, weakened, and demoralized.

When fighting broke out between the British and the Americans in 1775, the Iroquois initially adopted a policy of neutrality, much like the one which had permitted them to maintain their independence from the French and the English in an earlier era. Both sides sought Indian aid without success. Then, in 1777, the British persuaded one of the Iroquois tribes—the Senecas—to join the fighting as allies of the King. For their part, the Americans sought and won the aid of the Oneidas and Tuscaroras. Soon the great Iroquois confederacy was seriously divided, and, when the Senecas (who supported the English) faced the Oneidas (who supported the Americans) at Oriskany in August 1777, the division intensified into outright enmity. The strength of the Iroquois tribes had always lain in their capacity to adopt a unified policy toward each of the various groups of whites whom they had encountered. The loss of that unity spelled disaster for them.

During the bitter struggle for control of New York in 1777–1778, combined Indian and British forces massacred an American settlement in the Wyoming Valley of Pennsylvania and destroyed an outpost at Cherry Valley, New York. But after the American victory at Saratoga, the Indians were suddenly without protection from their British patrons, who had shifted their efforts to the southern front. Washington seized the opportunity to revenge earlier defeats and to eliminate the Iroquois from the war. He sent Major General John Sullivan against the Iroquois in the Finger Lakes Region of New York. Sullivan undertook an all-out campaign of conquest and destruction. He burned forty Indian villages and 160,000 bushels of corn. The Sullivan campaign left Indian society in the area decimated and permanently scarred.

A similar pattern emerged in the South, where the British sought alliances with the Creeks and the Cherokees. When the Indians raided settlements in Virginia and the Carolinas, the Americans responded in 1776 with a campaign similar to Sullivan's against the Iroquois. In South Carolina, Colonel Andrew Williamson destroyed every Indian town and all the Indian corn that he could find, while Colonel William Christian performed similarly brutal tasks in Virginia. In 1780, Virginians and North Carolinians, afraid that the Cherokees might retaliate by aiding Cornwallis, burned over 1,000 Cherokee houses and 50,000 bushels of corn. The Creeks managed to escape such devastation, but the end of the war left them without the protection of their English allies. They were forced to cede much of their land to the United States, and the Revolution was as disastrous for them as it was for the Iroquois and the Cherokees. None of these great Indian confederacies emerged from the war capable of maintaining their territorial independence.

In addition, all the states offered incentives to white civilians to fight the Indians. They adopted a policy that royal governors had used earlier with some success: they offered cash bounties for Indian scalps. South Carolina, for example, paid £75 for every Cherokee scalp and £100 for every Cherokee prisoner. Other states pursued similar tactics. The combination of policies like these and outright conquest by American military units spelled the end of Indian resistance and opposition in the East. The American Revolution thus not only secured the independence of Britain's former colonies; it also paved the way for the extensive settlement of the trans-Appalachian West. In fact, Congress paid its soldiers by distributing almost 10,000,000 acres of land that had belonged to the Indians to veterans of the Continental Army. The Revolution was a tragedy for the Indians. White Americans purchased their political independence in part at the expense of the Iroquois, Cherokees, Creeks, and other eastern tribes.

Blacks and the Revolution

In 1776, 95 per cent of all black Americans were slaves. One of the most important consequences of the Revolution was to reduce this proportion considerably and create a sizable free black community. Many whites of the Revolutionary generation took the equalitarian principles of the Declaration of

Independence quite seriously, and the Revolution forced them to recognize the contradiction between their democratic professions and the practice of holding human beings in permanent bondage. As a result, in 1781, a Massachusetts court interpreted the state's constitution as having abolished slavery. The other New England states and Pennsylvania set gradual abolition in motion during the Revolution, and New York and New Jersey followed suit in 1799 and 1804. Of course, slavery was far less significant in these states than in the southern states. It is also true that the former states only abolished slavery; they did not prohibit their citizens from participating in the slave trade. Yet the Revolution unquestionably encouraged and gave moral force to the growing movement for the abolition of slavery. One reason for the growth of antislavery sentiment was the fact that about 5,000 blacks fought in the war for independence. They fought, not in segregated units, but side by side with white men. Moreover, slaves were drafted for military service in all states except Georgia and South Carolina.

In addition, many southern Revolutionary leaders — including Washington, Madison, Henry, and Jefferson — talked about freeing their slaves (though none of them actually did so) and expressed deep concern about the long-run implications of the institution for American society. Other Southerners, however, did more than talk. The number of voluntary manumissions increased markedly in the aftermath of the Revolution, particularly in Virginia and Maryland. By 1810, almost 25 per cent of the blacks living in Maryland were free. Furthermore, a large number of slaves escaped to the North in the confusion of the war, while others joined the British, who promised them freedom in exchange for military service.

Another effect of the Revolution on Afro-Americans was that it encouraged them to resist their condition by using the democratic rhetoric of their masters to highlight the contradiction of slavery. One group of Connecticut slaves petitioned the General Assembly for their freedom in 1779. They wrote that both natural law and Christianity guaranteed their freedom, and they asked "Whether it is consistent with the present claims of the United States to hold so many Thousands of the Race of Adam, our Common Father, in perpetual slavery?" They asserted that they would never be convinced that they were "born to be slaves" and demanded their freedom in uncompromising terms. Sentiments like these appeared in the South as well, and the Virginia slave rebellion led by Gabriel Prosser in 1800 was to some extent inspired by the democratic oratory of white Virginians. The Revolution thus opened freedom to a substantial number of blacks who would otherwise have remained enslaved.

Despite these gains, even free blacks suffered severe discrimination and oppression in every aspect of their lives. Special laws designed to regulate their behavior such as curfews and limits on the right to travel, restricted their freedom, and they were frequently denied the right to vote and other basic civil liberties. The very racism that tried to justify the enslavement of Africans in the first place also rationalized the legal and quasi-legal disabilities imposed upon them as free men and women. Moreover, the vast majority of black Americans remained in chains under a system that, in some ways, became even more oppressive after the Revolution. The American Revolution did provide many slaves an opportunity to become free, but it did little to end slavery where it was strongest, and most blacks continued to live as the chattel of their fellow human beings.

Women and the Revolution

Although men fought the battles of the Revolution, wrote the Declaration of Independence and led the Continental Congress, women both participated in the rebellion and were affected by it. During the decade before the fighting began, there were Daughters of Liberty in all the major cities and towns. During the war, many women did "men's work" while their husbands served in the Continental Army or the militia. Women ran businesses, tilled fields, and supervised family affairs until their spouses returned. Yet the leading woman of the era, Abigail Adams, was acutely conscious that the Revolution was primarily a male enterprise. In 1776, she wrote to her husband, John, that she hoped that the new government would "remember the Ladies." She went on to ask Congress to avoid placing "unlimited power into the hands of the Husbands." "Remember," she continued, "all Men would be tyrants if they could. If particular care and attention is not paid to the Ladies we are determined to foment a Rebellion, and will not hold ourselves bound by any Laws in which we have no voice, or Representation." Her husband replied: "We know better than to repeal our Masculine systems."

Abigail and John Adams carried on this exchange in an ironic, almost playful tone, but it contained a solid core of truth. Abigail Adams' apprehensions about the consequences of the Revolution for American women seem to have been justified. The Revolution did not advance the status of women; if anything, it eroded some of the rights that women already possessed. Divorces became more difficult to obtain; prosecutions for sexual crimes (like fornication and adultery) now focused only on the female, whereas previously both partners had been culpable; new restrictions were also placed on the right of women to hold, sell, and transfer property; and women's political rights did not advance at all.

Moreover, in the period which immediately followed the Revolution, American men composed elaborate theoretical justifications for the suppression of women's rights, both in the family and in society at large. Several male authors published handbooks which detailed what they said was the "proper," submissive behavior of women. By the time that the French aristocrat, Alexis de Tocqueville, came to America in the 1830s, he was astounded by the careful distinctions that Americans made between the social roles of men and women

Abigail and John Adams, by Benjamin Blyth. John Adams, later the second President of the United States, was one of the most brilliant men of the revolutionary generation. His wife, Abigail, was equally brilliant and maintained close intellectual relationships with many of the most important American leaders. (Courtesy of the Massachusetts Historical Society)

and by the extent to which democracy highlighted rather than blurred those distinctions. Thus, although Jefferson used the word "men" in its generic sense when he wrote "all men are created equal," whatever equality the Revolution helped to encourage ultimately applied more to men than to women.

Democracy, Equality, and the American Revolution

The men who led the American Revolution were conservatives. When the resistance movement began in the mid-1760s, they intended to do no more than secure the repeal of laws that they perceived as oppressive. As the movement progressed, however, some of them gradually adopted more radical views, while others balked at separation from the British Empire. Throughout the pre-Revolutionary decade, the middle- and upper-class leaders of the resistance continually expressed their concern lest their struggle against royal and parliamentary authority would unintentionally engender a struggle for power in their own society. As a result, they made every effort, not only to maintain their control of the resistance, but also of society at large. Even after independence had been declared, most of them did not foresee an alteration of the distribution of economic or political power within American society. They fully expected that the deference which they and their predecessors had always received from the "lower orders" would continue under the new governments that they established. They certainly did not expect to return land to the Indians, free the slaves, or advance the rights of women. They hoped that the Revolution would change the political relationship of America and England and little else.

For all their conservatism, however, the signers of the Declaration of Independence knew that they could not achieve their objective without help. If their movement was to succeed, it would have to enjoy wide popular support. Consequently, even while they hoped to control persons beneath them, they actively solicited the participation of ordinary people in the resistance. Such activity ultimately eroded, though it did not destroy, the dominance of the upper classes in American politics and made the political process more democratic and political opportunity more equal than it had been before.

For example, the revolutionary committees, the Sons of Liberty, and other revolutionary organizations all grew in size during the years immediately before the war. Not only did the number of people in positions of leadership rise, but socioeconomic status changed as well, for the average wealth of committee members declined steadily.

This "democratization" of the revolutionary movement was most dramatic in Philadelphia, but it was apparent everywhere. Moreover, the local and decentralized nature of the committee system further encouraged this broadening of political power. Radical leaders in Boston not only had to respond to the views of the city's working class; they also had to accommodate the wishes of local committeemen in the countryside. Once the war began, of course, this process continued as more and more people actually joined in the fighting, both as common soldiers and as officers. By the time that the peace treaty was ratified, a large number of "new men" had been brought into the political process, and they were determined not to surrender their newly acquired power easily or gracefully to those who presumed to be their betters. As we shall see in the next chapter, these new men would have a profound influence upon the political life of the new nation.

Developments like these did not always please the men who headed the Continental Congress or occupied positions of influence in the states. John Jay said that the Revolution was "giving rank and Importance to men whom Wisdom would have left in obscurity." When James Bowdoin, Governor of Massachusetts, looked around him, he could "scarcely see any other than new faces." John Adams, not the wealthiest of men, was worried because the Revolution had brought to power men who "will obtain an Influence, by Noise not Sense, by Meanness not Greatness, by Ignorance not Learning." Conservative as these men were, however, they shared the conviction that independence was worth the risks to their own position that were inherent in social and political change. The Loyalists, on the other hand, failed to support the Revolution precisely because they were unwilling to trade the costs of social upheaval for what they thought were the dubious benefits of independence. Ironically, the withdrawal of perhaps 100,000 Loyalist emigrés accelerated the very democratization that they feared by opening positions of power and influence to men who had previously been excluded from the highest echelons of the political system. In addition, the confiscation and resale of Loyalist property effected a moderate redistribution of some of the nation's wealth and opened economic opportunities for ambitious men.

But the Revolution was not an unalloyed triumph for democracy, even if we focus only on the experience of white males. Its consequences were both more subtle and more complex. Whatever else it may have been, the Revolution was not a class war—perhaps because those most likely to be the targets in such a war, the Loyalists, removed themselves from the scene. Yet many of the antagonisms—geographical, ethnic, and socioeconomic—that had characterized American society earlier in the eighteenth century continued to run at full force after the Revolution. Moreover, at the same time that American political life was becoming more inclusive, the new nation's economic life was becoming more exclusive. The social stratification and concentration of wealth that had been in progress before the Revolution continued and even accelerated in its aftermath, especially in the South and in the cities. As a result, the very same men who were making gains in the political sphere were frequently suffering losses in the economic sphere. In the long run, this loss of economic opportunity substantially undermined political opportunity and intensified the political struggles of the 1780s.

The results of the American Revolution were ambiguous. If the Revolution did not do all that it might have done to guarantee life, liberty, and the pursuit of happiness to everyone—red, black, and white, male and female, rich and poor—it still did something. Perhaps John Adams was correct when, late in his life, he wrote that the real American Revolution had not taken place on the battlefields, but in the hearts and minds of the American people—a change not so much in their society and politics as in their values and aspirations. Almost in spite of themselves, the conservatives who led the American Revolution set a new standard for human liberty and justice which, although not met either by them or by their successors, had profound repercussions for America and for the world. They began their struggle as subjects of an English King and emerged from it as Americans, citizens of an independent republic. The story of the 1780s, and, indeed, of all the rest of American history, is the story of a people seeking to come to terms with the meaning of that transformation.

SUGGESTED READINGS

The Declaration of Independence, a document whose impact upon the American imagination has been as great as its effect upon American government, is carefully dissected in several major books. Carl Becker, *The Declaration of Independence* (1922), has been criticized, but it has not been superseded. Garry Wills, *Inventing America* (1978), is a revisionist work which argues that the Declaration must be understood in light of the central role of Scottish Common Sense philosophy in the thought of Thomas Jefferson. Morton White, *The Philosophy of the American Revolution* (1978), on the other hand, emphasizes (as Becker did) the place of John Locke in the intellectual life of Jefferson and his contemporaries. In his way, Tom Paine was as important to the movement for independence as Jefferson, Franklin, and Adams were. Eric Foner, *Tom Paine and Revolutionary America* (1976), is a controversial but brilliant book on Paine's career and its significance, while David F. Hawke, *Paine* (1974), is the most comprehensive biography. John Adams, who hated Paine and alternately loved and hated Jefferson, has been the subject of several biographies. Two of the best are John R. Howe, Jr., *The Changing Political Thought of John Adams* (1966), and Peter Shaw, *The Character of John Adams* (1976). Apart from his *Autobiography*, the best short account of Franklin's life is Verner W. Crane, *Benjamin Franklin and a Rising People* (1954). With his usual flare, Edmund S. Morgan has provided brief portraits of Adams, Jefferson, and Washington in *The Meaning of Independence* (1976).

Discussions of motivation in the Revolution must almost necessarily be speculative since, except for the very small percentage of the population that left private papers and correspondence, the most intimate thoughts and feelings of the men and women of the eighteenth century have escaped our grasp. Any of the state studies and several of the more general works described in the bibliographical essay at the end of the last chapter can be used as guides to the motivation of the patriots. Kenneth S. Lynn, *A Divided People* (1978), is a sketchy and not altogether persuasive attempt to apply ego psychology to patriots and Loyalists and to discover the sources of their political behavior in their relationships with their fathers. The closing section of Philip Greven, *The Protestant Temperament* (1978), also contains some speculations on the relationship between individual psychological experience and public activity in the eighteenth century.

There are two good general studies of the Loyalists which concern themselves, at least in part, with the forces that impelled some people to remain loyal to Great Britain while so many of their contemporaries were in rebellion against imperial authority. William H. Nelson, *The American Tory* (1961), is relatively brief, while Robert M. Calhoon, *The Loyalists in Revolutionary America* (1973), is more encyclopedic. Wallace Brown, *The King's Friends* (1965), is a state-by-state quantitative analysis of the composition of the Loyalists; Brown's companion volume, *The Good Americans* (1969), summarizes his earlier work. Claude H. Van Tyne, *The Loyalists in the American Revolution* (1902), is still useful, while Mary Beth Norton, *The British-Americans* (1972), is a gracefully written and moving account of the Loyalists who fled to England. Other sources are the biographies of some of the major figures. Although unsatisfactory in some respects, Bernard Bailyn, *The Ordeal of Thomas Hutchinson* (1974), displays the remarkable fluency of Bailyn's writing, as well as his sensitivity to the human side of an epochal event. Carol R. Berkin, *Jonathan Sewall* (1974), is a suggestive portrait of a man who was a close friend of John Adams and whose experience was in some ways more typical than Hutchinson's.

The military history of the Revolution was long the province of antiquarians rather than historians. Due almost entirely to the influence of one historian, John Shy, contemporary scholars have come to recognize that warfare cannot be separated from the Revolution without losing an essential component of the Revolutionary experience. In *Toward Lexington* (1965) and in a series of brilliant essays collected in *A People Numerous and Armed* (1976), Shy has made it impossible to ignore the vital role that thoughtfully conceived military history can play in achieving an understanding, not only of the Revolution, but also of the rest of early American history as well. More standard treatments of the war are Don Higginbotham, *The American War for Independence* (1971), and Piers Mackesy, *The War for America* (1964). Both volumes are distinguished by meticulous scholarship and attention to detail. The essays in George A. Billias, ed., *George Washington's Generals* (1964), and *George Washington's Opponents* (1969), assess the role of military leaders on both sides of the rebellion. Ira D. Gruber, *The*

Howe Brothers and the American Revolution (1972), and Jonathan G. Rossie, *The Politics of Command in the American Revolution* (1975), deal with other significant aspects of the military history of the revolt.

The impact of the War for Independence on American society is not a subject about which historians agree. Jackson T. Main, *The Sovereign States* (1973), contains the best estimates of one of the most respected scholars in the field. Howard H. Peckham, ed., *The Toll of Independence* (1974), contains some startling statistics on the casualties in the war, and James A. Henretta, *The Evolution of American Society* (1973), proposes some tentative generalizations about the effect of the war on social and economic development. The classic statement of the social changes that the Revolution engendered is J. Franklin Jameson, *The American Revolution Considered As a Social Movement* (1926), a brief book that has been subjected to searching criticisms. William E. Nelson, *The Americanization of the Common Law* (1975), offers an arresting interpretation of the role of the Revolution in shaping American law and legal institutions.

The part played by women in the Revolution as well as the effects of the Revolution upon women's lives have received less attention from historians than they deserve. Mary Beth Norton, *Liberty's Daughters* (1980), is the only sustained scholarly account of the relationship between women and the movement for independence. The early chapters of Mary P. Ryan, *Womanhood in America* (1975), are a useful synthesis of our current knowledge, and Carol R. Berkin, *Within the Conjurer's Circle* (1974), is original and well-written. Nancy F. Cott's extraordinary book, *The Bonds of Womanhood* (1976), focuses on a slightly later period but has important implications for the Revolutionary era as well.

The Revolution was a catastrophe for the American Indian, but a general history of the Indian in the Revolution has yet to be written. Barbara Graymont, *The Iroquois in the American Revolution* (1972), is sensitive and thoughtful, and James H. O'Donnell, *Southern Indians in the American Revolution* (1973), is also helpful. Robert Berkhofer, *The White Man's Indian* (1977), is an excellent account of white attitudes toward the Indian, but much more needs to be done in this essential field.

The standard history of the place of black Americans in the Revolution is Benjamin Quarles, *The Negro in the American Revolution* (1961). Gerald W. Mullin, *Flight and Rebellion* (1972), attempts to show that the Revolution led slaves to resist their masters' authority and control. Arthur Zilversmit, *The First Emancipation* (1967), shows how and why independence encouraged antislavery activity and, eventually, abolition in the northern states. However, David Brion Davis, *The Problem of Slavery in the Age of Revolution* (1975), places both the Revolution and American abolitionism in a larger framework of intellectual, political, and legal transformation. In the later chapters of *White Over Black* (1968), Winthrop Jordan has a great deal to say about the attitudes of white Americans during the period, while Duncan J. MacLeod, *Slavery, Race, and the American Revolution* (1974), argues that the Founding Fathers ignored an opportunity to expunge slavery from the new nation. The concluding sections of Edmund S. Morgan, *American Slavery, American Freedom* (1975), attempt to interpret the contradictory spectacle of slaveholders fighting the first great struggle for political liberty in the modern West. Finally, several of the essays in Alfred F. Young, ed., *The American Revolution* (1976), deal with the effect of American independence upon women, Indians, and blacks. The essays in James K. Martin, ed., *The American Revolution: Whose Revolution?* (1977), are also useful.

The most detailed account of the negotiation of the Treaty of Paris is Richard B. Morris, *The Peacemakers* (1965). The treaty with France signed in 1778 is discussed in William C. Stinchcombe, *The American Revolution and the French Alliance* (1969). Samuel F. Bemis, *The Diplomacy of the American Revolution* (rev. ed., 1957), is a traditional history that is still valuable.

The Revolution was an event whose reverberations are still felt all over the world, but it was part of a series of similar movements that occurred throughout the West at the end of the eighteenth and the beginning of the nineteenth centuries. This international tide of political change is treated brilliantly in Robert R. Palmer, *The Age of Democratic Revolution*, 2 vols. (1959–1965), while Seymour Martin Lipset, *The First New Nation* (1963), and Richard B. Morris, *The Emerging Nations and the American Revolution* (1970), provide more long-range assessments. Insofar as the meaning of the Revolution in our national life is concerned, a recent book of essays edited by Larry R. Gerlach, *Legacies of the American Revolution* (1978), contains the work of several major historians and is a fine starting point. It is one of the fascinations of the Revolution, however, that its significance is constantly changing and can never be known completely.

CHAPTER 7
AMERICAN STATES, AMERICAN NATION

1. THE STRUCTURE OF GOVERNMENT IN REVOLUTIONARY AMERICA

Republican Principles

The formal cessation of British rule embodied in the Declaration of Independence required that the colonies, now states, devise a system of government that would at once guarantee their independence and protect their liberty. Although Americans differed about the precise form that their political institutions ought to take, they were in substantial agreement about the fundamental principles that ought to underlie such a system. First, few Americans wanted to duplicate the vagueness of the unwritten British Constitution in their new frames of government. After all, many of their troubles with the British had resulted from the inability of the two sides to agree about just what the Constitution was or ought to be. Americans feared that, without some clear statement of the rules of the political game, their new nation would be subject to the same forces of political fragmentation that had disrupted the British Empire. Virtually everyone agreed, therefore, on the need for written constitutions in the individual states as well as on the national level—constitutions that would set limits on the exercise of power and establish positive protections for liberty.

Beyond this, most Americans also shared the conviction that a republic was the only sort of government that would be appropriate to their changed political circumstances. The events of the pre-Revolutionary decade had persuaded them that monarchies were fatally flawed by the concentrated power that they placed in the hands of a single individual. Even a monarchy like Great Britain's, which attempted to balance monarchial and legislative power, was prone to corruption and abuse by the King. Americans had not declared their independence of the English King to submit to a new King of their own. In the British Empire, sovereignty—the capacity to exercise final authority in political affairs—rested with the King in Parliament. In the new republican states, however, the people would be sovereign. Such an assumption had far-reaching consequences, for it meant that the people of America—unlike the people of Great Britain—would not merely be the final check on arbitrary or tyrannical government. Rather, they would *be* the government itself and would exercise their sovereignty directly through their chosen representatives in institutions of their own devising. This transformation of the people from the passive objects of governmental power to the active wielders of that power was one of the signal theoretical accomplishments of the Revolution.

These two assumptions—that the new states and nation required written constitutions and that the people were sovereign—were central to the development of American republicanism in the years which immediately followed the Declaration of Independence. Americans were aware, of course, that history provided other examples of republican states; ancient Rome was one, the Italian city-states of the Renaissance were another. But the former colonists were convinced that they had a unique opportunity to correct the faults of previous republics that had failed because the people had been corrupted and thereby had sacrificed their liberty. Thus, a third political assumption to which most Americans subscribed was that written constitutions and popular sovereignty would be only the most fragile guarantees of liberty if they were not supported at every level of society by that virtue which was the ultimate bulwark against corruption and its inevitable companion, despotism. As usual, John Adams provided a succinct description of the American position: republics, he said, were the only governments "whose principle and foundation is virtue," and "there is no good government but what is republican."

Although most Americans could agree that their new governments ought to be republican, they did not agree on the precise form that those governments should take. What would be the relationship between the states and the new nation of which they were a part? How would power be exercised and distributed within the new governments? To these questions—and many others—Americans had a multitude of often contradictory answers. Apart from the defeat of the British, therefore, the most important task that Americans faced in the aftermath of independence was to create governments that would simultaneously embody republican assumptions and establish particular political institutions whose legitimacy would be generally acknowledged. Such a task was almost as difficult to accomplish as military victory, for it meant balancing conflicting ideals, such as liberty and order, and compromising the conflicting interests of the states and the nation.

The Articles of Confederation and the Structure of National Government

The most essential dilemma that Americans faced in framing a national government was to determine just how much power that government should have. On the one hand, their experience as colonists suggested to them that centralized power was to be feared, for it tended to interfere with the prerogatives of local government. Although Parliament was a "representative" institution, its treatment of the colonial assemblies hardly constituted a recommendation for the establishment of a central legislature that would be superior to the legislatures of the states. On the other hand, everyone acknowledged that the thirteen states could not survive as thirteen completely independent nations; some sort of national government was a necessity. Of course, some persons were afraid of centralized power, while others were disturbed by the potential chaos that might ensue if the national government was too weak. The first group was more concerned with exalting liberty as it was expressed in the institutions of the states, while the second hoped to insure order by creating a national government that would in all respects be superior to the states.

Despite this division, most Americans were still more loyal to their individual states than to the nation. The creation of a powerful national government required a leap of faith that most people were still unwilling to make. Thus, when a committee of the Second Continental Congress, headed by John Dickinson, drafted a plan for a strong central government that would be superior to those in the states, even those who leaned toward the centralization of power as a check on "excessive democracy" hesitated. As a result, Dickinson's draft was extensively revised, and, when it finally reached the floor of Congress late in 1777, it was a clearly anticentralist document called the Articles of Confederation.

The Articles of Confederation barely created any national government at all. Although they declared that the states were joined in a "perpetual union" and a "firm league of friendship," they also asserted that each state retained its "sovereignty, freedom, and independence." Moreover, Congress, while given the power to make laws, possessed no powers of enforcement or coercion. The national legislature was entirely reliant upon the voluntary compliance of the states and their citizens. In addition, there were no provisions either for an executive or a judicial branch, and Congress was permitted only to *request* funds from the states. It had no taxing power whatsoever. Finally, all thirteen states had to approve amendments to accomplish their ratification.

The Articles of Confederation thus reflected long-standing American concerns that were deeply embedded in their historical experiences as colonists under the rule of a British Parliament and King. When Congress sent the Articles to the states for ratification in May 1778, there was little reason to believe that even the most zealous guardians of state power would find much in the document that threatened local prerogatives. Yet the Articles of Confederation were not ratified by all thirteen states until March 1781.

The delay of three years in ratification was not due to fear of giving either too much or too little power to Congress. Rather, it occurred because of the difficulty in settling the potentially divisive question of ownership of the vast lands in the West. Massachusetts, Connecticut, Virginia, the Carolinas, and Georgia claimed land which extended to the Mississippi River by virtue of the "sea-to-sea" provisions in their colonial charters. George Rogers Clark strengthened Virginia's claim with his conquests in the Northwest. In addition, New York also claimed western land obtained through treaties with the Indians.

The other states had no western land claims because they bordered on neighboring states to the west, as was the case with Rhode Island and New Jersey, or because their western boundary was limited in their charter, as in the cases of Pennsylvania and Maryland. These landless states, led by Maryland, refused to agree to a general government until the others had surrendered to Congress their claims to lands west of the Alleghenies. The Maryland legislature acted under the powerful influence of the Illinois-Wabash Company, which had purchased land claimed by Virginia from the Indians at absurdly low prices.

New York led the way for the other states with western claims in 1780. Virginia relented and offered to give up her far better claims in January 1781. Massachusetts, Connecticut, and the Carolinas soon followed suit. (Georgia, on account of complications with Indians on her borders, did not surrender her claims until 1802.) By these cessions, the United States became the owner of an immense public domain. As soon as Virginia offered to give up her claims, Maryland voted to ratify the Articles of Confederation.

Constitution Making and the Structure of State Government

The process of framing new governments was more complex in the states than at the national level because there was much more power to be distributed within the state governments. The new state constitutions revealed that republicanism might encompass an extraordinarily broad range of different political systems. As in the national arena, the alignment of forces in the states set those persons who sought, above all else, to guarantee liberty against those who sought primarily to insure order. To put it another way, the divisions among Americans, which had been apparent throughout the resistance, continued in the struggles over the writing of state constitutions. At one end of the spectrum were radicals such as Thomas Paine, who hoped that the Revolution would effect a fundamental redistribution of power within American society. At the other end stood men like the Virginian, Carter Braxton, who feared the "licentiousness" of the lower classes and hoped that the Revolution would only secure independence, not alter the traditionally deferential patterns of American politics. Most men fell somewhere between these two extremes and advocated what John Adams called a "mixed republic," one that would reflect the popular will and simultaneously guard against the excesses of an unrestrained democracy.

The actual constitutions that emerged in the states reflected this variety of American opinion. Pennsylvania, where radicals had seized control of the resistance, adopted an extraordinarily "democratic" constitution. It provided for a unicameral legislature, abandoned all property qualifications for voting and officeholding, and virtually eliminated the council and governor as functioning arms of the government. In addition, it called for frequent elections to keep the representatives accountable to their constituents and reapportioned representation to give backcountry settlers a greater voice in the government. Conservative leaders in Pennsylvania and elsewhere in America abhorred the new constitution because it violated their principled commitment to deferential politics and destroyed the foundation upon which the power of their own elite had been based.

The radicalism of the Pennsylvania constitution was exceptional. In most states, conservatives had considerably more impact upon the shape of political institutions. Such men favored property qualifications for voting and officeholding, sought to maintain prevailing patterns of apportionment, desired strong executives and courts, and advocated bicameral legislatures, with an upper house to represent propertied interests against the claims of the poorer members of society. Ironically, such men achieved their most complete victory in one of Pennsylvania's closest neighbors, Maryland. For the most part, however, the state constitutions contained a mixture of democratic and elitist elements. Seven of them included explicit bills of rights to provide fundamental guarantees of individual liberty. Most also placed limits on the power of the governor by placing his election in the hands of the assembly or by reducing his term of office. Only the Maryland constitution gave the governor the power to veto legislation. In addition, most of the new state constitutions also extended the franchise by reducing or eliminating property requirements.

On the other hand, conservatives also won significant victories. In particular, the inequities of representation, which had permitted the coastal elites to dominate colonial politics, continued in the 1780s; and some states, such as New Jersey and South Carolina, imposed stringent property requirements for membership in the upper house. In sum, the state constitutions contained aspects of both the democratic and elitist programs. In most states, of course, one side or the other did get the upper hand. Pennsylvania and Maryland were only the most extreme examples. Generally, though, both members of the old colonial elites and the more radical democrats could both hope that their side might prevail in the day-to-day politics of the newly independent states. And, indeed, the competitive political climate from which the state constitutions grew continued to affect state government in the 1780s, just as the division between central and local concerns generated conflict in the nation at large.

Taken all together, the Articles of Confederation and the new state constitutions not only revealed significant conflict among different groups of Americans; they also indicated how fully the newly independent citizens of the United States continued to think in terms that were essentially English. Two characteristics of their new constitutional arrangements stand out above all others. The first was the severe limit that they placed on centralized power in the Articles; the second was their equally clear reluctance to exalt executive power in the state constitutions. The former grew from their experience with the imperious behavior of the King and Parliament before the Revolution; the latter resulted from their experiences with arbitrary colonial governors. Few Americans could yet conceive of either central or executive power exercised in the interest of liberty. But the unanticipated consequences of political conflict in the 1780s would soon permit many Americans to abandon their old English fears and adopt a new attitude. It would find room for the exercise of both central and executive power within more generous boundaries.

2. POLITICS IN THE 1780s

The Nationalists

In June 1783, George Washington sent a Circular Letter to the states in which he detailed the achievements of the American Revolution. The Revolution, he noted, had taken place at a time "when the rights of mankind are better understood and more clearly defined, than at any former period." Yet Washington also confessed that the citizens of the new nation might lose all that they had gained. "This is the time of their political probation," he wrote, "this is the moment when the eyes of the whole world are turned upon them. . . . This is the favorable moment to give such a tone to our federal government, as will enable it to answer the ends of its institution, or this may be the ill-fated moment for relaxing the powers of the Union, annihilating the cement of the confederation." Washington was afraid that the new government would simply not be strong enough to protect the great victory that the Revolution had won. Others agreed with Washington's view that a federal government which lacked the power to insure "faithful and pointed compliance" by the states would have "fatal consequences" for the liberty and independence of America. Although they were a minority in the early 1780s, the men who held this nationalist point of view were to have a critical impact on the nation's subsequent history.

The nationalist critique of the Articles of Confederation emerged even before the document had been ratified. In September 1780, Washington's young lieutenant, Alexander Hamilton, wrote a letter to James Duane in which he outlined a plan for "vigorous" government. Although he was only twenty-three, Hamilton revealed the incisive intelligence that was to be the hallmark of his public life. He argued that, unless ultimate and final authority was lodged in Congress, the new nation would collapse. Congress should have complete control over foreign affairs, the army and navy, coinage of money, and the various other matters entrusted to it by the Articles. But it also needed the power to levy and collect taxes, regulate commerce, establish banks, and compel the states to obey its laws. Instead of committees of Congress, there should be federal officials entrusted with real authority. These men should be heads of administrative departments in charge of foreign affairs, the treasury, the army, and the navy.

Washington and Hamilton were articulate spokesmen for the nationalist program, which tended to emphasize order rather than liberty, but its chief architect was Robert Morris, a wealthy merchant and financier who became Congress' Superintendent of Finance in 1781. Morris believed that what the national government required, more than anything else, was an independent source of revenue. When he came to power, the national debt to foreign and domestic creditors was enormous and still growing, but the states had proved that they could not be relied upon voluntarily to help pay the nation's creditors. Some mechanism had to be devised to place the public credit on a firmer footing, and Morris pressed Congress to amend the Articles of Confederation to permit the levy of a 5 per cent duty, or impost, on all imported goods. Once that was done, the door would be open to national taxation of all kinds. In addition, Morris, and many of those who supported him, had more in mind than the financial health of the national government. Morris, himself, was a public creditor and bought up government bonds at deflated prices in the hope that the passage of the impost amendment would bring him a tidy profit.

In any case, the Impost Plan did not pass. The amendment to the Articles to empower Congress to levy the tax of course required the unanimous consent of all thirteen states, and Rhode Island refused to go along. The key measure of their program eliminated, Morris and the other nationalists took more desperate measures early in 1783. The Continental Army, camped at Newburgh, New

York, was about to be demobilized, and Congress had done nothing to satisfy earlier promises of back pay and pensions. Nationalists in Congress, including Hamilton and Morris, joined in a scheme to threaten a military takeover of the government if the army's demands were not met. General Horatio Gates, who resented his position as Washington's second-in-command, also joined the plot. But Washington, himself, refused to cooperate with the attempted coup and used his personal prestige with his men to see that the so-called Newburgh Conspiracy did not succeed.

Domestic Problems of the Confederation

After the defeat of the Impost Plan and the collapse of the Newburgh Conspiracy, the nationalists quickly lost their edge in the Congress. But problems remained. The United States still owed a wartime debt of some $35 million to its own citizens and $7.8 million to the French government and Dutch bankers. In addition, the Confederation government needed a modest sum each year to meet its own operating expenses. Without the impost or other federal taxes, Congress received only $2.5 million in voluntary contributions from the states between 1781 and 1786. It was hardly enough to maintain a skeleton government, much less to meet interest payments on the national debt. By 1789, the arrears of interest amounted to $11.5 million on the domestic debt and $1.6 million on the foreign debt. Congress had been able to maintain a semblance of credit abroad only because Dutch bankers had been daring enough to lend an additional $2.3 million between 1784 and 1789. However, the Confederation government was almost totally bankrupt throughout its entire life.

In addition to its other difficulties, Congress could not stimulate foreign commerce because the Articles forbade it to make any commercial treaty which limited the right of the states to levy their own import duties. The states quarreled and fought among themselves over boundaries, debts, river rights, currency, and a hundred other matters. New York taxed firewood coming in from Connecticut and farm produce coming from New Jersey. Pennsylvania actually went to war to drive Connecticut settlers out of the Wyoming Valley, which Connecticut claimed. Congress was powerless either to prevent or to mediate these controversies, even though they were a hindrance to the revival of national confidence and trade.

Equally important, Congress could do little to ameliorate the severe depression that overtook the American economy in the mid-1780s. European merchants had extended considerable credit to Americans, who were eager to buy the luxury goods that had been unavailable to them during the war. Unfortunately, the massive importation of commodities from Europe was not offset by a comparable increase in American exports. Staple production fell off in the South, and New England merchants were cut off from many of their traditional markets in the British West Indies. The result was a disastrously unfavorable balance of trade which left currency in a shambles. With specie in short supply and creditors demanding payment in gold and silver, the entire economy fell into a tailspin characterized by inflation and unemployment. By 1786 and 1787, a sharp increase in domestic manufacturing, a rise in staple production, and the development of non-English markets for American shipping combined to bring a return to prosperity. In the meantime, however, Congress had been impotent. In dealing with economic problems, as in other things, the ineffectual character of national government was only too apparent.

Western Policy

The domestic failures of the Confederation government were real enough, but they should not be exaggerated. There were successes too. One of the most important was in the area of western policy, for which Congress did possess full constitutional responsibility and authority. More was involved than the question of how the western lands should be disposed of; also at stake was the more important question of whether the new western territories should remain subordinate to the original states and be treated like colonies or become equal, self-governing states. The future character of the United States depended upon the answer to the second question.

Thomas Jefferson drafted the first plan for the political organization of the western territories in 1784. It provided for the creation of a number of new states with high-sounding names like Assensipia, Polypotamia, and Pelisipia. They would be full-fledged members of the American Union after they had gone through a stage of somewhat limited self-government as territories. Jef-

The United States in 1787

ferson's plan also stipulated that slavery should not exist in any new territory or state after 1800. The southern states mustered enough votes to strike out the latter provision, and the plan was approved (although without Jefferson's name) as the Ordinance of 1784. It never went into effect, however, because new legislation soon took its place.

Congress next turned to disposition of the western territory north of the Ohio River that had been ceded by Massachusetts, Connecticut, New York, and Virginia. In the Land Ordinance of 1785, Congress ordered that the northwestern region be surveyed and laid out in townships six miles square. These were divided, by lines running north and south and other lines running east and west, into thirty-six sections. Each section was one square mile, or 640 acres. The land was to be sold for not less than a dollar an acre and in lots not smaller than a square mile. One section in each township was to be set aside for the support of education.

Congress adopted its final, comprehensive law for the political development of the Northwest on July 13, 1787. Known as the Northwest Ordinance, it placed newly created territories under an appointed governor and three judges. When the number of adult white male inhabitants in the territories had reached 5,000, they might elect a legislature and send a delegate to Congress, who might speak but not vote. Once the population of a territory numbered 60,000, it was eligible for admission to the Union as a state, on an absolutely equal footing with the original thirteen states. Not less than three nor more than five states were to be created in the Northwest.

The Northwest Ordinance also extended the ideals of the Revolution to the territories of the West by providing for religious freedom, full protection of liberty and property, and encouragement of education. It further mandated fair treatment of the Indians and — of great significance for the future — prohibited slavery in the new territories. The Ordinance furnished the pattern for the organization and self-government of the great regions already owned, and of those later acquired. It made possible the growth of an expanding Union of equal states.

Foreign Affairs under the Confederation

In addition to its numerous domestic troubles, the United States faced grave and difficult diplomatic problems in the 1780s, and it did not solve them. The decade which followed the Treaty of Paris was one of peace in Europe. As a result, America was not able to take advantage of Europe's distress, as she would do after the wars of the French Revolution, which began in 1793. Furthermore, the weak young republic had no bargaining power in negotiations with the great imperial nations. The absence of a strong central government made a bad situation worse. Thomas Jefferson, Minister to France from 1785 to 1789, wrote home that he could not get the French government to take Congress seriously. "We are the lowest and most obscure of the whole diplomatic tribe," he complained. An English clergyman wrote in 1781 that the idea that America would ever become a strong and united empire was "one of the idlest and most visionary notions ever conceived even by writers of romance."

The new nation's greatest diplomatic difficulties were with Great Britain. First, there was the question of trade with the British West Indies. Some British officials, immediately after the Treaty of Paris, favored courting American friendship. John Adams, the first American Minister to England, was warmly received by King George when he presented his credentials in 1785. But British shipping interests strongly opposed American participation in the West Indian trade. And the British ministers decided that it was not necessary to make concessions because the Americans would have to trade mainly with Britain anyway. Hence all of Adams' efforts proved to be fruitless. Indeed, when he first suggested such an agreement, the British Foreign Secretary sarcastically asked him whether England was expected to make thirteen treaties or one.

Another problem was Anglo-American rivalry in the Northwest. The British held on to a chain of fur-trading posts that extended from Lake Champlain to Lake Michigan. All were situated in territory awarded to the United States by the Treaty of Paris. Adams also pressed for the evacuation of these frontier posts, only to be told that the British would not evacuate them until Americans had paid their debts to British creditors. The failure of Americans to pay their British debts was yet another example of the Confederation government's inability even to enforce provisions of the peace treaty. But the real reasons for the British government's decision were its hopes both to keep control of the fur trade, which amounted to $1.5 million in value a year, and to maintain close relations with the Indians, whom the British wanted to use to slow American expansion into the Northwest.

The new nation also found itself embroiled in a difficult diplomatic confrontation with the Spaniards in the region west of the Appalachians and south of the Ohio River. Settlers were pouring into this area and numbered more than 100,000 by 1790. The only outlet for their produce was the Mississippi River. The Treaty of Paris stipulated that the Mississippi should be open to both American and British navigation. But Spain, now in possession of both banks of the river mouth and its commercial outlet, New Orleans, opposed the expansion of the United States and wished to keep the river trade in her own hands. Spain therefore closed the river to Americans—except those with whom she was plotting to detach the Southwest from the United States.

Spanish hostility to the United States increased when news leaked out of a secret clause in the Anglo-American treaty of 1783. It stipulated 32° 30′ northern latitude as the northern boundary of Florida—which cuts midway through the present states of Alabama and Mississippi—if Great Britain kept Florida, but 31°, the present boundary of the state of Florida, extended to the Mississippi River, if Florida should be returned to Spain, as it actually was.

John Jay, Secretary of Foreign Relations, began negotiations with Don Diego de Gardoqui, who came to Philadelphia as the first Spanish Minister in 1785. The Spanish government was absolutely adamant about its title to the disputed part of Florida. But this was something of an academic controversy, since Americans had not begun to move into the disputed territory. Much more pressing was the matter of the free navigation of the Mississippi River. But Jay was also eager to obtain commercial concessions for American merchants in the Spanish Empire, and he was convinced that Spain would not open the Mississippi River in any event. He therefore asked Congress for permission to sign a treaty, limited to twenty-five or thirty years, in which Spain would make commercial concessions and the United States would agree not to export products through New Orleans. Delegates from the northern states gladly voted to sacrifice western interests for the advantage of merchants of their own section. But southern delegates were all strongly opposed, and the Jay-Gardoqui treaty was never ratified. In sum, America was no more successful in international relations during the 1780s than it was in domestic affairs.

Divisions in the States

While the Confederation government limped along unable to deal effectively with many of the nation's most pressing problems, the state governments became the focus of intense political controversy and competition. Since the greatest share of political power was firmly lodged in the institutions of the several states, it was only natural that men of talent and ambition would turn to those institutions to realize their political goals. Moreover, remarkably consistent political alignments emerged in the legislatures—alignments that reflected divisions within American society that had been only temporarily abated by the need to present a united front against Britain. Although there was some variation, the nature of these alignments was quite consistent from state to state. The men whom one historian has called the "localists" took one side in the major issues of the day while those whom the same scholar has dubbed the "cosmopolitans" took the other.

Although neither localists nor cosmopolitans made any effort to coordinate their efforts on a national basis, the policies advocated by each group also varied little from one state to another. Localists tried to minimize governmental spending and tax burdens on those who could least afford to pay. Therefore, they advocated low salaries for state officials, lower property taxes, and higher excise taxes on luxury goods. In addition, localists backed the interest of debtors over creditors. They demanded such relief measures as "stay laws," which gave debtors additional time in which to discharge their obligations, and they supported an inflationary monetary policy in the form of state-issued paper money. Furthermore, they sought to aid Westerners over Easterners with low prices for vacant land and by moving state capitals from coastal areas into the interior. Finally, localists opposed the return of confiscated lands to former Loyalists. Generally speaking, localist views were those of agrarians who held small amounts of property and sought to protect their traditional way of life against the incursions of more modern and commercially oriented interests.

The cosmopolitans opposed the localists on virtually every issue. As representatives of the old established coastal elites, the cosmopolitans hoped to maintain the traditional apportionment of power within the states. Where the localists tended to emphasize liberty, the cosmopolitans tended to emphasize order. In the main, the cosmopolitans were oriented toward economic development and commercial expansion. They concerned themselves with issues of national and international importance as well as with local questions. They also sought to create an integrated national economy that could be controlled for the benefit of eastern commercial creditor interests. The cosmopolitans came almost exclusively from coastal areas, and their electoral strength declined in proportion to the distance from a given assembly district to the coast. The cosmopolitans also tended to live in densely populated areas that contained the wealthiest families, most newspapers, banks, educational institutions, and centers of commerce. In addition, cosmopolitans were about twice as wealthy as their localist colleagues. Cosmopolitans frequently owned slaves or had servants; they were often lawyers, merchants, or doctors; and their assets usually exceeded their debts. Finally, they were more likely to have served in the Continental Army than in the local militia during the Revolution.

The localists differed from the cosmopolitans as much in social background as in political viewpoint. More than 80 per cent of the localists came from sparsely settled inland counties that were distant from major market towns. Although they were not destitute, localists were rarely among the wealthiest men in a state, and their debts frequently exceeded their assets. The political divisions that emerged in the states thus reflected underlying social divisions. Moreover, these differences—social as well as political—had their roots in the societies of the pre-Revolutionary colonies. Although the Revolution had united Americans in a common cause, it did not magically ameliorate antagonisms which drew their vitality from fundamental socioeconomic conditions deeply rooted in the colonial past. The democratic thrust of the Revolution, which brought into government so many new men unattached to the older sources of political power, was embodied in the localist program. Many of the cosmopolitans had joined the Revolution reluctantly because they had recognized the potential threat that it posed to their own positions of political eminence. In the 1780s, that threat became a reality in the form of the localist bloc and its influence in state politics. Thus the political battles of the 1780s represented a continuation of, rather than a departure from, divisions that had been present in American society long before the Revolution began.

Significantly, however, the political conflict in the states during the Confederation period took place *within* institutions rather than *outside* of them. The intense, even bitter, struggle between cosmopolitans and localists did not end in the utter chaos and destructive violence that has so frequently attended other revolutions. In part, this was true because the class differences in American society were not so great as they were in French society, for example. It was also true, in part, because the rhetoric and principles of even the most conservative cosmopolitans would not permit them to exclude the localists from power altogether. In any case, just as the cosmopolitan-localist split echoed earlier conflicts in colonial society, it foreshadowed the coming struggle for a stronger national government and the political parties and controversies of the 1790s. Viewed in retrospect, state politics in the 1780s, despite their turbulence, demonstrated that republicanism was viable and that it need not degenerate into anarchy and despotism. But many contemporaries, particularly cosmopolitans in the states and nationalists in Congress, had a different perception of events, and it was from this perception that a new vision of the American nation ultimately drew its strength.

3. A FEDERAL CONSTITUTION

The Revival of Nationalism

By the middle of the 1780s, the nationalist movement, which had faltered earlier in the decade, began to regain its former vitality. A variety of causes contributed to this renewed momentum. The nation's economic troubles continued, and the debacle of the Jay-Gardoqui treaty seemed to plunge America's international prestige to a new low. Equally disturbing to many cosmopolitans was the fact that localists had won enough votes in seven states to issue paper money. Virginia permitted farmers to pay their taxes in tobacco receipts. Rhode Island, whose economic distress was perhaps most acute, issued paper money against the security of land. A debtor could pay his or her creditor through the courts with this currency, even if the creditor could not be found. This provision became necessary when creditors actually fled the state to avoid payment in worthless paper bills. Debtors in South Carolina organized a Hemp Club, which sent pieces of rope as warning of a possible hanging to creditors who refused to accept the state's paper money.

Even in states where localists had failed to gain control of the legislature, cosmopolitans were anxious about the future of stable government. Many of them had insisted on the primacy of state power earlier in the decade, but now they began to have their doubts. Perhaps a strengthened federal government might be the answer to their problems after all. Such thoughts became even more credible when an armed crowd surrounded the cosmopolitan-dominated New Hampshire legislature in 1786 and demanded that it issue paper. But it was in Massachusetts that antagonism between poor farmers in the West and their creditors in Boston generated a series of events that helped to crystallize support for the nationalist movement.

Late in 1786 and early in 1787, a virtual civil war broke out in the western counties of the Bay State. A force of 1,500 discontented and indebted farmers, who were frustrated by the state legislature's refusal to provide them with any relief, organized themselves under the leadership of a Revolutionary War veteran, Captain Daniel Shays. They prevented courts from sitting to foreclose mortgages, broke into jails filled with debtors, and freed the prisoners. They forced judges to promise not to act until the grievances of the people had been remedied. Finally, Shays' army attacked the United States arsenal at Springfield. Governor James Bowdoin, himself a nationalist, sent 4,000 troops under General Benjamin Lincoln, who defeated Shays and his ragtag band at Springfield on February 25, 1787.

By their actions, Shays and his followers indicated their belief that they were following the best traditions of the American Revolution. And indeed, in at least one sense, they were. When they failed to achieve redress of their grievances through petitions and institutional means, they turned, as their forebears had, to organized resistance. They had acted to defend liberty against irresponsible and arbitrary power. Yet to many persons, Shays' Rebellion was not so much a vindication of the Revolution as its ultimate perversion—the opening battle of the class warfare that conservatives had feared since the Stamp Act resistance of twenty years before. In fact, Shays' Rebellion was the climax of a series of popular uprisings and crowd actions that had occasionally closed Massachusetts courts throughout the 1780s, but it roused men of property and social position as no other event had. They had resisted the "excessive democracy" of the Revolution in Congress and in the governments of the states. In their view, the nation was clearly on the road to ruin.

By 1787, events seemed to prove to conservative propertied Americans that it had been folly to expect the unlettered masses to exhibit the public virtue that was necessary for a republic to function properly. As Washington put it, "We have probably had too good an opinion of human nature in forming our confederation." To put things right again would not be an easy task, but power had to be taken from those "whose ability or situation does not intitle them to it" and returned to those worthy of it. In other words, the democratic tendencies of the Revolution had to be halted by a return to a more aristocratic and hierarchical form of government.

It is against this background that the nationalists of the late 1780s — soon to be called the Federalists — must be understood. As they saw it, a "spirit of licentiousness" had broken loose and encouraged an unacceptable abuse of the very liberty that the Revolution had been fought to defend. Few of the great men of the Revolution — even those who would ultimately oppose the Constitution — looked very favorably upon Shays' Rebellion and the chaos that it seemed to portend. Even so ardent a localist as Samuel Adams, who had himself been known to organize resistance to government in his time, was appalled and demanded the death penalty for the rebels. James Madison wrote that the rebellion had done "inexpressible damage" to republicanism, and George Washington exclaimed that only a Tory or a Briton would have predicted such a catastrophe.

Only Thomas Jefferson was relatively undisturbed by the turn of events in Massachusetts. He saw Shays' Rebellion as a healthy expression of the American people's affection for liberty and suspicion of despotic power. From Paris, where he was serving as Minister to France, Jefferson wrote Madison that "a little rebellion now and then is a good thing, and as necessary in the political world as storms in the physical." Again, Jefferson wrote from Paris: "The tree of liberty must be refreshed from time to time, with the blood of patriots and tyrants. It is its natural manure." But most leaders were less optimistic than Jefferson. They believed, with Alexander Hamilton, that the people had to be protected from their own worst impulses. The only way to accomplish this objective was to revise, and perhaps abandon, the Articles of Confederation in favor of a new system that would strengthen the central government and place power in the hands of those best equipped to exercise it responsibly in the public interest. Even before Shays' Rebellion was over, therefore, the nationalists had begun to take the steps which would lead to the drafting of the Constitution.

The Great Convention

The chain of events that culminated in the meeting of the Constitutional Convention in Philadelphia on May 25, 1787, began in discussions between Virginia and Maryland over navigation of the Potomac River and oystering in Chesapeake Bay. Commissioners from the two states met at Alexandria in 1785 and then moved their meetings to Mount Vernon at Washington's invitation. In the course of their discussions, it became evident that Pennsylvania and Delaware were also interested. Soon afterward, the Virginia legislature invited all the states to send delegates to Annapolis, Maryland, the next year. Their task would be "to consider how far a uniform system in their commercial regulations" might "be necessary to their common interest and permanent harmony."

Only five states responded to Virginia's invitation to come to Annapolis in September 1786. This was too few to take any action, but one delegate, Alexander Hamilton of New York, took the opportunity to further the nationalist program that he had been supporting since the beginning of the decade. He

"Washington Addressing the Constitutional Convention," by Junius Brutus Stearns. It took the artist fifteen years to complete this famous painting because the heads are actual portraits of the people at the convention. (Courtesy of the Virginia Museum of Fine Arts. Gift of Colonel and Mrs. Edgar W. Garbisch)

proposed that the Annapolis delegates invite the states to send representatives to still another convention to meet in Philadelphia in the following May. Its purpose would be to do a great deal more than to draft a system of commercial regulations. Rather, it would be charged to "take into consideration the situation of the United States, [and] to devise such further provisions as shall appear to them necessary to render the constitution of the federal government adequate to the exigencies of the Union." This was an unusual and perhaps illegal proposal. Congress alone had the right to suggest any change in the Articles of Confederation, and, even then, all the states had to consent. Nevertheless, Congress tacitly accepted the Annapolis proposal. It called upon the states to appoint delegates to a convention in Philadelphia "for the sole and express purpose of revising the Articles of Confederation." However, Hamilton and his friends had in mind more than a simple revision, as events would soon demonstrate.

All the states except Rhode Island responded to the summons. They sent a group of fifty-five men who have rarely been surpassed in breadth of political experience and abilities and sophistication of political thought by any body of equal size. From Virginia came George Washington, Governor Edmund Randolph, James Madison, and George Mason. Pennsylvania sent Benjamin Franklin, James Wilson, Robert Morris, and Gouverneur Morris. Roger Sherman and Oliver Ellsworth came from Connecticut; Elbridge Gerry and Rufus King represented Massachusetts; John Rutledge and the Pinckneys, South Carolina. John Dickinson came from Delaware; Alexander Hamilton from New York.

Some of the men who had been in the front rank in the struggle for independence were absent. John Adams and Thomas Jefferson were serving abroad as Ministers to England and France, respectively. Patrick Henry refused to attend because, he said, he "smelt a rat." Sam Adams was ill, but like his old ally, Patrick Henry, he later opposed the Constitution. Both men feared that liberty would be in peril if the states parted with some of their power. But most men in the convention were more impressed with the danger of disorder and threats to property. Few of the delegates were men of humble origin, and they shared the fears and anxieties of their class. Most represented the cosmopolitan parties in their respective states and saw the convention as an opportunity to attack the power of the "new men" whom the Revolution had brought to power in the state legislatures. The primary weapon of that attack would be to exalt the power of the national government. In addition, many of the delegates stood to gain personally from a more powerful and stable federal establishment. Thirty of them owned public securities whose value would almost certainly be increased by the creation of a fiscally solvent federal government.

Despite their elite backgrounds and conservative social and political views, the members of the convention were not simply or solely concerned with advancing their own narrow interests. They genuinely believed that the republic for which many of them had fought in the Continental Army was in serious danger. They were persuaded that the only remedy for the problems that the nation faced was a radical redistribution of political power within the class structure, as well as between the states and the nation. Furthermore, they were convinced that the excesses of the state legislatures only proved the Revolutionary maxim that *all* concentrations of power tended to undermine the public interest and destroy liberty. In the flush of victory, Americans had erred in believing that their state legislatures, as representatives of the people, could not endanger the common weal. The delegates to the meeting in Philadelphia now sought to correct that error by seeing that no single institution of government—state or national—had the power to determine public policy alone. In other words, the convention members were not averse to advancing their private interests, but they believed that, if they did so, the public interest would ultimately be served also.

Conflicting Plans

Among the first decisions made by the convention was that its deliberations would be secret to protect the delegates against undue public pressure. Fortunately, James Madison preserved the substance of the debates for posterity. He took notes each day and wrote them out every evening as a journal. When he died, fifty years later, his widow sold the manuscript to Congress for $30,000, and it was published in 1840. Madison's notes provide a vivid portrait of the convention, which unanimously chose Washington, the hero of the Revolution, as its president. Although most of the men who met in Philadelphia in the hot summer of 1787 hoped to create a more powerful central government, Madison's meticulous records make it abundantly clear that they disagreed about precisely what form that government should take, and how powerful it should be.

Soon after the convention opened, Governor Randolph presented a plan designed to base the government on the people, rather than on the states, as the Articles of Confederation did. This "Virginia Plan," of which Madison was the primary author, proposed to divide the federal government into three separate branches, each of which would act as a check against the others. The legislative branch would consist of two houses of Congress; representation in the lower house would be proportionate to population, and this chamber would elect the members of the upper house. Congress would have broad legislative powers and the right to nullify state legislation which, in its opinion, violated the national constitution. Moreover, members of the House and Senate, as well as the President and federal judges, were to be servants of the United States, paid out of the national treasury, and not subject to the authority of any state. There was much debate as to how these officials would be chosen. No less than seven different methods were suggested for the election of the President alone.

But the Virginia Plan was not immediately accepted. The smaller states feared that they would be swallowed up by the more populous ones. They supported a counterplan introduced by William Paterson of New Jersey. This called for the continuation of the unicameral legislature established under the Confederation, although Congress would be given additional powers to tax and regulate trade. The representatives would still be chosen by the state governments, not the people, and they would fundamentally represent the states, not the people. Each state would still have only one vote in Congress.

The New Jersey Plan obviously proposed essentially a modification of the Articles of Confederation, while the Virginia Plan sought to create an entirely new structure. In a remarkable speech, Alexander Hamilton urged an even more "consolidated" national government than that of the Virginians. The President and senators, he said, should hold office for life, as did the English King and lords. And the executive should have the power to appoint governors of the states and to veto state laws. This plan aroused considerable curiosity about Hamilton's objectives—some said that his aim was to create an American monarchy and dispense with republicanism completely—but he gained little support.

Many of the members of the convention were disturbed by the direction that the debates were taking because they believed that, according to its instructions from Congress, the convention had the right to do no more than revise the Articles. Some of these men were so concerned that they left the convention. Governor George Clinton of New York was opposed to a new constitution because he knew that a more vigorous national government would undercut his own very substantial power. Through his influence, two men sympathetic to his point of view, Robert Yates and John Lansing, had been chosen as Hamilton's colleagues in the convention. They returned to New York when they realized the direction that the convention was taking. This left Hamilton powerless because the vote of his state could only be cast by a majority of its delegation.

Compromises

At times it seemed that the convention would go to pieces in the fierce debates over the division of power between the central government and the states, and between the large and small states. In addition, the sectional interests of the agricultural South and the commercial North frequently conflicted. But, as in the Revolutionary crises of the 1770s, the delegates chose to "hang together rather than separately," and they worked diligently to compromise the many different points of view that they represented. The compromise that finally settled the most stubborn impasse was introduced by Oliver Ellsworth and Roger Sherman of Connecticut. It broke the deadlock between the large and small states by giving something to both. To the large states went representation on the basis of population in the lower house, or House of Representatives. The small states received equal representation—two members to be elected by each state legislature—in the upper house, or Senate. No state could ever be deprived of its equal representation in the Senate without its own consent.

Other major compromises attempted to reconcile the differences between the North and the South. One permitted the southern states to count three fifths of the slaves as "population" in determining the states' representation in the House of Representatives. In other words, the Constitution defined each slave as being completely neither a person nor a piece of property. Rather, in its passion for compromising anything and everything, the convention absurdly defined slaves as being three-fifths human and two-fifths chattel! Another compromise granted Congress the power to regulate trade, as the commercial North wanted, but forbade Congress ever to levy duties on exports, on which the South depended for its wealth. A final compromise stipulated that Congress should not interfere with the importation of slaves for twenty years.

In order to protect property against future assaults, the authors of the Constitution were careful to include provisions which forbade the states to issue paper money or to pass any law which lessened the obligations of contracts. Both measures were, of course, boons to creditors who had been suffering under the rule of debtor-dominated state governments. Perhaps the happiest device of the whole Constitution was the skillful way in which it secured the obedience of the states and private citizens to the federal government. It did not authorize Congress or the President to interfere directly in state affairs or to use the army or navy to coerce the states. Instead, it declared that the Constitution, and all laws and treaties made "in pursuance thereof," were to be the supreme law of the land. It required officials in every branch of the *state governments* to take an oath to support the Constitution, and it provided for a system of federal courts throughout the country to enforce federal laws against private citizens, as well as against state officials.

The Constitution was thus the result of a series of compromises between the various groups represented in the convention. More than that, it made compromise the central principle of American government. The balancing of power among the three branches of the government and the distribution of power between the state and federal governments created a system in which compromise would be a necessity. What the Constitution failed to account for, of course, was that there might be some issues that simply could not be compromised. The tragedy of the Civil War demonstrated that slavery was one such issue and that, in the long run, the humanity of black Americans could not be compromised by legal technicalities.

Still, when the Constitution was completed on September 17, 1787, most of the delegates must have shared the feeling of Benjamin Franklin, their most senior colleague, that, although the document was not completely satisfactory, it did provide a workable plan for a new government. "On the whole," Franklin said, "I cannot help expressing a wish that every member of the Convention who may still have objections to it, would with me, on this occasion doubt a little his own infallibility—and to make manifest our unanimity, put his name to this instrument." Of the members still present in Philadelphia, only Mason and Randolph of Virginia and Gerry of Massachusetts did not heed Franklin's request. Thirty-nine delegates from twelve states signed the Constitution, which was then submitted through Congress to the states for ratification.

Federalists and Antifederalists

The convention realized that the state legislatures would be very reluctant to give up their sovereignty, and that the Constitution would not be sympathetically received by men whose power depended on strong state governments. Therefore, the convention shrewdly recommended that the Constitution be considered by special conventions elected by the voters in each state for that single purpose. The convention also provided in Article VII that when nine state conventions had ratified the Constitution it would go into effect in those states. This would force any dissenting state to choose between secession from the Union or ratification of the Constitution. The backers of the Constitution had played their cards cleverly, but ratification was by no means assured. Even before the elections to the state-ratifying conventions took place, a vigorous and frequently acrimonious debate began between the Constitution's supporters—now called Federalists—and its opponents—the Antifederalists.

The Antifederalists had many specific criticisms of the Constitution. Indeed, Antifederalist pamphleteers found fault with virtually every provision of the document. At the core of the Antifederalist critique, however, was the not entirely incorrect suspicion that, in the words of one writer, the friends of the new system were "the enemies of the Revolution." The consolidation of power in a national government, which the Constitution would institutionalize, would usurp the very prerogatives of local, state-based government for which the Antifederalists believed the Revolution had been fought. By removing government from the people—in physical as well as institutional terms—the Constitution would substitute order for liberty and aristocracy for democracy. The New York Antifederalist, Melancton Smith, wrote that a government such as that proposed by the Constitution would inevitably "fall into the hands of the few and the great." This would be "a government of oppression."

But there was more to the Antifederalist argument than vague fears and suspicions about the intentions of the Federalists. Opponents of the Constitution noted that, because the new frame of government would clearly supersede the existing state constitutions, it was even more serious that it contained no bill of rights. The Constitution would, therefore, provide no sure protection of the basic human liberties which had been the very heart of the Revolutionary creed. And the emasculated state governments would be powerless to prevent altogether the destruction of the liberty of the common people of America by an aristocratic despotism. Furthermore, the noted French theorist, Charles Louis de Secondat Montesquieu, had demonstrated that republics could not succeed in so large a country with so diverse a population as that of the United States. Rather, republics were best suited to smaller political entities like the states, where legislatures could more accurately reflect the opinions of the people and where legislators could be kept strictly and immediately accountable for their actions.

The Federalists believed that they, and not their Antifederalist opponents, were the true heirs of the Spirit of '76. The Revolution, they said, had been fought to establish a republic, not a democracy. The great defect of the Articles of Confederation was that it created thirteen separate republics—and excessively "democratical" ones at that. The Constitution, on the other hand, would be more in keeping with the true aims of the Revolution. To charges that the proposed government tended toward aristocracy and oligarchy, the Federalists answered that the Constitution clearly preserved the most critical component of republicanism: popular sovereignty. Indeed, the very first words of the Constitution—"We the people"—signaled its commitment to republican rule. Moreover, the popular election of the House of Representatives preserved a direct voice for the people in the federal government.

The most complete statement of the Federalist position appeared in a series of essays written by Alexander Hamilton, James Madison, and John Jay under the pseudonym of Publius. The essays, collectively titled *The Federalist*, were published in New York to persuade the people of the state that it was in their interest to support the Constitution. *The Federalist* remains to this day one of the most thorough and persuasive explications of the basic principles of American constitutionalism. Although its three authors provided a point-by-point defense of the entire Constitution, they also articulated a unique theory of social and political relations that marked a clear departure, not only from the ideology of the Revolution, but also from the best republican thinking of their day. Madison, in particular, identified a critical difficulty for which no previous writer had accounted adequately. In so doing, he came to terms with one of the central dilemmas of the entire American experience: how to maintain unity in the midst of diversity.

Madison argued in the *Federalist No. 10* that the fatal flaw to which all republics were prone was "faction." Society was inevitably composed of a large number of groups with different interests and different goals. Madison contended that it was folly to expect, as the Antifederalists did, that those groups would sacrifice their private concerns for the good of the public. Previous writers, such as Montesquieu, who recognized the problem had solved it by saying that republics could only succeed in small nations with a relatively homogeneous population. But Madison argued otherwise. Faction and diversity of interest would always exist, no matter how small the country and no matter how homogeneous the population. These were inherent traits in the nature of mankind. How then, Madison asked, might faction be eliminated? There were two possibilities. A government could either destroy liberty, which was morally untenable, or it could see that everyone had the same opinions and interests, which was impossible. In other words, the causes of faction could not be removed.

If the causes of faction were unavoidable, how might the problems created by diversity of interest be handled? Madison argued that the Constitution wisely focused on the effects of faction, which could be controlled, rather than upon its causes. The Constitution, he said, distributed power so widely that it would be impossible for any one group to gain control of the government and enforce its own policies to the detriment of the public and at the expense of liberty. Indeed, even a majority of the people would not be able to impose their will on a minority because the new government would provide political representation for all groups and grant political dominance to none. As a result, both liberty *and* order would be preserved, and the true public interest would

James Madison, dubbed "the father of the Constitution," is painted here by Gilbert Stuart, an outstanding portraitist of his era. (The Bettmann Archive)

be advanced. Madison's reasoning led to the conclusion that, despite Montesquieu's arguments to the contrary, liberty and order would be safest in a large and diverse republic where the largest number of factions could contend for power.

Madison's argument was not entirely original, of course. He relied to some extent on the work of the Scottish philosopher, David Hume. What was unique, however, was Madison's application of Hume's ideas to the peculiar situation of the United States. In addition to reversing Montesquieu's formulations in regard to small republics, Madison implicitly rejected the Revolutionary view that virtue was necessary for the maintenance of republican liberty. In fact, the Revolution's emphasis upon virtue represented a futile attempt to eliminate the causes of faction. For Madison, there was no point in hoping that a sudden revival of virtue would save the republic because he believed that most men, however good their intentions, would not be virtuous if given political power. Rather, the point was to make the inevitable lack of virtue irrelevant to government by making it impossible for any individual or group to gain control of every branch of government. The Constitution succeeded in this goal by distributing power among the various branches of the federal government and between the federal government and the states, rather than by concentrating it in the state legislatures, as the Articles of Confederation had done.

Despite their protestations to the contrary, therefore, the Federalists *were* counterrevolutionaries. The Constitution, by implication, dismissed the Revolutionary concept of virtue and removed power from the states. It, therefore, sought to reverse processes that the Revolution had both reflected and encouraged. The Federalists sought to limit the influence of the "new men" who had ascended to power in the states as a result of the Revolution. The Federalists also sought to return the reins of government to those members of society whom they believed were qualified to use them responsibly. The Antifederalist accusation that the Constitution was "aristocratic" was not without foundation, for the Federalists did hope to overthrow those for whom the Revolution had opened unprecedented political opportunities. To that extent, the Constitution was counterrevolutionary and the Federalists were, as their opponents charged, "the enemies of the Revolution."

In another sense, however, the Constitution was the natural outgrowth and culmination of the Revolution. The difficulties of the 1780s were real enough, and the Constitution did attempt to come to terms with them. Furthermore, the men who wrote the Constitution represented a conservative aspect of the Revolution that had always been present, even if it had not always been dominant. In addition, the Constitution was a peculiarly American document. It was not merely a refurbishing of the British Constitution, minus the King and Parliament. Instead, it was conceived with the unique problems of the United States in mind. More than that, it sought to reconcile the enduring tension between liberty and order with which Americans had been grappling since the earliest years of colonization. Subsequent history has shown that that reconciliation was far from perfect. However, in attempting it at all, the Federalists were acting within the republican tradition which the Revolution initiated. Moreover, they wrote a document which helped to insure that that tradition would be maintained.

The Federalist Triumph

In spite of the cogency of *The Federalist*'s defense, few of the Constitution's opponents were persuaded. They continued to attack the new government in all states, and they very nearly succeeded in preventing its ratification. Despite the severity of the struggle, the Federalists ultimately prevailed. The Delaware convention led the way by unanimously ratifying the Constitution on December 7, 1787. Pennsylvania, New Jersey, Georgia, and Connecticut soon followed. In Massachusetts, the outcome was very uncertain, but the hesitant support of John Hancock for the new government helped to insure ratification in that critical state. Maryland, South Carolina, and New Hampshire soon followed suit, and the nine positive votes necessary for the Constitution to go into effect had been achieved. But Virginia and New York were still outside the orbit of the new federal government, and few people believed that it could succeed without their participation.

The opponents of the Constitution were very strong in both Virginia and New York. Localists in both states insisted that they could never vote for a

Constitution that lacked a bill of rights. The Federalists were not exactly opposed to a bill of rights; they only regarded such a measure as unnecessary. Fortunately, they were willing to compromise, and they promised that a bill of rights would be added as soon as the Constitution had been ratified. This move, along with some shrewd politicking by Washington and the other supporters of the Constitution, succeeded in securing ratification in Virginia on June 26, 1788. The victory in Virginia brought strong pressure on the delegates to the New York convention and, by a very narrow margin, they, too, ratified the Constitution at the end of July.

Although North Carolina did not ratify until November 1789 and Rhode Island did not officially enter the Union until May 1790, the Federalist triumphs in Virginia and New York guaranteed that the new government would be adopted, since Rhode Island and North Carolina could hardly survive as independent nations. Yet the struggle had been a difficult one which set two fundamentally different conceptions of politics and society against each other. John Adams did not exaggerate the case when he said that "the Constitution was extorted from a reluctant people by a grinding necessity." The event itself, however, was hailed with rejoicing. Celebratory dinners, processions, fireworks, and commemorations of every kind followed. Once the issue had been decided, few seemed to regret the end of the old government under the Articles of Confederation. It was called the "sloop of anarchy which had gone ashore on the rock of Union."

With the adoption of the Constitution, the Confederation Congress expired. But before it did so, it instructed the states to elect senators and representatives to the new Congress created by the Constitution. The states were also to

Celebrating the ratification of the United States Constitution in New York City in 1789. This woodcut shows the ship Hamilton *passing the fort at Bowling Green where members of Congress greeted the procession. (The Bettmann Archive)*

appoint electors to choose the new President. Every elector wrote Washington's name first on his ballot; so the hero of the War for Independence would become the first President of the United States. John Adams received the second largest number of votes and thereby would become Vice-President. Washington's association with the new Constitution was one of its greatest assets. No leader of the Revolution was more widely known or admired than he. His willingness to serve as President gave the new government a legitimacy that it could not otherwise have enjoyed.

The first Wednesday in March was the date set for the inauguration. (That day fell on March 4 in 1789, so March 4 was set as the date for the inauguration of each new administration. It was changed to January 20 by the Twentieth Amendment, adopted in 1933.) In 1789, however, April was well advanced before enough congressmen had arrived in New York for a quorum. Then, on April 30, 1789, after a triumphant trip northward from Virginia, George Washington appeared on the balcony of Fredrick Hall in New York to take the oath of office. To the members of Congress, the President read his inaugural address in a voice "a little tremulous" with the sense of the responsibilities that rested upon him. "The preservation of the sacred fires of liberty and the destiny of the republican model of government," he said, "are justly considered, perhaps, as deeply, as finally, staked on the experiment entrusted to the hands of the American people."

As Washington so clearly recognized, his inauguration marked the beginning of an extraordinary experiment in republican government. But Washing-

This drawing by C. C. Reinhart is the only known contemporary representation of the first inauguration of George Washington in New York City on April 30, 1789. Washington was sworn into office by the Chancellor of New York, Robert Livingston. (The Bettmann Archive)

ton's presidency was an end as well as a beginning, for it marked the close of the formative era of American history. Across the years between the founding of Jamestown in 1607 and the drafting of the Constitution 180 years later, the physical and human landscapes of North America were quite literally transformed. The full extent of that transformation, like its cost in human suffering, is very nearly incalculable, but it had its origins in the thousands of collective and individual decisions through which Europeans, Africans, and Indians either chose to adjust or were forced to adjust to the realities of life in a world that was truly "new" to all of them. The ultimate result was a nation quite unlike any that the world had ever known—a nation that set a new standard of human liberty which neither it nor any other nation has been able to meet. And yet the creation of that standard must finally be counted as the most enduring accomplishment of the American Revolution. It was an event whose repercussions, for good and for ill, are still being felt throughout the world.

SUGGESTED READINGS

Since 1888, when John Fiske published *The Critical Period of American History*, scholars have been debating the essential character of the decade or so before the drafting and ratification of the Constitution. That debate continues today, and one of the most important participants is Merrill Jensen. His two books, *The Articles of Confederation* (rev. ed., 1959), and *The New Nation* (1950), have a very clear interpretive perspective, but they are also fine general histories that remain immensely valuable. Forrest McDonald, *E Pluribus Unum* (1965), has a different point of view on the period—especially insofar as the economy is concerned—and is also worth consulting. Edmund C. Burnett, *The Continental Congress* (1941), is a lively and impressionistic account of politics at the national level, but not all of Burnett's generalizations about divisions in the Congress are reliable. They should be compared to those emerging from the sophisticated quantitative analysis of H. James Henderson, *Party Politics in the Continental Congress* (1974). E. James Ferguson, *The Power of the Purse* (1961), is a thorough examination of public finance that can be supplemented by reference to Clarence L. Ver Steeg, *Robert Morris* (1954), a biography of the most important figure in the American financial community during the Confederation, and to Curtis P. Nettels, *The Emergence of a National Economy* (1962).

Constitution making in the states is covered in Elisha P. Douglass, *Rebels and Democrats* (1955), while the extension of suffrage in the aftermath of the Revolution receives careful consideration in Chilton Williamson, *American Suffrage from Property to Democracy* (1960). J. R. Pole, *Political Representation and the Origins of the American Republic* (1966), also contains some excellent discussions of developments in the states, as does

Jackson Turner Main, *The Upper House in Revolutionary America* (1967).

The central work around which the historiography of the Confederation and the Constitution revolves is Charles A. Beard, *An Economic Interpretation of the Constitution of the United States* (1913). Beard's conclusions as well as his methods have been severely criticized in Robert E. Brown, *Charles Beard and the Constitution* (1956), and Forrest McDonald, *We the People* (1958). McDonald's evidence in particular seems to disprove Beard's thesis. Certainly, it destroys permanently the notion that the Federalists acted as they did simply because they believed that the value of the public securities that they held would increase under a new federal government. However, Beard's more general contention that the struggle over ratification embodied social conflict of significant dimensions is still alive. Indeed, it has been brilliantly revived in the work of two historians whose approaches differ not only from that of Beard but from that of each other. Jackson Turner Main, *Political Parties before the Constitution* (1973), uses a rigorous quantitative analysis to demonstrate that the cosmopolitan-localist division in the states that is described in this chapter appeared throughout the country, partook of genuine disagreement over economic issues, and flowed directly into the conflict over ratification. In *The Creation of the American Republic* (1969), Gordon S. Wood, on the other hand, traces intellectual and ideological developments in the 1780s, and also discovers a deep rift in American thinking on the relationship between politics and society which, while not a class division in the narrow sense, did reflect social antagonisms of the most profound kind. Thus, for both Main and Wood, the argument between the Antifederalists and the

Federalists was more than a rarefied intellectual controversy over abstractions. It was, instead, the political expression of a more fundamental set of alignments within American society. Among those who seem to reject this view is Bernard Bailyn whose *Ideological Origins of the American Revolution* (1967) and subsequent writings reject any understanding of the Revolution, the Confederation, and the Constitution that emphasizes social conflict. Benjamin F. Wright, *Consensus and Continuity* (1958), has a similar view.

Ironically, the best history of the Constitutional Convention was published in the very same year that Beard's book appeared. Max Farrand, *The Framing of the Constitution of the United States* (1913), is marvelously detailed and eminently readable. Clinton Rossiter, *1787: The Grand Convention* (1965), is a good supplement, though not a replacement for Farrand, and also contains a fine section-by-section discussion of the final product of the meeting in Philadelphia. The best study of the Antifederalists is Jackson Turner Main, *The Anti-Federalists* (1961). Gerald Stourzh, *Alexander Hamilton and the Idea of Republican Government* (1970), is a fine intellectual biography. There is no comparable study of James Madison, although the essays of Douglass Adair in *Fame and the Founding Fathers* (1974) constitute an excellent beginning. For Washington's career and larger significance in American life, Marcus Cunliffe, *George Washington: Man and Monument* (1958), is brief, accessible, and interesting. Finally, Jack P. Greene, ed., *The Reinterpretation of the American Revolution* (1968), contains a fine historiographical essay by the editor as well as an outstanding collection of essays on the entire period from 1763 to 1789.

CHAPTER 8
THE FEDERALIST ERA

1. PROBLEMS UNDER THE CONSTITUTION

The New Experiment

The Great Seal of the United States includes the caption *"Novus Ordo Seclorum"* ("A New Order of the Ages"). Americans in the 1780s were very conscious that they were making a "new beginning for mankind." Among them were close students of Roman history who greatly admired the constitution of the Roman Republic. But they well knew that the first great republic in history had degenerated into a dictatorship and an imperial system that gradually destroyed ancient Roman liberties. Americans of the 1780s were determined to prove that republican government by representatives chosen by the people could succeed.

The American experiment started under generally advantageous circumstances. Primarily, it was neither radical nor revolutionary but was built solidly upon centuries of British traditions and 150 years of increasing local self-government. This foundation of freedom contrasted sharply with the background of the French Revolution—a long era of despotic feudalism which the French people had to uproot in 1789 before they could conduct their own democratic experiments.

No political venture in history was launched by more high-minded and dedicated leaders than the American founding fathers. George Washington was a remarkably selfless public servant, utterly devoted to the success of the experiment. Moreover, an overwhelming majority of the people supported him in his efforts. Even those persons who had opposed ratification were willing to give the new Constitution a fair trial. Finally, the new government had the good luck to be launched upon a rising tide of economic prosperity.

Nevertheless, the men who directed the new republic faced difficult tasks. They inherited almost nothing by way of structure from the Confederation government—only a dozen clerks who had not been paid for some time, an army of 672, and heavy debts. The President and Congress had to create machinery for raising money, for defending the country, and for dealing with the Indian tribes. The government needed to organize territories, establish federal courts, and regulate trade. There were a host of nagging, difficult diplomatic problems which had been left unsettled by the Confederation. The President had to make hundreds of appointments to executive, judicial, and diplomatic offices.

Washington Creates a Government

Washington took careful pains to appoint only Federalists—strong friends of the Constitution—to office. By this action, he did what he had never intended to do. He indirectly laid the basis for a national political party among officeholders who later proved loyal to Washington and his chief adviser, Alexander Hamilton. By following the rule that appointees be chosen first for their political loyalty and second for their ability, Washington also introduced the spoils system into national administration.

Washington chose his old friend and comrade in arms, Alexander Hamilton, to head what was then the most important department of government, the Treasury. Hamilton, an ardent nationalist, was eager to build a strong central government. Washington appointed another member of the Constitutional Convention, Governor Edmund Randolph of Virginia, as Attorney General. The War Department was entrusted to General Henry Knox of Massachusetts, a firm supporter of the new Constitution and a close friend of the President. Washington called Thomas Jefferson home from Paris, where he had been Minister since 1785, to become Secretary of State. Jefferson had been alarmed because the Constitution accorded the government such great powers. His friend, James Madison, won him over to lukewarm support of the new Constitution; however, Jefferson continued to insist on protection for the rights of the states and of the common people.

The Secretaries of State, Treasury, and War, along with the Attorney General, constituted the four heads of the "executive departments" referred to in Article II, Section 2 of the Constitution. They made up Washington's cabinet. There was a Post Office Department dating from colonial times, but the Postmaster General did not have a seat in the cabinet until Andrew Jackson's administration. From time to time, as the business of the government required, Congress would add new executive departments.

Hamilton's Financial Program

The commanding figure of Washington's first administration was the financial genius, Alexander Hamilton, only thirty-four years old in 1789 when he assumed control of the Treasury Department. His overriding objective was to place the finances of the country on a sound basis. He faced a national debt of $54 million, more than $11 million of which was owed to France and to Dutch bankers. The rest was owed to Americans. This domestic debt usually took the form of paper certificates which promised to pay the holder the amount named on the bond. Each of the separate states also had unpaid debts which, altogether, amounted to $25 million.

Hamilton, on account of his authorship of many of *The Federalist* papers and his leadership of the movement for ratification in New York, had done as much as any other person to assure ratification of the Constitution, but he had strong doubts about the future of the new constitutional system. Although he was illegitimate—John Adams later lashed him publicly as "the bastard son of a Scotch merchant"—Hamilton had married well and considered himself to be an aristocrat. He detested democracy as mob rule, and he worked out a financial program with one major objective—to give the propertied classes such a large stake in the success of Federalist policies that they would have to support them and the new government.

In his *Report on the Public Credit,* sent to Congress in January 1790, Hamilton proposed a plan to solve the nation's financial problem. He would pay the foreign debt in full, pay the domestic debt at face value, and assume the unpaid war debts of the states. Taxes would of course have to be levied to pay these debts. The program was aimed at restoring confidence in American credit and currency. The reaction to these proposals was decidedly mixed at first. Everyone agreed that the honor of the country required payment of the entire for-

Alexander Hamilton, painted here by Charles Willson Peale, was the man most responsible for the success of the government under the Constitution. The brilliant work of his compatriots at the Constitutional Convention came to fruition in large part because Hamilton managed to place the government on a sound financial basis. (Courtesy of The New-York Historical Society, New York City)

eign debt. But Hamilton's proposal to pay at its full face value the domestic debt incurred during the Revolution by the Continental Congress and the Confederation Congress set off fierce opposition. The certificates had fallen to a low price on the market because of a lack of faith that the government would ever pay them in full. Many patriotic men had been obliged to sell their certificates for whatever they could get for them during hard times, and speculators had bought some at prices as low as fifteen or twenty cents on the dollar. Indeed, no sooner had Hamilton submitted his report to Congress than speculators hurried to rural areas to buy up Continental securities at low prices, before news of Hamilton's refunding plan had reached their owners. Payment of the certificates in full would enrich these speculators. Nevertheless, Hamilton persuaded Congress that payment of the domestic debt was necessary in order to establish the credit of the United States.

On the problem of the unpaid war debts of the states, Hamilton posed two questions: had the war not been fought for the benefit of all the states? Hence, should not the whole debt be paid by the government representing all of them? Moreover, the federal government, by taking over the state debts, would both make them usable as capital for expanding the economy and bind the holders of the state debts closely to the federal government. There was great opposition to assuming these debts because the southern states had already paid most of theirs through the sale of land. The measure was defeated in the House by a vote of thirty-one to twenty-nine. But Hamilton persisted. He finally persuaded Jefferson to get several southern congressmen to change their votes. In return, Hamilton promised that the new capital of the republic would be built on the Potomac River in the South.

The total debt of about $75 million was then funded by the issuance of government bonds bearing interest, some at 6 per cent, some at 3 per cent. Scarcely any of the bonds were bought by people west of the Appalachians or by farmers in the uplands of the original states. The bonds were bought by persons who had money to invest—mainly bankers, merchants, and people of inherited wealth. The wealthier citizens were thus, from the beginning, attached to the government and interested in its success—precisely as Hamilton had planned.

The Hamiltonian Fiscal Program

The new government needed money to pay interest on its bonds, the salaries of its employees, and other expenses. Fortunately, it no longer needed to rely upon requests from the states. Congress now had power to levy and collect taxes. The first tariff act, adopted on July 4, 1789, placed small duties ranging from 5 to 15 per cent on more than eighty manufactured articles. It was not a protective tariff; its exclusive purpose was to raise revenue.

But for Hamilton, this was merely the beginning of his fiscal program. He was one of the most innovative political economists of his day and believed in a powerful central government that would work actively to increase national wealth and prosperity. He envisioned a great and powerful nation—a land of factories, mills, mines, and teeming cities. The United States was destined to become a great power in the world, Hamilton predicted, but that day would never come so long as European manufacturers, who paid low wages, undersold American manufacturers, who paid high wages. The solution to this problem, he said, was a protective tariff. In his *Report on Manufactures*, sent to

Congress on December 5, 1791, Hamilton recommended levying import duties high enough to guarantee the growth of American industries. Congress ignored the proposal, but Hamilton had laid down a program that would be taken up by future political parties.

In addition to receipts from the tariff and the sale of land, the Treasury had a third source of income from internal revenue (or excise) taxes, such as are found today on gasoline, furs, jewelry, and automobiles. One of these excises, adopted by Congress in 1791 at Hamilton's suggestion, was a tax on distilleries. Hamilton intended this tax to remind independent-minded western farmers, who often shipped their surplus grain in liquid form as whiskey, of the existence of the central government.

Opposition to this tax flared dangerously in western Pennsylvania in 1794, where farmers openly defied the government and refused to pay the tax. Not only that, they attacked federal revenue officers and tarred and feathered some of them. When Congress, during the summer of 1794, enacted a law to compel payment of the whiskey tax, a crowd of 500 men burned down the home of the chief tax collector. Washington overreacted. He called out the militias of Virginia, Maryland, New Jersey, and Pennsylvania and sent some 13,000 men to crush the "rebellion," which quickly evaporated. Two of the rebel Pennsylvanians were convicted of treason and then pardoned by Washington.

Engraving by William Birch of the first Bank of the United States, located in Philadelphia. The bank was built in the Roman style instituted by Thomas Jefferson. (Culver Pictures, Inc.)

Hamilton was delighted by Washington's quick use of force against western rabble. To Washington, however, the "Whisky Rebellion" was nothing less than defiance of the authority of the fledgling national government and, as such, had to be sternly suppressed. Best of all, from Washington's point of view, the rebellion was suppressed with the help of the states.

The capstone of Hamilton's financial program was a national bank. The Secretary of the Treasury persuaded Congress in February 1791 to charter the Bank of the United States for twenty years with a capital stock of $10 million. The government would own one fifth of the stock and appoint one fifth of its directors. It was a significant sign of future sectional divisions that nineteen of the twenty votes cast against the bank bill in the House of Representatives came from Southerners.

The bank would receive on deposit the money that came into the United States Treasury. It could use this money, like that of private depositors, for investment. Naturally, the profits would be shared by the stockholders, which included the United States Government. The bank could also issue notes, that is, promises to pay, which could be used for payment of taxes and other debts owed to the government. In return for these privileges, the bank would pay a certain sum to the government and do some of the financial business of the Treasury (such as collect taxes) free of charge. It would also lend the government money when it needed it.

Washington, troubled by doubts about the constitutionality of the bank bill, asked for written opinions on it from both Hamilton and Jefferson. The former defended the bank and argued that its authority was implied in the Constitution under the "necessary and proper" clause which reads that Congress may "make all Laws which shall be necessary and proper for carrying into Execution the . . . Powers vested by this Constitution in the Government of the United States." The bank, said Hamilton, would carry out the power of Congress to "borrow money on the credit of the United States" and to regulate the currency. Jefferson opposed the bank because the Constitution, he said, nowhere gave Congress the specific power to establish a financial institution. Moreover, he saw danger in the government going into partnership with the wealthy men who would control the bank and its policies. The government, through this legislation, would create a "paper aristocracy." Secretary Knox agreed with Hamilton; Attorney General Randolph, with Jefferson.

Hamilton's arguments persuaded Washington, and he signed the bill. Washington thus stood with persons such as Hamilton who believed in a loose construction, or wide interpretation, of the Constitution. State-righters agreed with Jefferson and demanded a narrow or literal interpretation of the Constitution. The bank's charter ran for twenty years, to be renewed by Congress in 1811. Its stock was offered to the public at $400 a share on July 4, 1791. Every share was sold within two hours after the subscription books were opened.

The Bank of the United States opened its main office in Philadelphia on December 12, 1791, and soon established eight branches in the major cities around the country. It more than fulfilled Hamilton's expectations. Its notes provided a sound currency and, because it was a clearing house for state-chartered banks, it exercised some restraint on them by refusing to accept their bills and notes if they were unsound. Finally, the bank provided a solid foundation for the new banking structure emerging in the United States.

Early Political Parties

The first national political parties took shape during the disputes over Hamilton's economic policies and were solidified by conflicting responses to the French Revolution and the European wars that followed it. Hamilton's measures—assumption and funding of the debt, the national bank, excise taxes, and the protective tariff—antagonized many persons who identified themselves with agricultural or debtor interests, or who feared that democracy in America would be strangled by a wealthy aristocracy. Few Americans, even among politicians who were obliged at least to take heed of it all, strongly opposed *every* feature of Hamilton's program. However, of those who disliked several of the measures, there were enough to comprise the nucleus of a political party. Two parties developed so gradually that it is impossible to fix the exact moment at which either came into existence. Leaders on both sides complained, often sincerely, about the growth of factions and factionalism. John Adams declared that the "division of the republic into two great parties . . . is to be dreaded as the greatest political evil under our Constitution." Nonetheless, competing politicians organized their forces to combat the offending "faction." Hamilton, who well understood the uses of political power, mobilized support for his program among congressmen much as an eighteenth-century British Prime Minister might have done in Parliament. Friends of the Hamiltonian program corresponded with one another and caucused on issues and candidates even before an organized opposition had emerged. They subsidized newspapers to win popular support for the Hamilton policies and distributed federal patronage in home districts to persons who favored a strong national program.

However, Hamilton's enemies, led by Jefferson and Madison, proved to be much more skillful politicians. At first they also neglected to organize a party except among congressmen and federal officeholders. They did found a newspaper in 1791, the *National Gazette,* to report on issues to the people from the people's point of view. Previously, the only newspaper in the United States offering full coverage of national politics had been Hamilton's organ, the *United States Gazette.* During the winter of 1791–1792, Jefferson and Madison adopted the name "Republican" for their group. Hamilton and his friends took the name "Federalist" in an attempt to brand their opponents with the term "Antifederalist"—the name that had been used for the largely discredited opponents of the Constitution.

During the next few years, Jefferson, Madison, and their supporters built a system of alliances with politicians in various states. Leaders in Virginia, Maryland, North Carolina, and Georgia could be counted on from the start. However, the Republicans needed allies in the North in order to bid for national power. Republicans became the dominant party in Pennsylvania after the imposition of the whiskey tax. Jefferson and Madison also cemented an alliance with Hamilton's enemies in New York, led by Governor George Clinton and Aaron Burr. The former controlled a large upstate vote, while the latter had built the Tammany Society into a formidable political machine in New York City.

Hamilton and Jefferson strongly disagreed in cabinet meetings, and their followers fought each other bitterly in Congress and in the press. Madison led the Republicans in the House of Representatives, and he was a vital force in the emergence of the Republican party. The Republicans charged Hamiltonians with aspiring to make the United States a monarchy. The Federalists declared that the Jeffersonians would wreck the government by turning it over to the mob. The respect and affection with which George Washington was regarded by almost all Americans, including Jefferson and Madison, prevented extreme measures. Party strife might otherwise have brought disaster to the government in its infancy.

Washington wished to retire to his home at Mount Vernon at the end of his first administration, but both Hamilton and Jefferson implored him to accept reelection in 1792. Washington was again the unanimous choice of the electors. John Adams, however, received only seventy-seven votes for Vice-President against fifty-five for George Clinton, the Republican candidate. Indeed, the Republicans elected a majority to sit in the next House of Representatives. The battle of the parties had begun.

2. INTERNATIONAL STRIFE

Washington's Indian Policy and Border Troubles

Domestic troubles alone did not persuade Washington to serve a second term. He was moved also, as he put it, by "the delicate posture of our foreign affairs." The United States had difficult problems with the three most important nations of western Europe — Great Britain, Spain, and France.

The British still refused to carry out the provisions of the Treaty of Paris concerning the Northwest. They continued to hold fur-trading posts within American territory, while their agents from Canada furnished arms and powder to the Indians and encouraged them to resist the advance of American settlers. Indian raids and massacres were frequent on the border as a result of continuing white encroachment into Indian lands. General Arthur St. Clair, the Governor of the Northwest Territory, was sent to punish the Indians, but his force of 2,000 men was depleted by desertions, and the remaining 1,400 were ambushed on the Wabash River on November 4, 1791. Only 600 escaped. This terrible defeat threatened to expose the whole territory to Indian attacks.

In order to settle the Indian problem, Washington and Secretary of War Knox formulated a national policy to "civilize" the Indians. They hoped eventually to absorb them into the Union. Washington said that he sought "to advance the happiness of the Indians and to attach them firmly to the United States." He, like other persons of his time, hoped that, with the application of this policy, the Indian would "cease his wandering ways," adopt the practice of private property as the white man understood it, farm like white Americans, educate his children, and embrace Christianity. Thus, frontiersmen were instructed not to attack the Indians; the frontiersmen should pursue a defensive policy only. The militia might be employed solely to ward off attacks.

This policy infuriated frontiersmen. It seemed to encourage Indian raids. Southern Indians began attacking settlers in Tennessee and Kentucky. The Spaniards — neighbors across the Mississippi River and along the shores of the Gulf of Mexico — still refused to allow American shipping to pass freely through New Orleans. After St. Clair's defeat in the Northwest, the Spaniards adopted an aggressive Indian policy and prodded the Creeks and Cherokees into active warfare with the frontier settlers. War with either Great Britain or Spain would have exhausted the strength of the new republic and crippled its reviving commerce. The United States would have to depend, temporarily at least, on peaceful diplomacy to settle its border disputes.

The French Revolution

France was not a North American neighbor like Great Britain and Spain. She was an ally—a fact that proved to be quite as embarrassing. Only five days after Washington's first inauguration, the Estates-General, the national assembly of France, met at Versailles and inaugurated the first stage of the French Revolution. Between 1789 and 1791, it accomplished sweeping reforms and abolished many age-old and oppressive privileges of the King, the nobility, and the higher clergy.

By resistance to these changes, the royalists and aristocrats brought on war. The government fell into the hands of the more radical Jacobins, who abolished the monarchy, established a republic, and beheaded Louis XVI and Queen Marie Antoinette for alleged crimes against the people. Within a few days after Washington's second inauguration (March 4, 1793), the lines of a great struggle all over Europe were clearly drawn. The Jacobins had not only embarked upon a thoroughgoing reconstruction of French society; they had also announced a pan-European crusade to destroy monarchy and privilege everywhere. War between France, on the one side, and Britain, Spain, Prussia, and Austria, on the other side, followed.

Scarcely a month after his second inauguration, Washington had to face the question of relations with the new French Republic. Its Chargé d'Affaires to the United States, "Citizen" Edmond Charles Genêt, landed at Charleston, South Carolina, on April 18, 1793. Genêt was welcomed in a series of banquets as he proceeded northward to the capital, then at Philadelphia. The Federalists, frightened by what they perceived as the wild excesses of the French Revolution, and particularly its attack against organized religion, did not want to receive Genêt as Minister.

Yet France was an ally. She had furnished the men and money that had helped to win independence from Great Britain. By the Treaty of Alliance of 1778, the United States had promised to help France to defend her West Indian islands if they were attacked by a foreign foe. The United States had also agreed to permit Frenchmen to bring into American ports ships that they captured in war.

Was the United States still bound by its treaty with France? Hamilton argued that the alliance had ceased to exist when the government of Louis XVI had gone out of existence. Jefferson replied that the United States was allied with the French *nation,* and that the Treaty of Alliance of 1778 was still in force. Washington agreed with his Secretary of State. However, there was no basic disagreement among the three men in charting a course. They all agreed that national self-interest, not sentiment, should be their guide. Participation in the European war on either side would be disastrous for the infant republic. Therefore, they had to avoid involvement almost at all costs. Hence Washington, on April 22, 1793, issued a Proclamation of Neutrality which announced that the United States would observe a scrupulous neutrality.

Genêt, however, ignored the proclamation. In childish letters, he scolded

Washington and the cabinet and appealed over the President's head to "true republicans" in America to support their "sister republic" across the sea. Furthermore, Genêt continued to enlist seamen and to equip vessels in American ports to prey on British commerce in the West Indies. His conduct became so insulting that even Jefferson, who was very sympathetic to republican France, agreed to demand Genêt's recall.

The discredited Chargé did not, however, return to France. The radical Jacobins controlled the French government and were guillotining members of the opposition party, the Girondins. Genêt had the misfortune to belong to this latter party. So, for his personal safety, Genêt was permitted to remain in the United States. He married a daughter of Governor George Clinton of New York and lived to a ripe old age on an estate along the Hudson River.

Preserving Peace with Britain and Accord with Spain

Genêt's mission and the war between Great Britain and France sharply increased the bad feeling between Federalists and Republicans. The Federalists were horrified, if not altogether surprised, by the violence of the French revolutionists. Also, northern merchants and capitalists wanted to preserve their valuable trade with the British Isles. Republicans, on the other hand, greatly distrusted the aristocratic British government and extravagantly admired the ideals, at least, of the French Revolution. Before long, politics in America degenerated to the point where Federalists referred to Republicans as "filthy Jacobins" and Republicans replied with epithets like "aristocratic snobs."

In spite of the Proclamation of Neutrality, the young nation barely escaped war with Great Britain. The British began to seize American cargoes going to French ports and to take sailors off American vessels to serve in the Royal Navy. In addition, there were reports that the British were encouraging the Indians in the Northwest to go on the warpath. Some Republicans demanded war with Britain. The Republican House of Representatives passed a bill cutting off all trade with the British; it was defeated in the Senate only by the tie-breaking vote of Vice-President Adams.

Washington was determined to have peace. In May 1794, he sent Chief Justice John Jay to London to negotiate a treaty. Jay was not a skillful diplomat, and his task was made all the more difficult by Hamilton, who was in secret communication with the British government through an agent in Philadelphia. One of Jay's few advantages was the threat that the United States would join a league of armed neutrality to protect its trade. Hamilton assured the British government that this was an empty threat. As a result, Jay's deficiencies as a negotiator were magnified. After a year's labor, he returned with a treaty by which Britain agreed to give up its fur posts in American territory by June 1, 1796. One reason for this concession was military necessity. General "Mad Anthony" Wayne had severely defeated a large British-supported Indian force in the Battle of Fallen Timbers on August 20, 1794. Wayne had then, in the Treaty of Greenville, forced the Indians to cede most of the present state of Ohio.

Great Britain also promised to submit to arbitration the question of disputed boundaries, the damage done to American shipping, and the pre-Revolutionary debts due by Americans to British merchants. (The United States later paid some £600 thousand in settlement of the debts; Great Britain, more than £1.3

million for illegal seizures of American ships.) But Britain would not open her West Indian ports to American vessels of more than seventy tons or permit them to carry any British West Indian products to Europe. Nor would she abandon the practice of searching American vessels at sea for sailors whom she claimed as British subjects.

News of the treaty set off a storm of wrath in the United States. Republicans accused Jay of selling out his country for British gold. Hamilton was stoned in the streets of New York for speaking in favor of the treaty. Effigies of "Sir John" Jay were hung by the neck throughout the country. Even Washington did not escape abuse. He decided, however, that acceptance of the treaty, unsatisfactory though it might be, was the only way to preserve peace. He was probably correct. He sent the treaty to the Senate, where it was barely approved by the necessary two-thirds vote.

Jay's treaty produced an unexpected diplomatic dividend. The Spanish government feared, quite groundlessly, that Jay had gone to London to negotiate an alliance for Anglo-American cooperation to drive Spain out of Florida and Louisiana. Suddenly the atmosphere in Madrid turned warm with friendship for the United States. Thomas Pinckney, American Minister to Spain, therefore took up the question of the navigation of the Mississippi. He found the Spanish Chief Minister, Manuel de Godoy (known as the "Prince of Peace") very sympathetic.

The result was the Treaty of San Lorenzo el Real, signed on October 27, 1795. Spain granted every point for which the United States had been contending for years: free navigation of the Mississippi, acceptance of 31° northern latitude as the southern boundary of the United States, and the right of deposit. The latter permitted American merchants to transfer cargoes at New Orleans from river boats to ocean-going vessels without payment of duty.

Thus, at the close of 1795, the United States was still at peace and more secure than ever before in its brief history. To be sure, Europe's distress and rivalries had worked to America's advantage. Except for the unfortunate Jay, the Washington administration had negotiated shrewdly, and it had used military force only where it could be effective—in the Northwest.

The Greatest Founding Father

Washington provided a model for all future Presidents. He exercised all his executive powers judiciously and wisely. He did more than any other man to establish the presidential office as a strong, creative force in order to provide the American people with the necessary leadership to promote their prosperity and happiness. No doubt he could have been reelected indefinitely. But he concluded that no President should serve more than two terms, lest the office become perpetual. As the election of 1796 approached, he determined to end his long service to his country. He therefore issued a farewell address (written earlier with the aid of Madison and Hamilton), to his fellow countrymen on September 19, 1796. He urged Americans to remain devoted to the Union and to the republican form of government. He also warned against "permanent alliances" with foreign nations, meaning France, and against political parties, meaning the Republicans. Neither Washington nor Hamilton considered the Federalists a party.

Nevertheless, Madison and Jefferson, who had resigned from the cabinet at the end of 1793, continued to build up the Republican opposition to the Feder-alist policies. In the election of 1796, Jefferson was put forward as the Republi-can candidate for President. The Federalists supported John Adams, who won a very narrow margin of electoral votes, seventy-one to sixty-eight. Jefferson, the runner-up, was elected Vice-President.

3. JOHN ADAMS AND THE END OF FEDERALIST SUPREMACY

Adams' Troubles

John Adams was sixty years old when he was elected President. His task was difficult — to guide a young nation torn with party strife at home and regarded with no great respect abroad. Adams' career had been distinguished before, during, and after the Revolution. He had helped to unify the colonists during the disputes with England that led to the Revolution and had served in the Continental Congress from the outset in 1774. It was Adams who had pro-posed that Washington be named commander in chief of the Continental Army and that Jefferson be designated to draft the Declaration of Independence. A member of the peace commission of 1783, Adams had also been the first Min-ister to the courts of Holland and Great Britain. All but the most fanatical Republicans acknowledged his patriotism, honesty, and courage, although the Republicans suspected him of aristocratic tendencies.

But Adams was somewhat irritable and obstinate and frequently demon-strated a lack of tact. He also always assumed the correctness of his own judg-ments, disliked partisan political activity, and made little attempt to harmon-ize conflicting views in his cabinet, in Congress, or in his party. To make his situation more difficult, he made the initial mistake of retaining the chief cabi-net members who were in office at the end of Washington's administration. Partly because of the pitifully low salaries paid to governmental officials, these men ranged in ability from mediocre to incompetent. Furthermore, they were all devoted followers of Adams' personal enemy, Hamilton. They almost open-ly took their orders from the latter until Adams, in 1799, discovered their dis-loyalty and dismissed them. On one occasion, Secretary of State Timothy Pickering actually apologized to Hamilton for his failure to block one of Adams' policies.

The XYZ Affair and Quasi-War with France

American relations with France deteriorated during the early part of Adams' regime. The so-called Directory had come into power in Paris in 1795. It was angered by the Jay treaty and by the recall in 1796 of the American Minister, James Monroe, who, in Washington's judgment, was too friendly toward France. The Directory, in retaliation, refused to receive Charles Cotesworth Pinckney, sent by Washington to replace Monroe. The Directory also un-leashed privateers from the West Indies against American commerce. By June 1797, they had captured some 300 American ships.

Adams called Congress into special session and declared that the United States had to convince France and the world that Americans were "not a degraded people, humiliated under a colonial spirit of fear." But he still wanted peace. Soon afterward, Adams announced that, at the invitation of the French Foreign Minister, Prince Talleyrand, he was sending John Marshall and Elbridge Gerry to join Pinckney in further negotiations with the Directory.

The envoys arrived in Paris in October 1797, just after the French had routed the Austrians and Russians at Austerlitz. Talleyrand arrogantly refused to receive the Americans. Instead, he sent three secret agents, referred to as X, Y, and Z in the reports that the American commissioners sent home. X, Y, and Z informed the Americans that no business could be done until an apology was forthcoming for Adams' message to Congress, a loan of $10 million from the United States to the French Republic had been promised, and the sum of $250 thousand had been slipped into the hands of the directors themselves.

The American envoys angrily refused to consider such insulting demands. "No, no, not a sixpence," Pinckney replied. Marshall and Pinckney immediately returned to America, where they aroused the people to patriotic fervor by the story of their treatment. Talleyrand persuaded the Republican Gerry to remain longer at Paris by warning that his departure might cause war between the two countries.

Adams, in early 1798, sent his envoys' reports to Congress and asked for measures to compel respect for the United States as a "great, free, powerful, and independent nation." For once in his life, John Adams was thoroughly popular. His fellow citizens, Republicans and Federalists alike, applauded his language of defiance. They shouted the new song "Hail Columbia!" and adopted as a slogan the toast proposed at a banquet to the returning hero, John Marshall: "Millions for defense, but not one cent for tribute!" Preparations for war

Cartoon of the XYZ Affair. The hydra-headed monster, a representation of the French government, is being refused its demand for money by Marshall, Gerry, and Pinckney. (Culver Pictures, Inc.)

were begun, and Washington was called back as commander in chief. Congress created an independent Navy Department and pushed completion of frigates under construction and ordered new ones. By the end of 1798, a force of fourteen American frigates was at sea.

There was no declaration of war, but Congress renounced the Treaty of 1778 and authorized American ships to prey on French commerce. Between 1798 and 1800, an undeclared state of war with France existed—a "quasi-war," it came to be called—and Americans captured more than eighty French ships.

Actually, neither country wanted war. When Talleyrand saw that he could not threaten or bribe the Americans, he hastened to assure the United States Minister to Holland that a new commission would be received with all due respect. And Adams resisted the clamor of the Hamiltonian faction for war and sent envoys to France to reopen negotiations. Four days after the envoys sailed, Napoleon Bonaparte overthrew the corrupt Directory.

Napoleon, intent upon consolidating his power, first in France, and then throughout Europe, wanted no trouble with the United States. In September 1800, therefore, he signed an agreement renouncing the Treaty of 1778. In return, the United States assumed responsibility for all claims of damages done to American shipping by French cruisers since 1793. The bargain enabled the United States to enter the nineteenth century both at peace and free from an alliance that had long outlived its usefulness.

The Crisis of the Alien and Sedition Acts

The Federalists seized the advantage of the public excitement that resulted from the exposure of the XYZ Affair and the naval war with France to put through Congress, in the summer of 1798, a series of measures deliberately aimed at silencing their opponents at home. The measures were made possible by a fear among the Federalists that the Republicans had engaged in a criminal conspiracy to bring the country to the side of the French revolutionists. Although both Adams and Hamilton contributed heavily to the creation of this atmosphere, neither specifically supported the anti-Republican legislation.

One of the measures was a new Naturalization Act, which increased from five to fourteen years the period of residence necessary for a foreigner to become a citizen. It was adopted because most recent immigrants had become Republicans. Two alien acts followed. They gave the President the power, for two years, to expel from the country any alien whom he thought dangerous to national security, and, in time of war, to deport or arrest aliens from an enemy nation.

The most serious menace to Republicans—and to the liberty of all Americans—was the Sedition Act. It punished with heavy fines or imprisonment any persons found guilty of "combining and conspiring to oppose the execution of the laws, or publishing false, scandalous, or malicious writings against the President, Congress or the government of the United States." The Sedition Act was to expire on March 3, 1801—late enough to check Republican criticism of the administration until after the next presidential election, but not too late to prevent Federalist criticism should the Republicans win. The legislation was so blatantly political and inimical to free speech that it lost the Federalists considerable popular support.

The administration moved against the most abusive Republican editors and leaders with a vengeance, brought some twenty-five men to trial, and secured convictions in ten cases. The longest jail term meted out was four years. The only reason that Adams failed to deport any objectionable aliens was the fact that the leading candidates for expulsion all fled the country before he could expel them.

By modern standards, the Alien and Sedition Acts did not inaugurate a "reign of terror." But to Republicans, the legislation, and the prosecutions that followed, threatened, not only liberty, but also the very foundations of the American political system. Jefferson and Madison prepared resolutions for introduction in the legislatures of Kentucky and Virginia. These declared that the Constitution was a compact among the several states. When the central government exceeded its constitutional power, the states had the right and duty to "interpose their authority."

The Kentucky resolution, which Jefferson had drafted, also declared the Alien and Sedition Acts "void and of no effect." The legislature not only adopted it, but also called upon the other states to join Kentucky to repeal the hated laws. When the invitation was rejected, the Kentucky legislature adopted another resolution. It maintained that the rightful remedy for an unconstitutional act of Congress was "nullification by the state sovereignties."

Jefferson and Madison, the authors of these protests, did not intend or want to destroy the Union. Indeed, Jefferson scolded an ultra-Republican of Virginia when he proposed that his state secede. Jefferson and Madison were attempting to grapple with the problem of how appropriately to protect the people when their basic liberties were jeopardized by the federal government. Today, such infringements would be taken to the courts; however, in 1798 the doctrine of judicial review had not yet been expounded by the Supreme Court. The Kentucky and Virginia resolutions, however, together with the Tenth Amendment, laid the foundations of the state-rights position. The resolutions would be heard again in other great crises of the Union.

The Election of 1800

As the election of 1800 approached, the Federalist party was split into two bitter, warring factions led, respectively, by Adams and Hamilton. On the other hand, Jefferson and his lieutenants had been skillfully consolidating Republican strength. The campaign of 1800 set a new record, even for rough-and-tumble American politics, for accusations and name calling. Republicans accused the Federalists of running the country in the interests of rich aristocrats. The Federalists replied that, if Jefferson was elected, the country would be turned over to a mob of Jacobins, who would then begin a reign of terror. When the votes were counted, the Republicans had sizable majorities in both houses of Congress. However, the vote in the Electoral College was so close—sixty-five for Adams and seventy-three for Jefferson—that no Republican elector dared to withhold a vote from Aaron Burr, Jefferson's running mate. Thus Jefferson and Burr each received seventy-three votes.

Every Republican elector had of course intended, when he wrote the two names on his ballot, that Jefferson should be President and Burr Vice-President. Nevertheless, the two men tied for first place. According to the Constitution (Article II, Section1), the choice between them now had to be made by the House of Representatives, where each state delegation would cast one vote each.

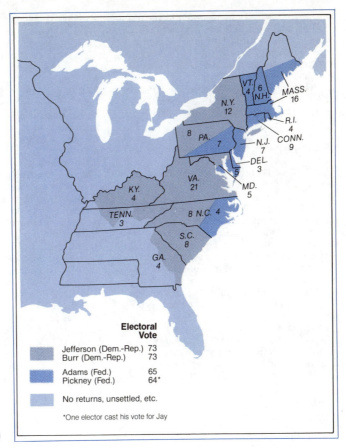

Electoral
Vote

Jefferson (Dem.-Rep.) 73
Burr (Dem.-Rep.)   73

Adams (Fed.)   65
Pickney (Fed.)   64*

No returns, unsettled, etc.

*One elector cast his vote for Jay

The Election of 1800

The Federalists controlled enough votes in the House to keep Jefferson out of the presidency even though they could not reelect Adams. They blocked Jefferson's election for thirty-five ballots. Finally, Hamilton broke the deadlock. He believed that the headstrong and temperamental Burr would be an even more dangerous President than Jefferson. Hamilton therefore persuaded some Federalists not to vote at all. This allowed Jefferson to be chosen by a vote of ten states to four. One outcome of this election was the adoption in 1804 of the Twelfth Amendment which requires electors to cast separate ballots for President and Vice-President. In a sense, the amendment recognized the existence of political parties and the operation of government through their interaction.

SUGGESTED READINGS

John C. Miller, *The Federalist Era* (1960), is a good survey of the period. Leonard D. White analyzes the administrations of Washington and Adams in *The Federalists* (1948), the first volume of his administrative history of the United States. Manning Dauer, *The Adams* *Federalists* (1953), covers the politics of that administration.

The development of political parties in the early national period has been one of the more fertile fields of historical investigation. Old but still valuable is Charles A. Beard, *The*

Economic Origins of Jeffersonian Democracy (1915), which describes an early party system based on class conflict. This thesis is contradicted by Joseph Charles, *The Origins of the American Party System* (1956). The controversy has been eschewed by Noble E. Cunningham, Jr., in his descriptive *The Jeffersonian Republicans* (1957). Another general account of the formation of parties is William N. Chambers, *Political Parties in a New Nation* (1963). Important for the first forty years of party history is Richard Hofstadter, *The Idea of a Party System* (1970).

The political conflicts of this period are discussed in Eugene P. Link, *The Democratic-Republican Societies* (1941). Irving Brant, *The Bill of Rights* (1965), is a comprehensive account of the framing and ratification of the first ten amendments. Leonard W. Levy, *Legacy of Suppression* (1960), challenges the belief that the authors of the First Amendment intended to guarantee freedom of speech. The Alien and Sedition Acts receive thorough treatment in J. M. Smith, *Freedom's Fetters* (1956), and John C. Miller, *Crisis in Freedom* (1956).

Early American foreign policy is skillfully analyzed in Felix Gilbert, *To the Farewell Address* (1961). Relations with France, and their effects on early American politics, are discussed in Alexander De Conde, *Entangling Alliance* (1958) and *The Quasi-War* (1966), and L. S. Kaplan, *Jefferson and France* (1967). Samuel F. Bemis' *Jay's Treaty* (1923) and *Pinckney's Treaty* (1926, 1960) remain the standard treatments, but Jerald Combs, *The Jay Treaty, Political Battleground of the Founding Fathers* (1970), adds valuable insights into early diplomatic history.

American political leaders of this period have been the subjects of an extraordinary number of biographies. Some are simply too massive for all but the most fascinated—or persevering—nonspecialists, for example, J. T. Flexner's multivolume biography of George Washington, Dumas Malone's vast study of Thomas Jefferson, and Irving Brandt's monumental biography of James Madison. Fortunately, a number of excellent shorter biographies of these men also have been written. John C. Miller, *Alexander Hamilton and the Growth of the New Nation* (1959), is exemplary, as is Broadus Mitchell, *Alexander Hamilton* (1957). Page Smith, *John Adams* (1962) is a fine biography. The best one-volume life of Jefferson is Merrill D. Peterson, *Thomas Jefferson and the New Nation: A Biography* (1970). A stimulating analysis of Jefferson's thought can be found in Daniel J. Boorstin, *The Lost World of Thomas Jefferson* (1948). Ralph Ketcham, *James Madison* (1970), is a serious and able study.

CHAPTER 9
A NATIONAL SOCIETY
TAKES SHAPE, 1790–1820

1. PEOPLE IN MOTION

Population and Immigration

Between 1790 and 1820, the population of the United
States increased from just under 4,000,000 to nearly
10,000,000. In 1800 fully one third of all Americans
were nine years old or younger, and two thirds were
under twenty-six. Also, this young and growing population was on the move. After 1790, the trickle of
American pioneers pushing westward beyond the
Appalachians became a mighty river.

The First Census of the United States, taken in
1790, showed a total population of 3,929,000, almost
evenly divided between the North and the South.
Virginia, with nearly 750,000 inhabitants, was easily
the most populous state. Although settlers had begun
to penetrate the bluegrass basins of present-day Kentucky and Tennessee just before the Revolution, census takers in 1790 could find only 109,000 persons in
the entire trans-Appalachian area. The American
people were, as they had been at the outbreak of the
Revolution, a mixture of almost all the peoples of
northern Europe, plus a large minority of West African descent. The first census takers estimated that
60.9 per cent of the white population were of English
origin, 8.3 per cent Scottish, 8.7 per cent German, 6
per cent Scotch-Irish, 3.7 per cent Irish, and 3.4 per
cent Dutch. The remainder was a scattering of nationalities. In addition, there were 757,000 Afro-
Americans, who constituted about 20 per cent of the
population. They were mainly slaves—657,000 of

them in the South and 40,000 in the North. Sixty thousand "free persons of color," as they were called, were almost equally divided between the northern and southern states. Americans still were mainly a rural people. In fact, the percentages of city and town dwellers had actually declined by one third during the Revolutionary era. In 1820, 7.5 per cent of the population lived in towns that had 2,500 or more inhabitants.

These, then, were the human resources out of which a new nation was to be built. The phenomenal increase in the population (almost 150 per cent between 1790 and 1820) came mainly from the natural growth of the native population, both free and slave. Immigration from Europe continued, but at a much slower pace than before—or afterward—on account of the wars of the French Revolution and Napoleon. We do not have reliable records on immigration before 1820, but experts have estimated that the annual flow from Europe could not have averaged much more than 7,000 persons between 1790 and 1815. Thereafter, the number jumped to about 30,000.

Immigrants between 1790 and 1820 came almost entirely from the Protestant countries of northern Europe that had peopled America during the colonial period. Thus white Americans in 1820 were still predominantly of northern European stock and mostly Protestant in religion, except for a few thousand Jews and about 40,000 Roman Catholics. The very slow pace of immigration between 1790 and 1815 greatly encouraged the further mixture of the various white national stocks. By the end of the War of 1812, that mixture, which had been developing for about a century, was virtually complete. There remained a substantial residue of cultural pluralism, but the passage of time and the pervasive blend of Revolutionary and evangelical ideology created a widespread sense of American cultural and national identity.

A steady stream of westward settlers traveling to the Alleghenies filled the Frederick Road west of Baltimore, Maryland, in the early nineteenth century. (Maryland Historical Society)

Blacks, meanwhile, were growing in numbers even faster than whites; they increased from 757,000 in 1790 to 1,772,000 in 1820. Among Afro-Americans, birth rates far exceeded death rates—a rarity among servile populations in the new world—but part of the increase was due to the continued importation of slaves from Africa, even after federal legislation banned the slave trade in 1807. In 1820, 1,538,000 Afro-Americans were slaves, who lived mainly in the South. There were by this date only 18,000 slaves (the residue of emancipation) who remained in the Northeast. The number of free blacks had been growing steadily and stood at 100,000 in the North and 134,000 in the South.

Transportation and Travel

Transportation and travel within the new nation were very much the same in 1790 as they had been a generation before. That is to say, it was still difficult and expensive to move passengers or freight for more than a few miles. This inadequate transportation network was more than an inconvenience; it was a major stumbling block to economic development. The new nation was connected by a network of roads, most of them unpaved. Poor though they were, the roads were filled with conveyances of all kinds—relatively comfortable stagecoaches, rude wagons pulled by oxen or horses, and huge Conestoga wagons for heavy freight. Roads were also choked with families on foot and herds of animals (including hogs and turkeys!) being driven to market. Stagecoaches, which traveled regular routes, usually covered thirty miles a day. Other forms of conveyance would be much slower.

It was the end of one era in transportation and the beginning of another. The new era actually began in the early 1790s with the construction of a network of paved turnpikes (toll roads). By 1820, New York, for example, had a network of 4,000 miles of turnpikes, while Baltimore attempted to tap the trade of its hinterland with seven roads to the west. However, the best highway of this period was the National Road, begun at Cumberland, Maryland, by the federal gov-

Early print of Robert Fulton's Clermont, *the first steamboat that moved "without appearance of sail, oar, pole, or any manual labor . . . within the secrets of her own mechanism." (I. N. Phelps Stokes Collection, The New York Public Library)*

ernment in 1811, which extended across southern Ohio and Indiana and reached Vandalia, Illinois, in 1838.

Canal building followed turnpike construction just before the War of 1812. Most early canals were very short and were designed to carry boats around the shoals of rivers. Major canals were abuilding by 1820, including the Erie Canal, which would link New York and the Great Lakes. But the full impact of canals on the nation's economy and on the patterns of community life would not be felt until the late 1820s and 1830s.

Finally, Americans traveled when they could by boats on inland waterways and along the coast. The monumental development in the field of water transportation was the invention of a workable steamboat. James Rumsey and John Fitch had demonstrated the feasibility of using steam power to propel a boat in the 1780s, but major credit for the invention must go to Robert Fulton. His *Clermont*, a sidewheeler that made the 146-mile trip from New York to Albany in 1807, proved that steamboats were practical, and it ushered in a new era in transportation history. The impact of steam power was felt most dramatically on the western rivers. The number of steamboats plying western waterways increased from fourteen in 1817 to sixty-nine in 1821. The economic stimulus of reduced freight rates, particularly for upriver traffic, sharply increased western farm income and stimulated the expansion of western commercial agriculture.

The Westward Movement: General Considerations

The one really dramatic event of this period of otherwise slow domestic change was the movement westward beyond the mountain barrier. Within a brief span of three decades, this migration doubled the inhabited area of the United States, created an empire of small farmers in the old Northwest, extended the kingdom of slavery to the Mississippi River and beyond, and transformed American national politics and diplomacy.

Families had of course been moving toward the setting sun since the first settlements were planted along the coast. Until the growth of cities and industries in the mid-nineteenth century, most Americans had no other way of surviving than by digging their living from the soil. The growth of families over time and the resulting subdivision of eastern farms meant that unless one was willing to live in misery on a small plot of land, or as a tenant, there was nothing to do but move to the West or stop farming. And move Americans did. By the outbreak of the Revolution, the line of settlement had reached the great Appalachian barrier beyond the Piedmont plateau and the eastern valleys. Settlers had even probed through that barrier into Kentucky and Tennessee. The "push" of crowded or worn-out land in the East was accompanied by the "pull" of economic opportunity. The availability of cheap land, coupled with the demand of world markets for American agricultural commodities, particularly between 1793 and 1807, made the potential benefits of western settlement substantial. The subsistence phase of frontier agriculture soon gave way almost everywhere to a mixture of subsistence and commercial farming. In 1806, cotton was selling for 18¢ per pound. By planting four acres of new land to cotton, a South Carolina farmer could net the tidy sum of $200 per annum.

The westward tide, to speak very generally, divided after the late 1780s into two great rivers of humanity, both with numerous tributaries. One flowed into the Northwest, the other into the Southwest. Along both frontiers the settlers were primarily yeoman farmers in search of cheap land. Settlers in both areas faced problems of clearing a wilderness in order to plant farms and begin communities. The two great rivers actually overlapped somewhat. The southern half of Ohio, Indiana, and Illinois was settled mainly by Virginians and North Carolinians.

But there were some striking differences in the way in which the two areas were opened up and in the kinds of people who settled them. The federal government owned much of the land in the old Northwest. It not only made careful surveys in advance of settlement; it also cleared Indian titles and provided military protection against Indian attacks. The settlers of the Northwest Territory were predominantly of New England stock. As they moved into Ohio from New England outposts in upper New York and northern Pennsylvania, they carried along with their earthly belongings some cultural baggage which included a zeal for orderly community development, an interest in education, and a devotion to pietistic Protestantism, usually expressed in Congregational or Presbyterian church polity. At least this was the ideal. In the rough and tumble of frontier life, squatters' rights and speculators' greed often prevailed over the neat grids on the surveyor's map. And the urgent appeals to plant churches and schools among the new settlements bespoke a fear that civilized life was endangered on the raw frontier.

In the opening of the southwestern frontier, the federal government exercised much less supervision than in the Northwest. Virginia owned Kentucky, and North Carolina gave away most of its land in Tennessee to veterans of the Revolutionary War before ceding the rest of its western land claims to the federal government. The settlement of much of the old Southwest proceeded on a helter-skelter basis and mainly by individual families rather than by communities. The burden of protection against the Indians fell entirely upon the settlers until very late in the period under discussion. The settlers of this region were predominantly the Scotch-Irish. Before the Revolution, they and their forebears had pushed down the great valley from Pennsylvania and settled the backcountry of Virginia and the Carolinas. In the decades after 1800, this restless breed, which included legendary figures like Daniel Boone and Davy Crockett, was on the "cutting edge" of the southern frontier from Georgia and Tennessee to Texas. Like the northwestern settlers, they imbibed the individualistic ideology of the Revolution and of evangelical Protestantism. However, they were a breed apart in their patterns of settlement and agricultural practices, which included the use of chattel slaves.

The Westward Movement: The Process

The opening of trans-Appalachia began about 1775 with settlements in the Kentucky bluegrass area, the Nashville basin, and the Watauga area of what is now eastern Tennessee. In the very summer that the statesmen at Philadelphia were framing the Constitution, a traveler reported that 900 boats had gone down the Ohio River from Pittsburgh. They carried 18,000 settlers with their horses, sheep, and cattle to take up new lands. Kentucky and Tennessee combined had a population of 110,000 in 1790. Thirty years later their number had increased to 1,000,000, and both areas had established flourishing political and social institutions.

Settlement of the old Northwest began in earnest in 1788, when the Ohio Company of Associates, a recently formed New England land company, planted a settlement at the junction of the Ohio and Muskingum rivers in the present state of Ohio. They named it Marietta. Settlement moved with lightning speed, especially after "Mad Anthony" Wayne's victory over the Shawnees at the Battle of Fallen Timbers and the signing of the Treaty of Greenville in 1795. There were only 51,000 settlers in the entire Northwest in 1800. By 1820, Ohio alone had over 500,000. The new states of Indiana and Illinois were also rapidly filling up, and even the Michigan Territory had 9,000 inhabitants.

Meanwhile, following the defeat of the powerful Creek Indians during the War of 1812, settlers surged into the Mississippi Territory. By 1820, that territory consisted of two new states, Mississippi and Alabama, with a combined population of over 200,000.

By 1820 the frontier had crossed the Mississippi River into the area of the Louisiana Purchase. Louisiana, with its well-established French population, came into the Union in 1812 with 76,000 inhabitants. Settlements in the northern half of the state doubled that figure in the next decade. Migrants also crossed the Mississippi River further north, into present-day Arkansas and Missouri. Indeed, the Missouri Territory, settled by pioneers from the Northwest and Kentucky, tripled its population between 1810 and 1820.

Some Consequences of the Westward Movement, 1790–1820

Westward expansion had a profound impact on many facets of American life. Politically, its chief effect was to create a new section, with peculiar interests and needs and an increasingly powerful voice in Washington. Economically, it extended and perpetuated agriculture as the way of life of most Americans. Among other things, this expansion of commercial agriculture would fuel the financial and technological bases of future industrialization.

The westward movement also helped to fasten slavery on the South. In the 1790s, the seemingly insatiable demand of the British textile industry for raw cotton and the invention of a practical cotton gin by Eli Whitney and his associates (see pp. 308–309) made possible the extensive cultivation of short staple cotton, a crop which was ideally suited to plantation slavery. Cotton culture, plantations, and slavery spread first into the upcountry of Georgia and South Carolina and then northward and westward all the way to Texas. The small kingdom of slavery was thereby transformed into an empire, with consequences that altered the course of American history.

In addition, the unrelenting pressure of western migration was leading toward the mass expulsion of Indians from ancestral lands east of the Mississippi. Early in the nineteenth century, the federal government vacillated between two policies regarding the eastern Indians: assimilation into an Anglo-American society and agricultural economy, or removal to unwanted lands further west. Republican sentiment and evangelical zeal led some persons to look forward, in the words of one missionary society, to the day when "the savage shall be converted to the citizen; when the hunter shall be transformed into the mechanic, when the farm, the work-shop, the School-House, and the Church shall adorn every Indian village." Some of the eastern tribes forcibly resisted this kind of assimilation. However, after the War of 1812, they could no longer count on any European support for their resistance, and, one by one, they were subdued. Even those tribes which chose the path of acculturation, most notably the southern Cherokees, found that the federal government could not protect them against those states and individual whites who coveted their land. By the early 1820s, forced removal loomed on the horizon, seemingly an inevitable consequence of Anglo-American expansion.

2. LAYING THE FOUNDATIONS OF ECONOMIC INDEPENDENCE

The Revival of Foreign Trade

Foreign commerce remained the lifeblood of the American economy in the late eighteenth and early nineteenth centuries. American foreign trade had been disorganized during the Revolution and was dealt a heavy blow by its exclusion from the British West Indian market. It was further dampened by a worldwide depression from about 1783 to 1786. But old foundations were being restored and new ones were being built even during the dark days when ships were rotting at their wharves. The tobacco trade had revived by 1783, and cotton became a major export crop soon thereafter. American merchants developed new markets which stretched from the Dutch and French West Indies (and, through smuggling, the British West Indies as well) to the Baltic states and China. In 1789, more than one third of the vessels that entered the Chinese port of Canton flew the American flag. The value of foreign trade in 1790 far exceeded that of any year before the Revolution.

This increasing foreign trade became a commercial boom once the Wars of the French Revolution broke out in 1793. Then the United States became a great source of food and raw materials for both Great Britain and France. Eighty per cent of all American exports were farm products, and lumber, naval stores, and fish accounted for most of the rest. American exports jumped from $21 million in value in 1792 to a peak of $108 million in 1807. Jefferson's Embargo and the War of 1812 caused severe cutbacks and demonstrated the tenuous nature of economic expansion based on foreign trade and the vicissitudes of international relations. But the return of peace brought an immediate revival of American exports, which, by 1818, had grown again to $93 million.

Along with growth in foreign trade went a spectacular increase in the shipbuilding industry and the size of the American merchant marine. European nations, at war with each other, relied on American ships. Consequently, the tonnage of the American merchant fleet grew to a peak of 1,425,000 in 1818. It was, next to the British merchant marine, the largest in the world.

Building the Infrastructure for Economic Development

Commerce and shipping both contributed to a rising national income. But still the new nation lacked the institutional structure of a modern economy. One of the missing ingredients was a domestic system of finance capable of organizing capital both for development and for short-term business operations. Americans had relied mainly on British merchant brokers for credit before the Revolution. The severing of the British connection forced Americans to strike out on their own. In 1781, Robert Morris, head of the Treasury in the Confederation government, founded the first bank in the United States, the Bank of North America, in Philadelphia. Banks were opened in Boston and New York in 1784. As we have seen, the federally chartered Bank of the United States began its operations in 1791. By 1811, there were eighty-six state-chartered banks in operation with note issues totaling $45 million. In addition, a federal mint, established in Philadelphia in 1794, turned out silver coins based on the decimal system adopted by Congress in 1797.

The emergence of an indigenous financial system based on banks, insurance companies, and securities exchanges, was one sign of a maturing economy. There were others. Even by the time of the Revolution, commercial market transactions had become the principal mechanism for mobilizing economic activity, particularly in the North. Furthermore, a thicket of law and custom had sprung up which provided governmental sanctions for business contracts and individual property rights. Government's involvement in economic affairs extended beyond giving an imprimatur to rational, dependable economic behavior. It also included direct or indirect subsidies to large-scale business undertakings whose establishment were deemed to be in the public interest. For example, a tariff bill passed in 1816 was designed to protect the nation's "infant industries" from foreign competition. State charters facilitated the rise of business corporations, and outright investment in canals and even manufacturing concerns provided needed capital for economic development.

By 1820, the economic system of the United States had become heavily commercialized and was becoming increasingly specialized. It was only beginning the transformation to industrialization which would mark its maturity, but the groundwork for that kind of growth was being laid. In that process, the "invisible hand" of the marketplace was steadied and strengthened by governmental policies which looked backward to mercantilism and forward to the modern mixed economy of the late twentieth century.

The Beginnings of American Manufacturing

By 1820, Americans were becoming less dependent on foreign manufactured goods than they had been during colonial times. The commercialization of the economy, under way since the eighteenth century, encouraged domestic production of all manner of goods. In 1816, the Secretary of the Treasury could report to Congress that the United States was entirely self-sufficient in the manufacture of wood products and furniture, hats, firearms and cannon, window glass, paper, and printing types. He could also report a substantial beginning toward self-sufficiency in coarse textiles, iron products, agricultural implements, spirits and ale, and pewter, tin, and copper products.

However, most manufactured goods were, as the name itself suggests, *hand* made. Manufacturing was still largely the province of the artisan and craftsman, and the home was still the basic unit of production. The output of these household industries, though small by modern standards, was nevertheless impressive. Household manufacturing had social advantages, which would only become apparent after the work place and the living place had been separated during the industrial revolution. Ties of family and community could be sustained, and the artisan-manufacturer, along with his neighbor, the yeoman farmer, could nurture a tradition of economic independence which would put its mark on the political life of the young nation. However, as one scholar has shown, the physically dispersed and economically independent artisan class was beginning to disappear even before the widespread introduction of factory production. Commercialization of the economy and transference of much of the manufacturing out of the countryside had already begun to produce an urbanized wage-earning class of workers by the 1820s.

The modern factory, with its churchlike bell tower and noisy machinery, did not begin to dominate the American landscape until the 1860s and 1870s. Before then, only in a handful of industries was there anything which resembled the modern factory system of production. Machinery was introduced early into the manufacture of wood products, including large-scale production of wooden clocks. Beginning around the turn of the century, the federal armory at Springfield, Massachusetts, pioneered many of the machine- and metal-working techniques, such as the use of interchangable parts, which would characterize modern factory production, as well as some of the management techniques of modern industry, such as cost accounting. Even though these techniques would later become commonplace, in the early years of the nineteenth century they were not cost effective and could be employed only because the armory worked under governmental contract and followed governmental specifications, regardless of cost.

A survey of manufacturing in 1832 revealed that large-scale factory production was then largely confined to the textile industry. This industry, more than any other, introduced the industrial revolution to America. Samuel Slater, an Englishman who had worked with the inventor of the spinning jenny, emigrated with plans of the British machinery indelibly etched in his mind. Slater built the first successful spinning mill in America in 1790. All of the earliest mills, including Slater's Rhode Island operation, engaged only in spinning. The yarn that they produced was *woven* by hand, either through the "putting out" system in which work was done in homes, or under the direct supervision of mill managers. In 1814, Francis Cabot Lowell, a Bostonian who had smuggled plans for the power loom out of England, established a mill at Waltham, Massachusetts, which combined mechanical spinning and weaving under one roof. Thus the modern integrated factory was first introduced to America. Lowell's firm, the Boston Manufacturing Company, was able to produce textile goods on a much greater scale than any other American manufacturer, and at a lower cost. His firm was thus able to withstand renewed British competition after the War of 1812. (Jefferson's Embargo Act of 1807 and the War of 1812 had temporarily given American manufacturers a protected market.) Lowell and his associates later moved their operation to a site on the more powerful Merrimack River, where they created one of the nation's first true factory communities. It included water-powered textile mills, shops to build and repair machinery, and dormitories to house the work force of young women recruited from rural New England. That town they called Lowell, a name which, in later years, would become synonymous with the social organization of work under the factory system.

3. THE EGALITARIAN MOMENT

The Democratization of American Society

Social classes remained in the new nation. Indeed, the economic developments already described caused a marked increase in the wealth and number of the upper classes. However, in almost every aspect of life there seemed to be a leveling, democratizing process at work. In truth, the nation was poised at an egalitarian moment, when the earlier dreams of sturdy independence seemed to mesh with the dynamic possibilities of an expanding nation. There was relatively little class consciousness or sense of class conflict. Most factory workers, for example, did not yet think of themselves as a laboring class, but identified themselves, along with their employers, as members of a particular craft or trade.

Was there a contradiction between the perception and the economic reality? For those who were white and male, the doctrine of egalitarianism had more than a little basis in fact in the early years of the century. The nation's rising prosperity *was* creating a kind of "leveling up," in which even the poorer classes saw real improvement in their standard of living. While *absolute* conditions improved for most persons, the *relative* gap between rich and poor, although growing, had not yet reached the mammoth proportions which it would attain after 1840. Furthermore, the old patterns of hierarchical and deferential relationships, which had earlier governed social intercourse, were giving way to relationships based on economic considerations and individual preferences. The institutions of family, church, and community, which had once bound people together in clearly delineated relationships, were now being transformed into voluntary associations. These traditional, localized institutions were now receding in importance in relation to new and impersonal relationships based on class, status, and personal choice. For some persons, these changes were causes for celebration. For others, they were signs of a dangerous rending of the social fabric and clear evidence of the need for social control.

One visible sign of the change in social relationships was the way that people dressed. In 1790, the upper classes continued to dress and act as if they were members of an aristocracy, albeit a republican aristocracy. For dress occasions, men wore scarlet coats, white knee breeches, silk stockings, and pumps with silver buckles; for more somber occasions, black coats and breeches. Wigs for men had given way to long hair tied in a queue in the back. Women wore silk hoop dresses, heavy cosmetics, and hair piled high on headdresses. Along with aristocratic dress went equally aristocratic manners and speech. One would have seen a perfect illustration of upper-class life at any of the weekly receptions that the Washingtons held at their home in Philadelphia.

The eighteenth-century style of dress vanished forever in the late 1790s. The Parisian upper class, trying, literally, to keep their heads, adopted simple dress. Men wore trousers and plain jackets, and cut their queues. Women cut their hair very short and put on simple dresses with straight lines. Americans followed Paris fashion even more then than now.

Dress has always been the most conspicuous status symbol in civilized society. The changes in dress, as well as in speech and manners, that occurred between 1790 and 1820 were, therefore, additional evidence of a general social upheaval. By the 1820s, the upper classes no longer tried to talk and act like a class superior and apart. And in the new republican simplicity can be seen a parallel to the leveling influences at work in politics.

Making Politics More Democratic, 1790–1820

The most important political event of the period between 1790 and 1820 was not the adoption of the Hamiltonian program or the victory of Thomas Jefferson. It was the broadening of political processes and institutions to permit participation by virtually all white males. When the period began, a conservative reaction against the so-called democratic excesses of the mid-1780s was in full swing. When it ended, most vestiges of aristocratic control over politics had been swept away, and the same spirit of egalitarianism and individualism, which was enlivening the economic and social life of the nation, had permeated politics.

Frederick Jackson Turner, in a very influential essay, "The Significance of the Frontier in American History," published in 1893, suggested one reason for this great change. He maintained that the main force working for political (as well as social) democracy was the frontier. Frontier-bred men, in their struggle to tame the wilderness, became self-reliant, resourceful, and courageous. Moreover, on the frontier one man was as good as another, politically and socially. The test of a man's worth, Turner said, was not his pedigree, but whether he could swing an ax, tame a horse, and bring down a squirrel with his long-barreled rifle.

Turner's frontier theory of American democracy dominated historical interpretation for nearly half a century and still has much to commend it. Certainly the availability of land for settlement in the trans-Appalachian West was a critically important factor in creating a democratic culture. Recent scholars, while they recognize that the frontier experience was an important factor, have given us broader understanding by pointing to other forces behind the progress of American democracy. First, the demographic, economic, and social transformations previously described underlay the democratization of politics. The *perception* that equality of economic opportunity was both a right and a fact in America (even if it was not always literally the case) inevitably altered the practice of politics. Second, nineteenth-century democracy was shaped by the historic political experience of the American people from earliest colonial times, and before that, the experience of the English people. Certainly definitions of "democracy" and even "the people" changed over time, but Americans by 1776 had political institutions, traditions, and practices which were already basically democratic. Third, Americans were still members of a larger European civilization, and they were very much influenced by European events. During the decades under discussion, a great democratic revolution was destroying feudalism and building the foundations of political democracy in western Europe. Americans were profoundly affected by this movement. Fourth, the changes in political institutions and practices that the leaders of the democratic movement in the United States worked for after 1790 were achievable, in part, because they were neither revolutionary nor vast. They were changes in details, not of basic structure. These can be summarized briefly as follows, noting that while most were achieved between 1790 and 1820, some were not won in certain states until the 1850s:

1. The three states that had retained some form of church establishment in 1783 disestablished the favored church—Virginia in 1786, Connecticut in 1818, and Massachusetts in 1833—thus recognizing the denominational and pluralistic shape of American religious life.

2. All states with religious tests and qualifications for voting and officeholding abolished them—for example, Massachusetts in 1821, North Carolina in 1835.

3. All states instituted universal suffrage for white male adults. The movement began in the 1790s and went forward steadily and rapidly. Kentucky,

admitted to the Union in 1791, was the first state to adopt white manhood suffrage. It should be added that the same wave of constitutional revision which led to universal suffrage for white males resulted in the disfranchisement of free blacks in most of the states, north and south, where they had previously been allowed to vote. North Carolina restricted the suffrage to whites in 1835, and Pennsylvania did so in 1838.

4. All states abolished property qualifications for officeholders, adopted the written ballot (except Virginia and Illinois), and took pains to have numerous polling places so that voting would be easy.

5. Most of the original seaboard states revised their constitutions to give western counties fairer representation in state legislatures.

6. Perhaps even more decisive than these institutional changes were changes in the basic popular assumptions about how democracy ought to operate and politicians should behave. Deferential political behavior gave way to aggressive, egalitarian democracy. It was assumed that every man (or at least every white man) should vote, that officeholders were emphatically servants of the people, and that offices were spoils that should be enjoyed by all. These assumptions were gaining wider acceptance all the time between 1790 and 1820, but they did not triumph until the 1820s and 1830s.

4. SHAPING THE CULTURE OF DEMOCRATIC AMERICA

Educating the Citizenry of the New Republic

American leaders well understood that democracy could neither succeed nor even survive without mass education. "A people who mean to be their own governors," said James Madison, "must arm themselves with the power which knowledge gives." Hence Thomas Jefferson had drafted a bill in 1779 to provide complete educational opportunities, from elementary school through university, for Virginia children. "America must be as independent in *literature* as she is in politics," said Noah Webster of Hartford, Connecticut, "as famous for *arts* as for *arms*." Hence Webster compiled the first American spelling books and grammars in the 1780s, and the first American dictionary in 1806, in order to help mold the American language and character and to stimulate nationalism.

In practice, progress in elementary and secondary education was slow between 1790 and 1820. An increasing number of states declared in their constitutions that it was the duty of the state to educate all children. This great principle was still more a dream than a reality in 1820. Indeed, no state had yet created anything like a modern school system. On the other hand, most states had made the necessary beginning by setting aside a part of their revenues for educational purposes. Moreover, old field and dame schools for young children and academies to prepare boys for college, both partially supported by public funds, grew rapidly in number between 1790 and 1820.

The more significant advances during this period were in higher education. In 1800, there were twenty-two colleges and universities in the United States. That number had increased to fifty-six by 1830. Moreover, one of the most important developments in the history of higher education in the United States—the founding of universities by the states—was well under way. North

Carolina took the lead by opening its state university in 1793. Then followed Georgia, South Carolina, the states of the old Northwest, and so on down through the nineteenth century. Jefferson did not get his public school system, but he did persuade the Virginia legislature to charter the University of Virginia in 1819. And he chose the faculty for what was probably the finest university in America in that day.

The period 1790–1820 is notable in education, finally, because it saw the laying of the first foundations for professional training in the United States. Andover Seminary in Massachusetts (1808) and Princeton Theological Seminary in New Jersey (1812) were the first of a growing number of theological schools. Medical and law schools spread with equal rapidity, not only in the East but in the South and West as well. Neither colleges and universities nor professional schools in the United States could yet compare with their European counterparts. However, American dependence upon Europe for college and professional training had decreased markedly by 1860. Even so, most American physicians, lawyers, and ministers still entered their professions through the apprentice system.

Religious Upheavals

American religious life and thought developed in two radically different directions during the decades between 1790 and 1820. Deism, which rejected orthodox Christianity and worshiped a God who revealed Himself only through nature and human reason, was greatly strengthened in the United States by the impact of both British and French rationalism. (A form of rationalism had permeated Anglican theology in the eighteenth century, and the radical French revolutionary party, the Jacobins, made a religious cult out of reason.) Thomas Paine's *Age of Reason*, published in 1796, summed up the beliefs of both deists and rationalists. These thinkers included many of the most influential intellectual and political leaders of the era, most notably Thomas Jefferson. The optimistic enthusiasm of the Revolution itself blended with the faith of the Founding Fathers in the abilities and perfectibility of humankind. This faith would have a lasting effect on the "civil religion" of the United States, even though organized deism was short-lived and had spent itself by the early 1800s.

The spirit of rationalism and free will (the latter identified with the theological position known as Arminianism) found new institutional form and life in Universalism, which preached a doctrine of universal salvation, and Unitarianism, which emphasized the humanity of Christ and the basic goodness of people. Both groups emerged out of New England Congregationalism around 1800. Despite (or perhaps because of) their support among the well-educated urban upper classes, neither became broadly based mass movements, but they had a strong impact on the intellectual life of the new nation.

At the very time when it seemed that deism and rationalism might capture the hearts and minds of Americans — or at least of the more urbane citizenry — other forces were at work to revitalize and strengthen evangelical Protestantism. A religious ferment, called the second Great Awakening, swept across the land in the 1790s and early 1800s and continued far beyond the period under discussion. Like the Great Awakening of the mid-eighteenth century, this new wave of revivalism began within the mainline churches; however, after

Lithograph of a nineteenth-century revival meeting after a painting by A. Rider. These camp meetings with hundreds "prostrate upon the earth before the Lord" were prevalent on the frontier. (Library of Congress)

1800 it would break the bonds of orthodox theology, traditional church order, and even acceptable social behavior.

The second Great Awakening began almost simultaneously in New England (particularly Connecticut) and in Kentucky. Between 1797 and 1801, New England towns experienced revivals of religion which revitalized churches and gave rise to organized missionary and benevolent activites. The revival in New England was a rather sober affair and lacked the emotional intensity which had accompanied the eighteenth-century Great Awakening. Such was not the case on the Kentucky frontier. The first of many frontier camp meetings was held in August 1801 at Cane Ridge in Bourbon County, Kentucky. A crowd of more than 10,000 persons sang, prayed, and were exhorted for six days and nights, and enthusiasm reached a fever pitch. Teams of ministers exhorted the multitude to repent and be saved. Many heeded the call, and, in the ecstasy of the moment, some of the participants shouted, danced, barked, and jerked uncontrollably. The outpouring of enthusiasm swept from Cane Ridge across the frontier and back into the settled areas of the East. Tens of thousands of persons became caught up in the excitement. This movement not only disrupted staid religious observances and practices; it even broke down sexual and racial barriers, since men and women and blacks and whites joined in the ecstatic fervor of the camp meetings.

The minister who organized the Cane Ridge meeting was a Presbyterian, but the ensuing enthusiasm either blurred denominational lines or caused the more socially conservative Presbyterians and Congregationalists to recoil in horror. However, the Baptists and Methodists—heretofore small and fairly insignificant groups—embraced the new enthusiasm. Both groups stressed the individual's ability to *choose* salvation and to play an active role in a personal experience of conversion. That is to say, they had moved theologically far beyond the strict Calvinism of old-line Presbyterians and Congregationalists. Furthermore, both Baptists and Methodists had organizational structures which enabled them to move quickly and aggressively to recruit into their local churches the mass of men and women who came under the influence of the second Great Awakening. Consequently, their number grew dramatically. The membership of the Methodist Church, for example, grew from 58,000 in 1790 to 258,000 in 1820, more than double the number of Presbyterians.

The second Great Awakening had aftershocks which rippled through the nineteenth century and fundamentally altered the social history of the United States. It is impossible to elaborate here all the changes that it wrought, but the most important of them can be mentioned. First, at the time of the Revolution, the fraction of the total population which was affiliated with some religious body had dropped to 7 or 8 per cent. These figures are deceptive, however, since they signify church membership only; actually a larger proportion of Americans were associated with churches in some way. By 1820, under the influence of revivalism, church *membership* had risen to 20 or 30 per cent; by 1860 it would rise to around 50 per cent. The Awakening was thus a tremendous *mobilizing* process, in which hundreds of thousands of individuals were brought into formal relationship with organized religion. Second, because it did mobilize such a great number of people, and influenced an even greater number, the Awakening served a nationalizing function and gave Americans of many communities and varied ethnic backgrounds a common set of values and a common idiom—one quite consistent with the individualistic and democratic spirit of the age. Third, the Awakening brought previously small religious bodies to positions of national prominence (the Methodists and Baptists) and created whole new denominations (most significantly, the Disciples of Christ). It also helped to establish denominationalism (the coexistence of somewhat competitive religious bodies within the over-all framework of Protestantism) as the dominant form of religious life in America. Fourth, the organizational success of the evangelical groups, particularly the Methodists, helped to establish the voluntary association as a basic mode of social organization in America. There had been voluntary associations in America before, such as scientific, agricultural, or professional societies, and Americans were familiar by 1800 or 1810 with specifically organized groups in England. However, the association of true believers, called out of the community at large, became a prototype of purposeful groups of like-minded individuals. Methodism, with its local "classes," disciplined itinerant clergy, subsidized press, and closely coordinated organizational structure, was particularly influential.

All kinds of voluntary associations sprang up at the beginning of the nineteenth century, many of them generated directly by the second Great Awakening, and almost all of them influenced by its methods of mobilizing people for action. Among such bodies were the first missionary societies, the American Bible Society, the American Colonization Society, the American Temperance

Society, Sabbatarian societies, and even a society for the assistance of "Poor, Infirm, Aged Widows, and Single Women, of Good Character, Who Have Seen Better Days." In later years, the voluntary association would become so common as to seem to be the method by which society naturally organized itself. However, it was in fact a creation of the early nineteenth century, and particularly of the second Great Awakening.

Although organized religion in the new nation was overwhelmingly Protestant, this era witnessed the formal organization of the Roman Catholic Church in the United States. There had been a few Roman Catholic congregations since the settlement of Maryland, but they had struggled for a century and a half without bishops or seminaries. They had done well to survive the hostility and outright persecution that had continued, even though Roman Catholics had repeatedly demonstrated their patriotism. One Roman Catholic, Charles Carroll, was a signer of the Declaration of Independence, and two others sat in the Constitutional Convention.

The Roman Catholic Church had its real institutional beginning in the United States when Pius VI created the Diocese of Baltimore, with John Carroll as first bishop in 1789–1790. Baltimore was made an archdiocese in 1808, and the new dioceses of Boston, New York, Philadelphia, and Bardstown, Kentucky, were established. Meanwhile, educational foundations were laid with the establishment of Georgetown College (now University) in 1789 and St. Mary's Seminary in Baltimore in 1791.

The Beginnings of an American Literature

There was also a striving for independence in literature and the arts during this period of transition from colonial dependence to national independence. Americans were keenly aware of their backwardness in literature. Ralph Waldo Emerson, the New England essayist and poet, said, for example, that between 1790 and 1820 "there was not a book, a speech, a conversation or a thought in the State [Massachusetts]."

Emerson's remark was not entirely accurate, although the underlying truth – the lack of excellence in American intellectual production – can hardly be denied. Those two vehicles of popular literature – the magazine and the newspaper – flourished as never before. Seventy-five magazines were published between 1783 and 1801, several hundred between 1801 and 1830. Newspapers spread like wildfire, particularly after the formation of political parties. They were usually bitterly partisan, and life was often dangerous for editors who did not restrain their pens. But newspapers were beginning to come out in daily editions and were trying to provide something like national news coverage. They were growing more numerous and influential all the time. Some 200 were being published in 1801. By 1830 their number had grown to about 1,200.

Emerson's indictment underrated only slightly the state of more traditional literature. Most fiction, poetry, and essays were either highly imitative of English models or heavily sentimental. The only epic poems produced by an American during this time were Joel Barlow's *The Vision of Columbus* (1787) and *Columbiad* (1807). These works not only lacked great literary quality, but they also were handicapped by excessive nationalistic sentiments. However, the work of Philip Freneau and Phillis Wheatley, a slave in Boston who was later freed, gave promise of a distinguished American poetry. Fiction writers

Monticello with its tall, white columns and broad porch is representative of the classical style used in many homes and public buildings. The designing of this and other structures has made Thomas Jefferson a notable figure in the history of architecture. (Historical Pictures Service, Inc., Chicago)

left few permanent contributions, but, during this period from 1790 to 1820, at last it became possible for an author to earn his living by writing fiction. One of them, Washington Irving of New York, was a novelist and short story writer of major stature (see p. 305).

The Flowering of American Genius

While American creative writers were struggling to lay foundations in poetry and fiction, American artistic talent flowered in two fields—painting and architecture. Gilbert Stuart, who returned to Philadelphia in 1793 after studying with Benjamin West in London; John Trumbull of Connecticut, who also studied with West; and Charles Willson Peale of Maryland were painters of great power whose works are treasured.

The great movement in architecture was toward a simple classical design. Thomas Jefferson introduced it when he designed the Virginia state capitol in Richmond after the Roman temple, the Maison Carée, in Nîmes, France. Jefferson remained the most influential architect of his time. His home, Monticello, and the University of Virginia (both of which he designed) are among the noblest creations of brick, stone, and mortar in the world.

There were numerous other practitioners of the new (what we now call neoclassical) style in building. For example, Benjamin Latrobe and Stephen Hallet designed the national Capitol. It was fitting, moreover, that Americans should have gone back to classical styles, particularly for their public buildings, for they were deliberately trying to build a constitutional republic based in part upon the ancient Roman model.

SUGGESTED READINGS

Two stimulating general studies which bear on the social history of this era are Rowland Berthoff, *An Unsettled People: Social Order* and *Disorder in American History* (1971); and James A. Henretta, *The Evolution of American Society, 1700–1815* (1973). Another useful, although flawed, interpretation is David J. Rothman, *The Discovery of the Asylum: Social Order and Disorder in the New Republic* (1971).

Information on population is available in Richard A. Easterlin, *Population, Labor Force, and Long Swings in Economic Growth: The American Experience* (1968). Aspects of early immigration are discussed in Marcus L. Hansen, *The Atlantic Migration, 1607–1860* (1940); and Maldwyn A. Jones, *American Immigration* (1960).

The construction of the American transportation network and its manifold economic effects receive exemplary treatment in George R. Taylor, *The Transportation Revolution, 1815–1860* (1951). Among the most important specialized works on the topic are P. D. Jordan, *The National Road* (1948); L. C. Hunter, *Steamboats on the Western Rivers* (1949); and Carter Goodrich, *Canals and American Economic Development* (1961).

Douglass C. North, *The Economic Growth of the United States, 1790–1860* (1961), is an important interpretive work, while Stuart Bruchey, *Growth of the Modern American Economy* (1975), and W. Elliot Brownlee, *Dynamics of Ascent: A History of the American Economy* (1979), are good recent surveys. Victor S. Clark, *History of Manufactures in the United States, 1607–1860*, 3 vols. (1929), still provides a useful over-all picture of that subject. Nathan Rosenberg, *Technology and American Economic Growth* (1972), interprets the relationship between technological innovation and economic development. Merritt Roe Smith, *Harpers Ferry Armory and the New Technology* (1977), is a model case study of the small arms industry, and C. F. Ware, *Early New England Cotton Manufacture* (1931), describes the crucially important textile industry. The most comprehensive treatment of the early labor movement in a single volume is John R. Commons *et al.*, *History of Labour in the United States*, 4 vols. (1918–1935), Vol. 1. The period is adequately covered, however, in a more generally available work by Joseph G. Rayback, *A History of American Labor* (1966).

Informative chapters on the early westward migration can be found in Robert E. Riegel and R. G. Athearn, *America Moves West* (1964), and in Reginald Horsman, *The Frontier in the Formative Years, 1783–1815*

(1970). Subsequent interest by historians in the West has been colored inevitably by Frederick J. Turner's *The Frontier in American History* (1920), which contains the famous essay of 1893, "The Significance of the Frontier in American History." A reassessment of Turner's thesis by a disciple is Ray A. Billington, *America's Frontier Heritage* (1966). A standard work on Indians and Indian-white relations during this period is Wilcomb Washburn, *The Indian in America* (1975).

The early nineteenth-century reform movements are described in Alice Felt Tyler, *Freedom's Ferment: Phases of American Social History to 1860* (1944); which should be supplemented by Clifford S. Griffin, *Their Brothers' Keepers: Moral Stewardship in the United States, 1800–1865* (1960); and Charles I. Foster, *An Errand of Mercy: The Evangelical United Front, 1790–1837* (1960).

The pioneer work on the history of Protestant revivalism is William W. Sweet, *Revivalism in America* (1944); but see also William G. McLoughlin, *Revivals, Awakenings, and Reform: An Essay on Religion and Social Change in America, 1607–1977* (1978). Two good regional studies of revivalism are Whitney R. Cross, *The Burned Over District* (1950), and John Boles, *The Great Revival in the South* (1972). The relationship between enthusiastic religion and reform movements is discussed in all the works cited above and also in Timothy L. Smith, *Revivalism and Social Reform: American Protestantism on the Eve of the Civil War* (1957). For a more general view of American religion during this period, see the appropriate chapters in Sydney E. Ahlstrom, *A Religious History of the American People* (1972).

Many surveys of cultural and intellectual history contain good sections on nineteenth-century American literature. The standard work is Robert E. Spiller *et al.*, *Literary History of the United States* (1963). Vernon L. Parrington, *Main Currents in American Thought*, 3 vols. (1927–1930), is an older work still worth the student's attention. More recent surveys include Merle E. Curti, *The Growth of American Thought* (rev. ed., 1964); and Russel B. Nye, *The Cultural Life of the New Nation* (1960). See also Henry F. May, *The Enlightenment in America* (1976).

CHAPTER 10
JEFFERSONIAN DEMOCRACY AND THE WAR OF 1812

1. JEFFERSON IN POWER

Moderation in the Transition

In the summer of 1800, the capital of the United States was moved from Philadelphia to the banks of the Potomac. There the foundations of the City of Washington, already planned by the French engineer, Pierre Charles L'Enfant, were being laid in the District of Columbia. The presidential mansion remained unfinished. More than a mile to the east, masons were at work on the wings of the Capitol. Pennsylvania Avenue, which now connects the Capitol with the White House, was then a muddy road, "scarcely more than a footpath cut through the bushes and briars." "We need nothing here," quipped Gouverneur Morris, "but houses, men, women, and other little trifles of the kind to make our city perfect."

The new President, Thomas Jefferson, with his democratic manners and ill-fitting, snuff-stained clothes, intentionally presented a striking contrast to the pomp and ceremony of Washington and Adams. Jefferson insisted that he walk to his own inaugural. He abandoned the coach and six horses and rode horseback or walked about in the streets of the capital. Rather than address Congress in person—a procedure he compared to the King speaking to Parliament from the throne—he sent a message instead to be read by the clerk. Woodrow Wilson, in 1913, revived the practice that Washington began; he read his messages directly to the Congress.

Jefferson replaced the formal weekly presidential receptions, or levees, with informal gatherings, and the public thronged to shake his hand. Jefferson shocked the British Minister, Anthony Merry, when he received him in his dressing gown with slippers worn down at the heels. (Actually Jefferson was deliberately snubbing the British envoy.) Merry's secretary compared the President to "a tall, large-boned farmer." The comment would have pleased Jefferson. Although he was,

Thomas Jefferson. This portrait, painted at the height of Jefferson's influence, popularity, and power, reveals the sense of serenity and intellectual optimism that made him a beloved President. The portrait was painted at the President's mansion in Washington in 1805 by Rembrandt Peale, the son of Charles Willson Peale. (Courtesy of The New-York Historical Society, New York City)

himself, a cultivated and highly sophisticated Virginia planter, Jefferson be-lieved that independent, sturdy farmers constituted the backbone of the na-tion.

It was soon evident that those who had predicted a revolution if Jefferson were elected had seriously misjudged him. The new President, in his inaugu-ral, promised "equal and exact justice for all men, of whatever state or persua-sion, religious or political"; friendship with all nations, but no alliances; re-spect for the rights of the states, yet preservation of "the general government in its whole constitutional vigor"; freedom of speech, of the press, and of elec-tions; and economy and honesty in the management of the country's finances. Jefferson continued in one of the most moving passages in American political history:

We are all Republicans, we are all Federalists. If there be any among us who would wish to dissolve this Union or to change its republican form, let them stand undisturbed as monuments of the safety with which error of opinion may be tolerated where reason is left free to combat it. I know, indeed, that some honest men fear that a republican gov-ernment cannot be strong, that this government is not strong enough; but would the honest patriot, in the full tide of successful experiment, abandon a government which has so far kept us free and firm on the theoretic and visionary fear that this government, the world's best hope, may by possibility want energy to preserve itself? I trust not. I believe this, on the contrary, the strongest government on earth. . . . Sometimes it is said that man cannot be trusted with the government of himself. Can he, then, be trust-ed with the government of others? Or have we found angels in the forms of kings to govern him? Let history answer this question.

Jefferson's moderation surprised his enemies and dismayed many of his friends. He said not a word against the Bank of the United States, and he worked just as hard as Hamilton to maintain the financial integrity of the fed-eral government. But there were some important changes during Jefferson's first term. Congress repealed the Naturalization Act and the tax on whiskey, which had set off the rebellion among the farmers of western Pennsylvania in 1794. Jefferson pardoned persons imprisoned or fined under the Sedition Act and permitted the measure to expire. He reduced the army from 4,000 to 2,500 men, and largely sold or dismantled the respectable little navy. Albert Galla-tin, Secretary of the Treasury, applied the savings resulting from a reduced mil-itary establishment to the payment of the public debt, which he estimated would be entirely paid off by 1817. Although his calculation was off by sixteen years, the national debt was reduced by half during the Jefferson administra-tion. However, these changes and reforms hardly constituted a "revolution."

Jefferson's Attack on the Judiciary

At one point, on the other hand, Jefferson made a direct attack on his defeated opponents. The Federalists—repudiated in the November elections for the presidency and Congress—tried to keep control of the judiciary. Their court-packing plan—the Judiciary Act of 1801—created sixteen new federal judge-ships and a number of minor judicial offices. These would, of course, be filled with Federalist appointees and would thereby maintain a strong Federalist in-fluence in the government. Because President Adams was still busy signing their commissions late in the evening of his last day in office, March 3, 1801, the new appointees were called "midnight judges."

The defeated Federalists outraged Jefferson by their attempt to retain "a dead clutch on the patronage." He sent word to the officials whose commissions had not yet been delivered to consider that their appointments had not been made. Then, in 1802, Congress repealed the Judiciary Act of 1801. But Jefferson and his colleagues were still not content. In 1803, they began impeachment proceedings against a federal judge in New Hampshire, John Pickering, who was extremely incompetent because of alcoholism. It was well understood that this was only the opening shot in a war against the Federalist judiciary. Pickering was later convicted and removed from the bench.

John Marshall of Virginia, a cousin of Jefferson whom Adams had appointed Chief Justice of the United States in January 1801, now struck back for the Federalists in a monumental decision. One of Adams' midnight appointees was William Marbury, named justice of the peace for the District of Columbia. Marbury brought suit against Secretary of State James Madison to compel him to deliver his commission, which was already signed and sealed. The suit, Marbury v. Madison, came before the Supreme Court in February 1803. Marshall severely scolded Jefferson and Madison for withholding the commission, but he refused to order its delivery. He did so on the ground that the section of the Judiciary Act of 1789 under which Marbury had brought his suit was unconstitutional and therefore null and void. The section was unconstitutional because the power to issue writs of mandamus (used in this case to compel Madison to deliver the commission) was not within the original jurisdiction of the Supreme Court as defined in Article III, Section 2, Paragraph 3 of the Constitution. Thus, for the first time the Supreme Court declared a provision of an act of Congress unconstitutional. This practice, called judicial review, enabled the courts to limit strictly executive and legislative power in the federal system.

John Marshall's attitude incensed Jefferson and his lieutenants in the House of Representatives. They now carried the war to the enemy by impeaching a member of the Supreme Court itself—Samuel Chase of Maryland, who was, incidentally, a signer of the Declaration of Independence. Chase had gone out of his way to denounce Republicans as Jacobins and revolutionaries during his charges to juries in cases under the Sedition Act. His trial began in the Senate in December 1804 and ended in acquittal on March 1, 1805. It also ended Jefferson's war against the judiciary, because there was now no hope that Marshall could be removed from his high office.

2. THE LOUISIANA PURCHASE

Warnings from the West

The Republican Congress very much desired to practice economy and limit federal power. At the same time, a Republican President took a step that cost the government more money at a single stroke than the Federalists had spent in any two years. Moreover, it stretched the federal power much further than any of Alexander Hamilton's measures had done.

Rumors reached Washington in late 1801 and early 1802 that Napoleon Bonaparte had forced Spain to cede Louisiana to France. This area included New Orleans and the whole western valley of the Mississippi River. Napoleon's possession of the western bank and the mouth of the great river posed great danger to the United States. It would reestablish on American borders a

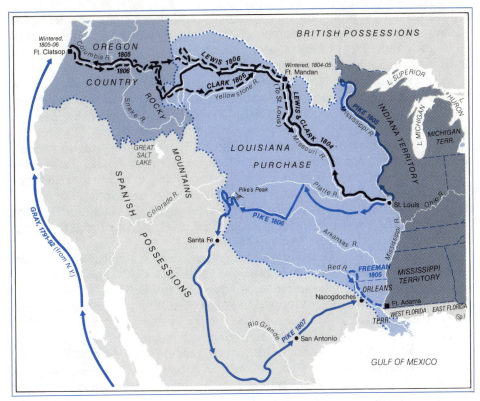

Exploring Louisiana

neighbor more troublesome than Britain and infinitely more powerful than Spain.

"The day that France takes possession of New Orleans . . .," Jefferson wrote to the American Minister in Paris, Robert R. Livingston, "from that moment, we must marry ourselves to the British fleet and nation." These were surprising words from France's champion in Washington's cabinet. His fears were confirmed when the news came, late in 1802, that the Spanish governor at New Orleans had closed the port to American shipping, thus breaking the Pinckney treaty of 1795.

It was a serious, almost desperate, situation. The country beyond the Appalachian Mountains was filling up rapidly. More than 200,000 settlers already lived in Kentucky, and Ohio was ready for statehood. The free navigation of the Mississippi River was crucial to these Westerners. Exports from the port of New Orleans in 1802 amounted to millions of dollars. It was the only outlet for the surplus produce of three eighths of the area of the nation. Westerners had supported the Republican party; now they threatened to march southward and seize New Orleans themselves.

Jefferson's Bargain

Congress authorized the President to call out 80,000 militiamen to support the Mississippi Valley farmers, but Jefferson moved confidently and quietly. He hoped to solve the problem by purchasing New Orleans from Napoleon. For this purpose, he sent James Monroe to Paris in March 1803 to aid Livingston in the negotiations. Upon their mission, Jefferson wrote, depended "the future destinies of this Republic." Jefferson authorized Monroe and Livingston to offer up to $10 million for New Orleans and West Florida. A few weeks later, Jefferson added the instruction that Monroe and Livingston should go to London to press for an alliance with Great Britain if the negotiations with Napoleon failed.

Before Monroe arrived at the French capital, however, the situation in Europe had changed, and Napoleon's interest in Louisiana had ended. France and Great Britain were about to renew war. Napoleon had planned to make a former French colony, Haiti, the basis of his colonial empire in America. But yellow fever and the stubborn resistance of the Haitians under the black leader, François Dominique Toussaint, called Toussaint L'Ouverture, destroyed the splendid army that Napoleon sent to conquer Haiti.

Napoleon knew that he could not defend Louisiana when war with Britain broke out anew. Haiti was lost forever. For these reasons, Napoleon suddenly decided to sell the whole province of Louisiana to the United States. The American envoys, who were prepared to offer $10 million for New Orleans and as much of the Gulf coast east of the city as they could obtain, were first stunned and then thrilled by this invitation to buy the entire province. The price set by the French Finance Minister, François, the Marquis de Barbé-Marbois, was somewhat less than $20 million. After some bargaining, the Marquis reduced his price to $14.5 million, and Livingston and Monroe accepted the terms. Of this sum, the United States would pay France $11.25 million in United States bonds. The Treasury of the United States would hold the remainder to satisfy the claims of its own citizens for damage to their trade by French cruisers. "We have lived long," Livingston said as he signed the treaty of cession on April 30, 1803, "but this is the noblest work of our whole lives . . . . From this day the United States take their place among the powers of the first rank."

Jefferson's Dilemma

Jefferson was in a dreadful quandary when the treaty reached Washington in mid-summer. He knew that his envoys had made an excellent bargain, but he could find no clause in the Constitution that authorized the President to buy foreign territory. First, he prepared an amendment to the Consitution so that the people might approve or disapprove the purchase. His friends in Congress persuaded him that this was unwise. Ratification of the amendment would take a long time; meanwhile, Napoleon might change his mind.

Without New Orleans, western settlers might seriously consider secession from the United States, and Jefferson might destroy the Union if he stuck rigidly to the letter of the Constitution. Consequently, Jefferson swallowed his constitutional scruples and appealed to the "good sense" of the people to approve an act that he had performed for their benefit. For the most part, the people supported him. The Federalist minority raised three objections to the treaty. It violated the Constitution—indeed, tore it to "tatters," they said; it was immoral and illegal, since Napoleon had promised the Spanish by treaty to restore the territory to them if he ever decided to get rid of it; and it was foolish to

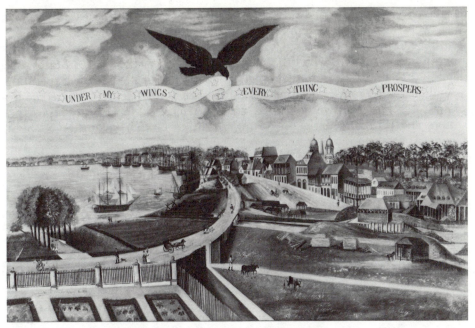

New Orleans in 1803, just after the Louisiana Purchase. The American eagle is pictured soaring above this busy port by the painter de Woiseri. (Chicago Historical Society)

pay so much money for a vast wasteland. But Federalist opposition was quite feckless. The Senate approved the treaty by a vote of twenty-four to seven on October 20, 1803. The House, eighty-nine to twenty-three, voted the $11.25 million in 6 per cent bonds.

The purchase of Louisiana added 828,000 square miles of territory to the United States at a cost of about three cents an acre. It relieved tension in the West by American acquisition of the whole Mississippi Valley. The great river became an undisturbed highway for the rapidly increasing products of the trans-Appalachian country, and New Orleans rose to be "the Queen City" of the South. More than a decade passed before Americans were rid of the troubles caused by British neighbors in the Northwest and the Spaniards in the Gulf area. But the danger was past that the pioneer communities of the West might secede from a nation that did not protect their interests.

3. EXPLORATION AND FURTHER EXPANSION

The Lewis and Clark Expedition

The Louisiana Territory excited widespread interest, for the great western expanse stretched 2,000 miles from the Mississippi River nearly to the Pacific coast. Jefferson, who was an ardent naturalist and geographer, was keenly interested in knowing more about the great empire that he had just purchased. He therefore persuaded Congress secretly to appropriate $2,500 "to send intelligent officers with ten or twelve men, to explore even to the western ocean." They were to study the Indian tribes, flora and fauna, and geology of the region. The expedition, after it passed the Rockies, would move into unknown and unoccupied territory beyond the western boundary of the United States. But this did not unduly trouble Jefferson; indeed, he hoped that the expedition would discover a route from the Missouri River to the Pacific. He selected his private secretary, Meriwether Lewis, an experienced explorer, to lead the expedition, and William Clark, the younger brother of the Revolutionary hero, George Rogers Clark, as his lieutenant.

Lewis and Clark, with a company of about forty men, started westward from the mouth of the Missouri River on May 14, 1804. They ascended the river to its source and crossed the Great Divide of the Rockies. Then they descended the Columbia River and reached the Pacific Ocean in the summer of 1805. A New England sea captain, Robert Gray, had sailed into the mouth of the Columbia in 1792, but Lewis and Clark laid the basis for the best American claim to the Oregon region.

About the same time, another explorer, Captain Zebulon M. Pike, traveled to the upper reaches of the Mississippi Valley. On a second expedition a year later, Pike moved through the lands of Indians and buffalo as far west as the Rockies, and thence into the Spanish territory of Mexico to the south. Maps and descriptions of these regions began to acquaint Americans with the vast territory west of the Missouri River.

Florida

Just what territory Jefferson had bought from Napoleon was far from clear. The treaty of cession stated that the Louisiana Territory had "the same extent that it now has in the hands of France, and that it had when Spain possessed it." When Livingston asked the French Foreign Minister, Talleyrand, what the eastern boundary was, Talleyrand could only say, "You have made a noble bargain for yourselves, and I suppose you will make the most of it." None of the negotiators seriously believed that the purchase included Florida, which still belonged to Spain. Nevertheless, Jefferson refused to admit that West Florida, at least, was not a part of Louisiana. He hoped that Spain at some future time might part with the territory, for Americans in what is now Mississippi and Alabama had access to the Gulf of Mexico only through rivers that drained West Florida.

The Barbary Pirates

The United States was at peace with the nations of Europe in the opening years of the nineteenth century. Commerce and wealth were increasing so rapidly that Gallatin had no difficulty in meeting payments for the Louisiana Purchase out of the ordinary receipts of the Treasury.

There was, however, one foreign problem that grew more serious as American commerce expanded. This was the behavior of the rulers of the Barbary states of Morocco, Algiers, Tunis, and Tripoli. For many years, they had seized ships that entered the Mediterranean Sea and held their crews for ransom. The European nations had paid tribute to these north African pirates and kidnapers as a cheap substitute for war, and the United States had done the same thing. In the decade 1790–1800, the American government gave the pirates "presents" amounting to some $2 million.

The crowning humiliation came in October 1800, when the ruler of Algiers compelled *U.S.S. George Washington*, which was bringing him tribute money, to haul down the American flag. Then he ordered the Americans to raise the Algerian ensign and to sail to Constantinople on an errand to the Sultan of Turkey. When the American commander objected, the Algerian replied, "You pay me tribute, by which you become my slaves."

Jefferson, as Minister to France, had ransomed American sailors from slavery on many occasions. No sooner had he been inaugurated President than the Pasha of Tripoli declared war on the United States in a move to force an increase in the blackmail payments. Jefferson was devoted to peace and economy, but the Pasha's declaration of war ended Jefferson's patience. He sent squadrons to punish the pirates. It was a costly business, for which Congress imposed a special 2.5 per cent tax on imports as a "Mediterranean Fund." The results hardly justified the sacrifice, for the war dragged on until 1805, and the peace with Tripoli, in January 1805, only reduced the rate of American payments to the Barbary rulers.

Then, during the War of 1812, Algerian pirates renewed their raids on American commerce. In 1815, Captain Stephen Decatur, a hero of the earlier war with Tripoli, returned with a fleet to the Mediterranean. He promptly seized two Algerian frigates and then forced the Algerian ruler to sign a treaty renouncing both raids and tribute. Decatur won similar guarantees from Tunis and Tripoli.

4. JEFFERSON TRIUMPHANT

The Decline of Federalism and the Beginning of a Second Term

The most striking political trend during Jefferson's first term was the steady and rapid erosion of Federalist power and influence. This tendency, of course, greatly strengthened the President's hand in dealing with Congress. Jefferson's popularity and that of the Republican party swelled even more in late 1803 and early 1804 as a result of the Louisiana Purchase.

But the more Jefferson's popularity increased, the more bitter grew the hatred and hostility of a group of extreme Federalists in New England. They were particularly incensed by the Louisiana Purchase because they were certain that the day would soon come when New England would be overshadowed and outvoted in Congress by new western states allied with the agricultural South. Not long after news of the purchase reached the United States, a small group, led by Senator Timothy Pickering of Massachusetts, began to plan to form an independent northern confederation of New England and New York. The conspirators were in close touch with the British Minister in Washington. They also turned to Alexander Hamilton, but he refused to cooperate. Then they approached Vice-President Aaron Burr. Jefferson had dropped Burr as his running mate for 1804 (Jefferson had chosen Governor George Clinton of New York instead), and Burr had decided to run for Governor of New York.

Burr agreed to bring New York into the northern confederation in return for Federalist help in electing him governor. Hamilton heard of the plot, denounced it to his friends, and helped to bring about Burr's defeat.

That ended a conspiracy that never could have succeeded in any event. The affair, however, had a tragic outcome. Hamilton's hostility to Burr in this scheme, which followed his success in keeping Burr out of the presidency in 1801, led the infuriated Burr to challenge him to a duel. The two men met at Weehawken Heights, New Jersey, on July 11, 1804, and Hamilton fell mortally wounded by Burr's first shot.

Meanwhile, Jefferson had been triumphantly reelected over his Federalist opponent, Charles Cotesworth Pinckney. The Federalists, in their vain opposition to the Louisiana Purchase and their earlier sponsorship of the Alien and Sedition Acts, had greatly declined as a truly national party. They had given the country its Constitution, launched the new national government, and led it for twelve years. But they slowly lost support as a national party because they distrusted the people and continued to believe in aristocracy and government by an elite. Meanwhile, the great majority of Americans were being caught up in the rising democratic movement.

The Federalists were a sectional, New England party, with scattered mercantile allies, before the presidential campaign of 1804 began. They were shattered in their own stronghold during the election. Jefferson had received only a single New England electoral vote (from Vermont) in 1800. But in 1804 he carried all the New England states except Connecticut. Indeed, he lost only one other state—Delaware—so sweeping was his victory. Of the 176 electoral votes cast, Jefferson received 162. It was a Republican landslide also in the elections for senators and representatives. The Ninth Congress, which would sit from 1805 to 1807, had 116 Republicans and twenty-five Federalists in the House of Representatives, and twenty-seven Republicans and seven Federalists in the Senate.

Few administrations in American history have been launched under more favorable auspices than Jefferson's second administration. Taking the oath of office again on March 4, 1805, Jefferson could congratulate his fellow countrymen that all was well for them both at home and abroad. He did not exaggerate. Foreign trade was booming. Except for the bickering with Spain over West Florida, relations with European nations were friendly. Americans, with supreme confidence in the future, were now pouring into the West. Nearly 10,000 settlers had gone to the new Mississippi Territory, established in 1798. Ohio, with a population of 55,000, was admitted to the Union as the seventeenth state in February 1803. In January 1805, a territorial assembly met in Indiana under the governorship of William Henry Harrison. And Congress created the new Territory of Michigan, with William Hull as governor. One spur to the westward movement was the Land Act of 1800, which had been supported by the Federalists in a vain effort to attract western votes. This measure provided for the sale of land in minimum-sized lots of 320 acres, at $2 an acre. The settlers might pay for their land in four annual installments. The minimum number of acres that could be purchased was reduced to 160 in 1804. This liberalized land policy was part of Jefferson's plan to make land available on easy terms as quickly as possible.

It was little wonder, then, in view of all the favorable signs, that the complaints of the few remaining die-hard Federalists were drowned in the general chorus of approval for Jefferson as he embarked upon his second term.

The Burr Conspiracy

Only one dark cloud appeared on the horizon in 1805. Soon after he retired from the vice-presidency, Aaron Burr set to work in one of the boldest and wildest intrigues in American history. Even now historians are not absolutely certain about Burr's intentions. Perhaps he hoped to seize New Orleans and establish an independent nation in the Southwest. Perhaps he planned to conquer northern Mexico and carve an empire out of Spanish territory. Perhaps, as he later claimed, he meant to plant an American colony on the Red River in western Louisiana. Or perhaps he had no precise intention and simply planned to take advantage of any opportunity that might arise.

At any rate, after Burr tried, unsuccessfully, to draw the British and Spanish Ministers into his scheme, he collected men, money, and arms on an island in the Ohio River owned by a romantic Irishman, Herman Blennerhassett. Burr persuaded several prominent Westerners, including one Tennessean, Andrew Jackson, to support him in what they supposed to be a campaign against the

Aaron Burr by John Vanderlyn, a painter who studied under Gilbert Stuart and copied some of his portraits. Vanderlyn, the first U.S. artist to study in Paris, had caught the attention of Burr, who became his patron. (Courtesy of The New-York Historical Society, New York City)

hated Spaniards. Burr also had the secret support of the American military commander in the West, General James Wilkinson, who had earlier been in the pay of the Spanish government.

Just as Burr was ready to move his expedition down the Ohio River, Wilkinson decided that it would be more profitable to betray his friend than to continue to cooperate with him. Wilkinson dispatched an urgent letter to Washington which warned Jefferson that a conspiracy was under way. Jefferson at once issued a proclamation ordering the arrest of "sundry persons" who were "conspiring and confederating together" to set on foot a military expedition against the dominions of Spain. Burr was seized while trying to escape into Spanish Florida and sent to Richmond for trial. The charge against him was treason, or levying war against the United States.

The eyes of the whole country were fixed on Richmond when the trial began in August 1807. Jefferson, eager to have Burr convicted, did everything in his power to aid the prosecution. But Jefferson's foes were in charge of the proceedings—Chief Justice Marshall, for example, was the presiding judge. Burr was acquitted of treason, but the verdict convinced few persons of his innocence. He lived on for nearly thirty years and finally died in poverty in New York in 1836 at the age of eighty. The most important outcome of the trial was the very strict definition of treason that John Marshall wrote into American law. Treason, the Chief Justice declared, consisted of *actual, overt* acts (not plans or conspiracies) to overthrow the government, and the acts had to be witnessed by at least two persons.

5. JEFFERSON TRIES TO PRESERVE PEACE

Troubles with Great Britain and France

Frigate *U.S.S. Chesapeake,* flagship of Commodore James Barron, weighed anchor at Norfolk, Virginia, on June 22, 1807, and sailed for the Mediterranean. Her guns were still unmounted, and her decks were littered with tackle and supplies. *H.M.S. Leopard* overtook her outside the capes and ordered her to stop to be searched for British deserters in her crew. Commodore Barron replied that he had no deserters and would not permit a search. *Leopard* thereupon poured a broadside of shot into *Chesapeake,* which killed three men and wounded eighteen more. Barron, unprepared to resist, struck his colors after firing a single gun. The British officers took four alleged deserters from *Chesapeake* and left her to limp back to Norfolk with her rigging torn, her hull riddled by solid shot, and her dead men lashed to the bow. The *Chesapeake* affair marked a turning point in American diplomatic history; thereafter, the United States Government would no longer permit its ships and seamen to be subject to the arbitrary actions of the British and French.

War between Great Britain and France had broken out on May 18, 1803, four years before the attack on *Chesapeake.* It was to engulf all of Europe and last until Napoleon's final defeat at Waterloo in 1815. In October 1805, Horace Horatio Nelson, Lord Nelson, destroyed the combined French and Spanish fleets off Cape Trafalgar. A few weeks later, Napoleon defeated the combined Austrian and Russian armies at Austerlitz. Great Britain was mistress of the seas; Napoleon was master of the continent.

In this deadlock, Britain and France each tried to strangle the other's commerce. The British issued Orders in Council that forbade neutral ships to trade with ports on the continent under Napoleon's control. Napoleon retaliated with the Berlin and Milan Decrees, which authorized seizure of ships that traded with the British Isles or permitted themselves to be searched by British cruisers.

The commerce of the United States seemed to be threatened with ruin. As it turned out, the prices of commodities and shipping rates rose so high that American merchants continued to make good profits in spite of losses through seizures. American exports increased in value from $45 million in 1803 to $108 million in 1807, while the tonnage of the American merchant marine grew from 949,000 to 1,269,000. So great was the demand for crews that sailors' wages trebled. Hundreds of foreign seamen, mostly British, took out American naturalization papers and went into service on American ships in order to enjoy the better pay, better food, and more humane treatment received on American vessels.

Napoleon had no more respect for American rights on the seas than the British did. The French seized American ships in continental ports and sold their cargoes for the benefit of Napoleon's treasury. But the French were unable to do as much damage as the British, simply because they lacked the cruisers to prey on American merchantmen.

Great Britain's survival in this death struggle depended upon the strength of her navy, and desertions were gravely sapping her naval strength. Lord Nelson estimated that 42,000 desertions occurred between 1793 and 1801. No doubt even more took place during the years of the Napoleonic Wars, 1803–1815. It mattered not at all to the British that seamen deserted from the Royal Navy because of brutal conditions. It mattered even less that deserters took out American naturalization papers. British law did not permit a subject of the King to transfer his allegiance to another country. Moreover, many of the naturalization papers were forgeries, which could be bought in any American port for about one dollar each.

The number of American citizens taken off American ships by British press gangs can only be estimated. Shortly before the United States went to war with Great Britain in 1812, President Madison sent to Congress a report listing more than 6,000 cases of American seamen who had been "impressed and held in bondage" by the British during the preceding three years alone.

The attack on *Chesapeake* and the impressment of four of her crew roused a storm of fury in the United States. Jefferson immediately issued a proclamation excluding British warships from American waters. He also sent orders to the American Minister in London, James Monroe, to demand an apology for the attack on *Chesapeake* and an end to impressment and the seizure of American ships.

The British knew that they were wrong and were prepared to admit it. But Jefferson demanded a complete end to impressment, and the British were in no mood to surrender unconditionally. A Tory Parliament, determined to let nothing stand in the way of crushing Napoleon, had recently been elected. Tory newspapers referred to America as "an insignificant and puny power," which could not be permitted to "mutilate Britain's proud sovereignty of the ocean." The reply of the British Foreign Secretary, George Canning, to Jefferson's demands arrived in Washington in December 1807.

Canning was eager to make amends for the attack on *Chesapeake.* Indeed, the admiral whose orders were responsible for that attack had already been dismissed from his command. But on the question of the right of search and impressment and controls over American shipping, the British ministry would not and could not yield an inch. On the contrary, a new Order in Council was issued making subject to seizure every neutral vessel that did not enter a British port and pay duties. Jefferson seemed faced with the alternative of submission or war.

The Embargo

Submission or war, however, were equally repugnant to Jefferson, for the tiny United States Navy was no match for the British fleet. Jefferson, therefore, determined to try a method of "peaceful coercion" to bring both Canning and Napoleon to terms. Both Great Britain and France depended on the United States, not only for food and raw materials, but also for shipping. If American trade was indispensable to the two great powers, Jefferson reasoned, then its interruption would force them to repeal their orders and decrees and respect American neutral rights.

Therefore, on December 17, 1807, Jefferson recommended to Congress an act prohibiting *any* American vessel from sailing for *any* foreign port. Congress immediately passed this, the Embargo Act. Support came from the South and West, while opposition came, naturally, from the shipping centers.

If strictly enforced, the embargo might have induced the British, who were more dependent upon American trade than were the French, to make large concessions. The chief defect of the embargo as a diplomatic instrument was that it could only work slowly, and then only if rigorously enforced. Meanwhile, it grew more unpopular at home every month after its adoption. Merchants complained that their trade was being ruined in order to punish Europe. Shipowners disobeyed the embargo. Town meetings in New England passed resolutions against it. There was even talk that New England might secede, as there had been five years before with the purchase of Louisiana. "I felt," Jefferson later wrote, "the foundation of the government shaken under my feet by

Cartoon on the Embargo Act. This wood engraving depicts a snapping turtle, Ograbme (embargo spelled backwards), trying to restrain a tobacco smuggler. (The Bettmann Archive)

the New England townships." Federalists told Canning's confidential agent in the United States that the embargo would send the Republicans down to defeat.

The South and West, which depended for their prosperity upon the export of food, tobacco, and cotton, were hurt nearly as much by the embargo as the mercantile areas. Yet Southerners and Westerners strongly supported the embargo because they were more nationalistic—perhaps even chauvinistic—than Easterners. They were historically anti-British and keenly resented impressment as an insult to American sovereignity. Westerners also had their own special grievances. They believed that the British in Canada were arming the Indians against them. The governors of the Indiana and Michigan territories reported on conferences between the British and Indians on the Canadian border in the autumn of 1807.

In the following summer, the Kentucky legislature adopted a resolution which pledged "our honor, our blood and our treasure" to protect the peace and dignity of the Union against "foreign invasion." It further resolved to "chastise and bring to reason our haughty and imperious foes." Frontiersmen in the Southwest were equally inflamed against the Spaniards in the Floridas for inciting the Indians to attack American settlements in the Mississippi Territory.

Politics also played its part in determining the fate of the embargo. The election of 1808 was just ahead, and Jefferson was determined that his Secretary of State, James Madison, should succeed him. He was able to secure Madison's nomination by the Republican caucus in Congress in spite of bitter opposition by members of his party from Virginia, Pennsylvania, New York, and New England, who supported James Monroe. It looked dark for the Republicans in the spring and summer of 1808, but the South and West stood by Madison in the presidential election. He defeated his Federalist opponent, Charles Cotesworth Pinckney, by 122 electoral votes to forty-seven. Yet Madison lost every New England state except Vermont. Moreover, the Federalists greatly increased their numbers in the House of Representatives. The Tenth Congress (1807–1809) had 118 Republicans and twenty-four Federalists in the House of Representatives, and twenty-eight Republicans and six Federalists in the Senate. The Eleventh Congress (1809–1811), elected in 1808, would have ninety-four Republicans and forty-eight Federalists in the House, and twenty-eight Republicans and six Federalists in the Senate.

It was obvious by now that the embargo was driving a wedge into Republican ranks and was greatly reviving the strength of Federalism. Hence the lame-duck Congress repealed the Embargo Act on March 1, 1809, three days before Jefferson left office. Congress substituted a Nonintercourse Act which permitted foreign trade with all nations *except* Great Britain and France. Furthermore, it authorized the President to reopen trade with either country if it should cease to violate American neutral rights.

6. THE COMING OF WAR

Madison's Weak Diplomacy

The new President was a profound philosopher and student of government, but he lacked the firm leadership necessary to control the factions in his cabinet and his party in Congress. Besides, he was so eager to preserve peace with

Great Britain and France that he permitted himself to be imposed upon by both nations. Madison's administration was only a few weeks old when a series of blunders made relations with Great Britain worse than ever before.

Canning instructed the new British Minister to Washington, David Erskine, to offer to withdraw the Orders in Council, but on the condition that the United States would still permit British cruisers to seize American ships that traded with countries obeying Napoleon's decrees. Erskine, a liberal Whig with an American wife, was eager to restore harmony between the two English-speaking countries. In a minor violation of his instructions, he signed a treaty which exempted American commerce from the penalties of the Orders in Council. Madison did not wait to see whether the London government approved. On the contrary, he issued a proclamation on April 19, 1809, which reopened trade with Great Britain on the tenth of the following June, as the Nonintercourse Act had authorized the President to do. American merchants thereupon dispatched to British ports some 600 ships filled with cotton, lumber, grain, and tobacco. They praised Madison as a statesman who had succeeded where Jefferson had failed. Then came the reckoning. The moment Canning heard what Erskine had done, he denounced the agreement and recalled the Minister. Madison was left with no choice but to issue a second proclamation restoring nonintercourse with Great Britain. This he did on August 9, 1809.

This unhappy episode was probably the fateful turning point in Anglo-American relations. British approval of the Erskine Agreement would have prevented war between the two countries and added a friendly power to the anti-French coalition. It still is not clear why Canning so hastily wrecked this opportunity for Anglo-American collaboration. In any event, this bungling diplomacy not only threw the United States into the arms of France, but also made an Anglo-American war almost inevitable.

The Nonintercourse Act expired in 1810, and Congress tried a new device — Macon's Bill No. 2 — which threw American commerce open to all the world. The act also authorized the President, in the event that either Great Britain or France should cease its depredations against American commerce before March 3, 1811, to revive nonintercourse with the other power. Napoleon lost no time in taking advantage of both the new law — and of Madison. On August 5, 1810, his Foreign Minister announced that the Berlin and Milan Decrees had been revoked and called upon Madison to revive nonintercourse with Great Britain. A careful investigation would have shown that Napoleon was still seizing American ships and was proclaiming the decrees to be "permanent laws of the Empire." The Marquess of Wellesley, who had succeeded Canning, warned accurately that Napoleon did not intend to keep his promise.

Yet Madison again jumped at the chance to coerce Great Britain by proclamation. He announced that, unless she repealed her Orders in Council before February 2, 1811, the United States would forbid all trade with the entire British Empire. The day came and went without any word from London. Madison issued his proclamation. A month later, on March 2, 1811, Congress confirmed his action by renewing nonintercourse with Great Britain.

Drifting into War

Meanwhile, a group of young, aggressive, and intensely nationalistic politicians, called "War Hawks," were winning power in the South and West. The

United States, they said, could not go on accepting insults and humiliations without destroying the pride, character, and morale of the American people. Therefore, the War Hawks demanded an end to weakness and caution in diplomacy and a firm defense of American rights, even at the risk of war. Their leader was Henry Clay, who had moved in his twentieth year (1796) from Virginia to the new state of Kentucky. Other War Hawks included John C. Calhoun of South Carolina, Felix Grundy of Tennessee, and Peter B. Porter from western New York. The War Hawks swept into power in the mid-term congressional election of 1810. When the House of Representatives assembled in November 1811, it elected Henry Clay as its Speaker.

The seizure of American ships and sailors angered Clay and his friends. But, as representatives of the frontier, they were equally angered by the encouragement that they believed that British and Spanish agents were giving to the Indians. The War Hawks were convinced that the West would never be free to develop its magnificent resources until the Indian danger was removed. They also believed that this objective could be achieved only when the British had been driven from Upper Canada and the Spaniards from Florida.

Meanwhile, before Congress met in November 1811, four events had driven the United States further down the road to war with England. William Pinkney, the American Minister to Great Britain, was tired of useless negotiations and quit London. He thereby left his government without official representation at the very moment when it needed it most. Second, on May 16, 1811, *U.S.S. President*, a frigate which was patrolling the coast to protect American sailors from impressment, met *H.M.S. Little Belt*, a British sloop, and forced her to surrender. The incident greatly stirred up war spirit in the United States. Third, the first steamboat made its appearance on the Ohio River, thus promising cheap and rapid two-way traffic between Pittsburgh and New Orleans. More than ever, it was believed to be necessary to free the whole Mississippi Valley from the Indian presence.

The fourth event was an explosion on the frontier that seemed to confirm the charge that the British were inciting the Indians to war on settlers in the Northwest. It was the battle of Tippecanoe that not only helped to propel the country into war, but also produced a future President of the United States.

Two able brothers of the Shawnee tribe, Tecumseh and the Prophet, decided to form a great Indian confederacy to prevent the whites from further encroachment on their hunting grounds. They established their headquarters on the Wabash River, near Tippecanoe Creek in the Indiana Territory, from which they defied Governor Harrison. Harrison moved with a force of 900 men near the Indian encampment.

The Prophet attacked on November 7, 1811, while Tecumseh was in the South urging the Creeks and Cherokees to join the confederacy. Harrison barely beat the Indians back; but the next day they abandoned their village, and Harrison burned it. Tecumseh fled to the British in Canada. Harrison's hard-fought encounter strengthened the belief of western settlers that British officials had been inciting the Indians on the frontier ever since St. Clair's defeat twenty years before. General Harrison reported the capture at Tippecanoe of new guns and "ample supplies of the best British glazed powder." These supplies evidently had been obtained from the King's stores at Malden, near Detroit. *"The War on the Wabash is Purely British,"* a Kentucky newspaper declared. The cry from orators and editors throughout the West ran, "Look to the

Wabash, look to the impressed seamen!" There is reason to believe that Westerners also looked to Canada, where they saw, not only the source of British aid to the Indians, but also a huge expanse of fertile land which, like Louisiana, could be added to the growing American empire.

7. THE SECOND WAR FOR AMERICAN INDEPENDENCE

Declaration of War

Another force which drove the American people into war with Great Britain was the psychological need to demonstrate once again that they had earned their independence and were determined to protect it. The insults that the nation had recently suffered at the hands of both the British and the French seemed to prove that the American experiment in liberty would not last long. Thus many Americans yearned to show the entire world that they could defend their freedom and would resort to war if necessary to gain the respect that they rightfully deserved as a sovereign, independent nation. War against both Great Britain and France would be absurd, but a successful war against the former would demonstrate American military power, stop impressment, solve the Indian problem, and possibly add Canada and Florida to the United States.

The war spirit grew steadily in the West and South during the winter of 1811–1812. Henry Clay left the Speaker's chair on several occasions to urge war in fiery speeches. Canada was ours for the taking, he exclaimed. A thousand riflemen from Kentucky alone could do the trick. Other War Hawks whipped up the confidence, pride, and patriotism of the people. The so-called Henry letters affair of March 1812 added to the excitement. A British secret

This engraving of Henry Clay caught some of the arrogance, self-confidence, and commanding presence of the "Great Pacificator." By T. Johnson from a daguerrotype by M. P. Simmons. (Historical Pictures Service, Inc., Chicago)

agent, John Henry, had been conniving with certain Federalist leaders in New England. Henry sold his correspondence with them to Madison, and the President laid the letters before Congress as proof of British infamy.

In response to the surge of war spirit, Congress voted to increase the regular army by 15,000 men, to accept 50,000 volunteers, to refit frigates *Adams, Constellation,* and *Chesapeake,* and to raise a loan of $11 million. Moreover, it was rumored (though denied by Clay) that the War Hawks were threatening to block Madison's bid for renomination if he refused to pursue a militant policy.

Madison was renominated by the Republican congressional caucus on May 18, 1812. On the next day, news arrived from England that the British ministry would make no immediate change in the Orders in Council. It had to be convinced that Napoleon had repealed his decrees in good faith. This dispatch, wrote Madison many years later, was "the more immediate impulse to the war." Americans were forced, he said, to choose between war and degradation.

Madison sent a message to Congress on June 1 reviewing "the injuries and indignities" which Great Britain had heaped upon the United States. Britain, he went on, was in a state of war against the United States. He would, however, leave the decision for peace or war to Congress. That body, by a vote of seventy-nine to forty-nine in the House and nineteen to thirteen in the Senate, declared for war on June 4 and June 17, respectively. This vote showed a far larger opposition than the votes which committed the United States to any other foreign war. Two days before the vote in the House of Representatives, the British government had announced that the Orders in Council would be suspended immediately. By the time that news of this announcement reached the United States, however, the two nations were already at war.

A Nation Unprepared

The United States was wholly unprepared for the war into which it had plunged. Although there were more than a million white male citizens of military age in 1812, the War Department could never put an army of more than 10,000 to 15,000 soldiers in the field. Less than 10 per cent of the 40,000 volunteers that the President was authorized to enlist responded to his call. American generals averaged sixty years of age, and some had seen no service since the Revolution. Several had never commanded even a regiment. A young army officer, Winfield Scott, spoke of the old officers as "sunk in sloth, ignorance, or habits of intemperate drinking . . . decayed gentlemen utterly unfit for military purpose whatever." In addition, the American navy consisted of less than twenty frigates and sloops, built in the days of Washington and Adams. It had 170 small gunboats, but these were intended for coastal defense and were useless on the high seas.

There was enough wealth in the country to finance the war easily, but it was concentrated in the commercial regions of the East, which were bitterly opposed to the war. New England bankers held half the money in the country. They refused to support "Mr. Madison's War" and subscribed less than $1 million of the $11 million loan of 1812. During the entire war, they contributed only $3 million of the $41 million paid into the Treasury.

Moreover, New York and the New England states refused to permit their militias to serve outside their own boundaries. Their legislatures and town meetings denounced the war, and their farmers sold produce to the British

Northwest Campaigns, 1812–1813

armies in Canada. The election of November 1812 showed the sharpness of the division in the country. The most powerful politician in New York, De Witt Clinton, had joined the Federalists to run against Madison as a peace candidate. Clinton carried all of New England, except Vermont, and several Middle Atlantic states, for a total of eighty-nine electoral votes. Madison carried the South and West, along with Vermont and Pennsylvania, for a total of 128 electoral votes. Only Pennsylvania's twenty-five votes saved Madison from defeat and the war from total repudiation.

War on the Canadian Frontier

The war began with a confident American campaign to conquer Canada. The attacks would be aimed at four points: at the St. Lawrence River and Montreal from Lake Champlain; at Kingston, where Lake Ontario narrows to the St. Lawrence River; and at both the eastern and western ends of Lake Erie. Every one of these plans failed because of poor teamwork, continual quarreling between generals, and the refusal of militiamen to leave their own states.

The series of disasters opened on the western front. There the aged Governor William Hull of Michigan Territory surrendered Detroit on August 16, 1812, to 700 British troops without firing a shot. Hull was tried by court-martial for

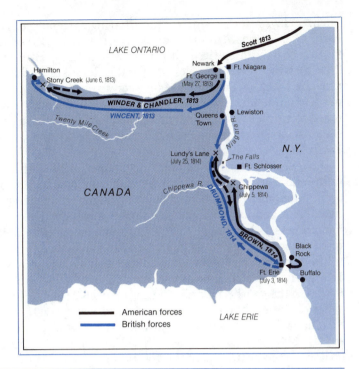

Niagara Frontier, 1812–1814

cowardice and condemned to death, but Madison pardoned him for his outstanding services to the nation during the Revolutionary War—and on account of his gray hairs. The fall of Detroit permitted the British to occupy the entire western frontier—from Lake Erie to the Mississippi River.

More than a year passed before the damage of Hull's surrender was repaired by the brilliant victory of Captain Oliver H. Perry's fleet over a British squadron on Lake Erie on September 10, 1813. "We have met the enemy, and they are ours," he reported. Perry's success forced the British to abandon Detroit and retire eastward along the northern shore of the lake. General Harrison then pursued the British with 10,000 Kentucky volunteers. Harrison overtook the British on the Thames River in Canada and routed them on October 5, 1813. The British commander barely escaped capture, and the great Tecumseh was among the slain. The Indian menace on the northwestern border was now ended.

The Naval War

When the war began, strategists believed that American troops would have little difficulty in conquering Canada, but that the tiny United States Navy would be powerless against the great British fleet. The strategists turned out to be almost entirely wrong for a time, mainly because the British fleet in American waters had recently been reduced to one ship of the line, seven frigates, and some smaller craft. The initial miserable failure on the Canadian border was offset by the deeds of frigates *President, United States,* and *Constitution* ("Old Ironsides").

Three days after his uncle's humiliating surrender of Detroit, Captain Isaac Hull, *U.S.S. Constitution*, met the British frigate *Guerrière* off the North Atlantic coast. In a spirited battle of half an hour, Hull reduced *Guerrière* to a floating wreck. Even the New England Federalists could not help rejoicing over this challenge to England's sea power at the beginning of the conflict. Other naval commanders, such as Stephen Decatur and William Bainbridge, hastened to emulate Hull. In six months, they forced three British frigates and two sloops to strike their colors, while they themselves lost only the eighteen-gun *Wasp*.

However, the enormous numerical superiority of the British fleet prevailed in the end. All but two of the American frigates were either captured or bottled up in ports, and British cruisers drew a tight blockade about the eastern coast from New London, Connecticut, southward. By the end of 1813, Americans had no vessels left at sea to defend their shores, and the British could land almost wherever they wished. Exports from New York fell from more than $12 million in 1811 to $200 thousand in 1814. Those from Virginia dropped from $4.8 million to $17.5 thousand. Foreign trade was paralyzed from Long Island Sound to the southern border of the United States.

On the other hand, swift-sailing American privateers attacked the British merchant marine on all its far-flung lines of world commerce. They captured some 1,300 ships and cargoes valued at about $40 million. The British had boasted at the beginning of the war that they would not let an American vessel cross from Manhattan Island to Staten Island. However, before the war was over, the British themselves were paying 15 per cent insurance on ships crossing the English Channel.

Great Britain Takes the Offensive

The British had been more concerned in 1812 and 1813 about fighting Napoleon in Europe than about the relatively minor war in America. But with Napoleon's abdication and exile to Elba in April 1814, the British were free to carry the war to the Americans.

The British worked out a grand plan of conquest with three prongs: amphibious raids on Washington and cities of the Atlantic coast; an invasion of New York State from Canada along Burgoyne's old route via Lake Champlain; and an expedition to seize New Orleans and detach the Mississippi Valley from the Union. Upon the outcome of this plan depended the fate of the young republic.

A large British amphibious force under Admiral Sir George Cockburn opened the offensive. He left Bordeaux, France, in June 1814, and sailed into Chesapeake Bay in August. The military commander, Major General Robert Ross, landed on the banks of the Patuxent River in Maryland with 4,000 Redcoat regulars and marines. He then marched on the undefended city of Washington. Ross' regulars easily swept aside a force of hastily gathered militiamen at Bladensburg, seven miles from the capital, on August 24, 1814. Madison gathered such valuables as he could and fled for refuge to Virginia. His wife, Dolley, managed to save many state papers and a portrait of Washington. The British set fire to the Capitol, the White House, and several other public buildings. This was in retaliation for the burning and pillaging of York (now Toronto) by American forces. The British troops were repulsed, however, in their next raid at Baltimore, where Ross himself was killed. Francis Scott Key,

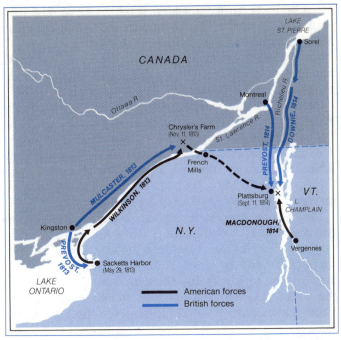

St. Lawrence Frontier, 1813–1814

who watched the bombardment, wrote the verses that were set to an old drinking tune and became "The Star-Spangled Banner."

While Ross' army approached Baltimore, General Sir George Prevost, in the second phase of the British offensive, was advancing from the Canadian border to Lake Champlain with 10,000 veterans. Prevost hoped to repeat with more success the march of Burgoyne in 1777. He arrived at the strong American fortifications at Plattsburg on September 6, 1814, and waited for the British fleet on the lake to enter Plattsburg Bay and help him to storm the American forts. But Captain Thomas Macdonough, a veteran of the Tripolitan War, was waiting for the British. Macdonough stationed his inferior fleet at the entrance of the bay and so skillfully outmaneuvered and outfought the British squadron that he gained as decisive a victory as Perry's on Lake Erie. On the following day, September 12, Prevost, unable to proceed because the Americans retained command of the lake, led his troops back to Canada.

Macdonough's victory was not only the most brilliant naval achievement of the war, but also the most important, because it came just when American fortunes were at their lowest point. The public buildings of Washington were in ashes, the Treasury empty. American warships had been driven from the seas, American coasts had been blockaded, and American commerce had been ruined. All New England, in addition to half a dozen other states, were discussing how they could secure the protection that the government at Washington seemed unable to provide.

Jackson Defeats the Creek Indians and the British

For the embattled Americans, the only heartening event in the land war during the early months of 1814 occurred in the Southwest. The Creek Indians in

Mississippi Territory, maddened by the never-ending theft of their lands by whites and stirred up by Tecumseh and Spanish agents from Florida, attacked 260 Americans at Fort Mims on the lower Alabama River above Mobile in 1813. Andrew Jackson, a Tennessee planter-politician, led a force of 2,500 militiamen that completely broke the power of the Creeks in the Battle of Horseshoe Bend, on the Tallapoosa River, on March 27, 1814. Jackson then forced the Creeks to sign the Treaty of Fort Jackson, by which they gave up two thirds of their land in Alabama and Georgia.

The Mississippi Territory was thus cleared of any immediate danger from the Indians. Jackson pressed on to occupy Mobile. Then, marching into Spanish East Florida to turn back a small British force there, he captured Pensacola on November 7, 1814. Jackson was raised to the rank of major general and given command of the District of the Southwest.

Meanwhile, American and British envoys had been hard at work on a peace treaty in Ghent, Belgium, since early August. The British were riding high after their victories over Napoleon (he was, they thought, safely put away in exile on Elba) and in North America. They demanded that the United States agree never to fortify its northern boundary, cede certain territory around the Great Lakes to Canada, and transform an enormous area south of the Great Lakes into a semi-independent Indian state under British protection.

The American commissioners, two of whom were Henry Clay and John Quincy Adams, packed their bags, but the British were able to prolong the

Southwest Campaigns, 1813–1815

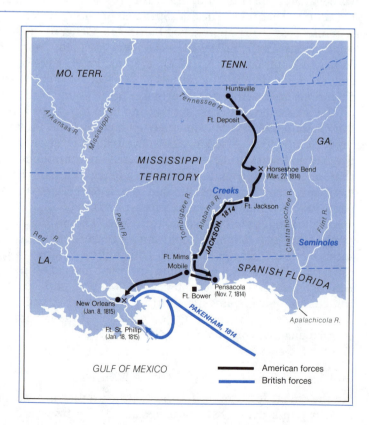

talks. They were certain that they would be able to dictate peace terms within a few months.

Great Britain's hopes were soon dashed in Chesapeake Bay and upstate New York. But the British still had high hopes for the third part of their campaign of 1814—the conquest of New Orleans and the Mississippi Valley. An army of nearly 10,000 men, half of them veterans of service against Napoleon's armies in the Spanish Peninsula, descended upon New Orleans in December 1814. Jackson hastened from his quarters at Mobile. He reached New Orleans a few days before advance British troops landed on the shore of Lake Borgne, only fifteen miles from the city. The Duke of Wellington's brother-in-law, Sir Edward Pakenham, was now in command of the British forces.

Pakenham's Redcoats scorned Jackson's hastily built fortifications of cotton bales and the men behind them and delivered a frontal attack on January 8, 1815. But deadly fire from the American artillery mowed them down like grain before a reaper. In a battle which lasted less than twenty minutes, the British lost their commander and more than 2,000 men, as against seventy-one Americans. Their shattered army reembarked on Lake Borgne and sailed eastward while Jackson, "the Hero of New Orleans," entered the city in triumph.

The Treaty of Ghent

Had the Atlantic cable existed in 1812, the war might not have begun. Had it been available in 1815, the battle of New Orleans would not have been fought. Also, Andrew Jackson might never have lived in the White House. For, on the evening before Pakenham arrived outside New Orleans—December 24, 1814— the British and American commissioners at Ghent had signed a treaty of peace.

By and large, the Treaty of Ghent provided simply for a return to the *status quo ante bellum.* Nothing was said about the American seizure of Mobile from Spain, and therefore the United States retained it. The British abandoned their demands for territory and an Indian buffer state, although the United States did agree (but did not honor the agreement) to return all lands seized from hostile Indians since 1811. The Americans gave up their demand that the British renounce impressment and the right to control neutral American commerce during wartime. The British agreed to reserve the question of fisheries and the navigation of the Mississippi River for future discussion. Most important, certain disputes over the Canadian-American boundary were referred to Anglo-American arbitral commissions. It was, altogether, a draw that turned into a peace of reconciliation because neither side had lasting resentments. The treaty reached Washington on February 14, 1815; the Senate approved it unanimously.

8. THE COMPLETION OF AMERICAN INDEPENDENCE

The Hartford Convention

Opposition in New England to "Mr. Madison's War" had begun even before the ink on the declaration of war was dry. Town meetings throughout Massachusetts denounced the war; clergymen thundered their opposition to it and set apart days for fasting and prayer. The discontent and disaffection verged on treason, as New Englanders traded quite freely with the enemy and urged their militiamen not to fight beyond the boundaries of their states.

The long discontent resulted in a call by Massachusetts to the other New England states for a convention to meet at Hartford, Connecticut, on December 15, 1814. It was "to unite in such measures for our safety as the times demand and the principles of justice and the law of self-preservation will justify."

Twenty-six delegates, mainly from Massachusetts, Connecticut, and Rhode Island, but with scattered representation from New Hampshire and Vermont, met at the appointed time and place. In secret sessions, they adopted resolutions which condemned Madison's administration and the war and recommended cooperation by the New England states in repelling British attacks. They demanded protection for New England citizens against unconstitutional acts by the federal government. In addition, the delegates proposed constitutional amendments to protect New England's sectional interests against the South and West.

Actually there was nothing "treasonable" in these propositions. The convention did not plan secession, as its enemies charged. However, the members made the mistake of opposing the war as a party measure, when it had become in reality a struggle for the survival of the nation. Three "ambassadors" from the convention arrived in Washington just in time to hear news of the Treaty of Ghent. There was nothing left for them to do but go home. The proceedings of the Hartford Convention were published a few years later, and the delegates to that convention spent the rest of their lives defending their personal honor and patriotism. On the whole, the country regarded them as unpatriotic.

Inconclusive though the Treaty of Ghent was, the War of 1812 is rightly regarded as the conflict that finally established American independence. Never again would European powers treat the United States with contempt. The Treaty of Ghent also ushered in an unbroken, if sometimes troubled, friendship with Great Britain, which enabled the United States to enjoy a century of freedom from European troubles and to concentrate upon the development of its own magnificent resources. Finally, success in fending off the greatest power in the world during the War of 1812 set off, as we will see, the kind of nationalism and pride that are, in a world of sovereign states, essential to the dignity and self-consciousness of power that underlie true national independence.

SUGGESTED READINGS

Marshall Smelser, *The Democratic Republic* (1968), C. M. Wiltse, *The New Nation, 1800–1845* (1961), and Marcus Cunliffe, *The Nation Takes Shape, 1789–1837* (1959), are exceptionally able surveys. Henry Adams, *History of the United States During the Administrations of Jefferson and Madison*, 9 vols. (1889–1891), a venerable and brilliant interpretation of the period, is available in a one-volume edition intelligently abridged by Ernest Samuels (1967). Noble E. Cunningham, Jr., *The Jeffersonian Republicans in Power* (1963), and David Hackett Fischer, *The Revolution of American Conservatism: The Feder-* *alist Party in the Era of Jeffersonian Democracy* (1965), explore the opposing parties of the era. Robert M. Johnstone, Jr., *Jefferson and the Presidency: Leadership in the Young Republic* (1978); Leonard D. White, *The Jeffersonians: A Study in Administrative History, 1801–1829* (1951); J. S. Young, *The Washington Community, 1820–1829* (1966); and N. E. Cunningham, Jr., *The Process of Government Under Jefferson* (1978), take different views on how well the Jeffersonians operated the government.

In addition to the biographical treatments cited in Chapters 7 and 8, there are four especially valuable studies of the influence exerted by Jefferson's political thought: Charles M. Wiltse, *The Jeffersonian Tradition in American Democracy* (1935); Adrienne Koch, *The Philosophy of Thomas Jefferson* (1943); Lance Banning, *The Jeffersonian Persuasion* (1976); and Merrill Peterson, *The Jeffersonian Image in the American Mind* (1960). For a negative view of Jefferson on the question of civil rights, see Leonard W. Levy, *Jefferson and Civil Liberties: The Darker Side* (1963). A provocative and controversial study of Jefferson by a psychohistorian is Fawn Brodie, *Thomas Jefferson* (1974). An excellent assessment of Federalist ideology during this Republican era is Linda K. Kerber's *Federalists in Dissent* (1970).

On the Louisiana Purchase, Alexander De Conde's *This Affair of Louisiana* (1977) is the best account. See also George Dangerfield, *Chancellor Robert R. Livingston of New York* (1960); Harry Ammon, *James Monroe and the Quest for National Identity* (1971); and Arthur P. Whitaker, *The Mississippi Question* (1934). The Lewis and Clark expedition is interestingly and thoughtfully evoked in Bernard DeVoto's *Course of Empire* (1952); and his edition of *The Journals of Lewis and Clark* (1953) makes exciting reading. For the Burr conspiracy, there are several fine studies: Thomas P. Abernethy, *The Burr Conspiracy* (1954); Nathan Schachner, *Aaron Burr* (1937); Francis S. Philbrick, *The Rise of the New West, 1754–1830* (1965); Ray Billington, *Westward Expansion* (1967); and Thomas P. Abernethy, *The South in the New Nation, 1789–1819* (1961).

In addition to the surveys of the period mentioned above, see John R. Howe, *From the Revolution Through the Age of Jackson: Innocence and Empire in the Young Republic* (1973), and Raymond H. Robinson, *The Growing of America: 1789–1848* (1973). Irving Brant, *James Madison: The President, 1809–1812* (1956), is the best study of that administration. The problems of American

neutrality are intelligently discussed in Harry Bernstein, *Origins of Inter-American Interest, 1700–1812* (1945), and Bradford Perkins, *The First Rapprochement: England and the United States, 1795–1805* (1955).

On the causes of the War of 1812, Julius W. Pratt, *Expansionists of 1812* (1925), stresses the desire of Southerners and Westerners for more land and their belief that the British were encouraging Indian attacks. This thesis is rejected by A. L. Burt in *The United States, Great Britain, and British North America from the Revolution to the Establishment of Peace After the War of 1812* (1940). Bradford Perkins, *Prologue to War: England and the United States, 1805–1812* (1961), and Reginald Horsman, *The Causes of the War of 1812* (1962), attempt to show that violation of neutral rights and impressment of American seamen were the most important causes. Readiness on the part of the Jeffersonians to defend America's unique republican form of government is suggested as the primary reason for the conflict in Roger H. Brown, *The Republic in Peril: 1812* (1964).

General accounts of the War of 1812 include H. L. Coles, *The War of 1812* (1965); F. F. Beirne, *The War of 1812* (1949); Reginald Horsman, *The War of 1812* (1969); and J. K. Mahon, *The War of 1812* (1975). For Andrew Jackson's role in the war, see Robert V. Remini, *Andrew Jackson and the Course of American Empire, 1767–1821* (1977). The classic study of naval operations is Alfred T. Mahan, *Sea Power in Its Relation to the War of 1812*, 2 vols. (1905). For an account of Madison's wartime leadership see Irving Brant's highly sympathetic *James Madison: Commander-in-Chief, 1812–1836* (1961). A good analysis of negotiations for peace is Samuel F. Bemis, *John Quincy Adams and the Foundation of American Foreign Policy* (1949). See also Bradford Perkins, *Castlereagh and Adams* (1964), and F. L. Engelman, *The Peace of Christmas Eve* (1962).

CHAPTER 11
AMERICAN NATIONALISM AND THE REVIVAL OF SECTIONALISM

1. NATIONALISM TRIUMPHANT

The Postwar Republican Program

One would have surmised that the United States had won a smashing victory over Great Britain, so intense was national pride following the War of 1812. Reports of Jackson's great victory at New Orleans, which came at the same time as news of the Treaty of Ghent, added fuel to the flames of nationalism. The War Hawks, still led by Henry Clay of Kentucky and John C. Calhoun of South Carolina, were now the undisputed leaders of the Republican party. They thought of themselves as the heirs and political sons of the Founding Fathers. The war had revealed a number of internal weaknesses, and the aggressive young Republicans were determined to remedy them and to make the nation as strong as it was proud. Furthermore, this generation of Republican leaders represented manufacturers as well as farmers who produced for world markets. These Republicans wanted internal improvements, tariffs, and sound and available credit.

Even President Madison responded to the new atmosphere. His Annual Message of December 5, 1815, was a ringing appeal for measures to strengthen "our highly favored and happy country." It called for liberal funds for national defense, new frigates for the navy, an increase in the regular army, national aid for roads and canals, a protective tariff, and reestablishment of the national bank. Alexander Hamilton himself could not have formulated a more Hamiltonian program than the one proposed by his old enemy. The country had changed, and the party of Jefferson and Madison had changed with it.

Congress responded heartily to Madison's appeal. First, a committee reported a bill to charter a Bank of the United States to be located in Philadelphia and to have a capital of $35 million. It was to have all the features of Hamilton's bank of 1791. Southern leaders, who had argued against the constitutionality of the old bank, now declared that any such discussion was "a useless consumption of time." Clay, who had fought the recharter of the bank in 1811, stepped down from the Speaker's chair to support the bill with Hamilton's own arguments. The bill passed both houses of Congress, and Madison signed it on April 10, 1816.

The creation of the new bank quickly remedied the most serious financial problems that had beset the country since the demise of the first Bank of the United States. Weak state banks had issued paper money without gold or silver backing and often with few assets behind it. The problem became particularly acute in 1814, when all banks, except those in New England, stopped redeeming their paper money in gold or silver. This currency quickly fell in value, but its value was not always easy to determine. Notes of New York banks circulated at 10 per cent below par, those of western banks often at 50 per cent below par.

The second Bank of the United States was established precisely to remedy this chaotic situation. As the great national banking clearinghouse, it could force state banks to toe the line by refusing to accept their notes and currency. Unfortunately for the country, the second Bank of the United States was recklessly managed from 1816 to 1819, and this greatly contributed to the heavy speculation of the period that ultimately led to a severe economic panic. The second bank narrowly escaped bankruptcy, was put under new management, and soon was fulfilling the objectives for which it had been established.

Madison signed another measure — the tariff act of 1816 — that gave further proof that he and his party had adopted Hamilton's economic policies. While foreign trade suffered from the embargo and war, large amounts of capital that had been invested in shipping were transferred to manufacturing. By the end of 1815, 140 cotton mills were operating within a radius of thirty miles of Providence, Rhode Island, and half a million spindles were humming throughout New England. Pioneer iron, woolen, and cotton textile factories were scattered throughout the Ohio Valley from Pittsburgh to Cincinnati.

British manufacturers, who had supplied the American market since colonial days, did not intend to lose it now. Even before the Senate approved the Treaty of Ghent, British ships were waiting off New York, loaded with goods. British exporters planned to dump them on the American market at lower prices than those at which the same goods could be produced in the new American mills and factories. In a single year, the British sent over $90 million worth of merchandise to undercut the fledgling American factories.

Congress responded with a tariff bill which Madison signed on April 27, 1816. Its duties averaged about 25 per cent. All sections of the country, except New England, contributed to the large majority by which the bill was passed. New England still engaged heavily in commerce and shipping. A second tariff measure in 1818 gave special protection to the iron industry and continued the duties of 25 per cent on textile goods to 1826. In order to strengthen the American merchant marine, taxes were levied on foreign vessels which used American ports. Only merchant ships of American registry were permitted to engage

*A view of Boston Harbor in the early nineteenth century. Although
export trade in ports like Boston thrived during the antebellum period,
New England's position on the tariff changed as its interest in manufacturing increased. By 1830 this transformation was complete. (Courtesy,
Museum of Fine Arts, Boston)*

in the American coastwise trade. No one wished to repeat the embarrassing
experience with the state militias during the war; Congress voted to maintain
a regular army of 10,000 men. The President appointed Jacob Brown and Andrew Jackson as major generals for the northern and southern districts, respectively. Jefferson's useless gunboats were sold, and Congress appropriated money for new warships to guard the coasts and shipping. Altogether, Congress
voted some $4.5 million to strengthen the national defenses.

Voters rendered a thundering approval of Madison's nationalistic program in
the presidential election in November. The decimated Federalists made only a
feeble attempt to recover control of the government; their presidential candidate, Rufus King of New York, spoke of his campaign as "a fruitless struggle."
"The Federalists of our age," he confessed mournfully, "must be content with
the past." Only Massachusetts, Connecticut, and Delaware cast their electoral
votes (thirty-four) for King. The 183 votes from the other sixteen states went to
the Republican candidate, James Monroe of Virginia.

The Revolution in Transportation

One of the lessons of the War of 1812 was the need for better means of transporting goods and troops. Calhoun, a prime mover behind the nationalistic legislation of 1816, came forward with a plan to help solve this problem in December of that year. It was the so-called bonus bill, which proposed to use for

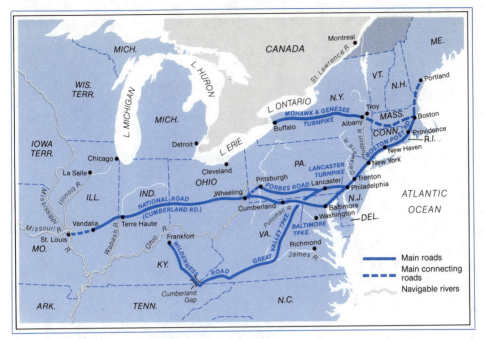

Rivers and Roads West before the Railroads

federal aid to internal improvements the $1.5 million bonus that the second national bank was to pay for its charter. The dividends that the government was to receive on its $7 million of bank stock would also go toward building roads and canals. Congress passed the bonus bill in February 1817, but Madison vetoed it. He did not disapprove of its purpose, but he thought that an amendment to the Constitution would be necessary to enable Congress to spend money on internal improvements that were not clearly interstate in character. Madison's successor, Monroe, had the same constitutional scruples.

Even though plans for roads and canals at national expense collapsed, the states undertook many such projects. The most notable was the Erie Canal, which connected Lake Erie with the Hudson River. The canal, completed in 1825, cost New York State $7 million. But it immediately reduced freight rates between Buffalo and New York from $100 to $15 a ton, doubled the value of farm products in western New York and the Ohio Valley, and stimulated the growth of cities on the lakes, such as Buffalo, Cleveland, Detroit, and Chicago. These became serious rivals of the river cities, Pittsburgh, Cincinnati, and St. Louis. The Erie Canal made New York City the nation's leading commercial metropolis, and its success set off a period of intense canal construction, particularly in the West. This canal boom flourished until the financial setback of 1837–1839. By the 1840s, railroads were beginning to bring the canal era to an end, although traffic on the Erie Canal continued to increase until the 1870s.

The coming of the steamboat and railroad and the building of roads, bridges, turnpikes, and canals produced a veritable economic revolution, as we have seen. And, as we have also seen, the social impact was also enormous. A steady

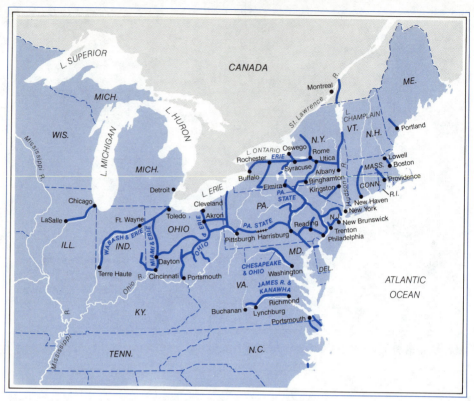

The Canal Boom, 1800–1850

stream of people moved more freely and quickly from one section of the country to another. A population once constricted to a narrow ribbon of land along the Atlantic seacoast now steadily expanded across a vast wilderness stretching thousands of miles.

Nationalistic Diplomacy

Young nations, proud of their new power, frequently adopt strident, aggressive diplomatic policies. Diplomatic chauvinism erupted in the United States following the War of 1812 and swept the country in two movements. One was a campaign, led by Henry Clay, to recognize the new republics of South America then struggling in rebellion against Spain. Many Americans thought that the least that they could do was to extend diplomatic assistance to Latin Americans who were following their own earlier example. Numerous private filibustering expeditions, moreover, sailed from New Orleans to carry men and supplies to the South American rebels. The second movement was the near hysteria that swept the United States when the Greeks rebelled against their Turkish masters in 1821. Ministers, poets, editors, and others caught the "Greek fever," and resolutions introduced into Congress urged the administration to recognize Greek independence.

That these movements did not get out of control was due largely to John

Quincy Adams of Massachusetts, son of the second President, who served as Monroe's Secretary of State from 1817 to 1825. Adams was as nationalistic as Clay, and almost as sympathetic with the desire of Latin Americans for independence; but he was also an experienced and shrewd diplomat who shared with the President the responsiblity for foreign policy. It would have been relatively easy to recognize the new Latin American republics. But Adams wanted to acquire East Florida from Spain, and he had to be careful not to spoil the chances for its acquisition by offending the Spanish government. Moreover, Adams resisted the demand for what would have been a premature recognition of Greek independence. Recognition was accorded in 1837, but only when Greek independence was secure.

As for Great Britain, it would have been both simple and popular to twist the lion's tail and hear him roar, but Adams knew that this would hardly cement friendly relations with the nation that the United States needed most as a friend, if not as an ally. Hence Adams, with the full support of Monroe, continued to temper nationalism with good sense.

Adams' first task in negotiation was to make new postwar arrangements with Great Britain. It was not an easy task, for the British at the end of the war planned to reestablish their naval supremacy on the Great Lakes. While Minister to Great Britain (1815–1817), Adams had taken the lead by proposing that both nations agree to disarm on the Great Lakes. Britain saw an advantage to its own interests in the proposal, and the outcome was an agreement negotiated in Washington in April 1817 between the British Minister, Charles Bagot, and Acting Secretary of State Richard Rush. In this treaty, which both nations have observed to the present day, Great Britain and the United States pledged that they would not keep warships on the Great Lakes. In the following year, 1818, Adams, now back in Washington as Secretary of State, negotiated a treaty which adjusted the boundary line between the United States and Canada. Henceforth it was to run along the forty-ninth parallel from the Lake of the Woods to the Rocky Mountains. The treaty also renewed American fishing rights off Newfoundland and Labrador. Finally, it provided for joint Anglo-American occupation of the Oregon territory from the Rockies to the Pacific for a period of ten years. These treaties marked a new beginning in friendlier relations between the United States and Great Britain. Both countries contributed substantially to this diplomatic change of attitude.

Adams also turned his attention to the problem of Florida, one made more difficult by the rising American demand for recognition of the Latin American republics. Periodic raids against American settlers by Seminole Indians in northern Florida, who were trying to protect their lands, also heightened Spanish-American tensions. While Adams resisted the movement for recognition of the Latin American republics, Monroe sent General Jackson to punish the Indians. Jackson took a very broad view of his instructions. He swept across East Florida in the early months of 1818 and captured Pensacola, Gadsden, and St. Marks in the process. He summarily hanged a British trader, Alexander Arbuthnot, and shot a former officer of the Royal Marines, Robert Ambrister, both of whom had been convicted of inciting the Indians to murder and pillage. When Jackson returned to Tennessee in May 1818, he left Florida a conquered province.

It was a delicate situation, especially since the United States was now more than ever eager to acquire Florida. An explosion of indignation rocked Great

Britain over the execution of the two British subjects, but the British ministry chose to ignore the incident. At home, the entire cabinet, except for Adams, wanted to disavow and censure Jackson. Adams had a plan—to use the episode in negotiations to force Spain to give up Florida—and Monroe permitted him to follow it. The Spanish Minister, Don Luis de Onís, protested against Jackson's raid. Adams took the offensive. Spain, he said, should thank the United States for going to so much trouble to subdue the Indians. Moreover, the continuation of Indian raids was proof that Spain was not able to discharge her international obligations in Florida. Spain should get out of this embarrassing difficulty by selling Florida to the United States. Otherwise, Adams warned darkly, the United States might have to solve the problem by military means.

The strategy worked, largely because the Spaniards feared Jackson and the possibility that the United States might recognize her rebellious colonies in Latin America. Hence Onís signed a treaty of cession with Adams in Washington on February 22, 1819. Spain ceded the Floridas outright to the United States. In return, the American government agreed to pay the claims—of about $5 million—of its citizens against Spain. The treaty also fixed the boundary line between the Louisiana Territory and the Spanish domain in the Southwest. That boundary, undetermined at the time of the purchase in 1803, was now drawn in a stairlike course from the mouth of the Sabine River in eastern Texas to the point where the forty-second parallel of latitude meets the Pacific coast. The Adams-Onís Treaty is frequently called the Transcontinental Treaty because in effect it recognized that the United States now stretched across an entire continent.

A few years later, Adams negotiated a treaty with Russia in which the Czar accepted the parallel of 54° 40′ as the southern boundary of his province of Alaska.

The New Nationalism in the Supreme Court

The nationalistic tendencies of the period were encouraged by a series of decisions by the Supreme Court, dominated by the great Federalist Chief Justice, John Marshall. In Fletcher *v.* Peck (1810), Marshall and his colleagues annulled a law of Georgia. In Martin *v.* Hunter's Lessee (1816), Marshall overruled the highest court of Virginia in its claim that the case could not be appealed to the Supreme Court. Three years later, in the Dartmouth College case, the Supreme Court annulled an act of the New Hampshire legislature which had changed the college's charter. Marshall maintained that the charter was a "contract," and that the Constitution (Article I, Section 10) forbade the states to "pass any law impairing the obligation of contracts."

In the same year, 1819, Marshall handed down one of his two most important decisions (the other was Marbury *v.* Madison, see p. 274) in the case of McCulloch *v.* Maryland. Maryland had levied a tax on the national bank's branch in Baltimore. "The power to tax involves the power to destroy," Marshall declared. No state, he said, had the right to tax or hinder in any way the operations of a national institution established within its borders. More important, the Chief Justice squarely faced the issue of the constitutionality of the act that established the second Bank of the United States. Congress, Marshall said, possessed all power necessary and proper to execute the authority delegated to it by the Constitution. One of the powers was control of financial af-

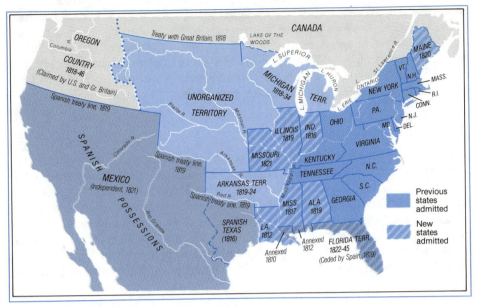

The United States, 1812–1822

fairs. Therefore, Congress had the right to establish a national bank. As Marshall put it, in a sweeping affirmation of the doctrine of implied powers: "Let the end be legitimate, let it be within the scope of the Constitution, and all means which are appropriate, which are plainly adapted to that end, which are not prohibited, but consist with the letter and spirit of the Constitution, are constitutional." Finally, in Gibbons v. Ogden, 1824, the court annulled the monopoly on steamboat traffic that the New York legislature had granted to Robert Livingston and Robert Fulton. Only Congress, and not the states, the court declared, could control interstate and foreign commerce.

The Supreme Court, under Marshall's powerful influence, had established the judiciary as an equal branch of the federal government. It had also established the principles that the courts had the last word as to the constitutionality of state and federal legislation, that the state courts were inferior to the federal courts, and that the implied powers of the federal government were virtually limitless.

An American Literature

Not the least important manifestation of the intense nationalism of the postwar era was the burgeoning of an authentic American literature. The foundations for this achievement had already been laid. The fact that the superstructure would be well begun was signaled by the founding of the *North American Review* in Boston in 1815. Between 1815 and the 1830s, a group of New Yorkers, called the Knickerbocker School, pioneered in creating an American literature based upon native themes and local color. Washington Irving had led the way with *Diedrich Knickerbocker's History of New York* (1809). His *Sketch Book* (1819) was a worthy sequel. James Fenimore Cooper was even more aggressively American in subject and spirit. His *The Spy* (1821) and *Leather-stocking Tales* (*The Pioneers*, 1823; *The Last of the Mohicans*, 1826; *The Prairie*, 1827) gloried in the American locale and history. The poet William Cullen Bryant ("Thanatopsis," "To a Waterfowl!") wrote odes to the beauty of nature in America. However, a sizable and distinctively American literature of high quality was not created until the 1840s and 1850s.

The Era of Good Feelings

Monroe, a few weeks after his inauguration, set out upon a tour of the North and West. His reception in New England was so enthusiastic that a witty writer compared it to "the adoration of the Wise Men of the East." Boston, the very center of Federalism, heaped honors upon this friend of Jefferson and supporter of "Mr. Madison's war." The Boston *Sentinel*, which had appeared with mourning borders when Jefferson was elected, now spoke of Monroe as the herald of "an era of good feelings." The phrase so pleased Monroe that he repeated it frequently on his tour. It caught the fancy of the American people at once.

Politically, however, it was anything but an era of good feelings. Many Republicans resented the nationalistic program of the postwar era and denounced it as an abandonment of true Jeffersonian principles. The Federalist party was virtually dead, and many former Federalists drifted into the Republican party. Soon there were sharp disagreements between two factions who called themselves Republicans but held to opposite philosophical views of government. A two-party system of government had degenerated into a one-party system; but that one party could not agree on what the federal government should do.

No serious rival candidate challenged Monroe in 1820. Monroe was reelected—despite the recent onset of a severe economic panic—with only one dissenting electoral vote cast by an elector from New Hampshire for John Quincy Adams. It was generally believed that this elector refused to vote for Monroe because, he said, only George Washington deserved to be unanimously elected to the presidency. Actually, he thought that Adams was the better man and so voted accordingly.

2. *THE REVIVAL OF SECTIONALISM*

The Panic of 1819

The near unanimity for Monroe gave an appearance of political harmony and national unity that actually had largely evaporated by 1820. In the roughest and most simplistic terms, the United States might be said to have consisted of three distinct sections by the time of Monroe's administration. These were the commercial and manufacturing East; the staple-crop plantation South; and the varied farming frontier of the West. Of course, each section had areas and communities with many types of inhabitants, occupations, and traditions unlike the dominant ones in the section as a whole. Nevertheless, the over-all sectional differences aroused conflicts on a great number of important national policies. Which were more important: agriculture, commerce, or manufacturing? What kinds of currency should be used, and what kinds of banks? Should the government at Washington help to develop the underdeveloped parts of the country, or should it leave them to shift for themselves? Did the federal government have the right to forbid slavery in territory west of the Mississippi?

Sectionalism had been a powerful force in American politics since colonial times. It would continue to divide the East from the West and the North from the South for at least another century. But sectional rivalries had been muted between 1815 and 1819. This was a time — or so it seemed — of roaring prosperity. It was also a time of frenzied speculation and reckless overextension, encouraged by the loose-money policies of the Bank of the United States and numerous new wildcat banks. They were called "wildcat" because they allegedly printed their notes in the wilderness, where only wildcats lived. Kentucky, Ohio, and Tennessee alone chartered forty new banks in 1817 and 1818. No sooner were these banks in business than they began to pour more cheap paper money into the economic bloodstream. By 1818, some 392 state-chartered banks operated throughout the country.

The bubble burst in 1819, as it had to do sooner or later. The Bank of the United States now began to call in its own loans. It also demanded that the state-chartered banks redeem their paper currency in gold and silver. Wild, unreasoning panic swept the country. Banks suspended payment in gold or silver and closed their doors. A depression in manufacturing, which had begun a year before, intensified as factory after factory went into bankruptcy. The bottom fell out of prices for agricultural commodities, lands, and slaves. Hardest hit were the South and West, where planters and farmers had bought land and slaves and built homes on credit after the removal of the Indian threat during the War of 1812.

Localism and sectionalism quickly asserted themselves in these unhappy circumstances. The "general interest" was forgotten as each section did what it could to persuade the federal government to promote its own particular interests. Thus practically all national measures — the very measures that had once drawn enthusiastic cooperation from most sections of the country — were bitterly disputed during the 1820s. The "era of good feelings" produced rancor and discord before it dissolved into the Age of Jackson.

Rival Sections

The economic changes caused by the War of 1812 in the Northeast have already been described. Capital switched from commerce, especially international trade, into manufacturing. New England and the Middle Atlantic states became the center of a manufacturing section that gradually extended westward into the Ohio Valley. For a time, the shipping interests of the seaport centers (such as Boston, New York, Philadelphia, and Baltimore) tried to encourage foreign commerce as against the development of manufactures. They wanted freedom of trade. Daniel Webster of Massachusetts, for example, voted against tariff bills until 1828. But manufacturing interests gained steadily, until they became the most powerful single economic group in most of the Northeast.

Until the 1840s, most manufacturers wanted, first of all, a high tariff to protect themselves against British competition. In order to have an abundant supply of laborers for their factories, they favored free immigration. By the same token, they opposed the rapid settlement of the West, which drew families off

The demands for easy credit in the West encouraged the development of wildcat banking years before statehood status was achieved. As the second Bank of the United States tightened its credit in 1819, it gathered up many western bank notes, such as the one above, and presented them to the banks for payment in cash. Lacking adequate reserves on hand (or at all), many of these banks were forced to close. Such fiscal irresponsibility helped precipitate the Panic of 1819. (Smithsonian Institute, National Numismatic Collection)

into the wilderness. Finally, most eastern manufacturers desired a sound currency and banking system to stabilize business, although a large minority wanted easy credit for expansion. The immediate effect on the Northeast of the Panic of 1819 (insofar as national policies were concerned) was to set off demands for tariff increases in order to save domestic industries.

The interests of the Lower South at this point were quite different from those of the North. The South's interests had been determined by the invention of a Connecticut schoolteacher named Eli Whitney, who had gone to Georgia as a tutor, and his patroness, Catherine Greene, widow of General Nathanael Greene. The tutorial position that brought Whitney south fell through, but Catherine Greene urged him to stay on at her Mulberry Grove plantation. Greene was impressed by Whitney's ingenuity in designing a new tambour frame for her embroidery, and she persuaded him to turn his talents to developing a machine that could strip the seeds from short-staple cotton and thus make it a profitable crop to raise. British demand for cotton at the time was so great that the State of Georgia had already established a commission to promote the invention of a workable machine. Greene's confidence in Whitney and her financial support encouraged him to work for six months behind locked doors in a basement room of the plantation house until, finally, in April of 1793, he announced that he had completed a working model of his engine, or "gin." Whitney's patent was secured in March 1794, but copies began to appear in Georgia almost immediately. There ensued a prolonged struggle to establish Whitney's rights to the invention. Catherine Greene continued to support him and his manufacturing partner, Phineas Miller, by committing her entire resources to their firm, but by the time Whitney reestablished title to his invention in 1807, his patent had expired, ending any hope of financial return.

In any event, the cotton gin was one of the most fateful inventions in history. It enabled one person to remove the seeds from 300 pounds of cotton in the same time that it had previously taken to clean a single pound by hand. This made the production of cotton so profitable that the plantation system, and therefore slave labor, became fixed in the South. Because cotton growing wears out soil rapidly, the planters looked constantly for fresh lands. "King Cotton" quickly spread into the fertile regions of the Mississippi Territory after Jackson's campaign. By 1821, more than one third of the cotton was raised west of the Appalachians.

Since the plantation system discouraged manufacturing in the South, there was no need for a protective tariff. On the contrary, the tariff was a burden upon the planter. The tariff raised the price of manufactured articles and benefited the northern manufacturer at the expense of the planter. The fact that the tariff made higher wages possible and so increased the buying power of workers was no argument in its favor to the planter. His laborers were slaves to whom he paid no wages but for whom he had to supply tools, clothing, and food. He was not particularly interested in the prosperity of cotton mills in New England. They used only about one fourth of the southern cotton crop. The planter's chief markets were in Europe. He wanted to exchange his cotton freely for the manufactured goods of Europe and the North at prices that were not increased 10, 20, or 30 per cent by the tariff. And the argument that the federal government should levy tariffs to aid one section of the country at the expense of another struck Southerners as patently unconstitutional.

The panic of 1819 struck most severely, among the South Atlantic states, in South Carolina. There the depression aggravated an already bad situation for planters who had been struggling to survive the competition of the newer and richer cotton area of the Southwest. South Carolina's discontent for a time — particularly during the nullification controversy of the 1830s — threatened the very existence of the Union.

By 1820, some 2,600,000 persons, or more than a quarter of the nation's population, lived in the states beyond the Appalachians. The greatest need of these western communities was for better transportation of their surplus products to eastern markets. They, themselves, were too poor to build the necessary roads and canals; hence they looked to Washington for help. After the Panic of 1819, the most immediate need of Westerners was for legislation to provide relief to farmers who had bought public land on credit. But, again, some staunch adherents of the Jeffersonian creed insisted that local public works by the federal government violated the Constitution. Internal improvements and relief laws, they argued, were purely matters for the state and local governments.

Clay's "American System"

Nationally minded Republicans, such as Henry Clay and John Quincy Adams, believed that constructive legislation could harmonize sectional claims and unite the country. Clay, especially, urged his fellow citizens to look no longer to Europe but to develop "a genuine American policy." He would encourage manufacturing in the North by a high tariff. This would create a large population of workers to use the farm products of the West and to spin and weave the South's cotton. Tariff duties on certain products would raise increased revenues, which Clay would spend generously to improve roads, canals, and river navigation. In turn, these lanes of transportation would bring the food products

of the West to the manufacturing centers of the North and the cotton and tobacco plantations of the South. Clay also viewed the second Bank of the United States as the guardian of a sound and uniform currency.

Clay's program would provide a platform for the Whig party in the future,
but it was impossible to achieve any such balanced national program in the
1820s as had been adopted in 1816. The continuing absolute predominance of
the Republican party, now infiltrated by former members of the defunct Federalist party, made agreement on controversial economic issues very difficult.
No stirring appeal could be made for party harmony. Even with a united party
behind him, it might have been impossible for Clay to achieve his American
System at this time. In the 1820s, the various sections were still too self-
conscious, too inward-looking, too concerned about their own problems, for
any two of them, or large segments in any two of them, to unite consistently to
form a solid majority in Congress.

The story of national legislation and politics in the 1820s can be written
largely in terms of competition between the Southeast and Northeast, with the
West holding the balance of power. Majorities for any federal legislation could
be found only when the West united with one of the older sections. This happened only upon a few occasions. Southern congressmen were able narrowly to
defeat tariff increases in 1820. But the Northeast and West combined in 1824
to increase average duties from the 25 per cent level of the act of 1816 to about
40 per cent. Significantly, in the House of Representatives, the middle Atlantic
and western congressmen voted eighty-six to nine in favor of the Tariff Act of
1824, the southern and southwestern representatives, seventy to six against it.
New England still was in a state of transition between a commercial economy
and a young industrial one, and its representatives remained divided over the
tariff until later in the decade. The western and southern states combined after
the Panic of 1819 to pass periodic laws for the relief of farmers who owed money to the federal government for land. They also combined in 1820 to adopt
new general land legislation. It abolished purchase on credit, reduced the price
of public land from $2.00 to $1.25 an acre, and reduced the minimum number
of acres that had to be purchased from 160 to eighty. On the other hand, majorities could never be found in the 1820s for federal aid to internal improvements.

3. THE SLAVERY QUESTION

The Slavery Question Rises in the West

At the precise moment that economic sectionalism began to assert itself, political sectionalism in its most dangerous form aroused such hostility between
the North and South as to threaten for a time the existence of the Union. It was
a controversy over the extension of slavery, and involved, in particular, the
admission of Missouri to the Union.

The tide of westward migration had crossed the Mississippi River into the
Missouri Territory—the name given to all the rest of the Louisiana Purchase
after the extreme southern part had been admitted as the state of Louisiana in
1812. By 1818, some 60,000 settlers had pushed up the valley of the Missouri
River. St. Louis had already become the center of the fur trade of the Far West.

More than fifty steamboats chugged up and down the Mississippi, doing a business of $2.5 million a year. In March and November 1818, the people of Missouri applied to Congress for admission as a state. No federal law had as yet been passed on the question of slavery in the territory west of the Mississippi. The majority of the settlers in Missouri were from the free-soil states north of the Ohio; but there were also about 10,000 slaves in the territory. No one assumed that this would make any difference when Missouri applied for statehood. Mississippi and Alabama had been admitted as slave states without much discussion about the institution of slavery. However, Congress deliberately had maintained an even balance between the slave and free states by admitting Indiana and Illinois to offset Mississippi and Alabama.

A bill to enable the people of Missouri to adopt a state constitution was reported in routine fashion to the House of Representatives in February 1819. Representative James Tallmadge, Jr., of New York immediately offered an amendment to the bill. It proposed that "the further introduction of slavery . . . be prohibited . . . and that all children of slaves born within the said state after the admission thereof into the Union shall be free at the age of twenty-five years." The House of Representatives adopted the amendment by a vote of ninety-seven to fifty-six, but it was promptly rejected by the Senate. The Fifteenth Congress expired on March 4, 1819, without acting on Missouri's request for statehood.

Tallmadge was apparently acting on behalf of a group of northern Republicans who keenly resented southern control of the federal government. The Northerners were disturbed in 1819 by the fact that the admission of Missouri with a slave constitution would give the slave states a majority in the Senate for the first time. (There were eleven free and eleven slave states in the Union in 1819.) As far as the future was concerned, the Tallmadge forces hoped to undermine southern power by limiting the extension of slavery. Opposition to slavery on moral grounds seems to have been only a minor motive behind the Tallmadge amendment. Southerners regarded the amendment as an unconstitutional assault on their fundamental rights as citizens. They regarded a slave as property, and they denounced as an attack upon their constitutional rights any action by Congress to restrict or control their property rights.

The Missouri Debate

The Missouri question went before the country as soon as Congress adjourned. Then a momentous fact, heretofore hidden, became immediately apparent: the country was divided along sectional lines on the basic issues of slavery. Previously, it had been generally assumed that most Southerners were opposed to the institution (or at least that the institution embarrassed them), and that the passage of time would take care of the problem. Even the movement of slavery into the Southwest had been regarded as the last extension of a dying institution. The southern states had all abolished the foreign slave trade during the Revolution, although South Carolina had reopened it in 1803. A southern President, Jefferson, had taken the lead in the adoption by Congress in 1807 of a law to close the foreign slave trade in 1808—the earliest date at which such legislation was permitted by the Constitution. There were many more emancipation societies in the South than in the North in 1820, and Southerners had taken the lead in 1817 in forming the American Colonization Society, which hoped to colonize freed slaves in Africa and did in fact develop a settlement in Liberia.

But the Missouri debates proved two very significant facts. There was much greater opposition in the North to slavery on religious and moral grounds than anyone had known. Up to this time, it had been mainly latent; hereafter, it would become organized and would spread. Also, southern opinion about slavery was slowly congealing in its favor by 1819 because of its profitability as a consequence of the cotton gin. In another ten years, that opinion would harden. Southern antislavery sentiment was confined to a small area—the Upper South. Even there, it did not by any means constitute the majority sentiment. Moreover, much southern antislavery sentiment was really anti-Negro. Racism, in both the North and in the South, greatly influenced political behavior. Even members of the American Colonization Society could not imagine a society in which whites and blacks lived in anything like equality. The only solution that they could imagine was to rid the country of blacks.

The Missouri debates demonstrated two additional facts: much of the opposition in the free states to the admission of Missouri stemmed from fear that southern predominance in Washington would mean continued blockage of measures like tariff increases; and the injection of a moral issue into a sectional controversy made its solution immensely difficult, if not impossible.

The Missouri Compromise

Passions were running high by the late months of 1819. The aged Jefferson wrote that the sudden strife awoke him like the alarm of a fire bell in the night. And Howell Cobb, a congressman from Georgia, would soon say on the floor of Congress that Tallmadge had kindled "a fire which only seas of blood could extinguish." There was much talk of disunion and civil war.

Congress took up the Missouri question again as soon as it reconvened in December 1819. Both houses were deluged with petitions for and against the Tallmadge amendment. The debate at this point shifted to constitutional issues. All of them boiled down to the single question: could Congress constitutionally prohibit the extension of slavery? Southerners argued that the Louisiana Purchase treaty of 1803 had guaranteed to the inhabitants of the territory "protection of their liberties, property and religion." Could Congress now, in fairness, deprive the planters of Missouri of their slave property by freeing all blacks born in the new state? Northerners replied that the Constitution gave Congress the power "to dispose of and make all needful rules and regulations respecting the territory or other property belonging to the United States." They pointed to the Northwest Ordinance of 1787—proof that Congress did indeed have the right to prevent the extension of slavery beyond the original states. The debate went on. Southerners argued that the issue was really whether new states should be equal to the old ones.

Miraculously, a solution was found. Maine had been a part of Massachusetts since 1677. Now it had the consent of Massachusetts to a separation. Accordingly, Maine applied to Congress for admission as a state in December 1819. The House at once approved an enabling act; that is, a measure to permit Maine's admission. But the Senate, after it received the Maine bill, incorporated it as an amendment to the Missouri bill. It also substituted for the Tall-

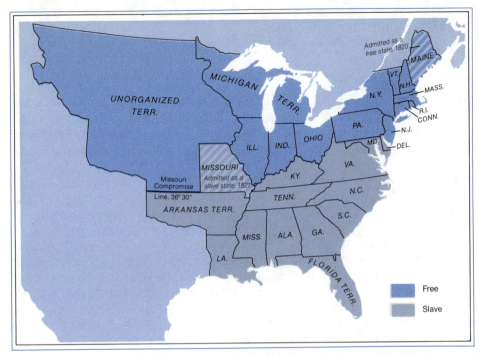

MICHIGAN TERR.

UNORGANIZED TERR.

Admitted as a free state, 1820

MAINE

VT.
N.H.
N.Y.
MASS.
R.I.
CONN.
N.J.
DEL.
MD.
PA.
OHIO
IND.
ILL.

MISSOURI
Admitted as a slave state, 1821

Missouri Compromise Line, 36° 30"

ARKANSAS TERR.

KY.
VA.
TENN.
N.C.
S.C.
MISS. ALA. GA.
LA.
FLORIDA TERR.

Free

Slave

The Missouri Compromise

madge amendment one introduced by Senator Jesse B. Thomas of Illinois. The Thomas amendment excluded slavery "forever" from the Louisiana Purchase north of the parallel 36° 30' (the southern boundary of Missouri), except for the state of Missouri itself. The House, by the close vote of ninety to eighty-seven, accepted this compromise, largely as the result of efforts by Henry Clay.

The country accepted the compromise with much relief. Northerners were pleased because the balance between the free and slave states had been maintained and Southerners had admitted the right of Congress to prevent the extension of slavery in the territories. A "permanent" solution of the slavery question—one making free soil of five sixths of the territory of the vast Louisiana Purchase—had been achieved. Southerners, more reluctantly, accepted the compromise because it maintained, at least for a time, their equality in the Senate. More important, an army survey team, recently returned from the Plains area of the northern part of the Louisiana Purchase territory, had reported that region to be a vast desert unfit for white settlement.

The compromise seemed to have averted the possibility of a civil war, which people in all sections contemplated with horror. But the compromise was only a stopgap. It did not end sectionalism, and it did not prevent fiercer controversies when the issue of slavery in the territories arose again in the 1840s. John Quincy Adams wrote prophetically in his diary: "I take it for granted that the present question is a mere preamble—a title-page to a great, tragic volume."

4. THE MONROE DOCTRINE

The Background

After Napoleon's final defeat at Waterloo in 1815, Russia, Austria, Prussia, and Great Britain formed the Quadruple, or Holy Alliance, in order to protect what they called the legitimate monarchies of Europe. Then the alliance (with an altered membership after the withdrawal of Great Britain and the addition of France) received a plea from Spain for help to recover its former colonies in the New World.

Meanwhile, Britain had developed a flourishing trade with Spanish America, which would end if Spain regained its colonies. In August 1821, George Canning, British Foreign Secretary, once again proposed to the American Minister in London that the United States and Great Britain combine to prevent the Holy Alliance from reimposing Spanish authority in the new world. Americans had been profoundly disturbed by the threat of European action against the new Latin American republics. Monroe asked Jefferson and Madison how he should reply to Canning's proposal. Both former Presidents urged him to cooperate with Great Britain. However, Secretary of State Adams strenuously disagreed. It would be more appropriate, Adams said, for the United States to take its own independent position. Anglo-American cooperation in this instance could only mean that the United States would "come in as a cock-boat in the wake of the British man-of-war."

A Warning to the Old World

Monroe agreed with Adams and decided to make his own pronouncement, but he rejected Adams' advice to put it in the form of a diplomatic note. Instead, he embodied it in his Annual Message to Congress of December 2, 1823, which included many other matters as well. The Monroe Doctrine contained four basic affirmations. First, the western hemisphere was no longer open to colonization by European powers. Second, the United States would consider any attempt on the part of European powers "to extend their system to any portion of this hemisphere as dangerous to our peace and safety." In other words, the United States would resort to war if necessary. Third, since the political systems and interests of Europe and of the western hemisphere were different, the United States recognized an obligation to refrain from intruding in European affairs in matters that did not concern it. Fourth, by the same token, Europe had to refrain from interfering in American affairs.

Nothing seemed more defiant than this blunt warning to the old world. Actually, Monroe and Adams knew very well that the British were determined not to permit the Holy Alliance to restore to Spain her former colonies in Central and South America. Indeed (although Monroe was ignorant of the fact), two months earlier, Canning had secured a promise from the French government that it would not participate in any effort to recover these colonies for Spain.

In announcing the "no-colonization" principle, Monroe established an important cornerstone of American foreign policy, namely that the entire western hemisphere was now under the care and protection of the United States. It would resist foreign intrusion. Whether European governments heeded it would depend for many years upon the might of the British fleet, and only later on the emerging power of the young republic in the West. At the time of its publication, most Americans paid no attention to the Monroe Doctrine, and it was soon forgotten. But President James K. Polk resurrected it some twenty years later (see p. 354), and it rightfully is regarded as one of the cornerstones of American foreign policy.

5. THE REPUBLICAN PARTY DIVIDES: ADAMS VERSUS JACKSON

The Favorite Sons

The presidential campaign and election of 1824 revealed, once again, the strength of sectional rivalry. It was not a contest of parties because, since the demise of the Federalists in 1816, the Republican party had stood without a rival in the field. The campaign of 1824 was, rather, a struggle between political factions. Each had a rough sectional basis; each sought to gain possession of the government; each championed its favorite son.

The congressional caucus was nearly defunct, and state legislatures made the presidential nominations in 1824. The New England states nominated the experienced John Quincy Adams of Massachusetts. Tennessee named her military hero, Senator Andrew Jackson. Kentucky put forward her brilliant orator and statesman, Henry Clay; the legislatures of Missouri, Illinois, Ohio, and Louisiana promptly approved him. South Carolina supported her most distinguished son, John C. Calhoun, although he later withdrew and ran unopposed for the vice-presidency instead. The more conservative wing of the Republican party supported William H. Crawford of Georgia, Secretary of the Treasury.

This early painting of John Quincy Adams was done in 1795 when Adams was twenty-eight years of age by John Singleton Copley, a Bostonian whose portraits revealed a distinctly American quality. (Courtesy, Museum of Fine Arts, Boston)

Long before the voting took place in November 1824, it was almost certain that no one of the four candidates would receive a majority in the Electoral College. As it turned out, Jackson had ninety-nine votes, a plurality but far less than a majority; Adams, eighty-four; Crawford, forty-one; and Clay, thirty-seven. According to the Twelfth Amendment, the House of Representatives had to choose a President from the three highest names on the list. Each of the twenty-four states had one vote, and a majority of the states—thirteen—was necessary for election.

Clay, since he was out of the race, threw his support to Adams. Adams agreed with Clay's views on the tariff, the bank, internal improvements, and other points of the American System. To Clay, Jackson was nothing more than a "military chieftain," unfit for the presidency. Finally, Clay came to an understanding with Adams that Adams would appoint him Secretary of State, the office which had traditionally led straight to the presidency. With Clay's support, Adams won on the first ballot in the House of Representatives; he received the votes of thirteen states; Jackson, seven; and Crawford, four.

The Corrupt Bargain Charge

The election of 1824–1825 (the election in the House occurred in February 1825) was perfectly constitutional. In fact, Jackson was one of the first persons to congratulate Adams on his election. However, when Adams appointed Clay as his Secretary of State, the Jackson men angrily charged that Clay had sold his support to Adams in return for the promise of the first place in the cabinet. They said that the Kentuckian had deliberately defied the will of the people and made a "corrupt bargain" with Adams in order to succeed him as President of the United States.

Adams' four years in the White House were something like an extended nightmare. Nothing that he proposed could please his enemies. The Republican party, which had seemed on the surface so united in the "era of good feelings," was now split into two factions. The Adams-Clay wing, called the National Republicans, continued to support the nationalistic American System. The Calhoun-Crawford wing reasserted the old state-rights doctrines of Thomas Jefferson.

The unpopular Adams was the victim also of his own stubbornness and political ineptitude. He would not dismiss officials who opposed him, even a member of his cabinet. The Senate, presided over by Vice-President Calhoun, held up his appointments. Congress frowned on his plans for internal improvements and a national observatory—Europe, he said had 130 of "these lighthouses in the skies"—and ignored his proposal for a great national university to be located in the city named for George Washington. They guffawed at his stupidity when he told them that they should not be "palsied by the will" of their constituents in passing legislation to strengthen the nation. The Governor of Georgia successfully defied Adams when the President courageously and honorably tried to defend the treaty claims of the Cherokee Indians to their lands within Georgia.

"The Tariff of Abominations"

The tariff question continued to cause the greatest trouble during the Adams administration. Northern manufacturers and northwestern commodity produc-

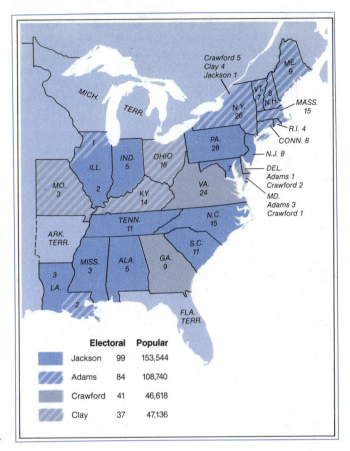

	Electoral	Popular
Jackson	99	153,544
Adams	84	108,740
Crawford	41	46,618
Clay	37	47,136

The Election of 1824

ers had obtained increased protection in the tariff bills of 1818 and 1824; but pressure for increased protection continued to grow and culminated in the meeting of a protectionist convention in Harrisburg, Pennsylvania, on July 30, 1827. It petitioned Congress for increases in the duties on woolen goods, iron and steel products, cotton textiles, hemp, and flax. Southerners were strongly opposed. Indeed, South Carolinians, now suffering more than ever from the competition of western cotton, were already beginning to talk seriously about withdrawing from the Union if tariffs were not lowered drastically.

The result was a tariff bill, which leaders of the antiadministration forces constructed and intended to use to attract votes for Jackson in those western states (such as Kentucky and Missouri) and northern states (such as Pennsylvania and New York) where the Hero needed them most. Martin Van Buren, Senator from New York, who led the Crawford Republicans into Jackson's political camp, and his lieutenant in the House of Representatives, Silas Wright, Jr., were the principal architects of this tariff. The bill, as reported, provided additional protection for raw wool, hemp, flax, and iron ore; however, woolen cloth, made chiefly in New England, a section committed to Adams' reelection, received little protection. Southerners voted for the tariff bill in the hope that it would be so distasteful to New England that, on the final vote, the New Englanders would join them in killing it. But enough New Englanders supported the measure, after Van Buren had deftly raised the rate on woolen cloth a trifle, to pass it in both houses of Congress by narrow margins. Adams signed it on May 19, 1828. Many Americans denounced this grotesque measure as a "Tariff of Abominations," but it probably won Jackson some votes in western and northern states.

Calhoun's Exposition and Protest

Opposition was particularly violent in South Carolina. Flags were flown at half-mast in Charleston when the tariff act was approved. Orators advised South Carolinians to boycott all trade with the protected states. George McDuffie, one of the state's leading politicians, called the Stamp Act of 1765 and the Tariff Act of 1828 "kindred acts of despotism." An excited journalist wrote that it was high time "to prepare for a secession from the Union."

The most significant protest came from Vice-President Calhoun. In an essay, *The Exposition and Protest of South Carolina*, published anonymously by the legislature of South Carolina in 1828, Calhoun argued that a protective tariff was unconstitutional because it penalized one section of the country for the benefit of other sections. He revived the idea of the Virginia and Kentucky Resolutions of 1798 when he declared that the states should be the ultimate

The Election of 1828

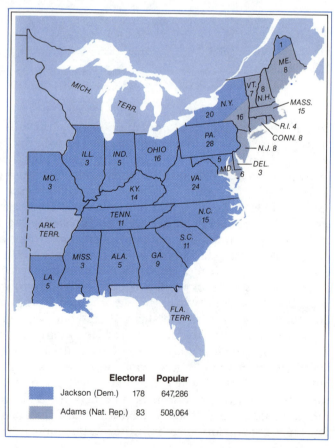

	Electoral	Popular
Jackson (Dem.)	178	647,286
Adams (Nat. Rep.)	83	508,064

Andrew Jackson by Asher Durand. This striking portrait of Jackson as President gives a realistic sense of the strong-willed, opinionated politician. The swept-back hair that seemed to be at attention like the man, himself; the powerful, hypnotic eyes; the angular nose and jaw constitute fitting features for a man who was to remake the presidency. Durand painted the portrait at the White House in 1835. (Historical Pictures Service, Inc., Chicago)

judges of whether or not Congress had exceeded its powers. Calhoun, however, went even further and said that any state might nullify altogether an act of Congress and appeal to its sister states for a verdict; if this occurred, Congress should submit an amendment giving it the power in dispute. If the amendment was ratified, the nullifying state could either yield or secede from the Union.

The Triumph of Andrew Jackson

The year of the Tariff of Abominations was also a presidential election year. The candidates were Adams, supported by Clay and like-minded Republicans, and Jackson, supported by the Crawford and Calhoun factions and most conservatives who desired a return to the state-rights doctrines of Jefferson.

Jackson won a complete victory. Every state west of the Appalachians and south of the Potomac gave him its entire vote. In addition, he won all the electors of Pennsylvania, twenty out of thirty-six in New York, and five out of eleven in Maryland—for a total of 178 to eighty-three for Adams. His popular tally was 647,286 to Adams' 508,064. Calhoun was reelected Vice-President, only this time as Jackson's running mate.

While the West celebrated its triumph noisily, the manufacturing North and the agricultural South stood facing each other in a hostile truce. The West had put an end to the dynasty of aristocrats and scholars from Virginia and New England and was sending a President to the White House for the first time. Andrew Jackson, who had once been a frontiersman, seemed to be a plain man of the people. This Indian fighter, who had given the nation its greatest military victory and possessed all the passions and prejudices of the untamed West, would sit in the chair of Washington, Adams, Jefferson, and Madison.

On inauguration day, the "common people" flocked from hundreds of miles around to invade the White House. They stood with muddy boots on damask-covered chairs and spilled orange punch on costly carpets. When the refreshments were moved outdoors to relieve the pressure inside the White House, people jumped through the windows to reach the punch bowl. They almost suffocated the Hero as they crowded around him to shake his hand. Dignified statesmen deplored this beginning of the reign of "King Mob." The gloomy former President slipped out of the White House on the evening of March 3 and refused to attend the inauguration of the "barbarian" who was taking his place.

SUGGESTED READINGS

George Dangerfield, *The Era of Good Feelings* (1952), actually describes an era of bad feelings, although without interparty strife or warfare. The same author's *The Awakening of American Nationalism, 1815–1828* (1965) takes recent research into account.

On economic change during the postwar period, there are several stimulating studies: George R. Taylor, *The Transportation Revolution* (1951); Douglass C. North, *The Economic Growth of the United States* (1961); and Stuart Bruchey, *The Roots of American Economic Growth* (1965). A valuable study on expansion is Frederick J. Turner, *The Rise of the New West* (1906). Ralph C. H. Catterall, *The Second Bank of the United States* (1903), and Walter B. Smith, *Economic Aspects of the Second Bank of the United States* (1953), are useful studies. R. E. Shaw, *Erie Water West: A History of the Erie Canal* (1966), is the best account of that subject. Also instructive is Nathan Miller, *The Enterprise of a Free People* (1962).

Dexter Perkins, *The Monroe Doctrine, 1823–1826* (1927), remains the basic work on that subject, but Ernest R. May, *The Making of the Monroe Doctrine* (1975), is a revisionist work. See also Arthur P. Whitaker, *The United States and the Independence of Latin America, 1800–1830* (1941). Glover Moore, *The Missouri Controversy, 1819–1821* (1953) is the standard account of that subject, as is Murray N. Rothbard, *The Panic of 1819* (1962), for the economic depression that hit the country after the War of 1812.

There are several excellent studies of John Marshall and the Supreme Court. Near classics include Albert Beveridge, *The Life of John Marshall*, 4 vols. (1916–1919); Charles Warren, *The Supreme Court in United States History* (1937); and Edward S. Corwin, *John Marshall and the Constitution* (1919). A more modern study is R. K. Newmyer, *The Supreme Court under Marshall and Taney* (1968).

On the politics and presidential elections of the period, see Shaw Livermore, Jr., *The Twi-*

light of Federalism: The Disintegration of the Federalist Party, 1815–1830 (1962); Robert V. Remini, The Election of Andrew Jackson (1963); and Norman K. Risjord, The Old Republicans: Southern Conservatism in the Age of Jefferson (1965).

Several biographies are important for an understanding of the politics of this period. Samuel F. Bemis, John Quincy Adams and the Union (1956), presents an excellent account of that President's administration. Charles M. Wiltse, John C. Calhoun, Nationalist (1944), is very sympathetic to its subject. Gerald M. Capers, John C. Calhoun—Opportunist: A Reappraisal (1960), is not. Glyndon G. Van Deusen, The Life of Henry Clay (1937), is still the best biography of "Harry of the West."

CHAPTER 12
THE JACKSONIAN ERA

1. THE NEW DEMOCRACY

Jacksonian Democracy

The period between 1829 and 1841 has been called by such names as the Age of Jackson, the Age of the Common Man, and the Age of Egalitarianism. The man who gave his name to an era also gave it to the broad and diverse movement for political, moral, and physical improvement known loosely as Jacksonian Democracy. This movement ran on different levels— local, state, and national—and included forces working against each other. It also included aspects of which Andrew Jackson disapproved and others that he ignored or knew nothing about. Nevertheless, Jackson adequately symbolized a series of political assumptions affected by a peculiar zeal. Although this was not a period in which the economic or social well-being of ordinary Americans increased faster than in other periods, earlier or later—indeed, a few recent historians have argued that it decreased—it was an era in which spokesmen of all kinds—literary, journalistic, but especially political—praised the common man for his virtue and commonsense wisdom. Jackson, the Hero of New Orleans, was widely believed to be the finest example of qualities so highly prized in ordinary people.

Jacksonian Democracy itself is most accurately defined as a convulsive movement that changed the style and some of the assumptions of American political life. To be sure, the movement toward egalitarianism began in the late colonial period. It reached a halfway point under Jefferson and was gaining great speed when Andrew Jackson came upon the national scene during the War of 1812. It finally triumphed in the Jacksonian Era.

It was, most fundamentally, aggressive, egalitarian democracy grounded on the assumption of the absolute political equality of all men (that is, all white men), regardless of wealth, rank, or education. It called for universal white male suffrage, and it had achieved it in most states by 1828. It insisted, not only upon political democracy, but also that everyone should have an equal opportunity to achieve success and good fortune. No one should have special privileges that worked to the disadvantage of others. Privileges, especially political and economic privileges—what the Jacksonians called "artificial distinctions"—had to be eliminated. The race for success must be a fair contest. The government, therefore, had to serve as an honest referee among all the classes in society and prevent any one of them from gaining an advantage over the others.

In addition, the leaders of this movement developed a new political style by appealing to the extremely politically conscious masses in the 1820s. These leaders sought votes by haranguing crowds in their own language. They held barbecues and gigantic torchlight parades, and sometimes issued demagogic appeals to class prejudices. In earlier times, candidates had "stood" for office

Engraving after The County Election *by George Caleb Bingham. More than any other artist of his time, Bingham caught in his pictures the shout, activity, sheer excitement, and festivity of Jacksonian America. (Courtesy, Museum of Fine Arts, Boston)*

and had given the impression that they were, to a large extent, favoring the people by permitting them to vote for them. Older politicians who could not change their attitudes, or at least their styles, were swept aside by practitioners of the new techniques.

The Dynamics of Jacksonian Democracy

The years after the return of peace in 1815 were a time of rapid social change and consequent political turmoil throughout the western world. The spread of factories and urbanization gave rise, for example, to a strong working-class movement in England called Chartism, which was not unlike a segment of the Jacksonian democratic movement in the United States. Social and economic conditions in the United States between 1815 and 1828 were even more tumultuous than in western Europe. The factory system and urbanization had not yet acquired as much momentum in the United States, it is true, but the westward movement created change in the United States just as swift as that caused by the beginning of industrialization in western Europe. The Panic of 1819, coming as it did in the midst of rapid change, greatly intensified social and economic distress. It set off or encouraged numerous movements for alleviation. One dynamic movement behind Jacksonian Democracy was the growing West's determination to share national political power with the older sections of the country. By 1828, nine of the twenty-four states of the Union lay west of the Appalachians. They contained more than one third of the inhabitants of the United States, and these people were determined to be heard. Jackson regarded himself as a Westerner, rather than a Southerner, and several of his closest advisers were also Westerners.

Another dynamic force — the emergence of a separate and somewhat politically self-conscious working class — was the product of the growth of factories. This group, swelled by immigration from Europe, was becoming conscious of its strength and was demanding social and economic legislation to benefit its interests. For example, labor groups demanded abolition of imprisonment for debt, free public schools, and means by which workers could force employers to pay wages owed. Skilled workers were much more effectively organized in the 1820s and 1830s than before. As enfranchised citizens, they also began to go directly into politics. In the year of Jackson's election, for example, the trade unions of Philadelphia organized a Workingmen's party, put up candidates for local offices, and founded the *Mechanics' Free Press,* the nation's first labor newspaper. There was an even stronger Workingmen's party in New York in the 1830s. It supplied powerful support for the radical faction in the Democratic party (the name adopted by the Jacksonians for their national party) in that state. Not all workers were solidly united behind Jackson or the democratic movement; indeed, most factory workers were still unorganized and and politically voiceless. However, the emergence of a degree of class consciousness among skilled workers raised new challenges that the major parties had to meet. During the mid-1830s, hundreds of strikes occurred throughout the country, many in support of a ten-hour day and higher wages. The federal government adopted the ten-hour day in 1840. An important labor victory was achieved in 1842, when Chief Justice Lemuel Shaw of the Supreme Court of Massachusetts ruled in Commonwealth *v.* Hunt that it was not a violation of the common law rule against restraint of trade for workers to form unions and strike in order to achieve their objectives. However, this doctrine did not obtain acceptance by all other state courts until several decades later.

Romanticism and Transcendentalism

Fundamentally, the Jacksonian age was a romantic one. The poetry and essays of such English writers as Samuel Taylor Coleridge and William Wordsworth, coupled with the philosophical ruminations of such German thinkers as Immanuel Kant and Johann Gottlieb Fichte, laid the groundwork for this new age. Although the old commitment to the ideas of the Enlightenment — such as the efficacy of reason and order — continued to persist, the romantic ideas of this new age began to sweep across the United States in the 1820s. Romanticism emphasized the sensate in mankind. The mind no longer ruled as the sole perceiver of truth and beauty. Now the emotions were acknowledged to be in partnership with the mind. Human feelings were no longer suspect; now they were to be enjoyed and obeyed. Romantics glorified nature as perceived through the senses; thus they stressed the intuitive powers; they emphasized the perfectibility of men and women; and they reasserted the importance of the individual.

Ralph Waldo Emerson, the essayist, poet, and "sage" of Concord, Massachusetts, said that "the demon of reform" had been loosed upon the land. Emerson, himself, contributed to this "demon" because of his involvement with Transcendentalism, which advanced the impulse of reform during the Jacksonian Era. It, too, was an expression of romanticism and was almost solely a creation of New Englanders. Transcendentalists preached the supreme worth of the individual. They proclaimed, not simply the goodness of men and women, but also their divinity. They urged self-reliance and the removal of all obstacles that impeded an individual's progress toward a better and higher life. They believed that the world comprised a variety of different beings, all united in the spiritual power of God, which Emerson called the oversoul. The oversoul was diffused in humanity and nature; and men and women, through intuitive contemplation, could hear the voice of God. In their approach to knowledge, Transcendentalists were mystics, for they believed that people could "transcend" experience and reason and, through their own intuitive powers, discover the wonders of the universe.

Since people were perfectible, they obviously were capable of governing themselves. Therefore, there must be no impediments to officeholding or participation in the affairs of government. In no way did any person need an authoritative government to tell him or her what to do or not to do and to exact penalties for refusal. Government had to be founded on good will. It should never coerce the individual against the sovereign dictates of his or her independent conscience.

Transcendentalists were concerned about social justice for both women and men, and they opposed social regimentation. They found society corrupted and a hindrance to the individual's full growth and development. So they preached reform. In his famous essay, "Man the Reformer," Emerson wrote: "What is man born for but to be a Reformer, a Re-maker of what man has made; a renouncer of lies; a restorer of truth and good, imitating that great Nature which embosoms us all?"

Other distinguished Transcendentalists were Henry David Thoreau, Bron-

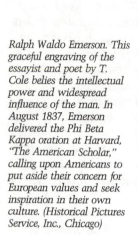

Ralph Waldo Emerson. This graceful engraving of the essayist and poet by T. Cole belies the intellectual power and widespread influence of the man. In August 1837, Emerson delivered the Phi Beta Kappa oration at Harvard, "The American Scholar," calling upon Americans to put aside their concern for European values and seek inspiration in their own culture. (Historical Pictures Service, Inc., Chicago)

son Alcott, Orestes Brownson, Nathaniel Hawthorne, Margaret Fuller, a strong advocate of freedom for women, and George Ripley. At first, they gathered at Ripley's home in Boston to discuss their ideas; later, a few of them founded a community called Brook Farm at West Roxbury, Massachusetts, where they could live together and put their ideas into practice. Although Brook Farm never numbered more than a hundred and fifty people, it drew thousands of visitors each year to study the extraordinary activities, particularly the experiments in education, that went on there. This experiment in communal living was not financially successful and was abandoned in 1847 after a fire.

Communitarianism

Antebellum reformers established many other communities to improve living conditions and form models of the good society. Some of these communities had a religious basis and were essentially sectarian in character. Others were attempts to reorganize society by creating new economic patterns of living. The latter were best represented by the "Fourierist groups," which advocated the creation of cooperative units for communal living called "phalanxes." These were first proposed by the French socialist, Charles Fourier, and permitted the members to work at tasks that they found most congenial. Presumably, such an environment would create a wholesome society and eventually achieve material equality for all. Albert Brisbane of New York propagated Fourier's ideas in the United States in his *Social Destiny of Man* (1840), which described the "vast and foolish waste which results from our present social mechanism and . . . the colossal economics and profits which would arise from Association and Combination in industrial interests."

Brook Farm was the most famous phalanx. Another communitarian experiment, distinct from the Fourierist idea, was founded by Robert Owen, a successful Scottish manufacturer known internationally for his humanitarian reforms. Owen came to the United States in 1825 and founded his community in New Harmony, Indiana. Cooperation, rather than competition, would be the motivating force behind the settlement. There would be political as well as economic equality, and everyone would have what he or she needed—and no more. Through collective ownership of property and cooperative labor, Owen expected to create an ideal society devoid of poverty and crime. But within two years, New Harmony had failed. Cynics found the reason in the basic depravity of human beings which defeats all efforts to ameliorate the "cruelties and miseries" of this "wretched world." More to the point was Owen's failure to devote full time to his experiment, the internal discord and conflict among the colonists, Owen's reputation as a "free thinker," and his unconventional attitudes about relations between the sexes.

Despite the failure of New Harmony, the idea of communal living to perfect the individual and improve social institutions persisted throughout the Jacksonian era. Frequently, the most successful communities had a religious basis. One example was the Shaker movement, founded by Mother Ann Lee, a poor woman who came to the United States from England and settled near Albany, New York, in 1776. She taught that God had a dual personality: the masculine, made manifest in Christ, and the feminine. Her followers claimed that she was the second incarnation of the feminine personality of God. Mother Ann drew heavily from the Quaker religion, but she added one element. She insisted that sexual lust was the root of all evil and that her followers had to be celibate. She was credited with miracles and drew many converts. By the 1840s, some 6,000 Shakers resided in two dozen communities scattered from Maine to Indiana. There they could live out their religious beliefs without exciting the distrust and resentment of others. Indeed, by the 1840s, the Shakers had overcome much of the hostility which their unorthodox beliefs and practices had aroused. Instead, they were widely praised for their simple style of life and the high quality of their workmanship in architecture, furniture, and other goods. Despite the difficulties caused by celibacy, the Shakers continued to attract new converts and to survive into the twentieth century in ever decreasing numbers.

Their unique practice—and the reason for their strange name—was the sacred Shaker dance in which the congregation would shake sin from their bodies. They formed lines, three abreast, and literally scampered around the room in a quick gallop, singing at the top of their lungs a wordless chant that went something like, "law, law de lawdel law." Soon they reached a state of ecstasy, and some of them fainted in hysterical convulsions to be caught in the arms of the other dancers.

The Society of True Inspiration, a pietistic sect, came from Germany. The members first settled in New York in 1843 and then moved to Iowa in 1855, where they founded the Amana Community. They held all property, except clothing and household goods, in common. The community eventually divided into seven villages or colonies, each with its own meetinghouse, store, school, and democratic government. The community drew few converts from outside society; most inhabitants came directly from Germany. The colorful Amana colonies are well preserved and thrive as a popular tourist area where fine furniture, clocks, wine, and textiles are produced by Amana craftsmen.

Not strictly communitarian, but by far the most important and influential religious group that experimented with the creation of new communities during the Jacksonian era was the Church of Jesus Christ of Latter-day Saints, better known as the Mormon Church. Its founder, Joseph Smith, was a poor but talented and imaginative young man born in Sharon, Vermont, in 1805, who grew up in central New York State. There he had a series of visions which convinced him that God had called him to restore the faith of early Christianity and to "translate" a set of golden plates which he claimed to have discovered. The result was published in 1840 as the *Book of Mormon*, which purported to be a continuation of the Old and New Testaments. The young Mormon Church grew slowly at first. Smith and his followers moved repeatedly to escape persecution — from New York to Ohio, to Missouri, and to Nauvoo, Illinois. In Nauvoo, along the Mississippi River, Smith established a religious community of more than 10,000 members.

The rapid growth of Mormon Nauvoo and the church's authoritarian structure provoked intense fear and hostility in surrounding non-Mormon areas. Smith was murdered in 1844 in Carthage, Illinois, and Brigham Young assumed leadership of the group. Young abandoned Nauvoo and led his people on a difficult trek across the Great Plains to the Rocky Mountains. In the arid region surrounding the Great Salt Lake, the Mormons found a haven where they could build their church on a lasting basis and create a cooperative commonwealth run as a theocracy. They also institutionalized the practice of polygamy as their marital ideal and practiced it until federal persecution and pressure forced official abandonment of polygamy in 1890. The Mormons played a key role in the settlement and development of the Rocky Mountain area. Their hard work, cooperative irrigation systems, and other settlement practices made the arid wastes of Utah and surrounding areas to "bloom as the rose." To this day, the Mormons remain a key force in the life of Utah and surrounding areas.

These communitarian experiments were some of the most important expressions of the vitality of the Jacksonian era. They demonstrated the willingness of many Americans to adopt new patterns of life in order to eliminate crippling social disabilities and to improve political, economic, and social institutions.*

Literature: Romanticism and Nationalism

The same energy that fueled activity in other fields during the Age of Jackson produced a literature that gave vent to all the stirrings and aspirations of the time. The most important literary renaissance occurred in New England among the Transcendentalists. Romanticism, individualism, and optimism characterized the writing of most of them. The leader was of course Emerson, whose essays and lectures called upon self-reliant Americans to build a new society divorced from European values. A fellow townsman and friend of Emerson was Thoreau, whose masterpiece, *Walden* (1854), emphasized the Transcendentalist themes of self-reliance and the goodness of nature. Among the Transcendentalist poets, the two giants were Henry Wadsworth Long-

*Other reform movements of this period are discussed in Chapter 14.

fellow of Cambridge and James Russell Lowell of Boston. Longfellow's romantic historical poems, *Evangeline* (1847), *Song of Hiawatha* (1855), and *The Courtship of Miles Standish* (1858) all glorified nature and human goodness. Lowell used his poetic skills in the campaign against slavery, most particularly in *The Biglow Papers* (1846–1848). No Transcendentalist, but very much in tune with their romanticism and nationalism, was Walt Whitman, whose *Leaves of Grass* (1855) drew high praise from Emerson and marked Whitman as the greatest poetic expounder of nineteenth-century American democratic hopes, values, and romantic nationalism.

A different kind of interpretation of individualism appeared in the writing of other Transcendentalists and persons affected by them. Hawthorne, in his greatest novel, *The Scarlet Letter* (1850), took a more pessimistic view of human nature than did his elders at Brook Farm. In New York, the prolific novelist, Herman Melville, wrote on the theme of the triumph of evil over virtue in this world in his two greatest novels, *Moby-Dick; or, The Whale* (1851) and *Billy Budd, Foretopman* (published in 1891).

There was also a literary awakening in the South, where the preeminent writer of the era was Edgar Allen Poe, romantic poet, writer of short stories, and inventor of the detective story. Poe was the first American to have a direct influence on European writers. The school of French poets called symbolists drew their inspiration directly from Poe. William Gilmore Simms of Charleston was the most prolific romantic historical novelist of the antebellum era. More important was the work of a group of Southerners—Augustus Baldwin, Joseph G. Baldwin, and Johnson J. Hooper—who began a new regional literature by depicting the lives of the common people in the South during the Age of Jackson.

2. THE NEW ADMINISTRATION BEGINS

Jackson as President

When he took office, Jackson did not have a national program to unite his diverse following throughout the country. He, as well as many of his followers and closest advisers and associates, were almost pure Jeffersonians in their attitudes toward national policies. They believed ardently in state rights, frugality, and government that conferred no favors on any groups. They wanted to restore what they romanticized as a long-lost Arcadia of small farmers, led by simple and honest governors.

Jackson, if he had had his way, would have served a single term undisturbed by any controversy. But he did not have his way. Events forced him to take strong positions. As he met crises and challenges not of his own choosing, he developed a style and program that made him a strong and popular President almost in spite of himself. Indeed, he transformed the American presidency.

Circumstances led Jackson into playing an essentially new role as President—that of serving as the spokesman and tribune of the people. Unlike most of his predecessors, Jackson was not the protégé of an administration, nor had he been nominated by a clique within Congress. State legislatures had advanced his nomination. He believed that he drew his power directly from the people, not from a party or from any faction operating within Congress. He was the first President to appeal directly to the people through statements, proclamations, and messages.

Circumstances also caused Jackson to break away from even the appearance of subservience to Congress. Former Presidents, even strong ones like Washington and Jefferson, had considered themselves to be executives in domestic matters, who would carry out the laws made by Congress. They had respected the checks and balances of the Constitution. But Jackson did not stand in awe of Congress. Was it not the House of Representatives that had kept him out of the presidency in 1825? So he vetoed more acts of Congress than all previous Presidents put together, and he was the first chief executive to use the pocket veto.* Nor did he hold any special veneration for the Supreme Court. He believed that the President had as much right as Congress or the Supreme Court to decide what laws were desirable or constitutional. He refused, for example, to sign one bill that he strongly believed unconstitutional even though the Supreme Court declared that it was constitutional. Later an apocryphal story made the rounds to the effect that he defied one Supreme Court ruling that he did not like with the remark, "John Marshall has made his decision: now let him enforce it."

Finally, Jackson's aggressive, assertive personality led him into conflicts in which he invariably played the role of presidential leader. He was combative by experience and nature and was seldom without a quarrel, personal or public. In such controversies, he naturally concluded that those who opposed him were enemies of the public good. Thus, the man who had only desired to serve his country in a time of political quietude found himself thrust into the forefront of battles that he said were battles for the people.

Jackson drew from those around him either intense devotion or intense hostility. To his opponents, Jackson was a selfish demagogue and an impulsive trigger-happy tyrant. They said that he would do anything necessary to please the mob in his desire for power. They called him "King Andrew" and feared that his warfare with Congress might result in the destruction of the constitutional system. To Jackson's enthusiastic supporters, he was a plain man of the people who carried out the people's will as a President should.

Jacksonian Policies

Jackson's official cabinet consisted mainly of second-raters, so the new President relied upon a group of informal advisers called the "Kitchen Cabinet." It included, among others, Secretary of State Martin Van Buren and Secretary of War John H. Eaton, and two editors, Amos Kendall (later Postmaster General in Jackson's cabinet), and Francis P. Blair, Sr. Although these men advised Jackson on many issues, the President himself formulated his own policies, both foreign and domestic.

Jackson's first major policy statement came in the form of a resounding veto on May 27, 1830. Clay had persuaded Congress to approve a bill granting federal money for the construction of a road between Maysville and Lexington, both in Kentucky. Jackson vetoed it. The Maysville road, he said, was a local road.

---

*An indirect veto by retention of a bill after Congress has adjourned and refusal to sign it.

The Constitution gave Congress no authority to support local internal improvements. His administration, Jackson warned, would respect state rights, practice frugality, and pay off the national debt.

When Jackson took office, he was convinced that the federal civil service was filled with corrupt and aristocratic officeholders. Thus he set about, as he put it, to clean the "Augean stables." No one has an inherent right to office, he said, and the public will be better served through a policy of rotation. For his efforts, Jackson was unfairly accused of introducing the spoils system into the federal government. The term came from a speech by Senator William L. Marcy of New York in which he said, "To the victor belong the spoils of the enemy." Actually the number of removals by the Jackson administration was less than 20 per cent, but the democratic principle of opening federal offices to everyone was established.

Removal of the Eastern Indians

Jackson, a Westerner and an Indian fighter *par excellence*, sincerely believed that Indians and whites could not coexist. He believed that the only hope for the survival of the Indians and of their culture was their removal to a distant territory beyond the Mississippi River. A policy of resettlement had in fact been begun during the Monroe administration; indeed, the idea of removal had originated with Thomas Jefferson. But President John Quincy Adams did not pursue the matter, and it remained for Andrew Jackson to drive the "Indian problem" to its tragic conclusion.

Indians signed treaties by which they exchanged their lands in the East for equivalent amounts in the West. If they balked, they were bribed or threatened. Considerable trouble ensued with the smaller tribes along the frontier. The Sauk and Fox, led by their noble chief, Black Hawk, tried to return to their homes in northwestern Illinois in 1832. The Governor of Illinois called out the state troops, who decimated the Indians in wanton slaughter. The Seminoles in Florida maintained a fierce resistance until 1842 in a war that cost the nation some 1,500 lives and millions of dollars. Even then, several thousand Seminoles remained hidden in swamps and were never resettled.

More difficult to deal with, because they were more numerous, were the four great Indian nations — the Chickasaws, Creeks, Choctaws, and Cherokees, who inhabited a broad region from western Georgia to Mississippi and northward to western North Carolina and eastern Tennessee. The Choctaws gave up in 1830; the Creeks and Chickasaws in 1832. The circumstances of their removal were horrible. Some of them were transported in the dead of winter, with no advance arrangements made to supply food or shelter. They died by the thousands. For the rest, they were taken to a new Indian Territory that is now part of the state of Oklahoma. The Cherokees, the most numerous and technologically advanced of the four tribes, sued in the Supreme Court to protect their rights, but they could not overcome the white man's determination to get rid of them. They finally gave in to superior force and were removed by the army to the Indian Territory in 1838. The long journey was an agony — a "trail of tears," they called it — in which one quarter of the Cherokee Nation died. A few hundred of them held out in the mountains of North Carolina.

Jackson has been severely criticized for his removal policy. Although he intended to rescue the Indians from certain destruction if they remained in their ancient lands he, in fact, succeeded in decimating them.

The Peggy Eaton Affair

It was difficult for "Old Hickory," as Jackson was affectionately called, to avoid controversy. Before many months of the new administration had passed, he was embroiled in a quarrel with Vice-President Calhoun that would have very serious consequences. It began with Jackson's disapproval of Mrs. Calhoun's part in a social feud that was raging in Washington. Secretary Eaton had married Peggy O'Neale, the attractive and sprightly daughter of a Washington tavern keeper. The wives of some of the cabinet members, led by Mrs. Calhoun, refused to recognize her socially. Jackson, whose own deceased wife had been slandered when he first entered politics, rushed to Mrs. Eaton's defense.

Calhoun's enemies seized this opportunity to discredit him with the President. Jackson had said that he would serve only one term, and it was generally assumed that the South Carolinian would succeed him. Calhoun's enemies dug up and brought to Jackson's attention the fact that Calhoun, as Secretary of War in Monroe's cabinet, had proposed to censure Jackson for his invasion of Florida in 1818. Jackson was highly sensitive about this matter and demanded an explanation, which Calhoun tried to evade with lame excuses. When Calhoun tried to defend himself by publishing several letters relating to the controversy, Jackson broke with his Vice-President, reorganized his cabinet, and excluded Calhoun's friends. The chief beneficiary of the affair was Van Buren, a widower who had no wife to participate in the conspiracy of cabinet wives against Mrs. Eaton. Van Buren emerged as Jackson's heir apparent.

3. THE NULLIFICATION CRISIS, 1830–1833

The Webster-Hayne Debate

Meanwhile, a dramatic debate in the Senate had set the stage for what would soon become the gravest crisis in the history of the nation up to this date. Samuel A. Foot of Connecticut proposed a resolution on December 29, 1829, which suggested the wisdom of restricting the sale of public lands. A lively debate ensued. Southern and western members of Congress attributed the Foot resolution to the selfishness of eastern manufacturers who, they said, wanted to stop migration to the West in order to have plenty of cheap laborers for their factories.

During the debate, Senator Robert Y. Hayne of South Carolina left the subject of public lands to launch a bitter attack against the North in general and against Massachusetts in particular for its selfish policy of sectionalism. In the course of a long speech on January 21, 1830, he set forth, for the first time in the halls of Congress, the compact theory of the Constitution. The states, Hayne insisted, had entered into a compact, or agreement, to create the federal government and had voluntarily surrendered certain powers to it. As the originators of the compact, the states were the proper judges of whether the federal government had gone beyond the powers granted to it or not. Otherwise, he said, liberty for all would be jeopardized. Calhoun, in his *The Exposition and Protest of South Carolina* (see pp. 318–319), had shown the way in which the states could use their authority to nullify laws of Congress that they thought were unconstitutional. Indeed, the Vice-President, presiding over the Senate, nodded in agreement as Hayne spoke.

Daniel Webster of Massachusetts replied to Hayne on January 26–27 in what was perhaps the most powerful speech ever delivered in Congress. Webster defended Massachusetts against the charge of selfish sectionalism. He then proceeded to defend the national government. It was no mere league of states, as Hayne claimed. Not the states, but the people, had created the Union. "It is, sir, the people's Constitution, the people's government, made for the people, made by the people, and answerable to the people." If Congress exceeded its powers, there was a judge created by the Constitution itself—the Supreme Court—to declare a law void. This authority could not be given to a state or group of states. Pennsylvania would annul one law, Alabama another, Virginia a third, and so on. Congress would become a mockery, the Constitution a mere "rope of sand." The Union would fall apart, and the states would return to anarchy. Then, in a magnificent summation, he reminded his listeners that, without the Union, there could be no liberty: "Liberty *and* Union, now and forever, one and inseparable."

Jackson, of course, could have no part in the great debate in the Senate. But a few weeks later an opportunity came for him to show where he stood on the question of the nature of the Union. The South Carolinians in Washington arranged a banquet to celebrate Jefferson's birthday on April 13, 1830. They planned to use the occasion to claim the author of the Kentucky Resolutions as the sponsor of the doctrine put forward by Calhoun and Hayne.

Jackson attended the dinner where, as President, he was called on for the first toast. He lifted his glass, looked Calhoun straight in the eyes, and said: "Our Union—it must be preserved!" The excitement was intense. All the company knew that Jackson's words were a direct challenge to Calhoun. "An order to arrest Calhoun where he sat," wrote one diner, "could not have come with more staggering, blinding force." The Vice-President accepted the challenge as he rose to give the second toast: "The Union—next to our liberty most dear!" Then, after a moment's delay, he added: "May we all remember that it can only be preserved by respecting the rights of the states and by distributing equally the benefits and burdens of the Union."

The issue was clear. For Calhoun, Hayne, and other South Carolinians, the Union threatened to endanger liberty, if not curbed by the higher authority of the states. For Jackson and Webster, the Union was superior to the states and was the supreme guarantor of liberty.

Nullification

Henry Clay pushed a new tariff bill through Congress in the summer of 1832, and Jackson signed it. It removed the crudities from the Tariff of Abominations but still left most duties at a high level. The South Carolina members of Congress reported to their constituents that high protection was now a fixed federal policy and that no relief was to be expected from Washington. Thereupon the people of South Carolina followed Calhoun's plan for nullification and elected a convention to consider resistance to the tariff legislation. The convention met at Columbia in November 1832 and declared the tariff acts of 1828 and 1832 null and void. It forbade South Carolinians to pay duties under these laws after February 1, 1833. At the same time, the convention declared that any attempt by the federal authorities to enforce the tariff laws in South Carolina would be a just cause for the secession of their state from the Union. The governor called for 10,000 volunteers to defend the state. When Union men warned the nullifiers that their course might lead to war, they contemptuously asked these "submission men" whether "the descendants of the heroes of 1776 should be afraid to fight?"

Jackson, who was hardly afraid to fight, answered the nullifiers on December 10 in a ringing proclamation to the people of South Carolina: "I consider, then, the power to annul a law of the United States, assumed by one state, incompatible with the existence of the Union, contradicted expressly by the letter of the Constitution, unauthorized by its spirit, inconsistent with every principle on which it was founded, and destructive of the great object for which it was formed." In another part of this proclamation, Jackson said: "The laws of the United States must be executed. I have no discretionary power on the subject. . . . Those who told you that you might peaceably prevent their execution deceived you. . . . Their object is disunion. But be not deceived by names. Disunion by armed force is *treason*." To the collector of the Port of Charleston, Jackson wrote: "In forty days I will have fifty thousand men in the state of South Carolina to enforce the law." Jackson told a Kentucky congressman that, if South Carolina took one more step, he would try Calhoun for treason and "hang him as high as Haman." Jackson also spoke ominously of other "examples." No one who knew Jackson or who had watched him dispatch mutineers in the army took these words lightly. Calhoun may have recalled Jackson's actions in Florida, particularly his executions of the British traders, Arbuthnot and Ambrister (see p. 303). Senator Thomas Hart Benton of Missouri, who had served under Jackson, remarked loudly in the Senate that "when Jackson speaks of hanging, you can send for the rope."

Civil Strife Averted

The situation at the opening of 1833 was extremely critical. Jackson had just been triumphantly reelected over Henry Clay. He was at the height of his power, and no one doubted that he would make good his threat to put down nullification by force, if necessary. But he acted with great caution to prevent unnecessary bloodshed. By alternating between conciliation at one moment and the threat of force the next, he kept the nullifiers off balance and unsure of his intentions. He exploited every opportunity to prod the nullifiers into abandoning their defiance.

Meanwhile, Calhoun had resigned the vice-presidency to carry his fight for state rights to the floor of the United States Senate. He took the seat vacated by Hayne, who had been elected Governor of South Carolina. But Calhoun was disappointed in the reaction of other states to nullification, particularly the reaction of the other southern states. Alabama's legislature declared that nullification was "unsound in theory and dangerous in practice." Mississippi denounced it as "subversive of the Constitution," and no southern state replied to South Carolina's appeal for cooperation. Clearly, the South rejected nullification as an instrument for the redress of grievances. But if South Carolina had seceded and Jackson had used force to compel submission, their response might have been different.

Calhoun saw that he had gone too far. At heart he loved the Union and had suggested nullification as a safety valve to avoid secession. Now his beloved South Carolina faced the awful prospect of invasion from without and civil war within (there were many Unionists in the state). In his anxiety, Calhoun turned to Henry Clay, the very man who had been most responsible for the tariffs that had driven South Carolina to defy the federal government. It was common enmity to Jackson that united Calhoun and Clay and caused the latter to move for a compromise.

It was a compromise in name only, but it gave South Carolinians an excuse to withdraw from a position in which they found themselves friendless before all the other states. In the bill drawn up by Clay and passed by both houses of Congress, tariff rates were only gradually reduced over a ten-year period. In fact, any real lowering of the schedule would not occur until the final two years. At the end of this ten-year truce, the general level of the tariff would be 20 per cent *ad valorem.* Jackson signed the bill on March 2, 1833; Calhoun, who needed a face-saving device to rescue his state from a bloodbath, pronounced it acceptable. The South Carolina convention quickly repealed the nullification ordinance, but reasserted its alleged constitutional rights at the same time by defiantly nullifying a "Force" bill that had been passed by Congress along with the compromise tariff. This measure had authorized the President "to employ the army and navy of the United States to collect duties in South Carolina." Jackson chose to ignore South Carolina's newest defiance as a means of helping the state to retreat from its embarrassment.

None of the fundamental issues plaguing the nation, such as sectional rivalry between sections, state rights, or the constitutional limits of federal authority was solved by the compromise. What was accomplished through strong executive leadership and a spirit of compromise and forbearance was the avoidance of armed conflict and the dismemberment of the Union. Twenty years later, the doctrines behind nullification would be revived in a sectional struggle far more serious than that over tariff rates.

4. JACKSON AND THE BANK WAR

The Bank War

The second Bank of the United States had prospered greatly since its reorganization in 1819, and especially since Nicholas Biddle of Philadelphia became its president in 1822. The Bank held not only $8 million of the government's money, but $6 million in private deposits as well. Besides the parent bank in Philadelphia, with its marble palace and hundreds of clerks, there were twenty-five branches throughout the Union. Foreigners owned many of its shares. The bank's notes were as good as gold, not only in every part of the United States, but also in all the financial centers of the world. But the bank's most useful function was to regulate the numerous state-chartered banks. It kept their notes and bills at par by refusing to accept those of poor quality.

The bank's charter would not expire until 1836. Hence Biddle was in no hurry to raise the question of a new charter. Although Jackson had openly expressed his dislike for all banks, Biddle hoped that a truce could be arranged with the President, who up to this point had made no moves against the Bank of the United States. But Henry Clay thought that he saw a chance to defeat Jackson on the bank issue in the presidential campaign of 1832. Clay had been unanimously nominated for the presidency by an anti-Jackson group, who called themselves National Republicans, at Baltimore on December 12, 1831. A few months later, he succeeded in getting a bill through Congress for the recharter of the bank. Clay believed that, if Jackson vetoed the bill, he would lose enough votes in the East to cost him the election.

Jackson and a majority of his party (now called the Democratic party) had come to fairly definite views on the banking question: banks and the state and federal governments should be absolutely divorced; the federal government should keep its funds in its own depositories; banks should be forbidden to issue paper money; and gold and silver should be the only circulating medium.

The recharter bill, an anti-Jackson measure to elect Henry Clay President of the United States, was naturally a personal and political challenge to Old Hickory. He went into action when the recharter bill was sent to the White House on July 4, 1832. Six days later he returned the bill to Congress with a veto that, in Biddle's words, "had all the fury of a chained panther biting the bars of his cage." Actually, it was one of the most important state papers in American history. Jackson virtually declared war against eastern financiers and their political spokesmen. He denounced the bank as a private business clothed with so much power by governmental favor as to make it a monopoly. The bank, he said, made the rich richer and the poor poorer. Worse still, the federal government, by its charter, helped the bank to perpetuate this inequity. Moreover, Jackson appealed to sectional passions by declaring that the bank drained money from the West to the East and to England. Webster, Clay, and Biddle were elated. They thought that Jackson had signed his own political death warrant; and they were foolish enough to distribute thousands of copies of the veto message as a campaign document!

Never were politicians more deluded. In the ensuing presidential election in November 1832, Clay won only six states, with a total of forty-nine electoral votes, to 219 for Jackson. William Wirt, the candidate of the first of the third parties in American history, the Anti-Masonic party, carried Vermont (see pp. 385–386).

The Removal of the Deposits

Had it not been for Clay's folly in precipitating the question of the bank's recharter four years before it was necessary, the bank might have weathered Jackson's unfriendliness and remained a steadying influence on the economy. But Jackson, who had been provoked to the battle and had won a decisive victory, became more determined than ever to put an end to "The Monster," as he called the bank. Its charter permitted the Secretary of the Treasury to discontinue placing the government's funds in the bank if he gave satisfactory reasons to Congress for so doing. It was not easy to find a Secretary of the Treasury who would give these reasons. Jackson had to promote one secretary to the State Department and dismiss another before he found, in Roger B. Taney of Maryland, one who would obey his orders.

On October 1, 1833, Taney announced that, after that date, the government would make no more deposits in the bank. Moreover, it would gradually withdraw the money that it had deposited in the bank for the payment of its current expenses. Governmental funds would henceforth be deposited in certain state banks, later called "pet banks" by Jackson's opponents. When Congress met the next month, the Senate declared that Taney's reasons for removing the deposits were "unsatisfactory." It refused to confirm his appointment as Secretary of the Treasury and spread on its minutes a censure of Jackson himself. Actually, the Senate had no constitutional right to censure the President, but was limited to trying him on impeachment charges brought before it by the House. Jackson's champion in the Senate, Thomas Hart Benton of Missouri, finally succeeded, on January 16, 1837—less than two months before Jackson left the White House—in having the offensive resolution expunged from the journal.

But Jackson himself let the Senate feel the full fury of his anger over the censure by sending the upper house a "Protest." It was really written for the American people, and again it was a major state paper. Jackson declared in the "Protest" that the President was "the direct representative of the American people." More than that, he was "elected by the people and responsible to them." In effect, Jackson recast the presidential office. The President was no longer equal with members of the other branches; he was the first among equals. He was the head of the government—the person who determined national policy. Unlike the other two branches, the President was the sole representative of all the people.

Biddle responded to the loss of governmental funds by calling in its loans, thereby wreaking havoc on business. He seemed intent to prove to the entire nation that the bank was indeed a "Monster." But his efforts failed. Upon the loss of the bank's federal charter, Biddle reorganized it under a charter granted by the state of Pennsylvania. Like many state banks, it failed to survive the economic depression that overtook the country in 1837.

Jackson as President

Theodore Roosevelt declared that Presidents were of two types. These were the Jackson-Lincoln type (with whom he classified himself) and the Buchanan-Taft kind. The former asserted their leadership in the name of the American people. The latter yielded to Congress and observed strictly the letter of the Constitution. Jackson was the first modern President. He strengthened the office, redefined its role, and profoundly altered its relationship to the people. He used the executive office for purposes of national leadership. Perhaps no other President has been so completely a master of the situation, in both domestic and foreign policies, as was Jackson in his second term. In diplomacy, he could be both conciliatory and forceful, according to the circumstances. His cautious, conciliatory negotiations with Great Britain won the removal of restrictions on American trade with the British West Indies. The more experienced John Quincy Adams had blundered by *demanding* that the British remove these restrictions. In a controversy with France, Jackson was forceful, almost blustering. He forced the government of King Louis Philippe to pay 23.5 million francs for long-standing claims of American citizens for property seized by Napoleon.

Andrew Jackson at the Hermitage. This painting by Ralph Earl, an artist highly favored by Jackson, is one of the few that exists which shows the Hermitage before it was severely damaged by fire. The primitive angularity of Earl's style dampen his popularity even yet, but his paintings attest to the disciplined, suffering, strong-willed Jackson. The large beaver hat worn in this painting is typical of the time and of Jackson, who used to keep notes and messages in it. (By permission of The Ladies' Hermitage Association)

At home, Jackson swept every opponent and rival out of his path. The aristocratic Biddle had scornfully written: "This worthy President thinks that because he has scalped Indians and imprisoned judges, he is to have his own way with the Bank. He is mistaken." It was Biddle, however, who was mistaken. Henry Clay had sought revenge for his defeat in 1832 by persuading the Senate to reject Taney as Secretary of the Treasury. But two years later, on Marshall's death in 1835, Clay saw Taney raised to the office of Chief Justice of the United States. Calhoun, who was smarting from Jackson's exclusion of his friends from the cabinet, had caused the defeat of Van Buren's nomination as Minister to England. But, in 1833, Calhoun saw that same Van Buren occupy his own former seat as Vice-President and preside over the Senate that had rejected his appointment to London.

From every attack on his policies, Jackson emerged victorious. In the eyes of the common people, he was almost superhuman. "General Jackson may be President for life, if he wishes," wrote William Wirt. But Jackson wanted only to retire to his beloved Hermitage, near Nashville. In the spring of 1835, a convention of his party met at Baltimore and, on his instructions, nominated Van Buren to succeed him.

5. *TOILS AND TROUBLES UNDER VAN BUREN*

The Election of 1836

Meanwhile, Jackson's enemies had formed a coalition against him under the name of "Whigs." In the beginning, the Whigs were held together by no stronger tie than a common dislike of "King Andrew." Several groups came under their banner: National Republicans, such as Clay and Webster, who favored a national bank, tariff protection, and federal aid to internal improvements; state-rights advocates, such as Calhoun and Senator John Tyler of Virginia, who resented Jackson's threats against South Carolina in the nullification controversy; and "Native Americans," who saw a danger in the number of easily naturalized immigrants who flocked to join the Democratic party.

The Whigs in 1836 held no national convention, published no platform, and put up no candidate against Van Buren. Instead, they adopted the favorite-son method of 1824 and let various state legislatures name their candidates in hopes of splitting the electoral vote. Thus the Whigs might prevent Van Buren from winning a majority and throw the choice into the House of Representatives.

But Jackson's influence was too strong. Van Buren carried fifteen states with a clear majority of 170 electoral votes. However, his running mate, Colonel Richard M. Johnson of Kentucky, who claimed to have killed Tecumseh, failed to receive a majority in the Electoral College. Opposition to him arose mainly because he kept a mulatto common-law wife and had two daughters by her. He introduced both daughters to society, and they married white men. So the choice of a Vice-President was, for the only time in American history, the responsibility of the Senate, which selected Johnson on the first ballot. In his inaugural address, Van Buren declared that he would "tread in the footsteps of illustrious men." It could almost be said that Andrew Jackson had been elected for a third term.

The Panic of 1837

Before Van Buren could go very far along the path of his illustrious predecessor, he ran into a storm that overwhelmed his administration and his party. The period of Jackson's second term had been one of reckless inflation, speculation, and overexpansion. Perhaps Jackson's own policies contributed to the speculative extravaganza, although some historians argue that they in no way contributed to the resulting economic panic. The federal government was completely out of debt in 1834, and custom duties were piling up large surpluses in the Treasury. Foreign trade in 1835 for the first time exceeded the figures of the great boom year of 1807. Proceeds from the sale of public lands, which were less than $2 million in 1830, rose to $24 million in 1836. Purchasers, or speculators, often paid for this land in notes of western state banks. Such money had multiplied rapidly since Jackson's attack on the Bank of the United States. Soon the Treasury was overflowing with this unsound currency. Congress made a bad situation worse when, in 1836, it distributed $36 million of the federal surplus to the states. Western states, particularly, were encouraged to

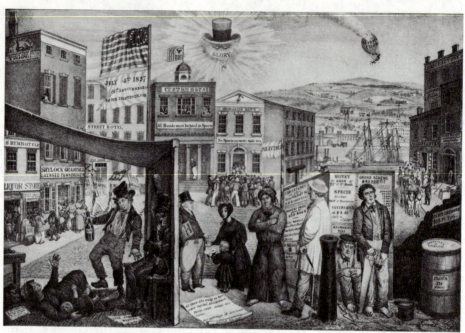

This lithograph by Edward Clay entitled "The Times" clearly reveals conditions during the Panic of 1837. (The Bettmann Archive)

go on with overly ambitious plans for internal improvements. Also, the death of the Bank of the United States opened the way for a reckless expansion of paper money by the 500-odd state-chartered banks. Bank notes in circulation increased from $48 million in 1829 to nearly $150 million in 1837.

Jackson tried to reduce the speculation and use of unsound currency by issuing a "specie circular" on July 11, 1836, which forbade acceptance of anything but gold and silver, called specie, or bank notes based thereon, in payment for public lands. A financial depression, only slightly connected with developments in America, hit Great Britain a few months later. It caused a sudden drop in cotton prices and an equally sudden decline in the export of British capital to the United States. The boom in America collapsed, and the Panic of 1837 was on. The proceeds from land sales dropped to less than $1 million. Building operations ceased. Canals and roads were left half finished in the western wilderness, and thousands of laborers were thrown out of employment.

By the end of May 1837, all banks in the country had suspended specie payment. By September, almost all factories in the eastern states were closed. More than 600 banks failed, including many of the eighty-nine "pet banks." A blight on the wheat crop sent the price of flour up to $12 a barrel. This started riots among hungry laborers, who broke into the warehouses of New York and Philadelphia. A brief recovery gave way to a new collapse in cotton prices, land values, and industrial activity in 1839. For four or five years, the country suffered one of the worst depressions in its history.

Martin Van Buren, the "Little Magician," was not half as bad as the reputation that he earned then and later. He was utterly loyal to Jackson's element in the country. But he was no man to be President in a time of national crisis. Personally, because of his earlier intrigues, he was leader of a faction, not of a party. He continued Jackson's tight-money policy and tried to ride out the storm. His one remedy—a subtreasury system in which the government could deposit its funds—was finally adopted in 1840. It was repealed in 1841 and reinstituted in 1846.

Diplomacy Versus Popularity

Severe economic depression was not the only strain on the country. The Texas problem caused concern, as well as relations with European nations. American settlers in Texas, under Stephen F. Austin and Sam Houston, had revolted against Mexico in 1835 and had won a shaky independence in the following year. Jackson had recognized Texan independence, but he had refused to support Texas' petition for annexation to the United States out of fear of splitting the Democratic party. Van Buren continued Jackson's policy, partly on the ground that the annexation of Texas would lead to war with Mexico. This earned him a reputation for cowardice in the eyes of expansionists.

Finally, Van Buren was accused of the unpardonable sin of yielding to Great Britain. During a Canadian rebellion in 1837, the English had seized and burned the American vessel *Caroline*, which had been illegally transporting men and supplies between New York and Canada on the Niagara River to aid the rebels. Some people on the border, who claimed that an American had been killed on *Caroline*, demanded war. By skillful diplomacy, however, Van Buren prevented trouble. A less courageous President might have seized upon war with either Mexico or Great Britain in order to escape domestic difficulties and gain popularity at home. "Little Van" (like Adams in the XYZ affair) refused to do so.

"Tippecanoe and Tyler Too"

Full of hope and confidence, the Whigs held their national convention in Harrisburg, Pennsylvania, in December 1839. Much to his surprise and chagrin, the Whigs passed over Henry Clay, the founder of the party. Instead, they nominated the aged military hero and political nonentity, General William Henry Harrison, the victor of Tippecanoe. In order to pick up southern state-rights support, the Whigs named Senator Tyler for the vice-presidency. Apart from his state-rights position, Tyler's only bond of sympathy with the Whigs was hatred of Andrew Jackson. The convention published no platform because the party could not agree upon anything except the defeat of Van Buren.

A Democratic newspaperman in Baltimore made a sneering comment on Harrison: "Give him a barrel of hard cider, settle a pension of two thousand dollars a year on him, and my word for it, he will sit for the remainder of his days in his log cabin by the side of a sea-coal fire, studying moral philosophy." The Whigs cleverly converted the sneer into a campaign theme. They praised the simple tastes and virtuous poverty of their candidate (who actually lived in much comfort on a 2,000-acre farm in Ohio). They contrasted Harrison's rugged frontier life to that of the allegedly aristocratic Van Buren, who, they said, enjoyed dainty foods and costly wines in the White House—indifferent to the sufferings that his misrule had brought upon the people.

Log cabins were erected for Whig headquarters, and barrels of hard cider were on tap at Whig rallies all over the country. Men and boys rolled huge balls from town to town to symbolize the majorities that would be rolled up for Harrison. They roared out their campaign songs of "Tippecanoe and Tyler Too," "Van, Van, Is a Used-up Man," and

Farewell, dear Van
You're not our man.
To guide the ship
We'll try old Tip.

It was a wild, rollicking campaign. There was no sober discussion of the tariff, the bank, state rights, and other serious issues of the day. None was necessary. Instead, the Whigs offered only boisterous appeals to emotion and prejudice. "We were sung down, lied down, drunk down," scornfully remarked a Democratic paper. But the voters had not forgotten the years of depression. Harrison and Tyler carried all but seven states, with 234 electoral votes to sixty for Van Buren.

In the excitement of the campaign, the appearance of a new party, which polled only 7,000 votes, passed almost unnoticed. It was the Liberty party, pledged to the extinction of slavery (see p. 353). This was the beginning of a political issue that would eventually shatter the Whig party and send the Democrats down to long-lasting defeat.

SUGGESTED READINGS

The student of Jacksonian America is fortunate in having the contemporary account of the astute French observer, Alexis de Tocqueville, in *Democracy in America*, 2 vols. (1835), many later edns. and translations. The analysis of another visitor to America, Francis J. Grund, *Aristocracy in America* (1839), offers conclusions which differ from Tocqueville's. Other foreigners who recounted their observations of the American scene in the Jacksonian era include Frances Trollope, *Domestic Manners of the Americans* (1832); Michel Chevalier, *Society, Manners and Politics in the United States* (1836); and Harriet Martineau, *Restrospect of Western Travel* (1838).

Three surveys of the period are of special interest: Arthur M. Schlesinger, Jr., *The Age of Jackson* (1945); Edward Pessen, *Jacksonian America: Society, Personality and Politics* (1978); and Glyndon G. Van Deusen, *The Jacksonian Era* (1959). It is perhaps misleading to call Schlesinger's interpretive work a "survey." It is a comprehensive analysis of the meaning of the term "Jacksonian Democracy." Other approaches to this problem can be found in Richard Hofstadter's short but incisive essay in *The American Political Tradition* (1948); John W. Ward, *Andrew Jackson: Symbol of an Age* (1955); Marvin Meyers, *The Jacksonian Persuasion* (1957); Lee

Benson, *The Concept of Jacksonian Democracy: New York as a Test Case* (1961); Edward Pessen, *Riches, Class, and Power Before the Civil War* (1973); and D. T. Miller, *Jacksonian Aristocracy: Class and Democracy in New York, 1830–1860* (1967). Most works concerned with the meaning of "Jacksonian Democracy" deal with the extension of suffrage. The best work on this subject is Chilton Williamson, *American Suffrage from Property to Democracy, 1790–1860* (1960).

There are several biographical studies of Jackson as President. John S. Bassett, *The Life of Andrew Jackson* (1916), is the most scholarly, while Marquis James, *The Life of Andrew Jackson* (1937), is the most readable. Robert V. Remini, *Andrew Jackson* (1966), is brief. Other important biographies for this period are Charles G. Sellers, Jr., *James K. Polk, Jacksonian, 1795–1843* (1957); William N. Chambers, *"Old Bullion" Benton: Senator from the New West* (1956); Thomas P. Govan, *Nicholas Biddle: Nationalist and Public Banker* (1959); Robert V. Remini, *Martin Van Buren and the Making of the Democratic Party* (1959); and Margaret L. Coit, *John C. Calhoun: American Portrait* (1950).

Leonard D. White, *The Jacksonians: A Study in Administrative History, 1829–1861* (1954), is the best introduction to the organization of Jackson's government. The partisan nature of this administration is the subject of Richard P. McCormick, *The Second American Party System: Party Formation in the Jacksonian Era* (1966). Valuable for its explanation of the western influences on the Jacksonian administration is Richard B. Latner, *The Presidency of Andrew Jackson: White House Politics, 1829–1837* (1979).

Robert V. Remini, *Andrew Jackson and the Bank War* (1967), is a comprehensive treatment. For the background of the controversy over the second Bank of the United States, see Bray Hammond, *Banks and Politics in America from the Revolution to the Civil War* (1957). Also useful are Peter Temin, *The Jacksonian Economy* (1969), and J. M. McFaul, *The Politics of Jacksonian Finance* (1972). A good survey of the Jacksonian Indian policy is R. N. Satz, *American Indian Policy in the Jacksonian Era* (1975). A highly controversial but most stimulating study is Michael P. Rogin, *Fathers & Children: Andrew Jackson & the Subjugation of the American Indians* (1975). William W. Freehling, *Prelude to Civil War* (1966), is a detailed study of nullification. The best analysis of the panic and depression of 1837 is still Reginald C. McGrane, *The Panic of 1837* (1924).

On the emergence of the Whig party, the most comprehensive account is E. M. Carroll, *Origins of the Whig Party* (1925). Also useful is G. R. Poage, *Henry Clay and the Whig Party* (1936). Robert G. Gunderson, *The Log-Cabin Campaign* (1957), is a good account of the election of 1840. For the Van Buren presidency see James Curtis, *The Fox at Bay* (1974). Irving H. Bartlett, *Daniel Webster* (1978), is the best biography of that leading Whig.

There are three surveys of the cultural and intellectual climate of the Jacksonian period: Merle Curti, *The Growth of American Thought* (1951); Russel B. Nye, *Society and Culture in America* (1974); and Clement Eaton, *The Mind of the Old South* (1964). On Transcendentalism, the standard account is O. B. Frothingham, *Transcendentalism in New England* (1876). However, see also Herbert W. Schneider, *History of American Philosophy* (1946), and William Hutchinson, *The Transcendentalist Ministers* (1959). On communitarianism, see Arthur Bestor, *Backwoods Utopias: The Sectarian and Owenite Phases of Communitarian Socialism in America: 1663–1829* (1950); Richard W. Leopold, *Robert Dale Owen* (1940); and Raymond Muncy, *Sex and Marriage in Utopian Communities: 19th Century America* (1973). On the Mormons, see Leonard J. Arrington and Davis Bitton, *The Mormon Experience* (1979), which is sympathetic, and Fawn M. Brodie, *No Man Knows My History: The Life of Joseph Smith, the Mormon Prophet* (1945), which is unsympathetic.

The standard survey of American writing during this period is Spiller *et al.*, *Literary History of the United States*, already cited. For more detailed (and splendid) studies, see Van Wyck Brooks, *The Flowering of New England, 1815–1865* (1936), and F. O. Matthiessen, *American Renaissance* (1941).

CHAPTER 13
MANIFEST DESTINY AND
THE MEXICAN WAR

1. FAR NEW HORIZONS

The Moving Frontier

The United States was on the verge of a vast westward territorial expansion near the end of Jackson's presidency. The frontier, roughly speaking, had reached the Mississippi River by 1836; beyond that landmark, portions of Missouri, Arkansas, and Louisiana were already settled, most of them snatched from the Indians. But the pressures of a growing population and the lure of new land, mineral wealth, and the fur trade were propelling the frontier westward at an amazing rate. Within a quarter of a century, Americans would settle the area between the Mississippi River and the Great Plains and surge beyond into the Southwest, California, and the Pacific Northwest.

There was, to be sure, nothing new about Americans moving toward the setting sun. What was new about the expansion of the 1840s and 1850s was the romantic rationalization for the aggressive plunge westward. Although they already possessed one of the richest expanses of territory on the face of the earth, Americans still craved more. As they looked beyond their frontiers to Texas, the Southwest, California, and the Oregon country, they yielded to the long-held notion that it was their destiny to inhabit and govern a continental empire which stretched from coast to coast. John L. O'Sullivan, in an article in *The Democratic Review* in 1845, said that this was the "Manifest Destiny" of the American people, and the phrase was immediately adopted by expansionists of the time.

Americans who did not intend to leave their homes in the East insisted upon their nation's right to settle western land occupied and governed by other people, especially land held by Mexicans, the British, and, of course, Indian tribes. A similar romantic nationalism affected many of the peoples of Europe during this period and was largely responsible for some of the violent efforts to establish nation-states in central, eastern, and southern Europe—for example, in Germany, Italy, and Hungary.

The Far West

At the end of the War of 1812, the trans-Mississippi region of North America consisted of three parts:

1. The Spanish territory, whose boundaries were redefined by the Adams-Onis Treaty of 1819, when the United States acquired Florida. This area included the present states of California, Nevada, Utah, Arizona, New Mexico, Texas, most of Colorado, and parts of Wyoming, Kansas, and Oklahoma.

2. The original territory of the Louisiana Purchase, which stretched from the Mississippi River to the Rockies, and from the forty-ninth parallel in the North to the boundary line of the treaty of 1819 with Spain in the South.

3. The Oregon country, which lay west of the Rockies, north of the forty-second parallel (the present northern boundary of California). This area included present-day British Columbia and the present states of Washington, Oregon, and Idaho, and parts of Montana and Wyoming. By treaties with Great Britain in 1818 and 1827, the United States had agreed to occupy this region on equal terms with the British.

There were only a few thousand white settlers in the Spanish domains. In Oregon, the English Hudson's Bay Company and the American Fur Company competed for furs from their posts on the Columbia River. Pelts went to China in exchange for silk, tea, and precious stones, which then were shipped to the major American cities in the East. American hunters and trappers, who ventured into the wilderness of the upper Missouri River, brought furs to St. Louis. These were floated down the Mississippi River and were destined eventually for European markets.

The "Indian Country"

Nomadic Indians inhabited the enormous Plains region between the Missouri River and the Rockies. Astride swift-moving ponies, they ranged over this extreme stretch of land. They lived primarily off the millions of buffalo that roamed the area. The Plains Indians were physically robust, warlike, and independent, and they resisted the steady intrusion of the whites. The most powerful of these tribes were the Dakota Sioux in the North and the Comanche in the South.

Major Stephen H. Long led an expedition through this area to the headwaters of the Platte and Arkansas rivers in 1819–1820. Back in St. Louis, he reported that the country was "almost wholly unfit for cultivation and of course uninhabitable by a people depending upon agriculture for their subsistence." "The scarcity of wood and water . . . ," he continued, "will prove an insuperable obstacle in the way of settling the country. . . . This region, however, viewed as a frontier, may prove of infinite importance to the United States, inasmuch as it is calculated to serve as a barrier to prevent too great an extension of our population westward."

Major Long's predictions were partially well-founded. In 1850, the entire Plains area contained hardly a thousand white inhabitants. Extensive settlement would not and could not occur until the introduction of the steel plow, the windmill, and barbed wire. They made it possible for farmers to break the tough soil of the Plains, to draw water from deep wells, and to fence in vast spaces (see pp. 516–517). But Long underestimated the daring of American pioneers; they would soon devise new ways to make the arduous journey across the Plains to Oregon and California.

The Santa Fe Trail and Oregon

Exciting news came from the Southwest the year after Long's discouraging report was published. Mexico joined the long list of Spanish-American colonies in the new world which threw off the rule of the mother country and estab-

Population, 1840

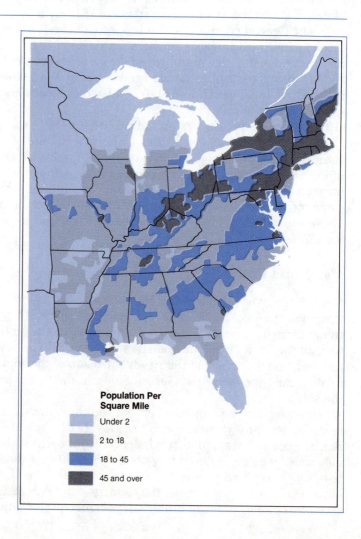

Population Per
Square Mile

Under 2

2 to 18

18 to 45

45 and over

lished independent republics. This meant that the strict Spanish law, which forbade foreigners to trade with her colonies, was at an end for Mexico.

A Missourian, Captain William Becknell, was quick to see the opportunities of trade with Santa Fe. For years, this town had had no outlet except the port of Veracruz, more than a thousand miles to the south in Mexico. In the autumn of 1821, Becknell opened the trade route known as the Santa Fe Trail. It ran from Independence, Missouri, across the broad plains of Kansas and a corner of Texas, to Santa Fe, in what is now New Mexico.

In 1828, a hundred wagons, carrying $100 thousand worth of merchandise, passed over the trail. President Jackson, in 1829, ordered four infantry companies to escort the caravan to the Mexican border, and the danger of Indian attacks abated. The profitable trade over the Santa Fe Trail continued until the eve of the war with Mexico (1846). Today the route of the Atchison, Topeka, & Santa Fe Railroad follows the trail in part.

Meanwhile, hardy explorers were risking the defiles and blizzards of the Rocky Mountains. They met attacks of Indian tribes and toiled through the arid wastes of sand covered with sagebrush and cactus. The pioneers threaded their way through the passes of the Great Divide and followed the courses of the turbulent rivers to the Oregon country. The movement of American settlers into Oregon began in the early 1830s. Four attractions combined to act as a magnet: the magnificent climate and natural resources of the area, excellent harbor facilities, the lure of trade with the Orient, and missionary zeal to convert the native Indians.

Nathaniel J. Wyeth of Massachusetts organized a trading company for the Columbia River Valley in 1831; he led a small group overland to Oregon the next year. His route became famous as the Oregon Trail. It led from Independence, on the Missouri River, up the Platte River and through the South Pass in the Rockies of Wyoming, to Fort Hall (Idaho), then down the Snake River to the Columbia River. A little west of the South Pass the trail forked, the lower branch leading southwestward through the salt plains of the Central Basin and over the Sierras to California.

Over the Oregon Trail went various missionaries. Jason and Daniel Lee, sent out by the Methodist Church, founded a mission on the Willamette River near the present site of Salem, Oregon, in 1834. Dr. Marcus Whitman and Henry H. Spalding, along with their wives, who were the first white women to cross the Rockies, went as representatives of the American Board of Missions in 1836. Father Pierre Jean de Smet, a friendly and learned Jesuit, established a mission in the Bitter Root Valley in 1840.

Dr. Whitman was a tireless worker for the development of Oregon. When there was some danger that the American Board would discontinue its mission there, he made the long trip back to the East during the winter of 1842–1843 to plead for the continuance of the station. Whitman also went to Washington, where he conferred with the Secretary of War and perhaps others. It was this trip that gave rise to a long-accepted legend that Whitman "saved Oregon" from the British by persuading the Washington government to press American claims to the Columbia River Valley.

By 1843, there were about a thousand American settlers in Oregon. Since Congress had made no move to extend jurisdiction over them, they followed the examples of earlier pioneers. They held a convention in an old barn, which belonged to one of the missions, and, on July 5, 1843, adopted a constitution "for the purpose of mutual protection and to secure peace and prosperity among ourselves . . . until such time as the United States of America extend their jurisdiction over us." The next year brought 1,500 new settlers. In the following year more than 3,000 others came. The government at Washington could not much longer neglect the distant "republic" of Oregon.

2. THE PROBLEM OF TEXAS

Americans in Texas

Long before the migrations to Oregon and Utah began, the constant lure of new land was drawing thousands of pioneers from the Mississippi Valley across the Sabine and Red rivers into the Mexican province of Texas. Two events encouraged this southwestward movement. First, Congress adopted an act in 1820 which required payment *in cash*, at $1.25 an acre, for public land, which had previously been sold on credit. This came just at the moment when the hard times caused by the Panic of 1819 were driving people to seek relief by moving to new lands in the West. Second, Mexico actively encouraged the settlement of Americans on Texan land during the 1820s. It granted large tracts to the leaders of the American colony, Moses Austin and his son, Stephen F., on the condition that they and their fellow American settlers recognize Mexican authority.

There were not more than 3,000 American colonists in Texas at the end of Spanish rule over the province. But in the single decade 1821–1830, more than 12,000 Americans emigrated. The distinguished French visitor, Alexis de Tocqueville, saw the trend in 1835. He wrote: "It may be easily foreseen that if Mexico takes no step to check this change, the province of Texas will soon cease to belong to her." The Mexican government had in fact already reversed its policy of generous welcome to American immigrants. By an edict in 1829, it forbade slavery in Mexican territory, although many of the American settlers were slaveholders from Tennessee, Alabama, and Mississippi. In the following year, Mexico prohibited all further immigration into Texas from the United States.

This treatment deeply angered the people of the province of Texas, who were mostly Americans. Texan leaders, encouraged by their American neighbors across the Sabine, met in convention at Washington, Texas, on March 1, 1836, and declared their independence from Mexico. General Antonio López de Santa Anna, then dictator of Mexico, led an army in person to punish the rebellious province.

Santa Anna's army suffered heavy losses during the siege of the Alamo (a mission building in San Antonio). Enraged, Santa Anna finally wiped out this garrison of some 180 Texans. Not even the sick in the hospital ward were spared. A little farther on, at Goliad, the American defenders were massacred after their surrender. On April 21, Santa Anna advanced to the San Jacinto River near the present city of Houston. Here a force of 750 Texas volunteers under General Sam Houston, a veteran of the War of 1812 and an ex-Governor of Tennessee, descended upon Santa Anna. The Texans, vastly outnumbered but thirsty for revenge and aided by superior weapons, routed the entire Mexican army. Santa Anna was captured as he hid in the reeds by the river. The independence of Texas was won. Texans at once adopted a constitution modeled upon the Constitution of the United States and elected Houston as President. The Texan constitution legalized slavery, but slaves could be imported only from the United States. Houston, the legislature, and the people of Texas at once asked for annexation to the United States.

The Problem of Annexation

Many Americans thought that it was a patriotic duty to give legal protection to a province so largely populated by fellow citizens; expansionists believed that it was the "manifest destiny" of the American flag to fly over the territory to the Rio Grande; purchasers of Texan land scrip knew that their investments would be safer under the protection of American law; and southern planters desired the fertile soil of Texas for the extension of their slave-based cotton culture.

John Quincy Adams had offered Mexico $1 million for Texas in 1825. Jackson had raised Adams' offer to $5 million. Had the Texans won the battle of San Jacinto and their independence at any time other than in the spring of 1836, their petition for annexation to the United States would probably have been accepted. But the abolitionist controversy was raging in 1836. It was a presidential year, and Jackson was determined not to endanger the chances of his candidate, Van Buren, by permitting slavery to become an issue. Moreover, the dangers of a war with Mexico were great. Mexico was as firm in refusing to acknowledge Texan independence as she had been in refusing to sell the province.

Just before he left office in 1837, Jackson extended diplomatic recognition to the Republic of Texas. The question of annexation was moot during the administration of Van Buren because he was opposed to the extension of slave territory. Besides, his attention was diverted by the devastating economic depression that began in 1837. Annexation of Texas was not an issue in the presidential election of 1840.

3. *JOHN TYLER AS PRESIDENT*

Tyler Disappoints the Whigs

The great Whig victory of 1840 soon began to look like a defeat. President Harrison caught cold during his inauguration and died a few weeks later. He had served as President for only one month. His one claim to fame as President is that he delivered the longest inaugural address in American history. Vice-President Tyler, who then entered the White House, was a state-rights Virginia Democrat. He would never have been put on the ticket by the Whig leaders if they had dreamed that he would do any more than preside over the Senate.

Henry Clay had expected to dominate the administration, with President Harrison as a sort of figurehead. In fact, Clay had declined Harrison's offer to appoint him Secretary of State because he preferred to remain as his party's leader and spokesman in the Senate. Clay had already drawn up an elaborate legislative program, which he called his "general orders to Congress." It included restoration of the national bank, a higher tariff, and distribution of money from the sale of public lands to the states for internal improvements. In short, Clay, at long last, hoped to achieve his American System in one great burst of legislation.

One Clay measure, the Distribution-Preemption Act of 1841, was mainly the result of long western agitation. It permitted settlers to stake out claims of up to 160 acres of public lands in advance of the sale of the land. When it was put up for sale, they could purchase this preempted land at the minimum price of $1.25 an acre. The act also provided for the distribution of the proceeds from the sale of public lands to the states for internal improvements. The distribution provision was repealed in 1842, but the preemption provision remained a great boon to settlers. It was probably more important in facilitating western settlement than the Homestead Act of 1862, which began a policy of free land grants.

To a degree, then, Clay briefly won federal aid to internal improvements for a period of only a few months. He also obtained passage and Tyler's approval of a tariff bill in 1842 that increased most rates. But Clay's hopes for his most important objective—a third national bank—foundered on the shoals of Tyler's constitutional scruples. Tyler twice vetoed a bank bill. He was thereupon read out of the Whig party, to which he had never really belonged. Angry Whigs called him "His Accidency." Clay resigned from the Senate in disgust in 1842, and all the Whig members of the cabinet, except Secretary of State Daniel Webster, also retired. However, Tyler, who was the first Vice-President to succeed to the presidency, firmly established the principle that a Vice-President who succeeds to the highest office *is* President with all the constitutional authority of the office.

The Webster-Ashburton Treaty

Webster remained at his post mainly because he was then engaged in important diplomatic negotiations with Great Britain. Relations with that country were more strained in 1841 than they had been at any time since the War of 1812. Bitter feelings still remained from the *Caroline* affair. An act of British authorities in the Bahama Islands had also angered southern planters. A shipload of slaves had mutinied on board the brig, *Creole*, killed the captain, overpowered the crew, and brought the brig into Nassau. The British had then set the slaves free. The stream of Americans who were moving into Oregon threatened to sweep away the equal rights of the British there—rights guaranteed by the terms of the treaty of joint occupation. Most important, fighting had broken out between lumbermen in Maine and New Brunswick, Canada, in 1839, in what is called the Aroostook War because it occurred along the Aroostook River. The cause of the dispute was disagreement over the northeastern boundary between the United States and Canada as defined by the Treaty of Paris of 1783.

A change in the British government in 1841 brought George Hamilton-Gordon, Earl of Aberdeen, a friend of the United States, into office as Foreign Secretary. He sent Lord Ashburton, a personal friend of Webster, to Washington in the summer of 1842. In pleasantly informal discussions, the two men settled most of the issues in dispute between their governments in the Webster-Ashburton Treaty. It fixed the northeastern boundary in its present location and divided the 12,000 square miles of territory in dispute almost equally between New Brunswick and Maine. It also provided that the United States and Great Britain would cooperate in suppressing the African slave trade. The Senate gave its consent to ratification on August 20, 1842, by a vote of thirty-nine to nine. With this accomplishment, Webster, who also disliked Tyler, resigned from the cabinet.

The Texas Question Reopened

After Webster's retirement, Tyler for the first time was master of his cabinet, even though he was still a President without a party. Tyler now took up the Texas question in the hope, his enemies charged, of winning reelection in 1844. His new Secretary of State, Abel P. Upshur of Virginia, began negotiations with the Republic of Texas. Upshur was killed early in 1844 by the explosion of a giant cannon, "Peacemaker," aboard *U.S.S. Princeton.* His successor in the State Department was John C. Calhoun of South Carolina, an ardent annexationist who nevertheless was worried about the effect that the addition of Texas would have on sectional animosities.

Meanwhile, the British had been hard at work wooing Texan friendship. An independent Texas republic under British protection could furnish Britain with plentiful supplies of cotton and a market for British manufactures not burdened by the tariff of the United States. Moreover, British antislavery forces, who had already won gradual emancipation in the British West Indies in 1833, hoped to persuade Texas to abolish slavery. Great Britain recognized Texan independence in 1840. Three years later, Britain went so far as to promise a large loan and support to secure Mexican recognition of Texan independence, if Texas would consent to remain an independent republic. The French government, which had recognized Texan independence in 1839, strongly supported British efforts to prevent the annexation of Texas by the United States.

**New States,
1836–1848**

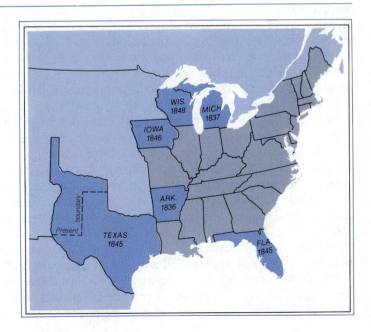

Some Texans were dazzled by the dream of a great new republic in the Southwest, but the overwhelming majority, led by Houston, was still eager for union with the United States. Moreover, Texans desperately needed the protection that only the United States could provide against an attempt by Mexico to reconquer what Mexicans still regarded as their lost province.

In April 1844, Secretary Calhoun, who by now was greatly worried about British intentions, signed a treaty with the Texan Minister in Washington. It provided for the incorporation of Texas, not as a state, but as a territory of the United States. Texas was to surrender her public lands. In return, the United States would assume the Texan public debt to a maximum of $10 million. It was well understood that Texas would remain slave territory. John Quincy Adams wrote in his diary on April 22: "The treaty for the annexation of Texas to this Union was this day sent in to the Senate; and with it went the freedom of the human race."

Adams' gloomy prophecy was somewhat premature. On June 8, the Senate rejected Calhoun's treaty by the decisive vote of thirty-five to sixteen. Only sixteen votes could be found for the treaty in a Senate that contained twenty-six members from southern states — evidence that the plan to annex Texas was not a southern conspiracy to add slave territory to the Union. The chief reason for defeat of the treaty was fear of war with Mexico. The Mexican President, Santa Anna, had formally warned the Washington government on August 28, 1843, that Mexico would consider American annexation of Texas as "equivalent to a declaration of war against the Mexican Republic."

4. MANIFEST DESTINY RAMPANT

The Election of 1844

Even while the Senate debated the Texan treaty, the national conventions were nominating presidential candidates. The Whigs unanimously selected Henry Clay at Baltimore on May 1. At Clay's own request, the platform was silent on the subject of Texan annexation.

The Democrats, reflecting an aggressive fever that was raging over the would be nominated. In fact, three fourths of the Democratic state conventions had instructed their delegates to support him. However, Van Buren had published a letter on April 27 which opposed the annexation of Texas; it turned many southern delegates against him. Van Buren had a majority of the votes on the first ballot, but he could not get the two-thirds vote then (and until 1936) necessary for nomination by a Democratic national convention. On the ninth ballot, the delegates unanimously nominated James K. Polk of Tennessee. Polk was a leading Jacksonian, second only to Van Buren among Old Hickory's lieutenants, but he had not been a candidate for the presidential nomination. He was thus the first example of the "dark horse" in a national convention. (The term was borrowed from the race track. A candidate who unexpectedly won the nomination was likened to a horse who was not expected to win and comes from behind and crosses the finish line first.)

The Democrats, reflecting an aggressive fever that was raging over the Southwest and West, were unashamedly expansionistic. Their platform announced that American title to the whole of the Oregon territory was "clear and unquestionable." The platform insisted that "the reoccupation of Oregon and the reannexation of Texas at the earliest practicable period" were "great American measures." "*Reoccupation*" and "*reannexation*" implied that the United States already owned Oregon and had purchased Texas from Napoleon in 1803. This clever combination of support for Oregon and Texas was intended to win the votes of both Southerners and Westerners for the ticket.

Clay had also published a letter on April 27 (when he thought that Van Buren would be the Democratic candidate), which opposed the annexation of Texas. However, when he found himself running against the annexationist Polk, Clay changed his mind. Now he wrote that he "would be glad to see Texas admitted on fair terms," and that "slavery ought not to affect the question one way or another." This turnabout caused antislavery Whigs in New York and Michigan to switch their votes from Clay to James G. Birney, candidate of the antislavery Liberty party. As a result, Polk carried those two states by narrow margins and won the election.

It was a bitter pill for the brilliant Clay to meet defeat in this, his third, campaign for the presidency, particularly because the election was very close, in spite of the vote in the Electoral College of 170 to 105. Polk's popular plurality was less than 40,000 in a total popular vote of nearly 3,000,000. Polk carried seven northern and western states to Clay's six, and eight southern states to Clay's five. It was the antislavery vote for Birney that defeated Clay. With New York's thirty-six electoral votes alone, the Kentuckian would have won by a margin of seven electoral votes.

The Annexation of Texas

Tyler, ignoring the narrowness of Polk's victory, announced that "a controlling majority of the people and a large majority of the states have declared in favor of immediate annexation." Tyler was still fearful that the British might win Texas as a satellite and was eager for the honor of joining Texas to the United States. He secured the passage of a joint resolution, which required only simple majorities in both houses, for the annexation of Texas to the Union in February 1845. Tyler signed the resolution on March 1, three days before he left office, and immediately sent a messenger to Texas with the offer. Texas was to be admitted as a state on condition that she frame and submit to Congress an acceptable constitution before January 1, 1846. She was to surrender all her public buildings, defenses, ports, and harbors to the United States and retain her public lands and her debts. She was to have jurisdiction over her coastal area for a distance of three leagues (10.5 miles) out to sea. Four additional states might be carved out of her immense area, but only with her consent. Slavery was to be prohibited in the small part of her territory north of 36° 30'.

The people of Texas ratified their new state constitution with fewer than fifty dissenting votes. Congress admitted the new state by large majorities, and Polk signed the act of admission on December 29, 1845.

"Young Hickory"

James K. Polk lacked Clay's oratorical brilliance and Andrew Jackson's ability to inspire personal loyalty and popular affection, but he was not called "Young

Hickory" by his contemporaries for nothing. He had been Jackson's chief spokesman in Congress as Speaker of the House of Representatives. He had also been the leader of the Democratic party in Tennessee and governor of that state. Polk's most notable trait was an absolute determination to achieve his objectives. In addition, he worked incredibly hard; in fact, he literally worked himself to death in the presidency and died only three months after he left the White House.

Long service in Congress well fitted Polk for the leadership of his party. The Democrats had a substantial majority in the House but only a narrow majority in the Senate in the Twenty-ninth Congress, which sat from 1845 to 1847. But his slight majority in the upper house did not prevent Polk from achieving every single feature of his domestic program. It included the Walker Tariff Act of 1846, which reduced the rates imposed by the Whigs in 1842, and the Independent Treasury Act of 1846, which restored the Independent Treasury system that the Whigs had abolished in 1841. Polk also vetoed, in 1846, a generous federal rivers and harbors bill. His veto succeeded, as did almost everything else that he undertook. But it alienated many northwestern Democrats and contributed to the beginning of the division of the Democratic party along sectional lines.

"Fifty-four Forty or Fight!"

Foreign affairs were of course all-engrossing from the beginning of the new administration. Once Texas was safely in the Union, Polk turned to the problem of Oregon. Many times before, the United States had proposed division of the territory along the line of the forty-ninth parallel. This would have given the United States most of the valley of the Columbia River. But the British had refused. Many times, also, the British had suggested the Columbia River as the boundary. The American government, in turn, had refused. Thus the only area in actual dispute lay between the forty-ninth parallel and the Columbia River, that is, the area, roughly speaking, of the present State of Washington.

Nevertheless, Polk, in his first Annual Message to Congress in December 1845, boldly claimed the whole of Oregon up to the boundary of Russian Alaska at 54° 40'. And he urged Congress to permit him to give notice to Great Britain that the United States would end the joint occupation. American rights to *all* of Oregon, he went on, could not be abandoned without "a sacrifice of both national honor and interest." Moreover, Polk revived the now almost forgotten Monroe Doctrine and insisted that the United States would not permit the planting of a future European colony on any part of the North American continent.

Congress gave the necessary authorization in April 1846. A month later, Polk sent formal notice to the British government of the termination of the Anglo-American treaty for joint occupation. There was much excitement in the United States and talk of "fifty-four forty or fight!" But neither Congress nor the President intended to go to war with Great Britain over a difference of five degrees of latitude in the northwestern section of a nearly unoccupied region, to which the United States had only a shaky title at best. This would have been foolhardy on the very threshold of war with Mexico over the annexation of Texas. In fact, the first armed clash occurred between Mexican and

American troops on the Rio Grande on the very day after Congress voted to end the Oregon agreement with Great Britain.

In spite of bold talk, therefore, Polk was ready for a compromise on Oregon. At a hint from the American Minister in London, the British Foreign Office submitted the draft of a treaty dividing Oregon on the forty-ninth parallel from the Rockies to the waters of the Pacific. Polk immediately sent it to the Senate, where consent to ratification was given by a vote of forty-one to fourteen. Expansionists raged at the "cowardice" of a government that marched its troops to the borders of a weak Mexico but retreated from Oregon in the face of a strong Britain. The alienation of many Westerners from the Democratic party also increased ominously.

Negotiations with Mexico

Relations with Mexico had been strained long before Polk came to the White House. The new Mexican republic had been torn by many revolutions, and foreigners had suffered heavy losses. Attempts to obtain payment to Americans for the loss of life and property had been fruitless. Jackson had actually broken off relations with Mexico in 1837 and had threatened to send a warship to Veracruz to enforce American claims. The aid furnished by Americans to secure and defend the independence of Texas did not endear the giant northern country to the Mexicans; nor did stories of Mexican atrocities in Texas please Americans.

Mexico's chief grievance, however, was the actual annexation of Texas to the United States. As late as November 1843, the Mexican Minister at Washington had warned the Secretary of State what would happen if the United States should "commit the unheard-of aggression" of seizing "an integral part of Mexican territory." He would consider his mission at Washington at an end, since his government was "resolved to declare war as soon as it received information of such an act." The Mexican government did not declare war when Tyler signed the resolution for the annexation of Texas, but it broke diplomatic relations with the United States at once.

Polk tried to renew negotiations in the autumn of 1845. He sent John Slidell of Louisiana to Mexico to adjust the long-neglected claims and the Texan boundary. Both Texas and the United States claimed that the Rio Grande River was the southern boundary of Texas. Mexico insisted that the Nueces River, much farther north, was the boundary. Polk, in addition, instructed Slidell to offer Mexico up to $30 million for a part of western Texas still claimed by Mexico, and for the Mexican provinces of New Mexico and California. Polk especially wished to acquire California with its excellent Pacific ports. For decades, Americans had traded with China; now China was being opened to more extensive trade with the West (see p. 415), and Polk and numerous other Americans believed that that trade would be of enormous importance in the future. But such an expanded trade with China demanded Pacific ports, which in turn meant a confrontation with Mexico. While the spirit of aggression pulsed throughout the United States, war fever ran high in Mexico. Candidates for the Mexican presidency assumed postures of defiance. Slidell was refused an audience, and Polk concluded that strong-arm tactics were necessary.

General Zachary Taylor, with 2,000 regular troops, was encamped near Corpus Christi on the Nueces River in the summer of 1845 to protect Texas against a Mexican invasion. News of Slidell's rejection reached Washington on January 12, 1846. On the following day, Polk ordered Taylor to advance to the Rio Grande River. Taylor built a fort opposite the Mexican town of Matamoros, trained his artillery on the town, and blockaded the Rio Grande. The Mexicans ordered him to withdraw to the Nueces River. When he refused, a Mexican detachment crossed the Rio Grande and ambushed an American scouting party. The Mexicans killed or wounded sixteen Americans on April 25, 1846.

5. THE MEXICAN WAR

The Declaration of War and Seizure of California and New Mexico

Polk was determined to force Mexico to recognize American claims in Texas to the Rio Grande River. He was equally determined to acquire New Mexico and California, even if the country had to fight for them. Indeed, he had already sent agents to California to incite an independence movement there, which he

The Mexican War, 1846–1848

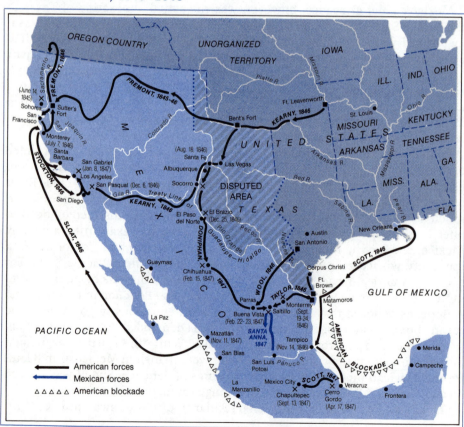

hoped would result in American annexation of the province. Moreover, not long after he heard that the Mexicans had refused to receive Slidell, Polk had begun to draft a message asking for a declaration of war against Mexico.

When he received news of the attack upon Taylor's troops, Polk tore up his first draft and wrote a new one. Now he declared that war already existed "by the act of Mexico herself," in spite of all his efforts to prevent it. What was more, Mexico had "passed the boundary of the United States . . . and shed American blood upon American soil." Polk asked Congress for recognition of the existence of a state of war and for soldiers and money to prosecute it.

On the same day that Polk sent his war message to Congress, May 11, 1846, the House passed bills which declared that a state of war existed between Mexico and the United States. They also authorized the enlistment of 50,000 men and appropriated $10 million for the war effort. The vote in the House was 174 to fourteen. The Senate approved the war resolution by a vote of forty to two on the following day, and Polk signed it on May 13. Except for New England, where the abolitionist spirit was strong, the country responded with enthusiasm to the call for troops. Soon 23,000 volunteers from western and southern states were in arms.

In June 1846, John C. Frémont, a young captain of engineers, was on one of those exploring expeditions in the Far West that won him the name of "Pathfinder." With secret aid from the American consul at Monterey, Frémont's band of frontiersmen set up a Republic of California under the "Bear Flag." When news of the outbreak of the war reached Frémont, he hauled down the Bear Flag and raised the Stars and Stripes. Meanwhile, Colonel Stephen W. Kearny, at Fort Leavenworth, Kansas, had received orders to invade New Mexico. He set out with 1,800 men and toiled over hundreds of miles of arid country. Kearny entered Santa Fe in August. A mixed Mexican and Indian force of 4,000 retreated before him without a show of resistance. Kearny raised the American flag and declared the territory of New Mexico "incorporated into the United States." A few days later, Kearny published a code of laws for the territory. Then he started for California, where he joined Frémont to complete the conquest of that beautiful Mexican province.

Carrying the War to Mexico

General Taylor, meanwhile, had mounted a successful invasion of the northern states of Mexico. Then the Washington government adopted a new plan to end the war. An expedition under General Winfield Scott was to land at Veracruz on the Gulf of Mexico and march directly upon Mexico City. Half of Taylor's army of 10,000 men was detached to Scott.

The Mexican President, Santa Anna, intercepted a letter that revealed how small Taylor's forces had become. He therefore swept northward with an "army of liberation," 20,000 strong, to drive Taylor's reduced forces back across the Rio Grande. Unfortunately for the Mexicans, their weapons were inefficient and most of their officers were even more so. The two armies met on February 22, 1847, near the ranch of Buena Vista. After two days of furious battle, the shattered Mexican army left the field under the shadow of night. Buena Vista was a decisive victory against the largest army that American troops had ever met. It also made Zachary Taylor the next President of the United States.

Meanwhile, Scott's troops had landed at Veracruz on March 9, 1847, and begun their march of 300 miles up through the mountains to the Mexican capital. Santa Anna, with an army of 13,000 men, had hastened back from Buena Vista to oppose Scott's advance. Santa Anna was driven from the heights of Cerro Gordo, on the road to Mexico City, however, by a brilliant flanking movement planned by Colonel Robert E. Lee. Thereafter Santa Anna's army ceased to be a menace; guerrilla bands only occasionally troubled the American troops.

Polk had sent Nicholas Trist, the chief clerk of the State Department, to join Scott as a potential peace negotiator. Trist was to offer peace and money at any moment that Mexico was ready to give up her claims to Texas, New Mexico, and California. Scott reached the outskirts of Mexico City in August and granted an armistice for the discussion of Trist's offer. Not only did the Mexican government refuse to part with its conquered northern provinces, but it also insisted that the United States pay damages for the invasion of its territory. These demands were morally justifiable, perhaps, but hardly realistic for a nation reeling on the brink of total defeat. Trist was ordered home, and the war was resumed.

As he stormed the strong defenses of Mexico City, Scott looked down, as Cortés had done three centuries before, upon the ancient and splendid capital now at his mercy. The Mexican troops withdrew, and the city council sent its surrender to the American headquarters. At dawn on September 14, 1847, troops "decorated with mud and the red stains of battle" entered the gates and raised the American flag above the palace. General Scott mounted the stairway of the "halls of Montezuma" to write his victory dispatch.

The Treaty of Guadalupe Hidalgo

The fall of Mexico City removed Santa Anna and brought to power a government eager for peace. On February 2, 1848, Trist, who had remained in Mexico in spite of his recall, concluded with new Mexican commissioners the Treaty of Guadalupe Hidalgo in which Mexico acknowledged American title to Texas, New Mexico, and California. In return, the United States paid Mexico $15 million and, in addition, assumed claims of its own citizens against Mexico of up to $3.25 million.

Secretary of State James Buchanan and other members of the cabinet wanted to take all or part of Mexico proper. Polk, however, held firmly to the line of the Rio Grande River. In the Senate, the treaty was opposed by expansionists who wanted more territory, antislavery men who wanted no territory, and Whigs who were chagrined that Polk should have completed his program so successfully just before a presidential campaign. The Senate gave its consent to ratification on March 10, 1848, by a vote of thirty-eight to fourteen, only three more votes than the necessary two thirds.

Opposition to the War

The Mexican War had been declared by an almost unanimous Congress, yet it was opposed more bitterly at the time and has been condemned more severely by later historians than any war in American history between the War of 1812 and the Vietnam War. The opposition stemmed partly from the strong moral objection of abolitionists to the acquisition of new territory that might be opened to slavery. Henry David Thoreau, the writer of Concord, Massachusetts, for example, went to jail rather than pay taxes to support a war of aggression. It also stemmed from the political jealousy of the Whigs, including, ironically, southern Whigs and Calhoun. The latter had refused to vote for the war resolution on the ground that it would result in the acquisition of a vast territory in which slavery could never thrive.

The Whigs did not hesitate to use their newspapers and speeches in Congress to encourage Mexican resistance to a war that was being successfully waged by a Democratic administration. Senator Thomas Corwin of Ohio, for example, said that he hoped that the Mexicans would "welcome the American soldiers to hospitable graves." Clay, Webster, and the other "Mexican Whigs" were accused of giving more aid and comfort to the enemy than if they "had arrayed ten thousand Mexicans against Scott." Abraham Lincoln, who served a single term in Congress (1847–1849), introduced "spot resolutions," which challenged Polk to name the spot of American soil on which Mexicans had shed American blood. That much of the Whig opposition to "Mr. Polk's war" may have had a partisan character is suggested by the fact that the Whig party soon chose both victorious Whig generals as presidential candidates—Zachary Taylor in 1848 and Winfield Scott in 1852.

It has to be said that the United States was guilty of gross aggression against Mexico. Many Americans, including Polk, coveted Mexican territory and were determined to obtain it—by force, if necessary. Perhaps the Mexican government would have been wise to accept Polk's original offer for these distant provinces over which it had little control. However, the area did belong legally to Mexico, and Mexico did not want to sell. And the United States did not have a monopoly on proud and nationalistic leaders or citizens. The Mexicans lost California and New Mexico, but the United States paid a heavy price—Mexican hatred of the United States, which persists to the present day. Moreover, the aggression of 1846–1848 tarnished American claims to the moral leadership of the world. Woodrow Wilson said in 1916 that not a day passed that he did not burn with shame at the thought of American aggression against Mexico in 1846–1848. But the biggest price that the United States paid was, as we will see, its own dreadful Civil War.

By fair means or foul, the United States had grown tremendously in four years. With the annexation of Texas (1845), the acquisition of Oregon to the forty-ninth parallel (1846), and the cession of New Mexico and California (1848), the continental boundaries of the United States had reached almost their present limits. A small strip of land south of the Gila River in Arizona and New Mexico was bought from Mexico in 1853 because, reputedly, it offered the best rail route to the Pacific coast. Some critics of the Mexican War regarded the large sum of $10 million paid for this, the so-called Gadsden Purchase, as "conscience money," paid to Mexico for the land that had been seized from her five years before.

6. THE PROBLEM OF SLAVERY IN THE NEW TERRITORIES

The New West

An area larger than either the United States in 1783 or the Louisiana Purchase became part of the United States between 1845 and 1848. The land varied greatly in terrain. Between the black land of Texas and the valleys of California there lay the arid plateaus and majestic canyons of the Rockies and hidden wealth of undiscovered minerals. In Oregon, fine timber and farm lands awaited settlers.

The new region, though thinly populated by white people, was not entirely unknown to Americans. Ever since the Lewis and Clark Expedition, mountain men, trappers, and wagon trains had been converting into roads the Indian trails to Santa Fe, Oregon, and California. Groups of settlers, who put into practice the American belief in self-government, had set up little "republics" on the Columbia and Sacramento rivers and on the Great Salt Lake. They waited for the United States to take them under its protection. In his Annual Message of December 1846, Polk had already urged Congress to make Oregon a territory. Then, with the acquisition of New Mexico and California, he recommended territorial governments for these former Mexican provinces as well.

The Wilmot Proviso and the Election of 1848

The question of slavery in the new territories came before Congress only three months after the Mexican War began, when Polk asked Congress for an appropriation of $2 million in order to open peace talks with Santa Anna. Antislavery congressmen, who knew that the United States would demand territory as a condition of peace with Mexico, persuaded David Wilmot, a Democrat from Pennsylvania, to offer an amendment to what was called the "Two Million Bill." The Wilmot Proviso, as the amendment was called, stated that "neither slavery nor involuntary servitude shall ever exist in any part" of territory that might be acquired in the future by treaty. Several other northern congressmen were ready to introduce similar measures had Wilmot not acted first, so this phase of the conflict over the extension of slavery certainly was inevitable.

The Wilmot Proviso passed the House several times in 1846 and 1847, only to be ignored or rejected by the Senate. It remained before the country, however, as the official demand of northern antislavery groups. Southerners well understood that the northern position would not only check the spread of slavery and the political power of the slave states, but that it also implied that slavery was immoral where it existed in the South, even if nothing could be done about it. This awareness added powerful emotions to the debates.

Southerners, led by Calhoun, denied that Congress had the right to interfere at all with slavery in the territories of the United States. They insisted that the territories were the common property of all the people. Congress had no right to discriminate against the private property (slaves) of Southerners. On the contrary, Congress had the constitutional duty to *protect* slave property in the territories. Slavery could be forbidden only when the territories had achieved statehood.

Between the extremes of the total exclusion of slavery and federal protection of slavery in the territories, there were several possibilities of compromise. The Missouri Compromise line of 36° 30' might be extended to the Pacific coast, or the question of slavery might be left to the settlers of the territories themselves. This last proposition was known as the doctrine of popular sovereignty. It was destined to play an important part in the controversies of the 1850s.

The two major parties in 1848 were more interested in winning the presidential election than in defending abstract theories. Polk refused to run for a second term, and the Democrats nominated Governor Lewis Cass of Michigan, an ardent expansionist who favored the principle of popular sovereignty. He is also said to have been the ugliest person ever to run for the presidency. The Democratic platform defended the Mexican War as "just and necessary." It denied the power of Congress to interfere with the domestic institutions (slavery) of the states. The convention shouted down every attempt to bring up the Wilmot Proviso.

The Whigs, in spite of their opposition to the war, nominated General Taylor, hero of Buena Vista. He was a Louisiana sugar planter and the owner of 300 slaves. Yet he opposed the extreme proslavery doctrine of Calhoun and of his son-in-law, Jefferson Davis of Mississippi. Taylor had had no experience in political affairs and had not even voted for some years. When asked for his opinions on the bank and the tariff, he replied frankly that he had had no time "to investigate" those questions. The Whigs counted on his war record to sweep him into office.

The old issues of bank, tariff, and internal improvements, on which Whigs and Democrats had formerly divided, had faded into the background. The lines of the new struggle over slavery, which cut across both parties, were not yet sharply drawn. Both parties in 1848 angled for votes by avoiding the main issues. The Whigs offered the bait of a Louisiana slaveholder, whose military glory commended him to the free West and North. The Democrats put forward a northern frontiersman, whose views on slavery were not offensive to the South.

Such straddling did not characterize a third party—the Free-Soil party—which was hastily organized and entered the campaign. It forthrightly endorsed the Wilmot Proviso, called for free homesteads to western settlers, and adopted the slogan "Free soil, free speech, free labor, and free men." The Free Soilers nominated former President Van Buren. He took enough votes in New York away from Cass to give its thirty-six electoral votes, and therewith the election itself, to Taylor. Taylor carried seven free states and eight slave states; Cass, eight free states and seven slave states. The electoral vote was 163 to 127; the popular vote was 1,361,000 for Taylor, 1,222,000 for Cass, and 291,000 for Van Buren. The Free Soilers won no state but elected thirteen members to the House of Representatives. They would hold the balance of power between the 112 Democrats and the 105 Whigs in the Thirty-first Congress (1849–1851).

The California Gold Rush

Polk's term ended on March 4, 1849, without any action by Congress for the organization of California and New Mexico. While Congress remained deadlocked over the question of slavery in the Mexican cessions, events on the Pacific coast made immediate congressional action necessary.

A few days before the treaty with Mexico was signed, gold was discovered in the Sacramento Valley of California. As news of the richness of the deposits spread, a wild rush to the gold fields began. Men from every walk of life abandoned their jobs to stake out claims in the "diggings." Thousands came by wagons across the plains and frequently left trails of broken wagons, dead animals, and human bones. Others traveled by sea and endured the discomforts of the six-month voyage around Cape Horn. Still others crossed the disease-ridden Isthmus of Panama to battle like crazy men for a place on the dirty, rickety steamers which went up to San Francisco. The influx in the year 1849 alone increased the population of California from 6,000 to more than 85,000.

The "forty-niners" were largely from the free states of the North. Consequently, when delegates elected by the California settlers met in a convention in September 1849, they drew up a state constitution and excluded slavery by a unanimous vote. Delegates from the South, however, were just as vigorous in opposing slavery as were Northerners, apparently because of hostility to blacks and fear of economic competition from slaves. When Congress met in December 1849, therefore, California was no longer waiting to be organized as a territory. She was asking for admission as a state with a free constitution.

7. THE COMPROMISE OF 1850

Clay's Compromise Proposal

There was no chance now that Congress would heed the new President's plea to "abstain from exciting topics of a sectional character." Northern and southern members had come to Washington determined to have their way on the issue of slavery in the territories. Heated resolutions on the "exciting topic" were introduced in the Senate, where the great triumvirate of Calhoun, Clay, and Webster sat for the last time. Disorder seemed to rule when Clay rose on January 29, 1850, to propose a set of compromise measures called the "Omnibus bill."

The Kentuckian had returned to Washington at seventy-three, after an absence of seven years, racked with the cough of advanced tuberculosis. The Omnibus bill that he presented in the opening speech of the greatest debate ever heard in the halls of Congress consisted of five main proposals:

1. California would be admitted as a free state.

2. Territorial governments would be established in the rest of the Mexican cession (Utah in the North and New Mexico in the South) without restrictions as to slavery.

3. The area of Texas would be reduced from 379,000 to 264,000 square miles. In return, Texas would receive $10 million to pay her public debt contracted before 1845.

4. The slave trade would be prohibited in the District of Columbia, but slavery itself should not be abolished in the district without the consent of Maryland.

5. A new fugitive slave law would be passed to make the recovery of runaway slaves much easier than under the old law of 1793.

Thus, Clay held out the olive branch to both sections. No sacrifice was too great to preserve the Union, he pleaded. Secession could only mean war.

Calhoun was to speak on March 4, but tuberculosis had weakened him so much that he could not take the floor himself. He listened while Senator James Murray Mason of Virginia read his prepared speech for him. Calhoun loved the Union and dreaded the word "secession." But the Union as it now existed, he said, was no longer a guarantee of the liberties of the South. The peace between the sections had already been destroyed by the attacks of the North. The North alone was to blame. The South asked only her plain rights under the Constitution; she had nothing to compromise or concede. It lay with the North to stop all agitation against slavery if the republic was not to be dissolved into warring factions. It was Calhoun's last speech; before the month had ended, he was dead.

Daniel Webster spoke to crowded galleries on March 7. He had gone on record many times as being opposed to the extension of slavery, "irrespective of lines and latitudes." But he loved the Union so much that he supported Clay's compromise at every point in order to save the Union. He said that there was no possibility that slavery would ever actually invade the deserts and plateaus of New Mexico. Of what use, then, was it to insist on the Wilmot Proviso, which the South regarded as a "taunt and a reproach?" As for the abolitionists, they "had produced nothing good or valuable in their operations for twenty years."

Denunciations of Webster as a traitor to the cause of human freedom rang across the North. The Quaker poet, John Greenleaf Whittier, called him "Ichabod" and wrote:

Let not the land once proud of him
Insult him now,
Nor brand with deeper shame his dim,
Dishonored brow.

However, the conservative businessmen of the North, eager for peace and stability, approved Webster's stand and circulated 200,000 copies of his speech. Two other notable speeches followed. William H. Seward, a new Whig senator from New York, appealed to "a higher law" than the Constitution, namely, the law of human freedom. Salmon P. Chase, Democrat of Ohio, denounced the compromise as a cowardly surrender to the South and denied Calhoun's charge that the North was the aggressor.

The Compromise of 1850

The great debate seemed no nearer its end in July than it had been in February. President Taylor, who was much under Seward's influence, would do nothing to hasten passage of the Omnibus bill. But Taylor died from acute gastroenteritis on July 9, 1850, after drinking too much lemonade and eating too many cherries on a hot day. His death brought a champion of compromise, Vice-President Millard Fillmore of New York, to the White House. Senator Stephen A. Douglas, Democrat of Illinois, vigorously took charge of efforts to pass compromise measures, and he succeeded where Clay and Webster had failed. Proposals similar to Clay's were adopted as separate bills and signed by the new President.

It is difficult to say which side profited most by the Compromise of 1850. By the admission of California as a free state, the North and West finally won control of the Senate, where the balance between free and slave states had been maintained for thirty years. Since the admission of Missouri and Maine in 1820–1821, the three slave states of Arkansas (1836), Florida (1845), and Texas (1845) had been balanced by the free states of Michigan (1837), Iowa (1846), and Wisconsin (1848). On the other hand, the new Fugitive Slave Act tacitly acknowledged the right of slaveholders to their human property and put the whole power of the federal government behind private attempts to obtain the return of runaways. The South gained admission for slaveholders into the territories of New Mexico and Utah. However, it was a region into which slavery was never likely to go. On the other side, the slave trade was abolished in the District of Columbia. This relieved antislavery congressmen from the painful necessity of having to view the spectacle of slaves being sold under the shadow of the Capitol.

Apart from the question of the gains to either side, it is altogether probable that the Compromise of 1850 postponed secession and civil war for a decade. At Calhoun's suggestion, a convention of delegates from nine southern states had met at Nashville, Tennessee, in June 1850. A majority of the delegates had declared that Congress had no power to exclude slavery from the territories. Some had denounced compromise of any sort and advised secession. With the passage of the compromise measures, however, the South in general agreed that the "sectional controversy" was finally settled. The status of slavery had now been determined in every square mile from the Atlantic to the Pacific. When Congress met in December 1850, Clay secured the signatures of forty members to a pledge that they would support no man for public office who refused to abide by the Compromise.

Both Parties Support the Compromise

The only chance to prevent the two great national parties from splitting into northern and southern factions was the acceptance of the finality of the Compromise of 1850. The Democrats, in their convention of 1852, pledged to abide by the compromise measures. They nominated Franklin Pierce of New Hampshire, a former congressman and senator and a brigadier general of volunteers during the Mexican War.

The Whigs were in a more difficult situation than the Democrats. Their great founder and leader for two decades, Henry Clay, was on his deathbed when the convention assembled. Daniel Webster had ruined his own chances with the antislavery element in the party by his speech in the Senate of March 7. It was not until the fifty-third ballot that General Winfield Scott, who had not been obliged to take a stand on any issue connected with slavery, won the nomination. The Whigs tried to straddle the slavery question in their platform. They "acquiesced in" the compromise instead of pledging, like the Democrats, to love, honor, and obey it.

But the Whigs failed to repeat the triumphs of 1840 and 1848 with their third military hero. The Whig leaders of the South suspected that Scott leaned toward free-soil principles, and they deserted him. He carried only the four states of Vermont, Massachusetts, Kentucky, and Tennessee, with forty-two electoral votes to 254 for Pierce.

Harmony was the key word of Franklin Pierce's inaugural address on March 4, 1853. The compromise measures of 1850, he said, were "strictly constitutional and to be unhesitatingly carried into effect." He sincerely hoped that no sectional ambition or radical excitement might again "threaten the durability of our institutions or obscure the light of our prosperity." Northerners who hated slavery, however, were not to be quieted by assurances that the compromise was constitutional.

SUGGESTED READINGS

Some of the general works on the West cited in Suggested Readings for Chapter 9 are relevant here. The most comprehensive treatment of westward expansion during this period is Ray A. Billington, *The Far Western Frontier, 1830–1860* (1956). See also Billington's *Westward Expansion: A History of the American Frontier* (1974). John A. Hawgood, *America's Western Frontier: The Exploration and Settlement of the Trans-Mississippi West* (1967), is an excellent study. On the motives for expansion, see Albert K. Weinberg, *Manifest Destiny* (1935), which should be supplemented by Frederick Merk, *Manifest Destiny and Mission in American History: A Reinterpretation* (1963). A stimulating interpretation of the West as an American symbol and myth is found in Henry Nash Smith, *Virgin Land* (1950). For a discussion of the diplomacy of expansion, see Frederick Merk, *The Monroe Doctrine and American Expansionism: 1843–1849* (1966). William H. Goetzmann, *Exploration and Empire: The Explorer and the Scientist in the Winning of the American West* (1966), is an outstanding study.

William C. Binkley, *The Texas Revolution* (1952), is a good account of the American occupation of Texas. R. L. Duffus, *The Santa Fe Trail* (1930), is a popular but useful history of southwestern expansion. Gloria G. Cline, *Exploring the Great Basin* (1963), contains a fine account of the fur trade and the opening of the Far West. The best general account of expansion in the Northwest is Oscar O. Winther, *The Great Northwest* (1947). See also the same author's *The Old Oregon Country: A History of Frontier Trade, Transportation and Travel* (1950). Robert G. Cleland, *From Wilderness to Empire: A History of California, 1542–1900* (1944), is the fullest treatment of American interest in California. The Mormon migration is the subject of Wallace Stegner's excellent *The Gathering of Zion* (1964).

Polk's role in the westward expansion is examined in Charles G. Sellers, *James K. Polk: Continentalist, 1843–1846* (1966). A fascinating account of the crucial year in this expansion is Bernard DeVoto, *The Year of Decision, 1846* (1943). On the annexation of Texas, see J. W. Schmitz, *Texas Statecraft, 1836–1845* (1945); it should be supplemented by David M. Pletcher, *The Diplomacy of Annexation: Texas, Oregon, and the Mexican War* (1973); J. H. Smith, *The Annexation of Texas* (1911); and Eugene C. Barker, *Mexico and Texas* (1928). For an account of the settlement of the Oregon dispute, see Melvin C. Jacobs, *Winning Oregon* (1938). Francis Parkman's classic *The Oregon Trail* (1849) and David Lavender, *Westward Vision: The Story of the Oregon Trail* (1963), make exciting reading. Brief one-volume accounts of the Mexican War include Alfred H. Bill, *Rehearsal for Conflict: The War with Mexico, 1846–1848* (1947); Robert S. Henry, *The Story of the Mexican War* (1950); and Otis A. Singletary, *The Mexican War* (1960). Rodman W. Paul, *California Gold: The Beginning of Mining in the Far West* (1947), and John W. Caughey, *Gold Is the Cornerstone* (1948), deal with the great gold rush.

Two general works contain stimulating analyses of the issues of slavery and territorial expansion in the Compromise of 1850: Allan Nevins, *Ordeal of the Union*, 2 vols. (1947), and Avery O. Craven, *The Growth of Southern Nationalism, 1848–1861* (1953). The most comprehensive study of the Compromise is Holman Hamilton, *Prologue to Conflict: The Crisis and Compromise of 1850* (1964).

Biographies of value to students of this period include Charles B. Going, *David Wilmot, Free-Soiler* (1924); Robert W. Johannsen, *Stephen A. Douglas* (1973); and Holman Hamilton, *Zachary Taylor: Soldier in the White House* (1951).

CHAPTER 14
LIFE IN THE ANTEBELLUM PERIOD

1. MODERNIZING AMERICA: POPULATION AND ECONOMIC GROWTH

A Growing and Changing Population

There was unprecedented demographic and economic growth in the United States between 1820 and 1860. Between these two decades, the population of the United States almost *doubled*. In the decade 1850–1860, alone, the number of Americans increased from 23,200,000 to 31,400,000. That was by far the largest numerical increase in any decade to this time, and it was due primarily to natural increase. Low infant mortality and the large proportion of the population of childbearing age more than offset the gradual decline in the birth *rate* which had begun as early as 1810. (Between 1800 and 1860, the birth rate declined from 55.0 to 41.4 per thousand.)

By the mid-1840s, this growing body of native-born Americans was being augmented by a huge new wave of immigrants. Between 1820 and 1840, the number of immigrants reaching American shores increased gradually from 8,000 to 84,000 a year. Then suddenly it seemed as if nature and politics abroad conspired to change the course of American social history. The net number of immigrants between 1840 and 1860 zoomed to 4,200,000 — a six-fold increase over the previous twenty years! It was a spectacular increase, to be sure, but it was only the beginning of a worldwide migration of peoples to the United States and other parts of the new world that would grow in volume until the outbreak of the First World War.

England, Scotland, and Wales sent 500,000 immigrants during the antebellum era, but the largest number of immigrants came from Ireland. In 1845 and 1846, a blight destroyed that country's potato crop—Ireland's chief food supply—and caused widespread famine. An estimated 1,000,000 men, women, and children died; another million—farm tenants and their families—were evicted from their cottages by landlords in the 1840s and 1850s. For millions of Irish people, emigration offered the only hope of survival. Between 1846 and 1860, 1,500,000 of them braved the perils of the North Atlantic passage to seek a new life in America. Ships which had sailed to Great Britain with American cotton, wheat, and timber in their holds returned with Irish families squeezed into steerage in conditions so filthy and overcrowded as to rival those of the old slavers.

Although the great majority of these Irish immigrants were agricultural laborers, only a few of them had enough money to take up land in the West, as many English, Scotch-Irish, and German farmers had earlier done. Instead, most of the Irish settled in the port cities of the East and Gulf coast and found jobs as servants, day laborers, and, above all, as workers on canals and railroads. They were openly discriminated against in hiring and shunned because they were Catholics, and they became America's first ghetto dwellers. But in their ethnic clusters within cities from Boston to New Orleans they recreated something of the communal life-style of the old sod and established a vital Irish-American culture.

Famine and political unrest also swept over western Europe in the late 1840s. Pulled by the prospect of material improvement and pushed by famine, overcrowding, and political-military uncertainties (including the threat of military conscription), many western and central Europeans joined the Irish

The United States at Midcentury

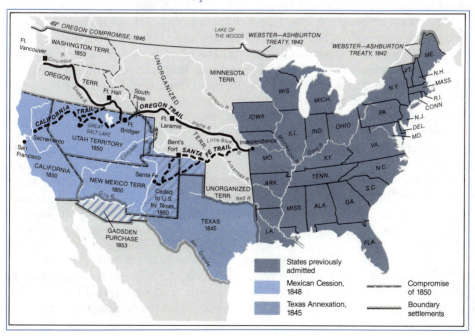

in the trek to the United States. Most numerous among them were the Germans, over 1,000,000 of whom came to the United States between 1848 and 1860. A few thousand of these Germans—the famous "forty-eighters"—were liberal intellectuals who fled as political refugees after the abortive German revolution of 1848. Most, however, were peasants and artisans in search of a new home in which to practice their vocations. The Germans for the most part were not quite so poor as the Irish and moved in large numbers to the growing cities of the West and to the northwestern frontier.

This flood of immigrants reduced substantially the chronic labor shortage of the northeastern and northwestern states. Many of them, particularly the Irish, had no marketable skills to offer, but they soon found their way into construction and service jobs and into semiskilled positions in the new textile mills. A much smaller but strategically important group of immigrants brought with them knowledge of scores of industrial processes and formed the backbone of America's skilled manufacturing work force, particularly before the 1840s. But equally important in their impact upon American industrial development were the thousands of skilled craftsmen in the textile, mining, and metal-making and metalworking industries, who found a ready market for their skills.

Two Frontiers for an Expanding Population

The rapid population increase produced two very significant changes in the spatial distribution of the American people. The first was the rapid growth of cities and towns. All in all, the proportion of urban dwellers increased, roughly, from 15 per cent to 20 per cent during the 1850s. More significant than the over-all increase in urbanization was its differing impact in the various regions of the country. The South remained overwhelmingly rural, but the urban population grew dramatically in the Northeast. In 1860, over one half of the people of Massachusetts and Rhode Island lived in cities and towns.

Old cities like New York and Philadelphia flourished, while new western metropolises sprang up. For example, Chicago and St. Louis battled each other for the commercial supremacy of the Midwest. And for every real metropolis, there were hundreds of towns which aspired to that status. Amid the flurry of land speculation and commercial development, who could predict which village or crossroads would become the next Chicago?

The population increase of the 1850s, however, had its most significant impact in building new pressures on the western frontier. Farmers in search of cheap land continued to pour into Iowa and Wisconsin, which had been admitted to statehood in 1846 and 1848, respectively. From these states they moved into Minnesota in such numbers that this territory became a state in 1858. Settlers also moved southward and westward—into the Nebraska Territory along the western bank of the Missouri River and into eastern Kansas. Kansas' admission to the Union was delayed only by the controversy over slavery.

Further to the south, the stream of Americans pouring into Texas almost trebled that state's population during the 1850s. And, every year, the wagon trains rolled westward across the plains, deserts, and mountains toward new far western agricultural frontiers. California was admitted to the Union in

1850; Oregon, in 1859. California's population increased from 93,000 in 1850 to 380,000 in 1860. The glamour of the gold rush obscured the fact that most settlers moved to California in search of farm land, not precious metals.

Farming in the Antebellum Period

The rapid settlement of western lands in the 1850s demonstrated the continuing importance of agriculture in the American economy. Farming was both a means of livelihood and a way of life for most Americans, even though the proportion of Americans who made their living from the soil declined from about 90 per cent in Washington's day to 60 per cent in the 1850s. The great majority of American farmers lived on family-sized farms and worked their own land with family help. This was especially true in the West, where liberal governmental policies made it easy to acquire land. In this region, farms averaged about 200 acres in the 1850s. Family farms were also prevalent in the South, despite the spread of the plantation system. Cotton and corn — the South's principal crops — could be grown profitably on small holdings as well as large. In this section about 80 per cent of the people were yeoman farmers — that is, small farmers who owned and tilled their own land.

In the antebellum period, many American farmers worked very much like their colonial forebears, and, for that matter, not much differently from farmers in Roman times. With only primitive plows that did little more than scratch the earth, they relied mainly on the hoe. Small farmers were so limited by crude technology, slow and expensive transportation, and a scarcity of hired labor that few of them existed above the subsistence level.

However, American agriculture, particularly in the North and West, was changing dramatically by the 1850s. Better and cheaper transportation was the key. The introduction of steamboats on western waterways after the War of 1812, the completion of the Erie Canal in 1825 and other major canals soon thereafter, and the building of railroads from eastern seaports into the West in the 1840s and 1850s, caused a virtual revolution in agriculture. Transportation costs dropped by as much as 90 per cent for western farmers, who now had access to lucrative new markets. Many eastern farmers, unable to compete with the cheaper grains and meat from the fertile western prairies, turned to raising sheep, dairying, growing fruit, and truck farming.

In the West, another revolution was under way, one which largely replaced manpower with horse-powered machinery. On the rich prairies of Indiana, Illinois, Missouri, Iowa, and Kansas the newly acquired access to markets made large-scale commercial agriculture feasible, if only the limitations of technology and manpower could be overcome. The tough prairie sod would not yield to iron plowshares and wooden moldboards. Harvesting the crops was a severe bottleneck for farmers with only primitive hand tools and a shortage of seasonal hired labor. One man with the traditional sickle could harvest only one half to three fourths of an acre of wheat a day. The hand cradle, introduced early in the nineteenth century, increased an individual's harvesting capacity to only two or three acres a day.

John Deere, in 1837, invented a steel plow that could slice through the prairie sod; it was in general use by the 1850s. Equally important was the wheat reaper, invented by Obed Hussey in 1833 and Cyrus H. McCormick in 1834, but not marketed on a large scale until the 1840s. By 1860, more than 100,000 reapers were in use in the West. Our hard-pressed wheat farmer, using the self-raking reaper, could now harvest ten to twelve acres a day.

Use of these technological innovations was largely restricted to the West, where chronic labor shortages stimulated the development of labor-saving machinery. In the Deep South, for reasons embedded in the economics of plantation slavery, the value of farm implements produced during the 1850s actually declined. In the West, by contrast, mechanization spurred the expansion of agriculture and at the same time stimulated the growth of manufacturing. The rise of Cyrus H. McCormick's farm-implement empire in Chicago was only one manifestation of the interaction between the modernization of western agriculture and the growth of manufacturing.

The Growth of Manufactures

The United States took its first significant steps toward industrialization in the two decades before the Civil War. Once the economy had recovered from the Panic of 1837, the rate of economic growth spurted upward. In part because economic statistics before 1840 are unreliable, scholars are still debating about whether this spurt represented a one-time "takeoff" into modernization or was merely one of several bursts of growth in the half century after 1790. Be that as it may, the growth which began around 1840 involved substantial increases in the manufacturing sector of the economy. The fraction of the total work force engaged in manufacturing increased from 13.9 per cent to 18.5 per cent between 1840 and 1860, while the manufacturing share of the total value added by commodity output grew from 17 per cent to 32 per cent in roughly the same period.

Behind these figures lie some of the fundamental features of America's impending shift toward industrialization. The 1,300,000 workers in industry in 1860 included skilled artisans lured from town and countryside in America and a substantial cadre of trained industrial workers who had migrated from Europe. The latter group also included a large number of unskilled and semi-skilled workers—the vanguard of an army of machine tenders who would man America's industrial system in years to come. The increase in value added by manufacturing, which outdistanced the proportional growth of the numbers of workers in industry, demonstrated that manufacturing was leading the economy's increase in productivity and would, in the years to come, be the most important factor in America's economic growth.

The significance of the 1840s and 1850s in America's industrial development can be seen, not only in statistics and upward-moving lines on a graph, but also in technological and organizational innovations which set the stage for full-scale industrialization after the Civil War. The United States borrowed technologies from England and adapted them to its own particular resources. The opening of large anthracite coal fields in eastern Pennsylvania in the 1830s made available, for the first time, a vast and inexpensive supply of coal. Anthracite was quickly applied to the metal-making and metalworking industries, and with dramatic results. By the 1850s, coal had replaced the more expensive charcoal and wood as the principal source of heat in the iron industry, and domestic iron manufacturing was flourishing. Readily available coal and iron stimulated machine making of various kinds. The 1850s witnessed the large-scale production of farm implements and sewing machines. Machine making depended, in a limited way, upon the technology of interchangeable parts, developed earlier in gun making. The factory system of production, formerly restricted to the textile industry, now spread to metalworking and other industries. The resulting demand for specialized machinery quickly created an American machine-tool industry. Coal not only transformed the heat-using industries, such as metal making, but also fueled the revolution in steam power. Here again, Americans borrowed and adapted British technology, both for transportation and manufacturing. Steamboats and, later, railroads quickly transformed inland transportation, and steam power more gradually supplanted waterpower in manufacturing, increased the productive capacity of manufacturing plants, and made possible the decentralization of plants away from the limited waterpower sites.

The beginnings of an industrial revolution involved not only innovations in the use of materials, but also advances in the organization of work. The factory system involved the subdivision of tasks as well as the use of specialized tools. By 1860, the factory system, at least in rudimentary form, had appeared in wood- and metalworking and in the manufacture of shoes, paper, glass, and textiles and in distilling. The continuous flow of goods through the production process—another hallmark of modern manufacturing—was beginning to appear in some industries, particularly food processing and operations involving liquids.

The increased speed and volume of production which this coal-powered, factory-based system of manufacturing generated required more complex and systematic forms of management than had previously been needed. Several industries, led by the railroads, began to develop the centralized, management-dominated pattern of business organization which would become another hallmark of modern industrialization.

Despite these dramatic changes, American industrialization still remained in its formative stages. Most manufacturing in the 1850s involved the processing of raw materials from farms and forests. For example, the milling of grain and lumbering stood first and third in order of importance in manufacturing in 1860; the second place was held by the textile industry. The technological and organizational innovations remained unfinished. For example, most "interchangeable" parts required some hand machining and hand filing until late in the nineteenth century. Furthermore, the modern, multi-unit organizational systems pioneered by the railroads in the 1850s were not adopted in most industries until much later.

Even in its early stages, manufacturing was centered in the Northeast. Although the South and West shared in the growth of manufacturing during the 1850s, the outlines of a regional specialization were clearly emerging in which the Northeast dominated the manufacturing sector of the economy, with the South and West leading in staple-crop production. By 1860, the Northeast was turning out two thirds of the nation's manufactured goods. Scholars have noted this regional specialization and have previously argued that the economic growth of the antebellum period was spurred by interregional trade among western foodstuffs, southern cotton, and eastern manufactured goods. However, there is now considerable evidence to suggest that the particular growth patterns of each region owed more to developments within the region than to interregional trade.

Revolutions in Transportation and Communication

As we have already noted, much of the economic expansion of the decades preceding the Civil War depended upon the development of cheap and efficient transportation systems. It would have done an Illinois farmer little good to raise a surplus of wheat and corn if he could not ship this surplus to eastern or European markets. It would profit the eastern manufacturer little to find sources of raw materials and to expand production unless he could sell his products cheaply in Illinois or Minnesota.

Promoters in New York, Pennsylvania, and Maryland had tried to build canals to tap western markets after the War of 1812. Maryland completed the Chesapeake and Ohio Canal to Cumberland, and Pennsylvania nearly completed the Pennsylvania Portage and Canal System between Philadelphia and Pittsburgh. But only New York really succeeded, with the completion of the Erie Canal which linked New York with the Great Lakes in 1825. Canal building came to a virtual halt in the East in the late 1830s. In the West, however, it continued apace until the late 1850s. Various canals afforded cheap internal waterways for what is now the Middle West. By the middle of the 1850s, products valued at nearly $600 million were being shipped on the Great Lakes alone. The tide of western commerce had already turned away from New Orleans toward New York.

Meanwhile, the railroads had already begun to change the face of America. It did not happen all at once. There was first a long period, from about 1800 to 1826, of experimentation in Great Britain and the United States with steam-powered locomotives running on fixed rails. The first line to begin actual operation in the United States was the Baltimore and Ohio, which ran trains over thirteen miles of track in 1830. Construction was painfully slow, and, even by 1840, only 3,328 miles of track had been laid, mainly in the Northeast and South. The 1840s saw the first substantial progress in construction and the vindication of the railroad as a serious competitor of canals. By 1850, more than 9,000 miles of track had been laid in the East and South.

Thus the foundations were securely laid, and a phenomenal craze for railroad construction swept the country in the 1850s. By the end of the decade, over 30,000 miles of track were in operation—9,500 miles in the Northeast, 10,050 in the South, and 11,100 in the West. Perhaps more important than the amount of track laid was the fact that, by 1860, four consolidated lines linked the Great Lakes region, Chicago, and even parts of the trans-Mississippi West securely to eastern ports. These railroads were the Erie, the New York Central, the Pennsylvania, and the Baltimore and Ohio.

Also binding the country together and speeding economic expansion was the electric telegraph, invented by Samuel F. B. Morse in 1840 and put into commercial use in 1844. By 1861, some 50,000 miles of telegraph wire sped news and business messages over the United States from New York to San Francisco. Meanwhile, in the Far West, the Pony Express had carried mail between Missouri and California at the then incredible speed of ten days! When the Pacific Telegraph Company completed its line to San Francisco, the Pony Express was all but driven out of business by a device that sent messages between the Atlantic and Pacific coasts in a few minutes.

The railroad and telegraph networks, which bound much of the nation together by the time of the Civil War, provided the fast, dependable, and rela-

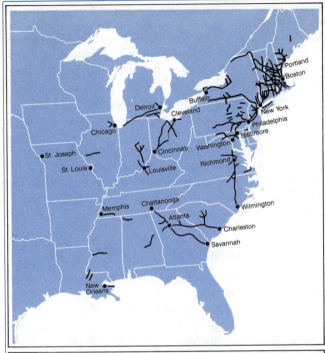

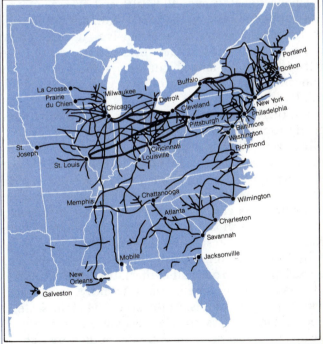

Railroads, 1850–1860

tively inexpensive transportation and communication which were essential for development of modern commercial agriculture and manufacturing. The railroad and telegraph companies were also the first firms which had to coordinate the activities of far-flung and technically complex operating units. The organizational solutions which they pioneered involved large staffs of full-time managers and became the prototype of modern corporate structures. Furthermore, the building of the railroad and telegraph lines directly stimulated American industry by creating a seemingly insatiable demand for American-made metal products.

The impact of the revolution in transportation and communication extended beyond the economic sphere. By connecting the nation's "island communities" with ribbons of iron rail and copper wire, they began to expand the boundaries of community life, and, as we shall see, to alter the very meaning of community in America.

A Land of Opportunity?

The over-all upsurge in wealth and economic development between 1820 and 1860 is abundantly clear, however one measures such things. But what of *individual* improvement and opportunity? Was this, indeed, the age of opportunity for the common man? The factual answers to these questions, as best we can reconstruct them, are more complex than popular legend would have it.

Unquestionably, *over-all* wealth and *average* income rose substantially during this period. And by the 1850s, ordinary Americans had available to them a wide range of relatively inexpensive—if fairly crude—consumer goods and tools, manufactured in the United States and marketed through commercial networks which fanned out across the country. Furthermore, there were enough genuine success stories to give some credibility to the rags-to-riches folklore.

But there was another side to the story. Blacks, both slave and free, were virtually excluded from this new prosperity, as were most Indians, many of whom were being forcibly removed from their ancestral lands. All women and certain immigrant groups, most notably the Irish, confronted systematic discrimination in employment. Even if we restrict our view to white males, there is strong evidence that wealth and the opportunity to acquire it were becoming less easily accessible, and that it was during this period that extremes of wealth and poverty began to emerge. The gap between the rich and the poor was greatest in the growing cities.

By 1860, according to the best estimates, 5 per cent of American families owned more than one half of the nation's wealth. And, despite individual cases of personal achievement, most wealthy people had been born with silver spoons in their mouths. At the other end of the scale, there clustered a growing body of propertyless, transient people, whose prospects for advancement were negligible. In between the extremes of the very rich and very poor, the range of opportunity available to most persons was modest. For every "common man" who rose to wealth and power, there were countless thousands of them who could look forward, at best, to moving up one step or two on the occupational ladder and to accumulating enough property and savings to ward off destitution in their old age.

Given this disparity between the optimistic individualism of the age and the limited opportunities actually available to most persons, one might wonder why so few Americans developed any significant class consciousness. To be sure, economic and social conflict abounded, particularly in the mushrooming industrial centers, but in fact the industrializing process in America did not engender the pervasive class conflict which it gave rise to in Europe.

Observers of this seeming contradiction, both then and now, have applied to it an analogy which was, at least metaphorically, appropriate to the age of industrialization. Society, they argued, was like a steam boiler to which heat was being applied. Unless the boiler (society) was fitted with some sort of "safety valve," it would eventually explode into revolution. The "safety valve," some argued, was the frontier, where there was abundant free or cheap land. To be sure, the westward migration reached mammoth proportions during this era, but, even by the 1850s, the cost and experience required to take up farming in the West negated it as a means of escape for most eastern industrial workers.

Recently, some scholars have identified another possible "safety valve" for nineteenth-century social unrest—the potential for both geographical and occupational mobility. By examining individual household records from the decennial censuses, scholars have determined that as many as one third of American families moved from one community to another from decade to decade. Similar research has shown that wage earners who did stay in one place tended to advance, at least slightly, on the occupational ladder. Do these findings prove the existence of a social "safety valve" which prevented a revolutionary explosion in nineteenth-century America? Not necessarily. Much of the geographical mobility resulted from the frequent layoffs which were a regular part of early industrialism. Many of the persons who moved, it now seems, were a kind of floating underclass, always on the move in search of better opportunity, but seldom finding it. In contrast, the "persisters," who put down roots in one place, may well have been the ones who were predisposed toward success.

Generally speaking, industrialization was accompanied by higher standards of living *for all classes of workers*, the skilled and the unskilled alike. That fact, along with the existence of the undeniable *possibility* of individual advancement no doubt softened the social and psychological impact of industrialization and the social stratification which accompanied it. And, as one student of industrial work has noted, by the time that such potentially divisive conditions had arisen, the movement for political democracy had given the vast majority of adult white males a sense of participation in community and national affairs. Finally, by the 1840s and 1850s, public attention was being increasingly focused on the sectional conflict revolving around the issue of slavery. Social tensions which might otherwise have turned inward could now be directed toward an external threat to liberty.

However, there were significant developments in the organization of labor during the antebellum period. There had long been local societies of printers, cordwainers (shoemakers), and other skilled craftsmen in American towns and cities. In the late 1820s, these societies, still organized along individual craft lines, began to restrict membership to journeymen, in recognition of a growing conflict of interest between practicing artisans and the entrepreneurial master craftsmen. These societies demanded higher wages, better working conditions, and shorter hours (a reduction from thirteen to ten hours per day). The journeymen and even some industrial workers—such as the women textile workers at

Lowell, Massachusetts—were not afraid to use the strike as a weapon to achieve their objectives. In the 1830s, the high demand for the services of skilled craftsmen and the relative shortage of industrial labor gave workers considerable bargaining power.

Although the group consciousness of skilled workers revolved around a particular trade, the early labor movement also moved toward cooperation among members of the various crafts to achieve more general goals. In 1827, journeymen from sixteen different crafts in Philadelphia banded together in a "union of the trades." Similar city-wide trades unions were established elsewhere during the 1830s.

Some unionists also supported broad-gauged social reform by joining the Working Men's parties which sprang up in various cities between 1828 and the early 1830s. These local political organizations of workers and reformers were, in the American political context, genuinely radical. They espoused, not only the ten-hour day and free public education, but also various socialistic communitarian schemes. These local Working Men's parties could not hope to compete on a large scale with the more broadly based political coalitions which were then taking shape, but they did represent a brief fusion of "bread-and-butter" unionism and political social reform—a fusion which would reappear in later farm and labor organizations. However, the Working Men's parties proved to be ephemeral, and even the journeymen's societies and trades unions suffered catastrophic reversals in the depression which began in 1837.

2. SOCIAL INSTITUTIONS IN A MODERNIZING AGE

Patterns of Community Life

Americans during the antebellum period faced the frightening prospect of reconstructing a stable social order in a world in which many of the familiar moorings of society were being swept away. The restless, acquisitive spirit of the age, romantic celebration of individual freedom, accelerating velocity of commerce and industry, and linking of towns and cities by new forms of transportation and communication—all these combined to transform the meaning of community and the terms of social relationships. However, they transformed but did not destroy. The family, the church, and the face-to-face community of neighbors and kin all survived and were joined by new forms of social organizations.

It might seem that, in an age of individualism and modernization, the bonds of community would be strained to the breaking point. Certainly the closely knit American community, as idealized in the colonial New England town, was subject to severe strains. Even so, for most Americans living in the 1830s and 1840s, the relationships which gave life meaning were still largely bound up in the daily and seasonal rhythms of local communities. What was beginning to change after the 1820s was the *balance* between the local, personal, and face-to-face ties of community, on the one hand and, on the other hand, relationships which were translocal, impersonal, and abstract—such as involvement in national or regional political parties, commercial networks, and professional organizations. This shifting balance—along with the persistence of a localistic orientation—can be seen explicitly in several different kinds of communities.

The transformation of community life was nowhere more striking than in the towns and villages which were touched directly by the transportation revolution. One such was Kingston, New York, situated in the Hudson River Valley between Albany and New York City. Kingston had been a sleepy agricultural village before the opening of the Delaware and Hudson Canal in 1828. The new canal put Kingston athwart a major transportation artery and transformed it into a small commercial city. By 1850, its population had swollen to include a large cluster of wage earners, many of them Catholic immigrants. The city not only grew larger; it also became more spatially diverse, with bustling commercial and wharf areas set apart from residential districts, which were themselves beginning to divide along class and ethnic lines. Yet Kingstonians were bound together by a shared cycle of community activities (social affairs in the icy winter, a return to harder work when spring thawed the canal) and by community organizations such as lodges, militia companies, baseball clubs, temperance and Bible societies, and churches. To be sure, membership in the various groups was self-selective, but, collectively, those organizations helped to define community on a personal and face-to-face basis for the city's residents.

A similar pattern of community life could be seen in the manufacturing centers which were evolving from preindustrial clusters of artisans. Lynn, Massachusetts, had been a center of shoemaking long before the industrial revolution. At first, journeymen shoemakers worked under the supervision of master

"Trial by Jury." The informality of the rural courtroom is clearly evident in this 1849 painting by A. Wighe. (Museum of Art, Rhode Island School of Design; Gift of Edith Jackson Green and Ellis Jackson)

craftsmen in homes scattered around the countryside. As production for commercial markets increased around the turn of the nineteenth century, shoemaking became more centralized under the entrepreneurs. Then, in the 1850s and 1860s, modern factories, which utilized the new sewing machine, began to dominate the shoemaking trade. Centralization and expansion of shoe manufacturing had transformed social relations among the men and women who worked at the trade and had created an industrial city. The transition from independent artisan to employee to factory worker engendered a tradition of class consciousness which earned Lynn a lasting reputation as a center of labor radicalism. The growing militancy of Lynn's shoe workers, a student of that subject has concluded, was grounded in the artisans' republican visions of community, older than the industrial revolution, which took concrete form in a succession of community-based organizations such as the Journeyman and Cordwainer's Society and the Knights of St. Crispin. In Lynn, as in Kingston, community life persisted, in altered form, amidst the great upheaval of modernization.

Even in new towns built specifically in response to the manufacturing, commercial, and agricultural needs of antebellum America, we can see this same persistence of community. On the midwestern frontier, "community" might seemingly refer to nothing more than adjacent tracts of land held together only by the wishful thinking of land speculators. Jacksonville, Illinois, was founded ("laid out" is the more descriptive term) in 1825 as part of the rectangular farming settlements then edging across the western prairies. It rapidly became a flourishing agricultural market center, although not the state capital or the "Athens of the West," as its boosters hoped. By the 1850s, booming Jacksonville had acquired the same kind of ethnically and economically stratified population as Kingston. Furthermore, its population, like that of many western towns, was incredibly transient. Only 27 per cent of the families living there in 1850 could be found again in the Census of 1860! And, yet, the boosterism of local promoters engendered pride in the town. The same kind of social organizations which were to be found in Kingston had created on the Illinois prairie what the town's historian has called a "voluntary community."

These patterns of community life would not be typical of American society much beyond 1860. The shape of the future could be seen in the eight American cities which, by 1860, had populations exceeding 150,000. By then, the takeoff in urban growth was gathering steam because fired by immigration and by the general expansion of commerce and industry.

American cities by 1860 had the high population density and the hum of activity which characterize modern urban life, but they *looked* very different from the cities of today. There were no skyscrapers in 1860, and most commercial and manufacturing establishments were rather modest in size. The scale was such that church steeples and the masts of sailing ships riding at anchor could still dominate the skyline. Another difference was the conglomeration of commercial and residential buildings. It was not unusual to find factories, shops, and homes of all kinds jumbled together within a few blocks. Indeed, in an era before urban public transportation, such mixing was essential. A modern observer would also be amazed at the residential mingling of ethnic groups and persons in various economic strata. To be sure, one could see the beginnings of residential segregation, but such was the exception rather than the rule.

Although the rich and poor might live near each other in the burgeoning cities, the urban areas were becoming increasingly stratified between the haves and the have-nots—more so than in the country as a whole. This kind of social stratification was doubly disturbing to many persons because it reflected a reversal of trends in the post-Revolutionary era, when there had been an increase in the power and prestige of artisans and workers in the cities. Not surprisingly, American cities were racked by collective violence in the antebellum period. There were riots between Protestants and Catholics, the native born and immigrants, and the rich and the poor. New York alone had eight major riots between 1834 and 1871.

America's major cities, as big and as stratified as they had become, could no longer be considered communities in the traditional sense, but they did *contain* communities of the kind found in Kingston, Lynn, and Jacksonville. The proliferation of these "voluntary communities" in the villages, towns, and cities across the land gave Americans familiar frames of references in an age of kaleidoscopic change.

Family, School, and Asylum: Shaping American Character

The transformation of community life was coupled with substantial changes in that basic building block of communities—the family. The commercial and industrial revolutions reduced the family's significance as an economic unit by shifting the locus of production from the home to the shop and then to the factory. As large numbers of children became less of an economic asset, family size began to decline. The narrowing of family functions was accompanied by a paradoxical shift in the family's role in shaping character. On the one hand, the popular literature of the day placed increasing emphasis on nurturing and socializing children within the home. Many persons saw the family as a haven within the rough, male-dominated society whose aggressive, individualistic tendencies were to be offset by the gentle nurture of women. The "cult of domesticity"—a redefinition of women's social role which focused on their ministrations within the family circle—had its origin in this redefinition of the family's social role.

Ironically, in the changed social and economic environment of antebellum America, the family could no longer bear as much of the responsibility for socializing the young and caring for the aged, infirm, and deviant as it had in the past. Formal institutions outside the home now took on greater significance in educating and caring for those groups.

The modern public-school movement, which began in the 1830s, grew out of concerns about the necessity to transmit social values in an unstable age and to produce an educated citizenry in an age of universal manhood suffrage. Educational reform paralleled the great movements to extend the franchise and reform American society. Educational reformers argued that the ability to read about and understand the problems of the day was the basis of responsible citizenship.

There had been free or almost free schools in various colonies and states since the seventeenth century. But no state had attempted to provide systematically for the education of all its children before the 1830s. Before this date, schools had sought only to prepare a small minority for academies and colleges.

The modern public-school movement began in Massachusetts under the leadership of Horace Mann, who was appointed secretary of the first state Board of Education in 1837. The next two decades saw the rise of a number of educational crusaders in other states. Like Mann, they planted schools, built teachers' colleges, and laid the solid foundations for the education of the masses. By the 1850s the movement was in full swing throughout the country. All the eastern and older western states had full-fledged public-school systems, and there was a substantial beginning in the South under the leadership of Calvin H. Wiley of North Carolina.

The results could be clearly seen by 1860. No state did much more than try to provide a common free elementary education by this date. Even so, about 60 per cent of all white children between five and nineteen years of age were enrolled in some kind of school. Public high schools were still rare in the antebellum period. There were only 300 free high schools in the nation, most of them in large towns and cities, as compared to some 6,000 private academies.

Colleges and universities were still primarily concerned to educate students in the classical curriculum. The number of institutions of higher learning grew

The lack of individual desks for students and the obvious assembling of different age groups into one room is clearly shown in this picture of a New England classroom by C. Bosworth. (Courtesy of the Massachusetts Historical Society)

rapidly in the 1840s and 1850s; in 1860 they totaled 467, with an enrollment of 56,000 students. Perhaps the most significant developments in higher education, after the founding and spread of state universities (see pp. 264–265), were the beginnings of coeducation at Oberlin College in 1837 and the founding of the first colleges for women—Mount Holyoke in Massachusetts and Wesleyan College in Georgia—in the 1830s.

The public-education movement was motivated by the twin beliefs that, with a proper environment and training, young people could be guided toward responsible adulthood, and that, in the absence of such nurture, the republic would soon be threatened with chaos. The same double-edged beliefs led to the establishment of institutions to deal with individuals deemed by society to be deviant or dependent. During the 1820s and following decades, state after state constructed large and elaborate penitentiaries, asylums for the insane and orphaned, and almshouses. All were hailed as agents of social betterment. They were intended to rehabilitate rather than merely to punish the criminal and remove the deviant and dependent from society.

Rehabilitation was possible, advocates of the penitentiary system proclaimed, but the methods required were drastic. Prisoners were to be separated from each other and from the outside world, both by architectural design and by elaborate regulations, which prohibited conversation and, in some cases, even outlawed congregating for meals, work, and exercise. To offset the lax and corrupt social environment, which presumably had created criminality, the penitentiaries imposed on inmates a strict daily regimen, which included mandatory labor and demanded of them strict adherence to the rules. This incredible discipline was rigorously enforced in some of the pioneering penitentiaries, notably in New York and Pennsylvania. But, elsewhere, practice did not always match the ideal. And, by the 1850s, even in the "better" prisons, the reformers' dreams were giving way to the grim realities of overcrowding and lax enforcement of the rules.

In the 1830s, however, penal reformers pushed for the application of the penitentiary model to institutions for the insane, debtors, and orphaned and wayward children. Penal reformers even argued that the well-ordered penitentiary was an appropriate model for the nation's burgeoning factories and schools. The enthusiastic chaplain of the Ohio penitentiary went so far as to proclaim: "Never shall we see the triumph of peace, of right, or Christianity, until the daily habits of mankind shall undergo a thorough revolution." How to achieve that aim? "Could we all be put on prison fare, for the space of two or three generations, the world ultimately would be the better for it." Such talk may seem to us more appropriate from candidates for admission to a mental or penal institution than from a proponent of their establishment. However, the chaplain's words, like the great stone penitentiaries and asylums which dotted the countryside after the 1820s, stand as monuments to the hopes and the fears of social reformers in antebellum America.

Revivalism and Reform

These same hopes and fears continued to spur the second Great Awakening which had begun in the late 1790s (see pp. 265–267). Two developments in the 1820s and 1830s caused a shift in the style and direction of American revivalism. First, revivalism was institutionalized in something like its modern form and brought into the mainstream of urban life. Second, revivalism was linked to social reform movements.

During the first Great Awakening, and even in the early phases of the second, revival of religion was perceived as an unpredictable occurrence, one caused entirely by the mysterious workings of the Holy Spirit. However, the doctrine of Arminianism, or of the freedom of the will, which, in the individualistic age of Jackson was sweeping away the vestiges of Calvinistic predestinarianism, might reasonably lead to the conclusion that human action could render revivals predictable and even necessary. This conclusion was stated baldly in 1835 by Charles Grandison Finney, the most successful revivalist of his day and the father of modern revivalism. As Finney put it: "Revival is not a miracle, nor dependent on a miracle in any sense. It is a purely philosophical [scientific] result of the use of the constituent means."

That may sound like a hypocritical manipulation of human emotions, but such was not Finney's meaning. He believed that each individual had the freedom to choose salvation, and that, if the proper methods were applied to facilitate that choice, then salvation would necessarily occur. Finney's methods, called "new measures" by his critics, included the use of protracted religious meetings which might last for a week or more; emotional prayer meetings, including prayers by women; direct, colloquial speech, such as calling sinners by name and urging them to repent; and the use of an "anxious bench" for persons who evidenced signs of being troubled about their souls.

The proof of the effectiveness of Finney's new measures was the number of his converts. He was the first of the successful traveling evangelists who combined careful planning, personal magnetism, and an entertaining style to win huge numbers of converts. Finney had been reared in the "burned-over district" of western New York, which at the time of his youth was being swept by wave after wave of religious enthusiasm. Finney was trained as a lawyer, but he gave up a promising legal career to become a traveling evangelist after an intense religious experience in 1821. In the 1820s, his revival meetings in the towns along the Erie Canal brought him national attention; in 1832, he was called to New York, where he conducted similar campaigns and presided over the Chatham Street Chapel. Finney's flamboyant style and disdain for systematic theology aroused opposition, not only from old-line Calvinists, but also from moderate revivalists like Lyman Beecher and Nathaniel W. Taylor. However, the success of Finney and others like him was so great, and they were so in tune with the temper of the age, that they ultimately prevailed and made their brand of revivalism the standard form of evangelical Protestantism for the balance of the nineteenth century.

Finney's optimism about the possibilities for human salvation was not confined to the cure of souls. It extended to the cure of society as well. Finney was an ardent champion of temperance, Sabbatarianism, and the abolition of slavery. In this regard, he typified the connection between revivalism and social reform which occurred in the North and West in the 1820s and 1830s. We have already seen how revivalism gave birth to a host of voluntary associations intended to spread the Gospel and reform society. In the 1820s and 1830s, this religious impulse for doing good took a rather more "secular" turn and included crusades to promote abstinence from alcohol, abolish slavery, and achieve equality for women. All of these movements, and many more besides, shared with revivalism a concern for lifting individuals from bondage of one sort or another. The humanitarian reformers believed that moral suasion could change society; however, they also came to understand the utility of the coercive power of the state.

The temperance reformers were remarkably successful in changing the social habits of many Americans and also in providing a model for organizing humanitarian reform. Americans had a serious drinking problem in the early years of the nineteenth century. As technological innovations in distilling made hard liquor readily and cheaply available, consumption increased dramatically in the United States and in England. According to one recent estimate, the annual per capita consumption of pure alcohol had reached about seven gallons by 1810; by 1830, it stood at ten gallons. Even if these figures are on the generous side, Americans, without question, drank much more in the 1830s than at any time before or since in their history.

Genteel reformers had launched a crusade against hard liquor (the poor man's drink) as early as the 1780s, but their efforts had not been particularly successful. However, when reformers began to link temperance to revivalism in the 1820s, the tide began to turn. In 1826, Justin Edwards established the American Society for the Promotion of Temperance. It began to use the techniques of the revivalists, with the single objective of extracting from individuals a pledge of total abstinence from the use of hard liquor. By the mid-1830s, 1,250,000 people had signed the pledge. By 1850, before prohibition laws began to appear in the states, per capita consumption had dropped to 2.1 gallons a year.

The linkage between temperance and evangelical Protestantism was the crucial factor in the success of the temperance movement. Abstinence from liquor (and eventually from beer and wine) became a preeminent expression of the ethical behavior expected of evangelical Protestants. And beyond that, it symbolized the kind of self-discipline which was supposed to characterize the life-style of progressive, middle-class Americans. Abstinence from alcohol, or at the least the appearance thereof, rapidly became a social necessity in mid-nineteenth century America.

The temperance movement took a more radical turn after 1837. The strictures against liquor were expanded to include beer and wine. Many Protestant denominations even discontinued use of sacramental wine in communion services. Then came demands for legal coercion. Maine adopted the first state-wide prohibition law in 1851, and other states followed suit.

The shift toward legal prohibition of all beverage alcohol reflected, among other things, a growing cultural cleavage between native-born Protestants and Catholic immigrants, particularly from Ireland and Germany, for whom the use of alcohol was as important an expression of cultural identity as was abstinence for many evangelical Protestants. Prohibition would remain a lively political issue at the local and state level throughout the nineteenth century and would sometimes attract as much attention as contests for high office. From zealous social reform to the symbol of cultural cleavage: such was the history of the temperance movement.

The army of temperance advocates in mid-nineteenth century included a great host of women, as did abolitionism and other reform movements. Out of the interlocking network of reform movements there emerged in the 1840s a genuinely radical crusade designed to end the particular form of bondage which was the lot of women in America. Given the long-standing history of the subordination of women, why did a vigorous women's movement occur at this particular time?

As we have said, the early years of the nineteenth century witnessed an increased emphasis on domesticity and the "cult of true womanhood." Women should be pious, pure, submissive, and domestic. This redefinition of the role of women in many respects represented a narrowing of the part that they were to play in society. However, two qualifications need to be made with regard to the impact of this redefinition. First, it applied primarily to upper- and middle-class women. Slave women, working-class women, and women on farms and the frontier continued to participate fully in the commercial economy. Even among the middle and upper classes, some women did work for which they were paid or managed property of their own, despite legal restrictions on property holding by females. Middle-class women were recruited as teachers in the new public schools, and the daughters of middle-class New England families flocked to the new textile mills, where they constituted a majority of the work force until mid-century. Second, even among women who were largely confined to the "female sphere" of home, church, and benevolent society, there were serious and successful efforts to redefine that sphere so as to give them a base from which to participate more fully in society. For example, women's missionary societies and women's branches of the various reform movements provided many women with their first opportunities to share their own feelings and ideas with others. The temperance movement, in particular, provided women not only with the means to share their experiences but to do something about them. Women were without legal remedies to protect themselves and their children from financial and physical abuse by a drunken spouse, and the temperance movement gave them a socially acceptable course of action. And, finally, the new public schools provided many women with greater educational opportunities—albeit still limited—than earlier generations had enjoyed.

For many women, the companionship of the church parlor and meeting hall were rewarding in themselves. For others, however, these outposts of the woman's sphere were way stations to a new world. Sarah Grimké of South Carolina, for example, discovered, while she worked to free the slaves, that women themselves faced a kind of slavery in which their legal rights were severely limited and their opportunities for advancement were circumscribed on the basis of sex. Women in the abolitionist and temperance movements—among them Susan B. Anthony—found that, even among the company of social reformers, they faced discrimination from males who either rejected the notion of female equality or were reluctant to disturb popular sensibilities concerning women's participation in public affairs. Women, for instance, were often not allowed to speak before, or even to be seated among, the male delegates to abolitionist and temperance conventions.

In 1848, more than 300 women and men who were veterans of various reforming crusades gathered in Seneca Falls, New York, the home of Elizabeth Cady Stanton, for a meeting to consider the status of women. They adopted a "Declaration of Sentiments," drafted by Stanton and modeled on the Declaration of Independence. It declared that "all men and women are created equal" and listed the particular grievances of women against a male-dominated society. These included the lack of the right to vote and hold property and discrimination in employment and education. The movement for women's

Elizabeth Cady Stanton, a well-educated, graceful writer and orator for women's rights, became conscious of the restrictions on women from an early age while observing her father's law practice. When she married a prominent abolitionist in 1840, she insisted that the word "obey" be dropped from the wedding vows. One of the most radical feminists of her time, Stanton took a bold stand not only on the woman question, but on abolition, religion, divorce, and birth control. (Historical Pictures Service, Inc., Chicago)

rights, of which the Seneca Falls meeting was only one manifestation, addressed itself to a number of fundamental questions, which included, not only the issues that the conference at Seneca Falls highlighted, but also to even more basic issues concerning the family and relationships between men and women. The women's movement was potentially the most thoroughly radical of the antebellum social crusades, but the issues which it addressed were so deeply embedded in the culture that it had even less chance to achieve its goals in the short run than the movement to abolish slavery.

Cultural Conflict and the Politics of Fear

We have noted at several points the nagging fears of social disorder and threats to liberty which tempered the optimism of antebellum America. These fears were linked to differences of class and also to ethnic and cultural differences. In an age of widespread participation in politics, it is not surprising that such conflicts should find political expression. In fact, two of the most virulent episodes of cultural conflict—the anti-Masonic and nativist movements—jolted the American political system at the beginning and end of an era dominated by the Whig and Democratic parties.

The period of Whig-Democratic competition, which was at its peak between 1840 and 1853, marked the rise of mass participation in political parties, complete with much of the pageantry and pyrotechnics which characterize modern politics. Although Whigs and Democrats sidestepped the most controversial national issues and concentrated on winning the presidency, both perceived political parties to be legitimate instrumentalities to express the will of "the people." That view of the political process was not limited to the major parties. Movements of social protest, which typically began with an enthusiastic concentration on a single issue, were transformed into political parties for the purpose of translating popular zeal into the election of sympathetic men to public office. They are conventionally characterized as minor parties, but they did, in fact, often tip the balance of power and even challenged the major parties.

Such was the case with the Anti-Masonic party in 1827–1834 and the American or Know-Nothing party in 1854–1855—two groups born of convictions that conspiracies were afoot which threatened to undermine the republic. Of the two, the Anti-Masonic party is probably less comprehensible to modern Americans. In the early nineteenth century, many people believed that Freemasonry, a secret society which numbered some of the nation's most notable men among its members, was a threat to American liberty.

Anti-Masonry began as a social movement in the "burned-over district." The catalyst for the movement was the disappearance (and presumed murder) in 1826 of one William Morgan, an ex-Mason, who had threatened to reveal the secrets of the order. The crusade which followed was based on the fear that Freemasonry was intent on manipulating the government and public affairs to the benefit of its well-to-do members and on promoting values antithetical to evangelical Protestantism. The movement was spurred by the revivalism then sweeping the area and by antiurban and egalitarian sentiments among the common people. The movement also provided a convenient rallying point in New York politics for opponents of Martin Van Buren. Politicians, such as Thurlow Weed and William H. Seward, latched on to the movement and helped to transform it into a political party which contested for elections, not only in New York, but in other northeastern states as well. For a brief time, the party actually dominated state governments in Pennsylvania and Vermont and had considerable strength elsewhere. As it spread, the Anti-Masonic party became a rallying point for opponents of the party of Andrew Jackson. Despite its leaders' efforts to broaden its popular base, the party was too much a single-issue party to create a national political coalition. By 1834, the popular excitement about Freemasonry had slackened, and the party which it spawned had been largely absorbed by the new Whig party.

The Anti-Masonic movement revealed that the enthusiasm of the revivals, coupled with underlying fears about elitist conspiracies against the liberties of the common people, could be translated into a powerful political force. The Anti-Masonic movement also revealed the vulnerability of such movements to manipulation by self-interested politicians. The party's presidential candidate in 1832, William Wirt of Maryland (who was nominated by the nation's first presidential nominating convention), had been a Mason and had opposed the attacks on Freemasonry almost until the Anti-Masonic party offered him its nomination. Wirt, like other politicians, saw the party as a convenient vehicle to oppose the Jacksonians.

The politics of fear showed itself most virulently in the outburst of nativism which culminated in the Know-Nothing party of the 1850s. This time the purported conspirator against liberty and Protestantism was the Pope. The nativism of the 1850s was both anti-Catholic and antiimmigrant (i.e., anti-Irish). It coincided with the large wave of Irish immigration, with a sharp recession which racked the economy in 1854–1855, and with an outburst of anti-Catholicism in England. Many native-born Americans regarded the Irish Catholics as the scum of the earth and competitors for scarce jobs. Many native-born Americans also detested the Roman Catholicism of the Irish. Like their colonial ancestors, many native-born Americans thought that the Roman Catholic hierarchy was plotting to undermine Protestantism, destroy democracy, and establish the temporal power of the Pope in the United States.

Anti-Catholic and antiimmigrant sentiments were interjected into politics in the 1850s in a particularly powerful way. Political nativism, prohibitionism, and the renewed sectional controversy shattered the balance between the Whigs and Democrats, which had remained remarkably stable for more than a decade. The nucleus of nativistic politics was a secret society called the Order of the Star-Spangled Banner, founded in 1849. When asked about the organization, its members supposedly responded "I know nothing," hence the popular name, "Know-Nothing." The new party, organized as the American party in 1854 (there had been earlier state parties), swept across the political landscape like a prairie fire. It actually gained control of state governments in much of New England and effectively replaced the Whigs as the major opponent of the Democrats in states all the way from California to the Deep South.

For a brief moment, political nativism eclipsed the nascent Republican party and seemed destined to become a national power. However, the Know-Nothings' popular base of support was narrow, and, even though the party could win impressive victories on the state and local levels, it could not assemble a broad political coalition, either in the nation as a whole (as the Whigs had done) or in one section of the country (as the Republicans were about to do). In 1856, when the sectional crisis radically changed the political situation, the Know-Nothing party began to fade from view and was quickly gone. However, the ethnic and cultural divisions which had brought it into being did not disappear, and would, in conjunction with related economic cleavages, remain a powerful force in American social and political life for decades to come. For the moment, however, these differences would be submerged in a different kind of conflict, to which we now turn.

3. THE SOUTHERN PLANTATION, SLAVERY, AND THE "OTHER SOUTH"

The Southern Plantation and Slavery

The plantation was an industrial unit in which capital was invested in land and labor for the production of staple crops at a profit. The owner-manager was the planter, who, along with his wife, had responsibility, not merely for business operations, but also for the welfare of the labor force as well. By the late antebellum period, a planter usually had to own at least twenty slaves before he could operate profitably, although there were many exceptions; farms with as few as one or two slaves earned profits. Only with a labor force of about twenty slaves, however, could the planter afford to hire an overseer to manage routine operations, effect an efficient division of labor among the slaves, and purchase machinery.

From romantic historical novels we often get a picture of an antebellum South dotted with huge plantations. In this picture, there is always a stately columned mansion, with whitewashed slave quarters to the rear of the "big house." There are servants galore, beautiful girls and dashing young men, a goateed colonel on the front porch drinking a mint julep, and hundreds of slaves singing in the cottonfields!

The picture, it is almost needless to add, is greatly overdrawn. Actually, as late as 1860, after a considerable expansion of the plantation area, there were only about 46,000 plantations with twenty slaves or more in the entire South. These, moreover, were heavily concentrated in a fertile area called the Black Belt. (The term here refers to that area of heaviest concentration of plantations and slaves, not to the particular area in Alabama and Mississippi sometimes called the Black Belt because of the color of its soil.) The life of the planter was as burdensome as any other isolated farmer's. The 2,312 planters who owned 100 slaves or more in 1860 might have had time and money for gaiety and leisure. But for the great majority of planters and their wives, who owned far fewer slaves and acres, the responsibilities of crop management and daily supervision of the blacks left little time for the pleasures of a carefree life.

Plantations varied in size, organization, and operation, but there were five major types in the antebellum period:

1. *The tobacco plantations.* As we have seen, the plantation system originated in eastern Maryland, Virginia, and North Carolina in connection with the growing of tobacco. The most important later development in tobacco production was its spread, along with the plantation system and slavery, into Kentucky, Tennessee, and Missouri in the nineteenth century. By the 1850s, about 15 per cent of the slaves engaged in agriculture were employed on tobacco plantations.

2. *The rice plantations.* Rice was grown in the antebellum period only in the coastal areas of North Carolina, South Carolina, Georgia, and along the Mississippi River in southern Louisiana. Rice plantations required large capital investments. They were, therefore, large in size and relatively few in number, and they employed only about 5 per cent of the slaves engaged in agriculture.

3. *The sugar plantations.* These were concentrated entirely (except for a tiny area in eastern Texas) in Louisiana and employed 6 per cent of the agricultural slave labor force in the 1850s. Because they not only grew sugar cane but also refined it into crude sugar, they combined manufacturing with agriculture and required a huge outlay of capital. In 1853, for example, there were a total of 1,481 sugar plantations in Louisiana. Capital invested in the 222 largest ones ran from $150 thousand to $350 thousand each. Even the smallest sugar planter had an investment of $40 thousand.

4. *The hemp plantations.* Limited to small parts of Kentucky, and to a larger area in northwestern Missouri, the hemp plantations were fewest in number and employed only 2.5 per cent of the slaves engaged in agriculture in the 1850s.

5. *The cotton plantations.* These employed nearly two thirds of the agricultural slave labor force and stretched from North Carolina to Texas. It was cotton that gave the plantation system and slavery a new lease on life at the end of the eighteenth century. At that time, it seemed as if both institutions were doomed to early extinction. However, the spread of the cotton kingdom after the War of 1812 into Alabama, Mississippi, Arkansas, Louisiana, and Texas fastened slavery firmly upon the South.

Although they were relatively few in number, the 46,000 large plantations were the dynamic and productive units in the southern agricultural economy.

BLACK BONDAGE

The high level of African civilization was evident in the city like Timbuctoo, a great city of the Songhai during the 15th and 16th centuries. This city served as an important trading conduit between the Moslem North and sub-Sahara Africa. The engraving here represents the impression of the first European traveler to reach this destination and return. (From Réné Caillié, Travels through Central Africa to Timbuctoo, *vol. 2. By permission of Frank Cass & Co. Ltd., London.)*

OF THE KINGDOME OF MELLI [At the beginning of the slave trade with Europe]

In this kingdome there is a large and ample village containing to the number of sixe thousand or mo families, and called Melli, whereof the whole kingdome is so named. And here the king hath his place of residence. The region it selfe yeeldeth great abundance of corne, flesh, and cotton. Heere are many artificers and merchants in all places: and yet the king honourably entertaineth all strangers. The inhabitants are rich, and have plentie of wares. Heere are great store of temples, priests, and professours, which professours read their lectures onely in the temples, bicause they have no colleges at all. The people of this region excell all other Negroes in witte, civilitie, and industry.

From The History and Description of Africa and the Notable Things Therein Contained, *by Leo Africanus, 1526.*

The king of Dahomey leading his female warriors into battle. (From A. Dalzel, History of Dahomey, 1793. Princeton University Library)

From the factors [agents] here we learned that the Ebo and Golo Kings had been at war, the latter of whom having been defeated, and a great part of his army had fallen into the hands of the conqueror, they therefore advised us to proceed . . . to the Ebo nation. . . .

On the 6th February we were visited by numbers of the natives, who offered to barter with us fruit and ivory for our hardwares; but finding after we had exchanged a few articles, that they belonged to a nation which had been before represented to us as thinly inhabited, and that we could not accommodate ourselves here as we wished, we made use of them to obtain information concerning the country of the Ebo king. We fortunately found an interpreter acquainted with that country and the trade, him we engaged, and an expedition was immediately determined upon by the captain. . . .

He proposed that I should go and see the prisoners; we accordingly crossed to the southeastern side of the rivulet, where at the lower side of the town, we found them confined in a large area within a thick stockade, on the outside of which was a trench: the inside was divided into parcels, and huts irregularly constructed, and the entrance as well as the whole circuit, was guarded by men with spears.

We commonly find ourselves impressed with emotions of horror or compassion, on entering places where our fellow men are doomed to punishment or thraldom. In the scene before me, the ear was not indeed dinned with the clanking of heavy fetters, but was horrible in its peculiar way. The captives were destitute for the most part of even their necessary covering, and bound indiscriminately together by the the hands and legs, the cords being again fastened to the ground by stakes; they were loosed a few at a time once every day, when each was permitted to eat the only meal they were allowed, consisting of rice and palm oil. Benevolence, however, sometimes broke through the rigours of a savage life, and occasionally alleviated the sufferings of the weakly, or the wounded with milk or other necessaries: their condition was on the whole deplorable.

From Voyage to the Coast of Africa, *by Joseph Hawkins, slave trader, 1797.*

*Chained slaves awaiting slave trader;
illustration from* Dahomey and the
Dahomans *(London, 1851), a journal
of two missions to the King of
Dahomey in 1849 and 1850, by
Frederick E. Forbes, commander in
the British Navy. (Princeton
University Library)*

*A slave coffle in America. (Culver
Pictures, Inc.)*

**The slaves are bought by the black traders at fairs, which are held for
that purpose, at the distance of upwards of two hundred miles from
the sea coast; and these fairs are said to be supplied from an interior
part of the country. Many negroes, upon being questioned relative to
the place of their nativity, have asserted that they travelled during the
revolution of several moons . . . before they have reached the places
where they were purchased by the black traders.**
From An Account of the Slave Trade on the Coast of Africa, *by Alexander
Falconbridge, surgeon on several slave ships, 1788.*

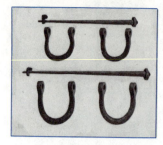

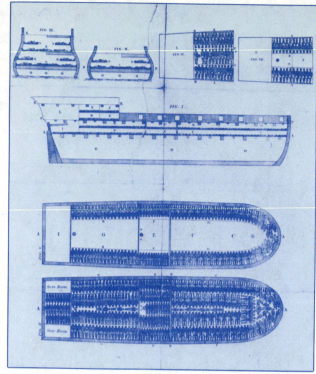

Cross section of a slave ship. (From the Rise, Progress and Accomplishment of the Abolition of the African Slave Trade by the British Parliament, 1808. (Courtesy of the New-York Historical Society, New York City)

Shackles and fetters used to confine slaves on the slave ship Vigilante. *(The Bettmann Archive)*

In some Years Slaves to the Amount of 2000, most of whom they say are Prisoners taken in War: they buy them from the different Princes who take them. . . . Their Way of bringing them is, tying them by the Neck with Leather-Thongs, at about a Yard distance from each other, 30 or 40 in a String, having generally a Bundle of Corn, or an Elephant's Tooth upon each of their Heads. . . . I cannot be certain of the Number of Merchants who follow this Trade, but there may perhaps be about an Hundred, who go up into the Inland Country with the Goods, which they buy from the White Men, and with them purchasing in various Countries Gold, Slaves and Elephants Teeth.
From Travels into the Interior Parts of Africa, *by Francis Moore, English factor on the Gambia River, 1734.*

One negro refused to eat. He was then whipped with the cat but this also was ineffectual. He always kept his teeth so fast that it was impossible to get anything down. We then endeavored to introduce a Speculum Oris between his teeth but the points were too obtuse to enter and next tried a bolus knife but with the same effect. In this state he was for four or five days when he was brought up as dead to be thrown overboard. . . . I finding life still existing, repeated my endeavours though in vain and two days afterwards he was brought up again in the same state as before. . . . In his own tongue he asked for water which was given him. Upon this we began to have hopes of dissuading him from his design but he again shut his teeth as fast as ever and resolved to die and on the ninth day from his first refusal he died.
Dr. Isaac Wilson, surgeon on an 18th-century slaver. As quoted in D. P. Mannix and Malcolm Cowley, Black Cargoes, *Viking Press, New York, 1962.*

The cargo of a vessel of a hundred tons or a little more is calculated to purchase from 220 to 250 slaves. Their lodging rooms below the deck which are three (for the men, the boys and the women) besides a place for the sick, are sometimes more than five feet high and sometimes less; and this height is divided toward the middle for the slaves lie in two rows, one above the other, on each side of the ship, close to each other like books upon a shelf. I have known them so close that the shelf would not easily contain one more.

The poor creatures, thus cramped, are likewise in irons for the most part which makes it difficult for them to turn or move or attempt to rise or to lie down without hurting themselves or each other. Every morning, perhaps, more instances than one are found of the living and the dead fastened together.

From Thoughts Upon the African Slave Trade, *by John Newton. captain of an English slaver, 1788.*

Africans crowded together on the slave deck of the bark "Wildfire," brought into Key West in April 1860. (From Harper's Weekly. 2 June 1860. *Courtesy of the Boston Public Library)*

Some wet and blowing weather . . . having occasioned the portholes to be shut and the grating to be covered, fluxes and fevers among the negroes ensued. While they were in this situation, I frequently went down among them till at length their rooms became so extremely hot as to be only bearable for a very short time. But the excessive heat was not the only thing that rendered their situation intolerable. The deck, that is, the floor of their rooms, was so covered with the blood and mucus which had proceeded from them in consequence of the flux, that it resembled a slaughter-house. . . . Numbers of the slaves having fainted they were carried upon deck where several of them died and the rest with great difficulty were restored. It had nearly proved fatal to me also. The climate was too warm to admit the wearing of any clothing but a shirt and that I had pulled off before I went down; notwithstanding which, by only continuing among them for about a quarter of an hour, I was so overcome with the heat, stench and foul air that I nearly fainted; and it was only with assistance that I could get on deck. The consequence was that I soon after fell sick of the same disorder from which I did not recover for several months.

From An Account of the Slave Trade . . ., *by Alexander Falconbridge. 1788.*

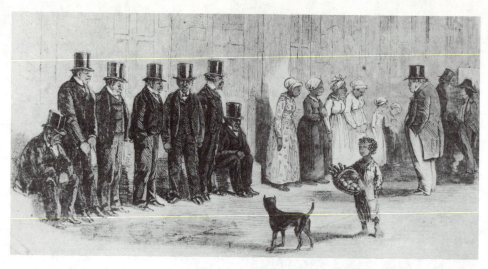

A slave-pen at New Orleans, before the auction. (Culver Pictures, Inc.)

The next day we proceeded to New Orleans, and put the gang in the . . . negro-pen. . . . In a short time the planters came flocking to the pen to purchase slaves. Before the slaves were exhibited for sale, they were dressed and driven out into the yard. Some were set to dancing, some to jumping, some to singing, and some to playing cards. This was done to make them appear cheerful and happy. My business was to see that they were placed in those situations before the arrival of the purchasers, and I have often set them to dancing when their cheeks were wet with tears. As slaves were in good demand at that time, they were all soon disposed of, and we again set out for St. Louis.
From The Narrative of William Wells Brown: A Fugitive Slave, *1847.*

Went on to the Exchange; a sale of men and women. Mr. Cole an acquaintance of Ryder's, told him they "had no feeling; they did not mind being parted from wife and children; they forgot it in a week. You see a cat when one drowns her kittens, she soon forgets it—it's just the same with the coloured people."
From the Diary of William Charles Macready, *an English actor visiting Mobile, Alabama, February 1844.*

My brothers and sisters were bid off first; and one by one, while my mother, paralyzed by grief, held me by the hand. Her turn came, and she was bought by Isaac Riley of Montgomery county. Then I was offered to the assembled purchasers. My mother, half distracted with the thought of parting forever from all her children, pushed through the crowd, while the bidding for me was going on, to the spot where Riley was standing. She fell at his feet, and clung to his knees entreating him in tones that a mother only could command, to buy her baby as well as herself, and spare to her one, at least, of her little ones. Will it, can it be believed that this man, thus appealed to, was capable not merely of turning a deaf ear to her supplication but of disengaging himself from her with such violent blows and kicks, as to reduce her to the necessity of creeping out of his reach, and mingling the groan of bodily suffering with the sob of a breaking heart? As she crawled away from the brutal man I heard her sob out, "Oh, Lord Jesus, how long, how long shall I suffer this way!" I must have been then between five and six years old. I seem to see and hear my poor weeping mother now. This was one of my earliest observations of men; an experience which I only shared with thousands of my race, the bitterness of which to any individual who suffers it cannot be diminished by the frequency of its recurrence while it is dark enough to overshadow the whole after-life with something blacker than a funeral pall.

Josiah Henson, a slave writing at the end of the 18th century. From Father Henson's Story of His Own Life. *ed. by Walter Fisher, Corinth Books, New York, 1962.*

Slave-pen in Alexandria, Virginia, c. 1865. (Courtesy of The New-York Historical Society, New York City)

We know better than others that every attribute of their [the Negroes] character fits them for dependence and servitude. By nature. the most affectionate and loyal of all races beneath the sun, they are also the most helpless; and no calamity can befall them greater than the loss of that protection they enjoy under this patriarchal system.

From a Presbyterian sermon delivered in New Orleans, 1860.

And to think old Abe wants to deprive us of all that fun! No more cotton, sugar-cane, or rice! No more old black aunties or uncles! No more rides in mule teams, no more songs in the cane-field, no more steaming kettles, no more black faces and shining teeth around the furnace fires! If Lincoln could spend the grinding season on a plantation, he would recall his proclamation.

From A Confederate Girl's Diary. *by Sarah Morgan Dawson. November 9, 1862.*

Old Master didn't have any overseer hired, but him and his boys looked after the place and had a Negro we called the driver. We-all sure hated that old black man but I forget his name now. That driver never was allowed to think up nothing for the slaves to do but just was told to make them work hard at what the master and his boys told them to do. White folks had to set them at a job, and then old driver would whoopity and whoopity around, and egg them and egg them until they finished up, so they can go at something else. He worked hard hisself, though, and set a mighty hard pattern for the rest to keep up with. Like I say, he been taught he didn't know how to think, so he didn't try.

Allen V. Manning, slave, born 1850. From Lay My Burden Down, ed. by B. A. Botkin. University of Chicago Press, 1945.

We raise de wheat,
Dey gib us de corn;
We bake de bread,
Dey gib us de cruss;
We sif de meal,
Dey gib us de huss;
We peal de meat,
Dey gib us de skin,
And dat's de way
Dey takes us in.
We skim de pot,
Dey gib us the liquor,
And say dat's good enough for nigger.
    Walk over! walk over!
    Tom butter and de fat;
    Poor nigger you can't get over dat;
        Walk over!

Traditional slave song, in My Bondage and My Freedom, by Frederick Douglas, 1855.

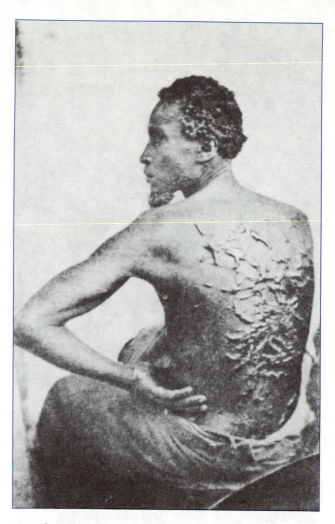

Massa have a great, long whip platted out of rawhide, and when one the niggers fall behind or give out, he hit him with that whip. It take the hide every time he hit a nigger. Mother, she give out on the way, 'bout the line of Texas. Her feet got raw and bleeding, and her legs swoll plumb out of shape. Then Massa, he just take out he gun and shot her, and whilst she lay dying he kicks her two-three times and say, "Damn a nigger what can't stand nothing." Boss, you know that man, he wouldn't bury mother, just leave her laying where he shot her at. You know, then there wasn't no law 'gainst killing nigger slaves.

An interview with Ben Simpson, former slave. From the Slave Narrative Collection, Federal Writers' Project, as quoted in **Lay My Burden Down**, *ed. by Botkin, 1945.*

*Drapetomania, or the Disease
Causing Negroes to Run Away*

Drapetomania is from [a Greek
word meaning] a runaway slave,
and [another Greek word
meaning] *mad or crazy*. It is
unknown to our medical
authorities, although its
diagnostic symptom, the
absconding from service, is well
known to our planters and
overseers. . . . The cause in
most of the cases, that induces
the Negro to run away from
service, is as much a disease of
the mind as any other species
of mental alienation, and much
more curable as a general rule.
With the advantages of proper
medical advice, strictly followed,
this troublesome practice that
many Negroes have of running
away, can be almost entirely
prevented, although the slaves
be located on the borders of a
free state, within a stone's throw
of the abolitionists. . . .

Before Negroes run away, unless
they are frightened or panic-
struck, they become sulky and
dissatisfied. The cause of this
sulkiness and dissatisfaction
should be inquired into and
removed, or they are apt to run
away or fall into Negro
consumption. When sulky and
dissatisfied with cause, the
experience of those [overseers
and owners] on the line and
elsewhere, was decidedly in favor
of whipping them out of it, as
a preventive measure against,
absconding, or other bad conduct.
It was called whipping the devil
out of them.
*Dr. Samuel Cartwright, University
of Louisiana. From his article
"Diseases and Peculiarities of the
Negro Race,"* De Bow's Review,
Vol. 11, September 1851.

*A slave takes his master's horse and
gallops to freedom. "Don't be afraid
to take the best horse," a group of
runaways advised their friends in
slavery, "you're entitled to it." (Culver
Pictures, Inc.)*

Nat Turner conspiring with his fellow slaves. (Culver Pictures, Inc.)

106. Any slave who shall wilfully and maliciously strike his or her master or mistress, child or children, or any white overseer appointed by his or her owner to superintend said owner's slaves, so as to cause a contusion or shedding of blood, shall be punished with death.

110. If any slave shall maliciously burn or destroy any stacks of rice, corn, or other grain, or produce, raw or manufactured, of this Territory, or shall set fire to, or willingly or maliciously burn or destroy any building or house, or shall wilfully or maliciously poison, or maliciously administer poison to any free man, woman, child, servant, slave, or shall commit a rape upon the body of any white woman or girl, such slave shall suffer death.

From The Consolidation and Revision of the Statutes of the State of Louisiana, *1852.*

. . . as it was my object to carry terror and devastation wherever we went, I placed fifteen or twenty of the best armed and most to be relied on in front, who generally approached the houses as fast as their horses could run. This was for two purposes—to prevent their escape, and strike terror to the inhabitants; on this account I never got to the houses, after leaving Mrs. Whitehead's, until the murders were committed, except in one case. I sometimes got in sight in time to see the work of death completed; viewed the mangled bodies as they lay, in silent satisfaction, and immediately started in quest of other victims.

From The Confessions of Nat Turner, the leader of the late insurrection in Southampton, Va., *ed. by Thomas R. Gray, 1831.*

Most of the havoc has been confined to a limited section of our county, but so inhuman has been the butchery, so indiscriminate the carnage, that the tomahawk and scalping knife have now no horrors. Along the road traveled by our rebellious blacks, comprising a distance of something like twenty-seven miles, no white soul now lives to tell how fiendlike was their purpose. In the bosom of almost every family this enemy still exists. Our homes, those near the scenes of havoc, as well as others more remote, have all been deserted and our families gathered together and guarded at public places in the county; and, still further, the excitement is so great that were the justices to pronounce a slave innocent, we fear a mob would be the consequence.

From a letter written to President Jackson by a committee of citizens in Southampton County, Virginia, August 29, 1832. As quoted in F. Roy Johnson, The Nat Turner Slave Insurrection, *Chapel Hill, 1966.*

Illustration from An Authentic and Impartial Narrative of the Tragical Scene Which Was Witnessed in Southampton County 1831, *by Samuel G. Warner: 1. A mother pleading for the lives of her children; 2. Nat and Will Turner attacking Joseph Travis; 3. John T. Barrow defending himself, so that his wife can escape. (Library of Congress)*

Harriet Tubman. In addition to helping hundreds of slaves win their freedom, she took part in the Civil War, directing Union raiding parties. She also built a home for ex-slaves too old or too ill to work; she herself lived to the age of ninety-three. (Library of Congress)

"The Resurrection of Henry Box Brown at Philadelphia." A former slave, Henry Box Brown was carried to freedom from Richmond, Virginia, in a box (3 feet long, 2½ feet deep, and 2 feet wide). The white Southerner who aided in the escape was sent to prison. (Library of Congress)

. . . I took my place in this narrow prison, with a mind full of uncertainty as to the result. It was a critical period of my life, I can assure you, reader; but if you have never been deprived of your liberty as I was, you cannot realize the power of that hope of freedom. . . .

From The Narrative of Henry Box Brown by Himself, Boston, 1849.

When Nalle was brought from Commissioner Beach's office into the street, Harriet Tubman, who had been standing with the excited crowd, rushed . . . to Nalle, and running one of her arms around his manacled arm, held on to him without even loosening her hold through the more than half-hour's struggle . . . to the dock, where Nalle's liberation was accomplished. In the *mêlée* she was repeatedly beaten over the head with policemen's clubs, but she never for a moment released her hold. . . .

True she had strong and earnest helpers in her struggle, some of whom had white faces as well as human hearts. . . . But she exposed herself to the fury of the sympathizers with slavery, without fear, and suffered their blows without flinching. Harriet crossed the river with the crowd, in the ferry-boat, and when the men who led the assault upon the door of Judge Stewart's office were stricken down, Harriet and a number of other colored women rushed over their bodies, brough Nalle out, and putting him in the first wagon passing started him for the West.

Witnessed by a crowd numbering in the thousands, Harriet Tubman helped free Charles Nalle in 1859. Martin Townsend, Nalle's white lawyer, describes the scene. From Harriet, The Moses of Her People, by Sarah Bradford, 1866.

Thomas Nast illustration for Harper's Weekly *showing "The Press on the Field" gathering "Contraband News," 1863. (Library of Congress)*

They [the escaped slaves] bring much valuable information which cannot be obtained from any other source. They are acquainted with all the roads, paths, fords and other natural features of the country and they make excellent guides. They also know and frequently have exposed the haunts of secession spies and traitors and the existence of rebel organizations.

Dispatch from a line officer to a Union army field commander, April 1862. From War of the Rebellion: A Compilation of the Official Records of the Union and Confederate Armies, *series 2, vol. 1.*

. . . it is a matter of notoriety in the sections of the Confederacy where raids are frequent that the guides of the enemy are nearly always free negroes and slaves.

District attorney of a Virginia county. From War of the Rebellion, *series 2, vol. 6, as quoted in James M. McPherson,* The Negro's Civil War, *Knopf and Random House, 1965.*

Abraham Lincoln entering Richmond, Virginia, April 3, 1865. (The New York Public Library)

"Marching on!"—The Fifty-fifth Massachusetts colored regiment singing John Brown's March in the streets of Charleston, S.C. February 1865. (From Harper's Weekly, 18 March 1865. Courtesy of the Boston Public Library)

Words would fail to describe the scene which those who witnessed it will never forget,— the welcome given to a regiment of colored troops by their people redeemed from slavery. As shouts, prayers, and blessings resounded on every side, all felt that the hardships and dangers of the siege were fully repaid. The few white inhabitants left in the town were either alarmed or indignant, and generally remained in their houses; but the colored people turned out *en masse.* . . . Cheers, blessings, prayers, and songs were heard on every side. Men and women crowded to shake hands with men and officers. Many of them talked earnestly and understandingly of the past and present.

. . . On through the streets of the rebel city passed the column, on through the chief seat of that slave power, tottering to its fall.
Colonel Fox of the Fifty-fifth U. S. Colored Infantry, describes the liberation of Charleston, South Carolina of February 17, 1865. From Charles B. Fox, Record of the Service of the Fifty-Fifth Regiment of Mass. Volunteer Infantry, Cambridge, Mass., 1868.

Nothing can exceed the rejoicings of the negroes since the occupation of this city [Richmond]. They declare that they cannot realize the change; though they have long prayed for it, yet it seems impossible that it has come. Old men and women weep and shout for joy, and praise God for their deliverance through means of the Union army. . . .

The great event after the capture of the city was the arrival of President Lincoln in it. . . . There is no describing the scene along the route. The colored population was wild with enthusiasm. Old men thanked God in a very boisterous manner, and old women shouted upon the pavement as high as they had ever done at a religious revival. . . .
Everyone declares that Richmond never before presented such a spectacle of jubilee. It must be confessed that those who participated in the informal reception of the President were mainly negroes. There were many whites in the crowd, but they were lost in the great concourse of American citizens of African descent. . . .
From the Philadelphia Press's field correspondent, April 4, 1865. As quoted in McPherson, The Negro's Civil War, 1965.

They employed more than half the slaves and produced two thirds of the cotton, two thirds of the tobacco, most of the hemp, and all the sugar and rice that went to market at home and abroad.

African slavery existed by law in Delaware, Missouri, and the thirteen states that are usually thought to make up the South. Slaves were defined as personal property and could be (and were) inherited, bought and sold, or given away. They could not own property and had no civil or legal rights, except the right, defined by law, to life and more or less humane treatment. All of the slave states adopted elaborate legislation to guarantee the subordination of the slaves and control their conduct. But it was the plantation owners who were primarily responsible for the slaves' conduct and welfare. All the owners had codes which governed personal behavior and provided for the punishment (usually by whipping) of disobedient or fractious slaves.

The Other South and Slavery

The vast majority of the southern white people were small farmers who owned no slaves at all. To be precise, there were some 384,000 slaveowners in all the fifteen slave states in 1860. Even if we count all these as heads of families, certainly not more than 2,000,000 men, women, and children, out of a total of some 8,000,000 southern whites in 1860, had any direct interest in slavery. Some 123,000 slaveowners, about one third of the total number, owned only one or two slaves.

In vast areas of the South—the upland Piedmont, the mountainous areas, and the valleys of the border states—plantations were virtually unknown and slavery itself was quite limited. Unlike the planters who concentrated on staple crops for export, the farmers of this other South lived in a semisubsistence economy and concentrated on producing food for their own families and conducted most of their limited commercial activities through barter in local markets.

How, then, did the plantation and slavery so dominate the economic life of the whole South? For one thing, although only a small percentage of white Southerners were planters, a much larger fraction—possibly one fourth of all white families—owned at least one slave, and many others saw slave ownership as a potential means to get ahead. Furthermore, the concentration of capital and labor made possible certain economies of scale on the plantation which the small farmer could not possibly achieve but which were often beneficial to him. The planter could probably afford to operate a cotton gin, grist mill, and other processing equipment. Because of his large volume of production, the planter also had ready access to marketing institutions. The planter would typically allow his neighbors, who were small farmers, to use his gin and grist mill (for a fee) and also permit them to add their one or two bales of cotton to the shipment which he was sending to market. Finally, most white Southerners, particularly the small farmers, feared the consequences of the abolition of slavery. Slavery was an almost perfect system of racial control to guarantee white supremacy. The great mass of white Southerners, unable to think in terms of the gradual absorption of blacks into the mainstream of southern life, could foresee only the breakdown of civilization in the South if slavery was not maintained. The slaveowners, themselves, did everything possible to keep these fears alive.

The Dilemma of the Profitability of Slavery

For decades, scholars have argued about whether plantation slavery was economically profitable. The debate is more than a matter of academic hairsplitting, particularly when, from hindsight, we can see the Civil War looming on the horizon. Was the institution economically unsound and doomed to internal collapse (thus possibly rendering the ghastly Civil War unnecessary), or was it economically viable, thus insuring an eventual collision between the North and the South? The best evidence now available suggests that slavery was indeed profitable, and that investment in slaves offered a greater return than other alternative forms of investment in the South. However, that profitability rested to a considerable degree on the large and growing demand of the British textile industry for southern cotton. That demand continued to rise throughout the antebellum era, but its relative decline after 1865 revealed that the planters were altogether vulnerable to market forces beyond their control.

Furthermore, while slavery was generally profitable for *individuals*, it did not encourage the economic development of the South as a whole. Plantation slavery offered little incentive for the kind of economic transformation which was then sweeping the Northeast. Where would be the mass market for southern-made manufactures if slaves and cash-poor whites could not buy them? And why would men of wealth mechanize agriculture or create the infrastructure of an industrial economy if the return on investment in slaves was greater than that on manufactures, banking, or whatever? To be sure, the South developed some manufacturing and built an impressive railroad network before the Civil War, but these factories and railroads were subservient to the interests of planters and were *relatively* insignificant. Slavery, then, secured great wealth for a few, but it did not secure for the region as a whole the kind of economic future that the industrial Northeast was building. However, the underlying structural weakness of the southern economy and its vulnerability to a long-term depression of world cotton prices was far from self-evident in 1860.

The World that the Slaves Made

Slavery was not only an economic and legal system; it was also a set of relationships between human beings, some of whom were masters and some of whom were slaves. The master-slave relationship rested on cruel exploitation, but it was at the same time so complex and ambivalent that, as Eugene Genovese has pointed out, "neither could express the simplest human feelings without reference to the other." There were, of course, varieties of slave experiences, and efforts to generalize about them are fraught with danger. The best evidence now available points toward "typical" patterns of behavior which represent neither the passive, docile "Sambo" type—totally traumatized by the repression of slavery—nor the industrious self-motivated worker, who internalized his master's driving concern for efficient labor, nor again the insurrectionary hero such as Nat Turner or Denmark Vesey, ready to lead the slaves in open rebellion. The more common pattern of relationships between master and slave was much more complex and subtle than any of these. Most slaves realized that the overthrow of slavery was beyond their control, but they did not passively accept their fate. On the contrary, the slaves tried to carve out a living space within the oppressive system in which they could preserve some degree of dignity and freedom.

The typical relationship between master and slave might well be character-ized as "paternalistic," although that term is loaded with ambiguity. Paternal-istic relations could involve both cruel and tyrannical treatment and genuine kindness and affection. Paternalism recognized reciprocal responsibilities even at the same time that it affirmed the domination of the master over the slave. Clearly, the slaves manipulated the masters' sense of paternalism to amelio-rate the harshest features of slavery. And in day-to-day work and social rela-tionships, the slaves themselves generally managed to maintain certain limits on the absolute power of the master and his representatives.

Furthermore, slaves were able to maintain institutions of their own which helped to shield them from the full force of enslavement and enabled them to develop a remarkably resilient sense of community. Religion and the family were critically important in this regard. Afro-American religion fused enthu-siastic evangelical Protestantism with powerful remnants of West African reli-gion. The result was a cultural force which was a bulwark against the dehu-manizing and debilitating potential of slavery and brought to the fore a leader-ship class of preachers and exhorters within the black community. The slave family, when permitted to survive, was a remarkably stable and vital institu-tion in the black community. Slave families typically included two parents and their offspring, and slave families had a strong sense of identity with and responsibility for the extended family network. Moreover the slave family re-tained considerable control over the socialization of slave children and the transmission of social values. Even so, the slave family was a very fragile in-stitution because of the ever present threat and fact of breakup on account of sale.

Subtle resistance in dealing with whites and withdrawal into a black com-munity enabled slaves to retain a sense of worth and communal solidarity. But this victory came at a great cost. It required continual compromise with an oppressive system and an acceptance of the basic fact of slavery. Thus, while resistance to slavery was ever present and varied, there were only isolated cases of open rebellion. The most important was the rebellion led by Nat Tur-ner in Southampton County, Virginia, in 1831, which resulted in the death of fifty-seven whites, the murder of about 100 blacks in a wild manhunt, and the subsequent execution of Turner and nineteen other blacks.

The Social Structure of the Old South

Southern social relations in general, like those between master and slave, were riddled by contradictions. On the one hand, the planter class had a highly de-veloped notion of itself as the rightful rulers of a hierarchical and deferential society. And the planters did dominate the region's politics and society as well as its economy. The paternalism which existed between masters and slaves extended, in a different form, to the women and children of their own families and to their communities as a whole.

Relative to the North, the South was indeed a hierarchial society, one in which the rich and the poor, the blacks and the whites, were bound together by certain patterns of deference and reciprocal obligation, which were in turn based in large measure on kinship ties and ascribed status. However, that was not the whole story. A very large percentage of the "plain folk" were landown-ing farmers and heirs of a proud tradition of independence. With the spread of universal white manhood suffrage early in the nineteenth century, they assumed considerable political power in the region. Even where planters retained political leadership, they had to take into account the wishes and needs of the numerous and potentially troublesome plain folk.

To a substantial degree, ordinary white Southerners accepted an identity of interests with the planters. For one thing, as we have seen, a large minority of the farmers had a small stake in slavery. Also, the solidarity between classes depended on the planters' care in attending to their side of the various reciprocal relationships — providing economic assistance, affirming the place of the small farmer in the local community, and, in many cases, acknowledging the web of kinship between himself and the yeomanry. In addition, racism, both among planters and plain folk, was a powerful social cement. It produced a remarkable degree of social solidarity among the whites, in spite of the deep-seated class and economic differences that existed among them.

At the bottom of the social ladder in the antebellum South were the "poor whites" and the free blacks. The former constituted about 10 per cent of the white population and lived in incredible squalor in the piney barrens and other submarginal areas. There were 215,000 free blacks in the South in 1860, who then constituted 44 per cent of the free blacks in the entire country. Some free blacks, notably in New Orleans, were well-to-do, indeed, several were prosperous planters. However, the great mass of southern blacks (like the free blacks of the North) were poor, disfranchised, and enjoyed only a precarious freedom.

The Crusade Against Slavery and the Revival of Sectional Conflict

Although the legitimacy of slavery had been tacitly acknowledged in the Constitution and openly affirmed in law and custom, the institution had long been under attack from various quarters. As we have seen, the sectional political controversy over slavery had come to focus on the issue of slavery in the territories. This controversy involved the old struggle between the North and the South for control of the Congress, fears that the "Slave Power" threatened the right of northern free labor to occupy the territories, and western interests in keeping blacks out of the territories altogether. At the heart of the controversy was a growing conviction that the North and South represented social systems whose values were fundamentally at odds with each other.

It was almost inevitable that conflict over slavery should occur. The ferment of Revolutionary ideals had caused gradual abolition to be set in motion in all the northern states by 1800 and had moved some individual Southerners to free their slaves. Indeed, in 1827, 106 of the 130 emancipation societies in the United States were located in the South. It was evident by 1830, however, that the southern antislavery movement had failed. The American Colonization Society had founded a colony for free blacks in Liberia in the 1820s, but colonization of more than a few thousand proved impossible. Far from being in retreat, slavery was now expanding at phenomenal speed into the Southwest.

By the 1830s, antislavery sentiment, never strong in the Lower South, was on the decline in the Upper South as well. The beginnings of radical abolitionism, Nat Turner's rebellion in Virginia, and the fear of similar uprisings, caused most Southerners who spoke about the subject to turn from apologies to aggressive defense of slavery. Ministers joined politicians and editors in extolling slavery as the divinely established cornerstone of southern civilization.

Part of what aroused Southerners' ire was the emergence of a radical anti-slavery movement in the North. Before 1830, most critics of slavery had advocated colonization and gradual emancipation. The new abolitionists, however, breathed the fire of revivalism. Slavery was a sin, they thundered, and must be rooted out immediately.

The ties between abolitionism, revivalism, and benevolent reform were extremely close. Some abolitionist leaders were themselves evangelists, most notably Theodore Dwight Weld, a protégé of Charles G. Finney. Others. most notably William Lloyd Garrison, had participated in the temperance crusade. The pioneers of radical abolitionism brought to their new movement, not only the zeal, but also the mobilizing techniques of revivalism and reform. Moral suasion, they believed, would carry the day against the "Slave Power." To that end, Garrison began publication in 1831 of his fiery newspaper, *The Liberator*. In 1833, he joined with other abolitionists to form the American Anti-Slavery Society, which, like other reform organizations and the revivalistic sects themselves, set out to mobilize supporters in local associations and to flood the nation with literature on the subject.

The abolitionist movement soon found that moral suasion was not going to exorcise slavery in an instant, and that support for the institution was deeply embedded in most American institutions. Faced with this situation, Garrison and others argued that they must sever all ties with institutions that compromised with slavery, be they political parties, churches, or the Constitution of the United States, which Garrison labeled "a covenant with death and an agreement with hell." In espousing such a position, Garrison reflected the perfectionist impulse of the revivalistic age, which called for men to repent and come out of the old corrupt institutions of this world.

Some other abolitionists, however, concluded that, if slavery were actually to be abolished, then they would have to work through the political process. This sentiment led to the establishment of two single-issue parties — the Liberty party, established in 1840, and the Free Soil party, established in 1848 (see pp. 342, 353, 361). The political approach, unlike Garrison's moral witness, required some compromises. The antislavery parties of the 1840s and the 1850s concentrated on efforts to eliminate slavery from the District of Columbia and to block the expansion of slavery into the territories. For the most part, political abolitionists chose not to dwell on the legal discrimination which confronted free blacks in the North. Thus they could attract support from the great majority of whites who would not accept the notion of racial equality but had a keen interest in limiting the spread of slavery.

The tactical dilemma of the abolitionists was the classical one of all radical protest movements. Garrison's perfectionism so threatened the security of American institutions that he and others like him faced howling mobs wherever they appeared in the North, and often the mobs were led by "gentlemen of property and standing." However, if abolitionists tried to work through established political instrumentalities, their cause might become so diluted as to lose its focus. This is not to suggest that all abolitionists were racial egalitarians. Black abolitionists often found themselves treated as second-class participants in the movement itself, and many white abolitionists tried not to offend the sensibilities of potential converts by limiting the public role of blacks in the movement.

The tactical dilemma of the movement, and its internal inconsistencies on racism, were keenly felt by black abolitionists, of whom there were many. David Walker, a free black man in Boston, published in 1829 a tract called *Walker's Appeal,* which was one of the most powerful and direct attacks on slavery ever written. Walker called upon slaves to rise up and win their own freedom by force. The best-known black abolitionist was Frederick Douglass, who escaped from slavery in Maryland and became a speaker for the Massachusetts Anti-Slavery Society. Like other abolitionist leaders, Douglass was mobbed and beaten, but he persevered. He lived to play a prominent role in the Civil War and Reconstruction, and to serve as United States Minister to Haiti. Douglass followed a course of nonresistant witness like Garrison until 1847. By this time, however, he and other black leaders, frustrated by racial discrimination within the movement and by its tendency to concern itself with other social reforms, began to speak of the need for blacks to work directly for an end to slavery, either through voting or through violent overthrow of the institution.

Garrison's brand of abolitionism—which called attention to racism wherever it appeared—never gained a mass following in the North. However, by the mid-1850s, the politically focused issue of free soil *was* gaining such support, and, in the process, was generating a widespread feeling in the North that the "Slave Power" represented a serious threat to American liberty and free labor.

In the heated political climate of the 1850s, any evidence of the growth of antislavery sentiment naturally exacerbated sectional tensions. Such evidence came from northern and midwestern resistance to the new Fugitive Slave Act. That measure provided that northern state and city authorities, and even plain citizens, had to assist in the capture and return of runaway slaves. Conservatives like Webster and Douglass begged Northerners to obey the law, but they pleaded in vain. State after state passed personal liberty laws which forbade state officials or private citizens to assist federal courts to enforce the Fugitive Slave Act.

In 1852, Harriet Beecher Stowe published a moving novel entitled *Uncle Tom's Cabin.* It pictured the inhuman cruelties practiced by a heartless overseer named Simon Legree, who, incidentally, was a Northerner, and it begged "the Christian and humane people of the North" to oppose the Fugitive Slave Act. The book sold by the hundreds of thousands and had a powerful effect upon the public. Partially because of it and similar literature, crowds of enraged citizens in Boston, New York, and other cities attacked federal marshals who took fugitives back to their masters.

Northerners showed their defiance of the Fugitive Slave Act most dramatically by expanding a secret organization known as the Underground Railroad. This was an elaborate network of "stations" (private homes or barns) along which "conductors" spirited runaways to freedom in Canada. Among the conductors were a number of blacks who literally risked their lives every time they set foot on southern soil. The most famous was Harriet Tubman, who had escaped from slavery herself and who is said to have made nineteen trips to the South and to have escorted more than 300 slaves to freedom. The routes of the Underground Railroad ran all along the border between the slave and free states. By the 1850s, it was assisting at least 1,000 runaways a year.

SUGGESTED READINGS

Most of the books on aspects of economic and labor history cited in Suggested Readings for Chapter 8 are also useful for this period. In addition, Paul W. Gates, *The Farmers' Age: Agriculture, 1815–1860*, (1960), is a good survey of that subject. Diane Lindstrom, *Economic Development in the Philadelphia Region, 1810–1950* (1978), demonstrates the importance of intraregional forces in American economic growth. One of several new studies which focuses on both technological and social dimensions of industrialization is Thomas Dublin, *Women at Work: The Transformation of Work and Community in Lowell, Massachusetts, 1828–1860* (1979). Still useful on that general topic is Norman J. Ware, *The Industrial Worker, 1840–1860* (1924). The significance of railroads in antebellum America has been analyzed, with differing conclusions, in the following: Robert W. Fogel, *Railroads and Economic Growth* (1964); Albert Fishlow, *American Railroads and the Transformation of the Ante-Bellum Economy* (1965); and Alfred D. Chandler, Jr., *Strategy and Structure: Chapters in the History of American Industrial Enterprise* (1962). See also Chandler, *The Visible Hand*, cited in Chapter 8.

Several excellent studies of antebellum community life have been published during the last decade. The discussion of that subject in this chapter relies on four of them: Thomas Bender, *Community and Social Change in America* (1978); Alan Dawley, *Class and Community: The Industrial Revolution in Lynn* (1976); Stuart M. Blumin, *The Urban Threshold: Growth and Change in a Nineteenth Century Community* [Kingston] (1976); and Don H. Doyle, *The Social Order of a Frontier Community: Jacksonville, Illinois, 1825–1870* (1978). Other major community studies include Stephan Thernstrom, *Poverty and Progress: Social Mobility in a Nineteenth Century City* (1964); Peter R. Knights, *The Plain People of Boston, 1830–1860* (1971); and Michael H. Frisch, *Town into City: Springfield, Massachusetts, and the Meaning of Community, 1840–1880* (1972). A useful introduction to the history of urbanization is S. B. Warner, Jr., *The Urban Wilderness: A History of the American City* (1972).

Stimulating studies of social institutions include Michael Gordon, comp., *The American Family in Social-Historical Perspective* (2nd ed., 1978); Philip Greven, *The Protestant Temperament: Patterns of Child-Rearing, Religious Experience, and the Self in Early America* (1977); Stanley K. Schultz, *The Culture Factory: Boston Public Schools, 1789–1860* (1973); and David

Rothman, *The Discovery of the Asylum: Social Order and Disorder in the New Republic* (1971).

The literature on revivalism and reform is voluminous. In addition to works cited for Chapter 8, see especially William G. McLoughlin, ed., *Lectures on Revivals of Religion*, by Charles Grandison Finney (1960); Dickson D. Bruce, Jr., *And They all Sang Hallelujah: Plain Folk Camp-Meeting Religion, 1800–1845* (1974); Ronald G. Walters, *American Reformers, 1815–1860* (1978); Norman H. Clark, *Deliver Us From Evil: An Interpretation of American Prohibition* (1976); and W. J. Rorabaugh, *The Alcoholic Republic* (1979).

The literature on women in antebellum society and on the early women's movement has grown substantially during the last decade and includes: Ellen DuBois, *Feminism and Suffrage: The Emergence of an Independent Women's Movement in America, 1848–1869* (1978); Nancy F. Cott, *The Bonds of Womanhood: "Woman's Sphere" in New England, 1780–1835* (1977); Ann Douglas, *The Feminization of American Culture* (1977); and Lois W. Banner, *Elizabeth Cady Stanton: A Radical for Woman's Rights* (1980).

Ethnocultural conflict and its impact on politics are discussed in Lee Benson, *The Concept of Jacksonian Politics: New York as a Test Case* (1965); Ronald Formisano, *The Birth of Mass Political Parties: Michigan, 1827–1861* (1971); and Michael F. Holt, "The Antimasonic and Know Nothing Parties," in *A History of United States Political Parties*, ed. by Arthur M. Schlesinger, Jr., Vol. 1 (1973).

The antebellum South continues to attract scholars, and much of their interest has focused on the plantation and Afro-American slavery. A careful new synthesis of recent scholarship is found in Idus A. Newby, *The South, A History* (1978), while the revision of an older general work is still useful in Clement Eaton, *A History of the Old South* (3rd ed., 1975).

The economic impact of plantation agriculture and slavery has been a subject of intense scholarly debate. A sensible treatment of that subject which draws on both the econometric and historical literature is Gavin Wright, *The Political Economy of the Cotton South: Households, Markets, and Wealth in the Nineteenth Century* (1978). A major study which has itself been the subject of searching investigation and considerable criticism is Robert W. Fogel and S. L. Engerman, *Time on the Cross: The Economics of American Negro Slavery*, 2 vols. (1974).

The best brief introduction to slavery is Kenneth Stampp, *The Peculiar Institution*

(1955). Ulrich B. Phillips, *American Negro Slavery* (1918), remains useful, despite its biases. Eugene Genovese, *Roll, Jordan, Roll: The World the Slaves Made* (1974), is a remarkably perceptive analysis of the interaction between the cultures of slaves and masters. Herbert G. Gutman, *The Black Family in Slavery and Freedom, 1750–1920* (1976), and John W. Blassingame, *The Slave Community* (2nd ed., 1979), also illuminate the slaves' world, as does Lawrence W. Levine, *Black Culture and Black Consciousness: Afro-American Folk Thought From Slavery to Freedom* (1977). Richard C. Wade, *Slavery in the Cities* (1964), and Robert S. Starobin, *Industrial Slavery in the Old South* (1970), describe lesser-known aspects of the peculiar institution.

Two standard works on intellectual history are Wilbur J. Cash, *The Mind of the South* (1941), and William R. Taylor, *Cavalier and Yankee: The South and American National Character* (1961). The role of plain folk in the Old South needs further investigation. The beginning point for any such investigation is Frank L. Owsley, *Plain Folk of the Old South* (1949), although many of its findings have been challenged. Various state histories of social relations shed light on this subject, as do several essays in O. Vernon Burton and Robert C. McMath, Jr., eds., *Southern Communities in the Nineteenth Century,* 2 vols. (1981).

A brief but excellent survey of the abolition movement is found in Louis Filler, *The Crusade Against Slavery* (1960), while Martin B. Duberman (ed.), *The Antislavery Vanguard: New Essays on the Abolitionists* (1965), brings the antislavery radicals into contemporary focus. Two major works by David B. Davis, *The Problem of Slavery in Western Culture* (1966), and *The Problem of Slavery in the Age of Revolution* (1975), provide a clear picture of the background of the antislavery movement. There are many useful biographies of abolitionist leaders, among them Irving H. Bartlett, *Wendell Phillips: Brahmin Radical* (1961), and John L. Thomas, *The Liberator: William Lloyd Garrison* (1963).

Leon F. Litwack, *North of Slavery: The Negro in the Free States, 1790–1860* (1961), chronicles the lives of semifree blacks, as does a newer companion study, Ira Berlin, *Slaves Without Masters: The Free Negro in the Antebellum South* (1974). The role of blacks in the antislavery movement can be followed in Benjamin Quarles, *Black Abolitionists* (1969), and Arna Bontemps, *Free at Last: The Life of Frederick Douglass* (1971). The literature on slavery, antislavery, and the sectional crisis is discussed in detail following Chapter 15, but two books which influenced the brief discussion of that subject in this chapter are Michael F. Holt, *The Political Crisis of the 1850s* (1978), and Eric Foner, *Free Soil, Free Labor, Free Men: The Ideology of the Republican Party Before the Civil War* (1970).

CHAPTER 15
A HOUSE DIVIDED

1. NATIONALISM UNLIMITED

Confident America

To most Americans in the early 1850s, it seemed an especially good time to be alive. The recent heated debate over the Wilmot Proviso had, it is true, raised dark warnings of the disruption of the Union, even of war. But in the compromise measures of 1850, good sense and devotion to the Union had once again prevailed over sectionalism, just as they had triumphed during the crises over Missouri in 1819–1820 and nullification in 1832–1833. Everywhere, in the South as much as in the North and West, men were relieved when it seemed that all sections would accept the Compromise as the "final" settlement of the vexing issue of slavery in the territories. This was true especially when, in 1851, hot fights over the Compromise in Georgia and Mississippi resulted in sweeping victories by the champions of the Union.

Of course there were dark clouds gathering just over the horizon during the antebellum period. Many Northerners were unwilling to accept one part of the Compromise, the Fugitive Slave Act. Some Southerners would not remain content with the exclusion of slavery from any part of the territories. Pent-up tensions would finally erupt in secession in 1861; but this future was invisible to all except a handful of far-sighted pessimists.

The 1850s was a decade of high and generally sustained prosperity, except for a setback in 1857. Gold from California swelled the money supply; the frontier was expanding westward at a rapid pace; foreign trade was growing by leaps and bounds. To a people who had just carved out a western empire and had fulfilled their "Manifest Destiny," no problem seemed too difficult to solve.

Expanding national pride and jaunty confidence were evident on all sides throughout the 1850s, even during the middle and latter years of the decade when sectional strife once again was menacing. Aggressive nationalism permeated popular literature and the speeches of politicians. It took form especially in the new twist that public spokesmen in the late 1840s and the 1850s gave to the older doctrine of Manifest Destiny. Before about 1848, Americans had conceived of their destiny in terms of expansion to the Pacific coast. Now they were beginning to think in bolder terms—of a mission to show the world, particularly decadent Europe, the superiority of democratic institutions; of a destiny, perhaps, to govern the entire western hemisphere!

Aggressive Diplomacy

Such confidence was reflected most vividly during the fifties in the statements of men who spoke for the United States abroad. When democratic revolutions swept over western Europe in 1848, the United States Government was quick to express its sympathies for peoples struggling for freedom. In December 1850, Secretary of State Daniel Webster sent a defiant message to the Austrian Minister in Washington. The latter had complained of the sympathy that the United States had shown to Hungary in her struggle for independence. "The power of this Republic, at the present moment," Webster boasted, "is spread over a region [which is] one of the richest and most fertile on the globe, and of an extent in comparison with which the possessions of the House of Hapsburg are but as a patch on the earth's surface."

Senator Stephen A. Douglas made a trip abroad in the summer of 1853, and probably expressed the sentiments of a large proportion of his fellow countrymen when he wrote: "Europe is tottering to the verge of dissolution." Henry Clay, on his deathbed, wrote to the Hungarian patriot, General Louis Kossuth, that "for the cause of liberty we should keep our lamp burning brightly on this western shore, as a light to all nations."

The climax of aggressive diplomacy came only a short time later, in the Ostend Manifesto concerning Cuba. Americans had long concluded that this rich Spanish colony guarding the entrance to the Gulf of Mexico should never be allowed to fall into the hands of any strong European power. As a consequence of harsh Spanish rule, Cuba was in a state of continual revolt during the mid-nineteenth century. It seemed that Spain either might have to withdraw or else sell Cuba to another country. In response to instructions from President Pierce, the American Ministers to Great Britain, France, and Spain (James Buchanan, J. Y. Mason, and Pierre Soulé) met at Ostend, then at Aix-la-Chapelle, Brussels, in the summer of 1854 to consider what the United States should do.

Instead of merely recommending, the three Ministers published a declaration—the Ostend Manifesto. It asserted to the world that the possession of Cuba was essential to the peace and security of the United States. It concluded with the startling statement that "if Spain, dead to the voice of her own interest and motivated by stubborn pride and a false sense of honor, should refuse to sell Cuba," then the United States would be "justified by every law human and divine in taking the island from her by force." It was bravado, and Secretary of State William L. Marcy at once disowned the manifesto. Yet, like Webster's note to the Austrian government, the manifesto gave sure evidence of unlimited confidence and national arrogance.

The Growth of Foreign Trade

Another cause of extravagant national pride was the phenomenal growth both of foreign trade and of the American merchant marine in the 1850s. Americans had been a seafaring, trading people since the earliest colonial times, but never so successfully as in the 1850s. For one thing, they had more to sell to Europe as their cotton plantations and corn and wheat fields spread westward. Consequently, the total value of all American exports increased from $152 million in 1850 to $400 million in 1860. In the latter year, cotton exports alone accounted for 60 per cent of the value of American products shipped abroad. Such figures caused Southerners to believe that the plantation system was the basis of the country's prosperity, and that cotton was king of the world's economy.

Americans not only sold more abroad in the 1850s, but also carried more of their products in their own ships. Between 1850 and 1860, the total tonnage of the American merchant fleet increased from 3,535,000 to 5,354,000 tons. In 1853, the tonnage of the American merchant marine topped that of Great Britain (heretofore the leading maritime power) by 15 per cent. And all through the 1850s, 70 to 75 per cent of the thriving foreign trade of the United States was carried in American vessels. One of the chief reasons for this success was the graceful and speedy clipper ship designed by Donald McKay of Boston, primarily for trade with California and the Orient. His *Flying Cloud*, launched in 1851, made the voyage from San Francisco around Cape Horn to New York in eighty-nine days, twenty-one hours.

Latin American and Far Eastern Treaties

Diplomacy and expanding foreign trade went hand in hand in the fifties. For one thing, the United States Government first began to think seriously about the construction of a canal across the Central American isthmus. The United States had already concluded one treaty in 1846 with New Granada (now Colombia) that gave the United States the right to build a canal across the Isthmus of Panama. Three years later, it made similar treaties with Nicaragua and Honduras. When it seemed that British and American canal ambitions might collide, the two governments concluded the Clayton-Bulwer Treaty in 1850; it provided for Anglo-American cooperation in the construction of any future isthmian canal. Half a century would pass before the American government took up the project in earnest.

Diplomacy was the handmaiden of trade, above all in the Far East. American merchants had plied the China trade on a small scale since the 1780s. That commerce grew slowly but substantially in volume after an American diplomat, Caleb Cushing, in 1844 concluded the Treaty of Wanghia with the Chinese government. It opened a number of ports to American ships. American exports to China increased in value from $2 million in 1844 to $9 million in 1860. American imports from China increased from $5 million in 1844 to $14 million in 1860.

In 1852, President Millard Fillmore sent a naval expedition under Commodore Matthew C. Perry to Japan to explore the possibilities of trade with that secluded country. Perry tarried only long enough on his first visit to awe the Japanese with the firepower of his steam warships, but he returned two years later. He then obtained a treaty opening two small ports to American vessels. It was the beginning of Japan's awakening to the modern era, and of what would become, in the 1870s, a thriving trade between the two countries.

2. THE KANSAS-NEBRASKA ACT AND THE RENEWAL OF SECTIONAL CONTROVERSY

Danger Signals

A deceptive calm pervaded the nation in the early 1850s. High prosperity, growing boastfulness in foreign policy, and widespread assertions of devotion to the Union all gave an impression of national harmony that did not really exist. Danger signals abounded and warned that the Compromise of 1850 had been only a truce. The older moderate leaders, who placed the Union before their own geographical sections, were fading away, one by one, and their places were being taken by impatient, fanatical hotheads—leaders such as Charles Sumner of Massachusetts and William L. Yancey of Alabama. Throughout the free states, many people proclaimed their determination to protect and assist runaway slaves—this despite the clear understanding that Southerners regarded the implementation of the Fugitive Slave Act as essential to the preservation of the Union. White Southerners grew increasingly apprehensive about the continued spread of antislavery sentiment in the North and West. They wondered aloud whether they could afford to remain much longer in the Union without serious danger to their domestic peace.

The Kansas-Nebraska Bill

Since the danger signals were waving at them in furious motion, politicians might have been well advised to sit tight and not stir up further trouble. But many of them disregarded the danger signals through stupidity, ambition, and misguided good intentions. As a result, the sectional controversy broke out again with unprecedented violence. It came when Senator Douglas moved to obtain a bill for the organization of the Nebraska Territory west of Iowa and Missouri. One undisputed reason for this provocative action was his desire to facilitate the building of a transcontinental railroad across the central section of the United States. The economic benefits to his section of the country, which trailed behind this railroad, naturally did not escape him. In order to win essential southern support for his measure, Douglas included a provision which stated that the Compromise of 1850 had supplanted the Missouri Compromise, and that the people of the Nebraska Territory should, therefore, determine for themselves whether or not they would have slavery.

At this point, Senator Archibald Dixon of Kentucky—Clay's successor—warned Douglas that the South demanded nothing less than an explicit repeal of the Missouri Compromise provision against slavery in the Louisiana Territory north of the line 36° 30′. Douglas knew that such a concession would cost him the support of many free-soil Democrats of the North, but he yielded and relied on the support of a prosouthern administration. Although Pierce came from New Hampshire, his sympathies were with the South. Jefferson Davis of Mississippi, the Secretary of War, and Caleb Cushing of Massachusetts, the Attorney General—the most influential members of the cabinet—were both strong state-rights and proslavery men. The secretaries of the Treasury and the Navy were conservative Southerners, while the Secretary of State, William L. Marcy of New York, studiously avoided the slavery question.

After a conference with Pierce and Davis at the White House, Douglas submitted, in place of the Nebraska bill, a Kansas-Nebraska bill. It created two territories divided by the fortieth parallel. The idea was that slavery might go into the southern one (Kansas), while the northern, larger one (Nebraska) would probably be free soil. The bill repealed the slavery restriction of the Missouri Compromise by declaring that it had been "superseded by the principles of the legislation of 1850."

The Triumph of Douglas

A storm of opposition in the North greeted this proposal to annul the Missouri Compromise. On the day after the Kansas-Nebraska bill was reported, anti-

Stephen Douglas, "the little giant," who asserted in his last debate with Lincoln that "this government can exist as they (our fore-fathers) made it, divided into free and slave states. . . ." (Historical Pictures Service, Inc., Chicago)

slavery men in Congress issued a protest against the measure. It was, they asserted, "a gross violation of a sacred pledge . . . a criminal betrayal of precious rights . . . part and parcel of an atrocious plot to exclude from a vast unoccupied region immigrants from the Old World, and free laborers from our own States, and convert it into a dreary region of despotism, inhabited by masters and slaves." The legislatures of half a dozen free states sent petitions to Congress in protest against its passage. Newspapers labeled Douglas a traitor, a Judas, and a Benedict Arnold, who had sold himself to the South in the hope of the presidential nomination. Douglas, himself, a short time before the passage of the Compromise of 1850, had spoken of the Missouri Compromise as "canonized in the hearts of the American people."

But insults and denunciation did not easily cower or silence the "Little Giant"—he was scarcely five feet tall. Aggressive, shrewd, and confident, Douglas rose to his greatest heights as a debater when the fight grew more intense. Practically unaided, he countered the arguments of the anti-Nebraska men on the Senate floor. He appealed for sectional harmony. He insisted that he did not care whether slavery was "voted up or down," and he begged Americans not to let their differences destroy the Union that he loved so deeply. Day after day, his vigor and tact won expressions of admiration even from his opponents.

On March 4, 1854, after a continuous session of seventeen hours, Douglas carried his bill through the Senate by a vote of thirty-seven to fourteen. In the House, the heavier concentration of northern and western representatives prolonged the battle for two and a half months. Finally, under the skillful management of Alexander H. Stephens of Georgia, the bill passed by the narrow margin of 113 to 100.

The New Republican Party

While the Senate debated the Kansas-Nebraska bill, a group of northern Whigs, anti-Nebraska Democrats, and Free Soilers met at Ripon, Wisconsin. There they resolved to organize a new party to resist the extension of slavery if the Kansas-Nebraska bill should be adopted. They suggested the name "Republican," which was popularized by Horace Greeley's New York *Tribune.*

The insurgents launched their party on July 6, 1854, at a meeting in a grove of oak trees on the outskirts of Jackson, Michigan. Its platform declared that slavery was "a great moral, social and political evil"; demanded repeal of the Kansas-Nebraska Act and the Fugitive Slave Act of 1850; and resolved to sink all political differences and unite in the battle against extension of slavery until the fight was won. The delegates nominated a full state ticket of Republican candidates, whom Michigan voters elected in November, together with four congressmen. During the summer and autumn of 1854, conventions in five other states—Maine, Vermont, Massachusetts, Ohio, and New York—met to organize Republican or Anti-Nebraska parties.

The elections in November revealed the dimensions of the political upheaval already in motion. The great Whig party suffered massive hemorrhages within its rank and file. Its northern members passed by the thousands into the Republican ranks, while its southern members drifted toward the Democrats. The Whig party never nominated another candidate for the presidency.

The Democratic party stood the shock better, but it, too, reeled under the blows of popular resentment. Of forty-two northern Democrats who voted for the Kansas-Nebraska bill, only seven won reelection to Congress in 1854. The Democratic majority of eighty-four in the House became a minority of seventy-five as a result of the election. Moreover, when Douglas had introduced his bill, the Democrats seemed secure in their control of the northwestern states—every one of the senators and all but five of the representatives from Indiana, Illinois, Michigan, Wisconsin, and Iowa were Democrats. The immense influence of Douglas helped to keep Illinois and Indiana in the Democratic column in the election of 1856, but Michigan, Wisconsin, and Iowa deserted to the Republicans. Worse reverses were yet to come.

"Bleeding Kansas"

When the Kansas-Nebraska bill became law, Douglas boasted that "the struggle over slavery was forever banished from the halls of Congress to the western plains." Although he underestimated tragically the staying power of the slavery question in Congress, Douglas predicted with deadly accuracy the next arena for the struggle. Since the settlers could choose for themselves between slavery and free soil, a rivalry for control of the territory began at once.

Free-soil emigrants from New England migrated to Kansas, and close behind them came shipments of Sharps rifles for their use. The rifles were called "Beecher's Bibles" in honor of the distinguished abolitionist clergyman, Henry Ward Beecher, who declared that it was a sounder moral argument to carry a rifle than a Bible in Kansas. The free soilers, opposed by armed proslavery men from Missouri, founded rival towns in Kansas. When Andrew H. Reeder of Pennsylvania, the territorial governor appointed by Pierce, arrived in the territory in October 1854, he found the stage set for bloody civil war. It was impossible to hold fair elections for the legislature or for a delegate to Congress. The election of a congressional delegate on November 29, 1854, for example, saw some 1,700 armed men from Missouri enter Kansas and vote illegally.

Violence was inevitable, and it came soon enough. A free stater attempted to assassinate a proslavery sheriff as he entered the free-soil town of Lawrence to arrest a man accused of murder. That did it. An armed band of Missourians rode into Lawrence on May 21, 1856, and sacked and burned the town. In revenge, the fanatical abolitionist, John Brown, led a small group of men, including his four sons, to a proslavery settlement on Pottawatomie Creek. There, on the night of May 24-25, they dragged five men from their beds in the dead of night and murdered them in cold blood. Bands of armed rioters rode up and down Kansas. Farmers with guns in hand traveled in groups to protect each other while they tilled their fields. More than 200 persons died in the armed clashes, and $2 million worth of property was destroyed.

Charles Sumner is Attacked in the Senate

The ashes of Lawrence still burned hot when tempers flared again over an atrocious act of violence committed on the floor of the United States Senate in May 1856. Charles Sumner of Massachusetts, a man of powerful intellect and immense vanity, had, on May 19–20, 1856, delivered a speech in the Senate called "The Crime against Kansas." The speech was filled with personal abuse, and Sumner fiercely attacked the proslavery men in Kansas and their supporters in the South. Sumner especially singled out for his criticism the aged Senator Andrew Pickens Butler of South Carolina, who was ill at the time and absent from his seat.

Two days later, Representative Preston Brooks of South Carolina, Butler's nephew, entered the Senate chamber. As Sumner bent over his desk attending to his work, Brooks struck him repeatedly over the head with a heavy gutta-percha cane. Sumner struggled to rise to his feet and in the process wrenched his desk from its strong bolting to the floor. Too dazed to resist his attacker, Sumner slumped to the floor unconscious as Brooks continued to rain blows on the prostrate form. Finally, other senators intervened and stopped the assault.

The House of Representatives censured Brooks, but a motion to expel him failed to win the necessary two-thirds vote. Thereupon he resigned and appealed to his constituents; they reelected him with only six dissenting votes. Brooks was toasted at banquets in the South and presented with souvenir canes. Meanwhile, the seriously injured Sumner was gradually restored to health by the skill of European doctors. Over three years passed, however, before he was willing or able to take his seat in the Senate. The empty seat served as a constant reminder of the closeness of bloody combat as the solution to the problem of slavery.

The Campaign and Election of 1856

The Democratic national convention met in Cincinnati on June 2, in the wake of the raid on Lawrence, the murders on the Pottawatomie, and the attack on Sumner. The delegates were careful not to nominate any candidate who could be held responsible for the strife in Kansas. They passed over both Pierce and Douglas and chose James Buchanan, a dignified and conservative Pennsylvanian, who had served as Secretary of State under Polk. Moreover, Buchanan had been absent from the country as Minister to England when the Kansas struggle started. His qualifications were based chiefly on two negative facts: He had no connection with Kansas, and he had no abolitionist leanings that would offend the South. Indeed he was known as a "dough-face"—a northern man with southern sympathies. Buchanan's running mate was John C. Breckinridge of Kentucky.

The first national convention of the Republican party met in Philadelphia on June 17. Its platform declared that it was "both the right and duty of Congress" to legislate for the territories of the United States, and to abolish in them "the twin relics of barbarism," slavery and polygamy. The reference to polygamy, was, of course, aimed at the Mormons. The Republican platform also called for the immediate admission of Kansas as a free state, condemned the Ostend Manifesto, and demanded construction of a railroad to the Pacific. Instead of choosing a man of political experience, like Seward or Chase, the Republicans nominated John C. Frémont of California. Frémont's career as the "pathfinder" of the Far West and the "Conqueror of California" had won him a reputation far greater than his abilities. Still the party's slogan, "Free Speech, Free Press, Free Soil, Free Men, Frémont," sounded well and had great appeal.

The Whig party had expired, but a third ticket emerged in the contest—the American, or "Know Nothing," party, formed in 1853 to combat the influence of immigrants, especially Roman Catholics, in politics. It derived its nickname from the reply, "I don't know," which its members gave to any inquiry about its activities. In the troubled early and middle 1850s, Know Nothings attracted a good many former Whigs and some Democrats to their ranks. The Know Nothings won control of Massachusetts and polled heavily in New York, Pennsylvania, Maryland, and several other states in 1854, in part because the Whig party was disintegrating in those areas. But while their candidate, former President Fillmore, polled 872,000 votes in the election of 1856, they carried only Maryland, which, ironically, had been founded as a haven for Roman Catholics.

There were frequent warnings that the election of a Republican President would mean the end of the Union. "To the fifteen states of the South," said Rufus Choate of Massachusetts, "Frémont's government will appear an alien government . . . a hostile government." On the other hand, every week that passed during the campaign saw new disturbances in Kansas, and every fresh disturbance added converts to the Republican ranks.

Despite the relatively weak and inexperienced candidate who represented the new Republican party, and the tireless campaigning of Douglas, the Democrats barely won the election. Buchanan carried the South and New Jersey, California, Illinois, Indiana, and Pennsylvania. His electoral vote was 174 to 114 for Frémont. A switch by Pennsylvania and either Illinois or Indiana would have put Frémont in the White House and might have precipitated secession and civil war in 1857.

The Republicans had made a remarkable showing in this, their first national campaign. They won eleven states and polled 1,340,000 votes to 1,833,000 for Buchanan, although they were not even on the ballot in the southern states. They closed their ranks and rallied for the next battle, cheered on by John Greenleaf Whittier's marching song:

Then sound again the bugles,
Call the muster-roll anew;
If months have well-nigh won the field,
What may not four years do?

The Dred Scott Case

Buchanan expressed the hope in his inaugural address that the long agitation over slavery was now "approaching its end." Two days later, March 6, 1857, the Supreme Court handed down one of the most fateful decisions in its history. Later it was discovered that Buchanan had helped to determine the timing, at least, of the court's action—a grave impropriety, to say the least and one which brought into question the court's independence and rectitude.

The basic facts in the case involved an army surgeon, Dr. John Emerson, who took his slave, Dred Scott, from St. Louis, where he was stationed, to the free state of Illinois and later into free Wisconsin Territory. Some years after their return to St. Louis in 1846, Dred Scott, with the help of a white patron, sued Dr. Emerson's widow for his freedom. Scott claimed that his residence in a free state and free territory had freed him. The Missouri Supreme Court denied his suit.

Then Scott was transferred to Mrs. Emerson's brother, John F. A. Sanford of New York. Sanford arranged for Scott, a Missourian, to appeal his case to a federal court on the ground of diversity of citizenship which means that, if a citizen of one state sues a citizen of another state, the case may be tried in a federal court (Constitution, Article III, Section 2). The case finally came up to the United States Supreme Court. Actually, the court had only to determine whether there had been any error in the procedure of the federal district court in Missouri, which had ruled that Scott was still a slave and, therefore, not entitled to sue. The court decided that there had not been any error, and there the case might well have ended. But Chief Justice Roger B. Taney of Maryland did not stop at this point. With the support of all but two of his colleagues, Taney went on to deliver an *obiter dictum,* or a ruling not required by the case, on the status of blacks and slavery in the territories. He hoped thereby to put an end to the slavery agitation, once and for all.

No black, Taney said, who was a slave or a descendant of slaves—even though free—could be a citizen of a state or of the United States, because blacks were not citizens when the Constitution was adopted. (This opinion, incidentally, was in defiance of the plain fact that free blacks had been voting citizens in some states in 1789.) Scott's residence in free territory was irrelevant since, Taney continued, he had been a slave in a slave state at the time that he sued. In any event, residence in territory made "forever free" by the Missouri Compromise would not have made Dred Scott a free man, because the Missouri Compromise's prohibition against slavery had itself been unconstitutional. And this was so because a slave was legal property, the Constitution forbade Congress to deprive citizens of property without due process of law, and the territories were the common property of all states.

Southerners rejoiced that, at last, the highest court in the land had endorsed the doctrines of Calhoun. There now seemed to be no barriers to the expansion of slavery into the territories except climate and geography. However, the enraged northern press spoke of the "soiled ermine of the judicial robes" and accused Taney and Buchanan of conspiring to settle the question of slavery in the territories in the South's favor. Northern anger at the decision helped to build the Republican party as the vehicle for the future reversal of the Dred Scott decision.

The Panic of 1857 and Renewal of the Kansas Troubles

A sharp if short-lived panic in the summer of 1857 added to the unrest caused by the Dred Scott decision. Overbuilding of railroads and overextension of bank credits played major roles in bringing on the crash. Banks failed, specie payments were suspended, factories closed, and thousands of jobless persons paraded and demanded "work or bread." The panic hardly touched the South, which proved to many Southerners the superiority of their institutions and economy.

An even more powerful disturbance to the national peace was the renewal of trouble in Kansas. The proslavery and free-soil extremists hated each other as much as ever. A convention met at Lecompton in September 1857 to draw up a constitution under which Kansas might come into the Union as a state. The proslavery men won control because the free soilers, who feared electoral frauds, refused to participate in the election for delegates. The proslavery delegates realized that the constitution that they had framed might be rejected; they therefore permitted a popular vote only on the question of whether the constitution should be adopted "with slavery" or "without the further introduction of slavery." Obviously, in either case Kansas would be a slave state.

The free soilers refused to go to the polls on December 21, 1857, and the Lecompton constitution was adopted. But the great majority of the people of Kansas really did not want slavery. A newly elected territorial legislature called for another election to permit a vote on the Lecompton constitution as a whole. Kansas voters rejected it by a huge majority on January 4, 1858.

3. THE EMERGENCE OF LINCOLN

Douglas Breaks with the Administration

In his inaugural address, Buchanan had pledged himself "to secure to every resident inhabitant of Kansas the free and independent expression of his opinion" on the subject of slavery. However, on February 2, 1858, he sent the Lecompton constitution to Congress with the suggestion that Kansas be admitted as a slave state—in spite of the recent overwhelming popular rejection of that document by the voters of the territory.

This was too much for Douglas, whose devotion to the principles of democracy may or may not have been greater than mere party loyalty. However, he certainly understood the danger to his reelection in 1858 posed by the strong feelings that the Kansas issue had aroused in the North and Middle West, including Illinois. He immediately protested against the President's proposal as a "travesty and mockery" of the doctrine of popular sovereignty. A new constitution had to be framed in Kansas and submitted to an honest vote of the people. The Washington government had no right to force either slavery or freedom upon them. That was a question for the people to decide. When Buchanan reminded Douglas of what Andrew Jackson had done to Democrats who broke with the administration, Douglas replied contemptuously, "Mr. President, General Jackson is dead."

Buchanan tried to crush Douglas by withdrawing all federal patronage from him, but the Little Giant stood his ground. On March 23, the Senate voted to admit Kansas under the Lecompton constitution. But Douglas rallied his friends in the House of Representatives, and a new measure, which permitted Kansas to vote again on the Lecompton constitution, passed both houses of Congress in April 1858. The Kansas voters rejected the Lecompton constitution for a second time by an overwhelming majority on August 2, 1858. Kansas remained a territory until the withdrawal of the southern members of Congress on the eve of the Civil War. On January 29, 1861, the tempestuous seven-year history of Kansas Territory came to an end with its quiet admission to the Union as a free state.

Lincoln and Douglas

Douglas returned to Illinois in the summer of 1858 to seek reelection. There he faced the most formidable challenge of his career from a rival who could match even Douglas in political craftiness and debating ability—Abraham Lincoln. The two candidates had known each other for twenty years. Both were poor men's sons who had come to Illinois early in their lives, gained reputations as great lawyers, and then entered politics. But here the resemblance ceased. Douglas had been in the United States Senate for more than ten years and had twice been a serious aspirant for the Democratic presidential nomination. Lincoln had served a single and undistinguished term (1847–1849) as a Whig member of Congress, and then had suffered defeat when he sought reelection.

In appearance and personality the men were exact opposites. Lincoln was very tall—about six feet four inches—lanky, awkward, reflective, slow in speech and motion. Douglas was, as we have said, scarcely five feet in height—thickset, quick, volcanic in speech, and forceful in gesture.

Neither was an extremist on slavery. Douglas was as far removed from the fire-eaters of the South as Lincoln was from the more doctrinaire abolitionists of the North. But the two men differed in one fundamental aspect. Douglas did not think that slavery was a moral question, and he did not seem to understand persons who did. As he said, he did not care whether slavery was voted up or down. Lincoln believed deeply that slavery was morally wrong. He insisted that the Union could not endure unless slavery eventually was abolished. In his speech before the Illinois Republican convention which nominated him for the Senate in June 1858, Lincoln declared: "A house divided against itself cannot stand. I believe this government cannot endure permanently half slave and half free. I do not expect the Union to be dissolved. I do not expect the house to fall, but I do expect it will cease to be divided."

Douglas misrepresented this long-range prophecy of Lincoln's as a plea for "war of the sections until one or the other shall be subdued." He criticized Lincoln's declared opposition to the Dred Scott decision and said that Lincoln's logic was an appeal from the judgment of the Supreme Court of the land to "the decision of a tumultuous town meeting." Lincoln, like most Northerners and Midwesterners, was no racial egalitarian. He could not foresee the day when blacks would live as free citizens in a free society, and he thought that the best solution of the race problem would be the resettlement of blacks in Central America or Africa.

Many eastern Republicans, including the influential Horace Greeley of the New York *Tribune,* thought that Douglas' reelection should be unopposed in Illinois because of his fight for popular sovereignty in Kansas. But the Illinois Republicans would not go back on their principles and support the author of the Kansas-Nebraska Act. They were as firmly opposed to Douglas' plan of letting the people of a territory determine whether or not they would have slavery as they were to Buchanan's attempt to force slavery upon Kansas. And no one did more to make certain that Illinois Republicans would not accept Douglas as their candidate than Abraham Lincoln.

The Lincoln-Douglas Debates

Douglas and Lincoln agreed, at the latter's invitation, to meet on the same platform in a series of debates. There were seven of them between August and October, 1858—one in each electoral district of Illinois. Their immediate object was to influence the people in the election of the legislature that was to choose one of them as United States senator.

The rivals spoke from platforms in the open air before thousands of persons, but the broader and more important audience was the people of the United States. Douglas constantly referred to Lincoln's "house divided" speech as an incitement to civil strife. He stressed the fairness, democracy, and "Americanism" of popular sovereignty, if honestly applied. Lincoln insisted that the territories must be kept as future homes for free white settlers. In this position, he

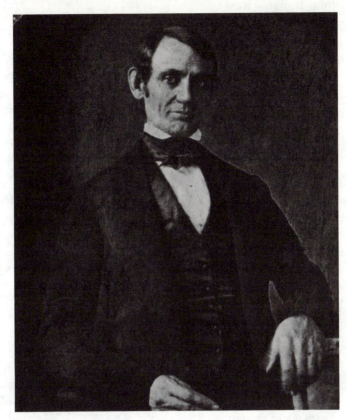

This, the earliest known portrait of Abraham Lincoln, was made from a daguerreotype taken in 1846 when he was 37 years old. At that time Lincoln served one term as congressman from Illinois. As a representative, he constantly reiterated his opposition to United States involvement in the Mexican War and the consequences this war would hold for the issue of slavery. (Library of Congress)

reflected the predominant western fear of the competition of black labor, not moral repugnance against slavery itself. In addition, Lincoln made it clear that he was opposed to interference with slavery in the states where it existed.

The high point of the debates came at Freeport, Illinois, on August 27. Here Lincoln asked Douglas whether the people of a territory could lawfully exclude slavery from its limits before the adoption of their state constitution and admission to the Union. Douglas was caught on the horns of a dilemma. If he answered "yes," he would seem to defy the Dred Scott decision. If he answered "no," he would repudiate his own doctrine of popular sovereignty. Douglas held firm to his faith in popular sovereignty. It was true, he admitted, that a territorial legislature could not outlaw slavery. The Dred Scott decision had settled that point. But, Douglas went on, slavery could not exist a single day in any territory unless the territorial legislature established and protected it by law. No one could force a territorial legislature to do this. Therefore, the territories could in effect decide whether or not to have slavery.

This soon became known as the Freeport Doctrine. Lincoln later summed it up in the witticism: "Then a thing may be legally driven away from a place where it has a legal right to be." Douglas won the senatorship by eight votes in the Illinois legislature, but he had ruined his chances of southern support for the presidency, just as Lincoln intended that he should. In contrast, the debates added significantly to Lincoln's political reputation throughout the North and West.

John Brown's Raid

By this time, intersectional tensions were rising dangerously high, and they were intensified further by one of those irrational events that often determines the course of history. John Brown, the murderer at Pottawatomie Creek in Kansas, believed that God had commissioned him to free the slaves. Brown collected some $4 thousand from abolitionist sympathizers and formed a band of about twenty followers. He planned to begin a slave insurrection in the mountains of Virginia, establish a "free state" there, and rally slaves throughout the South from his mountain stronghold. Accordingly, Brown and his band seized the United States arsenal at Harpers Ferry, Virginia, at the junction of the Potomac and Shenandoah rivers, on October 16, 1859. A detachment of United States marines under the command of Colonel Robert E. Lee battered down the doors of the arsenal and easily captured those members of Brown's band who had not been killed in the siege. Brown himself, severely wounded, was promptly tried for treason in a Virginia court. It was a strange indictment, since it was hardly possible for Brown to commit treason against a state of which he was not a citizen. He conducted himself with enormous dignity at his trial, but he offered no defense other than his divine commission. He was

This daguerreotype was taken during John Brown's visit to Boston in the winter of 1856–1857 to raise money for the abolition of slavery. (Boston Athenaeum)

condemned and hanged on December 2, 1859. Ralph Waldo Emerson said: "He made the gallows glorious like the cross."

Brown's courage and dignity in the face of death could not alter the fact that his raid at Harpers Ferry was the rash deed of a fanatic—if not a pyschotic. In the eyes of Southerners, Brown's raid was an abolitionist plot to incite a slave rebellion, and one supported by Republican leaders. More than any other single event of the prewar period, it convinced Southerners that they could not remain safely in the Union if the federal government ever fell into the hands of an antislavery party. If that happened, worried one Southern lady, "they will Brown us all." Southern nonslaveholders were even more agitated and alarmed than were the large planters who, as the largest property owners, had the most to lose economically in the event of war. Many Northerners also were appalled by Brown's raid. They realized that crazed fanatics were encouraged by the climate of events to go about the country and kill people. However, once the Civil War began, ordinary northern soldiers seemed to regard Brown as a predecessor. Northern regiments marched to the song:

John Brown's body lies a-moldering in the grave,
His soul goes marching on.

The Crisis Deepens

Congress met on December 5, 1859, three days after John Brown had been hanged. In the House, which contained 109 Republicans and 101 Democrats, a battle lasted two months over the choice of a speaker. The impasse occurred because John Sherman of Ohio, candidate of the Republicans, had spoken favorably of a book entitled *The Impending Crisis in the South and How to Meet It.* It was written by Hinton R. Helper, an antiblack poor white of North Carolina, and aimed to prove (by figures that were not always accurate) that slavery impeded the industrialization and agricultural progress of the South. Helper appealed to the great mass of nonslaveholders to join with the Republicans and get rid of slavery. (He later wrote three bitter racist tracts. One of them, *Nojoque*, 1867, advocated the forced deportation of American blacks to South America.) In the House of Representatives, insults were hurled across the aisle, and challenges to duels were exchanged. Many of the members went to the sessions armed with revolvers.

An even more important struggle raged within the Democratic party between the northwestern faction, led by Stephen A. Douglas, and the extremist southern faction, led by Jefferson Davis. Davis earlier had taken a position on slavery in the territories not remarkably different from Douglas' Freeport Doctrine. Now, however, he was determined to prevent Douglas' nomination in 1860. Partly in order to solidify southern Democratic sentiment against Douglas, Davis introduced a set of resolutions in the Senate on February 2, 1860. They declared that no state should interfere with the domestic institutions of any other state; that territorial legislatures should pass no antislavery legislation; that Congress had to protect slave property in all territories; and that personal liberty laws for the protection of runaway slaves violated the Constitution. The Senate approved the resolutions on May 24, 1860, after a bitter debate that greatly widened the breach in the Democratic party.

On the twenty-seventh of the same month in which Davis introduced his resolutions, Lincoln made a notable address at Cooper Union, an industrial school in New York City. The debates with Douglas, reported in newspapers throughout the country, had gained a national reputation for Lincoln. However, eastern Republicans had not yet given him a place among their leaders alongside Seward and Sumner. Lincoln's clothes were ill-fitting, his voice was high and thin, and his gestures were awkward. All these deficiencies, however, were forgotten when he began to speak.

Lincoln proceeded, accurately and clearly, to set forth Republican doctrine. He pointed to the fact that Congress had repeatedly made laws to control slavery in the territories and that the South had accepted such legislation. He emphasized that no shred of evidence could be adduced to show that the Republican party had had anything to do with John Brown's raids, and that the threat of the fire-eaters to break up the Union if a Republican President was elected had no justification. Lincoln concluded with a ringing appeal to the men of the free states to stand by their principles in the faith that "right makes might." The Cooper Union speech—a clear answer to the Davis resolutions— made Lincoln a leading candidate for the Republican nomination.

The Democratic Party is Split

The great conventions of 1860, which nominated candidates for the most important presidential election in American history, began with the meeting of the Democrats at Charleston, South Carolina, on April 23. The platform committee approved the Davis resolutions, but the majority of the delegates supported Douglas, who was the unanimous choice of northwestern Democrats. Thereupon the Alabama delegates, led by one of the leading southern fire-eaters, William L. Yancey, marched out of the hall. They were followed by the majority of the delegates from South Carolina, Georgia, Florida, Mississippi, Louisiana, Arkansas, and Texas. Since in the diminished convention Douglas failed to get the two-thirds vote then necessary for nomination, the members adjourned to meet again at Baltimore on June 18. There the convention again split. This time the "regulars" nominated Douglas and Herschel V. Johnson of Georgia, while the "bolters" nominated Vice-President John C. Breckinridge and Senator Joseph Lane of Oregon.

The Election of Abraham Lincoln

Meanwhile, the Republican convention had met at Chicago on May 16. Senator William H. Seward of New York, the favored candidate, confidently expected the nomination and led Lincoln by 173 votes to 102 on the first ballot. But Seward was handicapped in the East by his outspoken sympathy with abolitionists and his savage attacks on Know Nothings. Westerners, on the other hand, were very solidly behind their homespun hero, "Honest Abe." Lincoln was nominated on the third ballot, and western delegates went wild with joy. Lincoln's running mate was Hannibal Hamlin of Maine.

The platform reasserted the free-soil doctrine and condemned the Lecompton constitution and the Dred Scott decision. It appealed to Westerners as well as eastern businessmen by urging construction of a Pacific railroad, and to

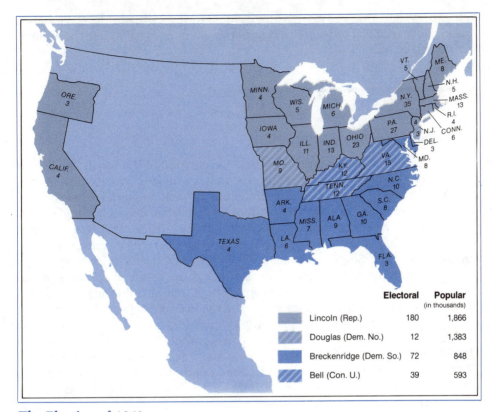

	Electoral	Popular (in thousands)
Lincoln (Rep.)	180	1,866
Douglas (Dem. No.)	12	1,383
Breckenridge (Dem. So.)	72	848
Bell (Con. U.)	39	593

The Election of 1860

manufacturers and workers in the crucial state of Pennsylvania with a plank which favored a protective tariff. To the western settler, it promised free homesteads and federal aid to internal improvements. Thus the Chicago "bargain," as one authority has called the platform, resembled a compromise between William Lloyd Garrison and Henry Clay. It had something for nearly everybody except slaveowners.

A fourth party also entered the contest—the Constitutional Unionists, made up chiefly of former Whigs, Know Nothings, and conservatives, who feared secession if Lincoln was elected. It sought to avoid the slavery issue and offered a platform which pledged "the maintenance of the Union and the Constitution and the enforcement of the laws." John Bell of Tennessee and Edward Everett of Massachusetts were chosen as its standard-bearers.

Lincoln carried the election by an overwhelming majority in the Electoral College. Nevertheless, he received only about 40 per cent of the popular vote, largely because he was on the ballot in only two southern states—Kentucky and Virginia—and received only 3,000 votes from both states combined. Douglas, although he was rejected by the administration and carried only Missouri and part of New Jersey, rolled up the very large popular vote of 1,383,000, compared to 1,866,000 for Lincoln. The three unionist candidates together polled four and one half times as many votes as Breckinridge. Even in the slave states, Breckinridge received only 45 per cent of the votes, or 115,000 less than Douglas and Bell combined.

4. THE SECESSION OF THE SOUTH

A Southern Confederacy Is Formed

It is only a slight exaggeration to say that the election in the South had been a mandate on the question of secession, and that the answer was decidedly negative. Yet leaders in South Carolina immediately went to work to dissolve the Union in spite of the fact that two unionist candidates, Bell and Douglas, had polled a majority of the southern popular vote. South Carolina was the only state in 1860 that chose its presidential electors by the legislature instead of by popular vote. The South Carolina legislature, after it chose its electors on November 6, remained in session until it heard the result of the vote in the other states. Then it called a convention, which met at Columbia on December 20, 1860, and, by the unanimous vote of its 169 members, adopted an Ordinance of Secession. This ordinance, which declared that "the union now subsisting between South Carolina and the other States, under the name of the United States of America, is hereby dissolved," repealed the act of May 23, 1788, by which the state had ratified the Constitution. Four days later, the convention issued a "Declaration of Immediate Causes" which justified this disruption of the Union. The most important cause, it said, was the triumph of a party dedicated to waging war against slavery "until it shall cease throughout the United States."

South Carolina sent emissaries to the other southern states, and Democratic leaders in the Deep South put into effect what seems to have been a prearranged plan. Within six weeks, Mississippi, Florida, Alabama, Louisiana, Georgia, and Texas had severed their connection with the Union. Even during circumstances that approximated panic, unionists in these states fought a hard rear guard action. The vote for secession was by no means overwhelming in some states. In the key state of Georgia, for example, the vote in the state convention was 164 for secession and 133 against; and it is very doubtful that a majority of the voters of Georgia favored secession.

Delegates from all these states (except Texas, where the secession ordinance had to be submitted to a popular vote) met at Montgomery, Alabama, on February 4, 1861, and organized the Confederate States of America. Jefferson Davis of Mississippi was chosen President, and Alexander H. Stephens of Georgia, Vice-President. The Confederate Constitution resembled that of the United States with these exceptions: First, the President was to serve a single term of six years; second, he could veto specific items in appropriations bills; third, cabinet members could speak on the floor of Congress; fourth, slavery was expressly legalized and protected; fifth, protective tariff duties were prohibited; sixth, Congress was given the right to levy taxes on exports; finally, and of crucial importance to the success of the new nation, the sovereign and independent character of the states was acknowledged in terms similar to those in the Articles of Confederation.

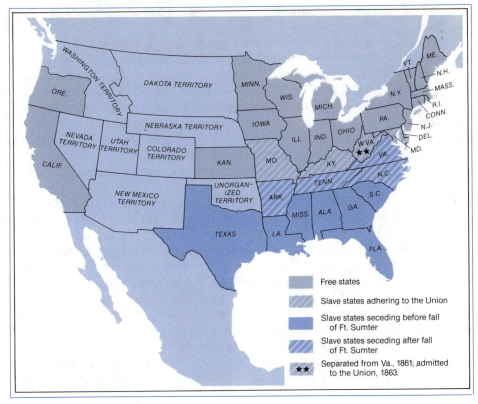

Alignment of States in 1861

Attempts to Prevent War

Meanwhile, great confusion reigned in Washington. President Buchanan had hoped that his term might come to an end before the storm broke. In his last Annual Message to Congress, on December 3, 1860, he denied the right of secession: "Its [the Constitution's] framers never intended to implant in its bosom the seeds of its own destruction. . . . Secession is neither more nor less than revolution." At the same time, Buchanan went on, the Constitution gave the national government no authority to coerce a state into submission, for "the power to make war against a state is at variance with the whole spirit and intent of the Constitution."

Buchanan's position was extremely difficult. He was, after all, a lame-duck President with only three more months to serve. Stern action by him might have precipitated a war that his successor would have to conduct. Moreover, public opinion in the North was divided and confused. The Mayor of New York City, Fernando Wood, actually proposed to his city council that New York City should secede from the Union. Abolitionists like Garrison and Wendell Phillips asserted that they were glad to see the slaveholding states out of the Union. Horace Greeley of the powerful New York *Tribune* advised letting the cotton states go in peace rather than wage a war to keep them in the Union. Buchanan tried to retain control of federal forts and arsenals in the

South without, however, running the risk of war. That decision he left to his successor.

Meanwhile, desperate attempts were being made in Congress to find a compromise to save the Union. Senator John J. Crittenden of Kentucky proposed a set of "unamendable amendments" to the Constitution. They would extend the Missouri Compromise line of 36° 30′ to California as the dividing line between slavery and free soil, forbid Congress ever to interfere with the domestic slave trade, and pledge the government to pay for escaped fugitive slaves. To these amendments were added resolutions that upheld the Fugitive Slave Act of 1850 but modified it to make it more acceptable to the North, recommended repeal of all personal liberty laws, and retained the ban on the African slave trade.

A congressional committee of thirteen, which represented all shades of opinion, discussed the Crittenden compromise earnestly, but they could not agree. The Republicans, backed by President-elect Lincoln, held firmly to their refusal to allow slavery to go into territories below 36° 30′. With them voted extremist Southerners, who just as firmly refused to exclude slavery above 36° 30′. This deadlock meant that compromise was no longer possible.

The only outcome of the long discussion was the recommendation of a constitutional amendment which legalized slavery forever in the states where it already existed. A two-thirds majority in both houses passed this proposed Thirteenth Amendment to the Constitution on February 28, 1861, and submitted it to the states. By that time, however, the Confederacy was already established, and only two states took the trouble to ratify the proposed amendment.

Lincoln and the Secession Crisis

The most serious crisis in the history of the nation confronted Abraham Lincoln when he took the oath as President on March 4, 1861. A rival government in the South had been in operation in Montgomery for a full month. Secessionists had seized all United States military installations in the seven Confederate states, except for several forts. Southerners were departing daily from federal offices in Washington and all through the North to join the cause of their states. Many voices in the North were bidding them Godspeed.

Meanwhile, Major Robert Anderson, with a little garrison of eighty-three men in Fort Sumter, in Charleston harbor, was writing to the War Department that his store of food was almost exhausted. Anderson had moved his garrison from Fort Moultrie to the stronger Fort Sumter a few days after the secession of South Carolina. The South Carolina authorities interpreted this as a warlike act and demanded that the garrison be sent back to Fort Moultrie. Buchanan refused to yield to commissioners from South Carolina who came to Washington to ask the government to surrender federal property in their state. Buchanan even sent a merchant vessel, *Star of the West*, with provisions for Anderson's garrison in Fort Sumter. The ship was turned back by fire from the guns on Morris Island on January 8, 1861. For the remaining two months of his term, Buchanan took no further step to disturb the "truce" in Charleston harbor.

Lincoln's inaugural address was a restatement of his kindly feeling toward the South and a plea for calmness and brotherly love. He declared that he had to hold the forts and property of the United States in the South and to collect

This cartoon of Lincoln, entitled "A Job for the New Cabinet Maker," is from Frank Leslie's Illustrated Newspaper (1861). Anticipating the difficult tasks before him, the new President insisted in his inaugural address that "we cannot separate." (Culver Pictures, Inc.)

customs duties in southern ports, as the law demanded. Yet he did not intend to disturb the institutions or invade the rights of the South. "In your hands, my dissatisfied fellow countrymen, and not in mine," he said, turning to his southern hearers, "is the momentous issue of civil war. The Government will not assail you. You can have no conflict without being yourselves the aggressors. You have no oath registered in heaven to destroy the government, while I shall have the most solemn one to 'preserve, protect, and defend it'." Finally, Lincoln appealed to the common memories of the North and the South, which, like "mystic chords . . . stretching from every battlefield and patriot grave to every living heart and hearthstone all over this broad land, will yet swell the chorus of the Union, when again touched, as surely they will be, by the better angels of our nature."

The Fall of Fort Sumter

Only a few days after his inauguration, Lincoln laid before his cabinet the critical situation in Charleston harbor. He opposed withdrawal from Fort Sumter both because it would destroy northern morale and because it would be regarded as recognition of the Confederacy. Also, he had sworn in his oath of office to uphold the laws and support and defend the Constitution, and he could hardly look the other way and permit federal property to be seized or a rival government exercise sovereignty over the southern states. Hence Lincoln was determined that Anderson should not be starved out; therefore, he notified Governor Francis W. Pickens of South Carolina on April 8 that he would send provisions to the fort. The Confederate government at Montgomery was likewise faced with a fateful decision. Should it blockade the fort until hunger forced a surrender, or order an immediate attack? General P. G. T. Beauregard at Charleston was ordered to demand the immediate surrender of Fort Sumter. Anderson refused to comply.

Just before dawn on April 12, 1861, Confederate batteries on Sullivan's, James, and Morris islands opened fire upon the fort. The bombardment lasted all day and at intervals throughout the night of rain and wind that followed. Cheering throngs lined the Battery along the Charleston sea front. For thirty-two hours, Anderson maintained the unequal contest. Then, on the afternoon of Saturday, April 13, with the fort in flames and his men tortured by heat and smoke, he surrendered.

The firing on Fort Sumter opened the Civil War. On April 15, Lincoln called on the states for 75,000 militiamen, who were needed, he said, to suppress resistance to the laws of the United States by "combinations too powerful to be suppressed by the ordinary source of judicial proceedings." None of the governors of the slave states heeded the President's call, but the response of the North was immediate. When President Jefferson Davis issued the momentous order to take Fort Sumter, Robert Toombs, his Secretary of State, warned, "It . . . will lose us every friend in the North." Exactly so. "The first gun at Fort Sumter," wrote James Russell Lowell, "brought all the free states to their feet as one man." Party lines dissolved. Douglas, the leader of a million and a half Democrats, hastened to the White House to grasp Lincoln's hand and pledge him his utmost support. Ex-Presidents Pierce and Buchanan, hitherto friendly to the South, became strong unionists. Editors such as Horace Greeley, preachers such as Henry Ward Beecher, and politicians such as Edward Everett, who only recently had opposed the use of force, now joined the call to arms.

The South was no less enthusiastic. Volunteers flocked to answer Davis' call for an army of 100,000. The Confederate Congress met in extra session to adopt measures for the military, financial, and industrial security of the Confederacy. So Americans of the North and the South confronted one another in arms.

Why the War?

Historians have long debated why it was that the worst of all possible wars, a "war of the brothers," broke out in the United States. There are no final answers, but this much can be said in summary:

1. Slavery, more than any other factor, contributed the most to the outbreak of war. The conscience of the North was aroused against slavery. It was probably only a question of time before a reckoning on the issue would come. In this respect, the war was perhaps "irrepressible," as William H. Seward said, unless Southerners should meanwhile abolish slavery voluntarily—an increasingly unlikely possibility. Related to slavery was the question of race. Racial tensions in the North and South contributed to the fears, anxieties, and emotional intensity of many whites who neither owned slaves themselves or necessarily were directly affected by it in any immediate way. Poor whites in the South, like poor whites in the North and West, resented and hated blacks for sociological, economic, and psychological reasons.

2. The slavery question also caused the controversy over slavery in the territories from 1846 to 1860 that brought that question to a head with Lincoln's election. The Republican party's emphasis upon free soil, free labor, and free men led to the growth of a powerful ideology which, inevitably, highlighted the socioeconomic differences between the slave states and the free states.

3. One of the causes was the wide difference that had developed between the southern and northern views of the nature of the Union. Many Southerners quite sincerely believed that the Union was a compact, and that they had a perfect constitutional right to secede. Northerners believed that the Union was indestructible, and that it was their constitutional duty to fight to preserve it. The significant fact is that these conflicting views of the Constitution had become sectionalized. Before 1815, groups in both the North and the South either had believed in the compact theory, or else had used it to defend their interests. But division polarized along geographical lines after 1815. The North was swept along by one current of nationalism, while the South (and particularly the Lower South) became more and more committed to state rights. Southerners had also become affected to some degree by a nationalism reminiscent of the romantic nationalism which appeared in the mid-nineteenth century among European peoples who attempted to secede from larger nations, such as the Austrian Empire. The crystallization of southern sentiment was in large part a result of the slavery controversy. It would be impossible to protect slavery, Southerners believed, against a powerful national government controlled by enemies of slavery.

4. Southerners in 1861 believed that the safety of their families, homes, and way of life was threatened now that the federal government was controlled by a sectional party, hostile to slavery. This unreasoned and unfounded fear was the immediate cause for secession in most of the southern states.

5. Old economic conflicts over the tariff, a national bank, and internal improvements played a minor role, if any, in bringing on the great crisis. Not since the Nullification controversy of 1832–1833 had an economic issue provoked violent discord between the two sections of the country. Even then, South Carolina had stood alone in resistance to federal authority. After the 1830s, tariff rates fell, powerful northern bankers lost interest in national intervention in the banking system, and Southwesterners and Northwesterners came to agree on the subject of internal improvements. In general, wealthy and influential Northerners sympathized with southern fears and usually sought to allay them. Tariff rates were increased, and a national banking system—although a system not remotely comparable to the first or second national bank—was created after the southern secession as a wartime measure; but, despite the war, this legislation was opposed by the most powerful northern business interests.

6. Finally, few Americans in 1860–1861 foresaw the consequences of failure to achieve a compromise. It is doubtful whether many persons on either side would have acted as they did if they had known that the result would be a bloody four-year conflict. When it became evident that war not only was possible, but also probable, leaders on both sides showed little skill in averting tragedy. Politicians in the mid-nineteenth century, even the most intelligent, were more adept at arousing emotions than at calming them, and better trained to tell voters what they wanted to hear than to admit the unpleasant truth. Nor-

mally, Americans are adept at compromise in resolving political controversy. This is part of their ongoing success in self-government. Only on one issue did they fail to compromise. Consequently, as Daniel Webster prophesied, the land was "drenched . . . in fraternal blood."

SUGGESTED READINGS

The best guide to this and the following two chapters is James G. Randall and David Herbert Donald, *The Civil War and Reconstruction* (2nd ed., 1961). Allan Nevins, *The Ordeal of the Union* (1947) and *The Emergence of Lincoln* (1950), is a full and masterful account of the political crisis of the decade of the 1850s; another masterful account is David M. Potter and Don E. Fehrenbacher, *The Impending Crisis, 1848–1861* (1976). Roy F. Nichols, *The Disruption of American Democracy* (1948), and Michael F. Holt, *The Political Crisis of the 1850s* (1978), offer more provocative views of the same series of events. For still other points of view, consult Avery O. Craven, *The Coming of the Civil War* (1942); Henry H. Simms, *A Decade of Sectional Controversy* (1942); and Dwight L. Dumond, *Antislavery Origins of the Civil War in the United States* (1939).

On the significance of the Kansas-Nebraska Act, see Roy F. Nichols, "The Kansas-Nebraska Act: A Century of Historiography, "*Mississippi Valley Historical Review*, XLIII (1956). James C. Malin, *The Nebraska Question, 1852–1854* (1953), and Paul W. Gates, *Fifty Million Acres: Conflicts Over Kansas Land Policy, 1854–1890* (1954), also contain useful information. Stephen B. Oates, *To Purge This Land With Blood* (1970), is the best modern study of John Brown, but C. Vann Woodward, *The Burden of Southern History* (1960), contains an excellent essay on Brown.

Eric Foner, *Free Soil, Free Labor, Free Men* (1970), is an important analysis of Republican policies and ideology. David Herbert Donald, *Charles Sumner and the Coming of the Civil War* (1960), and Martin B. Duberman, *Charles Francis Adams* (1961), offer views of the origins of the Republican party from the vantage point of New England antislavery politicians. An up-to-date biography of Lincoln is Stephen B. Oates, *With Malice Toward None* (1977). A short biography that is very useful is Benjamin P. Thomas, *Abraham Lincoln* (1952). On Lincoln's early career, see Don E. Fehrenbacher, *Prelude to Greatness* (1962). A fine analysis of the Lincoln-Douglas debates is Harry V. Jaffa, *Crisis of the House Divided* (1959). The Dred Scott case is splendidly illuminated in Don E. Fehrenbacher, *The Dred Scott Case: Its Significance in American Law and Politics* (1978).

The best general account of secession is Ralph A. Wooster, *The Secession Conventions of the South* (1962). A good description of events at the level of national politics is David M. Potter, *Lincoln and His Party in the Secession Crisis, 1860–1861* (1950). For the northern reaction, see Kenneth M. Stampp, *And the War Came: The North and the Secession Crisis, 1860–1861* (1950). Richard N. Current, *Lincoln and the First Shot* (1963), discusses the Sumter crisis. See also Steven A. Channing, *Crisis of Fear* (1970), and J. L. Roark, *Masters Without Slaves* (1977). For a view of secession as a consequence of the development of a southern culture in which violence was an important component, see John Hope Franklin, *The Militant South* (1956).

CHAPTER 16
THE CIVIL WAR

1. THE WAR IN THE EAST

The Confederacy Enlarged

Lincoln's call for volunteers precipitated Virginia's secession. The adherence of the Old Dominion to the Confederacy was the most important event of 1861. The Confederate capital was immediately moved from Montgomery to Richmond, and Virginia thereafter became the chief battleground of the war and the main arsenal of the Confederate armies. Moreover, Virginia's secession had a profound impact on the rest of the Upper South. At first, Virginia had voted against secession. On April 4, 1861, by a vote of eighty-eight to forty-five, the state convention voted to stay in the Union, and the other upper southern states followed suit. But Lincoln's call for volunteers forced the convention to choose between making war against other Southerners or joining the Confederacy. The Virginia state convention adopted an ordinance of secession on April 17. The rest of the Upper South followed immediately: Arkansas on May 6; North Carolina on May 20, and Tennessee on June 8.

Strong secessionist sentiment existed, too, in the Border States of Maryland, Kentucky, and Missouri. Lincoln resorted to military arrests in Maryland to end a secessionist majority in the legislature of that state. He used tact and patience and finally secured a unionist majority in the legislature of his native state of Kentucky. However, it required a little civil war to keep Missouri in the Union. In that state, "home guards" under Captain Nathaniel Lyon drove the secessionist governor, Claiborne Fox Jackson, from the capital and held the state for the Union. The loss of the Border States to the Confederacy would have been disastrous for the Union. It is a measure of Lincoln's stature as a statesman that he held them fast despite their large number of Confederate sympathizers.

Virginia not only brought most of the Upper South into the Confederacy; it also gave the struggling new nation its greatest general — Robert E. Lee. Son of the distinguished Revolutionary soldier, "Light-Horse Harry" Lee, Robert E. Lee was a brilliant field commander and a gentleman of spotless character — generous, deeply religious, and brave. Lincoln offered him the command of the Union army, but Lee could not lead a war against his own people and his native state, which he believed had "never parted with her sovereign right to demand the ultimate allegiance of her citizens." So Lee resigned his commission in the United States Army to accept command of the state troops of Virginia. A year later, he was made general of the Confederate forces in Virginia. Toward the end of the war, Davis appointed him general in chief of all Confederate forces in the field. Another Virginian, Winfield Scott, faced the same dilemma as Lee. But he chose the Union over his native state. The Civil War had remarkable and frequently conflicting effects on the men and women who fought and suffered through it. In large part, this explains its enduring fascination for the American people.

The Balance Scales

At first glance, it seemed that the Confederacy was doomed from the beginning. The Union enjoyed great superiority in everything necessary for an enormous military undertaking. The population of the free and border states totaled 22,000,000. The Confederacy had scarcely 9,000,000 people, and that number included slaves. In money, credit, manufactures, shipping, and the all-important factor of railroad transportation, the North far excelled the South. Once the North had mustered its resources and sent its armies pouring into the South, the Confederacy stood little chance of survival

On the other hand, in a short war, the Confederacy had enormous advantages of terrain, defense, interior lines, and fighting experience. In a quick, lightninglike war, the South might easily defeat its northern enemies. Southerners were more united in spirit at the outset because they were fighting a defensive war to protect their native states; they also probably began the struggle with better generals — or at least more energetic, more decisive generals. Furthermore, the Confederacy expected aid from three sources — all of which proved disappointing. The Confederate leaders believed that Great Britain and France, heretofore dependent on the South for their supplies of raw cotton, would recognize southern independence and break the blockade of southern ports that Lincoln decreed shortly after the fall of Fort Sumter. Southerners believed that northern Democrats, who had cast 1,370,000 votes against Lincoln, would refuse to support a Republican attempt to subjugate the South. Southerners also expected that Lincoln's call for troops would at once bring into the Confederacy all of the eight slave states — Virginia , North Carolina, Tennessee, Arkansas, Maryland, Delaware, Kentucky, and Missouri — which had not seceded. Only half the anticipated number seceded, and none of the other expectations was realized. Unfortunately for the Confederacy, the war dragged on for four years. Each year diminished the hope of eventual victory.

The First Battle of Bull Run

The Confederate Congress was called to meet at Richmond on July 20, 1861. Meanwhile, forty-eight counties in the western, mountainous part of Virginia voted against secession in May 1861. When Governor John Letcher sent troops to coerce them, they seceded from Virginia and set up the new state of Kanawha. Lincoln dispatched an army under General George B. McClellan, of the Department of the Ohio, to drive the Confederates out of the region. This

Major Campaigns of the Civil War

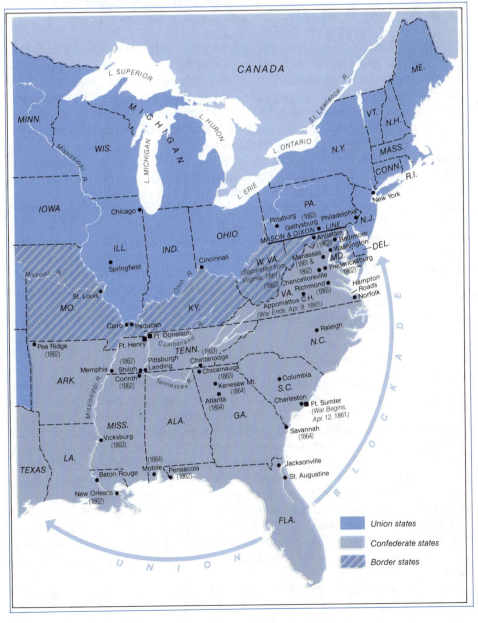

McClellan did with complete success. In 1863, Congress admitted the western counties of Virginia into the Union as the state of West Virginia. Strong pro-Union sentiment existed in other parts of the Confederacy, particularly in western North Carolina and eastern Tennessee. Mountaineers in these states hated slavery, slaveowners, and blacks. They were also fiercely loyal to the Union, and furnished at least as many fighting men to the Union army as to the Confederate army.

Overconfident Northerners, cheered by McClellan's success in clearing the rebels out of West Virginia, demanded that the war be ended before the Confederate Congress could meet. General Irvin McDowell had 30,000 troops at Washington. They were not yet properly organized or drilled, but their three-months' term of enlistment was about to expire. Lincoln and Scott yielded to the popular cry, and McDowell's "grand army" marched toward Richmond. It was accompanied by newspaper reporters and crowds who expected to see the rebellion crushed by a single blow.

McDowell met General Joseph E. Johnston's Confederate force of 22,000 on July 21 at Manassas Junction, a little town on Bull Run, or creek, about thirty-five miles southwest of Washington. The battle favored the Union side until early in the afternoon, and reports of victory were sent back to Washington. But both armies were exhausted by nearly ten hours of fighting; then fresh Confederate troops from the Shenandoah Valley arrived on the field and turned the tide. By sundown, McDowell's thoroughly defeated army was rushing toward Washington in wild flight and, to make matters worse, collided with panic-stricken civilians. For his firm stand at the critical point in this battle, General Thomas J. Jackson, Lee's ablest lieutenant, earned the nickname, "Stonewall."

The defeat at Bull Run sobered the North. Lincoln called for three-year volunteers, and tens of thousands of men poured into the camp of the Army of the Potomac. Southerners, elated by their victory, strengthened fortifications around Richmond and prepared to hold their far flung front. It extended westward to forts on the Cumberland and Tennessee rivers and to the middle of the Mississippi River. No other important battles occurred in 1861; each side was preparing for a long and bitter struggle.

Relations with Great Britain

The two sides in the American Civil War competed fervently for the support of the major European powers. The Washington government of course worked hard to prevent foreign aid to the rebels, because the Confederacy could not long survive without rifles, medicines, ships, and other supplies from abroad. The rival governments competed especially in Great Britain. Some persons in Great Britain, notably among the aristocracy, hoped to see the American democratic experiment fail. However, most ordinary Englishmen sympathized with the Union, especially after the Emancipation Proclamation appeared to recast the war into a crusade against slavery. At first Southerners believed that the British textile industry would come to a standstill without their cotton, but manufacturers in Great Britain had accumulated large inventories during the secession crisis and then substituted cotton from Egypt, India, and other countries.

As his Minister to Britain, Lincoln sent Charles Francis Adams, a son and grandson of former Presidents and a capable and resourceful diplomat in his own right. On the day of Adams' delayed arrival in England—May 13, 1861— Queen Victoria's government recognized the belligerency of the Confederacy, that is, its right to be treated according to the rules of warfare between two acknowledged powers. It meant that the Confederacy could purchase supplies, including munitions, in Great Britain.

The Lincoln administration resented even this form of recognition and formally objected. But the practical-minded Lincoln soon appreciated the need to treat so numerous and united a people as the Confederate States of America as a belligerent power. Indeed, by proclaiming a formal blockade of the Confederacy on April 19, 1861, he had recognized Confederate belligerency and had given the British government sound precedent for its action. Moreover, Lincoln approved the exchange of prisoners with the Confederacy and occasionally dealt with Confederate authorities through official channels.

The Trent Affair

A far more serious controversy threatened Anglo-American peace in the autumn of 1861. The Richmond government had appointed James M. Mason and John Slidell as commissioners to Great Britain and France, respectively, for the purpose of winning recognition of the Confederacy. Mason and Slidell slipped easily through the as yet ineffective blockade and boarded the British steamer *Trent* at Havana.

On November 8, Captain Charles Wilkes of *U.S.S. San Jacinto* stopped *Trent* on the high seas with two shots across her bow. Then Wilkes forcibly removed Mason and Slidell from *Trent* and brought them back to New York. The two commissioners were later sent as prisoners to Fort Warren in Boston harbor. The North rejoiced over Wilkes' deed, while the South hoped that this insult to the British flag would trigger a declaration of war. The angry British government at once sent 11,000 of its best troops to Canada. It was largely a symbolic gesture, but it was, nevertheless, a clear warning.

Lincoln and Secretary of State Seward realized that Wilkes had violated British neutral rights. The United States, itself, had gone to war with Great Britain in 1812 to defend these very rights. Naturally, the Washington government was not eager to take on another and more powerful enemy. Therefore, Seward apologized for the seizure and assured the British that Mason and Slidell would be "cheerfully liberated" and permitted to resume their voyage. But he also pointed out that, what England now protested, she had once defended as an incontrovertible right. The United States, said Seward, was happy to know that Great Britain had at last seen the light and agreed that forcible seizure on the high seas was a violation of neutral rights. The British government accepted Seward's explanation and apology, and the Union blockade of the southern ports remained unchallenged by the Royal Navy.

In general, the British government's willingness to recognize Confederate independence fluctuated with the fortunes of war, and the South never came close enough to demonstrating that it could hold out indefinitely to win British recognition. A possible serious crisis also arose between the United States and Great Britain in 1863, when the Confederacy contracted to have large ironclad rams (so-called because they had iron rams on their bows to splinter wooden ships), powerful enough to break the Union blockade, built in England. Again Adams' diplomatic skill proved effective. He bluntly warned the British Prime Minister, Lord Palmerston, that the building of these rams for the Confederate States constituted an act of war, and he prevailed upon the London government to block delivery of the rams.

The French government was strongly sympathetic to the Confederacy but did not dare to act in its behalf without British cooperation. French recognition of the Confederacy would have resulted immediately in a declaration of war by the United States. The French Emperor, Louis Napoleon III, was in a cruel dilemma—one created by his own folly. He had sent an army of 35,000 men to Mexico and put the Austrian Archduke, Ferdinand Maximilian, on a throne in Mexico City. He knew that the United States would never acquiesce in this flagrant violation of the Monroe Doctrine. Hence, he hoped to protect his Mexican flank by an alliance with a victorious Confederacy. But the British would not cooperate, and it was obvious after 1863 that the South could never win. (The sequel to the story of Louis Napoleon's Mexican adventure is related in the next chapter.)

However, British and other shippers and merchants maintained a thriving trade with the South in spite of the federal blockade. Fast, slim steamers violated the blockade almost at will during 1861. As the war progressed, the cordon of federal ships drew tighter around the South. Still, there were, all told, some 8,000 breaches of the blockade, and only one blockade runner in six was captured, on an average, during the entire period from 1861 to 1865. Blockade runners brought in at least 600,000 small arms and untold quantities of medicines, munitions, and civilian goods. Without these supplies, the Confederacy could not possibly have survived for four years.

The Virginia and the Monitor

The Confederates attempted to break the still thin blockade of their coasts in the spring of 1862. They salvaged *U.S.S. Merrimac*, which had been sunk at the Norfolk Navy Yard, and converted her into an ironclad by covering her sides with a sloping roof of four-inch iron plates. To her bow, they attached a powerful iron ram.

On March 8, this strange craft, renamed *C.S.S. Virginia*, entered Hampton Roads and proceeded to destroy the wooden ships of the federal fleet, whose shots glanced off her sides like pebbles from a sling. *Virginia* sank *U.S.S. Cumberland* and set *U.S.S. Congress* aflame with red hot shot. Then the tide forced *Virginia* to return to her moorings. She intended to finish the destruction of the Union vessels the next day and perhaps proceed up the Potomac to shell the city of Washington. Panic again swept through the national capital.

Before dawn, however, an even stranger craft steamed into Hampton Roads. She was *U.S.S. Monitor*, a true ironclad—not simply a wooden ship with iron plates nailed to her sides. She was designed for the Union navy by the Swedish-born engineer, John Ericsson. From the deck of *Monitor*, which was almost flush with the water, rose a revolving turret armed with two eleven-inch guns. The protruding turret on the flat surface made the vessel look like a "cheesebox on a raft." *Monitor* put herself between *Virginia* and the wooden ships, and a spectacular duel took place in which neither ironclad did much harm to the other. Finally *Virginia* withdrew to the navy yard at Norfolk.

The Union blockade was saved, but this first appearance in battle of iron-clad vessels reduced wooden ships to obsolescence forever. Neither of these queer looking vessels, however, was destined to last long. When the Confederates evacuated Norfolk in May, they blew up *Virginia. Monitor* sank in a storm off Cape Hatteras. Its location has since been discovered, but hope has been abandoned that it can be raised from the ocean floor.

Jefferson Davis Builds a Navy

The Confederate naval effort was still far from finished. An act of the British Parliament of 1819 forbade any subject of the realm to "equip, fit out or arm any ship to be employed in the service of a foreign state, to commit hostilities against any state at peace with Great Britain." But James Dunwody Bulloch of Georgia, Confederate agent in England (and also the uncle of a future President of the United States, Theodore Roosevelt), found a loophole in the law. In 1862, he had dummy firms arrange for the construction of ships without armaments. The vessels, built in England, were fitted and armed as warships beyond the three-mile limit and, as *C.S.S. Florida, C.S.S. Alabama,* and *C.S.S. Shenandoah,* roamed the oceans of the world. By 1863, about a score of Confederate commerce raiders sailed the high seas. They destroyed more than 250 merchantmen, and their havoc caused Union shipowners to transfer more than 700 vessels to foreign registries. In 1860, about 70 per cent of the foreign trade of the United States had been carried in American bottoms. By 1865, the figure had dropped to 26 per cent. *Alabama* alone destroyed more than sixty merchant ships. *U.S.S. Kearsarge* finally sank *Alabama* in a spectacular battle off the coast of France on June 19, 1864. *Shenandoah* was still roaming the Pacific Ocean when news reached her, several weeks after Lee's surrender, that the war was over.

After Adams blocked the Confederate government's effort to arrange for the construction of British ironclad rams, it turned to France, where contracts were let for four cruisers and two powerful rams. However, Louis Napoleon so feared American retaliation that he withdrew his approval of the contract, and only one of the rams ever sailed to American waters. It was too little and much too late for the Confederates.

The Peninsular Campaign

General McClellan was not yet thirty-five years old when he assumed control of the Army of the Potomac. He was a graduate of West Point, a magnificent organizer, a tireless worker, and the idol of his troops. Yet, in the spring of 1862, McClellan seems to have been almost paralyzed by the responsibility of commanding an army that had grown to nearly 180,000 men. He became obsessed with the belief that the smaller forces of Lee and Johnston actually outnumbered his own and berated the "imbecile" administration at Washington for not giving him more men.

McClellan paid little heed to repeated orders from the War Department and Lincoln to advance on Richmond. Not until the beginning of April 1862 did he begin to move. Then, instead of marching on Richmond directly, he ferried his huge army down the Potomac River and Chesapeake Bay to the end of the pen-

Major General George McClellan was dubbed "Little Mac, the Young Napoleon," after successfully driving the Confederates out of West Virginia. (Library of Congress)

insula between the York and James rivers. There he started a cautious movement up the peninsula toward the Confederate capital. By the end of May, he could see the church spires of Richmond, only five miles away.

For weeks, Davis, the Confederate cabinet, and a majority of the citizens of Richmond expected to hear federal batteries thundering at the city's defenses. But McClellan still thought that he faced an army of at least 100,000 men and clamored for reinforcements. Instead of attacking, he prepared for a desperate defense.

The reason why McClellan received no reinforcements, even from McDowell's corps of 40,000 men defending Washington, was due to Stonewall Jackson's remarkable campaign in the Shenandoah Valley in May and June. With only 17,000 men, Jackson defeated three times that number of federals under Generals John C. Frémont, Nathaniel P. Banks, and James Shields. He so threatened the capital that the eyes of the administration were drawn off the Army of the Potomac. "The fate of Richmond in 1862," asserts one historian, "was decided not on the banks of the Chickahominy, but by the waters of the Shenandoah."

McClellan was hard pressed by Johnston, Lee, and the dashing Confederate cavalry commander, J. E. B. ("Jeb") Stuart. They concentrated their forces on striking at the enemy's outnumbered flank. McClellan skillfully drew his men together on the southern side of the peninsula, where he beat off a furious attack at Malvern Hill on July 1. Then, in a magnificent retreat, he led his army back to the bank of the James River within the protection of federal gunboats. The Peninsular Campaign was at an end. McClellan had demonstrated his peculiar talents for organization, defense, *and* retreat. But the initiative in the war belonged to the South.

2. STALEMATE

Union Victories in the West

Meanwhile, McClellan's failure in Virginia had been offset by a series of Union successes on the Cumberland, Tennessee, and Mississippi rivers. These operations brought into prominence the North's greatest general, Ulysses S. Grant, a West Pointer who had served with credit in the Mexican War. The outbreak of the Civil War found him, at the age of thirty-nine, a clerk in his father's hardware and leather store in Galena, Illinois. Military success ultimately made him the hero of the Union and President of the United States.

Grant's first battle command of the war revealed his true qualities: a genius for discovering the weakest positions of the enemy; a silent, grim, cool courage in battle that mounted as danger and difficulties thickened; and a determination to press on to his objective, even after defeats that would have discouraged men like McClellan.

Forts Henry and Donelson, on the northern border of Tennessee, were Confederate strongholds which guarded the lower Tennessee and Cumberland rivers. Grant captured Fort Henry on February 6, 1862, with vital aid from a fleet of gunboats under Commodore A. H. Foote. Ten days later, in another joint military and naval operation, Grant compelled the surrender of the even stronger Fort Donelson and its 14,000 defenders.

General D. C. Buell then occupied Nashville without a blow, while Union gunboats went down the Mississippi River to the high bluffs of Vicksburg. Grant moved his army of 40,000 men up the Tennessee River to Pittsburgh Landing. Near there, at Shiloh, Mississippi, on April 6 he was suddenly at-

More than telegraphs, cannons, or guns, it was the leadership of General Ulysses S. Grant, photographed here by Mathew B. Brady, which won the war for the Union. (United Press International)

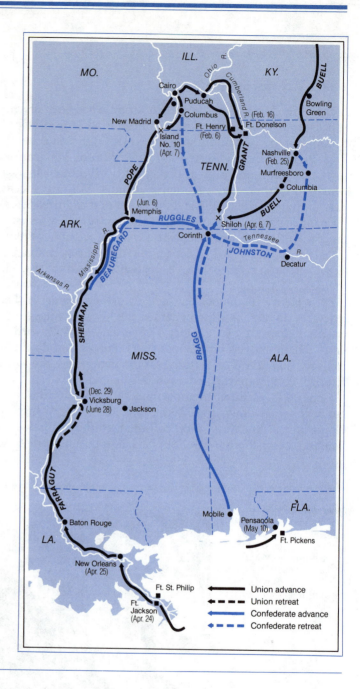

ILL.

MO.

Cairo

Puducah

Columbus

New Madrid

Island
No. 10
(Apr. 7)

Ft. Henry
(Feb. 6)

Ft. Donelson
(Feb. 16)

Ohio R.

Cumberland R.

KY.

BUELL

Bowling
Green

GRANT

Nashville
(Feb. 25)

Murfreesboro

Columbia

POPE

TENN.

(Jun. 6)
Memphis

RUGGLES

Shiloh (Apr. 6, 7)

ARK.

Corinth

BEAUREGARD

Mississippi R.

JOHNSTON

BUELL

Tennessee R.

Decatur

Arkansas R.

SHERMAN

MISS.

BRAGG

ALA.

(Dec. 29)
Vicksburg
(June 28)

Jackson

FARRAGUT

Baton Rouge

Mobile

Pensacola
(May 10)

FLA.

Ft. Pickens

LA.

New Orleans
(Apr. 25)

Ft. St. Philip

Ft.
Jackson
(Apr. 24)

	Union advance
	Union retreat
	Confederate advance
	Confederate retreat

**War in the West,
1862**

tacked by Albert S. Johnston, the Confederate commander in the West. The
Union forces were driven back to the river bank and, for a time, were in dire
straits. Then the reckless General Johnston was killed, and the tide turned
with the arrival of Union reinforcements. On the following day, Grant drove
the Confederates from the field.

Three weeks later, in a naval action, Union forces captured New Orleans. In
the blackness of the night of April 23, 1862, Captain David G. Farragut ran by
the forts at the mouth of the Mississippi and captured the city.

The Second Victory at Bull Run

These western victories made Kentucky safe for the Union and cleared the Confederates out of western Tennessee. Nevertheless, the Confederacy continued to hold its main defensive lines. On the eastern front, Lee with his Army of Northern Virginia and his great lieutenants—Stonewall Jackson, James Longstreet, Richard S. Ewell, A. P. Hill, Daniel H. Hill, and Jeb Stuart—outwitted, outfought, and turned back Union armies at every point. After McClellan's failure to take Richmond, the Union forces in the East were combined into the new Army of Virginia. General John Pope assumed command with a boastful confidence born of his recent successes on the Mississippi. But before Pope could march on Richmond and keep his promise to end the war, Lee and Jackson attacked him at Bull Run on August 29–30, 1862. Pope was as completely defeated as McDowell's green troops had been on the same field thirteen months before. With victorious Confederate troops nearby, Washington again felt panic.

Repeated reverses in battle were causing a strong reaction against the Lincoln administration. The war was costing $2 million a day and apparently was accomplishing nothing. Enlistments decreased steadily, while desertions increased. The half-billion issue of 6 per cent government bonds was not selling well, and congressional elections were approaching.

On the southern side of the Mason-Dixon line, hope of ultimate victory ran high in the late summer of 1862. It was the brightest point in Confederate history. The Confederate War Department planned a great offensive: Lee would invade Maryland, capture that state for the Confederacy, and then threaten Washington. Forces under Generals Braxton Bragg and Early Van Dorn would expel the Union troops from Kentucky, Tennessee, and Mississippi, and thereby regain control of the Mississippi River.

The Bloody Stalemate at Antietam

Lee crossed the Potomac River at Shepherdstown (now West Virginia) with his Army of Northern Virginia on September 4, 1862—55,000 seasoned troops who sang "Maryland, My Maryland!" McClellan, with 85,000 men, met him in the area around Antietam Creek, near Sharpsburg, Maryland. The battle swayed back and forth all day long on September 17. By nightfall, Lee, now reinforced by Jackson and his men, who had come up from Harpers Ferry after they had captured that town, still held his positions. But Lee's losses were so staggering that he could no longer continue the invasion. On September 19, he led his weary army back across the Potomac—except for the 11,000 men left dead and wounded on the battlefield. McClellan suffered even larger losses. He had checked Lee's advance in the bloodiest battle of the war, but Lincoln was keenly disappointed because McClellan had permitted Lee to escape.

3. EMANCIPATION AND CONTINUED STALEMATE

The Emancipation Proclamation

At the beginning of the war, Congress had resolved, and Lincoln had agreed, that the conflict was to be waged solely to preserve the Union, not to conquer the South or free the slaves. Lincoln had always believed that slavery was a curse, but he said, quite frankly, that the preservation of the Union was his "paramount object." He insisted that any action that he took regarding slavery would depend entirely upon its impact on the fortunes of the Union.

Even so, Lincoln was under constant and enormous pressure to make the war a crusade against slavery. The abolitionist wing of his own party continued to increase in power. Lincoln was obliged to rebuke two of his generals for issuing proclamations which freed slaves in their departments. His Minister to Spain, Carl Schurz, wrote home that the sympathy of Europe could be won only by a frank declaration that the object of the war was the abolition of slavery.

Lincoln had a keen ear for public opinion, but he believed that an open war for abolition would drive the loyal slave states of Missouri, Kentucky, and Maryland into the Confederacy. He tried his best to persuade these states to accept payments for their slaves in United States bonds; he also hoped that the seceded states would follow their examples. Lincoln proposed to pay $400 for each slave, and Congress voted to appropriate money for the purchase of the 430,000 slaves in the border states. This would have cost the government less than the expense of two months of war. Even if the Border States had consented, which they refused to do, it almost certainly would have had no effect on the Confederacy.

Congress abolished slavery in the District of Columbia in April 1862. In June, it prohibited slavery in the territories and thus disregarded, if it did not nullify, the Dred Scott decision. A month later, congressmen from the Border States rejected the plan for compensated emancipation. Lincoln then decided that an appropriate time had come to reap the advantages of seeming to fight a war to free the slaves. He prepared, as commander in chief, to declare the slaves of rebels free. Upon Seward's advice, however, he postponed such action until the North had won a victory in the field.

On September 23, 1862, only six days after McClellan had checked Lee at Antietam, Lincoln published the warning announcement. He declared that, on January 1, 1863, "all persons held as slaves within any State or designated part of a State, the people whereof shall then be in rebellion against the United States, shall be then, thenceforward, and forever free." Actually, the proclamation freed few slaves; it affected only slaves whose masters were "in rebellion against the United States," and in those parts of the Confederacy not under Union military control. Since almost all slaves were still behind the Confederate lines, Lincoln's action could be effective only if the North won the war.

The irony of Lincoln's announcement pointed up the dilemma of the President—indeed, of a majority of the people of the Union. Unlike the abolitionist minority, they were not ready to think in terms of absorbing black people as free persons into the mainstream of American life. Lincoln proclaimed liberty for slaves within the Confederacy, not principally because it was morally right, but, more directly, because it would help to win the war and accomplish his main objective—preservation of the Union. Insofar as Lincoln could see any hope for blacks, it still lay in their colonization in Africa.

Even so, the Emancipation Proclamation did give a new meaning to the war and a powerful lever to the abolitionists, who began to agitate for the enlistment of black troops. Negroes were taken into the service in small numbers in the autumn of 1862, but in subordinate positions and at lower pay than that

The President then announced that "the Ordinance of Secession has been signed and ratified, and I proclaim the State of South Carolina," said he, "an independent Commonwealth."

At once the whole audience broke out into a storm of cheers; the ladies again joined in the demonstration; a rush was made for the palmetto trees, which were torn to pieces in the effort to secure mementos of the occasion. As soon as the passage of the Secession Ordinance at St. Andrews Hall was accomplished, a messenger left the house and rode with the greatest speed to the camp of the First Regiment of Rifles, South Carolina Militia, Colonel Pettigrew, one mile distant, where in front of the paraded regiment the Ordinance was read amid the loud acclamations of the men. *From* The Genesis of the Civil War, *by Samuel Crawford, 1887.*

Facsimile of a Charleston newspaper extra, December 1860. (Culver Pictures, Inc.)

CHARLESTON

MERCURY

EXTRA:

___

Passed unanimously at 1.15 o'clock, P. M., December 20th, 1860.

AN ORDINANCE

To dissolve the Union between the State of South Carolina and other States united with her under the compact entitled " The Constitution of the United States of America."

We, the People of the State of South Carolina, in Convention assembled, do declare and ordain, and it is hereby declared and ordained,

That the Ordinance adopted by us in Convention, on the twenty-third day of May, in the year of our Lord one thousand seven hundred and eighty-eight, whereby the Constitution of the United States of America was ratified, and also, all Acts and parts of Acts of the General Assembly of this State, ratifying amendments of the said Constitution, are hereby repealed ; and that the union now subsisting between South Carolina and other States, under the name of "The United States of America," is hereby dissolved.

___

THE

UNION

IS

DISSOLVED!

*Recruiting in the New York City
Hall Park. (Culver Pictures, Inc.)*

*Poster for a war rally in Lacon,
Illinois, 1861. (Courtesy Chicago
Historical Society Library)*

An uptown New York City draftee sought to deceive the doctor by implanting a "tumor" on his side. His body was enveloped in swaths of gauze, which when removed, left a transparent patch covering the sore. The man was reluctant to remove the patch, but under the doctor's insistence did so. The surgeon examined the red swelling with great curiosity, and then told the draftee to re-swath his "tumor" and wait in the outer office. Soon a clerk brought out the following message:

Mr. ——— examined and found entirely healthy. Sound in brain, lungs, and limbs. No skin or other disease qualifying him for exemption. He wears, however, an ingeniously constructed tumor that does not interfere with his bodily strength, and can at any time be removed with a little hot water and scrubbing brush.
From a New York newspaper, 1863.

I was greatly amused while listening to the exploits of each [bounty jumper], as he in turn detailed them. One related, that at a certain period he left New York, and having enlisted at Albany, Troy, Utica, Buffalo, and Chicago, returned via Elmira, at which place he likewise enlisted. Another had enlisted at every rendezvous from New York to Portland, Maine; while a third boasted of the amounts he had received, and mentioned those paid to recruiting officers, surgeons, brokers, and detectives. The den in which I spent the evening was a favorite haunt of the bounty jumpers. It contained a wardrobe of wearing apparel, consisting of both soldiers' and citizens' outfits. The idea of this I easily comprehended; here the jumpers could assume whatever dress they pleased, to carry out their designs. Three times that night, before two o'clock, I saw the interesting operation performed.

I selected one of my assistants to experiment in this military lottery. He dressed himself in the appropriate apparel, and in one day enlisted three times; he was sent to the Island, bought himself off, and reported for duty the following day.

The scenes described were followed by numberless arrests of bounty brokers, bounty jumpers, and others in the business, and consequently by the disclosures of their crimes, which have since attracted much public attention.
From The Secret Service in the Late War, *by Lafayette C. Baker, 1874.*

[These] Negroes make good soldiers, . . . they are docile and quick to learn . . . and they have a decided advantage over our white soldiers in the fact that they are taught *obedience* to every command, especially when that command comes from a white man. The trouble with *our* [white] volunteers, is, that they have always been accustomed to do as they pleased and to have their own way about everything and it is very hard work to come under the yoke of army discipline. With the Negro it is right the reverse.

From a letter written during the Civil War by a white lieutenant in one of the colored regiments to his wife.

Sketch from Frank Leslie's Illustrated Newspaper *showing the assault of the Second Louisiana (Colored) Regiment on the Confederate defenses at Port Hudson, Louisiana, May 27, 1863. (Culver Pictures, Inc.)*

One of the most efficient officers was Capt. André Callioux, a man whose identity with his race could not be mistaken; for he prided himself on being the blackest man in the Crescent City. . . . This regiment petitioned their commander to allow them to occupy the post of danger in the battle [of Port Hudson, Louisiana], and it was granted. . . .

At last the welcome word was given, and our men started. The enemy opened a blistering fire of shell, canister, grape, and musketry. . . . At every pace, the column was thinned by the falling dead and wounded. . . . No matter how gallantly the men behaved, no matter how bravely they were led, it was not in the course of things that this gallant brigade should take these works by charge. Yet charge after charge was ordered and carried out under all these disasters with Spartan firmness. Six charges in all were made. . . . Shells from the rebel guns cut down trees three feet in diameter, and they fell, at one time burying a whole company beneath their branches. . . . The last charge was made about one o'clock. At this juncture, Capt. Callioux was seen with his left arm dangling by his side, — for a ball had broken it above the elbow, — while his right hand held his unsheathed sword gleaming in the rays of the sun; and his hoarse, faint voice was heard cheering on his men. A moment more, and the brave and generous Callioux was struck by a shell, and fell far in advance of his company. . . . Seeing it to be a hopeless effort, the taking of these batteries, the troops were called off. But had they accomplished anything more than the loss of many of their brave men? Yes: they had. The self-forgetfulness, the undaunted heroism, and the great endurance of the negro, as exhibited that day, created a new chapter in American history for the colored man.

From The Negro in the American Rebellion, *by William Wells Brown, 1867.*

A body of these, five or six hundred strong, gathered about one of the enrolling-offices in the upper part of the city [New York], where the draft was quietly proceeding, and opened the assault upon it by a shower of clubs, bricks, and paving-stones torn from the streets, following it up by a furious rush into the office. Lists, records, books, the drafting-wheel, every article of furniture or work in the room was rent in pieces, and strewn about the floor or flung into the street; while the law officers, the newspaper reporters—who are expected to be everywhere,— and the few peacable spectators, were compelled to make a hasty retreat through an opportune rear exit, accelerated by the curses and blows of the assailants. . . .

The work thus begun, continued,—gathering in force and fury as the day wore on. Police-stations, enrolling-offices, rooms or buildings used in any way by government authority, or obnoxious as representing the dignity of law, were gutted, destroyed, then left to the mercy of the flames. . . .

By far the most infamous part of these cruelties was that which wreaked every species of torture and lingering death upon the colored people of the city,—men, women, and children, old and young, strong and feeble alike. Hundreds of these fell victims to the prejudice fostered by public opinion, incorporated in our laws, which here and thus found legitimate outgrowth and action.
From What Answer? by Anna E. Dickenson, 1868.

*The riots in New York: a mob
lynching a Negro in Clarkson Street,
July 1863. (Culver Pictures, Inc.)*

Cold Harbor is, I think, the only battle I ever fought that I would not fight over again under the circumstances. I have always regretted that the last assault at Cold Harbor was ever made.
From Memoirs of U. S. Grant.

Suddenly we saw a magnificent brigade emerge in our front; they came forward in perfect order, a grand but terrible sight. At their head rode the commander, a man of fine physique, in the prime of life—quiet and cool as though on a drill. The artillery opened, the infantry followed; notwithstanding the slaughter they were closer and closer. Their commander [Colonel Rogers] seemed to bear a charmed life. He jumped his horse across the ditch in front of the guns, and then on foot came on.
Report of the assault on Corinth by an eyewitness.

In the brief space of one hour the bloody battle of the 3d of June was over, and 13,000 dead and wounded Federals lay in front of the lines behind which little more than 1000 of the Confederate force had fallen. . . .

A few hours afterward orders were sent to the corps commanders to renew the assault, and transmitted by them through the intermediate channels to the men. Then an event occurred which has seldom been witnessed on a battlefield, yet which testified most emphatically to the silent judgment of the men on the useless slaughter to which they had been subjected. Though the orders to advance were given, not a man stirred. The troops stood silent, but immovable, presenting in this unmistakable protest the verdict of the rank and file against the murderous work decided on by their commanders.
From Memoirs of Robert E. Lee.

Nursing at *The Old Theater*, on the front at Fredericksburg, Md.

From "Our Women and the War,"
Harper's Weekly. *(National Archives)*

*When there was so much to be done, I would do the most
needful thing first, and this was ridding the wounds of worms
and gangrene, supporting the strength of the men by proper
food, and keeping the air as pure as possible. I got our beef
into the way of being boiled, and would have some good
substantial broth made around it. I went on a foraging
expedition—found a coal-scuttle which would do for a
sloppail, and confiscated it, got two bits of board, by which it
could be converted into a stool, and so bring the great rest of a
change of position to such men as could sit up; had a little
drain made with a bit of board for a shovel, and so kept the
mud from running in at the side door; melted the tops off
some tin cans, and made them into drinking cups; had two of
my men confiscate a large tub from a brewery, set it in the
vestibule to wash rags for outside covers to wounds, to keep
off chill, and had others bring bricks and rubbish mortar from
a ruin across the street, to make substitutes for pillows.*

 *I dressed wounds! dressed wounds, and made thorough
work of it. In the church was a dispensary, where I could get
any washes or medicines I wished, and I do not think I left
a worm. Some of them were over half an inch long, with black
heads and many feet, but most were maggots. They were often
deeply seated, but my syringe would drive them out, and
twice a day I followed them up. The black and green places
grew smaller and better colored with every dressing. The men
grew stronger with plenty of beef and broth and canned milk.*

Jane Swisshelm, Half a Century *(Chicago, 1880), from Gerda Lerner,
ed.,* The Female Experience: An American Documentary, *Bobbs-
Merrill Educational Publishing, 1977.*

*Mounting casualties, demoralizing defeats in battle, and increasing taxes made
the services of women on both sides of the war ever more important. This
illustration recognized some of the vital contributions of American women
during the Civil War. Ironically, many people felt that women, who were
expected to handle matters of sickness and death in the home as a matter
of moral obligation, could not handle such matters in a hospital or in the
battle field. Particularly in the South, women fought opposition to their services
as nurses before and during their fight against death, disease, and filth.*

Columbia, South Carolina, ruins. Sherman turned northward after reaching Savannah, and the destruction in South Carolina is said to have been even greater than that in Georgia. Columbia fell on February 17, 1865, and most of the city was burned that night. (Library of Congress)

We have . . . consumed the corn and fodder in the region of country thirty miles on either side of a line from Atlanta to Savannah, as also the sweet potatoes, cattle, hogs, sheep and poultry and have carried away more than 10,000 horses and mules, as well as a countless number of their slaves. I estimate the damage done to the State of Georgia and its military resources at $100,000,000; at least $20,000,000 of which has inured to our advantage, and the remainder is simple waste and destruction. This may seem a hard species of warfare, but it brings the sad realities of war home to those who have been directly or indirectly instrumental in involving us in its attendant calamities.

Report from General Sherman to Washington, D.C., January 1, 1865. From War of the Rebellion: A Compilation of the Official Records of the Union and Confederate Armies, series 1.

Savannah, Georgia, 1865. Sherman's march to the sea ended in Savannah, which fell to him on December 22, 1864. (Library of Congress)

The top scene shows Richmond, Virginia, as it appeared the morning of April 2, 1865, shortly before that part of the city nearest the James River went up in flames. The bottom view shows the aftermath of the battle. Although southern cities were restored by the new economy of the "New South," twelve years of northern "reconstruction" failed to heal the more profound scars of the war. (Wide World Photos)

*The Bombardment of Port Hudson by Admiral Farragut's Fleet,
March 14–15, 1863.*

*The brilliant naval officer, David Glasgow Farragut, who first served as a
midshipman at the age of nine, organized the West Gulf Blockading squadron
during the Civil War. His blockade of the Red River cut off supplies to
Vicksburg and Port Hudson. With the eventual surrender of Port Hudson, the
Union army controlled the whole length of the Mississippi and split the
Confederacy. Port Hudson fell to Farragut in May with formal surrender
ceremonies in July.*

Sketch by J. R. Hamilton for Harper's Weekly. *(Personal collection)*

*Above: The Bombardment of Port
Hudson—The 100-Pound Parrott Gun
of the "Richmond" at Work. Sketched
by an officer of the navy for* Harper's
Weekly. *(Personal collection)*

Left: The Formal Surrender of Port Hudson. Drawn by J. R. Hamilton for Harper's Weekly. *(Personal collection)*

At the earliest dawn of the—now ever memorable—9th of July, the whole camp was necessarily in the highest state of glee and commotion, and the "Star-Spangled Banner," "Yankee Doodle," and "Dixie" came upon the morning air—never sounding sweeter.

At 7 o'clock General Andrews, Chief of the Staff of General Banks, made his grand entrance into the rebel fortifications, with Colonel Birge leading his brave storming column, whose noble services have thus been, happily for their friends, dispensed with, but to whom the country is no less indebted—taking the will for the deed. These were followed by two picked regiments from each division, with Holcomb's and Rawle's battery of light artillery, and the gunners of the naval battery.

The rebels were drawn up in line, and an immense line they made, their officers in front of them in one side of the road, their backs to the river. Gen. Gardner then advanced toward Gen. Andrews, and, in a few accompanying words, offered to surrender his sword with Port Hudson; but General Andrews told him, in appreciation of his bravery—however misdirected—he was at liberty to retain his sword.

Our men were then drawn up in two lines on the other side of the road, opposite to the rebels, and our officers placed themselves in front of their men. Gen. Gardner then said to Gen. Andrews: "General, I will now formally surrender my command to you, and for that purpose will give the orders to ground arms."—The order was given and the arms were grounded.

After that Gen. Andrews sent for the enemy's general officers, staff and field-officers. The line-officers were left with their companies and guard, composed of the Twenty-second Louisiana and Seventy-fifth New York, placed over them. These formalities over, the glorious old flag of the Union was unfolded to the breeze from one of the highest bluffs facing the river, by the men of the *Richmond*—a battery thundered forth its salute, which roled majestically up and down the broad surface of the Mississippi—and Port Hudson was ours!

It was with no little delight that I found myself riding at last over every portion of this long-forbidden ground, noting the havoc which our cannon made not only in the ramparts but over the whole internal surface. Not a square rood but bore some indisputable proof of the iron deluge that had fallen upon it, in earth plowed up, trees with the bark almost completely torn off by rifle-shot, and some—twice the bulk of a man's body—fairly snapped in two by some solid ball, as easily as a walking cane.

From the Times *as quoted in* Harper's Weekly, *August 8, 1863.*

The dead of the Twenty-fourth Michigan Infantry at Gettysburg, July 1, 1863. The unit lost 399 of its 496 men. (Library of Congress)

The dead in this war—there they lie, strewing the fields and woods and valleys and battle-fields of the south—Virginia, the Peninsula—Malvern hill and Fair Oaks—the banks of the Chickahominy—the terraces of Fredericksburgh—Antietam bridge—the grisly ravines of Manassas—the bloody promenade of the Wilderness— . . . Gettysburgh, the West, Southwest—Vicksburgh—Chattanooga—the trenches of Petersburgh—the numberless battles, camps, hospitals everywhere—the crop reap'd by the mighty reapers, typhoid, dysentery, inflammations—and blackest and loathesomest of all, the dead and living burial-pits, the prison-pens of Andersonville, Salisbury, Belle-Isle, &c., (not Dante's pictured hell and all its woes, its degradations, filthy torments, excell'd those prisons)—the dead, the dead, the dead—our dead—or South or North, ours all, (all, all, all, finally dear to me)—or East or West—Atlantic coast or Mississippi valley—somewhere they crawl'd to die, alone, in bushes, low gullies, or on the sides of hills—(there, in secluded spots, their skeletons, bleach'd bones, tufts of hair, buttons, fragments of clothing, are occasionally found yet)—our young men once so handsome and so joyous, taken from us. . . .

In some of the cemeteries nearly all the dead are unknown. At Salisbury, N.C., for instance, the known are only 85, while the unknown are 12,027, and 11,700 of these are buried in trenches. A national monument has been put up here, by order of Congress, to mark the spot—but what visible, material monument can ever fittingly commemorate that spot?
Walt Whitman, 1865.

given white soldiers. Then the continued need for manpower and the devotion of the black soldiers led to further enlistment and the use of blacks as fighting men. About 180,000 blacks had served by the end of the war. Thus, they, themselves, participated significantly in the fight for freedom in the United States.

Discouragement in the Confederacy

The year 1863, a decisive one in the terrible contest, opened darkly for both sides. The South had failed to win Maryland or to regain the ground lost in the West. Her hopes of recognition by England and France were fading fast. The blockade was depriving her of the food, clothing, munitions, and, particularly, the railroad equipment necessary for success. She was unable to raise by taxation or loans more than a fraction of the money needed to meet the current expenses of the war. In fact, she had already resorted to printing hundreds of millions of dollars of paper money, which declined in value so rapidly that, near the end of the war, it took $1 thousand to buy a barrel of flour and $400 to buy a pair of shoes. Finally, there was serious political opposition to President Davis, especially in the eastern seaboard states of the Confederacy. They clung to the doctrine of state rights, which they believed they had seceded to protect; they seemed unable to realize that a successful modern war can be waged only by a highly centralized government with unlimited power. At one point, the governors of North Carolina and Georgia, Zebulon B. Vance and Joseph E. Brown, respectively, even threatened to refuse to permit their soldiers in the Confederate army to serve outside their home states. Militiamen commonly were kept in their home states, despite pleas from Richmond for more men. Every kind of equipment—from shoes and uniforms to rifles and even food—was held in state warehouses, despite the desperate need of the Confederate army for all these items. Perhaps one of the most serious of all the dangers that threatened the southern cause was the growing conviction among common soldiers, who served under aristocratic officers, that this was "a rich man's war and a poor man's fight." The number of volunteers fell off alarmingly, and desertion became a major problem. Toward the end of the war, it was said that the strongest concentration of Confederate troops was the army of deserters who were hiding in northern Alabama. An unpopular conscription law, adopted in April 1862, increased opposition to the Davis government, both among the poor people and Governors Vance and Brown.

Defeatism in the North

The deadly military stalemate and mounting casualties also caused deep discouragement in the North. The first half of 1863 marked the lowest ebb in Union military fortunes. Lincoln finally replaced the slow-moving McClellan with the energetic General Ambrose E. Burnside. Burnside suffered a bloody defeat in a rash attempt to storm Lee's fortified position on Marye's Heights, above Fredericksburg, Virginia, in December 1862. Lee and Jackson badly mauled his successor, Joseph ("Fighting Joe") Hooker, at Chancellorsville, Virginia, in May 1863. Jackson, riding in the twilight with some of his staff officers, was mistaken by an overeager Confederate sharpshooter for a Union officer and fatally wounded. It was an irreparable loss for the Confederacy.

Increasing taxes, repeated defeats, and mounting casualty lists chilled the early northern enthusiasm for the war as much as the grim realities of war had chilled southern ardor. The Democrats, increasingly hostile to a continuation of the conflict, carried New York, Ohio, Pennsylvania, Illinois, and Wisconsin in the elections of 1862 and gained thirty-two seats in the House of Representatives. Carloads of civilian clothing were smuggled into the Union lines to aid deserters to escape. Voluntary enlistments fell so low that, in March 1863, the United States Government, too, was forced to resort to conscription. Draft riots occurred in many cities, most notably in New York. There, from July 13 to July 16, 1863, some thousand-odd persons (including many blacks lynched or beaten to death) were killed before the riots were suppressed by federal troops brought in from General George Meade's army in Pennsylvania. Obviously, what may have begun as a draft riot ended in a race riot. Clement L. Vallandigham, the "Copperhead," or Confederate sympathizer, congressman from Ohio, flailed the administration for the disasters of the war. "You have not conquered the South; you never will. The war for the Union . . . is a bloody and costly failure. Monies have been expended without limit, and blood poured out like water. Defeat, debt, taxation, and sepulchres—these are your only trophies." Burnside arrested Vallandigham, and Lincoln banished him to the Confederacy.

Civil Liberties during Wartime

Nations fighting for their lives are not usually inclined to respect civil liberties when exercise of those rights seems to endanger the security of the state. So it was in both the North and the South during the Civil War. Lincoln dealt with antiwar obstructionists mainly by military arrest and imprisonment without trial. On his own authority, he suspended the writ of *habeas corpus* on September 24, 1862, and instituted a quasi-military rule throughout the Union. The Constitution (Article I, Section 9) ambiguously declares that *habeas corpus* shall not be suspended "unless when in cases of rebellion or invasion the public safety may require it." But the Constitution does not say who has the power to suspend the right to the writ of *habeas corpus*.

Military arrests were so widespread that Congress, in the Habeas Corpus Act of 1863, tried to provide some safeguards for individuals. But Lincoln paid no attention to the measure; he arrested thousands of individuals and suppressed newspapers at will. He and his military commanders simply ignored civil courts when they tried to interfere. The Supreme Court, in *ex parte* Milligan, ruled that military arrests were illegal when regular civil courts were functioning. But this decision was not rendered until 1866. During the war, the Supreme Court, already discredited by the Dred Scott decision, declined to risk appearing to interfere with the Union military effort.

Davis had to move more cautiously because of the stronger state-rights sentiment in the South. But he, too (with the approval of the Confederate Congress), suspended the writ of *habeas corpus* in certain areas. This led to further serious conflict with Governors Vance and Brown. Their resistance to presidential authority was so strong that Davis and the Confederate Congress had to retreat.

Triumph of the American System

Wartime legislation laid the foundation for a new national political economy, despite the fact that few economic interests supported the measures as a whole. Although this legislation superficially resembled Clay's American System brought up to date, it was no longer as attractive to business interests as before. New England textile manufacturers, for example—by far the most important manufacturing group in the nation—predominantly opposed high tariffs, just as their British competitors did. British manufacturers, who wanted inexpensive raw and semifinished materials, and cheap food for workers, had obtained essentially free trade during the 1840s. In order to compete effectively in markets around the world, New Englanders wanted duty-free raw materials for construction and power, as well as for use in the direct production and dyeing of fabrics. New York bankers and importers also advocated low tariffs. Nevertheless, the American government's wartime need for revenue, especially for the gold in which import duties had to be paid, and the desire of certain struggling industries for protection, obliged Congress to reverse the low-tariff policy of the prewar period. By 1864, duties averaged 47 per cent.

Similarly, the country's greatest bankers were coerced into a national system almost completely against their will. The motivating force, again, was the federal government's need for gold to make purchases and interest payments abroad. As the war dragged on, major banks were reluctant to trade their dwindling supplies of specie for government bonds that immediately depreciated in value and which might never be redeemed. A National Banking System was conceived in 1863 by the Secretary of the Treasury and adopted by Congress. National bank notes would be issued to member banks in exchange for the government bonds that they purchased from the Treasury. Almost all the large eastern banks refused to join because they knew that the national system would destroy their local associations and empty their vaults of gold. The government then imposed a 10 per cent tax on notes issued by banks under their state charters, and the bankers were warned that, if necessary, the government would tax them into insolvency. It is hardly an exaggeration to say that almost all the major banks in the Union were dragged, kicking and screaming, into the National Banking System.

Other important economic legislation passed by wartime Republican Congresses continued policies supported by Democrats and Whigs alike before the war. The principle, already established, of providing cheap lands for settlers was extended a bit further, and Westerners finally obtained, with the adoption of the Homestead Act of 1862, their long-sought goal of free land grants of a quarter section, or 160 acres, to a family. As it turned out, the measure was not nearly as important in the settlement of the West as the Pre-emption Act of 1841 had been. Most of the good agricultural land of the Middle West had been preempted by 1862.

Railroad promoters and Westerners won federal charters for two transcontinental railroads. Again, opposition to such roads hardly existed before the war, although Northerners and Southerners had debated which route should be built first. The Union Pacific and Central Pacific railroads, chartered in 1862, were to build a line along the central route. The Northern Pacific Railroad, chartered in 1864, was to follow a route through the northern Plains and Rocky

Mountains. Congress continued a policy begun in 1850 of aiding the railroads by lavish land grants, as well as by loans, and also permitted the railroad construction firms to import cheap Chinese laborers under contract. The Morrill Land Grant Act of 1862 awarded large tracts of public lands to the states for agricultural and mechanical education. This marked the beginning of the present-day state universities which concentrate upon engineering and agricultural training. This body of legislation, passed in large measure because of wartime needs, nevertheless marked the victory of the ideas of Alexander Hamilton, John Quincy Adams, and Henry Clay in the long struggle for an American System to promote national economic growth. This program would become the cornerstone of Republican national policies until about 1901.

4. THE WAR REACHES A CLIMAX IN THE EAST AND IN THE WEST

The Battle of Gettysburg

Northern distress and the hope of receiving diplomatic recognition abroad led Davis and Lee in 1863 to launch their boldest stroke of the war—an invasion of the North. The French Emperor was working hard to persuade the British Prime Minister, Lord Palmerston, to join him in recognizing Confederate independence. Louis Napoleon even went so far as to offer mediation to the embattled American government in January 1863. Congress replied by warning that

The battle at Gettysburg as drawn by Thomas Nast whose cartoons and illustrations during the Civil War led Lincoln to call him "our best recruiting sergeant." (Culver Pictures, Inc.)

any such offer in the future would be regarded as a cause for war. Louis Napoleon, unwilling to risk such a conflict without assurance of British support, never intervened officially again.

Lee's victory at Chancellorsville in May revived the movement in Great Britain for full recognition of Confederate independence. Indeed, a motion for recognition was pending in the House of Commons, when Lee started his second invasion of the North.

Lee crossed the Potomac with a seasoned army of 70,000 men on June 15, 1863. He sought the great victory that would perhaps lead to the capture of Washington, wreck Lincoln's government, and certainly win foreign recognition for the Confederacy. By chance, Lee's soldiers met the advance forces of General George Meade's army of 80,000 men at the little town of Gettysburg, in southern Pennsylvania, and the opposing troops poured into the area to fight the greatest battle of the war from July 1 through July 3, 1863.

Lee had the advantage during the first day's battle because Meade's main units had not yet come up. But Lee was obliged to delay his attack while he waited for more troops to arrive. While he waited, Union troops occupied the

War in the East, 1863

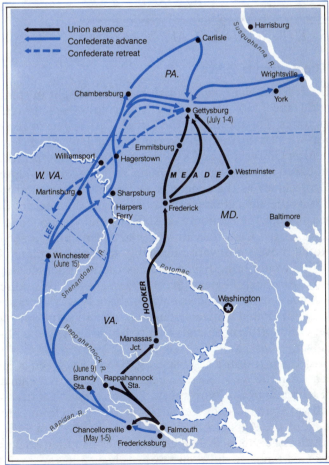

strategic positions. For the next three days, the Confederate Army unsuccess-fully assaulted Union positions on a series of hills mostly south of Gettysburg.

Lee made his last desperate bid for victory by sending three divisions of 15,000 infantrymen under the long-haired, dashing Major General George E. Pickett to break the center of the Union line. A hail of fire from the federal batteries decimated Pickett's men and left the ground "carpeted with the dead." By this time, more than 25,000 Confederate soldiers had been wounded or had died at Gettysburg. Lee's invasion of the North, begun with such high hopes, had ended in disaster.

During a pouring rain on the evening of July 4, the remnant of the shattered Confederate army began its retreat to the Potomac. Meade's army was too ex-hausted to pursue Lee. On the same day, General John C. Pemberton surren-dered the great stronghold of Vicksburg on the Mississippi River to Grant. Along with the city, Pemberton surrendered 170 cannon, 50,000 small arms, and 30,000 men. Five days later, Port Hudson, the last Confederate post on the Mississippi River, also surrendered. The South was now cut in two. The supply line, over which had come meat and munitions from Texas and Mexico, was closed. And, as Lincoln said, the Father of Waters now ran unhindered to the sea. These smashing defeats in both the East and the West left the South here-after unable to wage anything but a defensive war.

5. THE ROAD TO APPOMATTOX

The Anaconda Policy

Confederate war bonds, which had been bought in small quantities in England and France, sank from ninety-five to thirty-seven on news of the two Union victories. The motion in the British Parliament to recognize the Confederacy was withdrawn. Louis Napoleon did not dare to interfere alone.

After Gettysburg and Vicksburg, Lincoln and his military advisers adopted a so-called anaconda policy. Union armies would wrap themselves around the Confederacy as the anaconda wraps its coils around its victim and squeezes out its life. One great army would invade the heart of the South from Tennes-see, disrupt the economy of Alabama and Georgia, and then move northward through the Carolinas to Virginia. Meanwhile, a second great Union army would move southward inexorably toward Richmond. This meant total war, which would bring havoc and destruction upon civilians as well as combat-ants. Although General Scott had suggested this policy at the outset of the war and Lincoln had accepted it as the only way to wage a modern war, Lincoln only now found generals who were able to carry out the policy. By this time, too, the northern generals finally had armies trained to fight this brutal kind of war.

After his triumph at Vicksburg, Grant was given command of all the Union armies in the West. He then began operations that ended the Confederate siege of Chattanooga in November. The victory at Chattanooga—a vital southern railway center—made Tennessee safe for the Union, broke Confederate power west of the Appalachians, and left only the four old seaboard states of the South to be subdued. The Confederates had their backs to the wall. Never, af-ter Chattanooga, did their armies advance in the confidence of achieving the victory that would establish their independence. Southern leaders continued to talk bravely, but the realists among them knew that the war was lost.

Grant Moves on Richmond

Grant was made lieutenant general on March 9, 1864, and given command of all the armies of the United States. He made his headquarters with the Army of the Potomac and chose the brilliant and determined William Tecumseh Sherman to command the Union armies in the West.

Grant's army crossed the Rapidan River in northern Virginia on the night of May 3, 1864, and began to fight its way through the wilderness west of Fredericksburg. Northern losses were appalling, but Grant's men steadily hammered their way toward Richmond. "I propose to fight it out on this line, if it takes all summer," Grant telegraphed to General Henry W. Halleck, the chief of staff. Grant lost 12,000 men in a frontal assault on Lee's trenches at Cold Harbor, northeast of Richmond, on June 3. Lee's defenses of trenches and barricades were almost impregnable. Thus, Grant had to outflank Lee, and he swung his army southward across the James River and laid siege to the railroad junction of Petersburg. Meanwhile, Grant had been in constant violent contact with Lee's forces. In this campaign of forty days, Grant had lost 55,000 men to Lee's

Grant's Virginia Campaign, 1864–1865

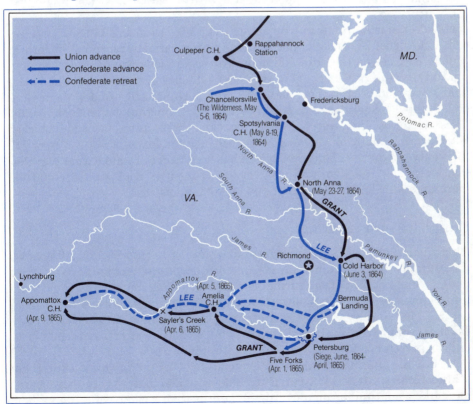

30,000, but Grant knew that such losses weakened the Confederacy far more than the Union. Here was one Union commander who did not permit his army to retreat when repulsed, or rest when victorious.

The Reelection of Lincoln

President Lincoln was renominated at Baltimore only four days after the slaughter at Cold Harbor. The name "Union party" was substituted for "Republican," and the Tennessee loyal Democrat, Andrew Johnson, former senator and military governor of his home state, was nominated for the vice-presidency in order to win the votes of Democrats who supported the war. The conflict did not seem to go well for the Union. Grant made no headway against Petersburg. Sherman, advancing slowly into Georgia, was repulsed at Kennesaw Mountain on June 27. The Confederate cavalry general, Jubal A. Early, who controlled the Shenandoah Valley, crossed the Potomac and threatened Washington on July 11; he actually drove to the outskirts of the capital before reserves repulsed him. Lincoln himself, thought in mid-August that his defeat in the coming election was "extremely probable."

The Democrats met in national convention in Chicago on August 29 and nominated General McClellan on a platform that contained one plank written by Vallandigham: "After four years of failure to restore the Union by the experiment of war . . . justice, humanity, liberty, and the public welfare demand that immediate efforts be made for a cessation of hostilities." McClellan repudiated this plank; nevertheless the Democrats, early in the campaign, at least, hoped to capitalize upon the war weariness that was sweeping across the North.

However, northern forces won enough victories to insure Lincoln's reelection. On August 23, a federal fleet under Admiral Farragut captured the forts at Mobile Bay, closed the port, and deprived the Confederacy of its last stronghold on the Gulf of Mexico. On September 2, Sherman entered Atlanta, after a hard and tortuous campaign. Six weeks later, a Union army under Major General Philip H. Sheridan drove Early's cavalry from the Shenandoah Valley. These victories, in Seward's words, "knocked the bottom out of the Chicago [Democratic] platform." Lincoln was reelected in November by a vote of 212 to twenty-one in the Electoral College. He carried every state except New Jersey, Delaware, and Kentucky. However, his popular vote was only 400,000 more than McClellan's in a total of 4,000,000 votes cast.

Sherman's March to the Sea

After the fall of Atlanta, the reckless General John B. Hood, who had replaced the cautious Joseph E. Johnston as Confederate commander in the West, tried to draw Sherman back from further invasion of Georgia by moving northward into Tennessee. Sherman's powerful army continued its invasion of Georgia; another Union army, under the command of a Virginian, General George H. Thomas, completely destroyed Hood's army in battles at Franklin and Nashville on November 30 and December 15–16, 1864.

Meanwhile Sherman, with 60,000 veteran fighting men, almost all of them Midwesterners, cut across Georgia in a 300-mile march to the sea that seemed more like a continuous picnic of three months than a campaign. The soldiers

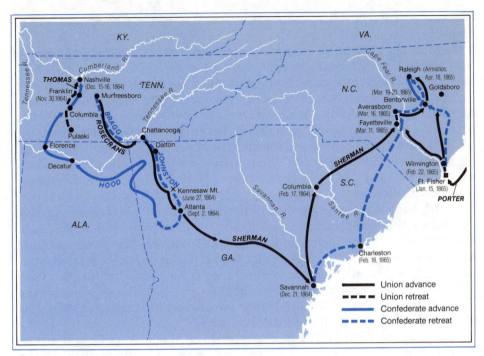

Sherman's Campaign, 1864–1865

lived off the newly gathered harvests of corn and grain and an abundance of chickens, turkeys, ducks, pigs, and sweet potatoes. They plundered as they marched and left a trail of destruction seventy-five miles wide.

Sherman planned the march with grim determination to make Georgia "an example to rebels": his troops burned public buildings, depots, and machine shops, destroyed stores of cotton, and confiscated 10,000 horses and mules. In short, he shattered the military potential of the area beyond repair. Sherman reached the coast in December and easily broke through the feeble defenses of Savannah. The militiamen, retained in Georgia by Governor Brown to protect the state, proved no match for Sherman's hardened troops. Sherman, on Christmas day, sent a telegram to Lincoln which announced "as a Christmas gift, the city of Savannah, with 150 heavy guns, plenty of ammunition and about 25,000 bales of cotton."

The Collapse of the Confederacy

The plight of the Confederacy was obviously desperate by early 1865. Desertions became even more frequent, food increasingly scarce. The Confederate government then began to make plans to enlist slaves in the army. Increasingly, leaders in Richmond realized that further resistance was useless. A delegation headed by Vice-President Alexander H. Stephens met Lincoln and Seward at Hampton Roads, Virginia, on February 3, 1865, to discuss terms of surrender. Lincoln insisted on two points: restoration of the Union and the abolition of slavery. The Southerners rejected these terms as "unconditional submission to the mercy of conquerors," and the conference broke up. "I can have no common country with the Yankees,'' declared Davis. Lee also advised continuation of the war.

Sherman and Grant now resumed operations with a vengeance. The former marched northward through South Carolina and left the state capital, Columbia, in ashes behind him. Slowly, systematically, the South was being ripped to shreds. Late in March, Grant renewed his attack on Petersburg. That stronghold fell on Sunday, April 2. Jefferson Davis, at worship in St. Paul's Church in Richmond, received a whispered message that the city must be evacuated. He hastily collected his papers and left Richmond for Danville with his cabinet and several of his staff officers. Union troops entered the ruined Confederate capital on the next day. They were followed by President Lincoln, who spoke words of kindness and reconciliation.

Lee tried to escape with his dwindling army of about 35,000 men to North Carolina, where he hoped to join forces with General Joseph E. Johnston, who was trying to stop Sherman near Raleigh. But Sheridan's men, who had come down from the Shenandoah Valley, blocked Lee's escape route. Lee faced Grant on one side and Sheridan on the other. On April 7, Grant wrote to Lee: "General, the result of the last week must convince you of the hopelessness of further resistance.'' There was no way out for Lee and his exhausted army; Lee consented to discuss Grant's terms of surrender.

The two great generals met in a farmhouse at Appomattox Courthouse on April 9. After a few minutes of friendly conversation, during which they recalled their comradeship in the Mexican War, Grant wrote out the terms of surrender. They were extraordinarily generous. The Army of Northern Virginia was to lay down its arms, but the officers might retain their sidearms and horses. The cavalry and artillery horses were also left, to be used "for the spring plowing,'' as Grant phrased it. Lee immediately signed the terms and graciously acknowledged their generosity.

The submission of the other Confederate forces followed quickly. Johnston surrendered his army of 37,000 men to Sherman near Durham, North Carolina, on April 26; Generals Richard Taylor in Alabama and Kirby Smith in Arkansas surrendered their armies to the Union commanders in the Southwest. All told, some 174,000 Confederate troops laid down their arms. Jefferson Davis was captured on May 10 at Irwinsville, Georgia, and imprisoned for two years at Fortress Monroe. After his release, he lived quietly in the South until his death on December 6, 1889; he never asked for pardon from the United States Government.

Thus ended a war which had cost at least 325,000 Union and 275,000 Confederate dead; hundreds of thousands of crippled men, whose lives would never be the same again; untold billions of dollars; the devastation of large portions of the South, and a legacy of bitterness and sectional hatreds that would live on long after the participants in the war were dead.

The Assassination of Lincoln

Lincoln attended Ford's Theatre in Washington to witness a performance of *Our American Cousin* on the evening of April 14, 1865. A mentally disturbed actor and Confederate sympathizer, John Wilkes Booth, stepped into Lincoln's box and shot him in the back of the head. Lincoln's assassination was part of a plot to kill several high officials of the government. Seward, who was then re-

Abraham Lincoln, as recorded by Mathew Brady's camera, not long before his assassination. In a eulogy to Lincoln, Ralph Waldo Emerson described how "by his courage, his justice . . . his humanity, he stood a heroic figure in the center of a heroic epoch. He is the true history of the American people in his time." (The Bettmann Archive)

covering from an accident with a runaway horse and carriage, was stabbed severely on the same night; he recovered. Grant, too, was marked for death, but the assassin lost his nerve after he jumped on the General's carriage step and saw his face through the window. Booth was trapped soon afterward in a barn in Virginia and shot. The other conspirators in the plot were caught and executed or sent to prison.

The dying Lincoln was carried to a private house across the street from the theater. There he lingered without regaining consciousness until a few minutes past seven o'clock the next morning, April 15, 1865. "Now he belongs to the ages," Secretary of War Edwin M. Stanton is alleged to have said as Lincoln breathed his last. His death meant that the best chance was gone that unrepentant Southerners and unforgiving Northerners could have been reconciled in support of reconstruction policies that were magnanimous toward whites and yet fair toward the black freedmen of the South.

SUGGESTED READINGS

Clement Eaton, *A History of the Southern Confederacy* (1954), is an adequate, one-volume study, but it should be supplemented by Charles P. Roland, *The Confederacy* (1960), and E. Merton Coulter, *The Confederate States of America, 1861–1865* (1950). Frank L. Owsley is the author of two older but still important works: *State Rights in the Confederacy* (1925) and *King Cotton Diplomacy* (1931). A sympathetic and detailed biography is Hudson Strode, *Jefferson Davis* (1955–1964). A shorter study is *Jefferson Davis* by Clement Eaton (1978). Rembert W. Patrick, *Jefferson Davis and His Cabinet* (1944), contains a good survey of Confederate administrative problems.

Of the many works on Lincoln, James G. Randall, *Lincoln the President*, 4 vols. (1945–1955), is probably the most important. Good single-volume biographies of Lincoln are Stephen B. Oates, *With Malice Toward None*, already cited, and Benjamin P. Thomas, *Abraham Lincoln*, also already cited. David Herbert Donald, *Lincoln Reconsidered* (1956), and Richard N. Current, *The Lincoln Nobody Knows* (1958), contain particularly stimulating interpretations. On Lincoln as a war President, see T. Harry Williams, *Lincoln and the Radicals* (1941) and his *Lincoln and His Generals* (1952); William B. Hesseltine, *Lincoln and the War Governors* (1948); and R. V. Bruce, *Lincoln and the Tools of War* (1956). Bruce Catton, *The Centennial History of the Civil War*, 3 vols. (1961–1965), makes for exciting reading. A good one-volume introduction to Lincoln's thought is *Abraham Lincoln: His Speeches and Writings* (1962), edited by Roy P. Basler.

Martin B. Duberman, *Charles Francis Adams* (1961), is a good introduction to the problems of northern diplomacy as well as the best recent biography of Adams. Wood

Gray, *The Hidden Civil War: The Story of the Copperheads* (1942), and George Fort Milton, *Abraham Lincoln and the Fifth Column* (1942), explore the problem of disloyalty in the North. Economic motivation is examined in Frank L. Klement, *The Copperheads in the Middle West* (1960). For economic policy and problems, see Robert P. Sharkey, *Money, Class, and Party* (1959). James G. Randall, *Constitutional Problems under Lincoln* (1926), is still the standard work on that topic.

On the drive to make abolition a war aim see James M. McPherson's excellent *The Struggle for Equality: Abolitionists and the Negro in the Civil War and Reconstruction* (1964). See also George M. Frederickson, *The Inner Civil War: Northern Intellectuals and the Crisis of the Union* (1965), and Benjamin F. Quarles, *The Negro in the Civil War* (1967).

The military history of the war is best recounted in Kenneth P. Williams, *Lincoln Finds a General*, 4 vols. (1949–1952), and Shelby Foote, *The Civil War: A Narrative*, 3 vols. (1958–1974). Bruce Catton's *Mr. Lincoln's Army* (1951), *Glory Road* (1952), and *A Stillness at Appomattox* (1953) are also excellent. For a general survey of naval operations, see Richard S. West, Jr., *Mr. Lincoln's Navy* (1957). A judicious one-volume biography is John Carpenter, *Ulysses S. Grant* (1976). Bruce Catton, *Grant Moves South* (1959) is also useful. Until an adequate one-volume biography of Lee is written, study of the great Confederate General will have to begin with Douglas S. Freeman, *Robert E. Lee, A Biography*, 4 vols. (1934–1935), which compensates somewhat for ite length with fine writing. The life of the common soldier has been described by Bell I. Wiley in *The Life of Johnny Reb* (1943) and *The Life of Billy Yank* (1952).

CHAPTER 17
THE ERA OF RECONSTRUCTION

1. STRUGGLES OVER RECONSTRUCTION POLICIES

The Status of the Southern States

The Civil War settled several old problems — forever. It determined that secession by one or more states from the United States was not only unconstitutional but also militarily impossible. The American people would rather go to war than permit the nation to be broken apart. It also ended the old debate about the nature of the Union and established the ultimate sovereignty of the federal government over the states. Finally, the Union victory put an end forever to slavery in North America. The Thirteenth Amendment, which abolished slavery, was approved by Congress, sent to the states before Lee's surrender, and ratified on December 18, 1865. On the other hand, the northern victory also raised difficult questions, many of which the nation was not yet prepared to answer. For example, what should be done about the former slaves? What was their status? How would they be integrated into American society? And the South? How were the seceded states to be handled? Were they states or not? These complex problems came before the nation during a period when minds — both in the North and in the South — were still affected by the searing emotions released during a brutal civil war.

The most immediate political question at the end of the war concerned the status of the former Confederate states. Had they become territories, as some congressmen argued, to be readmitted as states sometime in the future on conditions imposed by the federal government? Or was the South merely a conquered province, like New Mexico in 1848, for example, to be disposed of according to the will of the conquerors? Or were the former Confederate states still states of the Union, in spite of their desperate and bloody struggle to break away from it? If so, were they free to accept or reject the Thirteenth Amendment? Or had their defeat deprived them of that right?

Furthermore, who was immediately responsible for dealing with the South? If the war had been only a rebellion of numerous individuals against the United States, then the President, who had the power of pardon, was the person to act. If, however, the southern states had really separated themselves from the Union, their readmission became the business of Congress, which under the Constitution had the right, subject to the President's veto, to admit states to the Union.

Lincoln, from the beginning of the conflict, claimed that the war had been a rebellion of individual citizens and that the states, irrespective of their resolutions of secession, had never left the Union. Although Lincoln was not committed to any single plan by which to restore the Union, he proclaimed in December 1863 that, when at least 10 per cent of those persons who had voted in the election of 1860 in any of the seceded states took an oath of loyalty to the United States, these persons might then form a government without slavery, which he would recognize. Governments actually were established during the war under the so-called 10 per cent plan in Tennessee, Arkansas, and Louisiana.

But Congress rejected Lincoln's plan in 1864 and substituted its own conditions for readmission in the Wade-Davis bill. This measure provided that 50 per cent of the voters in rebellious states had to take the oath of loyalty. Moreover, it excluded Confederate leaders, officers, and soldiers from voting, and Confederate army officers and civilian officials above certain ranks from holding office. It also abolished slavery in the states affected. Lincoln killed the bill with a pocket veto and said that he thought that the measure was unwise and unconstitutional. This drew a fierce public rebuke in a "Manifesto" by Senator Benjamin F. Wade of Ohio and Representative Henry Winter Davis of Maryland, authors of the bill. Lincoln had to understand, they warned, that "the authority of Congress is paramount and must be respected; that the whole body of the Union men of Congress will not submit to be impeached by him of rash and unconstitutional legislation."

The war ended without any decision on basic reconstruction policies, except, of course, on the abolition of slavery and the restoration of national sovereignty throughout the former Confederacy. Lincoln, had he lived to finish his second term, might have had to fight tumultuous battles with members of his own party. However, Lincoln was a masterful politician and might well have maintained a congressional majority behind a fairly moderate program by strategic concessions. Certainly he would not have allowed himself to fall so far out of touch with the wishes of Congress and the electorate that his policies would be overwhelmingly repudiated at the polls, his vetoes overridden, and he, himself, nearly removed from office by Congress, which is what happened to his successor.

Andrew Johnson and the Radicals

Andrew Johnson of Tennessee succeeded Lincoln. Johnson, born in Raleigh, North Carolina, on December 29, 1808, was of humble origin and had scant formal education, like Lincoln. But Johnson lacked Lincoln's tact, sympathy, and political skill. Although a Southerner and a former slaveowner himself, Johnson hated the great planters who, he believed, had dragged the poor people of the South into a senseless war. And, although he was a state-rights Democrat, he was intensely devoted to the Union. In fact, he had been the only senator from the seceded states to remain in his seat in Washington in 1861. Lincoln had appointed him military governor of Tennessee and had put him on the Union ticket for the vice-presidency in 1864. This was done partly to reward him for his loyalty. It also helped to answer charges that the Republican party (renamed the Union party in 1864) was purely sectional.

Although no one has made a detailed survey of northern public opinion in the spring of 1865, there does appear to have been a high degree of unity within the dominant Republican party in support of a policy that would bring the defeated South back into the Union fairly quickly. This basic policy included a constitutional amendment affirming the sovereignty of the national government over the states and a guarantee of at least basic civil rights for the freed blacks. The most extreme element in the Republican party — the so-called Radicals — demanded a somewhat more thoroughgoing reconstruction of southern politics and society by the elimination of secessionist leaders from politics and by economic assistance, especially the grant of lands, to black people. A second Republican group — the so-called Moderates — perhaps more numerous within the party than the Radicals, did not want to go as far as the Radicals in social and economic reconstruction. Yet these Moderates, too, wanted to protect the civil and to some degree the political rights of the recently freed slaves.

The new President enjoyed a reputation as an extreme Radical and, during the first days of his tenure, indicated that he favored stern measures toward former Confederates. "I can only say you can judge of my policy by the past," he told a congressional delegation that visited the White House. "Everybody knows what that is. I hold this: Robbery is a crime; murder is a crime; *treason* is a crime; and *crime* must be punished. . . . Treason must be made infamous and traitors must be impoverished." And yet Johnson soon made it clear that he would follow a moderate, even a mild program of reconstruction. No one has ever satisfactorily explained his change of policy. Perhaps the presidential office itself sobered him; perhaps he thought that he was implementing Lincoln's program — to preserve the Union and Constitution in all their purity. Some cynical Republican politicians believed that he was trying to lay the basis for a coalition of moderate Republicans and Democrats, which he would lead. Others said that Johnson, a person of humble birth, was beguiled by southern aristocrats.

For whatever reasons, Johnson proceeded during the summer and autumn of 1865 — when Congress was not in session — to carry out his own plan. On May 29, 1865, he issued a proclamation of amnesty, or pardon, to all persons who had engaged in rebellion against the United States, except Confederate officers and persons with property worth more than $20,000. Even the exempted groups were invited to apply to the President for individual pardons, which would be "liberally extended." Next, Johnson appointed provisional civilian governors, after Lincoln's pattern, in the Carolinas, Georgia, Florida, Alabama, Mississippi, and Texas. He stipulated that constitutional conventions should be elected which had to repeal the ordinances of secession, frame new constitutions, and ratify the Thirteenth Amendment. Most of the southern states followed Johnson's instructions at once.

However, the suggestion by leading southern politicians that the federal government should assume Confederate debts received prominent attention in northern newspapers. The South Carolina constitutional convention refused either to repudiate the state's wartime debt or to ratify the Thirteenth Amendment. Southern voters elected many former Confederate officials to the United States Congress; they included the former Vice-President of the Confederacy, Alexander H. Stephens. Most galling of all to Northerners, southern legislatures began to adopt "black codes" which applied to blacks alone. They usually included vagrancy and apprentice laws which assigned blacks without jobs to "guardians"—sometimes their former masters—for work without pay. South Carolina's code made the theft of a mule or a horse or housebreaking by a black person a capital crime. The Mississippi black code was so notorious that one northern newspaper predicted that angry Northerners would descend on the state and convert it into "a frog pond." No southern state under the Johnson government permitted black men to vote or to hold office. To Northerners who felt some obligation toward the people freed by the Civil War, it seemed that the black codes were nothing more than a device to return black people to slavery. Almost every northern family had suffered some casualty during the terrible war. Now—despite the North's sacrifices for victory—Southerners appeared unwilling to acknowledge defeat and, instead, seemed intent upon retaining in peacetime much of what they had lost in war.

2. RADICAL RECONSTRUCTION

The Beginnings of Radical Reconstruction

Johnson failed to gauge northern public opinion, and he woefully underestimated the opposition that his program would arouse among congressmen. When the Thirty-ninth Congress convened in December 1865, Thaddeus Stevens of Pennsylvania, leader of the Radicals in the House of Representatives, obtained adoption of a resolution which instructed the clerk to omit from the roll call the names of the newly elected representatives from former Confederate states. The Senate, led by another Radical, Charles Sumner of Massachusetts, took the same course. Moderates and Radicals united behind these resolutions.

Immediately after the House of Representatives turned the Southerners away, Stevens called for the appointment of a special Joint Committee of Fifteen on Reconstruction to inquire into the right to representation of the states of the "so-called late Confederacy." Actually, the committee would try to find a new plan of reconstruction acceptable to northern opinion. The battle between Johnson and the Radicals was now joined in earnest. Moderate Republicans held the balance of power in Congress and in the North, Midwest, and West as a whole; victory would go to the side that won their support.

Stevens maneuvered skillfully and cautiously to win that prize. Within the Committee of Fifteen, he permitted policy to be determined by Moderate members. The committee's first measure was a bill to extend indefinitely the life of the Freedmen's Bureau. Congress had created this agency on March 3, 1865, to provide the freed slaves (and many whites as well) with food, clothing, and shelter. It helped freedmen to find employment at fair wages, founded thousands of schools and several colleges, and was primarily responsible for beginning free public education for black people in the South. The Freedmen's Bureau was, in some respects, the conscience of the North in action. Then Congress passed a civil rights bill, which granted citizenship to blacks and guaranteed the same civil rights to all persons born in the United States. Senator Lyman Trumbull of Illinois, one of the leading Moderates in Congress, prepared the bill after many interviews with Johnson. The Senator offered to revise the measure to meet any objections that the President might have; Johnson indicated that he had no objections.

The Joint Committee of Fifteen next turned to the problem of guaranteeing permanently the basic civil rights of blacks. Its solution was the Fourteenth Amendment, reported to Congress in April 1866. It declared that "all persons born or naturalized in the United States" were "citizens of the United States and of the state wherein they reside," and forbade any state to deprive such persons of their rights as citizens. It did not enfranchise black men—that came with the Fifteenth Amendment—but it required a reduction in the representation in Congress of any state that denied the vote to black men. It also forbade payment of the Confederate debt and guaranteed payment of the public debt of the United States. Finally, it disqualified former Confederate leaders from holding federal or state offices. This disqualification, however, could be removed by a two-thirds vote of Congress.

In retrospect, it seems that this was the minimum northern program for Reconstruction; Moderates insisted upon it as avidly as did Radicals. In light of the circumstances, it was extraordinarily lenient. It offered a speedy process of self-reconstruction by the southern states. Tennessee promptly ratified the Fourteenth Amendment and was restored to full statehood. It is only fair to assume that the other southern states would have been readmitted had they followed suit.

Now Johnson had to decide whether to accept this mild congressional plan or to insist upon his own. For reasons that probably had to do with his own defects of character—his stubbornness, arrogance, and political ineptitude—Johnson, in a speech from the balcony of the White House on Washington's birthday, 1866, attacked Stevens and Sumner by name. He accused them of seeking to enslave the white South, to invade the constitutional powers of the presidency, and even to encourage his assassination. His performance shocked both Congress and most people outside the South. Johnson carried the fight further in a ringing message that vetoed the bill that extended the life of the Freedmen's Bureau. He outraged Moderates by also vetoing the civil rights bill. Finally, he urged the southern states to refuse to ratify the Fourteenth Amendment. Congress rebuffed the assault by passing both the Freedmen's Bureau and the civil rights bills over Johnson's vetoes.

Radical Reconstruction Is Launched

The struggles over the Freedmen's Bureau bill, the civil rights bill, and the Fourteenth Amendment provided the issues for the crucial congressional campaign of 1866, in which the Fortieth Congress was elected. At the outset, important Republicans and many Democrats supported Johnson. But the President's opposition to the Fourteenth Amendment and, particularly, the refusal of most southern states to ratify that amendment, drove more and more

Moderate Republicans into the Radical camp. Then, in an effort to carry his fight with Congress to the people, Johnson undertook a long speaking tour through the East and Middle West. His speeches were filled with coarse invective, and his conduct was unbecoming of a President. He offended many people and added new recruits to the ranks of his foes. The voters in November returned a Congress with an overwhelming anti-Johnson majority. It would contain 143 Republicans and forty-nine Democrats in the House, and forty-two Republicans and eleven Democrats in the Senate.

The Radicals believed that they had a popular mandate, and, with the support of their Moderate allies, took complete control when the Thirty-ninth Congress returned to Washington for its short final session in December 1866. Congress moved rapidly and, on March 2, 1867, adopted — over Johnson's veto, of course — what was later called the First Reconstruction Act (there were supplementary acts in 1867 and 1868). The First Reconstruction Act wiped out the governments created under presidential reconstruction and grouped the ten southern states that had refused to ratify the Fourteenth Amendment into five military districts, each to be governed by a major general of the army. The military governments were to summon conventions in the states under their control to frame new constitutions. Blacks could vote freely for members of these conventions, while former Confederate leaders were disqualified from voting. State constitutions with a provision for black male suffrage had to be framed and then approved by Congress; in addition, the legislatures elected under these constitutions had to ratify the Fourteenth Amendment. Once this was done, the states would be received into the Union and permitted to send representatives to Congress.

The striking fact about this program was not its harshness, despite appearances, but its leniency. Some Radicals wanted to impose a thoroughgoing economic and social revolution upon the South. Stevens and other extreme Radicals, if they had controlled sufficient votes in Congress, probably would have confiscated the land of former Confederates and tried to establish a large class of independent black landowners. But Stevens did not have the votes for some of his more ambitious plans. Republican Moderates still held the balance of power, and they insisted that blacks receive the power to protect themselves at the polls. Beyond that, they were unwilling to go. Charles Sumner advised blacks to use the courts to sue for their rights — all their rights, not simply civil rights. Again, Moderates regarded such action as extreme and insisted that blacks had no claims beyond what had already been done for them.

Radical Reconstruction in the South

Governments had been established with the aid of federal soldiers in six southern states by the midsummer of 1868. By 1870, the four remaining states — Mississippi, Virginia, Georgia, and Texas — had ratified the Fourteenth Amendment and were back in the Union.

It is not easy to characterize the Reconstruction governments in the southern states because they varied so greatly. A few general statements, however, can be made.

1. Blacks participated enthusiastically as voters and officeholders, but it is completely inaccurate to speak of Reconstruction as a time of black rule or of black domination. Only in South Carolina did blacks ever constitute a majori-

Woodcut of freedmen voting in New Orleans in 1867. In imposing suffrage for black men upon the former Confederate states, the Radicals in Congress set in motion the forces behind the movement for national suffrage for blacks that resulted in the passage of the Fifteenth Amendment. (The Bettmann Archive)

ty of a state legislature. No black governor was elected, and only two black United States senators. Conservative native whites controlled Reconstruction governments in some states. Native whites, derisively called "scalawags" by some of their neighbors, cooperated with Reconstruction authorities when it served their interests to do so. The best example of this occurred in Mississippi, where many former Whigs moved into the Republican party and then withdrew when they could not control it. In no state did blacks ever use their power to try to dominate or punish their former masters. On the contrary, black political leaders worked very hard to conciliate the whites.

2. Many of the northern whites who had moved to the South (dubbed "carpetbaggers") and cooperated with blacks to control the Republican party in some states were not very well trained for political leadership. Many black officeholders had little education, since most southern states had made it a crime to teach slaves to read and write. Even so, Reconstruction governments in the southern states left a record of constructive work that has endured to this day: establishment of public schools for whites and blacks alike; establishment of the principle in state constitutions which mandated public support of education; the broadening of the suffrage and further democratization of state constitutions; improvement of transportation facilities and other public works; and expansion of state social and welfare services. Given the difficulty of the tasks, the wonder is that the Reconstruction governments were able to accomplish so much.

3. Many of the Reconstruction governments in the South were flagrantly corrupt. Officials stole and wasted much of the money that they could lay their hands upon. Legislatures increased taxes nearly to the point of confiscation, pledged the credit of their states to support fraudulent railroad bonds, and greatly increased the indebtedness of their states.

In this connection, three points should be emphasized: First, the postwar years were a time of general deterioration in public morality. Corruption permeated local, state, and national governments all through the Reconstruction era. Southern states had no monopoly on corruption. In New York City alone, Boss William Marcy Tweed and his friends in Tammany Hall stole more money from the taxpayers than all the state governments in the South combined! Second, no single party accounted for the corruption and public immorality of the period. Democrats in New Orleans, like those in New York, fed at the public trough every chance that they had. Third, corruption in the South was not confined to carpetbaggers and blacks. Southern white politicians were just as eager to profit—and did profit whenever they had the opportunity—from outright bribery. Furthermore, the major beneficiaries of bribery and other illicit operations during Reconstruction were not the politicians, but southern white businessmen and plantation owners who obtained the rights to railroad franchises, lands, and convict labor.

Moreover, "carpetbagger" and "scalawag" were epithets used by former Confederates to condemn those who helped former slaves—much as civil rights activists were condemned later. Unquestionably, there were many greedy carpetbaggers and scalawags concerned with nothing other than their own personal gain. But among the carpetbaggers were many sincere reformers from the North, who worked hard to heal the scars of war; and among the scalawags were thousands of Southerners who had opposed the war from the beginning and were now eager to help "bind up the nation's wounds."

The White South Strikes Back

Recent southern historians of Reconstruction have pointed out that most southern whites objected to the Reconstruction regimes, not so much because they were incompetent or corrupt, but mainly because they were based in large part upon black suffrage. It was perhaps asking too much of human nature to expect most white Southerners, who had been trained all their lives to regard black persons as inferior, to approve or even to accept the social revolution that seemed to accompany Radical Reconstruction. The older ruling class struck back violently in a number of ways, but especially in secret organizations. The chief of these was the Ku Klux Klan, organized in Tennessee in 1865. The Klan took advantage of the fears of black people to force them back into a position of social and political subordination. Bands of masked men on horseback, robed in white sheets, spread terror through Negro quarters at night. Klansmen burned fiery crosses and posted warnings of what would happen to all persons who aided the freedmen. They also whipped, tarred and feathered, and murdered at will. The Klan was lawless and irresponsible from the beginning, for its leaders could not control the more violent members. Its Grand Wizard, General Nathan Bedford Forrest, finally tried, in vain, to disband the organization.

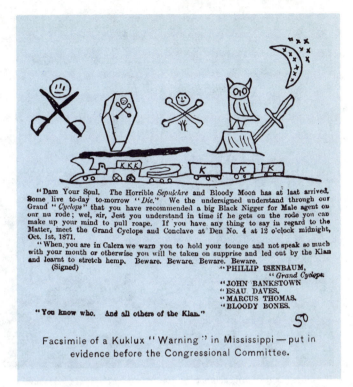

During Reconstruction, members of the Ku Klux Klan used such devices as warnings to bring terrorism to the South. (Picture Collection, The Branch Libraries, The New York Public Library)

"Dam Your Soul. The Horrible *Sepulchre* and Bloody Moon has at last arrived. Some live to-day to-morrow "*Die.*" We the undersigned understand through our Grand "*Cyclops*" that you have recommended a big Black Nigger for Male agent on our nu rode; wel, sir, Jest you understand in time if he gets on the rode you can make up your mind to pull roape. If you have any thing to say in regard to the Matter, meet the Grand Cyclops and Conclave at Den No. 4 at 12 o'clock midnight, Oct. 1st, 1871.

"When you are in Calera we warn you to hold your tounge and not speak so much with your mouth or otherwise you will be taken on surprise and led out by the Klan and learnt to stretch hemp. Beware. Beware. Beware. Beware.

(Signed) "PHILLIP ISENBAUM,
"*Grand Cyclops.*
"JOHN BANKSTOWN
"ESAU DAVES.
"MARCUS THOMAS.
"BLOODY BONES.

"You know who. And all others of the Klan."

Facsimile of a Kuklux "Warning" in Mississippi — put in evidence before the Congressional Committee.

Meanwhile, reports of this violence profoundly disturbed northern opinion. Congress, in 1870–1871, adopted laws to protect black voters and to outlaw the Klan. The President suspended the writ of *habeas corpus* in nine South Carolina counties in the summer of 1871, and a joint congressional committee launched a full-scale investigation. These efforts were on the whole ineffective. Emboldened whites continued to use force to intimidate and defraud blacks in order to deprive them of political rights. Such tactics were supplemented by economic coercion—an even more effective weapon of racial control. Congress had refused to establish and train blacks in economic independence, and had, in effect, left the former slaves to the mercy of white property owners. Most freedmen had no alternative but to work as sharecroppers or tenants on plantations.

The Impeachment of Johnson

The Radicals, not content with reducing Johnson to political impotence, were determined to drive him from the White House. On the same day that it passed the First Reconstruction Act, Congress adopted the Tenure of Office Act. This measure deprived the President of the right to dismiss members of his own cabinet (and all other officials whose appointment required confirmation by the Senate) without the prior consent of the upper house. It was designed, not only to prevent Johnson from removing adversaries within his administration,

The High Court of Impeachment in the Senate for the trial of Andrew Johnson with John A. Bingham, Chairman of the House Committee of Impeachment Managers, reading the Articles of Impeachment. This engraving is from Frank Leslie's Illustrated Newspaper *(1868). (Culver Pictures, Inc.)*

but also as a convenient trap in the event that Johnson should violate the law. The Act specifically defined any violation as a misdemeanor, and a President can be impeached only for committing high crimes and misdemeanors.

Johnson accepted the challenge. He dismissed Secretary of War Stanton, a virtual spy in the cabinet who was in close alliance with the congressional Radicals. Thereupon the House of Representatives impeached Johnson. The Senate, presided over by Chief Justice Salmon P. Chase, tried the case from March 30 to May 26, 1868. In spite of frantic efforts by Radicals to secure a conviction, seven Republican senators refused to vote as directed. They joined the twelve Democrats and voted for acquittal. The vote, thirty-five to nineteen, fell one short of the two thirds necessary for conviction.

3. NATIONAL POLITICS AND PROBLEMS

The Election of 1868

As the impeachment trial drew to an end, the Republican national convention met in Chicago and nominated General Grant for President on the first ballot.

Johnson and the Reconstruction acts were the main issues in the campaign that followed. At this time, the Republicans began the practice, which they long continued, of "waving the bloody shirt." The term came from an exhibition in Congress of a bloodstained shirt allegedly worn by a carpetbagger beaten by a Mississippi mob. Northern bitterness at the South was excited each time that the bloody shirt was waved, and Republicans continued the practice throughout the rest of the nineteenth century.

Grant won a decisive victory over his weak Democratic opponent, former Governor Horatio Seymour of New York. The General carried every northern and western state except New York, New Jersey, and Oregon, and every state of the reconstructed South except Georgia and Louisiana. The electoral vote was 214 to eighty. However, Grant's popular majority was only 306,000 in a total of 5,715,000 votes cast. Without the approximately 700,000 blacks who voted for him in the South, he would have fallen behind Seymour at the polls. These figures made it clear to the Radicals that it was absolutely necessary to retain the black vote, if the G.O.P. was to remain in power. Congress, therefore, in 1869 adopted and submitted the Fifteenth Amendment. It forbade the states to deny the right to vote to any citizen on account of "race, color, or previous condition of servitude." It was ratified on March 30, 1870.

Grant as President

An unkind act of fate put Ulysses S. Grant in the White House. Had he eschewed politics, he would be known to history as a brave and brilliant general and a compassionate human being. But Grant yielded to the flattery of his Radical friends and permitted his election to an office for which he was totally unprepared in experience and unequipped in temperament. A professional soldier with no political experience, he became little more than a puppet of the dominant faction of his party. Without a broad national vision or desire to exercise leadership, he was content to drift with the main tide. He was personally honest, but he was also gullible, naive, and so morally insensitive that he often could not tell the difference between an honest person and a rogue. He saw nothing wrong in accepting expensive presents from rich friends. In fact, he expected them as tokens of gratitude for his many services to the nation. He refused to believe that they were intended to gain an advantage. Consequently, he suffered repeated betrayals. His administration ended riddled by corruption and blackened by disgrace. Historians rate him one of the worst failures among American Presidents.

Fortunately for Grant, most of the important policies of his administration had already been adopted before he assumed office. By 1869, Radical Reconstruction was well under way. Grant tried faithfully to carry out Radical policies, and it was not necessary for him to devise new ones. The Republican program of free homesteads, protective tariffs, the National Banking System, and lavish assistance to western railroads seemed to enjoy the support of an overwhelming majority of the people. Except for controversies about paper money and taxes, the Democrats did not try seriously to challenge the Republican economic policies. Hence most partisan controversy revolved around Radical Reconstruction. The main body of Republicans continued to support it; the Democrats tried, unsuccessfully in 1868, to overturn it.

The Prostrate South

Significantly, no political leader seems to have given any serious attention to the nation's most important problem at this time – the economic reconstruction of the South. That section was devastated in 1865. It lay in ruins and remained so in 1869. Southern capital invested in slaves and Confederate bonds, or held in the form of Confederate currency, had evaporated. The real wealth of the South – buildings, railroads, livestock, factories, and roads – had been destroyed wherever it stood in the path of the furious war. Financial institutions suffered bankruptcy when the Confederate bonds and currency which they held turned out to be worthless, and when a high proportion of borrowers were obliged to default on loans. The greatest loss, however, was the 275,000 men who might have rebuilt the ravaged section had they not died for the Confederacy and the untold thousands of other men who were mutilated or rendered psychologically unfit for productive work.

Northerners were in no mood, during the Reconstruction period, to pay taxes to rebuild the South. Even if feelings had not been poisoned by arguments over Reconstruction policies, the United States in the 1860s was hardly a welfare state. Even the unfortunate former slaves received little in the way of material aid in exchange for their years in bondage. Except for the efforts of the Freedmen's Bureau, the blacks were left to shift for themselves – and so was the rest of the population of the former Confederate States of America.

Enough capital came from the North and Great Britain to put railroads in running condition, but manufacturing did not revive. Risks in the postwar South were too great, and opportunities elsewhere were more promising for northern and English capitalists. Planters, utterly devoid of capital, had to break up their plantations into inefficient small holdings farmed by sharecroppers. These tenants paid a part of their crop for food, seed, fertilizer, and rent of the land. They generally were in debt to the planter, and the planter was usually in debt at high interest rates to the village storekeepers and moneylenders, who, in turn, usually owed money at high interest rates to suppliers in the North. It would have been wise to grow a variety of crops, but cotton could not be stolen or eaten, and creditors therefore insisted on its cultivation to the exclusion of fruit or grain. Thus a one-crop system, immensely costly, both to human beings and the soil, was fastened, along with an expensive credit system, upon large sections of the South.

The Greenback Controversy

Besides the reconstruction of the southern states, the one issue that excited national controversy during the first Grant administration was monetary policy. It stemmed from the methods used by the federal government to pay for the war. Congress increased tariffs and excise taxes and levied an income tax; altogether, taxes contributed about $667 million to the cost of the war. The largest sum – more than $2 billion – came from the sale of government bonds. To provide additional money, Congress resorted to paper money, called "greenbacks." They were based, not on gold or silver, but on the good faith of the United States and were legal tender, or lawful money, for the payment of all debts except import duties. The government issued $250 million in greenbacks in 1862. Subsequent issues brought the total amount to about $450 million. Naturally, this currency rose and fell in value (as compared with gold) and depended upon the confidence of holders, both at home and abroad, in the successful outcome of the federal war effort.

The greenbacks had been issued as emergency currency. When the war ended, the government proposed to call them in for payment in gold or bonds. Consequently, the value of the greenbacks rose sharply. The Secretary of the Treasury had already begun this process when a cry went up from many debtors, including certain manufacturers, railroad builders, and many farmers, who wanted cheap paper money. They had borrowed depreciated paper and now found themselves obliged to repay in dear money or gold. As paper money disappeared into the federal Treasury, businessmen suddenly found that it was difficult to obtain loans.

Resentment against retirement of the greenbacks swept over the country, particularly the Middle West, in 1867. It found expression and a program in the so-called Ohio Idea, suggested by the Cincinnati *Enquirer* and embodied in a bill introduced in Congress in 1867 by Representative (later Senator) George H. Pendleton of Ohio. The bill directed the Secretary of the Treasury to redeem *in greenbacks* the Civil War bonds known as five-twenties (because they paid interest at 5 per cent for twenty years).

Arrayed against the Ohio Idea — and the idea of cheap money in general — were most of the National banks; creditors in general; exporters and importers, who had an interest in a stable currency; and academic economists. Most of the latter argued for a sound currency to stimulate economic growth and foreign confidence. And of course many of the devotees of hard money were not averse to the enhancement of their own economic interests.

Greenback sentiment permeated both major parties. The Democrats, desperate for an additional issue, endorsed the Ohio Idea in their platform in 1868. However, they refused to nominate Pendleton for the presidency and chose Seymour, a hard money man, instead. The Republican platform demanded payment of greenbacks and bonds in gold, and Grant supported this program.

Congress accepted the election returns as something of a mandate and provided for payment of United States bonds in gold in the Public Credit Act of March 18, 1869. When the Democrats, in the mid-term election of 1874, captured the House of Representatives for the first time since the war, the Republicans made haste in their lame-duck session to settle the greenback issue, once and for all. They adopted the Resumption Act, which reduced to $300 million the volume of greenbacks in circulation. Moreover, the Act stipulated that greenbacks might be redeemed in gold on and after January 1, 1879. Champions of cheap money put the Greenback party into the field in the presidential election of 1876. The Greenbackers won only about 80,000 votes. But demands for cheap money were only temporarily silenced. They would be heard again during the 1890s in the powerful agrarian demand for the free coinage of silver.

4. THE EAGLE SCREAMS

Nationalism Rampant Again

Curiously, there were few partisan divisions on foreign policy in the postwar era. On the contrary, bitter enemies in domestic controversies showed surprising willingness to forget partisan advantage when foreign policy was involved.

One reason for this near unanimity was the type of foreign policies pursued as a result of the widespread exhilaration in the North after its great military victory. Pride in their military power, and deep resentment at the nations that had tried to take advantage of American preoccupation with the Civil War, made Americans adopt a particularly chauvinistic stance when they turned to deal with those countries. The expansive nationalism rampant during the 1840s reappeared in both sections after the end of the violent controversy between the North and the South. Agreement on foreign policy was encouraged also by William H. Seward and Hamilton Fish of New York, two of the ablest Secretaries of State in American history. Seward remained loyal to Johnson on Reconstruction policies without, however, losing the confidence of Republican leaders in Congress. By bridging the gap between the warring ends of Pennsylvania Avenue, Seward was able to put into effect the first bipartisan foreign policy in American history.

Challenges to the Monroe Doctrine

America's distress during the Civil War had tempted Spain and France to throw down the first serious challenges to the Monroe Doctrine. Certain leaders of the revolution-torn Dominican Republic appealed to the Spanish government to reannex their country into the remains of the Spanish Empire in the new world. Secretary Seward sent a stern warning to Madrid. The Spaniards, aware of the distraction of the United States and its inability to take vigorous action at the moment, ignored the warning and took their former colony back into their empire in May 1861. But bloody confrontations with Dominicans, disease, and the eventual emergence of an aggressive and victorious North determined to enforce the Monroe Doctrine finally compelled the Spaniards to withdraw voluntarily early in 1865.

Much more formidable was the challenge of the French Emperor, Louis Napoleon. In 1861, the British, French, and Spanish governments sent a joint expeditionary force to Mexico to compel payment of debts owed to their subjects. But the Spaniards and the British lost interest in the project and withdrew. Not Louis Napoleon. He envisioned an expanded French Empire in the new world and set in motion a plan to establish a puppet government in Mexico. First, he dispatched an expeditionary force that occupied Mexico City on June 7, 1863. Next, he arranged for Mexican collaborators to offer the throne of a Mexican Empire to a candidate of his choice, the Archduke Ferdinand Maximilian of Austria. The Archduke was crowned a year later.

Seward watched events in Mexico with an apprehensive eye. He followed a cautious policy because he knew that any drastic move against France might drive Louis Napoleon into open alliance with the Confederacy. Once the Civil War had ended, however, Seward had 50,000 federal veterans under General Sheridan sent to the Mexican border. At this point, the Union army had become a military machine that no sane political leader in the world would challenge, especially in the western hemisphere. Seward spoke in increasingly menacing tones to the French government. Finally—on February 12, 1866—the Secretary of State sent a virtual ultimatum to Louis Napoleon to withdraw his troops from Mexico.

The Emperor realized his mistake. Liberals in his own country condemned his Mexican adventure; taxpayers howled their complaints. Across the Rhine, war between Austria and Prussia grew ever more likely, and France might be compelled to step in. Also, the Mexican rebel forces severely mauled the French army in Mexico. So Louis Napoleon recalled his troops in the summer of 1866 and abandoned Maximilian to Mexican patriots under Benito Juárez. The Mexicans captured the hapless Ferdinand Maximilian and shot him on June 19, 1867.

The Monroe Doctrine came of age with Seward's success in eliminating Spain from the Dominican Republic and France from Mexico. The doctrine had never been seriously challenged or defended before. Now the whole world knew that it was the keystone of American foreign policy and that the United States would fight to defend it. Europe did not soon forget this lesson.

A New Manifest Destiny?

A new movement for overseas expansion emerged in the United States during the immediate postwar era. As it turned out, it quickly subsided, and it probably had the support of only a small minority of Americans at any time. However, it was a harbinger of what would become—a generation later—a nationwide drive to achieve a new Manifest Destiny to extend American dominion and civilization beyond the seas.

Given greater support in the Senate, Seward might have gone far in this direction. Congress shot down his negotiations for a naval base in the Dominican Republic, for example, and the Senate rejected his treaty with Denmark in 1867 for the sale of the Danish West Indies to the United States for $7.5 million.

Seward's third effort at territorial expansion—a project for the acquisition of Russian Alaska—succeeded only because of an unusual sequence of events. Russia and the United States, in spite of their totally different political systems, had always enjoyed good relations. This friendship had been cemented in 1863, when Russian fleets had visited San Francisco and New York. Americans erroneously concluded that the Russian warships had come to indicate support for the Union side to Great Britain and France. Actually, the Imperial Russian government acted to get the Russian warships out of harm's way. It feared that the ships might be bottled up in the Baltic in the event of war with Britain and France. Thus, when the Russian Minister in Washington intimated, in the early months of 1867, that the Czar might be willing to sell his province of Alaska to the United States, Seward responded enthusiastically. After some mild haggling over the price, the Secretary of State signed a treaty on March 30, 1867, for the purchase of Alaska for $7.2 million—$2.2 million more than the Russians would have accepted. For a time it seemed that the Senate would reject the treaty. But Seward repaired his political fences in the upper house and won the support of the influential chairman of the Foreign Relations Committee, Senator Sumner. Besides, "Old Glory" had already been hoisted over Alaska, and several senators cringed at the thought of voting to lower it. The Senate approved the treaty on April 9 by an overwhelming majority. There was much public outcry against "Seward's folly," and condemnation of his seemingly frantic search for any available real estate. But the acquisition turned out to be an excellent bargain. The gold taken from the Yukon River Valley alone since

1897 has paid for the largest American state many times over. Later, the gas and oil resources discovered and exploited again proved the wisdom of Seward's action.

Settling an Old Score with Great Britain

The longest and most nagging diplomatic controversy of the postwar era involved American claims against Great Britain for damages done to American shipping by Confederate cruisers built in British shipyards. The House of Representatives, sputtering with outrage, actually passed a bill to change American neutrality laws to permit Americans to sell ships to nations at war. Let Great Britain beware! Johnson's Minister to England, Reverdy Johnson of Maryland, negotiated an agreement which provided for arbitration of claims on both sides without, however, mentioning *Alabama* and other cruisers. The Senate contemptuously rejected the treaty by a vote of fifty-four to one on April 23, 1869.

On that same day, Senator Sumner delivered a startling speech in which he totaled the claims of the United States against Great Britain. The items included $15 million for vessels actually destroyed by Confederate cruisers and $110 million for the American ships that had been frightened off the seas. To these claims, Sumner added $2 billion (one half of the cost of the war to the North!) for "indirect damages" because, he said, Great Britain had doubled the duration of the war by aiding the Confederacy. Sumner then modestly suggested that Great Britain might pay this staggering bill of $2.125 billion by ceding Canada to the United States! The British reacted with surprise and outrage; they made it plain that they would fight rather than negotiate on the basis of such monstrous terms.

Anti-British feeling still ran strong in the United States. It was, politically, both necessary and profitable to "twist the lion's tail" and make the beast scream with pain. But Sumner's speech and the favorable reaction that it evoked in the United States greatly complicated the problems of the new Secretary of State, Hamilton Fish. Fish negotiated patiently, and American and British commissioners signed a treaty at Washington on May 8, 1871. It provided for the settlement of an old fisheries dispute, arbitration of a boundary dispute which involved the San Juan Islands in Vancouver Bay by the Emperor of Germany, William I, and arbitration of the *Alabama* and other claims by a tribunal to meet at Geneva, Switzerland, in December 1871.

In addition to the British and American representatives, the tribunal included distinguished members from the governments of Switzerland, Italy, and Brazil. The American counsel, in order to curry favor with anti-British elements in the United States, at first presented Sumner's complete bill. Britons muttered threats of war when they heard about it, and the entire negotiations verged on collapse. Then, at the quiet suggestion of one of the American representatives, Charles Francis Adams, the tribunal decided to rule out all indirect damages. It next decided, unanimously in the case of *Alabama,* and by three-to-one and four-to-one votes in the cases of *Florida* and *Shenandoah,* that Great Britain had been guilty of breaches of neutrality in permitting these ships to go to the Confederacy. It awarded damages of $15.5 million to the United States on September 14, 1872.

The tribunal settled the other matters in dispute shortly thereafter. It awarded Great Britain about $2 million for injuries to the property and persons of her subjects during the Civil War. Britain also received $5.5 million for American violations of her fishing rights on the North Atlantic coast. Finally, the German Emperor awarded most of the San Juan Islands to the United States.

The peaceful adjustment of these claims and counterclaims of the two great English-speaking nations was one of the great diplomatic accomplishments of the nineteenth century. It remains a landmark on the road toward world peace, for it substituted discussion and compromise for an appeal to arms in disputes between nations.

Fish Restrains Grant

Fish's difficulties were multiplied nearly as much by a blundering President as by extreme nationalists like Sumner. A rebellion against Spanish rule broke out in Cuba in 1868, and Grant, encouraged by various interested groups, decided to recognize the belligerency of the Cuban rebel government. Fish knew that such action would bring on war with Spain and quietly sidetracked this project. The Secretary of State also succeeded, the following year, in heading off a congressional movement for recognition of the Cuban rebels. But the worst crisis came in 1873, when the Spaniards captured a Cuban-owned gunrunner, *Virginius*, and shot fifty-three passengers and members of her crew as pirates. There were Americans and Englishmen among the executed. Fish bombarded Madrid with severe demands, but he carefully avoided the point of no return. Without humiliating the proud Spanish authorities, he accepted payment for the American lives lost.

Fish now diverted Grant's attention toward another project—annexation of the Dominican Republic—in order to keep him from meddling in the Anglo-American negotiations. The Dominican government appealed to the United States for annexation. Grant responded eagerly, and an annexation treaty was signed. The Senate rejected the treaty on June 30, 1870, probably much to Fish's relief.

5. A NADIR OF NATIONAL POLITICS

The Campaign and Election of 1872

The victory for the United States at Geneva came just in time to help reelect Grant for a second term. It offset a very substantial revolt in the Republican party. Discontent with party leadership had spread in reaction against the apparent failure of Radical Reconstruction and its local excesses, signs of corruption in high places of government, the general low tone of public morality, and the mania for speculation that had swept the country from one end to the other.

A group of Republicans, led by Carl Schurz, began a movement for party reform in Missouri in 1870. The movement quickly gathered strength among Republicans throughout the nation. They advocated amnesty for the South, reduction of the tariff, and a thoroughgoing purge of the corrupt elements in the Republican party.

These Liberal Republicans, as they called themselves, held a national convention in Cincinnati on May 1, 1872. But dissension in their own ranks prevented them from nominating a strong candidate such as Charles Francis Adams. Instead, they chose Horace Greeley, editor of the New York *Tribune*, an ardent protectionist, and a champion of reconciliation with the South. The Democratic convention also nominated Greeley. The Republicans had meanwhile renominated Grant.

The campaign that followed was one of the most abusive in American history. Indeed, it led Greeley to say that he was not sure whether he should be running for the presidency or for the penitentiary. The Liberal Republicans had hoped to establish a new party. They disliked the amalgamation with the Democrats and gave Greeley only lukewarm support. Grant carried every northern and western state, together with eight of the former slave states. He received 3,597,000 popular votes to 2,843,000 for Greeley, and the Republicans retained control of Congress by comfortable majorities in both houses. Greeley died only three weeks after the election. His sixty-six electoral votes (as compared to Grant's 286) were cast mostly for his running mate, Benjamin Gratz Brown of Missouri.

Corruption Riddles the Grant Administration

Neither the confused President nor the patronage-hungry Republicans who dominated Congress exercised leadership in national politics. Thus, the second Grant administration failed to distinguish itself with much constructive legislation. It was notable mainly for a series of scandals that shocked the nation and nearly toppled the Republican party from its preeminent position. Congressional committees disclosed the grimy facts in one scandal after another. These investigations revealed the extent of the demoralization in public life caused by the greed, recklessness, and irresponsibility that had followed in the wake of the war.

The first major scandal broke at the very end of the presidential campaign of 1872. The managers of the Union Pacific Railroad had formed a company called the Crédit Mobilier to construct the line, and then had awarded themselves contracts for construction. They charged the railroad exorbitant prices and received huge profits from the arrangement. Moreover, they bribed Schuyler Colfax, Vice-President during Grant's first term, and several influential congressmen by the free distribution of stock in the construction company. The New York *Sun* first exposed the skulduggery, and a congressional committee uncovered the details early in 1873. The offending congressmen, however, showed about as much repentance as did Jefferson Davis and Alexander H. Stephens after the Civil War. One especially powerful congressman, when asked what his constituents would say when they learned that he had accepted a gift of stock in the Crédit Mobilier, replied that they would ask why he had not taken more.

In that same year there occurred the "salary grab," or "back-pay steal." Greedy congressmen not only voted themselves a 50 per cent increase in salary but also made the increase retroactive to the session just coming to an end. Public indignation forced Congress to repeal the law in 1874.

In 1875 came revelation of the so-called Whiskey Ring. A group of distillers and internal revenue officers had cheated the government out of hundreds of thousands of dollars in taxes. Grant's private secretary, General O. E. Babcock, was involved and escaped conviction only because the President intervened to save him from disgrace. But the most shocking scandal came to light the following year. Secretary of War William W. Belknap was charged with reaping large profits from the sale of licenses to corrupt agents who stole supplies destined for Indian posts in the West. When the House of Representatives impeached Belknap on March 2, 1876, he resigned on the same day to escape trial. However, the Senate went ahead with the trial; it voted for acquittal only because a number of senators believed that they no longer had jurisdiction because Belknap had resigned.

Scandal and corruption were not confined to Washington. In New York, Tammany Boss William M. Tweed plundered the city treasury of millions of dollars during the same period. Eventually he went to prison, where he died. Corrupt politicians all over the country sold public rights to businessmen who wanted control of such interests as natural resources, franchises for street railways, public utilities, and building contracts.

A severe panic in 1873 deepened the general mood of despair. The panic was caused by reckless speculation, an unstable currency, dishonest banking practices, excesses in railroad construction, and general get-rich-quick methods in business. The depression dragged on for about five years; it caused sharp and widespread distress all over the country. It was little wonder that the administration suffered a stunning defeat in the mid-term election of 1874. A large majority of Democrats were returned to the House of Representatives, which they controlled for the first time since the Civil War.

The Republican-controlled Fifty-third Congress (1873–1875) adopted two measures in its lame-duck session before passing out of existence: the Resumption Act, already discussed, and the Civil Rights Act, sponsored by Senator Sumner and approved on March 1, 1875. The Civil Rights Act prohibited discrimination on account of race in inns, public transportation facilities, and theaters. It forbade exclusion of blacks from juries on account of color. Many congressmen who voted for this bill did so as a sop to black voters and white advocates of civil rights, not as an expression of a national determination to abolish the color line then being drawn. The Grant administration made only feeble efforts to enforce the law. In the Civil Rights Cases of 1883, the Supreme Court declared the measure unconstitutional on the ground that the Fourteenth Amendment (on which the Civil Rights Act had been based) prohibited only official or state, not individual, discrimination against persons on account of race.

The End of Radical Reconstruction

Meanwhile, Radical Reconstruction gradually ended in one state after another. The Radical governments could not have lasted unless Northerners were prepared to support them indefinitely with armed force. But every year that passed after 1867 saw more and more lurid newspaper reports about the alleged incompetence and corruption of the Radical regimes. Fewer and fewer Northerners wished to continue the Reconstruction experiment. They lost interest in the perpetual problem of the South. Wartime idealism faded, and Northerners abandoned blacks to whatever fate awaited them. Every year a new crop of young white southern voters, to whom the disqualifying clause of the Fourteenth Amendment did not apply, appeared at the polls to vote and assume political control of their cities, counties, and states. At the same time, largely because of the Klan and its terroristic tactics, there was a marked decline of the black vote in the South, despite the Fifteenth Amendment.

The Democrats, in their platform of 1868, had already declared that the issues of slavery and secession were "settled for all time." They demanded the restoration of all the states to their former rights in the Union. Virginia, North Carolina, and Georgia were "redeemed," as white Southerners put it, from Radical rule between 1869 and 1871. In 1872, public opinion in the North compelled the Republicans to pass the Amnesty Act, which removed political disqualifications from all but about 500 former high-ranking Confederates. In 1875, Democrats won control of Alabama, Arkansas, and Texas. That same year Mississippi went Democratic after a notorious campaign of terror and intimidation against black voters. Thus only Louisiana, South Carolina, and Florida remained under Radical Republican rule in 1876. The turbulent drama of Reconstruction was nearly over.

The Election of 1876

The Republicans were in deep trouble in 1876. They might have nominated for President their leading contender, the brilliant and dashing Speaker of the House of Representatives, James G. Blaine of Maine, but his implication in a

The Election of 1876

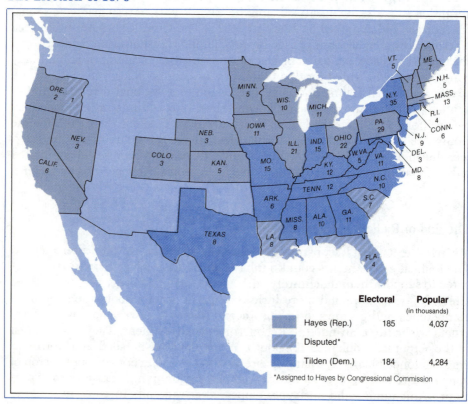

	Electoral	Popular (in thousands)
Hayes (Rep.)	185	4,037
Disputed*		
Tilden (Dem.)	184	4,284

*Assigned to Hayes by Congressional Commission

railroad scandal ruled him out of the running. Instead, the Republicans played it safe and selected Governor Rutherford B. Hayes of Ohio, a former Union general. A man of unquestioned honesty, Hayes also entertained conciliatory views on the southern question, and this added to his "availability." The Democrats nominated Governor Samuel J. Tilden of New York, whose one claim to fame was the national reputation that he had won for his exposure of the Tweed Ring.

The presidential election of 1876 was the most exciting one since the election of 1800. Late in the evening of election day in 1876, it seemed almost certain that Tilden was the victor. He had won enough states to give him 184 electoral votes—only one short of a majority. Hayes had carried states with a total electoral count of 165. Twenty votes were in dispute because the three southern states with federal garrisons—South Carolina, Louisiana, and Florida—each had rival election boards, one Democratic, the other Republican. Another disputed vote for Hayes came from Oregon, where it was discovered that the Republicans had put a postmaster on the list of electors; they had overlooked the provision of the Constitution that no person holding a federal office might serve as an elector.

The election hung on the returns from South Carolina, Louisiana, and Florida. Congress, with one house Democratic and the other Republican, had to decide which of the double sets of returns to count. The Constitution offered little help; it reads simply (Amendment XII): "The President of the Senate shall, in the presence of the Senate and the House of Representatives, open all certificates, and the votes shall then be counted." As weeks passed without a solution to the dilemma, it seemed that, for the second time in sixteen years, a presidential election would lead to a dire national crisis. Groups of war veterans began to talk of another civil war.

The Compromise of 1877

Conservatives in both parties, especially northeastern Republicans and southern Democrats, were determined not to repeat the mistakes of 1860, when excitable men had been allowed to have their way. After a series of meetings, congressmen agreed to create a commission of fifteen members to determine which of the disputed sets of returns should be accepted. The commission consisted of five senators (three Republicans, two Democrats), five representatives (three Democrats, two Republicans), and five members of the Supreme Court (two Republicans, two Democrats, and a fifth to be chosen by the other four). It was expected that Justice David Davis, an independent with Democratic leanings, would be chosen as the fifth member from the court. But Davis resigned his justiceship to accept election by the Illinois legislature to the United States Senate. As only Republican members were left on the Supreme Court, the commission finally consisted of eight Republicans and seven Democrats. Not surprisingly, in every case of the disputed twenty electoral votes, the commission voted, eight to seven, to accept the Hayes certificates.

But the crisis had not ended because both houses of Congress had to approve the commission's decision before a President could be inaugurated. Many northern Democrats wanted to hold out in the House of Representatives and thereby prevent Hayes' inauguration. However, a group of conservative southern Democrats in the lower house negotiated with spokesmen for Hayes and reached an informal understanding that the Southerners would vote to accept the commission's report. In return, the Hayes administration would remove the last federal troops from the South, include at least one Southerner in his cabinet, give conservative Southerners control of part of the local patronage, and support generous appropriations for internal improvements, particularly railroads, in the South.

Hayes himself did not take part in the negotiations, and no one knows to this day whether a formal bargain was made. But southern conservatives did join with Republicans in the House of Representatives to approve the commission's report on March 2, 1877 — only two days before the scheduled inauguration. The Republican Senate of course concurred at once, and the crisis ended. The other side of the alleged bargain, however, was not kept completely. Although administration forces tried, they were unable to persuade Congress to deliver the expected railroad subsidies for the South.

Did the votes of South Carolina, Louisiana, and Florida rightfully belong to Hayes or to Tilden? Committees of both parties that went to these states to investigate found evidence of fraud and intimidation on both sides. Republican election boards had undoubtedly thrown out Democratic ballots. And Democrats had forcibly prevented black Republicans from voting. It seems very probable, however, that the electoral votes from Florida belonged rightfully to Tilden, and that he should, therefore, have been President. If the popular will means anything, it should be recorded that Tilden received 4,284,020 votes and Hayes, 4,036,572.

The End of an Era

Hayes' inauguration signaled the formal end of the Reconstruction era. The new President withdrew the last of the federal troops from South Carolina, Louisiana, and Florida in April 1877. These three states immediately returned to what Southerners were fond of calling "home rule," that is, rule by white Southerners. To dramatize the end of Reconstruction, President Hayes decorated the graves of Confederate dead at Chattanooga, Tennessee, in May 1877.

The new administration quickly buried the bloody shirt, even though it would later be resurrected from time to time by Republican orators. Hayes named a former Confederate officer, David M. Key of Tennessee, as Postmaster General. The new President also set out to rebuild and reunite the Republican party. He named the distinguished lawyer, William M. Evarts, who had defended Johnson in the impeachment trial, as Secretary of State. Hayes appointed Carl Schurz, leader of the Liberal Republican movement of 1872, as Secretary of the Interior. And the entire administration applied itself vigorously to cleaning up graft and incompetence in the federal civil service, while Hayes pressed, unsuccessfully, for civil service reform.

The symbol of the new era was the Centennial Exposition held at Philadelphia during the summer of 1876 to celebrate the hundredth anniversary of the Declaration of Independence. Millions of visitors to the fair admired the many works of art from all over the world. Americans were most enthralled, however, by the whirling wheels in Machinery Hall. Giant engines — one of which generated the power of 1,600 horses — rapid home sewing machines, and amazing new inventions like the telephone all gave evidence that another era of economic expansion lay ahead.

Reconstruction and Afro-Americans in Retrospect

More than a century after the end of Reconstruction, historians are still debating its impact on blacks in the South. Did Reconstruction actually bring about fundamental changes in the political, economic, and social relationships which shaped the lives of Afro-Americans? The answer to that question is rather like the one about the bottle which was either half empty or half full.

When all was said and done, Reconstruction left much power in the hands of the southern landed aristocracy, which, by combining agribusiness with commercial and industrial pursuits, managed to dominate much of the South for generations. In such a situation, improvement in the status of the ex-slaves was inevitably limited. There was never any serious prospect of transferring economic and political control to blacks, even in those states where they were a majority. Nor did Reconstruction bring about social integration, except in rare cases.

Yet, by any measure, the gains registered during Reconstruction were remarkable. Between 1860 and 1880, the percentage of black children attending school rose from two to thirty-four. By 1870, over 1,000,000 blacks could vote, and 15 per cent of all public officials in the South were black, as compared with 3 per cent in 1979. Educational and political gains did not evaporate with the Compromise of 1877. Literacy rates and the number of black children in school continued to climb. And, contrary to popular myth, blacks continued to play a major role in southern politics until the end of the century.

How can we account for these gains? The simple but profoundly important fact of emancipation is the first part of the answer. It *did* make a difference that blacks were no longer slaves. The umbrella of federal protection and the stimulus of northern philanthropy allowed freedom to become more than the absence of slavery. Last, and perhaps most important, black institutions and community leaders emerged which enabled the freedmen to shape their own destiny. White Southerners were continually amazed during Reconstruction by the appearance of black preachers, teachers, and other community leaders. Quite often, these freedmen, and the network of kin and neighbors which they represented, were simply the "invisible" community of antebellum blacks, slave and free, coming into the open. These communities would prove resourceful and resilient bulwarks in preserving the blacks' circumscribed freedom, even after bargains had been struck between the white North and the white South.

SUGGESTED READINGS

In addition to Randall and Donald, *Civil War and Reconstruction*, already cited, there are a number of good general surveys of Reconstruction: Kenneth M. Stampp, *The Era of Reconstruction* (1964); John Hope Franklin, *Reconstruction: After the Civil War* (1961); Rembert W. Patrick, *The Reconstruction of the Nation* (1967); E. Merton Coulter, *The South During Reconstruction* (1947); David Herbert Donald, *The Politics of Reconstruction* (1965); and W. R. Brock, *An American Crisis* (1963). Several older works are worth mentioning here. William A. Dunning, *Reconstruction: Political and Economic, 1865–1877* (1907), is the representative work of the older racist interpretation. W. E. B. DuBois, *Black Reconstruction* (1935), is the classic, militantly problack reaction to the Dunning school. A good social and economic history of the period is Allan Nevins, *The Emergence of Modern America, 1865–1878* (1927).

Andrew Johnson receives sympathetic attention from Howard K. Beale, *The Critical Year: A Study of Andrew Johnson and Reconstruction* (1930). More recent studies have been extremely critical of Johnson. See, for example, Hans L. Trefousse, *The Radical Republicans: Lincoln's Vanguard for Racial*

Justice (1969); Eric L. McKitrick, *Andrew Johnson and Reconstruction* (1960); and LaWanda and J. H. Cox, *Politics, Principle, and Prejudice: 1865–1866* (1963).

On the problems faced and occasioned by the emancipated Negro, see George R. Bentley, *A History of the Freedmen's Bureau* (1955); Vernon L. Wharton, *The Negro in Mississippi 1865–1890* (1947); Willie Lee Rose, *Rehearsal for Reconstruction: The Port Royal Experiment* (1964); and Joel R. Williamson, *After Slavery* (1965). On the South's difficulties after the Civil War, see C. Vann Woodward, *Origins of the New South, 1877–1913* (1951), a stimulating analysis. On the Ku Klux Klan, the most recent work is Allen W. Trelease, *White Terror: The Ku Klux Klan Conspiracy and Southern Reconstruction* (1971). Thomas D. Clark and Albert D. Kirwan, *The South Since Appomattox* (1967), is an adequate general survey with an excellent selective bibliography.

There is no satisfactory survey of the Grant administration. The best introduction is Allan Nevins, *Hamilton Fish, The Inner History of the Grant Administration* (1936). Useful on the Grant presidency is William B. Hesseltine, *Ulysses S. Grant: Politician* (1935). The scandals associated with the era are described in David G. Loth, *Public Plunder: A History of Graft in America* (1938). On the disputed election of 1876, see C. Vann Woodward, *Reunion and Reaction* (1951), and Harry Barnard, *Rutherford B. Hayes and His America* (1954). Two excellent studies of the reform movement of the period are John G. Sproat, *"The Best Men": Liberal Reformers in the Gilded Age* (1968), and Earle D. Ross, *The Liberal Republican Movement* (1919). The description of Washington during the Grant administration in Henry Adams, *The Education of Henry Adams* (1918), is well worth reading.

CHAPTER 18
THE INDUSTRIAL REVOLUTION, 1850–1900

1. THE INDUSTRIAL REVOLUTION IN THE UNITED STATES

Causes of Industrialization

Most of the forces which triggered America's spectacular industrial growth were already in existence, at least in embryo, before the Civil War, even though their full impact would not be felt until much later. The story of America's role as borrower, adapter, and innovator in the technological processes of industrialization is a complicated one. Nevertheless, the major causes can be summarized briefly.

1. Steam, coal, and iron were basic ingredients of the new industrial system. In the antebellum period, the United States borrowed from Britain and adapted for its own needs the technology of steam power. Steam gradually overtook water as the principal source of power in manufacturing. By 1869, 52 per cent of the power used in American manufacturing was steam-generated, although waterpower remained important due to its widespread availability and to technological advances in its generation. (In New England the amount of power produced by water actually increased into the twentieth century.) In transportation, the conversion to steam was quicker and more complete than in manufacturing, first with application to western river traffic, and then to the new railroads. The steam revolution was fired by coal, a fuel not widely used in the United States before the 1830s. With the opening of Pennsylvania's anthracite fields, coal became available in large quantities, and by the mid-1840s its price had dropped from $10 to $3 per ton. The metal-making and

metalworking industries were among the first to take advantage of this new power source. With an abundance of iron ore and coal (usually found close to each other) the United States was able to adopt new British techniques for transforming iron into steel. A process invented at about the same time by the Englishman Henry Bessemer and the American William Kelly was first used in the United States in 1864 and was widely employed during the 1870s. It was largely replaced in the 1890s and 1900s by the open hearth method, which not only made better steel but was able to use American iron ores more efficiently than the Bessemer process. American steel production increased from about 15,000 tons in 1865 to 935,000 tons in 1879. Then, under the leadership of steelmakers such as Andrew Carnegie, production mushroomed. By the late 1890s *one* of the blast furnaces at Carnegie's huge J. Edgar Thompson works in Pittsburgh produced more steel than had the entire nation in 1879.

2. The expansion of the American railroad network was a vital stimulus to industrialization. By providing fast, regular, and relatively cheap transportation and communication, the railroads (and their companion, the telegraph) laid the groundwork for a continental market network, which in turn made possible the mass production and distribution of goods in the late nineteenth century. Railroads were the first American enterprises to face the problem of large and complex business operations. They developed the first modern system of business administration, and manufacturers and distributors, as they began to encounter similar problems, widely copied the railroads' management techniques.

3. Technological innovations and their "diffusion" or transfer made possible the exploitation of abundant raw materials, the generation of power to process them, and the creation of transportation systems to move them. Throughout the nineteenth century, machines replaced more and more hand operations, while factories replaced homes and small shops as the site of most manufacturing. Innovations appeared throughout the economy, but some of the most important were those in power generation, metal-making, and metalworking (which involve machines that shape, cut, grind, and mill metal). As one scholar has pointed out, the machine-tool industry was doubly important in creating a "machinofacture" economy; it not only solved many of the basic technical problems but also served to diffuse these solutions, in the form of skills and techniques, to other industries.

4. The unskilled and semiskilled labor needed to operate the new factories was available in abundance. An increasing flow of immigrants from Europe joined a stream of Americans moving from farms to towns and cities. The number of wage earners in industry increased from nearly 1,000,000 in 1860 to more than 5,000,000 in 1900.

5. Capital was generally abundant in this period. Beginning in the 1850s, British, German, and French investors purchased large quantities of American railroad securities. This infusion of foreign capital helped to centralize the American capital market in New York and bring into being the modern securities business. Life insurance companies also played an important role in gathering and lending capital. American banking resources grew from $1 billion in 1860 to more than $10 billion in 1900.

6. Government at all levels stimulated economic growth. Local, state, and federal governments subsidized private railroad construction, and federal improvements of rivers and harbors also helped to develop the transportation

network which was essential for industrial growth. High tariffs protected American manufacturers from foreign competition; at the same time, federal regulation of industry remained minimal. Federal and state governments subsidized agricultural research and education, and millions of acres of farm and timber land were transferred from public to private ownership. The notion that government in the nineteenth century took a "hands off" attitude toward the private economy does not square with the facts.

Railroads and the Beginnings of Big Business

Between 1860 and 1900, the American railroad system grew from about 30,000 miles of track to 200,000. In size and complexity, the railroads dwarfed other business institutions and agencies of the federal government. In 1891, the Pennsylvania Railroad alone employed more workers than the Post Office (the largest federal agency) and over twice as many as the army and navy combined. As late as the 1860s, American railroads were not sufficiently integrated to move goods over long distances without frequent unloading and reloading. But by the 1880s, due to physical expansion and managerial integration, goods could be moved across the continent without transshipment.

The growth of the railroad system was of two kinds—construction of new lines in the West and completion and integration of existing systems east of the Mississippi. In 1862 the federal government stimulated transcontinental

Drawing of railroad building on the Great Plains by A. R. Waud. Emerson observed that Americans took "to this little contrivance, the railroad, as if it were the cradle in which they were born." (Culver Pictures, Inc.)

railroad construction by chartering the Union Pacific Railroad to build westward from Omaha, and the Central Pacific Railroad to build eastward from Sacramento. Construction was to continue until their tracks met. The government subsidized construction through grants of land along the right of way and through long-term loans. But, even when government support was expanded in 1864, the project languished due to lack of capital and war-related construction problems. The first rail was finally laid on July 10, 1865; the last, held in place by a golden spike, was laid on May 10, 1869, when the two lines met at Promontory Summit, near Ogden, Utah.

The first through train from California to New York arrived at the Hudson River Terminal on July 20, 1869, after a run of six and a half days. The effects of binding the continent by ties of iron were felt immediately. Trade with China and Japan increased 100 per cent within three years. A "Pacific fever" invaded Congress, and the government granted land or subsidies to other western railroad companies. Altogether, federal, state, and local governments granted some 186,000,000 acres of land and over $600 million to western railroads. Wildcat financing, construction fraud, and the Panic of 1873 brought disaster to many of these enterprises. However, by 1900 six rail systems linked the West coast with the Midwest and thus to connections with the eastern seaboard.

Railroads and Cattle Trails, 1850–1900

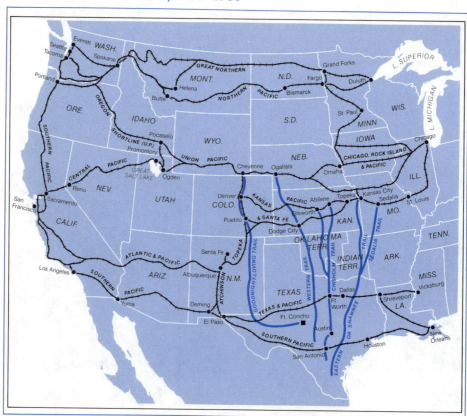

During this same era, the development of railroad systems in the more settled regions of the country equaled in importance, if not in drama, the building of the transcontinentals. The Pennsylvania, Baltimore and Ohio, New York Central, and Erie systems linked the eastern ports with the nation's heartland. Similar systems spread out from Chicago and St. Louis and accounted for much of the over-all growth in the rail network. In some cases, this expansion created duplication of services by competing systems, and the available rail traffic could not support all the lines that had been built.

The growth of American railroads in the second half of the nineteenth century brought with it two sets of problems for their managers. First, how were they to operate such giant enterprises safely and efficiently? (Not the least of their problems was to keep the trains from running into each other on the single-track lines). Second, with massive and sometimes artificially inflated fixed costs, how were they to deal with the "ruinous" competition between duplicating lines? To deal with the first set of problems, railroad managers established what we have called the first modern system of business administration, which included (1) an organizational structure that integrated many operating units in one firm, (2) cost accounting systems which enabled managers to measure precisely the unit cost of the services that they provided, and (3) a hierarchy of salaried managers, including a layer of "middle" managers, who came to dominate the railroads in place of the nominal owners. These methods of organizing economic activity have become so commonplace as to constitute a definition of the modern business firm. But before their development by the railroads in the 1850s, they simply did not exist.

Railroads in the South and East, faced with sharp competition for freight traffic in the 1870s, formed "pools," which were cartels designed to set rates among supposedly competing roads. Cooperating railroads pooled their profits or traffic in return for an agreed upon share. The sophisticated accounting and management systems, which the larger roads commonly employed by the 1870s, made it technically possible to set rates and distribute traffic according to an agreed upon formula. But the pools were simply gentlemen's agreements, not contracts enforceable in a court of law, and, in the absence of enforceable sanctions, the pools failed to prevent secret rate cutting. By the mid-1880s, cooperation through pools had clearly failed to limit "cutthroat" competition, and more of the major lines turned to outright consolidation in the form of huge interregional systems.

Until the 1890s, the railroads' efforts to limit competition through cooperation or consolidation were not uniformly successful. However, these efforts, along with the railroads' influence on government at every level, evoked the wrath of shippers and reformers of various persuasions. Consequently, the railroads became the first industry to face demands for governmental regulation, demands which led to the establishment of the Interstate Commerce Commission in 1887 (see p. 533).

The Evolution of Modern Manufacturing Technology

The automobile assembly line has come to symbolize modern manufacturing. Innovations in automobile manufacturing early in the twentieth century marked a giant leap forward in the mass production of manufactured goods, but these innovations also rested on the evolution of manufacturing processes in the second half of the nineteenth century. By 1880, the giant mill and factory had already become a familiar part of the American landscape, but mass production, as symbolized by the automobile plant, was still in the future. Its full development would depend on the perfection and combination of four technological processes. The complete integration of all four of them at Henry Ford's automobile assembly plant in 1913 marked the beginning of a new industrial age.

1. Specialized machines were used in the individual steps of the manufacturing process. In textile manufacturing, shoemaking, and all manner of wood- and metalworking operations, machines gradually replaced many hand operations, even before the Civil War. In 1854, a visiting team of British experts were so impressed by this "American system of manufactures" that they warned British industrialists to adopt it or lose out in competition with the upstart Americans.

2 Interchangeable parts were used in assembling manufactured goods. Machine-made parts were not necessarily interchangeable with each other. In fact, before the late nineteenth century, most parts had to be fitted together by skilled craftsmen using files and other hand tools. One historian has shown that, even in the manufacture of sewing machines and farm implements, two pioneering American industries, interchangeability was not widespread before the 1880s. Interchangeable parts were widely used prior to that time only in the manufacture of small arms; in that instance, it was governmental subsidies that made their use economically feasible.

3. There was a continuous flow of goods in the manufacturing process. This innovation, introduced in the milling of grain in the eighteenth century, was adopted by slaughterhouses ("disassembly" plants for beef and pork) in the 1860s. By the 1870s and 1880s, continuous flow techniques had been widely adopted in food processing, cigarette manufacturing, and petroleum refining; they were only beginning to make their way into the metalworking industries.

4. There was centralized, or "scientific," management. As late as 1900, the management of America's giant factories was typically decentralized. Individual foremen — skilled craftsmen who oversaw particular operations — still controlled production and employment to a substantial degree. Beginning in the 1880s, several efficiency-minded mechanical engineers and plant managers developed ways to standardize and centralize management of the industrial work place. The most influential of these innovators was Frederick W. Taylor. Taylor and his associates devised a plan of "scientific management," which included cost accounting, systematic purchasing, efficient plant design and layout of machinery, and — most controversially — the use of time and motion studies to capture on paper the details of the work process and to determine the most expeditious methods to carry out the specialized tasks of factory work. These studies, coupled with incentive wage systems, were designed to increase worker efficiency. They also transferred actual control over the work place from foremen and workers to central managers. As late as 1900, the old method of factory management still prevailed. However, by the First World War, scientific management, in one form or another, had become commonplace in American industry.

Combination and Consolidation in Big Business

Along with the increasing complexity and speed which technological innovation brought to American industry, there was a steady movement toward bigness and consolidation. There were obvious advantages of large size in many fields. Savings resulted when the various steps in the manufacture of a product were combined, as in the manufacture of steel. Greater size and concentration of capital also made possible control of patents, advantages in competition for raw materials, and exploitation of national and international markets. There were also other reasons for business concentration: high profits could be maintained by curtailing competition, and more predictability and stability could be brought into an industry than was possible with wide-open competition.

The railroad pools discussed above constituted one early effort to achieve centralized managerial control over an industry. In the 1870s and 1880s, single companies or groups of companies developed a more tightly knit instrument of concentration known as the trust or trustee device. In most instances, these combinations gained dominion over one phase of an industry and thus achieved "horizontal" control. The trust was an unchartered "corporation"

John D. Rockefeller, a ruthless fighter with a passion for perfection. This painting was described by the artist Deferraris as the "intimate portrait of Mr. Rockefeller." (Culver Pictures, Inc.)

that held the stock of the combined companies in trust and managed the new combination through a single set of officers and board of directors. Later, journalists, politicians, and the public at large began to apply the name"trust" to all corporations that enjoyed near monopolistic control of an industry.

The most important of the trusts was the Standard Oil Company. Toward the close of the Civil War, a young Cleveland commission merchant, John D. Rockefeller, saw the possibilities of the new oil industry, then centered in western Pennsylvania, and set out to become an oil refiner. At that point, over 300 companies were engaged in refining, and most of them were small and poorly managed. By 1870, Rockefeller's Standard Oil Company of Ohio controlled most of the refining business in the state. Within another five years, Rockefeller had absorbed large refineries in New York, Philadelphia, and Baltimore. Then, through the Standard Oil Trust, formed in 1879 and reorganized in 1882, Rockefeller combined some forty oil companies which controlled more than 90 per cent of the nation's refining industry and an almost equal portion of the oil pipelines.

Rockefeller achieved this preeminence by adopting careful management practices in a generally chaotic industry, by translating refining efficiency into lower prices, and by ruthlessly suppressing competitors. For a brief time, he possessed a particularly deadly weapon: As the greatest shipper of oil, he was able to force the oil-carrying railroads to charge Standard Oil a rate of 10 cents a barrel, and all other oil companies 35 cents a barrel. In addition, he compelled the railroads to give (rebate) to the Standard Oil Company 25 out of the 35 cents that they charged its competitors. The public outrage and demands for regulation that followed revelation of these agreements forced their cancellation.

The horizontal integration of industries through the trustee device proved to be a temporary, though important, phase in the development of modern business enterprise. The trust encountered legal difficulties, both as a violation of common-law doctrines against the restraint of trade and as the object of anti-monopoly legislation from federal and state governments. *Vertical* integration of industries superceded horizontal integration. In vertical integration, one firm combined mass production and mass distribution and thus administered the flow of goods from raw material, to manufacture, to purchase by the consumer. The organizational structure most commonly used in the drive for vertical integration was the holding company, a kind of legalized trust made possible by laws in New Jersey and other states which allowed one corporation to hold stock in another and thus legally to control its management.

In the 1880s, vertically integrated firms gained dominance in a few industries, including meatpacking (Swift and Armour), tobacco (Duke), and oil. As for the latter, Rockefeller's Standard Oil Company became a New Jersey holding company and diversified from refining backward into production of crude oil and forward into distribution of the finished product. The major depression which hit the country in 1893 slowed combinations for a time, but a tremendous spurt of vertical integration through merger and expansion began as the depression ended in the late 1890s.

None of the efforts at combination was more spectacular than the industrial giant which emerged in steel. By 1890, Andrew Carnegie dominated steel manufacturing and also controlled huge iron ore and coal deposits. By the end of the nineties, Carnegie (faced with the prospect of competition in primary steel manufacture from the producers of finished steel goods) threatened to diversify into that phase of the business as well, an event which would have touched off competitive warfare among the steel companies. At that point, J. Pierpont Morgan, head of the preeminent investment firm in the United States, intervened. Morgan had emerged during the depression of the 1890s as the leading American financier because of his success in reorganizing and consolidating bankrupt railroads. Morgan offered to buy out Carnegie's steel interests for close to half a billion dollars. Carnegie accepted the offer and retired to a life of philanthropy. Morgan then combined Carnegie's properties with the Federal Steel Company (which Morgan had organized in 1898) and several smaller firms to form the United States Steel Corporation. The company was capitalized at $1.4 billion and controlled 60 per cent of the American steel industry.

Within a short time, Morgan helped to establish many other giant consolidations, including the International Harvester Corporation and the General Electric Company, to say nothing of the banks, railroads, and insurance companies in which he had a powerful voice. In 1913, a congressional committee reported that the House of Morgan and its allies had 314 directorships in 112 corporations with aggregate resources of more than $20 billion.

The role of Morgan and other bankers in reorganizing and stabilizing American corporations around the turn of the century led many observers to conclude that bankers were replacing individual entrepreneurs as the dominant force in business. Such a conclusion ignores the increasingly important role of the army of salaried managers who actually operated the new multi-unit, integrated firms. Beginning with the railroads, and spreading to most American corporations, a hierarchy of professional managers assumed control of American industry. By the time of the First World War, this new breed of professional, technically trained managers, while they did not literally own the giant corporations, had come to dominate even high-level policy in most major corporations. With the ascendency of the manager and the spread of huge, vertically integrated corporations, the American economy no longer fitted Adam Smith's classic description of a system moved by the "invisible hand" of market forces. To a remarkable extent, those forces were replaced, in one historian's phrase, by the "visible hand" of the corporate managers.

Business, the Government, and the Public

Despite the radical departure from classical capitalism which characterized modern American business, the idea has persisted that the great economic expansion of the late nineteenth century was the exclusive work of heroic captains of industry, with no important role by government. There is just enough truth in this idea to give it the appearance of authenticity. Before the ascendency of the manager, this was an age of heroic enterprise, when daring, far-sighted, and sometimes ruthless men built a national railroad network and laid the foundations for a modern industrial economy. Moreover, the popularity of social Darwinism—the application of Charles Darwin's theories of natural selection to civilized societies—seemed to indicate widespread support for complete laissez faire. Social Darwinism, first developed by the English philosopher Herbert Spencer, found its popularizer in the United States in William Graham Sumner of Yale University. Some businessmen discovered that this body of thought corroborated their belief that governmental interference in economic life was both dangerous and futile, because it violated basic economic laws.

Superficial appearances were deceptive, for the postwar economic expansion was the result of a great national effort aimed at rapid modernization and industrialization. There were disagreements over the speed of development and whether one class or section was getting a fair share and equal treatment. These disagreements fueled the important political debates of the day. But most Americans gloried in their nation's technological and economic growth.

Moreover, much of the economic development was the result of direct or indirect governmental encouragement. The building of a national railroad network could not have occurred so quickly without massive public assistance to the railroad companies. Liberal land policies and governmental support of silver prices spurred the development of the West. High tariffs stimulated certain industries, such as steel, copper, and wool. Federal banking and monetary policies also stimulated the growth of a far-flung financial structure and encouraged investment, particularly from abroad.

Even the Supreme Court played an important role by insisting that railroads and corporations had certain rights which the states had to respect. That tribunal, in Munn *v.* Illinois (1877), had declared that the right of the states to regulate business enterprise was virtually unlimited. But the court did an about face in the Wabash case (1886) and related decisions. The court, in these rulings, declared that corporations were persons entitled to protection under the Fourteenth Amendment, and that states could not deprive them of property through regulation without due process of law. These decisions did not forbid the states to regulate railroads and corporations, but they did affirm that state regulations had to be reasonable, and that the federal courts would determine reasonableness in the final analysis.

The dominant philosophy of the period was not classical laissez faire. The governing doctrine was partnership between government and business enterprise. To be sure, the federal government did refrain from extensive regulation of business, but this was a deliberate policy with widespread support from people who believed that it would promote economic growth. We have already noted how governmental assistance contributed to economic development. The other side of the story is that businessmen participated widely in political processes. Railroads, manufacturing firms, and other corporations maintained lobbies in Washington to protect and advance their interests. Lobbyists also worked hand in glove with state legislatures and city councils to influence legislation and obtain favors. Businessmen contributed handsomely to the campaign funds of city, state, and national political parties, usually with the expectation that successful candidates would cooperate with their benefactors in the future. As we shall see, it was precisely this situation that various reform movements sought to change.

2. WORKERS IN INDUSTRIAL AMERICA

The New World of Work

The technological revolution, which gained momentum in the late nineteenth century, was accompanied by profound changes in the kinds of work done by

American men and women and in the social and economic relationships among working people. At the time of the Civil War, most American workers were engaged in agriculture and perhaps half were self-employed. However, by the early years of the twentieth century, the typical worker was a wage-earning employee engaged in manufacturing or mining.

The new world of work carried with it a host of contradictions. The standard of living for many workers rose dramatically, yet the gap also widened between the "haves" and the "have-nots." A broad range of Americans embraced the idea that material advancement was open to all who were willing to work. Yet the creation of a permanent body of industrial wage earners brought into being a new sense of working-class solidarity. The roots of these contradictions are to be found in both the material conditions of work and in the work-related ideas and values which Americans shared.

The factory system spread unevenly, but relentlessly, across the American economy in the late nineteenth century. In one industry after another, old ways of working and old ideas about work were pushed aside. With the coming of mechanization and division of labor, the artisan gave way increasingly to the semiskilled machine tender, and the place of work shifted from the crafts-man's home or shop to the large factory. Nowhere was this transformation more rapid and complete than in the shoe industry. In little more than a decade, shoemaking shifted from handcraft methods to factory operations based on the sewing machine and other technological innovations. During the 1860s, when the shift to factory production was in full swing, productivity tripled in the shoe industry.

Increases in productivity, which routinely accompanied the introduction of the factory system, were attributable, not only to new machinery, but also to new work habits and work discipline. For preindustrial artisans and farmers, work involved alternating periods of intense labor and idleness. The day's "work" in a craftsman's shop might well include lengthy periods of relaxation, complete with refreshments of all sorts, and the work week was often short-ened by the tradition of "blue Monday," which found workmen recovering from Sunday's entertainment.

This pattern of hard work mixed with recreation was a way of life for many people, and they resisted efforts to change it. But the dictates of factory and machine production required sobriety and, above all, steady attention to work over a fixed period of time. The factory bell, which summoned and dismissed the workers, symbolized the new order in which time replaced the specific task as the measure of work.

The craftsman's detailed knowledge of production processes had given him considerable control of the work place, even when he was nominally an employee. But, by the end of the century, routinization and division of labor, the perfection of machine tools, and the rise of professional management all had eroded traditional patterns of control by workers and foremen. Resistance to this loss of control and to assaults on other aspects of traditional work culture helped to stimulate the organization of skilled craftsmen in unions in the late nineteenth century.

Workers' Standard of Living

The evidence is mixed about the well-being of workers in industrializing America. Real wages rose sharply between 1860 and 1890, and the living conditions of American workers in the early stages of industrialization were better than those of their European counterparts. However, there was also widespread poverty among industrial workers. Wages in the soft-goods industries, such as textiles, lagged far behind those in iron, steel, and machine goods. Seasonal layoffs were a fact of life for most workers (which explains much of the geographical mobility of working-class Americans), and depressions caused widespread unemployment and wage reductions in 1873–1878, 1883–1885, and 1893–1897.

Furthermore, safety standards were lax, and workers were presumed to be responsible when accidents occurred. With unsafe conditions and long hours of work, the United States had one of the highest rates of industrial accidents in the world. Between 1880 and 1900, 35,000 workers were killed on the job each year.

Living conditions for workers and their families were often equally grim. Modern conveniences, such as public sewer and water systems, were slow to penetrate the crowded neighborhoods of the working classes, and most of the new labor-saving appliances for the home, including the washing machine, were priced out of the reach of most working-class families. And, yet, with the revolution in agriculture, which diminished the need for rural labor, most industrial workers found alternative employment opportunities limited or unattractive.

Women, Families, and Industrial Work

It has been previously noted that most manufacturing had shifted from the home to the factory by the end of the nineteenth century. It is often asserted that, as this process occurred, women withdrew from income-producing work and retired behind lace curtains to manage the home. To the extent that such a withdrawal occurred, it was largely a middle-class phenomenon. In many working-class families, the income of the mother was essential for survival. In absolute terms, the number of women in industry actually increased in the late nineteenth century. In 1900, women comprised 19 per cent of the total industrial work force and 48 per cent of all textile workers. To be sure, both percentages represented a decline from earlier decades, but this was due to the even larger number of men entering the work force, many of whom were immigrants who moved into fields formerly dominated by women. A growing number of women worked in "white collar" jobs, such as retail sales and office work, but the largest number of women employed outside the home (about 2,000,000) were in domestic or personal service.

Despite the rise of the factory system, women and men continued to do income-producing work at home. In addition to the women still engaged in farm work, many did "piece work" at home, particularly for garment and cigar industries. Boarding nonfamily members also provided income for numerous households.

The world of work and the world of family were not so separate for many nineteenth-century Americans as we might imagine. Home place and work place were usually not far distant before the rise of modern suburbs. Furthermore, the family unit often served as a source of recruitment and job placement in the days before professionalized personnel management. Families, voluntary associations, and ethnic groups helped to create a supportive environment for industrial workers. The vitality of these institutions both sustained the individual and made more difficult the formation of a self-conscious working class.

Thinking about Work

In the latter part of the nineteenth century, traditional American ideas about work collided with the new reality of factory and machine production. The so-called Protestant work ethic had shaped middle-class thinking about work for generations and had had a large, if indeterminable, impact on the nation as a whole. The Protestant reformers of the sixteenth century had elevated secular labor to the status of a divine calling. "In the things of this life" one reformer had proclaimed, "the laborer is most like to God." By the early nineteenth century, the work ethic in America had come to mean that individuals found meaning and freedom through constructive, self-directed toil. The corollary of this idea was that anyone who chose to work hard in America could get ahead.

In reality, however, workers in industrial America were losing their status as independent craftsmen, tradesmen, and farmers, and more and more found work as semiskilled wage laborers. The very idea of a large and permanent class of wage workers engaged in routine machine tending contradicted the American dream of upward mobility. People dealt with this contradiction in a variety of ways. Some simply continued to affirm the old idea that hard work was both a virtue and a ticket to advancement. However, much of the popular literature of the late nineteenth century added a new twist: success required not only hard work, but also self-advertisement, aggressiveness, and, as in the case of the novels of Horatio Alger, a measure of luck.

The undermining of workers' independence and creation of a permanent wage-earning class brought protests from many quarters. In the 1870s and 1880s, a variety of reformers called for cooperative production and distribution of goods as an alternative to private ownership. When the cooperative movement declined, a variety of other measures were suggested to give workers more control of their own lives than was possible in the factory.

Toward the end of the century, similar concerns led some Americans to embrace socialism. Although many of the first American socialists were disciples of Karl Marx, doctrinaire Marxism made relatively little headway among American workers. The brand of socialism which predominated in America owed more to Edward Bellamy than to Karl Marx. Bellamy's enormously popular novel, *Looking Backward* (1888), described the United States in the year 2000, by which time it had become a socialist utopia in which Christian ideals were practiced as well as preached. The idea that such a society could be established peacefully and governed reasonably apparently appealed to Americans, for hundreds of "Nationalist" clubs were organized to work for the creation of Bellamy's state. Bellamy and other non-Marxist radical reformers made socialism palatable enough to Americans for the Socialist party to become a major political force early in the twentieth century.

The Beginnings of Organized Labor

The growth of organized labor in the United States parallels that of the development of business enterprise. Both were local in character until after the

Civil War. Local unions of workers in the same craft had existed from the earliest days of the republic. As early as 1799, the shoemakers of Philadelphia conducted a strike; in 1836 the women textile workers of Lowell, Massachusetts, "turned out" in protest against changes in work rules. An attempt was made in New York in 1834 to unite workers from various crafts into a general organization of "the productive classes of the country." The time was not yet ripe for such a movement, however, and it failed.

Class consciousness developed very slowly among American industrial workers. At first, most of them refused to regard factory work as a career, or themselves as a separate class apart from employers and consumers. Hence they concentrated in the 1820s, 1830s, and 1840s less upon organization for collective bargaining than upon the generalized reform of society. Many of their objectives, such as liberal land policies and abolition of imprisonment for debt, were those of other reform groups as well.

The beginnings of a momentous change occurred in the 1850s. This decade saw the first important organization of trade unions primarily to improve wages and conditions of employment. Among these were the National Typographical Union, the International Union of Machinists and Blacksmiths, and the Iron Molders' International Union.

Although the direction of American trade unionism was to be away from generalized, utopian reform and toward collective bargaining in the interest of union members, the lines between these two activities were seldom clear-cut. Recent research by labor historians has revealed a lively and persistent interaction between reformism and "bread and butter" unionism throughout the late nineteenth century. For example, in the Brotherhood of Carpenters and Joiners—one of the most successful of the early trade unions—proponents of "business unionism" did not finally prevail over supporters of broad-gauged reform until after 1900.

Labor unions of all kinds increased fourfold during the Civil War and could claim a membership of 200,000 at its end. New strength fed an increasing class consciousness. This upsurge culminated in the National Labor Union (NLU), formed in 1866 under the leadership of William H. Sylvis, president of the Iron Molders' Union. The NLU was a loose confederation of trade unions, reform associations, labor parties, and even the Marxist International Workingmen's Association. At its peak, in about 1869, it enrolled between 200,000 and 400,000 workers—a substantial portion of the industrial work force.

The NLU was momentarily so successful that it attracted a variety of reform movements to its ranks. The reformers, many of whom, like Sylvis, were also trade unionists, advocated banking and monetary reform, the reconstitution of society through cooperatives, and even the abolition of industrial capitalism as it was then taking shape. The main purpose of the NLU, these reformers believed, was to help to achieve these goals by lobbying and by the education of the working classes. Despite its auspicious beginnings, the NLU began to decline in 1870. Members failed to find ways to separate their political and trade-union activities; as a result, disagreement over politics split the organization. The weakened NLU received a death blow from the depression of 1873–1878. Many of the newly formed trade unions collapsed along with the NLU, when widespread unemployment and a tough antiunion stance of management forced many workers to choose between jobs and a union.

Large-scale working-class organization next occurred in the mid-1880s, and this time the dominant organization was the Noble and Holy Order of the

Knights of Labor. It was first organized in 1869 as a secret society of Philadelphia garment cutters and remained essentially a local organization until the mid-1870s. The Knights survived the depression and reorganized in 1878 with the stated purpose of mobilizing all workers—skilled and unskilled—into one big union for mutual protection. Under the leadership of Terence V. Powderly, a machinist and trade unionist, the Knights embraced all "producers" and excluded from membership only bankers, lawyers, speculators, and stock brokers.

The Knights, due largely to a spectacularly successful strike against Jay Gould's southwestern railroad system in 1885, reached a peak of about 700,000 members in 1886. Most persons who joined were wage earners, although the organization also attracted a substantial number of farmers and a small but influential group of self-employed craftsmen and professionals.

The Knights, like the NLU, were not prepared to accept industrial capitalism as a permanent state of affairs. They worked for monetary reform, cooperatives, settlement of industrial disputes by arbitration rather than by strikes, the eight-hour work day, and the abolition of child labor. But the Knights suffered the same internal conflict that had plagued the NLU—a conflict between long-term, generalized reform and short-term benefits for union members. The Knights also came on the scene at a time of intense antiunion sentiment, both

Handbill for T. V. Powderly, leader of the Knights of Labor, who observed that "a deep-rooted feeling of discontent pervades the masses." (Culver Pictures, Inc.)

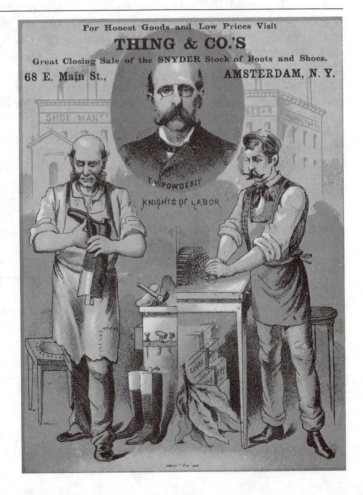

among employers and many middle-class citizens. Ironically, the internal crisis which helped to destroy the Knights came in 1886, the year of the organization's most spectacular growth. The Knights could not duplicate their victory of 1885 in a second strike against the Gould system, and the defeat exacerbated disagreements within the organization. The Knights collapsed as quickly as it had sprung up. By the early 1890s, it had shrunk to a fraction of its former strength.

The Rise of the American Federation of Labor

The organization that would eventually succeed in permanently organizing large numbers of workers was the American Federation of Labor (AFL). It was formed in 1886 by Adolph Strasser and Samuel Gompers of the Cigar Makers' International Union of New York. Gompers, elected president of the AFL every year but one from 1886 until his death in 1924, had long opposed the general reform wing of the labor movement. He was more interested in winning immediate increases in wages and reduction of hours of labor than in creating a utopian commonwealth. The AFL consisted largely of workers in the skilled trades and gave each constituent craft union within the federation considerable control over its own affairs. The AFL refused to take an active role in politics during the early years of Gompers' leadership.

The AFL focused, instead, on higher wages, shorter hours, job security, protection of women and children against exploitation and overwork, recognition of the legality of labor unions by legislatures and courts, and, above all, the right to bargain with employers, through strikes if need be. As it focused on these bread-and-butter issues, the AFL conceded the permanence of the wage labor system, rejected partisan politics as a direct concern of the labor movement, and cut the ties between trade unionism and intellectual and middle-class reformers.

At the turn of the century, neither the AFL's preeminent position within the labor movement nor its overwhelming commitment to business unionism were self-evident. In 1897, the AFL had 447,000 members, far fewer than the Knights of Labor had had at their peak. The craft unions which made up the AFL enrolled fewer than 5 per cent of America's wage earners and had failed to make inroads among the semiskilled workers of the new mass-production industries. Furthermore, members of many constituent unions rejected Gompers' disavowal of working-class politics.

However, unlike the earlier national groups, the AFL survived, and membership had risen to more than 2,000,000 by 1914. By then, the AFL spoke for a substantial proportion of the skilled workers in the United States. In the early years of the twentieth century, the AFL modified its stand on political activism. It entered the congressional campaign of 1906 and subsequently supported Democratic presidential candidates in 1908, 1912, and 1916. Unlike the general reformism of earlier labor politics, the AFL's political goals were narrowly focused on obtaining amendments to the Sherman Antitrust Act to exempt labor unions from that law's restraints. Court interpretation of the Sherman Act had severely limited union activities by declaring them subject to its prohibitions against illegal restraint of trade.

The AFL's brand of bread-and-butter unionism did not completely dominate organized labor in the first years of the twentieth century. In 1905, a small group of socialists and labor radicals formed the Industrial Workers of the

World. The "Wobblies," as they were called, rejected the AFL's conservative, craft-oriented approach and set out to organize the mass of unskilled workers in manufacturing, mining, and agriculture. The IWW never gained a mass following, but between 1905 and 1917 the headline-grabbing rhetoric of its militant leaders and their knack for appearing wherever violent strikes broke out, made the small, faction-ridden group appear to threaten public safety.

The Wobblies did call for the overthrow of industrial capitalism and the establishment of direct worker control of factories and mines. As the leading historian of this organization has said, they were, in this sense, syndicalists— cousins of the labor radicals in Europe who were at the same time challenging capitalism and rejecting political solutions to economic problems. Despite the Wobblies' widely perceived association with violent labor tactics, they were probably more sinned against than sinners in this respect. They were met by publicly sanctioned vigilantes at every turn. During the First World War, federal authorities crushed the union by breaking IWW strikes, infiltrating the organization with spies, and finally arresting most of its top leaders on charges of espionage, sedition, and obstruction of the war effort.

Violence in Labor-Management Relations

From the 1870s to the turn of the century and beyond, the industrializing process was accompanied by brutal conflict between workers and owners. It ranged from spontaneous and isolated outbursts to massive urban rioting, such as occurred during the railroad strike of 1877, pitched battles between workers and private armies employed by managers, such as took place during the strike against Andrew Carnegie's Homestead plant in 1892, and large-scale boycotts, such as happened during the Pullman strike of 1894.

The Pullman strike and boycott revealed the extent to which, by the 1890s, large corporations had both the will and the power to break strikes and unions and to employ not only their own private resources, but also the power of the federal government. The Pullman Company, manufacturer of railroad sleeping cars, cut wages for its workers five times within a year without, however, lowering rents on company-owned houses. The new American Railway Union (ARU), led by Eugene V. Debs, supported the Pullman workers in their fight against the company and launched a boycott against all trains which pulled Pullman cars. Rail traffic in the Midwest ground to a halt. With support from Attorney General Richard Olney, a former railroad lawyer, the railroads won a federal court injunction forbidding the ARU and Debs to interfere with the shipment of United States mail. Strikers greeted the announcement of the injunction with hoots and jeers. When the boycott continued despite the injunction, President Grover Cleveland sent 2,000 troops to Chicago. When the troops arrived on July 4, Debs appealed for order, but some of the strikers and a large number of unemployed workers could not be restrained. They ditched and destroyed trains and looted and burned buildings. Soldiers killed twelve of the rioters. In effect, the Cleveland administration broke the strike, while the federal court in Chicago sent Debs to jail for violating its injunction. The experience converted Debs to socialism.

With very few exceptions, the outbreaks of violence were not the work of organized terrorists or revolutionaries, nor were they necessarily touched off by ruthless businessmen eager to stifle the aspirations of labor. For the most part, workers and employees shared a common set of values, yet violent con-

The Homestead Strike, July 1892. Strikers at Carnegie's Homestead steel plant fired upon barges carrying 300 Pinkerton detectives. (Library of Congess)

frontation between them was endemic between the 1870s and the 1890s. Workers who struggled to maintain or win control of their own work place and to preserve the traditional structures and customs of community life found themselves in conflict with increasingly powerful business organizations. Workers, faced with an adversary organized on a national scale and backed by massive resources, including, at times, the authority of state and federal governments, took to the streets in a wave of violent outbursts. To many contemporary observers, these actions seemed to threaten the very social fabric of the republic.

3. THE SOUTH AND WEST IN THE AGE OF INDUSTRIALIZATION

Southern Agriculture after the Civil War

Despite appeals for Yankee-style industrialization, the South's economy remained predominantly agricultural and its people overwhelmingly rural. Rural life changed in the aftermath of the Civil War, but not as drastically as fiction has portrayed it. The hand- and hoe-culture of cotton production was unaffected by political upheaval. The war swept away slavery, but not its companion, the plantation. Cotton plantations, which had formerly been operated by slaves working in gangs, were "divided" into small plots worked by families of former slaves who now became sharecroppers for the plantation owners. The sharecropping system—a form of labor based on a division of the crop between the owner and tiller of the land—involved close supervision by the owner or his agent, a system of credit which often bound the cropper to the land year after year, and a set of laws designed to protect the interests of the planter rather than his tenant. The large number of former slaves who became enmeshed in the sharecropping system or, even worse, subsisted as casual agricultural laborers, found the fruits of freedom less enjoyable than they had dreamed. They were tied to an economic system that made them only half free, and faced a life of grinding poverty with little hope of material improvement so long as they remained in the southern countryside.

The agricultural transformation which faced white small farmers began differently from that of the slaves, but sometimes ended in the same way. The yeoman farmers, clustered primarily in the Piedmont region of the South, had been less dependent than the planters on cotton and other cash crops before the Civil War. Instead, they had concentrated on food crops for their own subsistence. But, after the war, many gambled on lifting themselves above bare subsistence through concentration on cotton. At first they were lured by the temporarily high prices of cotton; they were later encouraged by the new railroad-linked marketing systems which fanned out across the Piedmont. Cotton production involved not only the possibility of substantial profits, but also greater fixed costs, and the latter increased the chances of financial ruin. As cotton prices dropped in the 1880s, many small farmers lost their land and sank into the tenant classes. These small farmers, bitter at the prospect of losing the economic independence which they viewed as a birthright, were eager converts to the agrarian reform movements which swept across the South and West in the last three decades of the century.

The Dream of Southern Industrialization

In the early 1880s, Henry W. Grady, editor of the Atlanta *Constitution,* told and retold the story of a Georgia farmer who had been recently laid to rest. Even though the region around the cemetery where he was buried was rich in natural resources, the coffin, coffin nails, and tombstone had been manufactured outside the South, as had the suit of clothes worn by the deceased. "The South," Grady remarked, "didn't furnish a thing on earth for that funeral but the corpse and the hole in the ground." The point of Grady's story, and of similar homilies by publicists, preachers, and politicians across the region, was that Southerners should pull themselves and their region out of poverty through industrialization. As one evangelist said in Salisbury, North Carolina, "What this town needs most, next to the grace of God, is a cotton mill."

In fact, manufacturing was not unknown in the Old South. Modest textile and iron factories had flourished for decades, and, during the Civil War, Southerners even established government-owned factories to arm the Confederacy. In 1864, the world's largest state-owned powder factory was located in Augusta, Georgia. However, southern manufacturing was limited in scale and tied to the needs of plantation agriculture and, temporarily, to the needs of the Confederate army and navy. Much of the South's manufacturing capacity, along with much of the region's railroad network, was destroyed during the war.

The restoration of antebellum railroads and the recovery of agriculture were fairly complete by 1870, but industry was slower to recover and expand. Beginning around 1880, cotton mills and tobacco and furniture factories sprang up, often backed by local capital. Local entrepreneurs and a regional railroad company exploited the coal and iron of the Birmingham district. Birmingham was a corn field in the 1870s; by 1900 it was a flourishing center of iron production. Atlanta was rebuilt from ashes to become a center of transportation and commerce.

By the end of the century, advocates of an industrialized New South were citing all manner of statistics to show that their goal was being achieved. But, despite a substantial increase in the amount of manufactures, the South's share of the nation's total (by value added) remained virtually unchanged from 1860 at about 10.5 per cent.

The New West

After the Civil War, the underdeveloped and almost unexplored area between the fertile midwestern prairies and the Pacific coast offered obvious opportunities for development. In 1860, the frontier was an irregular line extending from western Minnesota to the Gulf of Mexico. Beyond lay an empire still largely uninhabited by Anglo-Americans except for settlements in New Mexico, Utah, and on the Pacific coast.

It was an empire not only dazzling in size and scenic splendor, but also immensely varied in soil and other natural resources. Beyond the frontier line of 1860, the well-watered prairies extended to about a line running from the central part of the Dakotas through central Texas. The black soil of the prairies was best suited to corn and, because of corn, which makes excellent feed for animals, to the production of livestock and hogs. Between the prairies and the eastern slopes of the Rockies lay the Great Plains, which were ideally suited for cattle because of rainfall insufficient for crops but enough for grass. Between the Rockies and the Sierra Nevada and Cascade ranges, further to the west, there was a vast arid or semiarid desert area suitable only for limited grazing unless irrigated. Finally, there were numerous valleys between the Sierra Nevadas and the Cascades and the Pacific coast ranges. These valleys were rich in minerals and potentially fertile, but they were well watered only from northern California to Washington State.

The western half of the United States was the area of greatest internal territorial expansion between the Civil War and the end of the nineteenth century. There were several different kinds of frontiers, not all of them agricultural. Beneath the soil lay some of the earth's greatest deposits of copper, petroleum, and other resources. These could be brought to the industrial centers of the East on the same trains that carried cattle and corn.

The Day of the Cowboy

The Homestead Act and cheap land sales by the railroads spurred the settlement of the western part of the prairies. This developed quickly between the

Civil War and the early 1870s. Meanwhile, a new frontier—the Cattle Kingdom on the Great Plains—had come into being. It started in Texas just before the Civil War, when cowboys rounded up the numerous wild Texas longhorns and stockmen began to domesticate them. Texans rounded up a herd of some 26,000 in 1866 and drove them to rail terminals in Sedalia, Missouri, and Abilene, Kansas. These cattle, after fattening, were sold to packers and shippers for the eastern market. In 1871, more than 600,000 cattle made the trek northward on the "long drive." By 1876, the Cattle Kingdom had spread up and down the Plains and even into New Mexico and Colorado.

Cattle raising and herding was a booming business from Texas northward into Canada during the 1870s and early 1880s. Profits were quick and large so long as the range remained open and beef prices were high. But a combination of severe winters, droughts, and low prices struck the cattlemen in the mid-1880s. Worse still for them, farmers and sheep raisers began to encroach upon the open range. They staked out claims and enclosed their farms. Bitter feuds and range wars broke out as cattlemen fought against those who settled on the range. There was much gunfire and not a little bloodshed before the cowboy gave way to the farmer, or became himself domesticated on large ranches. Meanwhile, the cowboy had become firmly embedded in American legend and song. At one point, at least, the legendary cowboy departs from reality. Unlike the movie and advertising versions, about one fourth of the real-life cowboys were black, as were a substantial number of soldiers stationed in the West.

Farmers Move into the Great Plains

The Great Plains, covering most of the area in western Kansas, Nebraska, Oklahoma, and the Dakotas, are treeless, windswept, and subject to extremes of heat and cold. The soil is so tough that it breaks wooden or iron plowshares. Yet the pressure on the agricultural frontier was so great in the early 1870s that farmers began to move into this inhospitable region.

Human courage and ingenuity enabled the settlers to make a start. For example, when they could not find wood, they built their first houses of sod. Or again, when settlers discovered, as they soon did, that it was impossible to make a living on a 160-acre homestead, they proceeded to ignore the Homestead Act and to stake out larger claims.

What really made agriculture possible on the Plains were the steel plow, barbed wire, and the windmill. The steel plow, invented in the 1830s to break the prairies, proved ideally suited to the hard soil of the Plains. Barbed wire, first produced about 1875, made an excellent substitute for wooden and stone fences. It enabled the farmer to fence in large areas easily and cheaply. Windmills, which could pump water from great depths, had been in limited use in the East since the 1850s. However, production in large quantities for use on the Plains began only about 1873.

An unusual amount of rainfall and relatively good prices for wheat and corn encouraged such rapid settlement that the Plains area underwent something of a boom in the 1870s and 1880s. Nebraska, for example, grew in population from 123,000 in 1870 to 1,063,000 in 1890; Kansas, from 364,000 to 1,428,000; and South Dakota, from 12,000 to 349,000. When a 3,000,000-acre tract in the Indian Territory, in what is now Oklahoma, was opened to homesteading in 1889, there occurred one of the most spectacular land rushes in all of American history. Oklahoma grew from no recorded white population in 1870 and 1880 to 259,000 in 1890 and 730,000 in 1900.

After he surveyed the results of the Census of 1890, the Superintendent of the Census wrote: "Up to and including 1880 the country had a frontier of settlement, but at present the unsettled area has been so broken into by isolated bodies of settlement that there can hardly be said to be a frontier line." The passing of the frontier seemed to mark the end of the long era of unlimited economic opportunity that stretched back all the way to Jamestown. As matters turned out, the announcement of the death of the frontier was somewhat premature. A frontier line beyond which there was virtually no white habitation was of course gone. But vast quantities of free or very cheap land remained to be opened up by railroads and later by automobile roads. Four times as many homesteads were taken up after 1890 than had been taken up during the entire period from 1862 to 1890.

The Miners' Frontier

Next to farming, mining was the most important industry of the New West. We have already discussed the California gold rush. It was only the first of many western rushes, which drew some 200,000 persons into the West between the late 1850s and 1880. The Appalachian gold deposits discovered early in the century, and the rushes which those discoveries touched off, were paltry in comparison. Every new discovery of gold, silver, copper, lead, or other minerals in the mountain ranges which stretched from Montana to Arizona had the same results. Each drew its crowds of prospectors, diggers, gamblers, and desperados to new mining towns.

Large-scale mining began when gold was discovered in the Pike's Peak district of Colorado in 1858. Before the end of the Civil War, Colorado had already sent more than $10 million in gold to the United States mint. Nevada was probably even richer in mineral wealth. The Comstock Lode at Virginia City was yielding $20 million worth of silver annually by the early 1860s. Gold was discovered in the Black Hills of the Dakota Territory, which set off another rush and gave rise to the famous mining towns of Lead and Deadwood. California, Colorado, and Nevada produced 90 per cent of the country's gold and 73.5 per cent of its silver in 1880. By that time, the West also produced most of the nation's copper and a growing proportion of its iron ore.

Assaults on Western Indian Lands and Culture

The advancing tides of cattlemen, farmers, and miners doomed the independence of the great Indian tribes that roamed the Plains and inhabited the mountains. In the North lived the Sioux, Crows, northern Cheyennes, and Arapahoes; in the South, the Comanches, Kiowas, southern Cheyennes, and southern Arapahoes; in the mountains, the Nez Perces, Apaches, and Utes. The Plains Indians, by far the most numerous, lived off the buffalo. From this shaggy beast they obtained their food, clothing, and shelter. Alone among the American Indians, they had domesticated the horse.

Between 1862 and 1890, Indians and whites clashed in a series of bloody confrontations, most of them triggered by the steady encroachment of white settlement. The worst outbreak occurred in 1876. The Sioux, outraged by the

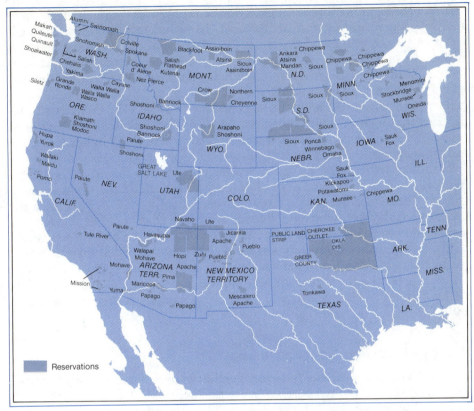

Indian Reservations in the West, 1890

movement of white miners and others into the Black Hills area of Dakota, which had been set apart "forever" as part of the Sioux domain, left their reservation, and it required a long and bloody campaign by the army to drive them back. The largest battle occurred at the Little Big Horn River in what is now Montana on June 25, 1876. General George A. Custer and his entire force of 264 men were wiped out when Custer recklessly attacked a huge force of Sioux under Chief Sitting Bull. However, the campaign ended, as did all the others, with the defeat of the outnumbered and outgunned red men.

Still, the Indians' final defeat was caused less by military conquest than by the relentless advance of European-style civilization, which brought with it railroads, fenced farms, and large, permanent settlements of whites. Most important, it brought the systematic destruction of the life-sustaining buffalo herds and diseases such as cholera, smallpox, and measles, which decimated the Indian population. The number of American Indians dwindled to a low of 220,000 in 1910, down from 600,000 at the time of the American Revolution. Many of the surviving western Indians were herded into reservations, often situated on land too poor to attract white settlers, and were stripped of all but nominal tribal independence. They either vegetated in a state of dependency or turned to religious rituals, such as the Sun Dance and Ghost Dance, which promised deliverance from the white man's rule.

By the 1880s, humanitarian and religious concern over the plight of the Indians was gaining momentum in the East. Unfortunately, the plans of well-meaning reformers coincided with the persistent efforts of those hungry for still more Indian land. Consequently, a series of governmental measures adopted in the 1880s almost eradicated Indian culture and tribal life. Missionaries and governmental agents pressed Indians to embrace Christianity and integrate into the American agricultural economy. In 1884, Congress actually authorized the suppression of Indian religions on the Sioux, Ute, and Shoshone reservations, and governmental agents worked to stamp out Indian languages and other manifestations of Indian culture.

Reformers argued that, for their own benefit, Indians should forsake tribal living in favor of individual assimilation into the American economic mainstream. Congress debated this issue for years; finally, in 1887, it passed the Dawes Severalty Act, which provided that tribal lands should be divided into family homesteads of 160 acres. Indians who accepted the homesteads would be given American citizenship. Ominously, the law provided that "surplus" tribal lands not allocated to Indians could be sold to whites. The results were predictable. Before the allotment program was ended in 1934, Indians had lost 90,000,000 of the 138,000,000 acres which had comprised the reservations in 1887.

The "New" Americans of the Southwest

The loss of Indian lands was tragically duplicated in the case of many Mexican Americans in the Southwest. The Treaty of Guadalupe Hidalgo, which ended the Mexican War in 1848, brought some 78,000 Mexican citizens under the American flag, supposedly with full rights of American citizenship and protection for their land titles. In California, home of 11,000 of these new American citizens, a small Mexican elite (Californios) dominated both the land and the government. But with the discovery of gold in 1849 and the subsequent realization of California's agricultural riches, Anglo squatters began challenging the land titles of the Californio ranchers. Biased arbitration boards and even less objective vigilantes forced many Mexican Americans off their land. By 1880, they had lost their dominant position in landholding.

In Texas, where Mexican Americans had come under Anglo control following the revolution of 1836, relations between Anglo-American Protestants and Mexican-American Catholics were even more hostile than in California and much more so than in neighboring New Mexico. In the Rio Grande Valley and other predominantly Mexican-American areas of southern Texas, land hunger triggered confrontations between the two groups. Again, both legal and extra-legal methods were employed to drive Mexican Americans off their land, curtail their voting rights, and relegate them to a segregated status. In Texas, as elsewhere in the Southwest, Mexican Americans resisted forcibly the takeover of their property, most often, through guerrilla-style banditry, but also by mob action.

Prior to 1900, most of the 300,000 Mexican Americans were descendents of people living in the Southwest before its annexation by the United States. By the turn of the century, loss of land, the breakup of traditional patterns of land tenure, and the curtailment of political and civil rights had reduced southwestern Mexican Americans to the status of a subservient underclass and had seriously eroded their own cultural values, which, like those of the Indians, had stressed the solidarity of the community and the extended family. As one scholar has written, "the Mexican-American community was ill-prepared for the American vision of progress and modernization."

SUGGESTED READINGS

Three general studies of the industrial era are John A. Garraty, *The New Commonwealth* (1968); Edward C. Kirkland, *Industry Comes of Age: Business, Labor and Public Policy, 1860–1897* (1961); and Thomas C. Cochran and William Miller, *The Age of Enterprise* (1942). Alfred D. Chandler, Jr., *The Visible Hand: The Managerial Revolution in American Business* (1977), assesses the development of modern business organization and finds the railroads to be critically important innovators in management as well as in technology. As a counterpoint, and for a spirited denunciation of railroad magnates, bankers, and other such capitalists, see Matthew Josephson, *The Robber Barons* (1934). In *Railroads and Regulation, 1877–1916* (1965), Gabriel Kolko argues that the railroads themselves spurred the movement for federal regulation. George R. Taylor and Irene D. Neu, *The American Railroad Network, 1861–1890* (1956), and John F. Stover, *The Life and Decline of the American Railroad* (1970), are useful surveys.

On Carnegie and the steel industry see Joseph F. Wall, *Andrew Carnegie* (1970), and Peter Temin, *Iron and Steel in Nineteenth-Century America* (1964). Conflicting views of *Rockefeller*, 2 vols. (1953), and Ralph W. Hidy in Allan Nevins, *Study in Power: John D. Rockefeller*, (2 vols. 1953); and Ralph W. Hidy and M. E. Hidy, *Pioneering in Big Business, 1882–1911* (1955). Harold C. Passer, *The Electrical Manufacturers, 1875–1900* (1953), is an excellent survey of this industry's technological, administrative, and corporate development. See also Matthew Josephson, *Edison* (1959), and Robert V. Bruce, *Alexander Graham Bell and the Conquest of Solitude* (1973). On technological innovation in general, see Nathan Rosenberg, *Technology and American Economic Growth* (1972), and Elting E. Morison, *From Know-How to Nowhere: The Development of American Technology* (1974).

Attitudes toward business and economic development are discussed in Robert G. McCloskey, *American Conservatism in the Age of Enterprise* (1951); Sidney Fine, *Laissez-Faire and the General Welfare State* (1956); and Daniel Rogers, *The Work Ethic in Industrial America, 1850–1920* (1978). The problem of monopoly can be viewed in the writings of contemporary social critics, including Henry George, *Progress and Poverty* (1879); and Edward Bellamy, *Looking Backward* (1888). Attempts at federal regulation of industry can be traced in H. B. Thorelli, *The Federal Antitrust Policy* (1954); and Ari Hoogenboom and Olive Hoogenboom, *A History of the ICC* (1976).

On industrial workers, see Melvyn Dubofsky, *Industrialism and the American Worker, 1865–1920* (1975); David Montgomery, *Beyond Equality* (1967); and Daniel Nelson, *Managers and Workers: Origins of the New Factory System in the United States, 1880–1920* (1975). Edith Abbott, *Women in Industry* (1910), remains a valuable introduction to that subject. On specific aspects of organized labor see Gerald N. Grob, *Workers and Utopia* (1961); Lloyd Ulman, *The Rise of the National Trade Union* (1955); and Philip Taft, *The A. F. of L. in the Time of Gompers* (1957). Two autobiographies worth consulting are Terence V. Powderly, *Thirty Years of Labor* (1889), and Samuel Gompers, *Seventy Years of Life and Labor*, 2 vols. (1925).

The standard account of the post-Reconstruction South remains C. Vann Woodward, *Origins of the New South, 1877–1913* (1951), although its conclusions about economic development are challenged in Jonathan Wiener, *Social Origins of the New South: Alabama, 1860–1885* (1978). In addition to the general surveys of frontier and western history previously cited, a superior work on this period is Howard R. Lamar, *The Far Southwest, 1846–1912* (1966). The transformation of the West from a frontier to an agricultural region is studied in James C. Malin, *The Grasslands of North America* (1947). Leo Marx, *The Machine and the Garden* (1965), analyzes the enchroachment of technology on the frontier "garden of Eden" and the effect that this had on American mythology. On the mythical laborer of the West, see Joe B. Frantz and J. E. Choate, *The American Cowboy: The Myth and the Reality* (1955). Fred A. Shannon, *The Farmer's Last Frontier, 1860–1897* (1945), is a good survey of the agricultural problems of this period, but it should be supplemented by Gilbert C. Fite, *The Farmer's Frontier, 1865–1900* (1966).

CHAPTER 19
POLITICS AND DIPLOMACY IN THE GILDED AGE

1. THE HAYES ADMINISTRATION

The Gilded Age in Perspective

The period between the end of Reconstruction and the late nineteenth century has been called the Gilded Age, largely because of the crass materialism common to the new class of wealthy businessmen, who often displayed their wealth blatantly. Historians have not been kind to the political leaders of the Gilded Age. It has been said that they reflected the businessman's concern for material things, fought sham battles in the political arena, and showed little wisdom in helping to solve the farmer's plight and new social problems such as the rise of city slums. The Presidents during this period, when mentioned at all, have not been compared favorably to Jackson and Lincoln.

These characterizations are somewhat overdrawn. It is true that the political leaders of the Gilded Age failed to devise a constructive program to meet the problems raised by drastic economic and social changes. But their failure was not due altogether to lack of effort or intelligence, although these were contributory factors. Change simply occurred too fast. People with a political philosophy suited to the needs of an earlier, simpler society perhaps could not be expected to work out satisfactory answers to the challenges of a new industrial age, especially when so many of the ablest people in the nation were unwilling to participate in politics. Nevertheless, political leaders wrestled earnestly with many important problems and in some cases succeeded in laying the foundations for far-reaching reforms in the future.

Hayes and the Silver Question

Hayes entered the White House without enthusiastic support, even within his own party. He had been nominated in 1876 only because the supporters of Grant and Blaine were hopelessly deadlocked. Neither of these factions wanted a reform administration. Hayes offended the conservative, professional Republican politicians—the Stalwarts—by withdrawing the last federal garrisons from the South. Democratic newspapers charged that he had stolen the election from Tilden, and the Democratic House of Representatives threatened to investigate his title to the presidency.

The new President had been in office only a few months when a railroad strike broke out. It turned into the most violent labor conflict in American history to that time. Before it ended, Hayes had to send federal troops to Baltimore, Pittsburgh, and other cities to restore some kind of order.

Hayes' most difficult problem, however, was dealing with the rising popular demand for increased currency through the free coinage of silver. The Resumption Act of 1875 made greenbacks redeemable in gold on January 1, 1879. The desire for a larger money supply led debtors and Westerners to demand a return to the free and unlimited coinage of silver.

Gold and silver had both been recognized as money since the beginning of the republic. The common ratio was one ounce of gold to about sixteen ounces of silver. By 1873, the price of silver had increased so much in relation to gold that silver miners preferred to sell their metal on the open market rather than to bring it to the mints for exchange at the official ratio. Few paid much

Rutherford B. Hayes, a temperate and cautious man, restored respectability and dignity to the presidency after the corruption of the Grant administration. Thoroughly uncomfortable in the high office, Hayes wrote in 1879: "I am heartily tired of this life of bondage, responsibility, and toil." (Library of Congress)

attention, therefore, when Congress, in the Coinage Act of 1873, provided that the government should no longer buy silver and coin it into dollars. Among the instigators of this action were Treasury officials and congressmen, who feared that the vastly increased production of silver from recently opened mines would flood the mint with metal and lead to a general depreciation in the value of the dollar. By 1877, rising output of silver from the mining frontier had caused its price in world markets to fall rapidly. The mine owners, naturally, demanded that the government take it all at the old ratio of sixteen to one. They called the demonetization of silver "the Crime of 1873," and were joined in their demands by farmers and debtors. The latter now saw in silver a vehicle for the expansion of the money supply much more respectable than green-backs.

Richard P. ("Silver Dick") Bland of Missouri thereupon introduced a bill into the House in December 1876, which provided for the unlimited, or "free," coinage of silver at the ratio of sixteen to one. The House of Representatives, dominated by easy money men, approved the measure, but the Senate did not act upon it. When Bland reintroduced it in the following year, the Senate added an amendment offered by William B. Allison of Iowa. It stipulated that the

This illustration from Frank Leslie's Illustrated Newspaper *(1877) shows office-seekers in the lobby of the White House awaiting an interview with President Hayes. It was Hayes who later advocated abolishment of the spoils system and encouraged civil service reform. (Library of Congress)*

Treasury should purchase and coin not more than $4 million and not less than $2 million in silver monthly. Thus amended, the Bland-Allison bill was approved by both houses in 1878 and was passed again over Hayes' veto. It only partially satisfied the popular demand for a larger money supply, and the issue would continue to cause the political pot to boil for many years to come.

The Spoils System

The great army of officials, clerks, and administrators who worked for the government make up what is called the civil service. It had been the custom, especially since Andrew Jackson's day, to give these positions to faithful party workers. "To the victors belong the spoils" was the motto of both parties. Indeed, every change of administration saw a wild scramble in Washington for positions. Moreover, the people rewarded with offices usually were assessed a percentage of their salary as a "voluntary contribution" to the party.

Abolition of the spoils system was the first great national reform movement of the postwar era. Many great problems cried out for solution by the federal government before the reform of the civil service. But democratic government could not become efficient government until the way was opened for the creation of a highly trained, professional corps of administrators.

A large body of thoughtful people, led by Carl Schurz, George W. Curtis, editor of *Harper's Weekly*, and E. L. Godkin, editor of *The Nation*, saw this fact clearly in the late 1860s. In the public press and on the lecture platform, they pleaded for modernization and argued that the spoils system inevitably was corrupt and inefficient. Under their pressure, Congress in 1871 authorized President Grant to appoint a Civil Service Commission; he named Curtis as its chairman. But the commission could do little in the face of opposition from the Stalwarts, who recognized the deadly threat to their political organizations. They sneered at the "snivel service" and called the reformers hypocrites. Grant was not interested, and Congress refused to appropriate funds for the commission's work. Curtis resigned in 1875 after his recommendations had been ignored repeatedly, and the commission disintegrated.

Civil Service Reform

Hayes' main task was to clean up the corruption left by the Grant administration. The new President forbade his Secretary of the Treasury, John Sherman of Ohio, to collect political contributions from employees in his department. Hayes also barred officeholders from taking part in the management of political campaigns. Moreover, Hayes appointed Schurz as Secretary of the Interior and supported him in thoroughgoing reforms in his department. Finally, the President removed two leading Stalwarts, Chester A. Arthur and Alonzo B. Cornell, from positions in the New York customhouse. They had been using their office to build up Senator Roscoe Conkling's New York state Republican machine.

Although Hayes was unable to obtain civil service legislation from Congress, his efforts for reform aroused widespread interest and sympathy. Civil service reform leagues were formed in more than thirty states during his administration. A national organization, the Civil Service Reform Association, was launched at Newport, Rhode Island, in 1881 to press the cause.

2. THE ELECTION OF 1880 AND THE TRIUMPH OF CIVIL SERVICE REFORM

The Presidential Campaign of 1880

Hayes had given the country an honest administration, which was more than Americans had come to expect; but he had declared that he would not accept a second term. Furthermore, his war against the Stalwarts had so alienated him from the Republican professionals that his renomination would have been difficult, if not impossible, to accomplish. Thus the Republican field was wide open for other presidential hopefuls.

One was none other than former President Grant, who had returned in 1879 from a trip around the world. On his journey, Grant had been received with royal honors by the sovereigns of Europe and Asia. The Stalwarts, who well remembered the free and easy days when the General sat in the White House, were determined to put him there again, in spite of the popular prejudice against a third term. A second presidential aspirant was Secretary John Sherman, one of the leaders of the powerful Ohio G.O.P. A third, more serious, contender was James G. Blaine, Senator from Maine.

Blaine was the most brilliant and magnetic politician of the age, and his followers were fanatically loyal to him. Until his death in 1892, they clung to the hope of putting him in the White House. Grant and Blaine ran neck and neck for thirty-five ballots in the Republican national convention. Then the deadlock was broken on the next ballot by the selection of a dark horse, James A. Garfield of Ohio. Garfield had managed Sherman's preconvention campaign and had electrified the convention with his speech nominating Sherman. To appease the Stalwarts, the convention nominated Chester A. Arthur of New York for Vice-President.

The campaign that followed was not notably exciting. The Democrats nominated General Winfield S. Hancock, a northern hero of the Battle of Gettysburg. Hancock was a totally lackluster candidate, and the Democratic platform differed from the Republican only in that it demanded substantial tariff reductions. Furthermore, what had promised to be an important development—the entry into the presidential race of the Greenback-Labor party—turned out to be of minor consequence. The Greenbackers had organized in 1878 and won more than 1,000,000 votes and elected fourteen members of Congress. The party nominated General James B. Weaver of Iowa for President in 1880. But the adoption of the Bland-Allison Act and substantial recovery from the Panic of 1873 deprived the new party of its issues and greatly reduced Weaver's potential vote.

The election of 1880 is often dismissed as unexciting. Actually it revealed four important, if not momentous, facts about American national politics at this juncture. First, the issues of Reconstruction were dead, and most Americans had reverted to traditional voting habits. Second, Republicans and Democrats were almost evenly balanced. Garfield won the election by an electoral vote of 214 to 155 for Hancock. But Garfield received a minority of the popular vote, and his plurality over Hancock was only about 40,000 out of nearly 9,000,000 votes cast for both men. This even balance in party strength would continue to be the most important fact of American political life until about 1900. Third, the return of white Southerners to power in their states had resulted in the creation of a "Solid South," at least in presidential elections, committed to the Democratic party. Fourth, Weaver's success in winning more than 300,000 votes revealed that agrarian discontent still survived, particularly in the Middle West. It was a warning that a third party might make a serious bid for power if farmers were struck by another economic depression.

The Assassination of Garfield Brings Arthur to Power

The election of Garfield brought no peace to the faction-torn G.O.P. Stalwarts such as Conkling had done much to secure his election, but Garfield refused to fulfill the promises that they claimed that he had made to them during the campaign. The President appointed Conkling's chief enemy, Blaine, as Secretary of State and removed the Collector of the Port of New York to make place for one of Blaine's friends. Garfield's new Postmaster General even went so far as to expose a nest of grafters in the Post Office Department. Conkling and Thomas C. Platt, stung by this "ingratitude," resigned from the Senate. They appealed, with Vice-President Arthur's help, to the legislature of New York for reelection. The legislature refused, and Conkling retired from politics and gave leadership to the New York Republican machine to Platt.

Factionalism had never been so high or bitter, and it soon culminated in tragedy. On July 2, 1881, Garfield was shot in the back in the Washington railroad station by a demented officeseeker, Charles J. Guiteau, who boasted, "I am a Stalwart and Arthur is President now." Garfield died on September 19, after lingering in great pain throughout the summer.

To the friends of good government, "Chet" Arthur's elevation to the presidency seemed to be the worst thing that could have happened. They feared that this former companion of bosses and spoilsmen might wink at graft and corruption. Yet Arthur, an extremely intelligent and scrupulously honest man, rose to the responsibilities of his great office and gave the country a vigorous and efficient administration.

The new President insisted on fair terms to China in an act of 1882 for the restriction of Chinese immigration to the United States. Thousands of Chinese had been brought over to work on the Central Pacific Railroad. By 1870, there were more than 70,000 Chinese in the country, nearly five sixths of them in California, where racial prejudice against the Chinese, stirred up by a powerful Workingmen's party, was intense. President Hayes had secured China's consent to the "regulation, limitation, or suspension" of Chinese immigration by the United States. Congress thereupon forbade the entrance of Chinese laborers into the country for twenty years. Arthur vetoed the bill because "suspending" immigration for twenty years was equal to forbidding it. He forced Congress to reduce the period to ten years. But at the close of the ten-year period, Congress renewed permanently the exclusion of the Chinese.

Arthur tried to prevent congressional raids on the Treasury by vetoing bills which appropriated huge sums for small harbors and unnavigable rivers. With congressional approval, he appointed a Tariff Commission in 1882 to investigate and recommend new rates. Congress reduced rates slightly in 1883 in response to its suggestions. Arthur also laid the foundation of the modern American navy by undertaking construction of steel cruisers to replace rotting wooden ships. Finally, he signed the act that has been called "the Magna Carta of Civil Service Reform."

Garfield's assassination shocked the American people into a realization of the desperate need for a cleanup in the civil service. Arthur took up the cause with vigor, and Congress responded by approving the measure introduced by Senator George H. Pendleton of Ohio. It provided for a bipartisan Civil Service Commission to classify the grades of the civil service and a merit system of competitive examinations to select candidates. The bill also forbade political assessments against federal employees and prevented removal from office for failure to make "voluntary" contributions to political campaigns.

Both houses of Congress passed the bill by large majorities, and Arthur signed it on January 16, 1883. But Arthur did not rest there. He appointed the secretary of the Civil Service Reform Association, Dorman B. Eaton, as chairman of the new Civil Service Commission and set up rules for the faithful execution of the act. Arthur immediately put about 15,000 federal employees into the classified service and continued his program of reform. By 1900, the professionalization of the federal civil service was substantially complete.

Foreign Policy at Low Ebb

American foreign policy during the eight years between Hayes' inauguration in 1877 and Arthur's retirement in 1885 was virtually nonexistent. The Secretaries of State during this period were capable, but the world scene was quiet. No serious threats to American security existed, no important objectives were sought, and, therefore, no significant policies were adopted.

The above would suffice to dispose of this subject had it not been for James G. Blaine, who served as Secretary of State from March to December 1881. Blaine was not merely a magnetic personality; he was that rare person in the State Department during the entire Gilded Age—a Secretary of State with an inventive mind and some understanding of the importance of foreign policy. He also was so energetic that he could not hold office without trying to accomplish something.

The announcement by a French company that it planned to construct an interoceanic canal across the Isthmus of Panama caused some mild alarm in the United States. It led Blaine to attempt, unsuccessfully, to persuade Great Britain to agree to the cancellation of the Clayton-Bulwer Treaty of 1850 which provided for joint Anglo-American construction of an interoceanic canal. Blaine wanted to clear the diplomatic road for unilateral American action at some future date.

Blaine's greatest interest was Latin America, where he hoped to promote stability, stimulate trade, obtain naval bases, and set under way construction of a canal across Central America. No sooner had he taken office than he tried to mediate both a border dispute between Mexico and Guatemala and the War of the Pacific between Chile and the allied forces of Bolivia and Peru. Both efforts failed; indeed, they earned considerable ill will for the United States throughout Latin America. But Blaine was not discouraged. He persuaded Garfield to approve the calling of a Pan-American conference, and invitations were sent. Acceptances were arriving when Garfield was assassinated, Arthur became President, and Blaine resigned. His successor in the State Department, Frederick Frelinghuysen promptly canceled the invitations upon President Arthur's advice.

Frelinghuysen was not totally inactive. He arranged for the United States to participate in the Berlin Conference of 1884 concerning the Congo, and signed a treaty with Nicaragua for possible construction of an interoceanic canal. But both actions, like all American foreign policies of this epoch, were of no great consequence. Indeed, the Senate refused to approve the treaty with Nicaragua.

3. THE DEMOCRATS RETURN TO POWER

The Campaign and Election of 1884

The way finally seemed clear in 1884 for Blaine to realize his great ambition for the presidency. Conkling, his bitter enemy, was out of politics. Platt, Republican leader of New York, announced that he would support the former Secretary of State. Arthur, unlike Hayes, was eager for renomination. He had southern delegates who were bound to him by patronage, but his support elsewhere was negligible, and the Republican national convention nominated Blaine for the presidency on the fourth ballot.

The smoothness of Blaine's nomination was deceptive. Signs of rougher times ahead appeared during the convention in the opposition of a sizable group of independent Republicans called Mugwumps. They did not like Blaine's shady railroad deals or his opposition to civil service reform. The Mugwumps had no candidate to put up against Blaine, but many of them worked to assure his defeat. These reformers included prominent public leaders, editors, educators, and clergymen in New York and New England, who denounced Blaine at conferences in Boston and New York. More important, the reformers invited the Democrats to nominate a candidate for whom citizens could vote without being ashamed of themselves.

The Democrats replied by nominating Grover Cleveland, Governor of New York. Cleveland was born in Caldwell, New Jersey, on March 18, 1837, the son of a Presbyterian minister of meager income. He had grown up in western New York and supported himself as best he could by tending a country store, teaching in a school for the blind, and acting as a clerk in a Buffalo lawyer's office. There he studied law, gained admission to the bar, entered politics, and slowly worked his way up to be elected Mayor of Buffalo in 1881. His administration of the office was so honest, able, and courageous that it brought him the Democratic nomination for governor the next year. Cleveland carried the state by a landslide. As governor, he was fearless in dealing with corrupt machine politicians.

The presidential campaign of 1884 was one of the bitterest and most disgraceful political contests in American history. Every nook and corner of the public and private lives of the candidates was searched for charges to smear their characters. The findings were then exposed in newspaper articles, pamphlets, cartoons, speeches, and sermons. Blaine was pictured as a scoundrel who had enriched himself by accepting bribes from railroad promoters and selling their worthless bonds to his friends. Cleveland was called a drunkard and a vulgar politician who had been transferred from a Buffalo saloon to the executive mansion at Albany. He also was accused of having fathered an illegitimate child, a charge he refused to deny, apparently because it was true.

The election on November 4 was so close that it turned on the key state of New York, which Cleveland won by 1,149 votes out of a total of 1,127,169. Blaine's followers claimed that dishonest count of returns in Brooklyn and on Long Island had cheated him out of the election, but Blaine accepted the result with good grace. He declared that the country's political fabric had been damaged enough by presidential elections during the past generation. The final returns gave 4,880,000 popular and 219 electoral votes to Cleveland, and 4,850,000 popular and 182 electoral votes to Blaine. Old General Benjamin F. Butler of Massachusetts, running as the last candidate of the Greenback-Labor party, received only 175,000 popular votes.

Cleveland as President

Grover Cleveland was not a dynamic leader, but he compensated for his lack of forcefulness by his flintlike honesty and dogged courage. He also was deeply devoted to political principles. He could have said, quite literally, that he would rather be right than President.

On the other hand, Cleveland ended his career as one of the worst failures in American political history. His fundamental trouble was his inability to grow into a national leader concerned about the problems and welfare of all the peo-

Grover Cleveland earned distinction as a President in his fight for tariff reform. He attacked high rates as "the vicious, inequitable, and illogical source of unnecessary taxation." (Library of Congress)

ple. He held firm to certain ideals. However, he had absorbed these ideals from the upper middle class of the East—honesty in government but no governmental support for special groups, even the underprivileged. Cleveland, as President, was totally unable to respond when southern and western elements in his party demanded legislation to help farmers and workers in the dismal 1890s. Another cause of Cleveland's failure was his rigid dogmatism that prevented him from recognizing that politics usually runs on compromise.

Cleveland's first term was a time of general prosperity, when social and economic discontent were running at low ebb. Hence there were no strong sectional tensions to challenge his leadership and threaten the unity of the Democratic party. During his first administration, Cleveland faced four great tasks: First, he had to demonstrate that the Democratic party, which had been out of national power since 1861, was capable of governing the country. Second, he had to preside over the return of Southerners, the largest element in his party, to national councils, without raising the specter of southern domination. Third, he had to complete the work of civil service and administrative reform begun by his predecessors. Fourth, he had to formulate a national program for the Democratic party. Cleveland attacked these problems vigorously, but with limited success.

Reunion, Reform, and Economy

Cleveland believed that the time had come to bury Civil War resentments forever. Moreover, as the leader of a party with its greatest strength in the South, he had no other choice but to welcome Southerners back into the federal government. It was, as they said, "the house of their fathers." Hence Cleveland appointed two Southerners to his cabinet and chose his diplomatic appointees equally from the North and the South. He later appointed one of his southern cabinet members, Lucius Quintus Cincinnatus Lamar of Mississippi, to the Supreme Court. For this policy of fairness to all sections, he was attacked as a friend of "rebels."

Cleveland wanted very much to extend the reform of the civil service. However, his party had been deprived of the spoils for a quarter of a century and thirsted for offices. Even so, Cleveland strongly supported the work of the Civil Service Commission.

Another problem was the burgeoning of expenditures for pensions to Union veterans. These payments had increased from $15 million in 1866 to $56 million in 1885; by 1885, nearly 350,000 names were on the pension rolls. When these names represented soldiers or sailors actually wounded or disabled in the war, the pensions were, as Cleveland said, "cheerfully approved by the people." He himself signed more pension bills than any previous President. But there was an immense amount of fraud in the system. More than 700 private bills for pensions to individuals were passed in Cleveland's administration, and he insisted on examining each one of them. Personal inspection of these bills led him to veto 233 of them. The Republicans said that he weighed the merits of the veterans "on an apothecary's scales."

Cleveland was also accused of "insulting" the army when he vetoed a Dependent Pension bill. This granted a pension of $12 a month to every indigent soldier and sailor who had served three months, regardless of whether or not he had suffered any injury or had even participated in a battle. Congress upheld his veto, however.

Cleveland's unpopularity with the officials of the Grand Army of the Republic, the powerful Union veterans' association, was increased by his "rebel flag order" of April 30, 1887. It instructed the Adjutant General to return to the southern states a number of flags that had been captured from Confederate units and had been lying in the attic of the War Office building. Cleveland was amazed at the storm of protest that arose over this act of charity to a beaten foe. On further thought, he realized that the disposal of the flags belonged to Congress, and not to the President. He therefore withdrew the order. More than twenty years later, a Republican Congress under Theodore Roosevelt voted unanimously to return the flags.

Cleveland's Fight for Tariff Reform

Cleveland wanted above all else to reform the revenue system. His purpose was "to relieve the people of unnecessary taxation . . . and prevent the accumulation of a surplus in the Treasury to tempt to extravagant waste." Because of thriving foreign trade and the high protective tariff, surplus funds were piling up in the Treasury at the rate of about $100 million a year. Hence, the tariff was the point of Cleveland's attack. It was the largest source of the government's income, since there was, as yet, no income tax; it was, he claimed, an outright subsidy to manufacturers.

Cleveland began his fight on the tariff in his first Annual Message to Congress, 1885, and he devoted his entire Annual Message of 1887 to the subject. Manufacturers replied that the high tariff made high wages possible. Cleveland insisted that it was more to the point that the high tariff made high prices possible. He showed that, according to the Census of 1880, only 15 per cent of workers were employed in protected industries. The other 85 per cent were burdened with artificial taxes on almost all the necessities of life, without any compensation by way of increased wages.

Not until July 1888 was Cleveland able to get the Mills bill for tariff reduction through the House. It reduced rates by 6 or 7 per cent and added new articles to the free list. However, the Republican Senate not only defeated the Mills bill but also adopted a new protective tariff bill of its own. This impasse between the two houses insured that the tariff would be the single major issue of the presidential campaign just ahead.

A Variety of Political Reforms

The presence of a Republican majority in the Senate throughout Cleveland's first term prevented the enactment of any Democratic program such as tariff reform. But a number of nonpartisan bills were passed, and most of them originated in the Republican Senate. The Presidential Succession Act of 1886 provided that, in the event of the death or disability of both the President and the Vice-President, the presidency should go to the members of the cabinet (State, Treasury, War, and so on) in order of the creation of their departments. Heretofore it had been the President *pro tempore* of the Senate and the Speaker of the House, who might both be of a different party from that of the President. An Electoral Count Act of 1887 made a repetition of the crisis of 1877 impossible.

It provided that, if more than one set of electoral returns were sent in, the set that had the seal of the governor of the state would be accepted. The Dawes Act of 1887 inaugurated a new federal policy toward the Indians, which, as we have seen, turned out to be a disaster for the Indians. In 1886, the remnants of the Tenure of Office Act of 1867 were repealed. Many persons regarded this as official vindication of President Andrew Johnson, who had been impeached for violating this very measure.

Ironically, Cleveland played very little part in the enactment of the one really consequential measure of his first term—the Interstate Commerce Act of 1887. The act was the result, first, of a growing popular demand for national regulation of railroads. The movement began in the states, but the failure of the midwestern Granger legislation of the 1870s (discussed in the next chapter) made it crystal clear that Congress alone was competent to deal with the problem. That conclusion was confirmed by the Supreme Court's decision in the Wabash case of 1886, which declared that state authorities had no jurisdiction over interstate rates and services. The Interstate Commerce Act was also the product of the desire of some railroad managers for an end to rate wars, rebating, and other competitive practices that kept rates unstable and reduced profits.

Senator Shelby M. Cullom, Republican of Illinois and chairman of a special committee on railroads, led the movement for national legislation. His committee traveled throughout the country in 1885 and heard the testimony of railroad officials, shippers, and farmers. The result of the committee's long labor was the Interstate Commerce Act, approved February 4, 1887. The measure, first of all, created an Interstate Commerce Commission of five members to enforce the law. The Act forbade special rates, rebates, and other favors to powerful shippers and stipulated that freight rates should be charged in proportion to distance, and should not be raised for short hauls on which no competition existed. It also outlawed pooling, or agreements between railroads to divide the profits of the total traffic among themselves according to a fixed ratio. Finally, rates had to be opened to public inspection; the railroads had to produce their schedules, waybills, and ledgers at the request of the commission; and violators of the law were made subject to heavy fines.

The huge majorities by which the Interstate Commerce bill was approved by both houses of Congress revealed that leaders in Washington were at last beginning to recognize the problems of the new industrial age. It came exactly one hundred years after the framing of the Constitution, and was the first act of Congress to attempt to regulate a major industry. It created the first of the many federal commissions and agencies that have since been established to deal with economic questions raised by the nation's changing and expanding economy.

4. HARRISON, THE ANTITRUST LAW, AND THE McKINLEY TARIFF

The Campaign of 1888

There was no secret why the Senate defied Cleveland and refused to approve the Mills bill for tariff reform. The national nominating conventions had been held while the bill was being debated in the House, and the Republicans had come out strongly in favor of a protective tariff. The issue would be decided at the polls, not in Congress.

Blaine might easily have had the nomination at the Republican convention in Chicago, but his poor health led him to decline the honor. At his suggestion, the convention selected General Benjamin Harrison of Indiana from among the dozen favorite sons who were seeking the nomination. Harrison was a former senator, an able lawyer, an honored veteran, and a grandson of the old Whig President, William Henry Harrison. The Democrats, who met in St. Louis, renominated Cleveland with cheers.

The campaign was waged almost wholly on the tariff issue. The Republicans concentrated their efforts on the two doubtful states of Indiana and New York, both of which had gone to Cleveland in 1884. These two states (the only ones which shifted their votes of four years earlier) were enough to give the victory to Harrison by an electoral vote of 233 to 168. Cleveland led in popular votes, however, by nearly 100,000, but only because of the disproportionate Democratic popular vote in the South.

A President Dominated by His Party

Benjamin Harrison took a very limited view of the presidential function. The Chief Executive, he thought, should carry out laws that Congress might enact, not give leadership to public opinion or to the lawmakers on Capitol Hill. Indeed, even in his own cabinet, Harrison was overshadowed by Blaine, whom he named as Secretary of State.

The most forceful among the Republican leaders in the Fifty-first Congress, which sat from 1889 to 1891, was the new Speaker of the House of Representatives, Thomas B. Reed of Maine. This big, jolly man, with a drawling voice and a gift for stinging sarcasm, was determined not to let the Democrats block the business of the House. When they refused to answer the roll call in order to prevent a quorum, Reed counted them present just the same. Even though they took refuge in corridors, cloakrooms, or the barber shop, he put them on the roll. When they made motions intended to delay business, he ruled them out of order. The Democrats, raging and storming, even rushed up to the Speaker's desk to shake their fists in his face and call him "czar" and "tyrant." Reed simply waited with a smile for the hubbub to cease and then went on with the business at hand.

The election of 1888 had given the Republicans narrow majorities in both houses of Congress. Tight party discipline enabled them to reverse some of Cleveland's policies and to enact new tariff legislation. In addition, bipartisan and sectional coalitions produced new laws to deal with two of the most important economic questions of the day.

Harrison and Congress were both bountiful toward veterans. Harrison's Commissioner of Pensions, "Corporal" James Tanner, welcomed applications, and shouted, "God help the surplus!" Moreover, Congress in 1890 revived the Dependent Pension bill to aid indigent ex-servicemen. As a result, applications for pensions rose from 36,000 in 1889 to 363,000 in 1891, while the outlays for pensions increased from $81 million to $135 million annually. This was a sum greater than the combined cost of the army and navy in any year of peace in the nineteenth century. Later, Republicans were unfairly accused of always having opposed the creation of a welfare state. However, it must be acknowledged that the early beneficiaries of charity under Republican administrations tended to be Republican voters.

The new Secretary of the Navy, Benjamin Tracy of New York, pushed the work begun under Arthur on construction of the new American navy. The United States had but three steel vessels in commission at the end of Cleveland's administration, and it was practically without modern coastal defenses. By the end of Harrison's term, nineteen new cruisers had been put into commission. Altogether, appropriations for the navy reached $30 million annually under Harrison. A a result, the United States advanced from twelfth to fifth place among the world's naval powers. At the same time, large sums were appropriated for coastal defenses, lighthouses, harbor improvements, and federal buildings.

The expenditures of the Fifty-first Congress totaled $1 billion. When the Democrats cried out against this "billion-dollar Congress," Speaker Reed replied that this was a "billion-dollar country." Indeed, the Eleventh Census (1890) revealed the astonishing prosperity of the United States at the end of its first century under the Constitution. Population was 62,500,000; national wealth, $65 billion. During the 1880s, the products of American mills and factories had increased in value from $5.3 billion to $9.3 billion, and the number of wage earners had risen from 2,700,000 to 4,300,000.

The Trust Problem and the Sherman Act

The most important problem which the Harrison administration faced was an overwhelming public demand for federal legislation to curb monopoly. Accompanying the formation of the trusts, there had been a rising public fear that these gigantic organizations were stifling competition, overcharging for their products, and preventing healthy economic expansion. Henry George had attacked the tremendous inequality of wealth in America in his very influential *Progress and Poverty* in 1879. Henry Demarest Lloyd's "The Story of a Great Monopoly" appeared two years later in *The Atlantic Monthly*; it was a scathing exposure of the methods of the Standard Oil Company. It was merely the first of what would later be called "muckraking" newspaper reports and articles.

Other investigations into the oil, sugar, and beef trusts added to the alarm. Owners of small and middle-sized business firms cried out for protection against allegedly unfair business practices on the part of big business. In response, twenty-seven states and territories had enacted legislation which outlawed trusts by 1890. But this did not quiet the public demand, since the huge firms, by incorporating as holding companies (see pp. 502–503) and changing their headquarters to more friendly states, made it obvious that the problem was national in scope.

The Republican party, which profited most by the campaign contributions of big business, was not eager to act against the trusts. However, popular agitation had reached such a high pitch by 1888 that both major parties incorporated antitrust planks in their platforms. When Harrison endorsed the demand in his Annual Message to Congress in 1889, Congress could not refuse to act.

The result was the adoption in July 1890 of the bipartisan Sherman Antitrust Act, one of the most important pieces of legislation in American history. It declared that "every contract, combination . . . or conspiracy in restraint of trade" was illegal and punished any violation of the law with a fine of $5,000 or a year's imprisonment. Moreover, it awarded triple damages to successful claimants. The language of the Sherman Act was sweeping yet clear, but it remained a dead letter for the next ten or twelve years, mainly because Harrison and his two successors did not really try to enforce it. Not until early in the twentieth century did Theodore Roosevelt revive the Sherman Act and make it a powerful weapon against monopoly.

The McKinley Tariff and the Sherman Silver Purchase Act

The Republicans passed the Sherman Antitrust Act in order to pacify public opinion. But the McKinley Tariff Act, adopted in the same year, was legislation much more to the G.O.P.'s liking. In April 1890, William McKinley of Ohio, Chairman of the House Ways and Means Committee, introduced a bill increasing duties on almost every import that competed with American products. It covered food, clothing, furniture, carpets, fuel, tools, kitchenware, thread, and hundreds of other items. Articles of necessity not produced at home, such as tea, coffee, spices, and drugs, were admitted free. Sugar was also put on the free list, but a bounty of two cents a pound was given to domestic producers of raw sugar in order to enable them to compete with lower cost sugar from Cuba and Hawaii. McKinley boasted that his bill, which passed the House on May 21, 1890, was "protective in every paragraph and American in every line and word."

Although the McKinley bill had fairly smooth sailing in the lower house, it was a different story when the measure reached the Senate. The first threat came from the western senators. North Dakota, South Dakota, Montana, and Washington had been admitted to the Union in November 1889. Wyoming and Idaho were added the next year. These new states were expected to contribute twelve senators and at least six representatives to the slim Republican majority in Congress and add eighteen Republican electoral votes in the next presidential election. But the newcomers brought embarrassment as well as strength to the G.O.P. They were silver-mining states, and their senators demanded something for silver before they would support the McKinley tariff.

Next, southern senators threatened to ally themselves with Westerners to kill the McKinley bill. They wanted to head off a Republican attempt to protect black voters in the southern states. On July 2, 1890, the House of Representatives passed a federal election bill. It provided that, on the application of 500 voters in any district, supervisors from Washington should have the right to inspect and verify the votes cast in a federal election. Southerners immediately charged that the purpose of what they scornfully called "the Force bill" was to restore "Negro rule" in their region. When the southern senators joined the Westerners to block the McKinley bill, the Republicans dropped the federal election bill.

The deadlock continued because the western silver senators would not vote for the tariff until their demands for free coinage of silver at the ration of sixteen to one had been satisfied. Since the adoption of the Bland-Allison Act of 1878, the Treasury had been purchasing silver at the rate of $2 million a month. Yet the price of the metal had steadily declined, lagely because of immense production from the recently opened mines, although the demonetization of silver by the United States, Germany, and other nations also contributed to the price decline. American silver production increased from 35,000,000 ounces in 1878 to 54,500,000 ounces in 1890. Nevertheless, the drive for the free coinage of silver at the ratio of sixteen to one continued. The Senate, in June 1890, actually passed a bill for free coinage. The House killed it only because Speaker Reed disapproved of the measure.

Although Republicans wanted very much to avoid free silver, they were even more eager to find the votes necessary to pass the McKinley bill. Therefore eastern Republicans reached a compromise with western senators which resulted in the Sherman Silver Purchase Act, approved July 4, 1890. It required the Treasury to purchase 4,500,000 ounces of silver a month at prevailing market prices—more than twice the amount bought under the Bland-Allison Act. In addition, the Sherman Silver Purchase Act provided for the issuance of a new currency—silver certificates—to pay for the silver purchased. The Sherman Silver Purchase Act was enough to win western votes for the McKinley Tariff bill. The Senate approved the latter measure, and President Harrison signed it on October 1, 1890, only thirty-five days before the mid-term elections.

The Democratic Landslide of 1890

Democrats had a heyday during the mid-term campaign of 1890. They pointed to the extravagance of the billion-dollar Congress, with its unusual pension bills and coastal defense measures, and the "tyranny" of "Czar" Reed. Democrats had the most fun, however, attacking the McKinley tariff. While the bill was being debated in the Senate, the Democrats were already issuing gloomy predictions that ruin would overtake the country if the bill was adopted. After its passage, Democratic politicians sent peddlers into rural districts to sell pots and pans to housewives at high prices. They asserted that these prices were required by the new tariff. Women shoppers in the stores, complained "Czar" Reed, "heard the clerks behind the counter explain how this article or that would not be sold hereafter at the former price, because of the McKinley bill." Then they went home and told their husbands, and their stories had a tremendous effect at the ballot boxes.

The returns in the congressional elections on November 6, 1890, were a landslide against the G.O.P. The Democrats returned 235 members to the House; the Republicans, only eighty-eight. McKinley himself, after serving seven terms in the House, went down to defeat. But, because most Republican senators were not up for reelection in 1890, the Republicans retained control of the Senate by a small margin. Thus Congress was deadlocked again, and no significant legislation came out of that body during the next two years.

5. EXPANDING HORIZONS, 1888–1893

An Old Secretary of State in a New Situation

James G. Blaine returned to the cabinet as Secretary of State in 1889 an older and less energetic man than he had been during his brief tenure eight years before. Blaine's first experience in this office had been frustrating and disappointing because of presidential and public apathy about foreign policy. But great changes had occurred in the eight intervening years. The United States had emerged as the chief industrial power in the world. A modern navy was under way. An increasing number of Americans were beginning to look outward and to believe that the United States should follow Europe in seeking new territories and markets. What one historian has called a new paradigm — a whole new way of looking at the world and the role that the United States should play in it — was coming into being. Thus Blaine, still a bundle of energy when compared with other Secretaries of State during this period, found much wider support for aggressive foreign policies during his second tenure than during his first. In Blaine's sometimes strident and not always wise policies we can see a young great power trying to make its voice heard in the councils of the world.

One of Blaine's first problems was a dispute with Great Britain over the seal fisheries in Bering Sea. The United States claimed that the sea, which was almost entirely enclosed by Alaska and the Aleutian Islands, was a *mare clausum* (closed sea), and hence should be under the jurisdiction of the United States, like Chesapeake Bay, for example. The British claimed that Bering Sea was a "high sea," over which American authority extended only to the ordinary three-mile limit from shore.

The seals were being rapidly exterminated by hunters from British Columbia. However, attempts to settle the question by an international conference failed through the opposition of the Canadian government. Blaine kept up a spirited correspondence on the subject with Lord Salisbury, the British Prime Minister and Foreign Secretary. Salisbury was equally insistent on not recognizing American rights either to police Bering Sea or to dictate to Great Britain the proper methods of seal hunting. After three years of argument and protest, the American government agreed on February 29, 1892, to submit the question to arbitration. The tribunal that met at Paris in the next year decided against the United States. Bering Sea was declared to be the high sea, beyond American jurisdiction, and the United States was assessed $473,000 damages for illegal seizures of Canadian vessels.

Blaine was more successful in his next effort — an attempt to forge a closer understanding between the United States and Latin America. Actually, Cleveland, with congressional approval, had issued the invitations to a Pan-American Conference in Washington. But Blaine was the dominant figure when the conference opened on October 2, 1889. He worked hard for a Pan-American customs union and arbitration treaty, but failed. However, he did succeed in persuading the delegates to create the Pan American Union to promote hemispheric unity and cooperation. Great international undertakings require many years for their realization. So it was with Blaine's projects for Pan-American cooperation. The Secretary laid the foundations for what would eventually become one of the more important regional organizations in modern history.

Quarrels and Crises

Blaine also was interested in extending American influence in the Pacific. During his first tenure in the State Department, he had taken steps to keep Great Britain from controlling the Hawaiian Islands. These he declared to be "a part of the American system." Now Blaine came into conflict with the German Chancellor, Prince Otto von Bismarck, over control of the Samoan Islands.

During strife between rival Samoan chieftains, the German consul raised his flag over Apia, and German sailors trampled the American flag. Then British, American, and German warships steamed into the harbor of Apia with their decks cleared for action. A battle appeared certain until Bismarck, who had no desire whatever to go to war with the United States, suggested that the three powers confer in Berlin. A terrific hurricane, which struck the Samoan Islands on March 16, 1889, capsized or drove on the coral reefs every warship in the area except one British cruiser.

Sobered by this disaster, American, British, and German delegates met at Berlin on April 29, 1889, and agreed to a joint protectorate over the entire Samoan archipelago. The agreement lasted during ten years of constant bickering. Great Britain withdrew from Samoa in 1899, in return for concessions in Africa, and the islands were divided between Germany and the United States. After the First World War, the German portion of the islands was awarded to New Zealand.

A nasty dispute with Italy followed in the spring of 1891. Eleven Italians were taken by a mob from the city jail in New Orleans and lynched for the alleged murder of the chief of police, who had been active in overcoming the local Mafia organization. The Italian government demanded that United States authorities punish the lynchers. Blaine sharply replied that, in the American federal system, the state, not the federal, authorities dealt with criminal cases. The Italian government recalled its Minister, and Blaine ordered the American Minister in Rome to come home. Still, diplomatic relations were not broken, and President Harrison adopted a conciliatory tone. He expressed his regret for the "deplorable incident." Further investigation revealed that only three of the murdered men were Italian citizens. Congress thereupon appropriated $25 thousand for the families of the Italian victims. The Italian government accepted these damages with thanks, and the incident was closed.

Much more serious was a quarrel with Chile, which nearly led to war. That country was torn in 1891 by a civil war between factions led by its President and Congress. The American Minister to Chile, Patrick Egan, a Blaine appointee, tactlessly took sides in the Chilean struggle, and, as further evidence of his poor judgment, supported the losers—the presidential faction. The United States further aroused Chileans by detaining a rebel ship that purchased arms in California and by turning it over to the loyalists. On October 16, 1891, after the rebels had finally triumphed, Chileans attacked a party of American sailors on shore leave from the cruiser *Baltimore* in a saloon in Valparaiso. The attackers killed two of the sailors and severely wounded eighteen others. The Chilean government not only refused to heed demands for an apology; it also accused the American sailors of starting the riot.

Blaine, who had been trying to promote Pan-American friendship, knew what the reaction in South America would be if the controversy was not handled carefully. He tried, unsuccessfully, to restrain Harrison. Prodded by jingoist newspapers and politicians (including young Theodore Roosevelt, who called for war), the President himself wrote an ultimatum that was delivered to the Chilean government over Blaine's signature on January 21, 1892. Harrison sent a special message to Congress four days later. It almost invited a declaration of war against Chile, a nation with one twentieth the population of the United States, and an especially weak army and navy. A squadron of eight cruisers stood ready in the Pacific. Fortunately, Chile's government had the good sense to yield quickly to the overwhelming military force that confronted the country. It apologized and paid an indemnity of $75 thousand to the families of the dead sailors and to the wounded sailors themselves. It would be many years, however, before Latin Americans would listen seriously again to announcements that the United States wanted friendlier relations with other nations in the hemisphere.

SUGGESTED READINGS

The best general surveys of this period are Morton Keller, *Affairs of State: Public Life in Late Nineteenth Century America* (1977); John A. Garraty, *The New Commonwealth, 1877–1890* (1969); and H. Wayne Morgan, *From Hayes to McKinley, 1877–1896* (1969). Matthew Josephson, *The Politicos, 1865–1896* (1963), is not kind to the politicians of the Gilded Age and should be balanced by reading David J. Rothman, *Politics and Power: The United States Senate, 1869–1901* (1966), and Robert D. Marcus, *Grand Old Party: Political Structure in the Gilded Age, 1880–1896* (1971). Two important regional studies are C. Vann Woodward, *Origins of the New South, 1877–1913* (1951), and Horace S. Merrill, *Bourbon Democracy of the Middle West, 1865–1896* (1953). On civil-service reform, see Ari Hogenboom, *Fighting the Spoilsmen* (1961). Leonard D. White, *The Republican Era: 1869–1901* (1965), is good on administration, but the classic works on American politics during the Gilded Age are Woodrow Wilson,

Congressional Government (1885, many later edns.), and James Bryce, *The American Commonwealth*, 2 vols. (1895). For a contemporary denunciation of the politics of the period, see Mark Twain and Charles Dudley Warner, *The Gilded Age* (1873).

Excellent studies of the Mugwump reformers are John G. Sproat, *"The Best Men,"* already cited, and Geoffrey Blodgett, *The Gentle Reformers: Massachusetts Democrats in the Cleveland Era* (1966).

Robert L. Beisner, *From the Old Diplomacy · to the New, 1865–1900* (1975), is the best survey of the diplomatic history of the period. But see also Walter LeFeber, *The New Empire: An Interpretation of American Expansion, 1860–1898* (1963). The following biographies are good for both the politics and diplomacy of the Gilded Age: R. G. Caldwell, *James A. Garfield: Party Chieftain* (1931); Allan Nevins, *Grover Cleveland: A Study in Courage* (1932); and Harry J. Sievers, *Benjamin Harrison*, 3 vols. (1952–1968).

CHAPTER 20
POLITICAL UPHEAVALS
OF THE 1890s

1. THE AGRARIAN REVOLT

Shaking the Foundations

From our vantage point in the late twentieth century, it is difficult to comprehend how seriously Americans of the late nineteenth century took their politics. Although voting was restricted largely to white males, within that segment of the population participation in the political process far surpassed modern levels. Voter turnout sometimes exceeded 80 per cent of the eligible voters. Personal identification with a political party was, for many Americans, a central means of self-understanding, almost as important as identification with one's family, community, and ethnic group. One old-line Alabama Democrat exaggerated, but did not completely distort, this sentiment when he wrote of his own son, a convert to the new Populist party: "I had rather see my son dead and in his grave than for him to become a Populist."

In this superheated political climate, challenges to the prevailing party system could set off shocks in society as a whole and create the impression that the foundations of civilization were crumbling. During the 1890s, two distinct but interrelated challenges sent just such shock waves through American society. First, the decades-old struggles of farmers for economic and political well-being culminated in the meteoric rise and fall of the Populist party. Second, the rough equilibrium that had existed between Democrats and Republicans for forty years collapsed in a major realignment of the two-party system. This realignment left

Republicans dominant most of the time until the 1930s and redefined the nature of mass participation in the political process.

Causes of the Farmers' Revolt

A storm was brewing in the South and West in the late 1880s because of depressed conditions. Farmers assembled in county courthouses and rural schools and churches to discuss common problems and means to solve them. Their spokesmen charged that railroad managers, bankers, and businessmen had conspired to keep farmers' costs high and farm prices low. Farm leaders accused both the Republican and Democratic parties of serving as agents of Wall Street. They demanded that the federal government pay attention to agrarian distress.

A complex set of economic problems set off the agrarian revolt. Fundamentally, almost every group involved — farmers, railroad men, factory workers, and even most industrialists — were caught in a system of fierce international competition that drove almost all prices, including over-all railroad rates, steadily downward from about 1867 to 1897. At the same time that the American West was being opened up after the Civil War, railroads were built into rich cotton, grain, and beef-producing areas around the world — from the Ukraine, Prussia, and Egypt to Canada, Argentina, and Australia. Ocean and rail rates dropped worldwide, and inexpensive farm products from all these areas flooded the channels of international trade. As a result, prices of American agricultural products sank rapidly. The price of wheat, for example, declined from about 90 cents a bushel in 1883 to 68 cents in 1886. Cotton, which averaged about 15 cents a pound in the early 1870s, fell to 11 cents a pound in 1881, and to about 7 cents in 1891. Prices fell close to and even below the average cost of production.

Everywhere, farmers with debts found them difficult to pay. Western farmers had borrowed money to expand production during the lush Civil War period. In the subsequent era of declining prices, a very high proportion were obliged to increase their indebtedness. Mortgages on farm property rose from $343 million to $586 million during the decade 1880–1890, despite the fact that land values in the South, especially, dropped so low that mortgage money became all but impossible to obtain. By the late nineties, 60 per cent of the farms in Kansas were mortgaged, 47 per cent in Iowa, 48 per cent in Michigan. In most of the Great Plains area, where second and third mortgages were common, there were more mortgages than farms in 1890. In the South, where long-term mortgages were less common, the crop-lien system bound many farm owners and most tenants to an annual cycle of crippling indebtedness. Merchants, planters, and bankers advanced supplies in return for a lien on the crop to be produced by the farmer. Effective annual interest rates under this system ran to 25 per cent or higher, and farmers had to concentrate their efforts on a cash crop, usually cotton. Within the crop year, prices were further depressed by the seasonal glut on the market at harvest time — precisely the time that tenants were forced to pay off their loans.

In the West, even the weather seemed to conspire against farmers during this troubled period. Exceptionally abundant rain in the middle 1880s tempted farmers to move westward into the Great Plains; they compensated for low prices by increasing production on cheap land. But high hopes were blasted and the entire Plains area from the Dakotas to Texas was plunged into depression and despair by a series of droughts that began in the summer of 1886. Thousands abandoned farms in western Kansas and Nebraska, and settlers who returned eastward decorated their wagons with slogans like "In God we trusted, in Kansas we busted." Eastern bankers and mortgage lenders, who had financed much of the western boom, began to foreclose right and left, although they had neither use nor purchasers for the drought-stricken land.

With some justification, farmers believed that political leaders, both in state capitals and in Washington, neglected agricultural interests and grossly favored bankers, railroad promoters, and industrialists. Farm spokesmen charged that, while farmers were forgotten, urban businessmen received subsidies, loans from government-chartered banks, lower railroad freight rates, and tariff protection. Not a little of the discontent was the normal resentment of a group once considered the pride of the republic. Farmers (like the prefactory craftsmen), once economically self-sufficient, had now lost both economic independence and political power to the new business classes.

The Farmers First Organize for Protest: The Grange

The farmers' movement that culminated in the organization of the Populist party in 1892 had behind it a twenty-year history which generated a culture of rural protest. Intellectually, the Populist party owed a great debt to the greenback, antimonopoly, and cooperative traditions which had enlivened much of the early labor movement (see Chapters 17 and 18). As an institution, however, the Populist party grew out of a series of farmer organizations which began with the Patrons of Husbandry, commonly known as the Grange. The Grange was organized in 1867 by Oliver H. Kelley, a clerk in the Department of Agriculture, to promote agricultural education and social fellowship among farmers. Farmers gathered in neighborhood Granges to listen to lectures on scientific farming and to enjoy each other's company. As part of their program of self-help, the Grangers established cooperative stores and marketing agencies, usually operated on the English Rochdale Plan, which required cash payment for goods. This requirement limited access to Grange cooperatives to farmers who were already relatively well off. With this restriction, Grange organizers made little headway among the poorest farmers and tenants. However, by 1875 the Grange had spread across the Midwest and South and claimed over 500,000 members.

Where farmers banded together for mutual advancement, the conversation inevitably turned to politics. The sharp decline of farm prices, which began with the Panic of 1873, coupled with discriminatory freight rates and other problems, led Grangers to demand governmental assistance. Like labor unions in the same era, they entered politics both as an interest group within the two major parties and as participants in splinter parties. Beginning in Illinois in 1870, the Grangers gained substantial influence in several midwestern and southern state legislatures. They instituted state regulation of railroads, promoted state agricultural colleges, and in various other ways fostered the interests of agriculturalists.

The failure of many Grange cooperatives in the mid-1870s, coupled with the internal dissension which accompanied political activism in the Grange, led to a sharp decline in membership. The Grange did articulate demands for needed reforms, and some of these were taken over by subsequent protest organizations. But the Grange lacked the mass support needed to translate demands into legislation on the federal level.

The Farmers' Alliance Movement

The story of organized agrarian protest in the late 1880s and early 1890s resembles the story of the Granger movement in some respects, except that the cooperative program was more ambitious, the organizational base more inclusive, and the demand for political action more insistent. The successor to the Grange—the Farmers' Alliance, which swept across the southern and Plains states in the late 1880s, grew out of several community-based farm organizations in the Southwest, particularly one established in frontier Lampasas County, Texas, in 1877.

Through mergers and an aggressive organizing campaign, which began in 1886, the Texas-based Alliance's membership grew to 1,500,000 by 1890. Most of them lived in the South and on the Great Plains, but the organization was active in over thirty states from New York to California. Membership in this, the so-called Southern Farmers' Alliance, was restricted to whites, but the organization maintained a loose affiliation with a parallel black organization, the Colored Farmers' National Alliance. Another Farmers' Alliance was established in Chicago in 1880 and has been credited with mobilizing midwestern agrarian radicals. In fact, the Chicago-based group flourished only briefly in

In this print from Harper's Weekly (1873), the Grange is seen awakening the sleepers to the greatest monopoly of the age. Determined to arouse agrarians from apathy to their own interests, the Grangers stressed the urgency of political action to curb monopolistic practices of the railroads. (Historical Pictures Service, Chicago)

the early 1880s and was almost moribund when the Southern Alliance moved in to organize farmers in Kansas and the Dakotas in 1887.

The Farmers' Alliance, like the Grange and the Knights of Labor, was a secret fraternal organization. It brought isolated farm families together in neighborhood assemblies (called suballiances) and in larger gatherings, including churchlike camp meetings. The local alliance functioned as a kind of community of the true believers. Here members could reaffirm their commitment to a common set of values and work to translate them into specific economic and political programs.

The program which enabled the Alliance to mobilize masses of southern and midwestern farmers was one of economic cooperation. Alliance cooperatives ranged from local schemes to "bulk" produce for sale to ambitious statewide purchasing and marketing exchanges. Perhaps the Alliance's most successful cooperative effort was a campaign in 1889 to break the "jute bagging trust" (the National Cordage Company), which had monopolized the manufacturing of binders' twine and cotton bale wrappers made from jute. What made the new Alliance cooperatives different from most Granger ventures was that they attempted to pool the credit resources of the members, and thus allowed cash-poor farmers and tenants to participate. Partially because of this feature, the people attracted to the Alliance represented more of a cross section of rural communities than had the Grange, although the poorest tenants were still underrepresented, and the movement was divided along racial lines in the South.

Despite some well-publicized individual successes, the Alliance's cooperatives could not overcome the harsh realities of the crop-lien and agricultural marketing systems. But the struggle against these systems raised the expectations of countless farmers, and the failure of the cooperatives radicalized many of them.

The Alliance in Politics

From its inception, the Farmers' Alliance was involved in politics as well as in cooperative enterprises. Indeed, the political, economic, and social functions of the organization were closely interrelated. In 1886, the Texas Alliance established a remarkably ambitious cooperative network and also adopted a platform of political demands which would, with some additions, form the ideological basis of Alliance and Populist political activism. The seventeen-point "Cleburne Demands" grew out of the greenbacker and cooperative movements of the 1870s, as well as out of the practical experiences of Texas farmers and alliancemen. Those experiences included, not only organization of cooperatives, but also battles with land syndicates and cooperation with the Knights of Labor in their strike against Jay Gould's southwestern railroad system. The demands included legal recognition of trade unions and producer cooperatives, governmental action to prevent monopolization of land by corporate syndicates, state and federal regulation of railroads, and reform of the nation's banking and currency systems. The latter demand concerning currency included coinage of both silver and gold and the issuance of greenbacks on a scale that would fluctuate with the needs of the economy.

Like the Grangers and the political activists within the early labor movement, alliancemen faced a choice about how to achieve their demands. Should they work within the two major parties, or should they take the route of political insurgency and form a new party? Grass-roots insurgency had cropped up throughout the rural South and West during the 1880s, but the Alliance at first largely avoided this approach. In the Plains states, farmers worked through the dominant Republican party, while in the South most alliancemen pressed their demands upon the reigning Democratic party. However, in 1890, southern and western alliancemen parted company in their political strategies. Alliancemen in Kansas and the Dakotas, rebuffed by entrenched Republican politicians, formed independent state parties. Most southern white alliancemen still shrank from deserting the Democratic party and concentrated their efforts on forcing Democratic nominees to endorse the Alliance demands. Both southern and western strategies seemed to work in 1890, for, by one means or another, farm protesters captured several state legislatures and governorships in the South and West, and three senators and some fifty congressmen elected that year were committed to support the Alliance's demands.

Despite these apparent successes in the South, events soon propelled many alliancemen toward insurgency in league with their western counterparts. Alliance cooperatives were beginning to go under by 1890–1891, and their failure convinced many persons that only governmental intervention in the economy could save the American farmer. Also, by that time the Alliance's political demands had become even more radicalized, and a sharp ideological line was being drawn between farm spokesmen and the two major parties. Of particular importance for southern alliancemen was the organization's endorsement of the subtreasury plan, which became both an economic panacea and a political litmus test for the Alliance. The subtreasury plan, brainchild of the Texas Alliance leader, Charles Wesley Macune, called for the federal government to establish commodity storage facilities in all counties which produced at least $500 thousand worth of agricultural products. The farmer could store his nonperishable crops in these warehouses and receive, in return, legal tender notes equal to 80 per cent of the value of the crops deposited.

When the subtreasury plan was put forth, one Alliance newspaper described it under the banner headline: "EUREKA! Key to the Solution of the Industrial Problem of the Age." To such supporters, the subtreasury plan seemed able to achieve for farmers precisely the benefits which the cooperatives had been unable to deliver, and also to reform the nation's currency system. It would create a flexible currency (the legal tender notes), which would expand to meet the increased seasonal demand for money at harvest time. It would also extend credit to farmers at low rates (2 per cent), based on the value of their stored crops. This would enable them to buy their year's supplies with cash, while they held their crop in storage in anticipation of higher prices. In short, promoters of the plan believed that it would break the stranglehold of bankers and merchants upon the countryside.

Most professional politicians saw the issue differently. To them, the subtreasury plan was a radical and unconstitutional departure from traditional governmental economic policy. Furthermore, it was a direct threat to party loyalty. By demanding that politicians either endorse what one of them called "that iniquitous subtreasury bill," or face reprisal at election time, the Alliance was planting the seeds of mass defection from the "party of the fathers."

Not surprisingly, most professional politicians either waffled on the subtreasury issue or openly opposed it. In the South, the result of this confrontation over the subtreasury was a split in the Alliance. Many members absolutely balked at political insurgency, but a large and vociferous faction of the Alliance concluded that enactment of the subtreasury and other demands was essential and could come only through the creation of a third party.

Formation of the People's (Populist) Party

The first step toward the creation of a new party to unite western and southern farmers came at a meeting in Cincinnati in May 1891. Veteran Alliance insurgents from the Plains states and Texas dominated the meeting. They were joined by a sprinkling of southern alliancemen and also by members of the Knights of Labor, greenbackers, and others. Together, they called for a national convention of a new People's party to meet the following year in Omaha.

By the time that the Omaha convention was gaveled to order in July 1892, the force of events and the maneuvering of radical Alliance leaders had prepared a substantial number of southern alliancemen to join with western farmers in an act of political insurgency. The platform that they adopted was a reiteration of Alliance demands developed over the past six years. The preamble to the platform, written by Ignatius Donnelly of Minnesota, sounded very much like Karl Marx's description of the last stages of capitalism. It declared:

We meet in the midst of a nation brought to the verge of moral, political, and material ruin. Corruption dominates the ballot-box, the Legislatures, the Congress, and touches even the ermine of the bench. . . . Business [is] prostrated, homes [are] covered with mortgages, labor [is] impoverished, and the land [is] concentrating in the hands of capitalists. . . . The fruits of the toil of millions are boldly stolen to build up colossal fortunes for a few. . . . We have witnessed for more than a quarter of a century the struggles of the two great political parties for power and plunder. . . . Neither do they now promise us any substantial reform. . . . They propose to sacrifice our homes, lives, and children on the altar of mammon.

The platform itself, which concentrated on the issues of transportation, land, and monetary policy, may seem in retrospect to be tame in comparison to Donnelly's rhetoric. However, it reflected a vision of what America should be which was sharply at odds with the views of the two major parties. The Populists demanded free coinage of silver at a ratio of sixteen to one, the subtreasury system, abolition of National Bank notes and the issuance by the federal Treasury of abundant legal tender currency, a graduated income tax, governmental ownership of railroads, telegraphs, and telephones, return to the government of unused lands granted to the railroads, restriction of immigration, the eight-hour day for labor, postal savings banks, and election of United States senators by popular vote.

The Populists planned to use the presidential election of 1892 to launch their party into national politics. Their most likely choice for a nominee had been Leonidas L. Polk of North Carolina, president of the National Farmers' Alliance, but Polk died only weeks before the Omaha convention. The party named as its standard-bearer James B. Weaver of Iowa, a former Union general and presidential candidate of the Greenback-Labor party in 1880. As his vice-presidential running mate, the Populists chose a former Confederate general,

James G. Field of Virginia. Thus the People's party set out to unite the North and the South, blacks and whites, and the city and countryside in a crusade to reshape the United States.

2. GROVER CLEVELAND AND THE PERILS OF THE PRESIDENCY

Political Parties and the Clash of Cultures

The party system which the Populists sought to overturn was dominated by Democrats and Republicans, as it had been since the 1860s. In the nation as a whole, the strength of the two parties was remarkably even. Although the Republicans won all but two presidential elections between 1876 and 1892, *never* did they win a majority of the popular vote, and only once did they win a plurality! In Congress, Democrats controlled the House of Representatives in seven out of eight terms but could organize the Senate only twice.

Despite the close over-all balance between the two parties, support for each tended to cluster around certain regional and cultural poles. The regional segregation of the two parties was a legacy of the Civil War and Reconstruction. Republicans remained strongest in the Midwest and Northeast, where the G.O.P. had begun as the party of "Free Soil, Free Labor, and Free Men." The Democratic party's strength lay with white Southerners and among immigrants and the working classes of the northern cities. The regional identity of the two parties was so clear-cut that a handful of "swing" states almost always determined the outcome of presidential elections between 1880 and 1892. New York and Indiana were crucial; New Jersey, Connecticut, and Illinois were also considered to be pivotal states. Not surprisingly, presidential and vice-presidential timber seemed to grow tallest in these states during the Gilded Age.

In addition to these sectional cleavages, party loyalties also followed ethnic and religious lines. Such divisions were of course never hard and fast, but in the Midwest and Northeast the Republican party continued to attract many old-stock evangelical Protestants. They tended to favor prohibition of alcoholic beverages and the rooting out of "un-American" cultures. In their minds, the business of government included the active promotion of morality and righteousness — as they defined those terms. In those same areas of the country, the Democratic party attracted many voters of recent immigrant stock, who tended to be Roman Catholics, members of other liturgical Christian communions, and Jews. For them, the suppression of the corner saloon or beer garden and threats to non-Protestant religions and immigrant cultures were denials of individual freedom. This kind of ethnocultural cleavage, though occasionally evident in presidential elections, was most pronounced at the community level. Here the battles over prohibition, public education, and other culturally related issues were waged.

The major parties were connected, though never completely, with sectional, religious, and ethnic subcultures, and, on occasion, with differing moral senses of what government's role in the economy ought to be. Thus distinguishable political cultures — sets of values and ideas — underlay the particularities of partisan politics. This helped to give meaning to the everyday existence of many Americans. The strength and persistence of these conflicting political cultures help to explain both the intensity of political participation and the long-term stability of the two parties in the late nineteenth century.

This equilibrium of sectional and cultural politics was upset in the 1890s. The most visible source of the disruption was the "movement culture" of Populism — ideally, a way of looking at the world which rejected sectional and ethnic divisions in favor of a broadly defined class consciousness. More fundamentally, the party system proved incapable of coping with the economic traumas of industrialization and commercial agriculture. The vicissitudes of the international market system compounded these traumas. Both the Populist challenge and the underlying problems of an industrializing nation came to a climax during the grim depression which began in 1893. However, the breakup of the old party system actually began in 1892.

The Election of 1892

The two major parties nominated familiar figures for President in 1892. The Republicans renominated the incumbent, Benjamin Harrison, in spite of a feeble attempt to stampede the convention in favor of James G. Blaine. The Democrats named Grover Cleveland for the third successive time. Machine politicians, under the leadership of Governor David B. Hill of New York, tried to prevent Cleveland's nomination, but he was so popular with the rank and file of the party that he won easily on the first ballot.

The campaign of 1892 would have been a dull affair, except for the effort by the Populists to build their party and make a good showing. Cleveland came out for sound money, but he made his fight mainly against the McKinley Tariff Act. Harrison straddled the money question and defended protection as a boon to labor. His claims that workers were prosperous and happy were undercut by a violent and bloody strike against Carnegie's Homestead plant in the middle of the campaign.

However, the main issue seems to have been the personalities of the candidates. Cleveland was not glamorous, but he was positively exciting in comparison to the icy Harrison. Voters eager for a change not only elected Cleveland by a large plurality; they also returned Democratic majorities to both houses of Congress for the first time in over a decade.

Weaver polled slightly over 1,000,000 votes (the largest number for a new party since 1856) and carried Colorado, Kansas, Nevada, and Idaho, with twenty-two electoral votes. However, in several western states the strong Populist showing was aided by "fusion" with the Democrats. Organized silver-mining interests played a major role in Populist campaigns in the mountain states of the West. No state east of the Mississippi and north of the Ohio River gave Weaver as much as 5 per cent of its vote — a portent for the Populists' dream to unite the industrial workers of the East with the farmers of the South and West.

In only one southern state — Alabama — did Weaver receive more than 25 per cent of the votes in the official tally. In the South, Weaver was vulnerable to the attacks of Confederate flag-waving Democrats, and the Populists were victimized both by widespread election fraud and by the beginnings of systematic disfranchisement of blacks and poor whites. Southern Populists also suffered from divisions within the farmers' movement. Whereas the Alliance had mobilized a huge cross section of rural Southerners, the call for alliancemen to foresake traditional party loyalties often fell on deaf ears. In only five southern states did Weaver's vote amount to more than one half of the Alliance's potential voting strength.

Even so the Populist party had established itself as a force to be reckoned with in the South and West. The new party elected three senators and eleven members of the House of Representatives. Moreover, it more than held its own in the mid-term congressional elections of 1894, when the Republicans once more regained control of the House. In 1894, few Democrats and Republicans would have dared to hope that the Populist movement had peaked. But it had.

The Panic of 1893

Like Martin Van Buren and Herbert Hoover, Grover Cleveland had the bad luck to be in the White House when a major depression hit the country. In fact, the financial panic which triggered the depression was touched off ten days before Cleveland took office by the bankruptcy of the Philadelphia and Reading Railroad and a panic-selling spree on Wall Street. The financial panic deepened into depression during the summer of 1893. By the end of the year, 500 banks had closed, and nearly 16,000 business firms and railway systems had gone into bankruptcy. Farm prices began a new plunge that did not reach bottom until 1896. By 1895, almost 3,000,000 workers were unemployed. The Populists' direst predictions seemed to be coming true.

Grover Cleveland struggled according to his lights to meet these challenges, but his policies alienated farmers and workers and disrupted his party. The country was suffering from a massive deflation, caused in part by rapid industrial expansion and an inelastic money supply. Instead of permitting expansion of the money supply through measures like the free coinage of silver and the issuance of new legal tender notes, Cleveland fought to defend the gold standard at the cost of further deflation. Workers and the unemployed were in desperate need. Instead of responding to their plight, Cleveland used force to break strikes and demonstrations and would not listen to proposals for federal relief. He won the respect of the eastern moneyed classes and lost the confidence of the masses.

The Repeal of the Sherman Silver Purchase Act

A major cause of the Panic of 1893 was the failure of the large British banking house of Baring Brothers, which forced many English investors to sell their American securities in order to obtain gold. Cleveland believed, however, that the depression had originated in a lack of confidence in the Treasury's ability to maintain the gold standard. The chief source of the drain on gold, Cleveland thought, was the Sherman Silver Purchase Act. By 1893, the Treasury was purchasing about $50 million worth of silver a year; at the same time, bankers and others were redeeming their silver certificates in gold. Consequently, the Treasury had lost about $132 million in gold and gained about $147 million in silver between 1890 and 1893. The situation was particularly acute by the spring of 1893. On April 21, the Treasury's gold reserves sank below the $100 million that had been maintained since 1882 as a metallic basis for the $350 million in greenbacks still in circulation.

Cleveland had two options at this point. First, he could permit the Treasury to go off the gold standard by default or congressional action. This would have caused some price adjustments, but it would not necessarily have led to profound dislocations and severe inflation. Second, he could defend the gold standard at all hazards. Actually, his choice was foreordained, given his belief that the dollar's integrity, and perhaps the nation's, depended upon the certainty that dollars could be redeemed for a certain amount of gold.

Cleveland called Congress into special session on August 7, 1893, and asked for immediate repeal of the Sherman Silver Purchase Act. The House voted for repeal by a large majority on August 28. The contest in the Senate, however, was long and bitter. Seven silver states of the West, representing only 2 per cent of the population of the country, sent fourteen of the eighty-eight senators to Congress. These silver senators were supported by the Populists and some other southern senators. Together they fought against repeal of the Sherman Act until the end of October. Repeal finally passed by the close vote of forty-eight to thirty-seven on October 30, 1893. Most Republicans voted for it, and most Democrats voted against, despite Cleveland's vigorous efforts on its behalf. Thus ended governmental purchase of silver and all hopes of Democratic unity.

The Morgan Bond Transaction

Although repeal of the Sherman Silver Purchase Act stopped the flow of silver into the Treasury, it had not added to the diminishing gold fund. The repeal was like plugging a leak that had been flooding the kitchen floor; now the floor had to be mopped up. The drain on the Treasury sent the gold reserve down to $70 million before the end of 1893. Twice during the next year, the Secretary of the Treasury sold $50 million worth of bonds for gold. This did not help the situation. In January 1895, the reserve was down to what Cleveland called the "frightfully low" figure of $41 million.

The explanation of this loss of gold is simple. The banks that subscribed to the bonds paid for them by presenting greenbacks or silver certificates to the Treasury to be exchanged for gold. This endless game not only left the government with no more gold, but actually cost it considerable interest on the bonds issued. Cleveland decided, therefore, that he must find gold somewhere that would stay in the Treasury.

Early in 1895, the President invited the investment banker, J. Pierpont Morgan, to the White House and asked for his help. Morgan and his European associates agreed to furnish $62 million in gold; half of this was to be brought from Europe and added to the domestic supply, in return for 4 per cent government bonds. Morgan made a profit of more than $6 million on the sale of the bonds. Populists said, bitterly, that Cleveland had entered into an unholy alliance with the bankers of New York and London.

Tariff Reform Is Defeated

Cleveland's vigorous action on monetary policy contrasts sharply with his lackluster efforts on behalf of another issue which he believed to be important—downward revision of the tariff. When the regular session of Congress met in December 1893, William L. Wilson of West Virginia, chairman of the Ways and Means Committee, introduced a bill for the removal of duties on many raw materials, including wool, iron ore, coal, copper, and sugar. The bill also provided for a considerable reduction in duties on such manufactures as china, glass, silk, and cotton and woolen goods.

The Democratic House promptly passed the Wilson bill by a vote of 182 to 106. However, Cleveland completely lost control of the measure in the Senate, mainly because of his own failure to exert any leadership. Special interests moved quickly into the vacuum. Senator Arthur P. Gorman of Maryland and other Democrats on the Senate Finance Committee added some 600 amendments to the Wilson bill. Even so, the Senate measure, which both houses approved as the Wilson-Gorman Tariff, put wool, copper, and lumber on the free list and reduced duties from an average of 49.5 per cent under the McKinley Tariff to 39.9 per cent. However, it imposed duties on imports of sugar, which struck a severe blow to the economy of Cuba. Finally, the Senate, at the insistence of Democratic agrarians, added a tax of 2 per cent on incomes of over $4 thousand per year. Instead of accepting the measure as a substantial beginning toward tariff reduction, Cleveland refused to sign it. He permitted it to become law without his signature. Furthermore, he denounced it publicly as a piece of "party perfidy and dishonor" and thereby further widened the split in the Democratic party.

Cleveland and the Poor

While Cleveland quarreled with his party leaders in the Senate, the country suffered through one of the worst winters in its history. One out of every six workers was unemployed. There were two dramatic confrontations between the federal government and the poor and unemployed in the spring of 1894, important both in themselves and for what they symbolized. Even more important were Cleveland's reactions, which further alienated rank-and-file Democrats.

The first incident was the march of an "army" of about 500 unemployed men under Jacob S. Coxey, a Populist reformer, from Massilon, Ohio, to Washington. They went to support a measure, already introduced in Congress, to provide for the issuance of $500 million in legal tender notes to be spent on road construction by the unemployed. Coxey and his followers arrived in Washington on April 29, 1894. They went to the Capitol on May 1, where a corps of policemen met them. Policemen arrested two marchers and then dispersed the rest with clubs. Other "armies" descended on Washington, only to be turned back by similar use of force. Thus Cleveland made indelibly clear his determination to deal sternly with demonstrations of protest, even peaceful ones.

Cleveland made his intentions even clearer in his brutal response to the second major eruption during 1894 — the strike and boycott that broke out against the Pullman Palace Car Company (see pp. 512–513). Cleveland and Attorney General Olney did indeed break the strike, as we have seen. But their action left ugly scars. Governor John P. Altgeld of Illinois, sympathetic to the strikers, condemned Cleveland for sending in federal troops over his objections and allegedly in contradiction of the Constitution. Altgeld believed that the state militia was fully able to handle the situation, as it had handled similar outbreaks in recent weeks. Many persons called Debs' imprisonment, without jury trial or conviction, tyranny. Even some conservatives called such "government by injunction" dangerous and unjust.

"Giving the Butt" by
Frederic Remington, a
Harper's Weekly *correspon-*
dent, who was at the scene
of what he called the "rape
of the government." In this
sketch of the Pullman
strike, he illustrates how
federal troops dealt with
the strikers. (The Bettmann
Archive)

The Cleveland Administration at Bay

On May 1, 1893, Cleveland pushed the electric button that opened the Columbian Exposition, or World's Fair, at Chicago. It was the only thoroughly popular act of his second administration. By the end of 1894, it seemed as if Cleveland had set out systematically to alienate all major groups in the country. He
had offended eastern industrialists by his attack on the protective tariff. He
had incensed Populists and other agrarians by his defense of the gold standard.
Cleveland had alienated organized labor by his use of troops to suppress the
Pullman strike. Businessmen blamed him for the Panic of 1893. Democratic
party leaders accused him of splitting his party in the tariff and currency fights
and of causing a landslide victory for the Republicans in the mid-term election
of 1894.

Three decisions of the Supreme Court in the spring of 1895 added to the general discontent.

1. The Supreme Court, in a five-to-four decision in Pollock *v.* Farmers' Loan
and Trust Company, killed the income tax provision of the Wilson-Gorman
Tariff Act on the ground that it was a direct tax. Therefore it had to be levied in
proportion to population (Constitution, Article I, Section 2, paragraph 3).
Moreover, the court, speaking through Justice Stephen J. Field, had labeled the
income tax, a short time before, as "an assault upon capital" and a "stepping
stone to others, larger and more sweeping, till our political contests . . . become
a war of the poor against the rich."

2. A week after this decision, the Supreme Court, in the case of *In re* Debs,
unanimously upheld the injunction under which Debs had been imprisoned at
the time of the Pullman strike, on the ground that the ARU's boycott had been
a conspiracy in restraint of trade and, therefore, a violation of the Sherman
Antitrust Act. By implication, all restraints of trade by labor unions fell under
the purview of the courts and their injunctive power.

3. At the same time, the court, in United States *v.* E. C. Knight Company,
declared that the Sherman Antitrust Act did not apply to combinations of
manufacturing concerns and thus gave the green light to further industrial
combinations.

These decisions set off mighty waves of protest from farmers and workers.

Foreign Affairs, 1893–1896

The Hawaiian Islands had long had a close and special relationship to the United States. American missionaries, merchants, and planters had been establishing families and making their fortunes in the islands since the 1830s.

In January 1893, a group of Americans—large planters, merchants, and others—with the help of marines landed from *U.S.S. Boston*, deposed the absolute monarch, Queen Liliuokalani, established a government, and declared the islands a protectorate of the United States. A few days later—on February 15, 1893—President Harrison sent a treaty of annexation to the Senate. Cleveland came to the White House before the Senate could vote upon the treaty.

It had all been too fast and irregular for the scrupulous Cleveland. He immediately withdrew the Hawaiian treaty from the Senate and sent a special commissioner to Honolulu to investigate. The commissioner reported what was true—that the American Minister to Hawaii had participated in the revolution and had guaranteed its success by calling in the marines. Cleveland sent orders

Queen Liliuokalani, last of the Hawaiian monarchs, who tried to free the islands of American influence in the government and was forced to abdicate. (Culver Pictures, Inc.)

that the American flag should be lowered from the government house in Hono-lulu. Cleveland also offered to restore the corpulent Queen to her throne if she would promise to take no reprisals against the revolutionists. She replied that she would cut their heads off. An embarrassed Cleveland simply withdrew, and the revolutionary government had no difficulty in maintaining itself in power until Congress, by joint resolution in July 1898, annexed the Hawaiian Islands to the United States. Congress granted the islands territorial status two years later.

Ineptness and stubbornness, which Cleveland had revealed in abundance since 1893, now led him into a controversy with Great Britain which might easily have resulted in a useless and dreadful war. The British claimed some 230,000 square miles of mineral rich land, which lay within territory the boundary of which had long been in dispute between Venezuela and British Guiana. The British government well knew that arbitrators usually split the difference in boundary disputes; thus they had rejected Venezuela's offer of arbitration on several occasions. American public opinion became greatly agi-tated when a paid Venezuelan propagandist published a pamphlet which ac-cused the British of violating the Monroe Doctrine by territorial aggrandize-ment in the western hemisphere. Congress, in February 1895, adopted a joint resolution urging the British to agree to submit the dispute to arbitration. No reply came from London. Then, on July 20, 1895, Secretary of State Richard Olney, with Cleveland's strong approval, dispatched a remarkable note to the British Foreign Office. The United States, Olney wrote, was "practically sover-eign on this continent." Its fiat was "law upon the subjects to which it con-fines its interposition." Under the Monroe Doctrine, the United States could not permit a European power to seize the territory of an American republic. In conclusion, Olney insisted upon a definite answer as to whether Great Britain would submit the Venezuelan boundary dispute to arbitration.

The haughty British Prime Minister and Foreign Secretary, Lord Salisbury, treated Olney's note with the contempt that it deserved by ignoring it for months. When he deigned to reply — on November 26 — he said that the Mon-roe Doctrine had no standing in international law; moreover, the boundary dispute was no concern of the United States.

Was Cleveland spoiling for a war in order to shore up his sagging political fortunes at home? It is possible. In any event, he fired off a special message to Congress on December 17. He asked Congress to empower *him* to establish an arbitral commission which would draw the boundary between Venezuela and British Guiana. (The British would have to accept the commission's decision or face the consequences.) "I am fully alive to the responsibility incurred," he ended, "and keenly realize all the consequences that may follow." Congress unanimously adopted the resolution that Cleveland had requested.

A wave of chauvinism swept the country; there was loud talk of war; and Cleveland enjoyed a fleeting moment of popularity. Then a sober second thought set in as Americans began to contemplate war over so trivial an issue with the best friend that they had in the world. British public opinion also re-coiled against the thought of war with the United States.

The British government was at this time involved in difficulties with the Boers in South Africa and faced other problems in Europe and the Far East. It had no desire for a war with the United States. Thus Salisbury accepted the American offer of arbitration and said that it would cooperate in every way possible. The arbitral commission began its hearings in Paris in 1899. Its award, ironically, was generally favorable to Great Britain.

One aftermath of the Venezuelan affair was a considerable improvement in Anglo-American relations. It was as if the two great English-speaking peoples, while standing on the brink of war, had realized that war between them was unthinkable. Moreover, the British, who now felt increasingly isolated and worried (especially by the rise of Germany as a naval power) began aggressively to woo the United States in the hope of winning a friend.

3. THE REALIGNMENT OF THE PARTY SYSTEM

New Actors on the Political Stage

Among the Democrats who lost their seats in Congress during the Republican landslide of 1894 was a young lawyer from Nebraska, William Jennings Bryan. He had remarkable oratorical powers and an infectious moralistic enthusiasm. Between 1894 and 1896, Bryan traveled tirelessly across the South and West, spoke on behalf of free silver, and pointed an accusing finger at eastern bankers and financiers. Bryan became a focal point of anti-Cleveland sentiment within the Democratic party; conservative Democrats and Republicans naturally thought that he was a dangerous demagogue and a radical. Cleveland described him as "a Populist pure and simple." In fact, Bryan was neither a Populist nor a radical, but his speeches did sound radical in comparison with the positions which prevailed in both major parties.

Like many Populists, Bryan believed that the eastern moneyed and business classes controlled the national government and used it to protect and promote their own interests. He believed in some degree of inflation and advocated free coinage of silver as one means of achieving it. Yet Bryan was not part of the great mass movement which produced the Populist party. He was not enamored of the thoroughgoing reforms advocated by the Omaha platform, and, as a professional politician, showed no inclination to desert the Democratic party for an uncertain career in the new Populist party. Radical Populists distrusted and even feared him, because he seemed capable of persuading farmers that free silver was *the* panacea for their problems.

The new star on the Republican horizon, William McKinley, was in some respects similar to Bryan. Both had served in the House of Representatives, and McKinley had lost his seat in the Democratic landslide of 1890. Both men were devout evangelical Protestants. McKinley, like Bryan, courted the labor vote. As Governor of Ohio in the 1890s, he had supported workers' rights to join a union and had promoted a system of arbitration of labor disputes. Moreover, McKinley's commitment to a protective tariff was popular with many of the iron and steel workers in his native northwestern Ohio, who shared his belief that foreign competition threatened American jobs and wages.

Despite his good relations with industrial workers, McKinley was not threatening to big business. His efforts in Congress on behalf of protection won him much business support, and his position on the money question (he favored "international bimetalism") was close enough to an endorsement of the gold standard to satisfy most "goldbugs."

McKinley caught the eye of a fellow Ohioan and would-be Republican king-maker, Marcus Alonzo Hanna, who headed a huge mining and shipping empire. Hanna was not ambitious for political honors himself, but he gave his time and money generously to the advancement of Ohio Republicans who sympathized with his ideas. He supported John Sherman for the presidential nomination in three conventions. Then he turned to William McKinley; from then on, he acted as McKinley's political and economic benefactor.

Just as Bryan was a very different kind of Democrat from Grover Cleveland, so McKinley and Hanna were new kinds of Republicans. Although they were clearly supportive of big business, they were not stridently antiunion. (During the Pullman strike, Hanna had favored arbitration between management and the union and had said of George Pullman, "A man who won't meet his men half-way is a God damn fool.") Although McKinley was a devout Methodist and a supporter of prohibition, he rejected the militant defense of evangelical culture which had been a hallmark of Republican politics since the party's inception. Instead, he sought to mute the ethnocultural issues which had cut the Republicans off from the mass of immigrant-stock Americans.

The Campaign of 1896

Just as Bryan and McKinley represented a new departure in national Democratic and Republican leadership, the presidential campaign in which they first met as adversaries was also a departure in national politics. The election of 1896 has been called the "Battle of the Standards," which means that it pitted free silver against the gold standard. To a substantial degree, monetary policy did dominate the speechmaking, but the real issues ran much deeper.

Hanna's careful work on behalf of McKinley paid off. Several months before the Republican convention met in St. Louis on June 16, Hanna had enough delegates pledged to McKinley to secure his nomination on the first ballot. Meanwhile, Bryan had been working tirelessly to rally the agrarian forces to wrest control of the Democratic party from Cleveland. In March 1895, just as he was leaving Congress, Bryan had secured the signatures of thirty-one members from the West and South to an appeal "to the Democrats of the United States." It invited them to unite behind free coinage of silver, take control of the Democratic party, and make it "an effective instrument in the accomplishment of needed reforms."

The task was easily accomplished. When the Democratic national convention opened in Chicago on July 8, 1896, the free silver forces were in complete command. They elected a free silverite as chairman and adopted a platform which advocated the free coinage of silver at the ratio of sixteen to one and expanded federal regulation of the economy. A motion praising the "honesty and courage" of President Cleveland was defeated by a vote of 564 to 357.

Bryan had come to the convention confident that he could win the party's nomination for President. He did so, on the fifth ballot, due in part to an electrifying speech that he delivered during the debate on the platform. "We are fighting," he cried, "in the defense of our homes, our families, and posterity. . . . Having behind us the producing masses of this nation and the world . . . we will answer their demand for a gold standard by saying to them: You shall not press upon the brow of labor this crown of thorns, you shall not crucify mankind upon a cross of gold." A tired and listless convention came to life as Bryan's speech progressed. Applause interrupted the orator at every sentence. It

William Jennings Bryan during the presidential campaign of 1896. He rallied the agrarian, silver forces behind him at the Democratic convention with these words: "You shall not press down upon the brow of labor this crown of thorns, you shall not crucify mankind upon a cross of gold." (The Bettmann Archive)

burst into a frenzy before the echo of the last defiant challenge had died. At the end, tears were streaming down many faces. Bryan's nomination was assured.

The silver issue split the two old parties and caused the virtual death of the Populist party in 1896. The Republican platform came out for sound money and against the free coinage of silver, "except by international agreement with the leading commercial nations of the earth." This caused many Republican delegates from silver-producing states to walk out of the St. Louis convention and to join the Democratic ranks. The Chicago convention's platform and its repudiation of Cleveland caused conservative Democrats to organize a gold, or National, Democratic party. Cleveland and all the members of his cabinet but one supported its nominees. But more conservative Democrats drifted into the Republican party rather than support the gold Democratic ticket.

The Populists were in a painful dilemma, because the Democrats had stolen their issue and nominated a candidate who at least sounded like a Populist.

For some time, one faction had worked to soften the party's demands. Specifically, they wanted to concentrate on the free silver issue as a way to attract mass support and as the first step in implementing the party's general program of reform. Many of these "silver Populists" assumed that neither major party would nominate a free silver advocate; this would leave the Populists in sole possession of a very popular campaign issue. Other silver Populists, most of them Westerners, favored cooperation with silver Democrats. To them, the nomination of Bryan represented an opportunity rather than a dilemma. The fact was that, in the western states, Populist-Democratic fusion had provided such victories as the party had enjoyed, and extension of this principle to the national level seemed quite sensible to many Populists.

On the other hand, southern and southwestern Populists did not want to be pushed back into the Democratic party, with which they had been locked in fratricidal conflict for four years. Many of these "midroad" Populists were old veterans of the Alliance movement; a few were urban radicals. They strongly opposed soft pedaling the more controversial planks of the Omaha platform.

The Populists met in St. Louis just two weeks after the Democrats had nominated Bryan in Chicago. The Populist convention was a bitter and almost bloody affair. Free silver advocates and fusionists battled more radical populists on every issue, and the fusionists prevailed in the end. They nominated Bryan for President by a narrow margin, but they then tried to preserve their party's independent identity by rejecting Bryan's Democratic running mate in favor of Tom Watson, the fiery Georgia Populist.

Bryan's nomination demoralized the Populist party. During the campaign, it virtually ceased to function as a viable national institution. The real battle was between Bryan, the Democrat (he never formally accepted the Populist nomination), and McKinley. Both men employed novel electioneering tactics which, in different ways, prefigured twentieth-century campaigning.

Bryan broke with tradition by campaigning personally and extensively for the office. Previously, presidential candidates had appeared to let the office seek them, rather than the other way around. Bryan lacked the money to maintain this fiction in a day of mass communication and well-oiled political machines. He took another approach. Like an itinerant evangelist, he traveled 18,000 miles throughout the country and made more than 600 speeches to an estimated 5,000,000 people. This was probably the most numerous audience that ever listened to a single voice before the invention of the radio.

McKinley's campaign appeared to be more traditional, but in fact it also broke with past practice. McKinley stayed at home in Canton, Ohio, and received delegations on his front porch. But while McKinley stayed at home, Hanna was hard at work raising huge sums of money for the first time during a presidential campaign. He collected millions of dollars from corporations (estimates vary from $3.5 million to $15 million, in contrast to the $1.5 million spent by the Republicans in 1892) and disbursed it to hire an army of campaign speakers and to flood the country with campaign literature. The $250 thousand which Hanna collected from Standard Oil alone almost equaled the Democrats' entire campaign fund.

The campaigning was intense and the rhetoric heated. Bryan's invectives against Wall Street and eastern business tycoons were matched by Republican charges that he was encouraging "the uprising of disorder in all its forms against the institutions of the American Republic." Wage earners in some eastern cities were given written notice, when they were paid off on the Saturday before the election, and told that they would not be needed if Bryan was elected.

The unprecedented vote on November 3 showed how stirred the people had been. Moreover, the vote revealed the sectional character of the struggle. McKinley carried the Northeast, the Middle West, and the border states of Kentucky, West Virginia, Maryland, and Delaware. This gave him a total of twenty-three states with an electoral vote of 271. Bryan's 176 electoral votes came from the Solid South and from the eight mining states of the West, plus South Dakota, Kansas, Nebraska, and Missouri—twenty-two in all. The popular vote, 7,102,000 for McKinley and 6,493,000 for Bryan, gave the Republicans a clear majority in a presidential election for the first time since 1868.

Significance of the Election of 1896

The presidential election of 1896 was one of the most significant in American history. It established the dominance of the Republican party, virtually reduced the Democrats to the status of a southern regional party, and killed the Populists. It marked the end, at least until the 1930s, of continuous efforts to win governmental support for an inflated currency for the relief of debtors. Furthermore, it indicated the emergence of the cities as a dominant force in national politics.

The Election of 1896

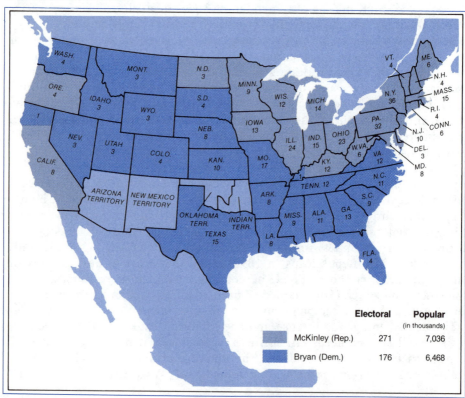

	Electoral	Popular (in thousands)
McKinley (Rep.)	271	7,036
Bryan (Dem.)	176	6,468

How can we explain these remarkable transformations? Some accounts suggest that the Republicans bribed and bullied their way to victory. Political chicanery did occur in 1896, but Republicans are not known to have monopolized the stuffing of ballot boxes in that era. Clearly, some industrial workers were intimidated into voting for McKinley, but this cannot account for the persistence of Republican support over the next thirty years. The fact is that, in 1896, the Republican party appealed to a broader constituency than either the Democrats or the Populists; the Republicans were also able to win a significant following among industrial workers. Under McKinley's leadership, the G.O.P. modified its evangelical image to take into account the cultural pluralism of the American electorate. It appealed to workers on the ground that Republican policies would bring them economic well-being. This new model Republican party could bill itself as the party of Progress, Prosperity, and Pluralism.

In contrast, by the time that Bryan took control, the Democratic party had already been blamed for the worst depression in the nation's history. The free silver crusade and even more radical inflationary proposals, such as the subtreasury plan, made little headway among urban workers, who feared substantial increases in the prices of consumer goods. Also, Bryan was personally unattractive to many urban workers. Many were put off by his antieastern and antiurban rhetoric, while many immigrants were suspicious of his evangelical style. As one historian has suggested, the Democrats now found themselves burdened with the "cross of culture."

As for the Populists, they were the victims of voter fraud, internal division, and, above all, the limited constituency to which they appealed. The Populists had been overwhelmingly a farmers' party, and, in the South, a white man's party. The Populists had dreamed of uniting all producers under one banner of reform. However, the reform measures which they promoted in the 1880s and 1890s — cooperatives, the subtreasury, free silver, and even political cooperation with organized labor — appealed to few nonfarmers.

Historians are still debating the relationship between Populism and the legal disfranchisement of southern blacks which occurred between 1890 and 1910 (see pp. 589–591). Did the defeated white Populists turn on the blacks whom they had tried to enlist in their cause, or were they both victims of a systematic effort to eliminate real or potential threats to Democratic hegemony in the South? The best work on this subject concludes that the latter was more nearly correct. It finds that Democratic politicians and members of the South's dominant socioeconomic class were the leaders in disfranchisement.

The Populists did indeed help to revive an old but dormant tradition in American politics — that it was the government's duty to be always active in promoting human welfare and economic democracy. They also spoke for a venerable American tradition of political democracy. For a time, they seemed to offer a serious challenge to capitalistic industrialism. Their demise at the end of the nineteenth century would limit the range of political discourse in the twentieth.

SUGGESTED READINGS

Shannon's *The Farmer's Last Frontier*, already cited, has chapters relevant to the farm protest movement and Populism. Lawrence Goodwyn, *Democratic Promise: The Populist*

Moment in America (1976), is now the standard history of Populism, but the older general study of the movement, John D. Hicks, *The Populist Revolt* (1931), remains useful. Norman Pollack, *The Populist Response to Industrial America* (1962), portrays the Populists as thoroughgoing radicals, a view which is disputed in Sheldon Hackney, *Populism to Progressivism in Alabama* (1969). The farm cooperative movement which led to Populism is described in Robert C. McMath, Jr., *Populist Vanguard: A History of the Southern Farmers' Alliance* (1975). Further insights into the agricultural problems of this period can be gained from the relevant chapters in Russell B. Nye, *Midwestern Progressive Politics: A Historical Study of Its Origins and Development, 1870–1958* (rev. ed., 1958), and Theodore Saloutos, *Farmer Movements in the South, 1865–1933* (1960).

Various aspects of politics in the late nineteenth century are discussed in H. Wayne Morgan, ed., *The Gilded Age* (rev. ed., 1970). The ethnocultural dimension of political conflict is discussed in Richard Jensen, *The Winning of the Midwest: Social and Political Conflict, 1888–1896* (1971); Paul Kleppner, *The Cross of Culture: A Social Analysis of Midwestern Politics, 1850–1900* (2nd ed., 1970); and Kleppner, *The Third American Electoral System, 1853–1892: Parties, Voters, and Political Cultures* (1979). The racial dimension of politics is discussed in J. Morgan Kousser, *The Shaping of Southern Politics: Suffrage Restriction and the Establishment of the One-Party South, 1880–1910* (1974).

Labor protest during the 1890s is studied in Donald L. McMurray, *Coxey's Army* (1929); Almot Lindsey, *The Pullman Strike* (1942); Ray Ginger, *The Bending Cross: Eugene V. Debs* (1949); Ginger, *Altgeld's America* (1958); and the accounts of labor history cited in the Suggested Readings for Chapter 18.

George H. Knowles, *The Presidential Campaign and Election of 1892* (1942), in addition to being a good account of the campaign and election, contains useful information on the depression. The crucial election of 1896 has been subjected to close scrutiny. In addition to the previously cited studies of Populism, useful treatments of the election include Stanley Jones, *The Presidential Election of 1896* (1964), and J. Rogers Hollingsworth, *The Whirligig of Politics: The Democracy of Cleveland and Bryan* (1963). For an analysis of the two contenders for the presidency in that election, see H. Wayne Morgan, *William McKinley and His America* (1963), and Paolo E. Coletta, *William Jennings Bryan,* 3 vols. (1964–1969). For an interesting firsthand account of the campaign see William Jennings Bryan, *The First Battle* (1897). On other important figures of the campaign see Herbert Croly, *Marcus Alonzo Hanna* (1912); C. Vann Woodward, *Tom Watson: Agrarian Rebel* (1938); and Francis B. Simkins, *Pitchfork Ben Tillman* (1944).

CHAPTER 21
THE WAR WITH SPAIN AND AN EMPIRE OVERSEAS

1. THE WAR WITH SPAIN

The Problem of Cuba

Cuba, separated from the United States by less than one hundred miles of water, seemed destined inexorably for some form of special relationship with its enormously powerful northern neighbor. Jefferson, after the purchase of the Louisiana Territory, considered a similar effort to annex Cuba. About twenty years later, John Quincy Adams postponed taking the island only because he was certain that the "laws of political gravitation" would naturally draw Cuba under the jurisdiction of the United States. The Ostend Manifesto of 1855 (see pp. 414–415) even invoked divine law in its call for the acquisition of Cuba by the United States.

Americans talked of intervention when Cubans revolted against harsh Spanish rule between 1868 and 1878; but war fever was not yet intense in the United States, and Spain suppressed the rebellion. The revolt that broke out on the island in 1895, however, was much more brutal, and rebel propagandists made more skillful appeals to American humanitarian feelings. The immediate cause of the uprising was the Wilson-Gorman Tariff Act of 1894, which destroyed the favored position enjoyed by Cuban sugar under the McKinley Tariff Act. Cuban exports to the United States fell precipitately because of the Wilson-Gorman Act's high duties and brought terrible poverty to the Cuban people. Cuban nationalists took advantage of widespread dissatisfaction to organize a new revolt. Bands of guerillas roamed the countryside, ambushed Spanish troops, and destroyed property owned by loyalists and foreigners—especially the large sugar plantations.

The repressive tactics that had worked in the past failed to discourage the determined revolutionaries in the 1890s. In desperation, the Spanish sent their most forceful commander, Captain General Valeriano Weyler y Nicolau to Cuba. He organized a system of concentration camps to deal with the problem of enemies who seemed to be peaceful farmers when Spanish troops passed them during the day, but who turned into guerillas under cover of night. The populations of whole villages were herded into insanitary camps; there the ill, the very young and very old, especially, died by the thousands from disease and malnutrition. American newspaper reporters, who wrote graphic descriptions of the camps, called Weyler "Butcher."

Americans had invested more than $50 million in the island's railroads, mines, utilities, and plantations. Moreover, trade between the United States and Cuba totaled nearly $100 million annually. American citizens with economic interests in Cuba naturally hoped that the United States Government would act to restore stability to the island. Their political weakness, however, was indicated by the unfavorable sugar tariff legislation that preceded the revolution. Furthermore, these investors and traders were far from certain that forcing the Spaniards out of Cuba would protect their interests. It was the rebels, after all, who were burning plantations and other property.

Cuban refugees in the United States were much more single-minded. Their clubs, or *juntas*, in New York and other cities not only collected money and bought guns and munitions for fellow revolutionaries in their homeland; they also spread very effective anti-Spanish propaganda. American newspapers throughout the country were more than willing to reprint this propaganda. In addition, the New York *World* and *New York Journal*, owned by Joseph Pulitzer and William Randolph Hearst, respectively, engaged in a fierce battle for readers with the aid of lurid descriptions of alleged Spanish atrocities against Cubans. These highly exaggerated accounts strongly stimulated the growth of popular demands for action to drive the Spaniards from the Caribbean.

Without benefit of atrocity stories, however, American political leaders, with strong public support, had brought the United States to the verge of war in recent years against Chile, Germany, and Great Britain. Pride in American wealth and military might played a part in encouraging this stridency in foreign affairs. In addition, many of the rising generation of political leaders had been deeply influenced by the application of social Darwinism to international relations. Men like Theodore Roosevelt and Henry Cabot Lodge were infected with a virulent strain of chauvinism; they also believed that war with Spain would toughen the national fiber and enhance the chances of American survival in a world that knew only the law of the jungle. However, the revulsion that a growing number of Americans felt against Spanish methods and a deep compassion for the plight of the Cuban people were the chief causes of American preoccupation with Cuba.

American feeling against Spain ran so high early in 1896 that the House of Representatives and Senate adopted a concurrent resolution in February and April which favored recognition of Cuban belligerency. Both major parties condemned Spanish misrule in Cuba in their platforms a few months later. Even Cleveland, who had stoutly resisted all pressure for war with Spain, devoted nearly one fifth of his last Annual Message to Congress, on December 7, 1896, to the Cuban situation. He warned plainly that the American people and government would not stand by idly if the slaughter in Cuba continued. Perhaps the time would come, he warned, when "our obligations to the sovereignty of Spain will be superseded by higher obligations, which we can hardly hesitate to recognize and discharge."

War with Spain

This was the situation that William McKinley inherited upon his inauguration in March 1897. The new President, a mild-mannered, well-meaning, deeply religious man, sincerely wanted to avoid war with Spain. "We want no wars of conquest," he announced in his inaugural address. "We must avoid the temptation of territorial aggression." He was strongly supported in this determination by the businessmen who were the main advisers and friends of his administration. But McKinley was also keenly sensitive to public opinion—so sensitive, in fact, that he was accused of cowardice. Theodore Roosevelt said that McKinley had "no more backbone than a chocolate eclair."

A liberal ministry came to power in Madrid in 1897. It recalled Weyler and granted limited autonomy to the Cubans. For a brief time, it seemed that the Cuban insurrection might end; however, the rebels by now would accept nothing less than full independence, and they intensified the war.

Two incidents early in 1898 set off what would become, for McKinley, an irresistible demand for war against Spain. One was the *New York Journal*'s publication on February 9 of a private letter written by Dupuy de Lôme, the Spanish Minister to the United States. The letter had been stolen by an insurgent spy and obtained by the Hearst newspaper. In it, De Lôme denounced the United States and described McKinley as a "cheap politician" and "bidder for the admiration of the crowd." The Spanish government immediately accepted De Lôme's resignation and apologized for his indiscretion.

The second incident was much more damaging to Spanish-American relations. *U.S.S. Maine*, in Havana harbor on a "friendly" visit, was sunk by a terrific explosion on February 15, 1898, with the loss of 260 officers and men. The American public, roused to fury by sensational headlines, was convinced that the battleship had been blown up on orders from Spanish officials. The popular cry in the United States for vengeance greatly increased when an American naval court of inquiry found convincing evidence that *Maine* had been sunk by a submarine mine, not an internal explosion. To this day no one knows who planted the mine (the Spanish government offered to submit the question of its responsibility to arbitration), although the most likely culprits would seem to be either the Cuban rebels, ruthless in their pursuit of American intervention; or else one of the groups of Spanish nationalists in Havana, whose rioting in protest against the softening of Spain's military policies had brought *Maine* into Havana harbor to protect Americans in the first place.

Neither McKinley nor the Spanish government wanted war. Nevertheless, Congress, on March 8, responded to the hysteria following the sinking of *Maine* by unanimously voting the President $50 million as "an emergency fund for national defense." Spain desperately appealed to the other European powers for help. Except for the British, the chief European governments were sympathetic, but they were willing to give Spain only weak verbal support.

The German Foreign Secretary was especially frank in his advice. "You are isolated," he warned the Spanish Ambassador in Berlin, "because . . . nobody wants to arouse America's anger. The United States is a rich country, against which you simply cannot sustain a war." On April 9, the Queen Regent of Spain yielded to the demands of the United States and the pleas of the Pope and made all the concessions that were possible without endangering the throne of her young son, Alfonso XIII. She revoked entirely the concentration policy and instructed her commander in chief in Cuba to stop all hostilities. The American Minister in Madrid, Stewart L. Woodford, immediately cabled that, if the Spanish government was given some time, he was sure that Cuban independence could be arranged during the armistice.

At this point, President McKinley failed to back up his pacific intentions with courageous actions. McKinley had already written a message to Congress in which he asserted that he had "exhausted every effort to relieve the intolerable condition" in Cuba—a statement quite open to question—and asked Congress for authority to use the armed forces to end the fighting. McKinley did not tear up this message and write a new one when the report of the Queen Mother's concessions arrived in Washington. Instead, he simply added a short paragraph which mentioned the concessions and sent the message to an angry Congress on April 11, 1898.

The House of Representatives, by a vote of 325 to nineteen on April 13, and the Senate, by a vote of sixty-seven to twenty-one on April 11, adopted resolutions that recognized the independence of Cuba, demanded the immediate withdrawal of Spain from the island, and authorized the President to employ the armed forces of the United States to carry out the resolution. At the same time, Congress adopted a second resolution, introduced by Senator Henry M. Teller of Colorado, which declared that the United States did not intend to annex Cuba. It would "leave the government and control of the island to its own people" once the Spaniards had been expelled. The Spanish government answered with a declaration of war against the United States on April 24.

Actually, further negotiations might not have prevented war. The Cuban rebels and the American people were now adamant on one basic demand—the complete withdrawal of Spain from Cuba. Autonomy, limited or otherwise, no longer sufficed. It is doubtful that Spain would have yielded on this point, and her refusal would probably have caused war with the United States. But we will never know how events might have turned out, for McKinley at the end had neither the nerve nor the will to continue the pursuit of peace.

Naval and Military Operations

Thanks to the naval construction and reorganization policies begun fifteen years before, the American navy entered the conflict in peak condition. When war broke out, the Asiatic Squadron of four cruisers and two gunboats, under the command of Commodore George Dewey, was at the British port of Hong Kong off the coast of China. As a belligerent, Dewey could not remain in a neutral port without facing the internment of his fleet.

Assistant Secretary of the Navy Theodore Roosevelt, acting while Secretary of the Navy John D. Long was out of his office on February 25, 1898, had instructed Dewey to attack the Spanish flotilla in the Philippine Islands as soon as war with Spain began. McKinley confirmed these instructions in a cable to

Dewey on April 24, 1898. A few hours later, Dewey's drably painted warships were steaming southeastward across the China Sea, bound for the ancient Spanish colony of the Philippines, nearly 630 miles away.

Dewey entered Manila Bay early on the morning of May 1 and attacked the poorly manned, decrepit Spanish vessels anchored off the navy yard at Cavite. By noon, every one of the Spanish ships was sunk or in flames. The land batteries of Cavite were silenced, and the city of Manila was at the mercy of Dewey's guns. Then the Admiral awaited transports from San Francisco with troops for land operations against the city.

As Dewey's vessels approached Manila, a Spanish fleet of four cruisers and three destroyers, commanded by Admiral Pascual Cervera y Topete, sailed westward across the Atlantic from the Cape Verde Islands. Cervera's destination was unknown, and there was a good deal of fear in the United States that he intended to bombard the unfortified cities of the Atlantic coast. The North Atlantic Squadron, under Rear Admiral William T. Sampson, including Commodore Winfield Scott Schley's so-called Flying Squadron, was patrolling the coast of Cuba, but Cervera slipped into the harbor of Santiago on May 19 without being discovered. There the small Spanish fleet was easily bottled up by a vastly superior squadron under Admiral Sampson, which blockaded the mouth of the harbor.

Meanwhile, about 17,000 troops, under the command of Major General William R. Shafter, had sailed from Florida to Cuba. The most picturesque and publicized unit of this army was the First Volunteer Cavalry Regiment, popularly known as the "Rough Riders." It was made up of cowboys, ranchers, Indians, hunters, and a number of graduates of eastern colleges. Colonel Leonard Wood commanded the Rough Riders, and Theodore Roosevelt resigned his post in the Navy Department to become their lieutenant colonel. The Rough Riders had to leave their horses in Florida; despite their inexperience as foot soldiers and their ineptness at landing operations, they managed to get ashore on June 20, 1898, east of Santiago—largely because the Spanish defenders failed to appear.

American troops stormed the fortified town of El Caney and San Juan Hill, just east of Santiago, on July 1. They won these strategic positions, but they were in a precarious situation. The men were clothed in winter uniforms and unused to the torrid heat. Moreover, illness had taken a far greater toll than the enemy's rifles. It would be weeks before reinforcements, needed to drive the Spaniards from Santiago, would arrive. The army's food supply was so low that a number of officers joined in a petition of protest to Washington. Indeed, General Shafter himself was ill with fever and gout in his camp several miles from the city. He considered the withdrawal of his army from the heights above Santiago, because he feared that his troops might be driven off by the guns of Cervera's fleet. Furthermore, the Spaniards, with about 200,000 troops in Cuba, might, if given enough time, concentrate their forces and overwhelm the Americans.

Then fortune smiled on the American cause. On Sunday morning, July 3, the Spanish fleet attempted to escape from Santiago. Cervera's ships steamed out of the harbor and started to run westward along the southern coast of Cuba. Admiral Sampson was absent at the time, in conference with General Shafter about the critical situation of the American army; Commodore Schley was the ranking officer. The American ships followed orders left by Sampson and

After landing at Daiquiri, American troops are seen under Spanish fire from San Juan Hill on July 1, 1898. Of the expeditionary force sent to Cuba, reporter Richard Davis wrote: "It was a most happy-go-lucky expedition, run with real American optimism and readiness to take big chances, and with the spirit of a people who recklessly trust that it will come out all right in the end . . ." (Library of Congress)

closed in on the Spaniards in a wild chase along the coast. The Spanish cruisers, one by one, disabled or in flames, turned and headed for the shore. The last of them, *Cristóbal Colón*, was driven on the beach forty-five miles west of the harbor of Santiago.

One American sailor was killed and another seriously wounded in the fray, but the enemy's fleet was completely destroyed—474 men were killed or wounded, and 1,750 were taken prisoner. American sailors rescued hundreds, including Cervera himself, from the burning decks and the wreck-strewn waters. A few days later, the Spaniards surrendered the city of Santiago and turned over their entire army. The war in Cuba was over, and the American army prepared to subdue Puerto Rico, the sole remaining outpost of the once great Spanish dominion in the new world.

The total loss of two fleets and of an army caused Spain to sue for peace. A preliminary treaty was signed at Washington on August 12. The news stopped General Nelson A. Miles' advance against the Spanish forces in Puerto Rico; but the Spanish governor immediately surrendered the island. It took longer for news of the armistice to reach the Philippines, where on August 13 an American army of some 11,000 men entered Manila and raised the American flag over the governor's palace.

U.S. troops marching in formation through the streets of Manila during the Philippine Insurrection, 1899–1901. Many Filipinos soon realized that the Spanish-American War had only made them pawns of another colonial power. Fighting for independence broke out and continued for several years in guerrilla fashion until U.S. forces were able to "pacify" the Islands. It was not until 1946 that the Philippines achieved independence from the United States. (Brown Brothers)

2. THE UNITED STATES BECOMES A COLONIAL POWER

The Treaty of Paris

The preliminary agreement provided that Spain should immediately evacuate and renounce all claims to Cuba and cede Puerto Rico and Guam, an island in the Pacific Ocean, to the United States. In addition, the United States would occupy the city, bay, and harbor of Manila "pending the conclusion of a treaty of peace which should determine the control, disposition, and government of the Philippines."

The American peace commissioners met their Spanish counterparts in Paris on October 1, 1898. More than two months passed before the Americans could persuade the Spaniards to accept their terms concerning the Philippines. The Spaniards reminded the American commissioners that the war had been undertaken for the liberation of Cuba, not of the Philippines. They pointed out that Manila had not been taken until the day *after* the preliminary peace treaty had been signed and hostilities suspended. The Spanish commissioners claimed, therefore, that the Philippines should remain in their country's possession and that the Americans should withdraw.

McKinley had been quite modest in his first instructions to his commissioners. He was inclined to ask only for the island of Luzon and equal commercial rights with Spain in the other islands of the Philippines. But various considerations gradually caused him to demand the cession of the whole of the Philippine archipelago to the United States. The President told a group of clergymen that he had been in a great dilemma about the Philippines and had prayed for divine guidance. The answer, he went on, came to him one night: "That we could not give them back to Spain — that would be cowardly and dishonorable; that we could not turn them over to France or Germany — our commercial rivals in the Orient — that would be bad business and discreditable; that we could not leave them to themselves — they were unfit for self-government . . . and that there was nothing left for us to do but to take them all, and to educate the Filipinos, and uplift and civilize and Christianize them, and by God's grace do the very best we could by them."

McKinley's explanation rather accurately reflected the thinking of certain important segments of American opinion. Like the President, some Americans believed that it was their moral duty to teach good government to their "little brown brothers." Commercial interests were also putting strong pressure upon the administration to take the Philippines for use as an entrepôt for what they thought would be greatly expanded trade with China. Imperialists like Secretary of State John Hay, Lodge, and Roosevelt argued that the United States should share in the spheres of influence that western European powers were rapidly establishing in the Far East. The Spanish commissioners resisted stubbornly. However, when the American commissioners made an offer of $20 million, Spain agreed to "sell" the islands to the United States.

The Philippine-American War

Meanwhile, an ugly situation had been developing in the Philippines. The Filipinos had been in revolt against Spain at the same time as the Cubans. Dewey made contact with the leader of the revolt, Emilio Aguinaldo, and Filipino troops entered Manila at the same time as the American army on August 13. The Filipinos had declared their independence of Spain on June 12 and proclaimed a provisional Republic of the Philippines, with Aguinaldo as President. Three months later, they moved their capital outside Manila.

It was clear by early February 1899 that the United States meant to occupy the Philippines, much as the Spanish had, without concessions to the Filipino insurgents, and certainly without recognition of the Philippine Republic. The Filipinos then prepared to renew the revolution against their new masters. Fighting broke out in the area of Manila between Aguinaldo's insurgents and American troops on February 4, 1899. The superior numbers, equipment, and training of the American army made victory in the open field very easy. But the Filipinos took to guerilla warfare in their swamps and jungles. Both sides resorted to atrocities. Some American officers admitted that they had resorted to the kind of brutal tactics that "Butcher" Weyler had used in Cuba. American superior power (the American army in the Philippines eventually totaled 70,000 men) prevailed in the end, but only at a terrible cost of human lives — 1,000 Americans and tens of thousands of Filipinos. Aguinaldo was finally captured—on March 23, 1901—in his mountain retreat by a party of American scouts disguised as insurgents. Two months later, he issued a proclamation that acknowledged American sovereignty over the islands.

Even this acknowledgment did not end the insurrection. It was not until April 1902 that the last rebel surrendered and the Philippines were officially declared "pacified." Aguinaldo himself came to accept American rule in the Philippines after the victors promised eventual independence to his country. Aguinaldo lived to see American promises finally honored and the Philippine Republic proclaimed on July 4, 1946.

The Debate over Imperialism

By a narrow two-thirds majority of fifty-seven to twenty-seven, the Senate consented, on February 6, 1899, to ratification of the Treaty of Paris. The United States was thus launched upon a "new and untried" course of overseas expansion. As had been noted, the United States had annexed the Hawaiian Islands on July 7, 1898; it then added the smaller Pacific coaling islands of Guam, Wake, and Baker. It had undertaken responsibility for establishing an orderly government for Cuba. It had also adopted nearly 1,000,000 subjects of Spanish and black ancestry in Puerto Rico. Finally, the United States had become the master of 8,000,000 people in the Philippines. They ranged from the highly civilized Tagalogs of Manila to the naked Negrito dwarfs, the headhunting Igorots, and the Moros of the Sulu peninsula.

Many Americans were distressed and angry. This use of brute force to impose American rule on peoples different in language, race, and customs, the antiimperialists argued, was no different from the imperialistic policies of European states that most Americans had loudly condemned. Floods of pamphlets criticized this alleged violation of the principles of the Declaration of Independence. Thomas B. Reed retired from the Speakership of the House of Representatives in disgust and referred to the treaty as "buying ten million Malays at two dollars a head."

The battle was taken up at once by all the advocates of overseas expansion. Manufacturers and bankers were among those who wanted markets for surplus goods and investment of surplus funds. Sympathetic, too, were many moralists like McKinley. They quoted the British poet, Rudyard Kipling, to argue that Americans had a sacred duty to "take up the white man's burden" and help to civilize the "backward" natives, "half devil and half child." A small group which included Theodore Roosevelt and Captain Alfred T. Mahan of the navy, argued that the United States could never be a great power until it had acquired naval bases far from its own shores.

The Election of 1900

Americans had an opportunity to vote on imperialism in the election of 1900. The Republican national convention, which met in Philadelphia on June 19, renominated McKinley by acclamation. Theodore Roosevelt, now a popular war hero, was drafted for the vice-presidency in spite of his well-grounded belief that the Republican bosses of New York were effectively putting him on the shelf. Roosevelt had been elected Governor of New York in 1898 and had proved himself to be both a natural vote-getter and a threat to the well-entrenched state Republican organization headed by Thomas C. Platt. Hence the effort by the New York politicians to get rid of him with the seemingly unimportant position of Vice-President of the United States. But, once nominated, Roosevelt threw himself into the campaign with characteristic vigor. He traveled around the country and denounced as weaklings and "mollycoddles" those who would "scuttle" out of the Philippines.

The Democrats unanimously renominated William Jennings Bryan. Although the Democratic platform remained faithful to free silver, it made imperialism the paramount issue of the campaign by demanding independence for the Philippines. A huge American flag hung from the rafters of the convention hall. The motto, "The flag of a Republic forever, of an Empire never," bordered the hall.

Antiimperialist leagues sprang up all over the country, and leading spokesmen emphasized the political and moral evils of the attempts to govern alien peoples against their wills. Support was given to their arguments by the Philippine insurrection, which was at its height during the summer of 1900. The Republicans angrily denied that they were imperialists. They claimed to be the liberators, not the oppressors, of the Filipinos.

It is impossible to know whether the voters endorsed overseas expansion in the election of 1900 or not. Most historians regard the returns more as a repudiation of Bryan and free silver than as a mandate for imperialism. McKinley's vote fell off in New England, where the antiimperialists were strongest, although he carried most of the West, including Bryan's home state of Nebraska. McKinley received 7,220,000 popular and 292 electoral votes; Bryan, 6,358,000 popular and 155 electoral votes. For better or worse, Americans were in the business of running a colonial empire.

The Reorganization of Cuba

The McKinley administration had already begun to establish governments for Cuba and Puerto Rico. The United States Government, by the Teller Resolution, had obligated itself to turn the government of Cuba over to Cubans after the restoration of order. The military governor, General Leonard Wood, oversaw, from 1899 to 1902, the repair of wartime destruction, the restoration of towns and cities, and the organization of an educational system. Through the brilliant work of Major Walter Reed of the Army Medical Corps, the mosquito that carried the yellow fever virus was discovered and destroyed, and the disease that had made Havana a pesthole was stamped out.

In the summer of 1900, General Wood ordered an election for delegates to a convention to frame a constitution for the Republic of Cuba. While the convention was in session, Secretary of War Elihu Root insisted that certain provisions be included in the Cuban constitution as a recognition of the special interests and responsibilities of the United States in the island. Root demanded that Cuba agree to make no treaties that impaired its independence or permitted any foreign power to acquire Cuban territory. Cuba should not contract debts whose interest could not be paid out of current revenues. Cuba should sell or lease coaling and naval stations to the United States. Most important, Cuba should allow the United States to intervene whenever the Washington government thought that such action was necessary to preserve Cuban independence or internal order.

Cuban nationalists, having fought bitterly for independence from Spain, naturally had no desire for their new republic to become a permanent ward of the United States. The Cuban constitutional convention therefore wrote a constitution patterned on that of the United States, but with no mention of the provisions demanded by Root. Thereupon, Senator Orville H. Platt of Connecticut wrote these provisions into an amendment to the army appropriation bill of 1901. It authorized the President to withdraw American forces only after the Cubans had accepted Root's terms. The Cuban constitutional convention sent a formal protest to Washington, but it had no alternative, yielded in the end, and incorporated the Platt Amendment in the Cuban constitution. The Cubans then held their election and chose Tomás Estrada Palma as their first President. He took over the government with a surplus of $7 million in the Cuban treasury. The American army withdrew from the island, and the Platt Amendment was embodied in a Cuban-American treaty in 1903.

In the years that followed, the United States felt obliged on several occasions to intervene in Cuba under the provisions of the Platt Amendment. For example, a revolution broke out there in 1906 on the reelection of President Estrada Palma. The American army restored order, and an American administered the government of Cuba until 1909. Again, in 1912 and in 1917, the American government landed marines on the island to prevent civil war. Four years later, the Liberal party of Cuba appealed to President Warren G. Harding to send American troops to supervise elections. In all cases, the United States acted to protect upper- and middle-class Cubans against leaders of the lower classes.

Puerto Rico

Puerto Rico, fourth in size among the islands of the West Indies, with a population of almost 1,000,000, for the most part came willingly under the rule of the United States. It did not seem possible at the time to give statehood or even full territorial status to the island. Some 83 per cent of the inhabitants could neither read nor write; no Puerto Ricans had had any experience in self-government. The Foraker Act of April 1900 gave Puerto Rico a status between that of a colony and that of a territory. It empowered the President of the United States to appoint a governor and a council of eleven, of whom five should be Puerto Ricans. A legislature of thirty-five members was to be elected by the citizens. Spanish courts were entirely swept away and replaced by a judicial system like that of the United States. The new government at once began to concentrate on sanitation, education, roads, and agricultural development.

The Jones Act of 1917 gave Puerto Rico full territorial status and American citizenship to her inhabitants. One result of this change was to give Puerto Ricans control of both houses of the territorial legislature. But the most drastic—and interesting—change occurred in 1952. In that year, Congress adopted a resolution that approved a new Puerto Rican constitution which made the island a self-governing commonwealth, free to choose independence if it so desired. Puerto Ricans voted overwhelmingly to remain within the American Union.

The Philippines

Governance of the Philippines was the hardest test of American abilities at colonial administration. Nearly 8,000,000 people, who inhabited a group of islands 7,000 miles from American shores, had been turned over to American rule against their consent. An armed rebellion against American authority was in process that would, as we have said, eventually cost the United States 1,000 lives and $135 million. In the absence of congressional legislation, President McKinley, as commander in chief, exercised full power over the Philippines. He delegated this power in 1900 to a commission of five members, headed by Judge William Howard Taft of Ohio. The commission proceeded at once to build a civil government and an educational system.

The Spooner Amendment of 1901 gave the President of the United States as absolute a power over the Philippines as any proconsul ever exercised over a distant province of the Roman Empire. The President then appointed Taft as governor of the islands. The Philippine Government Act, approved on July 1, 1902, provided for the faint beginnings of self-government. The Act called for the appointment of a civilian Philippine Commission, to be headed by a civilian governor-general. The commission should take a census of the islands as soon as the insurrection was declared officially to be at an end. Two years later, the commission was to hold elections in the Christian provinces for a Philippine assembly. The commission would be the upper house of the Philippine legislature; the assembly, the lower house. The right to vote was to be given to all males who were twenty-three years of age or over and had held municipal office, or possessed property, or paid taxes of a certain amount, or were literate in either the Spanish or English languages. The literacy test disfranchised a majority of male Filipinos, who were literate in their native languages but were not literate in Spanish or English.

Elections held in 1907 resulted in the choice of an assembly of eighty-one members. About three fourths of these were Nationalists, or supporters of Philippine independence. Meanwhile ex-Governor Taft had won great popularity by his fair, friendly, and forward-looking administration. He went to Manila in person (he was now the Secretary of War) to open the first session of the new assembly in October 1907. Congress had already, in 1902, permitted Philippine products to enter the United States at a reduction of 25 per cent from prevailing tariff rates. Free trade between the Philippines and the United States was established by the Underwood-Simmons Tariff Act of 1913.

Although both the Republican and Democratic parties were committed to eventual independence for the Philippines during this period, the Democrats were more honest in their promises. President Woodrow Wilson was able partially to redeem these promises in the Jones Act, or new Organic Act, of 1916. Although the Jones Act reserved ultimate sovereignty to the United States, it created an elected Senate to supplant the commission as the upper house of the Philippine legislature. It lowered suffrage requirements and required the American governor-general to appoint most heads of executive departments with the consent of the Philippine Senate. Filipinos were far along the road to full self-government by the end of the Wilson administration in 1921; indeed, it was obvious by then that independence could not be long postponed.

The Open Door in China

Victory over Spain and the acquisition of a colonial empire marked the end of American isolation, whether most Americans realized that fact or not. But many Americans did realize it. They became more conscious of events in Asia;

and American manufacturers, merchants, and shippers dreamed once more of potentially enormous markets, particularly in China.

The American government found itself involved in Asian problems almost immediately after the Treaty of Paris had been ratified. China had been badly defeated by Japan in a war in 1894–1895. The great powers then proceeded to carve China's territory into spheres of influence, and Great Britain, France, Germany, Japan, and Russia forced the Chinese government to grant them "leases" of certain areas. The United States took the Philippines just at the time that the European nations and Japan seemed about to agree on a permanent division of China.

The prospect of new markets in the Far East made Americans eager to preserve equal opportunities for trade in China. In addition, Americans already had begun extensive missionary and educational work in China and desired to see her treated fairly. Finally, the British government, whose subjects had the biggest stake, urged the American government to join it to try to preserve equal economic opportunity in China.

Secretary of State John Hay, therefore, had wide support at home and in London when, on September 6, 1899, he circulated what is called the first Open Door note to the powers that were then busy dividing up China. The first Open Door note asked them not to interfere with freedom of trade in the twenty-two ports in China, not to disturb the regular collection of the Chinese customs,

"Marines Defend Peking Legation during Boxer Rebellion." This painting by a U.S. Marine Corps artist depicts the Boxers, a group of Chinese Nationalists, attempting to rid the country of "foreign devils" and thus end the ruthless exploitation of China. (Wide World Photos)

and not to discriminate against other nationals in their spheres of influence in railroad rates or harbor dues.

None of the governments which received Hay's note wished to appear more grasping than the rest. Russia politely declined to give any pledges, but the other nations answered by accepting the terms of the note on condition that all the other governments concurred. Hay, in a gigantic bluff, announced that all the powers had agreed, finally and definitively, to respect the Open Door in China. It was a futile effort to achieve a diplomatic objective—protection of American merchants and investors in China—cheaply, without any commitment, or even threat, of force. Like most such attempts, the Open Door did not work. The powers continued systematically to close their spheres.

Meanwhile, the exploitation of China by Europeans and the social changes caused by the rapid introduction of capitalism had aroused fierce anger among the masses of the Chinese people. Millions of them joined a semireligious patriotic society called the "Righteous Fists of Harmony" (abbreviated to "Boxers"). The Boxer movement spread quickly and violently over the northern provinces of China. A determined army of Boxers besieged the Chinese capital of Peking in 1900, and some 400 persons, including members of the diplomatic corps and their families, took refuge in the enclosure of the British legation. This they fortified with trenches and barricades against the Boxers, who kept them under continuous fire. Of the defenders, sixty-five were killed and 135 were wounded. Finally, an army of American, British, French, German, Russian, and Japanese troops captured the city of Peking. The imperial court fled, and the foreign troops brutally plundered the great city.

Hay feared that the victors would take revenge by overthrowing the Chinese government and dividing the territory of China among themselves. Therefore, he addressed a second circular note to the powers involved on July 3, 1900. It announced that it was the purpose of the United States to preserve Chinese territorial and administrative integrity. This, the second Open Door note, committed the American government, at least in principle, to an important international objective—although again Hay did not promise action if American wishes were ignored. The note may have had some effect, because the powers did not even discuss a division of Chinese territory. Instead, they imposed an indemnity of $334 million upon the Chinese Empire. Half of the American share of $24 million sufficed to satisfy the claims of United States citizens, and the balance was returned to Peking. The Chinese government, 'profoundly impressed with the justice and great friendliness of the United States," used the money for the education of hundreds of young Chinese in American colleges and universities.

3. PROSPERITY AND THE DEATH OF McKINLEY

The Return of Prosperity

While these events were taking place abroad, the United States was entering a period of remarkable prosperity at home. New gold discoveries in Alaska and Canada, and increased production of gold in South Africa, added new money to the stream of currency throughout the world, as well as in the United States. The result was a mild inflation, beginning in 1897, that enabled farmers to sell their cotton, corn, and wheat at higher prices. Farmers began to paint their barns, pay off their mortgages, and put money in the bank. Orders for steel and other industrial products picked up quickly. In 1897, the Republican Congress tried to insure high profits for American manufacturers by passing the Dingley Tariff, which increased rates to the unprecedented level of 52 per cent. The Gold Standard Act of 1900 not only established gold as the single standard; it also provided for the creation of more national banks in small towns.

President McKinley agreed with his friend Mark Hanna that the success of business was the best measure of the country's progress and welfare. Therefore, he initiated no suits under the Sherman Antitrust Act against the growing number of industrial combinations, nor did he take action to regulate the railroads.

It was no accident that American interest in new markets and sources of raw materials across the sea grew with the development of big business. So long as Americans remained chiefly an agricultural people, their surplus crops had gone to feed the industrialized nations of Europe. But the rapid growth of manufacturing had brought a profound change. Now important sectors of American industry needed supplies of raw materials that were unobtainable at home;

President McKinley and party at the U.S. Government Building at the Pan-American Exposition, 1901. This is the last known photograph of McKinley before he was struck down by an assassin's bullet the next day. (Culver Pictures, Inc.)

among these were various metals and ores, rubber, silk, dyewoods, and drugs. The tropical countries could furnish such materials and, at the same time, their peoples could be educated to buy and use American manufactured goods.

Increasingly, it worked out that way after 1900. American exports increased from $1.4 billion in 1900 to nearly $2.5 billion in 1914, while imports rose from $850 million to $1.8 billion during the same period. More important was the change that was taking place in the character of exports and imports. In 1900, agricultural products constituted 60 per cent of the nation's exports; manufactured products, only 35 per cent. But by 1914, manufactured products accounted for nearly 49 per cent of American exports, although a large proportion of these products went to other industrialized nations, especially Canada and the western European countries. American investment abroad grew even faster than foreign trade. By 1898, Americans had invested only $685 million abroad. The figure stood at $3.5 billion on the eve of the First World War.

The Assassination of McKinley

Fortune seemed to smile on McKinley as he took the oath of office for the second time on March 4, 1901. The country had just given his administration a vote of confidence, and he left Washington with members of his cabinet at the end of April for a grand tour of the country.

On September 5, McKinley spoke at the Pan-American Exposition at Buffalo, New York, and advocated reciprocal trade agreements to promote American foreign trade. The next day, as he was holding a reception in the Temple of Music, he was shot by a young anarchist named Leon Czolgosz, whose emotions had been aroused by attacks against "Czar McKinley" in sensational journals. After a week of suffering, McKinley died. He was the third American President to fall by an assassin's bullet.

SUGGESTED READINGS

For excellent general works on the war with Spain, see Beisner, *From the Old Diplomacy to the New*, already cited; Foster R. Dulles, *America's Rise to World Power* (1955) and *The Imperial Years* (1956); and Margaret Leech, *In the Days of McKinley* (1959). More specialized but very significant are Ernest R. May, *Imperial Democracy* (1961); Julius W. Pratt, *The Expansionists of 1898* (1964); and LeFeber, *The New Empire*, already cited.

Walter Millis, *The Martial Spirit* (1931); Frank Freidel, *The Splendid Little War* (1958); and M. W. Wilkerson, *Public Opinion and the Spanish-American War* (1932), are all excellent. R. S. West, Jr., *Admirals of the American Empire* (1948), covers naval operations.

For expansionism in general, see Edmund Morris, *The Rise of Theodore Roosevelt* (1979), and W. D. Puleston, *Mahan* (1939).

The late nineteenth-century mood can best be caught by reading two very influential books: Josiah Strong, *Our Country* (1885), and Alfred T. Mahan, *The Influence of Sea Power upon History* (1890).

There is a very large literature on the anti-imperialists. Some of the best books on their crusade are E. Berkeley Tompkins, *Anti-Imperialism in the United States, 1890–1920* (1970); Robert L. Beisner, *Twelve Against Empire: The Anti-Imperialists, 1898–1900*; and Sondra R. Herman, *Eleven Against War* (1969). For the Philippine Insurrection, see Leon Wolff, *Little Brown Brother* (1961). Julius W. Pratt, *America's Colonial Empire* (1950), is splendid on the Treaty of Paris and the subsequent administration of American dependencies.

CHAPTER 22
THE AMERICAN PEOPLE AT THE END OF THE CENTURY

1. PEOPLE IN MOTION, VALUES IN TRANSITION

The Growth of the City

The industrial and transportation revolutions which transformed the American economy in the second half of the nineteenth century caused profound demographic and social changes. In the last decades of the century, the urbanization of the United States began in earnest, and the nation received a new wave of immigrants. Urbanization and immigration, along with industrialization itself, brought into focus the outlines of modern mass society. In the process, Americans were forced to reconsider many old and cherished conclusions about what constituted the good society. By the time of the First World War, this reconsideration had advanced so far that the social values of the preceeding half century would seem quaintly archaic to many forward-looking Americans. And, yet, the values of an older America, tied to the community, family, church, and ethnic group, would persist into the new century and would often conflict with "modern" thinking.

At the turn of the century, more Americans lived outside of large towns and cities than in them; less than 14 per cent were foreign-born, and three out of four lived east of the Mississippi River. However, the demographic landscape was already undergoing drastic changes. For one thing, the westward movement was continuing apace, despite the widely heralded "closing" of the frontier in 1890. There was the further settlement of Texas and the Plains states. In addition, an ever growing stream of people moved to California and the other states of the Pacific coast. Even more consequential than the west-ward movement was the migration of people from the country and small towns to the large cities. In response to the growing need for workers in commerce and industry, rural Americans flocked to the cities by the millions every year. By 1910, more than 46 per cent of the people would live in cities and towns; ten years later, the United States would be primarily a nation of city dwellers. Finally, immigration was not only increasing at the turn of the century but was also changing profoundly in character. To a large extent, immigrants were settling permanently in cities, both the older seaports and the newer inland metropolises, such as Chicago, St. Louis, and Milwaukee. The cities seemed to represent a new frontier which drew immigrants from the country-side and foreign shores with the promise of a better life.

Growth and Physical Transformation

Cities had long been the centers of American commercial, cultural, and polit-ical life, and there had been an identifiably urban way of life since the seven-teenth century. What was different about the last decades of the nineteenth century was the dizzying rate of urban growth, the expanded role of cities in the nation's economy, and the altered physical configuration of the cities themselves.

In the last part of the nineteenth century, New York City more than doubled in size to 3,400,000. Chicago grew from less than 300,000 in 1870 to 2,700,000 in 1920. By 1920, the nation had twenty-five cities with populations over 250,000. Most of the large cities were in the Northeast and Midwest, but the rise of Birmingham and Atlanta in the South and Denver, Los Angeles, and Seattle in the West emphasized that the urbanization process was affecting the entire nation. Hundreds of smaller cities and towns, many of them called into being by the rail lines which crisscrossed the nation, were also an important part of the urban network.

The reasons for this population shift are not hard to find. Urban growth was almost entirely the result of industrial, financial, and commercial develop-ment. The railroad network, which was virtually complete by the turn of the century, made many of the large cities into the principal "nodes" of a vast na-tional transportation and market system. In addition, on the coasts, and at crit-ical points on inland waterways, cities became the connecting links between that national market system and the lanes of international commerce. Conse-quently, cities became the locus of manufacturing to a much larger extent than had been the case in the early days of the industrial revolution. To name the burgeoning cities of the late nineteenth century is to see these processes at work: railroads (connecting with Great Lakes waterways) plus meat packing and steel manufacturing made Chicago into the metropolis of the Middle West by 1900. Iron and steel made a large city out of old Pittsburgh and gave birth to Birmingham, where a corn patch had stood in 1870. The garment industry and great expansion of domestic and foreign commerce, banking, and in-surance promoted New York's extraordinary growth. While a handful of giant cities diversified into the full range of manufacturing and commercial endeavors, scores of smaller ones specialized in one or a few lines of goods for sale in the national market. Richmond relied on cigarettes; Schenectady, on electrical machinery; Fall River, Massachusetts, on cotton textiles, and so on.

While the size and economic function of cities were being altered in the late nineteenth century, so, too, was their physical layout. For one thing, cities became easier to get around in, and thus earlier constraints on urban size were lifted. This made possible the urban sprawl which has come to characterize modern cities. Horse-drawn conveyances, first, then steam railways and electric trolleys gave city dwellers more mobility. Trolley systems, which were in common use by the end of the 1890s, freed urbanites and the cities themselves from the old scale of the "walking city," which had a radius of about two and one-half miles. Trolleys and interurban railroads made possible the appearance of a new species of American—the suburban commuter. Movement within cities was also facilitated during this era by the construction of steel suspension and truss bridges across the rivers which often divided cities or separated neighboring towns. Among the most monumental of these was the Brooklyn Bridge; it was 1,600 feet in length and completed in 1883, and it spanned the East River between Manhattan and Brooklyn. Smaller truss bridges, virtually mass produced by bridge-making firms, served similar functions in countless towns across the land by the end of the century.

Not only were cities growing *out*, but they were also growing *up*. The development of high quality steel, available for building use by the late nineteenth century, was a crucial cause of this phenomenon. In the 1880s, a group of Chicago-based architects developed steel-framed high-rise buildings which were structurally capable of surpassing the maximum height of traditional masonry-walled buildings. Chicago's Home Insurance Building, designed by William Jenny and completed in 1885, was the first such building. Louis Sullivan moved beyond Jenny in pioneering the now familiar skyscraper, with its smooth functional lines, plain thin walls, and large glass windows. Beginning with the Tacoma Building in Chicago (1888), Sullivan and his protégés (who included Frank Lloyd Wright) led the way in transforming the skylines of America's largest cities. The soaring height of the commercial skyscrapers reflected not only the technological breakthrough of steel-frame construction and the costliness of urban land, but also the expanding scale of American commercial and industrial enterprise. The same was true of many new factories, which dwarfed older buildings in order to accommodate the increased scale of industrial production. The age of big business became the age of big buildings.

Increasingly, these giant industrial structures were located at the outer edge of the metropolis or in segregated industrial corridors, or even in "satellite cities," such as Pullman, Illinois, or Gary, Indiana, both built near Chicago in the late nineteenth century. Rapidly disappearing was the older urban pattern in which small commercial, manufacturing, and residential buildings were side by side. At the end of the century, American cities were fast becoming segregated along functional lines.

At the same time, residential areas were becoming more and more segregated along class and ethnic lines. In Chicago, as in most major cities, one could discern the now familiar radial pattern of residential segregation, with a decaying core inhabited by the poor, surrounded by rings where the more well to do lived. The segregation of American cities along lines of economic function and of class in the late nineteenth century is not surprising, given their increasing size and complexity. However, this spatial transformation (and it *was* a departure from past practice) would bode ill for the economic and social well-being of the nation's major urban centers.

The City and American Democracy

When Lincoln Steffens, one of the great journalists in American history, published a book on the government of American cities in 1904, he could find a no more accurate title than *The Shame of the Cities*. As Steffens described it, municipal administration everywhere was characterized by waste, inefficiency, and, above all, corruption.

Perhaps it could not have been otherwise. The government of cities had been organized for the most part during the high tide of Jacksonian democracy. City founders had deliberately diffused power among mayors, aldermen, and numerous boards and agencies, but in most cities the formal government was a mere facade. Shrewd observers, such as Steffens, found that the real government was the "machine" headed by a boss and numerous lieutenants. They were usually not officeholders, but were simply in business for the profit that officeholding would yield. Unlimited profits were to be made — from the sale of franchises for street railways and utilities, for protection against enforcement of all sorts of municipal regulations, and the like.

This bribery, or "boodle," as Steffens called it, was the oil that lubricated the machines. The votes of newly enfranchised immigrants often supplied their political power. The machines, with their political clubs and friendly societies, were the one great assimilating and unifying force in the large American cities in the late nineteenth century. Moreover, the machine maintained its political base by providing all kinds of social services for its constituents — finding work for newly arrived immigrants, providing fuel and food for hungry families, and acting as intermediary between immigrant families and a host of unfamiliar public institutions. These services were usually delivered by the same neighborhood functionaries who got out the vote on election day.

There were periodic campaigns by local reformers to organize the "better" elements (usually they were the commercial elite) and to overthrow corrupt machines in the cities. But campaigns for municipal reform were sporadic and usually only temporarily successful before the end of the century. The National Municipal League, founded in 1894, would later become a major clearinghouse of information on methods to promote efficient and honest government in the nation's cities.

Many thoughtful and influential Americans saw that the cities were beset by social and economic ills which threatened the very foundations of democratic society. But their perceptions of what the problems *were* varied sharply. Some persons were preoccupied with political corruption and individual vice (they usually meant drunkenness and prostitution), and some saw the cities as a potential battleground of the class warfare which seemed to loom on the horizon. They argued that stern measures were needed to turn back the rising tide of anarchism. At the height of the urban rioting which accompanied the railroad strikes in 1877, one respected journal of opinion, *The Independent*, proclaimed: "Bring on then the troops — the armed police — in overwhelming numbers. Bring out the Gatling guns. Let there be no fooling with blank cartridges."

Others began to see the problems of the cities differently and focused less on confrontations in the streets than on the quieter crises of overcrowding and inadequate medical care, sanitation, and fire protection within the impoverished sections of the cities. Out of this discovery of urban poverty and deprivation would come a wide variety of humanitarian reform crusades, often linked to the campaigns to reform city government. We will return to the story of these urban reform movements in the next chapter.

The Transformation of Community Life in Urban America

Many Americans feared that life in the sprawling new cities would undermine the social cohesion which had presumably characterized small communities. Until the middle of the nineteenth century, the lives of most Americans were rooted in a place, or series of places, within which social networks of family, kin, and neighbor created a powerful sense of communal solidarity. The unceasing westward movement certainly weakened the bonds of those social networks, but people often moved as families or neighborhood groups; and, even in the new settlements throughout the West, the "voluntary communities" of churches, benevolent societies, and fraternal orders had provided surrogates for community ties based on blood, marriage, and long association.

But the primacy of these "island communities" in American life was fading by the 1870s, as railroads and telegraph lines strung together villages and towns into vast regional and national marketing networks, and burgeoning cities expanded the scale of urban life far beyond the physical limits of the face-to-face community. At the same time, the "wholeness" of community life — the union of work, play, and worship — was splitting into specialized segments (work life *vs.* family life, for example), each with different and even conflicting values. More and more, Americans found themselves living in two worlds, the small, private world of family and community, and a larger, public world in which one's identity lay with an abstract group, such as a profession, trade, or class.

However, these physical and cultural changes by no means spelled the end of face-to-face community life in America. On the contrary, the *transformation* of community life, which had begun before the Civil War, continued apace: social relations which were entirely rooted in a particular locality became relatively less important than translocal social networks. And even the most closely knit of all communities — the family — changed in response to the modernizing influences of urbanization and industrialization discussed in Chapter 18. In short, community life was not bulldozed out of existence by the forces of modernization. It was sometimes reformulated and sometimes forced into tense coexistence with impersonal, modern social relationships, but it did not collapse.

There also emerged at the end of the nineteenth century "communities of interest," which brought together individuals from different localities who shared a particular professional or business interest. Like the voluntary associations which Americans had been forming since the beginning of the nineteenth century, these occupational groups were formed for specific and instrumental purposes, but they also carried some of the overarching cultural meaning which characterized community life.

By the 1880s and 1890s, forward-looking lawyers, doctors, educators, and engineers were beginning to shape their respective professions into something which resembled their present form. They began to use professional associations, such as the American Medical Association, to modernize and regulate their respective occupations. For this new breed of professionally minded individuals, accredited competence in a particular specialization (such as medicine, engineering, or law) was at once the source of power and status and of their ability to render service to society. They aggressively developed their new regional and national organizations to further both of those ends. Increasingly, this new breed of professionals, along with progressive counterparts in business, labor, and agriculture, perceived their own role in society to be based more on their professional skills and their affiliation with forward-looking colleagues than on their status within a particular local community. All together, they formed a new "middle class," whose standing as a class was based more on their professionalism and cosmopolitan attitudes than on wealth or income. For better or for worse, they would lead the way in reforming government, society, and business in the early years of the twentieth century.

2. IMMIGRATION, ETHNICITY, AND ETHNIC CONFLICT

The "New" Immigration

From the beginning of American history, the character of the United States has been determined by the shifting tides of immigration to its shores. Between 1860 and 1900, almost 14,000,000 immigrants came to the United States, and another 14,500,000 followed between 1900 and 1915. The most important fact of this huge movement was not its size, but the radical change in the origins of the immigrants. A shift in the tide of immigration from northern Europe to southern and eastern Europe began quietly in the 1880s and then gained speed in the 1890s and early 1900s. In the first decade of the new century, nearly three quarters of all immigrants coming to the United States were from southern and eastern Europe. Most of the rest came from northern Europe and Canada, with a relatively small number entering from Japan, China, and Mexico.

These "new" immigrants were not only pulled by the promise of a better life in the United States; they were also pushed by economic, social, and political pressures in parts of Europe which threatened traditional cultures and, for some, even life itself. In the late nineteenth century, sharp population increases in rural Europe fragmented landholdings which were already hard pressed to support the existing population. Competition from American agricultural commodities after the 1870s depressed grain prices for farmers in central and southern Europe, and industrialization rendered obsolete the skills of many peasant craftsmen. Religious and political persecution, particularly against eastern European Jews, made migration a virtual necessity for many persons.

For whatever reason they came, Europeans who came to the new world in 1900 found the voyage itself to be much less hazardous, less time-consuming, and less expensive than had been the case for earlier immigrants. Although immigrants were still typically crowded into steerage and confronted with indignities at many points along the way, they now had dramatically greater prospects of surviving the voyage, and the cost was low. In 1911, the fare from Naples to New York was as low as $15.

The shifting tide of immigration to the United States (and to other countries in the new world as well) clearly reflected European conditions at the turn of

An Italian family arriving at Ellis Island in 1905 by Lewis Hine, the reformer-photographer who earned a fine reputation for his studies of immigrants. The story of American immigration contains motives that were "a mixture of yearning—for riches, for land, for change, for tranquillity, for freedom, and for something not definable in words." (Collection of International Museum of Photography at George Eastman House)

the century. Nearly 3,000,000 Italians migrated to the United States between 1901 and 1915, mainly from impoverished southern Italy and Sicily. Between 1880 and 1915, about 6,000,000 persons came from the two empires of Russia and Austria-Hungary. There were Poles, Slovaks, Croatians, south Serbs, Ruthenians, and many other ethnic and national groups. The eastern European migration included about 2,750,000 Ashkenazic Jews, whose religious orthodoxy and Yiddish culture set them apart from most of the 250,000 German Jews who had already settled in the United States.

For the most part, the "new" immigrants were people of the land—property-holding peasants and landless agricultural workers. For them, ties of family and village were vitally important. Except for the Jews, most of them were Roman Catholic, Eastern Orthodox, or communicants of ethnically and nationally identified Catholic churches. The cultural heritage which they brought with them to the new world (and through which they maintained ties with the old) was both a source of strength and a barrier to full participation in the life of their adopted country.

The "New" Immigrant in America

Although most of them were of rural origin, the "new" immigrants flocked to the cities of America. The high cost of taking up land and the declining need for farm laborers blocked their access to the countryside. The cities, on the other hand, held out some hope of employment and of maintaining ties with their own people. Indeed, many had come because friends or relatives in the United States or agents of American companies had promised them jobs and paid their passage. They went to stockyards in Chicago; to steel mills in western Pennsylvania, Ohio, and Indiana; to mines in Pennsylvania, West Virginia, and Colorado; and, among the Jews, to garment factories in New York and other large cities. Others, who could not find jobs in manufacturing or construction, eked out a living as street peddlers or domestic servants, or in similarly low paying jobs. Even in industry, the jobs open to most immigrants were low paying. Although their labor made possible the rise of the United States to industrial and economic power between 1880 and 1910, the immigrants received only a tiny portion of the wealth which industrialization generated.

Most of the immigrants who were thrust into urban America at the turn of the century came from communal societies, in which kinship networks and the seasonal rhythms of village life had framed their very existence. Their experience in adjusting to a strange new world obviously differed from place to place and from one group to another. However, in general, families survived the temporary separations and the trauma of migration, and they retained many of their old world functions in the new. Extended families, and even groups of families from the same village or region, clustered together in neighborhoods in American cities. This promoted social cohesion and economic security. Family and village ties persisted, as was evidenced by the steady flow of money from the United States to family members who stayed behind, and by the return to the old country of many immigrants who had intended only to earn enough money in the United States to secure the economic well-being of themselves and their children. Many immigrants also found a sense of national identity in their new home through ethnic parishes and voluntary associations, such as fraternal orders and mutual benefit societies. Taken together, these various social institutions created remarkably cohesive cultural enclaves within the anonymity of American cities.

As for the economic fortunes of the "new" immigrants, that matter has to be discussed in the context of the immigrants' own cultural heritage, since definitions of "success" are by no means culture-free. Most of the "new" immigrants began at the bottom of the economic ladder, since they had access to only the most menial and low paying jobs. There were differences in the rate at which various ethnic groups moved up the ladder. Some groups, particularly those which placed a premium on education, moved rather quickly into the middle class. In other groups, upward occupational mobility was valued less highly than the maintenance of stability and order within the ethnic community, and these groups tended more often to maintain working-class status.

The economic condition of the "new" immigrants should also be viewed within the over-all context of affluence and poverty in urban-industrial America. At the end of the century, the gap between the haves and the have-nots continued to widen. In 1910, 1 per cent of the people owned 47 per cent of the na-

View from the south terrace of Biltmore, the country house of George W. Vanderbilt. Situated near Asheville, North Carolina, it was designed by Richard Morris Hunt, an architect who modeled fashionable homes for the wealthy businessmen after French chateaux. These large and elaborate estates were built of heavy stone and generally had high, steep roofs, turrets, and towers. (Culver Pictures, Inc.)

tional wealth and received 15 per cent of the annual income. In the days before income and inheritance taxes, a small number of individuals were able to build unbelievable fortunes. For example, by 1900 John D. Rockefeller's income was about $100 million a year (a dollar in 1900 would be worth almost four dollars today). The very rich lived on a scale that rivaled, if it did not surpass, that of the wealthiest monarchs of Europe, and the ostentatious social life of rich Americans was reported in the popular press in the manner of royalty. At the same time, some of the very rich shunned such conspicuous consumption, and many of them were pouring millions into various charitable causes. Philanthropy became almost as necessary for social acceptance in some upper-class circles as formal dinners, tours of Europe, and the presentation of one's daughters at the proper debutantes' balls.

Things were different at the other end of the scale. As late as 1915, the United States Industrial Commission found that between one third and one half of all American workers in mining and manufacturing earned less than enough to buy the food, shelter, and clothing needed by their families. Conditions were even worse in some rural sections, particularly in the South, where declining prices and the ubiquitous sharecropping system locked millions of black and white farmers into grinding poverty. Everywhere, the lot of the very poor included drab surroundings, poor or nonexistent educational opportunities, exceptional health hazards, and shortened life expectancy.

The opportunity for poor people to move into the emerging middle class varied from place to place. For example, the rigid class and caste systems of the rural South severely limited upward mobility. On the other hand, a sizable proportion of those who stayed in industrial communities for several years advanced from blue collar to white collar jobs. However, we do not know what happened to those who left (many were unquestionably part of a floating underclass of unskilled workers). Opportunities for economic advancement certainly existed at the turn of the century, and countless families persistently hoped to create a better life for their children, but the pervasiveness of poverty did not change. In addition, periodic convulsions of the economic system — most notably the depressions of the 1870s and 1890s — created even more misery than usual in the form of massive wage cuts and unemployment.

Racism and the Immigrants: Nativism and the Drive for Exclusion

The rapid infusion of immigrants, coupled with hard times, created severe social tensions in America at the turn of the century. It was neither the first nor the last outburst of nativism in the United States (witness the wave of anti-Catholic hysteria which greeted the Irish in the 1840s and 1850s and, in the late 1970s, the mixed reception of the Vietnamese boat people). But the coming of so many millions of people of backgrounds radically different from those of old-stock Americans, in such a short period, seemed to raise insoluble problems. Because the new immigrants were very different in language, political backgrounds, and social customs, many Americans wondered whether they could ever be assimilated into the mainstream of national life. They were usually poor and often (except for the Jews, Syrians, and Armenians) unable to read and write in their native languages. Their self-contained ethnic communities, which the immigrants saw as a source of strength and protection, were perceived by others as proof of their unwillingness to become "100 per cent Americans."

Some Protestants resented the fact that a high percentage of the "new" immigrants were Roman Catholics and Jews. Others were sure that the immigration of so many "foreigners" threatened the country with revolutionary upheavals. Many frightened Americans thought that the "new" immigrants were inferior "racially" and that their assimilation would weaken the dominant "nordic" stock. This popular view was reinforced by the prevailing scientific and scholarly thought of the day, whether it emanated from biologists, sociologists, or historians.

Such hostilities and fears provoked movements that were themselves alien to the most highly valued American traditions. They bore various names — such as United Order of Deputies, the American League, and the Minute Men of 1886. But the most powerful nativist group during this period was the American Protective Association, organized in 1887 to rally Americans for a fight against Catholicism. It grew with startling rapidity after the onset of the Panic of 1893 and stirred hostilities that would weaken the society for decades to come.

Not all the animosity directed toward the "new" immigrants came from

Americans of British or northern European extraction. Old-world hostilities between and among national and ethnic groups were brought to America. For example, northern Italians had for ages looked down upon southern Italians, and the small northern Italian community in the United States transferred those feelings to the great wave of immigrants from southern Italy. Similarly, American Jews of German extraction, many of whom practiced reform Judaism and strove for assimilation, looked askance at the newly arrived eastern European Jews, whose strict orthodoxy and Yiddish culture set them apart. And eastern European Catholics, for whom religion and ethnicity were intertwined, received a less than cordial welcome in many American parishes, where Irish or French clergymen and parishioners treated them as second-class communicants. No wonder, then, that many of the recent immigrants found that American society upset the equilibrium of their lives at least as much as their presence distressed the old-stock Americans.

Many Americans who believed that there was an "immigrant problem" saw its solution in reducing the numbers coming to the United States. One method proposed was to require that immigrants be able to read and write. Organized labor and other groups pressed hard for a literacy test all through the late 1890s and early 1900s. Congress adopted such a measure three times, only to have it vetoed by Presidents Cleveland, Taft, and Wilson. Finally, in 1917, Congress passed the literacy test over President Wilson's veto. Other forms of restrictive legislation began in the 1880s. In 1882, Congress excluded Chinese immigrants, convicts, and the insane. Subsequent laws denied entry to certain "undesirable" types of individuals, including immigrants under contract, paupers, anarchists, and people with communicable diseases. The exclusionary legislation would culminate, as we shall later see, with the National Origins Act of 1924, which reduced the flood of immigration to a trickle.

Racism and Afro-Americans: Disfranchisement and Segregation

Despite the nominal equality afforded blacks by the Thirteenth, Fourteenth, and Fifteenth Amendments to the Constitution, and by federal legislation, the freedmen had continually to deal with a virulent strain of racism similar to that which confronted the "new" immigrants. The presumption of black inferiority was widespread and constant among white Americans throughout the nineteenth century. What was new at the end of the century was the institutionalization of racism. Southern states and localities legally disfranchised and segregated blacks, and the federal government and national public opinion acquiesced in those processes.

Even after the Republicans lost control of the various southern state governments, the G.O.P. — which still included many black voters — remained a force to be reckoned with in the South. To be sure, intimidation took its toll, but, as late as 1880, a majority of adult black males voted in the presidential election in every southern state except two. However, in the last two decades of the nineteenth century and the first decade of the twentieth, southern states and municipalities passed a series of ordinances which, without violating the letter of the Fifteenth Amendment, effectively disfranchised almost all southern blacks. Property requirements and cumulative poll taxes excluded many of the poor. Literacy and "understanding" tests screened out those who could not read and, when administered prejudicially, many of those who could. Along with these and other legal restrictions, outright terrorism was again used, as it had been in the Reconstruction era, to prevent blacks from voting.

In 1890 Congress failed to enact the so-called Force bill (see p. 536), which would have instituted federal supervision of elections in the South (and in many northern cities as well). In 1898, in the case of Williams v. Mississippi, the Supreme Court upheld the constitutionality of that state's thoroughgoing system of disfranchisement.

It is an interesting fact that the holders of political power in the South, who had not attempted to prevent black voting altogether at the end of Reconstruction, did just that at the end of the century. Some historians have linked disfranchisement to the movements of rural insurgency in the 1880s and 1890s, which culminated in Populism. However, the exact connection between disfranchisement and agrarian protest is still shrouded in controversy. Some scholars have argued that white Populists, who had tried and failed to establish an effective biracial coalition, revealed their underlying racism by turning on their erstwhile allies and leading the movement for disfranchisement. However, the same laws which removed most blacks from politics also sharply reduced voting among poor whites. In Virginia, for example, the over-all turnout in gubernatorial elections dropped from 81 per cent in 1885 to 27 per cent in 1905. The most thorough study of disfranchisement in the South concludes that it was engineered, not by the Populists, but by their archenemies, the conservative Democrats, who wished to stamp out lower-class insurgency and political opposition among both blacks and whites. The evidence on that point is substantial, and, yet, in many southern states the disfranchisement of blacks drew strong support from the very rural whites who were the natural constituency of Populism.

At the same time, southern states and municipalities enacted segregation ordinances which separated whites and blacks in schools, restaurants, hotels, theaters, railway cars, and even court rooms. South Carolina went so far as to provide separate Bibles for administering oaths to black witnesses. In practice, some degree of segregation had long existed between blacks and whites, in the North as well as in the South. But these new ordinances made segregation virtually universal in the South and backed it with the full force of the law.

As in the matter of disfranchisement, the federal judiciary chose to overlook the obvious affront to constitutional safeguards which de jure segregation represented. In 1883, the Supreme Court struck down the Civil Rights Act of 1875, which had prohibited segregation of public facilities. In the case of Plessy v. Ferguson (1896) the court established the doctrine of "separate but equal" and held that, so long as "equal" facilities were established for blacks and whites (in this case railroad accomodations), they need not be integrated. For over half a century, this principle governed civil rights cases. Neither in Plessy v. Ferguson nor in most subsequent cases did the court examine closely the actual conditions which were alleged to be equal.

De jure segregation and disfranchisement were accompanied by an upsurge of racial violence. In the first two years of the twentieth century, 214 blacks were lynched in the United States. Violence was collective as well as individual. Urban mobs in Atlanta and elsewhere attacked blacks and black-owned property in 1906. Armed Democrats in Wilmington, North Carolina, in 1898 overthrew the duly elected Republican government, an event which, had it occurred elsewhere on the globe, would have been called a *coup d'état.* Instead, it is known in history books as the Wilmington race riot.

Historians do not really understand why this wave of racial repression and violence swept across the South when it did. It coincided with severe economic distress, and the two are somehow related. But it is also true that these repressive acts occurred within a climate of popular and scholarly opinion which found them at least tolerable and sometimes even justifiable. Only a few white Americans in either the North or the South possessed both the courage and the detachment from their own culture to protest. In the postemancipation era, this was truly the nadir of relations between blacks and whites.

Black Americans resisted as best they could, but for the most part the forms of their resistance resembled those practiced by their forebears in slavery times. A few fled to the West or the North, although the great exodus from the rural South would not begin in earnest until the First World War. Others employed the day-to-day resistance of the field hand; others, even after the turn of the century, risked life and property to protest openly such things as the segregation of street cars in southern cities.

Among the educated elite a few, like William Monroe Trotter, a Harvard graduate of Boston, still clung to the Reconstruction dream of full equality. Others, like Bishop Henry M. Turner, despaired of American justice and urged Afro-Americans to return to their ancestral homeland in Africa. However, the strategy which won the broadest support among the black elite (and probably among the masses as well) was that of Booker T. Washington, the ex-slave who founded Tuskegee Institute in Alabama and who preached a gospel of self-help and accommodation. Washington publicly urged blacks to defer hopes of political and social equality and to concentrate on economic self-improvement and bourgeois refinement. Privately, even secretly, Washington consulted with Presidents and leaders of business on matters relating to blacks. With strong support from wealthy white philanthropists, Washington exerted a powerful influence over the press, the pulpit, and the classroom in black America until his death in 1915.

Militant blacks denounced Washington before and after his death as a self-serving accommodationist (see pp. 606–607). Washington's preeminence owed much to the support of prominent whites who found his rhetoric reassuring. But Washington's strategy was double-edged. He called for *temporary* acquiescence in a bad, but virtually intractable situation. At the same time, he nurtured the cultural pride and interior resourcefulness which had sustained Afro-Americans during the long night of slavery.

3. CULTURAL CHANGE IN THE AGE OF INDUSTRIALIZATION

Old and New Currents of Social Reform

Throughout most of the nineteenth century, genteel and middle-class reformers had proposed all kinds of cures for the ills of American society. The great wave of reform which began early in the century had included the temperance crusade, the drives to abolish slavery and emancipate women, and the campaign to restore social order by the establishment of asylums and penitentiaries for the insane, the infirm, and the criminal. This antebellum reform crusade had involved fresh, original thinking about the needs of American society in a new age. At heart, it had been optimistic about the prospects of reforming individuals (and, through them, the whole society) by moral suasion.

However, the optimistic individualism of the antebellum reform movement did not fare so well in the age of urbanization, industrialization, and massive immigration. The temperance crusade gave way to tight-lipped prohibitionism. The asylum movement was conceded to be a failure before the end of the century. And even large elements of the abolitionist army could not see beyond individual emancipation to the structural barriers which confronted freedmen in American economic, social, and political life. Perhaps the women's movement most nearly retained its antebellum vitality and imagination, although even here the growing concentration on suffrage caused a narrowing of the movement's objectives.

The new breed of social reformers who emerged in the 1890s retained some of the religious fervor and optimistic individualism of their predecessors and a touch of the idealism of utopian and communitarian thinkers. However, social reformers in the 1890s also differed from their predecessors in their perceptions of social problems and how to cure them. For one thing, late nineteenth-century reformers were forced to look at the structural and environmental ills of the cities and of modern industry in different ways. In addition, they began to adopt a tactic of attack on social problems quite unlike the once-for-all utopian plans so common in the mid-nineteenth century.

By the end of the century, religious organizations and a new group of professional social workers were addressing themselves to problems of the urban poor. Protestant churches, greatly influenced by an earlier movement in Great Britain, began to awaken to the challenges to Christian ethics raised by slums, poverty, disease and human exploitation on a massive scale. New social attitudes emerged, quite different from the alarmed conservatism with which most church leaders had responded to the first waves of urban-industrial violence in the 1870s. This new perspective came to be known as the Social Gospel, and its most eloquent spokesmen included the Baptist minister Walter Rauschenbusch and the Congregationalist Washington Gladden. In Rauschenbusch's words, the Social Gospel was "the application of the teachings of Jesus and the total message of the Christian salvation to society, economic life, and social institutions . . . as well as to individuals." The Social Gospel took concrete form in institutional (community-oriented) churches, hospitals, missions, and social and relief work. The Salvation Army, founded by William Booth in England in 1880, spread to the United States in 1890 and concentrated its efforts on work with the urban poor. The Roman Catholic Church, which had been operating on the front lines in urban slums since the massive Irish. immigration in the 1840s, redoubled its ministrations to the poor. Moreover, Pope Leo XIII's encyclical of 1891, *Rerum Novarum*, put the Catholic Church squarely behind the European and American movements for social justice.

Ministers and priests were in the vanguard of efforts to improve life in city slums. A separate class of social workers, employed by city welfare departments and charity organizations, followed closely on their trail. Not only did they minister to the needs of the poor, but they also made intensive surveys of labor conditions, the causes of poverty and crime, and the means of alleviating social distress. One group of the social workers made a major contribution through the founding of settlement houses as social-service centers in the heart of the slums. Jane Addams' Hull-House, founded in Chicago in 1889, and Lillian D. Wald's Henry Street Settlement, founded in New York in 1893, were among these "spearheads for reform," as their historian has called them. To a greater extent than most other charity workers, participants in the settlement-house movement viewed the assimilation of the immigrant poor as a two-way street. They moved into the neighborhoods which they served and attempted to learn from the immigrants; at the same time, they sought to "uplift" them and introduce them to American ways of life.

The professionalization of social work (one of the few professions open to women at the turn of the century) was part of the larger trend toward professionalization described above. Whether in medicine, law, education, engineering, or a host of other occupations, these new college-trained professionals believed that knowledge and skill, not merely wealth and social standing, held the key to power in modern America, and also to the resolution of social ills. At the turn of the century, to a much greater extent than would later be the case, professional men and women believed that social reform *was* humanly possible and that the responsibility for its achievement was theirs. Economic and social problems, as well as the physical problems of urban overcrowding, rural isolation, and many other problems, could be reduced to their constituent parts and then be attacked rationally — "scientifically" — by experts in various fields. The persistent application of scientific and bureaucratic methods would, they believed, bring results where less practical approaches had failed. This new breed of reformers would coexist for some time with the older utopians, and even share some of their enthusiasm. But the future belonged to the experts.

Educational Innovations

The emergence of modern professionalism at the end of the nineteenth century was linked to important changes in American higher education. The antebellum colleges, relatively few in number and small in size, offered a single classical course of study (students did not *major* in a particular subject), which was intended to build character and provide a general education rather than to prepare individuals for a particular occupation (with the exception of training for the ministry). Beginning in the 1870s, major changes began to occur in college curricula and in the over-all purpose of higher education. Under Charles W. Eliot, Harvard led the way in broadening the classical curriculum, raising academic standards, and identifying university training more explicitly with the professions. The Johns Hopkins University, founded in 1876, brought to the United States the model of the German graduate and research institution. Other universities, both old and new, followed Hopkins' lead in promoting graduate training and scholarly research in a broad range of disciplines, including the new social sciences. Equally important was the proliferation of state-supported colleges of agriculture and engineering. These "land-grant" colleges — established with the help of land grants from the federal government under the Morrill Act of 1862 — were from the outset committed to broadening the social base and the academic content of higher education.

These developments had two important consequences for higher education. First, the older professions (medicine, law, and education) and many newer ones (such as engineering and business management) became more dependent on the university. Recognition as a profession now required a corresponding program of university study, and an individual's admission to the profession required certification by completion of such a program, either at the graduate or undergraduate level. One could no longer "read" medicine or law or learn engineering in the shop. The relationship between the universities and the professions was interactive. Practicing professionals, organized into national associations, had considerable influence over curricula related to their fields, and the universities not only conveyed the required knowledge to neophytes in each field, but also imbued many of them with the missionary zeal which made the professions a focal point of social reform at the turn of the century.

The transformation of the classical college into the modern university also affected the growing public-school systems. Widespread university training of high quality presupposed a broad network of high schools with similarly rigorous standards and a uniform curriculum. Before the end of the nineteenth century, no such network existed in America. In many parts of the country, particularly in rural areas, high schools were either nonexistent or substandard, and the content of their curricula varied widely. Colleges and universities led the fight for higher standards, a uniform curriculum, and state accreditation for public high schools. The high schools thus formed a link in the educational chain which was being forged at the end of the century, one between the new universities and also the expanding elementary school systems, which were just then being organized into a graded curriculum of eight years in duration.

At the turn of the century, the outline of our modern educational system had taken shape, but the structure was far from complete. By 1900, free public education (and inexpensive parochial schooling) at the elementary level was within reach of children in most parts of the country. The fledgling system of high schools, most of which were situated in towns or cities, enrolled only about 500,000 students, but the high schools were about to undergo a major expansion. Similarly, the colleges and universities, as influential as they were becoming, had a total enrollment of only slightly more than 100,000. However, that represented a sharp increase from the recent past, and much greater expansion was just on the horizon.

Main Trends in Literature

The turn of the century also found American literature in the midst of important changes. The period from 1865 to 1900 had witnessed the flowering of a new school of realism, whose writers endeavored to portray life as it was, whether bitter or sweet. William Dean Howells, already the "dean of American letters," had left Boston in 1881 for New York. He was convinced that the center of American life and letters had passed to the larger, more cosmopolitan city. In the 1890s, Howells, who had been affected by sustained contact with socialists and anarchists, young writers, and some less savory aspects of American life, wrote to his friend Henry James: "After fifty years of optimistic contentment with 'civilization' and its ability to come out all right in the end, I now abhor it, and feel that it is coming out all wrong in the end, unless it bases itself in a real equality." Howells' novels about the effects of industrialization and the rise of the new rich were stilted, almost devoid of passion; but they

An advertisement for two stories by Mark Twain, "Pudd'nhead Wilson"
and "Tom Sawyer Abroad." Convinced that Twain's literature
documented an entire epoch in American history, playwright George
Bernard Shaw once wrote to him: "The future historian of America will
find your works as indispensable to him as a French historian finds the
political tracts of Voltaire." (The Bettmann Archive)

were all the more effective because of his past acquiescence in the post-Civil
War changes in his country. However, his best novels in the 1880s and 1890s,
A Hazard of New Fortunes and *A Traveler from Altruria*, did more to encour-
age the younger realists than they did to edify the public.

Mark Twain, probably the greatest American writer of fiction of the period,
poked fun mercilessly at the pretensions of his fellow Americans. Only stories
published after his death, such as *The Mysterious Stranger*, revealed the full
extent of his bitterness. In *The Adventures of Huckleberry Finn*, *The Adventures of Tom Sawyer*, *The Gilded Age*, and *A Connecticut Yankee in King
Arthur's Court*, Twain created a host of memorable characters and hundreds of
uproariously funny scenes. His finest characters — Tom Sawyer, Huck Finn,
and the slave Jim — parodied accepted customs in their games and, in their
conversations, exposed the hypocrisy with which American life was rife.

Henry James, who almost defies classification (although he called himself a
realist), explored the contrast between mythical democracy in the United
States and the actual uneven distribution of power. However, his favorite
theme was the confrontation of the innocent American with the sophisticated
European culture. James' novels, especially *The American* and *The Ambassadors*, are still read, not so much for their realistic depiction of these problems,
as for their dramatic stories and the author's elegant prose.

Realism as a force in American literature was by no means dead at the turn of the century. Indeed, it would continue to be the major school of fictional writing for at least two decades to come. But realistic writing was becoming harsher and less optimistic, as the work of young novelists such as Hamlin Garland and Jack London in the West and Ellen Glasgow in the South revealed. Asked for love stories with happy endings, Garland refused: "No, we've had enough of lies. Other writers are telling the truth about the city . . . , and it appears to me that the time has come to tell the truth about the barnyard's daily grind." In addition, the turn of the century marked the spectacular growth of literature concerned frankly with political, social, and economic problems. This literature of protest, as it was called, would swell in volume and add much strength to the reform movements of the early years of the twentieth century.

Just beginning in the United States at the same time was a new school of fictional writing called naturalism. Its practitioners sought to portray man as a biological creature in his natural environment. The publication of Theodore Dreiser's *Sister Carrie* in 1900—a sympathetic, yet tragic story of a prostitute—announced the coming of naturalism from France to the United States; it would reach full flower in the 1920s with the advent of a host of brilliant writers such as Ernest Hemingway and John Dos Passos.

The realism of late nineteenth-century literature contrasted sharply with the dominant romanticism of an earlier day. The social origins of this intellectual shift included the growing perception by men of letters from old-stock, genteel families that the future, and even the present, belonged to people of a different class. But more was involved here than the anxieties of a declining elite. Educated Americans from many social levels were coming to see that, in the age of industrialization and urbanization, the romanticism and optimistic individualism of an earlier time could no longer suffice as a way of interpreting the world around them.

SUGGESTED READINGS

Two general studies which interpret social change at the end of the nineteenth century are Robert H. Wiebe, *The Search for Order, 1887–1920* (1967), and Samuel P. Hays, *The Response to Industrialism, 1885–1914* (1957).

Sam B. Warner, Jr., *The Urban Wilderness: A History of the American City* (1972), provides a good description of the physical development of American cities, while Arthur M. Schlesinger, Sr., *The Rise of the City, 1878–1898* (1933), remains useful as an introduction to the urban history of the period. American urbanization is placed in broad historical perspective by Lewis Mumford in *The Culture of the Cities* (1938), and *The City in History* (1961).

A number of recent works focus on social and occupational mobility and family structure in late nineteenth-century cities. Among them are Stephan Thernstrom and Richard Sennett, eds., *Nineteenth Century Cities: Essays in the New Urban History* (1969); Thernstrom, *The Other Bostonians: Poverty and Progress in the American Metropolis* (1973); Sennett, *Families Against the City* (1970); Michael Frisch, *Town into City: Springfield, Massachusetts and the Meaning of Community, 1840–1880* (1972); and Clyde Griffen and Sally Griffen, *Natives and Newcomers: The Ordering of Opportunity in Mid-Nineteenth Century Poughkeepsie* (1977). A thoughtful discussion of the changing meaning of community, and one which challenges the assumptions of many of the mobility studies, is Thomas Bender, *Community and Social Change in America* (1978).

A pioneering study of the experience of immigrants in the United States is W. I. Thomas and Florian Znaniecki, *The Polish Peasant in America*, 5 vols. (Boston, 1918–20). A more recent work, Oscar Handlin, *The Uprooted* (1951), has been subjected to serious criticism by later works, which have focused on immigrants and immigrant families in particular cities. Among these are Josef Barton, *Peasants and Strangers: Italians,*

Rumanians, and Slovaks in an American City, 1890–1950 (1975); Virginia Yans-McLaughlin, *Family and Community: Italian Immigrants in Buffalo, 1880–1930* (1977); and Thomas Kessner, *The Golden Door: Italian and Jewish Immigrant Mobility* (1977). John Higham, *Strangers in the Land: Patterns of Nativism, 1860–1925* (1955) remains the standard treatment of that subject. James Stuart Olson, *The Ethnic Dimension in American History* (1979), is a useful survey of various ethnic groups in America.

Among the common problems of urban and immigration history are the related ones of poverty and slums. Robert H. Bremner, *From the Depths* (1956), provides a fine introduction. Among contemporary comments on those problems, well worth reading are the works of Jacob Riis: *How the Other Half Lives* (1890), *The Children of the Poor* (1892), and *The Battle with the Slum* (1902). Jane Addams, *Twenty Years at Hull-House* (1890), gives a firsthand description of the settlement-house movement. The standard historical treatment of that subject is Allen F. Davis, *Spearheads for Reform* (1967). The most profound contemporary criticism of corruption in city governments is Lincoln Steffens, *The Shame of the Cities* (1904).

The role of religious organizations in dealing with social problems of urban-industrial America is discussed in Charles H. Hopkins, *The Rise of the Social Gospel in American Protestantism, 1865–1915* (1940); Henry F. May, *Protestant Churches and Industrial America* (1949); and Aaron I. Abell, *American Catholicism and Social Action: A Search for Social Justice, 1865–1950* (1960).

The Afro-American encounter with institutionalized racism in the late nineteenth century has been the subject of considerable research. John Hope Franklin, *From Slavery to Freedom* (5th edn., 1980) contains a good introduction to the subject. The rise of *de jure* segregation is discussed in a classic study, C. Vann Woodward, *The Strange Career of Jim Crow* (3rd edn. 1974), although some of its conclusions are challenged in Joel Williamson, *After Slavery: The Negro in South Carolina During Reconstruction, 1861–1877* (1965). The standard account of disfranchisement is J. Morgan Kousser, *The Shaping of*

Southern Politics: Suffrage Restriction and the Establishment of the One-Party South, 1880–1910 (1974). Booker T. Washington's early career is examined in the first volume of a projected multivolume biography: Louis R. Harlan, *Booker T. Washington: The Making of a Black Leader, 1856–1901* (1972).

Useful information on public education in this period is found in Lawrence A. Cremin, *The Transformation of the School: Progressivism in American Education, 1876–1957* (1961). For a thorough treatment of the movement to extend education beyond the classroom, see Robert O. Case and Victoria Case, *We Called It Culture: The Story of Chautauqua* (1958). On higher education, see especially Lawrence R. Veysey, *The Emergence of the American University* (1965), and Richard Hofstadter and Walter Metzger, *The Development of Academic Freedom in the United States* (1955). A humorous and stinging contemporary indictment of outside influence on the universities is Thorstein Veblen, *The Higher Learning in America* (1918).

On the art and architecture see Lewis Mumford, *The Brown Decades: A Study of the Arts in America, 1865–1895* (1931); Oliver W. Larkin, *Art and Life in America* (1949); Wayne Andrews, *Architecture, Ambition, and Americans* (1955); and John E. Burchard and Albert Bush-Brown, *The Architecture of America* (1961).

In addition to the general surveys of literary history already cited, a good survey of the period is Lazer Ziff, *The American 1890s: Life and Times of a Lost Generation* (1966). A good brief account is also found in Alfred Kazin, *On Native Grounds* (1942). Van Wyck Brooks, *New England: Indian Summer, 1865–1915* (1940), is a fine regional study. Everett Carter, *Howells and the Age of Realism* (1954), traces Howells' influence. The best treatment of Henry Adams is in Ernest Samuels, *Henry Adams: The Middle Years* (1958) and *Henry Adams: The Major Phase* (1964). Justin Kaplan, *Mr. Clemens and Mark Twain* (1966), is a generally satisfactory biography, but it should be supplemented by James M. Cox, *Mark Twain: The Fate of Humor* (1966). The greatest work on an American writer of this period is Leon J. Edel, *Henry James*, 5 vols. (1953–72).

CHAPTER 23
THE PROGRESSIVE MOVEMENT

1. BACKGROUND OF REVOLT

The Nature of the Progressive Movement

When Theodore Roosevelt succeeded McKinley in 1901, the United States was already in the first stages of the political eruption that historians call the progressive movement. Basically, progressivism was the response of the great majority of the American people to the problems raised by recent industrialization and urbanization. The most disturbing of these problems were the breakdown of responsible democratic government in city and state; the spread of slums, crime, and poverty in the large cities; the exploitation of workers, especially women and children; the growth of industrial and financial concentration; and, above all, the emergence of great economic interests—railroads, large corporations, and banking empires—that had the power profoundly to affect the destinies of the people and yet remained beyond popular control.

In actuality, progressivism was not one national crusade, but an aggregation of many movements for social, economic, and political reform. These movements. were enormously varied and sometimes mutually antagonistic, and this fact sometimes causes confusion in historical understanding.

There were two broad currents in what is loosely called progressivism during its early years—currents of reform and of reconstruction. Many Americans were reformers of the earlier Mugwump type in that they worked for honest, good, and efficient government, but some of them had no desire for any important reconstruction of political or economic life. They might believe strongly in businesslike administration of government, for example, and also regard the income tax or the subtreasury plan as pernicious class measures. Other Americans believed in both reform and reconstruction. To achieve the latter, they came to rely more and more upon concerted, purposeful, and democratic governmental action. The political and economic reconstructionists were the growing, dominant element among progressives after the Panic of 1893. It is these champions of the expansion of governmental power that will be referred to below as "progressives."

The Dynamics of Progressivism

All of progressivism's major components had their origins as recognizable movements in the 1890s. They were among the immediate responses to the economic distress caused by both the agrarian depression of that period and the industrial depression that followed the Panic of 1893. It is more difficult to explain why the movement gained its greatest momentum and achieved its most important triumphs between 1897 and 1920 — a period of expanding prosperity and national contentment. An understanding of this phenomenon requires study of the great variety of people involved in various aspects of progressive reform, their different objectives, and the many forms that their participation took.

Progressivism's roots lay deep in American traditions, but it had its immediate origins in a series of disconnected movements for reform and reconstruction during the 1890s:

1. The most obvious was Populism. The Populists, and then Bryan in 1896, failed to win national power because they remained essentially agrarian spokesmen and never won the support of either industrial labor or the urban middle classes, the groups that provided most of the motivating force in progressivism. However, as we have seen, Populism and Bryanism did shake the political foundations and caused an important major political realignment. More important, Populist propaganda publicized widespread distress at the same time that it succeeded in reviving the concept of governmental action to insure the people's economic well-being. In addition, the Populists' emphasis upon greater popular participation in and control of the political machinery paved the way for sweeping institutional reforms in the near future.

2. The sharp intensification of human distress during the Panic of 1893 dramatized for increasing numbers of urban Americans the wide contrast between the privileged position of the well-to-do and the plight of the poor. The impact was heaviest on the ministers, priests, and social workers who worked in the slums of the great cities. The Reverend Doctor Walter Rauschenbusch (whose *Christianity and the Social Crisis*, 1907, made him the leading prophet of the Social Gospel) said about the poor whom he saw in a New York settlement house during the depression of the 1890s: "They wore down our threshold, and they wore away our hearts. . . . One could hear human virtue cracking and crumbling all around." While the depression that began in 1893 was much less severe in the United States than the economic catastrophe of the 1930s, a larger proportion of the population lived at the subsistence level in 1893 than in 1929. For this reason, temporary unemployment had more serious consequences. The suffering connected with the depression of the 1890s stimulated

enormously the two movements that furnished much of the moral zeal for progressivism—the Social Gospel and the movement for social justice.

3. Americans in the 1890s, already convulsed by the hard-hitting indictments of the Populists and Bryan, were further agitated by a growing literature of exposure. As we have said, it began with Henry George's *Progress and Poverty* (1879), gained momentum with the publication of Edward Bellamy's utopian socialist novel, *Looking Backward* (1888), and came to fully developed form in Henry Demarest Lloyd's scathing indictment of the Standard Oil Trust, *Wealth Against Commonwealth* (1894). From 1894 onward, arraignment and exposure were the order of the day in American journalism. The introduction of the inexpensive magazine in the 1890s provided a new medium of vast circulation. Soon muckraking magazines, such as *McClure's*, *Everybody's*, and *The American Magazine*, and muckrakers, such as Lincoln Steffens, Ida M. Tarbell, Ray Stannard Baker, and Burton J. Hendrick, were exploring and exposing every dark corner of American life. The muckrakers did not set off the progressive movement. However, they fired the moral indignation of the middle classes by exposing the misery and corruption in American society and helped to make the progressive movement in the early 1900s a national uprising instead of a series of disconnected campaigns.

4. By the 1890s, economists, political scientists, sociologists, and other publicists were beginning to challenge successfully the philosophical foundations of the laissez-faire state—social Darwinism and classical economics—and the whole cluster of ideals associated with rugged individualism. Leaders of this revolt against laissez faire were young economists like Richard T. Ely and Thorstein Veblen and sociologists like Lester F. Ward and Edward A. Ross. Their ranks swelled in the early 1900s. Herbert Croly (*The Promise of American Life*, 1909), Walter Weyl (*The New Democracy*, 1912), and Walter Lippmann (*Preface to Politics*, 1913) worked out a sophisticated justification for the activistic welfare state. Gustavus Myers, in his *History of the Great American Fortunes*, (1909–1910), debunked the fabled captains of American industry by portraying them as freebooters and plunderers. Charles A. Beard, another muckraking historian, destroyed the halos around the Founding Fathers in his *An Economic Interpretation of the Constitution* (1913). Roscoe Pound and Louis D. Brandeis developed what was known as sociological jurisprudence; that is, a legal system based on economic and social facts, as well as upon abstract legal theories.

5. The growth of the urban middle classes accelerated the impact of these movements and the development of certain tendencies within these groups. Progressivism became largely an urban, middle-class movement after the waning of the agrarian revolt. Three profoundly important things happened to the urban middle classes in the 1890s and early 1900s. First, they grew so rapidly in numbers because of business expansion that they were able to wield the balance of political power in many sections of the country by 1900. Second, influential segments of these classes, molded by their specialized training and professional standards and affiliations, joined in insisting upon rationality and efficient administration in public affairs. Finally, because they were the best educated and most idealistic segment of the population, they were deeply affected by the exposures of corruption and accounts of economic and social distress. By the late 1890s they were building up a full head of steam of moral indignation. The boiler would soon explode, with very significant political repercussions.

2. THE MUNICIPAL REFORM MOVEMENT

Beginnings and Progress

The crusade for municipal reform marked the beginning, chronologically speaking, of progressivism as a *political* movement. It began sporadically in the early 1890s and became a widespread revolt about 1896–1897. Hazen S. Pingree, elected Mayor of Detroit in 1889, led the way by battling and subduing that city's trolley, gas, and telephone companies. Then an uprising occurred in Chicago against a corrupt city council that was busy selling franchises to Charles T. Yerkes, a utilities magnate. A Municipal Voters' League, organized by civic-minded businessmen, clergymen, and professional leaders, won control of the city council in 1896–1897 and helped to elect a reform mayor, Carter Harrison, in the latter year. Similar citizens' groups overthrew a notoriously corrupt administration in Minneapolis.

The dominant pattern of municipal reform, however, was redemption through the work of a single colorful and dynamic leader. There was a host of such city reformers, and only a few of them can be mentioned. Mark M. Fagan, elected Mayor of Jersey City in 1901, fought for, and won, more equitable taxation of railroads and public utilities in order to pay for his program of expanded social services and better schools. Also notable were Samuel M. ("Golden Rule") Jones and Brand Whitlock in Toledo.

This drawing of Lincoln Steffens by James Montgomery Flagg appeared in Harper's Weekly *(1914). The leading reform journalist during the early part of the twentieth century, Steffens wrote of municipal corruption in* The Shame of the Cities: *"Business men came almost as cheap as politicians and they came also at the city's expense."* (Culver Pictures, Inc.)

The most successful municipal reformer of this era was Tom L. Johnson of Cleveland. Johnson, elected mayor of that city in 1901, gathered around him some of the brightest young municipal administrators in the country. He made Cleveland, as Lincoln Steffens put it, the best-governed city in the United States. Johnson gained a national reputation for his fight against the Cleveland street railways. But he made his greatest contributions by reorganizing and streamlining the Cleveland city government and by proving that it could be efficient even while greatly expanding its services. He also won the support of the "new immigrants" and conclusively demonstrated that the big-city masses would follow reform leadership that understood their needs and would not always remain the pawns of the established, corrupt machines.

New Instruments for Municipal Democracy

All municipal reformers fought political officials allied with privileged business elements and the underworld. In addition, they all fought for efficient government, fair taxation, regulation of public service corporations, and better education and expanded social services for the poor. But the reformers soon learned that their victories would never be secure so long as the established leaders continued to control the party structures. Hence progressives in the cities joined hands with other groups to obtain new machinery which would assure popular control of political processes. This machinery included the direct primary for nominating candidates, the short ballot, and the initiative, referendum, and recall. These campaigns were carried out on the state level, and will be discussed in connection with the progressive movement in the states.

City governments were almost totally subject to state legislatures. Thus the city political organizations—usually powerful parts of state organizations—were often able to hobble the city progressives by voting down their reforms. Municipal reformers in most states, therefore, also battled to obtain home rule and an end to legislative interference in city administration. State legislatures dominated by rural and small-town representatives did not give up power willingly. Missouri, California, Washington, and Minnesota had granted home rule by 1900. Eight other states followed suit between 1900 and 1914, but only two of them—Ohio and Michigan—had cities of any size.

As it turned out, the most promising and successful institutional changes were two new forms of city government. The first—the commission form—originated and proposed by political scientists in the 1890s, was instituted in Galveston, Texas, in 1900, after a tidal wave inundated the city, and the old administration of mayor and aldermen proved utterly unable to cope with the emergency. Government of the city was vested in five commissioners, elected, after 1903, by the people.

The commission form was so successful in Galveston that soon Houston, Dallas, Fort Worth, Austin, and El Paso adopted it. It spread rapidly, particularly after the Iowa legislature, in 1907, adopted a more elaborate version of the Texas model. The Iowa Plan, or Des Moines Idea (so-called because Des Moines instituted the plan in 1908), provided for the election of five commissioners in a nonpartisan canvass. Each commissioner was responsible for a single administrative department, such as finance, public health, or public works. In addition, the Iowa Plan incorporated the initiative, referendum, and recall as part of the machinery of city politics. By 1914, some 400 municipalities, chiefly medium-sized cities in the Middle West, New England, and the Pacific states, had adopted the commission form.

The commission plan was a great advance over the old mayor-aldermen system because it concentrated responsibility in a small body, but experience soon proved that it offered no guarantee that commissioners themselves would be expert administrators. Hence, between 1908 and 1912, progressives refined a new idea—government by an expert city manager appointed by and responsible to a popularly elected city council. The city-manager plan, first adopted in its complete form by Dayton, Ohio, in 1913, after a disastrous flood, spread rapidly. More than 300 cities had adopted it by 1923.

It would be a gross exaggeration to say that all American cities had been politically redeemed before the outbreak of the First World War. But the accomplishments of the municipal crusaders were significant and in most cases more than temporary. The era of flagrant nationwide corruption was over. Even the old-fashioned organizations such as Tammany were being transformed by young leaders of urban democracy such as Alfred E. Smith and Robert F. Wagner. Cities not only were being governed more efficiently; they were also beginning to grapple successfully with economic and social problems. Moreover, a whole new class of professional municipal administrators was in training throughout the country. The city, while far from the bright hope of American democracy, was no longer its nemesis.

3. THE STRUGGLE FOR SELF-GOVERNMENT IN THE STATES

The Shame of the States

Different special-interest groups, often corrupt, reactionary, and blind in many respects to the welfare of the people, controlled the governments of most states around the turn of the century. There were state political machines, just like city machines, that governed behind the facade of the formal structure. What was called the System worked usually with relentless efficiency.

Missouri and New Jersey offer vivid if somewhat exaggerated examples of the System in operation. In the former, the real power in the state capital was a lobby which represented certain railroad and business interests. This totally nonpartisan lobby governed through the party caucuses and controlled them by bribery and favors. In New Jersey, the System worked through a corporation-machine alliance in which the corporate, railroad, and financial interests furnished the leadership, called the Board of Guardians, of the dominant Republican party. The railroad lobby, for example, in 1903 provided the chief justice of the state, the attorney general, the state comptroller, the commissioner of banking and insurance, and one of the members of the state board of taxation. Railroads in New Jersey, needless to say, paid very low taxes.

The Progressive Revolt in the States

The progressive revolt in the states was the product of earlier reform movements, both urban and rural. In the South and the West, agrarian radicalism gave way to progressivism after 1896, as urban spokesmen took leadership in the fight against railroad and corporation dominance. The Middle West, where conservative Republicans were firmly in the saddle until near the end of the century, was swept by a series of spectacular state revolts from about 1900 to 1908. Insurgent antiorganization Republicans such as Robert M. La Follette of Wisconsin, Albert B. Cummins of Iowa, and Joseph H. Bristow of Kansas transformed the Middle West from the bastion of conservative Republican power into the leadership of progressivism in the states.

State progressive movements in the East were more often the culmination of earlier municipal movements, but they were no less important than those in other sections. New York progressives came to power in Albany under the governorship of Charles Evans Hughes from 1907 to 1910. Woodrow Wilson's election as Governor of New Jersey in 1910 was the culmination of a movement begun largely by Republican progressives. In Ohio, progressivism won its most sweeping triumph with the adoption of a new constitution and the election of a Democratic progressive, James M. Cox, in 1912. Politics was equally convulsed on the West coast by the successful campaigns of reformers like William S. U'Ren in Oregon and Hiram W. Johnson in California.

It was nothing less than a nationwide revolt, one that profoundly affected American politics. The rebellion shattered the old political organizations, brought vigorous new leadership to power in many states, and transformed state governments into agencies more sensitive to economic and social needs. The most important cause of this upheaval, in the cities as well as in the states, was the sudden growth and emergence to power of the urban middle classes. Their spokesmen were quick to articulate and fight for their needs.

"Give the Government Back to the People!"

That fight proceeded first on the political front, in an effort to make institutions of government more susceptible to public control. Representative government had collapsed because old forms either had broken down or were too easily controlled by self-serving politicians. Hence new forms had to be found to help restore democracy. One such device was the direct primary, in which the people themselves, rather than a coterie of politicians in caucuses and conventions, would nominate party candidates. Mississippi, in 1902, was the first state to require nominations by the direct primary. The following year, Governor La Follette persuaded the legislature of Wisconsin to enact a similar law. The direct primary was widely adopted after this date. By 1916 only Rhode Island, Connecticut, and New Mexico still used the convention system for nominations.

The direct primary was merely the first step, and progressives won a variety of other innovations. One was the short ballot, which supposedly would enable voters to make intelligent decisions and concentrate responsibility. It was adopted most widely by cities in connection with the commission and city-manager forms of government. Another was stringent corrupt-practices legislation to limit campaign contributions and expenditures. Progressives also obtained the direct election of United States senators by the people instead of by the state legislatures.

The demand for the direct election of senators had originated with the Populists. It was further excited by the muckrakers, particularly by David Graham Phillips' "The Treason of the Senate," published in *Cosmopolitan* in 1906.

This article portrayed the upper house as the nerve center of the System in the United States. The Senate resisted the demand for popular election for many years, and state after state adopted the plan of permitting the voters to indicate their choice of a senatorial candidate in primary elections. By 1910, more than enough states to ratify a federal amendment had already instituted this indirect method of the direct election of senators. After a scandal in the senatorial election of William Lorimer, Republican boss of Illinois in that state's legislature, the Senate finally yielded in 1912 and approved the Seventeenth Amendment for the direct election of senators. It was ratified in record time in 1913. Another democratic innovation — the presidential preferential primary — enabled voters to express their choice for presidential candidates. It was first adopted by Oregon in 1910; a dozen states used it in 1912.

Finally, progressives championed measures to be used as a last resort, in the event that governments became irresponsible even under the new representative forms. Two such measures were the devices of the initiative and referendum, which enabled a certain percentage of the voters to initiate and submit legislation to the general electorate if the legislature refused to adopt it (the initiative), and to demand a special election enabling voters to repeal legislation enacted by the legislature (the referendum). Some twenty-one states had adopted the initiative and referendum by 1915. A further safeguard was the recall, which enabled voters to unseat unpopular or dishonest officials, including judges. It was adopted most widely in cities with the commission and city-manager forms, but nine states, most of them in the West, made state as well as local officials subject to the recall.

Experience since the adoption of these measures has cast some doubt on the usefulness of the initiative, referendum, and recall; but it has confirmed the soundness of the rest of the progressive institutional reforms. Progressives were not socialists; they did not desire or advocate sweeping fundamental changes in the American political, economic, or social systems. They simply wanted to make the capitalistic system socially responsible and democratic institutions more responsive to the needs and wishes of its citizens. In their efforts to achieve these goals, they enjoyed considerable success.

Toward the Regulatory-Welfare State

Progressives must be judged not so much by the institutional changes that they wrought, but on a basis of what they did with the political power that they won. Their achievement in modernizing the administrative structures of city and state governments was impressive in itself. Even more impressive were their accomplishments in social and economic reform. By 1914, every state but one had established minimum age limits for child labor which ranged from fourteen to sixteen. By 1917, some thirty-nine states had attempted to protect women workers by limiting the number of hours that they might work. The Supreme Court, in Muller v. Oregon, in 1908 had upheld the constitutionality of this legislation. Various investigations revealed that numerous women received wages entirely inadequate to maintain a decent standard of living. Beginning with Massachusetts in 1912, some fifteen states by 1923 had enacted some form of minimum wage legislation for women. In the latter year, the Supreme Court declared all such laws unconstitutional. Between 1911 and 1916, some thirty states established accident insurance systems for industrial workers and thus removed the burden of industrial accidents and deaths from the backs of both workers and employers. Under the leadership of the Women's Christian Temperance Union, the Anti-Saloon League, and the Methodist, Presbyterian, Baptist, and Congregational churches, state after state, particularly in the South and West, prohibited the manufacture and sale of intoxicating beverages. Three fourths of the American people lived in dry counties by 1917, while two thirds of the states had adopted prohibition. Although many Americans did not consider prohibition either progressive or a reform, the leaders of the movement were sincerely trying to improve the quality of American life. Most states that did not have them by the beginning of the progressive era established state railroad and public utility commissions to regulate rates and services. So effective had state regulation of railroads become by 1914 that the railroad managers were then begging Congress to save them from too harsh controls by state commissions.

Progressives, despite all their concern for vital democratic government, on the whole ignored America's greatest problem—the plight of the one tenth of Americans who were black. They remained economically submerged, socially ostracized, and, in large sections of the South, disfranchised as well. Faint glimmerings of hope did appear for black Americans. A small group of black intellectuals, led by William E. B. Du Bois, organized the Niagara Movement in 1905 to work for the advancement of blacks. But Du Bois' movement be-

Theodore Roosevelt speaking at a meeting of the National Negro Business League with Booker T. Washington on his left. Because of his belief that "the agitation of questions of social equality is the extremest folly," Washington's conservative and submissive doctrine was later rejected as "Uncle Tomism." (Culver Pictures, Inc.)

came mired in constant controversy with the blacks and whites who looked to Booker T. Washington, founder and head of Tuskegee Institute in Alabama, as the chief spokesman of black Americans. Washington gave the impression of being willing to accept segregation and a very gradual change in race relations. Actually, Washington was a canny politician, and he did much to cool the superheated racial antagonisms of the late 1890s and early 1900s, particularly in the South.

In any event, it was largely in protest against Washington's program of accommodation that a group of black and white educators, editors, clergymen, and social workers organized the National Association for the Advancement of Colored People in 1909, the year after a race riot in Springfield, Illinois. The N.A.A.C.P. kept the American democratic conscience alive, in part through its journal, *The Crisis*, which Du Bois edited; but it represented only a tiny minority even as late as the outbreak of the First World War.

In addition, a group of white and black social workers, sociologists, and philanthropists organized the National Urban League in New York in 1911. It worked with increasing effectiveness to find jobs for blacks and to improve their living standards in the large northern cities. Indeed, the National Urban League played an indispensable role after the migration of hundreds of thousands of blacks from the South to northern and midwestern urban areas began in 1915.

Blacks continued to struggle for education and reduced their illiteracy rate from 44.5 per cent in 1900 to 22.9 per cent in 1920. But their economic condition did not markedly improve during the progressive period, and their social condition actually worsened as racism and segregation spread throughout the North. As we have seen, the political and social condition of southern blacks had deteriorated earlier in the aftermath of the agrarian revolt. Lynching continued in the twentieth century to be an important means to control or intimidate blacks. More than 1,100 of them fell victims to lynch mobs between 1900 and 1914. Hardly any of the progressive leaders acted as though the terrible plight of black Americans was a problem that ought seriously to concern them.

Women and the Progressive Movement

Much of the generative power of progressivism came from what has to be called one of the most remarkable generations of women in American history. Middle-class women began to go in large numbers to college, particularly to the women's colleges that were founded during the last four decades of the nineteenth century (for example, Vassar, 1861; Smith, 1871; Bryn Mawr, 1885; Agnes Scott, 1889; Randolph-Macon College for Women, 1893). Some 2,500 women had graduated from college in 1890; that number had increased to nearly 8,500 by 1910.

A few brave women almost literally fought their way into graduate and professional schools, but they were rare exceptions. Many female college graduates, of course, went into elementary and secondary school teaching. Most of them married and devoted themselves full-time to their families, but a large number were filled with a zeal for social service and reform. Of this latter group, some took leadership in establishing settlement houses—social centers built in the midst of the slums of great cities that provided day-care services for children, classes for immigrants, and a wide variety of social services. To mention only two, Jane Addams founded Hull-House in Chicago in 1889 and became in the eyes of many persons the greatest woman of her generation. Lillian D. Wald founded the Henry Street Settlement in New York in 1895; she was also active in many other reform causes. Numerous women went into the new profession of social work. Others, such as Frances Willard, who founded the Women's Christian Temperance Union in 1874, led the fight against the saloon. Still others worked for child labor legislation and the regulation of the hours and wages of women and helped to organize female workers in the garment workshops. Margaret Drier Robins and Mary McDowell were the driving forces in the National Women's Trade Union League, founded in 1903. Josephine Goldmark organized the National Consumers' League in 1899 to work on behalf of saleswomen in department stores. Florence Kelley and Goldmark also assembled the data that Brandeis used in his brief in the case of Muller *v.* Oregon. Julia Lathrop became, in 1912, the first head of the United States Children's Bureau. These are only a few representatives of thousands of women who were in the forefront of the movement for social justice. That movement could not have succeeded without their energy, zeal, and moral commitment.

The Struggle for Woman Suffrage

The movement for woman suffrage, begun so bravely at the Seneca Falls convention of July 1848 by Lucretia Mott and Elizabeth Cady Stanton (see pp. 384–385), did not prosper as the Victorian period, with its emphasis on male supremacy and the "proper" role of women, wore on. Mrs. Stanton and a

Woman Suffrage before 1920

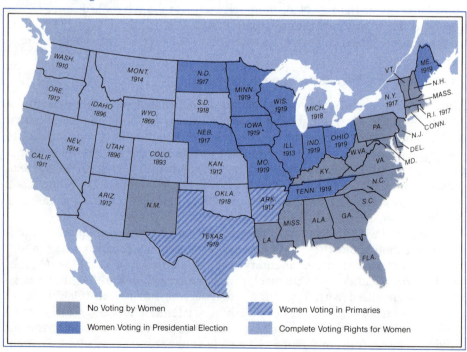

younger recruit, Susan Brownell Anthony, organized the National Woman Suffrage Association in 1869 to secure a Sixteenth Amendment; it was reorganized in 1890 as the National American Woman Suffrage Association (NAWSA). But woman suffrage reformers met abuse and ridicule, not only from men, but also from many Victorian women, who thought that political equality would lead to the destruction of the home and what women's magazines called the redeeming feminine influence. The real power and momentum of the campaign for female suffrage had to await the emergence of the new middle-class generation of women, about which we have just written. By 1900, only Wyoming (1890), Colorado (1893), and Idaho and Utah (1896) had granted suffrage to women, presumably because they had proved that they were equal to men in the arduous tasks of subduing the wilderness.

What had been a seemingly hopeless cause began to turn into a crusade with the election of Carrie Clinton Lane Chapman Catt as president of the NAWSA in 1900 and of Dr. Anna Howard Shaw to the same position in 1904. They turned the NAWSA from propaganda work to political action. Washington (1910), California (1911), Arizona, Kansas, and Oregon (all in 1912), and Montana and Nevada (1914) fell into line, and Illinois, in 1913, permitted women to vote in presidential elections. But resistance remained formidable, both from women and men in the South and the East. New Jersey, New York, Massachusetts, and Pennsylvania rejected woman suffrage in 1915. Moreover, the ranks of woman reformers divided when a militant group, led by Alice Paul, broke away from the NAWSA in 1914 and formed the Congressional Union (later the National Woman's Party). Paul and her associates announced that they had only one objective and would oppose *any* candidate who would not promise to vote for a federal woman suffrage amendment.

The Progressive platform of 1912 contained a plank vaguely favoring woman suffrage; the Democrats and Republicans were silent on the issue in that year. But this did not daunt Catt and Shaw. They began to bombard Woodrow Wilson with petitions and delegations of women once he was in the White House. Wilson at first refused to take a position. However, he voted for woman suffrage in New Jersey in 1915 and wrote a plank for the Democratic platform of 1916 that read: "We recommend the extension of the franchise to the women of the country by the States upon the same terms as to men."

Wilson seems to have become committed in principle to woman suffrage in 1916. To be sure, he would not go beyond the Democratic platform plank in the campaign of 1916, even though his Republican opponent, Charles Evans Hughes, came out in favor of a federal suffrage amendment. However, Wilson's letters and speeches during the campaign indicate that he deeply believed in suffrage for women and that, now, it was with him merely a question of political strategy — that is, whether he could muster the necessary two-thirds votes in both houses of Congress for a federal amendment. Also, Wilson recognized and was grateful for the votes of women which reelected him in 1916. He carried ten of the eleven states that granted complete voting rights to women by 1916.

For whatever reason, Wilson became a leading and the most important advocate of woman suffrage from this time forward and worked in close cooperation with Shaw and Catt. Women rallied to the war effort once the United States entered the First World War. Wilson said that they had earned the suffrage by their heroic sacrifices; but he also insisted that woman suffrage was "an act of right and justice." Under his pressure, the House of Representatives approved a woman suffrage amendment on January 10, 1918. Prospects for approval by the Senate seemed bleak, but Wilson only redoubled his campaign. When it seemed certain that the Senate would reject the amendment, Wilson went before that body on September 30, 1918, and eloquently appealed for its approval. It was the only time in American history that a President has ever addressed either house of Congress on behalf of a constitutional amendment. The Senate rejected the amendment on October 1, but Wilson would not give up. He twisted the arms of his personal friends in the upper house and sent a special message to Congress from the Paris Peace Conference on May 20, 1918. The Senate yielded on June 4 — with no votes to spare.

Wilson worked as hard for ratification as he had for congressional approval of what was now the Nineteenth Amendment. It was due entirely to his influence that Tennessee ratified the amendment on August 21, 1919, and made it a part of the Constitution.

The Nineteenth Amendment was one of the crowning achievements of the progressive era. It did not bring the millennium for women in the United States. They continued for decades to run into stone walls when they tried to enter the professions, particularly the medical and legal professions. They also continued (and still continue) to suffer wage and other discriminations. Thus, the Nineteenth Amendment marked the beginning, not the culmination of the fight for legal, social, and economic equality for women. But that amendment was *the* necessary beginning and the cornerstone of what would eventually become a powerful movement to recognize the dignity and simple human rights of more than one half of the American people.

4. SOCIALISM AND THE SPREAD OF LABOR UNREST

The Rise of Socialism

The spectacular growth of socialism after 1900 gave revealing, and to many persons, alarming, proof of the extent of discontent. Socialists united in the 1890s to form the Socialist Labor party under the dogmatic Marxian theorist, Daniel De Leon. They remained, however, a small minority of little influence. A new era began when the midwestern labor leader Eugene V. Debs founded the Social Democratic party in 1896. The anti-De Leon group in the Socialist Labor party, led by Morris Hillquit of New York and Victor Berger of Milwaukee, joined Debs to launch the Socialist Party of America in 1901.

The new party was torn by dissension until it finally divided between Communists and Socialists in 1919. On one side were doctrinaire Marxists and radical labor leaders like William D. Haywood of the Industrial Workers of the World (IWW). They wanted to work for revolution and a proletarian commonwealth. On the other side stood moderates like Hillquit and Berger, who advocated working through democratic processes to achieve a limited socialistic economy. The moderates triumphed, at least temporarily. In 1912, they obtained adoption of a resolution by the Socialist national convention that expelled advocates of crime, violence, and sabotage.

Meanwhile, the party's increasing commitment to democratic gradualism

A meeting of the militant Industrial Workers of the World (IWW) in
1910 in New York. Its members, called "Wobblies," denounced the
capitalist system and attempted to organize all workers into one
industrial union. (Culver Pictures, Inc.)

had attracted to its ranks a large number of clergymen, writers, and others who
believed that thoroughgoing reform was impossible through the major parties.
The Socialist party's membership of 58,000 in 1908 had increased to 126,000
by 1912. By 1912, Socialist mayors held office in Milwaukee, Schenectady, and
Berkeley, California. One Socialist sat in the United States House of Representatives, and another soon would join him. In the presidential election of
1912, the Socialist candidate, Debs, won 900,000 votes.

As the advanced guard, or left wing, of progressivism, socialism posed a real
challenge to the two major parties. Moreover, moderate, or reform, socialistic
ideas had a far greater impact upon progressivism than the record of socialist
political accomplishment would indicate. For one thing, Marxism had a strong
impact upon the leading American social scientists, particularly the economists. The most important among them avoided any open avowal of Marxist
beliefs because the public tended to associate Marxism with anarchism and
revolution. However, the founders of modern American social science—
among them, Ely, Henry Carter Adams, John R. Commons, Thorstein Veblen,
and Woodrow Wilson—were all profoundly affected by socialistic ideas. So
also was the Social Gospel, the chief propounder of which, Walter Rauschenbusch, was a socialist.

For a second thing, Americans, in general, have stubbornly refused to lie on
any ideological Procrustean bed. One of their responses during the progressive
era to the problem of controlling the things that affected them most vitally—
utilities—was to institute public ownership. By 1915, 3,045 cities owned their

own water works, as compared with 1,355 cities that had privately owned facilities. In 1917, 2,318 cities owned their own central electrical power stations—nearly half the number that used the services of private companies. St. Paul, Minnesota, established a municipal bank in 1913; North Dakota opened a large state bank—the bank of North Dakota—in 1919. San Francisco took over ownership of its street car lines in 1912; Seattle, in 1919; Detroit, in 1922. Other cities established municipal fuel yards, ice plants, ports, piers, and terminals, printing plants, markets, ferries, and so on. Not only this, but the trend toward municipal ownership greatly accelerated between 1890 and 1920. One conclusion can surely be drawn from these facts: the American people were not so wedded to the idea of private ownership that they were unwilling to undertake public ownership whenever they concluded that the latter would furnish essential services more efficiently and more cheaply than private companies.

Labor Unrest

The prevalence of labor unrest, particularly among the ranks of unskilled and exploited workers, was a further sign of social ferment. As we have seen, the AFL, under Gompers' leadership, had succeeded by 1914 in organizing most skilled workers. But the AFL was constantly thwarted by employers when it tried to organize the mass of industrial workers. Efforts in 1901 and 1909 to organize the steel industry resulted not only in failure, but also in the destruction of the steel workers' union. The United Mine Workers, an AFL affiliate, succeeded in organizing the older coal areas, but it failed in West Virginia in 1912–1913 and in Colorado during 1913–1914. Violence, even open warfare, broke out in these states. The worst episode was the so-called Ludlow Massacre in Colorado, when National Guard troops attacked a miners' tent colony on April 29, 1914, and accidentally killed eleven women and two children.

The most eloquent and frankly revolutionary voice of labor discontent was the IWW, which worked largely among western lumbermen and miners. In the East it organized unskilled workers, especially in the textile industry. The IWW seemed to be gaining strength just before the First World War, in spite of its advocacy of violence and sabotage when necessary in labor disputes.

The most important challenge to progressive leaders during this era, in addition to the plight of blacks, was the struggle for economic justice by millions of impoverished workers. Progressives were divided in their response. Most urban middle-class progressives remained either unconcerned or unsympathetic for various reasons, but they supported measures such as those for minimum wages, factory inspection, and workmen's compensation in the hope that these measures would prevent the spread of socialism and labor radicalism. Others, particularly leaders of the social justice movement, warned that American democracy could not survive if a large element of workers felt disinherited and powerless to shape their own destinies. These progressives asserted that the labor movement was the hope of the future, and that governments, state and federal, should encourage labor drives for unionization and collective bargaining. Leaders in Washington heeded their warnings to some degree during the Wilson administration and much more extensively during the New Deal of the 1930s.

SUGGESTED READINGS

Among the general works on the progressive movement, Richard Hofstadter, *The Age of Reform: From Bryan to F.D.R.* (1955), is the book most often read by students and also most often criticized by specialists in the period. Robert H. Weibe, *The Search for Order* (1967), is provocative, as is Samuel P. Hayes, *The Response to Industrialism* (1957), and John W. Chambers III, *The Tyranny of Change* (1980). Wiebe, *Businessmen and Reform* (1962), and Gabriel Kolko, *The Triumph of Conservativism* (1963), emphasize the role that businessmen played, although it must be said that the latter book is badly flawed. Excellent general works are Sidney Fine, *Laissez Faire and the General Welfare State* (1964); Eric F. Goldman, *Rendezvous with Destiny* (1953); John D. Buenker, *Urban Liberalism and Progressive Reform* (1973); James T. Timberlake, *Prohibition and the Progressive Movement* (1963); Russell B. Nye, *Midwestern Progressive Politics* (1951); and, for the South, Woodward, *Origins of the New South*, already cited.

Most of the words mentioned on reform movements in Suggested Readings for Chapter 20 are relevant here. Among the most significant specialized works are Morton White, *Social Thought in America: The Revolt against Formalism* (1949); Daniel Aaron, *Men of Good Hope* (1951); David W. Noble, *The Paradox of Progressive Thought* (1958); and Henry May, *The End of American Innocence* (1959). The best work on the muckrakers is David M. Chalmers, *The Social and Political Ideas of the Muckrakers* (1964), but there is no substitute for the writings of the muckrakers themselves, particularly Lincoln Steffens, *The Shame of the Cities* (1904) and *The Struggle for Self-Government* (1906).

The best state study on progressivism is David P. Thelen, *The New Citizenship: Origins of Progressivism in Wisconsin, 1885–1900* (1972). Other good local and state studies are Ranson E. Noble, Jr., *New Jersey Progressivism Before Wilson* (1946); George E. Mowry, *The California Progressives* (1951), which should, however, be supplemented by Olin C. Spencer, Jr., *California's Prodigal Sons* (1968); James B. Crooks, *Politics & Progress: The Rise of Urban Progressivism in Baltimore* (1968); Zane L. Miller, *Boss Cox's Cincinnati* (1968); and Melvin G. Holli, *Reform in Detroit: Hazen S. Pingree and Urban Politics* (1969).

There is now a growing literature on the movement for social justice. Robert H. Bremner, *From the Depths: The Discovery of Poverty in the United States* (1956), is the best general study. Excellent also are Allen F. Davis, *Spearheads for Reform: The Social Settlements and the Progressive Movement* (1967); Walter I. Trattner, *Crusade for Children* (1970); and Roy Lubove, *The Struggle for Social Security* (1968). For the contributions of women, see John C. Farrell, *Beloved Lady*, on Jane Addams (1967), and Josephine C. Goldmark, *Impatient Crusader: Florence Kelley's Life Story* (1953).

There is a rich literature on the struggle for women's rights; some of the most important works on this subject are Eleanor Flexner, *Century of Struggle, The Woman's Rights Movement in the United States* (1975); Aileen S. Kraditor, *The Ideas of the Woman Suffrage Movement, 1890–1920* (1965); and Anne Firor Scott, *The Southern Lady: From Pedestal to Politics, 1830–1930* (1971).

For socialism and left-wing unionism during the progressive era, see David A. Shannon, *The Socialist Part of America: A History* (1955); John P. Diggins, *The American Left in the Twentieth Century* (1973); Howard Quint, *The Forging of American Socialism* (1953); Ira Kipnis, *The American Socialist Movement, 1897–1912* (1952); James Weinstein, *The Decline of Socialism in America, 1912–1925* (1967); and Melvyn Dubofsky, *We Shall Be All: A History of the Industrial Workers of the World* (1969).

CHAPTER 24
THE ERA OF
THEODORE ROOSEVELT

1. THEODORE ROOSEVELT AND BIG BUSINESS

Roosevelt and the Progressive Movement

Theodore Roosevelt, only forty-three years old when elevated to the presidency by an assassin's bullet, was born in New York on October 27, 1858. His parents united northern and southern aristocratic traditions. His father was from a wealthy Knickerbocker family, his mother a member of a prominent Georgia family. After graduation from Harvard in 1880, Roosevelt spent two strenuous years on a ranch in North Dakota to rebuild his health. He denounced his genteel friends who refused to dirty their hands with political affairs, and he decided to make politics his profession. He served in the New York state legislature, on the national Civil Service Commission, and as president of the Police Board of New York City. He demonstrated independence from the other Republican reformers of his day by supporting the allegedly corrupt James G. Blaine for the presidency in 1884, rather than by joining the Mugwump revolt. McKinley appointed Roosevelt as Assistant Secretary of the Navy, but he soon resigned to help organize the Rough Rider regiment in the War with Spain. With the help of publicity about his battlefield heroics, Roosevelt won election as Governor of New York in 1898. Then he was nominated for the vice-presidency in 1900 at the insistence of the New York Republican boss, Thomas C. Platt, who was eager to speed Roosevelt's exit from the state.

Dynamic energy is the key to understanding Roosevelt's character from boyhood onward. The variety of his interests, activities, and accomplishments was incredible. Although not a professional historian, he wrote what is still the authoritative history of the naval war of 1812. He was a distinguished amateur naturalist and an accomplished explorer and big-game hunter. Although born to wealth, he chose his friends from all walks of life: cowboys, ambassadors, labor leaders, senators, clergymen, prize fighters, and journalists. People from widely different backgrounds were likely to meet one another in the reception room of the White House or to sit down at Roosevelt's table.

It would have been difficult for a man of Roosevelt's intelligence, interests, and energy to have continued the recent tradition of passive Presidents. Roosevelt, on the contrary, aggressively revived the presidency and made it an effective instrument of national leadership. In the process, he showed considerable sympathy for the poor and defenseless and an open contempt for exploiters of human and natural resources. Hence, even though fundamentally conservative, Roosevelt was keenly responsive to the rising demand for reform. Soon he took over leadership of the progressive movement in national politics and became the best publicity agent that progressivism ever had.

Roosevelt Reactivates the Sherman Act

Roosevelt found obstacles in every path that he took toward reform in his early years as President. Influential business interests had constructed an organization within the Republican party that could not be toppled by mere bugle blasts. That organization, commonly referred to as the Old Guard, controlled the Senate through men such as Mark Hanna and Senators Nelson W. Aldrich of Rhode Island and William B. Allison of Iowa. A somewhat different Old Guard coalition, oriented more toward local business interests, was almost as firmly entrenched in the House of Representatives. It ruled there with the help of the enormous power exercised by Speaker Joseph G. Cannon of Illinois. Unable to destroy the Old Guard, Roosevelt decided to work with it; meanwhile he would undermine its power and gain personal control of the G.O.P.

However, Roosevelt was keenly responsive to popular opinion. Americans in 1901 were alarmed about the rapid spread of industrial consolidations incorrectly called "trusts." The return of prosperity and business confidence in 1897 had prompted an extraordinary outburst of industrial and financial combinations, and cries of alarm rang loudly, especially throughout the Middle West. Roosevelt, in fact, had a fairly sophisticated understanding of the economic causes for the concentration movement. He never opposed giant corporations simply because of their size. Rather, he tended to apply subjective moral standards to differentiate between good corporations and bad ones. But he stood foursquare against monopoly in industry, and he believed that great corporations should be subjected to considerable regulation. He met the popular demand for action in his first Annual Message to Congress of December 1901; he declared that corporations engaged in interstate commerce should submit to full investigations of their business practices.

The financial community was startled a few weeks later to discover that the new President seemed to mean what he said. In February 1902, Roosevelt instructed Attorney General Philander C. Knox to bring suit under the Sherman Act for dissolution of the Northern Securities Company. This was a holding company that J. Pierpont Morgan had recently formed to control the Northern

Pacific and Great Northern railroads. James J. Hill, who controlled the Northern Pacific, had organized the combination in order to protect the securities of the two lines from the raids of Wall Street speculators, not to monopolize the traffic of the Northwest. But the federal court in St. Paul ordered dissolution of the Northern Securities Company in 1903, and the Supreme Court upheld the decision by a five-to-four vote in 1904.

The government's action in this case actually was more significant in its promise for the future than for its immediate practical accomplishments. It symbolized Roosevelt's determination to assert the nation's sovereignty over great concentrations of wealth, and it promised the beginning of a vigorous antitrust crusade on several fronts. Only a few months after the institution of the Northern Securities suit, Roosevelt began the activation of the Sherman Act against industrial corporations. The campaign opened with a suit against the so-called Beef Trust in late 1902. It reached its culmination with suits against the Standard Oil Company in 1907 and the American Tobacco Company in 1908. All told, the Justice Department during the Roosevelt administration instituted eighteen proceedings in equity and obtained twenty-five indictments under the Sherman Act. The Supreme Court supported the government in every case; it even went so far in the oil and tobacco cases in 1911 as to reverse the Knight decision (see p. 553) and to rule that the Sherman Act did outlaw monopolies in manufacturing.

Meanwhile, in the early months of 1903, Roosevelt moved on another front. He demanded enactment of a bill to create a Bureau of Corporations empowered to investigate all business practices and instructed to advise the Justice Department on antitrust proceedings. Immense opposition developed from big business interests, but Roosevelt won his measure by appealing over the head of Congress to public opinion. The Bureau of Corporations' reports on the Beef Trust, 1905; the Standard Oil Company, 1906–1907; the Tobacco Trust, 1909–1916; the steel industry, 1911–1913; and the International Harvester Company, 1913, furnished exhaustive details for future antitrust proceedings.

These forays alarmed conservatives, who from the beginning had wondered whether Roosevelt could be trusted to carry on the McKinley policies. Hanna had allegedly retorted, when Platt insisted upon Roosevelt's nomination for the vice-presidency, "Don't any of you realize that there's only one life between that madman and the White House?" But for every enemy that Roosevelt made in Wall Street or among the lobbies in Washington, he attracted thousands of devoted followers among the people at large. His declaration that government had to be "the senior partner in every business" was hailed as a warning that no business interest would be permitted to defy the law.

Roosevelt and the Anthracite Coal Strike

Roosevelt again asserted his leadership dramatically in the same year that he opened his antitrust crusade. Nearly 150,000 anthracite coal miners in Pennsylvania began a strike on May 14, 1902. John Mitchell, president of the United Mine Workers, tried in vain to persuade the mine operators to hear the workers' grievances or to submit their complaints to arbitration. The strike dragged on through the summer and into the autumn. Anthracite was the fuel used for heating most eastern homes, and its price rose from $5 to $30 a ton for those fortunate enough to find any. Roosevelt found the situation intolerable and decided to intervene.

On October 3, the President summoned Mitchell and the mine operators to the White House. Let the miners go back to work at once, he demanded. Meanwhile, he would appoint an arbitral commission to investigate and recommend a settlement. Mitchell sprang to his feet and accepted the plan, but the operators flatly refused; they insisted that there was nothing to arbitrate. George F. Baer, president of the Reading Railroad, which controlled a large number of coal mines, had earlier been reported to have written that the interests of the miners would be protected, "not by the labor agitators, but by the Christian men to whom God, in His infinite wisdom, has given control of the property interests of the country."

To the strong-willed President, the operators' refusal was nothing less than defiance of presidential authority and the national interest. He issued secret orders to the army to move 10,000 troops into the anthracite region, seize the mines, and operate them for the government. Next he sent Secretary of War Elihu Root to New York City to warn J. P. Morgan, who had large investments in the coal companies and great influence with the operators, of the impending seizure. Morgan and Root worked out a plan of mediation. The operators accepted it on the condition that Roosevelt would not name a labor leader to the arbitral commission. Mitchell accepted the plan but insisted that the President be free to name any arbiters he might choose. Roosevelt coolly named a former railway union official to the commission as a "sociologist." He greatly enjoyed the joke that he had played upon the operators.

The miners returned to work on October 23, 1902. A short time later, the arbitral commission awarded them a nine-hour day, a 10 per cent wage increase, the right to check on the weighing of coal, and a permanent board of conciliation. But the significance of the affair went far beyond the miners' immediate gains. For the first time in American history, the federal government had intervened in a labor dispute without automatically taking the side of management.

2. THE BIG STICK IN DIPLOMACY

Roosevelt as a Diplomatist

As we have seen, events already had thrust the United States into the arena of world politics by the time that Roosevelt entered the White House. Roosevelt decided that far-flung American interests necessitated even more forceful participation in world politics. He took part increasingly, with the same vigor that he showed in domestic affairs, and he justified his actions with what he said was an old African proverb: "Speak softly and carry a big stick, and you will go far." Roosevelt carried a big stick, but he did not always speak softly during his first years as President. Experience alone could teach him that force must be tempered with wisdom and used with restraint.

The Decision to Build an Isthmian Canal

Americans had dreamed for at least half a century of uniting the Atlantic and Pacific oceans by an interoceanic canal. A French company headed by Ferdinand de Lesseps, builder of the Suez Canal, obtained from Colombia in 1878 the right to dig a canal across the Colombian province of Panama. But De Lesseps' hopes were ruined by disease and engineering obstacles. The French company declared bankruptcy and abandoned work.

The War with Spain revived American interest in connecting the two oceans. The dramatic 14,000-mile voyage of *U.S.S. Oregon* from the Pacific Ocean to Cuban waters emphasized the strategic necessity of a canal in wartime. Also, the development of the West coast, anticipation of a large far eastern trade, and acquisition of distant Pacific colonies highlighted the economic and strategic needs. Therefore Congress, only a month after ratification of the Treaty of Paris, created an Isthmian Canal Commission and directed it to investigate the comparative advantages of routes through Nicaragua and Panama.

One diplomatic obstacle blocked the execution of any plans — the Clayton-Bulwer Treaty of 1850, by which both Great Britain and the United States had promised not to build a canal without the other's participation. The British government, eager to win American friendship, abandoned its rights under the Clayton-Bulwer Treaty in the first Hay-Pauncefote Treaty (1900), on condition that the United States should never fortify the canal. The Senate refused to accept the condition. Then the British, in the second Hay-Pauncefote Treaty (1901), withdrew their objection to fortification.

Discussion now focused on the best route. Roosevelt and the Isthmian Canal Commission favored a Nicaraguan route, and the House of Representatives concurred on January 9, 1902. Meanwhile, agents of the New Panama Canal Company (which owned the rights and property of the old French company) had been working desperately for the Panamanian route. They hastily cut their price from $109 million to $40 million. Roosevelt and the commission thought that this was a good bargain. Congress, in the Spooner Act of June 1902, authorized use of the Panamanian route, provided that the President could obtain a right of way from Colombia within a reasonable time. If not, he should use the Nicaraguan route.

Roosevelt and the Panamanian "Revolution"

There remained only the necessity of coming to agreement with Colombia. Secretary Hay concluded a treaty with the Colombian Chargé, Tomás Herrán, on January 22, 1903. The United States agreed to pay Colombia $10 million at once and an annual sum of $250 thousand beginning nine years after ratification of the treaty. In return, Colombia leased to the United States forever a strip of land six miles wide across the Isthmus of Panama. Colombia also promised not to conduct independent negotiations with the New Panama Canal Company; in other words, Colombia would not attempt to gain a share of the $40 million to be paid to that company.

The Colombian government rejected the treaty, chiefly because the rights of the French company would expire within a year, and Colombia could then demand payment to herself of the $40 million. Roosevelt was infuriated. It was, he said, as if "a road agent had tried to hold up a man." Colombians were entitled "to precisely the amount of sympathy we extend to other inefficient bandits." An angry President made plans to seize the Isthmus by force.

New and somewhat melodramatic events soon made unnecessary direct violent action by Roosevelt. Panamanian leaders, inspired and financed by Philippe Bunau-Varilla, chief agent of the New Panama Canal Company in the

United States, set plans in motion for a revolution. Roosevelt and Secretary of State Hay knew about the plot. They did not openly encourage it, but Bunau-Varilla received the impression that the United States Government would not permit a Panamanian revolution to fail.

The revolution took place in Panama City on schedule on November 3, 1903. To prevent it, some 400 Colombian troops had already been landed at Colón, on the Atlantic side of the Isthmus. But *U.S.S. Nashville* had, quite providentially, arrived at Colón on the preceding day. Its commander, under instructions from Washington, landed troops and forbade the Colombian general to march his troops across the Isthmus. The Colombians reembarked two days later and returned to Cartagena.

The United States recognized the independence of Panama on November 6. Bunau-Varilla, a French citizen, hastened to Washington as Panamanian Minister to the United States. On November 18, he signed with Secretary Hay a duplicate of the Hay-Herrán Treaty — except that the strip of land was widened to ten miles, and the United States obtained the right to intervene at any time in order to protect Panama City and Colón.

The Senate approved the Hay-Bunau-Varilla Treaty with great enthusiasm, but Americans gradually developed a very guilty conscience about the affair, and a committee of the House of Representatives in 1912 virtually accused Roosevelt of wrongdoing. Roosevelt never seemed to have any regrets. In a special message to Congress on January 4, 1904, he declared: "No one connected with this government had any part in preparing, inciting, or encouraging the late revolution of the Isthmus of Panama." Every action of his administration in the affair, he later wrote, had been "in accordance with the highest, finest, and nicest standards of public and governmental ethics." But Roosevelt came closer to the truth when he blurted out in 1911: "I took the Canal Zone and let Congress debate, and while the debate goes on the Canal does also."

Actually, work was held up while Colonel William C. Gorgas and his assis-

Always eager for adventure, Theodore Roosevelt is seen here at the controls of a 95-ton steam shovel at the Panama Canal. His frequent displays of great physical stamina, personal courage, and aggressiveness led Mark Twain to call him "the Tom Sawyer of the political world . . . always hunting for a chance to show off." (The Bettmann Archive)

tants cleaned up the Isthmus and destroyed the mosquitoes that carried yellow fever. Construction began under Colonel George W. Goethals and the Army Engineers in 1907. The first ship passed through the canal on January 7, 1914. It soon proved a tremendous boon to world trade, as well as a vital link in American national security. Whether the good accomplished justified the American government's aggression against Colombia remains a very doubtful question.

Waving the Big Stick at Great Britain and Germany

Roosevelt used the Big Stick impartially against large as well as small nations during the early years of his presidency. A sharp dispute between the United States and Canada and Great Britain broke out at the end of the nineteenth century over the boundary of the long finger of Alaska that runs from Alaska proper down the Pacific coast to the latitude 54° 40'. The State Department knew that arbitrators tend to split the difference in boundary disputes and refused to submit the dispute to arbitration. Roosevelt was sincerely convinced that the American claim was absolutely sound; he insisted that the matter be settled by an Anglo-American-Canadian tribunal. The British expressed willingness, and the tribunal, consisting of three Americans, two Canadians, and the Lord Chief Justice of England, met in London in September 1903. While the tribunal deliberated, Roosevelt sent word to friends in the British government that he would ask Congress for authority to determine the boundary line himself if the tribunal did not support the American position. This threat could not have failed to intimidate the British government; the Lord Chief Justice voted with the American members to uphold the American claim; and Canadians felt, justly, betrayed.

In that same year, 1903, Roosevelt spoke nearly as harshly to the arrogant and reckless German Emperor, William II. Britain, Germany, and Italy had instituted a blockade of Venezuela in December 1902 after that country's dictator, Cipriano Castro, had refused to pay Venezuela's debts to their subjects. Castro offered to submit the matter to the Hague Tribunal (a world agency created by the First Hague Conference in 1899), but the Germans replied by bombarding a Venezuelan fort and destroying the adjacent town. Roosevelt called the German Ambassador to the White House in February 1903 and told him that he had sent the Atlantic Fleet under Admiral Dewey to the West Indies for its annual maneuvers. American opinion was so aroused against the German action, Roosevelt continued, that, "regretfully," he would have to use force against the Germans if they tried to seize territory in Venezuela or anywhere else in the Caribbean area. The German government probably had no such intention, but it and the British government quickly agreed to arbitration of the Venezuelan debt issue.

The Roosevelt Corollary to the Monroe Doctrine and Its First Application

In its ruling on the Venezuelan debt controversy in 1903, the Hague Tribunal awarded first claim on Venezuela's debt payments to Germany, Britain, and Italy—the very countries that had used force to attempt to collect the debts. The ruling, therefore, seemed to suggest that the application of military force was the surest guarantee of collection of debts against Latin American countries. Roosevelt agreed that European creditors were due payment of just debts, but he believed that the American people would never again tolerate armed intervention by a European power in Latin America.

The problem of how to satisfy both European creditors and American public opinion faced Roosevelt in 1904, when the Dominican Republic defaulted on its foreign debt of $32 million. Roosevelt desired neither to annex the war-torn island republic, nor to assume responsibility for its finances. To prevent European intervention, he established (with full Dominican approval) an American receivership of the Dominican customs. American control of the main source of Dominican revenues removed the financial incentive to revolution, and the island prospered for a decade under American guidance.

By now Roosevelt was convinced that American sensitivity over armed European intervention in Latin America, and concern for the defense of the Panama Canal, demanded absolute American naval supremacy in the Caribbean. Partly to achieve this objective, he announced a new policy, soon called the Roosevelt Corollary to the Monroe Doctrine, in 1904. The Monroe Doctrine, Roosevelt stated, prohibited European use of force in the new world. Since the United States forbade European nations to intervene, it would itself take action to guarantee that Latin American nations paid their debts and performed their international responsibilities. The Roosevelt Corollary was based upon very bad history: no one had ever before suggested that the Monroe Doctrine forbade temporary European interventions. Nor was it clear that the United States possessed any right, other than that derived from superior military power, to collect the debts of Latin American countries and supervise their payments.

3. ROOSEVELT AND CONSERVATION

The Conservation Movement

Theodore Roosevelt came to the presidency with a concern, born during the years that he had spent in the West, for the conservation of America's enormous but dwindling supply of natural resources. His education as a conservationist was advanced by his friend and favorite White House boxing partner, Gifford Pinchot, chief of the Forestry Service in the Department of Agriculture. Pinchot had taken up the task of forest preservation in the same spirit that brought other wealthy progressive reformers into social work and the reform of city administration.

Roosevelt discussed the various aspects of conservation in his first Annual Message to Congress in 1901. The government had disposed of most of its unoccupied lands, he pointed out, in an era when few persons seriously considered the possibility that the supply might not be endless. Americans had proceeded to waste natural resources by the careless mining of coal, reckless cutting of forests, and exploitive use of semiarid land. It seemed clear, Roosevelt concluded, that America's natural riches could be handed down to posterity only if the present generation accepted its responsibilities. With aid from Pinchot and others, Roosevelt took up the work of conservation in a program with four main objectives. First, national forests should be enlarged, protected, and carefully exploited in order to guarantee that their yield would be perpetual. Second, irrigation projects should be launched to reclaim arid lands. Third, internal waterways should be improved and extended. Fourth, state governments should work in close partnership with the national government in the conservation programs.

Congress, in the Forest Reserve Act of 1891, had given the President power over "public lands wholly or in part covered with timber." He could withdraw these lands from sale and homesteading and establish them as forest reserves. Cleveland set aside the San Joaquin forest of 25,000,000 acres in California as a national forest. However, the total combined area of lands reserved by Harrison, Cleveland, and McKinley was less than 50,000,000 acres. Roosevelt added 148,000,000 acres. He also withdrew from the public domain more than 80,000,000 acres of mineral lands and 1,500,000 acres of water power sites. In 1905, he transferred control over the government's forest lands from the Public Land Office to Pinchot's Forestry Service.

The Carey Act of 1894 had authorized the President to allot to states with large areas of public lands within their borders 1,000,000 acres each for irrigation and reclamation. But little was done, since the public-land states lacked the financial resources to launch large-scale projects. Roosevelt inaugurated a new era of federal participation with the adoption of the National Reclamation, or Newlands, Act of 1902. Its generous provisions awarded almost all the proceeds from the sale of public lands in sixteen western states to finance irrigation projects. The irrigated lands were to be sold to settlers at reasonable prices on a ten-year installment plan. The proceeds constantly renewed the fund. The acreage of irrigated land, less than 1,000,000 in 1880, had increased to more than 20,000,000 by 1920. Arid land, formerly worth only a cent or two an acre for grazing, became worth hundreds of dollars an acre for agriculture. Fruits and vegetables came to eastern markets from Arizona and California farms which, a few years earlier, had been sandy wastes. Almost 10 per cent of the population of Mexico crossed the border and provided the labor that made this transformation possible. The great Roosevelt Dam on the Salt River in Arizona, completed in 1911, stands as a monument to the man who gave the greatest impetus to such projects. It was the forerunner of the huge flood-control and power projects constructed later on the Tennessee, Colorado, Missouri, and Columbia rivers.

A related aspect of the conservation movement was the improvement of transportation over the 26,500 miles of navigable rivers and canals in the United States. The rapid spread of the railroad network had condemned most canals to decay and reduced the importance of rivers as commerce carriers. Again, natural resources were being wasted. Roosevelt, in 1907, appointed an Inland Waterways Commission to study the possibility of developing rivers and canals into a great arterial system.

The Conference of Governors

The White House, Roosevelt said, was a "bully pulpit," and he used it to arouse public support for his policies. He used the "bully pulpit" with particular success in his campaign for conservation. The high point of that campaign was the Conservation Conference that he summoned to the White House in May 1908. So dramatic was Roosevelt's invitation that the meeting room was crowded with thirty-four governors, members of the cabinet and of the Supreme Court, congressmen, influential businessmen, labor leaders, and delegates from sixty-eight conservation organizations. For days the conference monopolized the front pages of newspapers throughout the country. It resulted in the appointment of a National Conservation Commission, headed by Pinchot, and forty-one state conservation commissions. Moreover, private citizens organized a National Conservation Association in 1909 to further the work of public education. It soon became one of the most powerful special-interest groups in the United States.

These programs, policies, and organizations laid the foundations for a great, coordinated national conservation effort. Further development of national policy beyond Roosevelt's achievement was delayed during the Taft and Wilson administrations by fierce public controversies over whether private capital should be permitted to develop resources in the public domain, and on what terms. However, these issues were finally resolved in 1920 with the adoption of the General Leasing Act and the Water Power Act. The former kept large oil reserves from private exploitation, but permitted the Secretary of the Interior to lease other public lands, which contained mineral and oil deposits, to private parties on terms that safeguarded the public interest. The Water Power Act established the Federal Power Commission. It was authorized to license the building and operation of dams and hydroelectric plants on navigable rivers and nonnavigable rivers within the public domain.

4. A NEW TRIBUNE EMERGES

The Election of 1904

Four Vice-Presidents had succeeded to the presidency during the nineteenth century, but none had been able to win nomination for a full presidential term. Wall Street and other big business interests eagerly sought Roosevelt's retirement in 1904. They preferred Mark Hanna, and Hanna seemed willing enough. At least he opposed a resolution of the Ohio Republican convention of 1903 which endorsed Roosevelt for nomination in 1904. But Hanna died on February 15, 1904, and no other prominent Republican dared to challenge Roosevelt's claim. In fact, Roosevelt had been using patronage quietly but very effectively to gain control of the Republican state organizations. By early 1904, he had so completely mastered the G.O.P. organizations and so mesmerized the rank and file of Republican voters that even Hanna could not possibly have prevented his nomination. The Republican national convention named Roosevelt by acclamation. For his running mate, Roosevelt chose Charles W. Fairbanks of Indiana.

The Democrats hoped to capitalize on conservative opposition to Roosevelt and nominated a colorless nonentity, Judge Alton B. Parker of New York. At Parker's insistence, the convention incorporated a plank in the Democratic platform which favored the gold standard. But the platform also denounced the "trusts" and called for more effective federal regulation of the railroads.

A dull campaign followed; it was enlivened only by Parker's charge, near the end of the campaign, that Roosevelt had blackmailed Wall Street into financing his campaign. Roosevelt blackmailed no one, but J. P. Morgan and other railroad, financial, and industrial leaders did contribute generously to the Re-

Banner for the Socialist party in 1904. Presidential candidate Eugene
V. Debs, who had become a national figure through his role in the
Pullman strike, ran for the presidency five times on the Socialist
party ticket. (The Bettmann Archive)

publican war chest. Then Roosevelt began to suspect that other Wall Street
interests were pouring money into the Democratic coffers, and he actually
feared defeat. In the end, the voters gave Roosevelt the largest popular majority
awarded a presidential candidate to that time. He won 7,629,000 popular and
336 electoral votes, to 5,084,000 popular and 140 electoral votes for Parker, and
402,000 popular votes for Debs, the Socialist candidate.

Intensifying the Fight for Reform

Roosevelt was momentarily stunned by the size of his popular mandate, but he
quickly grasped the significance of his victory. Progressivism and insurgency —
a revolt against conservative policies — was sweeping the country. Roosevelt
responded by taking leadership of the nationwide reform movement.

He began with a speech before the Union League Club of Philadelphia, a bastion of the Old Guard, in January 1905. Great corporations, railroads, and financial institutions had to submit to public control, Roosevelt warned. The
people particularly demanded effective control of railroads, and he would see to
it that this control was obtained. Roosevelt followed this blast by ordering the
Bureau of Corporations to make a thoroughgoing investigation of the meat-
packing industry.

The fight began in earnest when the Fifty-ninth Congress assembled in December 1905, for Roosevelt demanded a new railroad regulation law, pure food

and drug legislation, and other reforms. The fight for railroad legislation was long and hard, and Roosevelt had to make some minor compromises. However, he won all his essential objectives in the Hepburn Act, which he signed on June 29, 1906. The Act increased the membership of the Interstate Commerce Commission from five to seven; extended the ICC's authority to express companies, sleeping car companies, oil pipelines, bridges, ferries, and terminals; and tightened the provisions of the earlier Elkins Act of 1903 against rebating. Other provisions required advance notice of any change in rates and obliged railroad companies to open their books to inspection by the ICC. Most important, the Act gave the ICC power to reduce unreasonable rates on the complaint of shippers, subject to the review of federal courts. The Hepburn Act, in short, gave the ICC really effective power for the first time in its history. Ultimate control over rates was taken from private hands and given to an agency representing the people.

Roosevelt pressed on other fronts and won passage of three other reform measures. A Meat Inspection Act gave federal officials authority to see that all meat shipped in interstate commerce came from healthy animals and was packed under sanitary conditions. Passage of this measure was helped by the publication, a few months earlier, of a novel, *The Jungle*, by the muckraking novelist Upton Sinclair. Sinclair wrote the novel as a plea for socialism. However, as he declared later, *The Jungle* appealed to the stomachs of the American people, not to their hearts, for it revealed in revolting detail the insanitary conditions in the Chicago stockyards and meat-packing plants. The Food and Drug Act forbade the manufacture and sale of adulterated or poisonous foods, drugs, and liquors. Labels on patent medicines were required to show what the contents actually were. Finally, the Employers' Liability Act of 1906 established a system of accident insurance for workers in the District of Columbia and on interstate railroads.

The Panic of 1907 and the Revival of Roosevelt's Drive for Reform

A sharp decline on the New York Stock Exchange began in March 1907 and continued into the summer. It led to an increase in business failures, much public alarm, and runs on banks that caused a dangerous financial stringency, particularly after the closing of the Knickerbocker Trust Company of New York. For a brief period, Roosevelt relaxed his reform energies. Indeed, during the worst of the panic he permitted the United States Steel Corporation to purchase a large competitor in the South, the Tennessee Coal and Iron Company. He permitted this violation of the Sherman Act in order to prevent a dumping of the Tennessee Company's shares on the market and a deepening of the stock market decline. And, in any event, Roosevelt considered United States Steel to be a "good trust."

The panic produced one immediate legislative result—adoption in May 1908 of the Aldrich-Vreeland Act. This temporary measure enabled banks to obtain additional currency during financial emergencies; it also provided for the appointment of a National Monetary Commission to study American banking and currency needs. The commission, headed by Senator Aldrich, worked diligently until 1912. Its investigations and recommendations provided a starting point for the Wilson administration when it turned to the problem of new banking legislation.

Business confidence and prosperity returned rapidly in 1908, and Roosevelt resumed his drive for reform with gusto. He obtained little legislation from Congress during his last year in office, but, in a series of messages, he advocated an income and inheritance tax, tariff reduction, and more effective governmental control of business. "The nation," he warned, "will not tolerate an utter lack of control over very wealthy men of enormous power in the industrial, and, therefore, in the social, lives of all our people." He was in fact laying the foundations of a new, advanced progressive program of his own, which he would call the New Nationalism.

Hindsight makes it clear that Roosevelt was not a radical and certainly not a socialist, as his more violent critics charged. He believed in the free enterprise system, but he wanted to make it work for the benefit of all people, not just the privileged few. To him must go the credit for giving voice to popular demands for reform and, above all, for the first successful leadership of the progressive movement on the national level.

5. IMPERIAL DIPLOMACY

Mediating the Russo-Japanese War

Theodore Roosevelt was a different kind of diplomatist during his second term. Some historians say that the change was due to the wise influence of Elihu Root, who became Secretary of State in 1905 after Hay's death. Others say that experience made Roosevelt wiser and more cautious. Whatever the cause, a visible change occurred. Gone were most of the bluster and arrogant chauvinism. Now Roosevelt revealed some tact and restraint in the use of power, even as he emerged as a principal actor on the stage of world affairs.

This new style was first revealed when Roosevelt mediated the Russo-Japanese War. Japan had gone to war with Russia in 1904 to block Russian expansion into Korea and Manchuria—areas in which Japanese leaders hoped that their nation would obtain special economic, if not political, influence. The Japanese were victorious everywhere by 1905, but they were also financially exhausted, and the Japanese government appealed to the American President in April 1905 to mediate the conflict. Roosevelt earlier had supported the Japanese, even to the extent that he warned Germany and France that he would not sit idly by if they went to Russia's assistance. However, Roosevelt refused to intercede until the Japanese had agreed to respect the Open Door and return the captured province of Manchuria to China. Finally, the Japanese were obliged to consent to this condition, and, in August 1905, Roosevelt invited Japanese and Russian delegates to a peace conference at Portsmouth, New Hampshire. For his part in ending the conflict, Roosevelt was awarded the Nobel Peace Prize in 1906.

Roosevelt and the First Moroccan Crisis

Meanwhile, an even more dangerous situation had been developing in Europe. The German government deeply resented France's expanding control over the North African state of Morocco, which endangered German commercial interests. The Germans seized the opportunity to force the issue when France's ally,

Russia, was embroiled in war with Japan. The Germans demanded an international conference to protect the open door in Morocco. The French refused, and it seemed certain that war would ensue. Then the German Emperor appealed to Roosevelt to put pressure on the French to yield. Roosevelt supported the Emperor reluctantly and only because he feared that the United States could not avoid entanglement in a major western European conflict. The French yielded, and a conference of the major powers, including the United States, met in Algeciras, in southern Spain, in early 1906. The conference reached an agreement that averted war but did not prevent the French from closing the door in Morocco. German leaders then realized that they could obtain world political and economic power commensurate with their nation's relative wealth and military might only by force of arms. As a result, the Moroccan controversy helped to bring on the First World War.

Disputes and Accord with Japan

Roosevelt greatly admired the Japanese for their industry and progress in modernization. He looked to the island empire as a buffer against Russian aggression in the Far East. To cement good relations, he negotiated an Executive Agreement with the Japanese government in July 1905. It was the Taft-Katsura Agreement, which acknowledged Japan's supremacy in Korea and confirmed American sovereignty over the Philippines.

This good beginning was rudely interrupted only a year later. Japanese laborers had been coming to California at the rate of about 1,000 a year since the 1890s, and Californians were becoming greatly agitated by fearful predictions of a "Yellow Peril." The San Francisco school board, in the autumn of 1906, adopted an order requiring the segregation of all Oriental school children. It was an open insult to a proud and hitherto friendly people, and much demagogic war talk ensued in both countries. Roosevelt, however, acted with admirable good sense. He was prepared to use the army if necessary to compel the school board to rescind its order. Happily, he did not have to resort to such a drastic remedy. He called the members of the school board to Washington and persuaded them to revoke the segregation order. In return, the State Department negotiated a "Gentlemen's Agreement" with the Japanese government — an informal understanding that the Tokyo government would issue no more passports to peasants or workers who intended to go to the continental United States. Thus, Roosevelt reached amicable agreement with the Japanese and, at the same time, removed the chief cause of the fear of Californians.

Sending the Fleet around the World

Partly to let the Japanese know that he had not acted out of fear, Roosevelt decided in the summer of 1907 to send the main American battle fleet around the world. A fleet of twenty-eight vessels, including sixteen battleships, steamed out of Hampton Roads, Virginia, on December 16, 1907. The fleet circled the world by way of the Strait of Magellan, San Francisco, Hawaii, Australia, the Philippines, China, Japan, the Suez Canal, and the Mediterranean. The officers and men were received warmly at every port of call, and nowhere was there greater friendliness than at Yokohama and Tokyo. This was fortunate, for the Imperial Navy and shore artillery undoubtedly could have sent the fleet to the bottom of Tokyo Bay, once it anchored in Japanese waters. The Japanese government also responded warmly by instructing its Ambassador in Washington to open negotiations for a comprehensive agreement with the American government. The outcome was the Root-Takahira Agreement of November 30, 1908 — another Executive Agreement — in which both countries agreed to respect each other's territorial possessions and to cooperate in maintaining the Open Door in China and the territorial integrity of that country.

The fleet returned to Hampton Roads on February 22, 1909. As he looked back over his administration a few years later, Roosevelt concluded that sending the fleet on its 46,000-mile voyage had been his most important contribution to the cause of peace. Roosevelt exaggerated the voyage's effect, but one fact was indelibly clear in 1909: the American navy was an efficient, well-disciplined, and highly mobile striking force — a power to be reckoned with in the councils of the world.

6. REPUBLICAN TROUBLES UNDER TAFT

Roosevelt Dictates His Successor

After his election in 1904, Roosevelt had announced that he would not be a candidate again in 1908. As the national conventions of that year drew near, his friends and party leaders put enormous pressure on him to run again. But he stubbornly refused and said that, while he had enjoyed every minute in the White House and had tried to be a strong leader, he did not believe that one man should hold the presidency for more than a "limited time."

Roosevelt would have preferred to choose as his successor his brilliant Secretary of State, Elihu Root. Root's career as an attorney for major business firms, however, eliminated him as a candidate. Agitation against the "trusts" was so intense that any political opponent probably could have defeated Root simply by listing the huge corporations that he had represented. Roosevelt made overtures to Charles Evans Hughes, reform Governor of New York, but Hughes coldly rebuffed the President's approaches. Roosevelt then turned to his Secretary of War, William Howard Taft, who accepted the candidacy. Taft was nominated on the first ballot by the Republican national convention.

The Democrats turned again to Bryan, who was still leading the Democratic fight for progressivism, in spite of his party's nomination of Parker in 1904. The "Great Commoner" made his campaign largely on the tariff and trust issues, but he also frankly appealed for labor support by promising unions relief from injunctions. Gompers and the AFL departed from their policy of nonpartisanship for the first time and entered the campaign for Bryan.

In the election on November 3, Taft won 7,675,000 popular and 321 electoral votes to 6,412,000 popular and 162 electoral votes for Bryan and 421,000 popular votes for Eugene V. Debs, the Socialist candidate. However, it was more a victory for Roosevelt's candidate than for the G.O.P. Bryan increased the Democratic vote by 1,330,000 over 1904. Democratic governors were elected in several states that went for Taft. More significant for the near future was the marked increase in Republican insurgency in the Middle West. The midwestern progressive group in Congress, heretofore a small minority, would be a powerful force in both houses of the Sixty-first Congress.

Taft as President

William Howard Taft, born in Cincinnati in 1857, educated at Yale and the Cincinnati Law College, had enjoyed a distinguished career in the public service since the 1880s. A fine lawyer and model administrator, Taft was also the largest man, physically speaking, ever to sit in the presidential chair; his good humor matched his weight, and it was sheer delight to see him laugh. His laugh, it was said, began in the folds of his stomach and slowly worked its way up to his face.

In a normally quiet period of political life, Taft would have been a successful and beloved President. Unhappily for this man who wanted only to do well, the period of his presidency was highly abnormal. The country simmered in political revolt, and the Republican party was split between the rising insurgents and the Old Guard. Had Roosevelt been in Taft's place, he probably could have kept the G.O.P. together by bringing the insurgents under his control. Taft, for various reasons, not only was unable to keep peace within the party; he also contributed to its disruption. The new President thought himself to be progressive, and in many ways he was. He believed in tariff and tax reform, and

William Howard Taft campaigning for the presidency in 1908. A large, good-natured man, Taft had little interest in politics and once wrote: "Politics, when I am in it, makes me sick." His basic conservatism, complacency, and lack of vigor made him a weak and ineffective President amid the fervor and conflict of the Progressive Era. (United Press International)

he carried on Roosevelt's conservation policy by enlarging the forest reserves and setting aside additional mineral lands. He also pressed the antitrust crusade and instituted forty-six suits for dissolution, which included cases against the United States Steel and International Harvester companies.

Taft ran into increasingly grave difficulties for several reasons. His major problem was acute obesity. Carrying his 300-odd pounds required so much energy that Taft had little left over for affairs of state. He consequently was slow-moving, put off problems until it was too late, and gave the appearance of laziness. Thus he did not have the physical strength to be a strong President during a period when the public demanded vigorous leadership. Several failures could have been avoided if he had only given decisive leadership to his party in Congress. But his intervention was always too little and too late, and frequently misguided as well. Taft's judicial temperament also inhibited his progressivism. He had grave doubts about the wisdom of many advanced progressive measures, particularly those for governmental regulation by administrative commissions. He favored review of business activities by the courts, with their careful examination of the evidence in each case. Finally, Taft could not get on with the new insurgent leaders in his own party. He disliked and distrusted them; to him, they seemed fanatics and demagogues. Taft much preferred the company of the Old Guard and inevitably drifted toward the political attitudes of his conservative friends.

Off to a Bad Start

The Republican platform of 1908 pledged the new administration to revise the highly protective Dingley Tariff Act of 1897. The cost of living had increased some 40 per cent between 1897 and 1909, and most people assumed, incorrectly, that high tariff rates were responsible for the increase. To honor the platform pledge, and also because he believed sincerely in tariff reform, Taft called Congress into special session in March 1909 with the admonition, "The successful party in the late election is pledged to a revision of the tariff." The administration's bill was introduced in the House of Representatives by Sereno E. Payne of New York, chairman of the Ways and Means Committee. The Payne bill fulfilled the party pledge by enlarging the free list and substantially reducing rates on iron and steel products, sugar, agricultural implements, and lumber. It also included a new federal inheritance tax ranging from 1 to 5 per cent.

The Payne bill had easy sailing in the House and passed that body by a large majority. However, it was a different story in the Senate. The Finance Committee, headed by Senator Aldrich, simply collapsed under the pressure of various lobbies. The committee reported the Payne bill to the Senate with 847 amendments, more than 600 of which increased rates, and it deleted the inheritance tax. A wave of indignation swept the country, particularly after a group of midwestern insurgent Republican senators took leadership in the fight against the Aldrich bill. Their efforts failed, and the measure, now known as the Payne-Aldrich bill, passed both houses. Taft signed it in August 1909.

The Payne-Aldrich Act was a plain betrayal of party pledges. Yet, until the very end of the fight in Congress, Taft made no attempt to prevent special-interest lobbyists from making the bill a mockery of those pledges. He did persuade the conference committee to lower some rates. He also obtained a promise of support from Aldrich for the submission of an income tax amendment to the states. This—the Sixteenth Amendment—was approved by Congress on July 12, 1909, and was ratified in 1913.

In a speech in September 1909 in Winona, Minnesota, a center of insurgency, Taft foolishly called the Payne-Aldrich Act the best tariff measure that the Republican party had ever passed. However, angry public opinion disagreed. Even Republican newspapers published fiery editorials about the tariff "betrayal," and insurgent Republican leaders wondered whether Taft had deserted to the Old Guard.

The so-called Ballinger affair, which followed immediately afterward, turned a bad start into a debacle. An investigator in the Interior Department told Gifford Pinchot that Richard A. Ballinger, Secretary of the Interior, was showing favoritism to a private syndicate which had been formed to develop coal properties in Alaska. Pinchot urged the investigator to go directly to the President. He did so, but Taft accepted Ballinger's explanation and dismissed the investigator. Then Pinchot entered the controversy publicly with accusations against Ballinger; Taft at once dismissed Pinchot. A congressional committee later cleared Ballinger of wrongdoing, but the committee's investigation revealed that the Secretary was openly antagonistic to conservation. The affair widened the breach between Taft and the progressives, particularly the conservationists.

Everything seemed to go wrong during the regular session of Congress that opened in December 1909. Insurgents were angered when Taft did not help them in their successful attempt, led by Representative George W. Norris of Nebraska, to shear Speaker Cannon of his dictatorial powers over the House of Representatives. Progressives accused Taft of working hand in glove with Wall Street bankers in the passage of a bill to establish postal savings banks in 1910. They also accused Taft of favoring the railroads during discussion of a measure to increase the powers of the ICC. The outcome, the Mann-Elkins Act of 1910, was, in fact, a great victory for progressives, rather than for Taft. It empowered the ICC to suspend rate increases or to reduce rates *on its own initiative.* The act also strengthened old prohibitions against charging more for a short haul than for a long one, and forbade railroads to acquire competing lines.

Taft was convinced early in 1910 that the insurgents planned to prevent his renomination, even if it meant the disruption of the Republican party. The President therefore joined with Aldrich, Cannon, and other leaders of the Old Guard in a nationwide campaign to defeat the insurgents in the midterm Republican primaries. But the flames of insurgency continued to rage across the country, and the administration's candidates went down to defeat everywhere. By the summer of 1910, Republican insurgents were talking about organizing a new party if Taft won renomination in 1912.

Bungling Diplomacy

The years from 1909 to 1913 were a time of increasing tension in Europe. Unlike his predecessor, Taft had neither the will nor the ability to play a leading role in world affairs. He and his Secretary of State, Philander C. Knox, were notably unsuccessful in their limited undertakings in foreign policy.

The most important new departure was "dollar diplomacy." Taft and Knox desired above all to increase American security and influence in the Caribbean area; this they attempted to do by persuading American bankers to displace European creditors in that region. Taft explained the motivation behind "dollar diplomacy" in idealistic terms: "The diplomacy of the present administration has sought to respond to modern ideas of commercial intercourse. This policy has been characterized as substituting dollars for bullets. It is one that appeals alike to idealistic humanitarian sentiments, to the dictates of sound policy and strategy, and to legitimate commercial aims." However, implementing "dollar diplomacy" led, among other things, to American participation in a civil war in Nicaragua and the victory of the conservative party of that country. Equally ill-fated was the Washington government's proposal in 1909 for the internationalization of the railroads in Manchuria. This move drove Russia and Japan together in order to ward off American influence. Taft succeeded in forcing an international banking group, formed for the purpose of lending money to China, to admit American bankers. One of his successor's first actions was to withdraw American bankers from this consortium on the ground that the loan agreement seriously infringed on Chinese sovereignty.

Indeed, it seemed that Taft and Knox could not succeed even when they adopted statesmanlike policies. They negotiated treaties with Britain and France in 1911 for the arbitration of virtually all disputes. The Senate so emasculated the treaties in consenting to their ratification that Taft withdrew them in disgust. In 1911, the State Department negotiated a reciprocity agreement with Canada that would have enormously benefited both countries. Taft finally roused himself, fought hard, and won congressional approval — only to see the treaty killed by Canadian voters frightened by talk that the United States would annex Canada.

Repudiation of Taft

The revolt against the administration reached its first culmination in the midterm elections of 1910. Repudiation of the Taft policies seemed inevitable, so great was public indignation against the Payne-Aldrich Tariff Act, Pinchot's dismissal, and "dollar diplomacy." Taft tried to make peace with the midwestern insurgents, but to no avail. He blundered again by alienating Theodore Roosevelt.

Actually, that alienation had begun much earlier. Roosevelt, after Taft's inauguration, departed for Africa to hunt lions. He then made a triumphal tour through Egypt, Italy, Austria, Germany, France, Holland, and England. But he also followed events at home with a careful eye, with the aid of messages from friends like Pinchot. He returned to New York on June 18, 1910, convinced that Taft's betrayal of his policies had made a division in the Republican party inevitable. Still, Roosevelt was eager to do what he could to heal party wounds. However, Taft rebuffed his efforts at mediation. Roosevelt then set out upon a speaking tour in the summer, climaxed by a speech at Osawatomie, Kansas, on August 31. In this series of speeches, Roosevelt expounded his now fully matured advanced progressivism — the New Nationalism. He advocated strict regulation of large corporations, publicity of campaign funds, income and inheritance taxes, workmen's compensation laws, protective legislation of women and children in industry, and all the measures for the reform of political institutions that progressives were championing. Above all, he called for a powerful federal government to work, not only on its own initiative, but also in partnership with the cities and states.

Roosevelt's eloquent articulation of an advanced progressive program only emphasized the wide gulf between the insurgents and the Taft administration. It also contributed to the emphatic repudiation of Taft and the Old Guard that occurred on November 8, 1910. The Democrats won control of the House of Representatives for the first time since 1892. Old Guard strength in the Senate was so greatly reduced that a coalition of Democrats and progressive Republicans would control that body from 1911 to 1913. Moreover, Democrats elected twenty-six governors, including governors in the traditionally Republican states of Massachusetts, New York, New Jersey, and Ohio. The progressive movement was profoundly affecting American politics.

SUGGESTED READINGS

The best introduction to this period is George E. Mowry, *The Era of Theodore Roosevelt* (1958) and *Theodore Roosevelt and The Progressive Movement* (1947). But see also Horace S. and Marion G. Merrill, *The Republican High Command, 1897–1913* (1971).

Elmo P. Richardson, *The Politics of Conservation . . . 1897–1913* (1962); Frank W. Taussig, *Tariff History of the United States* (1931); Sidney Ratner, *Taxation and Democracy in America* (1967); and Hans Thorelli, *The Federal Antitrust Policy* (1954), are the standard works on these subjects. Albro Martin, *Enterprise Denied: Origins of the Decline of American Railroads, 1897–1917* (1971), argues convincingly that overregulation nearly destroyed the solvency of American railroads.

The biographical literature on the political leaders of this period grows increasingly richer. William H. Harbaugh, *The Life and Times of Theodore Roosevelt* (1963), is the best one-volume biography; but see also John M. Blum,

The Republican Roosevelt (1954). Henry F. Pringle, *The Life and Times of William Howard Taft*, 2 vols. (1938), is uncritical. Compare its treatment of the Taft presidency with Mowry, *Theodore Roosevelt and the Progressive Movement*, and Alpheus T. Mason, *Brandeis: A Free Man's Life* (1946). Richard W. Leopold, *Elihu Root and the Conservative Tradition* (1954); Merlo J. Pusey, *Charles Evans Hughes*, 2 vols. (1951); and John A. Garraty, *Henry Cabot Lodge* (1953), are all excellent biographies of distinguished Republican leaders.

For the diplomacy of the Roosevelt and Taft administrations, see Howard K. Beale, *Theodore Roosevelt and the Rise of America to World Power* (1961); A Whitney Griswold, *The Far Eastern Policy of the United States* (1938); Dexter Perkins, *The Monroe Doctrine, 1867–1907* (1937); and Dana G. Munro, *Intervention and Dollar Diplomacy in the Caribbean, 1900–1920* (1964).

CHAPTER 25
WOODROW WILSON AND THE TRIUMPH OF PROGRESSIVISM

1. REVOLT AT HIGH TIDE, 1910–1912

The Fight for Control of the G.O.P.

Republican insurgents did not wait long after the elections of 1910 to organize a fight for control of their party. Their leaders met at the Washington home of Senator La Follette in January 1911, formed the National Republican Progressive League, and adopted La Follette's "Declaration of Principles." Later, in the autumn of 1911, a conference of about 300 progressives, most of them Republicans, met in Chicago. The group endorsed La Follette as "the logical candidate for the Presidency of the United States."

The great enigma in the Republican situation was Theodore Roosevelt. He warmly supported the insurgents, but he was not at all certain about what he should do. Republican progressives were putting heavy pressure on him to enter the race against Taft for the presidential nomination. They admired La Follette for his courage and devotion to progressivism, but they admired Roosevelt even more, and they knew that only he could unseat an incumbent President. Roosevelt, by his hesitation, was not simply playing hard to get. He hated the thought of a personal battle against his old colleague, Taft. Moreover, Roosevelt despised the Democrats and did not want to destroy the Republican unity so essential to victory in 1912.

Roosevelt finally yielded to the pleadings of his friends, mainly because he was convinced that Taft's renomination would wreck the G.O.P. and lead to Democratic victory in 1912. Republican progressives, who included seven governors, met in Chicago on February 10, 1912, and begged Roosevelt to enter the race. Roosevelt replied on February 24: "I will accept the nomination for President if it is tendered to me." To reporters, he added, "My hat is in the ring."

The battle that ensued within the Republican party during the next four months was one of the bitterest in the history of American party politics. Roosevelt and his followers fought with incredible vigor. Taft's friends replied with personal attacks that soon brought the campaign to a very low level. Roosevelt, they charged, was a revolutionary, vulgar, unfaithful to friends, and the "first liar" who ever sat in the President's chair. Roosevelt and his spokesmen replied in kind, until the mutual abuse far surpassed normal name-calling between Republicans and Democrats. Before the preconvention campaign had ended, Taft had called Roosevelt a "dangerous egotist," "demagogue," and "flatterer of the people," and Roosevelt had replied that Taft was a "puzzlewit" and "fathead," with as much intelligence as a guinea pig.

The mass of Republican voters rallied to the man who remained their hero. Roosevelt won smashing victories in the states that held presidential primaries. Roosevelt defeated Taft even in his home state of Ohio and amassed a total of 1,157,397 primary votes to 761,716 for the President.

Yet the issue was still very much in doubt at the end of the Republican preconvention campaign. Roosevelt had barely missed winning a majority of the delegates. Taft had collected about one third, some of whom were southern delegates whose chief political function was to appear at national conventions every four years to pay for their federal jobs with their votes. All the rest of the Taft delegates were from northern states controlled by conservative organizations. The outcome depended upon the decision over 254 contested delegates. That issue, and, as it turned out, the fate of the Republican party in 1912, was settled in Chicago early in June, just before the opening of the Republican national convention.

Taft and the Old Guard controlled the Republican National Committee. Its credentials committee awarded nineteen of the contested delegates to Roosevelt and 235 to Taft—just enough to insure Taft a majority. With the aid of these delegates, the Taft managers were able to organize the convention, beat down all attempts to seat the Roosevelt delegates, and, finally, barely to renominate Taft.

Meanwhile, Roosevelt had come to Chicago to take personal charge of his forces. He was convinced that the bosses had stolen the nomination and was angrier than ever before in his political career. Immediately after the Republican convention, Roosevelt agreed to accept nomination on a third-party ticket. The rebels returned to Chicago on August 5, organized the Progressive party, and nominated Roosevelt and Governor Hiram W. Johnson of California to head their ticket. The delegates acted as if they were at a camp meeting rather than a political convention. They sang the Doxology and "Onward Christian Soldiers" and listened, enraptured, as Roosevelt announced in his acceptance speech, his "Confession of Faith," that they stood at Armageddon and battled for the Lord. Roosevelt also said that he felt as strong as a bull moose.

The Emergence of Woodrow Wilson

It seemed obvious after the elections of 1910 that, with new leadership, the Democratic party could be reconstructed and win the presidency in 1912.

Bryan admitted as much by announcing immediately after the elections of 1910 that he would not be a candidate. Party leadership and a chance for the highest office were open, therefore, and an all-out struggle for control followed. It was not as colorful as the one taking place within the Republican party, but it proved more decisive.

Woodrow Wilson had made a brilliant campaign for the governorship of New Jersey during the autumn of 1910. Then he had pushed a series of important reform laws through the state legislature in the first months of 1911. Wilson quickly emerged as the leading Democratic contender. Bold and aggressive, he was rapidly transforming himself into a true progressive. Furthermore, he was a new type of politician—a man who had stepped from the presidency of Princeton University into leadership in politics. Wilson began an exhaustive campaign in the spring of 1911 for the Democratic presidential nomination. He was so successful that, by the end of the year, it seemed that he would meet no serious resistance.

Strong opposition developed suddenly during the early months of 1912 in the candidacy of Champ Clark of Missouri, Speaker of the House of Representatives. He was a devoted follower of Bryan who had served without distinction in the House of Representatives since the 1890s. Clark was also completely mediocre. He is the only serious contender for the presidency ever publicly to endorse a patent medicine—a product called Electric Bitters. He probably liked it because of its high alcoholic content. Wilson campaigned widely but would make absolutely no promises to conservative state organizations. Clark remained in Washington and lined up the support of many state leaders and of William Randolph Hearst, the demagogic newspaper and magazine publisher, who was powerful in the Democratic party.

Clark was far ahead of Wilson in the race for delegates by the end of the pre-convention campaign. To make matters worse for Wilson, Oscar W. Underwood of Alabama, the leader of the Democrats in the House of Representatives, also entered the contest. Underwood drew off support in the South that, otherwise, probably would have gone to Wilson.

The Wilson cause, in fact, seemed hopeless when the Democrats assembled in their national convention in Baltimore on June 25, 1912. Clark won a majority, but not the two thirds then necessary for nomination, on the tenth ballot. The Wilson and Underwood delegates stood firm, and Bryan switched his vote from Clark to Wilson on the fourteenth ballot because Tammany Hall had thrown the votes of New York to Clark. Then there followed a long and harrowing battle in which the Wilson managers gradually wore away Clark's strength, much of which was superficial. Finally, Underwood's supporters threw their votes to Wilson, and the nomination went to the New Jersey Governor on the forty-sixth ballot. He chose Governor Thomas R. Marshall of Indiana as his running mate.

The New Freedom versus the New Nationalism

Taft made almost no effort to campaign and was never in the running. He was a candidate only in order to keep Roosevelt out of the White House. Socialist Eugene V. Debs made a hard fight and had some impact, but he never had a chance. However, in the two serious contenders—Roosevelt and Wilson—the people had candidates of superb intelligence, great capacity for leadership, and boldness of vision. Both men called themselves progressives, but important differences separated them. The campaign revealed, for the first time, a deep cleavage that had been developing in national progressivism.

The Democratic platform of 1912, drafted largely by Bryan, approved or demanded most of the then widely supported measures for political and economic reform, such as the direct election of senators, the adoption of a federal income tax, the strengthening of the Sherman Act, and immediate and drastic tariff reduction. On the great issue of 1912 — how far the federal government should go in promoting human welfare — the Democratic platform was vague and evasive. It gave scant encouragement to various groups who were working for economic and social justice. Indeed, its silence on specific social and economic welfare legislation indicated that the party still adhered to its traditional state-rights doctrines and a general policy of modified laissez faire on the federal level.

Wilson, following his party's platform, began by highlighting the tariff issue. But this thrust drew only an indifferent popular response. While he searched for a more dramatic issue, Wilson met Louis D. Brandeis, the "people's lawyer" of Boston, in August 1912. Brandeis quickly persuaded him that the most important national problem was the destruction and prevention of industrial and financial monopoly. Wilson developed the program that he called the New Freedom. He would unleash American economic energies through destruction of special privileges and the preservation of competition in the business world. And he would accomplish this great goal by reducing the tariff, reforming the banking and currency systems, and strengthening the Sherman Act. Thus he would release anew the individualism that had made America rich and powerful.

Theodore Roosevelt responded with what he called the New Nationalism. It was embodied in the Progressive platform, in Roosevelt's "Confession of Faith," and in other campaign speeches. The New Nationalism expressed advanced American political and socioeconomic thinking in a remarkable way. It included all the various proposals then advanced for the reform of political institutions and practices, such as woman suffrage and the recall of state judicial decisions which affected human rights. It embodied, moreover, Roosevelt's more recent thinking about the most effective way to deal with big business. Great corporations were here to stay, Roosevelt asserted, and they should be subjected to sweeping regulation by a federal trade commission. Finally, the New Nationalism demanded a graduated federal income and inheritance tax, a national child labor law, and other measures to erect strong safeguards between workers and farmers and the interests that exploited them. The Progressive platform laid down the guidelines for federal policies for at least a generation. It was the most significant such document between the Populist platform of 1892 and the Democratic platform of 1936.

The debate between Wilson and Roosevelt only emphasized the wide ideological gulf between the New Freedom and the New Nationalism. Wilson savagely attacked the New Nationalism. He charged that it would end in acceptance of monopoly by the federal government, domination of that government by big business, and, finally, enslavement of the American people by a paternalistic government dominated by great economic interests. Roosevelt replied as warmly. He asserted that the New Freedom was based on a state-rights philosophy and embodied a rural Toryism oblivious to the great social and eco-

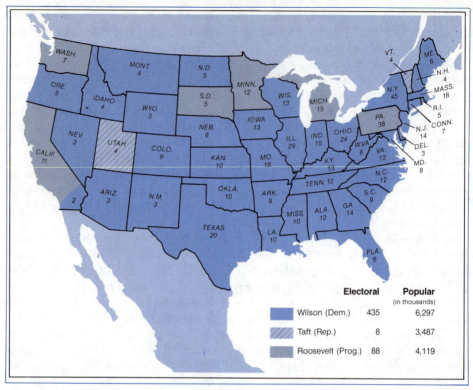

	Electoral	Popular (in thousands)
Wilson (Dem.)	435	6,297
Taft (Rep.)	8	3,487
Roosevelt (Prog.)	88	4,119

The Election of 1912

nomic challenges of the time. The New Freedom, he declared contemptuously, was really the very old economic freedom to cut your neighbor's throat.

Wilson and the Democrats swept the country on election day, November 2, 1912. The Democratic candidate carried forty states and received more electoral votes (435) than any previous presidential contender. For the first time in American history, many blacks, including Du Bois, supported a Democrat for President because of Wilson's promises of fair treatment and recognition. Yet, Wilson carefully avoided specifying exactly what blacks would receive. The Democrats also won control of the Sixty-third Congress, which would sit from 1913 to 1915, and elected governors in twenty-one of the thirty-five states that had gubernatorial elections in 1912.

But the election returns also provided the President-elect with material for sober thought. He had won slightly less than 42 per cent of the popular vote and would, in fact, be a minority President. He, and other Democrats as well, had won only because the Republicans were divided and because Roosevelt had failed to unite progressives of both parties in a majority reform coalition. Perhaps even more unsettling was the spectacular increase in the Socialist presidential vote to nearly 900,090, or about 6.5 per cent of the total, despite the fact that there were two other strong reform candidates on the ballot.

2. THE NEW FREEDOM

Woodrow Wilson and the Progressive Movement

Woodrow Wilson carried on the work that Roosevelt had begun in laying the foundations for the national political economy of our own time. Wilson also continued Roosevelt's reconstruction of the presidency into the powerful office that it is today.

Thomas Woodrow Wilson was born in Staunton, Virginia, on December 29, 1856, the son of a distinguished southern Presbyterian minister who had been born in Ohio. Wilson grew up in Georgia and South Carolina during the Civil War and Reconstruction, but from his youth he was an American nationalist, grateful for the abolition of slavery and the preservation of the Union. He early showed evidence of the quick, keen intelligence and incredible self-discipline that later would set him apart from other politicians. He attended Davidson College in North Carolina for one year and transferred to Princeton University, where he was graduated in 1879. He studied law at the University of Virginia and practiced for a year in Atlanta, the booming metropolis of the New South. He then went to the newly founded Johns Hopkins University in Baltimore for graduate work in history, political science, and economics and received the Ph.D. degree from that institution in 1886. He taught, successively, at Bryn Mawr College, Wesleyan University, and Princeton University between 1885 and 1902. He was elected president of Princeton in 1902 and soon earned a national reputation as a pioneer in the field of higher education.

The obsession of Wilson during all his adult life was the study of how leadership could make democracy work more effectively. He believed for many years that the chief, almost fatal, defect of the American constitutional system was the division of responsibility between Congress and the President. That division, he thought, made responsible leadership impossible. His remedy was some form of adaptation of the British cabinet system, which concentrates all responsibility in a ministry responsible directly to the legislature. Wilson expounded these views in his most famous book, *Congressional Government* (1885). However, the War with Spain and, particularly, Roosevelt's revivification of the presidential office caused Wilson to view the presidency in a new light in his last book, *Constitutional Government in the United States* (1908). The President, Wilson wrote, "is . . . the political leader of the nation, or has it in his choice to be. The nation as a whole has chosen him, and is conscious that it has no other political spokesman. His is the only national voice in affairs. Let him once win the admiration and confidence of the country, and no other single force can withstand him, no combination of forces will easily overpower him. . . . If he rightly interprets the national thought and boldly insists upon it, he is irresistible."

Wilson was himself so nearly irresistible in leadership that he literally transformed the presidency. Politicians since his day have studied his methods and profited from his example. Wilson succeeded, first, because he was a strong-willed activist, determined to be a strong leader. He took control of his party in Congress and became, in effect, its prime minister. He originated legislation, saw it through to passage, and, if necessary, used public opinion as a club over

Woodrow Wilson as president of Princeton University is shown here with Andrew Carnegie to his left at commencement exercises. Carnegie had recently become a Princeton benefactor. (Brown Brothers)

Congress. But he led and did not drive his forces in Congress. And he succeeded mainly because he was a person of complete integrity, who insisted only that congressmen and senators fulfill their promises to the people. Wilson succeeded, finally, because he was deeply immersed in the democratic, Judeo-Christian traditions that underlay the progressive movement, and, most of all, because he was able to express these traditions in speeches of unrivaled eloquence.

Power can become demonic, and Wilson has to be judged on the basis of how he used the power that he achieved. Although a latecomer to the ranks of progressivism, Wilson made his greatest domestic contribution by bringing the national progressive movement to its first full flowering. In brief, he united the hitherto divided forces of progressivism and laid the ideological foundations for later reform movements.

Wilson and the Triumph of Tariff Reform

Wilson, inaugurated on a bright March 4, 1913, announced his purposes in a typically moving address at his inauguration. He and his administration would provide honest and impartial government and be as fair to workers and farmers as to businessmen and bankers. He would continue the constructive policies of conservation begun by his predecessors. In short, he would be President of all the people, not just of certain powerful interest groups. In legislative policy, he promised tariff reform, the strengthening of the Sherman Act, and the reconstruction of the banking and currency systems. He also promised, less specifically, measures to advance social welfare.

The first item on Wilson's schedule was tariff reform, for the integrity and success of the Democratic party and the new administration depended upon revision of the Payne-Aldrich Act — that glaring symbol of the power of special-interest groups. Therefore, Wilson, on the very day that he was inaugurated, called Congress into special session. When it met, he went in person on April 8, 1913, to deliver a brief and forceful address. Thus, at the very beginning of his administration, he asserted his leadership in legislation; he also deliberately focused public attention on Congress. It was the first time since John Adams that a President had addressed a joint session of Congress.

The administration's bill, drafted under Wilson's supervision by Oscar W. Underwood and the Ways and Means Committee, fulfilled all the Democratic party's promises of tariff reform. It reduced duties on hundreds of articles and put sugar, wool, iron and steel products, shoes, agricultural implements, and other products on the free list. It included a provision for a slight income tax, which ranged from 1 to 4 per cent. The measure encountered no difficulties and passed the House of Representatives by a vote of 281 to 139 on May 8.

Many times earlier, the House had enacted sweeping tariff reductions, only to see its work wrecked by a Senate that yielded to tariff lobbies. That danger was particularly acute in 1913. Hundreds of lobbyists descended upon Washington to put pressure on the Senate Finance Committee, which would consider the Underwood bill. Futhermore, Wilson, by his insistence upon free sugar and free wool, had antagonized Democratic senators from the states that produced these commodities. Without their votes, the Underwood bill would fail, just as the Wilson and Payne bills had failed in 1894 and 1909. Wilson struck out boldly in a public statement that denounced the lobbyists who, he said, infested Washington. A senatorial investigation of Wilson's allegations failed to prove undue influence by lobbyists, but it uncovered the fact that many senators had large holdings of stocks in industries that would be affected by a reduction in the tariff rates. The consequent embarrassment caused several important shifts into the low-tariff camp. Wilson, moreover, put such heavy personal pressure on wavering Democratic senators that all but two of them fell into line. Wilson also had loyal support from the chairman of the Finance Committee, Furnifold M. Simmons of North Carolina.

The bill that the Finance Committee reported and the Senate approved on September 9 actually *reduced* the Underwood bill's rates. The Senate committee reduced average rates to about 29 per cent, as compared to the Payne-Aldrich Act's average of about 40 per cent. The Senate committee, in addition, *increased* the maximum income tax to 7 per cent. Both houses approved this version, and Wilson signed the bill on October 3, 1913.

The First World War broke out before the effects of the new rates could be felt significantly, but the Underwood-Simmons Act had an enormous political significance. Defeat in this first test of leadership would have been fatal to the new President. Instead, the victory of Wilson fastened his control over the Democratic forces in Congress and won the confidence of people still skeptical about the Democratic party's ability to fulfill its campaign promises.

The Federal Reserve Act

Wilson, who kept the pressure on Congress, went to the Capitol again on June 23, 1913, to demand thoroughgoing banking and currency reform. Everyone agreed that the banking structure and currency systems were antiquated and totally inadequate for the needs of the American economy in the twentieth century. Scholars, public leaders, and bankers had been seeking solutions since the 1890s. The Panic of 1907 had revealed two major flaws—the absence of a central bank to mobilize reserves and move them where needed in emergencies and a currency based upon inflexible supplies of gold and the bonded indebtedness of the United States (the basis for National Bank notes), rather than upon the real wealth of the country.

The National Monetary Commission had drafted a plan that Senator Aldrich, its chairman, introduced in the form of a bill in 1912. It proposed a great central bank, with branches, which would hold banking reserves and issue currency against gold and commercial assets. It would be owned and controlled by private banks, and its currency would not be an obligation of the United States Government. Both the Democratic and Progressive platforms of 1912 opposed the Aldrich plan for private control. Furthermore, popular fear of Wall Street increased early in 1913, when a committee of the House of Representatives revealed that the House of Morgan and its allies exerted powerful influence over the national economy and that a "money trust" might exist.

Perhaps the greatest challenge that Woodrow Wilson faced in domestic legislation was the drafting of a banking and currency bill. Most bankers wanted a reserve system and money supply controlled by private banks. On the other hand, Bryan and his followers, particularly Senator Robert L. Owen of Oklahoma, chairman of the Senate Banking Committee, wanted total public control of the reserve bank (or banks) and exclusive governmental issue of currency. Carter Glass of Virginia, chairman of the Banking Committee of the House of Representatives, however, demanded a decentralized reserve system under private control.

Wilson moved quietly but effectively and made the final decisions about the banking and currency measure called the federal reserve bill. A decentralized system of Federal Reserve Banks, to be owned and largely controlled by private banks, would mobilize reserves and perform other central banking functions. These Federal Reserve Banks would issue a new currency—Federal Reserve notes—based on gold and commercial and agricultural paper, in accordance with fluctuating needs. Moreover, Federal Reserve notes would be obligations of the United States Government. A Federal Reserve Board, composed entirely of presidential appointees, would, as Wilson put it, be the "capstone" of the Federal Reserve System. It would mobilize and shift banking reserves from one section of the country when needed, set interest rates, and, in general, determine the money supply of the country.

Glass introduced the federal reserve bill on September 9, and the House of Representatives approved it by a huge majority only nine days later. The fight in the Senate, in contrast, was long and harrowing on account of the frantic opposition of certain big-city banking interests. But Wilson would not yield on any major point and maintained relentless pressure on the Senate. He got his federal reserve bill, exactly as he wanted it on December 23, and signed it on the following day. "I cannot say with what deep emotions of gratitude I feel," he declared as he signed the bill, "that I have had a part in completing a work which I think will be of lasting benefit to the business of the country."

Wilson did not exaggerate the significance of the Federal Reserve Act. It was the crowning domestic achievement of his administration. The Federal Reserve System, with twelve regional banks united by the Federal Reserve Board, went into operation in 1914. It was a success from the outset, and, soon, the very bankers who had condemned the bill most violently were its strongest supporters. As a result of the collapse of the American banking system in the early 1930s, the Federal Reserve Board was reorganized and its powers were greatly enlarged in 1935. But our present-day banking and currency structures remain essentially those established by the Wilsonian legislation.

A New Solution for the Trust Problem

The last major item on the New Freedom schedule was legislation to strengthen the Sherman Antitrust Act. There was nearly as much controversy about new antitrust legislation, when Wilson went before Congress in January 1914 to ask for it, as there had been about banking and currency legislation. Many conservatives and legal authorities, including former President Taft, asserted that there was no need whatsoever for new legislation in view of the Supreme Court's recent clarification of the Sherman Act in the Standard Oil and American Tobacco Company decisions. Other conservatives admitted the need for new legislation, but they wanted merely to add new, clarifying provisions to the Sherman law. Advanced progressives, like Roosevelt, demanded a powerful federal trade commission with comprehensive control over business.

Wilson reaffirmed the stand that he had taken during the campaign of 1912 and came out firmly on the side of those who wanted merely to strengthen and clarify the Sherman Act. The original administration program consisted of three measures: First, an antitrust bill, sponsored by Representative Henry D. Clayton of Alabama, which contained severe provisions against industrial and financial interlocking directorates and practices used to suppress competition. Second, a bill introduced by Representative James H. Covington of Maryland, which established an interstate trade commission; however, it was merely a reorganized Bureau of Corporations, with no regulatory authority. And, third, a railway securities bill, written largely by Brandeis and sponsored by Representative Sam Rayburn of Texas, which gave the ICC authority over the issuance of new securities by railroads. The House of Representatives approved all three bills on June 5, 1914.

House approval only intensified the public furor. Businessmen, small and large, were up in arms against the draconian features of the Clayton bill. It also seemed impossible to define and prohibit, by statute, every conceivable means of restraining trade. Meanwhile, a close friend of Brandeis, Representative Raymond B. Stevens of New Hampshire, had introduced a bill to establish a strong federal trade commission. It would have free wheeling authority to issue cease-and-desist orders against businessmen accused of unfair trade practices. At Brandeis' urging, Wilson shifted ground, took up the Stevens bill, and made it the cornerstone of his antitrust program. Wilson signed the Federal Trade Commission Act on September 26, 1914.

Meanwhile, Wilson and his lieutenants had rewritten the Clayton bill. They softened somewhat its severest provisions. Even so, the measure that Wilson signed on October 15, 1913, greatly strengthened the antitrust powers of the government; moreover it made businessmen, personally, criminally liable for infractions. In addition, one provision of the Clayton Act explicitly declared that labor unions and farm organizations were not, per se, conspiracies in restraint of trade; and it also provided substantial relief from indiscriminate injunctions against unions engaged in strikes. Gompers and the

AFL had demanded complete exemption of all activities by labor unions that restrained trade, such as secondary boycotts and sympathetic strikes, but Wilson drew the line at granting such exemption on the ground that it would be class legislation.

The adoption of the Federal Trade Commission Act signaled an important new departure in antitrust policy. The federal government now had an agency — the Federal Trade Commission — whose business it was to protect competition and deter would-be monopolists before, rather than after, they had crushed competitors. The bill's adoption also demonstrated an important shift in the philosophy of the Wilson administration. Wilson had adopted much the same program of corporation control which he had condemned when it was advanced by Theodore Roosevelt as a central part of his New Nationalism during the campaign of 1912. Wilson was soon to demonstrate flexibility in other areas of domestic and foreign policy as well.

3. THE NEW FREEDOM ABROAD

Woodrow Wilson as a Diplomatist

Wilson, of course, had had no practical training in diplomacy before 1913. However, he was probably better prepared to conduct foreign relations, on account of his long study of history and international relations, than any President since John Quincy Adams. Wilson was also a "strong" President in the conduct of foreign relations. He believed that the people had vested their sovereignty in foreign affairs in him. Thus, even from the outset of his administration, he was deeply involved in foreign affairs. He made some mistakes at the beginning. However, he quickly learned, not only the skills of diplomacy, but also how to use power wisely and with restraint. By 1916 his was a major voice in world affairs. As Sir Winston Churchill put it, when he spoke of Wilson's influence during the First World War: "Writing with every sense of respect, it seems no exaggeration to pronounce that the action of the United States with its repercussions on the history of the world depended, during the awful period of Armageddon, upon the workings of this man's mind and spirit to the exclusion of almost every other factor; and that he played a part in the fate of nations incomparably more direct and personal than any other man."

New Freedom Diplomacy

Wilson was, in many respects, the pivot of democratic foreign policy of the twentieth century. He was the first effective decolonizer among statesmen of the twentieth century. As has been noted, the Jones Act of 1916, which Wilson sponsored, gave self-government and promised early independence to the Philippine Islands. His mandate system, embodied in the covenant of the League of Nations, promised eventual independence for many of the former German and Turkish colonies.

Wilson was also the most effective and certainly the most eloquent champion of human rights among all the statesmen of the twentieth century. As we will see, he used the power of the United States, wherever he could effectively do so, to protect weak nations against aggression by stronger powers. He was

Formal portrait of Woodrow Wilson, a masterful politician and an inspiring leader, who added strength and power to the presidency. While in office he made imaginative and aggressive use of power, and felt that "we have grown more and more inclined to look to the President as the unifying force of our complex system, the leader of both his party and his nation." (Princeton University)

also the most effective champion of self-determination, that is, of the right of peoples with a common language, culture, and history to govern themselves. He utterly detested the old European practice of bartering provinces and peoples about in the game of balance of power.

Wilson, additionally, was the first effective antiimperialist statesman of the twentieth century. He believed strongly in the free enterprise system and in a world united by trade and commerce. But he believed even more strongly that it was morally wrong for rich powers to exploit underdeveloped countries and colonies. As he once said, he would never permit dollars to be used to purchase other people's liberties. Almost singlehandedly, Wilson destroyed the imperialistic system in Mexico, where it had reached its apogee.

Finally, Wilson was the most ardent champion of peace and world unity among all the leaders of the twentieth century. He hated war and the use of force in international relations, although he did have to use force himself. He promoted vigorously, although unsuccessfully, a Pan-American pact to mutualize the Monroe Doctrine. And he was of course the chief architect of the League of Nations—the first organization in the history of the world devoted to the advancement of world unity and the prevention of war.

Wilson appointed William Jennings Bryan as his Secretary of State mainly because it was safer to have the "Great Commoner" inside the administration than on the outside. Actually, both Wilson and Bryan were Christian moralists who shared common assumptions about the proper goals of foreign policy. They embarked, therefore, upon various programs to further peace, restore the integrity of the United States in the eyes of the world, and advance the cause of human rights.

With Wilson's blessing, Bryan negotiated conciliation (not arbitration) treaties with thirty nations. These provided for a "cooling-off" period of six months or a year and an investigation of any disputes before nations in controversy could resort to war. Whether the treaties did much good is doubtful, but they were evidence of the dedication of the administration to the cause of world peace. Other policies were of more immediate practical significance.

The administration tried to make honorable amends for Roosevelt's aggression against Colombia in a treaty signed in Bogotá on April 6, 1914. The United States expressed "sincere regret" that anything should have happened to mar good relations between the two countries and agreed to pay Colombia $25 million for the loss of Panama. Publication of the treaty evoked a roar of rage from Roosevelt, and his friends in the Senate prevented approval of the treaty. But, in April 1921, after Roosevelt's death, a Republican Senate approved the treaty—with the expression of "sincere regret" omitted.

Wilson withdrew American bankers from the international group formed to lend money to China because he believed, correctly, that the loan agreement was a blatant instrument of "dollar diplomacy." He also recognized the new Republic of China in 1913, without insistence upon the concessions that the other great powers had laid down as the price of recognition. Furthermore, in 1915, when Japan tried to make China a virtual protectorate by imposing twenty-one "demands" upon her, Wilson intervened so strongly in China's behalf that the Japanese withdrew the "demands" that would have gravely impaired Chinese sovereignty.

Wilson settled a potentially serious dispute with Great Britain by going the second mile to preserve the honor of the United States. Congress, in 1912, had adopted a law which exempted American coastwise shipping from payment of tolls for use of the Panama Canal. The British government, in a formal protest, asserted that this exemption violated the Hay-Pauncefote Treaty, which promised that the canal would be open to the ships of all nations on equal terms. In a special address to Congress in 1914, Wilson admitted that the United States had possibly violated the treaty and demanded repeal of the tolls exemption, even though he knew that he was jeopardizing his leadership of the Democratic party in Congress. Wilson won repeal after a hard struggle; actually, his victory strengthened his leadership of congressional Democrats. Wilson also moved forcefully when a serious dispute broke out with Japan in the spring of 1913. The California legislature debated a bill to deny aliens "ineligible to citizenship"—in other words, Orientals—the right to own land in the state. This measure was aimed at Japanese families who had bought farms in the lush, newly irrigated valleys of the state and who bothered no one but their competitors for the land then in the marketplace. However, these competitors found it fairly easy to arouse a majority of California voters against the "yellow peril."

The Japanese government protested against what it said was invidious discrimination and an open insult to the Japanese people. Wilson sent Bryan to Sacramento to plead against adoption of the bill. He failed, and the Japanese government delivered a strong formal protest. Yellow newspapers, both in Japan and the United States, fanned ill feeling, and American naval leaders began to talk about the danger of war with Japan. Wilson sternly suppressed such discussions in official circles and kept the dispute on a diplomatic level. He was severely hampered in his negotiations by the fact that California had a good legal case, while the Japanese government had no case at all. The California legislation stated, explicitly, that any of its provisions contrary to the treaty obligations of the United States would be null and void. Actually, the California law did not violate any Japanese-American treaty. Moreover, Japanese law forbade aliens to own land in Japan.

Missionary Diplomacy in the Caribbean

The results of the policies of Wilson and Bryan in certain Caribbean and Central American republics reveal that good intentions do not always produce anticipated results. Wilson and Bryan carried on active diplomacy in the Caribbean region partly because of their concern to protect the Panama Canal. Hence the Wilson administration continued to support the conservative government of Nicaragua that Secretary Knox had helped to install. Wilson permitted Bryan, in addition, to negotiate a treaty with Nicaragua for a right-of-way for a canal in Nicaragua, in return for payment of $3 million. The treaty also permitted the United States to intervene in Nicaragua, if necessary, to protect order, property, and Nicaraguan independence. This provision was added at the strong urging of the conservative Nicaraguan government.

But the main objectives of the policies of Wilson and Bryan in the Caribbean—indeed, in all of Latin America—were maintenance of the peace of the western hemisphere and the development of orderly, democratic governments. Wilson and Bryan were, so to speak, missionaries of democracy, who sincerely hoped to help Latin American peoples to develop stable institutions and governments responsible to their peoples.

With these objectives in mind, Wilson and Bryan became entangled in the

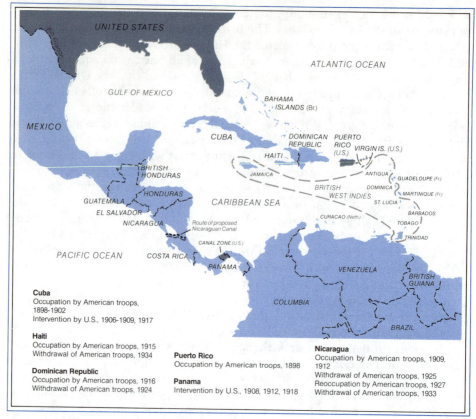

United States Armed Intervention in the Caribbean

Dominican Republic and Haiti, where recurrent revolutions occurred between 1913 and 1915. In their efforts to be helpful, Wilson and Bryan were drawn into the quagmire of local factional politics, particularly in the Dominican Republic. When their efforts failed to restore order, they had to use force to prevent anarchy and chaos. American marines and sailors occupied Port-au-Prince, the capital of Haiti, on July 28, 1915, and established a puppet government. This was really a rescue operation, which Wilson undertook reluctantly. American marines and naval forces seized Santo Domingo, the capital of the Dominican Republic, on May 15, 1916. They proceeded to govern the country themselves when they were unable to form a stable puppet regime. Both Haiti and the Dominican Republic were forced to become protectorates of the United States under treaties like the "Platt Amendment."

American control did bring many material benefits to these Caribbean nations. Money that had been wasted on recurring violent revolutions was used instead for sanitation, roads, schools, and hospitals. More orderly political conditions attracted American and other foreign capital to develop such resources as sugar, fruit, and coffee. Yet this experiment in "missionary diplomacy" did not succeed in the long run. Neither in the Dominican Republic, Haiti, nor Nicaragua did American administrators and diplomats succeed in training the peoples involved for effective self-government. Once American forces were withdrawn from these countries in the 1920s, military dictators again seized power.

Wilson and the Mexican Revolution

The acid test of Wilson's sincerity about advancing human rights abroad was the long, nagging problem of Mexico, where the first authentic socioeconomic revolution of the twentieth century broke out in 1911. The United States was vitally concerned, not only because Mexico was its nearest southern neighbor, but also because Americans had invested nearly $1 billion dollars in Mexican mines, oil properties, ranches, railroads, and public utilities. Some 40,000 to 50,000 Americans resided in Mexico. Increasingly, there were threats to these property interests and people as the Revolution moved from one bloody stage to even more violent ones.

The Revolution began hopefully when the middle-class reformer, Francisco I. Madero, ousted the aged Mexican dictator, Porfirio Díaz, and was elected President in 1911. Then, in February 1913, a cruel but able general, Victoriano Huerta, proclaimed himself to be President and had Madero and his Vice-President murdered. Huerta promised to accord full protection to foreign property, and Japan and the major European powers hastened to recognize his government. Business interests put great pressure on Wilson to grant recognition as soon as he entered the White House. Their advice was strongly endorsed by the American Ambassador in Mexico City, Henry Lane Wilson, who, incidentally, had helped to arrange Madero's overthrow. But President Wilson hesitated; he said privately that he would not recognize a "government of butchers." Moreover, in a public statement he declared, "We can have no sympathy with those who seek to seize the power of government to advance their own political interests or ambition."

Wilson announced his policy in mid-June 1913. He would seek to mediate between Huerta and his regime and the followers of Madero, called Constitutionalists, who had begun the Revolution anew under Venustiano Carranza, Governor of the northern state of Coahuila. Mexico should have early constitutional elections, and, in order to insure the possibility of a fair election, Huerta should not be a candidate for the presidency.

Huerta, encouraged by the British government (British subjects had large oil interests in Mexico and the Royal Navy depended on Mexican oil), replied with the dispersion of the Mexican Congress and the establishment of a military dictatorship. Wilson then went into action with grim determination. First, he virtually compelled the British to withdraw support from Huerta; Wilson made it plain that the British would have to choose between either American friendship or their ties with Huerta. Second, Wilson threw his moral support to the Constitutionalists and, in early 1914, permitted them to purchase arms in the United States. By this time, Wilson was emotionally committed to the cause of the Mexican Revolution. He believed that it, like the French Revolution, represented the struggle of an oppressed people for land and liberty.

However, by the spring of 1914, Huerta was consolidating his power. Wilson now resorted to military force. He found an excuse in a petty incident that occurred in Tampico. When Huerta refused to yield to Wilson's extreme demands, Wilson sent marines and sailors into Veracruz and seized that port on April 22, 1914. Wilson had expected the operation to be bloodless; indeed, he did not give the order for the occupation until the Mexican general at Veracruz had agreed to withdraw his troops to Mexico City. However, fighting broke out when cadets at the Mexican Naval Academy resisted the invaders; there were heavy casualities, particularly on the Mexican side. Wilson was appalled and quickly accepted an offer of mediation of the dispute by the Ambassadors to the United States of Argentina, Brazil, and Chile. But all through the mediation, Wilson insisted upon the triumph of the Revolution. Huerta, greatly weakened by the loss of revenues from Veracruz and hard pressed by the Constitutionalists, fled to Spain in July 1914.

Toward the Brink of War with Mexico and Back Again

Carranza's entry into Mexico City on August 20 seemed to mark the triumph of the Revolution. However, even worse difficulties were brewing at that very time. Francisco, known as Pancho, Villa, Carranza's most colorful general, began a new revolt only a few weeks after Carranza entered the Mexican capital. Another terrible civil war raged for more than a year. Carranza rapidly emerged as the head of the more democratic, modernizing forces in the Revolution; Villa, as leader of the wild and corrupt elements. But Villa shrewdly appealed for American support by promising to protect American property interests in Mexico. The State Department actually made plans for American military intervention in order to assure the victory of Villa's army. But Wilson had learned his lesson at Veracruz; he would not intervene in any way. The Mexicans, he said, were entitled to settle their problems in their own way. Thus he rejected the State Department's plan. And, after Carranza had dealt Villa several crushing defeats, Wilson extended *de facto* recognition to the Carranza regime in October 1915.

Mexican-American relations were unusually friendly during the following months. Then the cunning Villa, in order to provoke war between the United States and the Carranza regime, among other reasons, swooped down on the

This rare picture of a congenial group, taken in 1916 at the border in Nogales, Arizona, shows (left to right): General Alvaro Obregon, General Pancho Villa, and General John J. Pershing. A few months later, the three generals became enemies on the field when Pershing dashed into Mexico in pursuit of Villa. (Wide World Photos)

border town of Columbus, New Mexico, on March 9, 1916; he burned the town and killed nineteen inhabitants. Wilson, under tremendous pressure at home, sent a punitive expedition, under Brigadier General John J. Pershing, into Mexican territory to apprehend Villa. Villa cleverly drew Pershing deeper and deeper into Mexico until, by April, Pershing had advanced 300 miles below the border. Fighting broke out between Carranza's forces and American troops at Parral on April 12, 1916. This led Carranza to demand the immediate withdrawal of Pershing's command from Mexican soil. The American government replied in a stinging rebuke, and Wilson mobilized most of the National Guard and sent it to the Mexican border. Another sharp engagement between Mexican and American troops occurred at Carrizal, in northern Mexico, on June 21. The American officer in command was clearly the aggressor in this incident, but, without waiting for an accurate report, Wilson assumed that the Mexicans were responsible. He sent an ultimatum which demanded the immediate return of Americans taken prisoner at Carrizal. He also drafted a message which requested authority from Congress to occupy northern Mexico.

Both nations recoiled from the thought of war just as it seemed inevitable. Wilson, in an address at the height of the crisis, asked whether there would be any glory in conquering a poor people who were struggling for liberty. Carranza responded with a suggestion to appoint a Joint High Commission to try to settle Mexican-American differences, and Wilson accepted the suggestion at once. The commission met off and on during the summer and autumn of 1916. It failed because Wilson would not yield to Carranza's demand for complete and immediate withdrawal of American troops from Mexican territory. However, once Carranza had succeeded in decimating Villa's forces, Wilson withdrew Pershing in January 1917. Not only that, but Wilson also accorded full diplomatic recognition to Carranza's new constititional regime on April 21, 1917.

Wilson made many mistakes in his relations with Mexico. Most particularly, he tried, at least at first, to impose his own solution upon Mexico, and he permitted Pershing to go too far and stay too long. But Wilson was a sincere, even a dedicated, friend of the Mexican Revolution. He prevented Huerta from consolidating his regime with European support, and he helped the Constitutionalists to overthrow the dictator. Wilson also supported Carranza at a critical time. He never permitted American interests with property in Mexico to swerve him from support of the Revolution. Finally, during the dark days after Carrizal, when war seemed inevitable, Wilson never lost control of events. Along with the patient Carranza, Wilson preserved the peace until Mexican-American friendship could be built on solid foundations.

4. THE TRIUMPH OF THE NEW NATIONALISM

Wilson and the Dilemma of National Progressivism

The great dilemma of national progressivism was the question of how far the federal government should go in trying to promote economic security and social welfare. More cautious progressives adhered to the type of program that Wilson had advocated in 1912 and argued that the federal government should never favor one class or classes—whether workers, farmers, or businessmen.

Advanced progressives and spokesmen for workers and farmers replied that the national government should help to correct the injustices that it had helped to create by giving special protection now to the helpless, disadvantaged, and exploited. Labor unions wanted exemption from prosecution for acts that the courts had declared to be illegal restraints of trade. Farmers wanted the federal government to subsidize long-term loans to them. Labor leaders and many social workers demanded some form of immigration restriction. Social justice advocates pressed hard for federal child labor legislation and a new workmen's compensation act for federal employees.

Wilson resisted, or did not support, these demands during the first two years of his administration. As has been said, he refused to grant the kind of exemption demanded by the AFL when the labor amendments were added to the Clayton bill. He endorsed a federally chartered but privately owned and operated system of rural credits, but he threatened to veto a bill which provided for federal operation and subsidy. In 1915, Wilson vetoed the Burnett bill for restriction of immigration by the imposition of a literacy test. It should be said that social justice leaders were deeply divided on this measure and that many of them applauded Wilson's eloquent veto message. The Burnett bill was passed over Wilson's veto in 1917.

Wilson refused to fight for passage of a child labor bill, on the ground that it was unconstitutional, even after the House of Representatives approved it by a huge majority in 1914. He did sign the Seamen's Act, sponsored by Andrew Furuseth of the Seamen's Union and by Senator La Follette, but only because he decided that the measure conferred no special privileges. He even permitted his Secretary of the Treasury and Postmaster General to institute a limited segregation of black and white employees in their departments in 1913. This action provoked such a storm of protest that it was substantially reversed in 1914.

The first clear sign that Wilson was beginning to doubt that a limited progressivism would either satisfy public opinion or meet the problems of the modern age came when he accepted the proposal for a strong Federal Trade Commission. His switch revealed that his mind was open to new suggestions and that, in the future, he might not adhere rigidly to the ideology of the New Freedom.

The Triumph of the New Nationalism

Wilson became a convert to the New Nationalism in 1916. The longer he served as President, the more he became convinced that the federal government had to take leadership in social and economic reform. Moreover, by the summer of 1914, the Mexican Revolution and the Colorado coal strike had considerably radicalized him. The strike in Colorado had a particularly heavy impact on Wilson, on account of the refusal of the mine owners to accept his mediation. Also, he knew that he faced defeat in the coming presidential election unless he came out wholeheartedly for advanced reform. The Progressive party had virtually disintegrated by the early months of 1916. The Democrats were still a minority party, and Wilson knew that their only hope of success lay in attracting the support of a large number of Roosevelt's former followers. The Democratic party would have to be rebuilt from a southern party with northern and western allies into a great national party with strength among the urban middle classes and working people.

Wilson signaled his new departure by appointing Brandeis, perhaps the foremost champion of social justice measures in the country, to the Supreme Court on January 28, 1916. The Senate confirmed Brandeis, but only after a long and bitter battle in which Wilson backed his nominee with all his influence as Democratic party leader.

Next, Wilson came out in support of the same rural credits bill that he had earlier threatened to veto. It was adopted in July 1916 and established twelve Federal Land Banks. Moreover, it stipulated that the government should furnish funds for loans to farmers if private investors refused to buy the Federal Land Banks' bonds. At the same time, he pushed the federal child labor and workmen's compensation bills through Congress. The former (depending upon the products involved) forbade shipment in interstate commerce of goods manufactured in whole or in part by children under fourteen or sixteen. In one respect, it was the most important piece of American domestic legislation of the twentieth century. It marked the first effort by Congress to regulate conditions of labor *within the states* by use of its control over interstate commerce. As such, it was the forerunner of all such legislation in the 1930s and afterward. Again, Wilson had forced passage of legislation that he had earlier refused to support.

To avert a nationwide railroad strike, Wilson, in September 1916, persuaded Congress to adopt the Adamson Act, which established the eight-hour day as the standard for workers on interstate railroads. Finally, a few days after he approved the Adamson Act, Wilson signed a tax bill that greatly increased the income tax and imposed a new federal estate tax and taxes on excess profits, corporation income, and munitions manufacturers. It marked the triumph of Populist tax policy and was the first serious effort in American history to effect some redistribution of wealth through taxation.

SUGGESTED READINGS

The basic source for Wilson and his era is Arthur S. Link, David W. Hirst, John E. Little, et al., eds., *The Papers of Woodrow Wilson*, 35 vols. to date (1966–   ). The only general works on the Wilson era are Arthur S. Link, *Woodrow Wilson and the Progressive Era* (1954), and Frederick L. Paxson, *The American Democracy and the World War*, 3 vols. (1936–1948). The richest literature on Wilson's first administration is in the form of biographies. Arthur S. Link, *Wilson*, 5 vols. (1947–1965), covers Wilson's rise to political prominence, the campaign of 1912, and the first Wilson administration in great detail. Arthur Walworth, *Woodrow Wilson*, 2 vols. (1958), is a good personal biography. See also Charles Seymour, ed., *The Intimate Papers of Colonel House*, 4 vols. (1926–1928); John M. Blum, *Joe Tumulty and the Wilson Era* (1951); Frank Freidel, *Franklin D. Roosevelt: The Apprenticeship* (1952); Paolo E. Coletta, *William Jennings Bryan: Progressive Politician*

and Moral Statesman, 1909–1915 (1969); and Richard Lowitt, *George W. Norris: The Persistence of a Progressive* (1971).

For specialized studies, see Henry P. Willis, *The Federal Reserve System* (1923); John D. Clark, *The Federal Trust Policy* (1931); Stephen Wood, *Constitutional Politics in the Progressive Era: Child Labor and the Law* (1968); and George B. Tindall, *The Emergence of the New South, 1913–1945* (1967).

The second, third, fourth, and fifth volumes of Link's biography cover Wilson's Caribbean, Mexican, Latin American, and far eastern policies from 1913 to 1917 in detail. However, the following specialized works are extremely helpful: Munro, *Intervention and Dollar Diplomacy in the Caribbean, 1900–1920*, cited earlier; Kenneth J. Grieb, *The United States and Huerta* (1969); and Robert E. Quirk, *An Affair of Honor: Woodrow Wilson and the Occupation of Veracruz* (1962) and *The Mexican Revolution, 1914–1915* (1960).

CHAPTER 26
THE UNITED STATES AND THE FIRST WORLD WAR

1. THE STRUGGLE FOR NEUTRALITY

The Crisis of Europe

The First World War changed the course of human history, or at least greatly hastened events that might not have occurred for generations. It destroyed three mighty European empires, terribly weakened the economic and political foundations of western Europe, and unleashed forces that would continue to threaten the order and stability of the world for decades to come. The war, caused by the same western European military power and aggressiveness that had created the European world empires, now accelerated the erosion of that western domination.

Even the immediate origins of such great events are always deep and complex. It is clear, nevertheless, that conflicts over national boundaries, colonies, and markets had produced arms races and led to a number of incidents that threatened general war. By 1914, Europe was divided into armed camps. On one side stood the Triple Entente, composed of Great Britain, France, and Russia. On the other side stood the Triple Alliance, composed of Germany, Austria-Hungary, and Italy. So tightly knit were both alliances that it was almost impossible for a member of one to become involved in conflict with a member of the other without plunging all the major European powers into war.

The fuse that detonated the powder keg was the assassination of the Archduke Franz Ferdinand, heir to the Austrian and Hungarian thrones, on June 28, 1914. A Serbian nationalist shot him and his wife while they were driving through the streets of Sarajevo in the Austrian province of Bosnia. Serbians hoped to add Bosnia to their kingdom and feared that the popular Archduke might defeat their ambitions. Austria-Hungary claimed that Serbian revolutionary societies were responsible for the murders and issued an ultimatum. Serbia, strongly supported by Russia, refused to yield to the severe Austrian terms. The German govenment, eager for a preventive war against Russia, meanwhile egged on its Austro-Hungarian ally. Austria-Hungary declared war on Serbia and marched upon Belgrade on July 28.

The war might still have been localized. However, the other powers proceeded to mobilize their armed forces and to move them into positions according to long-standing war plans. Each nation feared that, unless it struck first, its enemies might gain a decisive early advantage. As the Russians prepared to march against Austria-Hungary, Germany struck first and declared war on Russia on August 1. This involved Russia's ally, France, which was preparing to meet her commitments when Germany declared war on her two days later. British leaders had secretly promised to come to France's aid; they needed some dramatic incident to arouse their nation. Germany provided this by sending her armies across neutral Belgium in order to strike a fatal blow at France before the massive Russian army could move into action on Germany's eastern flank. Since England was committed by treaty to defend the neutrality of Belgium, Parliament declared war on Germany on August 4.

Foreign ministers labored in vain during the last week of July to prevent the war; the system of alliances was now operating almost automatically. Bulgaria and Turkey joined Germany and Austria-Hungary—the Central Powers; Japan and Italy were lured to the side of the Entente—or Allies—by promises of territory. Eventually, in all of Europe, only Norway, Sweden, Denmark, Holland, Spain, and Switzerland were fortunate (or weak) enough to avoid involvement.

The Establishment of American Neutrality

As Americans faced the catastrophe, most of them recoiled in horror and disbelief and could not understand why Europeans had set out to slaughter each other. The brutal German invasion of Belgium particularly outraged many Americans. Probably a majority of Americans, influenced to some degree by British propaganda, were pro-Allied in sentiment and remained so until the United States entered the war. However, the Germans also conducted a skillful propaganda campaign in the United States and had many defenders among the large German-American and Irish-American elements. Most thoughtful Americans, however, realized that the causes of the war were complex and that no single nation was to blame. President Wilson shared this view. Americans in general, whomever they blamed for the onset of the war, remained doggedly neutralist and were determined to avoid entanglement if at all possible.

In the light of this widespread determination and Wilson's own passion for peace, any course other than neutrality was unthinkable for the American government. Following the custom practiced since the days of Washington, Wilson issued a proclamation of neutrality on August 4. Two weeks later, he added a personal appeal to his fellow citizens to be "neutral in fact as well as in name" and "impartial in thought as well as in action."

It was easy to set the ordinary machinery of neutrality in motion, but it was extremely difficult for the administration to work out the rules in complicated situations. Neutrality meant doing nothing that would give an undue advantage to either side. It also meant respect of legitimate belligerent rights, for example, the right of blockade. The Wilson administration always tried to be fair. It steadfastly resisted demands by German Americans and others for an arms embargo, for such an embargo would have denied to the British the advantage of access to American markets that their dominant sea power gave them. The administration did discourage American loans to the belligerents during the early months of the war. But it quietly reversed this policy before the end of 1914 and openly repudiated it when the British and French governments sought to float a public loan in the United States during the summer of 1915. To have denied any belligerent access to private credit markets would have been as unneutral as to deny any belligerent access to American commercial markets.

First Difficulties with the British

The British naturally were determined to use their great fleet to cut off the flow of vital materials from the United States to the Central Powers. Wilson

European Alliances in World War I

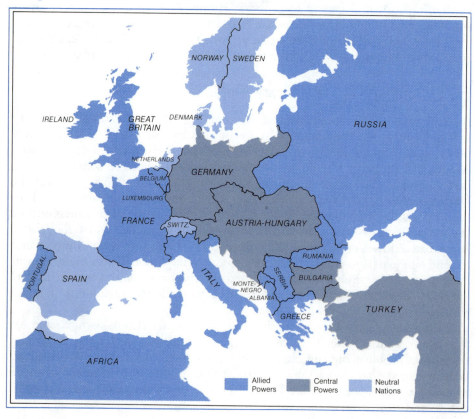

and his administration were equally determined to preserve as much freedom of trade as possible for American producers and merchants.

On the matter of the shipment to Germany of absolute contraband—munitions and articles destined for military use—there was no difference between the British and American governments. It was well established in international law that a belligerent had the right to seize and confiscate absolute contraband which was going to its enemy. But there were innumerable controversies over conditional contraband—articles that *might* be used by armed forces—and so-called innocent goods, destined for use by civilians. Controversies occurred also over certain British blockade policies. For example, the British established a long-range blockade of Germany instead of following the traditional policy of maintaining cruisers outside enemy ports. The British also forbade so-called broken voyages, that is, the shipment of contraband to the Central Powers by way of an intermediary neutral port.

The American government sent strong protests to London, but Anglo-American differences over the blockade were never acute, at least not before 1916, for a number of reasons: First, the British instituted their controls over American trade gradually, and usually with a keen regard for American property rights and interests. It was not until the Germans had declared an unprecedented submarine blockade that the British forbade all trade with the Central Powers. In doing so, the British could and did invoke the ancient right of retaliation. Second, the British government argued impressively that it was impossible to distinguish between types of contraband during total war. Specifically, food destined for civilian populations was as essential to a war economy as guns and bullets. Third, the British were also carful to avoid any open affronts to American sovereignty, at least before 1916. Finally, the British could say, quite accurately, that they, in their own extension of blockade practices, were simply following precedents established by the United States during the Civil War.

The United States and the Challenge of the Submarine

So long as the British controlled the seas and the Germans commanded the heartland of Europe, the American task of neutrality was relatively simple—to pursue the most impartial policies within this framework of power. But Wilson faced an entirely new situation when the Germans decided in early 1915 to challenge British control of the seas by using an untried weapon—the submarine. The German Admiralty announced on February 4, 1915, that all enemy vessels would be torpedoed without warning in a broad area around the British Isles, and that even neutral vessels would not be safe. Wilson responded quickly on February 10 that the United States would hold Germany to a "strict accountability" (a conventional diplomatic term) for illegal destruction of *American* ships and lives. The German government soon retreated from its threat against American ships, and submarine attacks against them were not a matter of serious dispute between the two governments before 1917.

Much more complex and difficult questions were involved when the Germans sank Allied ships on which Americans were traveling or working, and especially when these ships were armed. Wilson rarely adopted an inflexible position against the German submarine war. On the contrary, he did not desire to deprive the Germans of the advantage that came from the use of submarines, and he usually struggled hard to find policies of accommodation. Moreover, Wilson evolved his policies in response to particular situations; the result was that his policies toward submarine warfare underwent considerable change between 1915 and 1917.

The first German-American dispute involved the right of Americans to travel in safety on *unarmed* Allied *passenger* ships. It was first raised when a German submarine sank the British liner *Falaba* on March 28 and killed one American. Under strong pressure from Bryan, Wilson decided to make no protest at all. Then the German submarine *U20* sank the great British liner *Lusitania* without warning in the Irish Sea on May 7; nearly 1,200 persons, including 124 American citizens, perished. So overwhelming was the American revulsion against the deed that Wilson was no longer able to maintain silence. Most Americans were still opposed to intervention, and Wilson, who agreed ardently with them, chose to deal with the crisis by diplomacy. In a series of notes, he appealed to the German government to abandon its campaign of terror against *unarmed* passenger liners. The Berlin government responded evasively or negatively to each note from Washington. On August 19, 1915, a German submarine sank another British liner, *Arabic,* with loss of American lives. Wilson now made it plain that he would break diplomatic relations if Germany did not stop sinking unarmed passenger ships. The Germans had no alternative but to yield; they had so few submarines that it would have been foolish to have risked war with the United States over the issue. Actually, Wilson planned not to go to war after breaking relations, but to call a conference of the neutral nations and to enforce the rights of neutrals on the high seas, against both Great Britain and Germany.

One result of the *Lusitania* crisis was the loss by Wilson of Bryan as Secretary of State. The "Great Commoner" resigned on June 8, 1915, rather than sign the second *Lusitania* note to Germany, because he thought that it was not conciliatory enough. Bryan's successor was Robert Lansing, formerly Counselor of the State Department, an expert in international law and usage.

The Preparedness Campaign

The major domestic repercussion of the *Lusitania* and *Arabic* crises was the strong stimulus that they gave to demands for the rapid expansion of the armed forces of the United States. A small minority led by Theodore Roosevelt had been sounding dire alarms since the autumn of 1914. But Wilson, Congress, and the people did not respond until the submarine controversy had revealed that war with Germany was possible. When Congress met in December 1915, Wilson made preparedness the chief objective of his legislative program. He encountered bitter resistance from pacifists and progressives, who contended that money spent for defense would benefit only big business and Wall Street. Then Wilson went to the people to build support for his program. The outcome was a series of measures, some of which were compromises that pleased neither antiwar progressives nor Roosevelt and his friends.

The Army Reorganization Act of June 3, 1916, greatly expanded the National Guard forces of the states and brought them under strict federal control. The Act also provided for large increases in the regular army and authorized the War Department to establish summer training programs for civilians. Congress followed, in August 1916, with an act which authorized huge increases in the navy during the next three years. A month later, Congress also created a United States Shipping Board and provided it with $50 million to build, purchase, or lease merchant ships. The shipping bill was a personal triumph for President Wilson, for he had fought hard and unsuccessfully for a similar measure in early 1915. Wilson rounded out his preparedness program in October 1916 by appointing a Council of National Defense to advise the administration on problems of economic mobilization, if war should come.

The Purchase of the Danish West Indies

One by-product of the increased concern for national security was the purchase of the Danish West Indies, or the Virgin Islands. Secretary of State Seward had signed a treaty with Denmark in 1867 for the purchase of the islands of St. Thomas, St. John, and St. Croix, only to see it fail to win the approval of the Senate. Secretary Hay in 1902 had negotiated a second purchase treaty, which failed because of the refusal of the Danish government to ratify.

President Wilson took up the project with grim determination in 1915 after the American Minister to Denmark warned him that Germany might absorb Denmark—and the Virgin Islands along with the mother country—if she won the war. The Danes asked the exorbitant price of $27 million, but Wilson was not inclined to haggle after his naval advisers said that the United States could not safely permit a potential enemy to acquire the islands with their fine sites for naval bases. A treaty, signed in New York on August 4, 1916, provided for the transfer of the islands to the United States at the slightly reduced price of $25 million. Both governments promptly ratified the treaty, and the United States took formal possession on March 31, 1917.

Between 1916 and 1931, St. Thomas, St. John, and St. Croix were governed by an American naval officer appointed by the President of the United States, and by local councils. Administration of the islands was given to the Interior Department in 1931. Meanwhile, in 1927, the islanders received American citizenship. An Organic Act in 1936 greatly enlarged the electorate and self-government of the American Virgin Islands, but reserved final control over the affairs of the islands to the President and Congress of the United States.

Wilson's First Peace Moves

No sooner had the fighting started in August 1914 than men began to talk of peace. Wilson offered American "good offices," or mediation, to the belligerents immediately after the outbreak of hostilities. A short time later, he tried to prevent Japan's entrance on the Allied side. Failure in these first overtures did not deflect the eager would-be peacemaker from his course. (Indeed, all of Wilson's policies during the period of American neutrality had one ultimate goal—his mediation of the war in Europe.) He sent his close friend and confidential adviser, Colonel Edward M. House, to Europe in the early months of 1915 to explore further the possibilities of American mediation.

Up to this point, Wilson had been feeling his way rather cautiously. He moved more aggressively after the *Lusitania* and *Arabic* crises, because the British Foreign Secretary, Sir Edward Grey, indicated that his government might be willing to discuss peace terms with certain guarantees from the United States. Wilson sent Colonel House back to London in January 1916 to press for an Anglo-American plan for peace. Under the provisions of this plan, Britain and France would request the American President to call a peace conference. The United States would not only issue the invitation, but also would probably enter the war if Germany refused the call. If the peace conference met, the United States would cooperate with the Allies in demanding a reasonable settlement and the establishment of a league of nations to maintain peace in the future. If the Germans proved uncooperative at this point, the United States, again, would probably enter the war on the Allied side.

House, in his discussions in London, made it very clear that Wilson, when he talked about a reasonable settlement, had in mind a peace of reconciliation accompanied by substantial disarmament and the establishment of a league of nations. The United States would support the restoration of Belgium, France's claim to Alsace-Lorraine, and certain other Allied war aims. But House insisted that Germany would have to be compensated also, and at no time did he promise that the United States would go to war to achieve any particular Allied war objective. This, precisely, was the rub, insofar as the British leaders were concerned. Grey initialed a memorandum which embodied the Wilson-House plan on February 22, 1916, but the Foreign Secretary carefully stipulated that the British and French governments would decide when the plan was to be implemented.

The Sussex Crisis

While House was in London negotiating what is known as the House-Grey Memorandum, Wilson and Lansing were beset by a host of difficulties at home. One of them was the problem of armed ships. Late in 1915, the Allies began to arm both passenger liners and merchantmen. The Germans argued that it would be very dangerous for submarine commanders to surface their frail craft in order to demand that armed merchant ships stop and submit to search. Lansing, with Wilson's approval, on January 18, 1916, proposed to the Allied governments that they disarm their merchantmen in return for a pledge by the Germans that they would not sink ships without warning. This proposal enraged the British leaders and seriously endangered the continuation of House's negotiations. Wilson thereupon withdrew the proposal and announced that the American government would defend the right of Americans to travel on ships that were armed *defensively* and did not threaten the security of an attacking submarine. Wilson's announcement set off a rebellion in the House of Representatives that threatened to take control of foreign policy out of his hands. A resolution, introduced by Representative Jeff McLemore of Texas, forbade Americans to travel on armed foreign ships. A furious fight ensued, and the McLemore Resolution seemed certain to pass; but Wilson finally obtained the tabling of the resolution, although only by reassuring Congress that he did not intend to go to war if the Germans sank a ship that had acted aggressively toward an attacking submarine.

The controversy with Germany came to a new and threatening head soon afterward, when a German U-boat torpedoed the unarmed French Channel packet *Sussex* on March 24 with heavy loss of life. Americans were aboard, but none died. In the belief that the British were eager to implement the House-Grey Memorandum, Wilson delivered an ultimatum to the German government. He declared that the United States would break diplomatic relations if German submarines did not cease their attacks against merchantmen without warning. The German leaders capitulated, but at the same time they stated their own views. They threatened to resume the unrestricted submarine campaign against Allied ships if the United States failed to force the British to observe international law in their blockade practices.

Wilson Tries to Mediate and Fails

Wilson now lost no time in trying to put the House-Grey Memorandum into operation. In a speech in Washington on May 27, 1916, he announced that the United States was prepared to join a postwar league of nations. Next, Wilson and House began to apply heavy pressure on the British government to give its consent to American mediation under the House-Grey Memorandum. The British, actually, had never taken that memorandum seriously. They would never accept Wilson's mediation so long as they thought that they had a chance to win. During protracted negotiations, the British revealed that they did not intend to submit to what they considered a risky American mediation.

The London government's negative replies convinced Wilson that the British were fighting for unworthy objectives. A series of events in 1916 confirmed Wilson's suspicion and caused him and many Americans to turn sharply against the Allies. One of these events was the British army's severe suppression of a rebellion by Irish freedom fighters that broke out in Dublin on Easter Sunday. In addition, the British began to censor American mail which went to Europe and forbade their subjects to deal with American firms which maintained any trade with the Central Powers. These latter measures seem trivial in retrospect, but Wilson and many Americans deeply resented them as flagrant violations of American sovereignty and national dignity. Anti-British feeling ran so high, in fact, that Congress, at Wilson's instigation, authorized the Chief Executive to take severe retaliatory measures against the British in certain circumstances.

The Campaign and Election of 1916

Meanwhile, leaders in both parties had been laying plans for the presidential election. The Republicans were in a cruel dilemma. They had to nominate a candidate acceptable to such conflicting groups within the party as former Progressives, conservatives, the large antiwar midwestern Republican element, and advocates of a strong foreign policy against Germany. The Republican convention, which opened in Chicago on June 8, solved the problem by nominating Charles Evans Hughes, Associate Justice of the Supreme Court. As Governor of New York from 1906 to 1910, Hughes had earned the reputation of a strong progressive, but without loss of respect from conservatives. As a member of the Supreme Court since 1910, he had not said a word about foreign policy

There never was any doubt that the Democrats would renominate Wilson, and the Democratic convention, which met at St. Louis, named him by acclamation on June 14. Wilson, personally, wrote the platform. It eloquently expressed the ideals and embodied the objectives of advanced progressives. The big surprises of the St. Louis convention were the numerous demonstrations

for peace that followed every reference to Wilson's success in keeping the country out of war. Indeed, "He kept us out of war" was written into the Democratic platform as the slogan of the party.

Hughes stumped the country from New York to California and denounced
the administration for its alleged bungling diplomacy, weak Mexican policy,
and inefficiency. He repeatedly said that he stood for the "firm and unflinching
maintenance of all the rights of American citizens on land and sea." But when
asked what he would do if elected — whether he would compel Great Britain to
relax its blockade, or go to war with Germany — he fell silent. Wilson conducted a "front-porch" campaign from his summer home in New Jersey. Wilson
fully realized Hughes' dilemma and hit repeatedly on the issue of war or peace
by implying that the Republicans would take the country into the war. Moreover, Wilson eloquently defended his administration's progressive achievements and frankly said that the Democrats had taken over the Progressive
platform of 1912 and had enacted most of its planks into law. And when Hughes
called the Adamson Act a cowardly surrender to organized labor, Wilson replied that the eight-hour day should be standard for *all* American workers.
Labor and farm leaders, social justice champions, social workers, and many
former Progressives and Socialists responded by moving into the Wilson camp.
The new Democracy that Wilson had worked so hard to build was now in
existence. The two great streams of progressivism that had hitherto diverged
were now united, at least temporarily.

Even so, the election proved to be the closest in American history since the
Hayes-Tilden contest of 1876. Wilson arranged for Hughes' immediate succession if he should win. The plan involved Hughes' appointment as Secretary of
State, the resignation of Wilson and his Vice-President, and then the successful
candidate's immediate succession to the presidency.

Before midnight of election day, November 7, it was clear that Hughes had
carried virtually all eastern states, plus Indiana, Illinois, Michigan, and Wisconsin. The New York *World*, the leading Democratic newspaper in the country, conceded Hughes' victory. But Wilson's prospects grew brighter as returns
began to come in from the western states early in the morning of November 8.
By the following day, it was certain that Wilson had carried California by a
slim margin, and therewith the election. The electoral vote was 277 for Wilson
to 254 for Hughes; the popular vote, 9,129,000 to 8,538,000. Actually, Wilson's
triumph was one of the greatest achievements in the history of the presidency.
He increased his popular vote in 1916 by nearly 50 per cent over his popular
vote in 1912. And in some states, such as California, Wilson nearly doubled his
popular vote in 1916 over that of 1912.

Toward the Brink

Woodrow Wilson was a shrewd analyst of public opinion. By the end of the
election, he was convinced that the American people ardently desired to avoid
being drawn into the war over disputes with Germany about the right of Americans to travel on Allied ships, whether armed or unarmed. But Wilson also
knew that the European rivals were growing increasingly desperate. They
would so intensify the war on the seas that it might become impossible to
avoid entanglement. Wilson also wanted to play what he believed was the no-

blest role given to a leader — that of peacemaker. Hence in November he decided to strike out upon a course of independent mediation.

Wilson's first step, taken on December 18, 1916, was to send a moving appeal to all the belligerents. He implored them to think about peace and asked that they state the terms upon which they would be willing to conclude a settlement. The Germans, who had already issued their own call for a peace conference, returned an evasive reply to Washington. The Allies, egged on secretly by Secretary Lansing, announced sweeping terms such as could be achieved only by a smashing military victory. Wilson, undisturbed, moved to the second stage of his plan. He opened secret negotiations with the British and German governments for a peace conference in the immediate future.

While he waited for replies from Berlin and London, Wilson appeared before the Senate on January 22, 1917. There he explained the conditions on which the United States would "give its formal and solemn adherence to a league of peace" to be formed to help to enforce the peace settlement that would be made. The present war had to be ended first, he announced, but it had to be ended by terms that would create a peace worth guaranteeing. First of all, it had to be "a peace without victory," for victory "would mean peace forced upon the loser, a victor's terms imposed upon the vanquished. It . . . would rest, not permanently, but only as upon quicksand." Only a "peace between equals" could last. Wilson went on to list what he thought should be the terms: limitation of armaments; freedom of the seas; self-determination for peoples under alien domination, particularly the Poles; and security against aggression for nations great and small.

These noble words not only raised the hopes of war-weary peoples all over Europe; they also drew favorable responses from leaders in Britain and Germany. The British government sent word that it was prepared to go to the peace table. The German government could not return so positive a reply, for it had decided on January 9 to launch total submarine blockade against the British Isles and other areas. U-boats already were on their way to their stations.

So the Germans replied, first, by announcing that submarines would begin unrestricted operations on February 1. They would sink all ships — neutral as well as Allied — without warning. The Germans added that they would permit a limited number of American passenger ships to sail without danger; and they postponed attacks against American ships until mid-March. The Imperial German Chancellor, in a confidential message to the White House, also divulged some of the German peace terms, but not the most extreme ones, and begged Wilson to continue his efforts for peace.

Wilson broke diplomatic relations with the German Empire on February 3, mainly as a protest against the new German submarine decree. But Wilson made it clear, when he broke relations, that he would not go to war merely because the Germans sank Allied ships. He continued to hope and pray for peace. However, two events soon pushed him nearer to the brink of war. One was the disclosure by the British of a telegram (which British intelligence had intercepted) from the German Foreign Secretary, Arthur Zimmermann, to the German Minister in Mexico. In the message, Zimmermann invited Mexico to attack the United States in the event of war between the United States and Germany. In return, Germany would pay Mexico handsomely in money and in the restoration of her "lost provinces" in the American Southwest. The other event was the near paralysis of American foreign trade that occurred when American shipowners refused to send their unarmed vessels into the blockaded area.

Wilson responded on February 26 by asking Congress for authority to arm American merchant ships and to take other measures to protect American commerce. Strong opposition to the proposal developed at once in the House of Representatives, whereupon the President gave the text of the Zimmermann telegram to the newspapers on February 28. It was published on the following day and aroused such anger across the nation that the House of Representatives approved an armed ship bill at once. However, in the Senate the measure met the stubborn resistance of about a dozen men, headed by La Follette. They were not so much opposed to arming merchantmen as to giving the President power to wage what they feared would be an undeclared maritime war. They took advantage of the rule of unlimited debate to prevent the bill's passage until the mandatory adjournment of Congress on March 4.

Wilson bitterly criticized what he called this "little group of willful men, representing no opinion but their own," who had "rendered the great government of the United States helpless and contemptible." Upon the advice of the Attorney General and the Secretary of State, Wilson, on March 9, invoked the authority of an old piracy statute and instructed the Navy Department to put guns and gun crews on merchant vessels. The armed American liner *St. Louis* soon afterward left New York and passed safely through the submarine zone.

The Decision for War

Woodrow Wilson suffered intense agony during the first three weeks of March 1917 as he tried to decide between peace and war. In spite of everything that had happened, he still wanted desperately to avoid belligerency. He had no illusions about Allied war objectives; they were, he knew, punitive. He realized, too, that participation in a total war would cause grave damage to democracy at home. He would have preferred to follow a course of armed neutrality; but he felt drawn irresistibly to a decision for war, which he reached on about March 20, for the following reasons:

1. The Zimmermann telegram had caused Wilson to lose all faith in the German government. He believed that it proved that the military leaders were the true masters of Germany, and that these leaders had adopted policies that would inevitably bring the United States into the war.

2. Wilson concluded that armed neutrality could not protect American maritime rights against the German challenge. Armed neutrality did not provide sufficient protection to American merchantmen, and Wilson believed that it would eventually lead to declarations of war between the two countries.

3. Wilson was heartened by news of the Russian revolution on March 15, which drove Nicholas II from his throne. It would be easier, Wilson thought, to make a lasting peace with a democratic Russian government involved at the peace conference.

4. German submarines on March 16 sank three American merchantmen, one with heavy losses of American lives. Demonstrations and demands for war swept the country. These signs of a growing national sentiment for war, however, merely reinforced a decision that Wilson made on other grounds.

5. Most important, Wilson was convinced that Europe could not endure its

A Liberty Bond poster during the First World War. Highly successful advertisements to buy bonds, such as this one, helped to finance a major portion of the war. They appealed to patriotism, and were often printed in several languages to reach the immigrants. (Historical Pictures Service, Inc., Chicago)

agony much longer. The war was in its final stages, and American belligerency would hasten its end. Moreover, Wilson knew that he would have much greater influence at the peace conference as a belligerent leader than as a neutral outsider.

Thus Wilson, on the evening of April 2, 1917, went before a joint session of Congress to ask it to recognize that a state of war existed between the United States and the German Empire. Wilson reviewed the series of acts which proved that the German autocracy was not and never could be the friend of the United States. He asserted that the American people had no quarrel with the German people. He insisted that America's motives should be "not revenge or the victorious assertion of the physical might of the nation, but only the vindication of human rights," and he ended with a statement of liberal war aims.

On that same evening, resolutions were introduced into both houses of Congress which acknowledged that a state of war already existed between Germany and the United States because of German aggressions. After a heated debate, the Senate adopted the resolution by a vote of eighty-two to six on

April 4. The debate in the House lasted through the following day and night. Congressmen finally approved the resolution by a vote of 373 to fifty at 3 A.M. on the morning of April 6, and the President signed it on the same day. For the first time in more than a century, the United States was involved in a major European war, and, for the first time in their history, Americans were about to enter, militarily, upon the European stage.

2. THE AMERICAN PEOPLE AT WAR

The American Military and Naval Contributions

Most Americans, including Wilson and the members of his cabinet, believed, when they entered the war, that their contributions would be limited to naval cooperation and furnishing credit and supplies to the Allies. However, British and French delegations, dispatched to Washington in April 1917, made it clear that the Allies were scraping the bottom of their manpower reserves and that American reinforcements were desperately needed. In response, Wilson obtained quick approval by Congress of a Selective Service Act to raise a huge national army in the shortest possible time. Eventually, the army inducted 2,810,296 men; by the end of the war, some 4,000,000 men and women were serving in the military forces.

As supreme commander of the American Expeditionary Force, Wilson appointed General John J. Pershing, formerly head of the Punitive Expedition in Mexico. Pershing arrived in Paris on June 14, 1917, and had some 14,500 men under his command by the autumn of that year. A series of events catastrophic to Allied fortunes emphasized the desperate need for rapid and massive American reinforcements. In October 1917, the Italians suffered a crushing defeat at the hands of a combined German-Austrian army at Caporetto. In the following month, the Bolsheviks seized control of the Russian government and sued for an armistice with the Germans. As a consequence, forty German divisions were freed to be thrown against the exhausted Allied troops on the western front. There, in March 1918, the German army began a great offensive—the second Marne offensive—to break through the British and French lines and capture both the Channel ports and Paris before American men and munitions could turn the tide. In the process, the Germans conquered 3,000 square miles of territory and took 150,000 prisoners. But they failed to achieve either of their main objectives.

The American navy was fully mobilized and prepared for instant action when Wilson signed the declaration of war. The gravest threat to the Allies at this time was not on land, but on the seas, for it seemed that German U-boats might well succeed in reducing the British to starvation and surrender. The American government set aside plans for construction of battleships and large cruisers and concentrated upon the production of destroyers and other subchasers. In addition, all available destroyers steamed to British waters to help the British navy to convoy merchantmen. This convoy system, introduced largely at American insistence, turned the tide against the submarines in the last months of 1917. In addition, American vessels later laid down 80 per cent of an antisubmarine mine field which stretched from the Orkney Islands to the coast of Norway in the North Sea.

Some 112,000 Americans sacrificed their lives for the Allied-American vic-

Under German machine gun fire. Trench warfare, one of the distinctive features of the First World War, was described in the Independent *(1916) as an agonizing experience during which "the guns boom their awful symphony of death, and the bullets zip-zip-zip ceaselessly along the trench edge that is your sky-line—and your death line, too, if you stretch and stand up." (Wide World Photos)*

tory, as compared to 1,700,000 Russians, 1,385,300 Frenchmen, and 900,000 Britons. The Italians and Serbs also suffered huge losses. But the American contribution came in the nick of time, both on the seas and on the western front. It turned the tide against what might have been, without American help, an irresistible German assault.

American troops participated heavily in the land fighting when the 1st Division captured the strongly fortified town of Cantigny on May 28, 1918, at the height of the second Battle of the Marne. Three days later, the 2nd Division and several regiments of marines helped the French to stop the Germans at Chateau-Thierry on the Marne River, only forty-two miles from Paris. By mid-July, the German drive had been checked at all points. Marshal Ferdinand Foch, the Supreme Allied Commander, then began a counteroffensive that lasted four months. The American army in France, now more than 1,000,000 strong, participated significantly in this drive that brought the war to an end in November 1918, one year earlier than the military leaders had anticipated.

Mobilizing for Total War at Home

It had been a long time since the American people had fought a total war, and the organization of the war effort in 1861–1865 had been so inefficient as to furnish few guidelines for Wilson in 1917. Roughly speaking, the government's efforts at economic mobilization during the First World War went through two stages. The first, lasting from April 1917 to about the end of that year, saw the administration relying mainly on voluntary and cooperative efforts. During the second stage, after about December 1917, the administration moved firmly and relentlessly to establish sweeping and complete control over every important phase of economic life. During this second stage, Wilson acted under his emergency war powers and under authority of the Lever Act of August 1917 and the Overman Act of May 1918. These measures gave the President complete control over farm production and prices and industrial raw materials, production, and prices.

Farmers and housewives were mobilized by the Food Administration, headed by Herbert Hoover, who had already gained a reputation for efficiency as director of the Belgian Relief Commission. Hoover's efforts to increase production of wheat, corn, and hogs were hampered by adverse weather conditions, but his system of indirect rationing and voluntary reduction in home consumption of food was so successful that the United States was able to export three times as much food in 1918–1919 as in 1916. A Fuel Administration, working closely with the Food Administration, stimulated the production of coal by setting prices high enough to encourage the mining of marginal fields.

The adoption of the war resolution found many American railroads in a rundown condition, largely as a consequence of the ICC's refusal to permit the railroads to increase their rates to meet rising costs. Wilson took over the railroads on December 26, 1917, and named Secretary of the Treasury William G. McAdoo as Director-General. McAdoo abolished competition, pooled terminals and rolling stock, poured more than $500 million into long-needed equipment and improvements, and created an efficient nationwide railway system.

The government moved in various directions to build a "bridge of ships" to western Europe. A Shipping Board was in business when the United States entered the war, thanks to the adoption of the shipping bill of 1916. This board seized eighty-seven German ships in American ports; they totaled more than 500,000 tons. The Shipping Board also commandeered some 3,000,000 tons of merchant ships in process of construction, and later purchased about 500,000 tons of Dutch ships in American harbors. In addition, the Shipping Board's Emergency Fleet Corporation built ninety-four shipways designed to construct some 15,000,000 tons of new ships. However, these shipways had turned out only about 500,000 tons of ships when the war ended a year ahead of schedule.

All of the aforementioned efforts would have been in vain without a smoothly functioning and highly coordinated production of uniforms, guns, and all the other equipment needed by the armed forces. The administration tried hard all through the first months of the war to achieve industrial mobilization through the voluntary cooperation of businessmen and industrialists. These efforts collapsed in the face of a wild scramble for raw materials and goods, and Wilson on March 4, 1918, gave sweeping new powers to the already established War Industries Board. Bernard M. Baruch, new head of the board, soon brought order out of chaos, mainly by controlling prices and the allocation of scarce raw materials like steel. By the spring of 1918, the great American industrial machine had been tightly harnessed for a victory effort.

Labor and the War

Labor received consideration during the war such as it had never enjoyed before. Four million workers or potential workers were drained off into the armed forces, while immigration, which had totaled more than 1,000,000 in 1914, shrank to 110,000 in 1918. A million women new to the work force filled the gap to some extent, but a chronic shortage of labor was one of the difficulties with which the government had to wrestle. To prevent wasteful turnover in employment, the Department of Labor established a United States Employment Service that placed more than 3,700,000 workers in vital industries.

Organized labor rallied to the war effort, and the AFL agreed not to engage in strikes during the war. But strikes did occur, sometimes because employers would not recognize the AFL as a bargaining agent, sometimes because workers would not accept the terms that employers offered. Hence Wilson established a National War Labor Board in April 1918 to serve as a court of arbitration in labor disputes. A War Labor Policies Board, established the following month, set national standards for hours and wages. Some 1,500 cases were submitted to the National War Labor Board, and almost all of them were successfully arbitrated. In the few cases in which labor or management refused to accept the decision, Wilson commandeered the plants involved. Labor was held to its promise not to strike; but employers were forbidden to discharge workers for union activities and were encouraged to lower the hours of labor. As a consequence, total union membership grew from 2,722,000 in 1916 to 4,046,000 in 1919; and hours of labor declined from an average of 53.5 per week in 1914 to 50.4 per week in 1920. Moreover, as a result of high wages and overtime payments, most workers actually were in a better economic position at the end of the war than at the beginning. By 1918, labor's real income had increased, generally, 20 per cent above the prewar level.

Democracy with a Vengeance

The direct costs of the war to the American people by 1920 were about $33.5 billion. The greatest domestic struggles raged over the question of the amounts to be raised by loans and by taxation. Progressives and socialists demanded that the entire costs of the war be met by taxation, particularly upon the rich. Spokesmen of the wealthy naturally replied that most of the costs should be raised by borrowing. Wilson and his Secretary of the Treasury, McAdoo, on the whole supported advocates of heavy taxation.

It was not possible to raise the entire cost of the war without the disruption of the economy. However, the Revenue Act of October 1917 imposed heavy excess profits taxes, increased maximum income taxes on individuals and corporations to about 65 per cent, and increased estate taxes. The Revenue Act of 1918 increased the excess profits tax and increased maximum income taxes to 77 per cent. As a result, for the first time in American history, those persons most able to pay were saddled with the burdens of the costs of a war, while the real income of most farmers and workers actually increased during the wartime period.

Public Opinion, Anti-German Hysteria, and Civil Liberties

"Once lead this people into war," Woodrow Wilson told a newspaper editor just before the United States entered the conflict, "and they'll forget there ever was such a thing as tolerance. To fight you must be brutal and ruthless, and the spirit of ruthless brutality will enter into the very fibre of our national life, infecting Congress, the courts, the policeman on the beat, the man in the street."

To a large degree, Wilson's doleful prophecy came true. Ironically, it came true because the administration helped to contribute to a nationwide hysteria. Only seven days after he signed the war declaration, Wilson created the Committee on Public Information, headed by George Creel, a journalist, to generate public enthusiasm for the war effort. Such an agency was necessary, Wilson believed, because the American people at the outset were still bitterly divided over the wisdom of fighting Germany. Indeed, it is doubtful that a majority of the people really approved the war resolution. To convert what might have been a hostile public, Creel went to work on the biggest and most successful advertising campaign in American history.

The IWW and the Socialist party openly opposed participation in the war, and the IWW fomented strikes in the western copper mines. No government engaged in fighting a modern total war has ever been willing to tolerate open opposition to the war effort. As we have seen, Lincoln had suppressed opposition ruthlessly, mainly through military courts. Congress responded during the First World War with the Espionage Act of June 1917. It provided heavy punishment for any persons who willfully helped the enemy, engaged in espionage, and obstructed the draft. This measure also empowered the Postmaster General to deny the use of the mails to any materials which, in his opinion, advocated treason or forcible resistance to the war effort.

Hysteria, egged on by volunteer organizations that often acted like vigilante groups, mounted as prosecutions were announced, particularly when the government arrested and tried most of the leaders (including Eugene V. Debs) of the IWW and the Socialist party. Fear of internal subversion reached such a height that Congress, in the spring of 1918, adopted a Sedition Act very similar to the Sedition Act of 1798 (see pp. 249–250). The Act of 1918 empowered the federal government to punish persons guilty of disloyal, profane, or abusive language about the American flag, form of government, or uniform.

Postmaster General Burleson used his power over the mails severely and, at times, capriciously. On the whole, however, the federal government enforced the Espionage and Sedition acts with considerable restraint and due process. Only 2,000 persons were indicted under these measures; of these 1,000 were convicted. All of the European belligerents established military courts that shot alleged spies and opponents of the war. There was a tremendous demand in the United States in late 1917 and early 1918, led by Theodore Roosevelt, to establish military courts. Wilson headed it off definitively by a public statement that compared military courts with Prussian militarism and clearly implied that he would veto a measure for military courts then pending in the Senate. Consequently, no person was executed in the United States for alleged treason or sabotage.

Most of the public fury was turned against antiwar radicals and German Americans who did not satisfy the public demand for all-out support of the war effort. Many states forbade the teaching of the German language, while local citizens resorted to such absurdities as renaming sauerkraut "liberty cabbage" and German measles "liberty measles."

The Supreme Court had no alternative but to support the Espionage and Sedition acts since they were based upon the government's inherent wartime powers Justice Oliver Wendell Holmes, in Schenck *v.* the United States, 1919, upheld the Espionage Act on the ground that the government had a right to protect itself against internal threats to its security. However, Holmes, in this decision, tried to impose some limits upon governmental suppression of free speech by requiring the government to prove that such speech constituted a *clear and present* danger. But the Court, in Abrams *v.* the United States, 1919, gave the government *carte blanche* to move against seditionists even after the war had ended.

3. THE VERSAILLES TREATY, THE LEAGUE OF NATIONS, AND A SEPARATE PEACE

Wilson Proclaims a War for the Liberation of Mankind

Woodrow Wilson never deluded himself into thinking that intervention would be a blessing for the American people. However, once he made his decision for war, he tried to make the best of it. He attempted to rally all the peoples of the western world in an irresistible movement for a peace settlement that would remove the causes of future conflicts and establish machinery to preserve peace. Wilson had, in fact, begun his crusade before the United States entered the conflict. His posture and policies inevitably changed after American entry, but his long-range objectives – a peace of reconciliation and the reconstruction of the world community – did not change. He carefully dissociated himself from Allied war aims (he insisted on speaking of the United States as an "associate" of the Allies), and he waited for some move from Germany and Austria-Hungary to open peace negotiations. Wilson, however, failed to respond to two such moves in the summer of 1917. One was the adoption by the German Reichstag, or parliament, of a resolution favoring a peace of reconciliation. The other was a peace appeal issued by Pope Benedict XV on August 1. Wilson could not respond because of opposition at home and from the Allies to a discussion of peace terms until Germany was thoroughly defeated.

Wilson's eagerness to begin a public campaign for peace mounted all during the autumn of 1917. He did not miss the opportunity to speak out once the Bolsheviks had seized power in Russia. The Communists published some of the Allied secret treaties for division of the spoils of war and called upon workers and soldiers in the West to convert the war into a proletarian revolution.

Wilson announced his program to the world in his Fourteen Points Address to Congress on January 8, 1918. It was high time, he said, for peace-loving nations to avow their ideals and objectives. These Wilson summarized in a series of general points, which included "open covenants, openly arrived at," freedom of the seas, general disarmament, removal of artificial barriers to international trade, an impartial settlement of colonial claims, and the establishment of a league of nations. Two points – restoration of Belgium and self-determination for Russia – were, Wilson said, indispensable to a just settlement. Other points, including the return of Alsace-Lorraine to France, an independent Poland with access to the sea, and autonomy for the subject peoples of the Austro-Hungarian Empire, were desirable but presumably negotiable. As Wilson said, they "should," rather than "must," be achieved. There was, finally an implied fifteenth point – that the United States had no quarrel with the German people and no desire to continue the war for selfish ends.

The Fourteen Points Address was much more than an avowal of peace aims.

It was western democracy's statement in its first official debate with international communism. The Bolshevik leaders, Lenin and Trotsky, had appealed to a peace-hungry world for a universal class war to destroy western capitalism. Wilson appealed for peace in order to give modern western civilization a second chance.

Wilson's hopes for immediate peace discussions were cut short by the second Marne offensive. Moreover, the Germans rebuilt their strength by gaining control of large parts of eastern Europe as a result of the harsh Treaty of Brest-Litovsk imposed upon Russia in March 1918. The war, Wilson now believed, had to be fought to the bitter end. But even while the ever growing Allied armies fought with increasing ferocity, Wilson refused to yield to motives of hatred and revenge. On the contrary, in the Four Additional Points of July 4 and in the Five Additional Points of September 27, 1918, he set forth his liberal war aims more clearly and eloquently than ever before.

The Armistice and Preparations for the Peace Conference

A series of events in the summer and autumn of 1918 gravely impaired Wilson's opportunity to establish a new world order.

The first of these events was the Allied decision to intervene in the civil war which then raged in Russia between the Bolsheviks and various more conservative groups called Whites. Wilson strongly believed that military intervention in Russia would be futile, counterproductive, and wrong, because the Russian people had the right to determine their own institutions and form of government. However, under heavy pressure from the Allies, he reluctantly consented to a limited American cooperation with Allied plans. With the approval of the Bolshevik government, he sent a force of some four to five thousand men to northern Russia in order to prevent the Germans from seizing military supplies at the ports of Murmansk and Archangel. Wilson dispatched another force of 7,000 men to Siberia to guarantee a safe exit for a Czech army formed from Austro-Hungarian prisoners of war in Russia. More important, Wilson also wanted to keep a close watch on a large Japanese army that had moved into Siberia. Both American expeditions went with strict presidential orders not to intervene in the Russian Civil War.

The second blow to Wilson's hopes was the sudden collapse of the Imperial German Government in late October. Wilson wanted German participation in the coming peace conference, and he hoped that German military might would, to some degree, offset Allied military power at the conference table. The Germans appealed to Wilson in October for an armistice based upon the Fourteen Points, and the President forced the Allies to agree to peace on these terms, with two exceptions. But William II abdicated and fled to Holland, and German morale had collapsed by the time that the Armistice was signed on November 11. Germany was completely at the mercy of the Allies, and Wilson had lost one of his crucial bargaining weapons.

The third event was a very considerable diminution of Wilson's position as spokesman of the American people. On October 25, at the end of a hotly contested congressional campaign, Wilson appealed for the election of a Democratic Congress. His great mistake was to declare that world opinion would interpret a Republican victory as the repudiation of his leadership by the American people. For reasons almost entirely unrelated to the coming peace settlement, voters elected Republican majorities in both houses of Congress on November 5. As Wilson had predicted, his leadership was seriously undermined by the Republican victory.

Wilson, nevertheless, proceeded with preparations for the peace conference scheduled to meet in Paris in January 1919. He believed that only he could provide the leadership necessary for a permanent settlement; hence, he decided to go in person to Paris as head of the American Peace Commission. He ignored the results of the recent election and failed to name any prominent Republican to accompany him to the peace conference. This—the fourth event— would have serious repercussions in the near future—when a Republican-dominated Senate would review Wilson's handiwork at Paris.

The Paris Peace Conference

In spite of these handicaps, Wilson, accompanied by a large body of experts, went to Europe in late December 1918 with the determination to fight for a just peace. Wilson visited Paris, London, Rome, and other places before the

The "Big Four" at Wilson's Paris home during the peace conference at Versailles: Mr. Lloyd George, Signor Orlando, M. Clemenceau, and President Wilson. Regarding the peace conference, Lloyd George later told Parliament: "I am doubtful whether any body of men with a difficult task have worked under greater difficulties. . . ." (U.S. Signal Corps Photo, courtesy of Historical Pictures Service, Inc., Chicago)

conference opened; everywhere that he went he was hailed as a new messiah, come from the new world to redeem the old.

It was a different story when the conference opened in Paris on January 18, 1919. No representatives from the defeated powers or Russia were present. Wilson stood alone against the Allied leaders—Prime Minister David Lloyd George of Great Britain, Premier Georges Clemenceau of France, and Prime Minister Vittorio Orlando of Italy. These statesmen, under pressure from nationalistic majorities within their own countries, were determined to divide the territories of the vanquished and to make Germany pay the costs of the war. The American President held certain advantages in the uneven contest. Everyone acknowledged that he was the one disinterested statesman at Paris. Moreover, Wilson spoke for a great body of liberal opinion throughout the world. Finally, he had one weapon as a last resort—the threat to withdraw and abandon Europe to its own devices.

Wilson declared to his advisers on their voyage to Europe, "Tell me what's right, and I'll fight for it." He did indeed fight throughout the conference, heroically and doggedly, for achievement of the Fourteen Points. He made a number of compromises, such as to permit the Allies to acquire all former German colonies. Also, Japan received former German rights in the Chinese province of Shantung, and the peace treaty imposed a potentially huge bill for war damages upon Germany. But Wilson won many more of his Fourteen Points than he lost. Belgium was restored, Alsace-Lorraine returned to France. The former subject peoples of the Austro-Hungarian Empire won independence and self-determination. An independent Poland with access to the sea was established. In addition, Wilson would have nothing further to do with futile Allied plans to intervene militarily in the Russian Civil War. And Wilson, by dramatically threatening to leave the conference, prevented the French from annexing German territory west of the Rhine and establishing a Rhenish republic under French control.

Wilson's greatest victory, however, was the establishment of the League of Nations. He had come to Paris for the chief purpose of writing into the peace treaty the covenant, or constitution, of such an organization. He warned the delegates a month in advance of the conference that, unless they heeded the "mandate of mankind," they would make themselves "the most conspicuous and deserved failures in the history of the world." A few delegates, such as Lord Robert Cecil of Great Britain, Jan Smuts of South Africa, and Léon Bourgeois of France, were enthusiastic supporters of the League. But many leaders, particularly Clemenceau, regarded it with indifference.

Wilson, however, was determined that the League should come first. At his insistence, a commission of ten members was named on January 25, 1919, to draft the covenant of the League. The most important of provisions of the covenant concerned the reduction of armaments, guarantees of security for all member nations, arbitration of disputes, and measures to be taken against nations that went to war in violation of the covenant. Article X, which Wilson called the heart of the agreement, read in part: "The members of the League undertake to respect and preserve as against external aggression the territorial integrity and existing political independence of all the members of the League."

The League itself had, so to speak, a legislative body of two houses: an Assembly, in which all members were represented, and a Council of nine members, with permanent representatives from the United States, Great Britain, France, Italy, and Japan. In addition, a World Court would sit at The Hague to arbitrate disputes; and the League was to establish a number of commissions to foster international cooperation in many fields.

The treaty was completed and presented to German envoys in early May. The Germans protested strongly against the violations of the Fourteen Points; but they were in no position to renew hostilities. Therefore, after minor changes were made by the conference, the treaty was signed in the Hall of Mirrors in the Versailles Palace outside Paris on June 28, 1919.

The Fight for the Treaty: The Opening Phase

There were several signs long before the conference ended that Wilson would encounter strong opposition in the United States Senate if he insisted upon incorporating the covenant of the League of Nations into the Versailles Treaty. Wilson returned to the United States in late February 1919 to sign bills during the closing days of Congress. On this occasion, he conferred with the House and Senate foreign relations committees and heard criticism of the covenant.

Europe after the Versailles Treaty

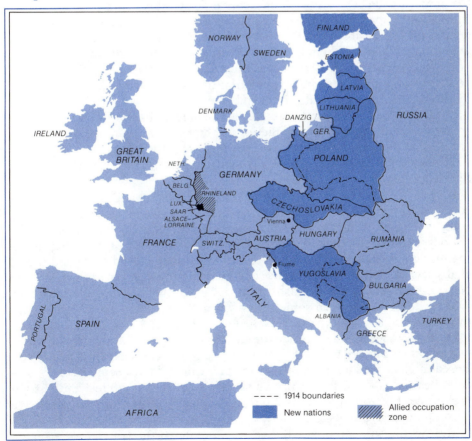

Critics noted that it contained no recognition of the Monroe Doctrine, did not exclude internal affairs from the jurisdiction of the League, and made no provision for the withdrawal of member nations.

Wilson defied his critics in a speech in New York just before he returned to France. He warned that senators would find the covenant so deeply embedded in the treaty that they could not cut it out. Henry Cabot Lodge of Massachusetts, the Republican leader in the Senate, responded with a statement signed by more than one third of the senators. The signers declared in effect that the upper house would never approve the treaty with the covenant in its present form. Consequently, Wilson set to work and obtained all of the changes that his critics demanded, even though the effort required him to make new compromises with the Allied leaders.

Wilson, immediately after his return to the United States in July 1919, presented the Versailles Treaty to the Senate in an eloquent and confident address. All superficial signs seemed to indicate that his confidence was well founded. To be sure, a few newspapers were already raising cries of alarm against what they called an entangling alliance. A small group of isolationist senators, called "bitter enders," led by Hiram W. Johnson and William E. Borah of Idaho, had announced that they would fight to the bitter end to prevent ratification of the treaty. But Wilson moved serenely in the confidence that the overwhelming majority of Americans was on his side.

Wilson did not know it, but Lodge, new chairman of the Foreign Relations Committee, had decided to kill the treaty if he possibly could do so. Lodge despised Wilson for many of the same reasons that had led his good friend, Theodore Roosevelt, to abhor the President. Lodge was, moreover, a bitter partisan, who did not intend to help the Democratic party earn credit for a successful peace settlement. Finally, Lodge was himself an extreme nationalist. As such, he disapproved of American participation in the League of Nations and preferred an alliance with Great Britain and France.

Lodge also was a wily strategist. He did not dare at first openly to oppose the treaty; hence, he used delaying tactics in order to give its opponents time to mobilize and get their message to the country. This the Massachusetts Senator did by reading aloud every word of the treaty to his committee, and by holding long hearings.

Wilson did what he could to win the support of Republican senators. His conferences revealed that the treaty was in danger, and he decided to go to the country in order, as he put it, to purify the wells of public opinion poisoned by the opponents of the League. To his physician, who warned that a long speaking tour could endanger his life, Wilson replied that he had to go and would gladly sacrifice his life for the cause of American membership in the League of Nations. He set out from Washington on September 3, traveled more than 8,000 miles, and delivered some thirty-seven major addresses to large and enthusiastic audiences all the way to the Pacific coast and back to Colorado. Altogether, the speeches were one of the great forensic efforts in American history, but they took a heavy toll of Wilson's limited physical reserves. He nearly collapsed after an eloquent address at Pueblo, Colorado, on September 25. His doctor canceled the rest of Wilson's speeches and sped the presidential train back to Washington. A few days later, on October 2, Wilson suffered a massive stroke that paralyzed his left side.

Meanwhile, on September 10, Lodge had reported the treaty to the Senate with a number of reservations and amendments. The amendments were voted down, whereupon Lodge offered fourteen reservations. Most of them were unimportant. However, the Senator's second reservation stated that the United States, upon ratifying the treaty, assumed no obligations under Article X of the covenant to preserve the independence and territorial integrity of member nations, and would not commit its armed forces to uphold the covenant unless Congress, by joint resolution in every instance, so provided. Wilson had announced his willingness to accept what he called "interpretive" reservations, but he absolutely refused to accept the second Lodge reservation on the ground that it nullified rather than ratified the treaty. Hence when the treaty came up for a vote in the Senate on November 19, 1919, most Democrats joined the "bitter enders" to defeat approval with the Lodge reservations. On a second vote, the Republicans and "bitter enders" combined to defeat approval without the Lodge reservations.

The Fight for the Treaty: The Debacle

Most Americans who had followed the peace negotiations were shocked and angered. They demanded that Lodge and Wilson reconcile their differences. Lodge wavered under the pressure, then stood firm. Wilson responded by saying that there could be no compromise on Article X, the "heart of the covenant." He also announced that the presidential election of 1920 should be a "great and solemn referendum" on the League of Nations. Wilson's stubborn stand caused public opinion to turn sharply against him, but he would not budge. When the treaty came up for a vote for a second time on March 19, 1920, Wilson again instructed Democratic senators to oppose approval with the Lodge reservations. Enough of them heeded Wilson's command to defeat approval.

Wilson has been accused of infanticide, of killing his own child — the League of Nations. It is certainly true that he prevented Senate approval on the final vote. As is true of all important decisions, the reasons for Wilson's decision not to permit approval of the Versailles Treaty with the Lodge reservations were mixed and various. First, he believed deeply that the question of the character of American participation in the League was so fundamental that it could not be compromised. As he had said repeatedly during his western tour, the United States should either enter the League without crippling reservations and provide leadership in building a new world order, or else the country should stay out of the League. Second, although Wilson's illness had not weakened his ordinary mental processes, it had gravely affected his temperament and ability to make decisions. In normal health, he, himself, would probably have worked out a compromise acceptable to a large majority of senators. Finally, Wilson was so isolated in the White House that he was out of touch both with the situation on Capitol Hill and with public opinion. Perhaps he refused to accept the Lodge reservations because he believed that the Senate would not dare to reject the entire treaty merely because it did not approve of every provision of the League Covenant.

Whatever the reasons, the treaty was doomed. It was returned to the White House with the formal announcement that the Senate had been unable to obtain the constitutional two-thirds majority necessary for consent to ratification. Shortly afterward, Congress adopted a resolution which declared the war with Germany at an end. This Wilson vetoed on May 27 as "an ineffaceable stain on the gallantry and honor of the United States." The House failed to pass the resolution over the veto. Thus the United States remained technically at war with Germany until July 2, 1921, when Wilson's successor approved a resolution for a separate peace.

4. THE AFTERMATH OF WAR

Demobilization

The signing of the Armistice occurred so unexpectedly that the conclusion of peace found the American government without any plans for a smooth transition from a wartime to a peacetime economy. Demobilization occurred almost overnight. As Wilson put it, "The moment we knew the armistice to have been signed we took the harness off." War agencies were quickly dismantled. More than two thirds of the American Expeditionary Force were back at home before the Versailles Treaty was signed. After January 1920, the only part of Pershing's forces which remained in Europe was a little American army of occupation at Coblenz.

There were urgent domestic problems that the administration and Congress had to face in spite of the overwhelming popular desire for a return to normal life. One problem was what to do with the railroads. The AFL and railroad brotherhoods urged the government to purchase the railroads and give workers a share in their management and profits. Wilson laid the problem before Congress on December 24, 1919, and warned that he would return the railroads to their owners on March 1, 1920, unless Congress decided otherwise. Congress responded with the Esch-Cummins Transportation Act of 1920. It rejected governmental ownership, but it vastly enlarged the powers of the Interstate Commerce Commission. The ICC was even empowered to supervise the sale of railroad securities and to consolidate competing lines into great regional systems.

Congress met another problem—disposal of the Shipping Board's fleet which now totaled 15,000,000 tons—with the Merchant Marine Act of 1920. It directed the Shipping Board to sell as many vessels as possible to private owners; however, it authorized the Emergency Fleet Corporation to operate vessels that could not be sold. Congress also approved three measures long advocated by the Wilson administration—the General Leasing Act, the Water Power Act, and the Nineteenth Amendment (see pp. 609–610, 623).

Meanwhile, the nation had embarked upon one of the most ambitious efforts at social reform in its history. This was the institution of nationwide prohibition of the manufacture and sale of intoxicating beverages. The long campaign against Demon Rum had begun in the early nineteenth century and was carried on after the 1870s by two powerful organizations, the Women's Christian Temperance Union and the Anti-Saloon League. The movement picked up strength from progressives who were eager to cleanse society of vice, from businessmen attracted by the idea of sober workers, and from conservatives who feared violence from blacks and the poor in general. By the end of 1918, over three fourths of the American people lived in dry states or counties. A prohibition amendment, the Eighteenth, was submitted to the states in 1917 and ratified in January 1919. In the following autumn, Congress adopted (over Wilson's veto) the Volstead Act, which defined alcoholic beverages as any which contained more than one half of 1 per cent of alcohol.

Postwar Inflation and Strikes

The administration was powerless to cope with perhaps the most urgent post-war domestic problem—a spiraling inflation in prices caused by a wild scramble of businessmen and industrialists for goods and raw materials. Wilson tried to stem the tide by establishing an Industrial Board to take the place of the War Industries Board, but the new board lacked any statutory authority whatsoever over prices and soon confessed its inability to halt rising prices. Consequently, the cost of living rose to 77 per cent above the prewar level in 1919 and to 105 per cent above the prewar level in 1920.

The most dramatic repercussion of inflation was an epidemic of strikes in 1919. All told, they involved 4,000,000 workers and cost $2 billion of loss in sales and wages. The strikes of 1919 began on November 1, when 435,000 bituminous coal miners laid down their tools. Winter was approaching, and coal supplies were short. Attorney General A. Mitchell Palmer broke this strike by obtaining an injunction from a federal judge which ordered the miners back to work on the ground that the strike violated the wartime Lever Act, which was still, technically, in effect. It is doubtful that Wilson, who was extremely sick at the time, knew about Palmer's action. A federal arbitral commission eventually awarded large pay increases to the miners, who had not received a wage hike since August 1917. At about the same time, some 350,000 steelworkers walked out after the steel companies refused to grant union recognition, wage increases, and the eight-hour day. The steel strike was accompanied by widespread violence and accusations of Communism against strikers; it ended in January 1920 in the complete surrender of the workers. Another strike—in Boston—seemed to lend credence to the widespread popular fear that the country was in the midst of a dangerous social upheaval. The police commissioner of Boston suspended nineteen policemen for organizing a union affiliated with the AFL. Thereupon, in September 1919, 90 per cent of the police force walked out. For two or three days, lawlessness threatened to engulf the city. Volunteers and guards from the Charlestown Navy Yard preserved order. Then Governor Calvin Coolidge mobilized the National Guard and backed the police commissioner's refusal to reinstate the striking policemen. When he received a telegram from Samuel Gompers, president of the AFL, urging him to show leniency to the discharged strikers, Coolidge wired: "There is no right to strike against the public safety by anybody, anywhere, anytime."

The First Red Scare and Racial Troubles

The churning events of 1919 induced an outbreak of hysteria against Communists that verged on a national madness. The hysteria began in earnest during February 1919, when workers in Seattle staged a general strike. The mayor of that city charged that the strike was the first step in a Bolshevik and IWW plot to paralyze the nation. A crude scheme to assassinate a number of prominent Americans was uncovered in April; then a bomb blew off the front of Attorney General Palmer's home in June, and other bombs exploded before public buildings. The culprits never were found; probably they were members of a tiny anarchist group. May Day riots in major cities required thousands of policemen and soldiers, and even tanks in one city, before they could be controlled. Americans, disconcerted by the wartime excitement, rocketing prices, gigantic strikes, revolutions abroad, and, now, bombs, riots, and talk of revolt at home, feared that they lived on the brink of catastrophe. When radical Socialists formed the American Communist and Communist Labor parties in August 1919, with the announced intention of promoting a proletarian revolution, otherwise sane Americans believed that these tiny, unarmed, disorganized parties threatened the national government.

Public alarm and demands from Congress for action were so great that the Labor Department rounded up 249 Russian Communists in November, loaded them on the army transport *Buford*—called the "Red Ark"—and shipped them to Russia. The popular excitement also affected Attorney General Palmer, who was a former leader of the most progressive wing of the Democratic party and was now eager for the Democratic presidential nomination. First, Palmer set the Justice Department's Bureau of Investigation—predecessor of the Federal Bureau of Investigation (F.B.I.)—to work to infiltrate and investigate Communist groups. To the radical division of the bureau, led by J. Edgar Hoover, was given the task of evaluating the extent of the Communist threat. When Hoover reported that revolution was imminent, Palmer urged Congress to approve a measure to punish persons guilty even of inciting sedition. Congress was more than willing to comply; representatives vied with each other for the privilege of attaching their name to this popular legislation. While the contest continued, however, no bill passed.

Palmer, hounded by critics who demanded action, organized a great federal dragnet to ferret out all alien Communists. On January 2, 1920, federal agents swooped down upon Communist headquarters all over the country and arrested well over 6,000 persons—American citizens as well as aliens—most without proper warrants. They were hustled off to jails and detention centers, where many were held for weeks and even months without the rights of bond or counsel. Eventually only 556 of them were deported as Communist aliens.

Further evidence of hysteria was the expulsion by the New York assembly in April 1920 of five members for no other offense than their election on the Socialist ticket. From this point on, however, public fear subsided rapidly. Prices fell sharply beginning in early spring of 1920, strikes virtually ceased, the Communist tide in Europe receded, and the bombing and riots in the United States ended completely, except for one later explosion in Wall Street. Palmer, on the advice of his Bureau of Investigation, warned of a great Red uprising on May Day, 1920. When it did not occur, the Attorney General became the laughing stock of the country.

American blacks were among the chief victims of the turbulence that followed the Armistice. The sudden decline in immigration in 1914 had created such a scarcity of unskilled labor in northern and midwestern cities that several hundred thousand blacks left the South to take advantage of employment opportunities opened to them for the first time. They had to crowd into slum areas and at once aroused the suspicion and hatred of white unskilled workers. Race relations deteriorated further during the war—ironically, because some 400,000 blacks served in the armed services, many of them overseas. Southerners, particularly, feared that Negro veterans would return home to demand some measure of equality. Lynchings increased from thirty-four in 1917 to more than seventy in 1919, and ten of the victims in 1919 were black veterans. A terrible race riot took place in East St. Louis, Illinois, in 1917.

Greater agony was in store for black Americans. The worst race riot in American history up to this time broke out in the national capital in July 1919, and an even more bloody conflict between black and white citizens erupted soon afterward in Chicago. Other race riots followed in Omaha and Knoxville, and a veritable race war raged around Elaine, Arkansas. All told, twenty-five riots left hundreds dead and caused property damage running into the millions. The most significant fact about all these riots was that blacks, determined to protect their families, fought back bravely and gave as much as they took.

The Campaign and Election of 1920

Fortunately, the country had regained a large measure of sanity by the early months of 1920, when the presidential campaign began. The leading contenders for the Democratic nomination were Wilson's son-in-law, William G. McAdoo, Attorney General Palmer, and Governor James M. Cox of Ohio. Wilson acted as if he wanted a third nomination, but he may have been striking this posture in order to prevent the nomination of McAdoo, who he did not think would make a good President. Palmer had incurred the everlasting wrath of labor leaders, and Governor Cox won the nomination at the Democratic national convention in San Francisco on July 5. He chose for his running mate Franklin D. Roosevelt of New York, a prominent Wilsonian and supporter of the League of Nations.

Republican hopes ran high in the spring of 1920. Senator Hiram W. Johnson tried to rally isolationists and former Progressives, but failed. Senator Warren G. Harding of Ohio was also "available," but he ran so poorly in the presidential primaries that he withdrew. The struggle then narrowed to a fierce and evenly matched contest between General Leonard Wood, Theodore Roosevelt's old friend, and Governor Frank O. Lowden of Illinois. Deadlock between the Wood and Lowden delegates ensued as soon as the balloting began at the Republican national convention in Chicago. A group of Republican leaders settled upon Harding, who was the most popular officeholder in the crucial state of Ohio. Harding won the nomination as a compromise candidate on June 12. Governor Coolidge, hero of the Boston police strike, was nominated for the vice-presidency.

Cox and Roosevelt visited Wilson at the White House immediately after their nomination and promised that they would continue the ailing President's fight for the League of Nations. They fulfilled their promise in a strenuous campaign. But they never had a chance because the coalition that had put Wilson back in office in 1916 was in shambles. The Wilson administration had alienated German Americans, Irish Americans, and radicals by entering the war. The administration had alienated businessmen by high taxes, western farmers by putting a ceiling on wheat prices, and labor by breaking the coal strike and a railroad strike early in 1920.

Harding, who read the political signs wisely, conducted a low-keyed campaign full of soothing but meaningless generalities. The main task of the Republican campaign managers was to neutralize the League of Nations as an issue. This they did by persuading thirty-one prominent Republicans to sign a statement which declared that Harding's election would be the best guarantee of American membership in the League of Nations. Not until the end of the campaign did Harding make it clear that he opposed American membership. By then it was too late for the Democrats to capitalize upon the issue.

The victory of Harding was the most smashing electoral triumph since the election of James Monroe in 1820. The Ohio Senator carried every state in the North, Middle West, and West, every border state except Kentucky, and broke the Solid South by carrying Tennessee. His 16,152,000 popular and 404 electoral votes dwarfed Cox's 9,147,000 popular and 127 electoral votes. The landslide also carried large Republican majorities into both houses of the next Congress.

The outcome, as one Democrat sadly described it, was a political earthquake, but the vote probably signified even less than Monroe's triumph one hundred years before. The election was not a mandate on the League of Nations; nor had the campaign seen a squaring off of progressives and conservatives. Harding won by a huge majority simply because he was able to add a large number of discontented voters to the ordinary Republican majority.

SUGGESTED READINGS

Link, et al., The Papers of Woodrow Wilson, and Link, Wilson, Vols. 3–5, both already cited, cover the period of neutrality and American entrance into the war in most detail. Link covers the same period in brief form in Woodrow Wilson and the Progressive Era, already cited, and all of Wilson's foreign policies in Woodrow Wilson: Revolution, War, and Peace (1979). Among the general studies, the best are Charles Seymour, American Neutrality, 1914–1917 (1935) and American Diplomacy during the World War (1934); Earnest R. May, The World War and American Isolation (1959); and Patrick Devlin, Too Proud to Fight: Woodrow Wilson's Neutrality 1974). Robert E. Osgood, Ideals and Self-Interest in America's Foreign Relations (1953), and John Milton Cooper, Jr., The Vanity of Power: American Isolationism and the First World War (1969), present good analyses of the reactions of the American people to the war in Europe.

For the American home front, 1917–1918, see especially Seward W. Livermore, Politics Is Adjourned: Woodrow Wilson and the War Congress (1966); Daniel R. Beaver, Newton D. Baker and the American War Effort, 1917–1919 (1966); and Stephen Vaughn, Holding Fast the Inner Lines: Democracy, Nationalism, and the Committee on Public Information (1980). H. C. Peterson and Gilbert C. Fite, Opponents of War, 1917–1918 (1957), and Zechariah Chaffee, Jr., Free Speech in the United States (1941), relate the suppression of civil liberties during the war period.

The best account of American military par-

ticipation is in Frank E. Vandiver, Black Jack: The Life and Times of John J. Pershing, 2 vols. (1977), but see also David F. Trask, The United States in the Supreme War Council (1961). On the American naval effort, see Elting E. Morison, Admiral Sims and the Modern American Navy (1942).

We now have an impressive literature on American diplomacy, 1917–1918: W. B. Fowler, British-American Relations, 1917–1918 (1969); Arno J. Mayer, Political Origins of the New Diplomacy, 1917–1918 (1959); George F. Kennan, Russia Leaves the War (1956), The Decision to Intervene (1958), and Russia and the West under Lenin and Stalin (1961); Betty Miller Unterberger, America's Siberian Expedition (1956); and Carl P. Parrini, Heir to Empire: United States Economic Diplomacy, 1916–1923 (1969).

For the early American movement for a league of nations, see Ruhl J. Bartlett, The League to Enforce Peace (1944). Lawrence E. Gelfand, The Inquiry: American Preparations for Peace, 1917–1919 (1963), is excellent. The best one-volume book on the Paris Peace Conference is Inga Floto, Colonel House at Paris (1980). Ray S. Baker, Woodrow Wilson and World Settlement, 3 vols. (1922), is especially important because Wilson was a secret co-author. Also important are N. Gordon Levin, Jr., Woodrow Wilson and World Politics: America's Response to War and Revolution (1968); Paul Birdsall, Versailles Twenty Years After (1941); and Herbert Hoover, The Ordeal of Woodrow Wilson (1958). Arno J. Mayer, The Politics and Diplomacy of Peacemaking: Containment and Counterrevolution at Ver-

sailles, 1918–1919 (1967), and John M. Thompson, *Russia, Bolshevism, and the Versailles Peace* (1966), highlight the Russian problem.

The best accounts of the fight over the Versailles Treaty are Denna F. Fleming, *The United States and the League of Nations* (1932), and Ralph Stone, *The Irreconcilables: The Fight Against the League of Nations* (1970), but see also the discussion in Link, *Woodrow Wilson: Revolution, War, and Peace,* already cited.

There is a growing literature on demobilization and the immediate postwar period. Mark Sullivan, *Our Times: The United States, 1900–1925,* 6 vols. (1926–1935), Vols. 5 and 6; the third volume in the Paxson series, already cited; William E. Leuchtenburg, *The Per-*

ils of Prosperity, 1914–1932 (1958); and Preston W. Slosson, *The Great Crusade and After* (1930), are all good introductions. Elliott M. Rudwick, *Race Riot at East St. Louis* (1964), and William M. Tuttle, Jr., *Race Riot: Chicago in the Red Summer of 1919* (1970), are both classics. For the Red Scare, see Chaffee, *Free Speech in the United States,* already cited; Robert K. Murray, *Red Scare: A Study in National Hysteria* (1955); Stanley Coben, *A. Mitchell Palmer: Politician* (1963); and Theodore Draper, *The Roots of American Communism* (1957).

The standard work on the presidential campaign of 1920 is Wesley M. Bagby, Jr., *The Road to Normalcy: The Presidential Campaign and Election of 1920* (1962).

CHAPTER 27
THE 1920s: ACCELERATED ECONOMIC AND SOCIAL CHANGE

1. PROSPERITY DECADE

A Population on the Move

During the decade between the Armistice and the onset of the Great Depression in 1929, economic and social change took place at a remarkably rapid pace in the United States. The movement of Americans from the countryside to the cities and their suburbs continued at an unprecedented rate. Farm population suffered a net decline during the decade for the first time in American history, and the percentage growth in population for the country as a whole was the lowest since the seventeenth century. More than 13,000,000 people moved from rural to urban areas between 1920 and 1930 and gravitated especially to the great metropolitan centers. The five cities with a population of over 1,000,000 grew more than 50 per cent during the 1920s, and most of their suburbs—with the aid of automobile transportation to shops and cities—grew even more rapidly. The traditional movement westward continued, and California became the prime beneficiary. Los Angeles absorbed a large bulk of the westward migration and spread horizontally into fragmented sections of chiefly single-family homes connected largely by automotive arteries and telephone wires. The resultant urban "sprawl" perhaps should have served as a warning of the megalopolis which would later develop on both coasts and in the Great Lakes region.

As late as 1910, a majority of the American population still lived on farms or in small villages. By 1930, however, 69,000,000 Americans lived in cities, compared to the less than 54,000,000 in rural areas. This shift and the various demographic changes which caused it would have political as well as social effects.

The "New Economic Era"

The postwar economic boom and price inflation ended abruptly in mid-1920. As has happened so often in American history, excessive optimism and speculation collapsed, to be followed by a sharp recession and declining prices. Recovery was achieved by 1923, with some help, perhaps, from lenient Republican tax policies. The following six years witnessed spectacular growth in some of the most visible sectors of the economy: total manufacturing, consumer goods, corporate profits, and stock market prices, for example. By 1927, businessmen, journalists, politicians, and economists were prophesying a "new economic era" of permanent prosperity and an increasingly higher standard of living for everyone.

Talk about a new economic era sounded hollow once the depression struck; but the American people did make mighty strides on economic fronts between 1919 and 1929. Total national wealth nearly doubled between 1914 and 1929, while per capita income, adjusted for the cost of living, increased from $620 in 1919 to $681 in 1929. Measured in the same dollars, per capita income had stood at $480 in 1900. This income, however, went largely to the wealthiest 5 or 10 per cent of Americans, and even the improvement in per capita income for the rest left most Americans near if not below the level of bare subsistence. However, most Americans always had been poor — and without enough nutritious food since the early stages of industrialization and the beginning of farm tenancy.

Farmers suffered most from the postwar recession and never fully recovered before the Great Depression dealt them even worse blows. Manufacturing industries increased their output by 60 per cent during the postwar decade; workers enjoyed an increase of 25 per cent in real income during the same period, although most of this went to a relatively small number of skilled or unionized workers. In addition, the construction industry prospered as never before as cities grew, suburbs spread, and roads were built. The value of materials used in construction increased from $12 billion in 1919 to $17.5 billion in 1928.

Financial resources grew apace with the output of goods and services. Even though the actual number of banks declined because of mergers and failures, total banking resources nearly doubled between 1919 and 1929, while the resources of life insurance companies and building and loan associations more than trebled.

Meanwhile, the United States became the world's leading banker. Western European nations incurred enormous debts during the war, while the supply of capital in America multiplied in the long, prosperous period from 1900 to 1929, and especially between 1914 and 1929. In 1914, American citizens had invested some $3.5 billion abroad but still owed Europeans a net debt of nearly $4 billion. Only five years later, Europeans owed Americans a net private debt of nearly $3 billion, and European governments owed the United States Government an additional $10 billion. An outpouring of about $1 billion in American credits and loans abroad each year between 1919 and 1929 only reinforced

New York's position as the financial center of the world. At the same time, the dollar displaced the pound as the chief medium of international exchange.

The Technological Revolution and Rise of New Industries

One of the main reasons for the American economic advance of the 1920s was a revolution in technology. Innovations helped to spawn new industries, and these industries, in turn, greatly stimulated the entire economy.

The technological revolution occurred largely because scientists and industrialists set out intentionally to develop new products, invent machinery, and devise methods of production that would increase productivity, or output per man hour. The success of American universities—larger in number than in any other industrialized nation—in giving advanced training to huge numbers of scientists and engineers made possible industrial research laboratories of a size, quality, and number that no other nation could rival. However, German chemical laboratories regained much of their prewar prowess with assistance from American investment capital. The new school of social engineers, begun by Frederick W. Taylor, continued to concentrate on teaching workers how to use machines more efficiently, and their success added to American industrial profits.

The greatest organizational breakthroughs of this era were the spread of the moving assembly line and the increasing use of interchangeable parts. The best measurement of the progress of the technological revolution is productivity. Between 1899 and 1909, productivity had increased by only 7 per cent in industry and by 6 per cent in agriculture. In contrast, between 1919 and 1929, productivity increased by 40 per cent in industry and by 26 per cent in agriculture. Several industries that had been in their infancy just before the First World War grew lustily during the 1920s. They not only stimulated the economy but also helped profoundly to change American life.

The Automobile and Its Impact

Europeans had developed the first gasoline-powered automobile in the 1880s. It was not until 1892–1893 that Charles and Frank Duryea of Springfield, Massachusetts, and Henry Ford of Detroit produced the first workable American "horseless carriage." Progress was so slow that only 4,000 automobiles were produced in the United States in 1900. Large-scale production began when Ford instituted the assembly line and started manufacturing the ugly but rugged Model T at cheap prices. Automobile production grew by leaps and bounds, except for a brief cutback during the war, to nearly 5,000,000 units in 1929.

Automobile drivers needed hard roads, gasoline, service stations, garages for maintenance, spare tires and parts, and a hundred other products and services. According to one estimate, the automobile industry in 1929 gave employment, directly or indirectly, to nearly 4,000,000 persons.

Through skillful use of advertising and automobile design, manufacturers began to sell a commodity that was much more than the simple transportation which Henry Ford had produced. By the mid-1920s, automobile manufacturers were merchandising comfort, power, beauty, luxury, status, and sex appeal. With the cooperation of American consumers, an automobile became an extension of a person's or even a family's personality; in many cases, the per-

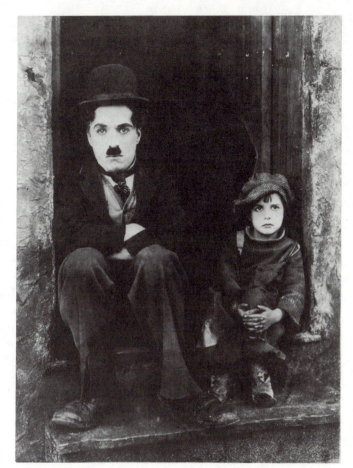

Charlie Chaplin and Jackie Coogan in The Kid, *1921. By the middle of the 1920s, immense movie theaters sprang up in all major cities, and millions of adoring fans flocked weekly to see their heroes—comedian Charlie Chaplin, the "it" girl, Clara Bow, and the glamorous Rudolph Valentino—on the screen. The motion-picture industry heralded a new moral code and helped to standardize American habits. Since 90 per cent of all films were made in the United States, motion pictures carried American speech and a rather distorted view of American culture around the world. The main themes, continuously repeated in predictable patterns, were sex, crime, broad comedy, and romantic adventure. (United Press International)*

sonality seemed to be derived from the car. General Motors played upon these nonutilitarian consumer needs most skillfully—so well, in fact, that in 1927 Ford was obliged to discontinue production of the efficient, much beloved Model T in favor of the more glamorous Model A, which was produced in a variety of colors and had other nonessential attractions.

The Electric Power and Radio Industries

The electric power industry grew from insignificance in 1900 into America's second most important economic interest by 1929, with a capital investment of $12 billion and an annual income of nearly $2 billion. Sixty-eight per cent of American homes were electrified by 1929. The increase in the sale of power was accompanied by the growing manufacture of electric turbines, motors, and home appliances. The value of the output of electrical machinery and appliances exceeded $2 billion in 1929.

Radio transmitters and receivers had been invented before the First World War, but their production on a large scale and the consequent development of a nationwide broadcasting industry did not occur until the 1920s. Before that time, the government had maintained a monopoly on the operation of radio transmitters. In 1929, the industry was turning out nearly 4,500,000 radios a year, and more than 10,000,000 families owned sets.

The Motion Picture Industry

The story of the rise of the motion picture industry is as dramatic as the saga of the automobile. Thomas A. Edison invented the first motion picture camera in 1896. Both technological progress and the development of the motion picture as an art form continued steadily thereafter, particularly after the production of the first "spectacular," *The Birth of a Nation*, in 1915. By 1930, more than 23,000 motion picture theaters were operating throughout the country, while the movie production industry itself had a capital investment of $2 billion and employed 325,000 persons.

The motion picture production industry eventually concentrated in Los Angeles. The weather there was conducive to year-round outdoor photography, and the topography lent itself to "westerns," which American audiences adored. A galaxy of great directors, actors, and actresses became a new species of American folk heroes. Charlie Chaplin, Rudolph Valentino, Clara Bow, John Gilbert, and Laurel and Hardy were as well known as leading politicians ever had been and probably were vastly more popular. Although situation comedies, westerns, and crime "thrillers" flourished, the motion picture industry was based even more firmly on a frank exploitation of sexual themes. Nudity and near nudity was not uncommon. Conventional sexual mores were broken by the dramatic heroes and heroines until a self-imposed censorship stopped, temporarily at least, the tendency toward increasingly blatant sexuality.

The Conquest of the Air

The most spectacular technological development in the United States during the 1920s was the growth of air transportation. Although the first successful flight in a heavier-than-air machine had been made by Wilbur and Orville Wright at Kitty Hawk, North Carolina, in December 1903, aviation made little progress in the United States until the First World War. But when the Armistice was signed, the United States had more than 800 planes at the battlefront and twenty-four plants capable of producing 21,000 planes a year. The air service had become a permanent and expanding branch of both the army and the navy. Moreover, air routes for mail, passengers, and cargo developed rapidly in the postwar decade, especially after the introduction of the all-metal Ford tri-motor plane in the late twenties. By 1930, 122 airlines operated over routes covering nearly 50,000 miles.

In the 1920s, aviation heroes gave a tremendous stimulus to public interest in flying. The entire world was thrilled on May 21, 1927, by the solo flight of a young American pilot, Charles A. Lindbergh. The "Lone Eagle" landed his monoplane, *The Spirit of St. Louis*, at Le Bourget Airport near Paris after a non-stop flight of thirty-three hours from New York. Another hero of the air was Commander Richard E. Byrd of the United States Navy. Byrd flew over the North Pole on May 9, 1926, and, with three companions, the next year flew from New York to the French coast. Byrd's greatest achievement was his exploration of the region of the South Pole. With a party of thirty scientists, he

Orville and Wilbur Wright and their "flying machine" at Kitty Hawk, North Carolina, December 17, 1903. In the first flight, by Orville, the craft remained aloft for 12 seconds and covered about 120 feet. Of the four flights made that day, Wilbur's flight of 59 seconds over a distance of 852 feet was the longest. (Library of Congress)

established his base at "Little America," on the Ross Ice Shelf of the Antarctic, on Christmas Day 1928. His equipment included four airplanes, a hundred dogs, ice tractors, and radio and motion picture apparatus. Flying 12,000 feet above the Liv Glacier, Byrd and his pilot crossed the South Pole on November 29, 1929. Before his return to Washington as rear admiral in March 1930, Byrd had made invaluable studies of the geography and climate of the vast continent of Antarctica.

One of the more interesting phenomena of the 1920s was the immense and long-lasting popularity of Lindbergh compared to that of Admiral Byrd. Something in "Lindy's" personality caught the American fancy. Perhaps it was the appearance and manner of an all-American boy that contrasted with the austere, uniformed Byrd. Perhaps it was his lonely conquest of space in a single-engine airplane compared to Byrd's well-equipped flight. For whatever reason, Lindbergh even surpassed the status of a movie star on the roster of celebrities in the 1920s.

Big Business

The movement toward consolidation and bigness in American industry proceeded inexorably during the first three decades of the twentieth century, in spite of antitrust legislation and prosecutions. By 1929, the 200 largest corporations controlled 49 per cent of all corporate wealth and received 43 per cent of all corporate income. In spite of this trend toward bigness, competition was livelier in 1929 than it had been in 1900. Most major American industries by 1929 were characterized by oligopoly, or control of the major share of production by a few large producers. These few producers, however, usually fought keenly among themselves, especially when major distributors — such as grocery chains and mail-order houses — could play one off against another.

Perhaps the most important change in American industry during this period was the continuation of the managerial revolution (see pp. 500–501). By 1929, most industries were run by professionally trained managers who did not and could not own the industries that they controlled. Thus, ownership had been almost completely divorced from control in most great American corporations. A growing class of executives and managers operated corporations in trust for owners interested only in increased profits and dividends.

The Decline of Organized Labor

Organized labor suffered heavy losses in spite of full employment and a shortage of skilled labor. The powerful railroad brotherhoods held their own, but membership in AFL unions declined from slightly more than 4,000,000 in 1919 to 2,770,000 in 1929. A number of factors caused this anomaly of declining union power during a period of high prosperity.

Employers had been frightened by the labor troubles of 1919. Many of them set out to alleviate labor discontent by instituting welfare programs of their own, including profit-sharing and group health and life insurance programs. Employers supplemented these welfare efforts by encouraging their workers to form unions under the company's sponsorship; at the same time, employers forbade the formation of more militant independent unions. These company unions, which had more than 1,500,000 members in 1929, drained much strength away from the AFL.

Many employers in the National Association of Manufacturers engaged, often successfully, in "open shop" drives to root out unions that already existed. Furthermore, the AFL itself increasingly came under the control of conservative trade unionists, who held attitudes similar to those of Samuel Gompers. They had little interest in risking the welfare of their skilled members by mounting costly campaigns to organize workers in mass-production industries.

Due to management's "welfare capitalism" and hostility to unions and the AFL's loss of militancy, the 1920s was the most peaceful period in labor-management relations since the 1870s. Strikes, in proportion to the number of American workers, declined and fell especially sharply from the postwar years, 1919–1920.

2. SOCIAL TENSIONS OF THE 1920s

The "Revolution in Morals"

Older Americans, as well as influential spokesmen for the younger generation, asserted persuasively during the 1920s that the country was living in the midst of a widespread rebellion against morality, religion, and traditional patterns of family authority. Significant changes in social life certainly did occur in the

1920s, but the word "revolution" is too strong a description for most of these changes.

The most important long-run shift took place in the appearance and status of women. Women bobbed their hair, wore short skirts, and began to smoke, drink, and discuss with men hitherto usually tabooed matters such as the stock market, baseball, and sex. Many of these changes in the behavior of women may not have been especially consequential in themselves. For example, women wore lighter clothing partly because the spread of central heating made changes in style possible. These changes in dress and manners, however, were part of a long-term rebellion, begun at a popular level in the late nineteenth century, against the Victorian standard of the absolute authority of fathers and husbands. Women not only started to vote throughout the nation in 1920; they also began to run for and win election to political offices. Women went to work in increasing numbers in the rapidly expanding services and professions (they constituted nearly one fourth of the nonfarm work force in 1930), and some were able, therefore, to support themselves. Increasing economic opportunities also brought increasing independence within the family. However, more often than not, the result was a new relationship of mutual respect and sexual frankness between young men and women and between husbands and wives. The divorce rate actually declined slightly between 1920 and 1930. However, the improvements in the status and opportunities of women during the 1920s were much less drastic than contemporaries believed. Within recent immigrant groups and among the poor, they may not have occurred to any great extent.

Young people also were allegedly in rebellion. To be sure, they did reject older and slower forms of dance in favor of the fast fox-trot and the Charleston, and some older Americans cried out in horror at what they called the "syncopated embrace." As the college population increased rapidly in the 1920s, the minority who drank to excess and lived what was considered a bohemian life attracted much wider public attention. Such descriptions of college life as those given by F. Scott Fitzgerald in his famous novel *This Side of Paradise* (1920) sent chills down the spines of parents. There is only slight and inconclusive evidence, however, that the moral standards of young people changed dramatically during the 1920s. Upon closer examination, Fitzgerald's college students seem rather staid, despite their tendency to talk, drink, dance, and vent their emotions more than their predecessors. Conventional marriage, business careers, and suburban families continued to be their ultimate objectives. Certainly Fitzgerald's heroines were rather pallid and restrained in comparison to the characters portrayed on the movie screens by Gloria Swanson and Clara Bow. However, these actresses appeared as fairly sophisticated urban women, not college girls. If shifts in popular morality were taking place, the major cities were obviously the areas most affected.

Nativism and the Rise of the Ku Klux Klan

One aftermath of the Red Scare of 1919–1920 was a large residue of nativism, or fear and dislike of elements in the population felt to be foreign. This nativism also was a manifestation of the resentment of Protestant Americans against the rising dominance of the cities, increasingly the home of blacks and non-Protestant immigrants. Nativists believed that, in the cities, long-established moral standards were being eroded, that crime went unpunished, and that minority groups led the way in this lawlessness, especially in the wide-spread refusal to obey the prohibition laws.

Among the consequences of the nativism of the 1920s was an increase in anti-Semitism and anti-Catholicism. Hostility to blacks, Hispanics, and Orientals probably never had decreased appreciably. New popularity was enjoyed by racist theories which proclaimed the superiority of so-called Nordic peoples to southern and eastern Europeans, Negroes, and Orientals.

The Knights of the Ku Klux Klan, the organization that had terrorized black people during the Reconstruction era, was revived in name by a Georgia mystic, William J. Simmons, in Atlanta in 1915. It spread very slowly through the Deep South between 1915 and 1920. After 1920, however, it moved rapidly throughout the Southwest, Middle West, and the Pacific coast area. At its peak in 1925, it probably had 5,000,000 members and was a powerful force in the politics of Texas, Oklahoma, Illinois, Ohio, Wisconsin, Indiana, Oregon, and a dozen other states.

Americans have always been a nation of joiners. Many Americans joined the Klan simply because it was a popular fraternal organization, and they were attracted by the Klan's regalia and high-flown ritual. However, the Klan was something more than just another secret fraternity, or even merely a racist or religious organization. The national leadership was openly anti-Negro, anti-Catholic, and anti-Jewish. National Klan officers avowed to keep Negroes "in their place," to boycott Jewish merchants and workers, and to diminish Catholic influence in politics. However, this new Klan, except at its very outset, engaged in little violent activity. It fed upon and encouraged the suspicion of rural and small-town America against the "alien" cities that supposedly were corrupting American life. In many areas, the local or state Klan dedicated itself more firmly to uphold the established morality — especially against sexual permissiveness and alcoholic indulgence — rather than to defend racial and religious ideals. Klan members often viewed as enemies, therefore, other Protestants, especially elite groups who valued business growth over the old moral certainties. Nevertheless, the organization had a strong appeal also to lower middle-class urban Protestants who objected to black, Catholic, and Jewish newcomers to their cities, especially in the Southwest and Midwest. In the East such individuals feared to expose themselves to Irish policemen and to powerful Catholic and Jewish politicians.

The majority of Americans eventually came to despise the Klan, and editors, clergymen, and other leaders fought courageously to destroy the organization. The Klan, moreover, was riddled by internal conflicts and was stripped of its chief leaders when they were jailed on charges of theft and immorality. It began to decline rapidly in membership about 1926 and had been reduced to a small though still militant organization by 1930.

The Antievolution Crusade

Another symptom of the reaction of rural and small-town Protestant America to the social changes of the 1920s was a crusade to forbid the teaching of evolution in public schools, colleges, and universities. The antievolution movement provided an excellent example of what sociologists call cultural lag. The Darwinian evolutionary hypothesis had caused some conflict between science and religion in the 1860s and 1870s, but theologians and urban churchmen had almost fully accepted the evolutionary hypothesis by 1900 and had long since ceased to regard it as any threat to Christian faith. Yet this was not true of rural fundamentalists, particularly in the South and Southwest. They deeply abhorred not only the evolutionary concept, but also what they called modernism and criticism of the Bible in any form. Battles for control between fundamentalists and "modernists" took place in every Protestant denomination. In every case, modernists won, although not always without some compromises.

Fundamentalist fears would probably only have simmered had it not been for William Jennings Bryan. The "Great Commoner," very much alarmed because he believed that the teaching of evolution was undermining the religious faith of schoolchildren and college students, opened a crusade in 1921 for adoption of antievolution laws. His call to battle was answered by numerous evangelists and ministers. Florida, North Carolina, and Texas took indirect action to prevent the teaching of evolution in public schools. Tennessee, Mississippi, and Arkansas adopted statutes which forbade the teaching of evolution in public institutions.

In 1925, John Thomas Scopes, a young biology teacher in Dayton, Tennes-

"The Silver Tongue Orator of the Platte." William Jennings Bryan quickly attained political popularity in the 1890's with his famous "Cross of Gold" speech and became the standard-bearer of the Populists and the Democrats in three presidential contests. Despite his promising beginning, Bryan reached the nadir of his career by defending the antievolutionary view of creation in the Scopes trial of 1925. Having become the object of national ridicule, Bryan died three weeks later, a rejected symbol of a bygone era. (Brown Brothers)

see, decided to test the validity of the act just passed by his state's legislature. He was arrested and tried. Bryan rushed to Dayton to join the prosecuting authorities, while the American Civil Liberties Union sent the famed trial lawyer, Clarence Darrow of Chicago, to defend Scopes. Newspapers throughout the country dispatched reporters to the small Tennessee town to describe the spectacle. The so-called "monkey trial" soon degenerated into a fierce verbal battle in which Darrow challenged Bryan's fundamentalist religious beliefs and, in the process, heaped scorn and ridicule upon him for his beliefs in the literal truth of the Bible. Scopes, who admitted that he had violated the antievolution law, received a light fine which was later revoked.

The antievolution forces earlier had formed an organization, the Supreme Kingdom, to fight for an amendment to the Constitution which forbade the teaching of evolution anywhere in the United States. However, Bryan's death shortly after the Scopes trial deprived fundamentalists of their only leader of national prominence. The antievolution crusade fizzled and sputtered almost to an end about 1928. However, antievolution laws remained in the statute books, and most teachers in the public schools in areas dominated by fundamentalists carefully avoided any mention of Darwin.

Struggles over Prohibition

No experiment in recent American history stirred higher hopes or began with greater fanfare than prohibition. At a victory celebration held in New York in 1920, Bryan, a leader in the movement for the Eighteenth Amendment, announced that the liquor issue finally rested as dead as slavery, and he clearly believed that the country was fortunate to be rid of both. Bryan spoke accurately in some respects about the beneficial effects of prohibition. During the first few years after ratification of the Eighteenth Amendment, the incidence of alcoholism, liver diseases, and other illnesses associated with drinking decreased significantly.

However, Bryan proved a very poor prophet in this matter. Passage of the prohibition amendment did not prevent millions of Americans from continuing to drink alcoholic beverages. Indeed, the new law seemed to make Americans thirstier than ever. Illegal distillers, smugglers, and brewers soon encountered no difficulty in keeping up with demand. Speakeasies (illegal saloons) flourished in the cities; and bootleggers, who sold liquor illegally, did a booming business. Urban populations, and often their policemen and elected officials, cooperated in what amounted to guerrilla warfare against federal prohibition enforcement agencies.

One of the more unfortunate results of prohibition lay in the stimulus that it gave to the growth of professional criminal gangs in large cities. The most infamous of these gangs, virtually a private army in Chicago led by Al Capone, did a $60 million business in liquor alone by 1927. This money enabled Capone and other mobsters to enter additional lucrative and illegal enterprises and some legal ones as well. The gangsters may have been the only really powerful supporters of prohibition in the cities—the laws acted something like tariff protection for their interests. Most other urban Americans, out of thirst or disgust with the results of the Eighteenth Amendment, favored its repeal. Except for many of the rural-born Protestants among them, residents in America's large cities also opposed state laws which forbade gambling and sporting

Dumping beer into Lake Michigan in 1919. Prohibition, called the "noble experiment" by Herbert Hoover, gave rise to massive violation of the law through the "bootlegger," the "speakeasy," and gangsterism. (United Press International)

events on Sundays. Prohibition became one of the leading political issues of the 1920s—further evidence of the struggle between those Americans who adhered to traditional nineteenth-century values and their cultural and often their political enemies. The latter included a "modernized" urban middle class, Irish Catholics, and recent immigrants and their children, who all tended to congregate in the nation's great cities.

The Black Nationalist Response

Partly as a result of the increase in racism between 1890 and 1919, black Americans developed (and rediscovered) ideas which promoted partial or full withdrawal from white society into their own cultural, social, and economic enclaves. The many conscious ties among these blacks led social scientists as well as many blacks to consider them a distinct nation within the United States. Disfranchisement, poverty, and physical abuse in the South, trauma associated with migration to the cold and unfamiliar northern cities, expectations of better treatment encouraged by governmental officials (who persuaded blacks to participate fully in the First World War), race riots, segregation, and other evidence that wartime promises would not be kept all stimulated further development of ideas which circulated among blacks about varieties of black nationalism.

Into this favorable situation stepped Marcus Garvey, already the leading black nationalist leader in the West Indies and Central America. When he arrived in the United States before American entrance into the war, Garvey merely intended to win American recruits for his Jamaican-based Universal Negro Improvement Association (UNIA). After the race riots of 1919, however, Garvey found the United States such a fertile recruiting ground for the UNIA that he moved his headquarters to Harlem. Probably a minimum of 100,000 (Garvey claimed millions) joined the American UNIA. Perhaps as many more attended meetings, subscribed to Garvey's newspaper, the *Negro World,* and bought stock in UNIA enterprises. They also contributed to Garvey's defense fund when the government prosecuted him for implying in advertisements that stock bought in the UNIA shipping line certainly would prove a profitable investment. Garvey's wide appeal, from New York to California (Louisiana contained more UNIA branches than any other state), owed much to his expressions of pride in his black skin. However, Garvey's plans to increase black strength everywhere by freeing Africa from white domination and his concept of black economic self-help exerted strong appeals also. We will never know how popular or powerful Garvey and his UNIA might have become, since he was prosecuted for mail fraud only a few years after his rise to leadership. The government won a conviction, sent Garvey to prison, and deported him.

3. THE MATURING OF AMERICAN CULTURE

Ferment and Maturing

The history of American intellectual life in the 1920s has long been written in terms of the invectives of its severest critics—a group of writers who considered that they belonged to what Gertrude Stein called the "lost generation." Critics like H. L. Mencken, editor of *The American Mercury,* railed at the "boobery" of the lower middle classes. Intellectuals like Herbert Croly, who had been leaders in the progressive movement of the prewar era, were disenchanted with democracy in general because of nativism, antievolution, and prohibition. Novelists such as Sinclair Lewis lashed out at the alleged prudery and hypocrisy of small-town life. Their indictment of the quality of American civilization was reasonably accurate, but its very persuasiveness tended to obscure cultural progress in areas which some of these writers failed to notice. Lewis himself described such progress, even in basically satirical novels such as *Main Street, Babbit, Arrowsmith,* and *Dodsworth,* all published during the 1920s.

School and Church in the Urban Age

The American people made greater educational advances during the 1920s than in any earlier decade in their history. The total expenditures on schools increased from a little more than $1 billion to $2.3 billion, and illiteracy declined from 6 per cent to 4.3 per cent. Two accomplishments of the 1920s stand out especially. One was the construction of a public high-school system which enabled almost every American child, for the first time, to obtain some secondary education. Poor children still tended to drop out of school in order to work or marry, but the sons and daughters of the middle class almost invariably tried to complete twelve years of formal education. High school enrollment doubled from 2,200,000 in 1920 to 4,400,000 in 1930.

The second especially noteworthy accomplishment was a tremendous expansion of American colleges and universities and an enrichment of their curricula. Students enrolled in institutions of higher learning increased in number from 598,000 in 1920 to more than 1,000,000 in 1930. At the same time, graduate and professional schools reached such a level of excellence that Americans, for the first time, were freed from dependence upon European universities for advanced training, except for training in advanced theoretical physics. It was during the 1920s that American universities trained the physicists, biologists, astronomers, mathematicians, chemists, and engineers who would soon make American science preeminent in the world, including the field of physics. It began with the great telescope erected on Mt. Wilson in California in 1917 and continued with the first atom smasher, which Ernest O. Lawrence conceived and built at the University of California at Berkeley in 1933.

Moreover, the wealth of the United States contributed enormously to the quality of research and advanced training, as American philanthropic foundations began to aid individual researchers. During the postwar decade, all of the following began programs of assistance: the National Research Council, the International Education Board, the General Education Board, the Guggenheim Foundation, and, for the humanities and social sciences, the American Council of Learned Societies and the Social Science Research Council. This financial aid enabled Americans to establish large-scale, long-range research programs and to use equipment unavailable elsewhere; but, perhaps even more important, it gave large numbers of potentially fine researchers time to think, master their fields, and develop as scholars. Consequently, the physical, life, and social sciences developed far more rapidly in American universities than in their counterparts abroad. Another result was enriched training for those scientists and engineers employed by American business, which, as has already been said, proved a vital factor in creating technological superiority for American firms which engaged in large research programs.

On the other hand, many critics of American mass education complained, accurately, that, despite the opportunity open to most citizens for learning and for high-level intellectual activity, standards in general remained low and probably even deteriorated as colleges were inundated with middle-class youths, most of whom were not vitally interested in academic education. Four years without serious responsibility and with a good job and a mate afterwards seemed to be the limited ambition of the average student. Visitors from Europe commented that sports stadiums and social clubs appeared to be the most important places in the colleges insofar as most students were concerned.

Meanwhile, American churches grew in membership faster than the population as a whole. There is no measurable evidence that the alleged revolution in morals undermined the religious faith of most Americans during the 1920s. On the contrary, some evidence suggests that religious faith may have increased. A poll taken in 1927 of 250,000 newspaper readers and 36,000 college students indicated that this sample of young people were even more certain about their faith than their parents. Churches not only increased their membership, but also continued to expand their ministries in urban areas. However, much of this church membership had social rather than purely religious causes, and ministers complained about members who preferred the golf course or a Sunday automobile drive to church attendance. Nevertheless, other members were as serious as participants in earlier religious revivals had been. Again, complexity and contradiction marked an aspect of life in the 1920s.

The Second Flowering of American Literature

American writers during the 1920s produced a literature of artistic excellence unrivaled in American history and not even approached since the pre–Civil War period. Although all literary forms took part in the renaissance, the writing of fiction enjoyed a special upsurge. Not only did the very existence of these authors belie their description of the United States as a cultural desert; they also provided an antidote for some of the deficiencies that unquestionably did exist. Americans, even in the dull midwestern small towns satirized by Sinclair Lewis, took much of the criticism seriously and responded to books like Lewis' *Main Street* with efforts at self-improvement that resembled earlier responses to disclosures by muckraking journalists. Among the other fine writers of the period, F. Scott Fitzgerald wrote elegantly about the hollow lives of the eastern and midwestern upper classes. William Faulkner began a series of penetrating novels about the decayed society and apparently cursed people of his native Mississippi. Thomas Wolfe, who would be one of the most prolific novelists of the 1930s, published his first and greatest novel in 1929, *Look Homeward, Angel.* The most important literary trend of the 1920s was the full development of the naturalistic school in the novels of Ernest Hemingway, John Dos Passos, Theodore Dreiser, and Sherwood Anderson. It is a commentary on the American literary achievement of the 1920s that three novelists— Lewis, Faulkner and Hemingway—and one dramatist, Eugene O'Neill, all began their significant work in the decade and later won Nobel prizes for literature.

The 1920s were also notable for remarkable advances in American poetry and drama. The old and great American tradition in poetry was carried forward in new forms by T. S. Eliot, e. e. cummings, Wallace Stevens, Robinson Jeffers, Edwin Arlington Robinson, Carl Sandburg, Robert Frost, and Ezra Pound, while a new school of southern poets developed at Vanderbilt University in the late 1920s. The most significant American literary event of the 1920s, however, was the burgeoning of a school of first-rate dramatists. Eugene O'Neill was the towering figure among this group, but a number of lesser playwrights, such as Maxwell Anderson, also enlivened the American stage.

For the first time, a group of writers in Harlem self-consciously attempted to create a black literature, partly in direct response to W. E. B. Du Bois' call in *The Crisis* for a black cultural "renaissance." In addition to demonstrating the talent that lay untapped among blacks, these writers hoped to establish both the foundations of a culture for blacks and a new image of them for whites. Among the more successful of these authors, along with Du Bois, were the young poets, Langston Hughes, Countee Cullen, and Claude McKay. McKay was also a successful novelist. James Weldon Johnson worked with both forms and wrote essays, songs, and history as well. Jean Toomer's mystical celebration of blackness and black culture in his impressionistic novel-poem, *Cane,* may have been the greatest single literary contribution from this group. Kelley Miller and Alain Locke contributed important essays and edited books to this body of work. Scholars of high accomplishment, such as E. Franklin Frazier, joined Du Bois in the front ranks of American sociologists. These middle-class writers, however, did not have the influence among blacks that they hoped for, and they lost much of their white audience early in the 1930s.

Music

America's original contributions to the world's store of music before the First World War had been limited largely to war songs, hymns, cowboy ballads, Negro spirituals, and other kinds of folk music, though black ragtime gave a hint of great innovations to come. The American tradition in popular music grew apace during and after the war with the work of many composers such as Cole Porter, Jerome Kern, George Gershwin, and Irving Berlin. The most important development in this field was the beginning of a native American musical form, jazz, a highly sophisticated form based largely on African traditions, though it drew on the black ragtime which had French, Spanish, and English elements. Jazz began among black musicians in New Orleans during the early years of the twentieth century, moved up the Mississippi Valley, and reached Chicago about 1916. It spread rapidly throughout the country and the world in the 1920s, although not without some loss of spirit, especially after Paul Whiteman, a popular band leader, and composer George Gershwin demonstrated that jazz could be expressed in a semisymphonic form.

This dilution of original forms for the benefit of white, middle-class audiences, however, did not prevent the survival of the driving rhythms that had originally emerged from the New Orleans brothels or of the lusty blues that continued to be a favorite among black audiences. Great musicians and singers, such as Louis Armstrong and Bessie Smith, both advanced the older forms of black jazz and blues and helped them survive. These artists' talents were so superior to that of many white jazz musicians that jazz and the blues, in their uninhibited black styles, began to thrive among a white audience. Later these forms would be combined with country folk traditions to create new, popular music styles such as rock and roll.

Almost as significant as these developments in popular music was the spread of more classical music in the 1920s. By 1930, practically every high school in the country offered some kind of musical training, and work done in conservatories and colleges and universities was of course even more advanced. By 1930, also, there were in the United States seventy-three permanent symphony orchestras, fifty-five chamber music groups, and 576 choral societies. American symphony orchestras had hired great European conductors such as Arturo Toscanini, Bruno Walter, and Serge Koussevitsky, who brought with them or attracted from Europe many fine musicians. Composers such as Aaron Copland and Samuel Barber were self-consciously creating an American style. If the United States was not already the center of the musical world in 1930, it soon would attain that position.

SUGGESTED READINGS

A lively romp through the period covered in this and the following two chapters is available in Frederick Lewis Allen, *Only Yesterday* (1931). William E. Leuchtenburg, *The Perils of Prosperity, 1914–1932* (1958), is equally readable and a much more careful attempt to make the period comprehensible. For an outline of a new emphasis among events and a different interpretive framework, see Stanley Coben, "The First Years of Modern America," in W. E. Leuchtenburg, ed., *The Unfinished Century* (1973).

George Soule, *Prosperity Decade: From War to Depression, 1917–1929* (1947), is a superior economic history. Business attitudes and practices are studied in James W. Prothro, *The Dollar Decade: Business Ideas in the 1920's* (1954). Useful information on the institutions of business will be found in Thomas C. Cochran, *The American Business System: A Historical Perspective, 1900–1955* (1957). Siegfried Giedion, *Mechanization Takes Command: A Contribution to Anonymous History* (1948), is a stimulating interpretation of the growth of industrial technology, but see also Elting E. Morison, *From Know-How to Nowhere: the Development of American Technology* (1974). For a detailed account of the decade's most famous industrialist, see Allan Nevins and F. E. Hill, *Ford: The Times, The Man and the Company* (1954), and *Ford: Expansion and Challenge* (1957). Adolph A. Berle, Jr., and G. C. Means, *The Modern Corporation and Private Property* (1932); Thomas Wilson, *Fluctuations in Income and Employment* (1948); and Emanuel A. Goldenweiser, *American Monetary Policy* (1951), are important specialized studies. Labor and widespread poverty in the twenties are examined in Irving Bernstein, *The Lean Years* (1960).

On intellectual currents, Edmund Wilson, *The Shores of Light* (1952) and *The American Earthquake* (1958), and the appropriate chapters in Kazin's *On Native Grounds* provide a good introduction. Among many fine literary portraits are Mark Schorer, *Sinclair Lewis* (1961); Cleanth Brooks, *William Faulkner: The Yoknapatawpha Country* (1963); Joseph L. Blotner, *Faulkner*, 2 vols. (1974); H. D. Piper, *F. Scott Fitzgerald: A Critical Portrait* (1965); and Carlos Baker, *Hemingway: The Writer as Artist* (1956), and *Ernest Hemingway: A Life Story* (1969). Max Eastman, *Enjoyment of Living* (1948), is a lively and perceptive autobiography.

George E. Mowry, ed., *The Twenties: Fords, Flappers and Fanatics* (1963), is an illuminating anthology of contemporary comment. Several excellent and even amusing retrospective essays on the period appear in Isabel Leighton, ed., *The Aspirin Age, 1919–1941* (1949). On college youth in the 1920s, see Paula S. Fast, *The Damned and the Beautiful* (1977).

Norman F. Furniss, *The Fundamentalist Controversy, 1918–1931* (1954), is a detailed account of a movement that divided American Protestantism during the twenties. Ray Ginger, *Six Days or Forever?* (1958), is the best description of the Scopes trial. On that subject, see also Lawrence Levine, *Defender of the Faith, William Jennings Bryan: The Last Decade, 1915–1925* (1965).

David M. Chalmers, *Hooded Americanism: The First Century of the Ku Klux Klan* (1965), is especially good on the twenties, but it should be supplemented by Kenneth T. Jackson, *The Ku Klux Klan in the City, 1915–1930* (1967), and Charles C. Alexander, *The Ku Klux Klan in the Southwest* (1965). On prohibition, Andrew Sinclair, *The Era of Excess* (1962), is readable and enjoyable, but the older accounts, Herbert Asbury, *The Great Illusion* (1950), and Charles Merz, *Dry Decade* (1931), offer valid viewpoints and additional information. More theoretical works about the meaning of prohibition are Joseph Gusfeld, *Symbolic Crusade: Status Politics and the American Temperance Movement* (1963), and Norman H. Clark, *Deliver Us From Evil: An Interpretation of American Prohibition* (1976). Clark presents what amounts to a modern defense of prohibition, and, to some extent, of the values it represented. Prominent figures associated with prohibition are the subject of a number of books, the best of which are F. D. Pasley, *Al Capone* (1930), and Virginius Dabney, *Dry Messiah: The Life of Bishop Cannon* (1949).

On the Harlem Renaissance, see Nathan I. Huggins, *Harlem Renaissance* (1971); Huggins, ed., *Voices From the Harlem Renaissance* (1976); and the chapters on that period in Gunther Schuller, *Early Jazz* (1968). The only good biography of Garvey is E. David Cronon, *Black Moses: The Story of Marcus Garvey* (1955). The Garvey movement has not yet been described adequately; but the Garvey papers are about to be published under the editorship of Robert Hill. Meanwhile, see Amy Jacque Garvey, *Garvey and Garveyism* (1963).

CHAPTER 28
THE POLITICS OF THE 1920s

1. THE REPUBLICAN RESTORATION

Ebb Tide of Progressivism

It is easy to get a distorted view of American national politics during the 1920s. All superficial signs point to easy generalizations: Harding's landslide victory in the presidential election of 1920, according to the conventional versions, marked a repudiation of progressivism and a return to McKinley-like policies of support of big business. The dominant Republican party, securely in the hands of financiers, manufacturers, and businessmen, enacted tariff, tax, and other legislation to benefit business, while it neglected labor and agriculture. In addition, probusiness Presidents and a property-minded Supreme Court worked to prevent the adoption, or to achieve the nullification, of progressive legislation.

There is some truth in these generalizations. Both of Woodrow Wilson's successors, Warren G. Harding and Calvin Coolidge, were conservative Republicans who believed that encouragement of business enterprise was the national government's first duty. They also packed federal regulatory agencies with men friendly to the industries that they were supposed to regulate. The most powerful voices in the Republican party were the spokesmen of financial and business interests. Moreover, the Supreme Court wrecked two of progressivism's most notable achievements. In Hammer v. Dagenhart (1918) and Bailey v. Drexel Furniture Company (1922), the court nullified the Child Labor acts of 1916 and 1919 on the ground that they violated the rights of the states to regulate wages and working conditions. The Supreme Court went a step further in Adkins *v.* Children's Hospital (1923) and outlawed all state attempts to set minimum wages for women workers.

Actually, the political developments of the 1920s were considerably more complex than the foregoing generalizations would imply. There can be no doubt that progressivism as a force in national politics was at ebb tide. On the other hand, the progressive movement not only survived but also expanded its objectives in the 1920s. How can the contradiction between the two statements be explained? The answer—and an understanding of the mild political upheaval that occurred in the 1920s—can best be found by seeing what happened to the progressive movement between the Armistice and the Great Depression.

Progressivism was gravely weakened by the desertion from its ranks of some intellectuals and writers who were disenchanted with democracy because of such popular movements as the prohibition and antievolution crusades. More important among the causes for the decline of progressivism was the widespread defection of the urban middle classes. These Americans, who had earlier provided numbers and leadership for various reform movements, were in a different mood after 1920. They were, perhaps, tired of successive calls to them to reform the nation and then the world; but that is not the full explanation of their change in mood. The middle classes were caught up in one of the greatest technological and economic revolutions in modern history, and they thought that they were building a new business civilization. It was to be a civilization based upon a whole new set of business values—mass production and consumption, short hours and high wages, full employment, and welfare capitalism. With such bright prospects, it was no wonder that the groups who constituted the urban middle classes, whether in New York, Atlanta, or Chicago, lost interest in rebellion or even in mild proposals for reform.

Progressivism, always a nonpartisan movement, had succeeded only when its forces captured a great national party. The movement was most seriously weakened in the 1920s because it was unable to find an acceptable political vehicle. During the presidential primaries of 1920, the Republican progressives, Hiram W. Johnson, Frank Lowden, and Leonard Wood, won almost all the contested states. However, at the convention, these three strongminded progressives refused to compromise, and Warren G. Harding, whom they all had easily defeated in Republican primaries, was nominated by a deadlocked convention. Then Johnson refused Harding's offer of the vice-presidential nomination, and the tired convention offhandedly nominated Calvin Coolidge, who, like Harding, previously had shown little ability to win votes outside his home state of Massachusetts. However, after Harding and Coolidge won easily, Republican leaders saw no reason to appease progressive voters. Real control of the G.O.P. remained in the hands of eastern and midwestern industrial, financial, and oil interests, as it had since 1910. Theodore Roosevelt had discovered the extent of their control in 1912.

There was always the hope of a third party. Numerous progressive groups came together under Senator Robert M. La Follette's leadership in 1924. Their ranks included insurgent midwestern Republicans, the railroad brotherhoods, the AFL, several state Farmer-Labor parties, and most of the country's politically active intellectuals who ranged from former New Nationalist Herbert Croly, to future New Deal Brain Trust member Rex Tugwell, and the Socialist party, still led by Eugene V. Debs. But these progressives soon discovered that

"The essence of the progressive movement, as I see it, lies in its struggle to uphold the fundamental principles of representative government. . . ." These are the words of Robert M. LaFollette of Wisconsin, one of the most militant of the progressives, who was called "Battling Bob" for his crusading methods in politics. (Culver Pictures, Inc.)

third-party movements in the United States are doomed to failure, except in extraordinary circumstances such as those of 1856–1860. However, the fact that La Follette won about 17 per cent of the total vote in the presidential election of 1924 in spite of a complete lack of a party organization (except for that of the Socialists), no money, inability to get his name on the ballot in any southern state, and a late start, indicated the potential strength of a progressive candidate. The Populists, with a nationwide campaign, had won only 5 per cent of the total presidential vote in 1892.

Thus the Democratic party remained the only vehicle through which progressives might work. However, that party was not capable of such service in the 1920s. It had lost Wilson's magnetic leadership. Indeed, it lacked national, unifying leadership of any kind. Worse still, the Democrats were so torn by conflicts between their eastern and midwestern big-city wing and their southern and western rural voters that they literally ceased to be a national political force. The party remained strong in its sectional and metropolitan parts, but it was so divided over issues such as prohibition, the restriction of immigration, and the Ku Klux Klan that it barely succeeded in nominating a presidential candidate at all in 1924. In 1928 it nominated a candidate from the urban wing, but at the cost of temporary disruption.

Nevertheless, progressive groups—both Republican and Democratic—were still strong enough to dominate Congress during most of the 1920s. However, they were so divided among themselves as partisans that they could not unite to capture the national government, as they had done so dramatically in 1912 and 1916. La Follette's death, soon after his disorganized campaign in 1924, demoralized those persons who had worked hard to build a progressive coalition which rural and urban dissident voters from both parties could support. As a consequence, the conservative groups that controlled the Republican party had little difficulty in winning the presidency and therefore in appointing the other executive and judicial officers of the federal government. This complex situation and series of accidents have given a misleading portrait of politics during the 1920s, and to some extent of the era as a whole.

The Travesty of Warren G. Harding

The history of the presidency has proved that a man of average education and adequate mental equipment can do well in the office if he has the desire to be a strong leader. Above all, he must possess integrity, reasonably good judgment, and the determination to rule wisely. Unfortunately, Warren Gamaliel Harding had barely average intelligence, no desire to be a strong President, and an abundance of defects of character. As President, he carried on much stock speculation and devoted a great deal of time to drinking and playing poker and bridge with his associates. He was physically lazy, morally undisciplined, and had a positive dislike of hard mental effort. Even his mistress in Marion, Ohio, eventually found him too intellectually and artistically limited for her tastes. As former editor and proprietor of the Marion, Ohio, *Star*, he had the world view of provincial, small town America. As an undistinguished member of the Ohio legislature and the United States Senate, he had no training for national leadership. Consequently, Harding as President simply refused to give leadership to his administration, to Congress, to the country, or even to his own friends and subordinates. Fortunately, this withdrawal did not ensue in a totally barren record for his brief administration. Several of his cabinet members, particularly Secretary of State Charles Evans Hughes, Secretary of Agriculture Henry C. Wallace, and Secretary of Commerce Herbert Hoover, were able to carry on vigorous and constructive policies. Nor were the Republicans without able leaders in Congress. They put through an impressive legislative program between 1921 and 1923. But in both cases neither initiative nor leadership came from the White House.

The "Ohio Gang"

It is difficult to imagine a more striking contrast than the one between the outgoing and incoming Presidents on March 4, 1921. On the one side stood Wilson, gravely weakened by his stroke and hobbling on a cane, but stronger than ever in his confidence that future events and the American people would vindicate his fight for the League of Nations. On the other side was his successor who was handsome, in full vigor, and looked every inch a President. In addition, there was a host of friends who crowded around the new Chief Executive on inaugural day. So many of them came from Ohio that they have been called the "Ohio Gang." They were Harding's own appointees and his personal cronies.

The leader of the group was Harding's old intimate from Ohio and the new Attorney General of the United States, Harry M. Daugherty. He had already

President Harding makes a recording in the early days of his administration. (Library of Congress)

earned a nationwide reputation as a corrupt politician and lobbyist. There were numerous other members of this group of buccaneers, incompetents, and ne'er-do-wells. They gathered regularly in a residence known as the Little Green House on K Street in Washington to trade favors, drink, and play poker. Harding's easygoing temperament and dogged devotion to these friends led to tragedy for both himself and the nation. With the possible exception of the Grant and Nixon administrations, the American government has never been so disgraced as it was during the two short years of Harding's tenure.

Colonel Thomas W. Miller, Alien Property Custodian, accepted a bribe for supporting false claims to the property of the American Metal Company, for which he was later sentenced to eighteen months in a federal penitentiary. Colonel Charles R. Forbes, previously a member of the executive committee of the American Legion in the State of Washington, stole an uncounted amount of money as head of the Veterans' Bureau before he was caught and sent to Leavenworth Prison. "Jess" Smith, an intimate of Daugherty, acted as collector and distributor of graft taken from persons who broke the prohibition and tax laws and who wished to buy immunity from prosecution or presidential pardons (which were recommended by the Attorney General). When Harding ordered him to return to Ohio, Smith committed suicide in the apartment that he shared with Daugherty. (Smith also shared a large bank account with the Attorney General.) Forbes' chief counsel, Charles F. Cramer, also killed himself rather than face investigation. Daugherty was tried in 1927 on charges of sharing bribes with "Jess" Smith and his brother, Mal S. Daugherty, but the indictment was dismissed after the jury twice failed to agree on a verdict, although in both cases a majority of the jurors voted to convict. Daugherty perhaps saved himself from conviction because he refused to testify and implied that, if he did so, he might have to implicate the still popular, though deceased, Harding in criminal activity.

The Oil Scandals

The most sensational scandal of the Harding administration was an attempted theft of some of the federal government's oil reserves. A group of wealthy oil men, including Jake Hamon, Republican national committeeman from Oklahoma, Harry F. Sinclair of New York, and Edward L. Doheny of Los Angeles, exercised an influence in the Republican convention of 1920 that rivaled that of the senatorial clique which represented big business interests.

Oil was a prime necessity for national defense. The oil-burning ships of the navy used 137,500 barrels in 1911 and 7,000,000 barrels in 1919. In 1912, the government had set aside, for the use of the navy, oil reserve No. 1 at Elk Hills, California; and, in 1915, reserve No. 3 at Teapot Dome, Wyoming. When wells in the neighborhood threatened to draw the oil from these reserves, the government considered pumping out its own oil and storing it in tanks for the use of the navy. Instead, it decided to lease the lands to private operators who would build storage tanks and supply the navy with fuel oil.

The leasing of public lands was a customary duty of the Department of the Interior rather than of the Navy Department. Hence, Secretary of the Interior Albert B. Fall, with the consent of Secretary of the Navy Edwin Denby, secured an Executive Order which transferred jurisdiction over the reserves from the Navy Department to the Interior Department. Fall then proceeded secretly, without competitive bids, to lease Teapot Dome to Sinclair, who had made a very large contribution to the Republican campaign fund in 1920, and Elk Hills to Doheny. Not long afterward, Fall's private fortunes, which had been in a bad way, began to show spectacular improvement. He paid up his back taxes, restocked his cattle ranch in New Mexico, and bought additional land.

News of Fall's actions leaked at once, and a special Senate committee headed by Thomas J. Walsh of Montana began a searching investigation in the autumn of 1923. Fall, Sinclair, and Doheny all denied that there had been any wrongdoing, but Walsh stayed on the trail, and the truth of the sordid business was fully revealed in 1924. Fall had accepted a "loan" of $100 thousand from Doheny at the time that the lease of Elk Hills was under negotiation. Sinclair had given Fall $223 thousand in government bonds, $85 thousand in cash, and a herd of cattle while the lease for Teapot Dome was being concluded. Sinclair and the presidents of four other oil companies had organized the Continental Trading Company to drill wells on Teapot Dome. This company had contracted to buy 35,000,000 barrels of oil from Sinclair's Mammoth Oil Company, which owned the lease on Teapot Dome, at $1.50 a barrel. And the presidents of the same oil companies had agreed to sell the same oil to their own companies at $1.75 a barrel. Thus they would realize for themselves a tidy profit of $8 or $9 million.

Sinclair and Doheny were brought to trial for conspiracy and bribery in 1926. They were acquitted, although Sinclair had to spend a term in the District of Columbia jail for attempted bribery of jurors in his case. In the following year, the government easily won its suit for cancellation of the leases. Fall, who had fled to Europe, was brought home and tried for conspiracy to defraud the government in 1929. He was convicted, fined $100 thousand, and sentenced to a year in jail. Fall, sent to the federal jail in Santa Fe, New Mexico, became the first corrupt cabinet member in American history to that date who received something like his just reward.

The Death of President Harding

Harding, his wife, and a large entourage set out upon a transcontinental tour in late June 1923. Harding was far from well when he left Washington. He was deeply depressed. He feared disgrace and political doom because he already knew about Forbes' corruption and suspected that Fall was also guilty of fraud. "I have no trouble with my enemies," Harding confided to a friend just before he left Washington. "I can take care of my enemies all right. But my damn friends. . . . They're the ones that keep me walking the floor nights!"

The trip through the Middle West brought no relief, for that section was in the midst of a searing heat wave. Harding and his party went on to Alaska from the Northwest. Secretary of Commerce Herbert Hoover joined the voyage at Tacoma, Washington, and found Harding extremely nervous and lonely. "As soon as we were aboard ship," Hoover recalled almost thirty years later, Harding "insisted on playing bridge, beginning every day immediately after breakfast and continuing except for mealtime often until after midnight."

On the return trip, Harding barely completed a speech in Vancouver before he collapsed. When he reached San Francisco, his condition became worse, although it was not considered critical. The country was, therefore, shocked when news came that he had died suddenly in the early evening of August 2, 1923.

Death came none too soon to release Harding from his troubles. Americans mourned for the distinguished President that they thought Harding had been. Friends began to raise money for a Harding Memorial Association to preserve his memory. However, it was not long before most of the truth about the scandals emerged, and Harding's own personal misbehavior was exposed to full view. So quickly was his reputation deflated that some people began to believe such wild rumors as one to the effect that Mrs. Harding had poisoned her husband because of his affairs with other women.

Calvin Coolidge and the Politics of Prosperity

The news of Harding's death arrived at the Coolidge farmhouse in Plymouth, Vermont, where Vice-President Calvin Coolidge was spending his vacation, early in the morning of August 3, 1923. The family was immediately aroused from bed and came down to the parlor. There, by the light of a kerosene lamp, John Coolidge, justice of the peace, administered to his son the oath of office as thirtieth President of the United States

Unlike his predecessor, the new President was no handsome, genial fellow, who was surrounded by cronies and exuded good spirits. Coolidge was a Puritan Yankee—plain and austere. He placed personal honesty, thrift, and individualism at the top of his list of virtues; and he was as rigid as the granite of his Vermont hills, although not nearly as silent as his reputation led people to believe. Coolidge, born in Plymouth, Vermont, on July 4, 1872, made his home in Northampton, Massachusetts, after he was graduated from Amherst College in 1895. He studied law in the old-fashioned way in the office of a successful firm. He entered local politics in 1899 and advanced steadily to election as Governor of Massachusetts in 1918. The Boston police strike of 1919 had made him a national hero and provided a reason for the tired delegates at the Republican convention of 1920 to nominate him for Vice-President—after better-known candidates had refused the dubious honor of running as Warren G. Harding's junior partner.

Coolidge had never been to Washington before he went there to take up his new duties in 1921. Indeed, he had scarcely been beyond the boundaries of Massachusetts and Vermont. Hence he had the world view of the rural, isolated sections of America. He was reared in the political traditions of the New England countryside. Scrupulously honest himself, he systematically cleaned up the mess left by the Harding scandals. He discharged Daugherty and appointed Harlan F. Stone, Dean of the Columbia University Law School, as Attorney General. Stone and the Justice Department were given full support in further investigations and prosecutions. Stone's reputation as an honest man and excellent attorney was well earned. However, he also was as bigoted against recent immigrants as was Coolidge and had worked hard to establish quotas against their admission to the nation's prestigious law schools. Stone was an appropriate choice for Coolidge, the only presidential candidate in 1924 who refused to condemn the Ku Klux Klan.

Coolidge was also heir to the eastern Hamiltonian, Whig, and Republican tradition of close relations between government, business, and finance. "The business of America is business," he said in his Annual Message to Congress in December 1923. Coolidge did not share Theodore Roosevelt's and Wilson's concern for the downtrodden. Nor did Coolidge have their faith in governmental regulation and participation in economic and social affairs. Coolidge believed simply in low taxes, encouragement of business enterprise, and as little governmental interference as possible. Hence he followed a policy of massive inaction—both legislative and administrative. When progressive groups in Congress combined to adopt legislation in the reform tradition, Coolidge relentlessly vetoed their bills. Indeed, he is unique among Presidents for having vetoed more important legislation than he signed.

2. PROBLEMS OF THE 1920s

The Course of American Politics, 1921–1928

The presence of do-nothing Presidents in the White House between 1921 and 1929 implies incorrectly that the American national political scene was untroubled during the 1920s. A severe decline in agricultural prices began before Harding's inauguration, and recession spread from the countryside to the cities in the spring of 1921. The dominant group in the Sixty-seventh Congress, which met in April 1921, was the midwestern insurgent Republicans. When the insurgents combined with the Democrats, they, rather than the administration, controlled Congress and determined legislative policies on many critical issues. Discontent was so strong that the Democrats narrowly missed winning both houses of Congress in the off-year election of 1922.

A new progressive revolt seemed to impend. The Republican national convention met at Cleveland on June 10, 1924, and ignored the danger signals; it nominated Coolidge for the presidency on a conservative platform.

It was a rare opportunity for the Democrats to go to the country with a strong candidate who could rally agrarian and labor discontent into a new progressive coalition. However, the Democrats seemed more intent upon fighting each other rather than conservative Republicans when they assembled in national convention in New York on June 24. Northern big city Democrats, who represented foreign-born and Jewish and Catholic constituencies, demanded condemnation of the Ku Klux Klan by name. Southern and rural Democrats, and state delegations controlled by the Klan, fought the resolution which condemned the Klan, either out of sympathy for, or fear of, the secret order. Northern Democrats demanded repeal of the Eighteenth Amendment or modification of the Volstead Act. Southern and rural Democrats, dominated by Protestant dry leaders, fought back bitterly and successfully.

All the tensions within the Democratic party came to a head in the struggle over the presidential nomination. The chief contenders were Governor Alfred E. Smith of New York and former Secretary of the Treasury William G. McAdoo. Smith was a Roman Catholic, a "wet" on prohibition, and a chieftain of the Tammany organization; McAdoo had the support of southern and western farmers, drys, and most Protestant Democrats. These included members of the Klan, whom he refused to criticize explicitly. Smith and McAdoo fought it out for 103 ballots, until the convention in desperation turned to John W. Davis. It was a sign of the paralysis of the party, for Davis, although a distinguished lawyer, was allied with great New York banking and industrial interests and was utterly incapable of leading any kind of revolt.

Convinced that both major parties were hopelessly reactionary, midwestern insurgents, politically inclined intellectuals, most Rooseveltian Progressive leaders who remained in politics, and some leaders of the railroad brotherhoods and AFL met at Cleveland on July 4. They formed a new Progressive party and nominated Senator Robert M. La Follette and Senator Burton K. Wheeler of Montana on their ticket. Their platform demanded nationalization of railroads, public development of hydroelectric facilities, and the right of Congress to override decisions of the Supreme Court. The model of most of the leaders of the new Progressive party was the British Labour party. The railroad brotherhoods actually sent La Follette to Europe at their own expense largely so that he could observe the British Labour government in action. However, Samuel Gompers, who had long fought Socialists in the labor movement and disliked social democrats, refused to support La Follette. Gompers thus prevented the formation of a new social-democratic party with long-term goals. Gompers even refused to open the AFL's treasury to La Follette, which left the Senator insufficient funds for travel or to pay campaign aides and other expenses. As a consequence, only a minority of Americans knew much about La Follette's proposed programs.

The campaign that ensued was enlivened only by La Follette's strenuous if ill-fated attempt to win that part of the country that he could reach with his message in a new crusade. On election day of 1924, Coolidge ran up a popular vote far larger than the combined vote of Davis and La Follette. The totals seemed to constitute a clear mandate for the continuation of Coolidge's policy of inaction. Actually, the election returns gave evidence of Democratic impotency as well as public apathy. Only 52 per cent of the voters bothered to go to the polls on election day in 1924. La Follette won almost as many popular votes as did Davis outside the South.

The next four years were prosperous, but there was not much peace in Washington. Republicans controlled the Sixty-ninth Congress, which sat from 1925 to 1927, by large majorities, and the following Congress by only a slight margin. However, the dynamic and controlling force on Capitol Hill was the coalition of midwestern Republicans and southern Democrats. The major struggles of these four years were between this coalition, which insisted upon certain reforms, especially to alleviate farm distress, and the conservative Coolidge administration.

Tariff, Tax, and Bonus Controversies

It is impossible to relate the legislative history of the 1920s in sheerly partisan terms, because alignments in Congress were usually sectional and economic, not political. There were three major groups in Congress during the decade: midwestern insurgent Republicans, who organized themselves into the so-called Farm Bloc in 1921; southern Democrats, who mostly represented agrarian constituencies and often cooperated with the Farm Bloc; and conservative Republicans and Democrats, mainly from urban areas. Since none of these three groups controlled a reliable majority at any time during the Harding-Coolidge administrations, legislation could be achieved only by coalitions. A fourth group, which gained in strength during this era, represented northern urban workers and included recent immigrants and black migrants from the South. Senator Robert F. Wagner and Representative Fiorello La Guardia, both of New York, were the leaders of this increasingly powerful interest group. By the 1930s — some historians say by 1928 — it constituted one of the major forces in American politics. It might even have emerged earlier, in 1924, if La Follette had received the money and had had the time to organize thoroughly in the cities, as his advisers had recommended.

The Farm Bloc and administration Republicans combined in 1921 to reenact a measure which increased tariff duties on meat and farm staples. Wilson had vetoed this bill a year earlier. These two groups cooperated again in 1922 to push through the Fordney-McCumber Tariff Act. It greatly increased duties on farm products and helped new industries like chemicals but provided only moderate increases for the great mass of industrial products. Actually, the framers of the Fordney-McCumber bill claimed that they tried to follow the Wilsonian policy of equalizing differences in costs of production in the United States and abroad.

Tax legislation was a very different story. All through the 1920s, the chief objective of the business interests and of Secretary of the Treasury Andrew W. Mellon was drastic reduction of the high wartime taxes. A midwestern-southern Democratic coalition wrecked Mellon's plan in 1921 by pushing through a tax bill that only slightly relieved the tax burden on the wealthy. Mellon renewed the struggle again in 1923. Again the midwestern-southern Democratic coalition rebuffed him by reducing income taxes significantly only for middle-income groups and by increasing the estate tax. Mellon finally had his way in the Revenue Acts of 1926 and 1928, which cut the maximum surtax on incomes from 40 to 20 per cent and slashed the estate tax in half. But the Secretary won adoption of his program only because surpluses were piling up in the federal Treasury. The country was prosperous, and the insurgents and southern Democrats could no longer justify punitive taxes on wealth. Meanwhile, Congress also defied the administration by adopting bonus, or adjusted compensation, measures for veterans. These bonuses were to recompense the men who had served in the armed forces at low pay during the First World War, while their neighbors were enjoying full employment and high wages. Harding vetoed a bonus bill in 1922, but Congress reenacted the measure in 1924 and passed it over Coolidge's veto.

The Farm Problem

The most important domestic problem of the 1920s was the agricultural depression which began in 1920 and continued off and on until about 1935. Although agricultural prices recovered somewhat in 1923, farmers operated at a net loss throughout most of the 1920s. Total farm income declined from more than $10 billion in 1919 to a little more than $4 billion in 1921. After some recovery, farm income ran between $6 and $7 billion a year between 1923 and 1929. Farmers received 16 per cent of the national income in 1919, but only 8.8 per cent in 1929.

The causes for distress in rural areas are not hard to find. Wartime demand had pushed up farm prices, and high prices caused farmers to increase acreage and purchase land and machinery at high prices. Once the war was over, millions of soldiers all over the world returned to their farms. Since American farm surpluses were sold abroad, the world market determined the prices received in the United States. Thus the American farmer had to compete with farmers in nations such as France, Argentina, and Canada. Canadian wheat output, for example, increased nearly 1,000 per cent in the postwar decade. The result was rapid deflation in agricultural prices in the immediate postwar years and generally low prices afterward.

The American farmer's woes did not end there. While prices for the products that he sold were declining, the prices that he paid for such items as tools, machinery, and clothing increased about 30 per cent between 1919 and 1929. Worse still, constantly mounting local taxes and interest charges on mortgages increased the farmer's burden of debt. Taxes on farm property, taking 100 as the index figure for 1914, were 130 in 1919, when farmers were prosperous, and 258 in 1927, when they were in semidepression. Mortgage indebtedness in the same period more than doubled. Finally, technological advances added to surpluses that were already smothering farmers. Improvements in farm machines, such as drillers, huskers, reapers, combines, and tractors, had made it possible to produce increasing quantities of staples with fewer workers. Furthermore, the number of gasoline tractors in use, which mostly replaced horses and mules, rose from 80,000 in 1919 to more than 800,000 a decade later. The effect on the market for hay and oats was of course disastrous.

The Second Agrarian Crusade

Agrarian distress in the 1920s set off the same kind of demands for governmental relief as it had produced in the late nineteenth century. The big difference between the first agrarian crusade and the second was that farmers by the 1920s had learned how to wield political power effectively. Senators and representatives from the midwestern states met in Washington in 1921 and formed the Farm Bloc to fight for the relief of agriculture. They won all their demands during the Harding administration. Midwestern farmers won high tariff protection for their products. Moreover, the Farm Bloc pushed through bills which prohibited certain kinds of speculation in grains. Other laws provided for stringent control of stockyards and packers by the Secretary of Agriculture, and the establishment of a new federal intermediate system of rural credit. Taken altogether, the farm bills of 1921–1923 were an impressive achievement. They completed the program begun by the Wilson administration and provided farmers with generous credit at low interest rates.

The main problem after 1923, then, was not lack of credit. Rather, it was how to prevent farm surpluses from depressing prices at home. George N. Peek and Hugh S. Johnson, farm machinery manufacturers of Moline, Illinois, offered an answer in 1922 in a pamphlet entitled *Equality for Agriculture*. Peek and Johnson said that the federal government should segregate the surplus and in effect guarantee minimum prices for agricultural products sold at home. Under their plan, federal agencies would purchase all major staples produced for the market at stipulated prices and would thus set a floor under them. These agencies would also sell the surplus on the world market at world prices, and would then recoup their losses on products sold abroad by levying so-called equalization fees against farmers at home.

The Peek-Johnson plan was embodied in a bill first introduced in Congress in 1924 by Charles L. McNary of Oregon and Gilbert N. Haugen of Iowa, chairmen of the agricultural committees of the Senate and of the House, respectively. The original McNary-Haugen bill applied only to midwestern farm products and failed in the House on June 3, 1924. However, the Midwesterners won southern allies in 1926 by including cotton, tobacco, and rice in the proposed system. The midwestern-southern coalition pushed a new McNary-Haugen bill through Congress in early 1927, only to draw a sharp veto from Coolidge. The southern-western coalition, failing to override the veto, pushed the measure through again in 1928 and evoked a second veto from Coolidge. This time the farm bloc and its allies came closer to the two-thirds vote needed to override Coolidge's veto. That illustration of strength, in addition to the refusal to approve Mellon's tax proposals for five years and the successful override of Coolidge's veto of the bonus bill, demonstrated the independence of Congress from presidential or party domination, and its rather progressive makeup.

Really effective farm legislation would have to await the inauguration of a President who was not so concerned as Coolidge and his successor about the alleged dangers of governmental participation in economic affairs. But the McNary-Haugen bill, even though it never was put into operation, had momentous significance for the American progressive movement. The espousal by farmers of this measure demonstrated that the best organized and most powerful political group had accepted the proposition that it was the federal government's duty to protect the economic security of all classes—and particularly of depressed groups.

The Power Controversy

One of the longest battles of the 1920s revolved around the disposition of two nitrate plants and the huge Wilson Dam and hydroelectric facility at Muscle Shoals on the Tennessee River in northern Alabama. The federal government had constructed them during the war in order to free the country from its dependence on imported nitrates. Before this struggle ended, it had become the focus of a larger, nationwide controversy over public development, ownership, or regulation of the entire electric power industry. More important still, the controversy gave additional evidence that the progressive movement not only survived in the 1920s, but was also expanding its horizons and objectives.

The end of the war found the nitrate plants at Muscle Shoals ready to go into full production, while Wilson Dam was not quite completed. One of the first acts of the Harding administration was to announce that it would lease the entire facility to any responsible private company that would complete the dam and guarantee a fair return to the government. Henry Ford excited the greatest enthusiasm by his offer. He promised to produce nitrates for cheap fertilizers and, moreover, to build an industrial complex seventy-five miles long in the Tennessee Valley.

Congress, in 1924, would have approved a bill which authorized the lease of

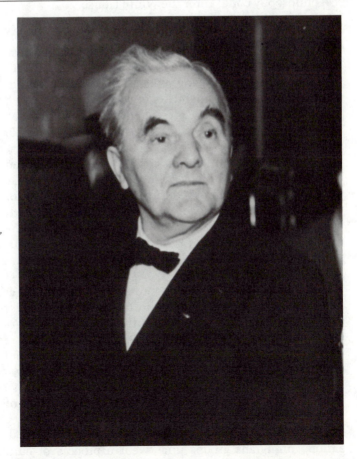

Senator George W. Norris, who had been at odds with both President Coolidge and President Hoover over private ownership and operation of public power, eagerly went on a coast to coast speaking tour on behalf of a new presidential candidate, Governor Roosevelt. Roosevelt had supported Norris and the progressives during the 1920s against the power trust which Norris called "the greatest monopolistic corporation that has been organized for private greed." (Wide World Photos)

the Muscle Shoals facilities to Ford if it had not been for the obstructionist tactics of Senator George W. Norris of Nebraska. Norris believed that Ford and other power and industrial interests were holding out the lure of cheap fertilizers for farmers in order to steal one of the nation's greatest natural assets — the hydroelectric resources of the Tennessee Valley. As early as 1922, the Nebraska Senator had begun to dream of a great federal agency that would build and operate a network of dams throughout the valley for flood control and the production of inexpensive electric power.

After he blocked the bill which authorized the lease to Ford, in 1924, Norris opened his own campaign for federal operation of the Muscle Shoals facilities. With strong southern support, he pushed a bill through Congress in 1928 to create a corporation to operate Wilson Dam and the nitrate plants. The lines between the champions of public power and the defenders of the private utilities were now clearly drawn, and it was well understood that federal development of the Tennessee Valley might well be only the first of such regional projects. Coolidge naturally took the side of the private interests and gave the Muscle Shoals bill a pocket veto. But Norris refused to give up and pushed another Muscle Shoals measure through Congress in 1931. Coolidge's successor, Herbert Hoover, vetoed this bill in a ringing message that denounced governmental operation of power facilities as socialistic. However, Norris had lost only two battles, not the war. He saved the waterpower resources of the Tennessee Valley from private exploitation until a President with a different political philosophy could enter the White House.

A New Immigration Policy

Congress, in several measures in the 1920s, effected a revolution in American public policies by decreeing an end to the centuries-old tradition of virtually free and unlimited immigration to the United States. Equally significant was the fact that this change was effected virtually without any partisan controversy or struggle between conservatives and progressives. Obviously, the country had come — temporarily, at least — to a fairly solid consensus on the subject, although different motivations contributed to this consensus.

Organized labor had long believed that a steady infusion of unskilled labor kept wages low and impeded the progress of unionization. The AFL and other unions had been working for restrictive measures since the 1890s. Some American labor leaders were as racially bigoted as most other restrictionists; but others responded mainly to the high unemployment rates, the low wages for unskilled and semiskilled workers, and the pressures on union members from employers during the period.

Many American sociologists and social workers were convinced that unlimited immigration created widespread social disorganization and insuperable problems of assimilation. By the outbreak of the First World War, these sociologists and social workers were in the vanguard of the movement for restriction. Meanwhile, the leading scholars in the field of sociology, especially those in the famous University of Chicago School of Sociology, had begun to disagree with the idea that immigrants caused serious problems of disorganization or assimilation. A common theme emerged in a series of books and articles, which began with William I. Thomas and Florian Znaniecki's *The Polish Peasant in Europe and America* (1918). After an initial period of cultural disorganization, immigrant groups underwent a process of cultural reintegration in

Immigrants arriving at Ellis Island. The narrowness and provincialism of Americans who had developed a dislike and distrust of foreigners became evident in the 1920s when quotas reduced sharply immigration from eastern and sourthern Europe and from Asia. (United Press International)

which "American" traits were combined with the most socially valuable of their old values and customs. According to these social scientists, these syntheses, in turn, enriched American society—much as elements of black and Mexican culture did, by adding elements which gave new vitality to American society. The leading American anthropologist of the 1920s, Franz Boas of Columbia University, and his students joined the Chicago sociologists in this view. However, as usual, popular ideas were based on the views of a previous generation of thinkers.

Most progressives (although not Woodrow Wilson) like other upper- and middle-class white Protestants, believed in the restriction of immigration. They also thought that the government should use immigration policies to create a homogeneous population. Finally, by 1914, most Anglo-Saxon residents of the West coast, who feared Oriental influences, were also restrictionists. The representatives in Congress of the aforementioned groups were strong enough to adopt bills which imposed literacy qualifications on immigrants in 1896, 1913, and 1915. Thwarted by presidential vetoes on these occasions, the restrictionists came back in 1917 to adopt a literacy test over Wilson's veto.

A startling change in the predominant American thinking about immigration occurred between 1917 and 1921. In short, a majority of Americans changed from restrictionists into virtually outright exclusionists, at least insofar as immigration from southern and eastern Europe was concerned.

The catalyst of this change was the fear in 1919 and 1920 that millions of poor and homeless Europeans, particularly in war-ravaged central and eastern Europe, were preparing to move to the United States. The postwar Red Scare severely intensified this fear of an uncontrollable inundation. Even employers of unskilled labor, who had earlier been the leading defenders of unlimited immigration, began to associate foreigners with Communism and moved into the exclusionist camp.

When some 1,250,000 immigrants poured into American ports in 1920–1921, it was no longer a question of whether Congress would act, but of what form the new legislation would take. Congress attempted to stem the flow in 1920 with a temporary measure which limited immigration to 3 per cent of the foreign-born elements in the United States in 1910. Wilson vetoed this measure, but Congress reenacted it in 1921, and Harding signed it. Congress then turned to the task of devising a permanent policy. It was embodied in the National Origins Act of 1924 and was severe enough to please all but the most extreme exclusionists. The measure abrogated the Gentlemen's Agreement with Japan by prohibiting the immigration of "persons ineligible to citizenship"—that is, all Orientals. The Act also limited the number of European immigrants to 2 per cent of the foreign-born, according to the Census of 1890. The use of the date of 1890 reduced the quotas from eastern and southern Europe to about one eighth of what they had been under the emergency act of 1921. It also boosted the quotas for the British Isles, Germany, and the Scandinavian countries. However, the National Origins Act of 1924 also stipulated that, after July 1, 1927, only 150,000 immigrants should be admitted annually. They were to be divided among the several countries in proportion to the numbers of their nationals in the United States according to the Census of 1920.

It took longer than had been anticipated to determine the national origins of the American people; indeed no reasonable person familiar with the problem even pretended that the result was anything more than a rough guess. But the experts had completed their work by 1929, and the new system was put into effect on July 1 of that year. President Hoover drastically reduced the quotas in 1931, largely in response to high unemployment, and the total net immigration for the decade of the 1930s was only 69,000. In part, this diminished net immigration (that is, total immigration minus migration from the United States) was caused by the Great Depression, which sent former immigrants—as well as many native-born Americans—back to the land, which at least provided them with some food. In the case of many recent immigrants, however, that land often was in the countries from which they had come (for example, Italy, Portugal, Jamaica, or Mexico), rather than in Iowa or Alabama. Those who had fled persecution, though, such as Jews or Armenians, remained in America and continued the struggle to bring in their relatives. The failure of Jews to overcome the many barriers of quotas helps to account for the huge number available for Nazi death camps in the 1940s.

3. THE UNITED STATES AND WORLD AFFAIRS IN THE 1920s

The Interwar Compromise

Most Americans in the 1920s desired only to be left alone by the rest of the world, although a minority still burned the Wilsonian torch of internationalism, if only faintly. Virtually all Americans were determined to defend the Monroe Doctrine and to brook no threat to the supremacy of the United States in the areas close to the Panama Canal. Moreover, the great majority of Americans were disillusioned by the results of their intervention in the First World War and by more recent events in Europe and were determined to avoid entangling obligations that might draw them into some future war.

Yet a powerful and wealthy nation cannot remain isolated merely by wanting to be left alone, unless, perhaps, it is both willing and able to leave matters alone in all other countries. The United States, however, was a great power in the 1920s with economic and political interests around the world. Moreover, the United States was also the hub of world trade and the source of much of the world's new capital for investment. Therefore, it was practically impossible for the Harding and Coolidge administrations either to withdraw completely from world affairs, or to ignore what was happening beyond American borders. Both administrations represented, among other constituencies, banks and industrial corporations with worldwide business dealings. Economic and political events in many other countries, therefore, affected the United States in a way that these two basically isolationist Presidents had to recognize.

Consequently, the United States played a more active and important role in international councils during the 1920s than it usually had during the century between the Monroe and Wilson administrations. However, clear limits were set to American foreign policy during the decade: The United States would cooperate in various endeavors for peace, but only upon its own terms. The most important of these terms was the understanding that the American government would assume no obligations whatever outside the western hemisphere.

The Washington Conference

Harding started rather blithely on his way in foreign policy by announcing in his inaugural, "We do not mean to be entangled." His Secretary of State, Charles Evans Hughes, the distinguished former Supreme Court justice and Republican presidential candidate in 1916, dutifully followed his chief's lead. For several months, Hughes refused to answer communications from the League of Nations out of fear of angering the extreme isolationists in the Senate. In addition, once Harding had signed a new congressional resolution which declared the war with Germany at an end, Hughes proceeded to negotiate separate peace treaties with Germany, Austria, and Hungary.

Harding and Hughes knew well, however, that the United States in 1921 was on the brink of an intense naval race with Great Britain and Japan. Moreover, relations with Japan had become embittered by controversies at the Paris Peace Conference and by the stationing of a large American fleet in the Pacific in 1919. Chauvinistic newspapers in both countries began to talk of war.

Few Americans wanted a naval race, and fewer still wanted war with Japan. Senator William E. Borah of Idaho, therefore, came forward on May 15, 1921, with an amendment to the nearly half-billion-dollar naval appropriation bill. Borah's amendment requested the President to invite Great Britain and Japan to a conference in Washington to discuss naval disarmament. Both houses of Congress approved the Borah resolution by overwhelming majorities. The British government, burdened by debt, was also eager for disarmament talks. In fact, the Foreign Office informed the State Department that it would move for a conference if the United States did not act soon. Under this pressure, Harding sent invitations, not only to Great Britain and Japan, but also to France and Italy as important naval powers. He also invited China, the Netherlands, Belgium, and Portugal, as nations with large interests in the Far East.

Delegates from these eight countries and the United States met at Washington on November 12, 1921. In his address of welcome, Hughes startled his listeners by proposing a ten-year "holiday" in the construction of battleships. A number of capital ships (warships of over 10,000 tons or carrying guns of over eight inches bore) either already built or under construction should be scrapped. The United States, Hughes went on, was ready to scrap thirty ships totaling 845,700 tons. Great Britain should scrap nineteen ships of 583,375 tons; Japan, seventeen ships of 448,928 tons. This would amount to a total reduction in the navies of the three major naval powers of about 2,000,000 tons and leave the ratio in capital ships at five for Great Britain, five for the United States, and three for Japan. Thus, the United States and its former mother country would continue to rule the world's oceans and military supply routes, but at a lesser expense than before, and without a naval building contest that might have required high taxes. However, the Japanese gained, for the first time, tangible recognition as the "great power" in the Pacific.

The Washington Treaties

Negotiations proceeded very smoothly, in spite of some difficulties in persuading France and Italy to accept definite and inferior tonnages. In fact, Hughes seized the opportunity offered by the cooperation of Great Britain and Japan to conclude a comprehensive series of treaties relating, not only to naval construction and tonnage, but to the Far East as well:

1. In the *Five-Power Treaty*, Britain, Japan, France, Italy, and the United States accepted Hughes' proposals relating to capital ships. France and Italy agreed to a tonnage allotment a little more than half that of Japan. In addition, the United States, Britain, and Japan promised not to fortify further their outlying possessions in the western Pacific.

2. *The Four-Power Treaty*, among the United States, Britain, Japan, and France, nullified the old Anglo-Japanese Alliance. More important, it bound its signatories to respect one another's possessions in the Pacific area and to submit to joint conference any issue that seemed likely to disturb the peace of the Far East.

3. *The Nine-Power Treaty*, signed by all the delegates at the conference, guaranteed the integrity of China and the preservation of the commercial Open Door in that country. It thus gave official sanction for the first time to the policy inaugurated by Secretary of State John Hay in 1899–1900.

4. Under Hughes' auspices, delegates from China and Japan signed a treaty providing for the return to China of Shantung Province, which the Japanese had seized from Germany during the war.

5. A final treaty by the signatories of the Five-Power Treaty prohibited the use of submarines as commerce destroyers during wartime and outlawed the use of poisonous gases. Within twenty years, only the prohibition against the use of poison gas remained unbroken by the nations which had signed the treaties.

Harding presented all the treaties that the American delegates had signed to the Senate and asked speedy approval to prove that American talk about peace was not so much hollow mockery. The Senate, without much ado, gave its consent to ratification, but with an important reservation appended to the Four-Power Treaty. It said that the United States, by the terms of that treaty, had assumed "no commitment to armed force, no alliance, no obligation to join in any defense." It was one of the clearest statements on record of American determination to cooperate whenever possible to promote world peace—but to assume no obligations whatever to defend that peace.

The Washington Conference was the first successful disarmament conference in modern history. The Five-Power Treaty was, obviously, a compromise, in which each nation gave up something. The United States gave up plans to build the largest navy in the world, although it is extremely doubtful that Congress would have appropriated the money necessary to realize this objective. Great Britain abandoned her historic policy of maintaining a navy equal to the combined strength of her two strongest possible rivals. However, this policy had become an intolerable financial burden, and the much wealthier United States now was a good friend. Japan gave up her foothold in China and an alliance with Great Britain that had been highly advantageous to her. Privately, though, Japanese expansionists reserved the right to regain their foothold in China, and, in fact, much more than a foothold, when such a change in policy again seemed advantageous to them. So the treaty really was a truce, temporarily expedient to the major powers. Through these mutual concessions, nevertheless, the conference stopped the naval race in capital ships and provided a political understanding that helped to preserve peace in the Orient for a decade. It was the chief accomplishment of the Harding administration.

It would have been well if congressmen and senators had remembered that international understanding constitutes a two-way street. On one side, Japanese friendship for the United States was already warm as a result of the negotiations in Washington. It was heightened in 1923, when a great earthquake devastated the island empire and Americans poured out millions of dollars in relief.

On the other side, Congress, in the National Origins bill of 1924, abrogated the Gentlemen's Agreement that had governed immigration from Japan to the United States since 1907. Worse still, Congress prohibited Oriental immigration in words that were humiliating to the Japanese, which proved to be a serious and very expensive error. Coolidge and Hughes both pleaded in vain for the deletion of provisions which insulted the Japanese nation. Coolidge reluctantly signed the measure on the ground that his signature was necessary if there was to be any immigration legislation at all. It was a terrible mistake. Reaction in Japan was so violent that it is no exaggeration to say that Congress' action, and Coolidge's approval of it, destroyed all the progress that Hughes and the liberal Japanese leaders had made since 1921 in restoring cordial relations between their two countries. Some Japanese military and political leaders now began to look forward to an opportunity for retribution. And they viewed all American actions concerning the Pacific Ocean area with suspicion. This was not a situation which would promote long-term peace between the two nations.

War Debts and Reparations

The necessity to work out some solution for the most vexing economic legacy of the war—the huge burden of war debts and reparations—gave additional proof that it was impossible for the American government to withdraw into blissful isolation.

The burden of intergovernmental debts was a great cancer on the body of the international economy. The British government had lent some $4 billion to seventeen nations during the war; the French had borrowed from the British and also lent to many countries. The Allied governments, principally Great Britain, France, and Italy, had borrowed more than $7 billion from the United States during the war, and another $3.25 billion immediately after the Armistice. Also, these nations, especially Great Britain, had sold a very high proportion of their assets in America—such as stocks in American corporations and United States government bonds—before they turned to borrowing. In addition, the Allied governments had stripped Germany of about $5 billion dollars from 1918 to 1920, and had then imposed a reparations bill of $33 billion on that vanquished nation in 1921. Therefore, the various national systems of credit repayment were stretched taut and were susceptible to any new or additional pressure. This turned out to be a very precarious and dangerous international financial situation, and one in which the United States was entangled whether Americans longed for isolation or not.

The Allies, from the Paris Peace Conference onward, proposed a mutual cancellation of Allied intergovernmental debts on the ground that they had been incurred in a common struggle against Germany. However, they were not at this time willing to reduce their reparations against Germany. Later in the 1920s, the former Allied governments tried over and over to tie German reparation payments directly to their own debt payments to the United States.

The Harding and Coolidge administrations followed the policy set by the Wilson administration (largely because of the adamant Allied stand on reparations) and insisted that the former Allies pay their debts to the United States in full. Congress established a World War Foreign Debt Commission in 1922, which eventually negotiated long-term funding agreements with Great Britain, France, and Italy. But developments soon proved that Allied debt payments depended unofficially upon German reparation payments, and that the latter, in turn, depended upon the flow of American capital to Germany, mostly for industrial development and redevelopment of industries injured financially by the war.

The entire structure of intergovernmental payments broke down temporarily when the German government—under the stress of making these unpopular heavy payments—defaulted on reparations payments in 1922. The French occupied the Ruhr Valley in retaliation, and the government in Berlin embarked, apparently intentionally, upon a course of wild inflation. Since all of Europe was heading toward economic chaos, Secretary Hughes intervened. A special committee headed by two American bankers, Charles G. Dawes and Owen D. Young, worked out a settlement which provided for an American gold loan to Germany and a scaling down of that nation's reparations burden. In 1929, a new committee, headed by Young, further reduced the German reparations debt to $2 billion, but the structure of intergovernmental payments remained still somewhat shaky. Indeed, it collapsed entirely when depression struck the world economy after 1929. The former Allies then abandoned the effort to collect reparation payments from Germany, defaulted on their own debts to the United States, and embarked upon policies of economic nationalism which aggravated the worldwide depression by disrupting almost all trade and financial exchange.

The Pursuit of Peace

Americans were in the vanguard of the pursuit of world peace—without accepting any obligations, however, for keeping that peace, beyond some reductions in armaments. Events abroad, particularly after the settlement of the Franco-German dispute over reparations, greatly encouraged hopes that the world had entered a new era. The League of Nations seemed to be functioning well, even without American participation. The democratic German Republic entered the League in 1926. Russia, renamed the Union of Soviet Socialist Republics (USSR, or Soviet Union) was controlled by a Bolshevik government hostile to the West, but that nation was so torn by internal convulsions that it offered no threat to its neighbors, much less to the world. A liberal government

President Coolidge signing the antiwar treaty, the Kellogg-Briand Pact, on January 17, 1929, after it had been overwhelmingly endorsed by the Senate. Just before Secretary of State Kellogg went to Paris to sign the agreement, the President clearly expressed the enthusiasm of the nation for it: "It holds a greater hope for peaceful relations than was ever before given to the world." (Wide World Photos)

in Japan sought understanding with China and cooperation with the United States and European governments.

American political leaders, for the most part, were not inclined to stand idly by when international relations seemed to be moving in new channels. The United States Government slowly established cordial relations with the League of Nations, sent unofficial "observers" to that organization, and participated in numerous League conferences. In 1923, Hughes, with Harding's approval, began a campaign for American membership in the League's judicial agency—the Permanent Court of International Justice, commonly called the World Court. Senate isolationists, led by Borah, blocked this campaign for membership in the World Court, which was carried on by every President from Harding to Franklin D. Roosevelt.

It is possible that the American people and their government would have come to maturity in international relations had it not been for the Great Depression and the collapse of the League of Nations in the early 1930s. These events caused Americans to turn inward in their concern for domestic problems. In any case, the American thrust into world affairs in the 1920s was both extremely cautious and naive because it was based on the assumption that the United States could play a leading role in the pursuit of peace without carrying commensurate responsibility. This was the assumption which underlay, for example, the Washington treaties and American cooperation with the League of Nations.

Leadership without responsibility was also the assumption of the most spectacular peace movement of the 1920s. This was a campaign to outlaw war, which American peace groups and isolationists like Borah supported. It culminated in the Pact of Paris, or Kellogg-Briand Treaty (so named because Secretary of State Frank B. Kellogg and the French Foreign Minister, Aristide Briand, were its chief negotiators and sponsors). The treaty was signed in the French capital on August 27, 1928, by representatives of all the great powers except the Soviet Union, which later signed it. "The High Contracting Parties," the pact said, "solemnly declare in the names of their respective people that they condemn recourse to war for the solution of international controversies, and renounce it as an instrument of national policy in their relations with one another."

The Pact of Paris was certainly a pious affirmation of good intentions, but it provided no penalties against nations which resorted to force. It excluded wars fought in "self-defense," a term which could be defined very broadly. At the request of the British, the treaty also did not apply in what were called "certain regions of the world" threatened with civil disturbances—presumably India and Egypt, but applicable elsewhere as well. Thus, the treaty contained enough holes and other weaknesses to satisfy any major nation. It did not prevent Japan from using force to seize Manchuria in 1931, or Italy from invading Ethiopia in 1935, or Germany and Russia from devouring Poland in 1939. However, the pact did provide one shaky legal basis for the trial and punishment of Nazi and Japanese war criminals following the Second World War. For his part in arranging this almost meaningless agreement, Kellogg won the Nobel Prize for his "contribution to world peace."

Coolidge continued the fight for naval disarmament by calling a conference of naval powers at Geneva, Switzerland, in 1927, to limit submarines and cruisers not covered by the Five-Power Treaty of 1922. The Geneva Conference was a complete fiasco, mainly because the British and American governments had failed to settle technical details beforehand. But a new conference in London in 1930 produced a complete understanding among Great Britain, the United States, and Japan. The Treaty of London extended the "holiday" on construction of capital ships for five years and provided for the scrapping of nine battleships. It also established definite limitations on submarines, destroyers, and cruisers.

The Beginnings of a Good Neighbor Policy

Fear of European intervention in the Caribbean and Central America had chiefly motivated the administrations of Theodore Roosevelt, Taft, and Wilson to establish the supremacy of the United States in those areas for protection of the Panama Canal. Various American efforts included customs receiverships, "dollar diplomacy," and outright military occupations. The removal of any threat to American supremacy in the 1920s permitted leaders in Washington to view developments in the Caribbean and Central American regions with less concern than at any time since the Venezuelan blockade crisis of 1902–1903.

First evidence that a new and more relaxed policy might be in the making came when Hughes permitted the people of the Dominican Republic, which had been administered by an American military government since 1916, to form a constitutional regime from 1922 to 1924. Hughes withdrew American troops in the latter year. He was also eager to call home the marines that Wilson had sent into Haiti in 1915, but an investigating commission warned that anarchy would follow an American withdrawal. Hughes therefore set aside his plan to restore self-government to the nearly all black population of Haiti.

Hughes, in 1925, also withdrew a force of marines that had been stationed in Nicaragua since 1909. However, when civil war broke out in that country soon afterward, Coolidge sent back the marines to maintain an unpopular, pro-American regime. This set off such violent criticism among antiimperialists in the United States that Coolidge hastily sent Henry L. Stimson, former Secretary of War, to mediate between the warring factions. Stimson's stern but honest mediation brought to power the antigovernment faction, which the United States not only supported but also helped to suppress a bandit faction. As peace returned to Nicaragua from 1931 to 1933, American troops were withdrawn. However, they left behind a family dynasty in control of Nicaragua, which ruled corruptly and violently, with the aid of American arms and military training for its troops, until 1979.

Dealing with small Caribbean and Central American republics was easy compared to the difficulties of following wise policies toward the larger and more sensitive population of Mexico—a country with a long history of antagonistic relations with the United States. Americans had invested about $1 billion in Mexican mines, oil fields, railroads, and other enterprises. Leaders of the Mexican Revolution had adopted a constitution in 1917, Article XXVII of which vested ownership of all oil and mineral resources in the Mexican people. All went reasonably well between the United States and Mexico so long as the Mexican government did not try to implement Article XXVII.

Dangerous friction developed when a strong nationalist, Plutarco Elías Calles, came to power in 1924. Two years later, the Mexican Congress passed laws for the enforcement of Article XXVII. Calles also embarked upon a bloody persecution of the Catholic Church that inflamed sentiment in the United States, where Catholics enjoyed considerable political power.

Coolidge and Kellogg, who had succeeded Hughes in 1925, reacted violently. They accused Calles of violating international law (a dubious interpretation of his actions) and also (unjustly) of establishing a Bolshevik-controlled regime in Mexico. However, tempers cooled on both sides of the border once the new American ambassador, the New York banker, Dwight W. Morrow, arrived in Mexico City in 1927. Through tact, understanding of Mexican pride and nationalism, and demonstrations of sympathy for Mexican ambitions, Morrow won the confidence of the Mexican government and people. He also won a new agreement on American-owned oil fields and persuaded Calles to halt his campaign against the Catholic Church. Mexican-American friendship was further strengthened when Charles A. Lindbergh landed at Mexico City on December 14, 1927, after a nonstop goodwill flight of 2,200 miles from Washington. This mood in Mexico lasted about ten years. In 1938, the Mexican government practically confiscated the remaining American oil holdings.

Meanwhile, the State Department had also undertaken a retreat from the Corollary to the Monroe Doctrine, which Theodore Roosevelt had enunciated in 1904 to justify intervention in the internal affairs of Latin American states. The United States was not yet ready to abandon the alleged right to intervene when it thought that its vital interests were at stake. Former Secretary of State Hughes made this clear at the sixth Pan American Congress in Havana in 1928. However, the State Department, in a memorandum prepared by Counselor J. Reuben Clark, admitted that intervention in the affairs of other countries could not be justified by appealing to the Monroe Doctrine. Coolidge's successor, Herbert Hoover, refused to intervene in Latin America during his tenure from 1929 to 1933, in spite of widespread repudiations and revolutions. Thus the way was well prepared for the full-scale launching of what would be called the Good Neighbor Policy of nonintervention and cooperation by Hoover's successor, Franklin D. Roosevelt.

SUGGESTED READINGS

In addition to the general works by Allen, Leuchtenburg, and Soule, mentioned in the Suggested Readings for the preceding chapter Arthur M. Schlesinger, Jr., *The Crisis of the Old Order* (1957), is a lucid interpretation of the decade. For a rather conventional political history, see John D. Hicks, *Republican Ascendancy* (1960). Two major problems of the period can be studied in the relevant chapters of Theodore Saloutos and John D. Hicks, *Agricultural Discontent in the Middle West, 1900–1939* (1951), and Randolph E. Paul, *Taxation in the United States* (1954). For a classic history of the South during this period see George B. Tindall, *The Emergence of the New South, 1913–1945* (1967).

The Harding scandals receive a thorough airing in Samuel H. Adams, *Incredible Era*

(1939), and Karl Schriftgiesser, *This Was Normalcy* (1948). Andrew Sinclair attempts, with little success, to redeem some part of Harding's reputation in *The Available Man* (1965). Robert K. Murray's *The Harding Era* (1968), although based on more original research than Sinclair's book, is an even less persuasive defense of its subject. Francis Russell arouses sympathy for and understanding of Harding somewhat more successfully in *The Shadow of Blooming Grove* (1968). J. Chalmers Vinson, *The Parchment Peace* (1950), is a good study of the Washington Conference. Dexter Perkins, *Charles Evans Hughes and American Democratic Statesmanship* (1953), is an exceptional study of the Republican Secretary of State. Calvin Coolidge is the subject of William A. White's entertaining, *A Puritan in Babylon* (1938). A more sympathetic, fuller, and somewhat more penetrating biography is Donald R. McCoy, *Calvin Coolidge: The Quiet President* (1967). Murray, *The Politics of Normalcy* (1973), although generally well informed, apparently seeks to rank Harding and Coolidge with Lincoln as constructive, intelligent Presidents. Those who agree with that appraisal will find evidence for it in the book, but that evidence seems highly selective.

Adequate, brief accounts of the election of 1924 can be found in Nye, *Midwestern Progressive Politics*, already cited. A more detailed analysis is provided in Kenneth C. MacKay, *The Progressive Movement of 1924* (1947). For a revisionist analysis of the thesis that the LaFollette candidacy possessed a potentiality that most "consensus" historians have ignored, see James Weinstein, *The Decline of Socialism in America, 1912–1925* (1967). For the election of 1928, see Edmund A. Moore, *A Catholic Runs for President* (1956), and, particularly, Allan J. Lichtman, *Prejudice and the Old Politics: The Presidential Election of 1928* (1979), which argues

convincingly that religion was *the* issue. The reorientation of the party out of power is analyzed in David Burner, *The Politics of Provincialism: The Democratic Party in Transition, 1918–1932* (1968). Burner's *Herbert Hoover* (1979), is a thorough scholarly defense of that President.

Several good biographies illuminate this period. Among them are Frank Freidel, *Franklin Roosevelt: The Ordeal* (1954); Matthew and Hannah Josephson, *Al Smith: Hero of the Cities* (1969); Oscar Handlin, *Al Smith and His America* (1958); Arthur Mann, *La Guardia: A Fighter Against His Times* (1959); Elting E. Morison, *Tradition and Turmoil: A Study of the Life and Times of Henry L. Stimson* (1960); William H. Harbaugh, *Lawyer's Lawyer, The Life of John W. Davis* (1973); and Richard Lowitt, *George W. Norris, The Persistence of a Progressive* (1971). Two autobiographical accounts of exceptional importance are Henry L. Stimson and Mc-George Bundy, *On Active Service in Peace and War* (1948), and George W. Norris, *Fighting Liberal* (1945).

CHAPTER 29
HERBERT HOOVER AND THE GREAT DEPRESSION

1. SUNNY DAYS OF HIGH PROSPERITY

The Election of 1928

President Coolidge, vacationing in the Black Hills of South Dakota, handed the following cryptic statement to reporters on August 2, 1927: "I do not choose to run for President in 1928." We know now that Coolidge would have welcomed a draft, although he did not relish the effort required to arrange his own renomination. However, the rank and file of Republicans were delighted to release him from the burdens of office. Tired of a do-nothing President, they demanded the nomination of Herbert Hoover, Secretary of Commerce since 1921, who enjoyed a reputation for vigor and moderate progressivism. The Republican national convention gracefully yielded to this popular desire by nominating Hoover on the first ballot. The Republican platform endorsed prohibition and tariff protection. It also promised farm relief but declared that the government should not engage in price fixing.

The Democratic party remained deeply split between its southern and eastern and its Protestant and Catholic wings. Southerners warned that the nomination of Governor Alfred E. Smith of New York would wreck the party. However, Smith was the only Democrat of national stature available in 1928. With the support of northern and western delegates (especially those from urban areas, or rural areas settled by Irish-American or recent immigrants), the New Yorker won the nomination easily at the Democratic national convention in Houston. Southerners were mollified somewhat by the defeat of a Smith-sponsored platform plank which demanded the repeal of the Eighteenth Amendment.

Never had the nation as a whole been more content with its present situation or more confident of its future than in the summer and autumn of 1928. Not since James Monroe had a presidential candidate faced so easy a campaign as Hoover. He made only half a dozen speeches and emphasized the general prosperity under Republican rule and promised its continuance. As he put it in his acceptance speech: "We in America today are nearer to the final triumph over poverty than ever before in the history of any land. The poorhouse is vanishing from among us. We have not yet reached the goal, but, given a chance to go forward with the policies of the last eight years, we shall soon, with the help of God, be in sight of the day when poverty will be banished from this nation." Moreover, Hoover made it plain that he stood foursquare against proposals like the McNary-Haugen bill, federal operation of power projects, and legislation that singled out organized labor for special benefits.

Smith had a long record as a defender of civil rights and as a champion of progressive legislation in New York. However, instead of trying to rally farmers and urban Americans in a new progressive coalition, he chose instead to make his campaign on the two issues of prohibition and religious toleration. Immediately after his nomination, Smith notified the Houston convention that he would feel free to advocate repeal of the Volstead Act, and perhaps also of the Eighteenth Amendment. Throughout his campaign, he attacked prohibition, which Hoover had defended in his acceptance speech as an "experiment

The Election of 1928

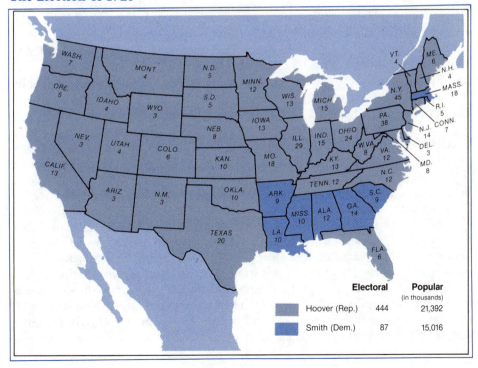

		Electoral	Popular (in thousands)
	Hoover (Rep.)	444	21,392
	Smith (Dem.)	87	15,016

noble in intent." Smith was goaded into discussion of the religious issue because of the numerous charges that he, a Roman Catholic, would move the Vatican to Washington and turn the government over to his church. Smith hit back hard at bigotry, but by so doing he helped to make religion the leading issue of the campaign.

It was evident long before election day, November 6, 1928, that Smith was struggling hopelessly against an overwhelming Republican tide. Few observers were surprised when Hoover won. He carried forty out of the forty-eight states; broke the Solid South by capturing Virginia, North Carolina, Tennessee, Florida, and Texas; and won 21,392,190 popular votes to 15,016,443 for Smith. Yet there were signs underneath the surface that profound changes had occurred in American national politics. The Solid South was gone forever, at least in presidential elections. No longer could the Democrats go into a presidential campaign absolutely assured of solid southern support. Of even greater significance for the future, Smith — the hero of the urban Democracy — made the Democratic party indisputably the party of the non-Protestant masses in the great cities. In contrast to Cox and Davis, who had done poorly in metropolitan centers, Smith carried the twelve largest cities and ran very well in all counties populated heavily by Roman Catholics and recent immigrants. He probably broke black ties to the party of Lincoln by winning about half of the black votes in the northern cities. Finally, Smith ran far better in the midwestern farm states than any Democratic candidate since Woodrow Wilson. In these respects, Smith benefited from the results of La Follette's coalition of these groups, which evidently turned much more to the Democrats than to the Republicans after La Follette's death in 1925.

Hoover and the American Dream

Herbert Hoover delivered his inaugural address on March 4, 1929, in a cold, drizzling rain. By contrast, his speech radiated bright hope for the future.

The man whom the American people had chosen to lead the way to permanent prosperity was a perfect symbol of old hopes of economic abundance and living proof of the vitality of the American tradition of success through character and hard work. Herbert Clark Hoover was born on a small farm at West Branch, Iowa, on August 10, 1874. He was orphaned at the age of ten and later worked his way through Stanford University. He gradually accumulated a large fortune as a mining engineer and investor in mining properties in many parts of the world. Hoover was director of the Belgian Relief Commission and devoted his superb administrative talents to the task of feeding the people of Belgium and northeastern France. When his own country entered the war in 1917, he returned home to become Food Administrator. He probably could have had the Democratic presidential nomination in 1920, but he decided that he was a Republican and refused all Democratic overtures. As Secretary of Commerce under Harding and Coolidge, Hoover raised his department to a major branch of the government. He tried to extend into peacetime the cooperation between government and industry which had been carried on so successfully by the War Industries Board and the Food Administration. He used industrial trade associations as vehicles for his objectives — an exchange of information intended to promote standardization and reduce costs. Because that ex-

*Calvin Coolidge and Herbert Hoover on March 4, 1929, en route to
Hoover's inauguration where the new President expressed his confidence
to the nation: "I have no fears for the future of our country. It is
bright with hope." (Wide World Photos)*

change included information about prices and wages, which tended therefore
to become uniform within an industry, the Attorney General warned Hoover
that he was violating the antitrust laws. When floods devastated the Mississippi valley in 1927, Hoover again demonstrated his abilities as director of a nationwide relief effort.

The American people had elected generals, lawyers, and politicians to lead
their government, but Hoover was the first and so far the only business executive of stature to occupy the White House. Hoover had never run for elective
office or engaged in mere politics. He was accustomed to directing great enterprises and to giving orders that would be obeyed without question. Such experience might be an advantage so long as the new President had comfortable
majorities in Congress and the strong support of public opinion. But his lack of
political experience, particularly the lack of experience in getting on with persons of opposing views, would place a heavy burden on Hoover's abilities as a
leader once the political tide turned against him. Still, the presence in the
White House of a successful businessman in 1929 seemed fitting. In the words
of the economist Stuart Chase, "the businessman had become the dictator of
our destinies and the final authority on the conduct of American society."

Prosperity Policies

In the prosperous early months of 1929, it seemed to political leaders, especially Republicans, that the only serious national problem was relief for agriculture. Soon after his inauguration, Hoover called the Seventy-first Congress into special session. Farm leaders still insisted that only something like the McNary-Haugen plan would afford a lasting solution, but the new President made it plain that he would not accept any far-reaching governmental intervention to maintain agricultural prices. Hoover's alternative—the Agricultural Marketing bill—was, at least in its original draft, perfectly tailored to fit Hoover's philosophy. It created a Federal Farm Board and gave it a revolving fund of $500 million to be lent to agricultural cooperatives to enable them to build warehouses and sell crops in an orderly way. However, midwestern Republicans and southern Democrats in the Senate changed the measure significantly. They added a provision which authorized the Federal Farm Board to establish corporations to purchase farm products in order to stabilize prices. Hoover reluctantly accepted the amendment in order to obtain his bill.

Hoover also urged Congress to give farmers additional tariff protection. High protectionist manufacturers, with their powerful lobbies, were in control when the House Ways and Means Committee, headed by W. C. Hawley of Oregon, began to draft a new tariff bill. Joseph Grundy, president of the Pennsylvania Manufacturers' Association, confessed that he was spending $2 thousand a month to boost tariff rates. Hence the Hawley bill, presented to the House of Representatives in May 1929, not only increased duties on agricultural products; it also included some 925 increases in the rates on manufactured goods. Senator Reed Smoot of Utah, chairman of the Finance Committee, pushed the measure through the upper house in May 1930 in spite of growing public opposition. One thousand members of the American Economic Association signed a petition which begged President Hoover to veto the Hawley-Smoot bill. What the world needed, they asserted, was freer trade, not economic nationalism. A reversion to McKinley-like tariff policies would start a cycle of similar actions by other nations.

Hoover not only signed the Hawley-Smoot bill, but also, long afterward, argued that it had had no significant effect on world trade. From a sheerly statistical point of view, Hoover was probably correct. The measure's increases in duties on agricultural products were meaningless except for meat and dairy products, since American farmers exported their surplus staples to the world market in any event. Moreover, the Hawley-Smoot Act's increased rates on manufactured products applied, aside from textiles and chemicals, largely to specialties traded in comparatively small quantities. Most American industrial products were unaffected by tariff increases; most other foreign producers could hardly compete with them in the world market, much less in the United States. However, the Hawley-Smoot Act was unfortunate in that it gave European countries an excuse for sharply increasing their own tariff rates. The British, for example, adopted protection and a system of imperial preference in 1932, in retaliation, they asserted, against American tariff policies.

Hoover believed that all problems could be solved by action based on careful investigation and study. Therefore, before he recommended action to strengthen the prohibition laws, the President appointed eleven distinguished citizens to a Commission on Law Observance and Enforcement, headed by former Attorney General George W. Wickersham. "No nation," Hoover said to the commission, "can long survive the failure of its citizens to respect and obey the laws which they themselves make."

The Wickersham Commission, after nearly two years of investigation, reported in January 1931 what everyone knew: enforcement of the Eighteenth Amendment had simply collapsed because of widespread public opposition, especially in urban areas. The commission as a whole did not recommend repeal of the amendment, but seven members attached individual opinions which favored either modification or repeal. Hoover, when he submitted the report to Congress, could only say lamely that he did not favor abandoning the "noble experiment." Ironically, the report of the Wickersham Commission was the death knell of the Eighteenth Amendment because it gave convincing proof that effective enforcement was impossible. Both parties came out in 1932 in favor of a return of the liquor problem to the states. Congress, with an almost audible sigh of relief, approved the Twenty-first Amendment in February 1933. It repealed the Eighteenth Amendment and forbade the shipment of alcoholic beverages into dry states. Repeal went into effect in December 1933. America's foremost growth industry during the 1920s — the production, smuggling, shipment, and sale of illegal liquor — therefore finally ended. The gangster empires that it had supported thus were forced to turn their accumulated profits into other industries, such as gambling casinos, and, finally, drugs.

2. THE GREAT DEPRESSION

Causes

Even in the most prosperous times, not all sectors of the American economy advance evenly; imbalances and weaknesses always exist, and it is relatively easy to discover them — years later. Some of the major weaknesses and imbalances in 1929 resulted from the fact that intellectual developments among businessmen and public officials in America did not keep pace with economic changes in all respects. Many otherwise sensible Americans believed, for example, that, in periods of economic setback, the government should cut expenditures and wait for the recession to run its natural course. The same men, strangely enough, frequently believed in taking immediate and drastic action to combat other kinds of disasters. Herbert Hoover provides a fine example of this type. Also, a great many influential Americans opposed governmental regulation on principle, even when it could be justified reasonably. In the early 1930s bankers, for instance, were obliged to watch their banks fail by the thousands for want of a simple protection such as federal deposit insurance.

Other important weaknesses in 1929 were more directly economic. The medium-term prospects for residential construction were adversely affected by the combination of a declining rate of increase in family formations and rising construction and land costs. Farmers were in difficulties because of the agricultural depression already discussed. This dried up part of the potential market for consumer goods in farm areas, and it weakened banks and other financial institutions with loans outstanding to farmers. Over 70 per cent of the American people lived at or below the Labor Department's estimate of a decent living standard. These people, who lacked savings, unemployment insurance, or other cushions, would be vulnerable to any economic adversity, especially if they had bought goods on credit as advertisements had urged them to do. And when they suffered, so, too, would the manufacturers and retailers who served them.

The economy was endangered also by a rickety system of international debts which depended upon an annual outpouring of American dollars for payment, and by the inflexibility of the gold standard upon which international trade was based. Some other alleged causes of the depression, such as the poor structure of the banking system, abuse of credit, and high incidence of dishonesty within the business community, were conditions that probably were no worse in 1929 than in most earlier periods of American history. However, the depression did bring out the terrible possibilities inherent in these endemic conditions.

The Great Crash

The most dramatic and obvious cause of the depression was the collapse of the stock market in the autumn of 1929. During the prosperous years between 1925 and 1929, stock market prices rose about 300 per cent. By 1929, the cycle of rising corporate sales, profits, dividends, and common stock prices had become so regular and pleasant that more than 1,000,000 American stock buyers were bidding up the prices of shares much faster than corporate profits increased. The process could not continue indefinitely.

In one terrible month, which started on October 23, 1929, prices on the New York Stock Exchange alone fell in value about $26 billion, and prices proceeded irregularly downward for two and a half more years. This catastrophe might have served as no more than an interesting example of the extremes to which Americans sometimes carry their affairs, except for its clear relationship to the nationwide disaster that followed. The loss of $26 billion in less than a month and of more than $35 billion in a year, on the New York Stock Exchange alone, takes on added meaning when compared to the American gross national product (GNP = the total of all goods and services produced), which was slightly over $100 billion in 1929, and $95 billion in 1930. It seems safe to assert that the enormous loss of wealth by individuals and institutions which held corporate stock played a major role in the subsequent failure of the American economy.

The Course of the Depression, 1929–1933

The depression passed through two distinct stages in the United States. The first, which lasted from the autumn of 1929 to the summer of 1931, might be called a severe recession. By the last quarter of 1930, for example, industrial production was only 26 per cent below its peak level of 1929, and unemployment ran only between 3,000,000 and 4,000,000 in 1930. The second stage was the severe depression that set in during the summer of 1931 and lasted, in the United States, until 1935 or 1936. This second stage was related, not only to domestic events, but also to serious financial stringencies in Germany, Austria, and Great Britain, which were induced primarily by a sharp decline in American investment, purchasing, and lending abroad. The German and Austrian governments were nearly bankrupt, and the British were forced off

THE GREAT DEPRESSION

The First National Bank of Melrose was the first [in the town] to go. There was no warning; in the middle of the banking day the doors were closed by the examiners. It was one of the oldest banks in the state, regarded as a branch of the United States Treasury. Within two or three hours everyone knew of the disaster. Depositors, stunned and disbelieving, gathered in small groups to read the notice on the door. . . . There was little public lamentation. The most shocking example was old Mrs. Gearman. She beat with her fists upon the closed plate-glass doors and screamed and sobbed without restraint. She had in a savings account the $2,000 from her husband's insurance and $963 she had saved over a period of twenty-five years from making rag rugs. Nothing was left but charity. For a week neighbors did not see her. A policeman found her sitting in the middle of the kitchen of her small, scrubbed house. They took her to the insane asylum a few days afterward.

The effect of the Depression on a small Midwestern city. From Marquis Childs, "Main Street Ten Years After," The New Republic, vol. 73, January 18, 1933.

Disappointed depositors in front of a New York bank. Following the national bank holiday, other members of the Federal Reserve System opened their doors again, but this bank had remained closed. (United Press International Photo)

A young man out of work, Washington, D.C., 1938. (Library of Congress)

Lineup for a free sandwich and cup of coffee, Times Square, New York City, February 1932. The free food was the gift of a New York newspaper. (Wide World Photos)

Such is the problem created by three years of increasing unemployment and two years of hand-to-mouth relief: city after city attempting to feed a half or a third or a quarter of its citizens upon gifts made from the reduced earnings, or from taxes levied on the overappraised homes of the other half or two thirds or the other three quarters; city after city maintaining the lives but not the health of its unemployed on a survival ration; city after city where the whole mechanism of relief has failed or is about to fail or has survived only by abandoning a major part of its task; and beyond the cities the mill towns and the coal mines and the 'cropper farms where relief is merely a name.

From "No One Has Starved," Fortune, *September, 1932.*

Jobless men sitting on a park bench, 1930. Photo by Lewis Hine. (Collection of International Museum of Photography at George Eastman House)

Crowds gathered in front of the employment office of the Pennsylvania Department of Labor and Industry to apply for jobs in President Roosevelt's dollar-a-day reforestation program. (United Press International Photo)

A few weeks ago, my city decided as a measure of relief to dig a little canal from some funds that they had left from another improvement. They advertised that they wanted 750 laborers . . . to do the hard, dirty work of digging and other laborious and unpleasant work. The men were to work 10 hours and to get $2 a day. They had over 12,000 registrations for those jobs, and they were supposed to be only men who live in my city.

Congressman George Huddleston, of Birmingham, Alabama, speaking before a Senate subcommittee hearing, 1932. From U. S. Congress, Senate, Subcommittee of the Committee on Manufactures, Hearings, Federal Aid for Unemployment Relief, 72d Congress, 1st Sess., on S. 174 and S. 262, Washington: U. S. Government Printing Office, 1932.

A policeman attempts to maintain order as 15,000 women turn out to apply for six Civil Service charwoman jobs, October 12, 1938. (United Press International Photo)

It is estimated that whereas one man in four is out of employment in the city generally, one man in two is unemployed in Harlem.
The New York Times, March 31, 1935.

Mr. Roosevelt, he could do something about all this, and the way white folks treat us. He gets power to mess with everything else, don't he? . . . But he ain't done a thing to help us, now has he?
From an interview with a Black working woman in Philadelphia by sociologist Charles S. Johnson, 1941.

Most of my customers were dressed as poorly as I. I think lots of them buy the apples to fill their stomachs, so they can skip a meal. Generally they start eating as soon as they get hold of the apple. Well-dressed people mostly hurry by as if they didn't want to look at you.
Apple seller in the business district of New York.

James Brown . . . has been a sandblaster in one of the pipe mills for over eight years. Everyone who knows him says that he is honest, reliable and a valuable worker. He has four children who, for the first time in their lives are suffering the pangs of real, stark hunger. Yet his plea is not for food, fuel or clothing, but WORK which this highly organized and efficient society fails to provide. He is given a permit to sell apples on the city streets. . . .
Report of an Urban League investigation of Negro conditions, Pittsburgh. From Opportunity, March 1931.

You see, when you get a shine kit it's a permanent investment, and it doesn't cost as much as a box of apples anyway. . . .
New York shoe shiner. From The New York Times, June 5, 1932.

Above: Fred Bell peddling apples on a street corner in San Francisco during the Depression. Once known as "Champagne Fred," he had been a near millionaire but lost his fortune when the stock market crashed. (Wide World Photos)

Left: Apple sellers on New York's 42nd Street. (Brown Brothers)

Free food at 52nd Street and Seventh Avenue, New York City, November 18, 1930. Meals were given to 1500 unemployed. (United Press International Photo)

A relief order from the city of Cleveland, May 12, 1938. The $2.99 was to feed a family of eight for one week. (United Press International Photo)

RELIEF ORDER	CITY OF CLEVELAND	SERIAL NO. D 445433
REDEEMABLE TO RELIEF CLIENT IN MERCHANDISE ONLY	EMERGENCY DIVISION OF CHARITIES & RELIEF 5716 EUCLID AVENUE	

DATE May 12, 1938   7-18-ok   CASE NO. 4513   NO. IN FAM 8   CODE F

VENDOR ANY CUYAHOGA COUNTY DEALER

NAME   Eugene Rocco   YOU ARE HEREBY AUTHORIZED TO ← DELIVER TO

STREET   7903 Dudley   CLEVELAND, OHIO

The following articles or services   Food   5/12-5/18   2|99   Two 99/100   AT A COST NOT TO EXCEED   DOLLARS ($ 2.99

SIGNED

I hereby certify that the money for the payment of this relief order has been lawfully appropriated for such purpose and is in the treasury or in the process of collection to the credit of the appropriated fund free from any previous encumbrances.   SIGNED   **G. A. GESELL**   DIRECTOR OF FINANCE

Our slip called for two dollars a week and [those in charge of relief] thought any woman could prepare forty-two meals a week on a dollar-fifty for two people. So we got fifty cents taken from the two dollars.

Those in charge of relief have never known actual hunger and want, have never lain awake at night worrying about unpaid rent, or how to make a few groceries do for the seemingly endless seven days till the next week's order of groceries. . . . It gives me the nightmare, but I'm used to it. . . .

But we are supposed to have faith in our government. We are told to keep cheerful and smiling. Just what does our government expect us to do when our rent is due? When we need a doctor? When we need clothes? We haven't had a tube of toothpaste in weeks and have to check off some item of needed food when we get soap. I can only do my washing every two weeks, because this is as often as I can get oil for the oil stove to heat wash water and laundry soap with which to do my washing.

But we are supposed to fall down on our knees and worship the golden calf of government when we are in dire need.

It is always the people with full stomachs who tell us poor people to keep happy. I should love to have some new clothes, and I should enjoy a radio the same as anybody. But try to get them!

No work, no hope; just live from one day to the next. Maybe better times are coming. Personally, I doubt it.
Resident of Muncie, Indiana, 1935. As quoted in Robert and Helen Lynd, Middletown in Transition, *Harcourt, Brace and World, Inc., New York, 1937, pp. 111–12.*

A curious social phenomenon has developed out of the present depression . . . the people whom our post offices label "address unknown". . . . Every group in society is represented in their ranks, from the college graduate to the child who has never seen the inside of a schoolhouse. Expectant mothers, sick babies, young childless couples, grim-faced middle-aged dislodged from jobs—on they go, an index of insecurity . . . the nomads of the depression.
From The New York Times, *December 11, 1932.*

Where can we sleep tonight?
Well, there's Hooverville on the edge of the river. There's a whole raft of Okies there.
He drove his old car to Hooverville. He never asked again, for there was a Hooverville on the edge of every town.
The rag town lay close to the water; and the houses were tents, and weed-thatched enclosures, paper houses, a great junk pile. The man drove his family in and became a citizen of Hooverville—always they were called Hooverville. The man put up his own tent as near to water as he could get; or if he had no tent, he went to the city dump and brought back cartons and built a house of corrugated paper.
And when the rains came the house melted and washed away.
From John Steinbeck, The Grapes of Wrath, *Viking Press, New York, 1939.*

The trek to California: car trouble and a sick baby bring the journey to a temporary halt. (Library of Congress)

I can count 23 farmers in the west half of this county that have had to leave the farms to give three men more land.

Was waiting to see what would be the outcome of my hunt for a place, and the outlook right now is that I will move to town and sell my teams, tools, and cows. I have hunted from Childress, Texas, to Haskell, Texas, a distance of 200 miles, and the answer is the same.

I can stay off the relief until the first of the year. After that I don't know. I've got to make a move, but I don't know where to.

From Texas Plains, June 20, 1938.

Refugee camp, Los Angeles. (Los Angeles Times Photo)

In the brush near Wasco, Calif., June 1938: squatters move in, all their possessions piled into open wooden trailers and atop their cars. (Library of Congress)

Below: The family shown here at their "home" in Bakersfield, Calif., were typical of thousands of American families who moved west to California seeking escape from drought, dust, and disaster in the 1930s. Here they were to eke out a meager existence through farm work. (Wide World Photos)

People just can't make it back there, with drought, hailstorms, windstorms, duststorms, insects. People exist here and they can't do that there. You can make it here if you sleep lots and eat little, but it's pretty tough, there are so many people. They chase them out of one camp because they say it isn't sanitary—there's no running water—so people live out here in the brush like a den o' dogs or pigs.
Tenant farmer with six children, who left Cook County, Texas, and moved to California in 1938. As quoted in Dorothea Lange and Paul Shuster Taylor, An American Exodus, *New York, 1939.*

Destitute pea pickers in California: a mother of seven children, age thirty-two, February 1936. (Library of Congress)

A duststorm rolling in on a Colorado farm. Once a productive agricultural area, the "Dust Bowl"—which encompassed eastern New Mexico and Colorado, the panhandles of Texas and Oklahoma, and western Kansas was dramatically transformed into a wasteland by the early 1930s due to extreme drought and high winds. (Library of Congress)

By midmorning a gale was blowing, cold and black. By noon it was blacker than night. It was a wall of dirt one's eyes could not penetrate, but it could penetrate the eyes and ears and nose . . . and the lungs until one coughed up black.

People were afraid, because they had never seen anything like this before. . . .

When the wind died and the sun shone forth again, it was on a different world. There were no fields, only sand drifting into mounds and eddies that swirled in what was now but an autumn breeze. There was no longer a section-line road fifty feet from the front door. In the farmyard, fences, machinery, and trees were gone, buried. The roofs of sheds stuck out through drifts deeper than a man is tall.
From Robert D. Lusk, "The Life and Death of 470 Acres," Saturday Evening Post, *August 13, 1938.*

I seen our corn dry up and blow over the fence, back there in Oklahoma.
Pea picker in California, February 1937. From Lange and Taylor, An American Exodus, 1939.

Above: Drought scene near Beaver, Oklahoma, 1935. (United Press International Photo)

Left: Cornfield, 1936. (Library of Congress)

National Guardsmen, armed with machine guns, are called in to keep peace in Le Mars, Iowa, as irate farmers protest the foreclosures of mortgages on their homes. The Guard was called in following an attack on a judge. (United Press International Photo)

Here's a paper [holds it up] made out fine and proper, seals and all. Aren't we foolish to think a little paper like that can take away a man's crop that he worked for? It's only a paper. A sheriff came with this crazy paper to take a neighbor's crop. We turned out with a hundred men and before we got through we had the paper and we had the crop. Why, he might as well have brought along a newspaper.

From a farmer's speech to the McKenzie County Holiday Association at Watford City, North Dakota, October 1934.

National Guardsmen, with bayonets, watch as a farm sale progresses in Iowa, 1933. (United Press International Photo)

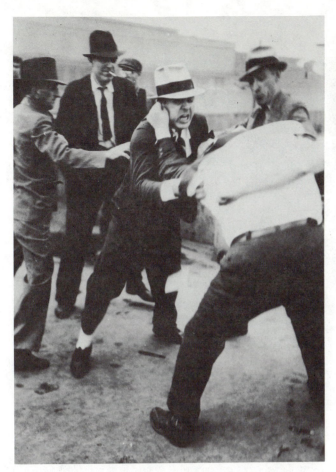

Above: Richard Frankensteen (right) and Walter Reuther, two organizers for the CIO's United Autoworkers, in Detroit on May 10, 1937, after having been badly beaten by unknown assailants. The two labor leaders accused Ford Company guards of the crime. (United Press International Photo)

A CIO organizer being beaten at the Ford plant in Dearborn, Michigan, May 26, 1937. (United Press International Photo)

. . . they had no lunch baskets and wore no badges. . . . After the pictures were taken we were approached by some of these men on all sides. . . . One called out that we were on private property and to get the hell off of there. Frankensteen and I turned to get off the bridge in obedience to the command. I had hardly taken three steps when I was slugged on the back of the head. I tried to shield my face by crossing my arms. They pounded me over the head and body. . . . I was knocked to the ground and beaten. . . .

They picked me up and threw me bodily on the concrete floor of the platform. Then they kicked me again and again. They tried to tear my legs apart. Seven times they raised me off the concrete and threw me down on it. They pinned my arms and shot . . . jabs to my face. I was dragged to the stairway. I grabbed the railing and they wrenched me loose. I was thrown down the first flight of iron steps. Then they kicked me down the other two flights. . . .

Walter Reuther, testifying before the National Labor Relations Board, May 1937.

Unemployed ex-soldiers heaving bricks and stones at Washington, D.C., police in an unsuccessful effort to keep themselves from being evicted from the city in 1932. They and other unemployed veterans had marched to Washington as part of the approximately 15,000-man "Bonus Expeditionary Force," to demand immediate payment of certificates entitling World War I veterans to bonus payments for their military service; the certificates were not scheduled to fall due until 1945. President Hoover called in troops to clear the marchers from Federal property. In 1936 an act of Congress made it possible for veterans to exchange their certificates for cashable bonds. (Wide World Photos)

The jobless throng gathered at 2 P.M. in Detroit. . . At the end of a six-mile walk they encountered a detail of fifty Dearborn police. . . . The police shouted a demand that the rioters turn back. The mob hesitated a minute, and then a woman shoved to the front. "Come on you cowards," she screamed. The mob rushed forward. The police let fly with tear-gas bombs and brought their nightsticks into play, but were thrown back. . . . The guards at the [Ford] plant threw open the gate and called to the marchers to turn back. The mob halted again for a moment, and then the woman who had led them into the first encounter leapt to the front and shouted, "Come on." Two volleys in quick succession from the police met the first advance. Two men in the crowd fell and the mob retreated.

From the New York Herald Tribune, *1932.*

A tall man with a tear-streaked face was marching up and down. "I used to be a hundred-percenter," he said, "but now I'm a Red radical. I had an American flag, but the damned tin soldiers burned it. Now I don't ever want to see a flag again. Give me a gun and I'll go back to Washington."

From Malcolm Cowley and Slater Brown, "The Flight of the Bonus Army," The New Republic, *August 17, 1932.*

the gold standard in September 1931. These developments, in turn, not only wrecked the system of international exchange but also drove international commodity prices to absurd depths. Repercussions were severe in the United States, especially on agricultural prices and on banks with extensive foreign holdings. Some 2,300 banks, with deposits of nearly $1.7 billion, failed in the United States during 1931.

Some of the dimensions of the awful economic catastrophe that befell the American people can be seen when we examine the statistical progress of the depression from 1929 to 1933. During these four years, national income declined from $87.8 billion to $40.2 billion. Per capita income, adjusted for the cost of living, shrank from $681 to $495. More than 100,000 businesses failed, with losses of nearly $3 billion. The number of unemployed, already at 7,000,000 in the autumn of 1931, swelled to about 14,000,000 in the early months of 1933. Gross farm income plummeted from nearly $12 billion in 1929 to $5.3 billion in 1932, while farm debts held up fairly well. Between 1929 and 1933, salaries decreased 40 per cent; dividends, nearly 57 per cent; and manufacturing wages, 60 per cent. Like farmers who had expanded landholdings or bought new equipment during more prosperous years, the debts of those who had bought cars, houses, refrigerators, and the like had to be paid at the original price and interest rate.

The Impact of the Great Depression

The trauma of the Great Depression was in many respects more devastating in its effects than the experience of fighting a great war. Two to three million persons moved from cities back to the country in the hope of being able to scratch a bare living from the soil. Family tensions multiplied as mothers lost their jobs, fathers gave up hope and remained at home all day, and relatives doubled up in houses and apartments. The number of marriages declined sharply, as did the birth rate. The worst result was the grinding poverty that millions had to endure with all its dire consequences. People suffered and some died from malnutrition, lack of clothing, fuel, and proper medical care. Despair came to millions who wanted work, could not find it, and had to accept charity or relief. Hardest hit were blacks ("the last to be hired, the first to be fired"), women workers, and recent immigrants in the large cities.

The foundations of America's two great social institutions—the church and educational facilities—were seriously eroded. Church membership and attendance decreased from 1929 to 1933, and donations to church causes plummeted sharply. Localities and states struggled heroically to save their schools and universities. In general they succeeded until about 1933, when the retreat on the education front turned into full-scale rout. Hardest hit were schools in the rural states, and in Michigan, where staggering unemployment in the automobile industry caused tax revenues to drop especially steeply.

One of the most significant long-term impacts of the depression was the change that it brought in attitudes toward business and government. Loss of popular confidence in the nation's business and financial leadership was almost complete by 1933. Mistrust increased particularly after several congressional investigations revealed the extent to which bankers had misused depositors' funds and manipulated the stock market during the 1920s. Indeed, the major investment bankers, along with President Hoover, became the chief scapegoats of the debacle.

Gradually the great majority of Americans began to look to the federal government for protection. The stage was set first in 1930, when private charitable organizations ran out of money, and further private efforts at alleviation failed. Persons in distress then turned to city and state relief agencies. Local governments struggled heroically during 1931 and 1932, when local governmental relief efforts collapsed for lack of funds. Then the unemployed, and the cities and states as well, turned to the federal government in Washington. The third stage occurred in the mid-1930s, when a majority of Americans finally concluded that the federal government should provide jobs for the unemployed whenever private business proved unable to do so.

Meanwhile, remarkably few people seemed to lose confidence in the capitalistic system. The Communist party made an intensive effort to take advantage of discontent, but it had only 12,000 members in 1932, as compared with 8,000 in 1928. On the other hand, the conviction spread among religious leaders, organized labor, agriculture, and even in the business community itself, that American capitalism had to change drastically. The old system of relatively unregulated free enterprise had to give way to a new system of governmental planning to assure the successful functioning of the economy. Even the United States Chamber of Commerce approved a plan, early in 1933, for business and governmental partnership in planning for full production and employment.

Surprisingly few eruptions of disorder occurred. Unemployed persons rioted in Dearborn, Michigan, in the spring of 1932, and a number of hunger marches took place. Throughout the Middle West, farmers banded together. They threatened to shoot bank and insurance agents who attempted to foreclose farm mortgages, and they went armed to auction sales to buy back their own foreclosed farms at low prices. In Le Mars, Iowa, a large crowd of enraged farmers dragged a foreclosing judge from the bench and beat him into unconsciousness.

Some officials in the Hoover administration feared that serious disorder would result from the descent of the so-called Bonus Expeditionary Force upon Washington in the spring of 1932. About 12,000 to 15,000 veterans and other unemployed persons built a shantytown on Anacostia Flats, just outside Washington. They demanded immediate payment of the soldiers' bonus by the issuance of $2.4 billion in paper money. About half the Bonus Army went home when the Senate refused to approve the bonus bill, but 6,000 to 7,000 remained. On July 28, 1932, a riot occurred, and two persons were killed when bonus marchers invaded a construction area in Washington. The District government, which apparently had been waiting for just such an opportunity, promptly declared that it could not control the situation, and Hoover just as promptly called upon the army to maintain order. General Douglas MacArthur, then Chief of Staff, led an armored force that burned down the shantytown and dispersed its residents with tear gas. Hoover blamed Communists and persons with criminal records for causing the trouble.

3. HOOVER AND THE CRISIS

Hoover and the Failure of Classical Economic Doctrine

The old partisan myth about President Hoover fiddling while the country burned has long since been discredited. He did not exaggerate when he claimed, during the campaign of 1932, that he had labored night and day to turn back the forces of economic disintegration and to restore national confidence. Moreover, he operated not blindly, but in harmony with a consistent philosophy based upon belief in the fundamental goodness of his fellowmen and in the power of democracy to correct social and economic injustices. No man ever came to the presidency with broader experience in world and domestic affairs than Hoover. Yet he failed to meet the challenge posed by the greatest crisis in the history of American capitalism.

Hoover was a prisoner of his own political and economic ideology; he was unable to consider seriously, much less to devise, new remedies to meet an unforeseen catastrophe. While the United States suffered from severe deflation, Hoover blindly followed deflationary policies that only aggravated the condition. The nation might have been set on the road to prosperity by well-coordinated fiscal policies: a large increase of the money supply, substantial relief and public-works programs, and encouragement of private investment. By 1932, concerted moves like these were being recommended by Republican businessmen as well as by Democratic critics of the President. The trouble, in Hoover's mind, was that such a program flagrantly violated sound economic theory. To the embattled Hoover, it seemed to be nothing less than economic heresy.

The questions of a balanced budget and preservation of the gold standard stood as the two most controversial political issues before the country during the last two years of the Hoover administration. An increasing number of leaders in Congress and the country pressed hard for monetary inflation and a huge relief and public-works program. To all such appeals, Hoover replied with stubborn determination. The only thing that could bring real recovery, he insisted, was popular confidence in the soundness of the dollar and business confidence in the integrity of the government. Both would be destroyed by inflation and wasteful expenditures for public works.

Combating the Depression

Hoover's antidepression policies went through two distinct stages. During the first stage of the crisis—the recession of 1929–1931—Hoover tried to mobilize a great national voluntary effort. He recognized the danger signals after the market crash and called business executives and labor leaders to the White House in the autumn of 1929. Hoover won their promise to maintain normal operations without severe wage reductions or strikes. At the same time, he called upon mayors and governors to increase expenditures for public works, and the Federal Farm Board went actively into the market to maintain farm prices.

For a time it seemed that the nation would get through the slump without major difficulties. When employers began to cut production (the industrial index fell from 96.3 in April 1930, to 84.6 in October of the same year), Hoover appointed a Committee for Unemployment Relief and requested local and private agencies to increase their relief assistance. The economy seemed, briefly, to be recovering. Indices of production, payrolls, and employment showed faint signs of recovery between February and June of 1931, although most had turned down again by June, even before international events aggravated the situation.

A storm of unprecedented magnitude broke over the world in the summer of

1931. It followed the breakdown of the world economy occasioned by the financial crisis in central Europe and the British abandonment of the gold standard. Hoover moved as quickly as he could to obtain a moratorium on war debts and reparations, but in vain. The most immediate consequence of the international breakdown of 1931 was the withdrawal of about $1.5 billion of foreign-owned gold from American banks. This, in addition to the dumping of securities on the New York Stock Exchange and large losses abroad by American banks, exaggerated further the dire crisis in the United States.

Hoover still hoped for miracles through voluntary efforts and called upon bankers to meet the crisis by cooperation. But the strain on private resources was too great, and the President reluctantly set to work to devise a federal program for recovery.

The chief antidepression weapon in Hoover's arsenal was the Reconstruction Finance Corporation (RFC), chartered by Congress on January 16, 1932, with a capital of $500 million and authority to borrow up to an additional $1.5 billion. It went to work at once to save banks, railroads, and other financial institutions. The RFC earmarked no funds for small businesses or for consumers who faced loss of their homes, possessions, health, and in some cases, their lives; but the RFC did protect most of the nation's large banks from closing. The Glass-Steagall Act of February 27, 1932, permitted Federal Reserve Banks to expand the currency and released about $1 billion in gold to meet continuing foreign withdrawals. A Federal Home Loan Bank Act made new capital available to building and loan associations, while the capital of Federal Land Banks was also increased. These measures brought new confidence and helped to save the financial structure from total collapse in 1932.

Meanwhile, the administration's efforts on the agricultural front were less successful. The Federal Farm Board was simply powerless to maintain prices after they dropped sharply on world markets in the summer of 1931. Wheat fell in price from 67 cents a bushel in 1929 to 39 cents in 1932; cotton, from 17 to 7 cents a pound; corn, from 80 to 32 cents a bushel. The Federal Farm Board tried to support prices through open market purchases and voluntary reductions in farm production. Both efforts failed miserably because the money made available for purchases caused only a small dent in the huge supplies offered for sale. Agricultural production actually increased in 1931, and the board had lost some $354 million in futile purchasing operations by 1932. The board confessed its impotence in December 1932 and urged Congress to institute an effective system to limit acreage and production as the only solution to the farm problem. Meanwhile, millions of Americans had gone hungry, and untold thousands of persons literally starved or died from diseases associated with malnutrition because they could not pay for food.

Fierce struggles took place in Washington during 1932 over relief and monetary policies. Progressives and inflationists in Congress combined in a nonpartisan bloc to demand immediate payment of the veterans' bonus by the issuance of paper money. They also urged adoption of a federal direct relief program. Hoover retained sufficient support in Congress to block these proposals. On relief, however, he did compromise by authorizing the RFC to lend an inadequate $300 million to the states to tide the unemployed over the winter. An additional $1.5 billion went to the states for self-liquidating public works such as airports, bridges, and tunnels. But these measures were mere palliatives for a terrible situation.

4. CHANGE OF COMMAND

The Political Impact of the Great Depression

The Great Depression was one of those profound internal upheavals that have fundamentally changed political alignments on several occasions in American history. One-party dominance has been the rule in American politics, and, except for brief interludes, the dominant party has been unseated only by some great convulsion. The Federalists gave way to the Jeffersonian Republicans because of the population movement to the West and the spread of democratic ideas. A Jeffersonian-Jacksonian Democratic coalition held sway until it was disrupted by the slavery controversy. The Republican party won supremacy during the great crisis of the Union, and Democrats only intermittently challenged Republican rule in the 1880s and 1890s. Populism and Bryanism again polarized American politics and further fastened control by the Republican party on the country from 1896 to about 1930. National Republican leadership (as contrasted with regional leadership, which was often in conflict with national party policies) rode high during the 1920s. Hoover coasted into the presidency by claiming that the Republican business leadership had brought permanent prosperity to the country. As the depression deepened, many Americans inevitably lost confidence in a President who had so closely identified himself with the business and financial classes, and with the party which bore responsibility for the end of relative prosperity.

The loss of confidence moved at about the same speed as the depression itself. The mid-term election of 1930 saw the election of the first Democratic Congress since 1916, but the results constituted no landslide. The Democrats controlled the Seventy-second Congress, which met in December 1931, by a bare majority in both houses, and some members of that majority held economic views as conservative as Hoover's. Extensive loss of confidence in the Hoover administration and in the Republican party did not begin until the autumn of 1931. The conviction then grew that Hoover was more interested in saving banks, railroads, and corporations than he was in saving people. Hoover became the object not merely of popular dislike, but also of contempt. Shanty-towns, erected by the poor on the edges of great cities, were named "Hoovervilles," while horse-drawn broken down automobiles were called "Hoovercarts." These terms were not altogether undeserved. Fortunately for his personal safety in 1931–1932, Hoover only later declared that thousands of Americans gave up good jobs during that period for the more lucrative one of selling apples on city sidewalks for up to five cents each.

The Democratic Fight for the White House

Democratic presidential fever rose rapidly between 1930 and 1932, as it became obvious that almost any breathing Democrat probably would win in 1932. Favorite sons abounded in number, but the decisive struggle for party leadership was between former Governor Alfred E. Smith and Governor Franklin Delano Roosevelt of New York.

Smith, desperately eager for a second nomination and popular vindication, had the support of the Tammany organization in New York and of Democratic organizations in New Jersey, Massachusetts, and other eastern states. However, the odds were heavily against Smith. Enemies resented his stand against prohibition and his emphasis upon the religious issue in the campaign of 1928. A greater liability for the former Democratic standard-bearer was the fact that he had never developed any strong support in rural areas. Furthermore, the Democratic party was not yet quite free of religious bigotry, and politicians could point out accurately, if not sincerely, that they had given Smith a chance in 1928 and that he had failed to win.

Smith's possibilities for a second nomination were imperiled most of all because the Democratic party now had another leader, Franklin D. Roosevelt. Roosevelt had suffered a severe attack of polio in 1921 but had gradually fought his way back to partial recovery by 1928. Meanwhile, he had maintained his political connections and friendships, without, however, engaging in any of the controversies that disrupted the Democratic party during the 1920s.

Roosevelt ran for Governor of New York in 1928 at Smith's urgent request in order to strengthen the national Democratic ticket in the state. Roosevelt was elected by a narrow margin in the face of the Hoover landslide and won reelection in 1930 by the largest majority ever given a gubernatorial candidate in the

Governor Franklin D. Roosevelt of New York, Democratic presidential nominee, outlines his plan for farm relief while campaigning in Topeka, Kansas. In the election of 1932, Roosevelt carried most of the agricultural West and South. (Wide World Photos)

history of New York. The magic of that majority at once made Roosevelt the leading contender for the Democratic presidential nomination in 1932. So successful were his managers, led on by James A. Farley and Louis M. Howe, who garnered support in the South, Middle West, and West that, by the early months of 1932, the Democratic preconvention contest had become a struggle of Roosevelt against the field.

A riotous, confident Democratic national convention opened in Chicago on June 27, 1932. Roosevelt had a majority of the delegates, but not the two-thirds majority then necessary for a Democratic presidential nomination. For the first three ballots, it seemed as if Smith's managers had succeeded in creating a solid anti-Roosevelt bloc that could prevent the New York Governor's nomination. The deadlock was broken on the fourth ballot, when John Nance Garner of Texas, Speaker of the House of Representatives and a strong favorite son, threw his support to Roosevelt in return for the vice-presidential nomination. Roosevelt disagreed with the conservative Garner on almost every major issue, but the vice-presidency seemed a small price to pay for almost certain election as President, especially because it removed Garner from the much more powerful position of Speaker of the House.

Roosevelt electrified the country by flying to Chicago to accept the nomination in person. He promised a "new deal" for the American people if they sent him to the White House, but neither his speech nor the Democratic platform, which he endorsed item by item, gave any promise of fundamental changes in federal policies. The platform demanded repeal of the Eighteenth Amendment. It promised to cut federal expenditures by 25 per cent and to balance the budget. It demanded the removal of government from all fields of private enterprise, "except where necessary to develop public works and natural resources." The Democratic platform also promised that the party would reform the banking system and maintain a sound currency "at all hazards." It proposed to lend money to the states to provide relief for the unemployed, and it approved social security legislation by the states. Finally, the platform promised tariff reduction and effective crop controls to restore agricultural purchasing power. Roosevelt had arranged to have this rather conservative document prepared by Wilsonians like Senator Cordell Hull of Tennessee and former Attorney General A. Mitchell Palmer, both of whom had been congressmen and Wilson supporters in 1912. Palmer had declared publicly that Wilson could have solved the nation's problems more satisfactorily than any live candidate in 1932.

Meanwhile, the Republicans had assembled in a gloomy national convention. They could not repudiate a President in office, so they duly renominated Hoover on the first ballot. The Republican platform, after it commended the President for his fight against the depression, approved federal loans to the states for relief, repeal of the Eighteenth Amendment, and cooperative efforts by farmers to limit production. On fiscal policy, the platform promised economy, defense of the gold standard, and reform of the banking system.

The Presidential Campaign and Election of 1932

Both Hoover and Roosevelt campaigned strenuously, but the contest was an unequal one. Actually, the two men said much the same things. Their main differences were over agricultural and public power policies. Hoover made it plain that he would not budge from his earlier opposition to federal crop controls and development of regional hydroelectric projects, which Roosevelt strongly supported.

The two candidates, however, *sounded* very different. While Hoover talked mournfully about his battles on a thousand fronts to stem the depression tide, Roosevelt exuded confidence in his ability to make things come out right, quickly. Moreover, Roosevelt hit hard at Hoover's alleged callousness about the suffering of the poor and promised that he would do anything to keep people from starving. Hoover's chances, and his public image, were also severely damaged by his use of military force to disperse the Bonus Army.

Roosevelt could hardly have failed to win in this unhappy year of depression. Also, his active, nationwide campaign convinced voters that he was physically fit for the burdens of the presidency and undoubtedly swelled the Democratic vote on election day. Hoover retained extensive business and upper-class support and did well in industrial centers that depended on tariff protection. He carried Maine, New Hampshire, Vermont, Connecticut, Delaware, and Pennsylvania, and won nearly 16,000,000 popular and fifty-nine electoral votes. Roosevelt swept the large cities and the rural areas outside New England, carried the rest of the states, and won nearly 23 million popular and 472 electoral votes. Democrats also elected majorities of 191 and twenty-two in the House of Representatives and Senate, respectively, in the Seventy-third Congress, which would sit from 1933 through 1934. The Socialists made their strongest effort since 1920, but their candidate, Norman Thomas, polled only 885,000 votes. The Communist candidate, William Z. Foster, trailed far behind with only 103,000 votes.

The final session of the Seventy-second Congress from December 1932 to March 1933, proved to be the last for "lame ducks." These were members of the House and Senate who had been defeated for reelection in November but continued to make laws in the three months still left before their successors took office. The Twentieth Amendment to the Constitution, sponsored by Senator George W. Norris of Nebraska, was ratified in January 1933. It provided that henceforth the Congress elected in November should begin its session on the third of the following January, and that the President should be inaugurated on January 20 instead of on March 4.

SUGGESTED READINGS

The surveys of the period cited in the previous two chapters end with accounts of the Hoover administration. The best accounts of that unfortunate era are Harris G. Warren, *Herbert Hoover and the Great Depression* (1959), and Albert U. Romasco, *The Poverty of Abundance* (1965). The administration is defended in Ray L. Wilbur and A. M. Hyde, *The Hoover Policies* (1937), Burner, *Hoover* (1979), already cited, and, in Herbert Hoover, *Memoirs: The Great Depression, 1929–1941* (1952). The *Memoirs* will be the most satisfactory introduction to Hoover's life until an adequate biography has been written. As of now, Burner's comes closest to appropriate

thoroughness and balance; but basically it remains a defense, with some important gaps in the negative aspects of Hoover's career and administration. For correction at a crucial point in history see Eliot A. Rosen, *Hoover, Roosevelt, and the Brains Trust* (1977), and Jordan A. Schwartz, *The Interregnum of Despair: Hoover, Congress and the Depression* (1970).

John K. Galbraith, *The Great Crash* (1955), is a superb account of that tragedy, written with a sparkling wit and a fine knowledge of the foibles of American businessmen. Thomas Wilson, *Fluctuations in Income and Employment* (1948), written from a business-cycle approach, and Milton Friedman and Anna J. Schwartz, *The Great Contraction, 1929–1933* (1965), a monetary history, are superior books, although Friedman's monetary theories should be read critically. The impact of the depression on American society is vividly portrayed in Bernstein, *The Lean Years*, already cited, David A. Shannon, ed., *The Great Depression* (1960), a book of poignant documents; C. Bird, *The Invisible Scar* (1966); Dixon Wecter, *The Age of the Great Depres-* sion (1948); and Frederick Lewis Allen, *Since Yesterday* (1940).

Good accounts of the campaign and election of 1932, in addition to the surveys already mentioned, appear in Frank Freidel, *Franklin D. Roosevelt: The Triumph* (1956); James McGregor Burns, *Roosevelt: The Lion and the Fox* (1956); Rexford G. Tugwell, *The Democratic Roosevelt* (1957); and William E. Leuchtenburg, *Franklin D. Roosevelt and the New Deal* (1963).

CHAPTER 30
FRANKLIN D. ROOSEVELT AND THE NEW DEAL

1. LAUNCHING THE NEW DEAL

Franklin D. Roosevelt and the Flowering of the Progressive Movement

An exciting era in American history began when Franklin D. Roosevelt took the oath of office shortly after noon on March 4, 1933. It commenced with a history-making special session of Congress, which in one hundred days laid the framework of a New Deal aimed to combat the depression. It ended in the victory of the United States and its allies over dictatorships that had all but enslaved the peoples of Europe and Asia.

The man who led the American people from depression into prosperity and from near defeat in war to global victory was born at Hyde Park, New York, on January 30, 1882. He received a proper patrician education at Groton and Harvard without revealing special promise or ambition. After a half-hearted study and practice of law, Roosevelt entered politics as an anti-Tammany Democrat. He won election to the New York State Senate in 1910 and fought Tammany and supported Woodrow Wilson for the Democratic presidential nomination. Wilson rewarded Roosevelt (and took advantage of the Roosevelt name) by appointing him Assistant Secretary of the Navy in 1913.

The young Roosevelt showed talent as an able administrator, but he was extremely ambitious and somewhat disloyal both to President Wilson and to his genial chief, Secretary of the Navy Josephus Daniels. The rising young politician made his peace with the Tammany organization, and he received the Democratic vice-presidential nomination in 1920 largely because he was the leading New York Wilsonian acceptable to Tammany.

Roosevelt can best be described politically as an old-fashioned democrat. A reporter once asked him to describe his political philosophy. "What do you mean?" Roosevelt replied. "Well, are you a Socialist?" the reporter asked. "No," Roosevelt said. "Are you a Communist?" the reporter went on. "Of course not," Roosevelt replied. "Are you a capitalist?" the reporter persisted. "No," Roosevelt answered. "Well, Mr. President, then what are you?" the reporter asked in puzzlement. "Why, I'm a Christian and a democrat," Roosevelt replied.

Hoover also was a Christian and a democrat. What set Roosevelt off from his predecessor was the fact that Hoover was trapped by his political and economic ideology, while Roosevelt possessed virtually no ideology. Hoover believed so strongly in voluntary cooperation, limited government, and the efficacy of classical economic doctrine that it proved impossible for him to cope successfully with the human problems raised by the Great Depression. Roosevelt, on the other hand, had no strong commitment to any particular method. This open-mindedness—some have called it lack of principle—made him willing and even eager to experiment. For example, although Roosevelt held an old-fashioned belief in sound money and a balanced budget, he tried new paths of

Hoover shaking hands with his successor, Franklin D. Roosevelt, just prior to the President-elect's inauguration. In his inaugural address, Roosevelt promised the American people: "This great nation will endure as it has endured, will revive and prosper. So, first of all, let me assert my firm belief that the only thing we have to fear is fear itself." (Wide World Photos)

economic policy without hesitation when conventional methods failed. Furthermore, Roosevelt, like his fifth cousin and uncle-in-law, Theodore, believed that government should play the leading role in organizing and leading the American economy and society.

Roosevelt was the greatest political campaigner in American history. He ran for office or nomination to office eleven times. He succeeded in nine tries and never suffered defeat in a general election when he ran on his own. He remains, not only the most successful politician in American history, but also one of the strongest leaders whom the United States has ever produced. These attributes did not exist accidentally, for Roosevelt, like his two great teachers— Theodore Roosevelt and Woodrow Wilson—believed in strong and responsible leadership as the most indispensable force in democracy. He believed in a strong President who alone spoke for all people, coordinated various departments of the government, and directed foreign affairs. He mastered the techniques of leadership as few Presidents in American history have ever succeeded in doing. Roosevelt also developed a keen understanding of public opinion and a canny sense of timing. He usually gave irresistible leadership to his party in Congress, precisely because he succeeded so well in interpreting the contradictions, nuances, and trends in public opinion. He also established direct communication with the rank and file of the people through addresses, press conferences, and the radio talks to the American people that he called "fireside chats."

Roosevelt possessed faults, of course. He was deficient as an administrator because he could not bear to dismiss a loyal but incompetent friend, and also because he carefully never permitted his subordinates to acquire much power. Some of his most important programs may have failed because he deliberately divided authority. He used his charm so successfully that he gave the impression (not altogether mistaken) of enjoying the game of manipulating people. His lack of any consistent guide to policies and methods served as a source of weakness as well as of strength, for it led him to place unmerited faith in experimentation for its own sake. This fault was exaggerated by Roosevelt's diffuse intellectual training, which sometimes made it difficult for him to evaluate various explanations of complex economic problems. Whether these defects proved so marring as to overbalance Roosevelt's positive personal qualities will, of course, remain forever a matter of personal opinion.

Roosevelt revitalized the progressive movement. He not only revived progressive faith in democracy; he also restructured the entire political economy of the United States so that the government could achieve the main goals of the progressive movement. These goals were protection for the underprivileged and economic security for all people. Roosevelt carried these policies much closer to their inevitable conclusion in a welfare state than Wilson or Theodore Roosevelt could possibly have done, given the political attitudes of Americans during their presidencies.

Prelude to the New Deal

The policies of the Roosevelt administration during its first year in office were influenced tremendously by the unique economic situation when Roosevelt was inaugurated. The history of the next eight years would have been very different if the worst single economic catastrophe in the history of the United

States—the banking panic of the early months of 1933—had not made emergency action of a drastic kind appear to be absolutely necessary.

The panic which occurred was the product of a chain reaction of irrational fear. One contributing factor was the widespread suspicion that Roosevelt, in spite of his campaign assurances, would abolish the gold standard and inflate the currency. The result of this suspicion became particularly visible during the week of January 18, 1933. Thousands of Americans hastened to withdraw bank deposits, purchase gold or tangible property, and sent their money abroad. Withdrawals of currency totaled $1.7 billion between February 8 and March 3, while the excess gold reserves of the Federal Reserve System declined from $1.5 billion in January to $400 million in March. Bank after bank was forced to close its doors, either permanently or temporarily. In order to afford relief, governors in various states began to declare bank holidays, that is, they closed the banks in their states for various periods in order to stop the withdrawals. By March 3, 1933, general closings had occurred in twenty-three states. During the early morning hours of March 4, the remainder of the governors followed suit under pressure from Treasury officials.

All banks were closed as Roosevelt rode to take the presidential oath. The economic life of the country was literally grinding to a halt, and the United States faced an economic paralysis such as no other civilized nation—except perhaps Germany—had ever confronted during peacetime. In accepting the nomination for President, Roosevelt had declared, "I pledge myself to a New Deal for the American people." Now, on March 4, 1933, in words of confidence he pledged himself to a dynamic program of action for the general welfare. Then Roosevelt asked the people to join him in a "national consecration" to the work of restoring prosperity through united and unselfish effort. Calling for faith and courage, he exclaimed:

This great nation will endure as it has endured, will revive and prosper. So, first of all, let me assert my firm belief that the only thing we have to fear is fear itself. . . . We face the arduous days that lie before us in the warm courage of national unity. . . . We do not distrust the future of essential democracy.

The President's Advisers

No President before in American history could call upon so many competent advisers as could Franklin Roosevelt when he took office. No President ever needed so many, so immense and complex were the problems that Roosevelt faced. In planning his early program, Roosevelt turned especially to Professors Raymond Moley, Adolf A. Berle, Jr., and Rexford G. Tugwell of Columbia University—the original "Brain Trust." Later, important advisers included Harry L. Hopkins, a former social worker, and Professor Felix Frankfurter of the Harvard Law School, whom Roosevelt appointed to the Supreme Court. Judge Samuel I. Rosenman served as Roosevelt's chief speechwriter and also wrote one of the best memoirs of the New Deal period. No previous administration drew so heavily upon the resources of American universities. Professorial experts, appointed to dozens of commissions, did much of the work involved in preparing for congressional action the hundreds of laws enacted between 1933 and 1940.

Several members of the Roosevelt cabinet also helped to shape the President's policies. Secretary of State Cordell Hull of Tennessee, a strong believer in inter-American cooperation and unshackled world trade, obtained substantial freedom in making foreign policy, especially before the Second World War erupted. Secretary of the Interior Harold L. Ickes, a follower of Theodore Roosevelt in 1912, revived the old crusade for conservation of natural resources. Secretary of Agriculture Henry A. Wallace of Iowa, a former Republican, carried on the work that his father had done as Secretary of Agriculture under Harding and Coolidge. Postmaster General James A. Farley skillfully dispensed the patronage, managed campaigns, and gave sound political advice. Secretary of Labor Frances Perkins, the first woman to hold a cabinet seat, was perhaps the most important person in the administration, aside from Roosevelt, in shaping labor policies and planning for economic security. Secretary of the Treasury Henry Morgenthau, Jr., Roosevelt's neighbor in upstate New York, exercised influence far beyond his own department. The budget director, Lewis Douglas, an advocate of balanced budgets (especially, by use of sales taxes, which struck particularly hard at the poor), also enjoyed access to the new President's ear. The most striking characteristics of the group around Roosevelt were creativity and variety—within a certain range. Roosevelt's advisers included Republicans and Democrats, conservatives and progressives, but very few who could, by any stretch of a reasonable person's imagination, be called "radical." Among those persons who influenced Roosevelt, probably only Tugwell, who favored some permanent type of centralized governmental planning, could be placed in that category. And Tugwell had not been considered especially radical among the Farmer-Labor supporters of La Follette in 1924.

2. THE FIRST NEW DEAL

The Concept of the Two New Deals

One of the oldest and most useful concepts for interpreting the New Deal era is the suggestion that there were in fact two New Deals, that is, two separate stages in legislative and administrative policies.

According to the "two New Deals" interpretation, the first New Deal operated during 1933 and 1934. It was based upon a coalition of all classes and interests that had united behind Roosevelt's leadership to fight the depression. During this period, the administration worked on the assumption that recovery could be achieved quickly and easily, mainly by the continuation and expansion of the Hoover policies.

Legislation and administrative action would strengthen the banking structure and clean up the securities markets, but all such activities would be aimed at securing private ownership and making financial institutions more secure in the future. The dollar would be devalued in order to bring prices up to a normal level; however, devaluation would not be accompanied by any massive countercyclical moves, such as large-scale deficit spending. Business and industry would be given a relatively free hand to work out their own salvation under federal supervision. Labor would be given new protections, but mainly through federal action for minimum wages and maximum hours, not through decisive governmental support of collective bargaining. As for relief, all that was needed was to extend further assistance to the states and to stimulate the construction industry with a federal public works program. Once recovery had set in, the federal government would get out of the relief business altogether. Finally, agriculture would be put on its feet by restriction of output through production controls.

Parts of this program worked well. However, according to the "two New Deals" interpretation, the first New Deal was in deep trouble by the middle of 1934. Recovery did not occur as planned. Various mass movements gave evidence that the first New Deal had failed to improve the lot or to assuage the discontent of workers, old people, small farmers, tenant farmers, and the unemployed. Then the first New Deal coalition fell apart in the spring of 1934, when the business classes deserted Roosevelt.

The first New Deal came to an end in the off-year election of 1934, according to the "two New Deals" scenario, when the voters repudiated conservative policies and sent a huge Democratic majority to Congress. The new members were very responsive to such groups as organized labor, the unemployed, and impoverished farmers. Roosevelt, who read the auguries shrewdly, veered sharply leftward and set about to launch a second New Deal to satisfy the demands of the new Left-of-Center coalition.

The "two New Deals" interpretation contains some major deficiencies. By magnifying the changes that did occur between 1933 and 1935, the interpretation gives the impression that the two New Deals were largely separated. Actually, the legislation of 1935–1938 was to a considerable extent a natural outgrowth of earlier programs. For example, the Banking and Holding Company acts of 1935 belong chronologically to the second New Deal but were, in fact, culminations of reforms originated early in the New Deal. Planning for social security legislation began soon after Roosevelt took office, but the complicated bills and payment schedules took time to prepare. The "two New Deals" interpretation also implies too strongly that Roosevelt, the master politician, deliberately tailored the entire second New Deal program in order to retain the support of segments of his new coalition. In many cases the coalition pushed him, rather than the other way around. For example, Roosevelt and Perkins did not support the most important labor legislation of the period – the Wagner Act – until the bill was about to be passed by Congress. Finally, the "two New Deals" interpretation incorrectly implies that the first New Deal was conservative, the second New Deal, progressive. Actually, no such sharp delineation existed. Yet the interpretation that assumes the existence of two New Deals is correct in its major outlines and provides helpful guidelines through the complexities of the Roosevelt era.

Financial Reinforcement and Reform

Roosevelt's first important move proved to be popular, effective, and dramatic. On March 6, he issued an order which closed all banks in the country for a four-day period. Then he summoned Congress to meet in extra session on March 9. On that same day, after four hours of debate, both houses passed the administration's Emergency Banking bill by overwhelming majorities. This measure approved Roosevelt's actions and authorized the Secretary of the Treasury to investigate the condition of all banks. The Secretary could permit them to reopen for business at his discretion.

Treasury officials went to work at once. By mid-summer, three fourths of the banks, holding 94 per cent of all deposits, were again in business with additional help from the RFC. Confidence in these institutions returned immediately. During the first month alone of the new administration, more than $1 billion flowed back to the banks.

Congress followed by adopting the Glass-Steagall Act, a banking reform measure. It increased the Federal Reserve Board's control over the credit system; required commercial banks to divorce themselves from their investment affiliates, which in some cases had been speculating with their depositor's money; and, at the insistence of southern and western Democrats, established the Federal Deposit Insurance Corporation (FDIC). The FDIC insured deposits in member banks up to $5 thousand (later increased to $100 thousand). All member banks of the Federal Reserve System were required to belong to the FDIC, and others could join if they met certain requirements. The American Bankers' Association denounced the FDIC as "unsound, unjust, and dangerous"; but the epidemic of bank failures ceased as soon as it became law.

To save embattled homeowners, Congress established the Home Owners Loan Corporation (HOLC) on June 13, 1933. During the next three years the HOLC lent more than $3 billion to some 1,000,000 homeowners. It turned back the tide of foreclosures for the first time since the onset of the depression.

There was considerable sentiment in Congress and the country for governmental ownership of banks and other financial institutions. Roosevelt spurned all such suggestions and restored and actually strengthened private ownership in the financial field. As Raymond Moley observed in 1939, "The policies which vanquished the bank crisis were thoroughly conservative policies. The sole departure from convention lay in the swiftness and boldness with which they were carried out."

Devaluation

Swiftness and boldness were also required to meet the problem of deflation. To use a somewhat homely metaphor, the American economic machine had four flat tires: First, purchasing power had declined tremendously, and, for millions of the unemployed, it had disappeared altogether. Second, prices had fallen because of a huge surplus of all kinds of goods and services compared to available money and buyers. Third, exports had plummeted for the same reason, plus the erection of the nationalistic barriers mentioned earlier. Fourth, debtors were finding it increasingly difficult to meet their obligations.

If the administration devalued the currency, inflationists argued, wages, prices, purchasing power, and exports would all rise, and it would be easier to pay debts. Then trade of all kinds could proceed at a more normal pace. The tires needed some inflation, but how much? That was the difficult question. Inflationists in Congress—probably a majority of that body—demanded the printing of billions in paper money. Economists argued that the answer lay in taking the country off the domestic gold standard and in sufficiently reducing the gold value of the dollar in international exchange to bring the domestic price level back to that of 1926.

Roosevelt turned a deaf ear to the pleas of paper-money inflationists and again adopted the more cautious course. On March 6, 1933, he took the country off the domestic gold standard, in the expectation that the dollar would fall precipitately in value on international exchanges. By October 1933, the dollar had declined in value by about 30 per cent, and domestic prices had risen by 19 per cent. This was not enough inflation to restore the price level of 1926, and Roosevelt instructed the RFC to purchase gold at increased prices, which resulted in further devaluation of the dollar. Finally, on January 31, 1934, Roosevelt used authority granted earlier by Congress to set the price of gold at $35 an ounce and the gold content of the dollar at 59.06 per cent of its pre-1933 value. According to the calculations of the commodity-dollar theorists, this action should have restored prices to their 1926 level.

The whole experiment in devaluation failed almost completely from beginning to end. Prices rose slightly as a result of Roosevelt's first steps in 1933, and because of anticipation of such policies; but they did not rise significantly in 1934 because devaluation was not accompanied by a significant increase in the domestic money supply and bank credits. Roosevelt put so much trust in the simple device of dollar devaluation that he intentionally wrecked all hopes of achieving international monetary cooperation toward stabilization at the World Economic Conference, which met in London in June 1933. Roosevelt recognized his mistake and approved conclusion of an agreement with Great Britain and France for international currency stabilization in 1936.

Protecting Investors

Meanwhile, Congress moved to protect the public from fraud in the purchase and sale of stocks and other securities. A Truth-in-Securities Act of 1933 compelled underwriters and brokers to furnish complete information about the true value of securities being offered for sale. The Securities Exchange Act of 1934 created the Securities and Exchange Commission (SEC). It was given power to license and regulate stock exchanges, to require basic data on securities listed, to oversee investment counselors, and to bring action against persons engaged in fraud. Similar regulations were later applied to the commodity exchanges.

The Completion of Financial Reform

Two important measures brought the New Deal's efforts at financial reorganization and reform to fruition. The first was the Banking Act of 1935 — the only fundamental revision of the Federal Reserve Act since its adoption in 1913. The Banking Act of 1935 was the kind of measure that Bryanites and agrarians had urged the Wilson administration to adopt. It concentrated immense power in a reorganized central board called the Board of Governors of the Federal Reserve System. The new board now had direct and complete control over interest rates, reserve requirements, and the open market operations of the Federal Reserve Banks. In addition, the measure created new classes of securities and commercial paper against which Federal Reserve notes might be issued. Populist demands for tight public control over the banking system and the money supply were finally satisfied.

The second measure was the Holding Company Act of 1935, the outcome of a long fight by Roosevelt to break up electric power holding companies that had pyramided company upon company in often irrational and uneconomical systems. Roosevelt wanted to destroy holding companies altogether in the field of electric power. The Holding Company Act, adopted over the bitter resistance and frenzied propaganda of the utilities companies, gave Roosevelt virtually everything that he wanted. It compelled the dissolution of large holding companies within five years, but permitted small holding companies, which controlled integrated operating systems, to survive. The measure also subjected the financial operations of holding companies to the control of the SEC.

Farm Relief and Recovery

The condition of American farmers had fallen to such a desperate state by the early months of 1933 that hardly anyone questioned whether the federal government should move swiftly to relieve agrarian distress; they disagreed only about how to proceed. The administration first acted by consolidating all farm credit agencies into a Farm Credit Administration. Large quantities of new credit became available to farmers through an Emergency Farm Mortgage Act. In addition, Congress, in 1934, adopted the Frazier-Lemke Farm Bankruptcy Act, which enabled farmers to recover foreclosed property on easy terms.

Such measures, of course, did not strike at the root of the problem—production in excess of consumption—that drove prices lower and lower, until by 1933 the income of farmers had fallen 60 per cent below that of 1929. Roosevelt said that he would approve any reasonable crop-control measure that farm leaders could agree upon. That bill was the Agricultural Adjustment Act, written by Secretary Wallace in conference with farm leaders, and approved by Roosevelt on May 12, 1933. The Act's objective was to raise the real income of farmers to the level that they had enjoyed in the five-year period, 1914–1919, when farm prices were supposed to have been at parity, or equality, with prices of manufactured goods. The measure assumed that the chief cause of low prices was overproduction. Hence it aimed to reduce surpluses by limiting production of major staples, milk, and meat by various devices. For example, the Department of Agriculture persuaded cotton growers to plow under about 30 per cent of their growing crop, or the equivalent of 4,000,000 bales of cotton. The Agricultural Adjustment Administration (AAA), established by the Act of May 12, 1933, bought 220,000 sows and 6,000,000 pigs and slaughtered them. For reducing their output, farmers received cash payments from the Treasury which were financed by a processing tax on industries that prepared raw agricultural products for the market. This farm program differed from the Mc-Nary-Haugen plan in that the latter invoked the government's help in disposing of farm product surpluses to a hungry world population, while the AAA sought to prevent such surpluses at their source.

A severe drought in the Middle West and Southwest cooperated with the AAA in reducing farm production in those sections. When cotton and tobacco farmers poured fertilizer on reduced acres and produced large crops in 1933, Congress imposed direct production controls on both staples in 1934. Altogether, the administration's credit assistance, the AAA, bad weather, and international economic recovery worked a quick miracle. Net farm income rose 250 per cent between 1932 and 1935, and the farm mortgage load decreased some $1.5 billion during the same period. Moreover, the principle of equality for agriculture was not only written into American law, but also was nearly achieved. The ratio of prices that the farmer paid for manufactured products to the prices that he received for his products rose from 58 per cent in 1932 to 88 per cent in 1935. To be sure, the AAA program contained major deficiencies.

For example, it benefited mainly large farmers and planters, and largely ignored tenant farmers and sharecroppers. However, the AAA saved the great bulk of American farm owners from bankruptcy through purposeful planning. That was no small achievement.

An Experiment in Industrial Recovery

Industry was in about as desperate a situation as were agriculture and banking when Roosevelt took the helm in 1933. Millions of men and women, who with their families made up fully a third of the population, were out of work. How to bring about business recovery and to employ this army of jobless workers posed a tremendous problem for which no one was prepared when the New Deal was launched.

Indeed, Roosevelt and his advisers had no specific plan at all for industrial recovery in early March 1933. Spokesmen of organized labor in Congress, led by Senator Hugo L. Black of Alabama, pressed for a measure to limit hours of work in industry to thirty a week. Convinced that the Black bill would impede recovery, Roosevelt and his advisers hastily sought an alternative. They worked it out in conference with the United States Chamber of Commerce in the form of the National Industrial Recovery Act (NIRA), approved on June 16, 1933.

This measure created the National Recovery Administration (NRA), headed by Hugh S. Johnson, to establish so-called code authorities for various branches of industry. These groups, composed of representatives of industry, the government, unions, and consumers, were empowered to prepare codes (reminiscent of those less official codes established under the jurisdiction of Hoover's Commerce Department) to establish production goals and determine fair prices for their particular industries. In addition, the code authorities were directed to eliminate child labor and to establish minimum wages and maximum hours for workers. The codes were to be exempt from the antitrust laws and were to have the force of law once they were approved by the President. At Secretary Perkins' insistence, Section 7a, which affirmed labor's right to organize and to bargain collectively, was inserted into the bill at the last minute. Also incorporated at the end was Title II, which appropriated $3.3 billion for a Public Works Administration (PWA) under Harold L. Ickes to stimulate the construction industry. The administration expected PWA expenditures to provide much of the consumer buying power to purchase the goods whose prices NRA would raise.

Johnson went about his job with tremendous enthusiasm. He prepared a blanket code for all industry until specific codes could be worked out, held NRA parades, and devised an emblem — the Blue Eagle — which employers who cooperated could display. Then code authorities, working from the autumn of 1933 through 1934, prepared 557 basic and 208 supplementary codes which covered every phase of trade and industry in the United States. Partly because of the administration's haste, large corporations, which gained disproportionate influence within the code authorities, set standards, wages, and prices which best suited their interests. Hundreds of codes, indicative of the attitudes of both businessmen and New Deal authorities toward women, contained provisions for lower wages for females than for males who did exactly the same work. Code makers rationalized this disparity by claiming that most women workers represented a second family income because their husbands worked, too.

Bitter opposition to the NRA soon developed. Small businessmen and manufacturers were in revolt by the spring of 1934 because, they said, the code authorities were dominated by big business. Although these allegations contained a good deal of truth, many of the small employers also resented the fact that the NRA had deprived them of their traditional competitive weapons of low wages, long hours, and cutthroat prices. Section 7a was widely disregarded, except in a few major industries, as an unnecessary concession to labor. Large corporations proved difficult to police, and they objected to governmental intervention in their labor relations. When the NRA attempted to discipline violators of the codes, the courts became jammed with cases, and enforcement broke down completely. Johnson, worn out from arguments, grew increasingly erratic and authoritarian and resigned under heavy fire. Roosevelt then abolished the office of administrator and substituted a National Recovery Board in September 1934. Meanwhile, the cautious Ickes, fearful of wasting governmental funds, spent virtually none of the PWA's $3.3 billion to fuel consumption under the NRA. Therefore, the country suffered from increased prices when few consumers received new jobs at sufficiently high incomes to buy the higher priced goods. Eventually, when sites for major construction had been carefully selected, and architects had completed their tasks, the PWA spent heavily. However, that occurred much too late to save the NRA.

The NRA flag being unfurled atop the R.C.A. building. Employers who agreed to follow the codes set up by the National Recovery Administration were able to display the blue eagle symbol—modeled on the Indian thunderbird—with its slogan "We Do Our Part." (United Press International)

As the only peacetime effort at national industrial planning, the NRA was a significant experiment. It wiped out child labor in industry and went a long way toward eliminating sweat shops and substandard wages and working conditions. However, the NRA not only failed to encourage recovery but probably impeded recovery. The NRA and the entire series of early New Deal policies assumed that the country was suffering from industrial overproduction and that the government must, therefore, limit production to actual need. It was an absurd assumption. The United States was suffering from severe underconsumption in 1933 because of unemployment and the decline in wages and in farm and business income. The country needed most of all a vast injection of purchasing power.

Relief under the First New Deal

Roosevelt was personally responsible for the Civilian Conservation Corps (CCC), which enrolled some 300,000 young men in camps throughout the country and engaged in reforestation and other work in national parks. Both the strenuous outdoor work and the conservation objectives appealed to Roosevelt's system of values, which in this respect, at least, resembled those of his Uncle Theodore. Aside from this successful exception, all the relief policies of the first New Deal continued policies begun by the Hoover administration. The Federal Housing Authority, established in 1934 to provide long-term credit at moderate rates for home repairs and new housing, continued a Hoover pol-

These young men, photographed at a CCC camp in Wisconsin, fought forest fires and cleared brush and trees. The camps, started by the Civilian Conservation Corps in 1933, took men off the bread lines during the time of economic depression and provided healthy, outdoor jobs for thousands. (Wide World Photos)

icy, but broadened its scope enormously. Between 1934 and 1940, this agency insured 554,000 loans which totaled $2.3 billion for new housing. The Federal Emergency Relief Act of May 12, 1933, appropriated $500 million for assistance to the unemployed to be disbursed by the states.

A sharp increase in industrial production and employment took place during the summer of 1933, because employers raced to produce as much as they could before the NRA codes were to go into effect. But the indices of production and employment slumped again in the autumn. As a harsh winter seemed to be fast approaching, Roosevelt created the Civil Works Administration (CWA), with Harry L. Hopkins as administrator, and took $400 million from the dilatory PWA to enable the CWA to provide temporary jobs for some 4,000,000 unemployed. Roosevelt liquidated the CWA in the spring of 1934 and then returned to the policy of providing relief assistance to the states through the Federal Emergency Relief Act.

Regional Resources Development

Roosevelt, always an ardent conservationist, gave personal leadership to a broad movement in the 1930s for federal development of regional multipurpose projects. These promoted flood control, river navigation, irrigation, and production of hydroelectric power. Roosevelt would happily have signed bills for regional projects in every section of the country. However, he obtained congressional approval for development only of the Tennessee Valley. He also

Wilson Dam, Muscle Shoals, Alabama, was one of the many dams in the TVA system. This New Deal agency was commissioned to construct and operate dams in the Tennessee Valley and to advance "the economic and social well-being of the people living in the said basin." The creation of the TVA meant the successful conclusion of George Norris' long struggle to prevent private development of the great water resources of the Tennessee River. (United Press International)

secured completion of the Boulder, later called the Hoover Dam on the Colorado River in Arizona; construction of the Fort Peck Dam on the Missouri River in Montana; and of the Bonneville and Grand Coulee dams on the Columbia River. The latter dam, completed in 1942, was the largest masonry structure in the world.

The New Deal's work in the Tennessee Valley fired the imagination of the world. Congress, at Roosevelt's suggestion, created the Tennessee Valley Authority (TVA) in the spring of 1933. Congress directed the new agency to improve the navigation of the Tennessee River, to provide for flood control, and, generally, to improve the agricultural and industrial development of the Tennessee Valley. The TVA built twenty new dams and improved five old ones and achieved a nearly perfect system of flood control and an inland waterway stretching from the Ohio River into the heart of the Appalachians. The authority also operated the electric power facilities at Wilson Dam in Alabama and installed turbines at its other dams. The TVA gradually purchased private power distribution facilities and established a monopoly on the production and sale of electric power in the entire Tennessee Valley. It built over 5,000 miles of transmission lines and charged consumers rates low enough to encourage wide use of electric power by farmers and urban households, as well as by industry. The TVA served as the major factor in transforming an economically backward, chronically impoverished area into one of the more heavily industrialized and wealthier sections of the nation.

People came from all over the world to see the wonders worked by the TVA and allied governmental agencies. They saw forests replanted, erosion halted, and worn-out soil restored to fertility by the use of cheap TVA-produced fertilizers. Moreover, industry now thrived in what had been one of the poorest sections in the country. Among the TVA's most significant achievements was its success in encouraging cities, states, and private cooperative groups to work together for the improvement and prosperity of the region.

3. LAUNCHING THE SECOND NEW DEAL

Prelude to the Second New Deal

Powerful forces of discontent destroyed the first New Deal coalition of all classes and divided the country, roughly speaking, into a Right and a Left during the months just before the mid-term election of 1934.

With notable exceptions, the manufacturing, business, and financial classes turned against the administration. They charged that Roosevelt was destroying constitutional government, coddling labor, and spending the Treasury into bankruptcy. Leadership in the conservative revolt was taken by the American Liberty League, which was formed by conservative Democrats in August 1934 and allied with big business and Wall Street. The league's avowed purpose was to capture control of the Democratic party.

Roosevelt, thus battered by conservatives, also felt the wrath of demagogues and radicals who accused him of being a tool of Wall Street. Among these critics were the Communists and Senator Huey P. Long of Louisiana, a ruthless, twentieth-century style populist from the poverty-stricken northern hill country of his state, who proposed to divide the national wealth and give every

American family a $2,500 guaranteed annual wage. In addition, there were Father Charles E. Coughlin, a priest from Detroit with fascist tendencies, a hatred of eastern bankers, and a large radio audience; and Dr. Francis E. Townsend of California, who organized a national movement among old people for federal pensions of $200 a month to every person over sixty. These demagogues and numerous others worked hard to stir the discontent of workers, small farmers, the unemployed, and the aged. Signs that they were succeeding disturbed Roosevelt more than the revolt of the conservatives. Long, especially, seemed to pose a real threat to Roosevelt's reelection. A poll conducted by the Democratic National Committee revealed that, if Long ran as an independent candidate in 1936, he could take three to four million votes from Roosevelt. Jim Farley consulted his own network of friends and acquaintances throughout the country; they verified Long's potential strength, even in New York City.

Perhaps fortunately for the moderate President, the revolt of the conservatives coalesced the lower classes and a large portion of the middle class into a solid New Deal front. In the congressional election on November 6, 1934, the Democrats increased their already large majorities in both houses of Congress. However, among this majority there now sat a significant number of congressmen who viewed Roosevelt's attempts to aid workers and struggling farmers as inadequate.

Launching the Second New Deal

"Boys," said Harry Hopkins, a leader of the welfare-state advocates in the Roosevelt circle, to his friends after the election, "this is our hour. We've got to get everything we want." It was not difficult to persuade Roosevelt to take a new tack, for he well understood the meaning of the election returns. He boldly assumed leadership of the new Left-of-Center majority coalition that had come into being and virtually jettisoned much of the First New Deal in his Annual Message to Congress of January 4, 1935. At the same time, he demanded that the federal government assume direct responsibility for the economic security of the masses of people.

The spearhead of the second New Deal was the $5 billion-work-relief program authorized by the Emergency Relief Appropriation Act of April 8, 1935. Roosevelt at once established the Works Progress Administration (WPA), with Hopkins as director. Hopkins immediately began to provide jobs for unemployed and needy workers, professional people, musicians, writers, actors, college students, and even historians, among others. Between 1935 and 1941, the WPA spent a total of $11.4 billion and gave work to a monthly average of 2,112,000 persons.

Signs that the Supreme Court might call a halt to social-welfare legislation had appeared even before the launching of the second New Deal. In January 1935, the court nullified a section of the NIRA that gave the President power to prohibit interstate transportation of oil produced in excess of quotas imposed by the NRA code. The vote was eight to one, and the decision seemed to imperil the entire NRA itself. On May 6 the court, in a five-to-four decision, nullified the Railroad Retirement Act of 1934 in language that appeared to doom any general social-security legislation. The court delivered its heaviest blow on May 27, 1935, in a decision in A.L.A. Schechter Corporation *v.* United

States which tested the constitutionality of the NIRA. The justices unanimously nullified that measure and the NRA as well, some on the ground that the NIRA delegated too much legislative authority to the executive branch, others because the measure permitted the federal government to regulate commerce that was purely intrastate in character.

New Laws for Old

The Schecter decision shocked both the nation and the President. In a press conference a few days later, Roosevelt spoke of the members of the Supreme Court as living in the "horse and buggy" days. The decision also plunged the administration into considerable confusion about its future course. Roosevelt had just urged Congress to extend the life of the NRA for an additional two years, even though that agency had been far from successful in most respects. After the Schechter decision, Roosevelt obviously had to abandon the enterprise, and for a short time it seemed that he was uncertain where to go.

Roosevelt quickly recovered his balance and sense of direction and decided to proceed at full steam with his program, in spite of threatened new reversals by the Supreme Court. Senator Robert F. Wagner had been working almost single-handed on a National Labor Relations bill. Roosevelt had opposed the Wagner bill on the grounds that it was better to provide protection for labor through the NRA. Roosevelt's paternalistic and naive ideas about such "protection" may be gauged by the fact that he and Secretary Perkins had practically negated the effectiveness of NIRA's Section 7a by interpreting collective bargaining units to include company-created and managed unions, and even units of one or two individuals in an industrial plant. After the election of 1934 and the Schechter decision, however, Roosevelt took up the Wagner bill and helped to give it the final push through Congress in July.

The National Labor Relations Act (NLRA) was by far the most important piece of labor legislation in American history. It strengthened and broadened Section 7a of the NIRA by affirming the right of workers to bargain collectively through representatives of their own choosing. The NLRA outlawed a number of so-called unfair practices by employers and established the National Labor Relations Board (NLRB). The NLRB was empowered to prevent unfair employer practices by issuing "cease and desist" orders, which courts were ordered by law to enforce. Most important, the NLRB was empowered to hold collective bargaining elections, when workers in a company or a plant petitioned for one, and to compel employers to bargain with unions once a majority of the workers had voted to join one. This latter provision all but destroyed the company unions established by the hundreds during the 1920s and approved by Roosevelt in certain interpretations of Section 7a.

The first session of the Seventy-fourth Congress passed a number of other history-making laws before it adjourned in the autumn of 1935. The Guffey-Snyder Coal Conservation Act reenacted the bituminous coal code of the old NRA in language carefully tailored to meet the Supreme Court's objections. Another measure revived the liquor code. New railroad retirement and mortgage moratorium acts replaced those declared unconstitutional by the court in May. The Revenue Act, or wealth tax bill, increased the surtax on incomes to the highest level in American history, and the federal estate tax to a maximum of 70 per cent. The measure was a direct assault on concentrated wealth. Attorneys and accountants devised means of avoiding these taxes to a large extent; however, that should not obscure the New Deal's intentions, or the fear and anger that they aroused among wealthy Americans.

The Social Security Act

The most far-reaching law adopted in the summer of 1935 was the Social Security Act, approved by the President on August 14, 1935. The Social Security Act was significant not only for what it did, but for what it symbolized. It marked the end of old American traditions of individual self-help. At the same time it marked the beginning, on a national scale, of the kind of system to protect economic security that virtually every European nation had possessed for half a century. The Social Security Act was divided into three main parts:

1. It provided a federal system of insurance against poverty in old age. A compulsory old-age insurance fund, contributed to by employers and employees alike, was to provide retirement pensions for workers after the age of sixty-five.

2. The Act established a system of unemployment insurance and levied a 3 per cent tax on payrolls to provide unemployment payments through the states.

3. The Social Security Act provided financial assistance to the states for a variety of welfare programs. The federal government, for example, offered to match state appropriations dollar for dollar up to a certain amount to provide old-age assistance to needy persons over sixty-five who could not benefit from the old-age insurance provision. The Act provided similar assistance for needy children, blind persons, the physically handicapped, widows with dependent children, and for various public health purposes.

The Social Security Act was weak in that it provided no coverage for agricultural workers, domestic servants, public servants, and professional people. Roosevelt and the authors of the measure were the first to admit that it was experimental and inadequate, but they knew that the Social Security system would be enlarged and strengthened in the future. That process began in 1937 and has continued to our own time.

4. THE ELECTION OF 1936 AND THE COURT CONTROVERSY

The Campaign and Election of 1936

Republicans turned their backs on former President Hoover in 1936 and nominated the progressive Governor of Kansas, Alfred M. Landon. They named Colonel Frank Knox, newspaper publisher of Chicago and former follower of Theodore Roosevelt, as Landon's running mate. The Democrats renominated Roosevelt and Garner by acclamation. They also repealed the rule which required a two-thirds vote for the nomination of a presidential candidate. Roosevelt's acceptance speech amounted to a declaration of war against "economic royalists" and was an eloquent call for national dedication: "This generation of Americans has a rendezvous with destiny. . . . We are fighting to save a great and precious form of government for ourselves and for the world."

The Socialists again nominated Norman Thomas, while their bitter enemies, the Communists, named Earl Browder. A new party appeared in the field under the banner of the Union for Social Justice. It consisted of the followers of Dr. Townsend and Father Coughlin, and the heirs of Senator Long, who had been assassinated in 1935. The party nominated Representative William Lemke of North Dakota for the presidency. Without the charismatic and clever Long, however, the Union party could not mount a real threat to Roosevelt.

The campaign was one of the most unequal presidential contests in American history. Landon made a game fight, but he was an inept campaigner and failed utterly to arouse the voters. Moreover, he suffered from two other crippling handicaps. The first was his own progressivism and the fact that the Republican platform of 1936 endorsed all the basic legislation of the New Deal. Landon could only say that he would carry out New Deal programs better than Roosevelt. Second, substantial recovery was in progress during the summer of 1936, after agonizingly slow improvement in economic conditions between 1933 and 1936. Production, employment, and real per capita income were all nearing their 1929 levels by the middle of 1936, and the upswing obviously did not help Landon's ailing campaign.

To make the situation almost hopeless for the Republicans, Roosevelt was at his best as a campaigner in 1936. He stumped the country as if the contest was close and appealed frankly for the support of the common people, as Jackson had done in 1832. On the basis of a much publicized poll of its readers, the weekly magazine, *Literary Digest*, predicted a Republican victory. However, when the votes were counted Roosevelt had carried every state except Maine and Vermont, with nearly 28,000,000 popular and 523 electoral votes, as compared to nearly 17,000,000 popular and eight electoral votes for Landon. The

The Election of 1936

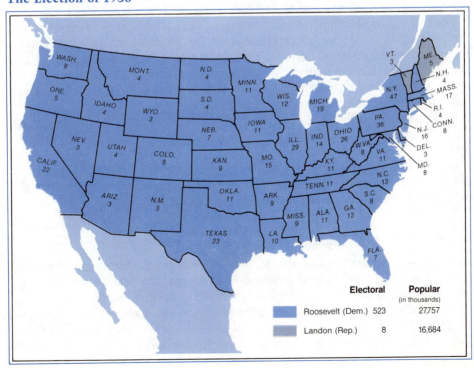

	Electoral	Popular (in thousands)
Roosevelt (Dem.)	523	27,757
Landon (Rep.)	8	16,684

landslide also reduced the Republicans to a corporal's guard of eighty-nine in the House of Representatives and twenty-one in the Senate. The Socialist, Communist, and Union parties combined received a little over 1,000,000 votes. *The Literary Digest* became the laughingstock of the nation — comparable to the experts who had promised an economic boom in 1930 — and soon went out of business.

A great majority of the American people obviously had given a strong mandate for the continuation of the New Deal. Keen analysts discovered three other developments in the returns: organized labor had played a significant part in the Democratic victory, while an overwhelming majority of blacks had voted for a Democratic presidential candidate for the first time in American history. Also, the white ethnic groups, who still formed a majority of the urban poor, voted almost completely for Roosevelt.

The Constitutional Crisis

It was extremely doubtful at the end of 1936 whether Roosevelt could carry out his mandate, for the Supreme Court had created a constitutional crisis comparable in significance to the breakup of the Union in 1860 – 1861. A bare majority of the Supreme Court had almost paralyzed the ability of Congress and the President to deal with national economic problems.

The essential issue in 1936 was whether Congress could use its taxing power and its power over interstate commerce to control economic activities that had traditionally been defined as intrastate or local in character. The conservative majority of the Supreme Court gave its answer in two key decisions in 1936: United States *v.* Butler nullified the Agricultural Adjustment Act on the ground that the production of foodstuffs was local and not interstate commerce; and Carter *v.* Carter Coal Company nullified the Coal Conservation Act on the ground that the mining of coal was a local activity.

The court, once it had deprived Congress of basic control over manufacturing, mining, agricultural production, and, by implication, labor relations, struck at social legislation again. In Morehead *v.* New York *ex rel.* Tipaldo, the justices denied that the states could regulate the hours, wages, and conditions of labor, because such regulation was a violation of the freedom of contract guaranteed by the Fourteenth Amendment.

Progressives in both parties were up in arms and demanded that the Supreme Court be curbed. Some suggested that such an extraordinary majority as six to three be required before the court could declare an act of Congress unconstitutional. Others proposed to permit Congress to override court decisions by a two-thirds vote. Still others wanted Congress to deprive the court of the right of judicial review altogether.

Roosevelt Breaks the Impasse

Neither the Democratic platform of 1936, nor Roosevelt during the campaign of that year, had given any intimation of an impending assault upon the supreme tribunal. However, the President virtually declared war on the Supreme Court's conservative majority soon after his triumphant reelection. On February 5, 1937, he sent to Congress the draft of a bill for the reorganization of the federal judiciary. It provided for a number of procedural reforms and a retirement system for federal judges. It also authorized the President to appoint up to fifty new judges when incumbents failed to retire upon reaching the age of seventy. Six of these judges might be added to the Supreme Court. In an accompanying message, Roosevelt justified his proposal mainly on the ground that insufficient and infirm judicial personnel had caused crowded dockets and intolerable delays.

For the first time in his career, Roosevelt made major errors in both strategy and timing. He had failed to inform his leaders in Congress of his plan. More important still, he had grossly underestimated the power of the traditions of the separation of powers and the independence of the judiciary in the federal system. To make matters worse, Roosevelt had also failed to be frank with Congress and the people. Once the battle began, Roosevelt came out in the open and asserted that his plan was necessary to save the country. But he could not repair the damage already done — the divisions among his supporters, especially among the Democratic members of Congress. Progressives joined conservatives in attacking the judicial reorganization bill as an attempt to pack the Supreme Court and to destroy the independence of the entire judicial branch.

We will never know how the battle would have come out had not the constitutional crisis been resolved in an unexpected way. Roosevelt might well have won a modified version of his judicial reorganization bill. However, the Supreme Court itself ended the quarrel, and, with it, Roosevelt's court plan. While the controversy raged at its height, the case of West Coast Hotel v. Parrish, which involved the constitutionality of a minimum wage law of the State of Washington, came before the court. The court not only reversed the Tipaldo decision of the year before; it also approved the Washington statute in language that left room for any reasonable state regulation of wages, hours, and working conditions. Two weeks later, an even more important case — National Labor Relations Board v. Jones and Laughlin Steel Corporation, which involved the constitutionality of the National Labor Relations Act of 1935 — came before the court. The justices now said that the Wagner Act of 1935 was constitutional because Congress' power over interstate commerce was absolute and extended to every economic activity that affected the manufacture of goods.

Roosevelt obviously had lost the battle and won the war. He accepted a watered down measure called the Judicial Procedure Reform Act. This measure was rushed through Congress and signed by Roosevelt on August 26, 1937; it instituted the procedural reforms that Roosevelt had requested. It also permitted federal judges to retire at full pay after they reached the age of seventy, but it did not provide for the appointment of new federal judges and Supreme Court justices.

Retirements from 1937 onward soon enabled Roosevelt to fill the Supreme Court with men closer to his own political and economic philosophy. The new "Roosevelt Court" subsequently upheld the constitutionality of every important New Deal measure.

5. STRENGTHENING THE SECOND NEW DEAL

The Rise of the CIO

In retrospect, it is clear that the New Deal effected a near revolution in American life by stimulating the growth of a labor movement politically self-conscious and capable of bargaining on more or less equal terms with management in most major industries.

These profound changes were not, of course, all of Roosevelt's making. In 1934 and 1935, a group within the AFL, led by John L. Lewis, president of the United Mine Workers, and Sidney Hillman and David Dubinsky, presidents of the garment workers' unions, made some changes of their own. They demanded that the AFL organize industrial unions (that is, unions which combined all workers in a single industry, regardless of their craft) in such still unorganized industries as steel, automobiles, and rubber. A majority of the leaders of the AFL were old, conservative, and still hostile to the very concept of industrial unionism. Lewis and his colleagues, rebuffed by the national convention of the AFL in 1935, formed the Committee for Industrial Organization. It became the separate, independent Congress of Industrial Organizations (CIO) in 1937.

The CIO in 1936 launched a campaign to organize the steel industry, the citadel of antiunionism since about 1900. It won this crucial struggle in early 1937 and turned next to the automobile industry. The union organizers won the right to bargain for workers in General Motors and Chrysler in 1937, and in Ford in 1940. In some of these fights for recognition, unions used sit-down strikes, that is, they refused to leave factories until managers agreed to negotiate fairly with their representatives. Roosevelt denounced these tactics, although he also declined to send troops to end them. He infuriated John L. Lewis, who refused to support him politically thereafter. Because the Wagner Act omitted so many categories of workers, and the CIO encountered so much opposition, only 28 percent of the nation's nonagricultural workers had been unionized by 1940, and only a slight proportion of agricultural workers belonged to even the small and isolated unions in their industry.

However, the CIO organized virtually every mass production industry in the United States and had grown in membership to about 5,000,000 by 1941. A revived AFL had reached a membership of 4,569,000 by this time. To be sure, labor won these gains mainly by its own efforts and sacrifices, but the sometimes reluctant support of the administration, particularly of the NLRB in drives for recognition, played a crucial role in labor's success. In turn, this powerful new labor movement became an indispensable source of political power for the second New Deal.

Completing the Second New Deal

Roosevelt's Annual Message and second inaugural of January 1937 were clarion calls for new legislation to benefit the "one third of a nation ill-housed, ill-clad, ill-nourished." These calls constitute an informative commentary upon the statistical information available to Roosevelt and his advisers and upon their standards of what it meant to be ill-housed, ill-clothed, and ill-fed. By the standards of Americans who live in 1980, at least two thirds of the population in 1937 lived on incomes less than what was then necessary for an adequate though poor existence. Nevertheless, the New Deal legislation of 1937–1938 provided the first large-scale effort to help the "invisible" people near the bottom of the nation's economic structure.

The fight over the judicial reorganization bill diverted congressional energies and temporarily disrupted Democratic unity. However, Roosevelt drew his forces together again in 1937 and 1938 and won most of the measures that he said were necessary for completion of his program. Assistance came to Roosevelt from an unexpected source. A sharp recession occurred in early 1938 — the result of the administration's slashing of expenditures in 1937 as a consequence of Roosevelt's efforts to balance the budget at the same time that new taxes for Social Security were collected. Industrial output fell 33 per cent, while unemployment again rose rapidly. Once more, stock market prices collapsed. Congressmen and senators, with nervous eyes on the impending midterm election, suddenly became very ardent New Dealers, eager to renew the spending program.

1. The Farm Tenancy Act of 1937 established the Farm Security Administration. It provided various kinds of assistance, particularly credit for the purchase of land, to tenants, sharecroppers, and migratory farm laborers who had benefited hardly at all from the AAA.

2. The National Housing Act of 1937 created the United States Housing Authority and furnished it with large sums to begin the first serious war on urban slums.

3. The Agricultural Adjustment Act of 1938 replaced the temporary and ineffective Soil Conservation Act, which Congress had adopted in 1936 when the Supreme Court invalidated the first AAA. The second Agricultural Adjustment Act continued soil conservation payments to farmers and permitted producers of the major staples to limit production by a two-thirds vote. The act provided for an "ever-normal granary" by keeping farm surpluses off the market in fat years and releasing them in lean years.

4. The Fair Labor Standards, or Wages and Hours Act of 1938 rounded out the second New Deal's comprehensive structure of labor legislation. The measure established a minimum wage of 25 cents an hour, to be increased to 40 cents, and limited hours of labor to forty a week.

5. A frightened Congress made some $3 billion available to the WPA, launched a huge public-works program in cooperation with the states, and greatly expanded the lending power of federal credit agencies.

6. Congress, in response to a special request from the President, established the Temporary National Economic Committee to study the American economy with a view to increasing price competition with new antitrust legislation. Roosevelt, influenced by Louis D. Brandeis and his disciples, much as Wilson had been in 1912, returned to the idea that large business combinations keep prices artificially high and restrict consumption.

6. THE PASSING OF THE NEW DEAL

The New Deal Comes to an End

The forward motion of the New Deal slowed down perceptibly between 1938 and 1939 as the result of developments both at home and abroad. The most important of these developments was the completion of Roosevelt's program for reform and reconstruction. With the exception of Roosevelt's plan for executive reorganization, and his desire for further "trust-busting," Roosevelt's ideas had all been turned into legislation. It would remain for the next generation to expand liberal objectives to include real urban revitalization, medical insurance, and full civil rights for blacks. A widely supported civil rights crusade, such as would occur in the 1960s, simply was not possible in the 1930s.

By 1938–1939, many signs indicated that the majority of Americans were eager for a breathing spell and believed that the time had come to digest and perfect the reform gains of the past six years. This feeling had important political manifestations. During the summer of 1938, Roosevelt set out to prevent the renomination of several Democratic congressmen and senators who had opposed some of the administration's measures. With a single exception (a congressman from New York), Democratic voters defeated Roosevelt's candidates in primary elections and renominated the men whom he had attempted to purge. What is more, the Republicans gained eighty-one seats in the House of Representatives and eight seats in the Senate in the mid-term election on November 8, 1938. They also elected thirteen additional governors; one of them was Thomas E. Dewey in Roosevelt's home state of New York. By joining with Democratic conservatives, Republicans now had the power to prevent further enactment of New Deal legislation.

Finally, Roosevelt was trying to build congressional support for a stronger policy of resistance to Nazi Germany's aggressions. In order to accomplish this end, Roosevelt had to avoid alienating conservative southern Democrats, who were the most consistent internationalists in Congress.

The New Deal in Retrospect

The New Deal tried to achieve economic recovery as well as extensive economic and social reform. Even now it is difficult to say whether the Roosevelt administration achieved its first objective. A certain measure of recovery did undoubtedly occur, for per capita real income exceeded the 1929 level in 1940, before the full effect of the Second World War had stimulated the economy. Yet substantial unemployment remained until 1941. Some economists believe that New Deal measures actually slowed down the return of normal economic activity by raising the prices of construction materials disproportionately, and, in general, by causing dislocations and discouraging corporate investment. In any event, it is difficult for a nation to engage in thoroughgoing reform and recovery at the same time, for the reform of basic institutions frightens the business and investing classes.

The Lasting Significance of the New Deal: An Evaluation

1. The New Deal effected sweeping administrative and regulatory reforms. For the first time since the industrial revolution, the American people and their leaders faced most of the challenges that were raised by industrialization and urbanization. The New Deal's answer was a vast increase in the power of the federal government to guide and promote general social and economic welfare. Theodore Roosevelt and Woodrow Wilson had laid the foundations for a modern regulatory and welfare state; but Franklin D. Roosevelt completed the superstructure of that state, and he built so well that the following generation could concentrate upon perfecting the edifice that he had erected.

2. The New Deal greatly strengthened the system of free-enterprise capitalism. To be sure, New Deal legislation put many restraints upon business and finance in order to guarantee that they would be socially responsible. But, while it subjected private economic institutions to new regulation, the New

Deal left most important economic decisions to individuals and groups of individuals. The New Deal also gave to hitherto submerged groups, such as farmers and workers, a large share in decision making, and hence a profound stake in the successful operation of the new economy. Some Americans in the 1930s—and not only the wealthy—thought that the New Deal was radical. Many of these objected to the erection of a vast bureaucracy and of regulatory agencies which intruded into their lives. Some still believed that aid to the poor and handicapped would destroy the spirit of individual initiative upon which American industry had depended in the past. Any evaluation of the New Deal must take into consideration such attitudes, which surfaced every time that economic conditions improved. They remain strong in the 1980s, but they were much more powerful during the 1930s. Most Americans would now agree with Roosevelt's claim, made in 1937, that he was in fact a conservative. As he put it: "To preserve we had to reform. Wise and prudent men—intelligent conservatives—have long known that in a changing world worthy institutions can be conserved only by adjusting them to the changing time. In the words of the great essayist, 'The voice of great events is proclaiming to us, "Reform if you would preserve."' I am that kind of a conservative."

3. The New Deal restored faith in democracy at a time when democracy seemed on the verge of extinction almost everywhere else in the world. It proved that men of good will could deal with serious national problems without revolution, violence, dictatorship, or a slave state.

4. Finally, Roosevelt helped to revive confidence in the human spirit itself by his own example in overcoming a catastrophic illness and continuing to fight for the principles in which he believed. No doubt he was thinking about himself when he uttered the following words during the presidential campaign of 1936:

It is not the critic who counts, not the man who points out how the strong man stumbled, or where the doer of deeds could have done them better. The credit belongs to the man who is actually in the arena; whose face is marred by dust and sweat and blood; who strives valiantly; who errs and comes short again and again; who knows the great enthusiasms, the great devotions, and spends himself in a worthy cause; who at the best knows in the end the triumphs of high achievement; and who at the worst, if he fails, at least fails while daring greatly; so that his place shall never be with those cold and timid souls who know neither defeat nor victory.

5. As a comparison of the paragraph above with New Deal programs reveals, Roosevelt's conception of "daring greatly" contained significant limitations. It hardly applied to the social and economic position of blacks and Hispanics, and Roosevelt rejected socialistic remedies altogether. Nor did New Deal leaders address themselves to the economic and legal inequities faced by women. Unskilled workers of all kinds received only enough help to prevent the great majority from outright starvation. Therefore, vast social and economic inequalities remained after the New Deal. Roosevelt truly had reformed in order to preserve.

However, Roosevelt had "entered the arena," as he put it, and had fought to improve somewhat the lives of those ordinary Americans who existed in the bottom levels of America's economic and social pyramid. Despite violent attack and criticism, he had "dared."

SUGGESTED READINGS

Arthur M. Schlesinger, Jr., *The Coming of the New Deal* (1959), and *The Politics of Upheaval* (1960), offer the most comprehensive treatment of the period covered in this chapter. An excellent one-volume account is Leuchtenberg, *Franklin D. Roosevelt and the New Deal, 1932–1940*, already cited. Other good political commentaries are Basil Rauch, *History of the New Deal* (1944); Dennis W. Brogan, *The Era of Franklin D. Roosevelt* (1951); Dexter Perkins, *The New Age of Franklin Roosevelt* (1957); and Burns, *Roosevelt: The Lion and the Fox*, already cited. Wecter, *The Age of the Great Depression*, and Allen, *Since Yesterday*, already cited, are good social histories. The biographies cited in the preceding chapter should also be consulted. All the books mentioned above regard the New Deal favorably and often uncritically. For more negative views from the Right, see Edgar E. Robinson, *The Roosevelt Leadership, 1932–1945* (1955); for another thoughtful criticism, see Paul Conkin, *The New Deal* (1975).

Biographies and memoirs constitute a significant part of the literature on the New Deal. Robert E. Sherwood, *Roosevelt and Hopkins*, (rev. ed., 1950); J. Joseph Huthmacher, *Senator Robert F. Wagner and the Rise of Urban Liberalism* (1968); T. Harry Williams, *Huey Long* (1969); and John M. Blum, *From the Morgenthau Diaries* (1959, 1960), are illuminating. A "collective biography" of the old progressives in this period is provided in Otis L. Graham, Jr., *Encore for Reform* (1967). Most opposed the New Deal. Some of the memoirs and personal accounts which ought to be consulted are Frances Perkins, *The Roosevelt I Knew* (1946); *The Secret Diary of Harold L. Ickes*, 3 vols. (1953–1954); James A. Farley, *Behind the Ballots* (1938); Hugh S. Johnson, *The Blue Eagle* (1935); Samuel I. Rosenman, *Working with Roosevelt* (1952); and Eleanor Roosevelt's indispensable *This I Remember* (1949). Less sympathetic accounts are Raymond Moley, *After Seven Years* (1939) and *The First New Deal* (1966). *The Public Papers of Franklin D. Roosevelt*, 13 vols. (1938–1950), contain fascinating material.

There are many specialized studies of the New Deal. On the divergence of New Deal from Hoover's policies, and what might be called the ideology of the New Deal, see Rosen, *Hoover, Roosevelt, and the Brains Trust*, already cited, and Rexford G. Tugwell, *The Brains Trust* (1968). For economic policies and their effects see Broadus Mitchell, *Depression Decade* (1947), and Kenneth D. Roose, *Economics of Recession and Revival* (1954). A subtly humorous and keen analysis is Thurman Arnold, *The Folklore of Capital-*

ism (1937). Ellis W. Hawley, *The New Deal and the Problem of Monopoly* (1966) is an adequate treatment. David E. Lilienthal, *The T.V.A.* (rev. ed., 1953), contains useful information on that regional development. New Deal agricultural policy is discussed in Christiana M. Campbell, *The Farm Bureaus: A Study of the Making of National Farm Policy, 1933–1940* (1962); Richard S. Kirkendall, *Social Scientists and Farm Politics in the Age of Roosevelt* (1966); Gilbert C. Fite, *George M. Peek and the Fight for Farm Parity* (1954); and Sidney Baldwin, *Poverty and Politics* (1968). Leonard Baker, *Back to Back: The Duel Between FDR and the Supreme Court* (1967), is the most comprehensive account of that subject, but Edward S. Corwin, *Twilight of the Supreme Court* (1934), *Court over Constitution* (1938), and *Constitutional Revolution* (rev. ed., 1946), and Alpheus T. Mason, *Harlan Fiske Stone: Pillar of the Law* (1956), are valuable.

Incisive essays on social history can be found in Isabel Leighton, *The Aspirin Age* (1949). Good studies of the Left are David A. Shannon, *The Socialist Party of America* (1955); Daniel Bell, *Marxian Socialism in the United States* (1967); Earl Latham, *The Communist Controversy in Washington* (1966); Robert W. Iverson, *The Communists and the Schools* (1959); Murray Kempton, *Part of Our Time* (1955) and Daniel Aaron, *Writers on the Left* (1961); a contemporary account of the Right is Raymond Gram Swing, *Forerunners of American Fascism* (1935). Huey P. Long, *Every Man a King* (1933), is a fascinating introduction to southern radicalism, and to Long; but also see T. Harry Williams' excellent biography of Long, already cited; David H. Bennett, *Demagogues in the Depression: American Radicals and the Union Party, 1932–1936* (1969); and Charles J. Tull, *Father Coughlin and the New Deal* (1965).

The conservative reaction to the New Deal is discussed in George Wolfskill, *The Revolt of Conservatives* (1962), and Wolfskill and John A. Hudson, *All but the People* (1969), and in James T. Patterson, *Congressional Conservatism and the New Deal* (1967). Samuel Lubell, *The Future of American Politics* (1952), is a pathbreaking analysis of political changes during the period. Lubell's chief themes, however, remain questionable and unproved.

The New Deal's comparative neglect of black Americans is examined in Raymond Wolters, *Negroes and the Great Depression* (1970), and in the essays in Bernard Sternsher, ed., *The Negro in Depression and War* (1969).

CHAPTER 31
THE UNITED STATES AND THE SECOND ROAD TO WORLD WAR

1. JAPANESE EXPANSION

A Decade of Turmoil

Depression, hunger, and domestic violence assaulted the populations of the nations of Europe and the Far East at the same time and with almost the same ferocity as they did in the United States. The American people not only absorbed the rude shocks; they also met these challenges without significant harm to their democratic institutions. Other nations throughout the world, which lacked America's lengthy democratic heritage, gave way to political or military leaders who promised economic security in exchange for liberties. Half the governments in Latin America, for example, toppled during the early 1930s without elections. During this worldwide chaos, several major industrial powers fell into the hands of groups which envisioned economic salvation and national aggrandizement through conquest.

The Japanese, utterly dependent upon commerce disrupted by tariffs and trade boycotts caused by the depression, permitted an oligarchy of militarists and imperialists to subvert weak democratic institutions and to turn their island empire upon a course of expansion. The Germans, in their anger against the Versailles Treaty, despair about economic conditions, and fear of Communism, turned to Adolf Hitler and watched the Nazis destroy the remnants of German democracy. Hitler and his followers, with their messianic plans for a "Greater Germany" and their fanatical anti-Semitism, plunged their nation into an abyss of terror.

Some of the legitimate aspirations and claims of the dictatorships might well have been satisfied through ordinary diplomacy. Unhappily for the world, the men and parties who led the expansionistic nations eventually became impatient with the slow course and unsatisfactory results of normal negotiations. Many of their aims conflicted with those of other major powers. In their efforts to achieve their objectives through violence, the leaders of Germany and Japan, especially, plunged the world into a decade of turmoil, crisis, and war. As the 1930s ended, whole continents were involved in a death struggle between huge contending armed forces.

The Manchurian Crisis

The first critical challenge to the postwar peace structure occurred in 1931, when Japan wrested Manchuria from China in open violation of the covenant of the League of Nations.

Manchuria had been Japan's most important area for investment and development since the 1890s. Fear that China under its new leader, Chiang Kai-shek, would succeed in reasserting control over Manchuria prompted the leaders of the Japanese Kwantung Army in Manchuria to attempt to settle the question before Chiang had an opportunity to do so. The Kwantung generals manufactured an incident to serve as a pretext, defied their home government, and attacked Chinese forces throughout Manchuria on September 18, 1931. Civilians in the Japanese cabinet proved unable to regain control over the army, and, in a campaign of about eight weeks, the Japanese troops occupied all of Manchuria.

The blow fell at the very moment that leaders in Washington and London floundered in the depths of the international financial crisis, which had just forced Great Britain to abandon the gold standard. Western leaders reacted slowly and cautiously. While they debated about an appropriate response, the liberal government in Tokyo gave way in December to a coalition of military officers and imperialistic politicians. Clearly, Japanese aggression in Manchuria would be but a prelude to further military adventures.

The League of Nations could have responded forcefully, but only if the two great naval powers, the United States and Great Britain, had been willing to go to war, if necessary, to defend the covenant. Since the British were unwilling to take the initiative, that task fell upon the United States. Hoover and Secretary of State Stimson would take no steps, such as an economic boycott, that carried any chance of war with Japan. One reason for their reluctance to act was the reaction of their fellow citizens. Americans in all walks of life understood that Japanese aggression imperiled the peace structure. However, the war seemed far away, and public opinion polls showed that most Americans believed that they—a peaceful people—had been tricked into entering the First World War by a combination of domestic creditors of warring countries, munitions makers, and foreign propaganda. Most Americans told poll takers that they did not want the country's young men to die again in the wars abroad, unless the United States was attacked directly. So, while they condemned Japan, a majority of American political leaders in both major parties opposed risking war to force the Japanese to obey the League covenant. They felt certain that verbal condemnation would suffice anyhow, and President Hoover, a Quaker and a true pacifist, agreed with them.

In these circumstances, Stimson used his only available weapon—moral suasion. On January 7, 1932, he warned both the Chinese and Japanese governments that the United States would not recognize any territorial or political changes brought about in the Far East by force. Stimson enunciated this policy of nonrecognition more plainly in a public letter to Senator Borah on February 23. The League of Nations endorsed the Stimson policy, but appeared helpless to act when Japan created the puppet state of Manchukuo in Manchuria and withdrew from the League of Nations.

2. THE COLLAPSE OF EUROPEAN STABILITY

Trying to Save the Versailles System

After the international economic collapse of 1931, leaders in western Europe and the United States, thrashing about in considerable confusion, tried last-ditch efforts to save the Versailles system. It soon became evident that one part of the Paris settlement—war debts and reparations—could not be salvaged. It would have been wise for Hoover to have agreed to mutual cancellation of all intergovernmental obligations which stemmed from the First World War. However, fear of reactions at home again paralyzed the President, hence the European nations took matters into their own hands. Representatives of the western European governments met at Lausanne, Switzerland, in 1932 and agreed in effect to cancel Germany's reparations debt. The following year, all governments which owed war debts to the United States, except Finland, defaulted on their payments. In the same year, 1933, leaders of western Europe tried to build the foundations for a revival of world trade at the London Economic Conference. On this occasion, however, President Roosevelt prevented agreement on the first step, monetary stabilization. As we have seen, Roosevelt was intent upon further devaluation of the dollar.

It cannot be said, therefore, that the United States, either under Hoover or under Roosevelt during his first year in office, gave any leadership in reconstruction of the world economy. The American government did, however, do all that it could to save the peace system through international land disarmament. A World Disarmament Conference finally opened in Geneva in 1932 after years of discussion and preparation. Hoover proposed a plan for the destruction of all offensive weapons and the reduction by one third of all naval and ordinary military forces. When Roosevelt took office, he not only supported Hoover's proposal, but also promised American participation in a new collective security system. In addition, France and Britain agreed that the Versailles Treaty should be revised to give Germany equality in land armaments.

Unhappily, this concession came too late. Adolf Hitler became Chancellor of Germany on January 30, 1933. He wanted, not equality in armaments, but military superiority in order to carry out his plans to dominate Europe. He therefore withdrew German delegates from the World Disarmament Conference and the League of Nations in October 1933.

Hitler's and Mussolini's Challenges

Europe careened from one crisis to another during the next six years as Hitler and the Italian dictator, Benito Mussolini, destroyed both the Versailles treaty system and the League of Nations.

Hitler made the first move on March 16, 1935. He denounced the provisions of the Versailles Treaty for German disarmament and began a military build-up. When Britain and France took no action to halt German rearmament, which they could easily have done, Mussolini launched an attack on Ethiopia. The League of Nations condemned this aggression, but Britain and France prevented any effective retaliation by the League out of fear that it would drive Mussolini into an alliance with Hitler.

Cheered on by Hitler and Mussolini, Spanish army leaders headed by General Francisco Franco in 1936 launched a civil war to destroy the liberal government in Madrid. Powerful industrialists, landowners, and Roman Catholics supported Franco; the former felt unsafe under a democratic regime. France and Britain stood by while Franco's armies destroyed the Spanish republic between 1936 and 1939.

In the same year that the Spanish Civil War began, Hitler sent his armies into the demilitarized German Rhineland. Again the French and British did nothing. Hitler then encouraged the Nazi movement among ethnic Germans in Austria and occupied that country in March 1938. At the same time, he concluded a military alliance with Italy and Japan.

Prime Minister Neville Chamberlain grasping the hand of Chancellor Adolf Hitler as a gesture of friendship between England and Germany after the Munich Conference in 1938. Chamberlain returned home confident that he had preserved "peace in our time." (Wide World Photos)

Europe came to the brink of war in the autumn of 1938. Hitler threatened to invade Czechoslovakia when that country refused to hand over to Germany its Sudetenland, which contained more than 3,000,000 inhabitants of German ancestry. The Czechs, relying on help from Great Britain, France, and Russia, mobilized, but neither Britain nor France was willing to go to war to save the Czech republic, and Russia would not act alone. Instead, Prime Minister Neville Chamberlain of Great Britain and Premier Edouard Daladier of France met Hitler and Mussolini at Munich on September 28, 1938. There, in a classic act of appeasement, Chamberlain and Daladier agreed to the dismemberment of the one surviving democracy east of the Rhine River. The British Prime Minister reported this agreement to the House of Commons as a guarantee of "peace in our time." Meanwhile, Hitler occupied the Sudetenland and soon destroyed the remnant of the Czech republic.

The United States Chooses Isolation

Concerted and only slightly bold action by Great Britain and France could have stopped Mussolini and Hitler in their tracks at any time before 1938.

New Yorkers march up Fifth Avenue in a "No More War" parade. In the mid-1930s, most Americans were alarmed over the threatened aggressions in Europe and Asia but were determined to stay out of all impending wars. They felt that internationalism had failed and they must resort to isolationism to maintain the peace. (Wide World Photos)

However, these democracies were unwilling to run even a slight risk of war. Great Britain and France had been bled white by the First World War. The British and French leaders were, moreover, so afraid of Communism that they did not look altogether with disfavor upon the rise of the militantly anti-Communist Nazi regime.

Americans viewed events in Europe from 1935 to 1938 with mixed emotions. Most Americans abhorred Hitler, especially for his brutal persecution of German Jews. American sympathies went out to beleaguered Ethiopia in 1935–1936, and to the Loyalists fighting to preserve the liberal Spanish Popular Front government. But almost all Americans assumed that, if it came to war, the British navy and the supposedly great French army would make short work of Hitler and Mussolini. This assumption affected all American thinking about developments in Europe at this time. It led straight to one conclusion and one policy: the bridling of Hitler and Mussolini was primarily Britain's and France's job, and the United States could safely avoid the responsibility of entanglement in another terrible European war.

Other developments in the mid-thirties made this choice by Americans virtually a unanimous one. Obsession with recovery and reconstruction of their own institutions caused Americans to turn inward in the belief that their most important tasks were domestic, not foreign ones. Second, many thoughtful Americans believed that, in Hitler and Mussolini, the former Allies had got only what they deserved for their vindictiveness and imperialism at the Paris Peace Conference. Repudiation by Great Britain and France of their war debts to the United States confirmed the American suspicion that the European democracies were selfish, faithless, and dishonest. Third, an investigation of armaments manufacturing led by Senator Gerald P. Nye of North Dakota confirmed millions of Americans in their belief that bankers and munitions makers had manipulated the country into the First World War, although, in reaching his well-publicized conclusions, Nye relied largely on his own beliefs to this effect rather than on solid evidence. Nye's charge was echoed by so-called revisionist historians, who concluded that American participation in the First World War had been a ghastly mistake. Finally, an organized peace movement rose to its height in the United States. Waves of pacifism swept through the churches and college campuses. Movies and plays embellished the theme that war was a grand illusion—the delight only of idiots.

American sentiment for noninvolvement grew as war clouds gathered in Europe and Asia. Congress in 1935 and 1936 prohibited the shipment of arms to Italy or Ethiopia, or to either side in the Spanish Civil War, and refused to distinguish between military aggressors and established governments which defended themselves. Furthermore, Mussolini's and Franco's armies did not need American arms, while the Ethiopian government and the Spanish republic did. A third and more comprehensive Neutrality Act of May 1, 1937, prohibited the shipment of arms or munitions, or the extension of loans, to *any* belligerents. The act of 1937 also included a cash-and-carry provision which stipulated that *all* belligerents had to pay cash for nonmilitary goods purchased in the United States and had to carry them away in non-American ships. In addition, the law warned Americans that they would travel on belligerent ships at their own risk. Finally, the Act empowered the President to determine when a state of war existed and to place an embargo on other exports besides munitions at his own discretion. The policies that allegedly had sucked the United States into the vortex of the First World War thus would not be repeated.

Isolationism ran so rampant that Roosevelt and Hull were virtual prisoners of public opinion in working out policies toward Europe and the Far East. The President and Secretary of State thought that the neutrality legislation was ill-timed and unwise. They realized that strict American neutrality usually favored aggressor nations, such as Japan and Italy, which possessed war supplies that their victims lacked.

Although Roosevelt and Hull worked to modify neutrality legislation so as to give the President more discretion in the application of the laws, the politically astute and still ambitious Roosevelt signed the bills even though they made no concessions to the administration's wishes. Moreover, the State Department, under pressure from conservatives and pro-Franco Roman Catholic groups, took the initiative in applying the neutrality laws to the Spanish Civil War. On one occasion, Roosevelt sent up a trial balloon to see whether the winds of public opinion were changing. In a speech in Chicago on October 5, 1937, he said that the time had come for peace-loving nations to quarantine aggressors. The violent public negative reaction made it clear that Americans were, if anything, more strongly isolationist than before.

British and French reluctance to stand firm would have made a strong American foreign policy difficult to execute, even if American public opinion had encouraged Roosevelt and Hull to follow one. For example, they eagerly wanted to cooperate with the League of Nations in applying an oil embargo against Italy during the Ethiopian crisis. However, the French government prevented effective action on this occasion. In late 1937 and early 1938. Roosevelt sought British and French cooperation in the calling of a world conference to find a basis for new international cooperation. His efforts were frustrated by Prime Minister Chamberlain, who had decided to try to appease Italy, and also by a cabinet crisis in Great Britain. In such circumstances, Roosevelt and Hull could only follow Britain and France's lead and hope for the best. Roosevelt, therefore, reluctantly supported Chamberlain's policy in Munich. Again, on April 14, 1939, Roosevelt asked both Hitler and Mussolini to promise to refrain, for at least ten years, from attacking any one of the thirty-one nations that the President listed. In return, he would ask these nations to promise not to attack Italy or Germany. Hitler replied with a sarcastic, abusive, two-hour speech before the German Reichstag in which he tried to justify his recent aggressions.

The United States Fails to Meet New Aggressions in Asia

The Japanese army on July 7, 1937, began a full-scale war to wrench the five northern provinces of China from the control of Chiang Kai-shek's government at Nanking. To deal with this clear-cut case of aggression, the League of Nations suggested that the signatories of the Nine-Power Treaty meet to consider what should be done. The United States Government endorsed the proposal, and a conference was scheduled for Brussels in early November 1937.

The Brussels Conference was doomed even before it could assemble. The British government was not eager to take strong action against Japan, but it informed the State Department that it would support any program that the

United States put into effect. However, American public reaction in the wake of Roosevelt's quarantine speech paralyzed the Washington government. In these circumstances, the Brussels Conference could issue only a harmless statement. The Japanese air force replied on December 12, 1937, by bombing *U.S.S. Panay*, a gunboat, and three American oil tankers in the Yangtze River. The reaction of most Americans was to demand that their government withdraw its small military and naval forces from China. The State Department accepted Tokyo's probably sincere apologies for the attack and payment of damages. The Japanese government still could not control its military forces — an ominous sign for the future.

3. THE GOOD NEIGHBOR

The Good Neighbor in Economic Policy

Secretary Hull was an old-fashioned internationalist from Tennessee who believed profoundly that the United States should take leadership in reconstructing the world economy through currency stabilization and liberal trade policies. Economic nationalists overshadowed Hull during the first months of the Roosevelt administration, but Hull patiently bided his time. He was able to take the initiative once the President, late in 1933, had decided on stabilization. With Roosevelt's blessing, Hull persuaded Congress to adopt the Reciprocal Trade Agreements Act in June 1934. It authorized the President to negotiate trade agreements, which would go into effect without congressional approval, and in these agreements to lower or raise the existing Hawley-Smoot rates by as much as 50 per cent. Moreover, American tariff reductions would apply to all nations that accorded the United States the status of a "most favored nation," that is, those which gave the United States the benefits of their own lowest tariff rates.

Hull had negotiated trade agreements with thirteen nations, including Holland, France, and Canada, by 1936. Congress renewed the Trade Agreements Act the following year. Hull then worked hard to persuade the British to lower their tariff barriers. He achieved some success in the Canadian-American and British-American trade agreements of 1938. By 1940, when the Trade Agreements Act was again renewed, Hull had concluded agreements with twenty-one nations. However, while the depression lasted, Roosevelt refused to consider agreements on goods which competed with those produced by American farmers and factories.

Hopes of stimulating a lively trade with Russia played an important part in the administration's decision to extend diplomatic recognition to the Soviet Union. Thoughtful Americans, including most representatives of large business corporations, had long asserted that it was foolish not to recognize a great power simply because one did not like its form of government. While the United States remained mired in depression, the Soviet economy grew rapidly in response to a five-year governmental plan. Russia appeared to American businessmen as one area where goods, especially factory and agricultural machinery, could be sold in large quantities. The Soviet Foreign Minister, Maxim Litvinov, came to Washington to promise that, in exchange for recognition by the United States, his government would negotiate a settlement of the old czarist debt to the United States and would refrain from propaganda activity in the United States. Roosevelt extended recognition on November 16, 1933, and a short time later established the Export-Import Bank to facilitate Russian-American trade. However, hopes both for friendly relations and for a flourishing Russian-American trade did not materialize until Germany attacked Russia in 1941. Soviet leaders soon made it plain that they did not intend either to pay past Russian debts or to cease to conduct their propaganda in the United States through the Communist Party of America.

Economic motivation also prompted the United States to wind up its experiment in colonialism in the Philippine Islands. American sugar and tobacco producers, represented by powerful southern Democratic congressmen, disliked the low tariffs on Philippine sugar and tobacco, because it meant tough competition and low prices. If the Filipinos obtained independence, the tariffs could be raised. In 1933, Congress, under the pressure of these and other American business interests, adopted an act which forced independence upon the Philippine Islands after ten years. The Filipinos rejected the measure and asked for dominion status instead. They feared the Japanese and wanted to remain within the American customs union. However, Congress and the agricultural and business competitors of the Filipinos won their way with passage of the Philippine Independence Act in 1934. Filipinos adopted a new constitution and elected Manuel Quezon President of the Philippine Commonwealth in 1935. July 4, 1946, was set as the date for the full-fledged independence of the Philippine Republic.

The Good Neighbor and Latin America

In his inaugural address, Roosevelt announced that the United States would try to play the role of a good neighbor in foreign affairs in general. A few weeks later, in an address on Pan-American Day, he used the phrase "good neighbor" again and this time applied it specifically to the Latin American policy of the United States. Roosevelt completed the retreat from intervention and occupation already begun by the preceding Republican administrations. Roosevelt and his advisers put a policy of genuine Pan-Americanism into effect. They sincerely believed that all the republics of the western hemisphere should stand on a basis of equality, and that mutual respect and cooperation should replace the unilateral domination of the United States. However, even while they implemented their Good Neighbor policy, Roosevelt and Hull kept in mind the self-interest of the United States. They believed that the United States would desperately need good friends in the western hemisphere if the old world succumbed to Nazi and Fascist terror. The way to win such friends, they believed, was to act like one to their Latin American neighbors.

As evidence of these neighborly intentions, Roosevelt withdrew American marines from Haiti. He also surrendered treaty rights to interfere in the internal affairs of the Dominican Republic, Haiti, and Panama. Although a revolution broke out in Cuba in 1933, Roosevelt refused to interfere. When a conservative regime took over the Cuban government in 1934, Roosevelt negotiated a treaty with it which abrogated the right of the United States to intervene in Cuban affairs under the Cuban-American treaty of 1903 (see pp. 572–573).

At the same time, the soft-spoken Hull took leadership at Pan-American conferences in building a new hemispheric system of mutual understanding and collective security. The Montevideo Conference of 1933 adopted a "Convention on Rights and Duties and States." It was sweeping affirmation of earlier Latin American claims, proclaimed the equality of states, and firmly embodied the principles of mutual nonintervention. A special inter-American conference, in Buenos Aires in 1936, adopted a "Convention for Collective Security" and a "Convention to Coordinate, Extend and Assure the Fulfillment of Existing Treaties"—treaties which pledged the signatories to consult with one another if war should threaten the peace of the western hemisphere. Another convention, approved at Buenos Aires, pledged the American republics to settle all disputes peacefully. It also outlawed territorial conquests, the collection of debts by force, and interference by one state in the affairs of another state. The Declaration of Lima, adopted by the Eighth Pan-American Conference in 1938, affirmed the determination of the American republics to resist jointly any Fascist or Nazi threat to the peace of the new world.

The Good Neighbor policy reaped large dividends in Latin American cooperation when war broke out in Europe in 1939. At a special conference in Havana in 1940, Hull won unanimous approval of a warning that an attack on any single American state would be considered to be an attack on all of them. The Havana Conference also established an Inter-American Commission for Territorial Administration to take control of any European colonies in the new world that seemed about to fall into Nazi hands. Once the United States had entered the war, all Latin American states, except Argentina and Chile, at once broke relations with, or declared war upon, the Axis nations. Chile and Argentina later broke relations with them also, though not until Nazi defeat seemed certain. Brazil not only provided airfields for the use of the United States, but also sent a division to fight alongside the Allies in Italy.

The climax of Roosevelt's and Hull's long efforts to build a new inter-American system was the Act of Chapultepec, adopted by a special conference at Mexico City on March 3, 1945. This treaty completed the transformation of the Monroe Doctrine from a policy supported in self-defense by the United States alone into one supported by all American republics. The Act of Chapultepec declared that any attack upon the territory or sovereignty of one American state would be met by the combined forces of all of them. Succeeding inter-American conferences created and used the Organization of American States to defend the peace and security of the western hemisphere. This unity deteriorated during the 1950s and 1960s, when, as will be described later, the United States Government again began to intervene in Latin American affairs, attempted to overthrow governments that it considered radical, and protected conservative dictatorships—all in the supposed interest of combating "international Communism."

The Good Neighbor and Mexico

Certain policies by the Mexican government put the Good Neighbor policy to the acid test. Beginning in 1934, the new administration of President Lázaro Cárdenas began to expropriate American-owned estates in order to provide land for the Mexican peons. Repeated inquiries from the State Department brought repeated answers from the Mexican Foreign Ministry that payment would be made in the future.

One act brought matters to a crisis. On March 18, 1938, Cárdenas announced that the Mexican government would expropriate all foreign oil properties. These holdings of seventeen British and American companies were valued by the companies at $459 million. Although compensation was promised, as in the case of the expropriated farmlands, it was clear that Mexico could not pay even a small fraction of what the oil companies demanded. The British government protested in such a manner as to cause the Mexican government to break diplomatic relations with the London government. But Roosevelt, Hull, and the United States Ambassador in Mexico City, Josephus Daniels, knew that the Mexicans were a proud people. Bluster and force would only provoke bitter resistance. Furthermore, the Americans knew that all of Latin America was watching to see how the Good Neighbor met this crucial test.

Friendly but firm negotiations led to the conclusion on November 19, 1941, of a full settlement of land and oil claims by the United States, which had meanwhile been greatly reduced. Moreover, the United States also promised to help to stabilize the Mexican peso and to provide funds to promote Mexican-American trade. Thus the Roosevelt administration won some degree of friendship from the Mexican people, gained a valuable ally during the Second World War, and demonstrated to doubting Latin Americans that the Good Neighbor meant what he said.

4. THE SECOND WORLD WAR, 1939–1941

The United States and the "Phony War"

Adolf Hitler set out upon a collision course in March 1939 by invading Prague and taking over the remnants of the Czech Republic. Mussolini invaded Albania in the following month. By this time, the British and French were aroused to the enormity of the Nazi peril. They hastened to conclude treaties with Poland that guaranteed the security of that nation, next on Hitler's list of victims.

The British and French also turned to the Soviet Union for help in stopping Hitler, but the Soviets instead concluded a nonaggression pact with the German government on August 23, 1939. The pact's secret provisions gave western Poland to Germany, while Russia might occupy Estonia, Latvia, eastern Poland, Bessarabia in Rumania, and later, Lithuania. Hitler thus protected Germany against a two-front war, while the Russian dictator, Josef Stalin, gained almost two years in which to prepare his country against possible German attack. And if attack should come, Russia had gained territories to absorb the first shock.

Hitler sent his armies into Poland on September 1, 1939. Britain and France declared war on Germany two later. Stalin's armies invaded Poland on September 17, and that helpless nation was partitioned between Germany and Russia on September 29. Europeans had turned upon each other again, almost exactly twenty-five years after the outbreak of the "war to end wars."

Roosevelt analyzed events correctly during the late spring and early summer of 1939. He begged Congress either to repeal the arms embargo, or else to permit the European democracies to purchase war supplies under the cash-and-carry provision of the Neutrality Act of 1937. In spite of the President's plea that such action would help to prevent war, both houses refused to act.

The Second World War

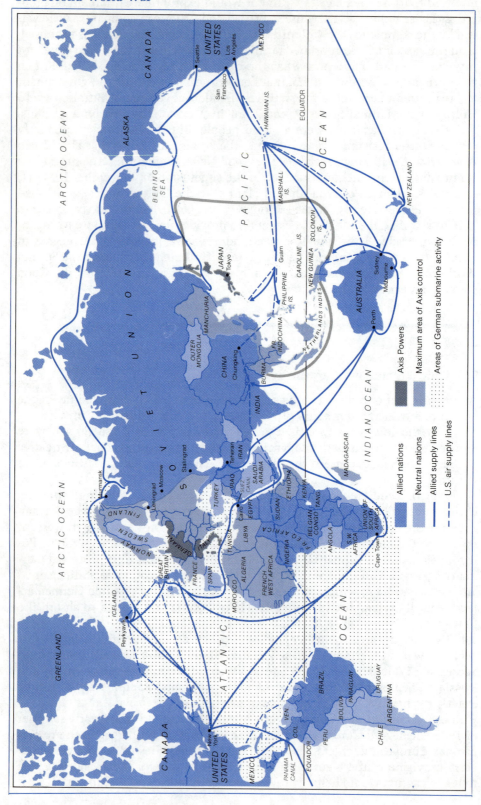

Legend:
- Axis Powers
- Maximum area of Axis control
- Areas of German submarine activity
- Allied nations
- Neutral nations
- Allied supply lines
- U.S. air supply lines

Once war had broken out in Europe, Roosevelt called Congress into extra session for September 21. Again Roosevelt asked Congress to amend the Neutrality Act to permit Allied purchases of arms and munitions in the United States. The many voices raised in protest included those of Senator Borah and Colonel Charles A. Lindbergh, but Roosevelt now had the support of southern and eastern Democrats. He also had behind him a number of Republicans, including Henry L. Stimson and Frank Knox, and also an organization called the Non-Partisan Committee for Peace through Revision of the Neutrality Law. William Allen White, a respected editor of Kansas, headed this group. After a sharp debate, the Senate voted to repeal the arms embargo and also to impose new restrictions on American shipping. The House quickly concurred, and Roosevelt signed the repeal measure on November 4, 1939.

Americans reacted angrily when Russia invaded Finland in November. To the west, quiet reigned as the German and French armies faced each other in their fortified Siegfried and Maginot lines. During this period of what press and radio commentators misleadingly called the "phony war," Americans continued to view events in Europe with calm detachment. They felt secure in the belief that the Royal Navy would strangle the German economy and that the French army would crush its foe, once large-scale fighting broke out.

Roosevelt Rallies the American People to Defense of the Free World

Under cover of the "phony war," Hitler spent the winter of 1939–1940 in frantic preparation for a spring offensive. He launched a blitzkrieg, or lightning war, on April 10, 1940, invaded and overran Denmark, Norway, Holland, Belgium, Luxembourg, and France. In all these attacks, Hitler used an overwhelming combination of tanks, dive bombers, airborne troops, and motorized infantry. To these were added the advantages of surprise and treachery by Nazi sympathizers, or fifth columnists, in the nations being attacked. Paris fell on June 16, and the Germans soon occupied all northern and western France. Southern France — one third of the nation — was left to the rump government of the aged Marshal Henri-Philippe Pétain, who agreed to act as the symbol of partial French independence. Pétain, a fervent anti-Communist, evidently wished for true cooperation with Germany in its war against the Soviet Union, an attitude which, later popular myths to the contrary, enjoyed wide popularity in France. Pétain appointed Pierre Laval, who had been Premier of the French republic four times during the 1920s and 1930s, as his deputy. Laval advocated joining the Germans in war, not only against the Soviet Union, but against Britain and, later, the United States as well.

Neville Chamberlain resigned as Prime Minister of Great Britain on the day that the Germans hurtled into the Low Countries and was succeeded by Winston Spencer Churchill. Churchill's main weapons for defense of the realm consisted of swift fighter planes and iron courage, for the British army of over 335,000 men, miraculously evacuated from Dunkirk, France, had returned home without armor and heavy equipment. Almost every English vessel that could float, including small fishing boats and barges, took part in this rescue effort under continuous fire from German planes, artillery, and infantry machine guns and rifles. Churchill promised his people nothing but "blood, toil, tears, and sweat" — and ultimate victory. He hurled defiance at the Nazi hordes which massed across the English Channel: "We shall defend our island, what-

Prime Minister Winston Churchill visiting residents of Bristol, England, after heavy attack by German bombers. Churchill told the victims, "We shall let them have it back." (United Press International)

ever the cost may be. We shall fight on the beaches. . . . We shall fight on the fields and in the streets. . . . We shall fight in the hills; we shall never surrender." These words still seem brave as well as eloquent, but they might now seem empty without some luck and Hitler's fickle character.

In reply, Hitler sent a vast fleet of bombers to rain devastation and death upon London and other British cities night after night, month after month. Fortunately for the British, the Germans did not have enough vessels available to carry their vastly superior army across the English Channel. Hitler had been unprepared for the rapidity of the German triumph in France, and he had neglected to consider sufficiently what the needs of the German armies would be for an amphibious assault. Furthermore, he expected the British to come to terms without a necessary bloody invasion. Mussolini entered the war as France was collapsing; he thus extended the hostilities to the Mediterranean and Africa. Then Hitler unexpectedly turned to the Balkans, made satellites out of Rumania and Bulgaria, and conquered Yugoslavia and Greece. But he did not attempt an invasion of England.

Alarm, even terror, seized the American people while these events unfolded. Only a tiny minority wanted the Nazis to win, but the great majority of Americans who loathed Hitler remained deeply divided over the wise course for the United States. The noninterventionists united in a nationwide organization called America First. Its supporters included Senators Nye, Wheeler, Bennett Champ Clark of Missouri, and Hiram W. Johnson of California. Charles A. Lindbergh was also a leading member. The America First group favored arming for defense, but it declared that the United States could not save western Europe and should not waste its resources in an attempt to do so.

In opposition stood the so-called internationalists, united in William Allen White's reorganized and expanded organization now called the Committee to Defend America by Aiding the Allies. Internationalists believed that a Europe

Franklin Delano Roosevelt in what was said to be his favorite portrait. He served longer than any U.S. President and led the country out of the depression and to victory in World War II. Shaping the office to himself, he greatly enlarged the powers of the presidency. (Historical Pictures Service, Inc, Chicago)

dominated by Hitler would be a dangerous threat to the security of the United States. They refused to agree that totalitarianism was "the wave of the future," as Lindbergh's wife, Anne Morrow Lindbergh, put it.

All through the spring and summer of 1940—indeed, all through the period of American nonbelligerency—noninterventionists and internationalists carried on their bitter debate. Americans listened and then changed their minds as the arguments of the internationalists and the lessons of events struck home. By July 1940, 69 per cent of the persons queried in a public opinion poll at last replied that they thought that a German victory would imperil American security.

The prime mover in this change in American public opinion was Roosevelt himself. He cast all political caution aside and put himself at the head of the movement to rally Americans to the peril of a Nazi victory. A month before the fall of France, he called for the production of 50,000 planes a year and a vast expansion of defense expenditures. In the belief that the British would not go under, he acted on his authority as commander in chief to rush every available rifle, cartridge, and artillery piece to the British Isles. In September, Roosevelt transferred fifty old but useful destroyers to Britain to enable the Royal Navy to convoy merchantmen and hunt down German submarines. In return the United States received the use of eight naval bases ranging from Newfoundland to British Guiana, and the assurance that Great Britain would not surrender her fleet even if invaded and conquered. The most important—and controversial—part of Roosevelt's defense program was a selective service bill. It was introduced on June 20, 1940, and passed both houses of Congress in September by large majorities.

The Campaign and Election of 1940

Politics continued also, because 1940 was a presidential election year, but not politics of the usual sort. Early in 1940, it seemed certain that one of the three leading Republican noninterventionists—Senator Robert A. Taft of Ohio, Senator Arthur H. Vandenberg of Michigan, or Governor Thomas E. Dewey of New York—would win the presidential nomination. But the Republican national convention met in Philadelphia in the middle of the panic set off by the fall of France, and the delegates took control out of the hands of the party managers. They nominated Wendell L. Willkie, president of the Commonwealth & Southern (utilities) Company, a former Democrat and, most important, an ardent proponent of all-out aid to Great Britain. In a bid for the farm vote, the Republicans nominated Senator Charles L. McNary of Oregon for Vice-President.

Roosevelt almost certainly had decided to run for a third term long before the preconvention campaign began. In a message to the Democratic national convention in Chicago on July 16, he said that he would accept a third nomination if the delegates insisted. Although party leaders would have preferred another candidate, they had to go along with the majority of delegates in renominating Roosevelt on the first ballot. Roosevelt then forced the nomination of the sometimes radical Secretary of Agriculture, Henry A. Wallace, as his running mate.

It was soon apparent that the rugged and forceful Willkie was the first dynamic Republican candidate since Theodore Roosevelt. Willkie tried to capitalize upon the strong tradition against a third term, but he was severely handicapped by his substantial agreement with Roosevelt's domestic and foreign policies. Indeed, Willkie had generously supported the selective service bill and endorsed the transfer of the destroyers to Great Britain. Faced with defeat, Willkie suddenly shifted gears in early October and began to attack Roosevelt for allegedly leading the country into the war. Roosevelt replied that he would not send American boys into any "foreign" wars.

In the election on November 5, 1940, Willkie polled 45 per cent of the popular vote, but he carried only ten states with eighty-two electoral votes, to Roosevelt's 449 electoral votes. The election made little change in the relative strength of the two parties in the Seventy-seventh Congress, which would sit during 1941 and 1942.

Lend-Lease

Roosevelt left for a Caribbean cruise—a much needed vacation—aboard *U.S.S. Tuscaloosa* soon after the election. On December 9, 1940, a seaplane delivered a long letter from Prime Minister Churchill to the President. Great Britain was rapidly approaching a crisis, Churchill explained, because she had spent almost all her available dollars for supplies in the United States. Britain would be unable to conduct any offensive operations if she could no longer obtain airplanes, munitions, and other supplies from the United States. Moreover, Churchill continued, Britain desperately needed American help in keeping the North Atlantic supply lanes open in the face of a mounting German submarine threat.

Roosevelt devised a solution during the next few days, which he announced at a press conference on December 17 and in a fireside chat twelve days later. Because Great Britain was fighting America's fight, Roosevelt declared, the United States would lend or lease to her the equipment and supplies necessary for victory over the common foe: "We must be the great arsenal of democracy," Roosevelt concluded in his fireside chat. ". . . I call upon our people with absolute confidence that our common cause will greatly succeed."

The lend-lease bill, introduced into Congress on January 9, 1941, received full and frank debate. Congress and the entire country well understood its momentous significance. Passage of the measure would mean nothing less than full-scale American commitment to the defeat of Germany, by aid to Britain if possible, and by American military participation if that was necessary. The Senate approved the lend-lease bill by a vote of sixty to thirty-one on March 8; the House, by a vote of 317 to seventy-one three days later. Roosevelt signed the Lend-Lease Act at once and recommended an appropriation of $7 billion for production of lend-lease materials. Congress voted the money two weeks later.

Toward the Brink of War

Roosevelt was still eager to avoid full-scale military participation, but, like a growing majority of the American people, he intended to do everything necessary to assure Germany's defeat, no matter what the risks. Above all, he was determined that crucial lend-lease supplies should get through to Britain. Consequently, during the spring and early summer, he seized ninety-two ships in

American ports which belonged to German, Italian, French, Dutch, and Norwegian owners; froze German and Italian assets in the United States; occupied the Danish islands of Greenland and Iceland; and extended the American "neutrality" patrol to the mid-Atlantic. When German armies invaded Russia on June 21, 1941, the President sent his now closest personal adviser, Harry Hopkins, to Moscow to assure the Russian leaders that they would receive lend-lease assistance as soon as possible.

In August 1941, Roosevelt met Churchill aboard *U.S.S. Augusta* off the coast of Newfoundland. They agreed upon eight principles upon which they said that they based their hopes for a better future for mankind. This declaration, known as the Atlantic Charter, called for the restoration of self-government to peoples oppressed by dictators. It also demanded equal access to raw materials for all nations, freedom of the seas, a peace with justice, and relief from the crushing burden of armaments.

Now that American naval vessels in fact convoyed British ships to Iceland, clashes between American warships and German submarines were inevitable. A submarine attacked the destroyer *Greer* on September 4, but the torpedo missed its mark. On Ocober 17, the destroyer *Kearney* was hit and badly damaged, with the loss of eleven lives. Then, on October 31, a German submarine sank the destroyer *Reuben James* with the loss of half her crew.

Roosevelt did not ask Congress to declare war, but he publicly denounced the "piratical" acts of Nazi submarines. Moreover, he instituted an undeclared naval war with Germany by ordering American naval vessels to "shoot on sight" at any submarine which appeared in waters west of Iceland. In November 1941, Congress authorized American merchantmen to arm and to sail through war zones to British ports. Congress renewed the Selective Service Act in August and eliminated the prohibition in that measure against sending draftees outside the western hemisphere. The United States thus became a full member of a new alliance in every respect except a declaration of war against the common enemy. Admiral Harold R. Stark, Chief of Naval Operations, confided to his diary that Hitler had been given "every excuse in the world to declare war on us now," but, with his armies already fully occupied, Hitler refrained from official war with the United States.

SUGGESTED READINGS

Textbooks on American foreign policy are not strong on early New Deal diplomacy, perhaps because it was overshadowed by domestic events. Allan Nevins, *The New Deal and World Affairs* (1951), is a brief survey. Charles A. Beard, *American Foreign Policy in the Making, 1932–1940* (1946), is an isolationist account which is refuted by Basil Rauch, *Roosevelt: From Munich to Pearl Harbor* (1950). William L. Langer and S. E. Gleason, *The Challenge to Isolation* (1952) and *The Undeclared War* (1953) are excellent, comprehensive studies. For an interesting account of the debate over neutrality, see Robert Divine, *The Illusion of Neutrality* (1962). On Roosevelt's problem with isolationists, see also Wayne S. Cole, *America First* (1953) and Ger-

ald P. Nye and American Foreign Relations (1962); John K. Nelson, *The Peace Prophets: American Pacifist Thought 1919–1941*;and Manfred Jonas, *Isolationisim in America, 1935–1941* (1966). James M. Burns, *Roosevelt: The Soldier of Freedom* (1970), is a worthy sequel to his study of Roosevelt as a domestic leader. For a recent thorough survey of Roosevelt's foreign policy, see Robert Dallek, *Franklin D. Roosevelt and American Foreign Policy, 1932–1945* (1979).

On more specialized problems, see Bryce Wood, *The Making of the Good Neighbor Policy* (1961); Howard C. Cline, *The United States and Mexico* (1953); and E. David Cronon, *Josephus Daniels in Mexico* (1960). Robert P. Browder, *The Origins of Soviet-Ameri-*

can Diplomacy (1953), is the best work on American recognition of the USSR. Dorothy Borg, *The United States and the Far Eastern Crisis of 1933–1938* (1964), is the fullest treatment of that subject. Paul W. Schroeder, *The Axis Alliance and Japanese-American Relations, 1941* (1958), and Robert J. C. Butow, *Tojo and the Coming of the War* (1961), are instructive but do not replace Herbert Feis, *The Road to Pearl Harbor* (1950). Warren Moscow, *Roosevelt and Willkie* (1968), covers adequately their presidential campaigns and later cooperation during the war. Early sections of John Costello, *The Battle of the Atlantic* (1977), deal with the "undeclared war." Winston S. Churchill's *The Gathering Storm* (1948) and *Their Finest Hour* (1949), and Hans L. Trefousse, *Germany and American Neutrality* (1951), are helpful in placing American policy in a global context.

On French negative and positive contributions to the Allied war effort, see Robert O. Paxton, *Vichy France* (1972); Alan Milward, *The New Order and the French Economy* (1970); H. Stuart Hughes, *The Obstructed Path* (1968); Peter Novick, *The Resistance Versus Vichy* (1968); R. O. Paxton, *Parades and Politics at Vichy* (1966); and Charles de Gaulle, *Memoirs*, 3 vols. (1954–1959). We still lack a balanced biography of De Gaulle, or a study of the Free French effort without obvious biases.

CHAPTER 32
THE UNITED STATES IN THE SECOND WORLD WAR

1. THE ATTACK ON PEARL HARBOR UNITES THE NATION

The Road to Pearl Harbor

In view of the growing commitment of the United States to Great Britain by late 1941, it probably remained only a question of *when*, not of *whether*, full-scale fighting would break out with Germany. As events turned out, the United States was plunged into active belligerency, not by any incident in the North Atlantic, but by the action of Japan.

Even though the Japanese continued their aggression against China and occupied northern Indochina after the fall of France in 1940, the United States Government followed a restrained policy toward Tokyo out of fear that too much pressure might cause the Japanese to attack Siberia or the East Indies. Roosevelt, however, issued a sharp warning on July 26, 1939, by renouncing the Japanese-American Commercial Treaty of 1911. According to the terms of that treaty, the American government could now limit or halt entirely trade between the two countries within six months. Such action would cut off Japan from its major source (the United States) of scrap iron, oil, and other materials necessary for either offensive or defensive war.

The attitude of leaders in Washington hardened rapidly during the autumn of 1940 in the wake of what seemed to be new signs of hostility from Tokyo. In September, the Japanese, German, and Italian governments concluded the Triple, or Axis, Alliance, which appeared to be aimed directly at the United States.

Moreover, leaders of the Japanese government made it clear that they meant to establish what they called a Greater East Asia Co-Prosperity Sphere, which meant, essentially, Japanese dominance over the entire Far East. Certain powerful Japanese leaders made it plain also that they would press forward with their plans in spite of the risk of war with the United States. For example, Foreign Minister Yosuke Matsuoka told the Japanese Diet, or parliament, on January 26, 1941: "There is nothing left but to face America. . . . Japan must demand America's reconsideration of her attitude, and if she does not listen, there is slim hope for friendly relations between Japan and the United States."

Japanese military leaders and the more militaristic of the Japanese political leaders hoped to take advantage of German victories in Europe and seize the relatively unprotected French, British, and Dutch possessions in Asia. However, they also wanted to end successfully their war with China, which was causing a terrible drain on their manpower and resources, and most of them still wanted to avoid hostilities with the United States.

As a preparatory step—in order to seal off supply lines to China and provide bases for possible future expansion southward—the Japanese occupied bases in southern French Indochina. Roosevelt and Hull interpreted this action as the opening move in a campaign of conquest. Their response was to freeze Japanese assets in the United States in July 1941; they also clamped an embargo on the export to Japan of oil, steel, aviation gasoline, and other materials. The British and Dutch in the East Indies followed suit immediately.

Authorities in Tokyo were now in a desperate dilemma. Half their supplies of oil, iron, and steel came from the United States. Without these supplies, it would be impossible to maintain the Japanese economy—or war machine. Some way had to be found to resume normal trade with the United States or else to find vital raw materials elsewhere. Since all but the most extreme military leaders in Tokyo continued to oppose war with the giant of the West, Japanese diplomats turned to Washington in the hope of finding some compromise arrangement.

Japanese-American negotiations had started in the early months of 1941. After an interruption caused by the embargo, they resumed in the summer and dragged on into the autumn. The Japanese offered many concessions. They promised to make no move southward and not to attack the Soviet Union. They declared also that they would not feel bound by the Triple Alliance to go to war against the United States if America became involved in hostilities with Germany. The more the Japanese conceded, the harder Secretary Hull turned the vise in the mistaken belief that the Japanese had to cave in and ultimately would do so. In the final analysis, the one sticking point was China. The Japanese demanded that the United States stop all aid to Chiang Kai-shek. Hull not only refused to abandon the Chinese, or to make any compromising concessions which would have postponed if not avoided war; Hull also insisted that the Japanese withdraw from China at once. The Japanese were faced with the alternative of either enormous blows to their pride and their new empire, on the one hand, or war, on the other hand. They reluctantly chose the latter course. This choice was made a bit easier by the Nazi attack on the Soviet Union, which removed a potential threat to the Japanese northern flank.

Pearl Harbor

On the morning of Sunday, December 7, 1941, three waves of bombers from Japanese aircraft carriers suddenly struck the great American naval and air bases at Pearl Harbor and elsewhere in the Hawaiian Islands. Their rain of destruction completely surprised all American leaders, despite warnings that a Japanese attack somewhere might be imminent. An American code analyst had broken the Japanese top-priority diplomatic code, and Americans had also deciphered the Japanese intelligence code. Furthermore, United States agents had monitored the movements of a huge Japanese fleet moving through the South China Sea. Despite this and other evidence indicating what was to occur (such as intensive Japanese mapping of Pearl Harbor), and when it would take place (intelligence officials estimated that an attack would take place about December 7), American leaders, including Roosevelt and Hull, the two officials with access to the fullest knowledge of Japanese plans and activities, as well as top American intelligence experts, refused to believe that a Japanese carrier flotilla could reach Pearl Harbor. Therefore, they neglected to keep naval and army commanders in Hawaii up to date on events, or to impart urgency to their messages.

Magazine of U.S.S. Shaw *exploding during the Japanese raid on Pearl Harbor, December 7, 1941. In this spectacular view, the destroyer had just been struck by a wave of bombers that blew off her bow and sunk the dock. Yet the damage was so slight from the bridge to the stern that* Shaw *was rebuilt and later rejoined the fleet. (United Press International)*

Altogether, the Japanese sank or disabled nineteen ships, including eight battleships; in addition, they destroyed 120 planes on the ground and killed more than 2,300 men. Their success exceeded the most optimistic Japanese hopes. Their task force even escaped without detection by American planes or ships. The Japanese also blasted naval and air bases in the Philippines, Guam, Midway, British Hong Kong, and the Malay Peninsula. The American air force in the Philippines suffered near annihilation when its planes were caught on the ground at the military airfield close to Manila. This occurred even though military leaders in that area were well aware of the earlier attack on Pearl Harbor. This negligence almost defies rational explanation. It does seem, however, that American political and military leaders, from Roosevelt and Hull to General Douglas McArthur, commander of American forces in the Philippines, simply underestimated the military capabilities of the Japanese. However, McArthur, at least, should have known better, because he had served in the Pacific area for a considerable period of time. It was the most devastating military disaster that the United States had ever suffered.

Roosevelt appeared before Congress on December 8, 1941, to ask for a declaration of war against Japan. It was voted with but one dissenting voice (of Jeannette Rankin of Montana, who had also voted against the war resolution in 1917) in the House and unanimously in the Senate. Three days later, Germany and Italy somewhat reluctantly honored their agreement with Japan and declared war on the United States on December 11. The American government replied in kind on the same day.

General George C. Marshall served as Army Chief of Staff from 1939 to the end of the war. Admiral Ernest J. King was named commander in chief of the fleet in December 1941 and, a few months later, was also appointed Chief of Naval Operations. Later these leaders received the new five-star ranks of General of the Army and Admiral of the Fleet.

Uniting for Victory

Not since the Civil War had the American people faced such stupendous military tasks as in 1941. In the Second World War, they were called upon to fight two major wars on two far-flung fronts at the same time. Never had Americans been so united as they were during the period of their belligerency in the Second World War. Their leaders, skeptical of excessive idealism, did not proclaim a second crusade to make the world safe for democracy. It was, they said, rather, a fight for the survival of American institutions and the American way of life; and leaders in Washington went about the job at hand with relentless determination to finish it as quickly as possible.

The government rounded up the small number of open Nazi sympathizers and later tried them, unsuccessfully, for sedition. At Roosevelt's instructions, the army apprehended all inhabitants of Japanese ancestry, citizens and noncitizens alike, on the West coast, although no evidence existed (or does now) to show that they were anything but loyal to the United States. Nevertheless, the army transferred them to makeshift camps in the interior. The evidence is unmistakable that Caucasian Californians took advantage of the panic after Pearl Harbor to persuade federal authorities to "settle" the Japanese-American "problem" once and for all. Thus California authorities, including Attorney General Earl Warren, were primarily responsible for one of the most disgraceful episodes in American history. Thousands of Californians of Japanese ancestry lost their homes, farms, and other businesses, and most of their possessions. In what can best be described as "concentration camps," many persons lost their health and some their lives. Yet thousands of young men in the camps volunteered to fight for the United States in the war against Japan as well as against Germany. However, even decorated Japanese veterans of the war's most bitter battles often could not recover their lost property or jobs after the war.

Nor were persons of Japanese ancestry the only group persecuted in the West during the war, particularly in California. Mexican-American youths became the victims of increasing violence which culminated in the so-called "Zoot-suit riots" of 1943 in Los Angeles. Mobs of servicemen roamed at will through downtown Los Angeles and stabbed and beat Mexican Americans, particularly young men.

Further steps to regiment or solidify the people were not deemed necessary, nor did the government launch a large propaganda campaign at home. Americans were united because the one potentially subversive group of any importance, the Communists, stood wholeheartedly behind the war effort. Russia and the United States were fighting a common enemy.

Mobilizing Manpower and Resources for Victory

Young men rushed to recruiting stations after Pearl Harbor, but the main task of raising an army and navy fell upon the Selective Service authorities. All told, they registered some 31,000,000 men, of whom nearly 10,000,000 were inducted into service. A total of more than 15,000,000 men and women (including volunteers) served before the end of the war. There were more than 10,000,000 men and women in the army, 3,884,000 in the navy, nearly 600,000 in the marines, and 242,000 in the Coast Guard. It was by far the largest mobilization of manpower in American history, but it was not exceptional compared to the mobilization of 22,000,000 in the Soviet Union, 17,000,000 in Germany, and 12,000,000 in Great Britain, the dominions, and the British Empire.

American casualties numbered 253,573 dead and 65,834 missing, 651,042 wounded, and 114,205 prisoners. However, these figures were remarkably low considering the numbers involved and the length and ferocity of the fighting. For this fact, American fighting men could thank recent medical advances such as penicillin and the use of blood for transfusions. Technology also provided new and superior medical equipment.

Industrial mobilization went through several stages, just as it had done during the First World War. In January 1942, with the creation of the War Production Board, Roosevelt first tried to institute effective controls. The failure of the War Production Board to gain control of raw materials led Roosevelt, in October 1942, to establish the Office of Economic Stabilization, with former Supreme Court Justice James F. Byrnes at its head. Byrnes successfully imposed priorities that assured an uninterrupted flow of raw materials to war industries. In May 1943, Roosevelt made Byrnes head of the new Office of War Mobilization, with near dictatorial authority over the entire economy.

Next in importance to mobilizing men for the armed forces and assuring a steady supply of materials to the battlefronts came the task of preventing runaway inflation, which could have seriously impeded the entire war effort. Roosevelt established an office of Price Administration (OPA) in April 1941, but it lacked authority to prevent price increases. Accordingly, the cost of living rose at the rate of 2 per cent a month during the next year. However, the OPA received statutory authority from the Emergency Price Control and Anti-Inflation Acts of 1942. Thereafter, the OPA and Office of Economic Stabilization fought successfully to hold the line in the face of pressures for increases in wages and farm prices. The cost of living increased less than 1.5 per cent between the spring of 1943 and the summer of 1945, despite the severe scarcity of consumer goods (no cars were made during the period, for example) and the huge increase in the number of Americans employed and in their incomes. The government's success in stabilizing prices was a remarkable achievement, which could have been accomplished only with wide cooperation from the American civilian population.

The lifting of production controls was all that was necessary to achieve abundant food production, in spite of a decline in the number of agricultural workers during the war. The index of farm production rose from 108 in 1940 to 123 in 1945, and the increases in food crops were even more striking. There was never any threat of food shortages, and the rationing of scarce items such as sugar and meat to the public assured a plentiful supply of these items to the armed forces.

The growing demands of war industries pushed domestic civilian employment up from 46,500,000 in 1940 to 53,000,000 in 1945, despite the induction of millions of men into the fighting services. The government had no such difficulty manning new shipyards and assembly lines during the Second World War as it had experienced during the First, because the United States went to war in 1941 with about 7,000,000 unemployed workers. They were quickly trained and absorbed into the labor force and provided the core of the new labor required. Women who might otherwise have remained at home constituted another huge pool of workers that was tapped to fill wartime needs. In April 1942, Roosevelt created a War Manpower Commission, which helped to direct the flow of labor into war industries. The United States never suffered a serious shortage of workers; thus the country was spared the necessity of having to institute severe manpower controls, such as the conscription of labor.

The main task in the mobilization of labor was to see that strikes did not slow down the war economy. The War Labor Board, created by Roosevelt in January 1942, went to work at once to establish guidelines for wages, hours, and collective bargaining. Employers, workers, and unions cooperated with an unprecedented show of unity. Under the protection of the War Labor Board, union membership grew to nearly 15,000,000 by 1945. The weekly earnings of persons engaged in manufacturing increased by 70 per cent from 1941 to 1945, while the cost of living rose by 23 per cent (mostly before the Anti-Inflation Act of 1942). There were numerous irritating work stoppages, but most were short-lived and caused a loss of only one ninth of 1 per cent of total working time. Even the British, with much more rigorous controls, did not exceed this record.

Blacks and the War Effort at Home

The Second World War was a dividing line in the history of race relations in the United States. Open segregation still prevailed throughout the South, to be sure, but blacks acquired a new sense of participation in national affairs from the knowledge that 1,000,000 of their number were serving in the armed forces. Resentment continued, however, against governmental policies that kept black soldiers in segregated units. Also, some black Americans remembered that their reward for participation in the First World War included increased lynchings and mob beatings of blacks throughout the country and a series of terrible race riots (see pp. 680–681).

American blacks also benefited more than any other single group in the country from the expanded opportunities that came with wartime full employment and prosperity. More than 1,000,000 black men and women left the South to find jobs in war industries in the North, Middle West, and the Pacific coast area.

Black demands for employment opportunities and the dire need for labor combined to cause Roosevelt, on June 25, 1941, to issue Executive Order 8802 that forbade discrimination in defense hiring on account of color. However, it had taken the threat of a gigantic march by blacks on Washington, issued by A. Philip Randolph, head of the pullman porters' union, to cause Roosevelt to act. Roosevelt, at the same time, established the Fair Employment Practices Committee (FEPC) to investigate charges of economic discrimination on account of race. This first federal agency dedicated to the protection of the rights of blacks since the Freedmen's Bureau worked ineffectively until 1943; then Roosevelt gave the FEPC real authority to enforce Executive Order 8802. By the beginning of 1945, nearly 2,000,000 blacks were at work in war plants throughout the country. In some areas, the influx of black workers led to mob violence. In Detroit, for example, a "riot" in June 1943 left twenty-three blacks and nine whites dead, and many more injured.

Production for Victory

Most American businessmen and economists thought that Roosevelt was dreaming when he talked in 1940 and 1941 about producing 100,000 planes and 50,000 tanks a year. As it turned out, Roosevelt overestimated only moderately how productive the American economy could be once it received stimulus from unlimited governmental credit, wartime demand, and effective organization. American factories turned out a total of 275,000 military aircraft, 75,000 tanks, and 650,000 pieces of artillery. American shipyards built 55,239,000 tons of merchant shipping. A brand new synthetic rubber industry, built during 1942 and 1943, produced 762,000 tons in 1944 and 820,000 tons in 1945. Some idea of the dimension of the achievement on the home front can be seen in the fact that the total value of all goods and services in the United States increased about 75 per cent between 1939 and 1945. Moreover, war-related goods never amounted to more than one third of America's industrial production. With the possible exception of Soviet Russia, no national economy in the world was so carefully planned and managed. The Germans, far behind American economists in econometrics and in applying theories of input-output models, suffered from staggering industrial and transport inefficiency.

Furthermore, American scientists, organized under the Office of Scientific Research and Development, at least matched their German counterparts, who enjoyed a lengthy head start, in devising weapons which may have been decisive in the war. American scientists developed highly effective radar with British assistance. Radar detected enemy ships, submarines, and planes, and accurately directed shells against them. Proximity fuses detonated explosives just as they reached their targets. Rockets increased enormously the firepower of planes, ships, and tanks, although German research went even further in this area. Fortunately, the German program to develop an atomic bomb came nowhere near matching American success, or the war might have had an entirely different ending.

The Costs of the War

Federal expenditures, virtually all of which went for the war effort, totaled a little more than $321 billion from 1941 to 1945. This sum was twice as large as all federal expenditures between 1789 and 1941, and ten times as large as expenditures during the First World War.

The government met 59 per cent of these costs by borrowing. As a result, the gross national debt increased from $49 billion in 1941 to $259 billion at the end of hostilities. The American people, already faced with greatly increased taxes in a bill passed in September 1941, accepted with little grumbling a new Revenue Act in October 1942 that more than doubled the tax burden. Tax receipts between 1941 and 1945 totaled about $131 billion and paid for 41 per cent of the costs of the war. It was the highest percentage of expenditures raised by taxes during any major war in American history. Moreover, this aspect of excellent cooperation among the great majority of the American people helped significantly to combat price inflation and to prevent handing to future generations a huge burden of debt.

2. FIGHTING A WAR ON TWO FRONTS

The African Campaign

The first massive operation in which American forces played a leading role was the campaign to drive the Italians and Germans from North Africa and to break their stranglehold on the Mediterranean supply line. The Italians had bogged down in their drive for the Suez Canal and the oil fields of Arabia. Hitler's Afrika Korps, commanded by the dashing "Desert Fox," General (later Field Marshal) Erwin Rommel, poured into North Africa and fought the British for possession of Egypt. American ships, forced to take the long route around southern Africa, arrived with tanks at Alexandria, just in time to help stop the Nazis. Then, on October 23, 1942, General Sir Bernard Montgomery and his British Eighth Army launched a great counteroffensive. Montgomery defeated Rommel at El Alamein and then drove the Italians and Germans 2,000 miles westward to the borders of Tunisia. At this point, the Americans struck at the enemy's rear through Morocco and Algeria.

On November 8, 1942, a huge Anglo-American force, in 500 transports convoyed by 350 warships, landed on the northwestern coast of Africa. The campaign was directed by General Dwight D. Eisenhower, new American commander in the European theater of operations. It had been planned by Roosevelt and Churchill to aid the Russians by diverting German troops and equipment from their crucial campaign against Stalingrad.

The German and Vichy French forces were caught unready for the attack. Within three days, the Anglo-American armies had gained the whole of French North Africa up to the border of Tunisia. They succeeded in bottling up the

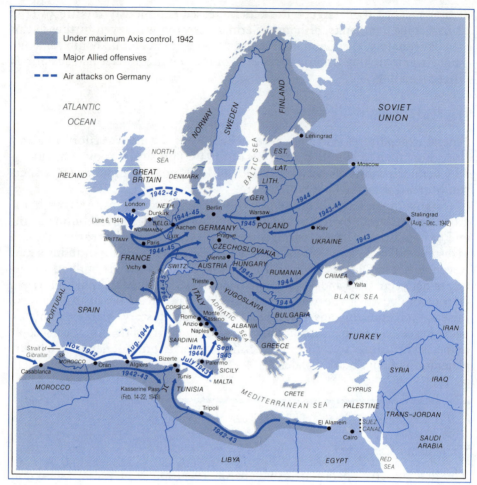

World War II in Europe and North Africa

Germans in the narrow Tunisian salient while Montgomery's Eighth Army moved in from the east. The Germans continued the fight all through the winter, but their losses were heavy because the Allies controlled both the sea and the air. Tunis was captured on May 7, 1943, after a bitter struggle, and the Axis army surrendered five days later. The entire campaign had cost the Axis more than 349,000 men killed or captured, in comparison to only 70,000 casualties for the Allies.

The victory at Tunis ended the Axis threat to the Mediterranean. This strategically important sea was now safe for Allied ships from Gibraltar to the Suez Canal. In the meantime, Soviet armies had captured an entire German army at Stalingrad and raised the siege of Leningrad.

Carrying the War to Italy

From Africa, the Anglo-American forces launched an attack on Italy. General George S. Patton's American Seventh Army and General Montgomery's Eighth

Army invaded Sicily on July 10, 1943, and captured the island on August 17 after bitter fighting. While the battle for Sicily raged, momentous events were transpiring in Rome. The Italians were thoroughly sick of the war, of the Nazis, and of Mussolini. The Fascist Grand Council deposed the Dictator on July 25, and King Victor Emmanuel appointed Marshal Pietro Badoglio as head of a new non-Fascist government. Mussolini was arrested but was rescued by German paratroopers, who took him to Lake Como in northern Italy. There he established a rump Fascist government.

Meanwhile, Allied armies prepared for the conquest of Italy. They landed on the toe of the peninsula on September 3, 1943, and made their way slowly northward against mud, rain, mountainous terrain, and desperate resistance by the Germans. The Italian government, on September 3, 1943, signed an armistice which permitted it to become a cobelligerent of the Allies. Nevertheless, the American and British armies in Italy endured a grueling test against the heavily reinforced Germans. Americans suffered heavy losses at the Gulf of Salerno, south of Naples, and at the Anzio beachhead near Rome—a foolish attempt to outflank a well-trained army whose generals were ready for just such a move. GIs (American troops), congregated on the beach after landing, were mowed down by German machine guns, artillery, and bombing and strafing from the air. Then the Americans ran into one clever ambush after another as they attempted to move inland. The GIs paid dearly when they stormed the towering monastery of Monte Cassino, south of Rome, which the Germans had heavily fortified. However, the Allied armies finally entered the Italian capital on June 4, 1944. The Germans hung on doggedly to the northern part of Italy and still held that area when the Nazi armies surrendered in May 1945. Meanwhile, the Americans had lost more than 70,000 men during their campaign in Italy.

From Disaster to Victory in the Pacific

During the six months after the attack on Pearl Harbor, the Japanese engulfed more than 1,000,000 square miles of the area of the Pacific Ocean. They captured the Philippines, Thailand, Burma, the Malay Peninsula, the great British naval base at Singapore, New Guinea, and the Dutch East Indies. In addition, the Japanese occupied hundreds of islands from which they hoped to cut the Allied supply lines to the South Pacific and to capture Australia and New Zealand as well. The United States, crippled by the losses at Pearl Harbor and in the Philippines, required several months before it could bring sufficient military and naval strength to the Pacific to try even to stop the onrushing Japanese.

Two huge naval-air battles turned the tide. In the great Battle of the Coral Sea, southeast of New Guinea, fought on May 7–8, 1942, both sides suffered heavy losses, but planes from the American carriers *Lexington* and *Yorktown* repulsed a large Japanese armada on its way to attack Australia. Soon afterward, the Japanese made a bold bid to cut American communications in the Pacific by sending a large invasion force against Midway, an outpost of the Hawaiian Islands. American experts had broken the Japanese secret military code, and the fleet under Admiral Chester Nimitz was ready and waiting when the Japanese warships neared Midway on June 3. In a furious battle that lasted until June 6, American carrier planes sank four of the enemy's finest carriers, a heavy cruiser, and three destroyers. The battle dealt a death blow to Japanese

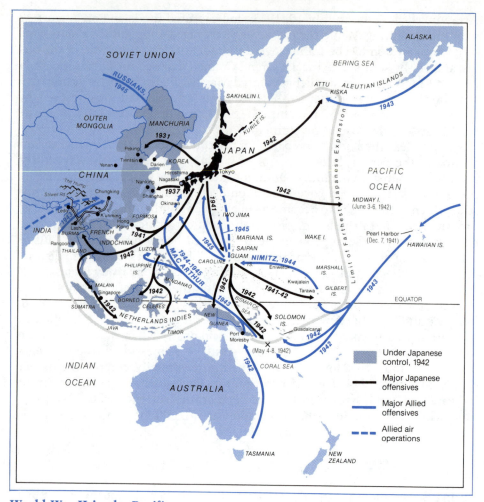

World War II in the Pacific

naval aviation. The balance of naval power thereafter rested in American hands, although the Japanese navy and army remained very strong.

American land operations began on August 7, 1942, when the 1st Marine Division went ashore on the steaming island of Guadalcanal in the Solomon Islands. Then began a two-year struggle to regain other islands, which the Japanese had heavily fortified and defended with extraordinary courage. American losses were, therefore, high in the capture of Tarawa in the Gilberts in November 1943. Kwajalein and other islands in the Marshalls, and Guam and Saipan in the Marianas, fell in 1944. It took a month of desperate fighting— from February 19 to March 16, 1945—at the frightful cost of 24,000 men, before marines planted the American flag on Mount Suribachi on Iwo Jima and rooted out the last defenders. An even more furious battle followed when marine and army forces attacked the island of Okinawa, only 350 miles south of Japan itself, in April 1945. The battle for Okinawa ended on June 21, and American naval and air forces were now within easy striking distance of the Japanese homeland.

By this time in 1945, the Pacific Fleet, under Admirals Nimitz and William F. Halsey, had grown to twenty-four battleships, twenty-six heavy cruisers, sixty-four escort carriers, fifty-two light cruisers, and 323 destroyers. In addition, twenty army divisions and some 15,000 combat aircraft were in the Pacific area. The Japanese fleet had been almost totally destroyed. Japanese merchant ships were being sunk by airplanes and submarines at so fast a pace that Japan faced starvation in the near future.

The Liberation of the Philippines

To Americans, the most gratifying of all operations in the Pacific was the liberation of the Philippines After the Japanese invaded the islands in early 1942, the American commander, General MacArthur, was ordered to Australia to take supreme command of Allied forces in the South Pacific. He left with the dramatic parting prophecy "I shall return." General Jonathan Wainwright commanded American and Filipino troops on Luzon in a heroic defense of Bataan and the rock of Corregidor. Japanese troops forced them to surrender on May 6, 1942.

It took two and a half years before MacArthur could redeem his promise. He first fought his way up the eastern and northern coast of New Guinea; he then assembled huge land, air, and sea forces for the counterinvasion in October 1944. It began on October 20, as Americans, under naval and air cover, swarmed ashore at Leyte Island in the southeastern part of the archipelago. The Japanese navy made one last suicidal bid for victory in the great Battle of Leyte Gulf and then withdrew. Again and again, the Japanese tried to land reinforcements on the islands, but the American navy frustrated every such attempt. American troops landed on the main island of Luzon on January 9, 1945, and fought their way southward to Manila. They took the city on February 4; organized Japanese resistance in the islands ended in March 1945. All told, the Japanese lost more than 400,000 men and 9,000 planes in the Battle for the Philippines.

MacArthur turned the government of the Philippines over to President Sergio Osmeña in March 1945. The independence of the Philippine Republic was proclaimed on July 4, 1946, in accordance with the Philippine Independence Act of 1934. In March 1947, the United States and the new republic signed a treaty which gave the United States military and naval bases in the islands.

From Normandy to the Siegfried Line

The crucial operation of the entire Second World War was termed, for secret communications purposes, OVERLORD — the long-awaited invasion of France and Hitler's *Festung* (Fortress) *Europa.* Early in the morning of June 6, 1944, some 11,000 American and British planes began to pound German coastal defenses in northern France. Then three airborne divisions landed in the fields of Normandy. Soon afterward, at 7:30 A.M., Anglo-American forces under the command of General Eisenhower, now Supreme Allied Commander in Europe, poured out of more than 4,000 transports and war vessels to assault five beaches on the Cotentin Peninsula. Altogether, it was the greatest amphibious landing ever undertaken. Fortunately for the invaders, Hitler ignored the advice of

General Rommel, who had calculated correctly where and when the invasion would take place, and had ordered the best German fortifications built and the finest German troops placed elsewhere. Hitler believed the misinformation deliberately fed to the Germans by the Allies because his favorite astrologer believed this wrong information.

For weeks the Allied armies battled against the stiff resistance of German forces under Field Marshals Rommel and Karl von Rundstedt. However, the Allies enjoyed complete control of the air, and the Germans had to divide their forces in expectation of attacks elsewhere. A huge hole was opened in the German lines at Saint-Lô on about July 25. Soon General Patton's tanks were pouring through by the thousands. French underground forces rose openly to aid their liberators, and, up from the Mediterranean, came the American Seventh Army under General Alexander M. Patch to join the eastward-moving troops. Paris was freed on August 25, Brussels and Antwerp a few days later. Units of General Courtney Hodges' American First Army entered the "sacred soil" of Hitler's Third Reich on September 12, 1944. Soon six Allied armies, which totaled more than 2,000,000 men, faced the great Siegfried Line which extended the whole length of Germany's western border from the Netherlands to Switzerland.

The Presidential Campaign of 1944

By constitutional stipulation, the United States held its quadrennial presidential campaign, even though the time was hardly propitious for ordinary political debate. The Republicans had done so well in the mid-term election of 1942 that a spirited contest took place among their leaders for the presidential nomination. Wendell Willkie at first seemed the favorite for the G.O.P. nomination, but he was soon vanquished in state conventions and primary elections by the young and energetic Governor Dewey of New York. Dewey won the nomination easily on the first ballot. The Republicans adopted a platform endorsing the basic New Deal programs. The platform also promised Republican cooperation in the movement then under way for the creation of an international agency to preserve peace in the postwar era.

Even though Roosevelt was in ailing health (he suffered a heart attack in June 1944), and it was doubtful whether he could survive the rigors of a fourth term, he was determined to direct the war effort through to victory and to take the lead in establishing a lasting peace. The Democratic national convention, which met at Chicago on July 19, had no alternative but to name Roosevelt as its standard-bearer for a fourth time. However, there was a bitter fight over the vice-presidential nomination. Democratic leaders were determined to unseat Vice-President Wallace because of his alleged temperamental defects. Some feared Wallace's egalitarian social and economic ideals; others worried about the political unorthodoxy of the man who might succeed the ailing President. Roosevelt did not insist upon Wallace's renomination and indicated that he would accept a number of other running mates. After much skirmishing, Roosevelt and the party managers settled upon Senator Harry S. Truman of Missouri. Truman, an ardent New Dealer, was acceptable to labor, Southerners, farmers, and workers.

Dewey put up a good fight, but the voters were more interested in the smashing Allied victories in Europe and the Pacific than in the New York Governor's speeches. Moreover, Roosevelt's health and spirits improved visibly as the campaign progressed. He won a decisive victory on November 7, 1944; Roosevelt garnered 25,600,000 popular votes and 432 electoral votes, against 22,000,000 popular votes and ninety-nine electoral votes for Dewey. In addition, the Democrats gained twenty seats in the next House of Representatives and elected governors in key states, including Ohio and Massachusetts.

The Battle of the Bulge

Costly sacrifices were still necessary before the Germans could be beaten. Von Rundstedt took advantage of bad weather, which grounded Allied planes, and of the rough terrain of the Ardennes Forest to launch a powerful counterattack on December 16, 1944. It was a final, desperate attempt to split the Allied lines and reach the Channel ports. The attack caught the Americans, who bore the brunt of the assault, by surprise. Generals Eisenhower and Omar N. Bradley had taken a calculated risk; they had left the Ardennes Forest area lightly guarded and concentrated heavy forces north and south of it. The German reserves, spearheaded by armored divisions, penetrated sixty miles, almost to the Meuse River near the Belgian-French border. They were finally stopped near Dinant by Patton's and Montgomery's armies. In this battle, the American 101st Airborne Division under General Anthony C. McAuliffe made a heroic stand at the vital rail junction and road center of Bastogne. McAuliffe and his men, although completely surrounded, disrupted the German timetables and transportation until relieved by the American Third Army.

Counterattacking Allied forces pinched off the Bulge on about January 21, 1945. Allied losses had been high—there were 77,000 American casualties alone—but the battle had cost the Germans 120,000 of their best reserves and untold quantities of war supplies.

The German Surrender

The Allies now closed in for the kill. On March 7, 1945, the American First Army crossed the Rhine River over the bridge at Remagen just before it was to be blown up by the retreating Germans. All Allied armies were across the Rhine by April 1.

At this point, the Allied high command faced a difficult choice. One alternative, fervently urged by Churchill, was a direct drive to seize Berlin before the Russians could enter the city. The other was to let the Russians enter Berlin first.

Eisenhower chose the second alternative, largely because of military considerations. He divided his army and sent Patton into Bavaria to prevent the escape of the German army to mountain strongholds in that state. Also, according to rumors, the Germans were attempting to produce an atomic bomb in Bavaria. Eisenhower knew that the American, Russian, and British governments had agreed earlier on postwar occupation zones in Germany. He did not consider the capture of Berlin worth the loss of American and British lives.

At this point, Churchill pleaded that Patton be sent into Prague to save Czechoslovakia from Russian domination. Eisenhower ordered Patton to take

Allied Victory in Europe

Prague but then reversed his decision after receipt of a strong protest from Stalin. In all these critical decisions, Eisenhower had the full support of General Marshall and of Roosevelt.

Meanwhile, the Russian armies steadily advanced from the east on a march of 2,300 miles from the Volga River. American First Army units met Soviet troops at Torgau, on the Elbe River, on April 25, 1945. Soviet troops then entered Berlin and fought their way from house to house through the heaps of rubble to which Allied planes and Soviet cannon had reduced the city. The German capital surrendered on May 2.

Instead of dying in defense of his country, as he had pledged that he would, Hitler committed suicide in his bunker beneath the chancellery in Berlin. Other leading Nazis who had not killed themselves or disappeared in the post-war confusion later were brought to trial before a four-power tribunal at Nuremberg. Robert H. Jackson, a justice of the United States Supreme Court, presided over the trial. Ten German leaders were hanged, and others received life or long-term prison sentences for crimes against humanity.

Hitler's successor, Grand Admiral Karl Doenitz, ordered all German sea, air, and land forces to surrender on May 7. On the following day, German delegates signed terms of unconditional surrender at Eisenhower's headquarters in the French city of Rheims.

Allied War Conferences

During the Second World War, Roosevelt, Churchill, and other Allied heads of state met from time to time to coordinate their war efforts and to plan final peace settlements. As we have seen, Roosevelt and Churchill met to draft the Atlantic Charter in 1941, even before the United States entered the war. The Anglo-American leaders later met at Washington, Quebec, and Hyde Park to plan common strategy. Early in January 1943, they again came together at Casablanca, Morocco, to plan the invasion of Italy.

In November 1943, Roosevelt and Churchill met with the Chinese leader, Chiang Kai-shek, at Cairo. They agreed that Japan should be driven from the Asiatic mainland and from the islands that she had seized since the beginning of her expansion in the Pacific. From Cairo, Roosevelt and Churchill flew to Teheran to meet Stalin and his advisers. There they discussed plans for an Anglo-American second front in Europe.

Throughout the first two and a half years of their association, Roosevelt and Churchill worked together in remarkable friendship and accord. To be sure, personal difficulties existed, and they did not always agree on policy. Roosevelt seems to have been jealous of Churchill's commanding position as the chief spokesman of the free world. Roosevelt and his advisers were always more eager than Churchill to open a second front in France. Churchill was more concerned about political objectives, such as the protection of the Balkan countries and other strategic areas from Soviet domination. But discord did not seriously mar the warm relationship between the two statesmen until about the time of the Teheran Conference. From this time forward, relations were occasionally strained by differences over specific problems.

Both Roosevelt and Churchill agreed that one of their prime tasks was to win Russian friendship and cooperation in the postwar world. Attainment of this objective had become imperative by early 1945, for the war obviously was coming to a close. The Russians had already indicated their intention to control the countries of eastern Europe which their armies were overrunning. Consequently, Roosevelt, Churchill, and Stalin met with their respective entourages in the Crimean city of Yalta from February 4 through February 11, 1945. The following is a brief summary of their agreements on crucial issues:

1. *Germany.* Roosevelt, Churchill, and Stalin approved the boundaries of the

Defeat of Nazi Germany was close, and cooperation seemed assured between the Big Three when Churchill, Roosevelt, and Stalin met at Yalta in February 1945. Yet, undercurrents of trouble were evident. Churchill later admitted, "Our hopeful assumptions were soon to be falsified"; and Roosevelt, who was gravely ill at the time, died two months later leaving many problems unsolved. (Wide World Photos)

postwar zones of occupation in Germany already drawn by an Allied commission in London. Germany was to be administered by an Inter-Allied Control Commission in Berlin. Russia and Poland were to receive territory in eastern Germany, and Germany was to pay reparations.

2. *Poland and eastern Europe.* The Russians had already installed a puppet Communist government in Poland. Churchill and Roosevelt accepted a compromise by which Stalin agreed to include democratic leaders in the Polish government and to permit free elections to determine the future of the country. The three leaders also signed a declaration which promised the free election of democratic governments in the other countries of eastern Europe.

3. *The United Nations.* Stalin promised to cooperate with Roosevelt and Churchill in creating a new international security agency along the lines already drawn by the American government.

4. *The Far East.* In a secret agreement between Roosevelt and Stalin, the latter agreed to come into the war against Japan within two or three months after the surrender of Germany. Stalin also promised to support the government of Chiang Kai-shek. In return, Roosevelt agreed that the Russians should acquire the Kurile Islands and all rights and territory lost to Japan at the end of the Russo-Japanese War. This meant the transfer of the southern half of the island of Sakhalin to Russia, Soviet control of the Manchurian ports of Dairen and

Port Arthur, and Soviet-Chinese operation of the Chinese Eastern and South Manchurian railroads. Roosevelt's military advisers strongly urged him to make these concessions in order to assure Russian help in subduing Japan.

Churchill believed at the time of the Yalta Conference that Roosevelt was physically and mentally incapacitated, and that he, therefore, made too many concessions to Stalin. Churchill's belief had some justification, but in retrospect it is difficult to see how Roosevelt could have acted differently. As Churchill later put it in his *Triumph and Tragedy:* "Our hopeful assumptions were the only ones possible at the time." In any case, Stalin, who had been surprised by Hitler's invasion of Russia, did not intend to permit his country to be overrun by western invaders again. In establishing eastern Europe as a buffer zone, Stalin took no more than he could have taken at any time without incurring the danger of American or British interference. Even if Roosevelt had obtained the "more specific" language about eastern Europe that many critics believe he should have insisted upon at Yalta, blame for the "loss" of eastern Europe would have been laid upon his successor.

The Death of Roosevelt

Roosevelt sought relief from his tremendous labors in a brief vacation early in April 1945 at Warm Springs, Georgia. He was sitting for a portrait in his cottage there on the afternoon of April 12 when he complained of a severe headache. Two hours later he died of a cerebral hemorrhage. Most Americans, regardless of race, creed, social status, or political persuasion, responded with a spontaneous expression of mourning that bespoke the loss of a great man. Roosevelt's body was brought to Washington, and he was soon afterward buried with simple ceremonies at his ancestral home at Hyde Park, New York. On the day before his death, he had been preparing a radio address for Jefferson's birthday, April 13. In it, he had written his last message to the nation that he led for so long: "The only limit to our realization of tomorrow will be our doubts of today. Let us move forward with a strong and active faith."

The Atomic Bomb

The tremendous task of concluding the war in the Pacific and planning for peace now fell to Roosevelt's successor, Harry S. Truman. Truman, utterly unprepared to deal with Churchill's proposal for the capture of Prague, supported Eisenhower and Marshall in their decision not to move against the Czech capital. However, Truman did not conceal his anger at Russian violation of the Yalta accords when he met with Stalin, Churchill, and Clement Attlee, Churchill's successor as Prime Minister, at Potsdam, Germany, from July 17 through August 2, 1945. The Allied leaders, in spite of differences over eastern Europe, did unite on July 26 in issuing the Potsdam Declaration. It called upon Japan to surrender unconditionally and threatened "prompt and utter destruction" if she did not.

Truman was emboldened to resist Stalin and to join in issuing the Potsdam Declaration because he knew that the United States now possessed a new weapon of incredible destructive power — the atomic bomb. Scientists had long known that immense energy could be produced by splitting the atom. Roosevelt had been persuaded of the vast military potential of atomic power.

There were reports that Hitler was trying to develop an atomic bomb, and the American government had spent $2 billion on its development. An Anglo-American scientific team, headed by Dr. J. Robert Oppenheimer, a theoretical physicist from the University of California, Berkeley, made the first test on July 16, 1945, in a desert area near Los Alamos, New Mexico. The bomb, on a high steel tower, exploded with a force equal to that of 20,000 tons of TNT. It sent a column of fire and smoke five miles into the air and shattered house windows 100 miles away. The terrible heat fused the desert sand into a substance like glass. In all of history, no such frightful weapon had ever been put into human hands.

We now know that the Japanese, under massive assault from American warships and planes, could not have continued the war much beyond the summer of 1945, even if the atomic bomb had not been used against them. Truman and his military and scientific advisers, apparently unaware of this fact, wrestled with the moral problems involved in using such a fearful weapon. Truman decided to drop the bomb because he was convinced that, by doing so, he would end the war and save perhaps the million Japanese and American lives that would otherwise be lost in an invasion of the Japanese homeland. Some scientists argued that a demonstration of the bomb's terrible destructiveness in an

Two civilians walking through the ruins of Hiroshima. In a radio address to the nation in August 1945, President Truman presented his justification for use of the atomic bomb: "We have used it against those who attacked us without warning at Pearl Harbor. . . . We have used it in order to shorten the agony of war, in order to save the lives of thousands and thousands of young Americans." (Wide World Photos)

uninhabited area for the benefit of Japanese observers would end the war without further deaths; other scientists said that the United States should not bear the stigma of being the first nation to use atomic weapons—and against largely civilian targets. These arguments were brushed aside. Only two atomic bombs were immediately available, and military and political leaders were convinced that both might be needed to force Japan to recognize the hopelessness of her position.

A lone B-29 Superfortress, winging its way over the Japanese island of Honshu, dropped an atomic bomb on the city of Hiroshima on the morning of August 6. A blinding explosion, followed by roaring balls of fire, completely demolished four square miles of the city. It killed close to 80,000 persons and wounded at least that many others. (American air force planners chose Hiroshima because of its many combustible wooden residential structures among which fires would spread quickly.) Three days later, a second bomb was dropped on Nagasaki and turned it into an inferno, in which many thousands died immediately. Thousands more died slowly from radiation poisoning in both Hiroshima and Nagasaki. Children conceived by survivors continue to suffer from the genetic effects of radiation. On the same day that the atomic bomb exploded over Nagasaki, Russia declared war on Japan and sent troops into Manchuria.

The Surrender of Japan

The Japanese government, faced with the choice of annihilation or surrender, gave up the struggle on August 14. Before the end, however, an extremist military group invaded the imperial palace and tried, unsuccessfully, to prevent the broadcast of Emperor Hirohito's declaration of surrender. Two weeks later, air transports landed the first Americans on the island of Honshu. On September 2, MacArthur received Japanese delegates aboard Halsey's flagship, *Missouri*, in Tokyo Bay, for the formal signing of surrender terms.

Hirohito, although permitted to remain on his throne, was forced to renounce the ancient Japanese legend that he was of divine origin. The Supreme Commander of the Allied Powers in the Far East, MacArthur, was vested with full power over Japan, and the Emperor was made subject to his orders until a treaty of peace had been concluded.

Thus ended the most destructive war in history.

3. THE UNITED NATIONS

The Declaration of the United Nations

American leaders remembered vividly the events of the 1920s and 1930s and were determined that their country should not repeat the tragic error of refusing to take leadership in a postwar international organization to preserve peace. Roosevelt and Hull, both veterans of the Wilson administration, shared this conviction. They were also determined to avoid Wilson's mistake of making a partisan issue out of peace, but they did not want to frighten the public by pushing their plans too fast. So, even though Roosevelt and Hull had a new postwar organization in mind from the outset, they moved very slowly.

Roosevelt's and Hull's first step along the road to international cooperation was the Declaration of the United Nations, signed in Washington on January 1, 1942, by representatives of twenty-six countries, including the United States, Great Britain, the Soviet Union, and China. This declaration was a pledge of partnership "in a common struggle against savage and brutal forces seeking to subjugate the world." The signatories—members of what Churchill would later call the Grand Alliance—agreed to accept the principles of the Atlantic Charter. They also pledged their full resources to the defeat of the common enemy and promised not to make a separate peace. From time to time, other nations joined the alliance, until, by 1945, it represented almost the entire population of the non-Axis world.

From the Fulbright Resolution to Dumbarton Oaks

Many signs indicated that Congress was eager for the United States to cooperate with other nations in planning for the postwar world. For example, in September 1943 the House of Representatives overwhelmingly adopted a resolution introduced by J. William Fulbright of Arkansas which endorsed American participation in the creation of international machinery "with power adequate to establish and maintain a just and lasting peace."

In October 1943, Hull flew to Moscow for a conference with the Foreign Ministers of Great Britain and the Soviet Union. The fourth paragraph of the declaration which emanated from their conference asserted that they recognized "the necessity of establishing at the earliest practical date a general international organization, based on the principle of the sovereign equality of all peace-loving states, and open to membership of all such states, large and small." A few days later, this paragraph was incorporated, verbatim, in a resolution introduced in the Senate by Tom Connally, chairman of the Foreign Relations Committee. The Senate approved the resolution on November 5, 1943, by a vote of eighty-five to five.

The American course was, therefore, well charted by the time that American, British, Soviet, and Chinese delegates met at the colonial mansion of Dumbarton Oaks near Washington on August 21, 1944, to consider a tentative plan for a new international agency. They agreed in principle upon the basic structure of a new organization to be called the United Nations. Certain disagreements over membership and voting procedures were later settled at Yalta, when Stalin accepted the American point of view.

Formation of the United Nations

The Conference on International Organization, approved at Yalta, opened on schedule at San Francisco on April 25, 1945. President Roosevelt had appointed the American delegation shortly before his death. It consisted of Cordell Hull, who had resigned as Secretary of State on November 21, 1944, and his successor, Edward R. Stettinius; the chairmen and ranking minority members of the Senate Foreign Relations Committee and House Foreign Affairs Committee; and various leaders in education and public life. More than 200 delegates from fifty nations assembled at the War Memorial Opera House in San Francisco. It was not a peace conference, for the war continued on all fronts. It was, rather, a conference to help keep the peace when it should come.

The charter of the United Nations, completed after two months of hard work and controversy, was to go into force when ratified by the United States, Great Britain, Russia, France, and China, and by a majority of the other forty-five member nations. Truman made the closing speech to the conference on June 26 and almost immediately sent the charter to the Senate. He expressed his confidence that "the overwhelming sentiment of the people and of their representatives in the Senate" favored immediate ratification. Truman did not misjudge American sentiment. The Senate gave its consent to ratification of the charter by a vote of eighty-nine to two on July 28, 1945, and the charter went into effect about three months later.

SUGGESTED READINGS

The most useful survey of this period is A. Russell Buchanan, *The United States and World War II*, 2 vols. (1964). Interesting but polemical accounts of governmental and business cooperative operations during the war can be found in Bruce Catton, *The War Lords of Washington* (1948), and Eliot Janeway, *The Struggle for Survival* (1951). Robert H. Connery, *Navy and Industrial Mobilization in World War II* (1951); Lester V. Chandler, *Inflation in the United States, 1940–1948* (1951); and James P. Baxter III, *Scientists Against Time* (1946), are good studies of the domestic front. Jack Goodman, ed., *While You Were Gone: A Report on Wartime Life in the United States* (1946); Ruben Hill, *Families Under Stress* (1949); and Richard Polenberg, *War and Society, The United States, 1941–1945* (1972), are adequate accounts of American society during the war; see particularly John M. Blum, *V was for Victory: Politics and American Culture During World War II* (1976). On the status of black Americans, see N. A. Wynn, *The Afro-American and the Second World War* (1976). The tragic story of Japanese Americans is told in Roger Daniels, *Concentration Camps U.S.A.: Japanese-Americans and World War II* (1971); Michi Weglyn, *The Untold Story of America's Concentration Camps* (1976); and Dorothy S. Thomas *et al.*, *The Spoilage* (1946). For the politics of the period, see Jonathan Daniels, *Frontier on the Potomac* (1946), and Roland Young, *Congressional Politics in the Second World War* (1956).

Multivolume accounts of military, naval, and air operations have been published by the Department of the Army, Office of the Chief of Military History. A better introduction to the battles and strategy, however, would be Fletcher Pratt, *War for the World* (1951); Martha Byrd Hoyle, *A World in Flames: The History of World War II* (1970); Samuel E. Morison, *Strategy and Compromise* (1958); or Kenneth R. Greenfield, *American Strategy in World War II, a Reconsideration* (1963). For a rather sympathetic account of the American

failure to interpret its intelligence information correctly before the attacks on Pearl Harbor and the Philippines, see Roberta Wohlsetter, *Pearl Harbor: Warning and Decision* (1962). The overriding role of General Marshall in devising American military strategy and Marshall's training for that role are described in Forrest C. Pogue, *George C. Marshall: Education of a General* (1963), and *George C. Marshall: Ordeal and Hope, 1939–42* (1966). On the European theater, see Chester Wilmot, *The Struggle for Europe* (1952), and the memoirs of Dwight D. Eisenhower, Omar N. Bradley, W. Bedell Smith, and Henry H. ("Hap") Arnold. For the Pacific theater, see Herbert Feis, *Japan Subdued* (1961); J. K. Eyre, *The Roosevelt-MacArthur Conflict* (1950) and the memoirs of Douglas MacArthur, Robert Eichelberger, and William F. Halsey. D. Clayton James, *The Years of MacArthur*, 2 vols. (1970), and Gavin Long, *MacArthur as Military Commander* (1969), are severely critical of MacArthur's general strategy in the war against Japan; William R. Manchester, *American Caesar: Douglas MacArthur, 1880–1964* (1978), in contrast, is almost wholly admiring. The war of the common soldier is described by Ernie Pyle in *Here is Your War* (1943), *Brave Men* (1944), and *The Story of G.I. Joe* (1945). Important fictional treatments include Norman Mailer, *The Naked and the Dead* (1948); James Jones, *From Here to Eternity* (1951); and Joseph Heller, *Catch-22* (1961).

Herbert Feis has written excellent accounts of the diplomacy of the war: *Churchill, Roosevelt, Stalin* (1957), *Between War and Peace* (1960), *The China Tangle* 1953), and *Japan Subdued* (1961). William L. Neuman, *After Victory* (1967); Edward R. Stettinius, *Roosevelt and the Russians—The Yalta Conference* (1949); and Milton Viorst, *Hostile Allies: FDR and Charles de Gaulle* (1965), are some of the books that illustrate the complexity of the diplomacy of war and peace. Gabriel Kolko, *The Politics of War* (1968), from a New Left perspective harshly indicts United States foreign policy during the Second World War for its anti-Soviet bias.

There is a large and growing literature on the atomic bomb project. Among the most valuable books are Robert Jungk, *Brighter than a Thousand Suns* (1958), Nuel Pharr Davis, *Lawrence and Oppenheimer* (1969), and Martin J. Sherwin, *A World Destroyed: The Atomic Bomb and the Grand Alliance* (1975). John Hersey's *Hiroshima* (1946) resembles a novel in its dramatic impact.

CHAPTER 33
POLITICS AND PROBLEMS
OF THE TRUMAN ERA

1. THE NEW PRESIDENT

Truman

When news of Roosevelt's death reached Washington on April 12, 1945, Vice-President Truman was presiding over a session of the Senate. That same evening, at 7:09 P.M., he was sworn in as President By Chief Justice Stone.

Harry S. Truman (1884–1972), born and reared in a small Missouri town, worked as a bank clerk and farmer after he finished high school. He never attended college. Truman served in the field artillery during the First World War and rose to the rank of major. The business that he entered when he returned home failed during the recession of 1921. Then Truman went into politics with the help of the notorious Kansas City Democratic organization headed by Tom Pendergast. Truman was elected to the Board of County Commissioners of Jackson County in 1922 and served as head of that board from 1926 to 1934.

With Pendergast's backing, Truman was elected to the United States Senate in 1934, and again in 1940. There he gained a reputation for loyalty to the New Deal and conscientious attention to duty. He won national prominence as the efficient and fair chairman of a special Senate committee that investigated defense contracts and saved the government billions of dollars.

The country knew very little about Truman when he succeeded Roosevelt; but it soon became apparent that he had defects that impaired his leadership. Combative by nature, Truman gave the appearance of a fierce partisan in the rough and tumble of politics. He was keen to resent a slight and often spoke impulsively—in a manner that many Americans felt was unbecoming to a President of the United States. But his strengths far outweighed his weaknesses. When he dealt with large matters, he possessed uncommon good sense, and his diligent study of American history gave him a great store of knowledge about the problems that he faced. In times of crisis, he seemed to know almost instinctively what the circumstances demanded. He was determined to provide vigorous leadership both at home and abroad; consequently he left the presidency as strong an institution as he found it. He had a deep sense of fair play. Hence, for a while at least, he defended and tried to expand civil liberties at a time when some of the most ferocious assaults in American history were being made against these cherished rights. This early stand and later circumstances should be kept in mind when studying the period during which Truman surrendered to political pressure and to his own fears of world Communism (his administration eventually carried out policies that violated traditional civil liberties). Also, Truman fought for a wide program which defended the civil rights of blacks far beyond anything that Franklin Roosevelt had ever dared to suggest. He soon developed a broad world view, and, once he found his bearings, he gave bold leadership to the West and its allies in Asia. Above all, Truman was courageous. More than once as President, he overcame seemingly insuperable odds—in dismissing a popular general, for example, and in running for reelection when almost all polls predicted that he would be defeated by a huge margin.

Staggering Problems

The day after he took the oath of office, Truman met reporters for his first news conference. With simple frankness, Truman said to them, "Last night the moon, the stars, and all the planets fell on me."

Truman's first tasks were to conclude the war both in Europe and in the Pacific, to carry through for Roosevelt on the organization of the United Nations, and then to give leadership to the relief and reconstruction of war-torn lands. For these tasks, Roosevelt had done almost nothing to prepare his Vice-President. Furthermore, Truman had to establish his personal control over a cabinet and administration of strangers—of men whose loyalty belonged to Roosevelt—and, even more difficult, to establish himself as the chief leader of the Democratic party and of the American people. These were not easy tasks. Americans, who were accustomed to regard Roosevelt as indispensable, found it hard to imagine another President in the White House. Moreover, Truman came to the presidency without a distinctive style such as the one that had won immediate confidence for Roosevelt. Indeed, Truman gave the impression of being overwhelmed and confused.

The New Leader of American Progressivism

Truman was so engrossed by military and foreign affairs during the spring and summer of 1945 that many Democratic politicians assumed that he would be content to serve as caretaker while a postwar reaction dismantled major portions of the New Deal. The truth is that Truman, slowly and quietly, decided domestic policy on his own, just as he did in the field of international affairs. He startled Congress on September 6, 1945, by calling for an expansion of the New Deal. He asked for extension of the Social Security system, an increase in the minimum wage, national health insurance, revival of the war against urban slums, and new regional developments similar to the TVA. Truman also called for federal guarantees of full employment and prosperity and maintenance of economic controls through the period of conversion to a peacetime economy. "It was on that day and with this message," Truman later wrote in his memoirs, "that I first spelled out the details of the program of liberalism and progressivism which was to be the foundation of my administration."

2. PROBLEMS OF DEMOBILIZATION AND RECONVERSION

Demobilization and the Care of Veterans

To get the boys back home without delay was the reigning passion of the American people in 1945. The United States would need strong military power in the years ahead, but the demand for immediate demobilization was so powerful that leaders in the executive branch and in Congress did not dare to ignore it. Therefore, the great army and navy were dismantled, until, by midsummer of 1946, the army had been reduced to 1,500,000 men and the navy to 700,000 men. In the light of America's postwar international problems, as one writer put it, "the rush to disarm in late 1945 was surely one of the most expensive economies . . . in which the United States ever indulged."

In most respects, the government prepared well for the homeward rush of former servicemen. Congress had made provision beforehand by passing the Servicemen's Readjustment Act, better known as the "G.I. Bill of Rights," or simply as the G.I. bill, in June 1944. When the tide of demobilized veterans poured home from local camps and far-flung battlegrounds, a grateful nation was ready with measures to help most of them make the transition to civilian life. However, black soldiers in the South and Japanese-American veterans in the West, especially in California, much too often found themselves greeted rudely, and even violently, as though the society to which they returned feared them — or feared that they would now demand equal civil rights. The Veterans' Administration (VA) rapidly expanded its hospitals to care for the sick and wounded. By 1950, some 159 veterans' hospitals served an average of 108,000 patients daily. Vocational rehabilitation centers provided guidance clinics and helped more than 610,000 disabled servicemen to discover their aptitudes and find appropriate jobs. Unemployed veterans received unemployment compensation for a full year, while special privileges were accorded servicemen who entered the civil service. Financial assistance and priority were given for the purchase of homes, farms, and businesses. Finally, veterans who wanted them received free tuition, books, and expenses for job training, college, or other advanced education.

Altogether, it was the largest assistance program undertaken by any government in history. The expenditures of the VA increased from less than $1 billion in 1944 to about $10 billion in 1950. Between 1945 and 1952, the VA spent $13.5 billion for the education and training of nearly 8,000,000 veterans, and $4 billion for unemployment benefits and self-employment help. Additionally, the VA insured nearly $16.5 billion of loans to veterans for homes, farms, and businesses.

Reconversion

In the late summer of 1945, the American economy resembled a great over-heated steam engine about to explode. Per capita disposable income stood at an all-time high. Individuals and corporations had amassed savings of $48.5 billion, and state and local governments had surpluses totaling more than $10 billion. Demand, which had been pent up for four years, was tremendous. The trouble was that not enough automobiles, appliances, homes, meat, and countless other commodities existed for sale to satisfy the demand. When Congress reduced taxes some $6 billion in November 1945, it only expanded consumer demands and placed even greater pressure on prices.

Republicans and conservative Democrats in Congress, led by Senator Robert A. Taft of Ohio, said that American businessmen and farmers could produce in abundance only if freed from crippling controls. In order to spur production, the administration quickly disposed of most government-owned war plants, which possessed 29 per cent of the industrial capacity of the country. However, Truman insisted upon rigorous price controls to dam up inflationary pressures until output could satisfy demand. The OPA, which still operated under wartime authority, held the line against price increases remarkably well in 1945–1946. However, when Truman vetoed a price-control bill in June 1946, on the ground that Congress had weakened it to the point of ineffectiveness, prices rose wildly.

Congress adopted another price-control measure in July, but, as Truman predicted, it proved ineffective, and the President ended most price controls in November 1946. As a consequence, the general consumer price index rose by almost 34 per cent between 1945 and 1948.

Troubles on the Labor Front

The end of the war found leaders of organized labor troubled by fears of inflation, unemployment, and the possibility of a postwar depression. Unions now boasted 14,600,000 members, and their leaders were determined to maintain wartime gains and to seek wage increases sufficient to hold their own against the rising cost of living. But higher wages gained from favorable contracts added to increased costs, which meant higher prices, which in turn stimulated strikes for higher wages. The spiraling cycle went on until about 1948.

In October 1945, the Office of War Mobilization agreed that a general wage increase of 24 per cent could be granted by industry without endangering either profits or price controls. A month later, Truman called a National Labor-Management Conference to work out a strike-prevention program. It failed, and 180,000 automobile workers, 200,000 electrical workers, and 750,000 steelworkers all went out on strike. A wage compromise was worked out upon the basis of recommendations made by a presidential fact-finding board. This set the pattern of wages for most of American industry and gave hope of peaceful industrial relations.

However, conflicts in two major industries upset the balance in the spring of

1946. After a nationwide railroad strike threatened to paralyze the economy, Truman seized the railroads on May 17, 1946. Then he offered a compromise settlement that was accepted by eighteen unions. But when the engineers and trainmen walked out, Truman asked Congress for power to declare a state of national emergency whenever a strike in a vital industry under federal control endangered national security. Workers who continued to strike would lose all benefits of seniority. They would also be drafted into the army, and their leaders could be fined and imprisoned. The House of Representatives approved the bill, but the Senate buried it because the striking railway workers returned to their jobs.

Meanwhile, John L. Lewis had led his United Mine Workers out on strike for higher wages and a number of so-called fringe benefits, such as improved safety regulations. After fruitless negotiations, the government took over the mines to protect the national interest. The government granted most of Lewis' demands, but he made new ones in October 1946. The government, supported by a federal judge's injunction, stood firm. Lewis defied the injunction and called a strike, only to draw fines of $10 thousand against himself and $3.5 million against his union. A new contract, which conceded most of Lewis' demands, ended the impasse in June 1947. The Supreme Court then reduced the fine against the union to $700 thousand.

A second round of nationwide strikes broke out in the autumn of 1946, but from then until 1950 labor and management settled most of their differences over the bargaining table. In the process, however, workers obtained additional wage increases, which contributed to further increases in prices.

Legislative Achievements, 1945–1946

The fierce struggles between Truman and Congress over price controls and labor policies gave the impression of a general political breakdown that in fact did not exist. On the contrary, Truman and the Democratic Seventy-ninth Congress cooperated to enact two epochal pieces of legislation.

One—the Employment Act—approved in February 1946, fulfilled a major pledge in the Democratic platform of 1944. Liberal Democrats wanted the government to take major responsibility for new investment and full employment. Conservative Democrats and most Republicans opposed statutory governmental responsibility for these matters. The act of 1946—a compromise between the extreme points of view—established a Council of Economic Advisers to study the economy and advise the President and Congress on measures best calculated to promote prosperity. The Act also directed the President to make an annual Economic Report to Congress and created a congressional Joint Committee on the Economic Report to study and propose appropriate legislation.

The most significant section of the Employment Act was its assertion that the federal government bore chief responsibility for maintaining prosperity. As Edwin G. Nourse, the first chairman of the Council of Economic Advisers, declared, the measure established machinery for "mobilizing all our organizational resources, public and private, within our system of free enterprise, for a sustained high level of national production." Both Truman and his successor used the Council of Economic Advisers only sparingly, but, in the 1960s, the council finally became what the framers of the Employment Act of 1946 had intended it to be. It grew into an expert body which exercised vital influence, because it was able to marshal knowledge accumulated by the science of economics to promote sound economic growth, and because new data-gathering techniques, econometric models, and high-speed computers made available timely statistical information about the entire economy and the likely courses of its components.

The second epochal piece of legislation was the Atomic Energy Act. Approved on August 1, 1946, it laid the foundations for postwar development of atomic energy. The Act retained the prevailing governmental monopoly on fissionable materials and vested complete control of research and production in a new five-man Atomic Energy Commission. The measure gave to the President alone power to order the use of the atomic bomb in warfare. It prohibited the divulgence of important atomic information to foreign governments.

The Election of 1946 and Its Aftermath

Popular discontent rose high in the early autumn of 1946 because of skyrocketing prices and a shortage of essential commodities, particularly meat. Public anger against organized labor grew because of what seemed to be union irresponsibility. Americans, already annoyed by railroad and coal strikes, were irritated further by Communist infiltration of the leadership of a number of key unions, racketeering in certain unions, and the widespread use of what many persons believed were unfair practices. In 1947, more than thirty states outlawed the most important of these practices: featherbedding (demanding the employment of more labor than was necessary); jurisdictional strikes (strikes that resulted from the warfare of rival labor unions), and secondary boycotts (the refusal of members of a union to handle nonunion goods). In addition, Congress in 1946–1947 outlawed featherbedding and tried to stamp out labor racketeering.

The Republicans capitalized upon this discontent, used the slogan "Had enough? Vote Republican!", and swept to victory in the mid-term election on November 5, 1946. They won control of both houses of Congress for the first time since 1928 and captured governorships in twenty-five of the thirty-two nonsouthern states.

The major aftermath of the Republican landslide was the adoption by the new eightieth Congress of the Labor-Management Relations, or Taft-Hartley Act. It was passed over Truman's angry veto in June 1947. Taft, the measure's chief sponsor, wanted to strike heavy blows at union power, principally by banning industry-wide bargaining; but Taft had to accept a compromise measure despite the solid Republican majorities in both houses of Congress. The Taft-Hartley Act outlawed the closed shop—an arrangement by which only members of a union could be hired by an employer. It forbade "unfair" union practices, such as refusal to bargain in good faith, secondary boycotts, jurisdictional strikes, and pay for work not performed. The Taft-Hartley Act also permitted employers to sue unions for breach of contract, to petition the NLRB for elections to determine bargaining agents, and to speak out during union organizational campaigns. In strikes which endangered the national health and safety, the Act provided for cooling-off periods and for use of temporary injunctions by the President. The measure also compelled union officers to sign anti-Communist affidavits in order to bring their cases before the NLRB. The Act required unions to register with and to submit annual financial reports to the Secretary of Labor. Finally, the measure prohibited union contributions to political parties.

Organized labor bitterly attacked the Taft-Hartley Act as "slave legislation" aimed at the destruction of the labor movement. The Taft-Hartley Act did, to be sure, represent the popular conviction that big labor, irresponsible and uncontrolled, could be as dangerous to the national interest as big business or big finance. The measure tried to rectify what a majority of Americans in 1946 thought was the prolabor bias of the National Labor Relations Act of 1935. However, the fact that unions continued to bargain effectively under the Taft-Hartley Act provided substantial proof that labor was functioning merely in harness, not in chains. The measure did have one strong side effect: union members who had wandered away from their Democratic loyalties, and had voted for Republican candidates, now repented and returned to the Democratic fold.

Bipartisan Domestic Achievements

Truman's accusations against the Eightieth Congress during the campaign of 1948 have left the impression of constant warfare between the White House and Capitol Hill. To the contrary, the two branches of government cooperated during 1947 and 1948 very much as they had before those years. They not only launched the United States upon bold leadership of the non-Communist world; they also cooperated to enact several important domestic measures.

By far the most important product of this bipartisan collaboration was the National Security Act of July 26, 1947, the result of a long struggle to overhaul America's defense structure. The lack of communication between the various armed services at Pearl Harbor had dramatized the need for unification of the forces. The army favored unification; but the navy, which feared the elimination of the Marine Corps and the eventual domination by a land-based air force, fought unification bitterly. The National Security Act provided for a single cabinet department and a single Secretary of Defense and Joint Chiefs of Staff. It also established an independent air force and three noncabinet departments of the Army, Navy, and Air Force. Finally, the measure created a National Security Council and a National Security Resources Board to advise the President and Congress, and a new Central Intelligence Agency (CIA) to take supreme command of the nation's intelligence work.

Congress also responded when Truman requested a change in the presidential succession. According to the law of 1886, which remained in effect, the next officer in line for the presidency after the Vice-President was the Secretary of State, followed by the other cabinet members in the order of the creation of their offices. The Presidential Succession Act of 1947 fixed the succession after the Vice-President, first in the Speaker of the House, and then in the presiding officer of the Senate. Cabinet members were then to follow in the same order as before. On its own volition, Congress passed the Twenty-second Amendment, which limited the tenure of Presidents after Truman to two terms. It was ratified on February 26, 1951.

The second session of the Eightieth Congress sat from January 6 to June 30, 1948. It was an election year, and Truman submitted seventeen major measures, eight of which Congress approved: first, a bill to draft men from nineteen to twenty-five years of age for twenty-one months of service in the armed forces (it supplanted a weak Selective Service Act adopted in 1946); second, appropriation of $6 billion for foreign aid; third, temporary support of farm prices at 90 per cent of parity; fourth, extension of the Reciprocal Trade Agreements Act for one year; fifth, a bill that increased Social Security benefits for the aged, the blind, and dependent children; sixth, extension of rent controls; seventh, admission of 205,000 displaced persons into the United States during the next two years; and, eighth, extension of governmental credit for veterans' homes and cooperative housing projects.

3. THE BEGINNINGS OF THE COLD WAR

Deadlock after Potsdam

The Potsdam Conference directed the Foreign Ministers of the United States, Great Britain, France, and Russia to draw up peace treaties with Germany, Italy, and former Axis satellites in Europe. Repeated meetings of the Foreign Ministers served only to reveal their conflicting claims. Disagreements were particularly acute over Germany. That powerful country in the center of Europe, with its population of 70,000,000, was in desperate condition. Many of its cities had been bombed into rubble and its industries crippled or destroyed. Its territory had been divided into four zones, each controlled by a military governor appointed by Russia, Britain, the United States, and France. The capital city of Berlin also had been divided among the four powers, but it was surrounded by Soviet-controlled territory. The western powers continued to call for the establishment of governments elected by the people in eastern Europe, while Soviet leaders continued to fear the presence of allegedly anti-Soviet nations along their borders. Much of the Soviet Union lay in ruins because of the second great German invasion of Russia in less than thirty years. Soviet officials, and especially Stalin himself, were determined that Germany must not be allowed to grow strong enough for a third such invasion.

Secretary of State James F. Byrnes, who succeeded Stettinius in 1945, made seven trips to London, Paris, and Moscow in vain efforts to find a definitive settlement satisfactory to the Truman administration. The Foreign Ministers finally agreed on treaties for Italy, Finland, Bulgaria, Rumania, and Hungary. These treaties, signed at Paris on February 10, 1947, confirmed western supremacy over Italy and her former African colony of Libya, and Soviet supremacy over Hungary and Russia's neighbors — Finland, Rumania, and Bulgaria. But then all progress came to a halt. On the all-important question of a settlement with Germany, the by now antagonistic Foreign Ministers could make no progress. Consequently, the western powers took steps to unify their three zones, while the Russians began to erect the apparatus of a separate East German government.

Russian-American differences were also acute in 1945–1946 on the overshadowing issue of disarmament and the international control of atomic energy. In June 1946, Bernard M. Baruch, on behalf of the American government, submitted a plan to the Atomic Energy Commission of the United Nations. This, the so-called Baruch Plan, created an International Atomic Development Authority under the UN, with a worldwide monopoly on the production of atomic energy and the right to inspect atomic plants anywhere in the world. Moreover, the Authority should not be subject to a veto in the UN Security Council. The Russians accepted all features of the plan except the one which forbade use of the veto. The United States Government then insisted that effective international control would be impossible. Hence the Baruch Plan, like all proposals for the unification of Germany, foundered upon the shoals of Russian-American mutual suspicion.

The Truman Doctrine

The Grand Alliance had obviously broken up by 1946, and the Soviet Union and the western powers had come to an uneasy truce for the division of Europe. What destroyed the truce and set off in earnest what was called the Cold War were certain clear signs that the Soviet Union intended to expand its influence into areas that the West deemed vital to its security, while the United States hoped to reduce Soviet influence throughout Europe, indeed, to turn it back in western Europe.

George F. Kennan, counselor of the American Embassy in Moscow, had warned as early as February 1946 that Stalin and his government were implacably hostile to the West. Events of the next twelve months seemed to confirm Kennan's warnings. The Russians attempted to create a puppet regime in northern Iran and withdrew their troops from that country only after Truman sent a blunt personal warning to Stalin. Furthermore, the Russians demanded that Turkey cede territory and permit them to build naval bases in the Bosporus. At the same time, the Russians supported a Communist-led rebellion against the government of Greece.

The crisis came to a head on February 24, 1947, when the British government informed the State Department that it could no longer maintain military and naval forces in Greece and the eastern Mediterranean. Truman reacted quickly. On March 12, he asked Congress to appropriate $400 million for military and economic aid to Greece and Turkey. Going further, the President announced what soon was called the Truman Doctrine: "I believe that it must be the foreign policy of the United States to support free peoples who are resisting attempted subjugation by armed minorities or by outside pressures." Truman's implied assumption—that only Communists used military force or "outside pressures" to overturn results of free elections—turned out to be quite mistaken. However, it should be remembered that he spoke out of the heritage of the New Deal "Good Neighbor" policy and the prewar American avoidance of foreign conflicts.

Many Americans still hoped for peaceful collaboration with the Soviet Union. Truman's request, therefore, especially his request for military assistance, met strong opposition in Congress. Some members argued that the United States should work through the United Nations, not alone. Truman replied that Russia could easily paralyze action by the U.N. with her veto. Arthur H. Vandenberg of Michigan, Republican spokesman on foreign policy and chairman of the Foreign Relations Committee, then solved the dilemma. He proposed an amendment which stated that the United States would cease its unilateral aid to Greece and Turkey as soon as the Security Council gave evidence of willingness and ability to act. The Greek-Turkish Aid bill was approved by large majorities in both houses of Congress in May 1947.

The President, when he enunciated the Truman Doctrine, and Congress, when it approved it, signaled a radical new departure in American foreign policy. Henceforth, the United States would not sit by idly while Europe attempted to recover from the Second World War and the Soviet Union expanded its influence. The United States would attempt to contain Soviet expansion whenever it was possible to do so through cooperation with the governments of the nations involved.

Generous assistance totaling some $350 million enabled the Turks to withstand Russian pressure. The struggle to rid Greece of domestic Communist rebels was more difficult, but American aid and military cooperation turned tha tide, and the Greek civil war ended in 1949. The new American policy to check the expansion of Communism by military force, as well as by economic assistance, would soon be put to much more severe tests in Asia.

The Marshall Plan

The near eastern crisis paled into insignificance when compared with the crisis that was developing in western Europe. The United States had poured $11 billion into Europe since the end of the war in relief, loans, and assistance of various kinds. Even so, Great Britain, France, Italy, Germany, and other western European nations were literally on the verge of bankruptcy, and there seemed to be danger of Communist party takeovers in Italy and France. It was clear to the Policy Planning Staff of the State Department, headed by Kennan, that western Europe could be saved from chaos and possibly Communism only by immense American aid. The new Secretary of State, George C. Marshall, discussed the matter with Truman, who agreed with his ideas. Then, in a speech at Harvard University on June 5, 1947, Marshall announced that the United States stood ready to help European nations (including Russia) to rebuild their economies, provided only that these nations themselves contribute as much as they could to general European recovery and prosperity.

The Russians condemned Marshall's offer as a cloak for American imperialism. They also forbade their satellites to join in the pan-European effort that Marshall had proposed. Delegates from sixteen non-Communist nations (Fascist-ruled Spain was excluded) met at Paris on July 12, 1947, to prepare estimates of both their needs and their abilities to contribute to European recovery. Their Committee of European Economic Cooperation (CEEC) submitted a master recovery plan two months later. It called for $22.4 billion in assistance from the United States.

Congress debated the European Recovery Program (ERP), as the Marshall plan was called, for ten months; Vandenberg led the discussion and mustered votes for the administration. Seizure of the government of Czechoslovakia by that country's Communists in February 1948 assured congressional approval of the ERP. The Senate approved the bill by a huge majority on March 13, and the House concurred by an equally overwhelming majority on March 31. President Truman signed the measure on April 3, 1948. In its final form, the ERP bill appropriated $5.3 billion for the first twelve months, with the understanding that the total American appropriation would come to about $17 billion.

Between April 1948, when the Marshall Plan began, and December 1951, when its tasks were taken over by the Mutual Security Agency, the United States poured some $12 billion into Europe through an Economic Cooperation Administration. At the same time, the CEEC distributed the money and began numerous projects for European cooperation. As early as 1950, western Europe had not only recovered its prewar levels of production, but it was well along the road to a much more substantial prosperity. Industrial production had risen by almost two thirds, to a total above prewar levels, and Communist parties throughout western Europe had become weaker and quieter.

From the Berlin Crisis to the North Atlantic Treaty

All investigations during the long period of discussion over the ERP pointed to one all-important conclusion: West Germany, the industrial heart of Europe, was the key to European recovery. Hence the American and former Allied governments not only decided to include West Germany in the ERP, but also to create a separate West German state. First steps toward West German unification, taken in February 1948, culminated the following June in the formation of a West German Federal Republic and its inclusion in the ERP.

The Soviet Union retaliated at once by limiting Allied and German access to Berlin and then, on June 23, by blocking all traffic into Berlin from the western zones. The Soviets made no secret of their intention to force the western powers either to abandon Berlin and accept the permanent division of Germany, or to abandon all plans for a West German state.

The thought of retreat seems never to have entered the mind of the stubborn Missourian in the White House. In collaboration with the British and French governments, Truman responded with a decision to supply beleaguered Berlin by airlift. If the Russians desired war, they had only to shoot down one of the thousands of planes that, day and night, regardless of weather, winged their way through narrow air corridors across the Russian zone to and from Berlin. Clearly, the Soviet government did not want war, for it did not interfere with the airlift. The giant cargo carriers flew 2,500,000 tons of fuel, food, and raw materials to Berlin in defiance of the Communist blockade. Emboldened by the western refusal to retreat in the face of Russian pressure, leaders of West Germany met at Bonn on October 20, 1948, to draft a constitution for the new Federal German Republic.

The Soviet leaders soon began to retreat. In February 1949, Stalin expressed his willingness to lift the Berlin blockade if the western powers would agree to resume the Foreign Ministers' conferences. They agreed; the blockade came to an end on May 12, 1949; and the Foreign Ministers met in Paris eleven days later for another futile discussion of the German problem.

Meanwhile, the movement for European economic cooperation and the growing threat from the East had also spurred a movement for the common defense of western Europe. Representatives of Britain, France, Belgium, the Netherlands, and Luxembourg signed a fifty-year treaty of economic cooperation and military alliance at Brussels on March 17, 1948. The Brussels Union was reconstituted in January 1949 as the Council of Europe and was enlarged to include Italy, West Germany, Ireland, Denmark, Norway, and Sweden.

Leaders of western Europe now turned to the United States to fulfill the Vandenberg Resolution of June 11, 1948, which had promised American cooperation with a western European military alliance. Out of the discussions that ensued came the North Atlantic Treaty, signed in Washington on April 4, 1949, by representatives of the United States, Great Britain, France, Italy, the Netherlands, Belgium, Canada, Iceland, Luxembourg, Denmark, Norway, and Portugal. The treaty was later signed by West Germany, Turkey, and Greece.

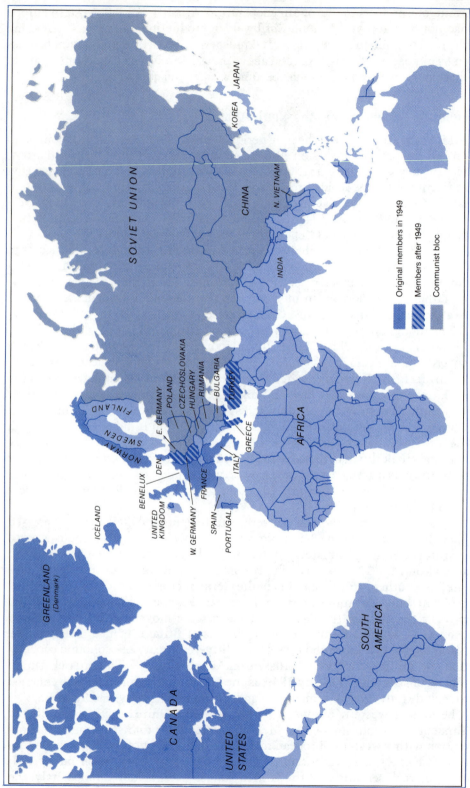

North Atlantic Treaty Organization

The key article of the treaty declared that an attack upon any one of the signatories would be considered an attack upon all, and would be resisted by all with armed force. Another article looked forward to the creation of joint military forces.

Senate debate on the North Atlantic Treaty was sharp but not prolonged. In the highly charged atmosphere of that time, even those senators who remained doubtful that the United States should involve itself deeply in European affairs were reluctant to join American Communists in opposition to the treaty. The Senate gave its consent to ratification by the bipartisan vote of eighty-two to thirteen on July 21, 1949.

4. THE ELECTION OF 1948 AND THE FAIR DEAL

Rising Republican Hopes

Republican hopes of capturing both Congress and the presidency were running higher in early 1948 than at any time since Herbert Hoover's nomination two decades before. Republicans were reasonably well united and believed that they could go to the country with considerable pride in the work of the Eightieth Congress. But more auspicious auguries of Republican victory appeared in the Democratic camp, where President Truman had come under violent attack within his own party.

One revolt was brewing in the South. In 1946, Truman had appointed a Committee on Civil Rights. In the following year, this committee issued an epochal report, *To Secure These Rights*. It called for a systematic campaign—including a permanent FEPC and antipoll tax and antilynching legislation—to root out discrimination on account of race. Against the wishes of many southern legislators, Truman urged Congress to implement the committee's recommendations, but without much success.

Another revolt against Truman brewed in the Left wing of the Democratic party. This faction had been alienated by Truman's measures to rally the western world against the Soviet Union, and particularly by his dismissal in 1946 of Secretary of Commerce Henry A. Wallace, a leader of the Democratic Left. Wallace had warned that Truman's Cold War policies could lead to another, even more terrible, world war.

With prospects for victory so alluring, many candidates wanted the Republican presidential nomination. Senator Robert A. Taft, Governor Harold E. Stassen of Minnesota, Governor Earl Warren of California, and Governor Dewey were all eager for the honor. Considerable sentiment existed for drafting General Eisenhower, but he refused to be a candidate. The Republican national convention of 1948 nominated Dewey on the third ballot. Its platform approved the basic New Deal reforms and the bipartisan foreign policy but promised that the Republicans would run the government more efficiently. Governor Warren received the nomination as Dewey's running mate.

Democratic Quarrels Seem to Assure a Republican Victory

The Democrats remained in deep gloom all through the spring of 1948. Party leaders tried, unsuccessfully, to persuade Truman to withdraw and General Eisenhower or Justice William O. Douglas to accept the Democratic nomination. Big-city bosses felt certain that the party would fail with Truman, and public opinion polls gave them grounds for pessimism. But Truman insisted on running. The Democratic convention could find no alternative but to nominate the incumbent and his choice for the vice-presidency, Senator Alben W. Barkley of Kentucky. After a bitter floor fight, a coalition of northern liberals and urban bosses drove through a strong civil rights plank which demanded a permanent FEPC and federal legislation against lynching and poll taxes.

Upon the adoption of the civil rights plank, thirty-five members of the Mississippi and Alabama delegations, waving the battle flag of the Confederacy, marched out of the hall. Delegates from thirteen southern states held their own convention at Birmingham on July 17 and organized the States' Rights Democratic party. The so-called Dixiecrats waved Confederate battle flags, sang "Dixie," and nominated Governor J. Strom Thurmond of South Carolina and Governor Fielding Wright of Mississippi for the presidency and vice-presidency. The Dixiecrats did not, of course, expect to win the presidency, but they did hope to win enough southern states to throw the election into the House of Representatives. They then hoped to strike a bargain with the Republicans.

Only five days after the eruption of the southern revolt in Birmingham, the Democratic Left wing met in Philadelphia and organized the Progressive party. The convention nominated Wallace and Senator Glen Taylor of Idaho on a platform which demanded further New Deal social reforms, gradual nationalization of certain basic industries, and a policy of friendship with the Soviet Union. Communists appeared well represented in the new party and may have gained a large measure of control before the campaign was over. Actually, Wallace represented rural values and stood closer in ideology to the Populists of 1892 than to Communists. However, he allowed Communist party members and fellow travelers of note, such as the great black singer and actor, Paul Robeson, to take a prominent part in his campaign.

The Campaign and Election of 1948

Public opinion polls all predicted a sweeping Republican victory, and Governor Dewey conducted a leisurely campaign while he made plans for his inauguration and new administration. The final makeup of Dewey's cabinet seemed, at times, to be one of the campaign's more exciting issues. Truman was undaunted and acted as though he had not heard about his impending defeat. He set out upon a whirlwind, whistle-stop campaign by railroad in which he gave 351 speeches to an estimated 12,000,000 people. Truman took the advice of a group of shrewd observers of American politics, led by the liberal Washington attorney, Clark Clifford, and concentrated on the great metropolitan areas, where the New Deal coalition remained strong. He did not neglect depressed farm sections, however, where he could blame poor economic conditions on the Republican-dominated Congress which had rejected his program for aid to farmers. In both areas, he stressed the continuity of his own programs with the New Deal, a theme which Clifford insisted would win him the votes of those who had supported Roosevelt. Truman also called Congress into special session and urged it to carry out at least the Republican platform by adopting civil rights and other progressive legislation. When it did not, Truman castigated the Republican Eightieth Congress before audiences of workers and

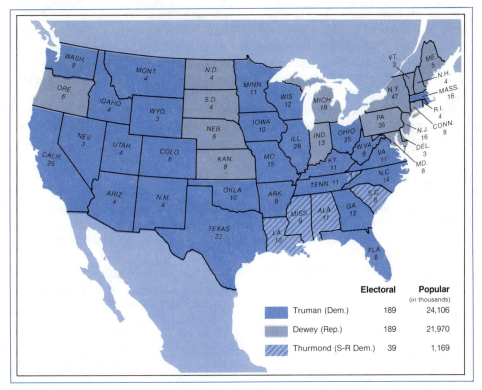

The Election of 1948

		Electoral	Popular
			(in thousands)
	Truman (Dem.)	189	24,106
	Dewey (Rep.)	189	21,970
	Thurmond (S-R Dem.)	39	1,169

farmers as a "do-nothing Congress." Soon these crowds began shouting: "Pour it on, Harry!" and "Give 'em Hell, Harry!"

Election day, November 2, 1948, found Truman still fighting and all pollsters and commentators agreeing that Dewey would win by a landslide. The outcome seemed so certain that the Chicago *Tribune* ran large headlines which hailed Dewey as the next President. In the most surprising upset in American political history, Truman won 24,106,000 popular and 303 electoral votes, to 21,969,000 popular and 189 electoral votes for Dewey. The Democratic tide also carried into office a Congress with substantial Democratic majorities in both houses. New Democratic senators included Lyndon B. Johnson of Texas, Hubert H. Humphrey of Minnesota, and Estes Kefauver of Tennessee.

Truman's victory does not seem so surprising in retrospect as it did in 1948. The revolts of the Dixiecrats and of the Left wing actually proved great boons to the Democrats. For one thing, the southern rebellion convinced blacks that southern segregationists did not dominate the Democratic party. Also, the revolt of the Left wing made it difficult (although the Republicans tried) to accuse the Truman administration of being soft on Communism. Moreover, the Dixiecrat and Left-wing revolts fizzled. Thurmond polled only 1,169,000 popular and thirty-nine electoral votes in Deep South areas with high levels of black population and of black disfranchisement. Pollsters showed a correspondence between areas which supported Thurmond and those which had voted heavily for secession in 1860–1861. Wallace received 1,156,000 popular and no electoral votes. The Democrats won aggressive labor support by their demand for repeal of the Taft-Hartley Act. The Democrats also gained midwestern farm support by coming out for retention of price supports at 90 per cent of parity, while the Republicans talked only about "flexible" price supports. Thus Truman held together the groups which had provided the basic support for the New Deal. Finally, the country was at peace and prosperous as never before. In such happy circumstances, the voters do not usually turn out a party in power, although William Howard Taft remains an example to complacent politicians.

The Fair Deal

Truman interpreted his victory as proof that the American people wanted to intensify the march of domestic reform. He outlined his program, which he called the Fair Deal, in his inaugural address of January 20, 1949, and in later messages to Congress.

During the next two years, before the attention of the country was diverted by a war in the Far East and other problems of foreign policy, the President won adoption of some Fair Deal measures. They included: first, an increase in the minimum wage from 40 to 75 cents an hour; second, extension of the Social

Harry S. Truman and Alben W. Barkley waving after their inauguration as President and Vice President. Polls had forecast a Republican victory, but Truman later noted: "My one-man crusade took effect. . . . I never doubted that they would vote for me." (Wide World Photos)

Security System to 10,000,000 new beneficiaries, with large increases in benefits to retired workers; third, the extension of rent controls until March 31,
1951; fourth, a Housing Act for the construction of 810,000 units for low-in-
come families; fifth, expansion of irrigation, water-control, and hydroelectric
activities of the Reclamation Bureau, plus increased appropriations for the
TVA, the Rural Electrification Administration, and the Farmer's Home Administration; sixth, a new Displaced Persons bill in 1950 to admit 400,000 refugees; seventh, the Agricultural Act of 1949, which set agricultural price supports at 90 per cent of parity through 1950; and, eighth, incorporation of the
Bureau of Internal Revenue, reorganized as the Internal Revenue Service, into
the civil service system.

Truman, however, failed to obtain certain important parts of his Fair Deal
program. He could have achieved substantial modification of the Taft-Hartley
Act, but threw away his chances for amendments by refusing to accept anything less than outright repeal of the law. Truman's other Fair Deal legislation—for civil rights, national health insurance, the St. Lawrence Seaway, and
federal aid to education—fell victim to the opposition of powerful interests
groups. Thus, most of what Truman obtained constituted an expansion of New
Deal programs. Legislative variations, such as those in the areas of civil rights,
health insurance, and educational aid, went down to defeat. However, these
later programs became the basis of Lyndon B. Johnson's Great Society program
of the 1960s. Truman did, nevertheless, use his independent executive power
to accomplish some of his objectives in the field of civil rights. He strengthened the Civil Rights Division of the Justice Department, began to abolish segregation in the federal civil service and the armed forces, and appointed a
number of blacks to high offices.

Modernizing the Government

Another noteworthy accomplishment—the reorganization of the executive
branch—was the product of unusually successful bipartisan cooperation. Congress and Truman had accomplished much in streamlining the government
even before 1949. The National Security Act of 1947 created a systematic defense structure for the first time, a need demonstrated, for example, by squab-
bles during the Second World War and by the tragic failure to coordinate intelligence from various sources before the Japanese attack on Pearl Harbor. Of
course, even coordinated intelligence and military orders need not necessarily
be used by field commanders, as General Douglas MacArthur soon demonstrated during the Korean War. Congress, in the Legislative Reorganization Act
of 1946, streamlined its own committee structure and instituted other reforms,
such as requiring lobbyists to register. Then, in 1947, Truman appointed former President Hoover to head a blue-ribbon commission on executive reorganization.

In the early months of 1949, the Hoover Commission issued eighteen reports. These recommended a reduction in the number of federal departments
and agencies from sixty-five to twenty-three. They also called for the establishment of a Department of Welfare to combine federal activities in the fields of
public health, social welfare, and education. Finally, the Hoover Commission
advocated a complete reorganization of the Post Office Department. Congress

responded in June 1949 with the Reorganization Act which authorized the President to submit plans for reorganization that would go into effect unless Congress specifically disapproved. Truman submitted thirty-six plans within a year. Only one of them — for a Department of Welfare — was rejected.

5. THE FALL OF NATIONALIST CHINA, THE SECOND RED SCARE, AND THE KOREAN WAR

The Return of Partisanship

The nation divided into warring camps from 1949 to 1952, as a second Red Scare spread throughout the United States. Although the division was not altogether a partisan one, leading Republicans, including Senator Taft, attempted to reap political benefit from it by attacking the patriotism and even the loyalty of the Truman administration, and of the Democratic party in general. In the process, the G.O.P. shattered bipartisanship in foreign policy and almost destroyed the mutual confidence necessary for the successful functioning of the two-party system.

The "Fall" of Nationalist China

American confidence in the peace of the postwar world, already shaken by the onset of the Cold War in Europe, was disrupted again by the fall of Nationalist China to Communist rebels, who took advantage of the widespread corruption and inefficiency in General Chiang Kai-shek's regime to defeat an enemy with superior firepower.

The American government had extended enormous military aid to the Nationalist government immediately after the Japanese surrender. American airplanes had even transported Nationalist troops into the provinces surrendered by the Japanese. Chiang faced awesome problems of inflation, political corruption, poverty, and disorganization. His most serious problem, however, was the threat from a large and well-disciplined group of Chinese Communists led by Mao Tse-tung in the northwestern provinces. Civil war broke out between the Nationalists and Communists in late 1945. Truman sent General Marshall to mediate the civil war and to persuade Chiang and Mao to form a unified government — one in which the Communists would occupy a subordinate position. Marshall tried hard but failed. When he returned to the United States in early 1947, Marshall reported that he could do no more to prevent the renewal of the Chinese civil war. He blamed both the Communists and Chiang's government; both sides believed that they would win control of the whole country.

War broke out again soon after Marshall's departure from China. The Nationalists enjoyed an initial advantage in manpower and supplies, but they soon collapsed under the assault of the better-disciplined and more determined Communist troops. By the summer of 1947, it was obvious that nothing less than full-scale American military participation in a Chinese land war would turn the tide in favor of the Nationalists. The Truman administration concluded that the American people would never approve participation in a Chinese civil war, and that such participation would be extremely foolish in any event.

The United States Government, therefore, did not intervene directly while the Chinese Communist armies overran China and drove Chiang and his government to Formosa in October 1949. Moreover, in January 1950, Truman made it clear that the United States would not fight to prevent a Communist seizure of Formosa. A week later, the new Secretary of State, Dean Acheson, announced that the United States would defend Japan and the Philippines, but would not attempt to protect Korea, Formosa, and southeastern Asia from Communist revolution or attacks.

The Second Red Scare

The fall of China occurred at a time when the American people were already in shock over revelations of Communist subversion at home. In 1946, a Canadian Royal Commission had reported the existence of a far-flung Soviet spy ring that had been engaged in stealing and sending atomic secrets to Moscow. The report was so sensational that it set off an intense security drive in the United States. On March 22, 1947, Truman issued an Executive Order which directed the FBI and the Civil Service Commission to investigate the loyalty of all federal employees. Within the next four years, 3,000,000 employees were cleared, about 2,000 resigned, and 212 were dismissed because they were considered bad security risks. The investigation was not only thoroughgoing, but also completely successful in its objectives. After the Republicans came to power in 1953, numerous investigations by various congressional committees, the Justice Department, and security officials turned up only one Communist in the government, and that one in a very subordinate job in the Government Printing Office.

A nationwide alarm did occur after a series of dramatic cases revealed that, prior to 1947, Communist agents had infiltrated the Anglo-American team that developed the atomic bomb. This led to the trial and conviction of three American Communist couriers, two of whom—Julius and Ethel Rosenberg—were executed in 1953. The FBI and various other branches of the government, evidence revealed, had been infiltrated as well. The most publicized of these cases involved Alger Hiss, who had held a position of trust in the State Department and was president of the Carnegie Endowment for International Peace. In 1948, Whittaker Chambers, a former Soviet courier, accused Hiss of having furnished him with valuable classified documents, which had been photographed by Communist agents and then returned to official files. Hiss denied the charges under oath, and character witnesses in his defense included some of the highest officers in the government. His indictment and trial, and his conviction on charges of perjury on January 21, 1950, shocked the nation.

By this time, certain Republican spokesmen were already charging that the federal government was honeycombed with Communists. More particularly, the Republicans charged that Communists in the State Department and the Foreign Service had been responsible for the administration's failure to do anything effective to halt the Chinese Communists. This kind of demagoguery reached new depths when Senator Joseph R. McCarthy of Wisconsin took up the anti-Communist cause less than a month after Hiss' conviction. McCarthy made headlines throughout the country by announcing, in a speech on February 9, 1950, that he held in his hand a list with the names of 205 card-carrying Communists in the State Department. When this statement was proved false, McCarthy went on to attack a number of American political leaders; among them were General Marshall, whom McCarthy called the leading American traitor. As chairman of a Senate investigation committee in 1953–1954, McCarthy hounded and bullied federal employees and a wide variety of other individuals, but discovered only one Communist in an insignificant job. The Wisconsin demagogue went too far, however, when he turned his bitter attacks against members of the Eisenhower administration, which had come into power in 1953, and even against Eisenhower himself. For his reckless, abusive actions, and even more for his political error in attacking Republican as well as Democratic officials, the Senate censured McCarthy in 1954 by a vote of sixty-six to twenty-two. Before the Senator's death in 1957, the term "McCarthyism" had become firmly established in the American vocabulary as a synonym for demagoguery, intentionally false accusations, and other loathsome political practices.

Meanwhile, the Truman administration had been swept along to some degree in the anti-Communist hysteria. In 1948, eleven Communist leaders were indicted, tried, and sentenced to prison under the Smith Act of 1940 for conspiracy to *teach* the violent overthrow of the government. The Supreme Court, on June 4, 1951, in Dennis *et al. v.* the United States upheld the constitutionality of the Smith Act—and the conviction of the Communist leaders—by invoking the clear-and-present-danger doctrine of the Schenck case of 1919 (see pp. 670–671). Nearly 100 state and regional Communist leaders were tried, convicted, and imprisoned under the Smith Act for allegedly *advocating* the violent overthrow of the government, not for any criminal acts.

Congress reflected the panic of the second Red Scare much more sensitively than the executive branch. The chief contribution of the legislative branch to the drive against Communism was the McCarran Internal Security Act of 1950. This measure required Communist organizations to register with the Attorney General and to furnish membership lists and financial statements. Membership in the Communist party was not made a crime, but the employment of Communists in defense plants was forbidden. A provision of the McCarran Act, which prevented former members of totalitarian organizations from entering the country, was opposed by the Department of Justice and the Central Intelligence Agency because it removed incentives for Communist agents to renounce their party and seek refuge in the United States. Truman vetoed the bill on this and other grounds, but Congress adopted it over his veto. Congressional eagerness to be seen by voters as striking at Communism was reflected also in the McCarran-Walter Immigration and Nationality bill of 1952, also passed over Truman's veto. It rectified an old injustice by permitting the annual admission of some 2,000 Orientals on a quota basis, but its provisions for the exclusion and deportation of aliens from southern and eastern Europe, and those with "wrong" political views, were very severe.

The Korean War: First Phase

The explosion of war in Korea in June 1950 drew the United States into the far eastern vortex in spite of the administration's desire to remain uninvolved. Korea had been annexed by Japan in 1910 and surrendered by her to the Allies in 1945. Russian troops penetrated as far as a line drawn across the Korean peninsula at 38° northern latitude, while American troops occupied the area south of that line. It was assumed, of course, that Korea would not only be united but would also be free of foreign domination. In fact, the UN held elections in South Korea in 1947, but a Communist government in the North refused either to participate or to permit UN personnel to enter its territory.

However, the Republic of Korea was established in the south in 1948, with dictatorial Syngman Rhee as President. The new government was recognized by the UN General Assembly, the United States, and thirty other UN members; the United States then withdrew its troops from Korea. Just a year later, on June 25, 1950, an army from North Korea invaded the Republic of Korea without warning. The move was approved by the Soviet Union on the assumption that the American withdrawal and Secretary of State Acheson's statement of January 1950 signified that the United States would not fight to defend South Korea.

News of the invasion reached Truman at Independence, Missouri, in the evening of June 24. Truman rushed back to Washington and instructed Acheson to bring the issue before an emergency meeting of the UN Security Council. The Russians had stalked out of the Council six months earlier, after that body had refused to seat a delegate from Communist China. Free of the Russian veto, the Council lost no time in adopting, by a vote of nine to nothing, a resolution which condemned the invasion as aggression and demanded the immediate withdrawal of North Korean troops from South Korea.

Meanwhile, Truman met with his civilian and military advisers and ordered the Seventh Fleet to protect Formosa. General MacArthur (still in Japan as Supreme Allied Commander) was to furnish arms and air and naval support to the South Koreans. Truman called Democratic and Republican congressional leaders to the White House and informed them of his determination to stop the North Korean aggression. Not only were they heartily in accord, but members of the House of Representatives stood and cheered when they heard the news of Truman's action. However, this precedent of going to war without a congressional declaration of war, or debate about one, would come back to haunt the American government during the 1960s and early 1970s. The Constitution, of course, grants to Congress, not to the President, the power to declare war (Section 8, Article 1).

The Security Council, on June 27, called upon all members of the UN to assist the Republic of Korea in every way possible. It also established a United Nations Command and invited the American government to name a Supreme Commander of UN forces. Truman nominated General MacArthur. Nineteen nations eventually sent troops to fight under the UN flag; however, in June 1950, the emergency had to be met with the forces at hand—two divisions of American occupation troops in Japan. These were rushed to Korea, where they fought a brilliant delaying action against overwhelming odds. The troops were hard pressed for a time to defend their last foothold on the peninsula at the port of Pusan, but the tide turned on September 15, 1950, when MacArthur's forces made a daring flank attack by sea at Inchon. McArthur then captured Seoul and UN forces reached the thirty-eighth parallel on about October 1.

On October 3, the Foreign Minister of the Chinese People's Republic told the Indian Ambassador in Peking that, if United States or UN forces crossed the thirty-eighth parallel, China would send troops across the Korean frontier to defend North Korea. Few leaders in the West took the warning seriously. The UN General Assembly, on October 7, called upon MacArthur to take all steps

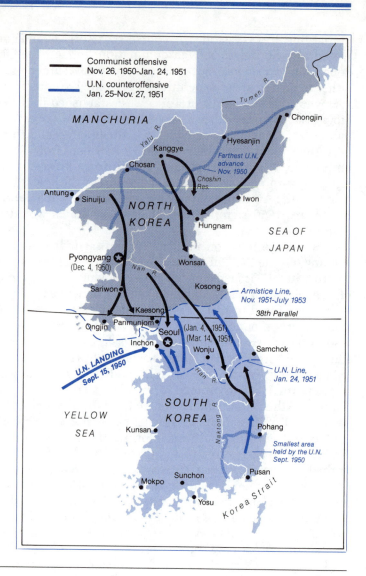

The Korean War, 1950–1953

necessary to establish the control of the UN over all of Korea. MacArthur himself informed Truman on October 15 that his intelligence organization had found little danger of Chinese intervention. If the Chinese did intervene, the General promised, they would be slaughtered. Intelligence officials in Washington collected evidence to the contrary, but there was little that they could do about MacArthur's decisions. Some governmental officials apparently feared being called "Communist dupes." Hence the UN forces were soon driving the North Koreans toward the Yalu River—the boundary between Korea and Manchuria. On Thanksgiving Day, MacArthur launched a great offensive to push the enemy beyond the Yalu and, as he announced, to finish the war before Christmas. The General unknowingly drove his troops into a huge trap set by about 1,000,000 Chinese troops already in North Korea. It required several weeks of desperate fighting and severe casualties before the retreating

American forces could extricate themselves and stabilize a defensive line along the thirty-eighth parallel.

As General MacArthur put it, UN forces now found themselves in "an entirely new war." He urged that the United States blockade the Chinese coast, bomb the Chinese mainland, use atomic bombs if necessary, and help Chiang Kai-shek to invade China from Formosa. The Joint Chiefs of Staff in Washington refused. To General Omar N. Bradley, chairman of the Joint Chiefs, a war with China would be "the wrong war, at the wrong place, at the wrong time, and with the wrong enemy." No one knew what the immediate future would bring, but the dangers appeared clear enough. There was the danger, first, that the Soviet Union would come to the aid of its Chinese ally, for the two nations had signed a mutual defense alliance in early 1950. There was also the danger that the Soviets would turn against western Europe while American forces were preoccupied in the Far East. Also, even MacArthur had warned Americans against getting bogged down in a land war against a huge, hostile Asian population. He estimated correctly that such a war could not be won.

Europe or Asia?

Congress was, at this very time, in the midst of a heated debate over whether American troops should be sent to bolster the defenses of Europe. American forces were asked to participate in a North Atlantic Treaty Organization (NATO) combined army, created in 1950, with General Eisenhower as supreme commander in Paris. The debate over Truman's recommendation of United States participation broke out with considerable bitterness in Congress on January 8, 1951. Senator Kenneth Wherry, Republican of Nebraska, offered a resolution to the effect that no ground forces be sent to Europe until Congress had rendered a decision on the matter.

It seemed for a moment that the administration had lost control of foreign policy to its opponents in Congress led by Senator Taft. These men, most of them midwestern and western Republicans, were not isolationists, for they demanded an all-out military effort against Communism in the Far East, but they were prepared to choose Asia over Europe if the choice had to be made. General Eisenhower rushed to Washington from Paris to plead against the abandonment of Europe. On April 4, 1951, the Senate adopted a resolution that approved the dispatch of four divisions to support American commitments to NATO. However, the Senate warned Truman not to send additional troops without further congressional approval.

The MacArthur Affair

The Truman administration, meanwhile, had made its own decision to limit military operations in the Far East. The Chiefs of Staff, in January 1951, ordered MacArthur and General Matthew B. Ridgway, commander of the American Eighth Army in Korea, to limit their activities to the defense of the Republic of Korea and to avoid a general war with China. MacArthur and Ridgway were to meet Communist attacks against their entrenched positions along the thirty-eighth parallel with a fire so deadly as "to break down not only the morale but the trained fabric of the Chinese armies." This is precisely what the American-UN armies under the successive commands of Generals Ridg-

President Truman is greeted by Douglas MacArthur upon his arrival at Wake Island where he received a firsthand briefing from the General. When Truman asked MacArthur about the chances for Soviet or Chinese interference in Korea, the General tragically miscalculated: "Very little. . . . Now that we have bases for our Air Force in Korea, if the Chinese tried to get down to Pyongyang, there would be the greatest slaughter." (Wide World Photos)

way, Mark Clark, and James A. Van Fleet proceeded to do. Communist Korean and Chinese casualties rose to more than 1,000,000.

MacArthur was in fundamental disagreement with this defensive strategy. In a letter to Representative Joseph W. Martin, Republican minority leader in the House of Representatives, MacArthur called for a victory offensive against China. "We must win," the General wrote. "There is no substitute for victory." MacArthur's letter, read to the House by Martin on April 5, 1951, was a direct challenge to the administration's foreign policy, and the Republicans made the most of it. Truman replied at once by relieving MacArthur of his command. "I could do nothing else and still be President of the United States," Truman wrote on April 10. "Even the Chiefs of Staff came to the conclusion that civilian control of the military was at stake, and I didn't let it stay at stake very long."

Truman's act was both courageous and necessary, but it set off wild excitement and demands for his impeachment. MacArthur came home for triumphal tours and an equally triumphant appearance before a joint session of Congress. Then the Senate Armed Services Committee began a long investigation of recent far eastern policies and MacArthur's recall. Even MacArthur was obliged to admit that he knew nothing of the government's global strategy. His demands had been based solely upon his estimate of the local situation in Korea. After listening to testimony from military as well as political leaders, the Senate hearings ended in the vindication of the administration and the discrediting of MacArthur. All three members of the Joint Chiefs of Staff, after studying the whole military situation, had, it turned out, advised Truman to take exactly the positions that he had adopted, including the dismissal of MacArthur.

Meanwhile, the vast resources of the United States had been deployed to meet the threat of a Russian attack in Europe. Four American divisions were sent to General Eisenhower, while military supplies in ever-growing volume flowed to the NATO countries. In addition, the United States constructed a system of air bases in Great Britain, France, Italy, North Africa, and Turkey within easy striking distance of strategic Soviet centers. The objective was to make a Soviet attack on western Europe too costly to be undertaken, should Stalin or his successors consider such a suicidal action.

Pacific Security Treaties

While it fought a limited war to win limited objectives in Korea, the Truman administration also worked to build a system of security pacts in the Pacific area comparable, at least in terminology, to those in the North Atlantic. A mutual defense treaty between the United States and the Philippines was concluded on August 30, 1951. Two days later, Australia, New Zealand, and the United States signed the Tripartite Security Treaty known as the ANZUS Pact.

A few days later—on September 8—Japan and forty-eight of her former enemies concluded a peace treaty in San Francisco. It was largely the work of John Foster Dulles, Republican adviser to the State Department, and it seemed a generous settlement. True, Japan was required to give up her overseas empire. But the treaty contained no provisions for punitive reparations or economic restrictions, and it restored full sovereignty to the Japanese people. On the same day, the United States concluded a security treaty with Japan that granted the American government the right to maintain land, sea, and air bases there. Thus the former enemy of the United States became the cornerstone of the American security system in the Far East. Japanese security, however, depended entirely on the willingness of the United States to fight to protect that country against Soviet or Chinese encroachments.

6. THE ELECTION OF 1952

Bitter Battles in the G.O.P.

Republican hopes for victory in the coming presidential campaign increased in the early months of 1952. McCarthy's unceasing attacks had raised grave doubts in wide quarters about the ability of the Truman administration to protect the country from internal subversion. Vastly exaggerated charges of corruption in Washington aroused further doubts. A jump in wholesale prices of 13 per cent between 1950 and 1952 hurt many persons who lived on fixed incomes or on Social Security. Finally, millions of Americans were tired of and frustrated by the Korean War, which continued intermittently without any end in sight, even though peace talks had been going on since the summer of 1951.

The Republicans, while hopeful, were also bitterly divided. The more conservative and isolationist (or Asia-first) wing, with strong support in the Middle West, was determined to end what Senator Taft called Dewey's "metooism." Taft proposed to give the American people a clear-cut alternative to the New Deal and Fair Deal, although he never made it clear how far he would go in dismantling the reform structure created by the Roosevelt and Truman administrations. Standing in opposition to Taft and his forces were Senator Henry Cabot Lodge of Massachusetts (grandson of Woodrow Wilson's foe), Governor Dewey, Governor Warren, and others. They accepted the New Deal and Fair Deal and considered NATO to be the cornerstone of American foreign policy.

Taft swept the Middle West and South so completely during the early stages of the Republican preconvention campaign that he seemed irresistible. Without a strong candidate to head off Taft, the Republican moderates and Europe-firsters felt hopeless. But their despair turned into elation when General Eisenhower agreed to accept the Republican presidential nomination—mainly, he said, to defeat Taft. The battle was fully joined when Eisenhower resigned his NATO command and returned home in June to fight for the nomination.

Eisenhower almost made his decision too late, for the Taft forces seemed to dominate the Republican national convention that opened in Chicago on July 7, 1952. However, the overconfident Taft managers made the error—inconceivable from this distance—of permitting the seating of most of the Eisenhower delegates in contested delegations from Texas, Georgia, and Louisiana. These delegates provided a bare majority for Eisenhower on the first ballot. For his running mate, Eisenhower chose young Senator Richard M. Nixon of California, who had gained a national reputation by helping to expose Alger Hiss. Nixon had also already won a reputation for his fierce attacks during political campaigns on the loyalty of Democratic politicians and a nickname among Democrats—"Tricky Dick." The Republican platform promised maintenance of basic New Deal-Fair Deal programs at home and a dynamic new foreign policy abroad.

The Campaign of 1952

The Democrats, assembled in national convention in Chicago on July 21, were badly split between southern opponents of civil rights legislation and the progressive-labor forces from the large cities. Before the convention met, Vice-President Barkley and Senator Kefauver of Tennessee appeared to hold the lead among the major contenders for the presidential nomination. However, Barkley withdrew after leaders of the AFL and CIO decided that he was too old to run. Truman and the party leaders then drafted Governor Adlai E. Stevenson of Illinois, who received the nomination on the third ballot. Stevenson chose Senator John J. Sparkman of Alabama as his running mate.

The campaign that followed was more exciting than any presidential contest that the country had seen since Franklin D. Roosevelt began to dominate American national politics. Stevenson easily ranked as the most eloquent American political leader since Franklin Roosevelt. The Illinois Governor, in a series of addresses, attempted to educate the people for their responsibilities in the complex mid-twentieth-century world. While Stevenson made few original suggestions, he did promise to extend the New Deal and the Fair Deal by further measures to expand and protect civil rights for blacks. He also spoke of

Republican presidential candidate Dwight D. Eisenhower is besieged by a crowd in Long Island, New York, on one of his many whistle-stops during the campaign of 1952. Eisenhower's roots lay in the rural life of a simpler era and contributed to his image as a humble, honest American. A symbol of victory during the war, he described his campaign as a "Great Crusade for honest government at home and freedom throughout the world." (United Press International)

increasingly complicated world problems with which the United States would have to deal. Stevenson promised no easy solutions and warned that the struggles ahead would be dangerous and difficult.

Eisenhower's campaign was very different from Stevenson's, but it was, politically, much more adept. Eisenhower, endowed with immense magnetism, went before the country like a conquering hero. He called upon Americans to join him in a crusade and promised to clean up what he referred to as the "mess" in Washington. Eisenhower conciliated conservatives by placating Taft. The General promised to stop "creeping socialism," but he did not specify which of the New Deal-Fair Deal programs he would repeal or curtail. Eisenhower also stood aside while McCarthy carried on a vicious personal campaign against Stevenson. Eisenhower even remained silent while McCarthy attacked the loyalty of General Marshall, the man most responsible for raising Eisenhower to his high command during the Second World War. Eisenhower actually deleted words of praise for Marshall's great contributions to his country rather than offend McCarthy and his supporters. However, Eisenhower's most effective stroke was a promise, made in Detroit on October 24, that he would go to Korea in person and bring the Korean War to "an early and honorable end."

More than 61,000,000 Americans went to the polls on election day and swept Eisenhower to victory. The General carried thirty-nine states, including four in the South, and amassed a total of 33,824,000 popular and 442 electoral votes. Stevenson polled 26,584,000 popular and eighty-nine electoral votes.

The victory, however, was more a nationwide approval of America's most popular wartime hero and of his dramatic campaign than a victory for the Republican party and program. In sharp contrast to the impressive Eisenhower majority, the Republicans won control of Congress by the margin of one vote in the Senate and eight in the House of Representatives. This slight majority could easily be accounted for by the people who voted a straight Republican ticket to elect and aid Eisenhower. The results constituted also a vote of impatience with the deadlocked Korean War, for which Republican orators, including Nixon, persistently blamed the Democratic party.

SUGGESTED READINGS

Eric F. Goldman, *The Crucial Decade, and After* (1960), is a casual survey relevant to this and the following two chapters. For the Truman administration, see Cabell Phillips, *The Truman Presidency* (1966); Alonzo L. Hamby, *Beyond the New Deal: Harry S. Truman and American Liberalism* (1973), a sympathetic account; and Robert J. Donovan, *Conflict and Crisis: The Presidency of Harry S. Truman* (1977), and Bert Cochran, *Harry Truman and the Crisis Presidency* (1973), which are more critical. For a radical critique, see Barton J. Bernstein and A. J. Matusow, eds., *The Truman Administration: A Documentary History* (1966). For biographical information on Truman, see Jonathan Daniels, *The Man from Independence* (1950), and *Memoirs by Harry S. Truman*, 2 vols. (1955–1956). Truman's political origins are discussed in Lyle W. Dorsett, *The Pendergast Machine* (1968).

Most of the works cited on diplomacy in the preceding chapter are relevant to the origins of the Cold War. These should be supplemented by John L. Gaddis, *The United States and the Origins of the Cold War, 1941–1947* (1973), and *Russia, the Soviet Union, and the United States* (1978); Walter LaFeber, *America, Russia, and the Cold War, 1945–1966* (1967); Herbert Feis, *Contest over Japan* (1967) and *From Trust to Terror: The Onset of the Cold War* (1970); Daniel Yergin, *Shattered Peace: The Origins of the Cold War and the National Security State* (1977); Lisle A. Rose, *Roots of Tragedy: The United States and the Struggle for Asia, 1945–1953* (1976); Thomas G. Patterson, *Soviet-American Confrontation: Postwar Reconstruction and the*

Origins of the Cold War (1974); William H. McNeill, *America, Britain and Russia: Their Cooperation and Conflict, 1941–1946* (1953); Martin F. Herz, *The Beginnings of the Cold War* (1966); and Paul Seabury, *The Rise and Decline of the Cold War* (1967). Gar Alperwitz, *Atomic Diplomacy: Hiroshima and Potsdam* (1965), a New Left analysis, has been subjected to sharp scrutiny and criticism. On this matter, also see the books by Jungk, Davis, and Sherwin cited in the Suggested Readings for the preceding chapter. An interesting survey is George F. Kennan, *American Diplomacy*, already cited. The Truman Doctrine and the Marshall Plan are discussed in Joseph Jones, *The Fifteen Weeks* (1955). Other important memoirs and personal accounts include Dean Acheson, *The Pattern of Responsibility* (1952) and *Present at the Creation* (1969); Walter Millis, ed., *The Forrestal Diaries* (1951); Arthur H. Vandenberg, Jr., ed., *The Private Papers of Senator Vandenberg* (1952); and Robert A. Taft, *A Foreign Policy for Americans* (1951).

The American occupations can be studied in Lucius C. Clay, *Decision in Germany* (1950); Jean Smith, *The Defense of Berlin* (1963); Edwin O. Reischauer, *The United States and Japan* (1957); and William J. Sebald, *With MacArthur in Japan* (1965). Further American involvement in Asia is surveyed in John K. Fairbank, *The United States and China* (1958), and Ellen Hammer, *The Struggle for Indochina* (1954).

Trygve Lie, *In the Cause of Peace* (1954), and J. G. Stoessinger, *The United Nations and the Superpowers* (1965), adequately cover the early years of that organization.

Carl Berger, *The Korea Knot, a Military-Political History* (1957), and Malcolm W. Cagle and F. A. Manson, *The Sea War in Korea* (1957), are the best general surveys. The best account of the Truman-MacArthur conflict is John W. Spanier, *The Truman-MacArthur Controversy and the Korean War* (1959). Richard H. Rovere and Arthur M. Schlesinger, Jr., *The General and the President* (1951), is another reasonably balanced analysis. Trumbull Higgins, *Korea and the Fall of MacArthur* (1960), is a military history hostile to the General; William Manchester, *American Caesar*, cited earlier, presents a favorable portrait of the man and the general, at times ignoring the disastrous consequences of MacArthur's military achievements.

An analysis of general political tendencies can be found in Lubell, *The Future of American Politics*, cited earlier. C. Vann Woodward, *The Strange Career of Jim Crow* (1957), and Arnold M. Rose, *The Negro in Postwar America* (1950), are good on the growing concern for Negro rights. Some of the better special studies of Truman's domestic policies are William C. Berman, *The Politics of Civil Rights in the Truman Administration* (1971); Allen Yarnell, *Democrats and Progressives* (1974); Edward S. Flash, Jr., *Economic Advice and Presidential Leadership* (1965); Richard Davies, *Housing Reform during the Truman Administration* (1966); and R. Alton Lee, *Truman and Taft-Hartley* (1967). Jules Abels,

Out of the Jaws of Victory (1959), and Irwin Ross, *The Loneliest Campaign: The Truman Victory of 1948* (1968), are good on the election of 1948. There is no satisfactory analysis of the election of 1952, but the interested student will find useful information in Kenneth S. Davis' *The Politics of Honor: Adlai Stevenson* (1967), and particularly in John Bartlow Martin, *Adlai Stevenson of Illinois* (1976) and *Adlai Stevenson and the World* (1977). James T. Patterson, *Mr. Republican: A Biography of Robert A. Taft* (1972), is indispensable for Republican politics during this period.

Edward A. Shils, *The Torment of Secrecy* (1956), is a good analysis of the growth of wild fears about national security. The danger to civil liberties posed by this attitude is the subject of Francis Biddle, *The Fear of Freedom* (1951), and Sidney Gook, *Heresy, Yes—Conspiracy, No.* (1953). On this topic also see Richard M. Freeland, *The Truman Doctrine and the Origins of McCarthyism* (1972); Earl Latham, *The Communist Controversy in Washington: From the New Deal to McCarthy* (1966); Allen P. Harper, *The Politics of Loyalty* (1969); and Robert Griffith, *The Politics of Fear* (1970). Allen Weinstein, *Perjury! The Hiss-Chambers Conflict* (1977), makes a persuasive case for Hiss' guilt, as does the earlier Alastair Cook, *A Generation on Trial* (1950).

CHAPTER 34
THE AMERICAN PEOPLE SINCE THE SECOND WORLD WAR

1. SOCIAL TRENDS

Changing Attitudes toward the Future

It is reported on dubious authority that, as Adam and Eve were leaving the Garden of Eden, Adam remarked to his wife: "My dear, we are now entering an era of transition." The human family has been in transition since its beginning: that is, after all, the stuff of history. But never has the *pace* of change been more accelerated than in the decades since the end of the Second World War, which itself set in motion much of the change.

In the United States, the combined impact of social, economic, geopolitical, and scientific-technological change produced a series of transformations so sweeping that they left many Americans with a sense of discontinuity with their own past. Ironically, the shock of historical change seems to have diminished the ability of individuals to see their own lives as part of a continuum in which the past, present, and future are part of one social process. It is now more difficult than ever before to view "the future as history."

In this era of rapid change, the attitudes of many Americans toward their own society and its future have fluctuated rather sharply. The history of these changes seems to divide itself naturally into three time periods, although such a division hides a considerable amount of historical continuity. During the first period—roughly 1945 to 1963—most Americans seemed satisfied with the direction and quality of their society. Economic growth proceeded at a rapid pace. A large fraction of the population moved into the middle class and adopted many aspects of what had been considered middle-class life-styles. They enjoyed steadily rising incomes, which they tended to use to support larger families and to buy the conspicuous accoutrements of suburban family life. The most noticeable complaints came from nonwhites, who still did not share equally in the postwar prosperity, and from cultural dissidents (called "beatniks" before anyone applied the term "hippie" to practitioners of a bohemian life-style), who protested against a stiffling conformity in ideas, tastes, and behavior. A milder form of protest, which foreshadowed the youth revolution of the 1960s, was the advent of rock-and-roll music, an event which transformed the entertainment industry and struck dismay into the hearts of many adults.

In the early 1960s, the scattered cries of dissatisfaction increased in number and volume, and, before the end of the decade, much of America was swept by protests of all sorts. During this second period, the first concerted protests came from persons who said that American democracy had failed to provide freedom, equality, and justice for blacks and other ethnic minority groups. As had happened in the 1830s and 1840s, concern for the well-being of oppressed minorities heightened awareness of the unequal treatment of women in American society and led to a movement to eliminate that form of discrimination. Finally, pervasive dissatisfaction appeared among American college-age youths. The principal catalyst of their protest movement was the war in Vietnam, which, by the late 1960s threatened to involve many of the male college students. The youth protest, however, went beyond the self-interest of middle- and upper-class students who sought to avoid the draft. The movement set itself against the entire structure of American society. Students pointed to the failure of the American people and government to live up to the nation's highest professed ideals in almost every important area of American life. While some students adopted a radical political stance in their communities and schools, thousands simply dropped out of what they despised as a stultifying, materialistic, authoritarian, and absurd society.

Compared with the turbulent 1960s, the social conflict during the third period, the 1970s, seemed tame. The end of the war in Vietnam and of most large-scale street warfare in this country, general acceptance of some manifestations of the counterculture, and an increase in "careerism" among students all helped to soften the line which had so sharply divided the American people into warring factions in the latter part of the 1960s. It is easy to overstate the fluctuations in attitudes which seem to have coincided with decadal breakpoints since the 1950s. Young people throughout the era have been concerned to find jobs and to find themselves. Similarly, movements for social justice, while undergoing changes in direction and intensity, have persisted. Both the fluctuations and the continuities will be discussed following an analysis of the social and economic structures of the United States since the 1940s.

Shifting Population Trends

The generation of young people that produced so many outspoken rebels became newsworthy even before most of them could talk. Falling birth rates during the 1920s and 1930s had led experts to predict that the American population would level off about mid-century and then decrease during the 1960s and

1970s. The findings of the Census of 1940 seemed to justify this prediction, for the population increase of 7.2 per cent for the decade 1930–1940 was by far the smallest proportionate increase in American history.

Instead, both the birth and marriage rates rose sharply during the 1940s. (Actually, the birthrate turned upward in 1939.) The number of births soared when veterans returned to build homes and start families in 1945–1946. Americans in the postwar period were having children at about the same rate as their grandparents before the First World War. The consequence was a population increase of 14.5 per cent between 1940 and 1950 and an additional 28 per cent increase between 1950 and 1965, to a total of about 193,000,000. This growth occurred mainly because of the increase in the birth rate, not because of significant additions through immigration, even though the number of immigrants to the United States increased by more than two-fold during the 1950s. By the end of the 1950s, one person was added to the growing ranks every twelve seconds. At this rate, the nation was adding a population equal to that of Richmond, Virginia, every month.

Beginning in 1957, however, the rate of population growth began to slacken, and, by the late 1960s, both the birth and marriage rates were falling in much the same fashion as they had during the 1920s. By 1972, the fertility rate (the number of children per family) dropped below the point of "zero population growth." Not until 1977 did the birth rate go up, and then only very slightly. Total population stood at about 230,000,000 in 1980.

To a large extent, the widespread availability of contraceptives helps to explain this decline. By the end of the 1960s, it was estimated that 70 per cent of American families were using some form of contraception. In addition, attitudes toward marriage and child rearing were changing. Both marriage and the birth of first children were being postponed by many persons, and it became more socially acceptable for couples to have fewer children or no children at all. As always, economic conditions and expectations had a major impact on the birth rate. Couples faced with rapidly rising costs of rearing children and with diminished prospects of meeting their own economic expectations increasingly decided to postpone or even forego parenthood. The same demographic results followed when more and more married women entered the work force, either because of personal preference or because of family necessity.

The Revolution in the Family and Life-Styles

Changing patterns of marriage and childbearing since 1960 pointed toward a more generalized transformation of the American family. Prescribed roles within families were challenged, and even the *forms* of household and family life became more variable, particularly since the late 1960s. Between 1970 and 1977, the number of adults living alone increased seven times faster than the number of households with both husband and wife. Between 1960 and 1980, the number of single-parent families rose at a similarly rapid rate in comparison with two-parent families. Perhaps most striking was the increase in cohabitation among unmarried couples. By the end of the 1970s, there were an estimated 1,000,000 such couples, and their number was expected to treble during the 1980s. None of these developments indicated, by the beginning of the 1980s, that traditional values or family patterns were on the verge of extinction.

Unquestionably, however, there had been major changes in sexual practices during the preceding two decades and an equally significant shift in the society's acceptance of differing life-styles.

People Still on the Move

One of the greatest growth industries after the Second World War was the business of moving household goods. One out of every five Americans moved *each year*. Where were they all going? There was, first, a continued exodus from the farms. Between 1940 and 1964, the number of dwellers on farms dropped from 23.2 per cent of the total population to 6.8 per cent. By the mid-1970s, it had dropped below 4 per cent. But the movement of people was not, as it had been in the past, toward the center of the great cities. By the mid-1970s, more people lived in the suburbs (38 per cent) than lived in the central cities (30 per cent).

The movement to the suburbs was encouraged, even subsidized, by the federal government, which helped to make available low-cost loans for home construction and underwrote the building of a new system of superhighways which provided easy access between the central city and its suburbs via private automobiles. The new suburban rings beyond the central cities were characterized by single-family homes, new community shopping centers, and a predominantly white, middle-class population. As suburban property tax bases soared, the relatively affluent and well-educated residents demanded and received improved public services, particularly better schools than those in the central cities. As it helped millions of Americans to fulfill their dream of owning their own homes, the federal government had, unwittingly, contributed to the increased segregation of American society along both racial and economic lines. To suburbanites, poverty became less and less visible, simply because they rarely saw poor people anymore.

The outward sprawl of the cities did not abate, despite the movement to renovate older residential neighborhoods. By the early 1980s, the highest rate of growth was still in the "exurban" areas—the small towns and nonfarm rural areas beyond the rims of the great metropolitan centers. It remains to be seen whether this outward push will be sustained in the face of gasoline shortages and escalating fuel costs. There is a growing indication that young adults, especially those without children, are moving back to the cities to take advantage of the many cultural and other opportunities provided there.

Americans also moved from region to region at a quickening pace. The Second World War accelerated the growth of the Pacific and Gulf coast states, for here were located, not only many of the huge military bases, but also most of the industrial plants which produced war material. After the war, many servicemen returned to those areas to live, and new industries joined the defense plants in locating near the growing labor pool and markets beyond the old industrial regions of the Northeast. In the South, new industries were lured by promises of local governmental subsidies and prospects of nonunion work forces.

Not only the young and adventurous but also the elderly and infirm sought the gentle climate and informal life of Florida and California. The Pacific states, for example, grew in population by about 140 per cent from 1940 to 1965; most of the migrants went to California, which became the most populous state in 1964. By 1970, 20,000,000 people—one tenth of the country's entire population—lived in California. By the mid-1970s, the populations of the southern and western states were growing at a rate double that of the nation as a whole. This shift of jobs and population to the so-called "sunbelt" had profound political implications, already felt by 1972, when the northeastern states lost and the sunbelt states gained in the decennial reapportionment of seats in the House of Representatives.

One other population movement of major proportions was the exodus of blacks from the southern countryside to urban centers. Until the 1970s, that shift was largely a movement out of the South. At late as the mid-1930s, 80 per cent of black Americans lived in the southern states. The mass migration from the South, which had begun before the First World War, reached major proportions during the Second. It grew during the prosperous postwar era, until, in 1960, slightly more than one half of all American blacks lived outside the former Confederate states, mainly in northern and midwestern cities. The regional flow reversed slightly during the 1970s, with the result that a bare majority of blacks was again living in the South by 1980. But in that region, as in the North, cities had become the magnet. Atlanta, Houston, and other urban centers absorbed much of the reverse migration, although not a few black emigrés, like many European and Caribbean immigrants, returned in their old age to their native communities.

An Aging Population

Americans were also living longer by the middle and latter decades of the twentieth century. The reasons included improved standards of living and fantastic advances in medical knowledge. Between 1900 and 1960, life expectancy had increased by twenty-one years for men and twenty-five years for women. Much of that increase was attributable to declining rates of infant mortality. However, the number of persons over the age of sixty-five also rose sharply, until, by 1977, 10.8 per cent of the population was in that age bracket.

The increased numbers of the aged brought a host of new social and economic problems. The upsurge in pension and retirement systems, as well as the extension of Social Security coverage, reflected a new concern for elder citizens and the growing strength of "gray power" in American politics. The growth of both private and governmental programs for the elderly also reflected the loosening of family ties and the gradual erosion of family responsibility for the eldest members—phenomena that had been under way throughout the twentieth century, but especially since the 1920s.

2. AFFLUENCE AND UNCERTAINTY IN THE AMERICAN ECONOMY

Unprecedented Economic Expansion, 1945–1965

Anyone who might have predicted in 1940 what lay ahead for the American economy during the next twenty-five years probably would have been regarded as insanely optimistic. Similarly, at the mid-point of the 1960s, anyone who

Maggie Kuhn, organizer of the Gray Panthers, addressing the Second Biennial Gray Panthers convention in Chevy Chase, Maryland, October 1977. The Gray Panthers works to eliminate age discrimination against all people, not just the aged. (Photo by Julie Jensen)

suggested that the economic boom might not go on forever might have been thought of as sourly pessimistic. However, events at home and abroad since the late 1960s demonstrated that hopes for never ending prosperity were premature. In 1980, the average American still enjoyed a standard of living which was the envy of much of the rest of the world, but American economic invincibility had come to an end.

By 1940, per capita income and the Gross National Product, or GNP (total value of goods and services produced) had returned to 1929 levels, but it was the massive war spending of the period from 1940 to 1945 that caused the wheels of the economy to spin at a dizzy speed. Brief business recessions occurred in 1949 and 1954, a longer and more serious one in 1957–1958, and a brief one again in 1960–1961. (By definition, a recession occurs when the GNP declines for two consecutive quarters.) However, during each of these recessions it seemed that the country was merely catching its economic breath and was not in serious trouble. Unemployment, which had reached 25 per cent during the Great Depression, averaged 4.6 per cent during the 1950s. Business recovered and went on to new heights with only moderate stimulus from governmental fiscal and monetary policies.

In the early 1960s, the federal government, influenced by neo-Keynesian economists, used its economic leverage more aggressively than before to counteract any slowdown of the business cycle. Tax reductions, increased welfare spending, and aids to business were all used to stimulate the economy. These policies followed, more or less, the precepts of John Maynard Keynes (1883–1946), the influential British economist, who had argued that, in a depression or recession, government could stimulate the economy through deficit spending. The results of these policies were spectacularly successful. The GNP, spurred by governmental action and by organizational and technological innovations in industry, rose by 25 per cent between 1960 and 1965—the largest half-decade increase ever recorded.

The economy's behavior during the period 1945–1965 can perhaps best be illustrated by a few summary statistics. The GNP increased from $314 billion in 1945 to about $570 billion in 1965. Per capita income, before taxes, increased by some 120 per cent. The median income for all families, which had been about $3 thousand in 1947, rose to $6 thousand in 1965. Such aggregate statistics certainly hide from view the extreme poverty at the bottom of the economic scale, but Americans as a whole had never before known such prosperity and economic growth, for so long a time, without a major depression.

The causes of this postwar prosperity were numerous and complex, but four stand out as particularly significant:

1. In 1945 a huge, pent-up demand existed for housing and for all the consumer goods—such as automobiles and electrical appliances—that had not been manufactured during the war. Huge savings had been accumulated by potential consumers, including millions of Americans who, before the war, had subsisted in abject poverty. Pent-up demand, backed by widespread ability to purchase, gave the economy a tremendous stimulus once civilian production was resumed.

2. The new army of consumers included, by the 1950s, the first wave of the postwar baby boom. As the demographic bulge created by this bumper crop of babies moved through childhood and adolescence in the 1950s and 1960s, it increased the demand, not only for consumer goods, but also for services, most notably, schools.

3. Governmental spending continued to stimulate the economy after the war. Military expenditures, including those for the Korean conflict in the early 1950s, remained high. Federal subsidies to farmers, veterans, and homeowners spurred over-all growth, as did the massive federal funding of a new system of interstate highways. In June 1956, Congress authorized the expenditure of $33 billion (later increased to $40 billion) for a 40,000-mile network of superhighways. This action caused expansion in the automobile and trucking industries, contributed to the postwar growth of suburbs, and, along with the federally induced growth of the airline industry, contributed to the decline of the railroads as a means of public transportation. Increased governmental expenditures at the state and local level, both for construction of highways and schools and for the expansion of social services, helped to bring over-all governmental spending to a level equal to 20 per cent of production in the private sector, which was higher than at any time during the New Deal.

4. Perhaps the most significant cause of the postwar prosperity was the extremely high rate of the increase in productivity on farms and in factories from the end of the Second World War through the 1960s. The increased productivity in the quarter century after the Second World War derived primarily from

the application of new technologies and the extension of efficient organizational techniques into larger and larger segments of the economy. We will discuss these developments later in this chapter.

Uncertainties in the American Economy Since 1965

By 1966, rapid expansion was straining the American economic system. One immediate source of the strain was federal fiscal policy. Under President Lyndon Johnson, the government expanded military spending (to finance the war in Indochina) and increased spending on domestic social programs—both at the same time, without increasing taxes. The resulting deficits in the federal budget sharply expanded the money supply and contributed to rapid inflation. During the 1950s and early 1960s, the annual inflation rate had rarely exceeded 1 per cent, but between 1965 and 1969 it jumped from 2.1 to 6 per cent; it stood at 13 per cent in 1979 and 18 per cent in early 1980. By 1980, the dollar was worth less than half its value in 1967.

Domestic inflation contributed to the weakening of the dollar as the basis of international exchange and trade. However, even before inflation had become a problem, the United States was experiencing significant deficits in its balance of payments. A declining share of worldwide trade in manufactured goods, coupled with American military expenditures overseas and direct private investment abroad, created deficits in the balance of payments that rose from $2.8 billion annually in 1960–1964 to $3.4 billion in 1965–1969. By 1980, the world economy had become so flooded with dollars, and the dollar had so declined in value, that the western European nations and the oil-rich middle eastern states were looking for alternative units of exchange.

The declining value of the dollar and the increased price of American goods sold abroad encouraged the Oil Producing and Exporting Countries (OPEC), an Arab-dominated cartel, to quadruple crude oil prices in 1973–1974. The price increases and the OPEC embargo of the United States during the Arab-Israeli war of 1973 demonstrated the growing dependence of the United States on expensive foreign sources of energy and raw materials. The disruption of Iranian oil supplies to the United States and the continued escalation of OPEC prices in 1979 and 1980 awakened many Americans to this, the rudest fact of their life. The problem was not restricted to oil. By the mid-1970s, American industry was dependent on foreign supplies for six of the thirteen most needed raw materials.

In searching for an explanation of America's economic woes, many economists, business leaders, and politicians focused on the nation's declining rate of productivity. The rate of increase in productivity gradually slipped in the 1970s; in 1979, productivity itself actually declined by 2 per cent. While no one could deny the fact of declining productivity, experts disagreed about its causes. One explanation was that people simply were not working as hard as they had worked earlier. This may have been true. However, a more important reason for the decline in productivity in the 1970s was the decrease of investment in new plants and machinery and a sharp decline in expenditures for research and development. An increasing amount of such capital investment had to be spent for environmental, safety, and health equipment mandated by governments on all levels. Other factors contributed to the decline. The bulge of young and inexperienced workers who entered the labor force played a part, as did the fact that "service" industries accounted for an ever increasing portion of the GNP (46 per cent in 1979 as compared to 31 per cent in 1950). It has proved more difficult to improve the efficiency of a doctor, policeman, or a college professor than that of a worker on the assembly line.

The inflationary spiral of the 1970s was particularly troubling because it was accompanied by high unemployment and recessionary swings in the business cycle. The country, in 1974–1975, suffered its sharpest recession since the Great Depression and entered another sharp recession in 1980. The over-all rate of unemployment during the 1970s ranged between 4 and 9 per cent, but unemployment among nonwhites was double that of the population as a whole, and the rate among young black males ran as high as 40 per cent— almost double the national rate at the depth of the Great Depression.

In the decades after the Second World War, economists had been numbered among the most trusted advisers of high governmental officials, and their role in governmental decision making had been written into law in the Employment Act of 1946 (see p. 829). During the early 1960s, the apparent success of the neo-Keynesian economists in "fine-tuning" the economy had secured the preeminence of their school. But by the end of the 1970s, the neo-Keynesian remedies—deficit spending, lowering taxes to stimulate demand, and wage and price "guidelines" to check inflation—simply were not working. A new breed of conservative economists called for stimulation of production rather than demand, through tax incentives to business and a lessening of governmental regulation. While these conservative economists and many business leaders were criticizing the neo-Keynesians from the Right, other economists and many union leaders were assailing them from the Left.

The Organization of Modern American Business

During and after the Second World War, integrated multidivisional corporations, operated by salaried managers and technologists, became even more powerful and widespread in the American economy than before. The demands of wartime mobilization and the opportunities of the postwar mass market and technological revolution virtually guaranteed this development. Now, as in the early days of its history, the overriding concern of this kind of business organization was to create a stable, predictable environment, in order to replace the "invisible hand" of the market with the "visible hand" of managerial planning. In these integrated firms, group management largely replaced the leadership function of the individual entrepreneur, and decision making was dispersed throughout a huge network of highly trained specialists—the "technostructure," as John Kenneth Galbraith has called it.

The pervasiveness of oligopoly and managerially planned development in many leading sectors of the economy attested to the success of managerial capitalism in achieving its objectives. A free market continued to function in some sectors of the economy, but in such key industries as energy, steel, automobiles, and communications, a combination of corporate and governmental planning had largely replaced the dynamics of the marketplace.

A particular variant of the multidivisional firm appeared in the 1960s—the conglomerate. Examples of this new type of firm were Ling-Temco-Vaught, International Telephone and Telegraph, Litton Industries, and Gulf and Western Industries. Unlike earlier diversified firms, which had typically expanded into new product lines related to their original lines, the conglomerates absorbed existing companies which were often in totally unrelated fields. The conglomerates were fundamentally *financially* oriented—that is, their major concern was capital appreciation through an increase in the value of their stock.

Many of the conglomerates, along with many of the older multidivisional firms, had become multinational in their operations. American investments abroad skyrocketed, particularly after the creation of the European Common Market in 1958. By the mid-1970s, American-based multinational firms constituted the third largest economic power in the world and trailed only the national economies of the United States and Russia. Although those firms were American in origin, they became increasingly free of the American domestic market and of control by any government.

The Continuing Technological Revolution

During and after the Second World War, technological innovations stimulated old industries and created new ones. Research and development (R & D) were incorporated into the routine operations of large corporations and of the government itself. The wartime development of nuclear power for military purposes and its subsequent commercial adaptation for generating electricity were prime examples of this kind of organized research. There were major innovations in the petrochemical industry. They began with the war-mandated development of synthetic rubber and also included plastics, fertilizers, and synthetic fibers. Lightweight metals, particularly aluminum, but also magnesium and titanium, were being manufactured in such expanded quantities after 1945 that they can justly be included among the new industries.

Television sparked the growth of the electronics industry after the war. Television sets in use in the United States jumped from 7,000 in 1947 to 54,000,000 in 1960. At the end of the 1970s, the television industry was poised on the brink of another revolution; expanded transmission of television signals by cable and satellite greatly increased the quantity and variety of national programming. Two-way television, made possible by linking cable transmission and home computers, was being test marketed by the end of the 1970s. Other innovations of the 1960s and 1970s in the field of communications included Xerography, lasers, and fiber optics. The latter two are key components in the telephonic communication systems of the future.

The modern computer, born in the era of vacuum tubes, came of age after the invention of transistors in the late 1940s and of large-scale integrated circuitry (silicone chips) in the 1970s. These two electronic innovations made possible phenomenal increases in the speed and capacity of computers. They also reduced their size and cost. Consumer applications of integrated circuitry and computers burst on the scene in the 1970s in the form of pocket calculators, digital watches, and electronic games. In 1979 one expert prophesied: "In the future you're going to get computers as prizes in breakfast cereal. You'll have to throw them out because your house will be littered with them." If one allows for some partisan hyperbole, his statement accurately reflected the trend in consumer uses of the computer.

Prior to this time, computers had already transformed business and industry through data processing and the automation of manufacturing. The application of computer technology to continuous flow and assembly-line manufacturing made it possible to program machines to give commands to other machines and thus to carry out the handling, machining, fabricating, and inspection of goods in a self-contained and self-correcting system, without the intervention of human hands.

Stunning innovations in the biochemical and genetic realm followed the discovery of deoxyribonucleic acid (DNA) in 1953 by Francis Crick and James Watson at Cambridge University. Comprehension of the genetic "code," which their discovery entailed, had profound technological and ethical implications. Their basic breakthrough led to the development of a technique for "splicing" genes from one organism to another (recombinant DNA), a technique through which technologists can "program" organisms to manufacture compounds as diverse as human insulin and alcohol. The full effects of genetic engineering are yet to be felt, but its impact is potentially as revolutionary as the chemical, mechanical, and electronic innovations of the period since the Second World War. The ethical and safety issues raised by this new technology are as complex and serious as any other by-products of human creativity.

The *organization* of R & D since the war is as significant as the particular innovations which it has created. Large, impersonal, and lavishly financed research laboratories and centers increasingly replaced the individual scientist and inventor as the sources of innovation. Such research centers were in some instances linked directly to industry (Bell Laboratories, for example), in other cases to universities, and in some cases, as with the National Aeronautics and Space Administration (NASA), operated directly by the federal government. This kind of highly organized R & D work has been heavily concentrated in the aerospace, electronic, chemical, and machine industries. Furthermore, close to half of all R & D expenditures since the war have been tied to military development and the space program.

Total expenditures for R & D in the United States had reached $40 billion by the late 1970s; the federal government had supplied over half that amount. But, when adjusted for inflation, the level of federal expenditures actually declined by 5 per cent between 1969 and 1979, while at the same time such expenditures increased steadily in other industrialized nations. At the end of the 1970s, there was, therefore, a growing concern about the relative decline of the United States in technological superiority. It should be noted that the decline was a relative one, and that the United States still led the world in over-all technological innovation. The narrowing gap in technology, as in productivity, was a natural result of the revitalization of the European and Japanese economies, a process which the United States facilitated.

Technology and the Ecosystem

As the pace of technological development accelerated, so did the level of related social and environmental problems. The social impact of mechanization, automation, and urban sprawl, and the biological effect of chemical, nuclear, and genetic innovations were often inadequately considered before they were implemented. Sometimes the consequences were tragic, or nearly so, as in the case of a partial "core melt-down" in a commercial nuclear reactor at Three Mile Island, Pennsylvania, in 1979. Perhaps even more threatening than the potential for individual catastrophes was the pervasive pollution of air and water by chemical effluents, both in manufacturing and agricultural processes and by automobile emissions. At the same time, predictions of the imminent depletion of nonrenewable resources, particularly petroleum, sounded to some like the death knell of the affluent, mobile life-style which most Americans had come to take for granted.

In response to these signs of impending ecological disaster, there emerged an environmental movement which was heir to the conservation movement of the progressive era. This latter-day movement heightened public awareness of the problems and helped to mobilize support for new governmental action. In the 1960s and 1970s, Congress passed a series of laws designed to clean up the nation's air and water and to curtail future pollution. The new Environmental Protection Agency used these statutes, along with the long-ignored Refuse Act of 1899, in an effort to curb pollution. Despite serious constraints on both federal and state environmental programs, substantial gains were made in some areas. Automobile emissions of carbon monoxide and hydrocarbons declined, and some heavily polluted waterways were reclaimed.

However, the cost of the antipollution campaign was substantial. Direct costs were passed along to consumers in the form of higher prices. Regulatory acts, when translated into administrative guidelines, necessarily curtailed individual and corporate freedom. And, as had happened before, efforts to protect the environment and to conserve natural resources triggered conflicting claims for use of the nation's land and water and the store of riches beneath them.

Environmentalism, along with the radical protest movements of the 1960s, evoked a critique of modern industrialization and its "high" technology; out of this emerged a search for technological alternatives to the nation's large-scale, energy-intensive system of production. Proponents of "appropriate" or "alternative" technologies stressed the need for renewable, nonpolluting sources of energy (including solar, geothermal, and biomass) and for a decentralization and reduction in scale of production, both in manufacturing and in agriculture. Clearly, this movement represented more than a dissenting opinion about the "how-to" of modern technology. It also articulated *values* which clashed with prevailing views about economic growth and mankind's relations with the natural environment. The movement's best-known spokesman proclaimed, "Wisdom demands a new orientation of science and technology toward the organic, the gentle, the non-violent, the elegant and beautiful."

By 1980, the force of world events had compelled acceptance of some features of the movement for an alternative technology, most notably the search for environmentally safe alternatives to fossil fuels. But as a radical critique of the centralized, growth- and consumer-oriented economic system, alternative technology still occupied a position in American society not unlike that of the nineteenth-century utopian communities, which set out self-consciously to demonstrate the appropriateness of their newly found solutions to mankind's ills, even in the face of a "reality" very much at odds with their own vision of the good society.

The American Worker

The technological innovations described above, along with the bureaucratization of work, changed the profile of the American work force significantly in the postwar period. The number of farmers and farm laborers continued to decline in the face of mechanization. The number of production workers stayed fairly constant after 1950. This indicates that, while automation reduced the fraction of the total work force needed in manufacturing, it did not cause the mass dislocation compelled by the mechanization of agriculture. The greatest change in the labor force from 1940 to 1980 was the enormous expansion of employment in "service industries," such as trade, finance, and government. After 1970, clerical workers formed the largest single category of workers. Clerical jobs in the huge bureaucracies of both the public and private sectors of the economy multiplied because of the seemingly insatiable demand of modern organizations for paper work and computer-related tasks. Although clerical workers were formally categorized as "white collar," many of the jobs in the modern, factorylike offices were routine and low-paying. The ambiguous position of many clerical, sales, and service workers in this respect called into question the oft-repeated assertion that white collar ("head") workers replaced blue collar ("hand") workers as the majority in the American work force. One change, which was not at all ambiguous, was the increased participation of women in the work force. Between 1960 and 1977, their percentage rose from 37.1 to 47.8 of the total.

By the time of the Second World War, labor unions had won legal sanction and achieved considerable political and economic power. In the Truman era, the AFL and the CIO won new objectives, such as improved pensions, more paid holidays, longer vacations, and medical insurance. In addition, many contracts from 1948 onward provided for automatic annual wage increases of 2 to 2.5 per cent to give the workers the benefit of increased productivity. An innovation of the late 1950s was the so-called guaranteed annual wage, whereby company payments supplemented unemployment benefits for a certain period.

In December 1955, the great division that had torn the labor movement apart in 1935 was finally healed when the AFL and CIO came together to form one big union, the AFL-CIO, with more than 15,000,000 members. George Meany, president of the AFL, became president of the new organization, and Walter Reuther, president of the CIO, was elected vice-president.

By 1970, all of organized labor counted about 19,000,000 members in its ranks, but, as a percentage of the total work force, it had actually been declining for a number of years. By 1974, only 26.2 per cent of all nonfarm workers belonged to unions. Organized labor suffered from the relative decline in the number of production workers and from the migration of many firms to the South, where the tradition of unionism was weaker. Also, the unions failed to make large inroads among the expanding body of professional and service personnel, with notable exceptions among public employees and teachers.

How well off were American workers in the postwar era? Has the United States succeeded in creating a classless society? The answers are "better" and "no." Real wages of factory workers increased steadily between the 1940s and 1960s. As late as 1929, the last year of "prosperity" before the Great Depression, about 60 per cent of Americans lived at or below the subsistence level. By 1977, that figure had been reduced to 11.6 per cent. Moreover, after the Second World War there was a dramatic increase in the percentage of blacks and other minority group members in the middle class and in professional and managerial positions.

Yet chronic and systemic inequities persisted. Despite the rise of a black middle class, the percentage of nonwhites who lived at or below the poverty level remained almost three times as high as the percentage of whites throughout the 1970s. Sex-based wage differentials for similar jobs also persisted, despite laws which prohibited them. Since the war, the distribution of before-tax income has changed very little: the top one fifth of American families

The plight of such children as these, the real victims of poverty in Appalachia, was brought to national attention in the 1960s. This home is near Hazard, Kentucky, in Appalachia, an area largely bypassed by economic development. (Wide World Photos)

received over 40 per cent of the income and the bottom one fifth received about 5 per cent. Similar figures on *wealth* are even more skewed.

Late twentieth-century American society seemed to harbor a "hard core" of poverty and unemployment that refused to yield to governmental programs or private efforts at amelioration. Despite published exposés of poverty and hunger in America (most notably Michael Harrington's *The Other Americans* [1962]), and massive investment of governmental funds, the problem persisted. The war on poverty, proclaimed by President Johnson in 1964, won some important battles—for example, a marked improvement in the level of nutrition among poor children—but the war dragged on, with no victory in sight in 1980.

3. AN AGE OF SOCIAL PROTEST

The "Silent" Generation

As has been noted earlier, most Americans from the time of the Second World War through the 1950s accepted the direction in which their society seemed headed. This sense of well-being sprang from the relative affluence of postwar America, the proliferation of consumer goods of all kinds, and the rise of a mass culture which the advent of television accentuated. Many social scientists claimed to have found evidence in the 1950s of fundamental changes in the American character. Americans, these social scientists concluded, were increasingly concerned with social acceptance and economic security, and less inclined to take chances. They were becoming "other-directed," in the phrase of the sociologist, David Riesman. College students allegedly had lost interest in "causes" and were concerned only with personal gain, other writers said. Women had accepted the "cult of domesticity" instead of continuing the struggle for equal rights. The prototype of the new American male, one observer said, was the "organization man"—the business executive whose social and political life was shaped by the large-scale organization of which he was a part.

These characterizations were certainly overdrawn and hardly applicable to the 1950s alone. Alexis de Tocqueville had observed similar traits in the 1830s. But there was some basis for the lamentations of the 1950s: college students, along with many other ambitious young people, did give the impression of a silent, uncommitted generation who were fearful of even the appearance of being unconventional. This impression did not last long, for young people, ethnic minorities, and women transformed the 1960s into a period of social protest. As we shall see, the roots of their various protest movements lay precisely in the era of the so-called silent generation.

The Afro-American Revolution: From Civil Rights to Black Power

A new movement among Afro-Americans broke the silence of the 1950s. In fact, the drive for racial equality had never died since Reconstruction, but it gained new momentum in the 1940s and 1950s. Blacks participated in both the military hardships and economic gains of the Second World War, albeit on an unequal basis with whites. Out of that experience came rising expectations for an end to racial discrimination.

Postwar prosperity enlarged the black middle class, and the courts chipped away at the wall of legalized discrimination which had been erected half a century before. In 1954, the Supreme Court handed down an epochal decision which required an end to school segregation, and during the 1950s both Congress and Presidents took some steps to end discrimination (see pp. 837, 841, 903–904, 906–907). But the pace of change was slow. The court's ruling produced only token integration of public schools, and other public facilities in the South remained tightly segregated.

Direct confrontation had been used to challenge segregation as early as the turn of the century, but nonviolent direct protest became a major tactic in the struggle in 1955. In Montgomery, Alabama, a black woman, Rosa Parks, refused to give up her seat on a bus to a white passenger and was arrested for violating a city ordinance which required her to do so. This touched off a boycott against the bus line which was led by a young Baptist minister, Martin Luther King, Jr. The Montgomery boycott was the beginning of a sustained effort by southern blacks to proclaim their dignity as human beings and to end segregation by their own efforts.

The civil rights movement of the late 1950s and early 1960s was community-based and nonviolent. Nonviolent civil disobedience was for King and others a philosophical imperative. It was also an effective tactic for dramatizing grievances in the age of television. Again and again, Americans witnessed on their television sets confrontations between passive resisters and enforcers of segregationist laws, who often fitted the national stereotype of bigoted white Southerners. To a considerable extent, television made the civil rights

BLACK AMERICANS IN THE TWENTIETH CENTURY

The black men of America have a duty to perform, a duty stern and delicate—a forward movement to oppose a part of the work of their greatest teacher. So far as Mr. [Booker T.] Washington preaches Thrift, Patience, and Industrial Training for the masses, we must hold up his hands and strive with him, rejoicing in his honors and glorying in the strength of this Joshua called of God and of man to lead the headless host. But so far as Mr. Washington apologizes for injustice, North or South, does not rightly value the privilege and duty of voting, belittles the emasculating effects of caste distinctions, and opposes the higher training and ambition of our brighter minds—so far as he, the South, or the Nation does this—we must unceasingly and firmly oppose them. By every civilized and peaceful method we must strive for the rights which the world accords to men, clinging unwaveringly to those great words which the sons of the Fathers would fain forget: "We hold these truths to be self-evident: That all men are created equal; that they are endowed by their Creator with certain unalienable rights; that among these are life, liberty, and the pursuit of happiness."
W. E. B. Du Bois, 1903. From his work The Souls of Black Folk, *Fawcett, New York, 1964.*

William E. Burghardt Du Bois, 1868–1963, Black educational leader and writer. (Library of Congress)

New Orleans, La.
May 2, 1917.
Dear Sir: Please Sir will you
kindly tell me what is meant
by the great Northern Drive
to take place May the 15th
on Tuesday. It is a rumor all
over town to be ready for the
15th of May to go in the
drive. The *Defender* first
spoke of the drive the 10th of
February. My husband is in
the north already preparing
for our family but hearing
that the excursion will be
$6.00 from here north on the
15th and having a large
family, I could profit by it if
it is really true. Do please
write me at once and say is
there an excursion to leave
the south. Nearly the whole
of the south is getting ready
for the drive or excursion as
it is termed. Please write at
once. We are sick to get out
of the solid south.
Letter to the Chicago Defender, *a
Black newspaper. From* Journal of
Negro History, *1919, as quoted in*
In Their Own Words, A History
of the American Negro, *ed. by
Milton Meltzer, New York, 1967.*

*. . . they take, say, a seven-
room apartment, which rents
for $50 a month to whites,
and cut it up into seven small
apartments, of one room
each; they install one small
gas stove and one small sink
in each room. The Bosses of
the Buildings rent these
kitchenettes to us at the rate
of, say, $6 a week. Hence, the
same apartment for which
white people—who can get
jobs anywhere and who
receive higher wages than
we—pay $50 a month is
rented to us for $42 a week!
And because there are not
enough houses for us to live
in, because we have been
used to sleeping several in a
room on the plantations in
the South, we rent these
kitchenettes and are glad to
get them. These kitchenettes
are our havens from the
plantations in the South. We
have fled the wrath of Queen
Cotton and we are tired.*
*Richard Wright, Black author.
From his work* 12 Million Black
Voices, *Viking Press, New York,
1941.*

*Above: A black family, just arrived
in Chicago from the South, during
the World War I migration. (Reprinted
from Allan H. Spear,* Black Chicago:
The Making of a Negro Ghetto,
1890–1920, *by permission of The
University of Chicago Press, 1967.)*

*Top: Gathering cotton near Dallas,
Texas, 1907. Photo by E. W. Kelley.
(Library of Congress)*

If We Must Die

If we must die, let it not be like hogs
Hunted and penned in an inglorious spot,
While round us bark the mad and hungry dogs,
Making their mock at our accursèd lot.
If we must die, O let us nobly die,
So that our precious blood may not be shed
In vain; then even the monsters we defy
Shall be constrained to honor us though dead!
O kinsmen! we must meet the common foe!
Though far outnumbered let us show us brave,
And for their thousand blows deal one deathblow!
What though before us lies the open grave?
Like men we'll face the murderous, cowardly pack,
Pressed to the wall, dying, but fighting back!

Claude McKay, written after the Washington, D.C., race riot, summer 1919. From Selected Poems of Claude McKay, *copyright by Twayne Publishers, Boston; 1953.*

Scene of a stoning during the Chicago race riot, summer 1919. (Courtesy Chicago Historical Society)

Dear Sir,
The Washington riot gave me the *thrill that comes once in a life time.* I . . . read between the lines of our morning paper that at last our men had stood like men, struck back, were no longer dumb driven cattle. When I could no longer read for my streaming tears, I stood up, alone in my room, held both hands high over my head and exclaimed aloud: "Oh I thank God, thank God." . . . Only colored women of the South know the extreme in suffering and humiliation.

We know how many insults we have borne silently, for we have hidden many of them from our men because we did not want them to die needlessly in our defense . . . , the deep humiliation of sitting in the Jim Crow part of a street car and hear the white men laugh and discuss us, point out the good and bad points of our bodies. . . .

And, too, a woman loves a strong man, she delights to feel that her man can protect her, fight for her if necessary, save her.

No woman loves a weakling, a coward be she white or black, and some of us have been near thinking our men cowards, but thank God for Washington colored men! All honor to them, for they first blazed the way and right swiftly did Chicago men follow [during the 1919 race riot]. They put new hope, a new vision into their almost despairing women.

God grant that our men everywhere refrain from strife, provoke no quarrel, but that they protect their women and homes at any cost.
        A Southern Colored Woman

Letter to The Crisis, *November 1919.*

We younger Negro artists who create now intend to express our individual dark-skinned selves without fear or shame. If white people are pleased we are glad. If they are not, it doesn't matter. We know we are beautiful. And ugly too. . . . If colored people are pleased we are glad. If they are not, their displeasure doesn't matter either. We build our temples for tomorrow, strong as we know how, and we stand on top of the mountain, free within ourselves.

. . . to my mind, it is the duty of the younger Negro artist, if he accepts any duties at all from outsiders, to change through the force of his art that old whispering "I want to be white," hidden in the aspirations of his people, to "Why should I want to be white? I am a Negro—and beautiful!" *Langston Hughes, 1926.*

Incident

Once riding in old Baltimore,
   Heart-filled, head-filled with glee,
I saw a Baltimorean
Keep looking straight at me.

Now I was eight and very small,
   And he was no whit bigger,
And so I smiled, but he poked out
   His tongue and called me, "Nigger."

I saw the whole of Baltimore
   From May until December:
Of all the things that happened there
   That's all that I remember.

A Song of Praise

My love is dark as yours is fair,
   Yet lovelier I hold her
Than listless maids with pallid hair,
   And blood that's thin and colder.

We like your "Jim Crow" laws, in that they defend the purity of races and any person married to any but a Negro cannot become a member of our organization. We are not members . . . of that class who are spending their time imitating the rich whites . . . studying Spanish so as to be able to pass for anything but a Negro, thereby getting a chance to associate with you. We are not ashamed of the Race to which we belong and we feel sure that God made black skin and kinky hair because He desired to express Himself in that type. *From a letter to the mayor of New Orleans from the Women's Auxiliary of the Universal Negro Improvement Association, 1923. From the Chicago Defender, March 31, 1923, as quoted in E. D. Cronon, Black Moses, University of Wisconsin Press, 1955.*

Top: Black Cross nurses marching in mammoth parade signaling the start of a U.N.I.A. convention in New York City, August 1922. A "back to Africa movement" was part of the U.N.I.A.'s program. (The Bettmann Archive)

Left: Marcus Garvey, 1922. (United Press International Photo.

Black men, you were once great; you shall be great again. Lose not courage, lose not faith, go forward. The thing to do is to get organized; keep separated and you will be exploited, you will be robbed, you will be killed. Get organized, and you will compel the world to respect you. If the world fails to give you consideration because you are Negroes, four hundred millions of you shall, through organization, shake the pillars of the universe and bring down creation, even as Samson brought down the temple upon his head and upon the heads of the Philistines.
Marcus Garvey, 1923.

A black mother and her children, surrounded by their belongings, wait to be moved to a new home by the FSA, June 1938, southeast Mississippi. (The Bettmann Archive)

Where is your husband?

"He worked in the steel mills for four-five years and was a good man. The mill closed and he was laid off. He went out early every morning and walked the streets until night, looking for work. Day after day he done this ever since last June. Once a man told him that he needn't trouble looking for a job as long as there is so many white men out of work. I guess us colored folks don't get hungry like white folks. He just got discouraged and one day he went out and didn't come back. He told me once that if he wasn't living at home the welfare people would help me and the kids, and maybe he just went away on that account. . . ."

A middle-aged Black woman in Pittsburgh, 1931. From Urban League Report, Opportunity, *March 1931, as quoted in* In Their Own Words, *Meltzer.*

I tried keeping books one year, and the man kept worrying me about it, saying his books was the ones he went by anyhow. And nothing you can do but leave. He said he didn't have no time to fool with no books. He don't ever give us no rent notes all the time. They got you 'cause you have to carry your cotton to his mill to gin and you better not carry your cotton nowhere else. I don't care how good your cotton is, a colored man's cotton is always second- or third-grade cotton if a colored man sells it. The only way you can get first prices for it is to get some white man to sell it for you in his name. A white man sold mine once, and got market price for it.

We haven't paid out to Mr. —— in twelve years. Been in debt that long. See, when a fella's got a gun in your face you gotter take low or die.

A Southern sharecropper. As quoted in Charles S. Johnson, The Shadow of the Plantation, *University of Chicago Press, 1934.*

Now the poor white folks is them that ain't got nothing, but thinks they is somebody. They like to pick on Negroes. They cheat them, 'buse them and meddle with them. An aristocratic white person is more decent about it. 'Course they cheat Negroes too, but they's nice about the way they do it.
Black laborer in Mississippi. As quoted in Johnson, Growing Up in the Black Belt.

Often the oppressor goes along unaware of the evil involved in his oppression so long as the oppressed accepts it. So in order to be true to one's conscience and true to God, a righteous man has no alternative but to refuse to cooperate with an evil system. This I felt was the nature of our action. . . . I conceived of our movement as an act of massive noncooperation. . . .
Dr. Martin Luther King, Jr., on the bus boycott of 1955, Montgomery, Alabama.

Ain't nobody tell me how to act around them [white people]. I just knowed how to tend to my business and let them tend to theirs. I knowed if I didn't, there'd be trouble. I was scared of white folks when I was small. I thought they had the rule. I don't know the reason why I thought that. I can't remember nobody telling me that. I don't never fight with no white people, and I don't play with them neither. Some of them call me "nigger." I don't do nothin'. I just keep going. I know that's what I is—a nigger—so I keep on. I don't get mad. I know that's what I'm supposed to be, and it don't make me mad.
Eighteen-year-old Black boy in Madison County, Alabama. As quoted in Charles S. Johnson, Growing Up in the Black Belt, Schocken Books, New York, 1941.

The crowd was quiet. I guess they were waiting to see what was going to happen. When I was able to steady my knees, I walked up to the guard who had let the white students in. He too didn't move. When I tried to squeeze past him, he raised his bayonet and then the other guards closed in and they raised their bayonets.

They glared at me with a mean look and I was very frightened and didn't know what to do. I turned around and the crowd came toward me.

They moved closer and closer. Somebody started yelling, "Lynch her! Lynch her!"

I tried to see a friendly face somewhere in the mob — someone who maybe would help. I looked into the face of an old woman and it seemed a kind face, but when I looked at her again, she spat on me.

Elizabeth Eckford, one of nine Black students who integrated Little Rock [Arkansas] Central High School in 1957. As quoted in Daisy Bates, The Long Shadow of Little Rock, *David McKay, New York, 1962.*

Top: Elizabeth Eckford, fifteen-year-old black girl, braves the insults of white students as she marches down a line of National Guardsmen, who blocked the main entrances of Little Rock's Central High School and would not let her enter, September 1957. (Wide World Photos)

Don't strike back or curse if abused;
Don't laugh out;
Don't hold conversations with floor workers;
Don't block entrances to the stores or aisles;
Show yourself courteous and friendly at all times;
Sit straight and always face the counter;
Remember love and non-violence;
May God bless you.

From a card carried by members of CORE during sit-ins.

I have a dream that one day down in Alabama with its viscious racists, with its Governor having his lips dripping with the words of interposition and nullification—one day right there in Alabama, little black boys and black girls will be able to join hands with little white boys and white girls as sisters and brothers.

I have a dream today. . . .

And if America is to be a great nation, this must become true. So, let freedom ring from the prodigious hill tops of New Hampshire. Let freedom ring from the mighty mountains of New York. Let freedom ring from the heightening Alleghenies of Pennsylvania. Let freedom ring from the snowcapped Rockies of Colorado. Let freedom ring from the curvaceous slopes of California. But not only that, let freedom ring from Stone Mountain of Georgia. Let freedom ring from Lookout Mountain of Tennessee.

Let freedom ring from every hill and molehill of Mississippi. From every mountainside, let freedom ring. And when we allow freedom to ring, when we let it ring from every village, from every hamlet, from every state and every city, we will be able to speed up that day when all of God's children, black men and white men, Jews and Gentiles, Protestants and Catholics, will be able to join hands and sing in the words of the old Negro spiritual: "Free at last! free at last! thank God almighty, we are free at last!"

Dr. Martin Luther King, Jr., in a speech to civil rights marchers, Washington, D.C., August 1963.

I woke up this morning with
   my mind
Stayed on freedom, I woke up
   this morning with my mind
Stayed on freedom, I woke up
   this morning with my mind
Stayed on freedom, Hallelu,
   Hallelu, Hallelujah!

We shall overcome
We shall overcome.
We shall overcome someday.
Deep in my heart I do believe
We shall overcome someday.
Civil rights songs.

Don't ride the bus to work, to town, to school or anyplace Monday, Dec. 5. . . . Another Negro woman has been arrested and put in jail because she refused to give up her bus seat. . . . Don't ride the buses to work, take a cab, or share a ride, or walk. . . . Come to a mass meeting Monday at 7:00 PM, at the Holt St. Baptist Church for further instruction.

From a leaflet concerning the bus boycott, prepared by Dr. Martin Luther King, Jr., and others, December 1955.

A wild mob of men and women, uncontrolled by police, pounced on newsmen and then on a group of nineteen Negro and white students who alighted today at the Greyhound bus terminal here after a ride from Birmingham to test segregated intrastate bus practices. . . . "Get those niggers," one dark-haired woman, primly clad in a yellow dress, shouted. Using metal pipes, baseball bats, sticks and fists, the mob surged on the small group of Freedom Riders, clubbing, punching, chasing and beating both whites and Negroes. When some of the bus riders began to run, the mob went after them, caught them and threw them to the ground.

Montgomery, Alabama. From the New York Herald Tribune, *May 20, 1961.*

Top: After stopping near Anniston, Alabama, because of a flat tire, this Freedom Riders' bus was trapped by a mob and went up in flames when a fire bomb was tossed through one of its windows, May 1961. The Freedom Riders had been testing bus station segregation in the South. The bus's passengers escaped without serious injury.

   The bus was to remain a significant test and tool in the civil rights movement throughout the sixties and seventies. Enforced busing of schoolchildren to meet affirmative action programs to desegrate schools around the country is still a volatile issue in many communities. (Wide World Photos)

As I approached the intersection I saw the police arrest Don Harris . . . (a Negro, football captain at the Fieldston School, graduate of Rutgers University, now with SNCC) Police then began to wade into the crowd of demonstrators with clubs, driving them back down the street with me, while someone in plain clothes stood at the intersection firing a pistol in the air. . . . Then the city marshal charged me from across the street and hit me a couple of times on the back and shoulders. . . . I then noticed another white SNCC worker, John Perdew, as the marshal attacked him. After beating Perdew up . . . he came after me and hit me twice on the head with a billyclub. . . . Then he said, "When I say run, you'd better run, you nigger-lovin' son-of-a-bitch. . . ." My head was streaming blood. . . . Don, John, and I were charged with "inciting an insurrection," a capital offense.

Account of the demonstration (intended to be peaceful) in Georgia, August 1963.

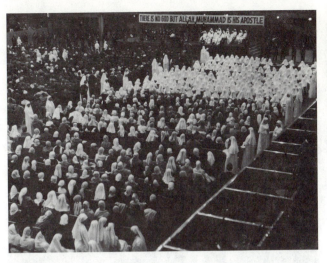

Today, their [the white race's] wealth is great upon the earth. Their sciences of worldly goods have sent them, not only after the wealth of other than their own people, but even after the lives and property of their own kind. They have tried to re-people . . . the earth with their own kind, by skillfully killing off the black man and mixing their blood into the black woman. . . .

. . . To see you trying to integrate with the very enemy of yours, and God, shows . . . that you don't know yourself nor your enemies; or rather are lost in love for our enemies, I know you, who love your enemy, don't like that I tell you this truth. But, . . . God has put upon me this mission, and I must do His will or burn.

From Elijah Muhammad, Message to the Blackman in America, *Chicago, 1965.*

For the white man to ask the black man if he hates him is just like the rapist asking the raped, *or the wolf asking the sheep, "Do you hate me?" The white man is in no moral position to accuse anyone else of hate!*

Why, when all of my ancestors are snake-bitten, and I'm snake-bitten, and I warn my children to avoid snakes, what does that snake sound like accusing me of hate-teaching?
Malcolm X, 1964. From "The Ballot or the Bullet," Malcolm X Speaks: Selected Speeches and Statements, *New York, 1965.*

Opposite, bottom: Civil rights demonstration leader Jerry Pogue is dragged to a police van, Mobile, Alabama, June 1968. Pogue was cut on the forehead by a metal eagle on the staff of an American flag he was carrying; police subdued him with Mace. (Wide World Photos)

Above: Elijah Muhammad, Black Muslim leader, speaking before a convention of his followers in Chicago, February 1961. Since Elijah Muhammad was succeeded by his son, Wallace, a more open attitude to both world Islam and the white community has been adopted. The group is now open to white members, and the name of the organization has been changed to The World Community of Islam in the West.

Don't nobody respect us, because all that we ever get is what somebody give to us. They give us our freedom, and they give us our civil rights, so they figure they give us what they please, and what they don't, they won't. We gonna have to take it, baby! We gonna have to get up on our hind legs, and take it! We gonna have to do just like Mr. Charley do with his Boston Tea Party. We gonna have to have our own uprising!
Nineteen-year-old participant in the Watts riot, 1965. As quoted in Robert Conot, Rivers of Blood, Years of Darkness, *Bantam Books, New York, 1967.*

Right: Malcolm X speaking before a convention of Black Muslims in Chicago, February 1963. Malcolm X broke away from the "Lost Nation of Islam" in 1964 to form the Organization of African-American Unity. Possibly because of his departure from total separatism, he was shot and killed on February 21, 1965. (Wide World Photos)

For too many years, black Americans marched and had their heads broken and got shot. They were saying to the country, "Look, you guys are supposed to be nice guys and we are only going to do what we are supposed to do—why do you beat us up, why don't you give us what we ask, why don't you straighten your-selves out?" After years of this, we are at almost the same point—because we demonstrated from a position of weakness. We cannot be expected any longer to march and have our heads broken in order to say to whites: come on, you're nice guys. For you are not nice guys. We have found you out.
Stokely Carmichael, in a speech delivered in Chicago, July 1966.

There is in America today a generation of white youth that is truly worthy of a black man's respect, and this is a rare event in the foul annals of American history. From the beginning of the contact between blacks and whites, there has been very little reason for a black man to respect a white. . . . But respect commands itself and it can neither be given nor withheld when it is due. If a man like Malcolm X could change and repudiate racism, if I myself and other former Muslims can change, if young whites can change, then there is hope for America. It was certainly strange to find myself, while steeped in the doctrine that all whites were devils by nature, command by the heart to applaud and acknowledge respect for these young whites—despite the fact that they are descendants of the masters and I the descendant of slave[s]. The sins of the fathers are visited upon the heads of the children—but only if the children continue in the evil deeds of the fathers.
From Eldridge Cleaver, Soul on Ice, Dell, New York, 1968.

Black people in America have no time to play nice, polite parlor games—especially when the lives of *their* children are at stake. Some white Americans can afford to speak softly, tread lightly, employ the soft-sell or put-off (or is it put-down?). They own the society. For black people to adopt *their* methods of relieving *our* oppression is ludicrous. We blacks must respond in our own way, on our own terms, in a manner which fits our temperaments. The definitions of ourselves, the roles we pursue, the goals we seek are *our* responsibility.
From Stokely Carmichael and Charles V. Hamilton, Black Power: The Politics of Liberation, 1968.

With all its faults, the American political system is the freest and most democratic in the world. The system needs to be improved, with democracy spread to all areas of life, particularly the economic. All of these changes must be conducted through our established institutions, and the people with grievances must find political methods for obtaining redress.
Eldridge Cleaver, "Why I left the U.S. and Why I am Returning," New York Times, November 18, 1975.

[A democratic black-oriented movement] must extend to every member of the black community the opportunity to have a say in who gets what from whom. It must cast its votes in a unit, it must deal with problems on a local, regional, national, and international basis, and it must decide that freedoms not enjoyed in Watts or Sunflower County cannot be enjoyed in Westchester or Los Angeles County. It must declare itself in the interests of laboring people, but not become the mistress of organized labor. It must pay as much attention to a street light in a fifty-foot alley as it does to national legislation involving millions of people, and international complications involving the future of the world. It must maintain a militance and aggressiveness that will earn it the respect of those it challenges.

Julian Bond, in The Black Man in American Politics: Three Views, *Kenneth B. Clark, Julian Bond, Richard G. Hatcher, New York, 1969. As quoted in Thomas L. Blair, Retreat to the Ghetto, New York, 1977, p. 213.*

You've had us in your lock,
   tight as a cage
and now you're
   acting shocked, we're in a
   rage.
Us on the bottom with you on top.
That's a game that we aim to stop.
That's all over now, Mighty Whitey.
That's all over now.

Muhammad Ali, from an interview in Black Scholar, *June 1970.*

Another kind of fighter, Georgia State Senator Julian Bond, was one of the founders of the Student Nonviolent Coordinating Committee in 1960. He served in the Georgia state House of Representatives from 1965–75 and won a long fight for the Senate seat in 1975. Bond is representative of a growing movement toward sophisticated participation in, rather than overthrow of, the political process—what one black scholar calls "the Americanization of Black Power." Though blacks are still represented in token numbers, such organizations as the Southern Elections Fund in Atlanta, chaired by Bond, have been instrumental in significant election victories. (Photo © Lionel Delevingne/Picture Group)

Muhammad Ali lands a right to George Foreman during his title bout in Zaire on October 29, 1974. Ali, an early member of the Black Muslims, remains a prominent symbol of the drive for black identity and celebration of racial pride. (United Press International Photo)

Shirley Chisholm, the first black woman elected to Congress, ran as a presidential candidate in 1972. Her first campaign slogan, "Fighting Shirley Chisholm—Unbought and Unbossed," still applies. Chisholm won reelection to Congress in the 1980 election in spite of tremendous Republican gains. (United Press International Photos)

Charles Evers (right) is shown here being sworn into office as Mayor of Fayette, Mississippi, by Justice of the Peace Willie Thompson in July 1969. Evers became the first black mayor of a Mississippi town since Reconstruction. Bloc voting by blacks in urban areas across the country made possible the election of increasing numbers of black officials in the 1970s. (United Press International Photos)

Cleveland Mayor Carl B. Stokes, who became one of the first black mayors of a major American city (1967), here calls for a "black political strategy" at Black Expo in September 1971. Among other black mayors of large cities elected within a ten-year period were Richard Hatcher of Gary (1967); Kenneth Gibson of Newark (1970); Tom Bradley of Los Angeles, Coleman Young of Detroit, and Maynard Jackson of Atlanta (1973); and Walter Washington of Washington, D.C. (1974). (United Press International Photos)

From the beginning I felt that there were only two ways to create change for black people in this country—either politically or by open armed revolution. Malcolm defined it succinctly—the ballot or the bullet. Since I believe that human life is uniquely valuable and important, for me the choice had to be the creative use of the ballot. I still believe I was right. I hope America never succeeds in changing my mind.
Shirley Chisholm, Unbought and Unbossed, *Boston, 1970.*

. . .a segmented labor market currently provides vastly different mobility opportunities for different segments of the black population. On the one hand, poorly trained and educationally limited blacks of the inner city, including that growing number of black teenagers and young adults, see their job prospects increasingly restricted to the low-wage sector, their unemployment rates soaring to record levels . . . their labor-force participation rates declining, their movement out of poverty slowing, and their welfare roles increasing. On the other hand, talented and educated blacks are experiencing unprecedented job opportunities in the growing government and corporate sectors, opportunities that are at least comparable to those of whites with equivalent qualifications. The improved job situation for the more privileged blacks in the corporate and government sectors is related both to the expansion of salaried white-collar positions and to the pressures of state affirmative action programs.
From William Julius Wilson, The Declining Significance of Race: Blacks and Changing American Institutions, *University of Chicago Press, 1978, p. 151.*

Fresh from his landslide reelection as Mayor of Atlanta in October 1977, Maynard Jackson raises his glass in a toast to his new bride. The couple were married two days after the election. (United Press International Photos)

An anxious young fireman pauses to glance over his shoulder while the fires from a three-day race riot in Miami continue. The rioting was triggered in late May 1980 by a verdict of not guilty from an all-white six-man jury in the trial of several Dade County policemen accused of fatally beating Arthur Lee McDuffie, an insurance company official. The riot in Miami prompted speculation on a renewal of the ghetto insurrections of the 1960s. (United Press International Photos)

No, Arthur McDuffie won't bury easy—black poor Miami made sure of that. And their outrage makes many of us who were his peers take painful stock of our lives, and our goals. If you're part of the black middle class, for the most part you live [an] illusion. . . .

During the seventies that meant believing in "mainstreaming." Miami makes us pause and reexamine that belief. And although we may come away still committed to economics and education as the solutions, we know it doesn't prevent Arthur McDuffie from dying in that street, doesn't ensure against a verdict of not guilty.
Marcia Gillespie, "What the Miami Riots Mean to All of Us," MS, October 1980, p. 87.

Two major figures in education, each in his own way. Professor John Hope Franklin (Left), preeminent scholar, teacher, and author, is past-President and now member of the Council of the American Historical Association and has been appointed to numerous professional and governmental advisory posts. One of the Reverend Jesse Jackson's (Right) programs developed under the educational branch of his Operation PUSH (PUSH for Excellence, or EXCEL) honors Professor Franklin. The John Hope Franklin Club draws high school students together to interview black celebrities and newsmakers from across the country. (Photo of Professor Franklin, courtesy of the University of Chicago; photo of Rev. Jackson, © 1979 Robert J. Izzo/Picture Group)

The architects of political and racial repression draw upon an enormous amount of knowledge and experience, and they expend an inordinate amount of time and energy to perpetrate it. If they are to be confronted and defeated, it will take more than indignation and outrage. It will take a skill and deftness that are grounded on a sure knowledge of how repression operates and how it can be destroyed. This requires more than romance. It requires hard work and diligent study as well as courage and fortitude.
From John Hope Franklin, "The Retreat from Excellence," speech before the 1980 Operation PUSH/ PUSH-EXCEL national convention. As quoted in The Voice of Excellence, *September 1980, p. 6.*

The new challenge is to move up. Upward mobility is the issue. Our struggle has shifted from the horizontal to the vertical. . . . The Merediths, the Hunters, and the Holmeses excelled because they served the need of their generation by busting down the barriers to opportunity. . . . But the challenge of this generation is to match opportunity with effort. . . .

We must EXCEL because resistance to our upward mobility has increased. Bakke and Bakkeism have convinced white America, erroneously, that blacks are making progress at white expense. The mass media have conveyed to white America that blacks have gained too much too fast and have come too far in their quest for equality. . . .

We must EXCEL because competition is keener. The exportation of jobs to the cheap labor base of the Third World; the increased competition in the world market from Japan, Western Europe, and the Middle East; and cybernation and automation have forced us to compete for jobs requiring greater knowledge. . . .

Our goal is educational and economic equity and parity. The goal is to close the gap between black and white, rich and poor, male and female. We are behind in the race, and the only way to catch up is to run faster.
From Jesse L. Jackson, "In Pursuit of Equity, Ethics, and Excellence: The Challenge to Close the Gap," Phi Delta Kappan, *November, 1978.*

movement a *national* phenomenon and thrust people like King into the lime-light.

The direct protest movement caught fire in 1960, when four black college students in Greensboro, North Carolina, sat down at a lunch counter reserved for whites and refused to move. During the following months there were many such "sit-ins" throughout the urban South. In 1961, black and white youths began taking "freedom rides" to test segregation on interstate buses and in bus stations in the Deep South. Violent opposition from whites in Mississippi and Alabama attracted national attention to the freedom rides and contributed to a decision by the Interstate Commerce Commission to begin to enforce its own regulations against segregation.

The movement gained additional momentum in 1962 and 1963. Young blacks applied for admission to the segregated universities of Mississippi and Alabama. At the same time, King lent his prestige and leadership to a campaign in Birmingham to end discrimination in access to public accommodations and employment. The movement literally filled the streets of Birmingham with peaceful protesters, young and old. Local police arrested thousands of blacks and dispersed even more with dogs and fire hoses. The spectacle, conveyed to the nation by the unblinking eye of television, forced President Kennedy to support federal legislation to bar discrimination.

Disfranchisement—the other side of the coin of legal segregation—also came under fire from the southern civil rights movement. Laborious efforts to register blacks to vote paid some dividends, despite violent resistance in the form of beatings and the murder of civil rights workers. However, it was the last of the large integrated mass demonstrations, centered in Selma, Alabama, that riveted national attention on the issue of voting rights. Open resistance to black registration by authorities in Selma provoked a march to the state capital of Montgomery, where King addressed a throng of 25,000 supporters. With national support for the movement running at full tide, President Johnson endorsed voting rights legislation which would finally end the legal disfranchisement of southern blacks.

Just as the movement seemed to be sweeping away centuries of racial discrimination, the fragile coalition of blacks and white reformers was jolted by the cry of "black power," and the black ghettos in scores of cities erupted into flames. The causes of this dramatic turn of events were to be found in places as different as the rural communities of the Deep South and the inner cities of the North.

Out of the first wave of sit-ins in 1960 came a new protest organization, the Student Nonviolent Coordinating Committee (SNCC). SNCC members participated in the sit-ins and freedom rides of 1960 and 1961. In 1962 they shifted their energies to an even more difficult and more important task—the mass registration of black voters in the Deep South, particularly Mississippi. The entrenched and sometimes violent resistance which these college students encountered in the small towns and rural communities, coupled with the seeming unwillingness of federal authorities to intervene, convinced many of them that King's dream of peaceful integration was unattainable and even undesirable. Within the organization itself, tensions between white and black workers, heightened by "battle fatigue," contributed to a demand for black separatism rather than integration. The enthusiastic response of some blacks in 1966 to the militant Stokely Carmichael's cry of "black power" stemmed from the radicalizing experience of SNCC's voter-registration drive.

Other voices, many of them outside the South, were also demanding black self-determination and the celebration of Afro-American culture. The black novelist James Baldwin predicted in *The Fire Next Time* (1962) that, unless the nation granted "the unconditional freedom of the Negro," there would be violence and destruction. Baldwin's words proved to be prophetic. Between 1964 and 1968 the nation's large cities were swept by rioting and burning; the riots began in Harlem and spread to Los Angeles, Detroit, Cleveland, Washington, and Newark. Following major riots in 1967, President Johnson appointed a group of distinguished citizens to a Commission on Civil Disorders to find the causes of the violence. Early in 1968 the Commission reported:

This is our basic conclusion: Our nation is moving toward two societies, one black, one white—separate and unequal. Segregation and poverty have created in the racial ghetto a destructive environment totally unknown to most Americans. What white Americans have never fully understood—but what the Negro can never forget—is that white society is deeply implicated in the ghetto. White institutions created it, white institutions maintain it, and white society condones it.

Indeed, the civil rights movement and the legislation which it spawned had left untouched the basic problems of the inner city. There segregation, although virtually as pervasive as in the South, was a matter of custom and housing patterns, not of law, and thus more difficult to attack. The root problems of the inner city were economic. In an age of rising expectations, lack of jobs and lack of control over the economic institutions which govern everyday life made the ghetto a tinder box, ready to be ignited by the smallest spark.

King was assassinated in April 1968; in the aftermath of that tragedy, one more wave of rioting erupted. Thereafter, the urban rioting subsided, although not because the problems described by the presidential commission had been resolved. King's objectives of gaining access to public accommodations and to the ballot box had been largely achieved by the time of his death. But the more stubborn problems of segregated urban housing and lack of economic opportunity for the mass of black people remained unsolved. In the 1970s, the use of busing to desegregate urban schools and of affirmative action programs to improve job opportunities for blacks triggered a backlash on the part of some whites. Many underlying causes of racial discrimination remained unresolved at the end of the 1970s, but substantial gains had been made. The civil rights movement and the drive for black identity had swept away the legal barriers of segregation and had contributed to a new awareness by Afro-Americans of their rich cultural heritage. Also, the struggles of the 1960s brought political power to southern blacks for the first time in the twentieth century, a development which, in the 1970s, would be felt from city halls to the White House.

The Emergence of the Hispanic Community

The struggle for black equality was paralleled by the rising aspirations of Hispanic Americans. By 1979, this group numbered about 18,000,000. It included (natives or their descendants) 1,000,000 Cubans, 2,000,000 Puerto Ricans, and 15,000,000 Mexicans. Although they were linked by similar ethnic roots and by a common language and religious heritage, the American experiences of these three groups had differed in significant respects.

The vast majority of the Cubans in the United States emigrated after the rise to power of Fidel Castro in 1959. The first wave came predominantly from the middle and upper classes and saw themselves as political exiles. They became a self-conscious ethnic community concentrated primarily in southern Florida, but they also blended into American business and professional life to a considerable extent. A second wave of 100,000 came in 1980 when Castro temporarily loosened his ban on emigration.

Relatively few Puerto Ricans migrated to the mainland until the Second World War, when poor economic conditions on the island and the lure of jobs in northeastern cities set off a large migration. Puerto Ricans, like American blacks, migrated to the cities just when the number of available jobs was declining. Those who did find work were often trapped in menial tasks. In the 1970s, over 40 per cent of all Puerto Rican families in the continental United States had incomes below the poverty level. In the 1960s, the concentration of Puerto Ricans in New York gave them, like earlier immigrant groups, some political leverage. For example, Herman Badillo, a Puerto Rican American, was elected borough president of the Bronx in 1965 and remained an important political figure in New York.

The Mexican-American community grew rapidly in the twentieth century, despite major efforts in the 1930s and 1950s to expel those suspected of being illegal immigrants. The federal *bracero* program brought in over 5,000,000 Mexican workers on a temporary basis between 1942 and 1964, mainly for seasonal labor in agriculture. A much larger number of *majados* (illegal aliens) immigrated after the 1940s and found their way initially into unskilled and low-paying jobs.

Ninety per cent of the Mexican-American people, called Chicanos, remained clustered in the Southwest. There, particularly since the 1940s, Chicano protest movements sought to preserve the Hispanic cultural heritage and to combat various forms of discrimination. As with blacks, rising expectations since the war created a new sense of purpose, even militancy, as was evidenced in the 1960s by the emergence of such groups as the short-lived *Alianza Federal de Mercedes* which, under the leadership of Reies Tijerina, demanded the return of lands seized long ago from Mexican Americans in violation of the Treaty of Guadalupe Hidalgo.

The most influential Mexican-American leader of the 1960s and 1970s was César Chavez, son of migrant farm workers, who formed a union of California agricultural laborers, the United Farm Workers, in 1962. Chavez used strikes and national boycotts against the fruit- and vegetable-raising agribusinesses and won a contract with California grape growers in 1970. As important as the victories of the United Farm Workers were, both in an economic and a cultural sense, the union could not become a major organizational base of the Mexican-American population as a whole. By the 1970s, 90 per cent of them lived in cities, and, as the 1980s began, sophisticated new farm machinery was reaching into Chavez' stronghold and rendering superfluous the labor of many who had joined his union. By the 1970s, Mexican Americans were the fastest growing ethnic group in the nation. With roots in Hispanic and Indian cultures, the Chicano spirit was taking its place along with black pride as a major manifestation of the new ethnicity in American life.

Student Protest

The struggle for racial equality helped to generate the student movement of the 1960s known as the "New Left." Less ideologically oriented than earlier Leftists, these protesters shared with the civil rights workers an idealistic commitment to righting the injustices of American society. The New Left's appeal for "participatory democracy," which in practice became an almost anarchistic distrust of organization and structure, was intended to reclaim a sense of community amid the impersonal, bureaucratized mass culture which industrialization had helped to create. The movement was self-consciously youth-oriented. "Don't trust anyone over thirty" became a rallying cry. The youths in question were part of the huge postwar generation, who, by the 1960s, were extending their education (and their "youth") beyond high school in unprecedented numbers. They were, in the words of the movement's own manifesto, "bred in at least modest comfort, housed now in universities, looking uncomfortably to the world we inherit."

Although, at its height, the New Left student movement could attract mass attendance at rallies, probably no more than 5 per cent of college students were directly involved in New Left organizations. However, the movement attracted some of the brightest students and was concentrated in the nation's most

Students on campus at the University of California, Berkeley, in 1960. At that time, universities were receiving massive amounts of federal, state, and private funds for teaching and research. Young people flocked to the universities in record numbers seeking certification that would lead to well paying jobs, and the nation as a whole looked to those same institutions for solutions to social and technological problems. By the end of the 1960s, however, both funds and student enrollment were declining, the optimism attached to higher education was dissipating, and some of the most prestigious campuses, including the one at Berkeley, had become battle grounds in the student protest movements. (Wide World Photos)

prestigious universities. At first, the movement viewed universities as havens from which to attack injustices in the society at large. But student protesters came to view the universities themselves as part of the oppressive "system" and students as part of an oppressed class. This transformation occurred first in the events which shook the University of California at Berkeley in 1964 and 1965. In the fall of 1964, the administration blocked student efforts to disseminate political materials on the campus. Student radicals mobilized a mass protest and used the confrontational tactics of the civil rights movement and the community-organizing techniques of the Students for a Democratic Society (SDS). The protests, which were sparked by the specific issue of freedom of speech, escalated to a more general challenge in which students demanded fundamental changes in the governance and mission of the school. American universities, they believed, had become impersonal, socially irresponsible institutions, which served the needs of the "military-industrial complex" more than they did the educational needs of students. Mario Savio, a leader of the Free Speech movement and a veteran of SNCC's Freedom Summer, expressed the views of many protesters: "When the operation of the machine becomes so odious . . . you've got to put your bodies upon the gears . . . and make it stop. And you've got to indicate to the people that run it, the people who own it, that unless you're free, the machine will be prevented from working at all."

Antiwar demonstrators and police in brutal confrontation at the Conrad Hilton Hotel in Chicago during the Democratic convention in August 1968. Police used rifle butts, tear gas, and clubs to battle the demonstrators. Police reaction, often caught by television cameras, to the taunts and rock throwing of demonstrators was later described by an official investigating committee as "police riot." (United Press International)

Over the next half decade the battle of Berkeley was fought again on campuses across the country, most notably at Columbia University. In 1968 disputes over issues, which ranged from Columbia's involvement in military research to its relations with the adjacent black community of Harlem, led to a bloody protest which came to be known as the Battle of Morningside Heights.

Beginning in 1968, the New Left's principal institution, the SDS, was splintered by ideological factionalism. Its vision of a student-worker coalition was in shambles; the SDS, confronted with governmental persecution, disintegrated into competing bands of ideologues and urban guerrillas.

The New Left's ideology overlapped with that rejection of middle-class values called the counterculture. It also overlapped with and gave some leadership to the movement to end American involvement in Vietnam. When President Johnson escalated American involvement in the war in 1965, there was an immediate outpouring of protest from the campuses. Teach-ins and campus rallies were followed by massive public demonstrations, most notably in Chicago in 1968 and Washington in 1969. In 1970, after President Nixon's announcement of an American incursion into Cambodia, there was one last wave of campus demonstrations and strikes. In the one at Kent State University in Ohio, National Guardsmen killed four students and wounded nine. (See pp. 983–987.)

In the minds of many Americans, the antiwar movement, the New Left, and the counterculture were all one uprising—a large and serious threat to the nation's values and security. In fact, the antiwar movement transcended the New Left and encompassed not only radicals and traditional pacifist groups but also nonradicals and a large number of young men and their families who had a personal stake in the issue. However, during those troubled times, the student New Left movement was less effective in convincing the unpersuaded of the moral bankruptcy of the United States than in setting in motion the processes which would change the structures and course of American politics.

The Women's Movement

The simultaneous appearance of a women's movement in the 1960s with other reform movements was a case of history repeating itself. Before the Civil War and during the progressive era, the movement for women's rights had had a close, but not always congenial, relationship with other reform movements. Like the crusade to achieve equal rights for ethnic minorities, the women's movement was spurred by profound social and economic changes since the Second World War.

As feminist writers pointed out, the popular literature and journalism of the 1950s had nurtured a "cult of domesticity" that conditioned women to content themselves with passive roles as wives and mothers rather than to challenge men for positions in the world of work and politics. Yet, as one historian has noted, this stifling emphasis was hardly new in the postwar era. Two profound changes did occur after the Second World War. First, by the 1960s fully 40 per cent of all adult women had entered the work force, including half of those with school-age children. This development blurred traditional male-female roles in the home. Middle-class boys and girls who grew up in postwar America were more likely than their forebears to have a "working" mother. By the 1970s, that cohort of young people had been conditioned to accept even greater changes in the traditional roles of the mother and the father. In addition to changes in the status and expectations of many women, there appeared a cogent feminist assessment of women's existing inequality and a demand for change. That assessment began in earnest with the publication of Betty Friedan's book, *The Feminine Mystique*, in 1963. Friedan criticized the stereotypes perpetuated by women's magazines, behavioral scientists, and the advertising industry which locked housewives into dreary and unrewarding lives.

The women's movement which emerged in the mid-1960s, like most social movements, was far from monolithic. The National Organization for Women (NOW) was founded in 1966, with Friedan as president, and quickly became the country's largest women's rights organization. A moderate reformist group, NOW fought institutionalized discrimination, sought liberalization of abortion and birth-control laws, and fostered "consciousness raising" among women and men. Other participants in the movement, often organized only in small, unstructured groups, sought, not just an end to formal discrimination, but also a revolution in the relationships between men and women. As presently constituted, they argued, marriage and the family were a form of slavery from which women had to liberate themselves.

Many feminists were veterans of the civil rights, antiwar, and student movements. For them, even participation in radical organizations had been demeaning, for they often found themselves consigned to the roles of secretaries, cooks, and sexual partners for the males who dominated the movement. Stokely Carmichael had shut off debate on the issue of women's rights within SNCC by asserting that "the only position for women in our movement is prone." Similar statements, even more blunt, came from male leaders of the SDS and other radical groups.

The women's movement had a substantial political impact in the 1960s, although some early victories were later reversed. Many states liberalized abortion statutes and laws which governed property rights of women. The federal government, through court rulings, executive orders, and legislation, took some steps to end sex-based discrimination, particularly in hiring, wages, and admission to graduate and professional schools. The equal rights amendment to the Constitution (ERA), which had been tied up in a congressional committee for forty-seven years, was finally passed by the House of Representatives in 1970 and by the Senate in 1971. However, by 1980 the amendment was still three states short of ratification by the required thirty-eight states, despite an unprecedented action by Congress to extend the time limit for ratification.

Resistance to the ERA from women as well as men, along with the controversy which raged over legalized abortion in the 1970s, clearly demonstrated the complexities of the liberation movement. In the 1960s that movement had primarily attracted white, middle-class college students and graduates, and, even among that group, its support was far from unanimous. Although the movement encountered apathy and resistance from many people in the 1970s, its base of support expanded dramatically. Third World women, organized labor, religious groups, and increasing numbers of men entered the movement in supportive and active roles. The struggle for and against the ratification of the ERA constituted a major course of education for large numbers of women on how to use political instrumentalities and economic pressure. The political sensitizing of large numbers of energetic, civic-minded women was an event whose ramifications would be felt for decades to come. Along the spectrum of women's points of view during the 1970s were the political commentaries of Gloria Steinem, the anti-ERA agitation of Phyllis Schlafly, the powerhouse behind "Stop ERA," and the ideas of Marabel Morgan's best-selling *The Total Woman* (1973). The total woman, Mrs. Morgan wrote, "caters to her man's special quirks, whether it be in salads, sex, or sports." The women's movement was still very much alive in 1980, with many new role models for young women to emulate.

In summary, there were substantial and significant changes since the Second World War in the social roles of both men and women. Massive entries of women into the work force dictated changes in sex roles. The sexual revolution, described above, ushered in an era of tolerance for diversity in life-styles for both men and women. Even the American language, which, as a bearer of culture reflects the sexual biases thereof, has felt the impact of the movement for women's liberation. The role of government in rooting out sex-based discrimination, while still ambiguous in some respects, opened access to jobs and other activities previously closed to women.

4. THE SEARCH FOR IDENTITY IN A MASS SOCIETY

Cultural Pluralism in a Technological Age

Social and political protest was by no means the sole source of personal and cultural identity during the unsettling postwar era. Despite, or perhaps because of, the uncertainties of the times, many Americans preserved bonds of mind and spirit which transcended the cultural homogeneity that the mass media attempted to impose. Amid the pervasive mass culture of the television age, there flourished a diversity of life-styles, religions, and ethnic communities. At its worst, this diversity bred polarization and bigotry; at its best, it nurtured a robust and tolerant cultural pluralism. A few examples will illustrate the juxtaposition of the new and the old cultures.

From Youth Culture to Counterculture

As has been noted previously, the sheer numbers of the generation born in the 1940s and 1950s made it inevitable that they would attract unusual attention. In late adolescence and early adulthood, they participated in the political upheavals of the 1960s, but the particular rebelliousness of youth in that decade was also expressed in cultural terms — in a rejection of prevailing values.

Popular music was the principal transmitter of the youth-oriented cultural revolution. Beginning early in the 1950s, young Americans gradually lost interest in music by swing and jazz bands and in sentimental lyrics. They adopted instead the rock-and-roll style which fused elements of black rhythm and blues and white southern folk music. The new music suited an enormous generation of teenagers who were just awakening to their own sexuality and increasingly conscious of themselves as a cultural minority. Whether the new popular singers were black, like Chuck Berry and Otis Redding, or white, like Elvis Presley and Jerry Lee Lewis, parents and teachers thought that their stage movements and the words of many of their songs were very threatening to moral standards.

The early 1960s witnessed a folk music revival. This ballad style, although a more familiar and less threatening genre than rock and roll, served as a vehicle for social protest. Bob Dylan, with his hard-driving song, "The Times They are a-Changing," expressed the growing alienation of many young people.

Rock and roll again dominated popular music after 1964 when the Beatles burst on the American scene. The message which this British rock group conveyed was by no means one of political radicalism, but the Beatles did express an infectious cultural rebelliousness. That was even truer of groups such as the Rolling Stones, the Jefferson Airplane, and the Doors, whose overt sexuality and identification with the drug culture made them the symbols of a small but highly publicized counterculture and the heroes of many more young people, who identified with it in one way or another.

This ill-defined antiestablishment movement embraced hedonism, eroticism, and unbridled individual freedom. Public expressions of this culture included rock music, long hair, communal living, sexual promiscuity, and the use of marijuana and drugs, such as the hallucinogen, LSD. Unlike the New Left, the counterculture reflected a withdrawal from political action. The admonition of Timothy Leary, high priest of the drug cult, to "tune in, turn on, and drop out" was heeded by many who despaired of reforming the "system."

The "hippie" culture which emerged in 1965 and 1966 in urban neighborhoods such as the Haight-Asbury district of San Francisco and in communes in cities and the countryside was too fragile to survive the combined assaults of repression by authorities, coverage by the news media, and commercialization of its life-style. The counterculture faded from public view after the late 1960s. The giant Woodstock Music Festival, held in 1969, was supposed to usher in a new Age of Aquarius. Actually, it coincided with the decline of the counterculture. Yet this cultural rebellion not only left behind pockets of aging "hippies" but also altered the life-styles of millions of persons who had not been part of the counterculture itself. By the early 1970s, long hair, blue jeans, and the use of marijuana had become so commonplace that they no longer aroused the ire of most "straight" Americans.

Religion in Modern America

The mysticism of the counterculture coincided with an upsurge of religious consciousness in the 1970s. Actually, there have been two periods of intensified religious fervor in America since the Second World War. Between 1940 and 1955, membership in churches and synagogues rose from 43 per cent to 61 per cent of the total population. Many social scientists (who assess the social impact of religion, not its ultimate truth) interpreted this interest in religion as a way to establish identity in a rapidly changing world. A religious scholar noted that to label oneself as Protestant, Catholic, or Jew was to claim an authentically American heritage and identity.

The religiosity of the 1950s involved an increase in church membership but did not alter traditional *forms* of religious expression. Among evangelical Protestants, the numerical growth was spurred by itinerant revivalists such as Billy Graham, whose urban "crusades" had antecedents in the labors of evangelists dating back to Charles G. Finney in the 1830s.

Many thoughtful church leaders were alarmed by what they described as unfortunate side effects of this renewed enthusiasm. Organized religion, some feared, occupied a comfortable niche as part of a generalized "civil religion" which deified the American Way of Life. However, the tradition of the Social

Philip (left) and Daniel (right) Berrigan, both then Roman Catholic priests, in a dramatic antiwar action, May 17, 1968. Nine people (five of them priests) removed and burned draft board records from the Selective Service office in Catonsville, Maryland, and were subsequently arrested. This event brought the Berrigans instant notoriety as leaders and symbols of the protest movements of the 1960s, a role that has changed only with the concerns and tempo of the 1970s. Both Philip, no longer a priest, and Father Dan are activists in the disarmament and antinuclear movements. Father Dan, in addition, has turned much of his attention to the terminally ill and to writing poetry and teaching. (United Press International Photo)

Gospel also remained alive after the Second World War. During the 1960s, religious leaders of many persuasions participated in movements for social justice, in particular the civil rights crusade. Their social action was accompanied by a renewed ecumenical spirit which swept through American Christianity, partially as an outgrowth of the Second Vatican Council, which Popes John XXIII and Paul VI convened in Rome in 1962 and 1965.

Religious institutions lost some support during the 1960s. Church attendance and membership dropped, particularly among young people, as religious institutions were affected by the general disillusionment with social institutions during that decade. However, beginning about 1970, membership in churches and synagogues stabilized.

The dramatic religious development of the 1970s had less to do with the number of worshippers than with the variety of their experiences. There was a wave of interest in eastern mystical religions, and new Christian or quasi-Christian sects emerged, as did a host of introspective "human potential groups," such as Transcendental Meditation, which functioned more or less as religions. Within established Christian bodies, ranging from Catholic and Episcopalian to evangelical Protestant churches, there appeared charismatic movements which featured speaking in tongues and faith healing. This charismatic movement became a source of renewed vitality for some persons, but it also threatened the routinized patterns of authority within the churches and thus produced institutional strains in both local parishes and national religious bodies.

One other feature of the religious revival of the 1970s was increased political activism, on religious grounds, for culturally conservative causes and candidates. Militant lobbying campaigns were mobilized in opposition to legalized abortion, the ERA, and aspects of modern school curricula, particularly sex education and the teaching of evolution.

The New Ethnicity

For many Americans, religious identity remained linked to an ethnic heritage. That ethnic identities could persist at the end of the twentieth century is perhaps surprising, given the forces of assimilation which have been at work even among relatively recent immigrant groups. The use of non-English languages other than Spanish declined sharply; suburbanization diluted or wiped out old ethnic neighborhoods; television's mass culture permeated all but the most resistant of ethnic communities; and intermarriages became commonplace.

Nevertheless, ethnic ties persisted, and there were even renewed signs of ethnic militancy and conflict in the 1970s. Native Americans sought to renew their tribal identities, which had been weakened in the 1950s by yet another effort at assimilation. Some militant Indian groups, including the American Indian Movement, fought for the return of tribal lands; and, at the end of the 1970s, litigation was in progress which involved millions of acres formerly held by Indians. In the East, the land in question included large parts of central Massachusetts, much of Cape Cod, and most of the State of Maine.

A sense of community remained strong among many white ethnic groups, including those from southern and eastern Europe. In the 1970s, several of these groups clashed with blacks in northern cities over such issues as school busing, open housing, and job quotas. Even a recent immigrant group, the Vietnamese, found themselves in conflict. More than 100,000 Vietnamese were resettled in the United States after the fall of Saigon in 1975, and a second wave arrived after the expulsion or flight of many ethnic Chinese from Vietnam in 1979. Although they were dispersed throughout the country in a planned resettlement program, these new arrivals sometimes encountered hostility and even violence, particularly when jobs or other scarce resources were at stake.

The new awakening of ethnicity in the 1970s was further stimulated by the television dramatization of Alex Haley's book, *Roots*. Encouraged by Haley's experience in tracing his ancestry to a west African village, Americans of various ethnic backgrounds filled the reading rooms of libraries and archives in search of information about long-lost ancestors. Without question, as the United States entered its third century of independence, ethnicity remained a vital component of self-understanding for many Americans.

The Crisis of Identity and the Renewal of Community

The term "identity crisis" is, appropriately, a creation of the postwar era. Erik Erikson, a psychologist, applied it to the personal anxieties which accompany the transition from one stage of human development to another. The concept could also be applied to much of American society during the tumultuous postwar epoch.

Much of the popular literature of the time voiced longings for personal identity and individual freedom in a world governed by large and impersonal forces. Norman Mailer's powerful novel of the Second World War, *The Naked and the Dead* (1948); J. D. Salinger's story of rebellious adolescence, *The Catcher in the Rye* (1951); and Joseph Heller's *Catch-22* (1960) all described a human condition in which freedom is circumscribed and personal identity is impossible to maintain in the "sane" world.

The search for selfhood in this kind of world has given rise to what some scholars have called a "psychiatric world view," one characterized by constant self-examination and self-doubt and by a preoccupation with self-gratification in the present moment. Christopher Lasch has written most passionately about the cultural malaise which this world view entails. In *The Culture of Narcissism* (1979), Lasch set out to probe the collective psyche of Americans in an "age of diminishing expectations." Lasch concluded that the nation, and for that matter the western world, was being swept by a debilitating, self-centered malaise. "The new narcissist," Lasch writes, "is haunted not by guilt but by anxiety. He seeks not to inflict his own certainties on others but to find a meaning in life. Liberated from the superstitions of the past, he doubts even the reality of his own existence."

President Jimmy Carter was one who came to share such a view. He was influenced by polls which showed an alarming increase in public pessimism about the nation's future and used a highly publicized television address to the nation in July 1979 to warn of a growing "crisis of confidence"—a cultural malaise which was sapping the nation's will and ability to act.

Not all Americans would agree with such a gloomy assessment, although few would deny that, particularly in the 1970s, Americans had acquired a more realistic understanding of their own limits and that there was some pessimism about the future. However, many Americans were either more satisfied with their own lives or more certain about the objects of their dissatisfaction than the victims of the debilitating narcissism which Lasch described. Furthermore, many Americans, although no longer optimistic about saving the whole world from its various maladies, were busily engaged in efforts of reform and reconstruction on a more modest scale.

In the 1970s, participants in a "neighborhood movement," which one observer has called "a kind of invisible saga of the decade," were engaged in community-based cooperative action of all sorts. The neighborhood movement confounded the traditional political categories of Left and Right and included groups engaged in such disparate activities as opposing school busing, encouraging interracial cooperation, fighting governmental and corporate bureaucracies, and resisting increasing increases in property taxes. While some neighborhood activists provided an organizational base for such new-style politicians as Mayor Jane Byrne of Chicago, others have turned their backs on politics and concentrated their energies on such things as alternative technologies and alternative marketing systems. The direction and impact of this movement for the remainder of the twentieth century are impossible to predict, but its vitality in the 1970s was a hopeful sign for the future of democracy at the grass roots in America.

SUGGESTED READINGS

The standard reference for up-to-date social and economic data is the *American Almanac* (formerly *Statistical Abstracts of the United States*), which is published annually. See also summary volumes of the decennial census. Scholarly studies of demography and social changes include John L. Shover, *First Majority—Last Minority: The Transformation of Rural Life in America* (1976), and Jean Gottman, *Megalopolis: The Urbanized Northeastern Seaboard of the United States* (1961).

The scholarship on the family in modern American is voluminous. Three recent and important studies are Kenneth Keniston *et al., All Our Children: The American Family Under Pressure* (1977); Christopher Lasch, *Haven in a Heartless World: The Family Besieged* (1977); and Joseph F. Kett, *Rites of Passage: Adolescence in America, 1790 to the Present* (1979).

General economic trends can be followed in W. Elliott Brownlee, *Dynamics of Ascent: A History of the American Economy* (1979). The structure of economic life is discussed in Alfred D. Chandler, Jr., *The Visible Hand: The Managerial Revolution in American Business* (1977); John Kenneth Galbraith, *The New Industrial State*, 2nd ed. (1972); and Robert Sobel, *The Age of Giant Corporations: A Microeconomic History of American Business* (1972). The role of American based multinational firms is discussed in Richard J. Barnet and Ronald E. Muller, *Global Reach: The Power of the Multinational Corporations* (1974); and C. Fred Bergsten, *Toward a New International Economic Order* (1975). The underside of economic development is described in an influential study, Michael Harrington, *The Other America: Poverty in the United States* (1963).

Elting E. Morison, *From Know-How to Nowhere: The Development of American Technology* (1974), is useful. The human side of America's most spectacular technological accomplishment—the manned space flight program—is treated with insight (if not with reverence) in Tom Wolfe, *The Right Stuff* (1979).

Changing sex roles and the women's movement are discussed in William H. Chafe, *The American Woman: Her Changing Social, Economic, and Political Roles, 1920–1970* (1972); Betty Friedan, *The Feminine Mystique* (1963); Jo Freeman, *The Politics of Women's Liberation* (1975); and Peter Filene, *Him/Her/Self: Sex Roles in Modern America* (1975).

Gunnar Myrdal, *An American Dilemma* (1944), provides essential background information on the transformation of Afro-American life since the Second World War. Of the general treatments of Afro-American history, the best is John Hope Franklin, *From Slavery to Freedom*, 5th ed. (1978). Important studies of black leaders and black movements for equality and liberation include Martin Luther King, Jr., *Stride Toward Freedom* (1958); David L. Lewis, *King: A Critical Biography*, 2nd ed. (1978); Peter Goldman, *The Death and Life of Malcolm X* (1973); and August Meier and Elliott Rudwick, *CORE: A Study in the Civil Rights Movement, 1942–1968* (1973). White opposition to social change is described in Numan V. Bartley, *The Rise of Massive Resistance: Race and Politics in the South During the 1950s* (1969). The urban upheavals of the 1960s are analyzed in Joe R. Feagin and Harlan Hahn, *Ghetto Riots: The Politics of Violence in American Cities* (1973).

The Hispanic experience in America is summarized in James S. Olsen, *The Ethnic Dimension in American History* (1979). The largest segment of the nation's Hispanic population is the subject of Matt S. Meier and Feliciano Rivera, *The Chicanos: A History of Mexican Americans* (1972). The economic struggles of Mexican-American laborers in the Southwest are discussed in Ronald B. Taylor, *Chavez and the Farm Workers* (1975). The cultural awakening of Native Americans is articulated in Vine Deloria, Jr., *Custer Died for Your Sins: An Indian Manifesto* (1969).

The search for cultural identity and "the American Character" has not lacked its chroniclers. David Reisman, *The Lonely Crowd* (1950), and W. H. Whyte, Jr., *The Organization Man* (1956), decried the conformity of the 1950s. William L. O'Neill, *Coming Apart: An Informal History of American Life in the 1960s* (1971), gives a good account of the youth movement and counterculture of that decade. In *The Culture of Narcissism: American Life in an Age of Diminishing Expectations* (1979), Christopher Lasch describes a debilitating cultural malaise which he believes is sweeping the United States and the western world.

The best general treatment of religion after World War II is found in Sidney E. Ahlstrom, *A Religious History of the American People* (1972). See also D. F. Wells and J. D. Woodridge, eds., *The Evangelicals* (1975); and Marshall Frady, *Billy Graham* (1979). Literary trends can be followed in Robert E. Spiller, *et al., Literary History of the United States*, 3 vols. (1963); and Alfred Kazin, *Bright Book of Life: American Novelists and Story Tellers from Hemingway to Mailer* (1973).

CHAPTER 35
THE MIDDLE OF THE ROAD
UNDER EISENHOWER

1. THE MIDDLE ROAD

Eisenhower and the Presidency

The election of Dwight David Eisenhower in 1952 gave new proof that the American people still loved military heroes. Eisenhower, born in Denison, Texas, on October 4, 1890, grew up in Abilene, Kansas. His appointment to West Point began a military career that culminated in leadership of the Anglo-American military forces which defeated Germany in 1945. No American was more popular than "Ike" in the joyous days following the end of the Second World War. His welcome home in New York City exceeded that of Charles Lindbergh after his flight to Paris, both in the numbers of persons who lined the streets and in the amount of confetti thrown at the returning hero. Eisenhower remained in the army as Chief of Staff until 1948, when he accepted the presidency of Columbia University. Three years later he was called back into public service as the first supreme commander of NATO forces in Europe. He resigned his command on June 1, 1952, to return home to campaign for the Republican presidential nomination. The American people respected Eisenhower for his qualities of leadership, but they elected him to their highest office because they admired him as a person who stood above ordinary political conflict. They also trusted his judgment in an era when charges of corruption and subversion and even treason reverberated throughout the land, and they liked his friendly smile.

It seems safe to say that Eisenhower will not be

ranked as a great domestic leader among the Presidents of the United States. His background and personal temperament appear to be most responsible for his shortcomings. Eisenhower wasted opportunities for constructive leadership unparalleled since the darkest days of the Great Depression. He resisted criticism from political enemies and pleas from his moderate Republican friends to take action in critical areas ranging from civil rights to air and water pollution (which he dismissed as a peculiarly local problem). He refused to recommend governmental action to counter industrial and technological stagnation, or to relieve hard-core unemployment. And he declined to change the Cold War assumptions which governed all foreign policy. A popular idol, he had at his disposal a reservoir of good will and loyalty such as few Presidents in American history ever possessed. He had behind him a resurgent party with many creative elements. His presidency coincided with a period of general prosperity. Finally, he came to national leadership at the end of a period of intense partisanship, when the great mass of people were yearning for domestic quietude. Yet Eisenhower did not take advantage of his opportunity to give the dynamic leadership needed by the country and that can be exercised through the presidential office. He served during a period when most Americans virtually pleaded for a strong President to follow Truman; but Eisenhower failed or refused to respond.

Part of Eisenhower's deficiencies stemmed from his view of the presidency — one that put heavy emphasis upon the principle of the separation of legislative and executive functions. He was convinced that Roosevelt and Truman had concentrated too much power in their own hands; hence, Eisenhower never tried to establish personal leadership over Congress, nor even over his own party. Moreover, Eisenhower thought that leadership consisted almost exclusively of conciliating differing points of view, not of planning and working for programs and causes. Of necessity, he had played this role — and played it well — in mediating among the nations which made up first the Allied war armies and then those of NATO. But the most important reason for Eisenhower's failure as a leader was his fundamental lack of interest in and knowledge about American politics, probably because he had been a professional soldier for so long. Although a magnificent campaigner, he did not enjoy the quest for votes and tired easily of crowds and adulation. Mere politicians, with their quarrels over party policies and patronage, bored him. He far preferred golf games with businessmen. Therefore, he failed to rebuild the Republican party, although many of his associates urged him to organize and lead the progressive and internationalist wing that had obtained his nomination in 1952. The Republican party actually was weaker at the end of his tenure than it had been in 1952, because it remained bitterly divided between conservatives and progressives and isolationists and internationalists.

Nevertheless, Eisenhower made some important contributions to American political traditions, if not to the presidency itself. In foreign policy, Eisenhower not only guided the government through a series of crises without resort to violence, but he also maintained firm continuity with the American diplomatic policies of the 1940s. He helped to heal deep wounds in the body politic by his own simple decency and fair play. It was a tribute to the reconciling effect of his leadership that Americans in the important presidential election of 1960 were once again able to demonstrate that they could disagree and even fight hard for control of the federal government without using destructive tactics.

Finally, Eisenhower helped to consolidate and strengthen the New Deal's economic and social programs. Eisenhower won Republican support for the extension of Social Security, public housing, and aid to education, and thus made such welfare measures the common property of both parties. This was a significant accomplishment. Of Eisenhower as a domestic leader, it can be said that he accomplished most of what he set out to do.

The Middle of the Road

Some Democrats rather gloomily predicted that Republicans, once in power, would try to turn the clock of history back to the 1920s. However, throughout his eight years as President, Eisenhower tried to follow domestic policies that would appeal to the moderate majorities in both parties. He once characterized these policies as follows: "When it comes to dealing with the relationships between the human in this country and his government, the people of this administration believe in being what I think we would normally call liberal, and when we deal with the economic affairs of this country, we believe in being conservative." This, Eisenhower explained, was "dynamic conservatism." (Adlai Stevenson quipped that Eisenhower apparently meant that he would advocate liberal measures to build school rooms, and then conservatively refuse the grant money to use them.) However, the evidence shows that Eisenhower protected New Deal and Fair Deal programs for human welfare and even extended some. His "dynamic conservatism" implied caution and conservatism in financial policies, not use of those policies to choke established social welfare programs. In other words, "dynamic conservatism" meant staying in the middle of the political road and avoiding the extremes or even the near extremes of both radicalism and reaction.

Promises and Performances

As a candidate in 1952, Eisenhower had put himself at the head of a great crusade to clean up the "mess" in Washington, and he had called upon all good Americans to join him in the effort. Yet he arrived in Washington only to discover that his predecessor had done a thorough job of cleaning up whatever "mess" formerly existed. The crusade was quickly adjourned, and Eisenhower did not mention it again, particularly since he suffered considerable embarrassment from minor scandals in his own administration, even within the White House circle. Eisenhower also talked much in 1952 about the evils of centralization in federal governmental functions at the expense of local and state power. However, he took not a single effective step as President toward diffusing federal power, and the federal system was, if anything, more centralized when he left office than when he entered the White House. The presidential candidate in 1952 discoursed on the utter necessity of what he called "fiscal integrity," of not spending more than one received in revenue. And yet the federal deficit in 1959 bulged to the largest in American peacetime history to that time, and there were deficits in other years as well. There was much Republican talk in 1952 — not by Eisenhower, to be sure — about cleaning the Communists out of Washington. Yet frantic investigations discovered only one Communist on the federal payroll, a typesetter in the Government Printing Office. Eisenhower did institute new security standards, and their severe application resulted in the dismissal of 3,002 so-called security risks. But the costs, both to individuals and the nation, were high because the new standards were so rigorous. Even distinguished individuals, whose loyalty was not questioned, but who were deemed to be security risks because they once knew friends or acquaintances who were Communists, were excluded from federal employment.

Less Government in Business

One promise — to reverse the tide of direct governmental participation in business and manufacturing — Eisenhower carried out to a considerable degree. Almost at the outset of his term, the new President ended all price and wage controls imposed during the Korean War. He let the Reconstruction Finance Corporation, which had lent about $40 billion since its founding by Herbert Hoover in 1932, go out of business. In April 1953, Eisenhower obtained authority from Congress to sell to private industry government-owned and government-operated synthetic rubber manufacturing plants capable of producing some 800,000 tons per year. And in August 1954, Eisenhower obtained amendment of the Atomic Energy Act of 1946 to permit private industry to participate more widely in the development of atomic materials and facilities.

Significant though all these actions were, they passed without much notice or debate. What did stir great and sometimes violent controversy were Eisenhower's determined efforts to halt the trend toward governmental development of natural resources. These efforts led to three major conflicts:

1. *Offshore oil lands.* The discovery of evidently vast oil deposits off the coasts of California and the Gulf states raised the question of the ownership of these coastal areas. Twice, in 1946 and 1952, Congress had passed bills giving title to the claiming states. On both occasions, Truman blocked such action with ringing vetoes. Eisenhower denied such sweeping national claims and gladly signed a compromise measure on May 22, 1953. It transferred title to submerged coastal lands to the states, but only within their historical boundaries. The Supreme Court, in May 1960, set these at the usual three-mile limit, except for Texas and Florida. Their historical boundaries were said to extend ten and a half miles into the sea.

2. *The development of Hell's Canyon.* Between 1953 and 1955, a bitter battle took place between the privately owned Idaho Power Company and certain advocates of public power development. The power company wanted to build three dams in the Hell's Canyon area of the Snake River. Advocates of public power fought back and pleaded for one large dam to be built and operated by the federal government. Eisenhower supported the power company, which won approval of its plans in 1955.

3. *The Tennessee Valley Authority.* Eisenhower revealed his opposition to further extension of public power most significantly in his attitude and policies toward the TVA. In 1953, he referred to the Authority as an example of "creeping socialism." Although he later retracted the remark, it revealed his fundamental opposition to governmental development when private utilities could do the same job. In 1954 he directed the Atomic Energy Commission to sign a contract with certain private power companies, the Dixon-Yates group, to supply 600,000 kilowatts of power to the TVA. This was to replace an equal amount of power to be delivered by the TVA to the AEC's plants at Paducah, Kentucky. The opposition grew so strong and bitter, and evidence of irregular activity in the contract negotiations so pervasive, that Eisenhower finally admitted defeat, and the contract was later canceled.

The Farm Problem

One of the most stubborn problems which faced the Eisenhower administration was the serious decline in farm income that occurred after 1952. Between that date and 1960, farm income fell 23 per cent, while the national income as a whole increased by 43 per cent. There were several reasons for agricultural distress. The most important one was a tremendous increase in production which resulted from the use of machinery, hybrid corn seed, and fertilizers.

Everyone agreed that overproduction was the basic problem after 1952, but considerable disagreement existed over the best means to curtail production and to maintain something like fair prices. Spokesmen of the farmers pled for maintenance of high price supports, such as the 90 per cent of parity level provided by the Agricultural Act of 1949. They also suggested that the government should use surpluses to combat hunger throughout the world. In contrast, Eisenhower's Secretary of Agriculture, Ezra Taft Benson of Utah, urged Congress to adopt low and flexible price supports. The government, Benson insisted, could never solve the problem of mounting surpluses until it stopped paying farmers to overproduce.

The tug of war between the farm spokesmen and the administration continued throughout the Eisenhower era. The alignment did not always follow partisan lines. However, the Democrats tended increasingly to support what most farmers wanted, while the Benson program drove more and more farmers out of the Republican camp.

Neither side had had its way completely by the end of the Eisenhower administration. Benson could point to the progressive lowering of price supports — from a flexible scale of 82.5 to 90 per cent under the Agricultural Act of 1954, to a general scale of 65 per cent under the Agricultural Act of 1958. Congressional representatives of the farmers could point to the program initiated by the Act of 1954 to use American agricultural surpluses abroad. Between 1954 and 1960, agricultural products with a total market value of nearly $4.5 billion were sold for foreign currencies.

Neither side, however, could claim credit for any solution. Farmers produced more every year, despite lower price supports — or perhaps because of them. Farm income continued to decline, in spite of an outpouring from Washington of about $4 billion in 1959 and of $2.6 billion in 1960 in subsidies of one kind or another. Surpluses so huge as to be almost unmanageable continued to burden the warehouses and granaries. By the end of 1960, the government still owned more than 1,000,000,000 bushels of wheat and nearly 1,500,000,000 bushels of corn, much of which was rotting in federally owned or rented warehouses.

Expanding Economic Security

During the campaign of 1952, one commentator quipped that the best hope for the survival of the New Deal and Fair Deal was the election of a Republican President. He meant simply that a Republican administration would have no choice but to continue the Democratic programs for economic security and that talk of repealing these programs would end once both parties could claim credit for them.

This turned out to be an accurate appraisal. Eisenhower and his party leaders never contemplated turning back the clock of economic and social reform.

Such an undertaking would have been too risky politically, for the American people obviously were determined to preserve the gains of the preceding twenty years. Repeal of the New Deal-Fair Deal laws would not have been possible anyway, for Democrats controlled both houses of Congress by increasing majorities from 1955 to 1961, and conservatives did not have a working majority in the Republican-controlled Congress from 1953 to 1955.

In any event, a fundamental part of Eisenhower's middle-of-the-road policy was not only to preserve, but also to strengthen and extend, programs for social and economic security. The only differences between Republicans and Democrats in Congress, or between Democrats in Congress and the President, involved the questions of cost and speed.

The President and Congress agreed in 1954, and again in 1956, to increase Social Security benefits and to broaden the system to include an estimated 10,000,000 new workers. In 1955, Congress and Eisenhower compromised on a new minimum-wage law that increased the minimum from seventy-five cents to $1 an hour. Greater disagreement took place between the two branches of government over providing low-cost public housing for poorer workers. Democrats wanted generous measures and were disappointed when forced to accept administration bills. Even so, the Housing Act of 1959 provided most of what the Democrats demanded. Thus, despite Republican occupancy of the White House, federal expenditures for public housing continued. Between 1953 and 1961, the federal government spent some $1.3 billion for slum clearance and public housing.

In health and medical welfare, as much as in housing and slum clearance, Eisenhower carried forward the programs begun by Roosevelt and Truman. On April 1, 1953, Eisenhower signed a bill (earlier proposed by Truman) which raised the Federal Security Agency to cabinet rank as the Department of Health, Education, and Welfare. Although Eisenhower opposed Truman's plan for broad national health insurance, he asked Congress in 1954 to provide federal support for the nonprofit health insurance plans that had been growing rapidly since the 1940s. A Republican Congress refused this request, but bills which provided federal funds for medical research and hospital construction were adopted with little opposition throughout the 1950s. In 1960, the federal government spent $80 million on hospital construction alone, and Congress passed the Kerr-Mills bill, which authorized the federal government to match state funds on a three-to-one basis to provide medical assistance for needy people over sixty-five years of age.

Eisenhower, who recognized that immigration policies affect the public welfare in a vital way, appointed a commission to study the entire program of immigration and naturalization. This commission recommended complete revision of the McCarran-Walter Immigration and Nationality Act of 1952. Congress refused to alter the basic features of American immigration policy, but it did adopt the Refugee Act of 1953, which permitted an additional 214,000 immigrants to enter during the next three years. Thousands more were admitted under special provisions when Russia suppressed a revolt in Hungary in 1956.

The Civil Rights Crusade Gains Momentum

Truman, who failed to win civil rights legislation, used every executive power at his command to launch a national war against Jim Crow laws and customs.

Eisenhower carried this program forward from the White House with mild determination and no great personal enthusiasm. But presidential action could provide only limited effectiveness in any event. Only Congress held the power to strengthen civil rights by legislation, and threats of a filibuster by southern senators prevented civil rights bills even from coming to a vote before 1957. The log jam was finally broken in that year in a most unexpected way. Senator Lyndon B. Johnson of Texas, Democratic majority leader in the Senate, persuaded administration Republicans and northern and western Democrats to accept a limited bill that sought only to protect black Americans' right to vote in the southern states. In return, southern senators permitted the measure to pass without a filibuster. Johnson possessed national political ambitions, a genuine wish to help poor blacks and Mexican Americans (who hardly were much poorer than he had been as a boy), and a near genius for persuading fellow legislators to vote his way. Officially, the bill passed as an Eisenhower administration measure, sponsored originally by the President and his Attorney General, Herbert Brownell. Actually neither felt much enthusiasm for it; the achievement belonged to Lyndon Johnson.

The Civil Rights Act of 1957 created a bipartisan Commission on Civil Rights with power to subpoena witnesses and authority to investigate violations of civil rights. It also provided for a new Assistant Attorney General to initiate suits in federal district courts when these rights were interfered with, and it authorized federal courts to issue injunctions and begin civil contempt proceedings to secure compliance with orders to cease discrimination. The Civil Rights Act of 1957 was a landmark—the first federal civil rights legislation since 1875. In 1960, Congress adopted a second bill to provide additional protection for blacks who attempted to vote. This measure empowered federal courts to appoint referees to consider state voting qualifications whenever a petitioner had been deprived of the right to register or vote on account of race.

Beginnings of the Judicial Revolution under the Warren Court

Chief Justice Frederick M. Vinson, author of the decision in the Dennis case of 1951 that upheld the imprisonment of Communists under the Smith Act, died in September 1953. Eisenhower unwittingly ushered in a new era in the history of the Supreme Court by appointing Earl Warren as Chief Justice of the United States. It was, Eisenhower later said, the "biggest damnfool mistake I ever made."

The appointment, however, appeared, in 1953, to be eminently safe and expedient. Warren, although a Republican in the predominantly Democratic State of California, had won a reputation as the most popular governor in the history of the state; Democrats had hardly bothered to oppose him when he was elected governor three times. As Attorney General of California in 1941, he had approved the internment of the Japanese Americans. Warren had also opposed reapportionment plans which would have given cities such as Los Angeles, San Francisco, and Oakland representation in the state legislature consistent with their proportion of the state's population. Finally, Warren had also accused the Truman administration of "coddling" Communists.

However, Warren's record masked what soon became activated, once he was no longer under the pressures of running for office: a burning social conscience and passion for justice. Moreover, Warren was a skillful politician who

The United States Supreme Court in 1962. Front row, left to right:
William O. Douglas, Hugo Black, Earl Warren, Felix Frankfurter, Tom
C. Clark. Back row: Potter Stewart, John M. Harlan, William J.
Brennan, Jr., and the newly appointed Byron White. Three of the
major figures behind the early landmark decisions of what is called
the "Warren Court" were Justices Douglas, Black, and Frankfurter, all
appointed by President Roosevelt in the late 1930s. The judicial
revolution that Warren presided over and helped to expand during his
sixteen years as Chief Justice involved critical cases in the areas of
race relations, free speech, fairness in the criminal justice system, and
fairness in legislative apportionment. (Historical Pictures Service, Inc.,
Chicago)

used his personal moral force to persuade a majority of the court to follow his
lead. Consequently, from 1953 until his retirement in 1969, Warren forged a
liberal majority on the supreme bench and led it in a judicial revolution that
made the Supreme Court the most important instrumentality for political and
social change in the United States during the 1950s and 1960s.

The Warren Court moved slowly but surely in cases relating to internal security to restore traditional constitutional protection to individuals. In Pennsylvania v. Nelson, 1956, it barred enforcement of state sedition laws on the
ground that Congress had preempted antisubversion legislation. However, in
the following year the court struck boldly in defense of civil rights in Yates v.
United States. In this decision, the court overturned the decision in the Dennis
case. The Smith Act, Warren said in the Yates decision, had forbidden only
conspiracies and overt acts to overthrow the government by force, not the
teaching or advocacy of the overthrow of government as an abstract principle.
Thus, without openly invalidating the Smith Act, Warren made it a dead
statute.

Desegregation and the Schools

The Supreme Court, from 1944 to 1953, had already begun to chip away at the legal bases of segregation. The Court had ruled, first, that blacks could not be excluded from state primary elections on account of race; second, that persons could not be excluded from jury service on account of race; third, that so-called restrictive covenants (agreements by buyers of houses not to sell them to persons of certain races and religions) were unenforceable; and, fourth, that segregation was illegal in the District of Columbia, in interstate transportation, and in public recreational facilities.

The Supreme Court, under steady pressure from lawyers representing the NAACP, principally Thurgood Marshall, had also begun to face the question of the constitutionality of enforced segregation in public schools and state colleges and universities. For example, the Vinson Court, in 1950, had ruled in Sweatt v. Painter that a recently established state law school for blacks in Texas could never provide a legal education equal to the one offered by the Law School of the University of Texas at Austin and had ordered the latter to admit the claimant, Herman M. Sweatt. However, in this and other cases, the Supreme Court had refused to overturn Plessy v. Ferguson, the bastion of legal segregation, which had said that public facilities could be separate so long as they were equal (see p. 590).

However, Marshall and his associates continued their relentless attacks against Plessy v. Ferguson; and the day of reckoning on the "separate but equal" doctrine could not have been postponed for any long period. Warren decided that that day had come when Brown v. Board of Education of Topeka and several related cases, all of which involved the legality of segregation in public schools, came before the court in 1953. Warren's first objective was to obtain a unanimous decision. This objective won, the Chief Justice read the decision in the Brown case on May 17, 1954. It decreed that compulsory segregation in public schools on account of race violated the Fourteenth Amendment's guarantee of equal rights to all citizens. Segregated schools, Warren said, specifically repudiating Plessy v. Ferguson, were inherently and inevitably unequal because, among other things, enforced segregation stamped black children as inferior and denied them equal protection under the law. It was a landmark in American constitutional history because it was the hardest blow yet struck against racist segregation and in fact blasted all legal bases for discrimination based on race.

A year later the Supreme Court clarified the application of Brown v. Board of Education and instructed federal district courts to require local authorities to show "good faith," to "make a prompt and reasonable start toward full compliance," and to move with "all deliberate speed" toward desegregation of all public schools.

School desegregation was fairly well accomplished in the District of Columbia and the Border States by 1957. By the same date, a beginning toward school desegregation had been made in North Carolina, Tennessee, Arkansas, and Texas, while more than half of the formerly all-white publicly supported colleges and universities in the South had opened their doors to blacks.

However, intense and massive resistance developed at the same time in Virginia and the states of the Deep South. Their legislatures adopted resolutions which denounced the Supreme Court's ruling as unconstitutional and then enacted laws which closed their public schools if desegregation was forced upon them. The first outright defiance of the federal courts occurred in Little Rock, Arkansas. Violence broke out there in September 1957, when the local school board attempted to implement its plan for desegregation of the high school. Governor Orval E. Faubus used National Guard troops to prevent the entry of black pupils. However, Eisenhower, who privately deplored the Brown decision, could not brook such defiance of federal authority. He called the National Guard of Arkansas into national service and also sent in federal soldiers to reopen the school and to preserve order in the area. For the first time since Radical Reconstruction, the federal government demonstrated that rights guaranteed to blacks by the Constitution would be protected by military might, if necessary. Violators of these rights were notified that, if they intended to continue to oppose black equality in all areas of political and social life, they might eventually have to express this opposition in armed conflict with federal troops.

Another fortress of the antiintegrationists fell early in 1959. Virginia, heretofore the leader in "massive resistance" to desegregation, permitted its local school boards to obey federal court orders if they wished to continue their public schools. Perhaps the most significant breakthrough occurred in 1961, when the Georgia legislature, after it had earlier vowed to resist to the bitter end, permitted Atlanta to begin limited desegregation. By the end of the Eisenhower administration in 1961, only South Carolina, Alabama, and Mississippi still maintained all-out resistance to at least a limited desegregation, and their resistance would be neither as strong nor as permanent as people thought at the time.

This combination of decisions, which insisted upon desegregation and protected basic civil liberties, earned Warren widespread anger, if not hatred. Calls for his impeachment appeared on billboards, fences, and car bumpers throughout the country, but especially in the South and the Southwest. The court was accused of making law rather than interpreting it—which was true to some extent—although Warren replied that the laws that the court had overturned were contrary to the higher law of the United States Constitution. Still, plain concern for simple justice also appeared to play a large role in forming some of the court's decisions. Also, in a period when President Eisenhower appeared reluctant to move off dead center in making decisions, and Congress remained unable to form a consensus on most important issues, the Supreme Court's decisions seemed more dramatic and extreme than they would have in eras of reform such as those over which Woodrow Wilson and Franklin Roosevelt had presided.

2. THE "NEW LOOK" IN FOREIGN POLICY

Secretary Dulles and the "New Look"

John Foster Dulles, long-time leading Republican spokesman on foreign policy, from 1953 until 1959 was one of the most controversial Secretaries of State in American history. Dulles was supremely confident both of his abilities and of his moral righteousness; in shaping foreign policy, he relied heavily upon

As U.S. delegates to the United Nations, John Foster Dulles and Eleanor Roosevelt here listen to Russian Foreign Minister Andrei Vishinsky call Dulles one of the nine leading "warmongers" in the United States, September 9, 1947. Despite Dulles' gift for forceful speech, he later proved to be capable of both restraint and diplomacy as Secretary of State. Eleanor Roosevelt's distinguished service as delegate to the UN included a major role in drafting and securing the adoption of the Universal Declaration of Human Rights in 1948. After she resigned her post in 1952, she promoted the work of the UN and other causes in her constant travels over the next decade. (Acme Photo)

his own ideas, intuition, and knowledge, and upon consultation with President Eisenhower. Dulles, nephew of Wilson's Secretary of State, Robert Lansing, had played a role in conceiving and carrying out American foreign policy during the Paris Peace Conference and between the two world wars. His views and pronouncements as Secretary of State arose from the confidence that comes with experience in a political role, as well as from deep personal belief. Dulles apparently began to decide, shortly after the First World War, that a nearly monolithic "world Communist movement" represented, in his words, "an unholy alliance of Marx's communism and Russia's imperialism"; and events after 1945 only strengthened this belief. Also, to understand Dulles' words and actions, it should be remembered that part of his job consisted of protecting Eisenhower and the administration's foreign policy from criticism which might be directed at it by politicians on the Republican Right wing—such as Senator Joseph McCarthy. Dulles tried always to balance his own moralistic beliefs and political responsibilities. The result, cast in Dulles' peculiar mold, inevitably caused criticism from all sides; but it won grudging agreement, also, from almost all American politicians.

Some of the controversy that Dulles provoked arose because he found it hard to resist the temptation to use his undeniable gift for coining catchy phrases and slogans. In the Republican platform of 1952, he inserted a promise that a Republican administration would repudiate all "secret understandings," such as the Yalta agreements, and find a substitute for the "negative, futile, and immoral" policy of containment. Dulles implied that the United States could somehow win the Cold War against the Soviet Union. He later talked about the liberation of "captive peoples" under Soviet domination (he evidently referred to eastern European and Baltic peoples) and about the use of "massive retaliation" against the Soviet Union or Communist China if they committed serious aggression. He gave audiences and newspaper reporters the impression that "massive retaliation" meant the use of atomic bombs and enough of them to lay waste the whole Soviet Union, if necessary. Another threat was that of "unleashing" Chiang Kai-shek so that his already defeated army could attack the Chinese mainland from Formosa. Meanwhile, there would be "agonizing reappraisals" of American foreign policy; and in some cases Dulles talked about carrying the country to "the brink of war" (giving rise to the term "brinkmanship") in order to preserve the peace of the world. The implied meaning of "the brink," of course, was that the United States would go over it if that policy failed and use "massive retaliation" against its enemy.

It was unfortunate that the Secretary of State possessed such a talent for phrasemaking. His slogans frightened the allies of the United States, who took them seriously for a while. His statements scared a good many Americans as well. They also obscured the really important facts about the foreign policies of the Eisenhower administration. First, Eisenhower, not Dulles, made almost all important decisions in the field of foreign affairs. On several important occasions, the President overruled his Secretary of State. However, the two men shared the fundamental beliefs that underlay American foreign policy in this period—firm commitment to a continuation of the Cold War, certainty of the moral superiority of the American position in this conflict, and the precedence of European affairs over problems that arose elsewhere. Second, Eisenhower and Dulles carried forward policies whose foundations had been firmly laid by Roosevelt and Truman. Third, Dulles, in spite of his bombast, was a cautious and resourceful diplomat, and his accomplishments were considerable. Among these was the protection of Eisenhower from harmful political criticism from the Republican Right wing—McCarthy, Senators Barry Goldwater and William Knowland, and others.

The Korean Armistice and New Crises in the Far East

The first task in foreign policy which faced the Eisenhower administration was the conclusion of the war in Korea. The Chinese and North Koreans had opened armistice negotiations with General Ridgway in the summer of 1951. The discussions proceeded until October 1952, when North Korea broke them off.

One of Dulles' first important acts as Secretary of State was to send a message to the Chinese leaders that the United States would open a wholesale offensive, perhaps against China as well as North Korea, if the North Koreans did not bargain in good faith. Something about this "brinkmanship" apparently worked. Eisenhower, of course, would never have risked the stability of the United States by an invasion and occupation of China, and certainly neither would Dulles. Negotiations were reopened, and the combatants finally signed an armistice at Panmunjom, Korea, on July 27, 1953. It provided for the return of prisoners on a voluntary basis and established a demilitarized buffer zone along the battle line not far from the thirty-eighth parallel. Thus, in this case, Dulles' reputation as a hard-core, devout Cold Warrior, ready to take extreme risks for his cause, served his country well.

In spite of some American criticism because there had been no clear-cut victory, the Korean War at the time seemed to be a significant achievement for the United Nations. Invaders from North Korea, later fully supported by Communist China's finest armies, had attempted to conquer the UN-sponsored Republic of Korea. The aggressors had been defeated with terrible losses to themselves. American aid had made it possible for the infant world organization to win its first major test at arms. More than 1,500,000 American soldiers participated during the three years of fighting in Korea, and of this number 54,246 gave their lives.

No sooner had peace talks begun in Korea than a new crisis broke out to the south. Communists in northern Indochina had been leading an independence movement against French colonial authority since 1946. With the conclusion of the war in Korea, the mainland Chinese government greatly increased its aid to the Communist rebels in Indochina. In the spring of 1954, the hard-pressed French appealed to the United States for support. Again Dulles, supported by Vice-President Nixon among others, wanted to take the nation to the "brink of war" by American air strikes against the Indochinese. The British government, however, warned that it could not support this action, since it might lead to general war in the Far East. With public opinion clearly lukewarm for American military participation, Eisenhower vetoed plans for the air strike. The result was the calling of a Foreign Ministers' Conference in Geneva in May 1954. Dulles left the meeting when it became evident that Vietnam, one of the new independent states created out of what had been French Indochina, would be divided, like Korea, between a Communist North and a non-Communist South.

Dulles, who feared that all of Asia might soon fall under Communist control, called a conference of non-Communist nations to meet in Manila and consider the threat of further aggression. Delegates from Australia, Britain, France, New Zealand, Pakistan, the Philippines, Thailand, and the United States signed the Manila Pact on September 8, 1954, which created the Southeast Asia Treaty Organization (SEATO). Like the North Atlantic Treaty, the Manila Pact pledged joint action in the event of aggression against any member nation, and it provided special protection for Cambodia, Laos, and South Vietnam.

The American security system in the Pacific was completed, if not strengthened, in December 1954, when Dulles signed a mutual defense treaty with the Chinese Nationalist government on Formosa. It provided protection against aggression by mainland China, as had a similar mutual security treaty that Dulles signed with South Korea in October 1953.

The Decision to Rearm Germany

Just as crises shook the Far East, so a controversy in the West threatened to split NATO. It involved the question of whether to rearm Germany and incorporate this former enemy state into the western defense system. Truman had made such a suggestion as early as 1950. France, Italy, Belgium, the Netherlands, Luxembourg, and West Germany had signed a treaty on May 27, 1952, which provided machinery for the formation of a European Defense Community (EDC) as soon as the parliaments of each nation approved. The important feature of the EDC was its plan for a tightly integrated western European army with German contingents.

Trouble soon developed because no majority could be found in the French Chamber of Deputies for any plan to put rifles in the hands of German soldiers. Dulles entered the fray by warning that continued French refusal to ratify the EDC treaty would force the United States to make an "agonizing reappraisal" of its foreign policy—in other words, perhaps to abandon NATO. The threat, empty at best, only further angered the French, who replied by rejecting the EDC treaty again in August 1954.

Fortunately, a solution proposed by the British Foreign Secretary, Anthony Eden, resulted in the signing of the Paris Pact on October 23, 1954. In this treaty, the western powers gave full sovereignty to the Federal Republic of Germany. The Brussels Treaty Organization was expanded to include West Germany and Italy. West Germany was admitted to NATO and permitted an army of 500,000 men to serve under NATO command. Finally, the United States and Britain promised to keep troops on the continent so long as the Brussels Treaty Organization wanted them to remain.

The First Summit Conference

The Soviet dictator, Stalin, died in 1953, and a new government, headed, first, by Georgi Malenkov and, soon afterward, by Nikolai A. Bulganin, came to power in Moscow. For a time, at least, these new Soviet rulers seemed to want sincerely to reduce the tensions of the Cold War. Eisenhower met suggestions for a summit conference of the leaders of the great powers with some enthusiasm. Like Franklin D. Roosevelt, Eisenhower believed that he could accomplish much by personal diplomacy. The conference met at Geneva in July 1955, in an atmosphere of strained cordiality. Although the chiefs of state (of the United States, Russia, Britain, and France) adopted no concrete measures to end the Cold War, they did refer four major problems to their Foreign Ministers for further discussions. These were European security, disarmament, German unification, and increased communication across what was called the "iron curtain" separating the western and eastern blocs. The "spirit of Geneva" quickly evaporated when the Foreign Ministers returned to that Swiss city in October 1955. Since both sides were still determined to have their way on all issues, the conference broke up without a single agreement.

The St. Lawrence Seaway

The relations of the two North American neighbors, the United States and Canada, presented a different story. Their main problem at the beginning of the Eisenhower administration was cooperation in building a great seaway from the St. Lawrence River to Lake Ontario. The seaway would open the Great Lakes to large freighters and passenger ships and make possible the development of vast new hydroelectric power.

Both Roosevelt and Truman had tried to win congressional approval for the project, and both had failed because of opposition from the eastern states and railroads. Finally, in May 1954, Congress yielded to pressure from the new President (and from Canada, which threatened to go ahead on its own); and digging for new locks and dams began almost at once. The seaway, completed in the spring of 1959, was formally opened by Elizabeth II and Eisenhower.

3. POLITICS STILL IN MODERATION

1956: The Eisenhower Landslide

Two events caused Democrats to look to the presidential election of 1956 with increasing confidence. The first was the somewhat surprising result of the mid-term election in 1954 — the election of a Congress with small Democratic majorities in both houses. The second event shocked the country. On September 24, 1955, Eisenhower suffered a heart attack while visiting Denver. He soon emerged from danger, but for several months all observers took it for granted that he would not run again. However, the President's recovery was almost complete by early 1956, and he announced on February 29 that he would be a candidate for reelection. The President and Vice-President Nixon were renominated by acclamation by the Republican national convention.

The Democrats had met in Chicago only a week earlier. Ex-President Truman tried to rally old-line liberals behind Governor W. Averell Harriman of New York. However, Adlai E. Stevenson, who this time made a spirited and successful fight in the presidential primaries, easily won the nomination on the first ballot. Senator Estes Kefauver of Tennessee, Stevenson's chief rival in the preconvention campaign, obtained Stevenson's endorsement as his running mate.

Both parties conducted short, intensive campaigns with much use of television. The Republicans had the advantage of Eisenhower's enormous popularity and of continuing prosperity. "Everything," Republicans exclaimed, "is booming but the guns!" Democratic hopes lay in better local organizations and in support from labor and blacks. In the final analysis, the campaign was a popularity contest between a candidate who did not seem able to rouse the voters and a President who remained a hero to many Americans. The differences on issues between the two party platforms and the two candidates were narrow, indeed.

Eisenhower's victory was never in doubt, and the expolosion of war in the Middle East in late October (see pp. 916–918) created a sharp crisis that turned many wavering voters to the President's side. He polled 35,590,000 popular votes and carried forty-one states. In contrast, Stevenson won only 26,023,000 popular votes and seven states. It was an endorsement, however, only of Eisenhower and not of his party. The Democrats actually increased their majorities in Congress and elected governors in several hitherto Republican states. Not since 1848 had the party that won the presidency lost both houses of Congress in the same election.

Combating the Recession

The most urgent problem confronting Eisenhower and the new Eighty-fifth Congress was a business recession that threatened to turn into a full-fledged depression. It began with a sharp decline on the stock market in the summer and autumn of 1957. The recession received further stimulation from a cutback in spending for new plants and machinery in the United States and by a decline in commodity prices and trade throughout the world. By January 1958, unemployment in the United States had reached a postwar high of nearly 4,500,000.

There never was any serious disagreement between the President and Congress as to whether the government should act to reverse the downward economic trend. Gone forever were the days when Americans would accept depressions as something that they could do nothing about. However, sharp disagreement existed between the White House and Capitol Hill over the weapons to be used. Many Democrats urged drastic tax reductions and large federal spending in order to increase consumer purchasing power. However, Eisenhower and his Council of Economic Advisers were convinced that the government need not go so far. They stood firmly behind a more limited program of increased credit, encouragement to home construction, a 7 per cent increase in Social Security benefits, extension of unemployment insurance payments, and some expansion of federal spending for highways, hospitals, housing, and schools. The administration had its way, mainly because a powerful group of Democratic senators who followed Majority Leader Lyndon B. Johnson also favored moderate policies.

The so-called built-in antidepression machinery worked perfectly during this recession. By May 1958, the economic downturn had ended, and the economy was growing at normal speed again by the beginning of 1959. However, some Democrats pointed to a retarded growth rate in the 1950s, as compared with the rate of the 1940s, and to persistently high unemployment of about 6 per cent of the labor force, as proof that stronger countercyclical devices should have been used in the recession of 1957.

Sputnik and Fears about National Security

The development of missiles had been proceeding in Russia and the United States since the end of the Second World War, and Americans confidently believed that they were far ahead in the race for new weapons. Then, in October 1957, a new star appeared in the sky. It was Russia's Sputnik I, the first earth-launched satellite. Americans suddenly realized that, if the Russians had rockets powerful enough to launch satellites, they possessed rockets powerful enough to bombard the United States with nuclear weapons. The Russians had exploded an atomic bomb in 1949 and a hydrogen bomb in 1953, not long after the first American hydrogen bomb had been detonated. A second Russian Sputnik appeared in the sky a month after the first one. The successful launching of the first American satellite, Explorer I, in January 1958 did not quiet

This ceremony took place in front of Iolani Palace, the seat of Hawaii's government in March 1959 after Congress took action that would make Hawaii the fiftieth state within five months. Honor Guards of the Army, Navy, Marines, Coast Guard, and Air Force lined up with flags while spectators joined in the National Anthem. (Wide World Photos)

American fears that the Russians were considerably ahead in the rocket race. And Democrats and aerospace corporations encouraged widespread talk and fear of a "missile gap"—a period when the Soviet Union would command vastly more intercontinental missiles than the United States. The leading Cold Warrior physicist, Edward Teller, "father" of the hydrogen bomb, when asked by reporters what Americans would find should they ever reach the moon, replied: "Russians."

Therefore, Congress met in a state of high excitement, not to say alarm, when it assembled in January 1958. Eisenhower presented the largest peacetime budget in American history, which called for expenditures of nearly $74 billion. Congress increased this sum to more than $76 billion and provided an additional $4 billion for rocket and missile development and the conquest of outer space. (Appropriations for defense ran at the same level of about $40 billion during the next two years.) In addition, at Eisenhower's request, the lawmakers amended the Atomic Energy Act of 1946 to permit the sharing of atomic secrets with America's allies; created a National Aeronautics and Space Administration (NASA) to coordinate research and development; gave the Secretary of Defense much greater direct control over the three branches of the armed services; and adopted the National Defense Education Act, which granted funds to schools for special programs in science, mathematics, and foreign languages. This made possible the teaching of atomic structure and the biology of DNA in high schools, as well as the "new math" of set theory, and it subsidized the acquisition of language laboratories; liberals had been requesting all of this for over a decade.

Alaska and Hawaii were especially important to American defenses. Bases near Anchorage, Kodiak, and Fairbanks, and the Distant Early Warning (DEW) Line of radar outposts stood guard to signal possible attacks across the Arctic. The great naval base at Pearl Harbor in Hawaii controlled the vast Pacific to Formosa Strait. Alaska contained huge natural resources, including some of the world's most magnificent scenery. Hawaii, too, ranked among the earth's most beautiful regions. Nevertheless, Alaskan and Hawaiian pleas for statehood had repeatedly died in Congress; but the rocket and jet plane had annihilated the "too far from the mainland" argument. In June 1958, Congress paved the way for the admission of Alaska, and it entered the Union as the forty-ninth state on January 3, 1959. Nor was Hawaii's admission long delayed. After action by Congress in March 1959, it entered as the fiftieth state on August 21, 1959.

1958: The Democratic Landslide and Its Aftermath

All signs seemed to point to a modest Democratic victory in the mid-term election in November 1958. Three developments turned what might have been a moderate Democratic gain into a landslide. First, a congressional committee discovered that Eisenhower's chief assistant, Sherman Adams, had been receiving gifts from a businessman in return for favors rendered. Eisenhower refused to discuss Adams and would not accept his resignation until September. Second, Republicans made open-shop, or "right-to-work," laws the main issue in many states and thus aroused the vigorous participation of organized labor on the Democratic side. Third, farmers blamed Republicans for the Agricultural Act of 1958 which cut price supports. A combination of these developments, together with some popular disillusionment about Eisenhower, resulted in a landslide victory that gave Democrats two-to-one majorities in both houses of the next Congress.

Democrats who expected to ride roughshod over the President in the Eighty-sixth Congress, which met in January 1959, underestimated Eisenhower's skill, popularity, and veto power. With the resignation of Sherman Adams and the death of Secretary Dulles in May 1959, Eisenhower began to exercise a more direct leadership in domestic and foreign affairs. By the end of the first session of the new Congress, the President could claim as many victories as could his Democratic opponents.

The most important legislative accomplishment of the last two years of the Eisenhower era was a bipartisan one—the Labor-Management Reporting and Disclosure, or Landrum-Griffin, Act of 1959. It grew out of the recommendations of a special Senate committee headed by Senator John F. Kennedy of Massachusetts. For several years, the committee had been probing deeply into racketeering and corruption in some labor unions, especially the Teamsters' Union. An aroused public opinion demanded preventive legislation, and the Landrum-Griffin bill passed Congress by overwhelming majorities.

The new law required union officials to submit detailed financial reports to the Secretary of Labor. It also required employers to report on any payments to union officers and to labor-relations consultants. To protect union members who opposed their officers, a "bill of rights" guaranteed to members the right to vote in union elections and to speak up against union policies. Moreover, unions were required to hold regular elections. Finally, the Act strengthened previous restrictions on secondary boycotts and blackmail picketing. These provisions hardly affected the powerful Teamsters' Union. It continued to contribute campaign funds liberally to key members of both parties.

4. TO THE SECOND SUMMIT AND BACK AGAIN

The Suez Affair Threatens Western Unity

Except for the Korean armistice, the Eisenhower administration could claim no great diplomatic victories during its first years in power; nevertheless, until mid-1956 it could say at least that the United States had suffered no major reversals and had more or less held its own in world affairs. Spokesmen of the administration could not make even these modest claims at the end of Eisenhower's tenure. The last four years, 1956–1960, were not only tumultuous but also full of reversals for the United States abroad. Even in Latin America, where the Good Neighbor policy had earlier won a host of friends, developments turned unfavorable after 1955. Vice-President Nixon's goodwill tour of Latin America in the spring of 1958 was marred by an outbreak of violence in Caracas, Venezuela. Moreover, in Cuba the victory of Fidel Castro and his band of revolutionaries in early 1959 brought to power a regime soon bitterly hostile to the United States. The question of whether Castro came to power as a dedicated Communist, or was pushed toward dependence upon Soviet Russia and its official ideology by the American administration's hasty opposition to his reform rule, including several efforts to overthrow or assassinate him, remains a mystery which perhaps only Castro himself can clarify. A repetition of the State Department's and CIA's coup, which helped to oust a pro-Communist government in Guatemala in 1954, could not be carried out immediately in the larger and more important Cuba, where it would have attracted worldwide scrutiny; but intensive planning for intervention began with Eisenhower's approval.

What seems to have been a chain of events in the Middle East began just before Eisenhower's smashing second electoral triumph. Israeli armed forces, goaded by Arab border raids and threats of destruction, attacked Egypt on October 29, 1956. Within four days, the Israelis had smashed the armies of President Gamal Abdel Nasser and had driven through the entire Sinai Peninsula. France and Britain had been angered by Nasser's aid to rebels against French rule in Algeria and by his recent seizure of the Suez Canal. Without the approval or knowledge of the American government, the British and French governments resolved to intervene to overthrow Nasser and regain control of the Suez lifeline. By a prearranged understanding with Israel, Britain and France demanded that Egypt and Israel stop fighting and withdraw from the area of the Suez Canal. When Nasser refused, the British destroyed what remained of the Egyptian air force and occupied the northern third of the canal.

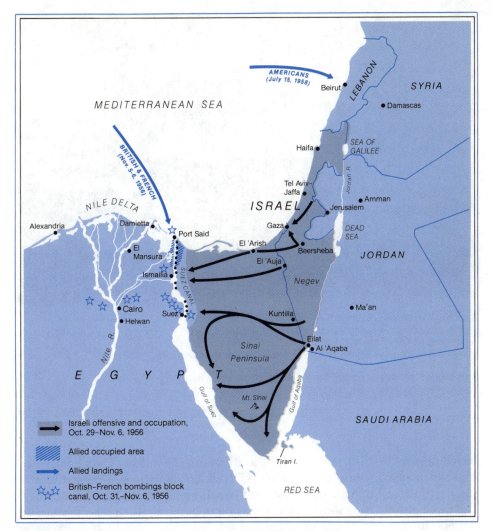

The Suez Crisis, 1956

The Soviet government was at this very moment suppressing an anti-Communist revolution in Budapest. Soviet leaders sought to draw the spotlight of world opinion away from the Russian tanks, which were shooting down Hungarian workers, by condemning Britain, France, and Israel as aggressors in Egypt. The new Russian leader, Nikita S. Khrushchev, acted as the protector of the Arabs. Khrushchev threatened to send "volunteers" to help Egypt and to blast Britain and France with rockets carrying nuclear bombs.

The United States Government did not rush to the defense of its allies. On the contrary, Eisenhower and Dulles were personally angered by the independent Anglo-French military action. In addition, they thought that it was morally wrong because it smacked of old-fashioned imperialism, and unwise because it might drive the entire Arab world with its great, American-leased

Burnt out Russian tanks that were set afire by Hungarian students while fighting continued in the streets of Budapest in 1956. During the uprising, Premier Nagy repudiated his country's military alliance with Russia and declared Hungary to be neutral. To cease this dual process of de-Russification and de-Communization, Soviet forces overwhelmed the Hungarians in bloody fighting and replaced the Nagy government with Soviet puppets. (Wide World Photos)

petroleum fields, into the arms of the Russians. Therefore, Eisenhower and Dulles supported a resolution in the UN which demanded a cease-fire and quick withdrawal of British, French, and Israeli forces from Egyptian territory. The three powers, threatened by Russia and opposed by their ally, decided to comply. In contrast, the Soviets ignored a UN resolution which called upon them to withdraw their troops from Hungary.

The Suez affair shook the western alliance to its foundations. France, especially, proceeded to reconsider its dependence upon American military protection. The American government tried to restore some measure of unity and supplied economic aid to clear the Suez Canal. It also gave Britain and France credit to purchase huge quantities of oil from the United States until the Suez route was restored. Next, Eisenhower conferred with the new British Prime Minister, Harold Macmillan, in Bermuda in March 1957. They agreed that the United States should build intermediate-range missile sites in Great Britain. These advanced bases would provide some deterrence to Russian rockets. And, when disarmament talks with Russia during the summer failed, the NATO Council agreed, in December 1957, that the United States should negotiate with other NATO members for construction of additional missile sites in western Europe. Meanwhile, the American government continued its mutual security assistance to NATO nations and others. By 1960, annual expenditures for this assistance were running to nearly $3.5 billion.

New Turmoil in the Middle East and Far East

The chief danger to world peace in 1957 was the turmoil in the Middle East that followed the Suez affair. American policymakers searched for a way that the United States could recover its influence in this oil-rich region. In an address to Congress on January 5, 1957, Eisenhower gave an answer in what was soon called the Eisenhower Doctrine. The United States, he announced, would help any middle eastern country to resist communist military aggression and, in addition, would undertake aid programs for economic development.

Events soon revealed that the Eisenhower Doctrine contained two fundamental weaknesses. The main threat to peace and American influence in the Middle East was not open Communist aggression, but the subversion of existing governments. Second, the doctrine could not be put into operation unless some government asked specifically for help. By sending some 14,000 marines into Lebanon at the request of the President of that country in July 1958, Eisenhower helped to prevent the overthrow of a government friendly to the United States. But the Eisenhower Doctrine provided no remedy when a much more serious crisis erupted in Iraq within the same week. There a group of army officers murdered the King and Prime Minister and knocked the props out from under the West's defensive system in the Middle East. America's only hope was that the new Iraqi government would at least remain neutral in the conflict between the great powers and not fall under the control of a pro-Soviet Communist clique. The same kind of threats which climaxed in Iraq existed in Syria, Iran, and virtually every other middle eastern nation.

No sooner had a kind of peace returned to the Middle East than the threat of war broke out on the other side of the globe. In August 1958, the Chinese Communists began to shell islands off the mainland held by the Nationalists. Eisenhower warned that the United States would join the fighting if Communist seizure of the offshore islands was part of a larger campaign against Formosa. To back up his words, Eisenhower sent the powerful Seventh Fleet into Formosa Strait. This action was probably decisive; in any event, the threat of Communist invasion of the offshore islands had passed by November 1958.

The Berlin Crisis

A more severe test of diplomatic strength began on November 27, 1958, when the Soviet government submitted notes to Britain, France, and the United States which proposed that West Berlin be evacuated by Allied troops and be made a free city. Russia warned that it would sign a separate peace treaty with the East German regime unless the western Allies pulled out of Berlin within six months. If this happened, the western powers would have to make arrangements with East Germany for entry into Berlin; and if the East Germans forbade the Allies to enter the former German capital, they would presumably have the military backing of their Soviet ally.

It was an obvious attempt either to split NATO or to force the western powers to abandon Berlin. The French, British, and American governments replied almost at once; they rejected Soviet demands and suggested a four-power meeting to consider the German problem. But how and when such a meeting could take place, no one seemed to know. Dulles, resolute in his opposition to a second summit meeting, proposed a conference of Foreign Ministers. Khrushchev, on the other hand, insisted upon a meeting of the heads of state to consider all the problems of the Cold War. The British Prime Minister, who visited Moscow and Washington in February and March 1959, tended to agree with Khrushchev.

The impasse was broken in a dramatic way not long afterward. Dulles died of cancer on May 24, 1959. He had been succeeded a month earlier by former Governor Christian A. Herter of Massachusetts. Eisenhower now took personal direction of foreign policy, and there were immediate results. In July, he sent Vice-President Nixon on a goodwill tour to Russia and Poland. In August, Eisenhower announced that he and Khrushchev would exchange visits. In the same month, Eisenhower flew to western Europe for conferences with leaders there; then, in mid-September, Eisenhower received Khrushchev. After he traveled to the West Coast and back, Khrushchev conferred again with Eisenhower in late September. The result was an agreement that seemed to promise an early end to the Berlin crisis: Khrushchev agreed to settle the Berlin question by negotiation and withdrew his six-month time limit, while Eisenhower made it plain that he would go to a summit meeting in the near future.

The Second Summit and Afterward

During late 1959 and early 1960, all signs seemed to point to a solution of the Berlin crisis and a revival of American influence throughout the world. Eisenhower continued his efforts at personal diplomacy and made triumphal tours of eleven European and Asian nations in December 1959 and of four Latin American countries in February and March 1960. Secretary Herter and the Japanese Premier signed a new treaty of mutual security on January 19, 1960. It bound the United States and Japan in alliance and gave the former a continued right to maintain armed forces in Japan. Leaders of the western powers met in a presummit conference in Paris on December 19, 1959, and invited Khrushchev to join them in a meeting during the coming spring. Negotiations with the Russians soon yielded agreement on May 16 as the date and Paris as the place of the conference.

At this point, bungling, bad luck, and bad temper spoiled all chances for an East-West understanding. On May 5, 1960, Khrushchev announced that, four days earlier, Soviet forces had shot down an American U-2 observation plane over the Soviet Union, but he gave no further information about the incident. Authorities in Washington immediately declared that the plane, on a routine meteorological mission, had strayed from its course. Two days after his original announcement, Khrushchev, who may have expected a prompt apology from the United States, now charged that the plane had been on an espionage mission over the Soviet Union. The pilot had been captured and had confessed. The Soviet evidence was so conclusive that Herter admitted the charge and implied that the espionage flights would continue. Eisenhower, in a television address, accepted personal responsibility for the aerial spying and, moreover, defended it. The atmosphere, consequently, was highly charged when the heads of state assembled in Paris in mid-May for the long-awaited summit meeting.

That conference actually never occurred. Khrushchev undoubtedly was genuinely upset by the U-2 incident. Perhaps he was determined already, as some

Enraged by repeated booing from the audience, a furious Nikita Khrushchev shakes his fist while delivering an abusive tirade during a press conference in Paris in May 1960. Referring to the U-2 incident earlier that month, the Soviet Premier compared President Eisenhower to "a thief caught red-handed in his theft." (United Press International)

American diplomats suspected, to wreck the Paris conference because he realized that he could not have his way on Berlin. Certainly, when Eisenhower presented him with an opportunity to vilify the American government, he was unwilling to pass it up. In any event, at the first meeting on May 16, Khrushchev made a violent personal attack on Eisenhower for continuing the spy-plane trips over the Soviet Union while he planned his meeting with Khrushchev; also he blamed the President for his attempt to justify their continuation rather than to apologize (as Khrushchev had requested) for the violation of Soviet air space and security. The Soviet leader also denounced the American lies about the U-2 plane when its crash was first announced, and he suggested that such untruthful announcements could have been made only with Eisenhower's consent. Khrushchev withdrew his earlier invitation to the President to visit Russia and announced that he would attend no more meetings until Eisenhower apologized for the U-2 incident. Eisenhower refused either to engage in personal recrimination or to apologize, and the conference broke up before it could begin.

Even though Khrushchev soon indicated that he was not prepared to force the Berlin issue, the unfortunate events at Paris were hard blows to hopes for the relaxation of tensions—and also to American prestige in the world. More bad news came in the months ahead. Eisenhower set out upon a visit of good-will to Japan on June 12 and got as far as Manila. The Japanese government felt compelled to ask Eisenhower to cancel the tour after rioting mobs, which prob-ably consisted mainly of Socialists and Communists, seemed to threaten his personal safety if he came to Tokyo. The Soviet delegation walked out of an East-West disarmament conference at Geneva on June 27, 1960, when the American delegates refused to accept a Russian plan. A civil war rocked the newly proclaimed Republic of the Congo in July 1960, as mutinous Congolese troops went on a campaign of rapine and pillage. The dispatch of a UN task force prevented threatened Russian intervention and a serious international crisis, but brought no long-term solution to the new nation's basic problems. Soviet-American tension was intensified when a Russian fighter plane shot down an American reconnaissance plane in the area of the Barents Sea on July 1, 1960. The American government charged deliberate destruction of an air-craft over international waters, while the Russians renewed the charge of spying and said that they would try the six American airmen whom they had captured alive. The pilot of the U-2 plane shot down over Russia was sen-tenced to a ten-year term in August 1960, after a trial in which he confessed to all charges. He was later exchanged for an important Soviet spy held by the United States. The U-2 pilot repeated his confession after his return to Ameri-ca and reported also that he had refused to take the capsule containing deadly poison provided by the air force so that there would be no confession in case of capture.

5. THE ELECTION OF 1960

Candidates and Conventions

It was during the turmoil just described that the parties began to prepare for the presidential campaign of 1960. It soon became evident that the Republi-cans, forced by the Twenty-second Amendment to seek a new leader, would not be torn by violent struggles for the presidential nomination in 1960, as they had been eight years earlier. There were only two serious Republican con-tenders at the outset of the preconvention campaign, Nelson A. Rockefeller and Nixon. Rockefeller, elected Governor of New York in the face of the Dem-ocratic landslide of 1958, represented the progressive elements in the G.O.P. Rockefeller, convinced that he could not win the nomination without splitting his party, withdrew from the race on December 26, 1959. The road was cleared for the Right wing's candidate, Nixon. His triumph was assured when Eisen-hower endorsed his candidacy on March 16, 1960.

Meanwhile, the Democrats had been hard at the game that they seemed to enjoy most—fighting among themselves for the leadership of their party. By the end of January 1960, four candidates openly contended for the nomination, while several others, including Stevenson, would not have refused a call. At first, the contest seemed to lie between Senator Hubert H. Humphrey of Min-nesota, who hoped to rally New Dealers and Fair Dealers, and Senator John F. Kennedy of Massachusetts, a young leader of the eastern, urban wing and the first Roman Catholic to make a serious bid for the presidency since 1928. The

Kennedy forces drew up a well-prepared booklet, complete with statistically sophisticated graphs and charts, which showed that much of Eisenhower's support in the northern industrial states had come from the Catholic voters who had deserted the Democratic party. All party leaders and potential delegates received copies of the booklet. The turning point of the battle came in the presidential primary in West Virginia on May 10. Kennedy polled 60 per cent of the votes in that predominantly Protestant state, and Humphrey withdrew from the race. From this point on, it was a question of whether Lyndon B. Johnson, who was sweeping the South and Southwest, and favorite-son candidates could prevent Kennedy's nomination on the first ballot. It also remained to be seen whether party leaders would risk running a Roman Catholic, despite the potential gain in votes from Catholics.

The questions were quickly answered at the Democratic national convention on July 11. With only token opposition from Southerners, the Democrats adopted the strongest civil rights platform in their history. They proceeded with surprising speed to nominate Kennedy for the presidency on the first ballot. In a move that startled the convention as much as it did the country, Kennedy requested and obtained Johnson's nomination as his running mate.

Republicans gathered in Chicago ten days after the Democrats left Los Angeles. For a moment it seemed that conflict would break out over the platform, for Rockefeller threatened to take the fight to the floor and perhaps be a candidate himself if Nixon did not support his demands for a more progressive platform than had been drafted. Rockefeller had his way, and Nixon was named for the presidency almost unanimously on the first ballot. At Nixon's request, Henry Cabot Lodge, Ambassador to the UN, was drafted for the second place on the Republican ticket. "To your hands," President Eisenhower wrote to the G.O.P.'s new standard-bearer, "I pray that I shall pass the responsibility of the office of the Presidency."

Ordeal by Television

Dramatic events distracted American attention from the presidential candidates during the first weeks of the campaign. The Cuban government grew increasingly hostile to the United States and now turned openly for moral and material assistance to the Soviet Union. Then Khrushchev led a procession of heads of governments—including Castro—to the UN General Assembly that opened on September 20. For several weeks he both appalled and puzzled Americans by his antics, such as taking off his shoe and beating it on his desk in the General Assembly, as a means of protest against the proceedings.

Once it began, the presidential campaign became an exciting affair. Each candidate enjoyed certain advantages at the outset. Nixon benefited from Eisenhower's active support and had the advantage of having been much in the public eye for eight years. Nixon's supporters claimed that his great experience made him the logical man to "stand up" to Khrushchev. Also, a huge amount of anti-Catholic literature was distributed by Nixon supporters, although not by the Nixon campaign organization itself. Many of those who received it seemed responsive, according to pollsters. Kennedy enjoyed the advantage of greater party strength, better organization, personal attractiveness, and an electric personality. Also, Catholics, angered at the campaign against Kennedy's religion, did return in large numbers to the Democratic fold. At the begin-

Senator John F. Kennedy and Vice President Richard M. Nixon as they appeared in the fourth and final television debate in New York City. The 1960 presidential campaign was marked by a series of televised debates during which the candidates were asked questions by newsmen before an estimated audience of 70,000,000 viewers. Self-confident and well-informed, Kennedy was able to cast aside his image of being too young and inexperienced in comparison to Nixon. (Wide World Photos)

ning of the campaign, the Democratic candidate tried, as he had done during the preconvention struggle, to eliminate the religious issue altogether by reaffirming loyalty to the historical American tradition of separation of church and state.

The turning point in the campaign came when the voters had an opportunity to judge the candidates in a series of four television debates between September 26 and October 24. It was the first time that presidential candidates had ever been brought face to face. The two men found it hard to grapple with issues, both for lack of time and because they agreed so much on fundamental principles. Consequently, they often discussed meaningless issues, such as American popularity abroad, or else questions that should never have been discussed in public, such as the defense of the Chinese offshore islands. Even so, Kennedy scored heavily by demolishing the Republican charge that he was inexperienced and badly informed. Moreover, Kennedy succeeded far better than his opponent in giving an impression of boldness, imagination, and poise.

A Long Night for Politicians

No one, not even the pollsters, knew what the result would be on election day, November 8, 1960, since there was a surge in Nixon's strength at the end of the

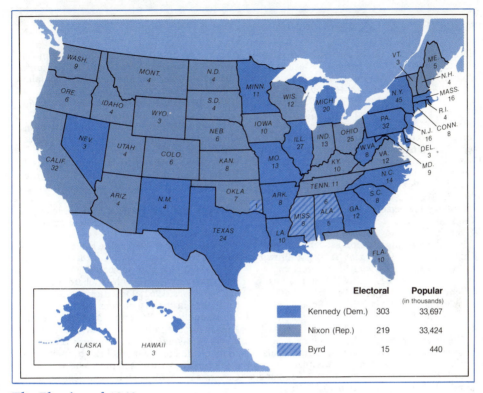

The Election of 1960

campaign. First returns from the eastern states and big cities indicated a Kennedy landslide. Kennedy held his lead in the Northeast and most of the South Atlantic states, but, as election night passed into the morning of the next day, Nixon, who had carried most of the Middle West and West, whittled away at Kennedy's lead in the crucial states of Illinois, California, and Texas. Not since 1916 had a presidential election been so long in doubt. California finally went to Nixon after the absentee ballots were counted, while Illinois and Texas went to Kennedy by 9,801 and 45,264 votes, respectively. All told, of the nearly 68,500,000 popular votes cast, Kennedy won 34,227,000 and Nixon 34,108,000. Kennedy's popular majority of two-tenths of 1 per cent was the smallest in the history of American presidential elections. The vote in the Electoral College was 303 to 219. The Democratic tide in the vote for congressmen and senators receded somewhat in 1960, but the next Congress would have Democratic majorities of sixty-four to thirty-six in the Senate and of 238 to 154 in the House of Representatives.

The election of 1960 had far-reaching meaning, to be sure, but the most significant result that could be read in the returns was the elimination of the religious issue—at least temporarily—as a decisive factor in American presidential politics. This is not to say that Kennedy's Roman Catholicism had not been a disturbing issue to many voters, but other issues probably were more important, and people who voted for and against the Democratic candidate because of his religion probably canceled each other out.

SUGGESTED READINGS

Herbert S. Parmet, *Eisenhower and the American Crusades* (1972); Charles C. Alexander, *Holding the Line: The Eisenhower Era, 1952–1961* (1975); Richard H. Rovere, *Affairs of State: The Eisenhower Years* (1956); and Robert J. Donovan, *Eisenhower, The Inside Story* (1956), are good surveys. The most complete accounts are by Eisenhower himself — *Mandate for Change* (1963) and *Waging Peace* (1965). Sherman Adams, *Firsthand Report* (1961); Lewis L. Strauss, *Man and Decisions* (1962); and Ezra T. Benson, *Cross Fire: The Eight Years with Eisenhower* (1962), are interesting personal accounts, while Emmet J. Hughes, *The Ordeal of Power* (1963), is a revealing discussion of the President and his administration as well. Richard Kluger, *Simple Justice: The History of* Brown v. Board of Education *and Black America's Struggle for Racial Equality* (1975), is an excellent book. On the period's legislation, the most valuable work is James L. Sundquist, *Politics and Policy: The Eisenhower, Kennedy, and Johnson Years* (1968).

The defense policy of the Eisenhower administration has been analyzed in numerous works. The best are Henry A. Kissinger, *Nuclear Weapons and Foreign Policy* (1956), and Samuel P. Huntington, *Changing Patterns of Military Politics* (1962). Conflicting opinions on John Foster Dulles can be found in Emmet J. Hughes, *America the Vincible* (1959); John R. Beal, *John Foster Dulles: A Biography* (1957); Michael A. Hugin, *John Foster Dulles: A Statesman and His Times* (1972); and Townsend Hoopes, *The Devil and John Foster Dulles* (1973). Hugh Thomas, *The Suez Affair* (1967), is a good account of that crisis. For the problem of the underdeveloped nations, see Barbara Ward, *The Rich Nations and the Poor Nations* (1962).

Most of the works cited in the Suggested Readings for Chapters 33 and 35 are relevant to the domestic issues of the Eisenhower administration.

The election of 1960 is the subject of Theodore H. White, *The Making of the President 1960* (1961). A highly subjective analysis of that campaign is offered by Richard M. Nixon, *Six Crises* (1962). Other important political figures in the Eisenhower Administration can be studied in Patterson, *Mr. Republican,* already cited, and John W. Anderson, *Eisenhower, Brownell and the Congress* (1965), a study of the President and his Attorney General's relations with each other and with Congress concerning civil rights legislation.

CHAPTER 36
NEW FRONTIERS, THE GREAT SOCIETY, AND THE VIETNAM WAR

1. THE KENNEDY ERA BEGINS

New Frontiers

It snowed heavily in Washington on January 19, 1961, and the following morning dawned clear and bitterly cold. But Democrats were rejoicing too warmly to mind the biting western wind. They had controlled both houses of Congress since 1955; on January 20, they would take possession of the White House as well. The world was about to witness democracy's most impressive drama — the peaceful transfer of control of the presidency of the United States from one person to another of a different party. Perhaps the country soon would see movement, too, toward the New Frontiers about which the successful candidate had talked so much during the campaign.

The inaugural procession moved slowly from the White House down a Pennsylvania Avenue that had been swept bare of snow. The presidential party, led by the tall, handsome forty-three-year-old President-elect and his beautiful, fashionably dressed, thirty-one-year-old wife Jacqueline, walked briskly to the stands at the east front of the Capitol and faced the assembled throng. After the usual rituals, Chief Justice Warren administered the oath of office. The United States had a new and vigorous President; the western world, perhaps a new leader.

Tens of millions of Americans watched as John Fitzgerald Kennedy began his inaugural address. He began by reminding his fellow countrymen that they were heirs to the first successful constructive revolution in history. "Let the word go forth from this time and place, to friend and foe alike," he continued, "that the torch has been passed to a new generation of Americans." He called for a "grand and global alliance" against "the common enemies of man: tyranny, poverty, disease, and war itself"; he also pledged strong support to the United Nations and generous assistance to underdeveloped countries. He concluded:

In your hands, my fellow citizens, more than mine, will rest the final success or failure of our course. . . . In the long history of the world, only a few generations have been granted the role of defending freedom in its hour of maximum danger. . . . The energy, the faith, the devotion which we bring to this endeavor will light our country and all who serve it—and the glow from that fire can truly light the world. And so, my fellow Americans: ask not what your country can do for you—ask what you can do for your country.

The New President

John F. Kennedy was born in Brookline, Massachusetts, on May 29, 1917, into a large Irish-American, Roman Catholic family. His grandfathers on both sides had been prominent in Irish Democratic politics in Boston. Kennedy's maternal grandfather, John Francis "Honey Fitz" Fitzgerald, was a legendary former Mayor of Boston and a long-time "friendly" contender against James M. Curley for leadership of the Boston Democratic party. John F. Kennedy's father, Joseph P. Kennedy, had made a large fortune in business and finance and had served as Ambassador to Great Britain from 1937 to 1940. Young John F. Kennedy was graduated with honors from Harvard in 1940. After distinguished war service, he entered politics and was elected to the House of Representatives in 1946 and to the Senate in 1952 and 1958. His opportunity for success in representing, first, an Irish-American congressional district, and, then, the State of Massachusetts, owed more to sentimental recollections of "Honey Fitz," which helped him gain access to voters in their homes, and to local civic and church groups, than to his father's money or political connections. John F. Kennedy owed most, however, to a group of Irish-American veterans of the Second World War whom he gathered around him as advisers and trusted aides. Kennedy ran unsuccessfully for the Democratic vice-presidential nomination in 1956. No sooner had he failed in this bid than he began an unrelenting campaign for the presidential nomination in 1960.

It was obvious, well before the campaign of 1960 was over, that a new star had risen on the American political horizon. Kennedy was not only the youngest man ever elected to the presidency, but he was also one of the most fascinating. With reporters, he was relaxed, candid, and witty. To the people at large, he gave the impression of youthful vigor infused with intelligence.

To young Americans, especially, Kennedy seemed to promise a new quality of leadership. "Style" was the word most frequently used to describe the difference between Kennedy and the preceding generation of Presidents and presidential candidates. The new national leader possessed a sharp wit that effectively exposed the foibles of established institutions and politicians. He seemed imaginative and unconventional enough to be open to new ideas and to try new approaches. His presence in the White House gave hope to youthful citizens (who included some of the more rebellious ones) that they might still

This photograph was taken following President-elect John F. Kennedy's announcement that his brother Robert, who had served as his campaign manager, was to be Attorney General in his cabinet. In an early effort to unite the nation, John Kennedy urged: "I call upon you to join us in a journey to the new frontier. The voyage is a long and hazardous one, but we are all partners in a great and historic journey." (United Press International)

identify with their government and respect their country. This idealization of Kennedy was widespread enough for some to refer to it as a cult.

Kennedy was also a very human person, with weaknesses as well as strengths. Inexperience in the conduct of foreign affairs caused him to make costly blunders. His most striking weakness was his inability to establish his leadership of Congress in legislative policies. Circumstances over which he had no control were in part responsible. The acclaim that greeted his inaugural address gave the appearance of an overwhelming support for the new administration that did not exist. The Eighty-seventh Congress, which sat in 1961 and 1962, was at superficial glance solidly Democratic. However, Kennedy never had a reliable, working majority because many southern Democrats broke ranks to vote with Republicans on crucial bills. Kennedy and his aides never quite trusted Vice-President Johnson sufficiently to make good use of Johnson's remarkable skills at winning votes for legislation from reluctant southern representatives.

In addition, Kennedy suffered the consequences both of his own political philosophy and of his own political past. Despite the somewhat misleading rhetoric of his inaugural address, he believed that the day of passionate commitment to causes was over. The United States, he thought, had reached a solid consensus on domestic policies. Therefore, his chief role as President was to use the resources of the political and intellectual communities to work out the details of legislation, not to lead a new reform movement. Moreover, as a representative and senator, Kennedy had never won the respect of his colleagues or been a member of the inner congressional circle because he was something of a dilettante and obviously ambitious for higher office. As President, he demonstrated a striking inability to use the techniques and powers that a President must master in order to lead the men and women on Capitol Hill. He proposed legislation but allowed Congress to go its own way, without sufficient pressure from the White House or strong efforts on his part to rally public opinion. Kennedy was not a strong domestic leader, finally, because he was preoccupied with foreign affairs. With the exception of a few programs, he seemed to lack an intense interest in domestic policies.

Furthermore, Kennedy accepted most of the premises on which American foreign policy in the Cold War were based. If anything, he seemed more attached to aggressive anti-Communism than Eisenhower, whose war experiences had led him to suspect the value of violent solutions and to fear another major war. Kennedy was entranced, especially, by the possibilities of war conducted quietly by expertly trained special units. He seemed particularly enthusiastic about the role of the Green Beret troops, a crack antiguerrilla force.

It is only fair to add that this evaluation is based upon Kennedy's brief tenure as President. He served only his apprenticeship in the White House. Kennedy was giving evidence of greater wisdom in foreign affairs and firmer mastery of domestic politics before his untimely death in 1963. We will never know whether he would have fulfilled the promise that he did begin to show.

Slow Progress toward New Frontiers

Kennedy outlined his domestic program in a State of the Union address on January 30, 1961, and in additional later messages and speeches. He spoke boldly and called for measures to "get the country moving again," but he soon discovered that unexpected circumstances have a way of defeating even the best-laid plans. Perhaps his most ironical defeat was the failure of his ambitious federal aid-to-education bill. Kennedy, on February 20, 1961, proposed to spend more than $5.6 billion to enrich and equalize educational opportunities. The states would receive about $2.3 billion over a three-year period for public-school construction and teachers' salaries. The rest of the money would go to colleges and universities for scholarships to needy undergraduates over a five-year period. The bill passed the Senate easily enough. Then Roman Catholic bishops and leaders insisted that the measure be amended to provide aid to parochial schools. Kennedy would not yield, because he thought that their proposal was unconstitutional; and enough Roman Catholic Democratic congressmen joined the bipartisan conservative opposition to defeat the administration's bill in the House of Representatives. The measure met a similar fate when Kennedy sent it back to Congress in 1962. Moreover, a new bill to aid higher education also ran aground on the shoals of religious controversy in 1962.

Opposition arose to other administration measures. An ambitious plan called Medicare—to provide medical care for the aged through the Social Security system—did not even receive serious consideration because of violent opposition from the American Medical Association. A new Food and Agriculture Act to regulate production of wheat was adopted in 1962 after much hard work on Capitol Hill. Then the measure was rejected by wheat farmers themselves in a referendum in 1963.

But the new President was not always disappointed during his first two years in office. The Housing Act of 1961 was a major administration victory. It authorized the expenditure of $4.9 billion over a four-year period for local urban renewal projects. It also included a provision for college dormitory construction and liberalized terms for home mortgages. Under Kennedy's prodding, the Democrats also honored their campaign promise to increase the minimum wage. A law that went into effect on September 3, 1961, raised the minimum from $1 to $1.25 an hour and extended protection of the Fair Labor Standards Act to an additional 3,624,000 workers. An Area Redevelopment Act, approved May 1, 1961, provided $300 million in loans and grants for new industries and the retraining of workers in some 675 "distressed areas" of high unemployment. This was supplemented in 1962 by a Manpower Development and Training Act to help workers threatened by automation. Amendments to the Drug Act, adopted in 1962, imposed new controls upon the manufacture and sale of drugs. However, the administration could probably have obtained a stronger bill pushed by Senator Kefauver if it had fought for it. The Twenty-fourth Amendment, which outlawed the poll tax as a requirement for voting for federal officials, was approved by Congress in 1962 and ratified in January 1964.

The Eighty-seventh Congress did not disagree with Kennedy about maintaining powerful defenses against possible aggression abroad. Congress appropriated nearly $47 billion in 1961 and more than $48 billion in 1962 for defense. It also authorized the President to call 250,000 reserves into active service for a year. All leaders in Washington continued to push the missile program because it seemed to offer the best hope of enabling the United States to deter a war against the country. Americans could feel reasonably secure by the end of 1961 — and even more secure by 1965 — for the first time since Sputnik I sailed across the sky. The missile gap with Russia had been closed — if, indeed, it had ever existed. The United States owned a fleet of nuclear submarines (twenty-nine of them by 1965) armed with Polaris nuclear missiles. The United States also had an arsenal of Atlas intercontinental missiles in position, and (by 1965) more than 500 new solid-fuel Minuteman missiles in underground "silos." Altogether, it constituted an awesome array of power.

Kennedy also met enthusiastic response from Congress when he recommended a vast expansion of the space program begun by the Eisenhower administration. Congress applauded and appropriated generously when Kennedy, on May 25, 1961, requested approval of a program aimed at putting a task force on the moon by 1970. Progress in space flight continued uninterrupted from 1961 onward. The Gemini series of flights in orbit around the earth was completed in 1966 with the successful docking of one manned Gemini capsule with another, an unmanned capsule floating in space. In addition, NASA by 1967 had successfully photographed the moon by cameras landed on the moon's surface, and by others in a lunar satellite. The space agency also launched successfully the gigantic Saturn rocket that was scheduled to carry the first Americans to the moon and back. In July 1969, Neil Armstrong and Edwin Aldrin made a historic landing on the moon, which was witnessed by television viewers around the world. To mark their flight, Armstrong and Aldrin, the first humans to walk on the lunar surface, planted an American flag and left a plaque that read: "We came in peace for all mankind." After they had collected rock samples and performed experiments on the moon, the astronauts rejoined the mother ship, piloted by Michael Collins, and returned safely to earth.

On Dead Center

The country seemed to be on political dead center again by the summer of 1962. Congress was deadlocked on important domestic issues, much as it had been since the Truman administration. To be sure, events created excitement and some alarm on other fronts. Under strong pressure from Kennedy and Secretary of Labor Arthur J. Goldberg, the steel companies and the United Steel Workers concluded a new contract on March 31, 1962, which provided modest wage increases. Most of the nation applauded the administration's victory in holding the line against inflation. Then, on April 10, the president of United States Steel Corporation announced an increase of $6 a ton in the price of steel, and other companies followed suit. Kennedy was furious. He denounced the action in scathing words and moved to prosecute the steel companies for illegal price fixing. They retreated at once, but the incident and the vehemence of Kennedy's attack badly shook the confidence of the business community. On May 28, 1962, the stock market suffered its sharpest decline since the great crash of 1929.

The administration faced its first test of public confidence in the mid-term election of 1962. Kennedy campaigned hard for Democratic candidates, and it seemed that the Democrats would hold their own or else suffer only minor losses, for the stock market had recovered and most of the nation's population enjoyed unprecedented prosperity — rising wages, salaries, and business profits with a low rate of price inflation. Then the missile crisis with Russia exploded in late October (see pp. 937 – 938) and caused a general disposition to stand by the President. This, probably, contributed most to the Democrats' success in increasing their majorities in both houses of Congress.

Prelude to the Civil Rights Revolution

The Eighty-eighth Congress, which sat in 1963 and 1964, was politically top-heavy, with sixty-seven Democrats and thirty-three Republicans in the Senate and 258 Democrats and 176 Republicans in the House of Representatives. Still Kennedy could not find a majority to carry through his program.

It is clear in retrospect that Congress was fiddling while the country burned. Americans, or at least a majority of thoughtful people outside the South, were aroused by the brutal police suppression, in April and May 1963, of black civil rights demonstrations led in Birmingham by the Rev. Martin Luther King, Jr., and, in September, by the bombing of churches and the murder of black children in that same city. Blacks and whites alike joined in sympathetic demonstrations across the country to protest against segregation in housing and public accommodations. Demonstrations sometimes went beyond the bounds of law and order, and police authorities resorted to fire hoses, tear gas, clubs, and dogs. Some 758 demonstrations occurred between early May and the mid-summer of 1963, as blacks and their white supporters pressed to destroy the

A fifty-foot cross blazes against the sky at a rally of the Ku Klux Klan in Tuscaloosa, Alabama, in June 1963. The meeting was held outside this college city where two blacks were scheduled to enroll in the University of Alabama, an event which Governor George Wallace vowed he would try to prevent. The inverted cross image in the photograph is an optical reflection in the camera lens. (United Press International)

last vestiges of Jim Crowism on this, the one hundredth, anniversary of the Emancipation Proclamation. It seemed that a terrible showdown between whites and blacks in the South might be brewing.

Kennedy, heretofore, had shown no great zeal for bold new civil rights legislation. He had used troops to suppress a bloody riot in Oxford, Mississippi, in September 1962, when a federal court had compelled the admission of a black student by the University of Mississippi. He dispatched troops again to force the admission of blacks by the University of Alabama. In addition, Kennedy sent a mild civil rights bill to Congress in February 1963. But, despite increasing criticism from black leaders, he did not press the measure for fear of imperiling southern support in Congress for other New Frontier bills.

Kennedy finally was galvanized into action by the Birmingham disorders and the demonstrations that followed. Kennedy spoke to the nation by television on June 11, 1963. Eight days later he sent a strong new civil rights bill to Congress with the warning that continued federal inaction would cause leadership on both sides to pass "to the purveyors of hate and violence." The response throughout the country was electric. Protestant, Catholic, and Jewish leaders joined hands with civil rights groups and the AFL-CIO in a campaign to stimulate pressure at the grass roots on Congress. On August 28, more than 200,000 blacks and whites gathered before the Lincoln Memorial in Washington in a peaceful demonstration for the civil rights bill. There was some floundering and partisan wrangling on Capitol Hill in the late summer and early autumn of 1963, but the President and his brother, Attorney General Robert F. Kennedy, hammered out a revised bill with leaders of both parties in the House of Representatives in October; the new measure was then put on its way.

2. THE COLD WAR CONTINUES

The Same Frontiers Abroad

The style of American diplomacy changed somewhat after the succession in 1961. The new Secretary of State, Dean Rusk, gave the appearance of greater ability and assurance than his immediate predecessor, Christian A. Herter, and of greater caution than John Foster Dulles. Kennedy, too, seemed to be more vigorous and more of a natural diplomat than Eisenhower. However, events soon demonstrated that things are not always as they seem. Moreover, the substance of foreign policy did not change under the new administration; the foreign policies of the early 1960s were marked by an almost complete continuity with the policies of the 1950s. Actually, except for differences in age and Dulles' experience between the world wars, Dulles, Rusk, and Acheson were practically interchangeable in terms of ideas, values, affiliations other than political party, and goals of their foreign policies.

One fact, surely, had not yet changed: the seemingly unending global struggle between Russia and the United States for the loyalty of the uncommitted majority of the world and for predominance along the perimeters of the two great powers. Kennedy soon decided that the Russian Premier, Khrushchev, did not intend to change course simply because a new President had come to power. Khrushchev, for his part, soon found that the relatively young American relished leading the non-Communist nations in their Cold War course as much or more than had any of his predecessors.

Trouble broke out in Laos during the early months of the new administration, but, it turned out, for the time at least, not to be serious. The European area in greatest peril was still Germany, and, in Asia, Vietnam. Khrushchev's main target in Germany remained West Berlin, where the United States, Britain, and France continued to maintain a precarious position. Kennedy, in order to explore any possibility that the Russian leader might be willing to moderate his continued threats against Berlin, flew to Vienna for a meeting with the Soviet Premier in June 1961. It was not a summit meeting; the two men were simply taking each other's measure. We can only guess what Khrushchev thought of the young American. We know, however, that Kennedy was shocked by Khrushchev's belligerence and threats against Allied rights in Berlin. Conferences with President Charles de Gaulle in Paris and Prime Minister Harold Macmillan in London strengthened Kennedy's determination to stand and fight for Berlin if necessary, although Khrushchev had yet to show evidence that he thought that the issue merited actual warfare. Kennedy announced this decision to the world in a television address on June 28. A month later, he again went before the people to say that he was asking Congress for an additional $3.25 billion for immediate increases in the armed forces, especially to meet the Soviet challenge to Berlin.

Berlin, called by John Kennedy "the great testing place of Western courage and will," was divided by the East German government on August 13, 1961. Concrete block and barbed wire barriers often divide streets in the middle and prevent any contact between life-long neighbors. People living on the Communist side (at right) are forbidden to talk to anyone on the West, but some still communicate through signals. (Wide World Photos)

There could be no doubt now what the United States would do, and Khrushchev announced that he was willing to negotiate to see if a settlement of the Berlin question was possible. Meanwhile, to prevent the escape of thousands of East Germans to the West, the Communists, in August 1961, walled off their part of Berlin. Conversations between the American and Russian governments proceeded while American and Russian troops faced each other across this barrier. These conversations failed, as earlier ones had, and West Berlin continued to be a powder keg. However, after 1961 the Communists did not again seriously endanger the western position, and the powder keg, at least for a time, was without a fuse.

Fiasco at the Bay of Pigs

The hardest blow to American prestige and the gravest threat to world peace during the early 1960s occurred not in Europe, but in the Caribbean, where it was least expected. After the triumph of Fidel Castro and his revolutionary movement in Cuba, Castro's defiance of treaty obligations, confiscation of American property, and agreements with the Soviet Union strained Cuban-American relations to the breaking point during the last two months of the

Eisenhower administration. It was obvious by the end of 1960 that a Soviet ally existed ninety miles off American shores.

Eisenhower, in September 1960, approved a plan to dislodge Castro proposed by Allen W. Dulles, director of the C.I.A. and brother of John Foster Dulles. The plan involved the supply of arms and money to equip and train a force of anti-Castro Cubans in Guatemala. They would invade Cuba, establish a stronghold there, rally the mass of supposedly disaffected Cubans to their banner, and then sweep through the country to Havana. American planes would protect the landing force.

Preparations went forward during late 1960 and early 1961. Kennedy relied on the advice of his intelligence and military specialists and gave his approval for the invasion in early April 1961, but he would not agree to United States air cover for the invaders. Some 1,400 armed Cuban refugees left for their homeland on April 17. Castro's forces easily destroyed and captured the little army as it became bogged down in the marshes of the Bay of Pigs on the southern coast of Cuba.

For the United States, the ill-planned, ill-timed, and futile project was more than a fiasco. Khrushchev, on April 18, threatened to go to Cuba's assistance if the United States did not "call a halt to the aggression against the Republic of Cuba." Kennedy replied in a public address on April 20; he warned that the United States did not intend to permit the Russians to establish a military foothold in Cuba or elsewhere in Latin America.

New Confidence and New Horizons

The Cuban fiasco had unnerved the young President and his administration, and a pall of gloom hung over Washington. Then confidence slowly returned. However, Kennedy's conference with Khrushchev in Vienna made it clear that there were no quick and easy solutions to conflicts between the United States and the Soviet Union, and that the struggle with Russia might be prolonged and dangerous.

Kennedy's main reply to the Soviet challenges consisted of a foreign-aid program to help peoples in underdeveloped countries, particularly in Latin America. Overpopulation, underindustrialization, and poverty were acute in the Latin American countries, which had been much neglected by Truman and Eisenhower. Congress followed Kennedy's lead by approving a five-year Development Loan Fund of $7.2 billion. Next, on August 16, 1961, the United States worked through an Inter-American Conference at Punta del Este, Uruguay, and launched the Alliance for Progress. This program looked forward to the extension of some $20 billion in United States economic aid of various kinds over a ten-year period. The administration hoped that this aid would improve the relations of the United States with politically unaligned countries and would prop up the governments of these nations against radical revolutions, such as that which had occurred in Cuba. Unfortunately, many of the governments to which the United States sent this aid were repressive dictatorships unpopular with their populations as a whole, and some were so corrupt that little American aid reached poor sectors of the population.

Meanwhile, other signs indicated that the United States was seizing the initiative in its foreign policy. Soviet prestige suffered in some respects when the Russians resumed atmospheric testing of large nuclear bombs in the summer of 1961. People in other nations worried about the consequent increase in ra-

A Peace Corps volunteer from Ohio administers vitamins to an infant in Togo. The Peace Corps, the most successful and least expensive of Kennedy's foreign aid programs, trained and sent thousands of volunteers, mostly young people, to work in underdeveloped areas. (Wide World Photos)

dioactivity in their atmosphere. But they worried about offending the possessor of such bombs also. One of Kennedy's answers was the creation of the Peace Corps to train thousands of young Americans for voluntary educational, medical, and technical services to people in underdeveloped countries. The immediate, enthusiastic response of young people showed that idealism remained very much alive on American college and university campuses. The Peace Corps, aided by an obvious increase in idealism on American campuses, had become well established by the mid-sixties. Kennedy replied to the Soviet show of military might also by asking for and receiving from Congress higher appropriations than Eisenhower had requested for both nuclear and conventional armaments.

Duel at the Brink

All during the summer and autumn of 1962, the American government became increasingly alarmed at the buildup of Soviet arms in Cuba. Congress, in a joint resolution signed by Kennedy on October 3, warned that the United States was "determined to prevent by whatever means may be necessary, including the use of arms, the Marxist-Leninist regime in Cuba from . . . creation or use of an externally supported military capability endangering the security of the United States."

This warning went unheeded in Moscow and Havana. Aerial reconnaissance revealed to Kennedy unmistakable proof that the Russians were installing sites in Cuba for missiles capable of hitting nations in the western hemisphere, even targets in the United States. The Russian Ambassador, summoned to the White House, denied that missile sites were being built in Cuba. Kennedy and his advisers then decided to force a showdown at the risk of war. To some extent, at least, this decision was based on domestic politics. The young President could hardly afford another humiliation comparable to the fiasco of the Bay of Pigs. Kennedy announced his decision to the world in a dramatic television address on October 22, 1962. He denounced "this secret, swift, and extraordinary buildup of Communist missiles" and said that he had already ordered the United States Navy to begin "a strict quarantine on all offensive military equipment under shipment to Cuba," in other words, a blockade against Russian ships which carried such equipment. Kennedy also said that he was calling an immediate meeting of the Organization of American States to rally Americans to self-defense under the Rio de Janeiro Treaty of 1947. Furthermore, he announced that he was requesting an emergency meeting of the UN Security Council to consider a resolution to demand prompt dismantling and removal, under UN supervision, of all offensive weapons in Cuba. "It shall be the policy of this nation," Kennedy went on, "to regard any nuclear missile launched from Cuba against any nation in the Western Hemisphere as an attack by the Soviet Union on the United States requiring a full retaliatory response upon the Soviet Union." What was more, "Any hostile move anywhere in the world against the safety or freedom of peoples to whom we are committed — including in particular the brave people of West Berlin — will be met by whatever action is needed."

American naval vessels then began the sensitive and potentially dangerous task of turning back Soviet ships approaching Cuba. Khrushchev, who undoubtedly realized that he had overreached himself, responded promptly in a conciliatory tone. This led to an exchange between the President and the Premier; Khrushchev promised to dismantle and remove the offensive missiles (which he did), and Kennedy promised to launch no attack against Cuba. The bargain salvaged some Russian prestige and the peace of the world. However, it led also to vast increases in Soviet expenditures for naval vessels and nuclear missiles in an effort to prevent American threats from forcing the USSR to back down under superior force in the future. Thus Kennedy's rather arrogant actions, meant partly to salvage his reputation from the defeat at the Bay of Pigs, increased the possibilities of war in the future. The successful blockade of Cuba, by stimulating Soviet arms expenditures, also intensified the arms race between the two superpowers.

The Weakening of the Great Alliances

The Cuban missile crisis and subsequent increased armament expenditures revealed that the two superpowers soon would be tied in a nuclear deadlock.

Neither would be able to inflict serious injury on the other without suffering nearly mortal damage in return. Each, therefore, had to refrain from threatening the other's sphere of vital interest. This condition seemed likely to prevail — and control diplomacy — for decades to come. The approaching nuclear standoff also had immediate consequences.

For one thing, the coming stalemate, along with rapid economic progress throughout Europe, gave much greater diplomatic confidence and freedom to the smaller powers within the two alliance systems than they had known since the end of the Second World War. Fear of Russian attack had drawn the western powers into close alliance in NATO in 1949. Fear of German resurgence had kept eastern Europe dependent upon Russia. The waning of these fears inevitably encouraged nations hitherto under the shadow of the superpowers to assert independent policies.

Few persons in Washington read these signs correctly in 1961 and 1962. On the contrary, the Kennedy administration was working at this very time on what was called a Grand Design to draw the western community into closer association. Kennedy revealed the plan in his Annual Message of January 11, 1962. The United States, he declared, should join in economic partnership with the European Common Market by mutual slashing of tariffs.

The Common Market, established in 1957 by France, Germany, Italy, and the Benelux countries, had been working toward a customs union and had already stimulated the rapid economic growth of its members. Congress did its part at once by approving the Trade Expansion Act in October 1962. This measure permitted the President to reduce tariffs generally by 50 per cent, and to remove tariffs altogether on articles heavily traded by the United States and western Europe. The latter provision depended upon the entry of Great Britain into the Common Market.

However, President De Gaulle interpreted the Grand Design as a plan to fasten Anglo-American control on western Europe. He vetoed Britain's application for membership in the Common Market in January 1963. De Gaulle hoped to create a new power bloc — a Third Force — under French leadership; thus he proceeded to build his own nuclear weapons and strike force and greatly reduced French participation in NATO. The result was considerable disarray in the western alliance in 1963. Kennedy, who sought to prevent any widening of the breach, offered to give Polaris missiles to France and proposed to create a NATO naval force with nuclear weapons. De Gaulle would not accept the Polaris missiles and rejected the plan for a NATO naval force. This was because final control over use of the nuclear weapons involved would remain in the hands of the President of the United States. Great Britain did not like the plan for a NATO naval force, either; it feared that it was the first step toward putting nuclear weapons in German hands.

At the same time that NATO was coming apart at the seams, a similar loosening of bonds proceeded apace within the Communist world. Eastern European nations, particularly Poland and Rumania, were no longer content to be hewers of wood and drawers of water for Russia. Following Yugoslavia's earlier example, they struck out on their own projects of internal development and began to show diplomatic independence. But the great rupture in the Communist world took place between the Soviet Union and China. The proud leaders of China finally tired of acknowledging the Soviet Union's status as the dominant center of Communism. Therefore they ended their dependence on Soviet arms, machinery, and replacement parts, and thereby on Soviet political ideological orders. A series of subsequent quarrels led to the abrupt withdrawal of all Russian advisers from China in 1960. During the next two years, the two powers glowered at each other along their long common border. Russia supported India when China attacked that country in 1962. The Chinese Communists accused Russia of being a "paper tiger" after Khrushchev's retreat in the missiles crisis. Khrushchev, in return, accused the Chinese leaders of reckless insistence that the world could be communized by war. Beginning in the late 1960s, reports reached the West of sporadic fighting along the Chinese-Russian border. During 1969, China and the Soviet Union shifted large military forces to the frontier areas, and Chinese newspapers and posters warned of possible war with their former ally.

Beginnings of a Russian-American Détente

Tension between the United States and Russia lessened as their respective alliance systems were weakening. The leaders of both superpowers seemed to acquire a new respect for each other during the missiles crisis. They now realized that coexistence was the only alternative to mutual annihilation.

   The first sign of what diplomats call a détente, or relaxation of tension, came in 1963. Kennedy appealed to Khrushchev for a ban on all nuclear testing in the atmosphere and outer space and under water. After months of negotiation, such a treaty was signed; it was approved by the Senate on September 24, 1963, by a vote of eighty to nineteen. But neither France, which recently had exploded her own atomic bomb, nor China, which would detonate one in 1964, agreed to join the more than 100 nations that signed the treaty.

   By the autumn of 1963, a dark cloud on the American diplomatic horizon appeared in the form of a resumption of the mostly Communist-led revolution in South Vietnam. The United States had given massive economic assistance to the government of that rump republic since Vietnam's partition after Ho Chi Minh's nationalist rebels had defeated the French in 1954. Sporadic attacks by a South Vietnamese nationalist and largely Communist force, the National Liberation Front (NLF),* supported by Ho Chi Minh's Communist government in North Vietnam, began to burgeon into a full-scale civil war by 1961. This occurred despite the announcement by the South Vietnamese dictator, Ngo Dinh Diem, that his "political reeducation" program aimed at the rebels had "entirely destroyed the predominant Communist influence." Diem had at his disposal also a law which permitted the arrest of any person deemed to be dangerous to the state, suspension of habeas corpus, and a nationwide system of prison camps. The American government sent thousands of military personnel allegedly to train the South Vietnamese army. By the autumn of 1963, some 16,000 American military "advisers" served in South Vietnam. They also flew airplanes for South Vietnamese forces, helped to supply troops in the field, and led some of these troops in action. However, the domestic political situation in South Vietnam could best be described as chaotic, and the war against the National Liberation Front made little progress. Sooner or later, and probably sooner, Kennedy would be forced either to withdraw or else greatly to increase

---

*Called the Viet Cong by the South Vietnamese dictatorship and then by the Americans to imply that all NLF members were Communists.

American commitments to the beleaguered Asian nation. His friends claimed later that he planned to withdraw American forces altogether from Vietnam after his reelection in 1964. These reports may or may not be true; in any event, while he lived, Kennedy continued to build up American forces in South Vietnam.

The Death of President Kennedy

Relaxation of international tensions during the summer and early autumn of 1963 freed Kennedy to repair some badly broken political fences at home. He needed to build popular support for items in his unfulfilled program, such as the civil rights bill, a tax cut to stimulate the economy, Medicare, and federal aid to education. To do this, he embarked upon a speaking tour in mid-November, traveling first to Florida, then to Texas. The crowds were large and enthusiastic everywhere that he went. Nowhere were they more friendly than in Dallas, where he arrived just before noon on November 22, 1963.

The presidential entourage, which included Mrs. Kennedy, Vice-President

Lyndon B. Johnson is being sworn in as President by Judge Sarah T. Hughes on November 22, 1963, aboard the presidential airplane at Dallas, Texas, with Mrs. Johnson and Mrs. Kennedy at his side. He returned to Washington and expressed his intention to follow the whole agenda of the New Frontier with the theme "let us continue." (Wide World Photos)

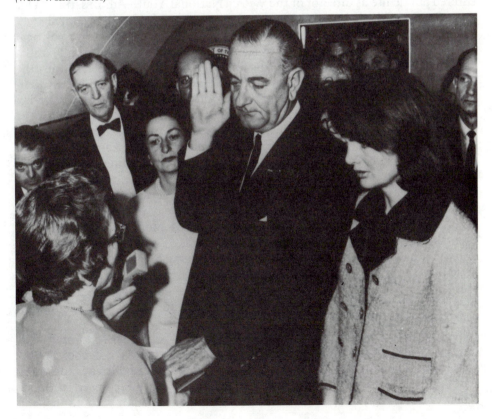

and Mrs. Johnson, and Governor and Mrs. John B. Connally of Texas, passed through cheering throngs on its way to the Trade Mart, where Kennedy was to deliver a luncheon address. Just as the presidential car turned into an expressway, bullets from a high-powered rifle ripped through Kennedy's body and seriously wounded Connally. Kennedy died before his car reached a hospital. His death is recorded officially as having occurred at 1 P.M., November 22, 1963. The assassin apparently was Lee Harvey Oswald, a neurotic, solitary miscreant bent upon wreaking vengeance on his country. Oswald was murdered in front of a television camera on November 24 by a Dallas nightclub owner.

John F. Kennedy was the fourth American President to die at the hands of an assassin. No single tragedy in American history, except perhaps the death of Lincoln, had ever caused such national trauma. Most Americans seemed genuinely shocked that a person so young and vital should have been struck down, and the entire nation and much of the world shared the feeling of bereavement and loss.

3. A NEW PRESIDENT MOVES TOWARD THE GREAT SOCIETY

The New President

Lyndon Baines Johnson, who took the presidential oath in Dallas soon after Kennedy's death, was born near Stonewall, Texas, on August 27, 1908. Johnson entered public life as director of the WPA's National Youth Administration for Texas in 1935. Elected to Congress in 1937, he served in the House until 1949 and in the Senate from 1949 to 1960. So formidable were Johnson's political talents that he was elected minority leader of the Senate in 1953, while still a freshman senator, and majority leader in 1955. He made a strong bid for the Democratic presidential nomination in 1960, only to be engulfed by the Kennedy tidal wave. Kennedy asked Johnson to be his running mate in part because the Texan's support was essential to party harmony and victory in the South and Southwest. Johnson accepted because he wanted to be a national, not merely a sectional, leader. Certain labor and liberal spokesmen objected, but the offer had been made and accepted, and Johnson became the vice-presidential nominee.

Few men outside of Congress really knew what the new President was like when he took the oath of office on that sad autumn day in 1963, but he would reveal his driving personality and political philosophy under the stress of events in the years ahead. Politically, Johnson was a New Dealer: Franklin D. Roosevelt had been the idol and mentor of his young manhood. This heritage, in addition to his own experience of growing up a poor boy in the Great Depression, imbued in Johnson a sympathy for the downtrodden and dispossessed. It gave him the strong conviction that governmental power should be used to improve the human condition.

Johnson also was a master manipulator of other politicians. No man ever came to the presidency with greater knowledge of Congress or deeper experience in managing it. In addition, he strongly believed that politics is the art of the possible. He usually had the uncanny ability to find and represent the consensus. He willingly accepted half a loaf if he could not obtain a whole one, and

THE MEXICAN-AMERICAN EXPERIENCE
by Ricardo Romo

This is the beginning of a social movement in fact and not in pronouncement. We seek our basic, God-given rights as human beings. . . . We are ready to give up everything—even our lives— in our struggle for social justice. . . .

Our wages and working conditions have been determined from above, because irresponsible legislators who could have helped us have supported the argument that the plight of the farm workers was a "special case." They saw the obvious effects of an unjust system, starvation wages, contractors, day-hauls, forced migration, sickness, illiteracy, filthy labor camps, and sub-human living conditions, and acted as if they were irremediable. . . .

Now we will suffer for the purpose of ending the poverty, the misery, and the injustice, with the hope that our children will not be exploited as we have been.

From Cesar Chavez, "The Plan of Delano," United Farmworkers of America.

Cesar Chavez, the charismatic farmworker organizer and human rights activist, delivers a speech at a rally. (United Farm Workers of America. Photograph by Cathy Murphy.)

One of Carl Nebel's most famous lithographs, "Scott's Entrance into Mexico." President James K. Polk directed General Winfield Scott to capture the Mexican capital by an amphibious operation. Six months after landing his troops at Vera Cruz, Scott marched into Mexico City. The Mexican American War had come to an end. (Courtesy Amon Carter Museum, Fort Worth, Texas)

In 1836 the Mexican forces led by Mexican President Santa Ana battled with the Anglo-Texans under the leadership of Sam Houston. Defeated in this confrontation, Santa Ana signed away the Texas Territory to the Anglo-Texans. Here the fighting is portrayed in a painting done in 1898 by H. A. McArdle entitled "The Battle of San Jacinto." (Photo by Alan Pogue, Austin, Texas)

The cession to the United States by Mexico of the Provinces of New Mexico and the Californias . . . would be more in accordance with the convenience and interests of both nations than any other cession of territory which it was probable Mexico could be induced to make. . . . The Bay of San Francisco and other harbors along the California coast would afford shelter for our Navy, for our numerous whale ships, and other merchant vessels employed in the Pacific Ocean, and would in a short period become the marts of an extensive and profitable commerce with China and other countries of the East.[25]

From an address by President James K. Polk, December 7, 1847, as quoted in Glenn W. Price, Origins of the War with Mexico, *University of Texas Press, 1976, p. 91.*

We can easily defeat the armies of Mexico, slaughter them by the thousands, and pursue them perhaps to their capital; we can conquer and "annex" their territory; but what then? Have the histories of the ruin of Greek and Roman liberty consequent on such extensions of empire by the sword no lesson for us? Who believes that a score of victories over Mexico, the "annexation" of half her provinces, will give us more liberty, a purer Morality, a more prosperous Industry, than we now have? . . .

People of the United States! Your Rulers are precipitating you into a fathomless abyss of crime and calamity! Why sleep you thoughtless on its verge, as though this was not your business, or Murder could be hid from the sight of God by a few flimsy rags called banners. Awake and arrest the work of butchery ere it be too late to preserve your souls from the guilt of wholesale slaughter.

From an editorial in the New York Tribune, *May 12, 1846.*

The inhabitants of the Pueblo are of the better and wealthier class of Californians, and have always been strongly disposed towards the institutions of Mexico, and at the time of the conquest of California, they fought with a determined resistance against the naval forces of Commodore Stockton. They have now, however, become reconciled to the institutions of our country, and will, I doubt not, in a few years make as good a set of democrats as can be found in Missouri or Arkansas. They are very strongly attached to the Roman Catholic Church, and are probably the most "religious," in their acceptation of the term, of any people in California. Every morning the solemn toll of the church-bell calls them to mass; at noon it is rung again, and every Poblano at the sound doffs his sombrero, and remains reverently uncovered in the hot sun, while the bell reminds him that he is to mutter over a short prayer.

E. Gould Buffum, "American Takeover," in John and LaRee Caughey, Los Angeles: Biography of a City, *University of California Press, 1976, p. 120.*

To the people of California:

On my approach to this place with the forces under my command, José Castro, the commandant general of California, buried his artillery and abandoned his fortified camp "of the Mesa," and fled, it is believed, towards Mexico. . . .

The Territory of California now belongs to the United States, and will be governed, as soon as circumstances permit, by officers and laws similar to those by which other Territories of the United States are regulated and protected.

But, until the governor, the secretary, and council are appointed, and the various departments of the government are arranged, military law will prevail, and the commander-in-chief will be the governor and protector of the Territory.

Robert F. Stockton Commander in chief and Governor of the Territory of California, August 17, 1846, Los Angeles. As quoted in John and LaRee Caughey, Los Angeles: Biography of a City, *University of California Press, 1976.*

Above: Two Mexican-American miners in Texas loaded with eighty pounds of cinabar ore emerge from a quicksilver mine, 1916. Such men worked in twelve-hour shifts for $1.00 a day. (Smithers Collection, Humanities Research Center, The University of Texas at Austin)

Right, top: Two Mexican freighters load a wagon with ore in the early 1890s. (Smithers Collection, Humanities Research Center, The University of Texas at Austin)

Right, bottom: Shoemakers pose for a company picture in San Antonio, Texas, about 1916. (Goldbeck Collection, Humanities Research Center, The University of Texas at Austin)

I came under contract from Morelia
To earn dollars was my dream,
I bought shoes and I bought a hat
And even put on trousers.

For they told me that here the
dollars
Were scattered about in heaps;
That there were girls and theaters
And that here everything was good fun.

And now I'm overwhelmed —
I am a shoemaker by trade
But here they say I'm a camel
And good only for pick and shovel.

What good time is it to know my trade
If there are manufacturers by the
score,
And while I make two little shoes
They turn out more than a million.

From "El Enganchado," anonymous, as reprinted in Manuel Gamio, Mexican Immigration to the United States, *Arno Press, New York, 1969, p. 84.*

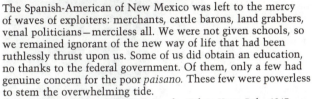

The Spanish-American of New Mexico was left to the mercy of waves of exploiters: merchants, cattle barons, land grabbers, venal politicians—merciless all. We were not given schools, so we remained ignorant of the new way of life that had been ruthlessly thrust upon us. Some of us did obtain an education, no thanks to the federal government. Of them, only a few had genuine concern for the poor *paisano*. These few were powerless to stem the overwhelming tide.

From George I. Sanchez, Forgotten People, *Calvin Horn, Pub., 1967, p. vii.*

When we arrived at Houston
We didn't find anything to do.
The times were very hard,
And didn't seem to want to get better.
When we arrived at Houston,
Working night and day,
They didn't give us anything to eat,
Nothing more than just watermelon.

From "The Beet Field Workers," anonymous, as reprinted in *Manuel Gamio*, Mexican Immigration to the United States, *Arno Press, New York, 1969, p. 85.*

Above: A wax maker and his family at mealtime in front of their home in Glenn Springs, Texas, 1917. (Smithers Collection, Humanities Research Center, The University of Texas at Austin)

Top: The Alamo City Employment Agency distributed bread three times a day to Mexican Americans who were in distress. (Summerville Collection, Humanities Research Center, The University of Texas at Austin)

Left: Mexican-American school children attended segregated schools in nearly every region of the Southwest. Here, children pose for a class picture in a segregated school in Carrizo Springs, Texas, in 1932. (Mexican American Library Program, The University of Texas at Austin)

Large-scale Mexican immigration to Chicago began in 1916 with the recruitment of 206 railroad track laborers from the Texas-Mexican border. The 1920 census counted 1200 Mexicans in Chicago, most of whom worked for the railroads, the steel plants, and the packing houses. Expanding steadily through the twenties, the Chicano community (Mexican and Mexican-American) reached 20,000 by 1930, establishing Chicago as a major center of Mexican settlement in the United States. Like the European ethnics who preceded them, they gathered in neighborhoods adjacent to the industries which recruited them: the Hull House area of the near West Side (railroads); South Chicago (steel plants); and Back of the Yards (packing houses). As ethnic newcomers they suffered the traditional hardships of limited and unstable employment along with cultural prejudice; as Mexicans they also suffered from racial prejudice. Although family formation was increasing, most of the Mexicans at the end of the decade were still young, male, and unskilled. Hoping to return eventually to their homeland, they remained Mexican rather than "American" in cultural as well as legal nationality.

Louise Año Nuevo Kerr, "Mexican Chicago: Chicano Assimilation Aborted, 1939–52," in Melvin G. Holli and Peter d'A. Jones The Ethnic Frontier, *William B. Eerdmans Publishing Co., 1977, p. 294.*

Mexican American workers at the Medina Dam construction site take a break from their work. During the 1920s thousands of workers from Mexico, such as the ones shown here, were recruited to perform unskilled labor in urban and rural communities. (Warren Roberts Collection, Humanities Research Center, The University of Texas at Austin)

Mexican American farmworkers loading a wagon in the early 1930s. (McGregor collection, Humanities Research Center, The University of Texas at Austin)

Field Poem

When the foreman whistled
My brother and I
Shouldered our hoes,
Leaving the field.
We returned to the bus
Speaking
In broken English, in broken Spanish
The restaurant food,
The tickets to a dance
We wouldn't buy with our pay

From the smashed bus window,
I saw the leaves of cotton plants
Like small hands
Waving good-bye
"Field Poem," by Gary Soto, The Elements of San Joaquin,
University of Pittsburgh Press, 1977, p. 23.

Mexican American workers preparing to board a train. During the early part of this century, labor contracting companies in the Southwest handled the distribution of Mexican workers to distant regions of the United States. (Goldbeck Collection, Humanities Research Center, The University of Texas at Austin, with the special assistance of Mary Ellen MacNamara)

The Mexican seemed, to the California power structure, to be the ideal answer to the state's agricultural needs. A docile, steady laborer who "knew his place"; a laborer who could be replaced easily; a laborer who neither created serious international problems nor raised the hackles of organized labor. When, in the lean years of the 1930s, many Mexican Americans in California cities begin to appear on the relief rolls, "voluntary" programs of repatriation were organized by various California governmental bodies. Los Angeles county, for example, with the cooperation of the federal government, shipped whole trainloads of Mexicans and Mexican Americans back to Mexico. Although there are no reliable figures for repatriation, probably more Mexicans crossed the border heading south during the depression years than came north.
Roger Daniels and Harry Kitano, American Racism, Exploration of the Nature of Prejudice, *Prentice-Hall, 1969, p. 70.*

Top: A farmworker family, living under substandard conditions, tries to cope without the amenities of modern society. (McGregor collection, Humanities Research Center, The University of Texas at Austin)

Above: Women pecan shellers in San Antonio averaged six cents an hour. The industry denied them the opportunity to earn even the minimum wage. (San Antonio Light Collection, Institute of Texan Cultures).

Left: Waiting while mother does the laundry. (Library of Congress, detail of photo by Russell Lee, 1936)

The Mexicans live concentrated on the Southside of El Paso largely, crowded into tenements, with the walls outside plastered with old Vote-for signs from years back and advertisements of Mexican movies at the Colón — the torn clothes just laundered waving on rickety balconies along Paisano Drive held up God knows how. Or if not, in the Government projects, which are clean tenements — a section for the Mexicans, a section for the Negroes. Politely. Row after row of identical box-houses speckled with dozens and dozens of children.
John Rechy, "El Paso del Norte," as quoted in Carlota Cardenas de Dwyer, Chicano Voices, *Houghton Mifflin, 1975, p. 57.*

In San Antonio we were under contract to go and pick cotton in a camp in the Valley of the Rio Grande. A group of countrymen and my wife and I went to pick. When we arrived at the camp the planter gave us an old hovel which had been used as a chicken house before, to live in, out in the open. I didn't want to live there and told him that if he didn't give us a little house which was a little better we would go. He told us to go, and my wife and I and my children were leaving when the sheriff fell upon us. He took me to the jail, and there the planter told them that I wanted to leave without paying him for the passage. The authorities would only pay attention to him, and as they were in league with him they told me that if I didn't pay they would take my wife and my little children to work. Then I paid them.
Personal narrative of an immigrant, as quoted in Manuel Gamio, The Mexican Immigrant: His Life Story, *Chicago 1930. Reprinted 1969 Arno Press, pp. 150–51.*

Textile workers in San Antonio. The garment industries of the Southwest have traditionally employed Mexican-American women. The hours were generally long, the wages low, and the working conditions poor. (San Antonio Light Collection, Institute of Texan Cultures)

Women involved in the Pecan Shellers' Strike in San Antonio line up for an allotment of food from the Union office. (National Archives)

The Mexican migrating to the United States worked for big business. His first masters were the agribusinessmen, the mine owners, and the railroad tycoons. The fact that he was intended to be a temporary supplement to white labor conspired against him from the beginning, for established labor wrote him off as a foreigner—and therefore not entitled to the protection given to U.S. workers. The pecking order within the labor community separated him from the other workers. Moreover, agriculture, which absorbed the largest number of Mexicans, was the most difficult area to unionize: the workers were dispersed, they were on the move, and, above all, agriculture ruled the Southwest.
From Rodolfo Acuña, Occupied America, Canfield Press, 1972, p. 154..

On the twenty-eighth day of April, at six o'clock in the morning,
we left on a labor contract for the state of Pennsylvania.

My beloved said to me, "I want to go on that job,
so I can wash your clothes, so I can cook your meals."

But the labor contractor told us, "Don't take your families along,
so you won't have any trouble in the state of West Virginia."

"Just to show you that I love you, leave me, then, in Forth Worth;
when you are settled and working, write me, wherever you are."
From "Pennsylvania," in Americo Paredes, A Texas-Mexican Cancionero, University of Illinois Press, 1976, p. 57.

Let's go back to Mexico, my compatriots,
because that is our own country
the Americans don't want us
and they are imposing immigration laws on us.

Dear friends, listen carefully,
the law of this great land that is imposed on foreigners
makes this a time of great trouble,
maybe there'll be compassion for the poor braceros, . . .

So, to avoid getting involved in business that's not our concern,
we will wait patiently for whatever befalls, . . .
From "The Immigration," (1928) in Guillermo Hernandez, Canciones De La Raza: Songs of The Chicano Experience, Berkeley, Calif., 1978, p. 40.

Top: A mother looks after her children in the farm camps of southern Indiana. (Gilbert Cardenas)

Above: Substandard living conditions for those who follow the crops persisted into the 1970s and '80s. These migrants are pictured at their current "home" in southern Indiana. (Gilbert Cardenas)

Right: Mexican Americans in fast-growing barrios of urban centers venture into a wide range of small business. Here, a tintorerta *(cleaners) in a Chicago barrio is in operation. (Gilbert Cardenas)*

"With the money that Mr. Thompson loaned us we can eat for at least three months. By that time we'll have the money from working in the beets. I hope we don't get too much in debt. He loaned me two hundred dollars, but by the time one pays for the trip almost half of it is gone, what with this business of having to pay half fare for children. And when I get back I have to pay back double the amount. Four hundred dollars! Interest is too high, but there's no way out of it; one can't fool around when one is in need. I've been told to turn him in because the interest rates are too high, but the fact is that he even has the trust deed to my house already. I sure hope everything goes well for us in the beet harvest; if not we'll be left homeless.
Tomas Rivera, "When We Arrive," as quoted in Carlota Cardenas de Dwyer, Chicano Voices, Houghton Mifflin, 1975, p. 152.

Oh what torment, oh what a
torment!
Is the famous cement work!

You take out stone and sand
To the stirring machine
For fifty cents an hour
Until the whistle blows.

In the famous wheelbarrow
More than four men gave out
And I, how could I stand it?
I preferred to wash dishes.

How remorseful, how remorseful
Am I for having come!

This work is honest.
Many Chicanos work at it
Although with the hot water
The hands get swollen a little.
From "The Dishwasher" by J. Osorio. As quoted in Nellie Foster, The Corride, MA Thesis, University of Southern California, 1939, p. 169.

The potential of this cohesiveness and unity is now being realized among Chicanos. Under the banner of *la causa* (the Chicano movement) Chicanos are increasingly identifying with other Chicanos across the region and nation. They recognize that they share a common past and future which transcends the regional variations that separate them. Thus we find urban Chicanos rallying to support *La Huelga*, the farm worker movement led by César Chávez, and rural Chicanos becoming increasingly aware of and supportive of urban efforts such as the Farah strike and demands for educational change. This surging sense of unity and realization of the importance of a united effort is increasingly obvious among Chicanos today. The incentive which many Chicanos have to end their depressed situation and earn their rightful place in American society is also very strong. This determination and group consciousness are very valuable political resources.

From F. Chris Garcia and Rudolph O. de la Garza, The Chicano Political Experience, *Duxbury Press, 1977, p. 70.*

Top; Cesar Chavez generated support for farmworkers and Mexican Americans in general in the '60s. Here, a UFW representative accepts a contribution from Andrea Martinez of the International Ladies Garment Workers' Union. (Alan Pogue)

Left: A mural in Las Vegas, New Mexico, manifests antiwar sentiment by noting that 15,000 Chicanos had lost their lives in the Vietnam conflict. (Gilbert Cardenas)

Above: Protest in the early '70s also took political form. Shown here is a segment from a march of 20,000 Mexican Americans through the barrio of East Los Angeles in 1970 to protest the Vietnam War. (Gilbert Cardenas)

A Mexican-American vaquero (cowboy) executes difficult maneuvers with the lariat (lasso). (Alan Pogue)

A ballet folklorico *group performs regional dances of Mexico for a festival in 1980. (Alan Pogue)*

Luis Valdes, producer and playwright, is the director and founder of the Teatro Campesino. Here he responds to questions from the audience at a workshop for Chicano theatre. (Gilbert Cardenas)

We developed what we call "actos": one-acts or skits, though skit is too light a word, dealing with the strike, the union, and the problems of the farm worker. Humor is our major asset and our best weapon: not only satire, but comedy, which is a much healthier child of the theater than tragedy or realism. Our use of comedy originally stemmed from necessity—the necessity of lifting the strikers' morale. We found we could make social points not in spite of the comedy, but through it. Slapstick can bring us very close to the underlying tragedy—the fact that human beings have been wasted for generations.
Luis Valdez, in Stan Steiner and Luis Valdez, AZTLAN: An Anthology of Mexican American Literature, *Knopf, 1972, p. 360.*

The twenty-third of October is a memorable day; a brave Mexican is honored in San Antonio.

The Mexican community cheers with both modesty and pride; Cleto Rodriquez honors us with a congressional medal.

In the state of Texas, so loyal and long suffering the Mexicans have already distinguished themselves in battle. . . .

Rodriguez went as a volunteer to show his courage; he killed 82 Japanese and he killed them without delay.
From "Cleto Rodriguez," in Guillermo Hernandez, Canciones De La Raza: Songs of the Chicano Experience, *Berkeley, Calif., 1978.*

CITY HONORS
MEDAL OF HONOR WINNER
With the city council chamber overflowing in corridors of two floors, San Antonio Tuesday expressed its gratitude to Cleto Rodriguez, the newsboy who went to war and returned a hero. City officials, khaki-clad buddies and mantilla-covered neighbors jammed the chamber to render official plaudits to the 22-year-old Congressional Medal of Honor winner and proclaim "Cleto Rodriguez Day."
From Raul Morin, Among The Valiant: Mexican-Americans in WWII and Korea, *Borden Publishing Co., Alhambra, Calif., p. 210.*

Alurista—poet, composer, and writer—sings a song of the Mexican revolutionary era. (Alan Pogue)

Professor Americo Paredes of the University of Texas is an internationally known collector of Mexican-American folklore. (Alan Pogue)

Reknown actor Anthony Quinn was born in Juarez, Mexico, of a Mexican mother and Irish father. He once worked in the fields of northern California as a farmworker. (Personal collection of Ricardo Romo)

He was a man, a Border man. What did he look like? Well, that is hard to tell. Some say he was short and some say he was tall; some say he was Indian brown and some say he was blond like a newborn cockroach. But I'd say he was not too dark and not too fair, not too thin and not too fat, not too short and not too tall; and he looked just a little bit like me. But does it matter so much what he looked like? He was a man, very much of a man; and he was a Border man. . . .

Not a gunman, no, not a bravo.[1] He never came out of a cantina wanting to drink up the sea at one gulp. Not that kind of man, if you can call that kind a man. No, that wasn't Gregorio Cortez at all. He was a peaceful man, a hard-working man like you and me. . . .

He was a vaquero, and a better one there has not ever been from Laredo to the mouth. He could talk to horses and they would understand. . . . And if an animal was lost and nobody could pick up a trail, they would send for Gregorio Cortez. He could always find a trail.

[1] BRAVO: fierce or ill-tempered man.

Americo Paredes, With His Pistol in His Hand, *University of Texas Press, 1958, p. 34.*

Black against twisted black
The old mesquite
Rears up against the stars
Branch bridle hanging,
While the bull comes down from the mountain
Driven along by your fingers,
Twenty nimble stallions prancing up and down the *redil* of
   the guitars.
One leaning on the trunk, one facing—
Now the song:
Not cleanly flanked, not pacing,
But in a stubborn yielding that unshapes
And shapes itself again,
Hard-mouthed, zigzagged, thrusting,
Thrown, not sung,
One to the other.
The old man listens in his cloud
Of white tobacco smoke.
"It was so," he says,
"In the old days it was so."
American Paredes, in Americo Paredes and Raymund Paredes,
Mexican-American Authors, *Houghton Mifflin, 1972, p. 51.*

Chicanos in the United States have almost no political representation at the local, state, or national level. The reason for this is that those with power never intended them to have representation. The Mexican is poor and, therefore, without a voice in the political process, which is predicated on campaign contributions and the ability to convince those in power that you deserve a share. Jess Unruh, a former Speaker of the California Assembly, graphically summed up the importance of money in politics when he stated that "Money is the mother's milk of politics." The Chicano, therefore, remains one of the few minorities in this nation that has not achieved political self-determination. As oppressed as the Black American has been, he has fared much better in politics than the Mexican, since in a few cases he has been included in the Democratic party's councils. Outside of New Mexico, the Chicano has been the victim of a conspiracy to keep him from gaining political representation and has been gerrymandered and managed for the benefit of a few politicos.

From Rodolfo Acuña, Occupied America, *Canfield Press, 1972, p. 247.*

Ruben Bonilla, national President of the League of United Latin American Citizens (LULAC), discusses the politics of equality at a Mexican American political rally. (Alan Pogue)

Grace Olivarez, the first woman to earn a law degree from Notre Dame University and former head of HEW's Community Service Administration, now teaches and works as a consultant for the United Way of America. (Gilbert Cardenas)

As a population force, Hispanic Americans have the lowest median age as well as the highest fertility rate, two statistics destined to make us the largest minority group in the early 1980's. Hispanics, however, must unite in order to maximize the attendant political power and influence that corresponds to growing population force in America. In recent months, several issues have surfaced which make LULAC's future work extremely important. The Bakke decision jeopardizes the concept of affirmative action in education and employment by its reference to mythical "reverse discrimination." Two, the growing hysteria and irrational emotionalism concerning the alien issue has made the Mexican-American and the Mexican alien the scapegoats of our nation's economic woes. Further, the dilemma — both tragic and compelling — of the maladministration of justice accorded the Mexican-American has certainly provided an urgent need to restore justice in the courts as well as in the streets. And finally, the "Proposition 13 Syndrome" has done little except to widen the gap between the "haves" and the "have nots," to the extent that Hispanics are becoming an expendable item in governmental budgetary deliberations. In 1979, as in 1929, the Spanish-speaking are still the last hired and the first fired.

Ruben Bonilla, Jr., from letter of February 17, 1979, for the League of United Latin American Citizens.

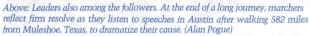

Above: Leaders also among the followers. At the end of a long journey, marchers reflect firm resolve as they listen to speeches in Austin after walking 582 miles from Muleshoe, Texas, to dramatize their cause. (Alan Pogue)

Top, right: Dr. Hector Garcia, founder of the American G. I. Forum and the first Mexican American to be appointed to the U.S. Commission on Civil Rights, delivers a speech in support of the farmworkers' cause at the state capitol, Austin, Texas, 1979. (Alan Pogue)

Right: Vilma Martinez, President and General Counsel of the Mexican American Legal Defense and Educational Fund (MALDEF). Photo courtesy of MALDEF.

I have interviewed hundreds of persons that we have either deported or dealt with, and, when you see the drive and ambition of someone who has walked two hundred miles across the desert to come here to take any job, you develop a great sense of respect for them and a great question about what this country is really doing.
Leonel Castillo, Commissioner, U.S. Immigration and Naturalization Service, February 24, 1978.

For all people, as with individuals, the time comes when they must reckon with their history. For the Chicano the present is a time of renaissance, of renacimiento. Our people and our community, el barrio and la colonia, are expressing a new consciousness and a new resolve. Recognizing the historical tasks confronting our people and fully aware of the cost of human progress, we pledge our will to move. We will move forward toward our destiny as a people. We will move against those forces which have denied us freedom of expression and human dignity. Throughout history the quest for cultural expression and freedom has taken the form of a struggle. Our struggle, tempered by the lessons of the American past, is an historical reality.
From "Manifesto," in El Plan de Santa Barbara, Analyses and Positions by the Chicano Coordinating Council on Higher Education, Oakland, Calif. 1969.

To grant equality to the Mexican American is to provide the nation with an incredibly rich human, intellectual and creative resource. It means the development of professionals who understand the problems of the urban ghetto, of the poor rural community— professionals who can use their education to help solve problems in these troubled areas of our nation. A well-educated Spanish-speaking community can promote diplomatic and economic ties with Mexico and with nations in Central and South American that are becoming increasingly important to the economic health of the United States.
Vilma S. Martinez, from a speech at Rice University, January 21, 1980.

Apprehension of Mexicans attempting to immigrate to the United States. U.S. Border Patrol agents used 2-way radios and a helicopter for this arrest in San Ysidro, California. (Copyright © 1980 by Len Lahman)

he seldom asked for more than he thought that he could get. His greatest deficiency, when he succeeded Kennedy, was lack of experience and knowledge in foreign affairs; he therefore had some distaste for an area in which he was obliged to rely heavily on the advice of others. This inexperience and dislike of foreign policy eventually cost Johnson his position as President and a large part of the fine reputation that his domestic achievements had won for him.

Johnson lacked Kennedy's suavity, wit, and flair; his ruggedness and his Texan manners and drawl reflected American rural, even frontier, traditions. His most striking personal characteristic—an almost superhuman energy that drove him, in spite of a severe heart attack in 1957, to herculean labors—might have made him a great President. However, his hypersensitivity to criticism deprived him of sound advice and advisers, and his mental rigidity, when events and facts failed to fit his preconceptions, prevented him from changing courses. This man of burning intensity, who was eager for approval and determined to earn a high place in the annals of the presidency, failed to earn that place. Johnson left the presidency under humiliating conditions; he was despised by the younger generation in his own party as a symbol of all that was wrong in American society. But he did not fail because he lacked lofty ambitions or the political skills and experience to carry them out—except in the crucial area of foreign policy, where, as we have said, he depended unduly upon the advice of others who supposedly knew more than he.

More Rapid Movement toward New Frontiers

The succession was carried out smoothly even while the nation mourned, and Johnson appeared before a joint session of Congress on November 27, 1963. He urged rapid completion of what he called the most urgent unfinished legislative business—tax reduction and adoption of the pending civil rights bill. Johnson did not hesitate to invoke the memory of the martyred Kennedy when he asked for passage by Congress of the administration measures, which had remained locked in committees while Kennedy lived.

Congress soon knew that it had a new rider—with sharp spurs. The large Democratic majorities in both houses also had their eyes on the coming election campaigns. Hence, in February 1964, they approved a bill that reduced taxes by some $11.5 billion over a two-year period. The reduction had more than proved its worth as a stimulant to economic activity by the end of 1966. Before the presidential election, Congress also provided funds for public housing. It continued the National Defense Education Act of 1958 for an additional three years and authorized more than $1 billion for a five-year program to improve college facilities. Furthermore, Congress established a food-stamp plan for families who received welfare assistance. After he brought all these Kennedy measures to fruition, Johnson submitted one of his own—the Economic Opportunity Act. This measure, approved August 20, 1964, authorized the expenditures of about $1 billion in the following year alone to inaugurate a massive, coordinated national war against the causes of poverty.

The most significant legislative event of 1964 was the adoption of the new Civil Rights Act. The House approved the bill on February 10. The Senate endured a filibuster by southern senators for eighty-three days and then adopted cloture (a rule ending debate, which requires a two-thirds majority) on June 10 and the bill itself on July 2. The Civil Rights Act of 1964 was one of the most ambitious and far-reaching pieces of legislation ever adopted by Congress. It forbade discrimination on account of race in most places of public accommodation; attempted to protect the right of blacks to vote; forbade (in Title VII) discrimination on account of race *or* sex by employers, employment agencies, and labor unions; created an Equal Employment Opportunity Commission, to begin its duties in 1965; forbade discrimination in any form in the use of federal funds by states and other local authorities; empowered the Attorney General to initiate cases to speed the desegregation of schools; and created a Community Relations Service to assist individuals and officials to deal with racial problems on the local level.

The Presidential Campaign of 1964

These mighty events on Capitol Hill served as a prelude to the battle for control of Congress and the presidency. The Democrats had not been as united behind a leader since 1944, in spite of the disaffection of many whites in the Deep South because of the Civil Rights Act. The Democratic national convention nominated Johnson by acclamation. It adopted a platform promising full-scale mobilization of national skills and resources to create what the President called "the Great Society." It thundered its applause when Johnson asked for a mandate to continue the war against poverty. The only question before the Democrats remained the choice of a vice-presidential nominee, and Johnson answered it while the convention reveled in Atlantic City. The President had already rejected Robert F. Kennedy and named Hubert H. Humphrey of Minnesota, one of the most ardent progressives in the Senate.

The Republicans, meanwhile, had been torn by dissension. The GOP suffered most from lack of available leaders and spokesmen of national stature. Nixon suffered a stunning loss while running for Governor of California in 1962. Therefore he appeared to be out of this presidential race. Most other Republicans of national stature knew that 1964 would be a Democratic year and refused to enter the contest for the presidential nomination. Only two serious candidates eagerly challenged the Texan in the White House. They were Governor Nelson A. Rockefeller of New York, a progressive, and Senator Barry M. Goldwater of Arizona, a conservative. Rockefeller ruined whatever chances he had by a divorce and a remarriage just before the campaign began. Goldwater, popular with most of the powerful state Republican organizations, and with the John Birch Society and other extremely conservative groups, won most delegations chosen in state conventions by Republican activists. When former President Eisenhower refused to rally the progressive and internationalist wing of the GOP against Goldwater, Governor William W. Scranton of Pennsylvania made a solitary and vain effort at the end of the preconvention campaign. Goldwater won the presidential nomination with ease on the first ballot at the Republican national convention. Conservative delegates heckled and booed progressive leaders when they tried to persuade the convention to denounce extremist groups. Goldwater widened the split by naming Representative William E. Miller of New York, an extreme conservative, as his running mate. Goldwater also alarmed moderates by saying in his acceptance speech that "extremism in the defense of liberty is no vice."

The Johnson Landslide

Not since 1936 had there been a presidential campaign in which the contenders were so unevenly matched. Johnson conducted a strenuous campaign. Concerning foreign affairs, he gave the impression of wisdom and restraint and warned that Goldwater's proposals about Vietnam might involve the nation in an Asian war—perhaps even in a third world war. On domestic issues, Johnson stood forthrightly behind the Civil Rights Act of 1964, the war against poverty, Medicare, and federal aid to education. The public response was overwhelming. Everywhere that the President went, he was engulfed by cheering throngs who wanted to shake his bruised, outstretched, and eager hand.

Goldwater, on the other hand, moved steadily downhill from the moment of his nomination. Most Republicans in Congress had supported the Civil Rights Act, and there had been strong Republican support for other Kennedy-Johnson measures. The majority of Republican voters differed little from the majority of Democrats. Most Americans clearly wanted the federal government to take the lead in meeting the changing problems of their day and differed only in details and on the speed of change. This consensus seemed to characterize American political attitudes more in 1964 than at any other time in American history, except, perhaps, in 1912.

However, Goldwater had promised the voters "a choice, not an echo." He had voted against the Civil Rights Bill, the Test Ban Treaty, and most of the Kennedy-Johnson welfare measures. During the campaign, Goldwater continued to oppose the very things for which a majority of his own party stood. He intimated that he would like to repeal the Social Security Act, sell the TVA to private investors, and wipe out as much progressive legislation as possible. He tried to repudiate his statement about Social Security when it aroused fear and outrage among low- and middle-income, middle-aged, and elderly Republican conservatives. He also gave the impression of believing that violent conflict with the Soviet Union was inevitable (for example, he referred to the Soviet Union as the "enemy"). Finally, he refused to denounce the support of the John Birch Society and other extremely conservative organizations which said that Eisenhower and Dulles, as well as Democrats, had been traitors to the United States.

Goldwater hoped to carry the segregationist South and what he believed to be the conservative Middle West and Far West. His strategy failed. The voters did not like the choice that he offered, and he probably lost a million votes every time he made a major address. The result was a Democratic landslide on November 3, 1964. Johnson and Humphrey amassed more than 43,000,000 popular and 486 electoral votes, to some 27,000,000 popular and fifty-two electoral votes for Goldwater and Miller. The Arizonan carried only five states in the Deep South and his home state. The Eighty-ninth Congress (1965–1966) would have sixty-eight Democrats and thirty-two Republicans in the Senate and 295 Democrats and 140 Republicans in the House of Representatives.

Toward the Great Society

Johnson's inauguration on January 20, 1965, seemed more like a second inaugural than the beginning of a first regular term, so entrenched in leadership was the President. However, the situation on Capitol Hill now appeared radically different. For the first time since 1938, a President had a firm working majority in both houses of Congress. For the first time since 1938, a Democratic President could obtain legislation without the help of conservative southern Democrats.

No one understood the significance of this fact better than Lyndon B. Johnson. With furious energy, he pushed through a willing Congress the most comprehensive domestic program since the high tide of the New Deal.

The President finally broke the logjam that had prevented a comprehensive education bill. The Education Act of 1965, adopted and approved in mid-April, authorized $1.3 billion for direct federal assistance to public schools. It sidestepped the religious issue by providing aid to parochial school children in a number of "shared services." The Education Act, Johnson said when he signed the measure, was "truly the key which can unlock the door to the Great Society." In addition, a Higher Education Act of 1965 authorized $650 million in federal aid to colleges and universities for scholarships to needy students and to strengthen teaching and research.

An Appalachian Regional Development Act, approved in March 1965, provided $1.1 billion for highways, health centers, and development to the poverty-stricken mountainous region which stretched from Pennsylvania to Alabama and Georgia. A Medicare bill, enlarged to include low-cost insurance against doctors' bills as well as against hospital and nursing expenses for all persons over sixty-five, was overwhelmingly approved by Congress and signed by the President on July 30, 1965. Medicare, administered by the Social Security Administration, effected the first fundamental change in the Social Security Act since its adoption in 1935. Congress approved the President's bill to cut excise taxes by $4.6 billion in several stages, which began in June 1965. The Housing and Urban Development Act of 1965 was the most important housing act since 1949. It provided assistance for the construction of approximately 240,000 units of low-rent public housing and authorized $2.9 billion in federal grants for urban renewal over a four-year period. A supplementary act of May 1966 provided funds to subsidize the rents of some low- and moderate-income families. In addition, Congress created a federal Department of Housing and Urban Development of cabinet rank. Robert C. Weaver, the first black ever named to the cabinet, was sworn in as head of the new department in January 1966.

Johnson and Congress also responded to growing popular demands that steps be taken to improve the ecological conditions in which Americans were forced to live. Legislation enacted in 1966 attempted to control both air and water pollution. Another measure gave the government authority to set safety standards for automobile manufacturers and on highways. Even the placing of advertising billboards, which adjoined new interstate highways, was rigidly controlled.

The Immigration Act of 1965 signified a fundamental change in American immigration policy. The National Origins Act of 1924 had provided for quotas that heavily favored immigration from northern Europe. The Immigration Act of 1965 put all nations on an equal footing by providing for the admission of some 170,000 "regular" immigrants annually with a limitation of 20,000 per year from any single country.

The Voting Rights Act of 1965

Johnson, meanwhile, had added another measure to his program in response to new convulsions on the civil rights front. Various organizations had begun campaigns to encourage black registration and voting throughout the South in 1964, and both were heavy in many southern states. But white reaction across a chain of black-belt counties in Mississippi and Alabama had been violent. Whites and blacks were murdered. Black churches, usually the centers of local political activity, had been bombed or burned, and local registrars had succeeded in preventing most blacks from registering. Local police seemed more intent upon obstructing efforts at registration than upon apprehending the arsonists, bombers, and murderers.

National indignation was at fever pitch by early 1965. Public outrage greatly intensified in March, when Alabama state troopers used clubs and tear gas to break up a demonstration in Selma, led by Dr. King. Some 400 ministers, priests, and rabbis flew at once to Selma to join the demonstrators. Johnson went before Congress in a nationally televised and impassioned address to denounce the denial of basic constitutional rights. He demanded adoption of a bill for federal registrars in all counties where blacks did not vote in normal numbers. These registrars would enroll blacks under rules so rigid that no person could be denied the right to vote on account of race.

This measure, called the Voting Rights Act of 1965, was put on its way to passage even while thousands of Americans took airplanes, cars, and buses to Alabama to join the marchers from Selma. Passage of the bill, probably already assured, was made inevitable by the murder of three civil rights workers near Selma. The measure quickly passed the House. Then it went through the Senate with unusual dispatch, for the majority in that body tolerated only a brief southern filibuster. President Johnson signed the bill on August 6, 1965.

The Supreme Court Continues Its Own Revolution

The Supreme Court, now completely under the influence of Chief Justice Warren, in the 1960s completed the revolution in constitutional interpretation that it had begun in the 1950s. This, actually, is an understatement. The court did nothing less than to effect a fundamental reinterpretation of laws which affected individual rights.

It is not surprising that the Supreme Court threw the weight of the entire American judiciary behind the civil rights revolution, for the court had been one of the principal originators of the revolution (see pp. 906–907). In Heart of Atlanta Motel v. the United States, 1964, the court upheld the Civil Rights Act of 1964 in sweeping language. In other cases, the court upheld the Voting Rights Act of 1965 and struck down local segregation statutes. It outlawed the poll tax as a requirement for voting in local and state elections and thus supplemented the ban against the poll tax in federal elections in the Twenty-fourth Amendment.

The Warren Court also struck death blows at another ancient political inequity—rural control of state legislatures in urban states, accomplished until then by the refusal of rural state lawmakers to reapportion voting districts to give equal representation to urban areas. Certain citizens of Tennessee brought suit in federal court to compel their legislature to grant to Tennessee's urban citizens representation equal to that enjoyed by the rural population. The Supreme Court, in Baker v. Carr, 1962, in effect declared that the federal courts should intervene in such cases to guarantee equal representation to all citizens in all states. Subsequent rulings, such as Westberry v. Sanders, 1964, and Reynolds v. Sims, 1964, compelled state legislatures throughout the country to reapportion both of their houses and their congressional districts on the principle of "one man, one vote."

At the same time, the court more clearly defined the First Amendment's affirmation of the principle of separation of church and state in Engel v. Vitale, 1962, and School District of Abington Township v. Schempp, 1963. These epochal decisions outlawed state or local laws which required Bible reading and prayers in public schools on the ground that they constituted establishment of religion contrary to the First Amendment.

Finally, the court threw up a variety of new safeguards for individuals accused of crime. In Gideon v. Wainwright (1963), the court ruled that a defendant too poor to hire an attorney had to be furnished one at public expense. The court, in Escobedo v. Illinois (1964), Miranda v. Arizona (1966), and other cases extended the right to be informed of self-incrimination, the option of silence, and rights to counsel and to confront prosecution witnesses in most categories of offenses, including juvenile delinquency proceedings.

Police representatives and some public officials like Governor Ronald Reagan of California complained that these decisions encouraged criminals and severely handicapped and demoralized law enforcement agencies. However, statistics since these decisions indicate a steady level of convictions and even of confessions. Most criminals, it was discovered, were convicted because of the collection of evidence and the testimony of witnesses, not by confessions.

Great Society Programs

The nation's concern about high crime rates and the Supreme Court's decisions prompted Johnson to appoint a Commission on Law Enforcement and Administration of Justice. The commission's report, *The Challenge of Crime in a Free Society*, submitted in February 1967, concluded that the major reasons for increased crime were conditions in urban ghettos: poverty, terrible housing, badly equipped and managed schools, and high unemployment, especially among young black males who seemed to be in a permanent state of economic depression. The commission suggested the utilization of new techniques to rehabilitate convicted criminals, including "half-way houses" and training for skilled jobs. It also recommended fair treatment of every individual before the law — the objective of the recent court decisions — and it suggested gun-control legislation. Congress, stimulated by the recent assassinations of Robert Kennedy and Martin Luther King, Jr., passed a gun-control measure in 1968; but it was so weakened by amendments demanded by gun lovers and their powerful lobby group, the National Rifle Association, that the bill's sponsor, Representative Emanuel Celler of New York, declared that it contained loopholes "as wide as the Grand Canyon." Most states also found it impossible to pass stringent gun-control legislation. In California, a group of Black Panthers armed with rifles entered the state capitol to protest against proposed gun limitations; the measure was also opposed by arch-conservatives, who insisted upon their right to protect their homes against unknown assailants, and by organized groups of hunters and marksmen.

Johnson's Great Society programs obtained a wide spectrum of support, which ranged from business leaders worried about deterioration in housing and smog in downtown urban areas, to blacks who demanded voting rights and access to decent homes and schools. Johnson seemed, early in his elected term, to have put together a progressive coalition at least as powerful as the one that kept Franklin Roosevelt in office. Then, in two years, a series of controversial decisions in foreign policy stripped needed funds from his domestic programs, shattered the consensus behind Johnson, and divided the country as bitterly as at any time since the secession of the southern states in 1861. Johnson's political career was one of the casualties.

Johnson and Foreign Policy

Since the introduction of the Good Neighbor policy during the 1930s, United States intervention in Latin America tended to be quiet; it depended on dollars rather than bullets, and it used friendly native leaders and United States-trained armed forces rather than American marines. Even the Bay of Pigs invasion conformed to this pattern to a large extent, although American participation was so obvious that Kennedy's refusal to use United States troops and planes served only to doom the expedition. Perhaps Johnson had that lesson in mind when civil war broke out in the Dominican Republic between forces led by army officers committed to the deposed democratic President, Juan Bosch, and other elements of the army led by conservative generals. Not even the participants knew who was winning when Johnson decided, on the basis of slight evidence, that a Communist conspiracy to take over the small Caribbean nation was about to succeed. Johnson did not even consult the Organization of American States before he sent more than 20,000 United States troops to intercede in the Dominican civil war. When it became obvious that Communists played hardly any role in the Dominican quarrel, and that the United States was attempting to install an unpopular military regime, the American government helped to work out a compromise between the warring factions. Meanwhile, United States troops had killed Dominican citizens. Latin Americans in general were furious, and many liberals in the United States began to worry about the possibility that a trigger-happy Texan occupied the White House.

Johnson reinforced the liberals' misgivings, and finally destroyed his political coalition, with his decision in favor of a massive land war in Asia. During the presidential campaign of 1964, Johnson had accused Goldwater of reckless statements about Vietnam and had assured the voters: "We are not going to send American boys nine or ten thousand miles away from home to do what Asian boys ought to be doing for themselves."

Vietnam and Further Complications

Early in 1965, the army of South Vietnam outnumbered its guerilla enemies, the NLF, by six to one. Nevertheless, thousands of American advisers and enormous amounts of American military equipment and financial aid barely

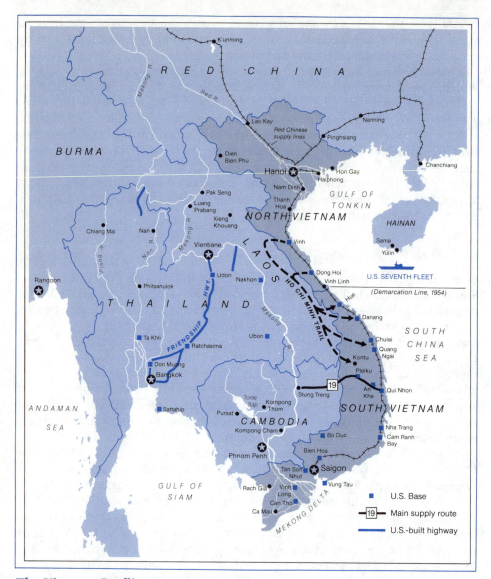

The Vietnam Conflict, 1966

enabled South Vietnamese forces to hold their own. Johnson and his chief policy planners decided that the "free world"—which actually included a number of nations run by dictators and military leaders, among them South Vietnam—faced a unified Communist threat and that Vietnam was only the immediate point of that expansionistic thrust. If Vietnam fell, they feared, then the monolithic Communist enemy would be encouraged to undertake further expansion. Many commentators referred to this idea as the "domino theory"—that is, if South Vietnam fell, neighboring countries, such as Laos, Cambodia, Thailand, Burma, Indonesia, India, and the Philippines inevitably would topple also. Johnson was impressed, too, with the arguments of military theorists, who confidently predicted that a calculated series of steps, which gradually enlarged the scope and intensity of a conflict, would sooner or later force an enemy to ask for peace. Johnson and his advisers also listened to optimistic advocates of counterinsurgency techniques and strategic bombing. Johnson, convinced that the war could be won, in February 1965 ordered the bombing of North Vietnam and sent units of American combat troops to South Vietnam. He had meanwhile received, in August 1964, congressional approval in a joint resolution adopted after North Vietnamese attacks upon American destroyers in the Gulf of Tonkin, off the coast of North Vietnam. The resolution, approved by overwhelming majorities in both houses, pledged full congressional support for action by the United States in Vietnam "to promote the maintenance of international peace and security in Southeast Asia."

A steady buildup of forces followed. But, just as steadily, reinforcements streamed down from North Vietnam to combat the Americans. Previously, the North Vietnamese had given the southern rebels little but training and moral support. By the time that Johnson left office, 535,000 United States soldiers were stationed in Vietnam and were assisted by 800,000 South Vietnamese regular troops, 200,000 South Vietnamese militia, and 72,000 allied troops. They opposed about 320,000 North Vietnamese soldiers and the remnant of the NLF. The bombing of North Vietnam, in an effort to disrupt the flow of men and materials southward, mounted to the dropping of 100,000 tons of explosives monthly. The tonnage of bombs dropped on North and South Vietnam by American planes by 1970 had already exceeded by over 50 per cent the total dropped in all theaters during the Second World War. Attempts to starve and expose the guerillas included chemical defoliation of almost 1,000,000 acres, which transformed South Vietnam from a major rice exporter as late as 1967 into a large-scale importer of rice in 1968, and into an impoverished area later.

Nevertheless, as United States casualties and expenditures in Vietnam increased, the Americans and South Vietnamese seemed no closer to victory, or even to a negotiated peace, than before the United States had intervened. A series of promises from American officials that triumph was near and American soldiers would soon be home accompanied each stage in the escalation of the war. Those who had doubted the wisdom of Johnson's policies from the beginning now pointed to the danger of continuing the costly battle. The war, Walter Lippmann wrote in December 1967, "is unwinnable in the sense that a horde of elephants cannot win a struggle with a swarm of mosquitoes, not because the mosquitoes are too brave or too fanatic, but because . . . no mosquito can surrender all the mosquitoes that can be bred in the marsh and no government or committee or general can surrender the revolutionary peasantry of the Asian continent." Even old friends of the President, such as Clark Clifford and Dean Acheson, found that Johnson refused to take advice to deescalate the war, and that he reacted with hypersensitivity to suggestions that he had made any kind of mistake. High officials who made such suggestions—like Secretary of Defense McNamara, who earlier had believed that intensive bombing would soon bring North Vietnam to its knees—were forced to resign.

Johnson learned somewhat tardily the limitations of his country's resources. Since the Vietnam War was costing over $20 billion annually, Johnson was obliged to reduce expenditures on domestic programs designed to alleviate poverty and urban unrest. Not only were Americans reluctant to tax themselves further to expand these programs, but international bankers and specu-

Helicopters, a distinctive feature in the Vietnam War, proved extremely useful for carrying infantrymen to remote and inaccessible points of the war front. In this 1968 photograph, U.S. infantrymen have landed on a dirt road southwest of Saigon and are wading into a rice paddy in search of Viet Cong. Intensive patrols of suspected hiding places are aimed at preventing another attack on the South Vietnamese capital. (Wide World Photos)

lators began to exchange dollars for gold and more stable currencies because of the inflation caused by the seemingly endless war. Incredible as it seemed to Americans, the dollar fell close to devaluation largely because of the expenses connected with a war in a tiny Asian nation.

Then, in January 1968, two separate series of incidents further exacerbated Johnson's problems. Early in the month, the NLF launched a major offensive— called the Tet offensive after the Vietnamese holiday on which it occurred— against almost every significant South Vietnamese town and city; they even invaded the center of Saigon and shelled the United States embassy there. Actually, the Tet offensive virtually decimated the NLF; but their ranks were now more than filled by North Vietnamese regulars. Late in the month, a United States intelligence ship, U.S.S. Pueblo, loaded with electronic spying equipment, was captured by North Korean patrol boats off the coast of that country. American officials angrily denounced the action and seemed to threaten reprisals. However, Johnson, fully aware by now that the country could not even afford the additional burdens on its currency and manpower demanded by American military leaders in Vietnam, wisely backed away from an additional conflict with an even more powerful enemy in Korea. North Korea possessed an air force many times larger and much more modern than the tiny air force of North Vietnam. Johnson's decision not to contest the seizure of *Pueblo* provided him finally with an opportunity to contemplate the overextended and vulnerable position in which he had placed the United States.

4. THE ELECTION OF 1968

McCarthy and the Peace Platform

In November 1967, Senator Eugene McCarthy of Minnesota announced his candidacy for the Democratic presidential nomination on a peace platform. At the time, McCarthy's action seemed a token gesture on behalf of the peace advocates, or "doves," within the Democratic party. Lyndon Johnson's renomination appeared to be a foregone conclusion. McCarthy, an able, moderate liberal, was virtually unknown in most of the country and really not even well known in the Senate, where he had introduced no important legislation and had often neglected to vote. His campaign suffered further from his subdued, whimsical speaking style, and from his refusal either to dramatize his differences with the administration or to appeal directly to ethnic groups. His campaign workers frequently found him diffident, almost unwilling to take actions necessary to win. This may, in fact, have reflected McCarthy's deep desire to avoid the overwhelming political and administrative problems that the next President would have to face.

Nevertheless, thousands of young Americans, almost all of them college students, grasped at the opportunity presented by McCarthy's candidacy to oppose actively Johnson's policies. Students on the East coast spontaneously descended upon New Hampshire, site of the earliest presidential primary, and swamped the local McCarthy offices. Quickly, and with little help from professional politicians, the students organized a thorough campaign. They also shaved their beards, cut their hair, and wore conservative-looking clothing. Those who refused to "clean for Gene" were set to work sealing envelopes and drawing maps in the basements of McCarthy headquarters. Bright, attractive, neat young men and women systematically canvassed the whole state and spoke casually to almost every registered Democrat and many Republicans about the necessity for a change in Washington. McCarthy found this informal, personal, and frank style of campaign congenial; he walked the main streets of New Hampshire's cities, chatted with passersby, and entered stores for an audience when he found no one outside.

Polls taken in New Hampshire, which earlier had predicted that McCarthy would win less than 10 per cent of the Democratic primary votes, now showed McCarthy gaining rapidly on Johnson, despite support for the President by the whole state Democratic organization. Johnson's supporters finally were reduced to accusing McCarthy of disloyalty to his country and to charging that McCarthy's campaign encouraged North Vietnamese to continue to kill American boys. Despite the polls, Americans were startled in mid-March 1968 when McCarthy won 42 per cent of the Democratic vote to 48 per cent for Johnson, with enough write-in votes for McCarthy on Republican ballots to make the two candidates almost even.

Politicians in Washington understood immediately the meaning of Mc-

Carthy's showing. National polls also reported widespread disenchantment with Johnson's policies, especially with his continuation of the Vietnam War. Newspapers and magazines such as *Time* and *Newsweek*, previously reluctant to express the reservations of their editors and reporters, after Tet began to criticize severely American participation in the Vietnam War.

Robert F. Kennedy, now senator from New York, heir to a large portion of his brother's political organization and to the "Kennedy cult," had refused for months to succumb to pressure from numerous friends and supporters, who had urged him to run against Johnson. Until the Tet offensive, Kennedy had opposed the Vietnam War strongly, but privately—apparently out of concern that public pronouncements would severely divide the Democratic party. After Tet, however, Kennedy decided to speak out, and at the same time he moved to the edge of entering the campaign. During a major speech in Chicago, before the New Hampshire primary, Kennedy declared that the United States was not winning the Vietnam War and should no longer attempt to do so. "Our enemy," Kennedy told the large audience, "has finally shattered the mask of official illusion with which we have concealed our true circumstances, even from ourselves."

As evidence mounted that Johnson could not muster dependable support from anyone but established Democratic politicians, and that the nomination might go to a political unknown who could easily lose the general election, Kennedy announced his active candidacy. Not only did Kennedy thus provide Johnson with truly formidable opposition—Kennedy's popularity, especially among blacks and Hispanic voters, may even have exceeded that of his older brother—but Johnson also now faced the possibility of losing to a man who had treated him with humiliating condescension when he served as Vice-President.

McCarthy's young campaign workers had already moved to Wisconsin, where hordes of midwestern college students—especially from the University of Wisconsin at Madison, a center of New Left and antiwar activities—helped to organize a statewide canvass similar to the successful New Hampshire venture. Polls in Wisconsin indicated that the Minnesota Senator, now a figure of national importance, would win an overwhelming victory over the President. Two days before the Wisconsin primary election on April 2, Johnson announced that, in the interest of national unity, he would not be a candidate for reelection. During the same speech, Johnson also announced an end to American bombing of a large portion of North Vietnam in the hope that this action would lead to early peace talks. An American mission headed by W. Averell Harriman met with North Vietnamese delegates in Paris in May for preliminary talks. Following Johnson's announcement of a total cessation of the bombing of North Vietnam on October 31, the negotiators in Paris began formal discussions in early 1969. However, peace remained as elusive as ever at the end of the Johnson administration.

Meanwhile, in the Democratic preconvention contest, Kennedy won every presidential primary that he entered, most by large margins, except for Oregon, which went to McCarthy. Just before the California primary, Kennedy predicted to an interviewer that an attempt would soon be made to assassinate him. He spoke with resignation of the unfortunate association of violence with manliness in the minds of many Americans. However, it was a young Jordanian immigrant, Sirhan Sirhan, mentally deranged and infuriated by Kennedy's statements favorable to Israel, who shot the Senator on June 5 at a victory celebration which followed Kennedy's triumph in the California primary election. Kennedy died on June 6, 1968.

The Democratic Convention

Kennedy's supporters and delegates were reluctant to swing behind McCarthy. Most of them tended to drift into the camp of either Vice-President Hubert Humphrey or Senator George S. McGovern of South Dakota, neither of whom had directly participated in the primaries. At the Democratic national convention in Chicago, which opened on August 26, Humphrey won the presidential nomination on the first ballot; he chose Senator Edmund Muskie of Maine as his running mate.

The attention of most observers at the Democratic convention focused not on floor votes, but rather on the battles which raged outside the convention hall between representatives of the nation's radicalized youth and the Chicago police. The protesters had no clear unifying purpose, except perhaps to express anger at a political system that obviously would ignore their strong wishes as well as the results of the primary elections. Words were exchanged with police; objects were thrown by demonstrators. Then television viewers were given a demonstration of what "police brutality" meant. Police used night sticks and tear gas indiscriminately. Members of the press, television and radio crews, and onlookers were assaulted along with the demonstrators. Stimulated by the excitement outside, guards inside the convention hall treated delegates roughly and even arrested a few who failed to display proper identification. Most of these events were captured by the ubiquitous eyes of the television cameras (see p. 889). Somehow Humphrey managed to keep smiling and in his acceptance speech termed the theme of his campaign "The Politics of Joy."

Nixon's Nomination and Other Candidates

The struggle for the Republican nomination in 1968 did not even last until the New Hampshire primary. Republicans opposed to former Vice-President Nixon, who again made a strong bid for Republican leadership, backed Governor George Romney of Michigan. However, Romney withdrew before the first primary, and the other possible candidates—Governors Nelson Rockefeller of New York and Ronald Reagan of California—did not campaign actively until just before the Republican convention. However, they acted too late, and Nixon won on the first ballot when the Republicans opened their national convention in Miami Beach on August 7. Nixon chose Spiro T. Agnew, Governor of Maryland, as his vice-presidential nominee. Agnew soon proved a distinct liability in much of the country and blundered into insults directed at a succession of ethnic groups.

Two minor parties also entered the contest. George Wallace, ex-Governor of Alabama, founded the American Independent party, a southern-based conservative organization, which obligingly nominated him for the presidency. As his running mate, Wallace named Curtis LeMay, retired air force general. On the Left, a coalition of pacifists and advocates of "black power" formed the Peace and Freedom party; they named the Black Panther leader, Eldridge Cleaver, to head their ticket. The Peace and Freedom group suffered from disorganization and internal squabbling from the beginning, and it soon became obvious that the American Independent party presented by far the greater threat to the two major parties.

The Campaign and Election of 1968

The presidential campaign of 1968 opened with Humphrey trailing far behind Nixon in the polls. Wherever he went in September and early October, student hecklers hounded the Vice-President. To these young people, Humphrey represented the Vietnam War, the suppression of the Chicago demonstrators, and, in general, the continuation of Johnson's policies. On the first major issue of the campaign—crime in the streets—Humphrey spoke of the need for "order and justice," rather than "law and order," and stressed that discrimination against black Americans had to end. On the second major issue—Vietnam—he encountered almost insurmountable difficulties. He badly needed the antiwar vote to win, but he could not repudiate Johnson without alienating many Democrats. When asked what changes he would make in Johnson's policies, Humphrey could not reply. Not until late September, in a speech in Salt Lake City, did the Vice-President appear to move away from the administration's position by calling for an end to all bombing of North Vietnam in order to make possible meaningful peace talks. By that time, however, Johnson also had decided that peace could best be attained by ending the bombing, as he

The Election of 1968

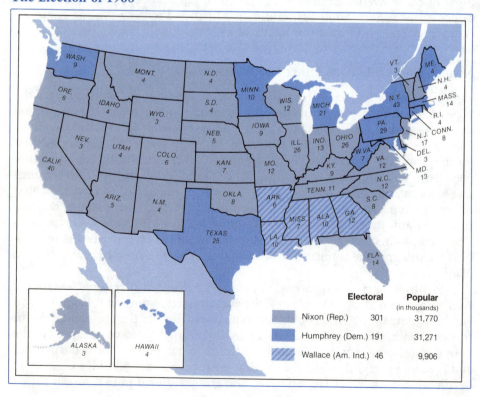

	Electoral	Popular (in thousands)
Nixon (Rep.)	301	31,770
Humphrey (Dem.)	191	31,271
Wallace (Am. Ind.)	46	9,906

publicly announced late in October. This declaration, coupled with Muskie's increasingly effective campaign, infused new vigor into the Democratic campaign.

In contrast to their opponents, the Republicans began their campaign confidently. Nixon, and particularly his running mate, Agnew, talked of "law and order" and the need to stop crime in the streets. Nixon also declared that he had a "plan for peace" in Vietnam but refused to divulge any particulars of it. Nixon increasingly stressed the need for national "unity." He spoke to a nation torn by racial animosities and deep disagreements over the Vietnam War and promised to end the war, without saying how, and to bring the American people back together again. These were widely shared desires, but Nixon said very little during the campaign about how he intended to accomplish these goals. It was very hard for the Democrats to attack him when he took no clear positions.

Meanwhile, Wallace attacked "pointy-head intellectuals" and "anarchists" and made law and order his major issue. Despite all the excitement generated by his flailing attacks and the prediction of the pollsters that he would receive about 20 per cent of the vote, it soon became apparent that he would poll a significant vote only in the South and would hurt Nixon more than Humphrey.

Humphrey's final push was aided by McCarthy's announcement that he would vote for the Vice-President and Johnson's announcement of a total bombing pause over North Vietnam on October 31. Indeed, it seemed that Humphrey might actually accomplish the impossible. Possibly Nixon, out of overconfidence, had been too vague concerning what he would do if elected. Americans spent election night, November 5, 1968, much as they had done eight years before. They watched the Northeast go Democratic and then waited for returns from the South, Midwest, and West. By the early morning of November 6, it was clear that Nixon had carried the crucial states of Ohio, Illinois, and California by small margins and had barely won the presidency.

The statistics show how close Humphrey had come to the prize. Nixon's popular vote of 31,770,237 was 43.4 per cent of the total; Humphrey's 31,270,533, 42.7 per cent. Wallace received 9,906,141 popular votes, or 13.5 per cent of the total, and carried Alabama, Arkansas, Georgia, Louisiana, and Mississippi. Analysts calculated that the Alabamian took two votes that otherwise would have been cast for the Republicans for each vote that he won from the Democrats. Only spirited campaigning by Agnew and Senator Strom Thurmond of South Carolina won a majority of the Border States for Nixon along with North Carolina, South Carolina, and Florida. Their electoral votes, in what had once been a solidly Democratic section, threw the election to Nixon. The final tally in the Electoral College was Nixon, 301; Humphrey, 191; and Wallace, forty-six.

SUGGESTED READINGS

Arthur M. Schlesinger, Jr., *A Thousand Days: John F. Kennedy in the White House* (1963), although distinctly partisan, is excellent as contemporary history and remains the most comprehensive and lively account of that administration. Theodore C. Sorenson, *Kenne-dy* (1965), is another good account. James M. Burns, *Kennedy: A Political Profile* (1959), although to some extent a campaign biography, nevertheless holds up well as a perceptive study of Kennedy as a politician. The literature on the assassinated President himself and his brief administration is already large and still growing. Special works on Kennedy's short administration include: Haynes B. Johnson, *The Bay of Pigs* (1964); John Kenneth Galbraith, *Ambassador's Journal: A Personal Account of the Kennedy Years* (1969); Robert F. Kennedy, *Thirteen Days: The Cuban Missile Crisis* (1969); Elie Abel, *The Missile Crisis* (1966); Henry A. Kissinger, ed., *Problems of National Strategy* (1965); Lewis J. Paper, *The Promise and the Performance: The Leadership of John F. Kennedy* (1975), a political scientist's evaluation; Carl M. Brauer, *John F. Kennedy and the Second Reconstruction* (1977). B. Miroff, *Pragmatic Illusions: The Presidential Politics of John F. Kennedy* (1976), deals with what may well have been Kennedy's basic intellectual weaknesses. In addition to the supposedly "objective" studies by Schlesinger and Sorenson, other members of Kennedy's staff whose memoirs now are in print include Kenneth P. O'Donnell and David F. Powers, *"Johnny, We Hardly Knew Ye"* (1972), which includes a fine account of the start and early years of Kennedy's political career; and Pierre Salinger, *With Kennedy* (1966). The official account of the Kennedy assassination is the Warren Commission, *Report* (1964). Among the many criticisms of this report, E. J. Epstein, *Inquest* (1966), remains the best. William R. Manchester, *The Death of a President* (1967), is a popular description.

The election of 1964 is the subject of Theodore H. White, *The Making of the President 1964* (1965). For an analysis of the problems of the Republican Party, see Robert D. Novak, *The Agony of the G.O.P. 1964* (1965).

Conflicting opinions on Johnson are offered by Rowland Evans and Robert Novak, *Lyndon B. Johnson: The Exercise of Power* (1966); William S. White, *The Professional: Lyndon B. Johnson* (1964); Eric F. Goldman, *The Tragedy of Lyndon Johnson* (1969); and Robert Sherrill, *The Accidental President* (1967). Doris Kearns, *Lyndon Johnson and the American Dream* (1976), is a highly personal analysis; Johnson gives his own version in *The Vantage Point* (1971). Johnson staff members with recollections now in print include Harry McPherson, *A Political Education* (1972), and Jack Valenti, *A Very Human President* (1975). Sar A. Levitan and Robert Taggart analyze the effects of Johnson's Great Society programs in *The Promise of Greatness* (1976). They produce a vast array of evidence that these programs have been much more beneficial to American society than is generally realized. Eugene McCarthy has offered his own history of his presidential campaign in *Year of the People* (1969); also see Jeremy Larner *Nobody Knows: Reflections on the McCarthy Campaign of 1968* (1970). Norman Mailer has written a fascinating piece of journalistic autobiography about the confrontation of police and demonstrators at the Democratic national convention of 1968 in *Miami and the Siege of Chicago* (1968). Philip L. Geyelin, *Lyndon B. Johnson and the World* (1966), is a sympathetic study of that President's foreign policy. More critical is J. William Fulbright, *The Arrogance of Power* (1966).

A blueprint for the Nixon Administration was presented by a young member of Attorney General John Mitchell's staff: Kevin P. Phillips, *The Emerging Republican Majority* (1969). A perceptive account of the election of 1968 can be found in Joseph McGinnis, *The Selling of the President* (1969). A more general account is Theodore H. White, *The Making of the President 1968* (1969), a rather naive description, especially of the "new Nixon."

The origins and early years of American intervention in Vietnam have received a great amount of attention. Among the better works are David Halberstam, *The Making of a Quagmire* (1965); Bernard B. Fall, *Viet-Nam Witness* (1966); and Townsend Hoopes, *The Limits of Intervention* (1969). The most comprehensive treatment can be found in Frances Fitzgerald, *Fire in the Lake* (1972). Those who wish to know more about the lies and staged deceptions of the Johnson administration, connected largely, but not solely, with Vietnam should read Neil Sheehan *et al.*, *The Pentagon Papers* (1971).

As with the Eisenhower administration, most of the works cited in the Suggested Readings for Chapter 34 are relevant to the domestic issues of this period. To this should be added Anthony Lewis, *Gideon's Trumpet* (1964), a provocative analysis of Gideon *v.* Wainright, and Robert G. Dixon, Jr., *Democratic Representation: Reapportionment in Law and Politics* (1968). For general studies of the Warren Court, see Stanley Kutler, *The Supreme Court and the Constitution* (1969); Archibald Cox, *The Warren Court* (1968); and Anthony Lewis, *The Warren Court: A Critical Evaluation* (1969).

CHAPTER 37
THE PRESIDENCY ON TRIAL

1. THE NIXON ADMINISTRATION BEGINS

The Tragedy of Richard M. Nixon

The biography of Richard Milhous Nixon might have been the epitome of the American success story. He was born on a small farm in California on January 9, 1913, and grew up in nearby Whittier, where his father owned a modest grocery store adjoining the railroad tracks. The Nixon family lived in rooms over the store. Richard M. Nixon was reared in the Quaker faith and seems to have been most influenced by his sensitive mother. Nixon's father barely made a living, but Richard worked his way through Whittier College and attended Duke University Law School on a scholarship. Then followed federal employment in Washington and service during the war as a naval supply officer. Back in California after the war, Nixon entered politics as a Republican and defeated a prominent Democratic liberal for the House of Representatives in 1946. Then came, as we have seen, election to the Senate in 1948 and nomination and election as Vice-President in 1952 and 1956, and, finally, election as President in 1968.

Personally, Nixon was shy, reserved, and, above all, insecure to the point of paranoia at times. He was extremely intelligent and hard working. He was also intensely patriotic; he loved his country and was grateful for the opportunities that it had given to him. Driven by insecurities, he was ambitious to the point of ruthlessness. Finally, as is so often true of persons ridden by insecurity, he enjoyed the trappings of power that sup-

President Nixon waves from his helicopter after his arrival in Washington from his world trip in August 1969. After his election, Nixon returned to a theme he had frequently touched upon during the campaign and asserted that "the great objective of this Administration at the outset" was "to bring the American people together." (Wide World Photos)

ported his weak ego, and was impelled by a drive for money, which, to him, symbolized success.

Nixon often said that his great objective was "to bring the American people together." He returned to this theme of national unity in his inaugural address and called for the reconciliation of blacks and whites and young Americans and old Americans. He also mentioned his strong desire for peace abroad.

Neither liberals nor conservatives, and certainly no radical Americans, could take Nixon's words seriously in 1969. Republicans had nominated him for Vice-President in the 1950s to placate the Right wing of the GOP and as a balance to the supposedly moderate and internationalist Eisenhower. During the presidential campaigns of 1960 and 1968, Nixon seemed eager to retain that conservative image, since he criticized Kennedy and George McGovern as reckless liberals, soft on the threat of worldwide Communism. Democratic politicians viewed Nixon as a slightly more cautious version of Senator Joseph R. McCarthy—as the relentless prosecutor of Alger Hiss and as the tireless campaigner who almost invariably attempted to tie Democratic opponents to years of alleged treason in high places. Democratic politicians, who viewed election campaigns as games to be forgotten when the returns were in, never forgave Nixon for breaking what they regarded as the cardinal rule of normal political behavior—that both major parties represented valid American positions.

Actually, Nixon was an opportunist who had adopted many Right-wing domestic positions only because they temporarily served him and his party well during a period of intense public concern about the Cold War. His fierce domestic anti-Communism represented a pragmatic pose more than it did a deep belief. A review of the campaign debates of 1960 shows that, even then, it was Nixon, rather than Kennedy, who suggested that attitudes of the Cold War might be outmoded and should receive a thorough review and revision. Nixon actually did wish to unify the country, and he wanted to bring to an end the era of severe Cold War tension with the Soviet Union and China. He realized that, as a proved extreme patriot, he enjoyed unique protection from rightist criticism and party revolt if he pursued such policies, and he intended to take full advantage of this position.

To some extent, Nixon's efforts toward domestic and international reconciliation met with remarkable success. And yet, when Nixon departed from the White House, he left behind a nation more divided than at any time since the Civil War. The damage that he inflicted, or permitted others to inflict, on the office of the presidency, on relations between the President and Congress, and on the faith of other nations in the United States Government placed his successors in almost impossible positions. The worldwide loss of faith in the American executive branch of government spread to the other branches also. Nixon, therefore, bequeathed to the Presidents who followed him a legacy of strife and a lack of trust within and of the federal government, and a deep belief (or at least an uneasy fear) that the President and his representatives could not be trusted. Nixon was not alone responsible for this legacy. Even so, the immense gulf between Nixon's opportunities and achievements and the terrible state in which he left the presidency constituted a tragedy of nearly classic proportions.

The New Administration

With few exceptions, Nixon appointed moderate or conservative Republicans to the cabinet and other important positions. John Mitchell, who was named Attorney General, immediately stood out as the most influential person in Nixon's entourage. Mitchell, Nixon's former law partner in New York and manager of his presidential campaign, had established and taken formal charge of the "brain trust" which had devised the strategy and tactics of Nixon's campaign. This group spoke often of a "new Republican majority" of middle-class white Southerners, midwestern and western conservatives, and conservatives in the labor movement and persuaded Nixon that that majority could be solidly consolidated at least by the time of the election of 1972.

During the campaign of 1968, upon the advice of these advisers, Nixon continually attacked Johnson's Attorney General, Ramsey Clark, for what he called softness toward criminals of all sorts—from muggers who made city streets unsafe to subversives in the antiwar and other dissident movements. Now, to Mitchell, had been entrusted the task of carrying out Nixon's promise to bring "law and order" to the country, and Mitchell accepted the task with great relish. Two other cabinet appointments for domestic affairs seemed important. Nixon persuaded his longtime California aide, Robert H. Finch, to give up a high state office and take charge of the gigantic Department of Health, Education and Welfare (HEW). Finch, a liberal on civil rights, provided some counterweight to the animosity aroused by Nixon's "southern strategy" (see pp. 992–993). As Secretary of the Interior, Walter J. Hickel, former Governor of Alaska, perhaps surprised Nixon by his enthusiasm for conservation and enforcement of regulations to protect the environment.

Nixon, as a nearly certain winner in 1968 (until Humphrey began to narrow the gap toward the end of the campaign), could and did remain vague about his proposed domestic policies as President. At the time, he appeared to be trying to project an image of a calm and judicious "new Nixon." It now seems clear that this vagueness resulted also from a lack of deep concern about domestic policy, except to the extent that it might significantly affect future elections. This partially explains why Nixon, as President, could often be persuaded to adopt liberal policies; it also explains why he just as easily lost interest when these policies aroused determined opposition.

Actually, Nixon imagined that he modeled himself after Woodrow Wilson, particularly after Wilson as *the* leader in foreign affairs. Foreign policy fascinated Nixon. He intended to use American power as a bargaining weapon for a reduction in the tensions of the Cold War. He also intended to take personal charge of these negotiations. Nixon had declared in a campaign speech in 1968: "I have always believed that this country could run itself domestically without a President. All you want is a competent cabinet to run the country at home. You need a President for foreign policy; no Secretary of State is really important. The President makes foreign policy."

Thus Nixon appointed as Secretary of State one of his early close advisers, William P. Rogers, Attorney General during Eisenhower's second term. Nixon said that Rogers' unfamiliarity with foreign affairs was an important asset because it would prevent him from interfering with the President's direction of foreign policy. Then Nixon proceeded to ignore or snub Rogers. Nixon's actual junior partner in making foreign policy was Henry A. Kissinger, whom he appointed as head of the National Security Council and Special Assistant to the President for National Security Affairs. Kissinger, a former Harvard professor and adviser to Nelson A. Rockefeller, had written books that criticized American Cold War foreign policies which he said were outdated by recent events, such as the split between China and the Soviet Union—an attitude that Nixon shared. Nixon also shared Kissinger's view that the Soviet Union remained a dangerous enemy because its leaders still intended to spread their system throughout the world. The Sino-Soviet rupture merely presented an opportunity to shift the global balance of power.

After Nixon's reelection in 1972, Kissinger's loyalty was rewarded with the post of Secretary of State, which he held thereafter concurrently with the position of National Security Adviser. Depite this superficial appearance of power, Kissinger remained in a situation which required nearly complete deference to Nixon. In fact, Kissinger's love of the personal benefits and publicity that came with his high rank, and his more private ability to act in a subservient manner, made him an almost perfect tool for Nixon.

Gyrating Domestic Policies

Nixon surprised both liberals and conservatives by advocating or accepting from Congress a wide variety of innovative legislation. He veered between Left and Right, partly in order to preempt the political center. Despite his unexpectedly open mind, Nixon's own policies seldom enjoyed success. He was not really interested in domestic legislation. Moreover, he was secluded behind a small group of trusted but inexperienced assistants. He was frequently absent from Washington in well-guarded homes in Key Biscayne, Florida, and San Clemente, California, and in the presidential retreat at Camp David, Maryland. His extreme shyness and suspicion of everyone but his completely devoted aides isolated Nixon from every possible critic, including the press and his own cabinet members. Nixon's closest assistants, H. R. (Bob) Haldeman and John R. Erlichman, totally lacked experience in the federal government or loyalty to anyone or anything in politics except the President and his reelection.

The experiences of Finch and Hickel illustrate how Nixon's domestic policy was formulated. Early in his administration, Nixon had permitted his old friend, Finch, great leeway in running HEW. Finch announced that HEW would withhold federal aid from school districts which made only token efforts at integration. Without interference from Nixon, Finch rejected every plan to slow school integration; these included "freedom of choice" rules, which obliged black students or their parents to request admission to white-dominated schools. When protests from southern politicians increased, Nixon suddenly called a halt to rapid integration and specifically granted Mississippi additional time to end its dual system for blacks and whites. Mitchell brought suits to delay integration in Mississippi. Within a few weeks, the Supreme Court decided that Mississippi had to integrate its schools "at once." Finch prepared to comply with the court's decision by cutting off federal funds to offending districts. Nixon then ordered Finch to permit delays in integration, the Supreme Court notwithstanding. Finch and his top aides in HEW soon resigned in anger and frustration. However, federal judges obeyed the Supreme Court's rulings and ordered prompt integration, with the use of busing when necessary. By the end of Nixon's first term, the percentage of southern blacks in all-black schools had declined from 80 to less than 20 per cent. Nevertheless, Nixon had made his own sympathies clear to Southerners.

Hickel issued a series of regulations to protect the environment, including one that halted the construction of the trans-Alaskan oil pipeline until a route less destructive to Alaska's natural terrain and wildlife could be found. Hickel also halted oil drilling in the Santa Barbara Channel after a well blowout filled the area's water and beaches with petroleum. Hickel banned billboards on federal land and even managed to shame the Justice Department into suing Standard Oil of California for the damage that its careless drilling had done in the Gulf of Mexico. Nixon not only permitted Hickel to undertake these and many other such initiatives; Nixon also called for an environmental program in his State of the Union message to Congress in 1970. By late 1970, however, business complaints about Hickel persuaded Nixon to withdraw his support from the Secretary of the Interior. Hickel promptly followed Finch into private life. Both former cabinet members complained that they had been unable to present their cases to Nixon because Haldeman and Erlichman had refused to give them appointments with the President and had evidently failed even to pass on their messages to Nixon.

Nixon's adviser on urban affairs, Daniel Patrick Moynihan, a sociologist who had served as an adviser to both Kennedy and Johnson, for a while enjoyed better access to Nixon than either Finch or Hickel. Moynihan owed his position largely to a speech which he had delivered in 1967 in which he had referred to "the limited capacities of government to bring about social change." Moynihan also advocated a shift in responsibility for social services from the federal government to the states. Both attitudes coincided with Nixon's. Therefore, Nixon responded favorably when Moynihan suggested a Family Assistance Plan (FAP), which would guarantee to a family of four an income of $1,600 a year, plus $800 in food stamps (a total equal to at least double that income in 1980 dollars). The amount suggested by Moynihan exceeded welfare payments in over twenty states, most of them in the South. Moynihan pleased Nixon by pointing out that he could thus aid the poor without interference from federal bureaucrats, and that Nixon could then end certain Great Society programs. These included the "Head Start" educational experiment for children in poor black and Hispanic families, especially, and free legal assistance to the poor.

Criticism quickly erupted from both liberals and conservatives. Democrats and black leaders complained that no family of four could live decently in an American city on $40 a week, and they demanded higher payments and the continuation of social services. Conservatives objected to such payments to persons who refused to work. Nixon responded to his conservative critics by insisting that every head of household who received FAP payments, except mothers of preschool children, either had to work or register for job training. Despite the misgivings of liberals, the Democratic House of Representatives approved the FAP early in 1973. However, Nixon, at the urging of Erlichman and other aides, announced that he no longer supported FAP. Both Democratic and Republican senators, already full of doubts about the FAP, dropped the measure also. Thus, the welfare system, which satisfied almost no one, continued in operation. And once again, Nixon, after showing a surprisingly open mind to new ideas, discarded them when apathy overcame his initial enthusiasm and opposition aroused his caution and that of his close advisers.

The most heralded part of Nixon's domestic program—revenue sharing by the federal government with the cities and states—also failed to meet any reasonable expectations. Congress approved Nixon's recommendation that the federal government transfer funds so that the cities and states could take over responsibility for what had been federal programs, and revenue sharing began in 1973 with the shift from Washington of about $5 billion. However, mayors of the big cities and governors of the urban states soon began to complain. Under revenue sharing, they said, their constituents received less money than they had previously received from the grants for specific projects and programs which the Nixon administration now reduced in size or ended, such as the Job Corps training centers, which Nixon ordered closed.

Nixon's attempts to reduce domestic expenditures, despite the fancy titles given to them, were motivated in large part by the need to control high rates of price inflation. This problem had arisen first largely because Johnson had vastly increased federal expenditures (and the money supply) for the Great Society and the Vietnam War and had not increased taxes. When reduced spending, tighter bank credit, and higher interest rates caused rising unemployment without checking inflation, Nixon asked Congress for authorization to impose wage and price controls. Although he received this authority in the Economic Stabilization Act of 1970, Nixon promised: "I will not take this nation down the road of wage and price controls, however politically expedient that may seem."

Nevertheless, a year later, continued inflation made controls seem necessary, and Nixon invoked his powers on August 15, 1971, to freeze wages and prices for six months. Then, when he set decontrol in motion in stages, prices began to rise again. With the presidential campaign of 1972 only months ahead, Nixon adopted policies that added fuel to the flames. He urged a willing Congress to reduce taxes and persuaded the Federal Reserve Board to lower interest rates and to encourage borrowing. Spending by governmental agencies increased by about $1 billion a month. The federal deficit for 1972 exceeded that of any year since the Second World War. Nixon's new policies had created tremendous pressure for a new inflationary surge in the future.

Mitchell and Law and Order

Nixon came closer to giving a free rein to Attorney General John Mitchell than to any other member of his cabinet. Mitchell built up a record of attempting to stifle civil liberties (as well as civil rights) which was unmatched since the actions of Attorney General A. Mitchell Palmer during the Red Scare of 1919–1920. Mitchell attempted unsuccessfully to prevent congressional extension of the Voting Rights Act of 1965. He even persuaded Finch to discharge the HEW official in charge of enforcing integration regulations because of that official's zeal for the task. Policies instigated largely by Mitchell caused a NAACP spokesman to declare: "For the first time since Woodrow Wilson, we have a national administration that can be rightly characterized as anti-Negro." (Actually, Mitchell's bigotry and assaults on civil rights far exceeded Wilson's.)

Mitchell's main objective was to stamp out dissent in the country. He apparently meant to bring "law and order" to the nation, no matter how many laws and constitutional safeguards he violated during this effort. Mitchell insisted that the Department of Justice could use wiretaps without obtaining court orders. He urged "preventive detention" for criminal suspects when evidence was insufficient for an arrest. Mitchell persuaded Congress to grant authority for "no knock" searches and to adopt a measure for mandatory prison sentences which obliged judges to ignore unusual circumstances and the mildness of certain offenses. He also instituted prosecution, under various "conspiracy" laws, of antiwar demonstrators and of prominent leftists present at the riots during the Democratic national convention in Chicago in 1968. The trial was a fiasco; all convictions were overturned.

On the surface, Mitchell failed also when he brought suit in 1971 to prevent publication of the Pentagon Papers, a forty-seven volume summary of evidence concerning the escalation of the war in Vietnam, which Secretary of Defense McNamara had ordered compiled when he evidently decided belatedly that the war had been a terrible mistake. The Supreme Court ruled that the *New York Times* could reprint the papers. However, these and many other actions by Mitchell intimidated dissidents, and his actions pleased that sector of the electorate whose votes or sympathies in 1968 had gone largely to George Wallace.

The "Nixon Court"

Nixon, on Mitchell's advice, promised to appoint southern justices to the Supreme Court. He also promised to appoint strict constructionists who, unlike members of the Warren Court, would "interpret the law, not make the law."

Warren resigned in 1969, and Nixon appointed as his successor Warren Burger, a Minnesotan with thirteen years experience on the United States Court of Appeals for the District of Columbia. Burger had publicly criticized the Supreme Court's concern for what he called the rights of criminals. He was quickly confirmed.

Soon thereafter, however, Nixon encountered unprecedented opposition in trying to fill vacancies on the high bench. He ran into trouble at once with his next nomination—a reward for Senator Strom Thurmond, Republican of South Carolina. Blacks accused the nominee, Clement Haynsworth, of bigotry; labor unions also opposed him. Evidence of conflicts of interest by the nominee while he had served as a judge led seventeen Republicans to join Democrats in rejecting the nomination. Mitchell then recommended another southern candidate, G. Harrold Carswell of Florida. Nine of the fifteen members of the faculty of the Law School of the University of Florida joined other legal authorities in testifying before the Senate about the candidate's lack of proper qualifications. Again the Senate rejected the nomination. Nixon charged senators with bias against the South and declared, "I understand the bitterness of millions of Americans who live in the South." He did not refer, of course, to the millions of black Americans in the South. After these symbolic actions and words, Nixon prudently nominated another experienced and competent Minnesota conservative, Judge Harry Blackmun, whose views on most subjects apparently resembled those of Burger. The Senate accepted Blackmun. After he nominated Blackmun, Nixon replaced two especially able liberal justices, Hugo Black and John M. Harlan, with Lewis F. Powell, Jr., of Virginia, a former president of the American Bar Association, and Assistant Attorney General William H. Rehnquist, a leading intellectual of the far Right from Arizona. These four new judges effectively changed the nature of the Supreme Court, although they did not make it predictably conservative. With the aid of occasional votes from other justices, however, they greatly slowed the activism of the Warren Court.

Those groups which had benefited most from the Warren Court's activism and had suffered especially from counterattacks generated by Nixon and Mitchell, now lost some aid which they had received previously from the Supreme Court. Criminal suspects lost the most; but the press, the poor, and minority groups also were deprived of rights and protections granted earlier. In a series of decisions, the Burger Court decreased the rights of criminal suspects and defendants; indeed, that court stopped just short of reversing the Miranda decision altogether. The court also approved police raids on newspaper offices in search of evidence and denied to reporters the right to keep their sources and notes confidential. In 1978, the Supreme Court ruled that a court could hold trials without admitting the public or the press if both the prosecution and defense approved. However, in 1980 the court reversed this decision. The court reduced the rights of poor people to appeal state and local welfare regulations and decisions. The court also permitted Congress to forbid Medicaid payments for abortion and thereby practically ended the former right of poor women to have legal abortions.

However, the court refused to reverse the Warren Court's major decisions. The central concept of the Brown decision—that segregation in public education had to end—was not repudiated. Affirmative action plans were upheld, although by slim majorities and with ambiguous majority opinions regarding the limits of such efforts. However, in 1980 the court explicitly approved federal affirmative action programs. Discharged employees were allowed to sue employers (including a congressman in one case), for sexual discrimination. The justices ordered the government to obtain court orders before employing wiretapping against suspected subversives. It disappointed Nixon terribly when the court ruled unanimously in 1974 that the President had to turn over tape recordings which contained damning evidence against him to a federal district court. Not only did the justices whom Nixon appointed retain greater independence than he had expected, but also the formerly conservative Blackmun moved increasingly toward liberal positions. Furthermore, the choice by Gerald R. Ford (Nixon's successor) of John Paul Stevens to replace the liberal William O. Douglas produced surprising results—for Ford and other conservatives, at least. They had evidently failed to note that Stevens held many liberal opinions, which he soon began to express as a Supreme Court justice.

2. NIXON'S VIETNAM WAR

Futile Efforts for Peace

Soon after he took office, Nixon promised the American people peace in Vietnam—"a peace we can live with and a peace we can be proud of." He failed to explain exactly what he meant. However, events soon made it clear that Nixon, like Johnson, hoped to end the Vietnam War without further large American casualties, and also without the surrender of Vietnam or any other part of Southeast Asia to the Communists. Ho Chi Minh and other officials in Hanoi and the National Liberation Front in South Vietnam, of course, refused to accept Nixon's definition of peace. Negotiations in Paris among representatives of the United States, South Vietnam, North Vietnam, and the NLF dragged on without evidence of progress toward agreement.

Meanwhile Nixon, with advice from Kissinger and Melvin Laird, the Secretary of Defense, adopted policies aimed to obtain the "peace we can be proud of." Laird encouraged Nixon to push "Vietnamization," that is, the development of the South Vietnamese military forces with huge supplies of American military equipment and intensive training, so that South Vietnam could take over completely the task of fighting. As part of this program, Nixon withdrew American troops. Compared to the 543,000 American soldiers in Vietnam in 1968, only 39,000 remained by the autumn of 1972. Nixon responded in part to a combination of public pressure from massive demonstrations for peace and public opinion polls which showed that a large majority of Americans wanted the war brought to a close.

However, Nixon was also responding to congressional action that limited his ability to continue the fighting. A Senate resolution, in 1969, advised the President that American armed forces could not be used abroad in the future without specific congressional approval. Congress (the House in December 1970 and the Senate in January 1971) repealed the Gulf of Tonkin resolution of 1964, which Johnson and Nixon had used as the legal justification to conduct an undeclared war in Vietnam, Cambodia, and Laos. When Nixon continued to order new American military activity, particularly in Cambodia and Laos, Congress passed a measure which set August 15, 1973, as the deadline for ending all United States military action in Indochina.

View of Washington, D.C., on Moratorium Day, November 15, 1969. The peace parade is passing along Pennsylvania Avenue from the Capitol to the Washington Monument for a rally. Mass protests such as this symbolized widespread opposition throughout the country to the Vietnam War. (Wide World Photos)

Although Nixon, Kissinger, and Laird announced periodically that Vietnamization was proceeding successfully, the poorly paid and badly led conscripts armed by the Americans under the program actually damaged Vietnamese villages much more than they did the well-trained North Vietnamese army or its NLF allies. American political and military leaders still seemed incapable of understanding the power of concealed NLF cadres in the villages of South Vietnam, or the slight public support that South Vietnam's dictator, Nguyen Van Thieu, enjoyed outside the capital city of Saigon and a few provincial capitals.

As the failure of Vietnamization became obvious, Nixon and Kissinger decided to use massive bombing attacks to persuade the North Vietnamese and the leaders of the NLF to negotiate seriously. The American leaders believed, correctly in this case, that their enemies would prefer a peace treaty which permitted them to occupy part of South Vietnam, rather than endure the terrible damage that huge amounts of American bombs and rockets could inflict. Stepped-up napalm bombing, the utter destruction of villages suspected of being enemy sanctuaries, and the burning of crops and the chemical defoliation of forests—all supposedly intended to harm the NLF—deprived ordinary Vietnamese of their homes and livelihood.

The Cambodian Affair

When NLF and North Vietnamese raids from bases in border areas of neutral Cambodia threatened the precarious stability of the Saigon government, Nixon, in April 1970, ordered American troops to invade Cambodia and destroy these bases. Enemy forces simply moved deeper into Cambodia, whose army was too weak to stop them. Kissinger then suggested the increased bombing of Cambodia and won approval of this policy from the National Security Council in April 1970. The elusive North Vietnamese suffered hardly at all from either the invasion or the tremendous bombing. However, the Cambodian government (at that point anti-Communist) and the Cambodian economy were wrecked. The bombing forced about 1,000,000 once prosperous and extraor-

A South Vietnamese Ranger keeps his finger on the trigger of his weapon as he watches a Cambodian woman and baby girl emerge from a bunker entrance following American air strikes near Cau Sap in Cambodia in early May 1970. The invasion of Cambodia by U.S. troops to clear out "sanctuaries" used by North Vietnamese and National Liberation Front forces increased opposition to the war at home, particularly as the devastating effects upon the Cambodian people and economy became known. (Wide World Photos)

dinarily peaceful Cambodians to leave their burning farms and villages and to wander toward the cities, where no homes or jobs existed for them. This mass destruction enabled a small but dedicated group of Communists—the Khmer Rouge—to take over the country and to start a bloody purge of both middle-class and pro-North Vietnamese elements of the population.

Nixon's announcement of the invasion (but not the ferocious bombing) of Cambodia set the American peace movement into violent eruption. It had grown quiet under the impression that Nixon was steadily reducing United States participation in the Vietnam War. Antiwar demonstrations occurred in May 1970 on hundreds of college campuses throughout the country, including many which had remained outwardly passive before. Protesters demanded "strikes" to close down colleges and universities as evidence of opposition to governmental policies. A more violent fringe of students burned and bombed school property and interrupted ROTC programs and recruiting efforts by corporations involved in war-related production. Police and national guardsmen who had been called to protect campuses often met angry rock-throwing mobs

A demonstration by students on the College Park, Maryland, campus of the University of Maryland on May 4, 1970. The antiwar demonstrators were dispersed by state police who threw tear gas into the crowd. (Wide World Photos)

of students. When tear gas failed to disperse the students, gunfire was used in a few cases.

Ohio National Guardsmen shot and killed four students and wounded eleven at Kent State University, and policemen killed two and wounded eleven students by firing without much cause into a dormitory at Jackson State University in Mississippi. These injuries and deaths led to larger demonstrations, which seriously disrupted classes at about 400 colleges and universities and closed down over 200.

Nixon seems to have thought seriously that a revolution was in the making. He arranged for taps on the telephones of thirteen high governmental officials, whom he suspected of leaking news of the Cambodian bombing, and on the

A wounded student on the campus of Kent State University, Kent, Ohio, receives help from other students following a confrontation between national guardsmen and antiwar demonstrators on May 4, 1970. National guardsmen, who had been called to the campus to control a series of demonstrations that had culminated in the burning of an ROTC building, resorted to tear gas and bullets. Four students were killed and several others were injured. (Wide World Photos)

telephones of reporters suspected of receiving such information. He attempted to establish a national security committee composed of FBI, CIA and Defense intelligence officials, led by J. Edgar Hoover, which would seek to end this dissent with the aid of wiretapping, electronic surveillance, secret break-ins, opening of suspects' mail, and infiltration of "subversive" groups, especially on campuses. This plan alarmed even J. Edgar Hoover, who feared that its blatant illegality would provide ammunition for the enemies of the FBI, and he refused to participate. Therefore Nixon reluctantly set aside the scheme, but only temporarily.

Nixon announced that the Cambodian invasion had been successful, although actually the North Vietnamese returned to their bases as soon as the Americans withdrew. Nixon expanded the war again with an invasion of Laos in February 1971, in another attempt to cut the supply lines of the North Vietnamese and to destroy their bases. The Defense Appropriations Act of 1970 prohibited Nixon from attacking Laos with American troops; Nixon used the opportunity to test Vietnamization by sending in 16,000 South Vietnamese soldiers who were aided by strong American air cover and bombing. This experiment in Vietnamization failed miserably. Nixon announced after the campaign had ended in April, "Tonight I can report that Vietnamization has succeeded," but the facts contradicted him. When the South Vietnamese troops met strong opposition from four North Vietnamese divisions, the South Vietnamese suffered casualties of over 50 per cent and finally retreated under the cover of heavy American bombing. Once more, American bombing of a neutral nation—this time Laos—killed thousands of innocent people and turned a large proportion of the population into refugees who crowded into already overpopulated cities.

Peace of a Sort

Nevertheless, Nixon and Kissinger got their main point across to the North Vietnamese and the NLF. If their resistance to American proposals at the Paris peace talks continued, the United States leaders would do anything—except permit large numbers of American troops to die—in order to end the war with an "honorable" peace. Had Vietnamization truly proved successful in Laos, Nixon probably would have ordered American support for an invasion by the South Vietnamese of North Vietnam. After the fiasco in Laos, however, Nixon was forced to rely almost entirely on air power to obtain an acceptable peace treaty. By 1971, the United States had already dropped more bombs on Indochina than it had in all the European and Pacific theaters during the Second World War. Now Nixon made certain that the North Vietnamese understood what a continued attempt to win total victory in the South would cost. He ordered a further escalation of the bombing, aimed without warning at South Vietnamese villages reportedly controlled by the NLF and at military installations in North Vietnam.

Meanwhile, South Vietnamese and American troops also understood that Nixon and Kissinger no longer hoped to win the war; they only hoped to get out without obviously losing. Desertions from the South Vietnamese army rose to 12,000 a month. The CIA reported in the autumn of 1970 that between 30,000 and 50,000 South Vietnamese officials were cooperating with the NLF. American troops, an increasing proportion of whom were black or

Hispanic draftees, realized that they risked death and mutilation in a futile war, and they carried on their own rebellion. Open warfare often broke out between black and white American soldiers; desertions and illnesses before combat missions rose dramatically; and enlisted men killed or disabled the officers who tried to push them too hard into dangerous fighting. The highest United States army commanders acknowledged in the spring of 1971 that at least 10 percent (almost certainly too low a figure) of American troops in Vietnam used heroin and that a much higher percentage smoked marijuana even while on active duty.

In these circumstances, Nixon and Kissinger, with the approval of army commanders in Vietnam, resorted to measures calculated to put still more pressure on the North Vietnamese and NLF negotiators. On May 8, 1972, Nixon ordered the mining of the chief North Vietnamese port of Haiphong, as well as of six other North Vietnamese ports. Nixon's objective was to stop or slow drastically the shipment of military supplies from China and the Soviet Union. Johnson had rejected suggestions for such action out of fear of retaliation from either of those countries if a mine sank one of their ships. However, Nixon and Kissinger were involved in negotiations aimed at more friendly relations with both China and Russia; in any case, Nixon needed progress in the peace talks to aid his chances for reelection in November. Nixon also ordered B-52 bombing strikes at targets near and in some cases on Hanoi and Haiphong—clearly a warning that no part of North Vietnam would escape destruction unless peace came soon.

Apparently, Nixon's policy succeeded. On October 26 (conveniently just before the presidential election), Kissinger announced that, as a result of talks that he had conducted personally with the North Vietnamese Foreign Secretary, Le Duc Tho, "Peace is at hand." The North Vietnamese government accepted the agreements reached by Kissinger and Le Duc Tho because they did not oblige it to evacuate most of the areas that it controlled in the South. However, after the election, South Vietnam's President Thieu demanded sixty-three changes in the peace treaty. Hanoi then demanded further concessions in an effort to force the Americans back to the October agreement. Yet Nixon chose to interpret the North Vietnamese demands as a signal that even greater pressure must be exerted.

On December 17, without warning, Nixon ordered the heaviest and most savage bombing of the entire war. Most of these B-52 bomber raids were aimed at targets in North Vietnamese cities. General Alexander Haig, Kissinger's military adviser, accurately described the bombing as the "brutalizing" of North Vietnam. The raids were directed largely at military targets, including factories, rail yards, docks, and power plants, but many of these were located near or in the midst of civilian residential areas. Schools, hospitals, and prisoner-of-war camps, as well as many homes, were hit by exploding bombs. So many B-52 bombing planes took part that North Vietnamese antiaircraft missiles shot down fifteen of them during the two weeks of around-the-clock bombing. Only one of these huge, high-flying bombers had been downed during the previous seven years of the Vietnam war. On December 30, Nixon announced that the North Vietnamese had agreed to reopen negotiations and that the bombing would cease, temporarily at least. The negotiations finally produced a cease-fire agreement that all parties signed on January 27, 1973.

The peace agreement—what Nixon called "peace with honor"—was basically the same as the one drafted—but not approved by Nixon—in October 1972.
It stipulated that the remaining American troops would leave and that all prisoners of war would be returned within sixty days. The agreement left the future
of South Vietnam vague. It referred to South Vietnam's right to self-determination, but also to the unity of Vietnam. Besides, it left the NLF in control of a
large portion of South Vietnam. Secretly, Nixon had promised Thieu renewed military aid if fighting resumed. Consequently, fighting in South
Vietnam continued, as did American military aid. To discourage further participation by American troops, Congress passed, over Nixon's veto, the war-
powers resolution of 1973. It stated that a President could not order troops
into action unless he reported the fact to Congress; that he must halt the
military action at once if Congress voted its disapproval; and that he must do
so within ninety days unless Congress voted its positive approval.

The Aftermath of "Peace with Honor"

In 1975, the North Vietnamese launched a powerful offensive across their border and sent the South Vietnamese army into hasty retreat toward Saigon. Kissinger urged Congress to honor Nixon's secret pledge to Thieu, but Congress
refused. Before enemy troops occupied Saigon, the 5,000 Americans who remained in Vietnam were evacuated, along with more than 100,000 of America's South Vietnamese allies, although more than that number of South Vietnamese who wished to leave had to be left behind. The Southeast Asian refugees—forerunners of many more to come—were settled first in refugee camps
in California, Florida, and Arkansas and then transferred to American communities where they found sponsors and jobs. As their number increased, the
Southeast Asians constituted a sizable new ethnic group, especially in California where over half of them eventually settled.

After more than a decade of American fighting in Southeast Asia, all of Vietnam, Cambodia, and half of Laos were in Communist hands. Casualties included 56,000 Americans killed, about 300,000 wounded, and an uncounted
but very high number addicted to drugs and psychologically disabled. Over
1,000,000 North and South Vietnamese troops had died, and about 5,000,000
had been wounded. Millions of refugees crowded camps for displaced persons
and the slums of the cities of Southeast Asia.

The war also left deep divisions in American society, comparable to those
caused by the Civil War. When Assistant Secretary of Defense John T. Mc-
Naughton suggested to McNamara in 1967 the "objective and encyclopedic"
study of events connected with Vietnam (published as *The Pentagon Papers*),
he had written to McNamara: "A feeling is widely and strongly held that 'the
Establishment' is out of its mind." This feeling spread and intensified during
Nixon's Vietnam War. Estimates of draft dodgers and deserters ranged up to
100,000, and probably over 10,000 young American men stayed in sanctuaries
such as Canada and Sweden after the war ended and Nixon refused to grant
them amnesty. Peace demonstrations and counterdemonstrations had fractured the nation. However, most Americans now realized that limits existed to
their ability to influence events in foreign lands, even with the use of America's great military strength. Furthermore, as the war-powers resolution of 1973
indicated, most Americans probably understood that some wars in which their
Presidents involved them might be mistakes that required prompt correction.

3. NEW INITIATIVES IN FOREIGN POLICY

Opening the Door to China

The achievement of friendlier relations with the People's Republic of China and the Soviet Union was one reason for Nixon's confidence that the United States could mine Haiphong harbor with safety and conduct the "brutalizing" bombing attacks on North Vietnam. By 1971, leaders of both huge Communist nations wished to end the drain on their resources caused by the Vietnam War. Moreover, after their split with the Soviet Union, Chinese leaders knew that they needed allies against their former protector. They also needed food for the Chinese people, who constituted one quarter of the world's population, and the United States was the world's greatest food producer. Access to American technology and capital goods was another reason for a friendlier Chinese attitude toward the United States. Nixon and Kissinger, both strong advocates of balance-of-power global politics, understood the advantage that improved relations with China would give them in negotiations or confrontations with the Soviet Union. Furthermore, for reasons not fully known, China fascinated Nixon.

The Chinese dropped numerous hints of their change in attitude before Nixon returned a favorable response by referring publicly to their country, early in 1971, as "the People's Republic of China," rather than as "Red" or "Communist" China, as he and most Americans had always done before. In response to an invitation by the Chinese Premier, Chou En-lai, Nixon sent Kissinger secretly to Peking, where he arranged for a visit to China by Nixon. Since 1949, few if any American politicians had opposed recognition of the Chinese Communist government, or had supported Chiang Kai-shek's regime in Taiwan, as forcefully as had Richard Nixon. Nixon, in fact, boasted that only he could have led the change in American policy toward China.

Nixon surprised the American people and shocked his more conservative supporters by announcing in July 1971 that he would visit the People's Republic of China. That visit, which occurred in February 1972, succeeded as a theatrical as well as a diplomatic event. American television cameras relayed to the United States Nixon's visits to the Great Wall of China and his meetings with the legendary Chinese Communist heads of state, Mao Tse-tung and Chou En-lai. Officials of the two countries agreed on various types of cultural, commercial, journalistic, and diplomatic exchanges. They postponed formal diplomatic relations, which would necessitate recognition of the People's Republic rather than Taiwan as the legitimate government of China, until the American public had grown more accustomed to the idea.

Détente with the Soviet Union

Nixon had wished to visit the Soviet Union in 1970 in the hope that important Soviet-American agreements would confound the peace demonstrators who were then protesting against the invasion of Cambodia. He expected to make North Vietnamese leaders more willing to sign a peace treaty by showing them that Soviet decision makers considered them expendable when larger matters were involved. Kissinger called Nixon's desire to visit Russia "a point of near obsession."

Four weeks after Nixon, in the summer of 1971, announced his forthcoming visit to China, Soviet officials invited him to visit Moscow. The agenda would include talks on the limitation of strategic arms (SALT) and cooperation in space exploration.

The agreements reached by Nixon in Moscow in May 1972 indicated that both the Soviet leaders and the American President were willing at least to attempt to reduce tensions between the two countries. The head of the Communist party, Leonid Brezhnev, seemed eager to slow down the arms race and to concentrate instead upon increasing Soviet capacity to produce food and consumer goods. Nixon and Brezhnev signed the SALT agreement, already hammered out by their subordinates. It severely limited emplacement of antiballistic missile systems, which, in any event, seemed unlikely to provide effective defense. The agreement also froze deployment of ICBMs by each side at the then existing number possessed by each country. The pact did not affect improvements in quality, and it was to last only for five years. The Soviet Union received the right to buy large quantities of American wheat, which American farmers eagerly sold them. After the presidential election, these sales produced sharply higher grain prices in the United States; meanwhile, however, both Brezhnev and Nixon had obtained what they wanted.

Brezhnev came to Washington in June 1973 for further bargaining. In a new agreement, Brezhnev and Nixon pledged never to engage in a nuclear attack and promised to hasten negotiations toward SALT II, which would halt the construction of offensive nuclear weapons. It seemed a promising beginning toward meaningful détente. In a toast that he offered to Brezhnev at a dinner before the Communist chief departed, Nixon asked: "Shall the world's two strongest nations constantly confront one another in areas which might lead to war, or shall we work together for peace?" Nixon, in the area that he considered the President's foremost responsibility—foreign policy—had tried, in dealing with China and the Soviet Union, to work for future peace and had enjoyed significant success.

4. WATERGATE AND THE DOWNFALL

The Campaign and Election of 1972

Like most Presidents, Richard Nixon began to run for reelection before his first inauguration; however, he did so with unusual skill and careful planning. During the campaign of 1968, Nixon's advisers had decided that a new majority coalition could be formed among the American electorate.

Its basis would be a combination of the regular conservative Republican minority and George Wallace's American party constituency of 1968. Wallace had won 10,000,000 votes, or about 13.5 per cent of the total cast in the election of 1968, despite the reluctance of many voters to "waste" their ballots on a hopeless third-party candidate. Wallace had also demonstrated earlier that a tremendous number of Democrats were dissatisfied with their party's dominant policies and presidential candidates. In the preconvention campaign of 1968, Wallace had won 43 per cent of the vote in the Maryland Democratic presidential primary and 34 per cent in the Wisconsin primary.

Some Nixon aides had spoken freely during the campaign of 1968 about presidential policies that would shift Wallace's supporters to Nixon during their candidate's first term in office. One of Nixon's clever strategists, Kevin Phillips, explained in *The Emerging Republican Majority* (1969) how the new majority would be created. Phillips used the term "middle Americans" to describe the former Democrats, Wallace supporters, and the regular Republicans who would form the new Republican majority in support of Nixon. Phillips further identified the members of the new majority as "the unyoung, the unblack, and the unpoor." Others preferred to use the phrase, "the silent majority," when they referred to essentially the same group.

Nixon and Mitchell aimed their "southern strategy" largely at middle-class southern whites. This was one reason for the nomination of two very ordinary southern judges to the Supreme Court and for the administration's efforts to halt or slow integration. To the former southern Democrats and the dependable conservative Republicans, Nixon strategists expected to add millions of votes from northern and western workers. Nixon and Mitchell used both rhetoric and policies to assure these particular "middle Americans" that the Nixon administration shared their distress and anger about crime in the streets, integration of their ethnic neighborhoods, mandated school busing, high taxes, inflation, welfare cheating, peace demonstrations, and certain life-styles associated with young people in the 1960s. Although such attitudes within the administration would antagonize many blacks, Hispanics, and some moderate Republicans, particularly in the Northeast, Nixon and his advisers concluded that the next presidential election could be won easily without them. Their new coalition, they believed, would destroy the Democratic majority created during the New Deal and make the Republican party dominant in the United States.

The Nixon strategists received unexpected aid in May 1972, when an attempted assassination left George Wallace partially paralyzed and eliminated Nixon's chief competitor for the votes of "middle Americans." The Democratic convention, which opened in Miami on July 10, provided further help. It nominated for President George S. McGovern, Senator from South Dakota, and the favorite of the party's antiwar and Left wing. Blacks, women, and young people constituted a much higher proportion of the delegates in the Miami convention than in previous Democratic conventions on account of the adoption of new rules for choosing delegates, proposed by a party committee headed by McGovern himself. Powerful elements within the Democratic party were antagonized by the sight on the convention floor of aggressive feminists, of blacks who, in 1968, had challenged the legitimacy of southern white delegations, and of young radicals who had demonstrated outside the Chicago convention in 1968. The rejection of Chicago's Mayor Daley as a delegate by the Democratic convention of 1972 revealed both the shift in power within the party and the alienation of traditional sources of Democratic votes. When Democrats such as Daley and George Meany, president of the AFL-CIO, withheld their active support from McGovern, they increased the chances for the successful execution of the plan of the Nixon strategists to form a new Republican majority coalition.

The Left-liberal positions which had won the nomination for McGovern — such as a guaranteed income for all Americans and immediate withdrawal from the Vietnam War — threw most of the center and Right of the American electorate to Nixon. McGovern's mishandling of a sensitive situation concerning his vice-presidential running mate, Senator Thomas Eagleton of Missouri, virtually ended whatever chances McGovern might have had. Eagleton admitted, soon after the presidential campaign began, that he had been hospitalized twice for psychiatric care. McGovern at first announced complete support for Eagleton. However, when public opposition to that position became clear, McGovern reversed himself and asked for Eagleton's resignation. (Sargent Shriver, a brother-in-law of John F. Kennedy, was named instead.) McGovern thus antagonized both those voters who sought stable leadership and those who had admired his integrity. At that early point in the contest, McGovern's campaign manager told him frankly that he would lose.

Nevertheless, McGovern stepped up his attacks on Nixon for continuing the war in Vietnam, which, McGovern charged, had caused the unnecessary deaths of 15,000 Americans since Nixon's inauguration. McGovern also made various strong charges of corruption against Nixon. Most of them were accurate but ignored. On the whole, McGovern failed to develop any programs or advance any domestic policies that excited the electorate.

Insecure and suspicious to the point of paranoia, Nixon and his campaign leaders jettisoned the Republican National Committee in 1971 and formed the Committee to Reelect the President (commonly called CREEP once its activities became known), under the leadership of John Mitchell, who resigned as Attorney General. CREEP collected a record $55 million to $60 million, much of it in large illegal contributions from corporations and individuals who had received or expected special favors from the federal government. During the preconvention campaign, CREEP used this money to finance highly imaginative "dirty tricks" intended to confuse and demoralize potentially strong opponents such as Wallace and the early leader for the Democratic nomination, Senator Edmund S. Muskie of Maine. One letter devised and circulated by CREEP moved Muskie to tears when he tried to refute it during the primary campaign in New Hampshire. At that time, polls showed Muskie leading Nixon. Pictures of Muskie weeping were published widely enough to harm his candidacy seriously.

Five CREEP agents broke into Democratic National Committee headquarters in the Watergate complex in Washington in May 1972, copied files, and placed a tap on the telephone of Lawrence O'Brien, chairman of the Democratic National Committee. At 2 A.M. on June 17, 1972, policemen, alerted by a security guard, arrested the same five men in the act of a second burglary of Democratic headquarters in the Watergate complex. The burglars again were engaged in placing "bugs" in the headquarters and in copying documents. Two accomplices were arrested soon afterward. One of them, James McCord, a former CIA agent, was a well-known official of CREEP.

Mitchell swiftly denied that the burglars had acted under orders from CREEP, and Nixon's press secretary called the break-in "a third rate burglary." Two months later, Nixon denied that he knew anything about the break-in. He declared that a careful investigation had revealed that "no one in the White House staff, no one in this Administration presently employed, was engaged in this very bizarre incident." (No such investigation actually had taken place.) Nixon also piously proclaimed: "This kind of activity, as I have often indicated, has no place whatsoever in our political process."

McGovern attempted to tie Nixon to the Watergate burglary, as well as to other evidence then coming to light of corruption in government; but few American voters took McGovern's charges seriously. Nixon left most of the

Republican campaigning to Vice-President Agnew, who railed against peace demonstrators and newspaper columnists and in favor of law and order and harsh punishment for criminals. After Kissinger announced that "peace is at hand" in Vietnam late in October, the only remaining question about the election was the dimension of the Nixon victory. Nixon won 60.8 per cent of the popular votes – the largest proportion obtained by any presidential candidate, except Johnson's 61.1 per cent in 1964. Nixon's majority in the Electoral College – 521 to seventeen – was the greatest in the history of the United States, except for Franklin D. Roosevelt's majority in 1936. McGovern won only Massachusetts and the District of Columbia. However, the Democrats retained control of both houses of Congress. The presidential election, therefore, constituted a glorious personal victory for Nixon and a public rebuke to the progressive McGovern.

The Cover-Up Begins

Meanwhile, the outwardly jubilant Nixon had been trying desperately to keep his administration and his career from falling apart. His personal counsel, John Dean, had told his closest aide, Haldeman, almost every detail about the Watergate break-in two days after it occurred, including the names of the persons arrested and their relation to the President's campaign. On the following day, June 20, after Nixon had returned from a visit to Florida, Nixon and Haldeman evidently discussed the arrests, their possible legal and political repercussions, and methods to prevent those consequences. During the remainder of the campaign, Nixon and his chief assistants devoted time almost daily to efforts to cover up the Watergate affair.

After his conversation with Nixon on June 20, Haldeman reported to him three days later: "We're back in the problem area because the FBI is out of control." Nixon ordered Haldeman to tell the Acting Director of the FBI, L. Patrick Gray – who had been appointed to the position after Hoover's death in May 1972 – "Don't go any further into this case, period." Haldeman and Erlichman met also with high CIA officials and left the director of the CIA with the accurate impression that Nixon was attempting to use the agency to prevent an investigation by the FBI. Mitchell resigned as head of CREEP two weeks after the Watergate burglary; he gave his wife's "psychological difficulties" as the reason. Gray and officials of CREEP destroyed huge quantities of records which related to the administration's illegal campaign activities. The leading Watergate defendants received promises of presidential pardons if they would agree quietly to serve short prison terms; over $400,000 was distributed to the defendants from CREEP campaign funds to pay legal fees, support families, and to pay bribes to buy their silence about the orders that they had received from above. Attorney General Richard Kleindienst announced that a massive FBI investigation revealed that no high administration officials had been involved in the Watergate burglary. Thus Nixon kept the matter fairly quiescent during the campaign.

The Downfall of Nixon

Nixon's administration and personal political career began to disintegrate at a rapid rate almost immediately after his second inauguration. The trial judge for the Watergate burglars, John J. Sirica of the district court of the District of

Columbia, was an Eisenhower appointee and a true law-and-order judge. He also was devoted to the Constitution. The trial of the Watergate burglars began in January 1973; on February 2, Sirica declared that he was "not satisfied" that the whole story was being told in court. Partly as a result of Sirica's demand for further investigation, the United States Senate established a special committee to investigate charges of illegalities during the recent presidential election. Another tough law-and-order advocate and an authority on constitutional law, Senator Sam Ervin, Jr., of North Carolina, was chairman of a committee dominated by Democrats. Of the three Republicans on the committee, only one had close ties to the Nixon administration.

After the prosecution had presented its case before Sirica, the Watergate defendants declined to testify and all pleaded guilty. Sirica then gave each defendant the maximum sentence allowed by law; however, he added that he would show leniency to any defendant who told the truth. McCord broke first. He presented to Sirica a letter which claimed that high administration officials had been involved, and he offered to testify before the Ervin committee. Dean, who had been running errands for Nixon which were connected with the cover-up, began to fear that he was being groomed for the role of chief victim. He, too, began to confess to the Watergate prosecutors. As evidence accumulated in the prosecutors' office, the records of the Ervin committee, and in newspapers—especially in the *Washington Post*—of widespread criminal behavior within the Nixon administration, the President sacrificed one aide after another to the investigators. However, he continued to pretend to be shocked at each revelation and to maintain his own innocence.

Gray resigned on April 27, 1973, after he admitted that he had burned documents concerning Watergate and other FBI investigations of the administration's activities. Three days later, Nixon announced in a major television address the resignations of Haldeman, Erlichman, Dean, and Kleindienst. Nixon also promised to continue to ferret out the facts. "The easiest course," he said, "would be for me to blame those to whom I delegated the responsibility to run the campaign. But that would be a cowardly thing to do. . . . In any organization the man at the top must bear the responsibility. I accept it. . . . There can be no whitewash at the White House. . . . God bless America. I love America."

Ervin's committee began televised hearings on May 17. A parade of witnesses connected or formerly connected with the administration confessed to criminal acts which aimed, first, to win the election of 1972, and, second, to cover up these acts by perjury and conspiracy to persuade others to commit perjury and to destroy evidence. In addition, there were revelations of attempts to interfere with judicial proceedings and of bribery, blackmail, promises of presidential pardons, burglary to collect material for use in blackmail, and numerous other offenses. "It's beginning to be like Teapot Dome," exclaimed Senator Goldwater.

During testimony before the Ervin committee, a White House official revealed for the first time on July 16, 1973, that Nixon routinely recorded on tape his conversations in the Oval Office. All through the following year, the Senate, Sirica, and federal prosecutors fought with Nixon for possession of these tapes. Although he continued to maintain, as he stated in one news conference, that he was not "a crook," Nixon knew that the tapes would prove otherwise. To give the appearance of an impartial investigation, Nixon had appointed men with reputations for independence and honesty to crucial positions. He had appointed his Secretary of Defense, Elliot Richardson, as Attorney General. Nixon had also agreed when Richardson — in response to the Senate's demands that he appoint a special Watergate prosecutor — chose a professor at the Harvard Law School, Archibald Cox, who had served as Solicitor General in the Kennedy and Johnson administrations. Nixon had also appointed William Ruckelshaus, the highly respected head of the Environmental Protection Agency, as acting director of the FBI.

Cox obtained an order from Sirica on August 29 for nine sections of tapes which would have incriminated Nixon. Nixon offered instead transcripts, which he would edit himself. Cox refused to accept the edited transcripts. Nixon then ordered Richardson to discharge Cox. Richardson resigned on Saturday, October 20, rather than carry out this order. Ruckelshaus, recently appointed Deputy Attorney General, also declined to discharge Cox, and Nixon dismissed Ruckelshaus. The Nixon appointee next in line for the position of Attorney General, Robert Bork, finally discharged Cox on Saturday night.

This, the so-called Saturday Night Massacre, aroused serious doubts about Nixon's innocence even among his own supporters in Congress. The House Judiciary Committee began to discuss whether the President should be impeached, and Republican congressional leaders warned Nixon that Republicans as well as Democrats were prepared to approve impeachment. Nearly a half million telegrams protesting the "Saturday Night Massacre" poured into the White House.

Another body blow to the administration came on October 10, 1973. Vice-President Agnew, that tireless campaigner for law and order and critic of judges who meted out lenient sentences to criminals, plea bargained for conviction on one count of income-tax evasion and surrender of the vice-presidency in exchange for an agreement by the government not to prosecute charges of soliciting, extorting, and accepting bribes. Evidence released by the Justice Department appeared sufficient to indict Agnew on at least fifty counts. Congress quickly confirmed Nixon's choice, Gerald R. Ford, the House Minority Leader, to succeed Agnew under the terms of the Twenty-fifth Amendment. Ford immediately began a series of speeches throughout the country. He defended Nixon and denounced the "few extreme partisans" who were persecuting him.

Nixon now tried desperately to squirm out of the legal nets cast about him by Sirica, the Ervin committee, Cox, and the House Judiciary Committee by delivering one emotional appeal after another over the heads of his tormentors to the American people. However, these appeals became less and less effective as new evidence came to light of Nixon's personal involvement in criminal activities during his administration and his campaign for reelection.

War broke out in the Middle East during October 1973, when Egypt, Syria, Jordan, and other Arab states launched a surprise attack against Israel. After the United States and many other nations expressed some degree of support for Israel, the Arab oil-producing nations reduced shipments of oil to these countries. The consequent sharp rise in oil prices caused a tremendous wave of inflation throughout the world. Nevertheless, the already embattled Nixon refused to call for the rationing of oil, measures for the conservation of energy, or other potentially unpopular actions to stem the tide of inflation. Nixon toured the Middle East in mid-1974 and visited Moscow soon afterward. As he had hoped, he received enthusiastic public receptions. However, Kissinger complained later that diplomacy with middle eastern nations and with Russia "was getting more and more difficult because it involved the question of whether we could, in fact, carry out what we were negotiating." The real question, of course, was whether Congress would permit Nixon to remain in the White House much longer.

By June 1974, Nixon had listened to all his tapes and realized that they provided evidence for criminal prosecution as well as impeachment proceedings against him. Therefore, when Cox's successor, Leon Jaworski, demanded access to some sixty-four tapes, Nixon ordered his attorneys to refuse on grounds of the constitutional privileges of the executive branch in its dealing with the judiciary and Congress. Nixon expected the Supreme Court, where his appointees formed nearly a majority, to concur in his refusal.

Impeachment

The Supreme Court gave Nixon a shocking reply on July 24, 1974. After it acknowledged that the executive could keep secret matters of national security, a unanimous court said that the Watergate events were "criminal proceedings," and that Nixon had to turn over the sixty-four tapes to Judge Sirica immediately. The pace of impeachment activity speeded, and opposition to it melted away.

By July 30, the House Judiciary committee had voted to impeach Nixon on

After hearing testimony for several weeks on impeachment charges against President Nixon, the House Judiciary Committee opened debate on the articles of impeachment on July 24, 1974, before a nationwide television audience. Three days later, the Committee voted by a margin of 27 to 11 to recommend the impeachment of Richard M. Nixon, 37th President of the United States. (Wide World Photos)

three counts. The first article of impeachment charged Nixon with obstruction of justice through the use of false statements, payment of "hush money" bribes, withholding evidence, interference with investigations, and lying in addresses to the American people. The second article accused Nixon of misusing the FBI, CIA, and Internal Revenue Service to spy on and otherwise oppress the American people. Efforts by Nixon's aides, who acted under his instructions, to intimidate Americans with burglaries, wiretaps, and the like were included in this article. The third article dealt with Nixon's refusal to turn over the tapes and other evidence to Congress, despite subpoenas to do so. The committee decided not to include articles which dealt with the bombing of Cambodia and the charge of misuse of public funds to enrich himself and his friends. The committee omitted these, not for lack of evidence, but because the other articles seemed virtually unassailable — and sufficient.

Resignation

Nixon finally turned over the last of the tapes demanded by Jaworski — those which were most incriminating to him personally — on August 5. Nixon admitted that he had concealed their existence from his own lawyers, but he still

Former President Richard M. Nixon waves farewell from Airforce One after his resignation. It is a crushing historical irony that the Nixon administration succeeded beyond belief in its campaign promise to unify the American people. The Watergate crisis not only brought the American public together in common outrage, but led to some of the most concerted Congressional action in the country's history. (Wide World Photos)

insisted that he was innocent of all charges against him. Nevertheless, Nixon did not wait to find out whether Congress would agree (which was highly unlikely in view of public statements about Nixon's guilt by many Republicans as well as Democrats in Congress). Instead, on August 9, 1974, Nixon resigned from office; he was the first President in the history of the United States to do so.

Members of the Nixon administration began a parade to grand juries, courts, and federal jails. In addition to the seven men connected directly to the Watergate burglary, over ten other Nixon administration and CREEP officials received jail sentences. The most prominent of these included the nation's chief law enforcement officer during the first Nixon administration, former Attorney General John Mitchell. Nixon's closest aides, Haldeman and Erlichman, soon followed Mitchell to prison. Still the nation waited for the truth about Nixon's role in crimes already discussed in court cases and signed confessions, as well as about other possible crimes which remained charges without much evidence. Now almost anything concerning governmental officials seemed credible to a high proportion of the American people as they awaited legal action against Nixon to follow the trial of almost all of "the President's men." Meanwhile, for the first time, the American people had a President whom they had not elected.

5. THE HERITAGE OF THE "IMPERIAL PRESIDENCY"

The Crisis in American Government

The misguided actions and deceptions of Johnson and Nixon and the illicit acts by their subordinates, which they encouraged or permitted, profoundly affected the attitudes of probably a large majority of American citizens. These deceptions and Nixon's lies about the Watergate cover-up made millions of Americans cynical about their government far beyond anything that Americans had experienced earlier — certainly more so than during the scandals of the Grant or Harding eras. In those earlier scandals, the President never had involved himself in the most despicable aspects, and widespread spying on citizens had never become deliberate and systematic national policy. Furthermore, the revelations of the 1970s came to people who still believed that their leaders differed significantly from the heads of totalitarian regimes, who obviously reported important matters untruthfully to their own people. This belief had survived attacks by the New Left during the 1960s and early 1970s on the basic premise that democratically elected political leaders could be trusted. The virtually indisputable evidence in the Pentagon Papers and the trials of Nixon's aides shocked a relatively trusting population and gave some credence to the New Left's charges, although not necessarily to the New Left's prescriptions for change. One symptom of this cynicism appeared in the growing belief in conspiracy theories about the assassinations of John F. Kennedy, Robert F. Kennedy, and Martin Luther King, Jr.,

Moreover, huge expenditures on the war in Vietnam, which filled the pockets of workers and the treasuries of corporations, helped to fuel a tremendous rise in prices which warped the American social and economic fabric. Also, enormous governmental spending for the Vietnam War deprived Johnson's ambitious Great Society program of sufficient funds and the attention needed to make it clearly successful. Money which might have made many parts of the program effective went instead to buy ammunition, tanks, helicopters, and personnel carriers. Funds which might have aided Great Society programs paid for the bombs which devastated Vietnam, Cambodia, and sections of Laos. Therefore, cynicism about the effectiveness of progressive governmental programs spread among the American public after the Great Society and parts of President Kennedy's New Frontier failed to deliver clear-cut results. Congress also suffered from the diminished confidence of the American people in their leaders. In fact, congressmen themselves demonstrated a loss of faith by removing powers formerly entrusted to committee chairmen who had failed to oversee properly the spending of public funds by the President, the CIA, the FBI, the Defense Department, and other agencies of the executive branch of government. Congress proceeded to distribute these powers to subcommittees. Perhaps the change increased the level of congressional scrutiny; it certainly decreased the ability of Presidents and other party leaders to gain legislative approval for broad programs, parts of which might be spread among a multitude of stubborn subcommittees. The courts suffered a lesser loss of prestige than the other two branches of federal government. The Supreme Court had, at least, permitted publication of the Pentagon Papers and had forced Nixon to surrender his tapes.

SUGGESTED READINGS

A sound, comprehensive analysis of the Nixon presidency remains to be written. Many interesting, informative, and often provocative biographies of Nixon have appeared, and some biographies, autobiographies, and what can best be described as defensive memoirs now are available, including some by Nixon himself. See Nixon, *Six Crises* (1962), for self-revelations about the man, some of which are unintentional. Nixon's presently definitive autobiography is *RN: The Memoirs of Richard Nixon* (1978). Garry Wills, *Nixon Agonistes* (1970), is perceptive, but lacks the perspective that knowledge of the rest of Nixon's presidency would have brought. The same might be said for Jules Witcover, *The Resurrection of Richard Nixon* (1970), and Rowland Evans and Robert Novak, *Nixon in the White House* (1971). Bruce Mazlish, *In Search of Nixon* (1972), is a dubious but sometimes enlightening psychobiography.

On Agnew, see Jules Witcover, *White Knight: The Rise of Spiro Agnew* (1972), unfortunately written before the "white knight's" fall. Witcover and R. M. Cohen remedy this deficiency in *Heartbeat Away* (1974). Kevin Phillips' fine book on the Nixon-Mitchell political strategy, *The Emerging Republican Majority* (1969), is also cited in the text. On the rise to power of Haldeman and Erlichman, see Dan Rather and Gary P. Gates, *The Palace Guard* (1974). Moynihan gives an account

of his intentions and his view of the probable effects of his guaranteed income plan, as well as an account of how he persuaded Nixon to adopt it, in *The Politics of a Guaranteed Income* (1972). Also see his *Coping* (1973). Other volumes on politics during the first Nixon administration include Arthur M. Schlesinger, Jr., *The Imperial Presidency* (1973), cited earlier; Frank Mankiewicz, *Perfectly Clear: Nixon from Whittier to Watergate* (1973), which is unsatisfactory as a whole biography, and Samuel Lubell, *The Hidden Crisis in American Politics* (1970). Theodore H. White's, *The Making of the President, 1972* (1973), is the least competent of White's series of books on presidential elections. Robert S. Anson, *McGovern* (1972), another campaign biography, almost does justice to its subject. Arthur M. Schlesinger, Jr., *Robert Kennedy and His Times* (1978), covers a wide period. Nixon's domestic policies are chronicled, again not quite satisfactorily, in R. L. Miller, *The New Economics of Richard Nixon* (1972). Richard Harris, *Decision* (1971), is an adequate treatment of one of Nixon's worst Supreme Court nominations—G. Harrold Carswell of Florida. The best general study of the entire Nixon presidency is Jonathan Schell, *The Time of Illusion* (1976).

Members of the Nixon administration have written about it in almost unprecedented numbers. Among the more informative is Henry Kissinger, *White House Years* (1979), which should be read as the work of a man still ambitious for high office and a leading role in the making of foreign policy. Moynihan's volumes are mentioned above. Walter J. Hickel, *Who Owns America?* (1971); William Safire, *Before the Fall* (1975); and Clark Mollenhoff, *Game Plan for Disaster* (1976), are useful. Memoirs by John Dean, James McCord, Jeb Stuart Magruder, Charles Colson, E. Howard Hunt, and Leon Jaworski reveal as much about the authors as about Nixon and his administration. The most valuable among these for students of history are John W. Dean, *Blind Ambition* (1976); Leon Jaworski, *The Right and the Power: The Prosecution of Watergate* (1976); Jeb S. Magruder, *American Life: One Man's Road to Watergate* (1974), and, particularly, John J. Sirica, *To Set the Record Straight* (1979).

In addition to the memoirs mentioned above, the Watergate scandals have given rise to numerous books. Among the best is Theodore H. White's *Breach of Faith: The Fall of a President* (1975), which compensates somewhat for gaps in his study of the election of 1972. Carl Bernstein and Bob Woodward, *All the President's Men* (1974), will remain a classic journalistic account of the uncovering of the Watergate scandal—in part—by the two *Washington Post* reporters who played major roles in that process. Bernstein and Woodward's *The Final Days* (1976) completes their particular story. Raoul Berger, *Impeachment: The Constitutional Problems* (1974), is a sound analysis of the problems presented by Nixon's actions.

In addition to Kissinger's memoir, mentioned above, other informative volumes on Nixon's foreign policy include: Marvin and Bernard Kalb, *Kissinger* (1974); Robert Osgood *et al.*, *Retreat from Empire?* (1973); Henry Brandon, *The Retreat of American Power* (1973); Lloyd Gardner, ed., *The Great Nixon Turnaround* (1973); Adam Yarmolinsky, *The Military Establishment: Its Impact on American Society* (1971); and Morton Halperin, *Defense Strategies for the Seventies* (1971). All these should be treated as tentative appraisals. More likely to be of lasting value are John G. Stoessinger, *Henry Kissinger: The Anguish of Power* (1976), although its author, another academician with policy-making experience and ambitions, overestimates Kissinger's influence over foreign policy; Schell, *The Time of Illusion*, already cited, which presents probably the finest analysis of Nixon's foreign policy as part of his overall presidential objectives; and John Newhouse, *Cold Dawn* (1973), on the shift in the relations between the United States and the USSR, especially concerning the SALT talks and agreement. Ted Szulc's *The Illusion of Peace* (1977) provides another comprehensive account of Nixon's foreign policies. Frances Fitzgerald, *Fire in the Lake* (1972), contains an excellent chapter on "Nixon's War"; but she may underestimate the effect of Kissinger's advice to Nixon that an enemy must be hit hard and swiftly to further negotiations aimed at peace. Finally, William Shawcross, *Sideshow: Kissinger, Nixon, and the Destruction of Cambodia* (1979), is a devastating indictment which Kissinger tried, unsuccessfully, to refute in *White House Years*.

CHAPTER 38
SINCE WATERGATE

1. THE FORD PRESIDENCY

The Legacy of Watergate

Vice-President Ford took the oath of office as President of the United States on August 9, 1974. On that same day, Ford announced reassuringly: "Our long national nightmare is over." He also reminded the American people that, during the ceremonies devoted to inaugurating him as Vice-President eight months earlier, he had stated: "I am a Ford, not a Lincoln." This evident awareness of his limitations and of the country's turmoil immediately established a favorable comparison of Ford with Nixon and won Ford wide though tentative support and popularity. Ford's selection of the veteran liberal Republican, Nelson Rockefeller, as his Vice-President seemed to demonstrate a desire to heal the nation's wounds. So, too, did Ford's regular consultations with his former colleagues in Congress — Democrats as well as Republicans — about potential presidential policies. The new President appeared open, amiable, and eager to compromise rather than to fight with opponents. He instituted what he called a "leniency" program for young Americans who had dodged the draft or deserted in order to avoid fighting in Vietnam. The program was vague and persuaded almost no young war opponents to turn themselves in; but it, too, seemed to indicate Ford's desire to heal the nation. Actually, Ford held much more conservative political views than Nixon, and his Cold War attitudes remained more rigid. For a while, however, these positions were virtually unknown to the public.

Then, only one month after his inauguration, Ford suddenly issued to his predecessor and benefactor a "full, free, and absolute" pardon for "all offenses against the United States" that Nixon had committed while President. Nixon continued to deny that he had committed any crimes, yet he hastily accepted the pardon. Rumors that Ford had agreed to some such deal as part of the price for his selection as Vice-President had circulated among the nation's politicians and national political reporters ever since Nixon unexpectedly elevated the genial but otherwise undistinguished House Republican leader.

During the hearings on his confirmation, a senator had asked Ford whether he would consider granting a pardon to Nixon if the President resigned. "I don't think the public would stand for it," Ford replied. In several respects the public did not stand for it. A majority found Ford's explanation unsatisfactory — that he wanted only to end "an American tragedy in which we have all played a part." Was Ford implying that he and others yet unnamed had played a part? Was he attempting to blame the American people for the behavior exposed in the Nixon tapes? For what crimes had Nixon been pardoned? Now the nation might never know. Why were Nixon's chief assistants — Mitchell, Haldeman, and Erlichman — on trial and probably on their way to prison, while the man who had issued their orders was enjoying the sea breezes at his mansion in San Clemente? Public confidence in Ford plunged.

Meanwhile, the Senate Select Committee on Intelligence began to reveal the evidence that it had uncovered of a long history of violations of constitutional rights and of international law by the CIA and the FBI. This evidence implicated the CIA in assassinations of a number of foreign political leaders in an effort to change policies in their countries. Bizarre but unsucessful efforts by the Kennedy administration to murder Fidel Castro — in one instance with a poisoned cigar — in which the CIA employed known gangsters, reopened the theory that Castro may have struck back in response by aiding in the assassination of President Kennedy. Castro found it necessary to acknowledge his annoyance, but to deny any complicity in the assassination. The committee revealed, too, that the CIA had spied on over 10,000 American citizens — including congressmen, governmental officials, and antiwar and civil-rights leaders. The CIA had thus violated the National Security Act of 1947, which had established the agency. That measure specifically forbade the CIA to undertake domestic internal security operations.

FBI misdeeds shocked the nation even more. Clearly illegal efforts to injure the reputations and careers of individuals disliked by J. Edgar Hoover were disclosed; so, too, were attempts to ruin organizations which had fitted Hoover's very broad definition of "subversive." Attorney General William B. Saxbe estimated that the FBI, in its attempts to disrupt the activities or destroy groups called "subversive" or "suspect" by Hoover, had carried out at least 2,370 covert actions in support of these objectives. Saxbe acknowledged in 1973 that these actions were "not something that we in a free society should condone." Directives from Washington had ordered field officers of the FBI to attempt to destroy the entire "insidious" New Left movement and the Black Muslims; yet some distinctly Fascist-type armed white organizations had been ignored. Hoover had directed an FBI campaign against the black pacifist, Martin Luther King, Jr., which exceeded in viciousness and perseverance anything that might have been expected from the Ku Klux Klan. Apparently Hoover had even approved an attempt to drive King to suicide. An FBI offensive against the

Black Panthers coincided with the shooting, evidently while they slept, of Chicago's Panther leaders by Chicago police who acted in cooperation with the FBI.

The Defense Department, investigations showed, also had committed outrageous offenses against American citizens. Soldiers had intentionally been placed dangerously close to atomic bomb explosions in order to study the effects of radiation. Clouds of potentially lethal bacteria had been released over cities such as San Francisco as part of Cold War "military research."

Thus Ford's pardon of Nixon eventually seemed to be one more dishonest act by the same government which had used deception to carry on the war in Vietnam and Cambodia, to spy on its citizens, to endanger their health, and perhaps to murder them.

Continuities in Foreign Policy

Ford retained Henry Kissinger as Secretary of State, and Kissinger continued to pursue the balance-of-power politics and shuttle diplomacy which had been his trademark under Nixon. In the Mideast, his efforts contributed to some easing of tensions between Israel and Egypt in the aftermath of the Yom Kippur War of 1973, but not to a resolution of the fundamental causes of Arab-Israeli conflict. Kissinger argued that the "fall" of Indochina in 1975, discussed in the preceding chapter, reflected an American failure of will. But there was much evidence that it reflected changed world conditions in which the vestiges of nineteenth-century colonialism were being swept away and in which the power of the United States was more severely limited than at any time since the Second World War.

The foreign policies of Kissinger, Nixon, and Ford had put great emphasis on détente with the two major Communist powers. Those efforts were partially frustrated during the Ford presidency. China, which for reasons of its own had responded to American diplomatic overtures in 1971 and 1972, now balked at establishing formal relations so long as the United States maintained diplomatic relations and military ties with Taiwan. United States-Soviet relations remained stable, but similarly inconclusive. Negotiations for SALT II dragged on, stymied both by mistrust and by continued technological innovations in weaponry. In July 1975, the United States and the Soviet Union, and thirty-one other nations, did sign a European Security Treaty. Ford and Brezhnev personally joined in the ceremonial signing of the treaty in Helsinki. The pact recognized the territorial status quo in Europe and pledged the signatories to protect human rights. However, the United States remained troubled by Soviet violations of the human-rights agreement, particularly the persecution of dissidents and of Jews who wanted to emigrate, and by indirect Russian intervention in Angola, the Horn of Africa, and other strategic areas.

Domestic Problems: Energy, Inflation, and Unemployment

In domestic affairs, as in foreign relations, old problems brought new troubles to the Ford administration. At no time in modern American history had the connection between domestic economic problems and foreign relations been more direct. The Arab oil embargo prompted by the Yom Kippur War in 1973 gave Americans a glimpse of the future. The embargo ended in March 1974.

More important, the quadrupling of OPEC oil prices in early 1974 and subsequent price increases saddled the world economy with another major inflationary force. Escalating oil prices, coupled with increased dependence on imported oil, put the American economy in a precarious and potentially cataclysmic position.

The sources of the oil crisis of the 1970s were many and complex, but underlying all of them was the fact that the world's finite reserves of oil—the lifeblood of modern economies—were being consumed at a prodigious rate. The United States was particularly profligate. With 6 per cent of the world's population, the United States consumed 33 per cent of the energy used worldwide. The oil would all be gone in the long run, but it was the short term which concerned Americans in the 1970s. Parties which shared some of the responsibility for the jump in prices included the OPEC nations, which had seen their earnings dwindle amidst worldwide inflation; the multinational oil companies, which had developed mechanisms for controlling world production and benefited from the new world market prices; and even the United States Government, whose oil policies had exacerbated the problem.

Faced with an energy crisis with strategic as well as economic ramifications, Nixon had proposed in November 1973 a "Project Independence" designed to make America self-sufficient in energy by 1980 through expanded domestic production of oil and gas, increased use of coal and nuclear power, and development of solar and geothermal energy. The results were not heartening. Old habits and old techniques did not readily yield to the imperatives of the future. As the decade waned, the nation actually became more dependent on imported oil than it had been in 1973. Not until 1979 did American oil consumption begin to decline. By the time that Gerald Ford took office, the shortages of oil had disappeared (although prices continued to climb), and there was little public support for stringent energy conservation or for massive diversion of public funds to energy research and development. Congress did pass a watered-down Energy Policy and Conservation Act in December 1975, but the bill was inadequate for the task at hand.

Oil price increases aggravated the troublesome inflation rates of the Nixon-Ford years. As we have seen, Nixon had reluctantly imposed a series of short-lived wage and price control measures in 1971. However, these controls failed to stop inflation. Ford relied on tight fiscal and monetary policy and on voluntary wage and price guidelines. These measures had little effect. Inflation did decline before the end of Ford's term, but it did so because of the worst recession since the Second World War. For several consecutive months in 1975, more than an additional 1,000,000 people joined the ranks of the unemployed. The over-all unemployment rate exceeded 9 per cent by the end of 1975—the highest since the 1930s—and Ford was forced to take steps to stimulate the economy despite the inflationary risks which such steps entailed.

In economic affairs, and in other aspects of domestic policy as well, Ford found himself at odds with a Democratic Congress which was flexing its muscles in the aftermath of Watergate. During his brief tenure, Ford vetoed fifty bills, almost two per month. Congress failed to override most of the vetoes, but it was able to block many of Ford's legislative proposals. By 1976, this legislative stalemate gave the impression of a government unable to deal with pressing affairs of state. There was blame enough to go around, but the presidency had become the most convenient target of such faultfinding. The seemingly ineffectual Ford bore the brunt of public criticism for the government's failure to make headway against monumental problems.

The Presidential Election of 1976

When Gerald R. Ford succeeded to the presidency in 1974, he seemed to have no further political ambition than to serve out the term to which Nixon and Agnew had been elected. Few Presidents have moved out of the White House voluntarily, and Ford was like the great majority of them. By early 1975, he was a presidential candidate in all but name. Yet the Republican nomination was not his for the asking. Ford was challenged by Ronald Reagan, former movie actor, former Governor of California, and the champion of the party's conservative wing. Reagan actually defeated the incumbent in several southern and western primaries and entered the Republican national convention with a chance of gaining the nomination. Ford won, but the narrow margin of his victory—in the convention sixty votes out of more than 2,000 cast—demonstrated his vulnerability.

The Democrats, excluded from the White House for eight years, smelled victory at last. The legacy of the Nixon-Agnew scandals, Ford's quick pardon of his predecessor and his lack of unified support in his own party, and the economic malaise of the nation made the Democratic party's chances bright indeed. One prominent Democrat remarked privately, "We could run an aardvark this year and win." The prospect of a Democratic victory attracted many well-known contenders for the nomination; they included Sargent Shriver, Representative Morris Udall of Arizona, and Senators Henry Jackson of Washington, Frank Church of Idaho, Lloyd Bentsen of Texas, and Birch Bayh of Indiana. In an astonishing upset, the nomination went to a relatively unknown "outsider," Jimmy Carter, former Governor of Georgia.

Carter's victory was no fluke. Like McGovern four years earlier, Carter had campaigned methodically and tirelessly for four years. His campaign strategy stemmed from a memorandum written in 1972 by his twenty-seven-year-old executive secretary, Hamilton Jordan. Following Jordan's plan and his own instincts for methodical campaigning, Carter cultivated friendships with shapers of public opinion both in and out of government. He and his small staff mastered the complex procedures for selecting delegates to the Democratic convention of 1976; Carter then set out on a grueling grass-roots campaign. Carter did not focus on a specific program of reform. He made *himself* the issue by emphasizing the need for honesty, managerial competency, and fresh ideas in Washington.

Carter's strategy paid off with early victories in the Iowa caucuses and the New Hampshire and Florida primaries. Following these successes, Carter's campaign attracted the kind of television and press coverage which can anoint candidates as "front runners" in modern campaigns. Carter's strategy of running in virtually all the state primaries also proved successful. He amassed enough delegates to lock up the nomination before the convention, despite a late challenge by Governor Edmund G. Brown, Jr., of California.

After the convention, Carter and his family resumed their grueling schedule of personal campaigning, while the Carter campaign managers used television

One of the remaining twenty "tall ships" (square-riggers with a mast height of more than 127 feet) as it prepared for the final stage of "Operation Sail," July 4, 1976. This barkentine was among the sixteen tall ships and more than 200 other sailing vessels from around the world that sailed up the Hudson River to the George Washington Bridge before more than 5,000,000 Bicentennial celebrants on the shores. Americans entered the third century of their national independence with growing misgivings about the future. Perhaps for that reason, the Bicentennial celebrations were more retrospective than had been the case in 1876, when anticipation of the new age of industry and technology competed for public attention with reflections on the nation's first one hundred years. (United Press International)

commercials to "sell" their candidate. Ford, using his incumbency to full advantage, spent much of his time in the White House carrying out the duties of his office—and attracting the daily news coverage that goes with such activities. Meanwhile, Ford and his associates jabbed at his opponent by questioning the wisdom of electing a man of unknown abilities. Ford's strategy seemed to work, for Carter's huge lead in the public opinion polls at the outset of the campaign had melted away by October. That month a series of televised "debates" between the incumbent and the challenger shed little light on substantive differences between them. However, they did reassure many voters that Carter was at least as well qualified as Ford to be President.

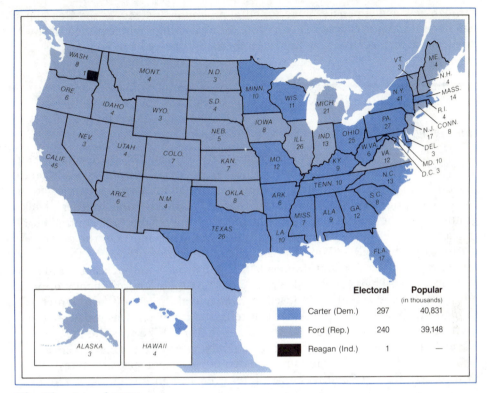

	Electoral	Popular (in thousands)
Carter (Dem.)	297	40,831
Ford (Rep.)	240	39,148
Reagan (Ind.)	1	—

ALASKA 3 HAWAII 4

The Election of 1976

The outcome was extremely close. Carter won 40,827,000 popular votes, or 51 per cent of the total, and 297 electoral votes; Ford, 39,146,000 popular (48 per cent) and 241 electoral votes. The sectional distribution of the electoral vote seemed to indicate a revival of traditional voting patterns. The Republican nominee carried every state west of Missouri, except Texas and Hawaii, while the Democrat carried the entire South, except Virginia, and won enough of the big industrial states of the East and Midwest to eke out a narrow victory.

Closer examination, however, revealed something quite new about Carter's "Solid South." His triumph in Dixie and in several industrial states would have been impossible without overwhelming support from blacks. Ironically, the Voting Rights Act of 1965 and the massive registration of black voters in the states of the former Confederacy helped to elect the first President from the Deep South since Zachary Taylor, a Virginia-born Louisiana slaveowner. Carter won over 90 per cent of the votes cast by blacks; Carter also won strong support from organized labor and did well among evangelical Protestants (including many black Baptists and Methodists), who shared his well-publicized religious beliefs.

Carter also benefited from the aura of corruption which, fairly or not, still clung to the party of Richard Nixon. As an outsider, Carter was free to capitalize on the public perception that the federal government was not coping with the country's great social and economic problems. Carter and his associates realized early that voters were suspicious of politicians who offered salvation through new and expensive governmental programs. Instead, as the Georgians had hoped, a majority was ready to vote for a candidate who extolled his own virtues as a manager and who promised them, "I'll never lie to you."

2. THE NEW PRESIDENT

"Jimmy Who?"

Despite his extensive personal campaigning and exposure by the media, Carter entered the White House unknown to most Americans. The press continued to label him an "enigma." In part, the uncertainty about Carter stemmed from his lack of prior visibility in Washington and from his rural southern background. But the confusion also reflected the ambiguous and contradictory images which he had projected during the long campaign. On the one hand, Carter called himself a "Populist" and championed the interests of the average citizen against the "special interests." On the other hand, he stressed his experience as an engineer (naval officer), businessman, and efficiency-minded governor. He consistently espoused an evangelical Protestant faith which, although firmly rooted in the American religious tradition, was unfamiliar and even threatening to millions of Americans in 1976. Who was the *real* Jimmy Carter—the "Populist" reformer or the efficiency-minded engineer/manager?

Carter's folksiness and his campaign denunciations of special interests gave him something of a Populist aura. Carter even had an intriguing, if tenuous, connection with the historical agrarian movement, for his maternal grandfather, Jim Jack Gordy, had been a Populist in southern Georgia. But Carter's Populism was more campaign rhetoric and strategy. The Populist label, vaguely associated in the public mind with reform, could help to establish Carter as a man of liberal credentials without antagonizing conservatives. At the same time, journalists and other political observers had applied the term Populist to southern champions of the "little man" (i.e., working class whites) such as Lester Maddox and George Wallace. Carter had to win a substantial following among Wallace supporters in both the North and the South if his long-shot candidacy was to succeed. And it did.

Like the historical Populists, Carter could identify himself with the aspirations of people who felt cut off from power. Yet his personal background, record as Governor of Georgia, and policies as President all suggest that he was not a Populist but a southern progressive. Progressivism in the South was predominantly a movement of the middle and upper classes, and its goals in the early twentieth century included efficient, "business-like" administration of government. Jimmy Carter, for all the talk of his humble origins, was the son of a small town rich man. Jimmy Carter was born near the small town of Plains in Sumter County, Georgia, on October 1, 1924. The Carters occupied a position of prestige and responsibility in Sumter County. The "best people" of the community had a sense of social responsibility, albeit a paternalistic one, and the young Jimmy Carter absorbed this feeling of responsibility. Carter's intensely personal religion also helped to instill in him a sense of responsibility for the underprivileged. By the late 1970s, American voters had become cynical about the political uses of religion. As a campaigner, Jimmy Carter certain-

President Carter and his family walking from the Capitol to the White House following his inauguration in 1977. Like Thomas Jefferson's unceremonious walk to his first inauguration in 1801, President Carter's gesture was an intentional contrast to the "imperial presidency" of the recent past. (United Press International)

ly used his religion to full advantage, but his evangelical faith was transparently genuine.

The chance for a college education uprooted Carter from Plains. That education broadened but did not fundamentally alter his notion of social responsibility. He attended the Georgia Institute of Technology and was graduated from the United States Naval Academy in 1946. His engineer's training, reinforced by service in the elite nuclear submarine service headed by Admiral Hyman Rickover, instilled in Carter habits of management and problem solving which encouraged diligent personal effort and the kind of systematic analysis that would identify the single objectively correct solution for the problem at hand. Once the right answer was determined in this engineering world, one need only explain it to others to persuade them of its correctness. This style of leadership had its limitations when transferred to the political and governmental arenas.

In the Georgia state house and in the White House, Carter's actions were shaped by a moderate, morally grounded reformism, coupled with an engineer's zeal for efficiency and rational problem solving. In the former respect, he resembled his southern predecessor, Woodrow Wilson. In the latter, he resembled his fellow engineer, Herbert Hoover.

As Governor of Georgia between 1971 and 1975, Carter pursued many of the same objectives and encountered many of the same difficulties which he would encounter as President. Carter rejected the segregationism of his predecessor, Lester Maddox. By Georgia standards, he was a social liberal; he was also a fiscal conservative. Rather than press for new and costly governmental programs, Carter sought to make existing programs work more efficiently. He upgraded the state's civil service and judiciary and reorganized the state bureaucracy. Carter experienced the same kinds of difficulties in getting his program through the state legislature that he would later encounter in dealing with Congress. He inherited a governorship weakened in its dealings with the legislature by the events of the recent past. He presented the legislature with a comprehensive and supposedly unalterable reorganization package and then refused to engage in the customary log rolling to get it enacted. When the legislators seemed ready to kill his favorite projects, he appealed over their heads to the public at large in a carefully orchestrated public-relations campaign. In the end Carter, by compromising on several key aspects of the program, created the appearance of being indecisive. But he won a reorganization bill substantially like the one he first introduced.

The programs of governmental reform which Governor Carter espoused did not evoke strong emotional support from any particular voting bloc or from the public at large, nor did Carter's personal style of leadership create a large and passionate body of supporters in the state. But most of his fellow Georgians believed that Carter had been a competent chief executive, and a handful of them were prepared to help him win the presidency.

The Carter Presidency

Carter's call for efficient management of governmental resources and his acknowledgment that government could not solve all of society's problems made him an appealing candidate for what one publicist has called the "age of diminishing expectations." Once in the White House, Carter's original inclination was to forego new spending programs (he promised a balanced budget by 1980) and to set about reorganizing and reforming the *structure* of government. His staff went to work, much as they had done in Georgia, on a plan to reorganize the federal bureaucracy. In January 1978, Carter proposed comprehensive reforms of the tax and welfare systems. All of these were long needed changes, but Carter was unable to steer them through the legislative maze.

In the post-Watergate era, Congress was determined to establish a stronger position relative to the President, *any* President. Furthermore, party discipline was weak among the unwieldy Democratic majority. Consequently, the administration had to cajole scores of "back bench" members who in earlier times would have meekly followed instructions of party leaders. The Carter administration, which at first prided itself on its distance from the Washington establishment, also proved unable or unwilling to play the game of legislation as it was customarily played on Capitol Hill. Carter vetoed "pet" water and flood control projects in the name of economy and prudence. His staff slighted, and infuriated, influential congressmen with real or imagined intent. More damaging still, Carter and his staff devoted their time and energy to devising comprehensive legislative programs without, however, giving adequate attention to the equally demanding task of shepherding them through Congress — a

AMERICAN WOMEN: TOWARD EQUAL RIGHTS

After having listened for hours to a discussion as to the reason why the profession of teacher was not as much respected as that of the lawyer, minister, or doctor, without once, as she thought, touching the kernel of the question, she arose to untie for them the Gordian knot. . . .

"It seems to me, gentlemen, that none of you quite comprehend the cause of the disrespect of which you complain. Do you not see that so long as society says a woman is incompetent to be a lawyer, minister, or doctor, but has ample ability to be a teacher, that every man of you who chooses this profession tacitly acknowledges that he has no more brains that a woman? And this, too, is the reason that teaching is a less lucrative profession, as here men must compete with the cheap labor of women. Would you exalt your profession, exalt those who labor with you. Would you make it more lucrative, increase the salaries of the women engaged in the noble work of educating our future Presidents, Senators, and Congressmen."

From Elizabeth Cady Stanton, Susan B. Anthony, and Matilda Joslyn Gage, eds., History of Woman Suffrage, *6 vol. (New York: Fowler & Wells, 1881), I, p. 514.*

Right: Susan Brownell Anthony, born into a large Quaker family in 1820, fought for woman suffrage and other major reforms throughout her life. She died fourteen years before ratification of what was known as the Susan B. Anthony amendment, but she is fully credited with the groundbreaking work that made its passage possible. (Historical Pictures Service, Inc., Chicago)

Above: Doña Marina, the brilliant interpreter and negotiator for Cortés who was given to him as a seventeen-year-old slave, is often pictured by early accounts as instrumental in his victory. Here, she interprets as Cortés is presented with a large number of "beautiful maidens" by his Tlaxcalan allies. The simultaneous illustration of woman as object and woman as subject makes this a richly symbolic depiction of the paradox peculiar to women throughout our history. Drawing from the Lienzo de Tlaxcala. (Historical Pictures Service)

The General Court of Massachusetts Condemns the Preaching of Mrs. Anne Hutchinson, c. 1634. The fate of women who dared speak publicly, let alone question the current convictions of male authority, was a harsh test of the courage of early American women. Engraving by Marsh. (Historical Pictures Service)

Mr. Cotton [*A leader of the Boston Church*]. . . . *I shall direct my speech to those who are Mrs. Hutchinson's sons and sons-in-law. Let me tell you from the Lord though natural affection may lead you to speak in defense of your mother, and to take her part, which may be lawful and praiseworthy in some cases and at some times, yet in the cause of God you are neither to know father nor mother, sister nor brother. You have not helped your mother by pleading for her but you have hardened her heart and encouraged her wrong opinion.*

Now let me speak to the sisters of our Congregation, many of whom I feel have been led astray by Mrs. Hutchinson. I warn you in the name of the Lord to look to yourselves and to take care that you accept nothing as Truth which has not the stamp of the word of God on it. Let me say this to you all, let not the good you have received from Mrs. Hutchinson make you believe all she says, for you see she is only a woman and many unsound and dangerous principles are held by her . . .

From Ezra Stiles, "Report of the Trial of Mrs. Anne Hutchinson," Proceedings of the Massachusetts Historical Society, Vol. IV, Series II (Boston, 1889), as adapted in We, the American Women, *ed. by Beth Millstein and Joanne Bodin, Science Research Associates, 1977.*

Top: Ridicule infused popular reactions to the first national Women's Rights Convention, held in July of 1848 in Seneca Falls, New York. Organized by Elizabeth Cady Stanton and the well-known abolitionist, Lucretia Mott, the Seneca Falls Convention is acknowledged as the formal beginning of the first wide-spread feminist movement in America. Harper's Weekly, *June 1859. (Historical Pictures Service)*

Above: Lady Clerks Leaving the Treasury Department at Washington. The Civil War created a hiatus in formal activities of the women's movement, but at the same time it spurred great changes in the lives of many women. Harper's Weekly, *February 1865. (Historical Pictures Service)*

The history of mankind is a history of repeated injuries and usurpations on the part of man toward woman, having in direct object the establishment of an absolute tyranny over her. To prove this, let facts be submitted to a candid world.

He has never permitted her to exercise her inalienable right to the elective franchise. . . .

He has compelled her to submit to laws, in the formation of which she had no voice. . . .

He has made her, if married, in the eye of the law, civilly dead.

He has taken from her all right in property, even to the wages she earns. . . .

He has denied her the facilities for obtaining a thorough education, all colleges being closed against her. . . .

From the "Declaration of Sentiments," in Elizabeth Cady Stanton, Susan B. Anthony, and Matilda Joslyn Gage, eds., History of Woman Suffrage, *6 vol. (New York: Fowler & Wells, 1881), I. pp. 70–71.*

The assemblage of rampant women which convened at the Tabernacle yesterday was an interesting phase in the comic history of the nineteenth century.

We saw, in broad daylight, in a public hall in the city of New York, a gathering of unsexed women—unsexed in mind all of them, and many in habiliments—publicly propounding the doctrine that they should be allowed to step out of their appropriate sphere, and mingle in the busy walks of every-day life, . . .

It is almost needless for us to say that these women are entirely devoid of personal attractions. They are generally thin maiden ladies, or women who perhaps have been disappointed in the endeavors to appropriate the breeches and the rights of their unlucky lords; . . .

From an editorial in the New York Herald, *September 7, 1853. As quoted in* Women Together, A History in Documents of the Women's Movement in the United States, *by Judith Papachristou, Alfred A. Knopf, Inc., 1976, p. 45.*

Mrs. Margaret Freeland, of
Syracuse, was recently
arrested upon a warrant
issued on complaint of
Emanuel Rosendale, a
rum-seller, charging her with
forcing an entrance to his
house, and with stones and
clubs smashing his doors and
windows, breaking his
tumblers and bottles, and
turning over his whisky
barrels and spilling their
contents. Great excitement
was produced by this novel
case. It seems that the
husband of Mrs. Freeland was
a drunkard—that he was in
the habit of abusing his wife,
turning her out of doors, etc.,
and this was carried so far
that the police frequently
found it necessary to interfere
to put a stop to his
ill-treatment of his family.
Rosendale, the complainant,
furnished Freeland with the
liquor which turned him into
a demon. Mrs. Freeland had
frequently told him of her
sufferings and besought him
to refrain from giving her
husband the poison. But alas!
she appealed to a heart of
stone. He disregarded her
entreaties and spurned her
from his door. Driven to
desperation she armed
herself, broke into the house,
drove out the base-hearted
landlord and proceeded upon
the work of destruction.
From The Lily, *June 1853,
reprinted in* History of Woman
Suffrage, *I, p. 475.*

"Dat man ober dar say dat womin needs to be helped into carriages, and lifted ober ditches, and to hab de best place everywhar. Nobody eber helps me into carriages, or ober mud-puddles, or gibs me any best place!" And raising herself to her full height, and her voice to a pitch like rolling thunder, she asked. "And a'n't I a woman? Look at me! Look at my arm! (and she bared her right arm to the shoulder, showing her tremendous muscular power). I have ploughed, and planted, and gathered into barns, and no man could head me! And a'n't I a woman? I could work as much and eat as much as a man—when I could get it—and bear de lash as well! And a'n't I a woman? I have borne thirteen chilern, and seen 'em mos' all sold off to slavery, and when I cried out with my mother's grief, none but Jesus heard me! And a'n't I a woman?

"Den dat little man in black dar, he say women can't have as much rights as men, 'cause Christ wan't a woman! Whar did your Christ come from?" Rolling thunder couldn't have stilled that crowd, as did those deep, wonderful tones, as she stood there with outstretched arms and eyes of fire. Raising her voice still louder, she repeated, "Whar did your Christ come from? From God and a woman! Man had nothin' to do wid Him." Oh, what a rebuke that was to that little man. "If de fust woman God ever made was strong enough to turn de world upside down all alone, dese women togedder (and she glanced her eye over the platform) ought to be able to turn it back, and get it right side up again! And now dey is asking to do it, de men better let 'em." Long-continued cheering greeted this. " 'Bleeged to ye for hearin' on me, and now ole Sojourner han't got nothin' more to say."

From History of Woman Suffrage, *I, pp. 515–17 As quoted in Judith Papachristou* Women Together: A History in Documents of the Women's Movement in the United States *Alfred A. Knopf, Inc, 1976, p. 36.*

Sojourner Truth, abolitionist, orator, preacher, and feminist. (Historical Pictures Service)

The parallel between women and Negroes is the deepest truth of American life, for together they form the unpaid or underpaid labor on which America runs.
Gunnar Myrdal, An American Dilemma, *New York: Harper and Brothers, 1944, p. 1077*

Above: Trimming Currency, Bureau of Engraving and Printing, Washington, D.C., 1907. As is still true, higher education for women often led to repetitive office work under the close supervision of men. (National Archives)

Right: An anatomy class at a medical college in Pennsylvania, dissecting cadavers, c. 1900. For a time, women seeking professional training fared better in segregated classes, away from the heckling of male students. (The Bettmann Archive)

"Do you know that the autopsy is on the genital organs?" "No," I answered; "but one part of the human body should be as sacred to the physician as another." Dr. Palmer here stepped back, saying: "I object to a woman's being present at a male autopsy, and if she is allowed to remain, I shall [leave]!" "I came here by written invitation," I said; "and I will leave it to a vote whether I go or stay; but first, I would like to ask Dr. Palmer what is the difference between the attendance of a woman at a male autopsy, and the attendence of a man at a female autopsy?" [The doctors voted her to stay and Dr. Palmer left. There were about forty or fifty spectators.]

. . . One of the doctors opened an old medicine case, and offered it to me. "You do not want me to do the work, do you?" I asked, in surprise. "Oh, yes, yes, go ahead," he said. I took the case and complied. The news of what was going on had spread to every house in town, and the excitement was at fever-heat.

I often jokingly remarked: "I wonder, as I look back now, that I was not tarred and feathered after that autopsy affair: I can assure you it was no laughing matter then to break through the customs, prejudices and established rules of a new country, which is always a risky undertaking, especially if it is done by a woman, whose position is so sharply defined. Only a few years before that date, the students of Jefferson Medical College [in Philadelphia] publicly "rotten-egged" the woman students, as they were leaving Blockly Hospital.

From Bethenia Owens-Adair, Some of Her Life Experiences (Portland, Oregon: Mann and Beach, 1906), pp. 58–50., as quoted in We, the American Women, ed by Beth Millstein and Joanne Bodin, SRA, 1977, pp. 64–65.

. . . Insanitary housing, poisonous sewage, contaminated water, infant mortality, the spread of contagion, adulterated food, impure milk, smoke-laden air, ill-ventilated factories, dangerous occupations, juvenile crime, unwholesome crowding, prostitution and drunkenness are the enemies which the modern cities must face and overcome would they survive. . . . To test the elector's fitness to deal with this situation by his ability to bear arms is absurd. These problems must be solved, if they are solved at all, not from the military point of view, not even from the industrial point of view, but from a third which is rapidly developing in all the great cities of the world—the human welfare point of view. . . .

From "Jane Addams Declares Ballot for Women Made Necessary by Changed Conditions," Chicago Sunday Record-Herald, *April 1, 1906. As quoted in* Up From the Pedestal, *Kraditor, p. 284.*

Top: Wash day in a tenement apartment, c. 1910. (The Bettmann Archive)

Bottom: The American dream. Palm Beach, Florida, 1913. (Library of Congress)

This world taught woman nothing skillful and then said her work was valueless. It permitted her no opinions and said she did not know how to think. It forbade her to speak in public, and said the sex had no orators. It denied her the schools, and said the sex had no genius. It robbed her of every vestige of responsibility, and then called her weak. It taught her that every pleasure must come as a favor from men, and when to gain it she decked herself in paint and fine feathers, as she had been taught to do, it called her vain.

From Carrie Chapman Catt, President's Annual Address (1902), as quoted in Up From the Pedestal, *ed. by Aileen S. Kraditor, New York, Time Books, p. 208.*

Top: The drive for solidarity in a Labor Day parade, 1914. (Historical Pictures Service)

Above: Carrie Chapman Catt, chosen by Susan B. Anthony as her immediate successor to the presidency of the National Woman Suffrage Association, called for the establishment of a League of Women Voters in 1919 in states where suffrage had already been won. She also collaborated with Jane Addams in founding the Women's Peace Party in 1915. (National Archives)

Right: Retouching an Old Masterpice, Life, July 1, 1915. (Historical Pictures Service)

Women are Jubilant: Antis Promise Appeal
Legal Fight Threatened Over Successful Outcome of Half-Century Suffrage Fight

Hailing the suffrage victory as bringing added opportunity and responsibility to American women, Mrs. Carrie Chapman Catt, President of the National American Woman Suffrage Association, applauded the Tennessee Legislature in a statement issued yesterday.

"Tennessee has thus closed sixteen years of woman's struggle for the right to have their prayers counted on Election Day," said Mrs. Catt. "The Ratification of the amendment is more than a victory for us. In the hour of victory there is but one regret and that is that every man and woman in the nation does not share our joy. Today there are those yet too blinded by prejudice to recognize the justice and inevitability of woman suffrage. But tomorrow we know that we shall work together for the common good of this great nation."

From The New York Times, *August 19, 1920.*

To the Editor of The New York Times:

The problem of finding employment for the returning troops is, without doubt, a very big one, and unless every possible effort is made to solve it the situation promises to become quite serious. Many steps have been taken already, but there seems to be one measure which has been largely neglected, and yet it is of the most vital importance. I refer to the numerous positions now held by women which were formerly filled by men. In not a few instances the women are retained because they work for something less. . . . A great many of these women are married and their husbands work also. On the other hand there is a tremendous shortage of female help for household services, and I venture to claim that a tremendously large percentage of these women are better qualified for domestic positions than for the situations they now hold. Therefore, as a matter of patriotism, employers should be urged to give men, particularly discharged soldiers, the preference.

From The New York Times, *March 30, 1919.*

Supreme Court Justice Harry F. Lewis said in a statement issued yesterday in his chambers that he deplored the apparent inroads of birth control propaganda in Brooklyn.

He also asserted that there was an "almost complete absence of real home life today in Brooklyn," ascribing this condition to "childless homes." "Birth control information," he said, "may have its good points but can truly be indicted on many counts, the least of which will be responsibility for unhappy marriages and a falling off in the census."

In sixty-four undefended divorce cases tried before him in one day he found that there was only one child for every two families and that the duration of each marriage averaged less than three years.

"Not long ago a home meant something." Justice Lewis said. "It was the location of our birth. It was the place where we entertained our friends and where we held all our family functions. Today we are born in hospitals, we entertain in our clubs, we eat in restaurants, we entertain our visiting friends in cabparlors. I cannot help but reach the conclusion that if our Brooklyn women had children there would be more happiness and fewer divorces.

"Presence of children attracts the husband to his home and keeps the mothers from the gossiping neighbors and bridge parties. Absence of children promotes discord. Their presence makes for harmony."

From The New York Times, June 10, 1930.

Top: Members of the Women's Land Army in World War I driving tractors near Toledo, Ohio. The Women's Land Army, organized by private women's organizations at first but directed by the government after the war, helped break down cultural barriers to hard, and rewarding, physical labor for women. (National Archives, photo no. 111-SC-9869)

Above: Woman working in a munitions factory during World War I. (The Bettmann Archive)

Top: Self-sufficiency as well as patriotic service in war jobs motivated women to expand their knowledge of technology. Here, a group of women are shown at work in a course in automotive mechanics, 1917. (The Bettmann Archive)

Bottom: A female gas station attendant checks the oil in a 1940s automobile. (The Bettmann Archive)

The OWI [Office of War Information] found that much of the resistance to women workers was due to male apprehension that women would continue in industrial jobs at war's end. To answer such objections, the OWI encouraged a deliberate policy of refuting such claims, and it urged the media to "reassure men that women will be only too glad to go back home and live a normal life after the war is over." Little recognition was given to the fact that thirteen million women had been in the labor force prior to Pearl Harbor, and these women could be expected to remain at the war's end. The Civil Service Commission boasted that its clerical jobs were war work "with a future," but few other employers made similar claims. A War Department brochure had concluded that "a woman worker . . . is a substitute—like plastics instead of metal," and womanpower literature assumed that men and women would be happy to return to traditional patterns of work and domestic responsibility as soon as the war emergency was over.

From War Department publication, You're Going to Employ Women, *Washington, D.C., p. 2.*

This has been a punishing year, in our legislative halls, for the good old institution of wedlock. There aren't enough jobs, and the newest and brightest solution advanced by an astonishing number of elected representatives of the people is to forbid married women to work if their husbands have jobs.

So hot has the fight become that the National Federation of Business and Professional Women's Clubs, in its recent national convention in Kansas City, designated the problem the most serious confronted in twenty years. The federation went after it, hammer and tongs, and will be carrying the fight to the legislators when they next convene. For although legislation to keep married women out of jobs was defeated in nearly every instance at the last series of legislative sessions, the battle continues.

From Kathleen McLaughlin, "Shall Wives Work?" The New York Times, *July 23, 1939.*

In the 1960s and early 1970s, protest action in the burgeoning women's liberation movement (the second wave of American feminism) sometimes took forms used by the Civil Rights activists of the '50s and '60s. Here police carry one of nine members of the Women's Liberation Front arrested for occupying the executive offices of Grove Press Publishing Company as a protest against the firm's "sexist editorial policy." About twenty-five women took part in the sit-in. (United Press International)

Last summer, Miss Morgan's authentic inventive genius found roots in the Women's Liberation. "From the beginning," she says, "it was clear to me that The Movement [the Movement for a Democratic Society which she had joined earlier] didn't really make room for women. A lot of women came in expecting a radically new scene. Like, here was a group of young people with a new politics, a new life style, a new sexual honesty and freedom. And still, the notion of a liberated woman was someone who is indiscriminate about whom she sleeps with, not a realization that women don't want to be objects. A lot of Movement women might just as well have gone to Scarsdale."

Robin Morgan, as quoted in Peter Babcox, "Meet the Women of the Revolution, 1969," The New York Times, February 9, 1969.

Billie Jean King, shown here in action in one of her many Wimbledon victory matches, has been instrumental, both as role model and by personal efforts, in promoting the current movement for equal rights for women in sports. Not the least of these accomplishments is a greater respect and commensurate salaries for the professional woman athlete. (United Press International)

The only reason the Company gave for not letting me have the job was that I am a woman. The job went to the only other bidder, a man with less seniority then me. . . . During the time I was waiting for a final decision I was criticized by both males and females. They seemed to think I was trying to take something from 'the breadwinner' while I was only trying to prove that all men aren't breadwinners and that a loaf of bread costs a woman as much as it does a man.
Lorena Weeks of Weeks *v.* Southern Bell, as quoted in "'A Unique Competence,' A Study of Equal Employment Opportunity in the Bell System," EEOC, 1971, pp. 143–44.

As the movement organized, protest marches quickly became as important a tool for modern feminists and movement supporters as they had been for suffrage activists. This scene from a Seattle parade of more than 2,000 in the mid-1970s highlights signs and placards that reflect some of the opinions represented in the march. (United Press International)

Again, of two deer, the buck has a special secondary sex-distinction in his towering antlers; but his power of speed, his love of speed, is not a sex distinction but a race distinction, common to both sexes. When the doe wishes to run far and fast, she is not "unfeminine," she is not "making a buck of herself." She likes to run, not because she is a doe, but because she is a deer, just as much of a deer as he is.
From Charlotte Perkins Gilman, "Are Women Human Beings?" Harper's Weekly, May 25, 1912, p. 11. As quoted in Up From the Pedestal, Kraditor, p. 328.

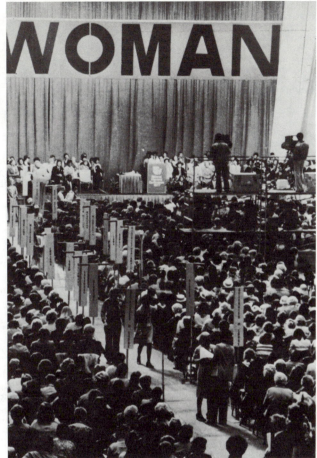

*We American women view
our history with equanimity.
We allow the positive
achievement to inspire us
and the negative omissions
to teach us.
We recognize the
accomplishments of our
sisters, those famous and
hallowed women of history
and those unknown and
unsung women whose
strength gave birth to our
strength.
We recognize those women
who were and are
immobilized by oppression
and crippled by prejudice.
We recognize that no nation
can boast of balance until
each member of that nation
is equally employed and
equally rewarded.
We recognize that women
collectively have been
unfairly treated and
dishonorably portrayed.
We recognize our
responsibility to work toward
the eradication of negatives in
our society and by so doing,
bring honor to our gender, to
our species, and to ourselves
individually.
Because of the recognition set
down above we American
women unfold our future
today.
We promise to accept nothing
less than justice for every
woman.
We pledge to work
unsparingly to bring fair play
to every public arena, to
encourage honorable behavior
in each private home.
We promise to develop
patience that we may learn
from our colleagues and
courage that we may attack
our opponent.
Because we are women, we
make these promises.*

*Above: Former first lady Betty Ford addresses a fundraising gathering in
support of the equal rights amendment on the eve of the National Women's
Conference in November 1977. (United Press International)*

*Left: Opening session of the National Women's Conference at the Houston
Coliseum, November 19, 1977. (United Press International)*

From What Women Want, *Simon
and Schuster, 1979, p. 58. This
1977 declaration of sentiments
was written by Maya Angelou,
poet, playwright, and one of the
Commissioners of the National
Women's Conference. The
declaration was signed by runners
whose continuous torch relay from
Seneca Falls, New York, to
Houston, Texas, linked
symbolically the two major stages
of the drive for equal rights for
women in America.*

Right: Barbara Jordan, in a photograph taken during her electrifying keynote address to the Democratic National Convention in 1976. Her career testifies to the power of role models; Jordan decided to become a lawyer after hearing a black woman lawyer, Edith Sampson, address a Careers Day program. After holding elective office in the Texas Senate and U.S. Congress, Jordan became a professor at the University of Texas at Austin. (United Press International)

Far Right: Eleanor Cutri Smeal, housewife President of the National Organization for Women, was largely responsible for gaining congressional extension of the time limit for ratification of the equal rights amendment. Having been a fulltime homemaker until her election to the NOW presidency in 1977, Smeal is also an outspoken advocate for homemakers' rights. In May, 1979, she brought to Congress NOW's proposal for a Homemakers' Bill of Rights similar in scope to the post-war G.I. Bill. (Photo courtesy of the National Organization for Women)

Last September, for the first time, women were enrolled in college in numbers proportionate to their numbers in the population. Small but significant numbers of young women are making inroads into traditionally male job fields. Today's young women marry later and have fewer children. Perhaps most significant of all, 41 percent of all the mothers with children under six are now working—and that figure would probably be much higher if we had an adequate program of child care.

The women in this younger generation still suffer discrimination, and I don't mean to minimize it, but they've been the beneficiaries of the legal and attitudinal changes of the past 10 years. And their future looks promising.

But for the woman of 35 or 50 or 65, the future *is right now*. And it is not a comforting one. . . . We have plenty of precedents in this country for government-aided reentry into the economic mainstream. We have programs for prisoners, and for alcohol- and drug-abusers—but nothing for the woman who's raised three children. It is 17 times more likely that any woman who gets pregnant today will die in childbirth in this country than it is likely that any man who joins the armed services will die in uniform. And yet that man has been entitled to on-the-job training, the G.I. Bill, and veteran's preference. A mother has no comparable benefits.

Marlo Thomas, testimony before the Senate Committee on Human Resources. February 1, 1979. As quoted in MS., *May 1979, p. 116.*

Right: Among honored guests as part of the vanguard for a march of more than 80,000 people in support of the equal rights amendment in Springfield, Illinois, May 1980, were Betty Friedan (often called the mother of the modern feminist movement), Addie Wyatt (a labor union leader from Washington, D.C.), and actress Jean Stapleton. The media reported that day that Phyllis Schlafly, head of Stop ERA, said that the march was so large because all of its participants had been paid $10 each to be there. (United Press International)

Top: Writer and publisher Gloria Steinem, a Commissioner for the National Women's Conference co-founded MS. magazine in 1972 and became a major leader in the women's movement. Her frequent speeches and political writings continue to inspire hardworking feminists around the world. (Photo © Christopher Brown/Picture Group)

The revolution didn't begin in Washington. It won't end there. **Reagan is not a majority President**. . . .*only about one fourth of all possible voters wanted Ronald Reagan in the White House. . . .*

The danger of a small, well-organized, and well-financed faction taking over one of the two major political parties has never been more clear than with this year's election. . . And most of the issues now espoused by Reagan and his ultraright-wing supporters are not futuristic, but outdated ideas of some "natural," sexual, and international order that has already been disproved or outgrown.

From Gloria Steinem, "Now That It's Reagan. . .," Ms., *January 1981, p. 28.*

Ratification of the Equal Rights Amendment continues to be essential to the attainment of equal rights for women and men under the law. In Federal statutes alone, the Commission has identified over 800 sections of the U.S. Code containing examples of substantive sex bias or sex-based terminology that are inconsistent with a national commitment to equal rights, responsibilities, and opportunities. State laws are replete with provisions that assign women, on the basis of their sex, to an inferior role. . . .

It is clear that existing constitutional guarantees will not mandate the changes that are needed. Judicial interpretation of these guarantees has allowed sex bias to survive. The Supreme Court has persisted in its view that sex-biased laws and classifications are more easily justified under the Constitution than are race-biased laws. As Justice Powell recently explained in *Regents of California* v. *Bakke*, the Supreme Court has never extended the full scrutiny of the 14th amendment to sex discrimination claims because the Court does not see such discrimination as inherently odious when compared to the lengthy and tragic history of race discrimination. But such a comparison of victims surely is neither appropriate nor required. The treatment of challenges to sex-based discrimination under existing law reflects the perpetuation of stereotypes and myths about women in American society, as well as a failure to recognize and understand the lengthy struggle of women to secure equal rights under the law.

From Statement on the Equal Rights Amendment, *by the United States Commission on Civil Rights, December 1978, p. 18–19,* body which proved more resistant to Carter's will than had the Georgia legislature.

During his first two years in the White House, Carter offered comprehensive legislative proposals relating to energy, welfare, and taxes; none of them was enacted in a form which resembled that proposed by the President. In April 1977, Carter sent to Congress an energy program which featured a substantial tax on crude oil. Although Carter's proposal passed the House more or less intact, it was gutted in the Senate. The series of bills which finally emerged from Congress in October 1978 gave Carter no more than a symbolic victory in his energy war. An even worse fate awaited the tax bill submitted in January 1978. Promoted as a plan to reduce taxes for the poor and to close "loopholes" for the rich, the income-tax cuts were largely offset by increases in Social Security taxes, while the taxes on capital gains were reduced rather than increased! Carter rejected appeals from liberal Democrats to veto the emasculated bill and signed it into law.

Carter's major accomplishments in the first two years came in the field of foreign affairs. He completed negotiations on two Panama Canal treaties in September 1977. The first provided that the United States should continue to operate and defend the canal until the year 2000, after which ownership of the canal would go to Panama. The second guaranteed the neutrality of the canal in peace and war. The Senate gave its consent to ratification in the spring of 1978 by only one vote to spare and only after adding a "clarifying" amendment and reservation that safeguarded the right of the United States to protect the canal, by the use of force if necessary.

In early 1979, thirty years after the Chinese Communists had gained control of the Chinese mainland, the United States and the People's Republic of China entered into formal diplomatic relations with an exchange of ambassadors. Carter also withdrew recognition of the Republic of China in Taiwan and renounced the mutual defense treaty between the United States and the Republic of China.

Carter and his Secretary of State, Cyrus R. Vance of New York, were not unmindful of geopolitical factors, but they were determined not to appear to use the Chinese-American détente to bludgeon the Soviet Union into new concessions. This was particularly true during the continuing negotiations over SALT II. They went forward steadily during 1978, and Carter and Brezhnev signed the treaty in Vienna on June 18, 1979. Its most important provision would have set a limit on long-range missiles that each country might possess and provided for a decrease in these awesome weapons by 1981.

Carter's most stunning achievement was a peace treaty between those two mideastern enemies, Israel and Egypt. Under pressure from Washington, President Anwar el-Sadat of Egypt and Prime Minister Menachem Begin of Israel exchanged visits in late 1977. The two leaders tried to reach an agreement, but negotiations were at an end by the early summer of 1978. Then Carter invited Sadat and Begin to Camp David in September and patiently and skillfully brought the two antagonists together. In spite of the opposition of the rest of the Arab world, Sadat signed with Begin a treaty of peace in the rose garden of the White House on March 26, 1979. It provided for gradual Israeli evacuation of the Sinai and for the establishment of normal diplomatic and trade relations. It was not a perfect settlement, for the troubling questions of the fate of Palestinians in the Gaza Strip and on the West Bank of the Jordan River remained

President Anwar el-Sadat of Egypt, President Jimmy Carter of the United States, and Prime Minister Menachem Begin of Israel at the signing of the peace treaty between Egypt and Israel on March 29, 1979. Carter's influential role in this tentative but significant step toward peace in the Middle East marked this occasion as a high point of his presidency.

unsettled. However, the Israeli-Egyptian Treaty did guarantee the security of Israel, at least for a time, and it gave Sadat an opportunity, with the assistance of the United States, to begin to address himself to urgent economic problems in his own country.

These were all impressive achievements, but many Americans were still frustrated by the realization that the United States no longer occupied the singularly dominant position in world affairs which it had held for a generation after the Second World War. Many persons were particularly disturbed by their nation's inability to influence events in the Middle East (except for Egypt), Africa, and other parts of the third world—areas which in an age of scarce natural resources had taken on new significance for the United States.

Foreign affairs intruded once again into the domestic economy in 1979 in the form of shrinking oil supplies and the skyrocketing prices of imported oil and in the continued decline of the value of the dollar overseas. In this inflationary situation, Carter had come to view inflation, not unemployment, as the nation's number one economic problem. Carter continued to rely on voluntary guidelines, but they had little effect on inflation. To deal with the renewed oil crisis, Carter proposed a $142.2 billion program which concentrated on the development of alternative sources of energy and on price-induced conservation of oil products. Funds for development were to be derived from a "windfall profits tax" levied against oil companies when prices were decontrolled.

As Carter's administration moved toward the end of its third year, to many Americans it seemed incapable of providing either the competent management of government which Carter as a candidate had promised or the decisive national leadership which foreign and domestic crises demanded. In a table-thumping speech in July 1979 (delivered after he had spent twelve days at Camp David contemplating the future of his presidency), Carter acknowledged that he had spent too much time managing the government and too little time leading the nation. To free himself for the tasks of leadership (not to mention the problem of reelection) and to reduce the appearance of disarray in his administration, Carter discharged several of his cabinet members and reassigned others, centralized more authority in the White House staff (as every President since Eisenhower had done), and installed his long-time aide, Hamilton Jordan, as chief of the White House staff.

Neither the new energy program nor the administrative shuffle bolstered Carter's sagging popularity. Gasoline prices had gone over $1 dollar per gallon by the early summer of 1979, and they continued to rise due to OPEC increases and the gradual deregulation of domestically produced oil. Carter finally won most of his energy program in the spring of 1980. It provided for the gradual deregulation of the prices of oil produced in the United States and a "windfall profits" tax on domestic production to finance a huge development of synthetic fuels and other forms of energy. However, even this achievement did not mollify critics for whom Carter, by this time, could do nothing right.

The sharp increases in oil prices in 1979 triggered still higher inflation rates. By the end of 1979, the Consumer Price Index was rising at an annual rate of almost 18 per cent. Carter firmly resisted the imposition of wage and price controls, although polls indicated that over half of the public favored them. Instead, with its wage and price guidelines in shambles, the government turned increasingly to federal budget cutting and restrictions on credit and the money supply. In October 1979, the Federal Reserve Board took steps to shrink the supply of money available for loans. Further restrictions drove bankers' prime interest rates to a high of 20 per cent by April 1980, while restrictions on consumer credit discouraged installment buying.

The clampdown on credit immediately depressed the housing and automobile industries and other industries dependent on them. Layoffs in these sectors of the economy led the surge in unemployment, which by July 1980 exceeded 8 per cent for the first time since the major downturn of 1974–1975. The long awaited recession had finally arrived. However, Carter's antiinflation program was also working, albeit at heavy social costs. And these costs, it must be said, were exacerbated by the American automobile industry's failure to foresee and plan to meet the demand for small fuel-efficient cars. One third of American automobile workers were out of work by the summer of 1980.

3. THE PRESIDENTIAL CAMPAIGN AND THE ELECTION OF 1980

Presidential Politics and International Crises

Carter had never left much doubt about his intentions to run for a second term. Yet during 1979 his popular support had steadily dwindled to the point where the elected incumbent appeared to be the underdog in the coming presidential campaign. Not only would Carter face strong Republican opposition in the general election, but, in late 1979, he also confronted the prospect of an uphill fight for the Democratic nomination. Potential challengers included Governor Brown and Senator Edward Kennedy of Massachusetts, whose presence had loomed over Democratic politics for over a decade and who now seemed interested in the nomination. A poll of Democratic voters taken on November 1,

1979, showed Kennedy leading Carter by 54 per cent to 20 per cent. One week later, both Brown and Kennedy formally announced their candidacies.

Even before the contest for the Democratic nomination began, it was transformed by events halfway around the world. On November 4, 1979, 500 young Iranians occupied the American embassy in Teheran and held 100 people as hostages, 65 per cent of whom were members of the American diplomatic mission. Two weeks later the student radicals released thirteen American women and black men but continued to hold more than fifty Americans hostage. Relations between the United States and Iran had been strained since the Islamic revolution which toppled the Pahlavi regime of the Shah early in 1979. Now the two nations were on a collision course. While Carter demanded the release of the hostages, the Iranians demanded that the Shah be extradited from the United States where he was receiving medical treatment. Neither the Shah's departure for Panama, nor the urgings of the United Nations, nor the Shah's death more than eight months after the hostages were seized persuaded the Iranians to release the hostages.

As often happens during an international crisis, the President's popularity rose sharply in the aftermath of the occupation of the embassy in Teheran. Carter's initial determination to obtain the safe release of the hostages without delivering the Shah and without resorting to force was generally applauded. Presidential contestants, most notably Kennedy, who openly criticized his stand, suffered politically as a result. In December 1979 another crisis—a Soviet invasion of Afghanistan to bolster an unpopular Communist regime—also worked to Carter's political advantage. His decisions to put an embargo on grain shipments to Russia and to discourage American athletes from participating in the Olympic games in Moscow in the summer of 1980 were well received, and his standing in the polls rebounded.

Carter's renewed strength became apparent in the early Democratic primaries and caucuses. He defeated Kennedy in Iowa, New Hampshire, and other states, and Brown trailed far behind. But Kennedy hung on by winning in his home state of Massachusetts and in Pennsylvania, New Jersey, and New York. As the crises abroad dragged on and the economy weakened, Carter's popularity sagged once again.

The persistence of the highly publicized hostage crisis was troublesome both for the United States and her European allies. Carter publicly pursued diplomatic options and pressed for worldwide economic sanctions against Iran. Privately, Carter authorized a military operation which he hoped would free the hostages and quickly end the crisis which had taken captive his own administration. On April 24, 1980, a daring commando raid was launched, but the mission had to be terminated, with eight lives lost, before the would-be rescuers could reach Teheran. Sadness and disappointment at the failure were mingled with questions as to whether the mission should have been attempted in the first place and as to whether the United States was now totally helpless to effect an end to the crisis.

At least for a time, Carter had been the beneficiary of international events which seemingly pointed to weaknesses in his own foreign policy. The United States Government had been taken by surprise by the Iranian revolution and had misjudged both its character and intensity. Similarly, the Soviet invasion of Afghanistan showed that, despite Carter's interest in easing East-West tensions, the Russians were still willing to advance their own interests by military force. Carter acknowledged, in the midst of the Soviet invasion of Afghanistan, that his perception of Soviet intentions had changed. So, too, had the mood of Congress. Senate action on the SALT II treaty was suspended, and Congress added funds to the military budget amidst talk of a new Cold War.

THE REPUBLICAN CHALLENGE

Even before the election year began, Carter's political vulnerability on both domestic issues and foreign policy had attracted a large field of would-be Republican challengers. Ronald Reagan, the precampaign favorite, repeatedly denounced Carter's foreign policy as one of "vacillation, appeasement, and aimlessness." Similarly, during the early primaries, most other Republican candidates aimed their barbs at the incumbent rather than at each other.

As the primary season progressed, Reagan's drive for the nomination began to look invincible, despite early losses to the Texan, George Bush, in Iowa and Massachusetts, and despite the highly publicized candidacy of John B. Anderson, congressman from Illinois. Anderson, whose record as a fiscal conservative was offset by his more liberal position on social issues, staked out a claim as the "moderate" alternative among the conservatives in the Republican field. Reagan and the other Republican candidates responded by attacking Anderson for being out of step with the party; in March, Reagan delivered a knockout blow to Anderson by defeating him in the primary in Anderson's home state.

One month later, Anderson withdrew from the Republican race and announced that he would run for President on an independent ticket. Unlike the environmentalist, Barry Commoner, who had accepted the nomination of the fledgling Citizens' party only a few days earlier, Anderson did not attempt to establish a new party. Rather, he intended to run a nonpartisan "campaign of national unity," one which he hoped would appeal to independents and the dissatisfied voters in both major parties. Public opinion polls taken at the time of Anderson's announcement showed that he would have the support of from 17 to 20 per cent of the voters in a three-way race with Reagan and Carter.

Meanwhile, Reagan's juggernaut forced his rivals from the field one by one and ended former President Ford's brief flirtation with the campaign. In May, George Bush withdrew, the last of the major challengers to do so, and the nomination was securely in Reagan's grasp.

Despite his age (sixty-eight at the beginning of 1980), Reagan had campaigned vigorously. In fact, he had never stopped running since his loss to Gerald Ford in 1976. In 1980, Reagan was able to maintain his base of support among the ideological purists of the Republican Right wing, while he added to that group an impressive number of voters, including many blue-collar workers who had never before been associated with the Republican party. Many of these new Reagan supporters were attracted by his conservative positions on social issues, his pithy attacks on big government, and his straightforward appeal to Americans to establish a "coalition of shared values" which would restore the presumed moral integrity and world leadership of an older United States.

With Reagan's nomination secure, the Republican convention, which opened in Detroit on July 14, took on the air of a coronation rather than of a political battleground. Only the question of Reagan's vice-presidential running mate remained as a point of contention between conservative and moderate delegates. Reagan tried to resolve that dilemma by enticing former President Ford to join the ticket. Ford had no interest in returning to Washington to assume the traditional and largely ceremonial duties of the vice-presidency, and he demanded something like a "co-presidency." This unprecedented and constitutionally dubious arrangement did not materialize when negotiations between Ford and Reagan broke down. Reagan then turned to his former rival, George Bush, who eagerly accepted the nomination.

Some persons viewed Reagan as the champion of a crusade to restore America to its former greatness; others saw him as a dangerously simple-minded reactionary. Neither view was entirely correct. As a frequent spokesman for conservative causes over the last twenty years and in campaigns for public office since 1966, Reagan had delivered snappy, one-line commentaries on all manner of public issues, and his comments had often been naive and erroneous.

Viewed only in the light of his public utterances, Reagan did, indeed, appear to be more conservative than any man who had sat in the Oval Office since Calvin Coolidge (whose style of governance Reagan proposed to emulate). However, Reagan had a record of public service as well as a record of public statements. Between 1967 and 1975, he had served as Governor of California, the most populous state in the Union. In campaigning for that office, he had preached a crusade against big government and against student protest on the campuses of the state university. However, Reagan's record in office was different from his campaign rhetoric. Although his doctrinaire approach at first produced stalemates with the state legislature, Reagan learned the art of compromise, and, during his second term, he worked effectively with the legislature in restructuring public programs in several areas, particularly in the field of mental health. Reagan attempted to hold the line on increased spending (although in the end both spending and taxes increased), and to streamline the state's government. But he did not dismantle state agencies wholesale, as his critics had feared that he would do.

In contrast to Governor Carter of Georgia, Governor Reagan's administrative style resembled more that of a chairman of a board than that of an active chief executive officer. Reagan depended on his staff to make all but the most important decisions, and he typically confined his office work to regular business hours. Reagan's public record and patterns of work as Governor of California could offer voters in 1980 some hints about how he might function in the White House and what his approach to domestic policies might be. However, they revealed nothing about the shape of a Reagan foreign policy. As one observer noted, California did not have the Bomb.

THE RACE FOR THE WHITE HOUSE

While Reagan was basking in his triumph in Detroit, Jimmy Carter was still struggling for his own renomination. By the summer of 1980, Carter's political windfall from the Iranian crisis had long since disappeared. Rising unemployment had caused wholesale defections among blue-collar workers. And, on the eve of the Democratic convention, revelations that Billy Carter, the President's brother, had engaged in questionable business dealings with the government of Libya raised fresh doubts about Jimmy Carter's capacity to govern, even within his own family. By early August, Carter trailed Reagan in the polls by fourteen to eighteen percentage points and faced an intraparty challenge from Kennedy supporters and others who wished to release convention delegates from their pledges to support particular candidates and thus open the way for the nomination of someone other than Carter.

When the Democrats gathered in national convention in New York on August 11, the "open-convention" movement was quickly snuffed out with adoption of a Carter-backed rule which bound each delegate to vote for the candidate to whom he or she had been pledged in their state primaries. Following the vote, Senator Kennedy conceded the nomination to Carter, but the party unity which Carter so desperately sought still eluded him. Kennedy addressed the convention to plead for the adoption of several liberal platform planks and nearly swept the convention off its feet; indeed, Kennedy's address sounded very much like an acceptance speech. Carter accepted most of Kennedy's platform planks in an effort to win the Senator's active support. In the end, Kennedy's endorsement seemed to be half-hearted, and some of his backers vowed to support Anderson rather than Carter, who they said had turned his back on the heritage of the New Deal.

The Democratic and Republican conventions reflected, in different ways, the changing nature of the presidential nominating process. Between 1960 and 1980, the number of primaries in both parties had doubled, as had the percentage of delegates selected by primary vote. Political "insiders," including an incumbent President, could no longer control the selection of delegates as easily as they once could. Victory in the all-important primaries required not only intensive organizing efforts in the states, but also cooperation with newly powerful single-issue groups, whose grass roots strength and ability to deliver votes could be crucial.

Pressure groups were very much in evidence at both conventions. At the Republican gathering, "Right to Life" and "Moral Majority" (right-wing evangelical Protestants and some Catholics) advocates helped secure the adoption of an antiabortion plank and the omission of approval of the Equal Rights amendment in the platform and also pressed Reagan in his vice-presidential selection. At the Democratic convention, whose rules now required that half of the delegates be women, feminists led a successful floor fight for platform planks which endorsed federally funded abortions and called for the Democratic National Committee to withhold campaign funds from candidates who did not support the ERA. After the conventions, the two candidates would downplay their parties' platforms. The adoption of those platforms had demonstrated that traditional party discipline at conventions was a thing of the past.

Although both platforms were largely ignored after Labor Day, the conventions did set the tone for the autumn campaign in another respect. To an even greater extent than is usually the case, the speechmakers at both conventions attempted to make the other party's candidate the central issue in the campaign. The Republicans charged Carter with incompetence and wrongheaded economic and foreign policies, while the Democrats resurrected extreme statements which Reagan had made over the years to suggest that he would dismantle the New Deal and lead the nation to war. Both candidates took up the same litanies. As one journalist noted, "Their most compelling boasts are that one isn't Jimmy Carter and the other isn't Ronald Reagan."

John Anderson's campaign strategy was based on the fact that he was neither Carter nor Reagan, and the widespread dissatisfaction with the two major party candidates seemed at first to work in his favor. In September, Anderson's standing in the polls was sufficiently high to win him an invitation to the presidential debates sponsored by the League of Women Voters. Carter refused to participate in a three-way debate without first meeting Reagan alone. Thus Reagan and Anderson ended up in a debate between the challengers. Although Anderson acquitted himself well, the debate, without Carter, did not give Anderson the boost in popularity which he had to have in order to be a credible candidate. By mid-October his standing in the polls had dropped below 10 percent.

As the campaign entered its last month, the two major candidates were virtually even in the polls, with one third or more of the voters having no strong preference. Reagan led in virtually all the western states which Ford had carried in 1976, while Carter led in most of the South, though not as securely as in his first race. As had often been the case in the past century, the election could be won or lost in the belt of industrial states stretching from New York to Illinois. These six states accounted for 157 electoral votes, 58 per cent of the total needed for victory.

The battle for the industrial heartland in 1980 shaped up as more than a contest between two candidates. It was, more fundamentally, a test of the vitality of the New Deal coalition which had kept the Democratic party preeminent in American politics since the 1930s. Shifts in voting patterns among blue-collar workers in that region in the 1890s and the 1930s had been crucial factors in the major political realignments of the past century.

In 1968 and in 1972, George Wallace and Richard M. Nixon had made inroads among blue-collar Democrats in the region, primarily through conservative appeals on social issues. Now, in 1980, a Republican nominee not only repeated those appeals, but also challenged an incumbent Democratic President on the bread-and-butter issues which had tied the blue-collar industrial workers to the party of Franklin Roosevelt for half a century. Like Roosevelt in 1932, Reagan could saddle his opponent with responsibility for high unemployment. And like William McKinley in 1896, he could proclaim to disgruntled blue-collar workers that their economic well-being would be best served by G.O.P. policies which would strengthen the large industrial firms of the region, and that Democratic policies threatened to undermine the vitality of those corporations. Regardless of whether or not either claim had a basis in fact, they were politically potent in a time of economic stagnation.

In the war for that blue-collar vote, the substantial difference over various policies between Reagan and Carter became obscured by claims and counterclaims about rival plans for "reindustrialization" and revitalization of the urban-industrial corridor. This much was clear: if Reagan's attacks on Carter's economic policies could substantially erode the usual Democratic majorities among blue-collar workers and among blacks and Hispanics (precisely the groups which had been hardest hit by the recession of 1980), then victory was within his grasp.

THE ELECTION OF 1980

In the final days of the campaign, the balance tipped dramatically toward Reagan, although all but the very last opinion polls failed to detect the shift. One week before the election, the two leading candidates met in the "one-on-one" debate which Carter had sought. But the televised confrontation actually stalled the President's drive to take the lead from Reagan. In the debate, the panel of reporters did not press Reagan to explain the inconsistencies in his policy statements or force Carter to justify his handling of the economy. However, Reagan succeeded in stopping Carter's momentum: Reagan avoided a major blunder and displayed a relaxed demeanor which seemed to belie the Democrats' characterization of him as a right-wing ideologue.

Along with the debate, the issue of the hostages gave Reagan a last-minute boost. Election day, November 4, was the anniversary of the capture of the American embassy in Teheran, and the stalemate epitomized for many Americans the loss of national power in world affairs. Carter, the incumbent, was the obvious target of such frustration. This frustration had its greatest impact on male voters. There was a swing (as compared with the election of 1976) of 20 per cent of the male voters from the Democratic to the Republican candidate. Two days before the election, the Iranian parliament finally stipulated its

President-elect Ronald Reagan and his wife, Nancy, wave to supporters November 4 after President Jimmy Carter conceded that Reagan had won the presidential election. Promising to "get America moving again," Reagan's campaign helped swing a nationwide move to the right among all levels of election. (United Press International Photo)

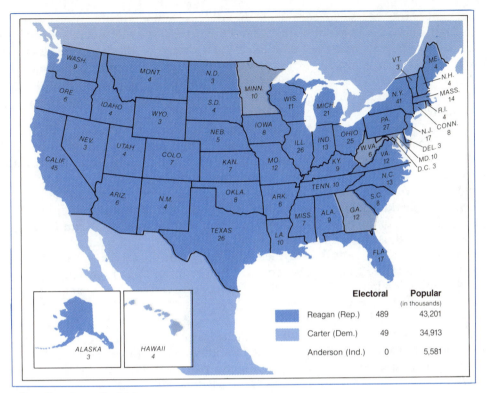

The Election of 1980

	Electoral	Popular
		(in thousands)
Reagan (Rep.)	489	43,201
Carter (Dem.)	49	34,913
Anderson (Ind.)	0	5,581

terms for the release of the hostages, but they still remained in captivity on November 4.

Reagan's victory was more decisive than any pollster had predicted. He captured 489 electoral votes to Carter's forty-nine. Reagan won about 43.5 million popular votes, or 51 per cent of the total; Carter 34.9 million popular votes, or 41 per cent of the total. Anderson failed to win any electoral votes and received just under 5.6 million popular votes, or about 7 per cent of the total. The twenty-year decline in voter turnout continued: only 52 per cent of those eligible to vote cast a ballot. Included among the 48 per cent of nonvoters were many persons on the west coast who walked away from the polling places or did not vote after they heard the television networks project Reagan as the winner soon after 8 o'clock, eastern time, and saw Carter concede defeat soon afterward.

Reagan's victory made one fact indelibly clear. There was no longer any Solid South, and Southerners would not vote for a presidential candidate simply because he came from their region. Reagan's sweep of the South (aside from Carter's native Georgia) actually reestablished the pattern to which Carter's showing in 1976 had been the exception. Since 1948, only in 1976 had the South given almost all its electoral votes to the Democratic presidential nominee.

All across the United States, the venerable New Deal coalition, which Carter had patched together in 1976, seemed finally to be coming apart. In 1976, 80 per cent of the voters who considered themselves Democrats supported Carter. In 1980, he won only about 60 per cent of the votes cast by Democrats. Reagan made huge inroads into the union labor vote; among blue-collar workers as a whole, he actually outpolled Carter. More Catholics voted for Reagan than for Carter, and Carter barely outpolled Reagan among Jews. Among the voting blocs which had historically constituted the New Deal coalition, only blacks remained solidly behind Carter. It was estimated that 82 per cent of blacks voted for him—about the same percentage that he had received in 1976. It is clear why such a reversal of accustomed voting patterns occurred in 1980. "Exit polls" conducted among voters as they left the polling places indicated that concerns about the economy and Carter's handling of inflation and unemployment were the key issues among the majority of voters. Reagan had succeeded in making Carter's leadership and his economic record the central issue. The issue of the hostages, as has been said, also played a role. Significantly, over half of those questioned in one poll said that they had little faith in *any* President's ability to deal with these problems. But Carter, as an incumbent who had promised to act decisively, bore the brunt of their frustration.

At a more fundamental level, the rejection of Carter, like the defeat of Gerald Ford, reflected the anxiety felt by many Americans throughout the 1970s about the nation's inability to shape its own domestic future. In the general election of 1980, Carter argued—with no little justification—that, in the years ahead, the freedom to act, both as a nation and as individuals, would be more circumscribed than had been the case in the boom years since 1945. Reagan, on the other hand, dismissed the possibility of an impending energy shortage and asserted that it was well within the power of the United States to reestablish its global economic and strategic superiority. In the end, his appeal to get America "moving again," reminiscent in a sense of Franklin Roosevelt's infectious optimism in 1932, probably contributed more to the Californian's success than any of his specific conservative proposals.

The Reagan victory was only part of the political upheaval of 1980. Veteran liberal Democrats in Congress went down to defeat in astounding numbers. Republicans gained twelve seats in the Senate, giving them control of that body for the first time since 1954. Democrats retained a solid majority in the House of Representatives, but lost thirty-three seats in that body.

Reagan's victory undoubtedly explained some of the Republican gains in Congress. All but four of the thirty-three Democratic Senate nominees received more votes than Carter did in their states, and some were undoubtedly pulled down to defeat along with him. However, an antiincumbent tide was running which involved more than the presidential race. A number of liberal Democratic senators had been "targeted" for defeat by various "nonpartisan" conservative groups, such as the National Conservative Political Action Committee (NCPAC), the Moral Majority, and various other groups. Three veteran liberal senators—Frank Church of Idaho, George McGovern of South Dakota, and Birch Bayh of Indiana—as well as freshman John Culver of Iowa, were obviously victims.

Republicans also won four additional governorships and four additional state legislative chambers. Democrats still controlled a sizable majority of state legislatures and a more modest majority of governorships. But the Republican advances, following on the heels of similar gains in 1978, left Democrats in fear of losing control of state houses everywhere but in the South. Even there, the "presidential Republicanism" of the last sixteen years was having some impact on state and local races.

Did all this add up to one of those "critical realignments" in the two-party system which has occurred once every half-century or so? We can only answer this question with any certainty in the future. But a few words of caution are in order before rendering even a preliminary answer. After each presidential election since 1964, the losing party has been diagnosed as terminally ill, only to make a miraculous recovery soon afterward. Democratic party registration in 1980 still exceeded that of the Republicans by a substantial margin. Finally, partisan identification among both Democrats and Republicans has been in decline for a number of years. What we may be witnessing, as one political scientist has observed, is not so much the realignment of the two-party system as its permanent fragmentation.

Whatever label one attaches to the dominant party or coalition in the coming years, it is not at all certain to represent a new conservative majority intent upon dismantling the New Deal. Candidate Reagan, unlike Goldwater in 1964, took pains to affirm his basic support for major components of the New Deal/ Fair Deal/Great Society programs. These programs are now, as recent Republican Presidents have discovered, part of the basic structure of government, and Reagan would have great difficulty in destroying them, even if he wanted to.

There has been, without question, a substantial shift to the right in American public opinion with regard to the proper role of government, and that shift can be traced over a number of years. But, upon close examination, the implications of this shift are ambiguous. As one writer has put it, "In the late seventies, the people of the United States were moving vigorously to the Left, the Right, and the Center, all at the same time." Traditional labels were confounded by surveys which revealed that majorities of the people believed that government was too powerful, but also that mandatory wage and price controls should be imposed; and that the government was spending too much money, but that is should also spend more on environment, health, and aid to the cities. Perhaps historians will look back to these years as a watershed in the nation's political philosophy, but the shape of that new political synthesis is not yet clear—indeed, it is not yet fully formed.

It may well be, as critics of both the Left and the Right have argued, that the progressive/New Deal synthesis, born in the first third of this century, is no longer adequate to deal with the problems of the last third. Whatever political philosophy might emerge to replace it may well be forged from the ideas of the "Left" and of the "Right." At this point one can only hope that such a philosophy will provide directions clear enough to enable the American people, through their leaders, to steer the republic safely through the stormy seas of the next decade.

SUGGESTED READINGS

Historical analysis of politics and government during the Ford and Carter years is just beginning. Much of the material for this chapter came from contemporary journalistic sources, including *Congressional Quarterly*, *The National Journal*, and major newspapers such as the *New York Times* and the *Washington Post*.

Several general studies of recent United States history include material on national politics and government in the late 1970s. The best brief account of energy and economic policies under Ford and Carter is found in Arthur S. Link and William B. Catton, *American Epoch, 1938–1980,* 5th ed. (1980). Richard S. Kirkendall, *A Global Power: America Since the Age of Roosevelt,* 2nd ed. (1980), is also useful for the Carter years.

Gerald R. Ford describes his own brief presidency in *A Time to Heal: An Autobiography* (1979). The role of Henry Kissinger in shaping American foreign policy under Nixon and Ford will be a matter of scholarly debate for years to come. The forthcoming second volume of Kissinger's memoirs will describe his years as Secretary of State.

The election of 1976 and the lengthy campaign which preceded it have already received book-length treatment from several political scientists and journalists. The most comprehensive journalistic account of the campaign is Jules Witcover, *Marathon: The Pursuit of the Presidency, 1972–1976* (1977). James T. Wooten, *Dasher: The Roots and the Rising of Jimmy Carter* (1978), is critical to the point of harshness.

Jimmy Carter's personality and background became grist for the journalistic mills with his sudden rise to national prominence. William Lee Miller, *Yankee from Georgia: The Emergence of Jimmy Carter* (1978), provides valuable insights, as do Carter's autobiography, *Why Not the Best?* (1975), and his celebrated interview with Robert Scheer in *Playboy* (November 1976) and the accompanying article by Scheer. The first study by a historian of Carter's gubernatorial career is Gary M. Fink, *Prelude to the Presidency: The Political Character and Legislative Style of Governor Jimmy Carter* (1980). It provides valuable clues for understanding Carter's method of operation in the White House. The first years of Carter's presidency are treated in a study by the veteran Washington reporter, Haynes Johnson, in *Governing America* (1980). The political upheaval which was so evident in the elections of 1980 reflected trends which had been emerging over the past several years and which had already become the subject of analysis and study by political scientists and journalists. William N. Chambers and Walter D. Burnham, *The American Party Systems,* 2nd ed. (1975), puts the electoral changes of the 1970s and 1980 in historical perspective. Michael Harrington, *Decade of Decision* (1980), and Kevin P. Phillips, *The Emerging Republican Majority* (1969), analyze from quite different perspectives the evidence on the apparent shift toward conservatism in American politics.

APPENDICES

THE DECLARATION OF INDEPENDENCE

When in the Course of human events, it becomes necessary for one people to dissolve the political bands which have connected them with another, and to assume among the Powers of the earth, the separate and equal station to which the Laws of Nature and of Nature's God entitle them, a decent respect to the opinions of mankind requires that they should declare the causes which impel them to the separation.

We hold these truths to be self-evident, that all men are created equal, that they are endowed by their Creator with certain unalienable Rights, that among these are Life, Liberty and the pursuit of Happiness. That to secure these rights, Governments are instituted among Men, deriving their just powers from the consent of the governed, That whenever any Form of Government becomes destructive of these ends, it is the Right of the People to alter or to abolish it, and to institute new Government, laying its foundation on such principles and organizing its powers in such form, as to them shall seem most likely to effect their Safety and Happiness. Prudence, indeed, will dictate that Governments long established should not be changed for light and transient causes; and accordingly all experience hath shown, that mankind are more disposed to suffer, while evils are sufferable, than to right themselves by abolishing the forms to which they are accustomed. But when a long train of abuses and usurpations, pursuing invariably the same Object evinces a design to reduce them under absolute Despotism, it is their right, it is their duty, to throw off such Government, and to provide new Guards for their future security. — Such has been the patient sufferance of these Colonies; and such is now the necessity which constrains them to alter their former Systems of Government. The history of the present King of Great Britain is a history of repeated injuries and usurpations, all having in direct object the establishment of an absolute Tyranny over these States. To prove this, let Facts be submitted to a candid world.

He has refused his Assent to Laws, the most wholesome and necessary for the public good.

He has forbidden his Governors to pass Laws of immediate and pressing importance, unless suspended in their operation till his Assent should be obtained; and when so suspended, he has utterly neglected to attend to them.

He has refused to pass other Laws for the accommodation of large districts of people, unless those people would relinquish the right of Representation in the Legislature, a right inestimable to them and formidable to tyrants only.

He has called together legislative bodies at places unusual, uncomfortable, and distant from the depository of their Public Records, for the sole purpose of fatiguing them into compliance with his measures.

He has dissolved Representative Houses repeatedly, for opposing with manly firmness his invasions on the rights of the people.

He has refused for a long time, after such dissolutions, to cause others to be elected; whereby the Legislative Powers, incapable of Annihilation, have returned to the People at large for their exercise; the State remaining in the mean time exposed to all the dangers of invasion from without, and convulsions within.

He has endeavoured to prevent the population of these States; for that purpose obstructing the Laws of Naturalization of Foreigners; refusing to pass others to encourage their migration hither, and raising the conditions of new Appropriations of Lands.

He has obstructed the Administration of Justice, by refusing his Assent to Laws for establishing Judiciary Powers.

He has made Judges dependent on his Will alone, for the tenure of their offices, and the amount and payment of their salaries.

He has erected a multitude of New Offices, and sent hither swarms of Officers to harass our People, and eat out their substance.

He has kept amoung us, in times of peace, Standing Armies without the Consent of our legislature.

He has affected to render the Military independent of and superior to the Civil Power.

He has combined with others to subject us to a jurisdiction foreign to our constitution, and unacknowledged by our laws; giving his Assent to their acts of pretended legislation.

For quartering large bodies of armed troops among us:

For protecting them, by a mock Trial, from Punishment for any Murders which they should commit on the Inhabitants of these States:

For cutting off our Trade with all parts of the world:

For imposing taxes on us without our Consent:

For depriving us in many cases, of the benefits of Trial by Jury:

For transporting us beyond Seas to be tried for pretended offenses:

For abolishing the free System of English Laws in a neighbouring Province, establishing therein an Arbitrary government, and enlarging its Boundaries so as to render it at once an example and fit instrument for introducing the same absolute rule into these Colonies:

For taking away our Charters, abolishing our most valuable Laws, and altering fundamentally the Forms of our Governments:

For suspending our own Legislature, and declaring themselves invested with Power to legislate for us in all cases whatsoever.

He has abdicated Government here, by declaring us out of his Protection and waging War against us.

He has plundered our seas, ravaged our Coasts, burnt our towns, and destroyed the lives of our people.

He is at this time transporting large armies of foreign mercenaries to compleat the works of death, desolation and tyranny, already begun with circumstances of Cruelty & perfidy scarcely paralleled in the most barbarous ages, and totally unworthy the Head of a civilized nation.

He has constrained our fellow Citizens taken Captive on the high Seas to bear Arms against their Country, to become the executioners of their friends and Brethren, or to fall themselves by their Hands.

He has excited domestic insurrections amongst us, and has endeavoured to bring on the inhabitants of our frontiers, the merciless Indian Savages, whose known rule of warfare, is an undistinguished destruction of all ages, sexes and conditions.

In every stage of these Oppressions We have Petitioned for Redress in the most humble terms: Our repeated Petitions have been answered only by repeated injury. A Prince, whose character is thus marked by every act which may define a Tyrant, is unfit to be the ruler of a free People.

Nor have We been wanting in attention to our British brethren. We have warned them from time to time of attempts by their legislature to extend an unwarrantable jurisdiction over us. We have reminded them of the circumstances of our emigration and settlement here. We have appealed to their native justice and magnanimity, and we have conjured them by the ties of our common kindred to disavow these usurpations, which, would inevitably interrupt our connections and correspondence. They too have been deaf to the voice of justice and of consanguinity. We must, therefore, acquiesce in the necessity, which denounces our Separation, and hold them, as we hold the rest of mankind, Enemies in War, in Peace Friends.

We, therefore, the Representatives of the united States of America, in General Congress, Assembled, appealing to the Supreme Judge of the world for the rectitude of our intentions, do, in the Name, and by Authority of the good People of these Colonies, solemnly publish and declare, That these United Colonies are, and of Right ought to be Free and Independent States; that they are Absolved from all Allegiance to the British Crown, and that all political connection between them and the State of Great Britain, is and ought to be totally dissolved; and that as Free and Independent States, they have full Power to levy War, conclude Peace, contract Alliances, establish Commerce, and to do all other Acts and Things which Independent States may of right do. And for the support of this Declaration, with a firm reliance on the Protection of Divine Providence, we mutually pledge to each other our Lives, our Fortunes and our sacred Honor.

THE CONSTITUTION OF THE UNITED STATES

We the people of the United States, in Order to form a more perfect Union, establish Justice, insure domestic Tranquility, provide for the common defence, promote the general Welfare, and secure tbe Blessings of Liberty to ourselves and our Posterity, do ordain and establish This CONSTITUTION for the United States of America.

Article I

Section 1. All legislative Powers herein granted shall be vested in a Congress of the United States, which shall consist of a Senate and House of Representatives.

Section 2. The House of Representatives shall be composed of Members chosen every second Year by the People of the several States, and the Electors in each State shall have the Qualifications requisite for Electors of the most numerous Branch of the State Legislature.

No Person shall be a Representative who shall not have attained to the Age of twenty-five Years, and been seven Years a Citizen of the United States, and who shall not, when elected, be an Inhabitant of that State in which he shall be chosen.

Representatives and direct Taxes shall be apportioned among the several States which may be included within this Union, according to their respective Numbers, which shall be determined by adding to the whole Number of free Persons, including those bound to Service for a Term of Years, and excluding Indians not taxed, three fifths of all other Persons. The actual Enumeration shall be made within three Years after the first Meeting of the Congress of the United States, and within every subsequent Term of ten Years, in such Manner as they shall by Law direct. The Number of Representatives shall not exceed one for every thirty Thousand, but each State shall have at Least one Representative; and until such enumeration shall be made, the State of New Hampshire shall be entitled to chuse three, Massachusetts eight, Rhode-Island and Providence Plantations one, Connecticut five, New-York six, New Jersey four, Pennsylvania eight, Delaware one, Maryland six, Virginia ten, North Carolina five, South Carolina five, and Georgia three.

When vacancies happen in the Representation from any State, the Executive Authority thereof shall issue Writs of Election to fill such Vacancies.

The House of Representatives shall chuse their Speaker and other Officers; and shall have the sole Power of Impeachment.

Section 3. The Senate of the United States shall be composed of two Senators from each State, chosen by the Legislature thereof, for six Years; and each Senator shall have one Vote.

Immediately after they shall be assembled in Consequence of the first Election, they shall be divided as equally as may be into three Classes. The Seats of the Senators of the first Class shall be vacated at the Expiration of the second Year, of the second Class at the Expiration of the fourth Year, and of the third Class at the Expiration of the sixth Year, so that one-third may be chosen every second Year; and if Vacancies happen by Resignation, or otherwise, during the Recess of the Legislature of any State, the Executive thereof may make temporary Appointments until the next Meeting of the Legislature, which shall then fill such Vacancies.

No Person shall be a Senator who shall not have attained to the Age of thirty Years, and been nine Years a Citizen of the United States, and who shall not, when elected, be an Inhabitant of that State in which he shall be chosen.

The Vice President of the United States shall be President of the Senate, but shall have no vote, unless they be equally divided.

The Senate shall chuse their other Officers, and also a President pro tempore, in the absence of the Vice President, or when he shall exercise the Office of the President of the United States.

The Senate shall have the sole Power to try all Impeachments. When sitting for that purpose, they shall be on Oath or Affirmation. When the President of the United States is tried, the Chief Justice shall preside: And no person shall be convicted without the Concurrence of two thirds of the Members present.

Judgment in Cases of Impeachment shall not extend further than to removal from Office, and disqualification to hold and enjoy any Office of honor, Trust, or Profit under the United States: but the Party convicted shall nevertheless be liable and subject to Indictment, Trial, Judgment, and Punishment, according to Law.

Section 4. The Times, Places and Manner of holding Elections for Senators and Representatives, shall be prescribed in each state by the Legislature thereof; but the Congress may at any time by Law make or alter such Regulations, except as to the Places of Chusing Senators.

The Congress shall assemble at least once in every Year, and such Meeting shall be on the first Monday in December, unless they shall by Law appoint a different Day.

Section 5. Each House shall be the Judge of the Elections, Returns and Qualifications of its own Members, and a Majority of each shall constitute a Quorum to do Business; but a smaller number may adjourn from day to day, and may be authorized to compel the Attendance of absent Members, in such Manner, and under such Penalties, as each House may provide.

Each House may determine the Rules of its Proceedings, punish its Members for disorderly Behavior, and, with the Concurrence of two thirds, expel a Member.

Each House shall keep a Journal of its Proceedings, and from time to time publish the same, excepting such Parts as may in their Judgment require Secrecy; and the Yeas and Nays of the Members of either House on any question shall, at the Desire of one fifth of those Present, be entered on the Journal.

Neither House, during the Session of Congress, shall, without the Consent of the other, adjourn for more than three days, nor to any other Place than that in which the two Houses shall be sitting.

Section 6. The Senators and Representatives shall receive a Compensation for their Services, to be ascertained by Law, and paid out of the Treasury of the United States. They shall in all Cases, except Treason, Felony, and Breach of the Peace, be privileged from Arrest during their Attendance at the Session of their respective Houses, and in going to and returning from the same; and for any Speech or Debate in either House, they shall not be questioned in any other Place.

No Senator or Representative shall, during the Time for which he was elected, be appointed to any civil Office under the Authority of the United States, which shall have been created, or the Emoluments whereof shall have been increased, during such time; and no Person holding any Office under the United States shall be a Member of either House during his continuance in Office.

Section 7. All Bills for raising Revenue shall originate in the House of Representatives; but the Senate may propose or concur with Amendments as on other bills.

Every Bill which shall have passed the House of Representatives and the Senate, shall, before it become a Law, be presented to the President of the United States; If he approve he shall sign it, but if not he shall return it, with his Objections, to that House in which it shall have originated, who shall enter the Objections at large on their Journal, and proceed to reconsider it. If after such Reconsideration two thirds of that House shall agree to pass the bill, it shall be sent, together with the objections, to the other House, by which it shall likewise be reconsidered, and if approved by two thirds of that House, it shall become a Law. But in all such Cases the Votes of both Houses shall be determined by Yeas and Nays, and the Names of the Persons voting for and against the Bill shall be entered on the Journal of each House respectively. If any Bill shall not be returned by the President within ten Days (Sundays excepted) after it shall have been presented to him, the Same shall be a Law, in like Manner as if he had signed it, unless the Congress by their Adjournment prevent its Return, in which Case it shall not be a Law.

Every Order, Resolution, or Vote to which the Concurrence of the Senate and House of Representatives may be necessary (except on a question of Adjournment) shall be presented to the President of the United States; and before the Same shall take Effect, shall be approved by him, or being disapproved by him, shall be repassed by two thirds of the Senate and House of Representatives, according to the Rules and Limitations prescribed in the Case of a Bill.

Section 8. The Congress shall have Power To lay and collect Taxes, Duties, Imposts and Excises, to pay the Debts and provide for the common Defence and general Welfare of the United States; but all Duties, Imposts and Excises shall be uniform throughout the United States;

To borrow money on the credit of the United States;

To regulate Commerce with foreign Nations, and among the several States, and with the Indian Tribes;

To establish a uniform Rule of Naturalization, and uniform Laws on the subject of Bankruptcies throughout the United States;

To coin Money, regulate the Value thereof, and of foreign Coin, and fix the Standard of Weights and Measures;

To provide for the Punishment of counterfeiting the Securities and current Coin of the United States;

To establish Post Offices and post Roads;

To promote the Progress of Science and useful Arts, by securing for limited Times to Authors and Inventors the exclusive Right to their respective Writings and Discoveries;

To constitute Tribunals inferior to the Supreme Court;

To define and punish Piracies and Felonies committed on the high Seas, and Offenses against the Law of Nations;

To declare War, grant Letters of Marque and Reprisal, and make Rules concerning Captures on Land and Water;

To raise and support Armies, but no Appropriation of Money to that Use shall be for a longer Term than two Years;

To provide and maintain a Navy;

To make Rules for the Government and Regulation of the land and naval forces;

To provide for calling forth the Militia to execute the Laws of the Union, suppress Insurrections and repel Invasions;

To provide for organizing, arming, and disciplining the Militia, and for governing such Part of them as may be employed in the Service of the United States, reserving to the States respectively, the Appointment of the Officers, and the Authority of training the Militia according to the discipline prescribed by Congress;

To exercise exclusive Legislation in all Cases whatsoever, over such District (not exceeding ten Miles square) as may, by Cession of particular States, and the acceptance of Congress, become the Seat of Government of the United States, and to exercise like Authority over all Places purchased by the Consent of the Legislature of the State in which the Same shall be, for the Erection of Forts, Magazines, Arsenals, dock-Yards, and other needful Buildings; — And

To make all Laws which shall be necessary and proper for carrying into Execution the foregoing Powers, and all other Powers vested by this Constitution in the Government of the United States, or in any Department or Officer thereof.

Section 9. The Migration or Importation of such Persons as any of the States now existing shall think proper to admit, shall not be prohibited by the Congress prior to the Year one thousand eight hundred and eight, but a tax or duty may be imposed on such Importation, not exceeding ten dollars for each Person.

The privilege of the Writ of Habeas Corpus shall not be suspended, unless when in Cases of Rebellion or Invasion the public Safety may require it.

No Bill of Attainder or ex post facto Law shall be passed.

No capitation, or other direct, Tax shall be laid unless in Proportion to the Census or Enumeration herein before directed to be taken.

No Tax or Duty shall be laid on Articles exported from any State.

No Preference shall be given by any Regulation of Revenue to the Ports of one State over those of another: nor shall Vessels bound to, or from, one State, be obliged to enter, clear, or pay Duties in another.

No Money shall be drawn from the Treasury, but in Consequence of Appropriations made by Law; and a regular Statement and Account of the Receipts and Expenditures of all public Money shall be published from time to time.

No Title of Nobility shall be granted by the United States: And no Person holding any Office of Profit or Trust under them, shall, without the Consent of the Congress, accept of any present, Emolument, Office, or Title, of any kind whatever, from any King, Prince, or foreign State.

Section 10. No State shall enter into any Treaty, Alliance, or Confederation; grant Letters of Marque and Reprisal; coin Money; emit Bills of Credit; make any Thing but gold and silver Coin a Tender in Payment of Debts; pass any Bill of Attainder, ex post facto Law, or Law impairing the Obligation of Contracts, or grant any Title of Nobility.

No State shall, without the Consent of the Congress, lay any Imposts or Duties on Imports or Exports, except what may be absolutely necessary for executing its inspection Laws: and the net Produce of all Duties and Imposts, laid by any State on Imports or Exports, shall be for the Use of the Treasury of the United States; and all such Laws shall be subject to the Revision and Control of the Congress.

No State shall, without the Consent of Congress, lay any duty of Tonnage, keep Troops, or Ships of War in time of Peace, enter into any Agreement or Compact with another State, or with a foreign Power, or engage in War, unless actually invaded, or in such imminent Danger as will not admit of delay.

Article II

Section 1. The executive Power shall be vested in a President of the United States of America. He shall hold his Office during the Term of four years, and, together with the Vice-President, chosen for the same Term, be elected, as follows:

Each State shall appoint, in such Manner as the Legislature thereof may direct, a Number of

Electors, equal to the whole Number of Senators and Representatives to which the State may be entitled in the Congress: but no Senator or Representative, or Person holding an Office or Trust or Profit under the United States, shall be appointed an Elector.

The Electors shall meet in their respective States, and vote by Ballot for two persons, of whom one at least shall not be an Inhabitant of the same State with themselves. And they shall make a List of all the Persons voted for, and of the Number of Votes for each; which List they shall sign and certify, and transmit sealed to the Seat of the Government of the United States, directed to the President of the Senate. The President of the Senate shall, in the Presence of the Senate and House of Representatives, open all the Certificates, and the Votes shall then be counted. The Person having the greatest Number of Votes shall be the President, if such Number be a Majority of the whole Number of Electors appointed; and if there be more than one who have such Majority, and have an equal Number of Votes, then the House of Representatives shall immediately chuse by Ballot one of them for President; and if no Person have a Majority, then from the five highest on the List the said House shall in like Manner chuse the President. But in chusing the President, the Votes shall be taken by States, the Representation from each State having one Vote; a quorum for this Purpose shall consist of a Member or Members from two-thirds of the States, and a Majority of all the States shall be necessary to a Choice. In every Case, after the Choice of the President, the Person having the greatest Number of Votes of the Electors shall be the Vice President. But if there should remain two or more who have equal votes, the Senate shall chuse from them by Ballot the Vice-President.

The Congress may determine the Time of chusing the Electors, and the Day on which they shall give their Votes; which Day shall be the same throughout the United States.

No person except a natural-born Citizen, or a Citizen of the United States, at the time of the Adoption of this Constitution, shall be eligible to the Office of President; neither shall any Person be eligible to that Office who shall not have attained to the Age of thirty-five years, and been four-teen Years a Resident within the United States.

In Case of the Removal of the President from Office, or of his Death, Resignation, or Inability to discharge the Powers and Duties of the said Office, the same shall devolve on the Vice President, and the Congress may by Law provide for the Case of Removal, Death, Resignation, or Inability, both of the President and Vice President, declaring what Officer shall then act as President, and such Officer shall act accordingly, until the disability be removed, or a President shall be elected.

The President shall, at stated Times, receive for his Services a Compensation, which shall neither be increased nor diminished during the Period for which he shall have been elected, and he shall not receive within that Period any other Emolument from the United States, or any of them.

Before he enter on the execution of his Office, he shall take the following Oath or Affirmation: — "I do solemnly swear (or affirm) that I will faithfully execute the Office of President of the United States, and will, to the best of my Ability, preserve, protect, and defend the Constitution of the United States."

Section 2. The President shall be Commander in Chief of the Army and Navy of the United States, and of the Militia of the several States, when called into the actual Service of the United States; he may require the Opinion, in writing, of the principal Officer in each of the executive Departments, upon any subject relating to the Duties of their respective Offices, and he shall have Power to Grant Reprieves and Pardons for Offenses against the United States, except in Cases of Impeachment.

He shall have Power, by and with the Advice and Consent of the Senate, to make Treaties, provided two thirds of the Senators present concur; and he shall nominate, and by and with the Advice and Consent of the Senate, shall appoint Ambassadors, other public Ministers and Consuls, Judges of the supreme Court, and all other Officers of the United States, whose Appointments are not herein otherwise provided for, and which shall be established by Law: but the Congress may by Law vest the Appointment of such inferior Officers, as they think proper, in the President alone, in the Courts of Law, or in the Heads of Departments.

The President shall have Power to fill up all Vacancies that may happen during the Recess of the Senate, by granting Commissions which shall expire at the End of their next Session.

Section 3. He shall from time to time give to the Congress Information of the State of the Union, and recommend to their Consideration such Measures as he shall judge necessary and expedient; he may, on extraordinary occasions, convene both Houses, or either of them, and in Case of Disagreement between them, with respect to the Time of Adjournment, he may adjourn them to such Time as he shall think proper; he shall receive Ambassadors and other public Ministers; he shall take Care that the Laws be faithfully executed, and shall Commission all the Officers of the United States.

Section 4. The President, Vice President and all civil Officers of the United States, shall be removed from Office on Impeachment for, and Conviction of, Treason, Bribery, or other high Crimes and Misdemeanors.

Article III

Section 1. The judicial Power of the United States, shall be vested in one supreme Court, and in such inferior Courts as the Congress may from time to time ordain and establish. The Judges, both of the supreme and inferior Courts, shall hold their Offices during good Behaviour, and shall, at stated Times, receive for their Services, a Compensation, which shall not be diminished during their Continuance in Office.

Section 2. The judicial Power shall extend to all Cases, in Law and Equity, arising under this Constitution, the Laws of the United States, and treaties made, or which shall be made, under their Authority; — to all Cases affecting ambassadors, other public ministers and consuls; — to all cases of admiralty and maritime Jurisdiction; — to Controversies to which the United States shall be a Party; — to Controversies between two or more States; — between a State and Citizens of another State; — between Citizens of different States, — between Citizens of the same State claiming Lands under Grants of different States, and between a State, or the Citizens thereof, and foreign States, Citizens or Subjects.

In all Cases affecting Ambassadors, other public Ministers and Consuls, and those in which a State shall be Party, the supreme Court shall have original Jurisdiction. In all the other Cases before mentioned, the supreme Court shall have appellate Jurisdiction, both as to Law and Fact, with such Exceptions, and under such Regulations as the Congress shall make.

The trial of all Crimes, except in Cases of Impeachment, shall be by Jury; and such Trial shall be held in the State where the said Crimes shall have been committed; but when not committed within any State, the Trial shall be at such Place or Places as the Congress may by Law have directed.

Section 3. Treason against the United States, shall consist only in levying War against them, or in adhering to their Enemies, giving them Aid and Comfort. No Person shall be convicted of Treason unless on the Testimony of two Witnesses to the same overt Act, or on Confession in open Court.

The Congress shall have power to declare the Punishment of Treason, but no Attainder of Treason shall work Corruption of Blood, or Forfeiture except during the Life of the Person attainted.

Article IV

Section 1. Full Faith and Credit shall be given in each State to the public Acts, Records, and judicial Proceedings of every other State. And the Congress may by general Laws prescribe the Manner in which such Acts, Records and Proceedings shall be proved, and the Effect thereof.

Section 2. The Citizens of each State shall be entitled to all Privileges and Immunities of Citizens in the several States.

A Person charged in any State with Treason, Felony, or other Crime, who shall flee from Justice, and be found in another State, shall on demand of the executive Authority of the State from which he fled, be delivered up, to be removed to the State having Jurisdiction of the crime.

No Person held to Service or Labour in one State, under the Laws thereof, escaping into another, shall, in Consequence of any Law or Regulation therein, be discharged from such Service or Labour, but shall be delivered up on Claim of the Party to whom such Service or Labour may be due.

Section 3. New States may be admitted by the Congress into this Union; but no new State shall be formed or erected within the Jurisdiction of any other State; nor any State be formed by the Junction of two or more States, or parts of States, without the Consent of the Legislatures of the States concerned as well as of the Congress.

The Congress shall have Power to dispose of and make all needful Rules and Regulations respecting the Territory or other Property belonging to the United States; and nothing in this Constitution shall be so construed as to Prejudice any Claims of the United States, or of any particular State.

Section 4. The United States shall guarantee to every State in this Union a Republican Form of Government, and shall protect each of them against Invasion; and on Application of the Legislature, or of the Executive (when the Legislature cannot be convened) against domestic Violence.

Article V

The Congress, whenever two-thirds of both Houses shall deem it necessary, shall propose Amendments to this Constitution, or, on the Application of the Legislatures of two-thirds of the several States, shall call a Convention for proposing Amendments, which, in either Case, shall be valid to all Intents and Purposes, as part of this Constitution, when ratified by the Legislatures of three-fourths of the several States, or by Conventions in three-fourths thereof, as the one or the other Mode of Ratification may be proposed by the Congress; Provided that no Amendment which may be made prior to the Year One thousand eight hundred and eight shall in any Manner affect the first and fourth Clauses in the Ninth Section of the first Article; and that no State, without its Consent, shall be deprived of its equal Suffrage in the Senate.

Article VI

All Debts contracted and Engagements entered into, before the Adoption of this Constitution, shall be as valid against the United States under this Constitution, as under the Confederation.

This Constitution, and the Laws of the United States which shall be made in Pursuance thereof; and all Treaties made, or which shall be made, under the Authority of the United States, shall be the supreme Law of the Land; and the Judges in every State shall be bound thereby, any Thing in the Constitution or Laws of any State to the Contrary notwithstanding.

The Senators and Representatives before mentioned, and the Members of the several State Legislatures, and all executive and judicial Officers, both of the United States and of the several States, shall be bound by Oath or Affirmation to support this Constitution; but no religious Test shall ever be required as a qualification to any Office or public Trust under the United States.

Article VII

The Ratification of the Conventions of nine States shall be sufficient for the Establishment of this Constitution between the States so ratifying the same.

Done in Convention by the Unanimous Consent of the States present the Seventeenth Day of September in the Year of our Lord one thousand seven hundred and Eighty seven, and of the Independence of the United States of America the Twelfth. In Witness whereof We have hereunto subscribed our Names.

Articles in Addition to, and Amendment of, the Constitution of the United States of America, Proposed by Congress, and Ratified by the Legislatures of the Several States, Pursuant to the Fifth Article of the Original Constitution.

Amendment I [1791]

Congress shall make no law respecting an establishment of religion, or prohibiting the free exercise thereof; or abridging the freedom of speech, or of the press; or the right of the people peaceably to assemble, and to petition the Government for a redress of grievances.

Amendment II [1791]

A well regulated Militia, being necessary to the security of a free State, the right of the people to keep and bear Arms shall not be infringed.

Amendment III [1791]

No Soldier shall, in time of peace, be quartered in any house, without the consent of the Owner, nor in time of war, but in a manner to be prescribed by law.

Amendment IV [1791]

The right of the people to be secure in their persons, houses, papers, and effects, against unreasonable searches and seizures, shall not be violated, and no Warrants shall issue, but upon probable cause, supported by Oath or affirmation, and particularly describing the place to be searched, and the persons or things to be seized.

Amendment V [1791]

No person shall be held to answer for a capital or otherwise infamous crime, unless on a presentment or indictment of a Grand Jury, except in cases arising in the land or naval forces, or in the Militia, when in actual service in time of War or public danger; nor shall any person be subject for the same offence to be twice put in jeopardy of life or limb; nor shall be compelled in any criminal case to be a witness against himself, nor be deprived of life, liberty, or property, without due process of law; nor shall private property be taken for public use, without just compensation.

Amendment VI [1791]

In all criminal prosecutions, the accused shall enjoy the right to a speedy and public trial, by an impartial jury of the State and district wherein the crime shall have been committed, which district shall have been previously ascertained by law, and to be informed of the nature and cause of the accusation; to be confronted with the witnesses against him; to have compulsory process for obtaining witnesses in his favor, and to have the Assistance of Counsel for his defence.

Amendment VII [1791]

In suits at common law, where the value in controversy shall exceed twenty dollars, the right of trial by jury shall be preserved, and no fact tried by a jury, shall be otherwise reexamined in any Court of the United States, than according to the rules of the common law.

Amendment VIII [1791]

Excessive bail shall not be required, nor excessive fines imposed, nor cruel and unusual punishments inflicted.

Amendment IX [1791]

The enumeration in the Constitution, of certain rights, shall not be construed to deny or disparage others retained by the people.

Amendment X [1791]

The powers not delegated to the United States by the Constitution, nor prohibited by it to the States, are reserved to the States respectively, or to the people.

Amendment XI [1798]

The Judicial power of the United States shall not be construed to extend to any suit in law or equity, commenced or prosecuted against one of the United States by Citizens of another State, or by Citizens or Subjects of any Foreign State.

Amendment XII [1804]

The Electors shall meet in their respective States and vote by ballot for President and Vice-President, one of whom, at least, shall not be an inhabitant of the same State with themselves; they shall name in their ballots the person voted for as President, and in distinct ballots the person voted for as Vice-President, and they shall make distinct lists of all persons voted for as President, and of all persons voted for as Vice-President, and of the number of votes for each, which lists they shall sign and certify, and transmit sealed to the seat of the government of the United States, directed to the President of the Senate;—The President of the Senate shall, in the presence of the Senate and House of Representatives, open all the certificates and the votes shall then be counted;— The person having the greatest number of votes for President, shall be the President, if such number be a majority of the whole number of Electors appointed; and if no person have such majority, then from the persons having the highest numbers not exceeding three on the list of those voted for as President, the House of Representatives shall choose immediately, by ballot, the President. But in choosing the President, the votes shall be taken by states, the representation from each state having one vote; a quorum for this purpose shall consist of a member or members from two-thirds of the states, and a majority of all the states shall be necessary to a choice. And if the House of Representatives shall not choose a President whenever the right of choice shall devolve upon them, before the fourth day of March next following, then the Vice-President shall act as President, as in the case of the death or other constitutional disability of the President.—The person having the greatest number of votes as Vice-President, shall be the Vice-President, if such number be a majority of the whole number of Electors appointed, and if no person have a majority, then from the two highest numbers on the list, the Senate shall choose the Vice-President; a quorum for the purpose shall consist of two-thirds of the whole number of Senators, and a majority of the whole number shall be necessary to a choice. But no person constitutionally ineligible to the office of President shall be eligible to that of Vice-President of the United States.

Amendment XIII [1865]

Section 1. Neither slavery nor involuntary servitude, except as a punishment for crime whereof the party shall have been duly convicted, shall exist within the United States, or any place subject to their jurisdiction.

Section 2. Congress shall have power to enforce this article by appropriate legislation.

Amendment XIV [1868]

Section 1. All persons born or naturalized in the United States, and subject to the jurisdiction thereof, are citizens of the United States and of the State wherein they reside. No State shall make or enforce any law which shall abridge the privileges or immunities of citizens of the United States; nor shall any State deprive any person of life, liberty, or property, without due process of law; nor deny to any person within its jurisdiction the equal protection of the laws.

Section 2. Representatives shall be apportioned among the several States according to their respective numbers, counting the whole number of persons in each State, excluding Indians not taxed. But when the right to vote at any election for the choice of electors for President and Vice-President of the United States, Representatives in Congress, the Executive and Judicial officers of a State, or the members of the Legislature thereof, is denied to any of the male inhabitants of such State, being twenty-one years of age, and citizens of the United States, or in any way abridged, except for participation in rebellion, or other crime, the basis of representation therein shall be reduced in the proportion which the number of such male citizens shall bear to the whole number of male citizens twenty-one years of age in such State.

Section 3. No person shall be a Senator or Representative in Congress, or elector of President and Vice-President, or hold any office, civil or military, under the United States, or under any State, who, having previously taken an oath, as a member of Congress, or as an officer of the United States, or as a member of any State legislature, or as an executive or judicial officer of any State, to support the Constitution of the United States, shall have engaged in insurrection or rebellion against the same, or given aid or comfort to the enemies thereof. But Congress may by a vote of two-thirds of each House, remove such disability.

Section 4. The validity of the public debt of the United States, authorized by law, including debts incurred for payment of pensions and bounties for services in suppressing insurrection or rebellion, shall not be questioned. But neither the United States nor any State shall assume or pay any debt or obligation incurred in aid of insurrection or rebellion against the United States, or any claim for the loss or emancipation of any slave; but all such debts, obligations, and claims shall be held illegal and void.

Section 5. The Congress shall have the power to enforce, by appropriate legislation, the provisions of this article.

Amendment XV [1870]

Section 1. The right of citizens of the United States to vote shall not be denied or abridged by the United States or by any State on account of race, color, or previous condition of servitude—

Section 2. The Congress shall have power to enforce this article by appropriate legislation.

Amendment XVI [1913]

The Congress shall have power to lay and collect taxes on incomes, from whatever source derived, without apportionment among the several States, and without regard to any census or enumeration.

Amendment XVII [1913]

The Senate of the United States shall be composed of two Senators from each State, elected by the people thereof, for six years; and each Senator shall have one vote. The electors in each State shall have the qualifications requisite for electors of the most numerous branch of the State legislatures.

When vacancies happen in the representation of any State in the Senate, the executive authority of such State shall issue writs of election to fill such vacancies: *Provided,* That the legislature of any State may empower the executive thereof to make temporary appointments until the people fill the vacancies by election as the legislature may direct.

This amendment shall not be so construed as to affect the election or term of any Senator chosen before it becomes valid as part of the Constitution.

Amendment XVIII [1919]

Section 1. After one year from the ratification of this article the manufacture, sale, or transportation of intoxicating liquors within, the importation thereof into, or the exportation thereof from the United States and all territory subject to the jurisdiction thereof for beverage purposes is hereby prohibited.

Section 2. The Congress and the several States shall have concurrent power to enforce this article by appropriate legislation.

Section 3. This article shall be inoperative unless it shall have been ratified as an amendment to the Constitution by the legislatures of the several States, as provided in the Constitution, within seven years from the date of the submission hereof to the States by the Congress.

Amendment XIX [1920]

The right of citizens of the United States to vote shall not be denied or abridged by the United States or by any State on account of sex.

Congress shall have power to enforce this article by appropriate legislation.

Amendment XX [1933]

Section 1. The terms of the President and Vice-President shall end at noon on the 20th day of January, and the terms of Senators and Representatives at noon on the 3d day of January, of the years in which such terms would have ended if this article had not been ratified; and the terms of their successors shall then begin.

Section 2. The Congress shall assemble at least once in every year, and such meeting shall begin at noon on the 3d day of January, unless they shall by law appoint a different day.

Section 3. If, at the time fixed for the beginning of the term of the President, the President elect shall have died, the Vice-President elect shall become President. If a President shall not have been chosen before the time fixed for the beginning of his term, or if the President elect shall have failed to qualify, then the Vice-President elect shall act as President until a President shall have qualified; and the Congress may by law provide for the case wherein neither a President elect nor a Vice-President elect shall have qualified, declaring who shall then act as President, or the manner in which one who is to act shall be selected, and such person shall act accordingly until a President or Vice-President shall have qualified.

Section 4. The Congress may by law provide for the case of the death of any of the persons from whom the House of Representatives may choose a President whenever the right of choice shall have devolved upon them, and for the case of the death of any of the persons from whom the Senate may choose a Vice-President whenever the right of choice shall have devolved upon them.

Section 5. Sections 1 and 2 shall take effect on the 15th day of October following the ratification of this article.

Section 6. This article shall be inoperative unless it shall have been ratified as an amendment to the Constitution by the legislatures of three-fourths of the several States within seven years from the date of its submission.

Amendment XXI [1933]

Section 1. The eighteenth article of amendment to the Constitution of the United States is hereby repealed.

Section 2. The transportation or importation into any State, Territory, or possession of the United States for delivery or use therein of intoxicating liquors, in violation of the laws thereof, is hereby prohibited.

Section 3. This article shall be inoperative unless it shall have been ratified as an amendment to the Constitution by conventions in the several States, as provided in the Constitution, within seven years from the date of the submission hereof to the States by the Congress.

Amendment XXII [1951]

No person shall be elected to the office of the President more than twice, and no person who has held the office of President, or acted as President, for more than two years of a term to which some other person was elected President shall be elected to the office of the President more than once.

But this Article shall not apply to any person holding the office of President when this Article was proposed by the Congress, and shall not prevent any person who may be holding the office of President, or acting as President, during the term within which this Article becomes operative from holding the office of President or acting as President during the remainder of such term.

Amendment XXIII [1961]

Section 1. The District constituting the seat of Government of the United States shall appoint in such manner as the Congress may direct:

A number of electors of President and Vice President equal to the whole number of Senators and Representatives in Congress to which the District would be entitled if it were a State, but in no event more than the least populous State; they shall be in addition to those appointed by the States, but they shall be considered, for the purposes of the election of President and Vice President, to be electors appointed by a State; and they shall meet in the District and perform such duties as provided by the twelfth article of amendment.

Section 2. The Congress shall have power to enforce this article by appropriate legislation.

Amendment XXIV [1964]

Section 1. The right of citizens of the United States to vote in any primary or other election for President or Vice President, for electors for President or Vice President, or for Senator or Representative in Congress, shall not be denied or abridged by the United States or any State by reason of failure to pay any poll tax or other tax.

Section 2. The Congress shall have the power to enforce this article by appropriate legislation.

Amendment XXV [1967]

Section 1. In case of the removal of the President from office or of his death or resignation, the Vice President shall become President.

Section 2. Whenever there is a vacancy in the office of the Vice President, the President shall nominate a Vice President who shall take office upon confirmation by a majority vote of both Houses of Congress.

Section 3. Whenever the President transmits to the President pro tempore of the Senate and the Speaker of the House of Representatives his written declaration that he is unable to discharge the powers and duties of his office, and until he transmits to them a written declaration to the contrary, such powers and duties shall be discharged by the Vice President as Acting President.

Section 4. Whenever the Vice President and a majority of either the principal officers of the executive department or of such other body as Congress may by law provide, transmit to the President pro tempore of the Senate and the Speaker of the House of Representatives their written declaration that the President is unable to discharge the powers and duties of his office, the Vice President shall immediately assume the powers and duties of the office as Acting President.

Thereafter, when the President transmits to the President pro tempore of the Senate and the Speaker of the House of Representatives his written declaration that no inability exists, he shall resume the powers and duties of his office unless the Vice President and a majority of either the principal officers of the executive department or of such other body as Congress may by law provide, transmit within four days to the President pro tempore of the Senate and the Speaker of the House of Representatives their written declaration that the President is unable to discharge the powers and duties of his office. Thereupon Congress shall decide the issue, assembling within forty-eight hours for that purpose if not in session. If the Congress, within twenty-one days after receipt of the latter written declaration, or, if Congress is not in session, within twenty-one days after Congress is required to assemble, determines by two-thirds vote of both Houses that the President is unable to discharge the powers and duties of his office, the Vice President shall continue to discharge the same as Acting President; otherwise, the President shall resume the powers and duties of his office.

PRESIDENTIAL ELECTIONS/1789–1980

Year	Candidates	Party	Popular Vote	Electoral Vote
1789	**George Washington**			69
	John Adams			34
	Others			35
1792	**George Washington**			132
	John Adams			77
	George Clinton			50
	Others			5
1796	**John Adams**	Federalist		71
	Thomas Jefferson	Democratic-Republican		68
	Thomas Pinckney	Federalist		59
	Aaron Burr	Democratic-Republican		30
	Others			48
1800	**Thomas Jefferson**	Democratic-Republican		73
	Aaron Burr	Democratic-Republican		73
	John Adams	Federalist		65
	Charles C. Pinckney	Federalist		64
	John Jay	Federalist		1
1804	**Thomas Jefferson**	Democratic-Republican		162
	Charles C. Pinckney	Federalist		14
1808	**James Madison**	Democratic-Republican		122
	Charles C. Pinckney	Federalist		47
	George Clinton	Independent-Republican		6
1812	**James Madison**	Democratic-Republican		128
	DeWitt Clinton	Federalist		89
1816	**James Monroe**	Democratic-Republican		183
	Rufus King	Federalist		34
1820	**James Monroe**	Democratic-Republican		231
	John Quincy Adams	Independent-Republican		1
1824	**John Quincy Adams**	Democratic-Republican	108,740 (30.5%)	84
	Andrew Jackson	Democratic-Republican	153,544 (43.1%)	99
	Henry Clay	Democratic-Republican	47,136 (13.2%)	37
	William H. Crawford	Democratic-Republican	46,618 (13.1%)	41
1828	**Andrew Jackson**	Democratic	647,231 (56.0%)	178
	John Quincy Adams	National-Republican	509,097 (44.0%)	83
1832	**Andrew Jackson**	Democratic	687,502 (55.0%)	219
	Henry Clay	National-Republican	530,189 (42.4%)	49
	William Wirt	Anti-Masonic ⎫	33,108 (2.6%)	7
	John Floyd	National-Republican ⎭		11
1836	**Martin Van Buren**	Democratic	761,549 (50.9%)	170
	William H. Harrison	Whig	549,567 (36.7%)	73
	Hugh L. White	Whig	145,396 (9.7%)	26
	Daniel Webster	Whig	41,287 (2.7%)	14
	W. P. Mangum	Whig		11
1840	**William H. Harrison**	Whig	1,275,017 (53.1%)	234
	Martin Van Buren	Democratic	1,128,702 (46.9%)	60
1844	**James K. Polk**	Democratic	1,337,243 (49.6%)	170
	Henry Clay	Whig	1,299,068 (48.1%)	105
	James G. Birney	Liberty	62,300 (2.3%)	

Because only the leading candidates are listed, popular vote percentages do not always total 100.

PRESIDENTIAL ELECTIONS/1789–1980

Year	Candidates	Party	Popular Vote	Electoral Vote
1848	**Zachary Taylor**	Whig	1,360,101 (47.4%)	163
	Lewis Cass	Democratic	1,220,544 (42.5%)	127
	Martin Van Buren	Free Soil	291,263 (10.1%)	
1852	**Franklin Pierce**	Democratic	1,601,474 (50.9%)	254
	Winfield Scott	Whig	1,386,578 (44.1%)	42
	John P. Hale	Free Soil	155,825 (5.0%)	
1856	**James Buchanan**	Democratic	1,838,169 (45.4%)	174
	John C. Frémont	Republican	1,335,264 (33.0%)	114
	Millard Fillmore	American	874,534 (21.6%)	8
1860	**Abraham Lincoln**	Republican	1,865,593 (39.8%)	180
	Stephen A. Douglas	Democratic	1,382,713 (29.5%)	12
	John C. Breckinridge	Democratic	848,356 (18.1%)	72
	John Bell	Constitutional Union	592,906 (12.6%)	39
1864	**Abraham Lincoln**	Republican	2,206,938 (55.0%)	212
	George B. McClellan	Democratic	1,803,787 (45.0%)	21
1868	**Ulysses S. Grant**	Republican	3,013,421 (52.7%)	214
	Haratio Seymour	Democratic	2,706,829 (47.3%)	80
1872	**Ulysses S. Grant**	Republican	3,596,745 (55.6%)	286
	Horace Greeley	Democratic	2,843,446 (43.9%)	66
1876	**Rutherford B. Hayes**	Republican	4,036,572 (48.0%)	185
	Samuel J. Tilden	Democratic	4,284,020 (51.0%)	184
1880	**James A. Garfield**	Republican	4,449,053 (48.3%)	214
	Winfield S. Hancock	Democratic	4,442,035 (48.2%)	155
	James B. Weaver	Greenback-Labor	308,578 (3.4%)	
1884 ·	**Grover Cleveland**	Democratic	4,874,986 (48.5%)	219
	James G. Blaine	Republican	4,851,981 (48.2%)	182
	Benjamin F. Butler	Greenback-Labor	175,370 (1.8%)	
1888	**Benjamin Harrison**	Republican	5,444,337 (47.8%)	233
	Grover Cleveland	Democratic	5,540,050 (48.6%)	168
1892	**Grover Cleveland**	Democratic	5,554,414 (46.0%)	277
	Benjamin Harrison	Republican	5,190,802 (43.0%)	145
	James B. Weaver	People's	1,027,329 (8.5%)	22
1896	**William McKinley**	Republican	7,035,638 (50.8%)	271
	William J. Bryan	Democratic: People's	6,467,946 (46.7%)	176
1900	**William McKinley**	Republican	7,219,530 (51.7%)	292
	William J. Bryan	Democratic: Populist	6,356,734 (45.5%)	155
1904	**Theodore Roosevelt**	Republican	7,628,834 (56.4%)	336
	Alton B. Parker	Democratic	5,084,401 (37.6%)	140
	Eugene V. Debs	Socialist	402,460 (3.0%)	
1908	**William H. Taft**	Republican	7,679,006 (51.6%)	321
	William J. Bryan	Democratic	6,409,106 (43.1%)	162
	Eugene V. Debs	Socialist	420,820 (2.8%)	
1912	**Woodrow Wilson**	Democratic	6,286,820 (41.8%)	435
	Theodore Roosevelt	Progressive	4,126,020 (27.4%)	88
	William H. Taft	Republican	3,483,922 (23.2%)	8
	Eugene V. Debs	Socialist	897,011 (6.0%)	

PRESIDENTIAL ELECTIONS/1789–1980

Year	Candidates	Party	Popular Vote	Electoral Vote
1916	**Woodrow Wilson**	Democratic	9,129,606 (49.3%)	277
	Charles E. Hughes	Republican	8,538,221 (46.1%)	254
	A. L. Benson	Socialist	585,113 (3.2%)	
1920	**Warren G. Harding**	Republican	16,152,200 (61.0%)	404
	James M. Cox	Democratic	9,147,353 (34.6%)	127
	Eugene V. Debs	Socialist	919,799 (3.5%)	
1924	**Calvin Coolidge**	Republican	15,725,016 (54.1%)	382
	John W. Davis	Democratic	8,385,586 (28.8%)	136
	Robert M. LaFollette	Progressive	4,822,856 (16.6%)	13
1928	**Herbert C. Hoover**	Republican	21,392,190 (58.2%)	444
	Alfred E. Smith	Democratic	15,016,443 (40.8%)	87
1932	**Franklin D. Roosevelt**	Democratic	22,809,638 (57.3%)	472
	Herbert C. Hoover	Republican	15,758,901 (39.6%)	59
	Norman Thomas	Socialist	881,951 (2.2%)	
1936	**Franklin D. Roosevelt**	Democratic	27,757,333 (60.8%)	523
	Alfred M. Landon	Republican	16,684,231 (36.5%)	8
	William Lemke	Union	891,858 (1.9%)	
1940	**Franklin D. Roosevelt**	Democratic	27,243,466 (54.7%)	449
	Wendell L. Willkie	Republican	22,304,755 (44.8%)	82
1944	**Franklin D. Roosevelt**	Democratic	25,602,505 (52.8%)	432
	Thomas E. Dewey	Republican	22,006,278 (44.5%)	99
1948	**Harry S. Truman**	Democratic	24,105,812 (49.5%)	303
	Thomas E. Dewey	Republican	21,970,065 (45.1%)	189
	J. Strom Thurmond	States' Rights	1,169,063 (2.4%)	39
	Henry A. Wallace	Progressive	1,157,172 (2.4%)	
1952	**Dwight D. Eisenhower**	Republican	33,936,234 (55.2%)	442
	Adlai E. Stevenson	Democratic	27,314,992 (44.5%)	89
1956	**Dwight D. Eisenhower**	Republican	35,590,472 (57.4%)	457
	Adlai E. Stevenson	Democratic	26,022,752 (42.0%)	73
1960	**John F. Kennedy**	Democratic	34,227,096 (49.9%)	303
	Richard M. Nixon	Republican	34,108,546 (49.6%)	219
1964	**Lyndon B. Johnson**	Democratic	43,126,233 (61.1%)	486
	Barry M. Goldwater	Republican	27,174,989 (38.5%)	52
1968	**Richard M. Nixon**	Republican	31,770,237 (43.4%)	301
	Hubert H. Humphrey	Democratic	31,270,533 (42.7%)	191
	George C. Wallace	American Independent	9,906,141 (13.5%)	46
1972	**Richard M. Nixon**	Republican	46,740,323 (60.7%)	520
	George S. McGovern	Democratic	28,901,598 (37.5%)	17
	John G. Schmitz	American Independent	993,199 (1.4%)	
1976	**Jimmy Carter**	Democratic	40,828,929 (50.1%)	297
	Gerald R. Ford	Republican	39,148,940 (47.9%)	240
	Eugene McCarthy	Independent	739,256	
1980	**Ronald Reagan**	Republican	43,201,220 (50.9%)	489
	Jimmy Carter	Democratic	34,913,332 (41.2%)	49
	John B. Anderson	Independent	5,581,379 (.066%)	21

THE VICE-PRESIDENCY AND THE CABINET/1789–1980

Vice-President

John Adams	1789–1797
Thomas Jefferson	1797–1801
Aaron Burr	1801–1805
George Clinton	1805–1813
Elbridge Gerry	1813–1817
Daniel D. Tompkins	1817–1825
John C. Calhoun	1825–1833
Martin Van Buren	1833–1837
Richard M. Johnson	1837–1841
John Tyler	1841
George M. Dallas	1845–1849
Millard Fillmore	1849–1850
William R. King	1853–1857
John C. Breckinridge	1857–1861
Hannibal Hamlin	1861–1865
Andrew Johnson	1865
Schuyler Colfax	1869–1873
Henry Wilson	1873–1877
William A. Wheeler	1877–1881
Chester A. Arthur	1881
Thomas A. Hendricks	1885–1889
Levi P. Morton	1889–1893
Adlai E. Stevenson	1893–1897
Garret A. Hobart	1897–1901
Theodore Roosevelt	1901
Charles W. Fairbanks	1905–1909
James S. Sherman	1909–1913
Thomas R. Marshall	1913–1921
Calvin Coolidge	1921–1923
Charles G. Dawes	1925–1929
Charles Curtis	1929–1933
John Nance Garner	1933–1941
Henry A. Wallace	1941–1945
Harry S. Truman	1945
Alben W. Barkley	1949–1953
Richard M. Nixon	1953–1961
Lyndon B. Johnson	1961–1963
Hubert H. Humphrey	1965–1969
Spiro T. Agnew	1969–1973
Gerald R. Ford	1973–1974
Nelson A. Rockefeller	1974–1977
Walter F. Mondale	1977–1981
George Bush	1981–

Secretary of State (1789–   )

Thomas Jefferson	1789
Edmund Randolph	1794
Timothy Pickering	1795
John Marshall	1800
James Madison	1801
Robert Smith	1809
James Monroe	1811
John Q. Adams	1817
Henry Clay	1825
Martin Van Buren	1829
Edward Livingston	1831
Louis McLane	1833
John Forsyth	1834
Daniel Webster	1841
Hugh S. Legare	1843
Abel P. Upshur	1843
John C. Calhoun	1844
James Buchanan	1845
John M. Clayton	1849
Daniel Webster	1850
Edward Everett	1852
William L. Marcy	1853
Lewis Cass	1857
Jeremiah S. Black	1860
William H. Seward	1861
E. B. Washburne	1869
Hamilton Fish	1869
William M. Evarts	1877
James G. Blaine	1881
F. T. Frelinghuysen	1881
Thomas F. Bayard	1885
James G. Blaine	1889
John W. Foster	1892
Walter Q. Gresham	1893
Richard Olney	1895
John Sherman	1897
William R. Day	1898
John Hay	1898
Elihu Root	1905
Robert Bacon	1909
Philander C. Knox	1909
William J. Bryan	1913
Robert Lansing	1915
Bainbridge Colby	1920
Charles E. Hughes	1921
Frank B. Kellogg	1925
Henry L. Stimson	1929
Cordell Hull	1933
E. R. Stettinius, Jr.	1944
James F. Byrnes	1945
George C. Marshall	1947
Dean Acheson	1949
John Foster Dulles	1953
Christian A. Herter	1959
Dean Rusk	1961
William P. Rogers	1969
Henry A. Kissinger	1973
Cyrus R. Vance	1977
Edmund Muskie	1980

Secretary of the Treasury (1789–   )

Alexander Hamilton	1789
Oliver Wolcott	1795
Samuel Dexter	1801
Albert Gallatin	1801
G. W. Campbell	1814
A. J. Dallas	1814
William H. Crawford	1816
Richard Rush	1825
Samuel D. Ingham	1829
Louis McLane	1831
William J. Duane	1833
Roger B. Taney	1833
Levi Woodbury	1834
Thomas Ewing	1841
Walter Forward	1841
John C. Spencer	1843
George M. Bibb	1844
Robert J. Walker	1845

Secretary of the Treasury (cont.)

William M. Meredith	1849
Thomas Corwin	1850
James Guthrie	1853
Howell Cobb	1857
Philip F. Thomas	1860
John A. Dix	1861
Salmon P. Chase	1861
Wm. P. Fessenden	1864
Hugh McCulloch	1865
George S. Boutwell	1869
William A. Richardson	1873
Benjamin H. Bristow	1874
Lot M. Morrill	1876
John Sherman	1877
William Windom	1881
Charles J. Folger	1881
Walter Q. Gresham	1884
Hugh McCulloch	1884
Daniel Manning	1885
Charles S. Fairchild	1887
William Windom	1889
Charles Foster	1891
John G. Carlisle	1893
Lyman J. Gage	1897
Leslie M. Shaw	1902
George B. Cortelyou	1907
Franklin MacVeagh	1909
William G. McAdoo	1913
Carter Glass	1919
David F. Houston	1920
Andrew W. Mellon	1921
Ogden L. Mills	1932
William H. Woodin	1933
Henry Morgenthau, Jr.	1934
Fred M. Vinson	1945
John W. Snyder	1946
George M. Humphrey	1953
Robert B. Anderson	1957
C. Douglas Dillon	1961
Henry H. Fowler	1965
David M. Kennedy	1969
John B. Connally	1971
George P. Shultz	1972
William E. Simon	1974
W. Michael Blumenthal	1977
G. William Miller	1979

Secretary of War (1789–1947)

Henry Knox	1789
Timothy Pickering	1795
James McHenry	1796
John Marshall	1800
Samuel Dexter	1800
Roger Criswold	1801
Henry Dearborn	1801
William Eustis	1809
John Armstrong	1813
James Monroe	1814
William H. Crawford	1815
Isaac Shelby	1817
George Graham	1817
John C. Calhoun	1817
James Barbour	1825

THE VICE-PRESIDENCY AND THE CABINET/1789-1980

Name	Year
Peter B. Porter	1828
John H. Eaton	1829
Lewis Cass	1831
Benjamin F. Butler	1837
Joel R. Poinsett	1837
John Bell	1841
John McLean	1841
John C. Spencer	1841
James M. Porter	1843
William Wilkins	1844
William L. Marcy	1845
George W. Crawford	1849
Charles M. Conrad	1850
Jefferson Davis	1853
John B. Floyd	1857
Joseph Holt	1861
Simon Cameron	1861
Edwin M. Stanton	1862
Ulysses S. Grant	1867
Lorenzo Thomas	1868
John M. Schofield	1868
John A. Rawlins	1869
William T. Sherman	1869
William W. Belknap	1869
Alphonso Taft	1876
James D. Cameron	1876
George W. McCrary	1877
Alexander Ramsey	1879
Robert T. Lincoln	1881
William C. Endicott	1885
Redfield Proctor	1889
Stephen B. Elkins	1891
Daniel S. Lamont	1893
Russell A. Alger	1897
Elihu Root	1899
William H. Taft	1904
Luke E. Wright	1908
J. M. Dickinson	1909
Henry L. Stimson	1911
L. M. Garrison	1913
Newton D. Baker	1916
John W. Weeks	1921
Dwight F. Davis	1925
James W. Good	1929
Patrick J. Hurley	1929
George H. Dern	1933
H. H. Woodring	1936
Henry L. Stimson	1940
Robert P. Patterson	1945
Kenneth C. Royall	1947

Secretary of the Navy (1798-1947)

Name	Year
Benjamin Stoddert	1798
Robert Smith	1801
J. Crowninshield	1805
Paul Hamilton	1809
William Jones	1813
B. W. Crowninshield	1814
Smith Thompson	1818
S. L. Southard	1823
John Branch	1829
Levi Woodbury	1831
Mahlon Dickerson	1834
James K. Paulding	1838
George E. Badger	1841
Abel P. Upshur	1841
David Henshaw	1843
Thomas W. Gilmer	1844
John Y. Mason	1844
George Bancroft	1845
John Y. Mason	1846
William B. Preston	1849
William A. Graham	1850
John P. Kennedy	1852
James C. Dobbin	1853
Isaac Toucey	1857
Gideon Welles	1861
Adolph E. Borie	1869
George M. Robeson	1869
R. W. Thompson	1877
Nathan Goff, Jr.	1881
William H. Hunt	1881
William E. Chandler	1881
William C. Whitney	1885
Benjamin F. Tracy	1889
Hilary A. Herbert	1893
John D. Long	1897
William H. Moody	1902
Paul Morton	1904
Charles J. Bonaparte	1905
Victor H. Metcalf	1907
T. H. Newberry	1908
George von L. Meyer	1909
Josephus Daniels	1913
Edwin Denby	1921
Curtis D. Wilbur	1924
Charles F. Adams	1929
Claude A. Swanson	1933
Charles Edison	1940
Frank Knox	1940
James V. Forrestal	1944

Secretary of Defense (1947-   )

Name	Year
James V. Forrestal	1947
Louis A. Johnson	1949
George C. Marshall	1950
Robert A. Lovett	1951
Charles E. Wilson	1953
Neil H. McElroy	1957
Thomas S. Gates, Jr.	1959
Robert S. McNamara	1961
Clark Clifford	1968
Melvin R. Laird	1969
Elliot L. Richardson	1973
James R. Schlesinger	1973
Donald Rumsfield	1975
Harold Brown	1977

Postmaster General (1789-   ) (since 1971 appointed by Postal Service Board of Governors)

Name	Year
Samuel Osgood	1789
Timothy Pickering	1791
Joseph Habersham	1795
Gideon Granger	1801
Return J. Meigs, Jr.	1814
John McLean	1823
William T. Barry	1829
Amos Kendall	1835
John M. Niles	1840
Francis Granger	1841
Charles A. Wickliffe	1841
Cave Johnson	1845
Jacob Collamer	1849
Nathan K. Hall	1850
Samuel D. Hubbard	1852
James Campbell	1853
Aaron V. Brown	1857
Joseph Holt	1859
Horatio King	1861
Montgomery Blair	1861
William Dennison	1864
Alexander W. Randall	1866
John A. J. Creswell	1869
James W. Marshall	1874
Marshall Jewell	1874
James N. Tyner	1876
David M. Key	1877
Horace Maynard	1880
Thomas L. James	1881
Timothy O. Howe	1881
Walter Q. Gresham	1883
Frank Hatton	1884
William F. Vilas	1885
Don M. Dickinson	1888
John Wanamaker	1889
Wilson S. Bissell	1893
William L. Wilson	1895
James A. Gary	1897
Charles E. Smith	1898
Henry C. Payne	1902
Robert J. Wynne	1904
George B. Cortelyou	1905
George von L. Meyer	1907
F. H. Hitchcock	1909
Albert S. Burleson	1913
Will H. Hays	1921
Hubert Work	1922
Harry S. New	1923
Walter F. Brown	1929
James A. Farley	1933
Frank C. Walker	1940
Robert E. Hannegan	1945
J. M. Donaldson	1947
A. E. Summerfield	1953
J. Edward Day	1961
John A. Gronouski	1963
Lawrence F. O'Brien	1965
Marvin Watson	1968
Winton M. Blount	1969
Elmer T. Klassen	1971
Benjamin F. Bailar	1975
William F. Bolger	1978

Attorney General (1789-   )

Name	Year
Edmund Randolph	1789
William Bradford	1794
Charles Lee	1795

THE VICE-PRESIDENCY AND THE CABINET/1789–1980

Theophilus Parsons	1801	Nicholas Katzenbach	1964	Henry C. Wallace	1921
Levi Lincoln	1801	Ramsey Clark	1967	Howard M. Gore	1924
Robert Smith	1805	John N. Mitchell	1969	William M. Jardine	1925
John Breckinridge	1805	Richard G. Kleindienst	1972	Arthur M. Hyde	1929
Caesar A. Rodney	1807	Elliot L. Richardson	1973	Henry A. Wallace	1933
William Pinckney	1811	Robert H. Bork (acting)	1973	Claude R. Wickard	1940
Richard Rush	1814	William B. Saxbe	1974	Clinton P. Anderson	1945
William Wirt	1817	Edward H. Levi	1975	Charles F. Brannan	1948
John M. Berrien	1829	Griffin Bell	1977	Ezra Taft Benson	1953
Roger B. Taney	1831	Benjamin R. Civiletti	1979	Orville L. Freeman	1961
Benjamin F. Butler	1833			Clifford M. Hardin	1969
Felix Grundy	1838	**Secretary of the Interior**		Earl L. Butz	1971
Henry D. Gilpin	1840	**(1849–)**		John A. Knebel	1976
John J. Crittenden	1841			Robert Bergland	1977
Hugh S. Legare	1841	Thomas Ewing	1849		
John Nelson	1843	Alexander H. H. Stuart	1850	**Secretary of Commerce and**	
John Y. Mason	1845	Robert McClelland	1853	**Labor (1903–1913)**	
Nathan Clifford	1846	Jacob Thompson	1857		
Isaac Toucey	1848	Caleb B. Smith	1861	George B. Cortelyou	1903
Reverdy Johnson	1849	John P. Usher	1863	Victor H. Metcalf	1904
John J. Crittenden	1850	James Harlan	1865	Oscar S. Straus	1906
Caleb Cushing	1853	O. H. Browning	1866	Charles Nagel	1909
Jeremiah S. Black	1857	Jacob D. Cox	1869		
Edwin M. Stanton	1860	Columbus Delano	1870	**Secretary of Commerce**	
Edward Bates	1861	Zachariah Chandler	1875	**(1913–)**	
Titian J. Coffey	1863	Carl Schurz	1877		
James Speed	1864	Samuel J. Kirkwood	1881	William C. Redfield	1913
Henry Stanbery	1866	Henry M. Teller	1881	Joshua W. Alexander	1919
William M. Evarts	1868	L. Q. C. Lamar	1885	Herbert Hoover	1921
Ebenezer R. Hoar	1869	William F. Vilas	1888	William F. Whiting	1928
Amos T. Ackerman	1870	John W. Noble	1889	Robert P. Lamont	1929
George H. Williams	1871	Hoke Smith	1893	Roy D. Chapin	1932
Edward Pierrepont	1875	David R. Francis	1896	Daniel C. Roper	1933
Alphonso Taft	1876	Cornelius N. Bliss	1897	Harry L. Hopkins	1939
Charles Devens	1877	E. A. Hitchcock	1899	Jesse Jones	1940
Wayne MacVeagh	1881	James R. Garfield	1907	Henry A. Wallace	1945
Benjamin H. Brewster	1881	R. A. Ballinger	1909	W. A. Harriman	1946
A. H. Garland	1885	Walter L. Fisher	1911	Charles Sawyer	1948
William H. H. Miller	1889	Franklin K. Lane	1913	Sinclair Weeks	1953
Richard Olney	1893	John B. Payne	1920	Lewis L. Strauss	1958
Judson Harmon	1895	Albert B. Fall	1921	Frederick H. Mueller	1959
Joseph McKenna	1897	Hubert Work	1923	Luther Hodges	1961
John W. Griggs	1897	Roy O. West	1928	John T. Connor	1965
Philander C. Knox	1901	Ray L. Wilbur	1929	A. B. Trowbridge	1967
William H. Moody	1904	Harold L. Ickes	1933	Maurice H. Stans	1969
Charles J. Bonaparte	1907	Julius A. Krug	1946	Peter G. Peterson	1972
G. W. Wickersham	1909	Oscar L. Chapman	1949	Frederick B. Dent	1973
J. C. McReynolds	1913	Douglas McKay	1953	Rogers C. B. Morton	1975
Thomas W. Gregory	1914	Fred A. Seaton	1956	Elliot L. Richardson	1975
A. Mitchell Palmer	1919	Stewart L. Udall	1961	Juanita M. Kreps	1977
H. M. Daugherty	1921	Walter J. Hickel	1969	Philip M. Klutznick	1979
Harlan F. Stone	1924	Rogers C. B. Morton	1971		
John G. Sargent	1925	Stanley K. Hathaway	1975	**Secretary of Labor**	
William D. Mitchell	1929	Thomas Kleppe	1975	**(1913–)**	
H. S. Cummings	1933	Cecil D. Andrus	1977		
Frank Murphy	1939			William B. Wilson	1913
Robert H. Jackson	1940	**Secretary of Agriculture**		James J. Davis	1921
Francis Biddle	1941	**(1889–)**		William N. Doak	1930
Tom C. Clark	1945			Frances Perkins	1933
J. H. McGrath	1949	Norman J. Colman	1889	L. B. Schwellenbach	1945
J. P. McGranery	1952	Jeremiah M. Rusk	1889	Maurice J. Tobin	1948
H. Brownell, Jr.	1953	J. Sterling Morton	1893	Martin P. Durkin	1953
William P. Rogers	1957	James Wilson	1897	James P. Mitchell	1953
Robert F. Kennedy	1961	David F. Houston	1913	Arthur J. Goldberg	1961
		Edward T. Meredith	1920	W. Willard Wirtz	1962
				George P. Shultz	1969

THE VICE-PRESIDENCY AND THE CABINET/1789–1980

James D. Hodgson	1970
Peter J. Brennan	1973
John T. Dunlop	1975
W. J. Usery	1976
F. Ray Marshall	1977

Secretary of Health, Education, and Welfare (1953–   )

Oveta Culp Hobby	1953
Marion B. Folsom	1955
Arthur S. Flemming	1958
Abraham A. Ribicoff	1961
Anthony J. Celebrezze	1962
John W. Gardner	1965
Robert H. Finch	1969
Elliot L. Richardson	1970
Caspar W. Weinberger	1973

Forrest D. Mathews	1975
Joseph A. Califano	1977
Patricia R. Harris	1979

Secretary of Health and Welfare

Patricia R. Harris	1980

Secretary of Housing and Urban Development

Robert C. Weaver	1966
Robert C. Wood	1968
George M. Romney	1969
James T. Lynn	1973
Carla A. Hills	1975
Patricia R. Harris	1977
Moon Landrieu	1979

Secretary of Transportation

John A. Volpe	1969
Claude S. Brinegar	1973
William T. Coleman	1975
Brock Adams	1977
Neil E. Goldschmidt	1979

Secretary of the Department of Energy

James R. Schlesinger	1977
Charles W. Duncan	1979

Secretary of the Department of Education

Shirley M. Hufstedler	1980

THE STATES

1. Delaware	7 Dec. 1787	18. Louisiana	30 Apr. 1812	35. West Virginia	19 June 1863
2. Pennsylvania	12 Dec. 1787	19. Indiana	11 Dec. 1816	36. Nevada	31 Oct. 1864
3. New Jersey	18 Dec. 1787	20. Mississippi	10 Dec. 1817	37. Nebraska	1 Mar. 1867
4. Georgia	2 Jan. 1788	21. Illinois	3 Dec. 1818	38. Colorado	1 Aug. 1876
5. Connecticut	9 Jan. 1788	22. Alabama	14 Dec. 1819	39. North Dakota	2 Nov. 1889
6. Massachusetts	6 Feb. 1788	23. Maine	15 Mar. 1820	40. South Dakota	2 Nov. 1889
7. Maryland	28 Apr. 1788	24. Missouri	10 Aug. 1821	41. Montana	8 Nov. 1889
8. South Carolina	23 May 1788	25. Arkansas	15 June 1836	42. Washington	11 Nov. 1889
9. New Hampshire	21 June 1788	26. Michigan	26 Jan. 1837	43. Idaho	3 July 1890
10. Virginia	25 June 1788	27. Florida	3 Mar. 1845	44. Wyoming	10 July 1890
11. New York	26 July 1788	28. Texas	29 Dec. 1845	45. Utah	4 Jan. 1896
12. North Carolina	21 Nov. 1789	29. Iowa	28 Dec. 1846	46. Oklahoma	16 Nov. 1907
13. Rhode Island	29 May 1790	30. Wisconsin	29 May 1848	47. New Mexico	6 Jan. 1912
14. Vermont	4 Mar. 1791	31. California	9 Sept. 1850	48. Arizona	14 Feb. 1912
15. Kentucky	1 June 1792	32. Minnesota	11 May 1858	49. Alaska	3 Jan. 1959
16. Tennessee	1 June 1796	33. Oregon	14 Feb. 1859	50. Hawaii	21 Aug. 1959
17. Ohio	1 Mar. 1803	34. Kansas	29 Jan. 1861		

TERRITORIAL EXPANSION

Louisiana Purchase	1803	Gadsden Purchase	1853	Guam	1899
Florida	1819	Alaska	1867	Amer. Samoa	1900
Texas	1845	Hawaii	1898	Canal Zone	1904
Oregon	1846	The Philippines	1898–1946	U.S. Virgin Islands	1917
Mexican Cession	1848	Puerto Rico	1899	Pacific Islands Trust Terr.	1947

POPULATION/1790–1980

1790	3,929,214	1840	17,069,453	1890	62,947,714	1940	131,669,275
1800	5,308,483	1850	23,191,876	1900	75,994,575	1950	151,325,798
1810	7,239,881	1860	31,443,321	1910	91,972,266	1960	179.323,175
1820	9,638,453	1870	39,818,449	1920	105,710,620	1970	203,235,298
1830	12,866,020	1880	50,155,783	1930	122,775,046	*1980	219,500,000

*Projection

THE CONGRESS/1789–1981

Congress	Term	Senate Maj.	Min.	Other	House Maj.	Min.	Other	Administration
1	1789–1791	Adm. 17	Op. 9		Adm. 38	Op. 26		Washington
2	1791–1793	Adm. 16	Op. 13		Adm. 37	Op. 33		Washington
3	1793–1795	Adm. 17	Op. 13		Adm. 57	Op. 48		Washington
4	1795–1797	Adm. 19	Op. 13		Adm. 54	Op. 52		Washington
5	1797–1799	F 20	DR 12		F 58	DR 48		J. Adams (F)
6	1799–1801	F 19	DR 13		F 64	DR 42		J. Adams (F)
7	1801–1803	DR 18	F 14		DR 69	F 36		Jefferson (DR)
8	1803–1805	DR 25	F 9		DR 102	F 39		Jefferson (DR)
9	1805–1807	DR 27	F 7		DR 116	F 25		Jefferson (DR)
10	1807–1809	DR 28	F 6		DR 118	F 24		Jefferson (DR)
11	1809–1811	DR 28	F 6		DR 94	F 48		Madison (DR)
12	1811–1813	DR 30	F 6		DR 108	F 36		Madison (DR)
13	1813–1815	DR 27	F 9		DR 112	F 68		Madison (DR)
14	1815–1817	DR 25	F 11		DR 117	F 65		Madison (DR)
15	1817–1819	DR 34	F 10		DR 141	F 42		Monroe (DR)
16	1819–1821	DR 35	F 7		DR 156	F 27		Monroe (DR)
17	1821–1823	DR 44	F 4		DR 158	F 25		Monroe (DR)
18	1823–1825	DR 44	F 4		DR 187	F 26		Monroe (DR)
19	1825–1827	Adm. 26	Op. 20		Adm. 105	Op. 97		J. Q. Adams (DR)
20	1827–1829	Op. 28	Adm. 20		Op. 119	Adm. 94		J. Q. Adams (DR)
21	1829–1831	D 26	NR 22		D 139	NR 74		Jackson (D)
22	1831–1833	D 25	NR 21	2	D 141	NR 58	14	Jackson (D)
23	1833–1835	D 20	NR 20	8	D 147	AM 53	60	Jackson (D)
24	1835–1837	D 27	W 25		D 145	W 98		Jackson (D)
25	1837–1839	D 30	W 18	4	D 108	W 107	24	Van Buren (D)
26	1839–1841	D 28	W 22		D 124	W 118		Van Buren (D)
27	1841–1843	W 28	D 22	2	W 133	D 102	6	W. H. Harrison (W) / Tyler (W)
28	1843–1845	W 28	D 25	1	D 142	W 79	1	Tyler (W)
29	1845–1847	D 31	W 25		D 143	W 77	6	Polk (D)
30	1847–1849	D 36	W 21	1	W 115	D 108	4	Polk (D)
31	1849–1851	D 35	W 25	2	D 112	W 109	9	Taylor (W) / Fillmore (W)
32	1851–1853	D 35	W 24	3	D 140	W 88	5	Fillmore (W)
33	1853–1855	D 38	W 22	2	D 159	W 71	4	Pierce (D)
34	1855–1857	D 40	R 15	5	R 108	D 83	43	Pierce (D)
35	1857–1859	D 36	R 20	8	D 118	R 92	26	Buchanan (D)
36	1859–1861	D 36	R 26	4	R 114	D 92	31	Buchanan (D)
37	1861–1863	R 31	D 10	8	R 105	D 43	30	Lincoln (R)
38	1863–1865	R 36	D 9	5	R 102	D 75	9	Lincoln (R)
39	1865–1867	R 42	D 10		R 149	D 42		Lincoln (R) / A. Johnson (R)
40	1867–1869	R 42	D 11		R 143	D 49		A. Johnson (R)
41	1869–1871	R 56	D 11		R 149	D 63		Grant (R)
42	1871–1873	R 52	D 17	5	D 134	R 104	5	Grant (R)
43	1873–1875	R 49	D 19	5	R 194	D 92	14	Grant (R)
44	1875–1877	R 45	D 29	2	D 169	R 109	14	Grant (R)

THE CONGRESS/1789–1981

Congress	Term	Senate Maj.	Min.	Other	House Maj.	Min.	Other	Administration
45	1877–1879	R 39	D 36	1	D 153	R 140		Hayes (R)
46	1879–1881	D 42	R 33	1	D 149	R 130	14	Hayes (R)
47	1881–1883	R 37	D 37	1	R 147	D 135	11	Garfield (R) / Arthur (R)
48	1883–1885	R 38	D 36		D 197	R 118	10	Arthur (R)
49	1885–1887	R 43	D 34		D 183	R 140	2	Cleveland (D)
50	1887–1889	R 39	D 37		D 169	R 152	4	Cleveland (D)
51	1889–1891	R 39	D 37		R 166	D 159		B. Harrison (R)
52	1891–1893	R 47	D 39	2	D 235	R 88	9	B. Harrison (R)
53	1893–1895	D 44	R 38	3	D 218	R 127	11	Cleveland (D)
54	1895–1897	R 43	D 39	6	R 244	D 105	7	Cleveland (D)
55	1897–1899	R 47	D 34	7	R 204	D 113	40	McKinley (R)
56	1899–1901	R 53	R 26	8	R 185	D 163	9	McKinley (R)
57	1901–1903	R 55	D 31	4	R 197	D 151	9	McKinley (R) / T. Roosevelt (R)
58	1903–1905	R 57	D 33		R 208	D 178		T. Roosevelt (R)
59	1905–1907	R 57	D 33		R 250	D 136		T. Roosevelt (R)
60	1907–1909	R 61	D 31		R 222	D 164		T. Roosevelt (R)
61	1909–1911	R 61	D 32		R 219	D 172		Taft (R)
62	1911–1913	R 51	D 41		D 228	R 161	1	Taft (R)
63	1913–1915	D 51	R 44		D 291	R 127	17	Wilson (D)
64	1915–1917	D 56	R 40		D 230	R 196	9	Wilson (D)
65	1917–1919	D 53	R 42		D 216	R 210	6	Wilson (D)
66	1919–1921	R 49	D 47		R 240	D 190	3	Wilson (D)
67	1921–1923	R 59	D 37		R 303	D 131	1	Harding (R)
68	1923–1925	R 51	D 43	2	R 225	D 205	5	Harding (R) / Coolidge (R)
69	1925–1927	R 56	D 39	1	R 247	D 183	4	Coolidge (R)
70	1927–1929	R 49	D 46	1	R 237	D 195	3	Coolidge (R)
71	1929–1931	R 56	D 39	1	R 267	D 167	1	Hoover (R)
72	1931–1933	R 48	D 47	1	D 220	R 214	1	Hoover (R)
73	1933–1935	D 60	R 35		D 310	R 117	5	F. D. Roosevelt (D)
74	1935–1937	D 69	R 25	2	D 319	R 103	10	F. D. Roosevelt (D)
75	1937–1939	D 76	R 16	4	D 331	R 89	13	F. D. Roosevelt (D)
76	1939–1941	D 69	R 23	4	D 261	R 164	4	F. D. Roosevelt (D)
77	1941–1943	D 66	R 28	2	D 268	R 162	5	F. D. Roosevelt (D)
78	1943–1945	D 58	R 37	1	D 218	R 208	4	F. D. Roosevelt (D) / Truman (D)
79	1945–1947	D 56	R 38	1	D 242	R 190	2	Truman (D)
80	1947–1949	R 51	D 45		R 246	D 188	1	Truman (D)
81	1949–1951	D 54	R 42		D 263	R 171	1	Truman (D)
82	1951–1953	D 49	R 47		D 235	R 199	1	Truman (D)
83	1953–1955	R 48	D 47	1	R 221	D 212	1	Eisenhower (R)
84	1955–1957	D 48	R 47	1	D 232	R 203		Eisenhower (R)
85	1957–1959	D 49	R 47		D 232	R 199		Eisenhower (R)
86	1959–1961	D 62	R 34		D 280	R 152		Eisenhower (R)

THE CONGRESS/1789–1981

Congress	Term	Senate Maj.	Senate Min.	Senate Other	House Maj.	House Min.	House Other	Administration
87	1961–1963	D 65	R 35		D 261	R 176		Kennedy (D)
88	1963–1965	D 67	R 33		D 258	R 177	1	Kennedy (D) / L. B. Johnson (D)
89	1965–1967	D 68	R 32		D 295	R 140		L. B. Johnson (D)
90	1967–1969	D 64	R 36	1	D 247	R 187		L. B. Johnson (D)
91	1969–1971	D 58	R 42		D 243	R 192		Nixon (R)
92	1971–1973	D 54	R 45	1	D 254	R 180	1	Nixon (R)
93	1973–1975	D 56	R 42	2	D 240	R 192	3	Nixon-Ford (R)
94	1975–1977	D 61	R 37	2	D 291	R 144		Ford (R)
95	1977–1979	D 61	R 38	1	D 292	R 143		Carter (D)
96	1979–1981	D 58	R 41	1	D 276	R 159		Carter (D)
97	1981–1983	R 53	D 46	1	D 242	R 191	2	Reagan (R)

INDEX

1980 election, 1038; *see also* Civil rights; Racism; Slavery
Black Death: *see* Bubonic plague
Black Hawk (Indian chief), 331
Blackmun, Harry Andrew, 982, 983
Black Muslims, **879, 880**
Black Panthers, 964–65, 1004–1005
Blaine, James Gillespie, 492, 526, 527–30, 534, 537–39, 549, 614
Blair, Francis Preston, Sr., 330
Bland, Richard Parks (Silver Dick), 524
Bland-Allison Act (1878), 525, 536, 537
Bleeding Kansas, 419
Blennerhassett, Herman, 281
Blitzkrieg, 795
Blyth, Benjamin: portraits of the Adams' by, **205**
Board of Trade and Plantations, 90
Boas, Franz, 715
Bonaparte, Napoleon: *see* Napoleon I
Bond, Julian, **881**
Bonilla, Ruben, **956**
Bonner, Jane, **73**
Bonneville Dam, 771
Bonus Army (Bonus Expeditionary Force), **748,** 750, 756
Bonus bill (1816), 300–301
Bonus bill (1924), 711
Book of Mormon, 328
Boone, Daniel, 257
Booth, John Wilkes, 470, 472
Booth, William, 592
Borah, William Edgar, 676, 717, 722, 795
Bork, Robert, 997
Bosch, Juan, 965
Bosnia, 655
Bosses, Political: *see* Machine politics
Boston, Mass: colonial period in, 78, 91, 123, 124, 128, 163; harbor view (1800s), **300**
Boston, U.S.S., 554
Boston Manufacturing Company, 261
Boston Massacre, 167–68, **168;** Revere poem on, 81
Boston police strike (1919), 679, 708
Boston Tea Party, 172–73
Boulder Dam: *see* Hoover Dam
Bourgeois, Léon, 674
Bow, Clara, **687,** 688, 691
Bowdoin, James (1726–90), 207, 222
Boxer Rebellion, **575,** 576
Braddock, Edward, 150
Bradford, William, 49
Bradley, Omar Nelson, 815, 847
Bradley, Tom, **882**
Bradstreet, Anne: poem by, 71
Bradstreet, Simon, **71**
Brady, Matthew B.: photographs

by, **445, 471**
Bragg, Braxton, 447
Brain Trust, 761
Brandeis, Louis Dembitz, 600, 608, 637, 643, 653, 779
Brandywine Creek, Battle of, 193
Braxton, Carter, 213
Breckinridge, John Cabell (1821–75), 420, 428, 430
Breed's Hill, 176
Brennan, William J., Jr., **905**
Brest-Litovsk, Treaty of, 672
Brewster, William, 49
Brezhnev, Leonid, 992, 1005, 1028
Briand, Aristide, 722
Bridge construction, 581
Bridgeman, John, **28**
Brisbane, Albert, 326
Bristow, Joseph Little, 604
Broadcasting industry, 687
Brook Farm, 326, 327, 329
Brooklyn Bridge, 581
Brooks, Preston Smith, 420
Brotherhood of Carpenters and Joiners, 510
Browder, Earl, 774
Brown, Benjamin Gratz, 490
Brown, Edmund Gerald (Pat), Jr., 1007, 1030, 1031
Brown, Henry Box, **402**
Brown, Jacob, 300
Brown, John, 419, **426,** 426–27
Brown, Joseph Emerson, 461, 462, 469
Brown, William Wells, **394**
Brownell, Herbert, Jr., 904
Brownson, Orestes, 326
Brown University, 137
Brown v. Board of Education of Topeka, 906
Brussels, Belgium, 814
Brussels Conference (1937), 789–90
Brussels Treaty Organization, 911
Brussels Union, 835
Bry, Theodore de, **18**
Bryan, William Jennings, 556, **558, 693;** as presidential candidate, 557-59, 572, 628, 636, 637; and Progressive movement, 599; and Federal Reserve System, 642; and "cooling off" treaties, 646; as Secretary of State, 646–48; and Caribbean diplomacy, 647–48; resignation of, 658; and Scopes trial, 693–94; and prohibition, 694
Bryant, William Cullen, 306
Bryn Mawr College, 607
Bubonic plague, 4
Buchanan, James: as Secretary of State, 358; and Ostend Manifesto, 414; and election of 1856, 420, 421; and Dred Scott case, 421, 422; and Kansas, 423; on secession, 431–32; supports Northern cause, 434
Buell, Don Carlos, 445

Buena Vista, Battle of, 357
Buenos Aires, Argentina, 792
Bulganin, Nikolai Aleksandrovich, 911
Bulgaria, 655
Bulge, Battle of the, 815
Bulloch, James Dunwody, 443
Bull Run, First Battle of, 439–40
Bull Run, Second Battle of, 447
Bunau-Varilla, Philippe, 618–19
Bunker Hill, Battle of, 176–77
Bureau of: *see* under the latter part of the name, such as, Corporations, Bureau of
Bureau of Investigation: *see* Federal Bureau of Investigation
Burger, Warren, 982
Burgoyne, John, 176, 192
Burke, Edmund, 168–69, 175, 182, 184
Burleson, Albert Sidney, 670
Burnett immigration bill, 652
Burnside, Ambrose Everett, 461, 462
Burr, Aaron, 242, 279–80, **281;** and election of 1800, 250–51; conspiracy and trial of, 281–82
Bush, George Herbert Walker, 1032, 1033
Business: growth of big business, 503–506, 689–90; managerial revolution in, 690; recovery under New Deal, 767–69; organization of modern, 862–63
Butler, Andrew Pickens, 420
Butler, Benjamin Franklin, 530
Byrd, Richard Evelyn, 688–89
Byrne, Jane, 896
Byrnes, James Francis, 806, 832

Cabinet, A16–A19; first, 237
Cabot, John, 33
Cairo Conference (1943), 817
Calhoun, Floride (Mrs. John C.), 332
Calhoun, John Caldwell, 287, 298, 300–301, 316, 339; and election of 1924, 315–16; tariff of abominations and, 318–19; and election of 1828, 320; and Peggy Eaton affair, 332; and states' rights, 333–35; and Jackson, 338; and Texas, 351, 352; on slavery, 360; and Compromise of 1850, 362–63, 364
California: and Mexican War, 356, 357; cession to the U.S., 358, 359, 360, **945;** gold rush in, 361–62; and Compromise of 1850, 362, 363; statehood, 368–69; population growth (1850–60), 369; and Mexican Americans, 520, **949;** Chinese in, 527; and woman suffrage, 609; and treatment of Japanese in,